Prolegomena
to All Future Cinema
Guy Debord (1952)

LOVE is only worthwhile in a pre-revo

I made this film when it was still the right time to talk about it.

It was about rising up with the greatest possible violence against an ethical order that later will be overcome.

Since I don't like writing, I lack the leisure activity to create an oeuvre that wouldn't be eternal: my film will remain among the most important in the history of the reductional hypostasis of cinema, made by a terrorist disorganisation of the discrepant.

The chiseling on the photo and the Lettrism (the given elements) are envisaged here as the very expression of revolt.

The chiseling blocks out certain moments of the film that are the eyes closed to the excess of the disaster. Lettrist poetry howls for a crushed universe.

The commentary is called into question by:

> *The censored phrase*, where the suppression of words (see "Appel pour la destruction de la prose théorique") exposes the repressive forces.

> *The spelled-out words*, a hint of an even more complete dislocation.

The destruction is followed by an overlapping of the image and of the sound with:

> *The torn visual-sound phrase*, where the photo overwhelms the verbal expression.

> *The spoken-written dialogue*, whose phrases are inscribed on the screen and which continue on the soundtrack. Then they respond to one another.

Finally, I secure the death of the discrepant cinema through the relation of the two non-meanings (perfectly insignificant images and words), a relation that exceeds the cry.

But all this belongs to an era that is finishing, and that no longer interests me.

Values related to artistic creation are being displaced by a conditioning of the spectator, with what I have called *three-dimensional psychology*, and the *nuclear cinema* of Marc,O., a cinema that begins another phase of amplification (*amplique*).

The arts of the future will entail the shattering of situations, or nothing.

Translated from the French by Sarah Clift

First published in *ION Centre de création*, Marc-Gilbert Guillaumin (ed.), no. 1, April 1952, Paris
http://www.chez.com/debordiana/francais/ion.htm

FUTURE CINEMA
The Cinematic Imaginary after Film

views from the exhibition
FUTURE CINEMA at the ZKM |
Center for Art and Media
Karlsruhe, 2003
photos © Franz Wamhof

Jean-Luc Godard
Le Mépris [Contempt]
1963
35mm film
color, sound
103 min
film stills

"The Cinema is an invention
without a future."
Louis Lumière

Electronic Culture
History, Theory, Practice
Timothy Druckrey, series editor

Ars Electronica
Facing the Future
edited by Timothy Druckrey with Ars Electronica, 1999

net_condition
art and global media
edited by Peter Weibel and Timothy Druckrey, 2000

Dark Fiber
Tracking Critical Internet Culture
Geert Lovink, 2002

Future Cinema
The Cinematic Imaginary after Film
edited by Jeffrey Shaw and Peter Weibel, 2003

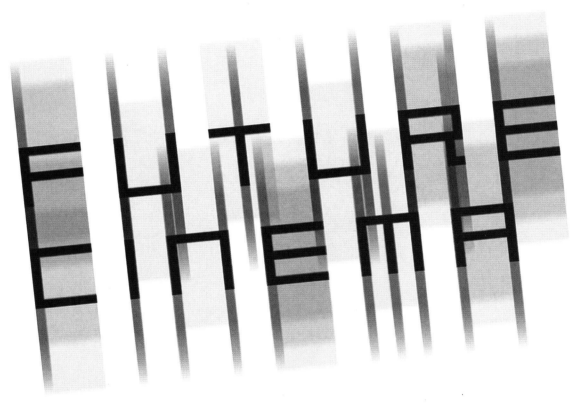

The Cinematic Imaginary after Film
Edited by Jeffrey Shaw and Peter Weibel

ZKM | Center for Art and Media Karlsruhe

The **MIT** Press
Cambridge, Massachusetts
London, England

FUTURE CINEMA The Cinematic Imaginary after Film

ZKM | Center for Art and Media Karlsruhe
16 November 2002 – 30 March 2003

Traveling to the following venues

Nykytaiteen Museo KIASMA /
Museum of Contemporary Art KIASMA Helsinki
28 June – 28 September 2003

NTT InterCommunication Center [ICC] Tokyo
2 December 2003 – 7 March 2004

Curators
Jeffrey Shaw and Peter Weibel

Curatorial Assistance and Project Management
Sabine Himmelsbach

Assistants
Anke Hoffmann, Katrin Kaschadt, Dominika Szope,
Leejone Wong

Exhibition Architecture
Ruth M. Lorenz. maaskant Berlin

Registrar
Regina Linder

Technical Manager
Martin Häberle

Construction Management
Christiane Ostertag, Ronald Haas

Construction Team
Werner Hutzenlaub, Gisbert Laaber, Mirco Frass,
Marco Sonntag, Claudius Böhm, Gregor Gaissmaier,
Volker Becker, Volker Möllenhoff, Jürgen Galli,
Lego Nainggolan, Oliver Klingel, Silke Fehsenfeld,
Martin Boukhalfa, Olaf Quantius, Manfred Stürmlinger,
Ines Gottwald, Marco Preitschopf, Thomas Linder,
Peter Gather, Werner Wenzel, Christian Wetzel,
Christine Müller, Reinhard Voss, Steffen Wolf, Karen Markert,
Joachim Hirling, Daniela Jacob, Sebastian Hammwöhner,
Predrag Zaric, Elke Cordell, Anna Reiss, Isabell Laske

Facility Management
Peter Futterer, Peter Kuhn, Klaus Wirth, Kurt Pfund,
Martin Braun, Hartmut Kampe, Michael Mack,
Christof Menold, Peter Kiefer, Karl Stumm

Media Library
Claudia Gehrig, Hartmut Jörg, Christiane Minter,
Julian Neville, Barbara Göhner

IT Support
Joachim Schütze, Uwe Faber

Institute for Visual Media, Technical Support
Jan Gerigk, Andrea Hartinger, Manfred Hauffen,
Katharina Klodt, Matt McGinity, Jeffrey Shaw, Keir Smith,
Silke Sutter, Christina Zartmann, Torsten Ziegler

Media Theater Program
Susanne Ackers

Corporate Design
Michael Throm

Public Relations
Andrea Buddensieg
Sabine Peters, Petra Meyer

Website
Silke Altvater, Heike Borowski, Arne Gräßer, Petra Kaiser

Museums Communications
Bernhard Serexhe, Marianne Womack,
Alicia Solzbacher, Harald Koch

Special Thanks to
all the lenders, museums, galleries and artists without whom such an outstanding project could never
have been realized. We wish to express our deepest
gratitude to

Annenberg Center for Communication,
The University of Southern California;
Art Production Fund;
Australia Council;
Australian Centre for the Moving Image, Melbourne;
Australian Federal Government's Art Advisory Body;
bitforms Gallery, New York;
Centre Georges Pompidou, Musée national
d'art moderne, Centre de création industrielle, Paris;
Chara Schreyer, Tiburon, CA;
Collection of Contemporary Art Fundación
"la Caixa," Barcelona;
Centre pour l'image contemporaine, Geneva;
CICV – Pierre Schaeffer (Patrick Zanoli);
CZech TV;
Deutsches Technikmuseum Berlin;
Donald Young Gallery, Chicago;
EPIDEMIC (Richard Castelli);
Eyebeam;
Film Victoria's Digital Media Fund;
Hosfelt Gallery, San Francisco;
iCINEMA Centre for Interactive Cinema Research,
University of New South Wales;
LFK-lafabriks (Jean-Luc d'Aléo, Nadine Febvre);
Victoria Miro Gallery, London;
Museums Dortmund;
NTT InterCommunicationCenter [ICC], Tokyo;
Postmasters Gallery, New York;
Sammlung Goetz, Munich;
Société des arts technologiques (SAT);
Street Vision Ltd., London;
Susan Hobbs Gallery, Toronto;
Thea Westreich Art Advisory Services, New York;
The Daniel Langlois Foundation for Art,
Science and Technology;
The International Academy for Media Arts
and Sciences (IAMAS);
Université de Montréal;
Z-A Production, Paris

A publication by the
ZKM | Center for Art and Media Karlsruhe
marking the exhibition

FUTURE CINEMA
The Cinematic Imaginary after Film

Edited by
Jeffrey Shaw and Peter Weibel

ZKM | Publication Program
Ulrike Havemann and Dörte Zbikowski, editors

Assistants
Jens Lutz, Alicia Solzbacher, Miriam Stürner

Catalog Design
Heidi Specker

Layout
Holger Jost

Copy Editor
Tom Morrison

Translators
Paul Bendelow, Alfred Birnbaum, Sarah Clift,
Pauline Cumbers, Gloria Custance, Michael Eldred,
Jeremy Gaines, Petra Kaiser, Matthew Partridge,
Steven Richards, Jaqueline Todd

Lithography
Karl Specht – Moderne Reprotechnik, Karlsruhe

Special Thanks to
Susanne Ackers, Nicole Blaffert, Karin Buol,
Nina Eberenz, Ernst Gärtner, Claudia Gehrig,
Martin Häberle, Marion Haimel, Brenna Jensen,
Jens Lill, Angela Lorenz, Katja Martin, Sabine Regh,
Margit Rosen, Ingrid Truxa, Franz Wamhof,
Christina Zartmann

First MIT Press edition published 2003.

Printed and bound in Karlsruhe, Germany by Engelhardt & Bauer.

Library of Congress Control Number:
2002113797

ISBN 0-262-69286-4

ZKM Partner

LB≡BW
Landesbank Baden-Württemberg

Partner der Staatsoper Stuttgart und
des Zentrums für Kunst und Medientechnologie Karlsruhe (ZKM).

Exhibition Sponsors

Main Sponsor

*la fondation Daniel Langlois
pour l'art, la science
et la technologie*

Sharp
Burger
Zumtobel Staff
CAN.media
Schwenk Betontechnik

Catalog Sponsors

**Gesellschaft zur
Förderung der Kunst und
Medientechnologie e.V.**

Kodak Polychrome
GRAPHICS

Contents

THE CINEMATIC IMAGINARY

SCREENINGS

THEATERS

CODES

REMAPPING

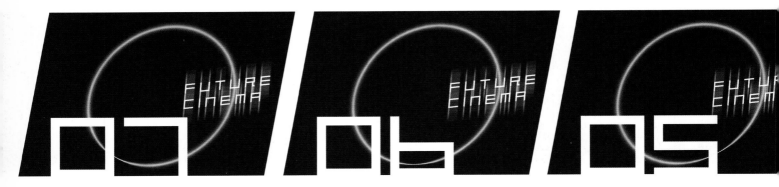

TRANSCRIPTIVE

RECOMBINATORY

NAVIGABLE

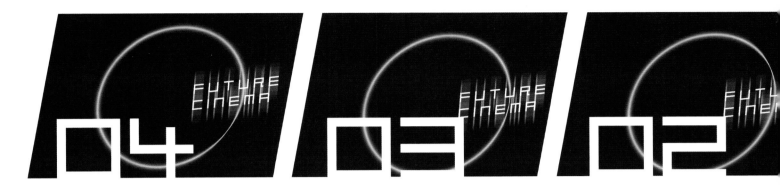

INTERPOLATED

IMMERSIVE

CALCULATED

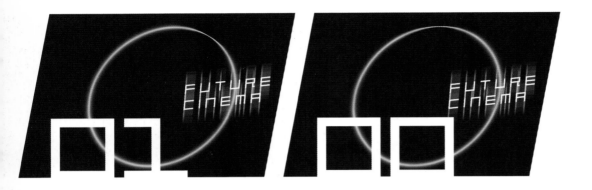

NETWORKED

SCREENLESS

APPENDIX

Jeffrey Shaw
EVE dome
FUTURE CINEMA at the ZKM|
Center for Art and Media
Karlsruhe, 2003
photo © Franz Wamhof

1 A survey of the basic apparatus for the video revolution was given by an exhibition at the Ars Electronica
in Linz (curators Woody and
Steina Vasulka, artist director Peter Weibel) and the
catalog *Eigenwelt der Appa-
ratewelt: Pioneers of Electronic Art*, David Dunn (ed.),
Oberösterreichisches
Landesmuseum Francisco
Carolinum, Ars Electronica,
Linz, 1992.

2 *The Cinematic Apparatus*,
Teresa De Laurentis,
Stephen Heath (eds),
Macmillan, London, 1980.

3 "… you are filming a parole
on a wall, but by filming it
you embed it into a specific
apparatus, constructed for
a certain purpose and having a certain ideological
structure …" – Marcelin
Pleynet, "Economique,
idéologique, formel …," in
Cinéthique, 3, 1969, pp. 10–11.

4 Jean-Louis Baudry, "Effets
idéologiques produits par
l'appareil de base," in
Cinéthique, 7–8, 1970, pp. 1–8.
See also Jean-Louis Baudry,
"Le dispositif. Approches
métaphysiques de l'impression de réalité," in *Communications*, 23, 1975, p. 56.

5 Christian Metz, "Le signifiant imaginaire," in *Communications 23, Psychoanalyse et
Cinéma*, 1975, pp. 3–55;
Christian Metz, "Le film de
fiction et son spectateur," in
*Communications 23, Psycho-
analyse et Cinéma*, 1975,
pp. 108–123.

6 Louis Althusser, "Ideology
and Ideological State
Apparatus," in *Lenin and
Philosophy and other Essays*,
New Left Books, London,
1971, pp. 127 ff.

One aspect of globalization is the development of a worldwide network of technological standards and production, distribution and presentation norms aimed at conquering new markets,
minimizing costs and maximizing profits on a global scale. The image industry is not exempt from
this economic pressure whose many side effects include enormous increased production costs
for movies that can be distributed on a mass global market. Although these production costs
also encouraged investment in new digital technologies, in general the price of globalization is
standardization. With its tendency to optimize existing formulas for success, the image industry
at the same time freezes the process of technological and expressive experiments. Digital media,
on the other hand, are providing an appropriate platform for the evolution of independent, experimental and personal cinema in the digital field. A new class of experts, those individuals formerly called artists, have developed technical competence enabling them to challenge a cinematic homogeneity supported by millions of dollars, and to rival and surpass Hollywood's innovative, narrative and expressive achievements. This book offers evidence of a surprising fact:
Even the technological and ideological apparatus of huge industries can be transformed by
individuals.

The transformation of classical cinema on the basis of apparatus took place in three phases:
The Expanded Cinema movement in the 1960s extended the cinematographic code with the cinematic elements itself, with analogous means. The video revolution in the 1970s with its electromagnetic basis allowed intensive manipulation and artificial construction of the image in a post-
production stage.[1] The digital apparatus of the 1980s and '90s created an explosion of the algorithmic image with completely new features like observer dependency, interactivity, virtuality,
programmed behavior, and so forth. This book focuses on the cinematographic code's expansion
into the digital field and concentrates on the apparatus-oriented approach. This emphasis on
technical innovation does not imply the exclusion of artistic or ideological content. On the contrary, we insist on the technical aspect because artistic and ideological functions of cinema are,
according to the apparatus theory of the 1970s,[2] inscribed in the cinematographic apparatus.
The apparatus (or, to use Foucault's term, "dispositif") is our platform. Each change of the technical apparatus also allows new artistic and ideological options. In 1969, Marcelin Pleynet queried
the ideology produced by the apparatus that determines the cinema.[3] In the 1970s, Jean-Louis
Baudry,[4] Christian Metz[5] and others used the work of Louis Althusser[6] and Jacques Lacan in
order to create an apparatus-oriented theory of cinema that combined psychoanalysis, Marxism
and cinema. The technical apparatus of the cinema is the ideological instrument. There is no neutral technology: "The machine is always social before it is technical."[7] Lacan developed an apparatus theory of the subject and demonstrated that the subject mistakes its true self (*je*) and
constructs instead an imaginary self (*moi*) that is offered from exterior to subject. This imaginary
self is the reflection of an imaginary other. In order to describe this process of the external constitution of the subject through an imaginary signifier,[8] Althusser uses the term "interpellation,"
by which a subject is addressed and positioned. This discursive method to address and position
subjects is ideology. Therefore, the function of ideology is not so much to reproduce social structures or classes as primarily to reproduce subjects who mistake themselves and are therefore
willing to reproduce the values and social order necessary for the survival of capitalism. The
apparatus theory of film shows that the cinema is an ensemble of discursive, material, formal

elements that construct not only a reality, but also a subject. We do not demonstrate a "fetishism of technique."[9] This book is therefore not inspired by "total cinema"[10] in André Bazin's sense of a total representation and mechanical reproduction of reality. The aim is to deconstruct the total apparatus of the cinema, to transform the cinematic apparatus, and create new technologies that allow different psychic mechanisms, that subjugate subjects in the cinema, that allow different relations between spectator and screen, different representations/constructions of reality and subjects, a critical relation to representation. The cinematic imaginary beyond film is the imaginary signifier in the digital field.

The genesis of this exhibition is closely related to the activities of the ZKM | Institute for Visual Media under Jeffrey Shaw's direction. For more than a decade this institute has been at the forefront of artistic, social and technological research into new forms of interactive digital media with an emphasis on the expansion of cinematic codes and techniques. Many of the world's leading digital practitioners have been artists in residence at the institute, and a majority of the installations in the "Future Cinema" exhibition present the groundbreaking works they produced in collaboration with the institute's team of experts. The exhibition also draws on the institute's achievements as an innovator in the field of interactive narrative through a seminal series of CD-ROM and DVD-ROM publications *artintact* and the *ZKM digital arts edition*.

An exhibition of this scope and complexity rests on the skills of the curatorial and engineering teams at ZKM. Led respectively by Sabine Himmelsbach and Martin Haeberle, these teams are specialized in organizing, installing and maintaining the public operation of highly complex works of electronic art in both the permanent ZKM | Media Museum collection as well as in an internationally acclaimed temporary exhibition program that has included "NewFoundLand" (1993), "surroGate" (1998), "video cult/ures" (1999), "net_condition" (1999), "The Anagrammatic Body" (2000), "Olafur Eliasson: Surroundings Surrounded" (2001), "CTRL [SPACE]" (2001) and "Iconoclash" (2002). The success of "Future Cinema" is also very much a result of the inspired cinematic luminosity of Ruth Lorenz' exhibition architecture. The editors have chosen a book design that graphically distinguishes the documented installation environments from the screenshots, which are slightly angled in order to show them as part of a time-based continuum. Furthermore, the artists' pages are illustrated in color, the essays in black and white.

That this catalog can join the series of influential publications produced by ZKM over the years is due to the unfailing patience and dedication of the ZKM editorial team, led by Ulrike Havemann and Dörte Zbikowski. We are also especially grateful to Roger Conover at The MIT Press, and to Tim Druckrey, the director of its Electronic Culture series, for their enthusiastic commitment and contribution to this project since its inception in 2000. Thanks are also due to Heidi Specker and Holger Jost, the graphic designers who responded so creatively to the editors' call for a new way of rendering the transitory, interrelated and heterogeneous nature of the images and writings that constitute this account of the past, present and future of the cinematic imaginary "beyond the frame."

7 Jean-Louis Comolli, "Machines of the Visible", in *The Cinematic Apparatus*, op. cit., p. 122. See also Jean-Louis Comolli, "Technique et idéologie," in *Cahiers du cinema*, nos. 229–231, 233–235, 241, 1971–1972.

8 Lacan's mirror image, the representation of the Other.

9 Christian Metz, "Le signifiant imaginaire," op. cit.

10 André Bazin, "Le mythe du cinéma total," in *Critique*, 1946 (English trans. "The Myth of Total Cinema," in *What is cinema*, vol. 1, Hugh Gray (ed.), University of California Press, Berkeley, 1967, pp. 17–22).

KINEΩ... *kino cine move - ⊙e moved ~ cosmic circle - merry go around* s

Tjebbe van Tijen

A Panorama of Pre-Cinematic Principles

2003
paginated visual scroll

le - mill a myth - ring a dance - pivot pirouette ~ twirl shutter flutter fly ~ keep o

Jeffrey Shaw
Introduction

I.

The history of cinema is a history of technological experiment, of spectator-spectacle relations, and of production, distribution and presentation mechanisms that yoke the cinema to economic, political, social and ideological conditions. Above all, it is a history of creative exploration into the uniquely variegated expressive capabilities of this remarkable contemporary medium. Despite cinema's heritage of technological and creative diversity, it is Hollywood that has come to define its dominant forms of production and distribution, its technological apparatus and narrative forms. But the hegemony of Hollywood's movie-making modalities is increasingly being challenged by the radical new potentialities of the digital media technologies, as evidenced by the rapid rise of the video game, the location-based entertainment industries, and new artistic practices. The new digital modalities for the production and presentation of cinematic content are setting up highly appropriate platforms for the further evolution of the traditions of independent, experimental and expanded cinema. This digital domain is above all distinguished by its broad range of new interaction methodologies. While many traditional forms of expression are also interactive to the extent that they must be interpreted and reconstructed in the process of apprehension, digital interactivity offers a new, immediate dimension of user control and involvement in the creative proceedings. As the growing spectrum of input-output technologies and algorithmic production techniques are applied in the creation of the digitally expanded cinema, this is a means whereby traditional cinema's compulsive spectator-spectacle relationship can be transformed.

The prodigious Chilean filmmaker Raul Ruiz 1 has criticized the compulsive attributes of the central conflict theory in the Hollywood cinema and calls for strategies whereby the autocracy of the director and his subjugating optical apparatus can be shifted towards the notion of a cinema located in the personally discoverable periphery. How exactly to achieve this is one of the challenges "Future Cinema" poses, and the exhibition is predicated on the conviction that a new poetics of narrative is being afforded by the new imaging/representation technologies.

1 See Raul Ruiz,
Poetics of Cinema,
Editions Dis Voir, Paris, 1995.

on turni... ...arve - track play - reel wheel ~ colours blur - dr...

A central research task is the conception and design of narrative techniques that allow the interactive and emergent features of that medium to be fulfillingly embodied. Going beyond the triteness of branching plot options and video-game mazes, one approach is to develop modular structures of narrative content that permit indeterminate yet meaningful numbers of permutations. Another approach involves the algorithmic design of content characterizations that would permit the automatic generation of narrative sequences that the user could modulate, for instance by using a genetic model of selection. And perhaps the consummate venture is the notion of a digitally extended cinema actually inhabited by its audience, who then become agents of, and protagonists in, its narrative development.

Although we are in the midst of this process of cinematic renewal, the curators of this exhibition have set out to identify some focal features of this emergent digitally expanded cinema as evidenced in contemporary media-art practice. These themes have been a core research focus of the ZKM | Institute for Visual Media for many years: the majority of its artists in residence have been working in this field, often making creative use of the new cinematic technologies developed at the ZKM. Given the unique character of the ZKM as an international center of convergence of artistic research, production, and presentation activities, this exhibition provides an appropriate opportunity to present the results of this concurrence of creative forces, as demonstrated by the works of Maurice Benayoun, Jean Michel Bruyère, Peter Cornwell, Dennis Del Favero, Masaki Fujihata, Tom Fürstner, Agnes Hegedüs, Perry Hoberman, Ian Howard, Norman Klein, George Legrady, Bernd Lintermann, Lev Manovich, Margie Medlin, Marnix de Nijs, Susan Norrie, Constanze Ruhm, Bill Seaman, Jeffrey Shaw, Peter Weibel, Christian Ziegler, and many others.

"Future Cinema" is an exhibition of current art practice in the domain of video-, film- and computer-based installations that embody and anticipate new cinematic techniques and modes of expression. The exhibition offers the context for bringing together a large number of highly significant cinematic installation, multimedia and Net-based works produced over the past ten years by both young and established international artists working in this field. At the same

clouds - *mirroring sky - lost in a gaze as boats pass by ~ speed ride - landscape f*

time, the exhibition premiers a large number of new works, some specially commissioned for this exhibition, and many actually produced at the ZKM.

One of the main curatorial emphases is on installations that diverge from the conventional screening formats, and explore more immersive and technologically innovative environments such as multi-screen, panoramic, dome-projection, shared multi-user, and on-line configurations. Another focus is on works that explore creative approaches to the design of non-linear narrative content by means of multiple points of view and/or interactivity. While the exhibition is a window on current artistic practice in the field of digitally expanded cinema, this catalog also sets out to document the historical trajectory of the variegated cinematic experiments that prefigure, inform and contextualize our current cinematic condition.

II.
The following thirteen chapters group the art works and essays under a set of thematic headings as a means of deciphering and interpreting some of the main features of the domains of the digitally expanded cinema. It should be made clear to both the reader of this catalog and the visitor to the show that these thematic clusters are generalized constructs, and many of the works simultaneously address more than one of the thematic arguments. Furthermore, by their very nature and the essential complexity of their formulation, works of art will always transcend (and even contradict) any such attempts at curatorial classification.

The first four chapters – THE CINEMATIC IMAGINARY, SCREENINGS, THEATERS and CODES – offer a general yet idiosyncratic cluster of theoretical statements that set the stage for an understanding of the variegated experiments embodied in the artworks themselves. Given that the exhibition is less concerned with established threads of cinema-theory discourse than with opening up for consideration the broader nature of the cinematic experience as a heterogeneous and renewable modality of artistic expression and public encounter, these writings are intended as frames of reference for the various issues that inform the cinematic research of the exhibiting artists. A further function of these essays is

landscape framed - landscape slides - pan & scope - pull a rope - stir eclipse & blind

to create an appreciation of the radical impact that the increasing shift to digital techniques of production and presentation is having on the nature of the cinematic experience.[2] Such an appreciation is often best achieved by a closer examination of the nature of the traditional, and even obsolete, means of production and presentation that have constituted cinema up to now. In this way we see more clearly the "differences" that the digital is offering, differences that more often than not are just other ways of going about achieving analogous artistic objectives, but with a different set of technical constraints and, consequently, of formal strategies. In the same sense, we can also include certain aspects of literature, painting, music, architecture and theater as "parents" of this undertaking, while the frustrations expressed by filmmakers with traditional cinematic forms expose deficiencies that the digital may, in often unexpected ways, be able to resolve.

REMAPPING shows a group of works that in one way or another make direct use of the actual filmic products of our cinematic heritage, taking these extant materials as the means to generate various forms of critical reflection upon the nature of the cinematic experience. This remapping process can be applied to the original material in various ways, for example by means of formal, temporal and/or spatial reconfigurations of the original data, or through reframings of its narrative and ideological components. While within cinema history (and, more paradigmatically, within music composition) there is an established tradition of referencing and recycling past examples, the artworks in "Future Cinema" offer more radical deconstructions of the original materials so as to place in question their very basic cinematic assumptions, and propose a completely new modality of apprehension.

TRANSCRIPTIVE covers the broad range of current experimentation that is challenging traditional notions of cinematic narrative. One enabler of this move towards more open narrative structures is the fact that in a museum or gallery the cinematic installation can be given temporal and environmental definitions wholly different from those which are obligatory (the norm) in traditional cinema-theater presentation. This opens the way for multiple screenings, multiple layering of narrative and, in the case of interactive works, the creation of navi-

2 The narratives in Ian Breakwell and Paul Hammond's captivating compendium of cinema-going *Seeing In The Dark* (Serpents Tail, London, 1990) focus the fact that the socio-environmental conditions of going to the movies is as much a part of the cinematic experience as the accounts of the films themselves. An understanding that the now ubiquitous cinema theater is merely one of the possible environmental (and ritualized) forms of the cinematic experience allows new cinematic practices to experiment with alternative strategies of manifestation and personal encounter.

dow cast - a phantom mind ~ flip leaves - skim a story - a voice from a picture rol

gable multi-branching narratives. The presence of computing techniques in these works may be more or less evident, ranging from simply the exactly synchronized playback of two or more video streams (from DVD players, for example) to an explicit interactive environment in which the viewer is engaged the manipulation of a programmed set of narrative options.

RECOMBINATORY is an extension of the transcriptive; its practitioners recognize the emergent narrative potentials of an interactively accessible database of audio-visual materials. Whereas transcriptive narratives are concerned with the re-assembly of defined sets of narrative paths (as is the case in most video-game scenarios), recombinatory narratives embrace the idea of an unascertainable complexity of path options, leading to an unforeseeable patterning of narrative conjunctions. At the same time these artworks are not random or chaotic narrative systems; each one has a meta-narrative identity embodied both in its selection of materials and in the underlying algorithms that determine the manifold combinatory permutations. It is here that the unique artistic definition of each work is being articulated.

The interactivity offered in many of the "transcriptive" and "recombinatory" artworks already carries with it the navigation function that viewers engage in when exploring their narrative options (behaviors). The artworks grouped as the NAVIGABLE are those that make the construction of a navigable narrative space their central feature, and in so doing create cinematic formalisms quite distinct from the types of representation we are used to in the cinema. On the most fundamental level, these works challenge the artificial optical properties of the camera lens with its perspectival framing constraints, and instead attempt to constitute an expanded model of representation that is truer to the way we actually apprehend the world. By creating virtual extensions of the image space that the viewer must explore in order to discover its narrative subjects, the navigable artwork allows the interactive viewer to assume the role of both cameraperson and editor, operations that in the traditional cinema are determined beforehand.

...re roll - animated as we scroll & stroll ~ procession cavalcade parade - frozen frie...

INTRODUCTION
Tjebbe van Tijen
Jeffrey Shaw

The varied works identified as **INTERPOLATED** all share an interest in conjoining conditions that are carefully separated in traditional cinema. The familiar boundaries between the factual and fictional, the actual and the virtual, are challenged by these "mixed reality" strategies that create paradoxical audio, visual, spatial and temporal interrelationships resulting in unexpected formations. In some works, these take advantage of the ability of digital methods to transpose one source of information and map this onto another data set. For example, spatial information can be merged with temporal coordinates, creating extended modes of representation different from those provided by traditional techniques that align themselves to the perceptual constraints of the human sensory organs.

IMMERSIVE environments are an important denominator of new-media research and practice. The objective, as in many forms of art, is an experience of physical and imaginative relocation that induces a totality of engagement in the aesthetic and dramatic construct of the work. Even via the smallest screens, there is an immersive condition resulting from our virtual dislocation into inhabited information spaces such as the Internet and cyber-games. The conventional cinematic mode of immersion derives from the darkened enclosure of the Movie Theater, in which it has striven, from Cinerama to Omnimax, to conjure representational equivalence with the real. The exhibited works demonstrate various experiments with new optical and environmental configurations, as well as drawing on techniques of stereoscopy, virtual reality and interactivity in order to achieve new levels of physical and imaginative assimilation of the viewer within the image space. And contrary to cinema's mere enlargement of the screen, these augmentations of the image space are sought after as a means of achieving semantic extensions of the narrative space.

CALCULATED covers the range of works which abandon, to various extents, the use of images captured from the real world and instead offer software-generated formations that may lead to representations that mimic the real world, or may constitute completely synthetic image structures. While the core qualities of these works derive from the algorithmic sophistication of their so-called "software engines," some have a hybrid nature, using real-world data

one will melt & flow while we stand still ~ move - be moved - cine... KINEΩ

Tjebbe van Tijen
*A Panorama of
Pre-Cinematic Principles*
2003
paginated visual scroll
©Tjebbe van Tijen

such as motion tracking or texture mapping to inform the design and/or behavior of their
meta-realisms. And others sidestep the effort of developing custom software by recycling
game-engine code as the platform for creating personal narrative formations.

The arrival of the Internet together with related low- and high-bandwidth telecommunication
technologies has already had enormous impact on the cinematic imaginary. All the specific
qualities of this new **NETWORKED** medium – including its economy of individual production,
its open distributed modalities of consumption, its ideological freedom and idiosyncratic formal
characteristics – has led to the proliferation of what is clearly now one of the main currents
driving future cinema. The technologies of video games and the Internet point to a cinema
of distributed virtual environments that are also social spaces, so that the people present
become protagonists in a set of narrative dislocations. The many catchwords in this field
of development (multi-user, distributed, mobile, ubiquitous, wearable and so on) are the real
technological underpinnings of what will be an increasingly broad range of experimental
cinematic undertakings.

The chapter entitled **SCREENLESS** looks at cinematic options that posit technical and
theoretic strategies of completely new forms of image-generation and image-reception
systems. In one instance, it is the already familiar but so far unrealized promise of holography
given a new twist. Others give tentative form to the again familiar but unrealized fantasy
of direct image generation into and out of the eyes and brain. And theoretically we begin to
conjure for the cinema futures that offer radical new territories of expression and experience
by foreseeing technologies and creation modalities of an order very different from those
currently being exercised.

III.
This brief overview of the exhibition and catalog contents must be followed by a few words
addressing certain areas of contemporary cinema culture whose coverage might appear
to be insufficient. The most obvious area is that of the transformations currently being

undergone by the film industry, with its shift towards digital methods of recording, storing, projection and distribution. One highly visible component is the proliferation of the usually sensational, sometimes subtle, digital effects that are invading our screens to the fascination of mass audiences around the world. This costly development seems to be especially welcomed, allowing as it does the articulation of plot, dialogue and character to be reduced to the most superficial levels required for the transnational commodification of cinema. The current boom in the video-game industry is likewise synergistically linked to this enormous surge in digital-image generation and processing technologies whose current pace of evolution surpasses even Moore's Law.

On these big and small screens the new media industry is exploring its own agenda of the cinematic imaginary. An overriding feature is its narcissistic fascination with the technological momentum that is underlying its own manner of making, namely self-reflexive products that conjure as their subjects the future of the future (and the future of the past). In these films, which are often prescribed (*Minority Report*), sometimes stimulating (*Blade Runner*), and very occasionally sublime (*2001: A Space Odyssey*), the problem usually evident is the fact that the industry is trying to summon a future in which the ideological underpinnings of its own interests remain unchallenged. No matter how fantastic and seductive the images seem, reactionary industrial (and political) paradigms of the cinematic experience remain intact. For that reason, "Future Cinema" has chosen not to locate its discourse in that territory but instead seek out all those fringe and often apparently eccentric individual artistic experiments pointing to a more radical and heterogeneous future for the cinema. That is also why the exhibition is acutely interested in the early history of the cinema. Hinting at a dynamic diversity of potential cinematic futures, the idiosyncratic individual experiments shown were conducted in an era before the industry instituted its narrative axioms and production/presentation techniques as the overriding, exclusive modality of cinematic experience. An internal affinity between current cinematic research and pre-cinematic experiments can also be seen in the work of many contemporary artists who recycle and/or reformulate earlier techniques as a renewable creative strategy.

Another area of synchronicity between pre-cinematic forms and current practice is the rebirth of the "cinema of attractions" in the context of "location-based entertainment" (LBE) centers. Typically, these are theme park and Expo type attractions that range from sophisticated interactive virtual-reality experiences to more prosaic ride films and game-arcade entertainments. DisneyQuest in Orlando, for example, demonstrates the first mass public implementation of VR technologies that were otherwise still at the prototype stage. Like in the case of the cinema, however, we are seeing LBEs become both low and high cultural phenomena, offering a heterogeneity that includes Las Vegas "gauche," Rem Koolhaas' Prada stores, the Guggenheim franchise, or Getty's new LA castle on the hill, as well as the proliferation in museums of new-media attractors signaled by the popular success both of Exploratorium-type "hands-on" exhibits and the aesthetic sophistication of current video-installation practice. The LBE may be also understood as a new urban phenomenon – its "E" offering in most cases Entertainment, in some cases Enlightenment – and as such it is a true child of the cinema as cultural phenomenon.

Frank Gehry's curvaceous excesses are analogous with the frantic twists and turns of the latest rollercoaster architectures. LBEs are also the test beds for some of the most interesting technological extensions of the cinematic experience, offering for example panoramic and 3-D full-dome projection environments as well as experimental kinesthetic, synaesthetic and simulatory experiences of various kinds. Their mass popularity signal the development of new forms of places of urban social activity, again echoing the radical social impact once generated by the arrival of the cinema theater and the ubiquitous social practice of "going to the movies." These large-scale, hi-tech, highly mediated mass social forums are the synergetic counterpart and partner of the parallel smaller-scale media developments in the domestic sphere as well as the micro scale of portable media devices. In the realm of the digital, the essential scalability and networkability of its codes allows the cinematic imaginary to be seamlessly distributed amongst these various forms, opening dizzying perspectives of creative interpolation on all levels and in all places.

As many of the essays make clear, the creative evolutions and transformations of the cinematic imaginary cannot be separated from the nature of the technologies that give it these opportunities. It is therefore completely understandable that throughout cinema history, and especially today, so much effort is dedicated to the creation of new technological resources as a means of enabling new modalities of expression and experience. In many ways this exhibition intends to testify to the cross-disciplinary genius of modern cinematic artists whose works conjoin technological and aesthetic dexterity in an inseparable and interdependent whole.

This interdependence of creative and technological advances causes some difficulties. For most people (including most cultural commentators) the technologies involved are esoteric, often incomprehensible, and the methods of production are hidden from view. This makes it problematic to decipher and describe the specific creative formulations that the artist has made, as distinct from (and in relation to) the formulations embedded in the technologies that have been used. On the other hand, technologies like the Internet and DVD have become so generic and ubiquitous that technological anxiety has pretty much disappeared in some fields of practice. For example, with the arrival of DVD players and digital projectors, all those old frustrations with damaged tapes, unreliable synchronization of multiple players and high maintenance projection have been resolved, so that the easily serviced video installation has at last made a triumphant entry into the mainstream of museums and galleries. In the same manner, the ubiquitous proliferation of networked video-game computers as a household appliance is laying the ground for the imminent arrival of the cinematic imaginary in everyone's home, while the mobile phone is setting a nomadic stage for the acceptance of distributed cinematic experiences.

Cinematic practice is predicated on a co-dependent relationship between the potentialities and constraints of its production/presentation machineries, and the filmmaker's desire to bring about specific embodiments of content. Cinematic practice in the twentieth century was forced to struggle with industrially designed, and highly predetermined, machineries. [3] Vilém Flusser [4] understood that it was therefore necessary to "hold the apparatus and its products in contempt," and that creative freedom "equals playing against the apparatus." This approach underlies the achievements of last century's "experimental" filmmakers. The digital machineries of the twenty-first century, while still very much determined by industrial agendas, are inherently more malleable and more open to reformulation at program level by the cinematographer. The latter can move beyond a strategy of "playing against the apparatus" towards procedures of actually transforming the apparatus, so that it can be made to embody idiosyncratic creative programs right down to the machine level. Raul Ruiz foresaw this new situation when he announced his central conviction that "in the cinema … it is the type of image produced that determines the narrative, not the reverse. No one will miss the implication that the system of film production, invention and realization must be radically modified. It also means that a new kind of cinema, and a new poetics of cinema are still possible." [5] Numerous works in the "Future Cinema" exhibition exemplify an artistic "reformulation" of industrial hardware and software architectures, especially those coming out of the video-game industry.

A full appreciation of any artwork includes an understanding of the extent to which it is a product and reflection of the technologies used in its making. At the same time the history of cultural production also shows us that the aesthetic arguments of an artwork are not necessarily subject to the short-term obsolescence of its manufacturing technology. Some technological developments/mutations themselves maintain the durability of established modes of representation, such as the perspectival congruity between the camera lens and the methods of Renaissance artists. And many current media visualization techniques are the progeny of traditional research into *trompe l'oeil*, anamorphoses, and immersive formations. On the cultural level, the spectacular but in fact often slight changes engendered by new media are clearly anchored in long-term discursive continuities and desires. [6]

"Future Cinema" announces and celebrates the immanent and increasing multiplicity of techniques of representation and intercommunication and the emergent expressive possibilities that derive from their invention and application, as well as the individual and social dynamics of these resulting new forms of experience. In the surmounting of the cinema's traditional constraints and the espousal of new media's new constraints, its practitioners are unearthing a profound and manifold territory of cultural renewal in accordance with Luigi Pirandello's standpoint that it is "compulsory to consider the cinema as an artistic problem endlessly in the process of being resolved, and not to trust ready solutions that in most occasions can only help those who found them and only for a brief span of time." [7]

Jeffrey Shaw

3 Brian Winston in *Technologies of Seeing* (BFI Publishing, London, 1996) exposes the cultural prejudices that informed the chemical composition of Kodachrome II color film. Eastman Kodak's scientists optimized it for a preferred whiteness in the rendering of Caucasian skin tones, resulting in the film's inability to give good black skin tones. Similarly, every computer-graphics software package on the market adopts Renaissance perspective as the axiomatic method of representing the world. Winston points out that this code of representation is largely a Western cultural contrivance, deriving from aesthetic strategies and preferences which he describes as its "addiction to realism."

4 Vilém Flusser, *Towards a Philosophy of Photography*, European Photography, Göttingen, 1984.

5 Raul Ruiz, op. cit., p. 8.

6 "But is there any other canonical way of viewing the future (whether one calls oneself serious in the profane or pataphysical sense of the word) than as a bouquet of Imaginary Solutions – that is, of potentialities?" ("Presentation of the Subcommittee's work in Dossier 17 of the Collège de Pataphysique," in Warren F. Motte Jr., *Oulipo*, Dalkey Archive Press, Illinois, 1998).

7 Luigi Pirandello, "Per il film italiano. Intervista con Pirandello," Testor (ed.), *La Stampa*, 9 December 1932. Quoted in Manuela Gieri, *Contemporary Italian Filmmaking: Strategies of Subversion*, University of Toronto Press, Toronto, 1995.

12

Werner Nekes
Media Magica

1995–1997
film series in 5 parts / 35mm film / color, sound / each film 55 min

Media Magica I – Durchsehekunst [Beyond the Image]
Media Magica II – Bewegte Bilder [Pictures come to Life]
Media Magica III – Vieltausendschau [Multi-Thousand Picture Show]
Media Magica IV – Bild-Raum [The Ambigous Image and Space]
Media Magica V – Wundertrommel [The Magic Drum]

Was geschah wirklich zwischen den Bildern?
[Film before Film]

1984
35mm film / color, sound / 83 min

Werner Nekes is one of the world's most dedicated and omnivorous collectors. He can be as excited by a 1930s trick postcard as by some rare sixteenth-century text, and will compete as relentlessly to secure it. His massive collection is living and changing: one part of it was acquired by the Getty Museum in California; but the gaps were soon filled. Some idea of its riches is conveyed by the series of videos Nekes has produced under the overall title of *Media Magica*.

The four hours and twenty minutes of total running time are less a conventional history of the archeology of moving pictures than a reflection of the individual philosophy that inspires the Nekes collection. He is above all fascinated by images, and all the magic that can be imparted to them by tricks of mechanics, movement or light.

It is a philosophy that is intrinsic to Werner Nekes' background and formation as a graphic artist and experimental film maker. As a film theorist with a special slant on art history, he has taught and lectured in numerous universities and film courses. He has directed more than fifty experimental films, ranging in length from one minute to two hours. Many of them, notably the experimental *Uliisses* (1981) and his earlier work on pre-cinematic devices *Was geschah wirklich zwischen den Bildern* [Film before

Film] (1984), have received international prizes. In 1992, he created a major exhibition on pre-cinema, "Von der Camera Obscura zum Film," in his native German town of Mülheim an der Ruhr, with an accompanying catalog; the following year, he arranged another exhibition on shadows at the Oberhausen Film Festival.

Media Magica records a wealth of pre-cinema artefacts to make the mouth of every collector water, but it goes far beyond the usual range. Nekes is particularly fascinated by images on paper, and the wonderful illusions that, over the centuries, have been produced in them.

The first of the five parts of *Media Magica* is titled "Beyond the Image" and begins by tracing the history of the camera obscura from the sixteenth-century writings of Cesariano and Della Porta, with illustrations of rare texts and actual examples of the camera. Nekes demonstrates how this device – along with the camera lucida, the Lorraine mirror and other helps to artists – played a role in advancing understanding of perspective and hence in the development of the perspective box or peepshow.

Interest in perspective conversely aroused the interest of seventeenth- and eighteenth-century physicists and artists in the distortion of perspective,

left to right

Giuseppe
Memento Mori
c. 1700
upside-down portrait
copperplate engraving
Italy
© Werner Nekes

The Perspective Viewers
engraving
in Abraham Bosse, *Manière
universelle de Mr. Desargues,
pour practiquer la perspective
par petit-pied*, Paris, 1648
© Werner Nekes

*The Human Skin
as an Anamorphosis*
engraving
in Juan Valverde de Hamusco,
*Vivae Imagines partium corporis
humani aereis formis expressae*,
Antwerp, 1566
© Werner Nekes

When viewed at a sharp angle
from below, the face of an old,
bearded man appears as an
optical anamorphosis.

and Nekes displays a rich exhibition of various forms of anamorphic art.

A second part of the video follows the thousand-year history of the shadow theater, with newly filmed sequences of shadow-theater exponents still carrying on their traditional shows in India, Thailand, China, Bali, Egypt, Turkey and Greece. Finally Nekes shows a staggering range of shadow toys from his own collection.

In "Pictures Come to Life" Nekes begins with a history of the magic lantern, culminating in demonstrations of moving slides. Especially thrilling for lantern enthusiasts is to see a water-tank slide and an elbow-polariscope in use, demonstrating spectacular physical, chemical and electrical processes.

In the second half of the video he shows how images printed or drawn on paper have been brought to life by mechanical means, by tricks of light (dioramic or translucent images) or by moving panoramas that imitated stage effects.

"Multi-Thousand Picture Show" develops Nekes' theory on various forms of multiplication and relationships of pictures that demonstrate how "many of the techniques of montage used by both computer and film, for example morphing, have a long visual tradition that reaches back to the sixteenth century." He illustrates his point with early anatomical diagrams, Humphrey Repton's folding montages made to demonstrate architectural and landscape improvements, and a wonderful display of trick books, changing pictures and Victorian erotic playing cards.

Looking forward to the holography of today, the installment "The Ambiguous Image and Space" looks at ways of creating special illusions through trick pictures, perspective theaters, folding peepshows and, from the nineteenth century, the stereoscope.

"The Magic Drum" examines "significant steps in the examination of the after-image and the stroboscopic effect" which are the basis of the modern moving picture. Again, every collector will envy the Nekes hoard of movement toys—thaumatropes, phenakistiscopes, zoetrope, praxinoscopes—along with flick books in ever more sophisticated forms like the mutoscope and the kinora.

David Robinson

First published in *New Magic Lantern*, vol. 8, no. 2, October 1997.

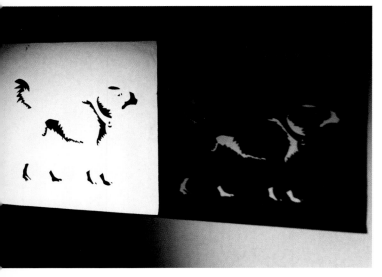

top left
coptography
c. 1800
paper
Holland
© Werner Nekes

When projected, the cut-out
negative motif produces a
positive image on the wall.

top right
hand-shadow game
c. 1900
postcard
France
© Werner Nekes

middle left
*Equestrian.
The Shadow as Caricature*
in Charles H. Bennett,
Shadow and Substance,
London, 1860
© Werner Nekes

One of the first moveable
picture books for children.

middle right
Jouets Séditieux
[Seditious Toys]
c. 1820
wood
France
© Werner Nekes

This lathework seal casts a
shadow resembling George
Washington.

bottom left
Catoptric Edition
c. 1720
twelve cylindrical and twenty-
four conic anamorphoses with
mirrors and wooden case,
attributed to the physical
workshop van Musschenbroek,
signed AvM, hand-colored
copperplate engravings
Leiden
© Werner Nekes

Only one set is known.

bottom right
Johann Michael Burucker
The Angel in Hell
c. 1760
catoptric pyramid anamorphosis
colored copperplate engraving
Nuremberg
© Werner Nekes

The figure of the angel in Hell
appears without the devils in
the pyramid mirror in the center
of the picture.

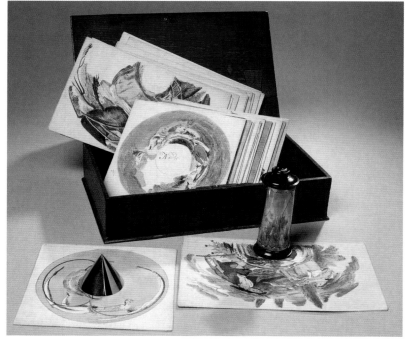

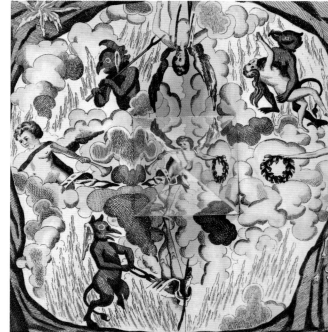

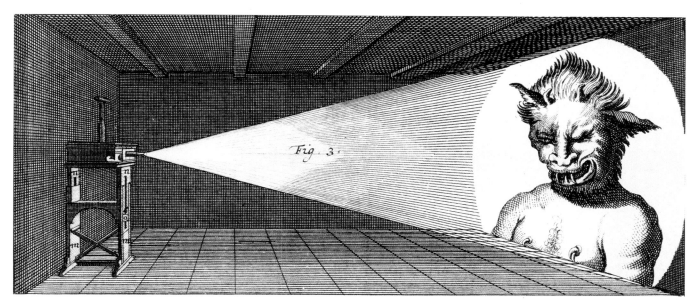

The Projection of the
Lamp of Terror
engraving
in Gulielmo Jacobo
s'Gravesande, *Physices
Elementa Mathematica*,
Geneva, 1748
© Werner Nekes

top
Louis Aubert (manufacturer)
Eiffel Tower
1889
magic lantern
France
© Werner Nekes

right
Diablerie Lanterne Magique
c. 1880
magic lantern
France
© Werner Nekes

The first magic lantern to use a
flexible, rollable film made of
Rhodoïd. Only two examples of
this lantern are known.

A. VAN DYCK

Fac-simile d'un portrait biographique en écriture microscopique, comprenant de 700 à 800 mots.

Anthony Van Dyck
c. 1900
micrography
postcard
France
© Werner Nekes

Un Bon Vivant
c. 1900
composite picture puzzle
postcard
France
© Werner Nekes

LOVELY LULU
THE PHANTOM NUDE

Stare, and concentrate your attention on Lovely Lulu's lips for one minute, then, stare with the same concentration at a plain white surface—the ceiling, for instance.

The Lovely Lulu appears—LIFELIKE!

(Beepee production, Copyright)

Lovely Lulu
c. 1920
afterimage
postcard
© Werner Nekes

If one looks for about a minute at the negative shown and then at a white surface, a positive afterimage appears.

Musical Mechanical Theater in the Cave
engraving
in Salomon de Caus, *Les Raisons des Forces mouvantes avec diverses machines tant utiles que plaisantes aus quelles sont adjoints plusieurs Desseings de Grotes et Fontaines*, Frankfurt, 1615, book I, plate 32
© Werner Nekes

First use of solar energy to produce movement with the help of lenses. The force of the vapor moves the theater's mechanism.

Sand animation
c. 1840
Paris
© Werner Nekes

When the box is turned three times, the running sand puts the figures into seemingly perpetual motion.

The Optic Marvel
c. 1860
illustration of optical toy to
demonstrate color fusion
England
© Werner Nekes

The Optic Marvel
c. 1860
illustration of optical toy to
demonstrate color fusion
England
© Werner Nekes

Around 1860, toys began to be
marketed in Europe as optical
toys that illustrated both the
phenomenon of color-blending
and the way bent wires could
draw shapes in space. With
the Optic Marvel, colored cards
were laid on the lower black
disc, and bent wires were
attached. When air was blown
in, the colored discs and the
wire rotated rapidly, making
the colors combine with one
another and the bent wire
appears as a virtual three-
dimensional stage.

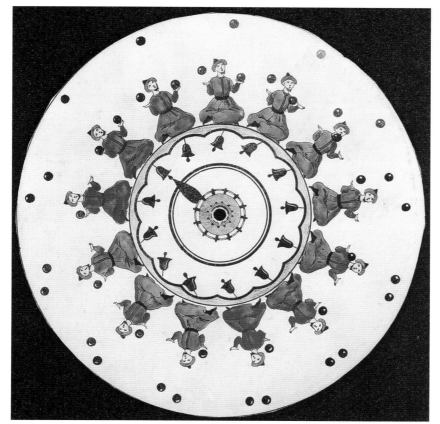

Ackermann (manufacturer)
The Juggler
after 1833
phenakistiscope disc after
Joseph Plateau
London
© Werner Nekes

The Phenakistiscope, also called
a stroboscope or Wheel of Life,
was the first device to show
continual movement in the
same way film does. Viewers see
a picture, then no picture, then
a slightly different second picture, producing in their minds
the illusion of movement. These
are the first animated phases
of movement ever published.

Eadweard James Muybridge
Man with Sulky and Horse
shot 1879
24 separate pictures mounted
on an albumin print
Palo Alto, USA
© Werner Nekes

Serial photographs taken with
24 cameras that were triggered when the sulky drove over
the strings connected with the
shutter release. Only five prints
were made from this subject.

top
Etienne-Jules Marey
Le Sauteur [The Jumper]
before 1890
chronophotograph
Paris
© Werner Nekes

right
The Human Gait as Sculpture
in Wilhelm Braune and Otto
Fischer, *Der Gang des
Menschen*, Leipzig, 1895
© Werner Nekes

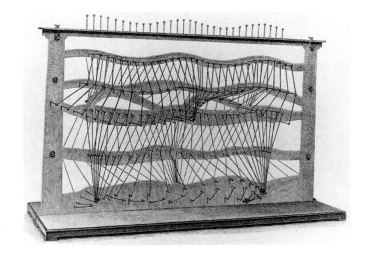

For geometric chronophotography, Marey dressed the walker in black and attached white
patches to the joints, tied on
with white thread. Braune and
Fischer aimed at giving these
results a more exact scientific
basis. They attached Geissler
tubes to the body and made
chronophotographs of the
walking motion. They translated
the photographs into a three-
dimensional sculpture.

Kinora for Two Viewers
c. 1905
England
© Werner Nekes

The film images, copied
onto paper, are flipped
through using a crank.

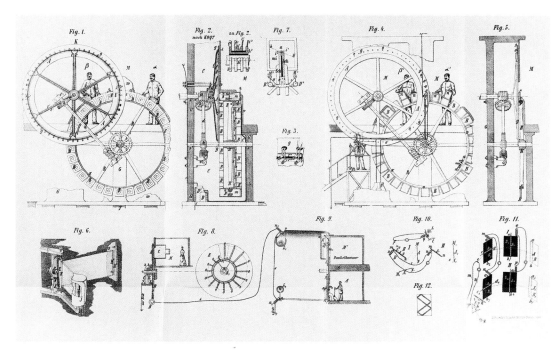

Vision of Television
plan for the technical
realization of television
by Major Benedict Schöffler,
in the k.u.k. Corps-Artillery-
Regiments Luitpold, Prince
Regent of Bavaria, Vienna
and Leipzig, 1898
© Werner Nekes

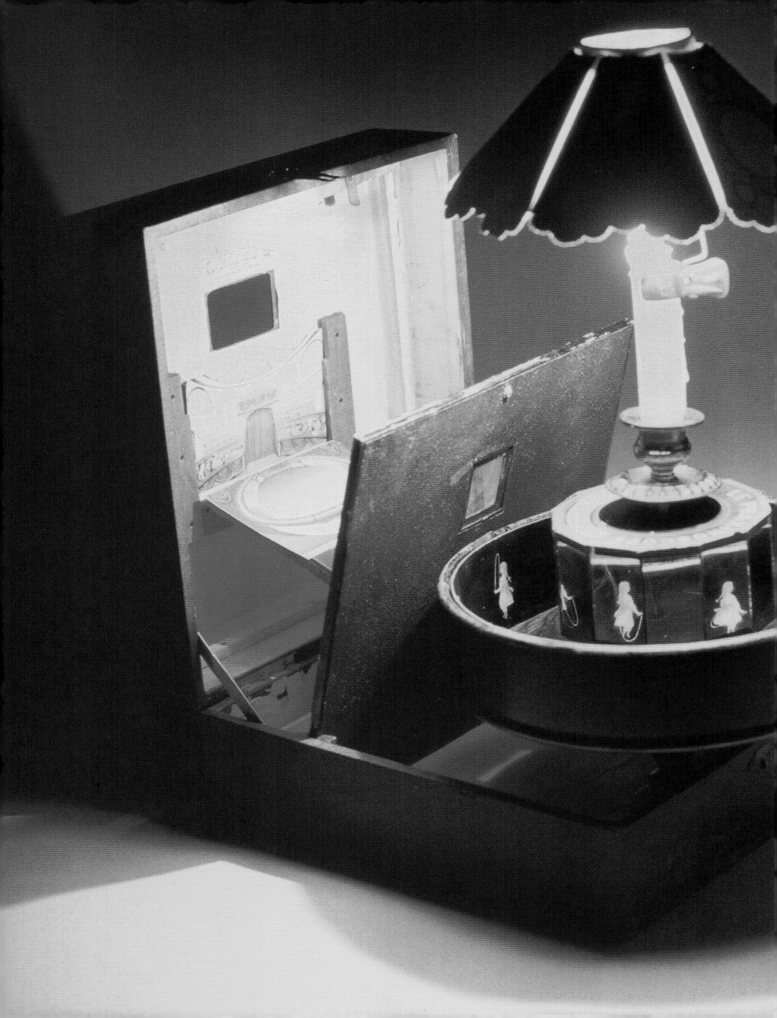

Emile Reynaud
Praxinoscope Theater
1879
Paris
© Werner Nekes

With the Praxinoscope, the illusion of motion is produced by looking in the mirrors, which are set up at an angle to each other. The moment in which the viewer's eye falls on the corner between the mirrors replaces the blank phase between the slots of the zoetrope and gives the viewer a much brighter picture. With the Praxinoscope Theater, one of several interchangeable sets of theater scenery is reflected in addition to the strip with the images, and the picture is viewed through a window set in the lid of the box.

Stefan Themerson
The Urge to Create Visions

[...]

PLATO? PTOLEMY? LUCRETIUS? BACON? PORTA?
HERSCHEL? ROGET? PLATEAU? FARADAY? SELLERS?
HEYL? MUYBRIDGE? ANSCHUTZ? MAREY? DEMENY?
GOODWIN? FRIESE-GREEN? LUMIERE? EDISON? PAUL?
JENKINS? PROSZYNSKI? LUBIMOV? SKLADANOWSKI?
TIMCHENKO? XXXXX?

You would like to know, dear Sir or Madam, who was the chap that invented the cinema?

Well, my dear Sir or Madam, as a matter of fact, it wasn't a chap. It was a girl. A girl from long ago:

"A girl from long ago took a handful of embers and threw them up into the air; and the sparks became stars."

(a Bushman tale)

[…]

The screen of the sky.

The screen was high up, the immense dome standing on the edges of the flat, circular floor of the Earth. It was enough to be willing to look, to be able to see a galaxy of dramas.

It's dawn. Look: Tama-nui-ki-te-Rangi, Great-Man-in-Heaven, plunges his hand into the ocean, pulls out the blazing sun, and hoists it up under the roof of his house. Immediately the screen of the sky is filled with cosmic heroes: here, Maui's lasso catches the ray of the Sun, as it runs over the Haleakala; there, his head grazing the sky, huge Ta-Iwo, whom neither rain nor heat can destroy, marches across the Earth; and now, at dusk, the King of the Fish swallows the glowing Manabozha who's pursuing his father-the Occident.

But the performance is not over yet.

Little by little the diaphragm of the lens stops down, narrows, until, with darkness, the Great-Daughter-of-Night, Hinenui-te-po, manifests herself. Now the screen fills with

| mysterious negatives | lyrical photograms | strange visions of the stars |

Chomette

Themerson

"The Coal Sack" in the Milky Way near the Southern Cross

Do you see up there, beside the Southern Cross, that yawning mouth exhaling darkness? That is "evil incarnate, Emu lying under the tree in wait for the opossum hidden among the branches."

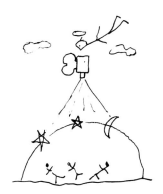

24 hours of continuous screening comes to its end.

Tama-nui-ki-te-Rangi, Great-Man-in-Projection-skyroom, throws on the concave screen the same lights over and over again. But the film is directed by the meek inhabitants of the Earth.

An Eskimo composes the script for a travel film about clouds surrounding the top of a mountain.

It would be absurd to say that Gutenberg built the foundations of poetry. It is equally wrong to think that the art of the cinema was born with Edison or Lumière. Poetry, long before we found a way of preserving it in written or printed characters, was recorded in human memory. Visions, long before we found a way of developing them on cinema film, were recorded in poetry.

Like hairdressers, or dentists, who immobilize their clients in their chairs, our film directors stand over the spectators and warn them: "Don't move! Look straight into the screen! I'll do all the shifting myself." The eyes of the spectator are immobilized. Not so the Eskimo's. His eyes are free to move. They shift in their orbits, follow the movements of his head. He is all by himself the director of his own film. He selects it from the infinity of others, enjoys it, and describes:

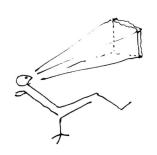

> "The high mountain Koonak there to the south
> I see her
> The high mountain Koonak there to the south
> I look at her
> The light that gleams there to the south
> I admire it.
> On the other side of Koonak
> something is spreading,
> the thing that surrounds Koonak
> from the side of the sea.
> Look how they (clouds) to the south
> sway and change;
> look how they, to the south
> make one another more and more beautiful.
> And he (the summit) enveloped from the side of the sea
> by floating clouds,
> enveloped from the side of the sea –
> and make one another more and more beautiful."

Scripts

Suppose you had found music scores written before the instruments of the orchestra had been invented. Yet that is what happened with film scripts, such as that one.

Loàkal

Cinematograph. Why not: *uedja* for silent shadows, and *loàkal – for sound ones?*

"The Arawacs use the same word for shadow, soul, and picture – *uedja*. The Abipons have only one word: *loàkal* for shadow, soul, echo, and picture."

F. & S. Themerson
The Adventure of a Good Citizen
1937

F. & S. Themerson
Europa
1932

The head in this study of eating
was shown horizontally. To break
the rules you must first have
them.

You can't break rules
unless
you
have
them

Once upon a time, when I was (not for long) a student of architecture, I designed, as an exercise, a cinema with a hemispherical screen. But, even then, I felt in my bones that by doing so one would lose more than one would gain. So long as we are earthbound (Eskimos or not), we need for our bearings the experience of straight vertical lines, and horizontal lines, the distinction between left and right, the notion of symmetry and of up and down.

Within the hemispherical screen, the spectator himself is the frame of reference. The rectangular screen provides an objective frame of reference both for "representational" and for "abstract" pictures.

Thus, the form and proportion of the screen is not something entirely arbitrary. In 1929, the Kodak Scientific Research Laboratory people (Rochester, USA) were trying to find the best proportions for the frame rectangle: which would be suitable for such subjects as landscapes, and which for mass scenes, or portraits. In 1930, Eisenstein "wanted to make the frame limit circular in form, and to change the sides in the course of projection. Rectangles of various proportions introduced into the circle would then completely satisfy the varied compositional needs that arise in the course of successive shots."[1]

Moholy-Nagy in the early 1920s was already full of ideas for large spherical screens and simultaneous projections in a "poly-cinema."[2] But it was Abel Gance who actually combined the free-to-move eye of the Eskimo with the advantages of the rectangular frame, by arranging 3 separate screens for the simultaneous projection of 3 separate scenes in his film *Napoléon*, 1927.

Abel Gance, *Napoléon*, 1927
16mm film, b/w, silent, 220 min, film still
© The Images Film Archive, Inc.; Zoetrope Studios

[…]

1 Vladimir Nilsen, *The cinema as a graphic art. On a theory of representation in the cinema*, Hill and Wang, New York, 1959, n.p.

2 László Moholy-Nagy, *Malerei Fotografie Film*, Langen, Munich, 1927, n.p.

Gargoyle on Notre Dame, Paris

The Middle Ages: Period of the Urge to Create Visions

The period of a great need for visions, and a burning urge to create them, was undoubtedly the Middle Ages. Carved in stone, cut in wood, whole sequences from the Old and New Testaments, fabulous beasts from across the oceans, the sharp focused anatomy of plants chiseled in huge close-ups, and other wonders of nature, formed a popular universal encyclopedia for the masses, just as film today forms a popular universal encyclopedia for the masses.

But it is not in order to show the cinema as a sort of contemporary *Biblia Pauperum* that I turn to the Middle Ages. I do so in order to salute across seven centuries the *doctor mirabilis* Roger Bacon and, three hundred years nearer to us, Giambattista della Porta.

Roger Bacon invented a darkened chamber in which, by means of a pin-hole in its wall, was projected the image of the outside landscape; called it *camera obscura*.

Giambattista della Porta invented an instrument for projecting illuminated and magnified transparencies on to a white screen; called it *laterna magica*.

From then on we can trace two ways of creating visions.

Two Ways of Creating Visions

1. *Camera obscura*: less or more fascinating vision of what a spectacle represents.
2. *Laterna magica*: less or more fascinating vision of an image itself.

Plateau Steals the Sun's Light

Five hundred years after Roger Bacon (1214–1294), two hundred after Giambattista della Porta (1542–1615), came Joseph-Antoine Plateau.

> "At the age of 20, he was imprudent enough to stare at the sun for twenty seconds without closing his eyes. It cost him his sight. He recovered it for a while, and it was then that he invented his famous *Phenakistiscope*, prototype of modern projectors. Later, appointed professor of physics at Geneva, he lost his sight for good at the age of 42, but didn't stop his scientific work. Under his direction, his family carried out experiments. Plateau's apparatus was extremely ingenious. By means of 16 pictures placed on the edge of a cardboard disc and lit from behind by an intermittent light source, he produced the impression of motion."[3]

The myth of a Prometheus possessed by heliotropism and blinded by the sun?

Franciscan Order – Adversary of the Xth Muse

Oh, if only the doctor mirabilis Roger Bacon had been allowed to do what Porta and Plateau did so much later, if the Friars of the Franciscan Order, instead of imprisoning him for dealing in the Black Art and Heresy, if they had themselves begun to draw and paint MOVABLE colored illuminations, the art of creating visions would today (1936) have a tradition and would be a "proper art," such as was imagined by Karol Irzykowski in the year 1913, when writing about the "MOVABLE PAINTING OF THE FUTURE":

> "… we would live to experience emotions more shattering than anything we are at present able to imagine, something of which the fantastic fairy-tale films of today give us but pale samples. Who knows? maybe there would arise a Michelangelo of the kinematograph, who would join together the drama of Humanity and the drama of Nature, and show us e. g. the *Last Judgment* not as a sort of a filmed *Quo Vadis*, this archeology plus tailoring pot-pourri of the novel, but conceived directly in the cinema's own innate material, a mighty cosmic tragedy which would leave the audience the impression of having lived all things …"[4]

[…]

Guillemin, *Forces of Nature*, Camera Obscura

s'Gravesande, Laterna Magica, 1746

Praxinoscope

3 W. Kaemffert

4 Karol Irzykowski, 1873–1944

Quo Vadis? 1911, after Henryk Sienkiewicz, Ambrosio, Italy

Michelangelo Buonarotti, *Giudizio Universale* [The Last Judgement], 1536–1541, fresco, 1080 cm x 1369 cm, Sistine Chapel, Vatican, Rome

Man Ray, *L'Etoile de Mer* [Star of the Sea], 1928,
16mm film, b/w, silent, 15 min, film strip,
© VG Bild-Kunst, Bonn 2003

Dziga Vertov, *Man with a Movie Camera*, 1929,
35mm film, b/w, silent, 75 min, film still,
© Kino Home Video

Len Lye, *Rainbow Dance*, 1936, 35mm film,
Gasparcolorfilm, 5 min, film still

In Praise of Slovenliness 2

Let me again praise slovenliness. A premeditated slovenliness; planned and consciously searched for. Better still: a constructive slovenliness. One which breaks the standard patterns and scrabbles among the tangled entrails of films running through the projector, and discovers the innate truth of this instrument for creating visions. I'm praising the avant-garde of the 1920s and 1930s, as I've praised a meter of scratched film scraps, whose zigzag lightning pulled the screen of the town of P. out of its passivity.

From the technician's point of view, it was slovenliness putting the camera too high or too low or askew on the tripod … but it was consciously developed into a new style of Soviet-Russian cinema, with its grasp of reality from different emotional angles;

it was slovenliness using a short-focus lens for photographing near objects … but in Germany it became a style of expressionist deformation;

it was slovenliness losing focus, underexposing, overexposing, etc … but all these became mediums of expression;

it was slovenliness (in the days of the handle) turning too fast or not fast enough … but it opened to our eyes new worlds of movement, never seen before;

it was slovenliness exposing more than one image on one frame, except for the purpose of ghost-raising … but it gave us simultaneous vision;

it was slovenliness to wobble the loose-fitting lense … but moving a condenser deliberately in front of a still photograph created such an effect that the censor cut out the picture;

for the technician, cutting the negative and joining separate scenes together was *malum necessarium* … but it developed into the art of "montage," "editing," "time-collage," of rhythm;

for him, it was sheer slovenliness scratching the print and dirtying it, as happened in the cinema of P. … but here was the origin of Len Lye's *Colour Box*, which was hand-painted directly on film.

for him, it was a waste of time turning frame by frame, unless for the purpose of cartoons or special "tricks," … but it is how to create movement in the most conscious and controlled way.

Thus, in spite of the intentions of their inventors, whose aim was the perfect reproduction of what their eye saw, the hidden potentialities of the ciné-camera and the projector were uncovered not by following, nor by rejecting, but by breaking the rules.

Jalu Kurek, *OR (Rhythmic Calculations)*, 1933

Jean Cocteau, *Le sang d'un poête* [The Blood of a Poet], 1930, film, b/w, silent, 55 min, film still, © VG Bild-Kunst, Bonn 2003

Oswell Blakeston, *I Do Like to be Beside the Seaside*, 1933

The Luminiferous Eye

Aboriginal mythography, medieval imagery, Joanna-Dorota's reverie, gave way to the new world of vision. The world of the fantasies of Meliès and the realisms of *La Zone*; the expressionisms of *Caligari* and the new realisms of *Changes of Streets*; the sur (?) realisms of René Clair, Jean Vigo, Buñuel, and the lyricism of Cocteau, Germaine Dulac, Blakeston, and Eisenstein's *Sentimental Romance*; the world composed of moving lines of Richter and Eggeling and Szczuka, and of light shapes of Chomette, and of mechanized blacks, grays & whites of Moholy-Nagy; the world of "pure" rhythms constructed from *non* pure realistic rushes, like Leger's mechanical ballet or Jalu Kurek's rhythmical calculations *(O.R.)*; the visions of the spirit of our age in Ruttmann's *Symphony of the Great City*, and of the ideas of our age in Bartosch's *L'idée*, and of the beauty of the world of Nature in Painlevé's *Hippocampus*, and of the beauty of the world of artefacts in Ivens's *Glassworks* …

Berthold Bartosch, *L'Idée* [The Idea], 1934

In their search for visions, some went the way of the *camera obscura*, some went the way of the *laterna magica*, – and the synthesis of both + the main element of this Changing World: motion. Nature gave us vocal cords but neglected to give us a light-producing organ. We had to build it ourselves: the projective luminiferous eye.

Yes, but …

"Yes, but what is it, actually, this new 'eye,' this apparatus for producing visions, this 'projector?' Where is it, where does it begin and where does it end in the complicated process of making a film?"

"Well, my dear sir or madam, what I'm talking about is much more than the piece of machinery in the projection room of a cinema. If Berkeley were alive today, and said that the reality seen on the screen is the idea in the mind of the film-maker, these words would define where our organ of lumination ends and where it has its beginning."

Jean Painlevé, *Hippocampe* [Seahorse], 1934

***

To sing images, like a luminous fish does in the dark depths of the ocean, not with a reflected but with one's own light.5

The Golden Calf of the Silver Screen

The film industry didn't like it. Oh, yes, its officiants would pinch here and there some avant-garde "gimmicks," "tricks," "knacks," and use them for their own "special effects" purposes, but they didn't like it. They had already succeeded in teaching people to accept the Hollywood (plus Hays Office) standards as an undisputed, sovereign, self-existent, absolute god, or – let's say – Golden Calf of the Cinema, they wouldn't like the worshippers to see any mad visions and have their acquired taste spoiled. […]

But let's go back to the silent avant-garde …

"The growth of the art of cinema can be compared with the growth of a plant buried under stones. The stones are Industry and Commerce which impose their own ways and means upon it. Cinema, to be born again, must withdraw for a moment into solitude, silence, into the very souls of those individuals who really do need it in order to express themselves, – Cinema must be given a breath of fresh air – become disinterested."6

The Trade was not alone in hating that sort of things. Consumers, including my dear Sir or Madam, hated it too.

Was it you, my dear Sir or Madam, who threw a bottle of ink at the screen of this Paris cinema showing Buñuel's *Le Chien Andalou*?

"No, but I understand why the person who did it did it."

Do you?

"Yes, I do. Because that's precisely what I felt like doing myself. And not only at Buñuel's film. At all the others you talk so glibly about, too. All those lights and lines and angles and rhythms … I'm fed up with all that."

Why?

"Because I'm fed up with things unreal."

And you want to be shown something real?

"Correct."

Meaning what?

"Well, real is real. Isn't it?"

Is it?

Is it?

[…]

6   Karol Irzykowski,
    Xth Muse, 1924.

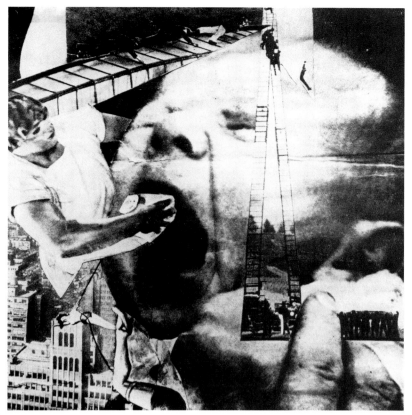

Stefan Themerson, photo-collage (a study for *Europa*), c. 1931, Warsaw

*

" … I do feel that one cannot make a distinction between content and form when actually making a film. For example, I can well imagine making an abstract film out of realistic rushes, and making a narrative film out of abstract elements. And I don't think now is the time to decide the content-or-form problem one way or another. Because the point is not whether we should stand here or there, the point is that we should move at last into an altogether different sphere. On to Parnassus? Why not? A fortnight's holiday on Parnassus, give us O Lord."7

*

A new avant-garde will come. And I know what I'd like them to do. I'd like them to do what I would like to see. And I would like to see some clear, rational, commonsense, visual statements. But what they should do is not what I want to see. What they should do is what their own URGE TO CREATE VISIONS will compel them to do.

[…]

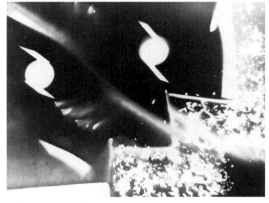

Stefan Themerson, photogram, 1928–1929

All images and text first published in Stefan Themerson, *The Urge to Create Visions. Essay on Film*, Gaberbocchus + De Harmonie, Amsterdam, 1983. For more information on the Themersons, their titles and ordering information see: http://www.gaberbocchus.nl

7 Interview with Stefan
   Themerson, from:
   Kurier Polski, Warsaw,
   10 September 1933.

William C. Wees
The Camera-Eye: Dialectics of a Metaphor

1 Gilette in Sidney Peterson's *Mr. Frenhofer and the Minotaur* (1949).

2 Quoted in David Douglas Duncan, "Prismatics: Photo-Data," *Prismatics: Exploring a New World,* Harper & Row, New York, 1972, n. p.

3 Dziga Vertov, "We. Variant of a Manifesto," in *Kino-Eye. The Writings of Dziga Vertov,* Annette Michelson (ed.), University of California Press, Berkeley and Los Angeles, 1984, p. 8. (Vertov's essay originally published in 1922)

4 Renato Poggioli, *The Theory of the Avant-Garde,* Harper & Row, Icon Editions, New York, 1971, p. 201.

5 Germaine Dulac, "The Aesthetics. The Obstacles. Integral Cinegraphie," in *Framework,* vol. 19, 1982, pp. 7, 9. (Dulac's essay originally published in 1927)

6 Jean Epstein, quoted in Ian Christie, "French Avant-Garde Film in the Twenties," in *Film as Film,* Arts Council of Great Britain, London, 1979, p. 38.

7 Jean Epstein, "Bonjour Cinema," in *Afterimage,* vol. 10, London, 1981, p. 13. (Epstein's essay originally published in 1921)

8 Louis Delluc, quoted in Stuart Liebman, "French Film Theory, 1910–1921," in *Quarterly Review of Film Studies,* vol. 4, no. 1, Winter 1983, p. 12.

9 Germaine Dulac, "The Essence of the Cinema: The Visual Idea," in *The Avant-Garde Film: A Reader of Theory and Criticism,* P. Adams Sitney (ed.), New York University Press, New York, 1978, p. 39. (Dulac's essay originally published in 1925)

10 Louis Aragon, "Du Décor," quoted in Liebman, op. cit., p. 6. (Aragon's essay originally published in 1925)

11 Louis Delluc, quoted in Jacques Brunis, "The Experimental Film in France," in *Experiment in Film,* Roger Manvell (ed.), Grey Walls Press, London, 1949, p. 70.

12 Jonas Mekas, [Interview], *Parachute,* no. 10, 1978, p. 24.

13 Stan Brakhage, lecture at McGill University, November 1970.

14 Ernie Gehr, "Program Notes for a Screening at the Museum of Modern Art," January 1971; revised December 1977, in Sitney, op. cit., p. 247.

15 Michael Snow, "An Interview," in *Form and Structure in Recent Film,* Vancouver Art Gallery, Vancouver, 1972, n. p.

"It's an obsession, really, of the eye.
He'd sell his own mother for a look."1

"Long ago, I pointed to the lens
and said the trouble was here!"2

"Everybody who cares for his art, seeks the essence of his own technique," said Dziga Vertov.3 This characteristically modernist "mystique of purity," as Renato Poggioli has called it, pervades the avant-garde tradition and produces the desire "to reduce every work to the intimate laws of its own expressive essence or to the given absolutes of its own genre or means."4 A typical exponent of the essentialist position was Germaine Dulac, who wrote in 1927, "Painting … can create emotion solely through the power of color, sculpture through ordinary volume, architecture through the play of proportions and lines, music through the combination of sounds." Thus, Dulac argued, it is imperative for film artists "to divest cinema of all elements not particular to it, to seek its true essence in the consciousness of movement and of visual rhythms."5

Probably the best known among the early candidates for cinema's "true essence" was Louis Delluc's *photogénie.* Jean Epstein declared, "With the notion of *photogénie* was born the idea of cinema art."6 But Epstein also admitted, "One runs into a brick wall trying to define it."7 The best description Delluc could come up with was, "[A]ll shots and shadows move, are decomposed, or are reconstructed according to the necessities of a powerful orchestration. It is the most perfect example of the equilibrium of photographic elements."8

The concept of *photogénie* simply did not get to the heart of the matter. It directed attention to the image – "the equilibrium of photographic elements" – but not to the properties or "elements" of the image itself. Not, in other words, to the "true essence" of cinema. Other avant-garde filmmakers and critics looked deeper and found cinema's basic principles in three interrelated elements: light, movement, and time.

"For cinema, which is moving, changing, interrelated light, nothing but light, genuine and restless light can be its true setting," said Germaine Dulac.9 Louis Aragon called cinema "the art of movement and light."10 And even the leading proponent of *photogénie,* Louis Delluc, wrote, "Light, above everything else, is the question at issue."11 Coming closer to the present, we find Jonas Mekas declaring, "Our real material had to do with light, color, movement."12 Stan Brakhage has called light "the primary medium" of film. "What movie is at basis is the movement of light," he has said. "As an art form really, the basis is the movement of light."13 For Ernie Gehr, "Film is a variable intensity of light, an internal balance of time, a movement within a given space."14 According to Michael Snow, "Shaping light and shaping time … [are] what you do when you make a film."15 For Peter Kubelka, "Cinema is the quick projection of light impulses."16

Although Kubelka, among others, has insisted that movement is merely an illusion produced by the "quick projection of light impulses," some filmmakers regard movement as, in the words of Slavko Vorkapich, "the fundamental principle of the cinema art: [cinema's] language must be, first of all, a language of motions."17 In a manifesto in 1922, Dziga Vertov called for "the precise study of movement," and added, "Film work is the art of organizing the necessary movements of objects in space." For Vertov, the recording of moving objects was less important than "organizing" their movement and if necessary "inventing movement of objects in space" through frame-to-frame and shot-to-shot relationships.18 These relationships – or "intervals" in Vertov's terminology – are temporal as well as spatial. They are the basis of what Snow calls "shaping time." As Maya Deren has put it, "The motion picture, though composed of spatial images, is primarily a time form."19

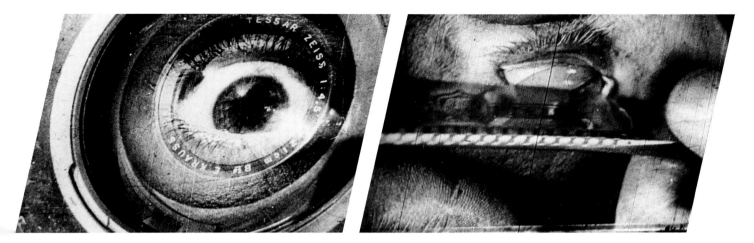

Dziga Vertov
Man with a Movie Camera
1929
35mm film
b/w, silent
75 min
film still
© Kino Home Video

The eye and lens superimposed.

Luis Buñuel, Salvador Dali
Un Chien Andalou
[An Andalusian Dog]
1928
16mm film
b/w, silent
17 min
film still
© Argos Films,
British Film Institute

A razor slices the eye.

"Light, color, movement," "the movement of light," "the quick projection of light impulses," "light and time," "a time form" – such phrases reflect the specific interests of individual filmmakers but taken together they specify film's "true essence" in terms appropriate to the avantgarde's "mystique of purity": "light-space-time continuity in the synthesis of motion," in Moholy-Nagy's neat formulation.20 What is most significant for our present purposes is that the same terms can be applied to visual perception. The basic requirements for seeing are also light, movement, and time. As one researcher has put it, "The eye is basically an instrument for analyzing changes in light flux over time."21 That succinct statement delineates a common ground for vision and film, and it points the direction I will take in seeking a perceptual basis for the visual aesthetics of avant-garde film.

When we look at the world around us, we do not, as a rule, see "changes in light flux over time." We see solid objects moving and standing still in a well-defined three-dimensional space (at least, that is what we see in the most focused, central area of our vision). Nothing would be visible, however, were it not for the "light flux" entering our eyes through the pupil and flowing over the photosensitive cells lining the back of our eyeballs. Experiments have shown that when the retinal cells receive a steady, unchanging light, when the stimulus is absolutely fixed and unvarying, the cells quickly "tire." They stop sending the information our brain needs to construct the visual world we see lying in front of our eyes.22 Thus there has to be a "flux," a movement of light over the retinal cells; otherwise, we see nothing at all. (If the sources of light do not move, the eye's own movements will keep the light moving across the cells.) "All eyes are primarily detectors of motion," R. L. Gregory points

out, and the motion they detect is of light moving on the retina.23 Only by these changing patterns of illumination can the world outside our eyes communicate with the visual processes of the brain. From that communication emerges our visual world.

Since light moving in time is the common ground of vision and film, perhaps it was inevitable that avant-garde filmmakers seeking the "true essence" of their medium would hit upon the "essence" of vision as well. Avant-garde filmmakers, especially the filmmakers of the 1920s, did not necessarily make a conscious effort to equate the basic elements of cinema with the basic processes of visual perception. Whether they did so or not, their work has been influenced by an implicit equation between cinema and seeing that this chapter is devoted to making explicit.

The superimposed eye in the camera lens in Vertov's *Man with a Movie Camera* (1929) and Man Ray's *Emak Bakia* (1926) is in fact an explicit depiction of that implicit equation. Less explicit references to the relationship of film and vision occur in many other images of eyes created by avant-garde filmmakers. What Steven Kovaks has called "the leitmotif of the eye" in *Emak Bakia* can be traced throughout the history of avant-garde film.24 To mention a few examples: the infamous sliced eyeball in *Un Chien andalou* (1928), the photograph of an eye operation in Paul Sharits' *T.O.U.C.H.I.N.G* (1968), the close-ups of Kiki's eyes in Leger's *Ballet mecanique* (1924), the oriental eye at the keyhole in Cocteau's *Blood of a Poet* (1930), the artist's escaped eyeball in Sidney Peterson's *The Cage* (1947), the Eye of Horus in Kenneth Anger's *Inauguration of the Pleasure Dome* (1954, revised 1966 and 1978) and *Invocation of My Demon Brother* (1969), and the "cosmic eye" created by swirling clouds of color in several of Jordan Belson's films. To end this potentially endless parade of avant-garde eyes are two

16 Peter Kubelka, "The Theory of Metrical Film," in Sitney, op. cit., p. 140.

17 Slavko Vorkapich, "Motion and the Art of Cinematography," in *Film Culture*, no. 40, 1966, p. 78. (Vorkapich's essay originally published in 1926)

18 Vertov, op. cit., pp. 8-9.

19 Maya Deren, "Cinematography: The Creative Use of Reality," in Sitney, op. cit., p. 69. (Deren's essay originally published in 1960)

20 László Moholy-Nagy, *Painting, Photography, Film*, The MIT Press, Cambridge, MA, 1969, p. 21. (Originally published in 1925)

21 Gunnar Johansson, "Visual Motion Perception," in *Scientific American*, vol. 232, no. 6, 1975, p. 76.

22 Alfred L. Yarbus, *Eye Movements and Vision*, Plenum Press, New York, 1967, passim.

23 Richard L. Gregory, *Eye and Brain: The Psychology of Seeing*, second edition, McGraw-Hill, World University Library, New York, 1973, p. 92.

24 Steven Kovacs, "Man Ray as Filmmaker," in *Artforum*, no. 11, November 1972, p. 79.

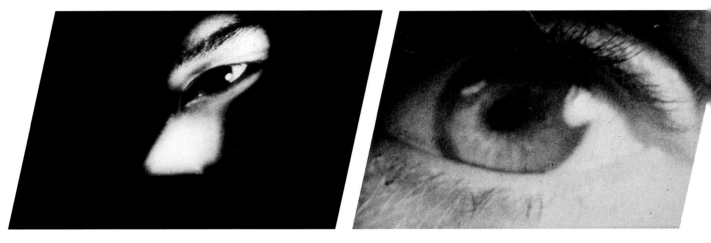

Jean Cocteau
Le Sang d'un Poête
[The Blood of a Poet]
1930
35mm film
b/w, silent
55 min
film still
© VG Bild-Kunst, Bonn 2003

The eye at the keyhole.

Willard Maas
Geography of the Body
1943
16mm film
b/w, sound
7 min
film still

The magnified eye.

especially pertinent examples: the extreme close-up of an eye at the beginning and end of Willard Maas's *Geography of the Body* (1943) and an eye superimposed over a reclining woman near the end of Brakhage's *Song I* (c. 1964).

   The eye in *Geography of the Body* alludes directly to the extremely close and (literally) magnified seeing that is the principal concern of that film – not the voyeur's secret sexual gratification but the explorer's fascination with the human body as terrain seen for the first time.[25] Brakhage's *Song I* also alludes to visual exploring, or what Brakhage would call the "adventure of perception," which should prompt all filmmaking. The eye in that film, which Guy Davenport has called "an overply, the flesh window," is seen in the world it sees, as it sees the world.[26] The Brakhagean eye is a participant-observer (perhaps the anthropologist rather than the explorer is the appropriate analogue). It refers specifically to the inseparability of seeing and filmmaking – as do Vertov's and Man Ray's images of the eye in the camera lens. As I pointed out in the Introduction, there are significant differences between Brakhage's emphasis on "the flesh window," of the human eye, and Vertov's and Man Ray's emphasis on the "mechanical eye" of the camera. But both make direct reference to the metaphor of the camera-eye and more indirectly to film as (in James Broughton's phrase) "a way of seeing what can be looked at."[27]

   To show that film is "a way of seeing," that it resembles visual perception in basic and specific ways, I will reexamine the metaphor of the camera-eye. Visualized directly through the superimposition of eye and camera lens, alluded to indirectly in many other variations on "the leitmotif of the eye," it is a

metaphor so intrinsic to the visual aesthetics of avant-garde film that despite (or perhaps because of) its familiarity, it requires close, careful explication.

   The metaphor of the camera-eye is constructed of synecdoches. That is to say, the eye and the camera are parts standing for the whole of their respective visual apparatuses. Vision is no more a product of the eye alone than pictures (especially the "moving pictures" of cinema) are made by the camera alone. In each case, what we see is the result of complex processes that only begin in the eye and the camera. No doubt it is because they house the beginnings of their respective ways of seeing that the eye and the camera have acquired their synecdochic weight. They are the outermost extensions of visual systems whose other structures and functions are hidden inside the skull and inside film labs, editing rooms, and projection booths. Even the crucial light-receptors of each system (the retina and the film) are hidden from view. An analysis of the camera-eye metaphor may properly begin with the eye and the camera per se, but if it is to demonstrate the metaphor's relevance to the visual aesthetics of avant-garde film, it must go on to seek other, less apparent correspondences between the two visual systems.

   The classic essay on the subject is George Wald's "Eye and Camera," published in *Scientific American* in 1950. Wald first asserts, "Today every schoolboy knows that the eye is like a camera," and summarizes these likenesses as follows:

   "In both instruments a lens projects an inverted image of the surroundings upon a light-sensitive surface: the film in the camera and the retina in the eye. In both the opening of the lens is regu-

25 Cf. Parker Tyler, "Willard Maas," in *Film Culture*, no. 20, 1959, pp. 53–54: "The film makers learned – with the thrill of discovering new land – that the anatomic parts, thus photographed, held mixed as well as ambiguous identities."

26 Guy Davenport, "Two Essays on Brakhage and His Songs," in *Film Culture*, no. 40, 1966, p. 10.

27 James Broughton, "Film as a Way of Seeing," in *Film Culture*, no. 29, 1963, p. 19.

lated by an iris. In both the inside of the chamber is lined with a coating of black material which absorbs stray light that would otherwise be reflected back and forth and obscure the image."[28] Wald goes on to point out similarities in the light-sensitivity of the film and the retina. Just as a fine-grained, "slow" film is designed for high intensities of light and a more coarsely grained, "fast" film for low intensities of light, so the retina has two kinds of receptor cells: the cones, which operate in bright light and provide the more sharply defined details of our visual world, and the rods, which work at lower light levels and are the source of the coarser, less sharply defined details in the peripheries of our visual world.

Moreover, the cones and rods are on the ends of minute stalks that respond to the light's intensity, so that when the light is dim, the rods are pulled forward and the cones pushed back; when the light is bright the cones move forward and the rods draw back. As Wald says, "One could scarcely imagine a closer approach to the change from fast to slow film in a camera." In subsequent layers of the retina, according to more recent research by Frank S. Werblin, the bipolar cells emphasize high contrast in the retinal image, while the amacrine and ganglion cells moderate contrasts. "It is as if," Werblin writes, "a camera system could switch automatically from a high-contrast film to a low-contrast film when it encountered a rapidly changing or a very contrasty scene."[29]

For Wald, the retina and photographic film offer another kind of analogy, because of their chemical response to light. The rods contain a pigment, rhodopsin, that bleaches in the light and is resynthesized in the dark. This led the nineteenth-century physiologist Willy Kuhne to devise an experiment in which he was able to take a picture with the living eye of a rabbit. First, the rabbit's head was covered to allow rhodopsin to accumulate in the rods. Then it was uncovered and held so that it faced a barred window. After a three-minute "exposure," the animal was killed, its eye removed, and the rear half containing the retina "fixed" in an alum solution, so that the bleached rhodopsin could not be resynthesized. "The next day," Wald reports, "Kuhne saw, printed upon the retina in bleached and unaltered rhodopsin, a picture of the window with a clear pattern of its bars."

Wald's own variation on this experiment was to extract rhodopsin from cattle retinas, mix it with gelatin on celluloid, expose it to a pattern of black and white stripes, then "develop" it in darkness with

hydroxylamine. The result was a "rhodopsin photograph" showing the same black and white pattern. Thus, just as exposure to the light produces a "latent image" in a film's emulsion, so, Wald argues, "light produces an almost invisible result [on the retina], a latent image, and this indeed is probably the process upon which retinal excitation depends. The visible loss of rhodopsin's color, its bleaching, is the result of subsequent dark reactions, of 'development'." It is now known that the cones also contain rhodopsin-like pigments that make color vision possible, which leads John Frisby to write, "So really the rods and cones are two distinct light-sensitive systems packaged together into a single 'camera' – the eye."[30]

If the vertical bands of light and dark gray make one think of the barred window that left its lasting impression on the retina of Kuhne's rabbit, it is an appropriate – if somewhat ironic – association, so long as one remembers that neither image duplicates actual vision. They are simply chemical traces of rhodopsin's response to the "light flux" that reaches the retina from the outside world; they are images of "the process upon which retinal excitation depends," as Wald put it. Nevertheless, Wald's and Kuhne's experiments show the eye to be more like a camera, and seeing more like photography, than is often recognized. They strengthen the metaphor of the camera-eye by grounding it in processes that can be scientifically verified. In Wald's words, "The more we have come to know about the mechanism of vision, the more pointed and fruitful has become its comparison with photography."

As convincing as that may sound, it is not a view all scientists of vision share. In Handbook of Perception R. M. Boynton offers a pointed and thorough rebuttal: "The eye most emphatically does not work just like a camera, and the differences are worth discussing. The eye is a living organ, while the camera is not. In a camera, light passes through the image-forming optics of high refractive index, and then back again into air before striking the film plane. In the eye, high-index media are encountered as light enters the eye at the outer surface of the cornea, but the light never again returns to air. The control of pupil size begins with the action of light upon the identical photoreceptors that initiate the act of vision, while the camera's photoelectric analog, when there is one, is located so that the light falling upon the photocell is not affected by the size of the opening in the iris diaphragm. The lens

28 George Wald, "Eye and Camera," in Scientific American Offprints, no. 46, 1950, p. 2. All subsequent citations of Wald are to this source.

29 Frank S. Werblin, "The Control of Sensitivity in the Retina," in Scientific American Offprints, no. 1264, 1973, p. 11.

30 John P. Frisby, Seeing, Illusion, Brain, and Mind, Oxford University Press, New York, 1980, p. 132.

surfaces in most cameras are sections of spheres, to which an optical analysis developed for spherical components can properly be applied. There is no spherical surface anywhere in the eye. The camera lens is homogeneous in its refractive index (or at most contains a few such distinct elements, each of which has this property). The lens of the eye is layered like an onion, with the refractive index of each layer differing slightly from the next. Cameras have shutters and utilize discrete exposures, either singly or in succession. The pupil of the eye is continuously open. Cameras must be aimed by someone; the eye is part of a grand scheme which does its own aiming. Images produced by photographic cameras must first be processed and then viewed or otherwise analyzed; the image produced upon the retina is never again restored to optical form, and the mechanisms responsible for its processing are perhaps a billionfold more complex than those used in photography."[31]

The list of differences "could be expanded," as Boynton says, but it is surely long enough to discourage anyone from turning to literal-minded scientists for validation of the camera-eye metaphor.

The fact that the eye does not work "just like a camera" is indisputable, but it is also irrelevant, since the significant similarities between the two are metaphorical, not literal. Boynton's effort to discredit the camera-eye metaphor is useful, however, for several reasons. First, it specifies the basic difference underlying the likenesses implied by the metaphor. The difference is between a machine and, in Boynton's words, "a living organ" – between Vertov's "mechanical eye and Brakhage's "flesh window." It is the basis of the dialectical relationship of eye and camera, from which the visual aesthetics of avant-garde film have emerged.

Second, Boynton repeats a common objection to equating the camera and the eye when he emphasizes the difference between the photographic image and the retinal image. It is true that the retinal image is "never again restored to optical form" and is nothing more than a stimulus for retinal cells at one of the earliest stages in the total visual process. What must be stressed, however, is that the production of an optical image in the camera and in the eye, though essential to both visual processes, is not in itself the basis of their most significant resemblances. Light moving in time – not images – is the "essence" they share.

A third point arises from Boynton's critique of the camera-eye metaphor. Like virtually all commentators on the camera and the eye, Boynton implies that the photographic image is the visible equivalent of the image cast by the lens on the film plane of the camera. In still photography this is more or less true (allowing for the inevitable differences created by the chemistry of processing and printing photographs), but in cinema, it is not. What the film viewer sees are not images on film but images projected on a screen. These images are created by light moving in time, and therefore they much more closely approximate the sources of seeing than do the images fixed in the emulsion of photographic film.

Cinematic images partake of the same "optical flow" described by Gunnar Johansson:

"The optical flow of images into the viewfinder of a camera (or into the camera itself when the lens is open) corresponds to the optical flow impinging on the retina during locomotion."[32]

In fact, since the eyes are always in motion, the image falling on the retina is always flowing over the retinal cells. Of course, cinematic images can not reproduce the same "optical flow" that entered the camera. There are too many intervening steps to permit the original "optical flow" to emerge from the projector unchanged (not to mention the fact that cinematic images may be made without the use of a camera at all). They can, however, represent the same kind of "flow" that impinges on the retina, the only difference being that their "flow" is shaped by the filmmaker through the materials and processes of the cinematic apparatus. Thus the camera-eye metaphor continues to be valid, if one takes into account the actual nature of the film image and conditions of film viewing.

A fourth point is suggested by Boynton's sentence "Cameras must be aimed by someone; the eye is part of a grand scheme which does its own aiming." The camera-eye metaphor should remind us that the camera, too, is "part of a grand scheme" that controls the way it is "aimed" at the world. Whether the camera is held in the hands of Stan Brakhage and "aimed" by Brakhage's intuitive response to his feelings and immediate environment, or attached to a motorcycle's handlebars and "aimed" by Vertov's cameraman as he steers around an inclined track, or perched atop Michael Snow's elegant remote-controlled machine and "aimed" at the Quebec landscape by electronic impulses scripted by Snow – the camera is integrated

31 Robert M. Boynton, "The Visual System: Environmental Information," in Handbook of Perception, vol. 1, Edward C. Carterette and Morton P. Friedman (eds), Academic Press, New York, 1974, p. 290.

32 Johansson, op. cit., p. 76.

Sidney Peterson
The Cage
1947
16mm film
b/w, silent
28 min
film still

The escaped eyeball of
an artist caught in a mop.

Kenneth Anger
*Invocation of
My Demon Brother*
1969
16mm film
color, sound
11 min
film still

The egyptian eye of Horus
superimposed on a human eye.

in "a grand scheme which does its own aiming."
Metaphorically, it is like the eye in its own "grand
scheme" of muscles, tissues, nerves, and brain cells.
Here, in fact, is another way of comparing the eye and
the camera as synecdoches representing a whole —
the "grand scheme" — of which each is a particularly
conspicuous but totally integrated part.

Despite the objections raised by Boynton, then,
the camera-eye metaphor not only continues to make
sense but gains strength and pertinence as it is given
closer scrutiny — so long as (1) it is understood to be a
metaphorical juxtaposition, not a literal equivalence,
producing a dialectical relationship of mechanical and
organic structures and functions; (2) its implied similarities between the retinal image and the photographic image are recognized to be less relevant than its
allusion to the flow of light essential to both visual
and cinematic perception; (3) it is treated as a comparison of interrelated parts and processes constituting the "grand schemes" of visual and cinematic
perception.

The camera's "grand scheme" includes taking in the
light (shooting), converting the light to images on film
(developing), arranging the images in a meaningful
order (editing), reproducing that order in combination
with all other visual effects (printing), and reconvert-
ing the images into a "light flux" (projecting), from
which the viewer's own visual system constructs the
cinematic image. The original "light flux" entering the
camera goes through a series of interactions and
transformations, so that the light emerging from the
projector will take on the shapes and rhythms imposed by the total filmmaking apparatus (in which the
filmmaker plays an important though not necessarily

the chief role). Only in this extended sense can one
properly call the cinematic image a representation of
what the camera "sees."

Only in an equally extended sense can one refer to
what the eye "sees." The visual world is a product of
the brain. The brain's building materials are electrical
impulses traveling through millions of cells in a network connecting many different parts of the brain.
No single line of cause-effect events (like those that
constitute the camera's "grand scheme") can be
traced from the eye to the completed visual world.
Many parts of the brain contribute to the eye's "grand
scheme," and at least some of those parts communicate with each other in an order that scientists have
been able to map.

A small area at the back of the brain called the
visual association cortex seems to pull together all
the information supplied by other parts of the brain.
Data on color, motion, and three-dimensionality probably come from the immediately adjacent prestriate
cortex which has already received information on
shape, size, and spacial orientation from the striate
cortex. The so-called hypercolumns of cells in the
striate cortex receive and coordinate data arriving
(after several intermediate steps) from the optic
nerves, whose ganglion cells make up the last of
four layers of cells in the retina. These cells have already begun to make preliminary discriminations between lighter and darker areas and their movements.
Their information comes from impulses produced by
the rods and cones as they respond to the retinal
image. The rods and cones, as we have already seen,
have their own specialized functions, the most obvious being the rods' response to the movement of
light and the cones' response to the wavelengths

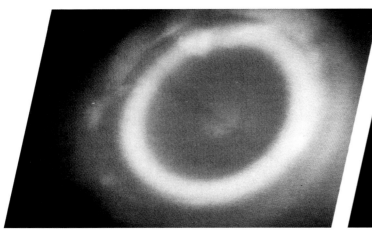

Jordan Belson
Infinity
1979
16mm film
sound
8 min
film still

The "cosmic eye."

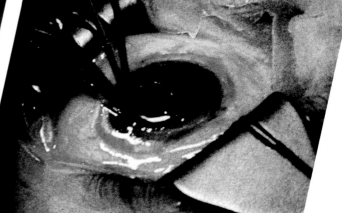

Paul Sharits
T.O.U.C.H.I.N.G.
1968
16mm film
color, sound
12 min
film still

An eye operation.

(i.e., color) of the light. Although some visual information also comes from nerve cells monitoring the movements of the eyes, it is reasonably accurate to say that the visual process begins when the rods and cones respond to the light moving over them.

(At this point, it should be remarked parenthetically that all visual activity is not initiated by light falling on the rods and cones. Much can be seen when the eyes are closed. There are phosphenes and other visual phenomena produced by the internal workings of the visual system, as well as dreams and visions that are seen as vividly as anything the eyes encounter in the external world. Similarly, not all cinematic images begin in the camera. Film may be exposed directly to the light, and it may be scratched, painted, or otherwise invested with shapes and colors that the projector's light will cast on the screen. Within both "grand schemes," in other words, there are alternative sources of seeing, about which much will be said in the chapters that follow. For the moment, one need only note that the "grand schemes" underlying the camera-eye metaphor do not necessarily require the presence of either a camera or an eye.)

Because light rays entering our eyes cross at the pupil, they produce a retinal image that is upside down and backwards, relative to the visual world as we perceive it. And because the eye moves – not only in large, intermittent movements, but also in minute and continuous jumps and tremors – the image darts this way and that across the retina. The retinal image is fluid and unstable; yet we normally perceive a solid and stable visual world. The retinal image spreads across a curved, two-dimensional surface; whereas, the visual world fills three-dimensional space. These transformations of retinal image into visual world are products of the eye's neural network in the brain.

Actually, the network begins in the eye itself. The cells of the retina develop from the same embryological tissue that produces the brain, and they function just like other brain cells. By surfacing in the eye, the brain makes direct contact with the "light flux." As the retinal cells make their preliminary discriminations, the brain is beginning to "think" about the visual world it will produce. The visual world is the completed "thought." Although it seems simply to be there, in front of our eyes, the visual world is, in fact, the product of what R. L. Gregory calls the "internal logic" of the brain's visual system, a system based on collecting, comparing, and drawing conclusions from data that is both "stored" in the brain and constantly arriving for the first time via the retinal image.[33] This process, which is still poorly understood, is not nearly as linear and hierarchical as my brief summary may seem to imply, and it is composed of nothing but electrical impulses traveling along millions of neural pathways at the same time. Shape, size, depth, movement, color, texture – all the components of the visual world are really millisecond-by-millisecond configurations of electrical activity in the brain.

Scientists of vision are careful to distinguish between what we see and the sources of our seeing. In one sense the source is the external world from which light flows to the eyes. In another sense, the source is the light itself, or the retinal image formed by the light. In still another sense, the source is the combination of electrochemical computations made by the millions of cells throughout the visual system of the brain. These sources produce what we see, but we do not see them. We see "an internal representation," as David Marr puts it, of what the eye's "grand scheme" has been able to derive from its encounter with "the light flux over time."[34]

33 Richard L. Gregory, *The Intelligent Eye*, Weidenfeld & Nicolson, London, 1970, pp. 24-25.

34 David Marr, *Vision: A Computational Investigation into the Human Representation and Processing of Visual Information*, W. H. Freeman, San Francisco, 1982, p. 3.

Likewise, what we see in cinema is the result of a complex process that begins with the external – or profilmic – world from which light streams into the camera's lens. Like the eye, the camera uses optical principles to form an image and photochemical principles to make that image available to subsequent cinematic processes. After that point, however, the camera's "grand scheme" operates quite differently from the eye's "grand scheme." In the latter, the photochemical transformation of the image on the retina produces changes in the voltage of the retinal cells. Those changes cause electrochemical impulses to pass from cell to cell through-out the brain's visual system until the final constellation of impulses creates what we see as the visual world.

In the camera, the incoming light changes the chemistry of the film's emulsion, producing a latent image that is made visible by chemical processing before it continues on to subsequent stages of analysis, modification, rearrangement, and reimaging within an optical-chemical system, not (as in the brain) a chemical-electrical one. Whereas the brain cells complete the eye's "grand scheme" without further reference to an image, the collective "brain" of the camera's "grand scheme" continues to work with images until the projector turns them back into the "light flux" received by the viewer's eyes.

The camera-eye metaphor should not be allowed to blur these distinctions, but neither should it be dismissed because of them. Clearly, its relevance varies according to which aspects of the two "grand schemes" are being compared. While the metaphor suits the light-gathering and image-forming capacities of the eye and the camera, it seems to have little relevance to their subsequent production of the visual world and the cinematic image. It can be applied, however, to their over-all function, which is to invest the originating "light flux" with a final, visual form. Neither "grand scheme" is simply a series of relay stations through which the external world sends along visible replicas of itself. Both schemes subject the light to mediating and transforming processes built into their respective visual systems. Looking at visible objects is not the basis of the camera-eye metaphor; rather, it is creating visual representations out of light moving in time.

The dialectic of eye and camera finds its synthesis, then, in the viewer's perception of these visual representations emerging from the "grand scheme" of cinematic production. While this is true of all film viewing, only avant-garde films call attention to that dialectical process and treat its synthesis as an aesthetic problem. As subsequent chapters will show, different avant-garde filmmakers have resolved that problem differently, but all in their own ways have responded to the dilemma raised in the two quotations that serve as epigraphs to this chapter.

In Sidney Peterson's *Mr. Frenhofer and the Minotaur* (1949), the model Gilette says of her lover, Nicolas Poussin, "It's an obsession, really, of the eye. He'd sell his own mother for a look." In an afterword to *Prismatics: Exploring a New World*, David Douglas Duncan recalls that while he was photographing Picasso in his studio, the artist said to him, "Long ago, I pointed to the lens and said the trouble was here!"[35] In these brief quotations we have the visual artist's obsession with seeing (probably the most extreme form of what Arnold Gesell has called "the visual hunger of cultural man") juxtaposed with the artist's deep suspicion of the camera and by implication the photographic process as a whole, because of its dispassionate and manufactured ways of seeing.[36]

Although both sentiments are attributed to painters, their relevance to avant-garde filmmakers should be apparent by now. The "leitmotif of the eye" testifies to the avant-garde's obsession with seeing. The camera-eye metaphor implies that film artists can satisfy that obsession through the apparatus of cinema. But to do so they must confront and resolve the "trouble" in the lens. Otherwise, the camera will shape their vision to suit its own limited ends. To appreciate the strategies avant-garde filmmakers have employed on behalf of their "obsession of the eye," we must take a closer look at the "trouble" Picasso pointed to. Where did it come from? How did it get built into the camera? What does it imply for a visual aesthetics of film?

First published in William C. Wees, *Light Moving in Time. Studies in the Visual Aesthetics of Avant-Garde Film*, University of California Press, Berkeley, Los Angeles, Oxford, 1992, The Regents of the University of California, pp. 11–30.

35 Pablo Picasso quoted in David Douglas Duncan, op. cit.

36 Arnold Gesell, *Vision: Its Development in Infant and Child,* Hafner, Darien, CT, 1974, p. 4.

Raymond Bellour
Battle of the Images

If there were an open polemic between today's competing image delivery systems, some light might at last be shed. As it is, all we have is incertitudes – slip-sliding, straddling, flickering, hybridization, metamorphosing, transition and passages between what is still called cinema and the thousand and one ways to show moving images in the vague and misnomered domain known as Art because it is what art school graduates do.

The convergence about to smack us in the face will mean you can use the same appliance to trade stock, watch a movie, e-mail or make toast. The bottom line is that from now on Intel's inside everything and our souls are networked, just as for so long "live" meant real-time television as opposed to real life. This means it's time to reconsider cinema with reference to the only thing that can really distinguish it both from what is now overtaking it and may succeed it and from that which existed before it was born. As Godard put it so succinctly in *Histoire(s) du cinéma*, cinema is film plus projection, i. e. a recorded image shown on a screen in a dark room. Barthes, not exactly a movie buff, was attracted by the movie house ambience, with its "anonymous, populated, dense darkness" and "the dancing cone cutting a hole in the dark like a laser beam." Daney, who did truly love motion pictures, was struck by the motionless silence in which viewers must sit, a state of "frozen vision" with its own history. All this would suggest that movies became what we know today with the advent of the talkies, i.e. the loss of the subtitles and intertitles that linked them to the theater and the novel, and of the pianist, not to mention the barker, a relic of still more ancient forms of entertainment. It took the first "death of cinema" twenty or thirty years ago to bring back and sanctify silent movies, and for the occasional orchestra or pianist to transform the movie theater into a museum. But above all, as Chris Marker, following Godard, said so well in his CD-ROM *Immemory*, where a second "death of cinema" is foretold, "Cinema is that which is bigger than we are, what you have to look up at. When a movie is shown small and you have to look down at

it, it loses its essence … What you see on TV is the shadow of a film, nostalgia for a film, the echo of a film, never a real film."

Movies were unrivaled and never anything but movies for only a generation or two, depending on when TV started in your local time zone. But since then, despite being surrounded, cinema has continually reinvented itself. And because film continues to be a mirror of the world, as the Lumière brothers and the first nineteenth-century moving picture machinery intended, a critic's job is not just to distinguish between good and bad movies but also to diagnose in certain symptomatic films whatever it is that remains of that intended essence and thus evaluate the state of the movies in relation to all the other image systems from which it is under siege. This was what Daney was doing when he pointed out the degree to which today's movies are cheating on cinema historically by unabashedly incorporating advertising iconography and hi-tech images. Thus *Gladiator* mixes whatever remains of *Spartacus* these days with synthetic dream sequences produced by Imagina software. But on the other hand, there also persists a stubbornly determined effort to make movies in the movie-making tradition, as if film were still alone in the world (the two extremes of this trend are marked by Straub-Huillet and Kiarostami). There are also those who bear ferociously despairing but joyful witness to the new deal, as noted by Daney, observing in Fellini and Godard a passage from "natural" motion pictures to motionless pictures, as the cinema experience becomes one of the spectator's virtual activity when faced with new, more or less immobile images. In *Smoking No Smoking*, Resnais gave us a fictional parallel of wired multiple reality and a narrative that mimics the possibilities of interactivity. With *Level Five*, Marker invented not the first movie to integrate IT (such firsts are necessarily American) but the first to integrate all the various levels of mutation brought about by the computer in terms of historical memory, subjective destiny and filmmaking.

Like Astruc with his "camera-pen," Marker evokes as lucidly as ever a "possible cinema" enabled by today's new tools, a "cinema of intimacy, solitude, a cinema worked out face-to-face with yourself, like a painter or a writer." But "you can't shoot *Lawrence of Arabia* like that, or *Andrei Roublev* or *Vertigo*." In other words, it rules out the best Hollywood-style block-buster tradition, great Russian cinema and the finest auteur movies. All of this may be doomed, because Marker's concept of "possible cinema" goes along with three gestures of acceptance, on his part, of the "honorable destiny" of the "death of cinema." The first is his commentator-filmmaker who acts as a guide to this death in the perspicacious and moving homage to Tarkovsky (*A Day in the Life of Andrei Arsenevich*), in contrast to Godard's approach in *Histoire(s)*. The second is Marker's long-term interest in video installations from *Zapping Zone* (for *Passages de l'Image*) to his homage to the Silent Movie. The third is his CD-ROM *Immemory*, a new genre of self-portrait, both installed in museums and sold like a book.

Or take Chantal Akerman. Twice now she has given in to some felt need to submit her films to the test of installation. With *D'Est (au bord de la fiction)*, she has done exactly the right thing, transforming this movie three times in order to create an installation that compares the three un-movie-like display systems through which nearly all films today are shown: museum pseudo-movie theaters, multiple video screens, and television at its best, as a box for experimentation and thought. Projection, circulation, mediation; viewer, stroller-visitor, contemplator – all these physical and mental positions at the service of a single content. Technically lighter but no less significant is her installation now on view in Paris at the "Voilà" exhibition, after Boston, New York, London and Brussels; *Self-portrait/Autobiography: a Work in Progress*. Here there are three monitors in front of which visitors station themselves — the *D'Est* principle again, but three monitors instead of the eight-times-three. Visitors can sit down in front of two screens to see Jeanne Dielman and the effect

is decidedly un-movie-like — each screen shows a different parallel narrative; and a single set-back monitor offers excerpts from *Toute une nuit* and *Hôtel Monterey*. A voice-over accompanies the whole thing, Akerman reading excerpts from her book *Une famille à Bruxelles*. This is a sort of a documentary about movies, as seen by the filmmaker herself, delivered up in space and transformable in keeping with place and time. This is all the more exciting when at the same time Akerman is presenting *La Captive*, her most pure and complete work of fiction, one of those films that seem increasingly unlikely these days, and in which cinema achieves a sovereign brilliance.

Such is the un-demarcated tension that calls for a response. When filmmakers give in to the temptation of installation, what is it that they are surrendering to? Raul Ruiz, Peter Greenaway, Atom Egoyan, Harun Farocki, Alexandr Sokurov and Raymond Depardon (I am deliberately skipping the already-classic installation films of seasoned experimental cineastes such as Snow, Sharits, etc.) – they all have their own unique form of spatialization, settings, objects and simultaneous projections with no time constraints. In a word, they invent one-off setups where, no matter how unique their films may be, each of them puts a little of the movies in the overall mechanism. Further, in the course of their exhibitions, their work is necessarily compared and contrasted with artworks of a different order, from photos to installations and all of the innumerable varieties of media and form now fully appropriated by the fine arts. Clearly filmmakers often give in to the wishes of curators. But that hardly alters the question and does nothing to solve the mystery of the mutating works themselves. Auto-biography of a man whose memory was in his eyes is one of the innumerable versions of Jonas Mekas' endless diary. But instead of seeing it in one of its possible continuous versions during a structured movie theater showing, in the exhibition at the Paris municipal modern art museum we see it redistributed in three small screening cabins organized around

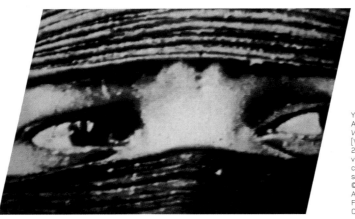

Yervant Gianikian,
Angela Ricci Lucchi
Visione del deserto
[Vision of the Desert]
2000
video
color, sound
screenshot
© Yervant Gianikian,
Angela Ricci Lucchi;
Fondation Cartier pour l'Art
Contemporain, Paris

three elements as if this were a CD-ROM. Even more
CD-like, outside these non-projection rooms stands
a vitrine stuffed with documentation. Or take another
small but perverse displacement, *Visione del deserto*
conceived by Yervant Gianikian and Angela Ricci Lucchi
for the "Déserts" show at the Fondation Cartier in
Paris. A row of seats in the back mimics the movies,
but in accord with the exhibition visitors' trajectory,
light comes in from the hall, spoiling the movie experience. To avoid it visitors can sit on the cushions piled
up along the wall and watch the film sideways. At the
entrance, show times have been posted, just like at
the movies. The film is the same and yet not really the
same as one would see projected in a real movie
house, or, for better or worse, recycled on TV.

On the other hand, there are some installations
that could not exist without the movies. Revisited,
remade, reworked and reduced to slivers, in these
pieces film is taken hostage by someone else's craving
for art. Such works comprise a real fantasy of what is
being lost, above all because of television, in both art
and the movies. But there are also enterprises that
evince a twisted and ridiculous desire to pump new
life into exhausted art by infusing it with movies in an
unsuccessful act of vampirization, a vain attempt at
mouth-to-mouth resuscitation between art forms.
Witness David Reed's insertion of one of his canvases
into a sequence form Hitchcock's *Vertigo*, as analyzed
by Arthur Danto in *After the End of Art*. There are also
works that through an insanely exaggerated fascination end up teaching us something about both art and
cinema — for instance, Douglas Gordon's take on
Hitchcock, from *Empire to Feature Film*.

Between filmmakers drawn to installation art and
"artists" for whom movies are raw material, there
pulsates an enormous and protean mass of all kinds
of installations (from Beat Streuli's photographic
dioramas to James Turrell's rooms of pure light). For
a long time they were dependent on the ideological
effects of television and the inherent nature of

Chantal Akerman
D'Est
[From the East]
1993
35mm film
color, sound
107 min
film still
© Eurimages

Chantal Akerman
La Captive
1999
35mm film
color, sound
112 min
film still
© Lemelle/
Corbis/Sygma

video itself. Using the most diverse approaches, many of them gradually drew closer to cinema, reappropriating certain elements of the machinery of the movies as well as cinematic modes of figuration and narrative postures – so much so that we can vaguely hypothesize the existence of an alternative cinema. Two noteworthy examples of this at the 1999 Venice Biennale were the pieces by Doug Aitken and Shirin Neshat. The latter's new work, *Rapture*, a more complex piece using the same principle of one monitor for each gender, was a hit at the Lyon Biennale. Faced with these shifts and media straddling, what is a poor critic to do? It would seem incumbent upon us to evaluate these works, in cases where that is worth the effort, from the point of view of dueling image delivery systems, at least in the implicit sense. For example, it is important to note that so far this year we have already seen two films where the sound track is designed to be created live during the projection, like certain experimental efforts of the 1920s. Manuela Morgaine's *Va*, about Casanova, comprises two shorts, one a talkie and the other silent, with the latter's sound effects added live in front of the screen (Morgaine defines this as "a kind of theater meant to take place in the front of a movie theater"). Dominique Gonzalez-Foerster's *Ipanema Theory*, a very long documentary about the urban environment, is accompanied by invasive music improvised in a sound booth by two new-genre DJs. It was astonishing, during the brief discussion that followed the screening, to hear Gonzalez-Foerster tell a theater full of people who had been sitting for two hours that her "film" would be equally suitable for an open-air night-time showing. This is a fascinating indecisiveness that indicates the degree to which things are slipping out of control.

Anyone who attends exhibitions and showings cannot fail to notice the migrations big and small resulting from various mixes of media and presentation systems. It seems a bit premature – you never know – to theorize this phenomenon. Certainly we could see a cautionary tale in the sorry fate of art theory since World War II, especially in the U.S., where the irresistible urge to concoct canons and labels in the name of painting or the so-called visual arts, of modernism or postmodernism, drew its self-justification from art history as if the latter were its own private reserve. It would seem wiser to stick to what Foucault called "the basic tasks of description." That means, today, more than ever, grasping all the arts as part of one single ensemble and analyzing each work in terms of its mix of different art forms, particularly in terms of media, or the artist's choice of confining oneself to one mechanism alone. What exactly, for example, is *Moments de Jean-Jacques Rousseau*, Jean-Louis Boissier's interactive CD-ROM? A film? A book? A picture album? This is an unmistakable sign of an aesthetics of confusion about which we still know very little. It seems that computers have gone way beyond the TV that they are about to subsume and are the first machines able to make use of all modes of language and expression, and to transform one into another and modulate them any way anyone wants. They can even simulate installations and play movies. Thus cinema – an impure art, as Bazin said, because it draws its inspiration from all the others and has nothing of its own to offer except reality – is, paradoxically, becoming gradually more pure insofar as its most active verity is becoming that of its mode of display. Cinema will forever be unique, in relation to all the modes that previously seemed similar and also to those that imitate it and parody it today. The most twentieth-century form of art, it is at once more crowded-in now than ever and more alone in its splendor.

First published in French and English "La querelle des dispositifs / Battle of the Images", in *art press*, no. 262, November 2000, pp. 48–52. Translated from the French by L.-S. Torgoff.

Timothy Druckrey

Fugitive Realities, Situated Realities,[1] "Situational Realities," or Future Cinema(s) Past

"Les arts futurs seront des bouleversements de situations, ou rien."[2]

Our theaters of the artificial have generated phantasmatic experiences whose effects strain to induce sensations of affinity with incredulous "realities." So deeply has the relationship to "photographic resolution" (a kind of epistemological plateau) engrained itself in the imaginary that even the "virtual" worlds of computer graphics substitute themselves – if fleetingly – for existing worlds untethered from history, unfettered by the forces of physics, and liberated from any banal correspondence to actuality.

The "cinema of attractions," and the "epic cinema" no longer capture or envelop the imagination. Now our "realities" are conjured and, often, coldly calculated (in both senses of the term). George Lucas suggests that this will be the time of "immaculate reality" – a reality stripped of the mystery of everything but its perfection, a reality that has passed from metaphysical to theological, a shift from a reality that recorded or narrated the intricacies of the world to a reality that renders the intricacies of possible worlds.

Certainly the "cinema century" – joined with four decades of video practice – has provided a range of practices that have merged with computers in forms with consequences that, on the one hand, merely replicate traditional cinematic strategies, and, on the other, has shattered the industrial and technical hierarchy whose stranglehold on independent production (and distribution) remains a contested arena. The melding of practices emerging in this electronic terrain has linked the re-evaluation of the history of cinema with an array of systems not just for an "expanded cinema" but for an exploded cinema.

Regis Debray, in the essay The Three Ages of Looking, outlined a broad framework for distinguishing the aspects of the history of seeing: Logosphere, Graphosphere, Videosphere, each corresponding to a different "regime" represented as "after writing," "after printing," and "after the audiovisual." And while there are problems in such sweeping historical characterizations, Debray identifies significant cultural issues concerning the "investment" in images. "Thus," he writes, "the artificial image would have passed through three different modes of being in the Western brain – presence (the saint present through his effigy); representation; and simulation (in the scientific sense), while the figure perceived exercised its intermediary function from three successive, inclusive perspectives – the supernatural, the natural, and the virtual."[3]

The three "regimes" of "presence," "representation," and "simulation" could roughly correspond to technologies of projection (before cinema), recording, rendering. Each of these stages created apparatuses for the creation of illusions or experiences that evoke "realities" that one could describe as fugitive, situated, and situational. Though innumerable technologies form the genealogy of modern representational systems, a few examples seem particularly pertinent in suggesting continuity between historical and contemporary formations of immersion.

I. Fugitive Realities

"It produces Effects not only very delightful, but to such as know the contrivance, very wonderful; so that Spectators, not well versed in Opticks, that could see the various Apparitions and Disappearances, the Motions, Changes and Actions, that may this way be presented, would readily believe them super-natural and miraculous [...]"[4]

Though it is a commonplace in the history of cinema to cite the shocked audiences – evidently unable to "suspend disbelief" – fleeing from the looming trains in the early Lumière films, the phenomenon of spectacular illusions actually preceded it by centuries in an abundance of "pre-cinema" technologies that ranged from the camera obscura and magic mirrors to peep shows and that were to extend into astonishing magic-lantern and Phantasmagoria flourishing during the seventeenth and eighteenth centuries. The programs for the one of the earliest Phantasmagoria performances (in January 1798) read (in part):

"FANTASMAGORIA at the Pavilion in the rue de l'Èchiquier, by citizen E-G Robertson: Apparitions of Spectres, Phantoms, Ghosts, such as they must have appeared or could appear in any time, in any place and among any people. Experiments with the new fluid known by the name of Galvinism, whose application gives temporary movement to bodies whose life has departed [...]"[5]

Robertson's use of rear-projection, of projection systems that allowed movement and thus the effect of "zooming," his projection onto smoke drew wild responses as the apparitions "mesmerized" growing audiences. The phenomenon of the Phantasmagoria spread quickly and was rapidly improved but its significance rested in the boundaries of the relationship between effects and credulity, on systems of illusion and on techniques (invisible to the audiences) that confounded common sense in the artificial light of an apparatus that could induce not just sensation but emotional fervor.

1   The title Situated Realities was provoked by the title of an exhibition at The Maryland Institute College of Art curated by Will Larson.

2   Guy Debord, "Prolégomènes à tout cinéma futur," in ION Centre de création, Marc-Gilbert Guillaumin (ed.), no. 1, 1952.

3   Regis Debray, "The Three Ages of Looking," in Critical Inquiry, vol. 21, no. 3, Spring 1995, pp. 536, 537. See too Regis Debray, Media Manifestos, Verso, New York, 1996.

4   Robert Hooke, Philosophical Transactions of The Royal Society, 17 August 1668, vol. 3, pp. 741–743.

5   Laurent Mannoni, The Great Art of Light and Shadow: Archaeology of the Cinema, University of Exeter Press, Devon, 2000, p. 150.

"We'll all be happy then," a 1911 prediction.

There's little doubt that the "immersive" environment of the darkened theater in which apparitions and spirits took eerie form so fascinated audiences that Phantasmagorias proliferated. What specific effect was realized with the use of Galvin's vitalistic principle is unclear, but was surely linked with the search for the "spark" that could bring the inanimate to life. It is not coincidental that the *Phantasmagoria's* animated spectacle stirred, or perhaps legitimated, notions of causation that defied common-sense and suggested that the ephemeral character of reality was inhabited by fugitive realities increasingly mediated through technologies that could, however fleetingly, materialize or represent worlds (if not hallucinations) imperceptible outside of the imagination.

II. Situated Realities

"The first true mass medium," Stephen Oetermann argues in his comprehensive history, *The Panorama: History of a Mass Medium*. The panorama is "the pictorial expression of 'symbolic form' of a specifically modern, bourgeois view of nature and the world" [...], it served both as "an instrument for liberating human vision and for limiting and 'imprisoning' it anew," it "assembles all segments of the horizon and collects all the details of visible nature, significant and insignificant [...] it puts an end to the uncertainty of relationships between details by claiming them all in one fell swoop," [...] it "was the first art form to attempt to fulfill the visual needs and desires of anonymous city dwellers" whose "entrance fees financed" artists and new projects. 6

6 Stephen Oetermann,
The Panorama: History of a Mass Medium, Zone Books, New York, 1997, pp. 7, 30, 45.

The panorama, with its "virtual" perspectives and experiential audiences, with its lush platforms and meticulous illusions, its grand scale and centrality (that would demonstrate its connection to Bentham's *Panopticon*), with its pedagogical and immersive pretenses, in the words of pre-cinema historian Laurent Mannoni, "hinted at the dream of a complete spectacle, of 'total cinema,' which some cinematograph pioneers attempted to realize at the start of the twentieth century, a dream finally realized in the 1980s and 1990s by large-scale systems such as *Imax*, *Omnivision*, and the 360-degree cinema." [7]

Richard Altick's impressive study, *The Shows of London*, found that in the panoramas "fidelity to fact was a prime consideration. Here the literate public repaired to visualize what it read about in the newspaper, with the same expectations with which, in the twentieth century, it would watch first newsreels and then newsreels' successors, television news programs." [8] "A substitute for travel and a supplement for the newspaper," says Scott Wilcox in *Panoramania!* invoking the linked fascinations of the nineteenth century – mobility, visibility, and information – with an "ultra-realism" that suggests the panorama as a "virtual world" engaged in producing the "reality effect," at once insulated from duration, yet paradoxically embedded in an inexhaustibly static temporality. [9]

While the panorama developed a singularly powerful public presence throughout the nineteenth century, it was joined (in the 1820s) by the momentous innovation of Daguerre and Bouton, *The Diorama*. In a culture already inebriated by spectacular visibility, the panorama, and an array of proto and pre-cinematic technologies – the Magic Lantern, The Phantasmagoria, Peep Shows, optical toys – the diorama linked the illusions of the image with theatrical lighting technologies and "special effects" that are undeniably the precursors of cinema – where illusion meets temporality. More theater than platform, the diorama's attraction was in the incorporation of temporal transformation. The diorama's "animated" transitions between reflected and transmitted light made for *passages* between day and night, interior and exterior, crowds and solitude. In essence it was a machine embedded in a bourgeois experience in which representation integrated the flow of temporality – the time-image as commodity.

Unlike the panorama, that positioned spectators in a discursive relationship to the fixed "image" [though there were a few "moving" panoramas], the diorama "fixed" the spectator as observers of duration in which a fluid process extended the perceptual field of the image into a cognitive field in which time was narrativized through extraordinary techniques that unhinged the frame of the image (through a blackening of the proscenium between audience and image creating a "visual tunnel," what Alfred Auerbach called an "aperture for looking through the picture" in which "it appears to the spectator to be unlimited." [10] As Wolfgang Schivelbusch writes in *Disenchanted Night: The Industrialization of Light in the 19th Century*, "The picture world of the new media offered endless opportunities for creating illusions, belonging as it did to a different existential sphere from the reality in which the audience was sitting." [11] This "unlimited" horizon (some panoramas gave binoculars

to their audiences) projected a universal gaze, suggested the image as inexhaustible, and anticipated the database! They also created an audience whose appetite for illusions was paralleled by a scientific frenzy to understand the physiology of optics and human vision as a central issue.

The twin technologies of the panorama and diorama were tuned to a burgeoning commerce in visuality and that institutionalized many media practices still functioning today. Their technologies necessitated the development of architectures suitable to their illusions and the staggering number of buildings devoted to their "performance" spread quickly throughout the world. These architectures, really these proto-media institutions, were dedicated to exploiting illusions and generating spectacles of sensation (visual and cognitive) and to claiming the "real" world, as photography would do (until its rendezvous with cinema technologies in the 1880s). As an effect of representational technology joined with a mass media they would drive a wedge into the high art pretenses of the parallel development of public museums, the bawdy origins of vaudeville, or the triumph of what Christine Boyer calls 'rational entertainment' – the visual mélange of the spectacular and the scientific" that "lies in the organizational heart of the great nineteenth-century exhibitions that turned the industrial world into one immense picture show" in which "things were replaced by a sequence of optical tableaux, an accumulation of weightless and fantastical images that floated about in a dream world." [12]

For a media reality already establishing what Peter Weibel calls "logocentric rationality," the intricately long development of the cinema comes as both radical possibility and industrial foreclosure. As Zielinski writes: the "culture industry has reified the audiovisual discourse in a number of arrangements, which thus also possess the characteristic features of a *dispositif*. From a media studies perspective, these arrangements are better comprehensible and explain more than considering isolated types of apparatus." In film culture, theory, and history approaches to the media apparatus emerged in the vigorous integration of "the triadic relationship of technology – culture – subject." [13] Tom Gunning suggests that though "the early history of cinema, like the history of cinema generally, has been written and theorized under the hegemony of narrative films," [14] it is the "harnessing of visibility" that "cinema before 1906 displays most intensely." But the "cinema of attractions," inheriting centuries of innovation, like today's technologies, did not possess the "*tabula rasa* assumptions of a new 'medium.'" [15] Surely technical limitations played a role in this fascination with the fleeting, transient, or spectacular, but the probing of this special effect went, in Gunning's term "underground" to be adopted by an avant-garde anxious to explore its potential. The early commercial cinema assimilated the spectators of illusion, the consumers of entertainment, the narratives of theater, the skits of vaudeville, and manufactured an empire of linear stories. The avant-garde discovered the "shock" value of interrupted narrative and shattered normalization – a heritage that continues to define artistic practice in the "new new media age."

7 Mannoni, op. cit., p. 176.

8 Richard Altick, *The Shows of London*, Harvard University Press, Cambridge, 1978, p. 176.

9 See Scott Wilcox, "Introduction," in *Panoramania!*, Ralph Hyde (ed.), exhib. cat. Barbican Art Gallery, Trefoil Publ., London, 1988.

10 Quoted in Wolfgang Schivelbusch, *Disenchanted Night: The Industrialization of Light in the 19th Century*, University of California Press, Berkeley, 1995, p. 217.

11 Schivelbusch, op. cit., p. 213.

12 Mary Christine Boyer, *The City of Collective Memory: Its Historical Imagery and Architectural Entertainments*, The MIT Press, Cambridge, MA, 1996, p. 257.

13 Siegfried Zielinski, *Audiovisions: Cinema and Television as Entr'actes in History*, Amsterdam University Press, Amsterdam, 1999, p. 20.

14 Tom Gunning, "The Cinema of Attractions: Early Film, its Spectator and the Avant-Garde", in *Early Cinema: Space, Frame, Narrative*, Thomas Elsaesser (ed.), BFI Publishing, London, 1990, p. 56.

15 Charles Musser, *The Emergence of Cinema: The American Screen to 1907. History of the American Cinema*, University of California Press, Berkeley, 1994, p. 16.

MULTIPLEX MAN

III. Situational Realities

There's no doubt that experimental film between the two "world-wars" was to exploit effects and shatter the normative status of a booming cinematic entertainment industry. From Duchamp's *Rotoreliefs*, the stunning works of montage Walter Ruttmann, Man Ray, Moholy-Nagy, etc., that the "cinema of attractions" could be extended beyond ephemeral effect and create dynamic cinema often abandoning optics altogther. And while the works of Dada and Surrealist cinema swirled and influenced generations involved with "future cinema," the film palaces grew in the scale of forums that could, on the one hand, exist as a revolutionary agora (in Benjamin's terms) and, on the other, could exist as spectacle in the "epic ideology" films of the 1920s – from Gance and Eisenstein to Murnau and Lang to DeMille and Hitchcock.

Indeed, Gance's *Napoléon* (1927) was filmed and, in very limited runs, shown, using *Polyvision*, a synchronized three-camera system that recorded and allowed projection on three screens that could be either synchronized in broad panoramic expansions or that could use the screens "to spectacularize his famous accelerated montage techniques, juxtaposing three different images [...]"16 In the late 1920s there were several attempts to commercialize wide-screen (including Henri Chrétien's *Hypergonar* lens he called

an "anamorphoser" that "compressed a wide horizontal view onto 35mm film" Paramount's Magnafilm, Fox's Grandeur (with 70 mm film), amongst many others).17

For all its possibilities, according to Belton, "wide-screen remained more of a novelty than a norm and other wide-screen processes avoided the gimmicky, image-expansion techniques of Polyvision and Magnascope and attempted to work with a fixed, 'theatricalized' playing space. Although it did transform the established spectator-screen relationship, filling the spectator's field of vision and refiguring passive distractions as engrossing attractions, the heterogeneous tradition of multi-event presentations in the theater continued to entertain audiences in pre-wide-film ways, and 'distraction' remained the dominant form of spectatorial engagement."18 Though technically feasible, early wide-screen cinema fell victim to an entertainment industry fervently attempting to standardize distribution and equipment, to economize on the enormous budgets for production, and to foreclose experiment.

The 1939 World's Fair brought bombastic and utopian visions of democracy and technology into a world on the verge of war (Hitler's invasion of Poland came four months after the opening). Of its numerous technological spectacles were the first American

16 John Belton, *Widescreen Cinema*, Harvard University Press, Cambridge, 1992, p. 39.

17 Belton, op. cit., p. 40.

18 Belton, op. cit., p. 51.

commercial television broadcasts from RCA (whose building was in the shape of a vacuum tube and displayed early home television sets), Westinghouse's robot *Elektro*, a rocket port in the Chrysler building, and, most notably General Motor's Futurama, no less the fair's icons the Trylon and Perisphere. Its interior featured rotating platforms from which on-lookers looked over a perfected phantasmatic city of the future (called *Democracity*), a model of efficient design, "immersed" in a spherical form that seemed a cross between panopticon, panorama, planetarium, and pantheon – and as much evoked the Masonic fantasy architecture of Etienne Louis Boulee's *Cenotaph to Newton* or Jean Jacques Lequeu's *Temple to the Earth* (from the late eighteenth century) as it did the *Cosmoramas*, *Cycloramas*, and *Globoramas* of the nineteenth century. As such it suggested not the "fidelity of fact" of the panorama, but of what was to become the omnipotent gaze. The projected sound and the film projections inside the Perisphere's spherical surfaces were worked on by Fred Waller (who served as a consultant and who also developed a project for Kodak's *Hall of Color* for the 1939 World's Fair) and whose post-war *Cinerama* was to revive wide-screen cinema.

John Belton's *Widescreen Cinema*, an exhaustive history of the *Cinerama*, cites numerous ways in which it replicated aspects of the panorama, became a tool of post-war technological prowess, and transformed the cinema into "an event." The *Cinerama* "sold itself through appeals neither to content or to form but to audience involvement. Ad copy promised that with Cinerama 'you won't be gazing at a movie screen – you'll find yourself swept right *into* the picture, surrounded by sight and sound.' […] And while 3-D slowly alienated its audience by throwing things at them, Cinerama drew them into the screen – and the movie theaters – in droves."[19] A number of films were made using Cinerama technologies: *This is Cinerama, Seven Wonders of the World, How the West Was Won, It's a Mad, Mad, Mad, Mad, World, 2001 – A Space Odyssey*. Recorded with three ultra wide-angle lenses and projected on a curved screen the horizontal angle of view was 146 degrees enveloping even the peripheral vision of the audience. Waller himself ultimately wrote that in many of the unique ways in which the optical "clues" resolved, that "cinerama re-creates reality."[20]

Soon Cinerama was supplemented by a number of adaptations – *CinemaScope, Vistavision, Panavision* – while its influence as a kind of a precursor to "immersion," a competitor to burgeoning 3-D, "widened" into the ideological spectacles of the popular World's Fairs of the late 1950s and 1960s. Touting industry, technology, democratic values, the fairs' pavilions strove to incorporate visions of the future that the 1939 fair failed to implement. "Widescreen" (in various forms) was everywhere. A sampling of some of the projects shows that not only corporations but artists were absorbing the possibilities of creating for what Belton a "new spectatorship," a kind of "epic of attractions" which revivified the multi-screen experiments of Gance, the montage of Eisenstein, the visual

frenzy of Vertov while exploring the use of enhanced optical technologies, broader projection techniques (the dome was particularly popular), computer controls, and even audience participation.

A few examples of the drive to incorporate spectacular visuality include: Disney's *Circarama* (shown at the Brussels World's Fair of 1958 along with the Philips Pavilion - more on this below), the *Spacearium* of the 1962 Seattle World's Fair (shot with fish-eye lenses and projected into a curved dome), *To Be Alive* from 1964 New York World's Fair, at Expo 67 in Montreal featured a stunning number of "immersive" screen experiments including: *Canada 67* – which utilized *Circle-Vision*, a 360 degree film made by The Disney Corporation, Roman Kroitor's *Labyrinthe* that proposed, in Kroitor's words, "a tight relationship between the movie and the architecture" (Kroitor quickly became involved in the development of IMAX),[21] Art Kane's multi-screen *A Time To Play* at the U.S. Pavilion, and a stunning array of works at the Czechoslovakia Pavilion including Radúz Çinçera's important *Kinoautomat* (that provided for audience feedback), *Polyvision: Czechoslovakia – The Automated Country* "completely controlled by electronic memory circuits (computer) that controlled the projector," *Diopolyecran a rapid-fire a 'slide show'* that presented "15,000 slides in the 11 minute show,"[22] and E.A.T.'s *Pepsi Pavilion* in Osaka.

While most of these projects evolved impressive projections systems, The Philips Pavilion at the Brussels World's Fair of 1958 represented a particular departure. Le Corbusier was engaged by Philips to construct a pavilion. "I will make you a *poème électronique*," he wrote, "everything will happen inside: sounds, light, color, rhythm […]"[23] Involved for some time in "visual acoustics," Le Corbusier, who also engaged Iannis Xenakis, wrote to Edgar Varèse (who was to compose a work to accompany the visual program): "the illumination will allow flashing drawings to be made from time to time, but occupying space with a striking presence […] It will be the first truly electric work with symphonic power."[24]

The Pavilion (with some two million visitors) "ultimately functioned as a giant speaker enclosure and screen for projection and illumination."[25] Varèse had a long familiarity with experimental music – from the Futurists and the work of Leon Theremin – to that of Bartók and Berg – and produced for the Pavilion his *Poème électronique*, a tape composition for some 425 speakers and 20 amplifier combinations. The speakers provided "a spectacle of light and sound [with] 'sound routes' to achieve various effects such as that of music running around the pavilion, as well as coming from different directions, reverberations, etc. For the first time, I heard my music literally projected into space."[26]

Familiar with the iconoclastic critique of the Futurists, Varèse was interested in "sound-producing (not sound re-producing)" means and his investigations led, as early as the 1920s, to contacts with Bell Labs (hoping for access to acoustic laboratories) and to work with René Bertrand's *Dynaphone* and the

19 Belton, op. cit., p. 98.

20 Fred Waller, "The Archeology of the Cinerama," in *Film History*, vol. 5, 1993, p. 297.

21 In Gene Youngblood, *Expanded Cinema*, Studio Vista, London, 1970, p. 354.

22 See http://naid.sppsr.ucla.edu/expo67/map-docs/cinema.htm

23 Joel Chadabe, *Electric Sound*, Prentice Hall, Upper Saddle River, 1997, p. 60.

24 Marc Treib, *Space Calculated in Seconds: The Philips Pavilion, Le Corbusier, Edgard Varèse*, Princeton University Press, Princeton, 1996, p. 6.

25 Treib, op. cit., p. 168.

26 Chadabe op. cit., p. 61.

Theremin (used in his work *Ecuatorial* in 1932). His works, *Ionisation*, *Density21.5*, *Hyperprisms*, evoke a scientific fascination with the oscillation between instrumental sound and mechanical-electronic "noises." Deleuze and Guattari write that "Varèse's procedure, at the dawn of this age, is exemplary: a musical machine of consistency, a sound machine (not a machine for reproducing sounds), which molecularizes and atomizes, ionizes sound matter, and harnesses a cosmic energy. If this machine must have an assemblage, it is the synthesizer."[27]

Indeed the synthesizer – no less the computer – was on the horizon while Varèse was working on *Poème électronique* and the transformation of sound/noise into equivalent forms of information heralded the shift from analogue to digital in which randomness, probability, computability, were to merge and extend the limits and reception of sound by dissolving sonic hierarchies, by detemporalizing sonic linearity, by obliterating the distinction between representation (or reproducibility) and calculability, by assenting to the possibilities of virtualization, by realizing that the signal/noise ratios of information theory could be implemented as analytical/critical/creative tools, by radicalizing the cybernetic.

Marc Treib's superb *Space Calculated in Seconds: The Philips Pavilion, Le Corbusier, Edgard Varèse,* is the only comprehensive study of the project. Treib called the pavilion "a collage liturgy for twentieth-century humankind, dependent on electricity instead of daylight and on virtual perspectives in place of terrestrial views […] a landmark in electronic media technology."[28] Philips' research in stereographic sound, not incidentally also related to the dimensional aural aspects of the "immersive" widescreen phenomenon, was to play a central role in the pavilion. The building was conceived as a "mathematical object," in the form of a hyperbolic parabola, within which a "a film (*écran*, literally "screen") presenting images illustrating the course of human civilizations and the threats to its prolongation" is projected. "The Philips *Poème électronique* would utilize electronic media to further the power of architecture in its quest for the unknowable," in Le Corbusier's words, "a boundless depth opens up, effaces the walls, drives away contingent presences, accomplishes the miracle of ineffable space." The projection of the visual images in *Poème électronique*, evoked themes that "emerge and re-emerge, for example, comic figures like Charlie Chaplin played against catastrophe (in a manner recalling the works of Samuel Beckett), human invention, tribal art and sophisticated technology, science gone amok, and order and chaos."[29] Not conceived as a spectacular surrogate cinema or as an open-system, the Philips Pavilion was a meticulously programmed "immersive" experience whose relationship to electronic media stands as exemplary.

Amid the whirling cinematic experiments of the 1960s, investigated in great depth in Gene Youngblood's pivotal *Expanded Cinema* (1970), came the introduction of video and soon synthesizers and early computing. Rapidly absorbed by a generation riveted by both cinema and television, the early phases of this *exploded* cinema turned away from sheer optical effects (though these were to return in the "synthetic" experiments of the 1970s) and integrated the possibilities for the creation of "event-spaces" into Happenings, performances, and installations (Stan VanDerBeek's *Movie-Drome*, that used film and not video, projected into a domed "intermedia" environment, Carolee Schneemann's *Night Crawlers*, that was performed at Expo 67, Aldo Tambellini and Otto Piene's *Black Gate Cologne*, 1968, Wolf Vostell's *Electronic Happening Room*, 1968, Nam June Paik's *Participation TV*, 1969, among many, many others).

In breaking the barrier between screen and space, in conceptualizing the electronic "image" as a relative phenomenon, this generation abandoned the passive viewer and posed fundamental questions about a future in which the significance of the experience of art was to become an aspect of communication, information, and calculation.

Conclusion

The many histories that are weaving their way through "Future Cinema" retrieve, reclaim, and reframe discourses and technologies with reverberating influences as both precedents and as models. The evolving systems for immersing audiences in "fugitive," "situated" and "situational" realities has come face-to-face with radically transformed expectations that can reframe the cinematic imaginary as one differentiated from localized "effects" and, instead, as complex configurations of intention and experience.

But by posing a "future" cinema merely as a kind of end-game in the history of representation suggests that it must obliterate the history it inherits or that it must perpetuate the crumbling passivity of its audience as "spectators of the spectacle" rather than reconceptualize itself in the face of radical new possibilities. Instead, the task is to reconsider cinema as itself an unfinished project, one which refigures the notion of cinema as an interface into realities only possible as cinema, cinemas that just do not coincide with an expectation that they verify a preexistent model, cinemas whose unpredictability strains the credulity of representation, cinemas whose strangeness evokes unanticipated transformations, cinemas whose uncanny-ness is a provocation, cinemas whose status lies precisely in an otherness disconnected from mere acknowledgment of the world, cinemas whose transience is only possible in the imaginary, cinemas whose temporality is not bound to the incidental, cinemas whose situations are not hopelessly confined to a reality that cannot conform with the now collapsed assumption that what we see is the effect of a cause, but perhaps its opposite.

27 Gilles Deleuze and Félix Guattari, *A Thousand Plateaus*, University of Minnesota Press, Minnesota, 1987, p. 343.

28 Treib, op. cit., pp. 3, 5.

29 Treib, op. cit., pp. 100, 118.

Vivian Sobchack
Nostalgia for a Digital Object:
Regrets on the Quickening of QuickTime

Whenever I watch QuickTime "movies," I find myself drawn into someone else's – and my computer's – memory. Faced with their strange collections, moving collages, and juxtapositions of image-objects whose half-life I can barely re-member, I tend to drift into a reverie not quite my own. Indeed, the form usually evokes from me the kind of temporal nostalgia and spatial intensity I feel not at the movies but before American artist Joseph Cornell's mysterious boxed relics. Both QT movies and Cornell boxes preserve "under glass" fragments of a "read-only" memory that is, paradoxically, "random access": that is, dynamic, contingent, associative. Both also refuse mundane space-time, drawing us into enclosed and nested poetic worlds far more miniature, layered, and vertically deep than we usually find in cinema. Both also salvage the flotsam and jetsam of daily life and redeem it as used material whose re-collected and re-member presence echoes with traces of an individual yet collective past. And both also construct "reliquaries" – cherishing "the ephemeral object as if it were the rarest heirloom."[1]

Both QuickTime movies and Cornell boxes contain "intense, distilled images that create a remarkable confrontation between past and present"[2] – a confrontation furthered by QT's stuttering attempts to achieve "real-time" movement, or to embrace the spatio-temporal lacunae that visibly mark its expressions. While cut-out statues and matted silhouettes float gracefully like collaged dreams across photo-realist backgrounds that effortlessly warp and melt, "live-action" balks and stiffens in contrast. Strangely static and consequently moving, full of gaps, gasps, starts and repetitions, QT movies intensify our corporeal sense of the molecular labor of human becoming – evoking not the seamlessly-lived animations of real-time and live-action movies, but, rather, the half-life of certain time-worn kinetic objects: wooden puppets with chipped paint, forsaken dolls with missing limbs, Muybridge-like figures in old flip books hovering with bravado and uncertainty between photography and cinema, images of nineteenth century strong men hand-cranked into imperfect action by old Kinetoscopes relegated to the dark corners of amusement arcades.

Given the pleasure I find in their fragmented temporality and intensely condensed space, I have no desire to see QuickTime movies get any quicker – or bigger. I don't want them to achieve the "streaming" momentum of real-time and live-action – measured against the standard and semblance of cinema.

Indeed, precisely because QT's miniature spatial forms and temporal lacunae struggle against (as they struggle to become) cinema, they poetically dramatize and philosophically interrogate the nature of memory and temporality, the value of scale, and the meaning of animation. In sum, I don't want them to become "real movies" at all. Nonetheless, they will – and have. It was just a matter of time, compression, memory, and bandwidth. Thus, it is a shame that QT movies were called "movies": so named, their extinction as a specifically computergraphic form of aesthetic expression was virtually preordained. Although QT is a "multimedia architecture," most developers and users quickly reduced it: "In QuickTime, a set of time-based data is referred to as a *movie*."[3]

Long ago, André Bazin argued in *The Myth of Total Cinema* that before the technology that made it possible, cinema was *preconceived* "as a total and complete representation of reality ... the reconstruction of a perfect illusion of the outside world."[4] Unfortunately this realist desire remains in force despite the emergence of a new medium – one that digitizes, integrates, and transforms all others. Belief in the myth of total cinema has led not only to the realization of sound, color, and relief, but also to the *primacy of cinema*, even as it is transformed into something else by a new medium. Thus, the aesthetic values of QT "movies" are measured against those of "cinema" – and the true computergraphic novelty of QT works becomes historically inverted as a false cinematic "primitivism." Hence the desire to make QT movies quicker and bigger rather than stopping to privilege the stalled and uncanny momentum of their animation and the poetic intensity condensed by their miniaturization and framing.

Indeed, I would have much preferred calling QuickTime works "memory boxes" rather than "movies" – for "memory box" evokes not only Joseph Cornell's work, but also the essential fundament of QT's existence: the *computer*. As well, referring to diverse containers from reliquaries to shoe boxes filled with photographs or souvenirs, "memory box" draws our attention to memory's historical transformations and the material conditions of its preservation. After all, in our technological moment, what is the computer but a fathomless "memory box" – one that collects, preserves, and allows for the conscious retrieval and visible re-collection of memories, all "cached" in an enormous, unseen network of past images, sounds, and texts.

1   Kynaston McShine, "Introducing Mr. Cornell," in *Joseph Cornell*, Kynaston McShine (ed.), The Museum of Modern Art, New York, 1980, p. 11.

2   McShine, op. cit., p. 9.

3   "Introduction to QuickTime," Developer Documentation for QuickTime 3, Apple Computer Inc., 1997, n. p.

4   André Bazin, "The Myth of Total Cinema," in *What is Cinema?*, André Bazin, Hugh Gray (eds), University of California Press, Berkeley, 1964, p. 20.

Memory Boxes and Databases

In *The Poetics of Space*, Gaston Bachelard writes of a character in a novel who basks in the solidity and order of his oak filing cabinet: "Everything had been designed and calculated by a meticulous mind for purposes of utility. And what a marvelous tool! It replaced everything, memory as well as intelligence. In this well-fitted cube there was not an iota of haziness or shiftiness."5 I often get the same feeling from my computer "desktop." It reassures me with hierarchy, clarity and order, with principled and logical menus, commands, and systems through which I can access vast amounts of information (if not intelligence or knowledge). While unseen, this information does not seem hidden to me; rather, it is "filed" away in "folders" and, more deeply, in "records" and "fields." It is rationally organized and always hypothetically available for retrieval and display. Indeed, my computer gives me access to what seems an infinite store of information – and I take comfort in the hierarchical logic of its "unhazy" and "unshifty" memory (of an order quite different than my own). Here is the logical – and official – organization of the office, catalog, library, museum, and stock room. Here, everything has been "designed and calculated by a meticulous mind for purposes of utility." Here, I've no sense of the secretive or unconscious: at worst, information gets bureaucratically "classified," misplaced, or erased (not repressed). Thus, the virtual "solidity" of my "desktop" and "files" refuses ambiguity or poetry – and any discomfort I feel in the face of mistakes, losses, or frustrations arises not from my "well-fitted cube" but from my own very human and irregular logic.

Human memory doesn't compute neatly. The orderly and hierarchical logic of the file cabinet and its database is not that of Cornell or QT memory boxes. Thus, as Bachelard writes: "A well-calculated geometric description is not the only way to write a 'box.'"6 Some other rationale informs these memory boxes: associative rather than hierarchical, dynamic rather than static, contingent rather than determined (even when "given" to us in "read only" form). Its search engines driven to the past by a present moment of desire (not utility), this is the eccentric, extensible, yet localized logic of the hyperlink that radically transforms the phenomenology of the file cabinet and its database. The file cabinet becomes charged with experience, temporality, and desire and its hierarchical order becomes jumbled by logically incompatible – if psychologically comprehensible – functions. Like Cornell's description of a preparatory file for one of his boxes, the file cabinet becomes "a diary journal, repository, laboratory, picture gallery, museum, sanctuary, observatory, key … the core of a labyrinth, a clearing house for dreams and visions."7 And the database? Its hierarchical order becomes labyrinthine – comprehensive but incomprehensible, a vast and boundless maze of images and sounds, dreams, and visions in which one follows, backtracks, veers off, gets lost in multiple trajectories, all the time weaving tenuous threads of association into the endless tele-

ology and texture of desire. Here, there is no fixed data or information requiring mere *re-collection*; here, from the first, are only unstable bits of experience, disordered as they are *re-membered*.

The poetic power of both Cornell's and QT's memory boxes emerge explicitly from their relation to a larger totality of material and memorial possibilities: they and their found objects exist not only as fragments of personal experience, but also as "emblem[s] of a presence too elusive or too vast to be enclosed in a box. These missing presences crowd the imagination."8 Thus, in differentiating QT's memory boxes from movies, it bears pointing out that watching a film, I usually don't have a profound sense of all the images left on the cutting room floor; watching a QT memory box, however, I always feel the presence of an elusive and vast absence, a sea of memories shifting below the surface and in the interstices of what I actually see. In other words, I am always aware of the database as *effluvial*.

Privileging both the fragment and the slightness and ambiguity of their associational links, both Cornell's and QT's memory boxes thus point to their own presence as the poignant and precious visible landmarks of an unseen, lost, and incomprehensible field of experience. What Carter Ratcliff says of Cornell's memory boxes is equally true of QT's: "[T]he mode is enchanted by fragmentariness itself, which serves as an emblem of a wholeness to be found in other times and places"; thus it produces "an aura of loss which is as perfect in its own way as reunion would be."9 Indeed, "the panic of loss gives way to nostalgia."10

Frames within Frames

Although "a mode enchanted by fragmentariness," Cornell and QT's memory boxes are themselves bounded *containers*. At the same time, their miniature size, collector's sensibility, and the discretion of their enclosures gain particular power from – and exist always against – their own *containment* by a larger and marked visual field. Both externally and internally, then, Cornell and QT works provoke a structural and poetic tension between two different logics: one represented by the hierarchical and rational organization of the "file cabinet" and computer "desktop" where everything has its place in some comprehensive master plan; the other by the associational organization that is the psycho-logic of the memory box and the "hyperlink" in which everything has a relative and mutable order that cannot be mastered as a totality. This tension is simultaneously *framing* and *framed*.

As a framing device, this tension exists in – and as – an *exterior* space (and logic) containing but juxtaposed to the associational logic of the Cornell and QT box. With Cornell's works, there is the museo-logic of the vitrine in which the box sits; with the QT memory box and its hyperlink logic, there is the hierarchical logic of the computer "desktop" upon which it is opened. That is, the larger frame of the vitrine or desktop allows the smaller frame of the memory box an intensified condensation and concentration of its

5 Gaston Bachelard, *The Poetics of Space*, Beacon Press, Boston, 1964, p. 77.

6 Bachelard, op. cit., p. 83.

7 Dawn Ades, "The Transcendental Surrealism of Joseph Cornell," in McShine, op. cit., p. 33.

8 Carter Ratcliff, "Joseph Cornell: Mechanic to the Ineffable," in McShine, op. cit., p. 43.

9 Ratcliff, op. cit., p. 59.

10 Ratcliff, op. cit., p. 43.

visible contents into an *aesthetic totality*: a poetically meaningful and contained microcosm nested within the dispersed and different order and meaning of the macrocosm that surrounds them. In this aspect, both Cornell and QT memory boxes take on the magnitude and function (if not the geometric size) of sixteenth and seventeenth century *Wunderkammern*, chambers of curiosities and art curated less on logic than on the personal sensibilities and desires of their wealthy collectors.

Writing of these condensed collections, Anthony Grafton wonders what contemporaneous visitors sought in them and concludes it was the experience of totality and plenitude: "They hoped … to encounter the universe in all its richness and variety, artfully compressed into the microscopic form of a single room that showed all the elements, all the humors, all the musical intervals, all the planets, and all the varieties of plant and animal creation."11 Obviously, these viewers of the *Wunderkammer* were not worried by the implications of its contingent arrangement or overwhelmed by its (to our eyes) chaotic clutter. Indeed, historicized, the *Wunderkammer's* totalizing impulse can be read as a celebration of mastery, order, and structural homology: that is, comprehension of the "universe in all its richness and variety" is represented mimetically in a single chamber complacently "nested" within the larger frameworks of both the master's residence and God's "master plan." We can find similar compressions and homologies articulated in the smaller *Wunderkammern* of Cornell and QT boxes as they emerge structurally and figurally nested – framing and framed within a larger field. But this compression of a homologous universe is apparent also in the *content* of these more contemporary memory boxes. Their multi-layered and rich imagery is marked repeatedly by maps, planetary and astrological charts; hourglasses and clocks and other measuring devices; diagrams and schematics of optical devices from the microscope to telescope; evolutionary and devolutionary biological images of microbes, spores, skulls and skeletons. Consistently asserting homologies of shape and structure across scale from the microscopic to the macrocosmic, much like the *Wunderkammern* these memory boxes position themselves as both framing and framed by larger cosmologies and cosmogonies.

Nonetheless, times and cosmologies change – transformed in and by historical sensibility. Thus, in Cornell's boxes, homologies between the micro- and macrocosmic are not emblematic of man's security and mastery – and, in QT boxes, they are used to foreground a relativism quite other than the comforting and nested unity of God's master plan. Cornell's boxes are nostalgic – indeed, elegiac – in relation to harmony and order. Homologies between mundane and cosmic objects thus provoke a sense of the great loss and mystery of "totality" and perfect "comprehension" – the boxes, as Ratcliff noted, generating "an aura of loss … as perfect in its own way as reunion would be." In QT memory boxes, homologies between the micro- and macrocosmic are also not about mastery, secu-

rity, or "nested-ness." Here, self-similarity across scale and structure constitutes the disconcerting relativism of "chaos," often evoking the vertiginous and non-hierarchical "totality" of "infinite regress" and "cosmic zooms," thus undoing a hierarchical history that frames and privileges the mastery and rationality of both God and Man. Indeed, in QT, it is not God's rational master plan framing or framed by the memory box opened on my computer desktop or browser; rather, these images of maps, measures, microbes, and constellations mimetically contain, figure, and point to the containment and mastering structure of a more contemporary – and secular – "main frame": the computer.

As suggested earlier, along with the poetic tension generated by the juxtaposed relation between the interior and exterior spaces of these contemporary memory boxes, poetic tension also emerges *framed within* the intimate space of the boxes themselves. Bachelard writes: "For many people, the fact that there should exist a homology between the geometry of the small box and the psychology of secrecy does not call for protracted comment."12 Nonetheless, it is worth noting that within both Cornell and QT memory boxes, we see such a homology dramatized again and again: the "secret" vagaries and "hyperlinked" debris of contingency, dream, and desire overlaid in palimpsestic relation to the geometry and hierarchy that governs the "orderly" order of the rational "file cabinet." Cornell's work evidences such internal tension in memory boxes that exist in taxonomic series titled "Jewel Cases," "Museums," "Pharmacies," "Aviaries," and "Habitats" which often, as Ratcliff notes, "tuck images into drawers and vials and grids."13 Compartments, drawers, slots, grids, and boxes within boxes: these displays of hierarchy and order point not only to potentially larger (and smaller) organizational frameworks so that scale, in Cornell's art, becomes "multiple,"14 such nesting also points to potentially uncontrollable fragments of temporality and experience that are infinitely extensible in their generation of secrecy, memory, and meaning.

The same is true of QT memory boxes. Frequently overlaying the image fragments and detritus of their re-membered experience are orderly grids and schematic diagrams, geometry in the form of mattes that segment and compartmentalize. And, specific to the particular medium, such compartmentalization and grid work points not only to the larger order and framework of the surrounding "desktop," but also to the smaller, hidden, and thus more "secretive" orders of the computer: microchips, bits, and bytes. Re-membered experience in QT is often explicitly "bit-mapped" and "pixel-ated." Boxed fragments of photorealist images are compartmentalized further into smaller boxes yet – dissolving the personal meaning and contours of human memory and re-solving them into the visible and controlled geometry that in-forms the underlying memory and structure of the computer itself.

There is, then, both without and within QT and Cornell memory boxes, a tension between two kinds

11 Anthony Grafton, "Believe It or Not," in *The New York Review of Books*, 5 November 1998, p. 16.

12 Bachelard, op. cit., p. 82.

13 Ratcliff, op. cit., p. 60.

14 Ratcliff, op. cit., p. 43.

Joseph Cornell
Jouet Surréaliste
[Surrealist Toy]
c. 1932
mixed media
2.2 x 10.4 x 9.8 cm
National Museum of American
Art, Smithsonian Institution,
gift of Mr. and Mrs.
John A. Benton
© The Joseph and Robert
Cornell Memorial Foundation;
VG Bild-Kunst, Bonn 2003
photo © National Museum of
American Art, Smithsonian
Institution

left
Joseph Cornell
*Object (Hotel Theatricals by the
Grandson of Monsieur Phot
Sunday Afternoons)*
1940
wood cabinet
mixed media
29.8 x 20 x 6.6 cm
Yokohama Museum of Art
© The Joseph and Robert
Cornell Memorial Foundation;
VG Bild-Kunst, Bonn 2003
photo © The Estate of
Peter Hujar 1973

right
Joseph Cornell
*Untitled (Penny Arcade Portrait
of Lauren Bacall)*
c. 1945–1946
mixed-media construction
Lindy Bergman Collection,
Chicago
© The Joseph and Robert
Cornell Memorial Foundation;
VG Bild-Kunst, Bonn 2003
photo © Art Institute of
Chicago 1996

Joseph Cornell
Untitled (Ludwig II of Bavaria)
c. 1940–1955
boxed dossier
mixed media
© The Joseph and Robert
Cornell Memorial Foundation;
VG Bild-Kunst, Bonn 2003
photo © Graydon Wood

of logic and order and between a desire to re-collect and to re-member. Memory is thus generated and enacted by both box and viewer as a multi-stable phenomenon – one echoed in a *palimpsestic* structure and imagery that together provoke a richly poetic ambivalence and ambiguity. On the one hand, the geometry of compartments, mattes, and pixels re-collect and contain the amorphous and ever-extensible material of experience. On the other, the composited and collaged accumulations and associations of this experiential material challenge the neatness of the re-collection by re-membering it – and we are reminded there is a radical difference between a "pharmacy" and a "treasure box," between a computer's memory and our own. In sum, Cornell and QT memory boxes gain their poetic power from the juxtaposition and layering of "two kinds of space"; as Bachelard suggests, "intimate space and exterior space ... keep encouraging each other, as it were, in their growth."15

"Little Movies": Miniaturization and Compression

Digital theorist Lev Manovich has used QT to make a series of what, with historical irony, he calls "little movies."16 All six use classic cinematic imagery as the raw material of an exploration that interrogates the differences between the cinematic and the digital. All also foreground and privilege the limitations of computer memory under which they are constructed and by which they are constrained – and, in various ways, all thus explore their *miniature size* and *compressed nature*. "A Single Pixel Movie" is particularly striking. To a quite literally "loopy" tune reminiscent of Laurel and Hardy's theme music and against a black background, we watch the small square of a primitive "movie" in which a strong man holding a pole does rote exercises, intermittently interrupted by the sound of a "blip" and a digitized circle of "light." With each blip, the image becomes smaller and smaller (and less and less audible) until both blip and "movie" are reduced to a single pixel on the screen. The effect is more compelling and poignant than the comical repetition of mechanical motion and see-sawing music would seem to warrant. We watch more and more intently as the already miniaturized image becomes smaller and smaller – and we become more and more aware of the increasing fragility and impending disappearance not only of the early cinema strong man but also of the QT "movie" presently being extinguished from our human sight.

It is no small thing that these "little movies" are "small" both spatially and temporally. Bachelard tells us in *The Poetics of Space*: "It must be understood that *values become condensed and enriched in miniature*."17 Thus, as Susan Stewart notes: "A reduction in dimensions does not produce a corresponding reduction in significance."18 Quite the opposite. Suggesting that "we should lose all sense of real values if we interpreted miniatures from the standpoint of the simple relativism of large and small," Bachelard points out: "A bit of moss may well be a pine, but a pine will never be a bit of moss. The imagination does not function with the same conviction in both directions."19

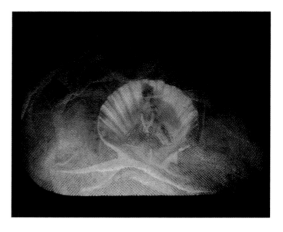

Joseph Cornell
Untitled (Ondine)
c. 1944–1946
box, electric light
private collection
© The Joseph and Robert
Cornell Memorial Foundation;
VG Bild-Kunst, Bonn 2003
photo © Richard L. Feigen
& Company

The "little movies" in QuickTime – or, as I prefer, QT "memory boxes" – not only emerge from and allegorize the objective necessities and constraints of data storage involving digital memory and compression, but they also accrue phenomenological and aesthetic value as an effect of these limitations. Objectively, the miniature is a compression of data in space, but phenomenologically and poetically, compression and condensation *intensify* the experience and value of the data, making it something rare and precious, something spatially intensified and temporally condensed that is "vast in its way."20 As Stewart suggests, "a constant daydream the miniature presents" is that "the world of things can open itself to reveal a secret life ... a set of actions and hence a narrativity and history *outside the given field of perception*."21 The miniature, then, is always to some degree secretive, pointing to hidden dimensions and unseen narratives. Its "nested-ness" within a larger whole draws us not only *beyond* its frame, but also *into* and *beneath* it. Thus, the miniature nature of QT's "little movies" or memory boxes exaggerates *interiority* – not only that of the individual perceiving subject, but also of the computer. Thus, whether in my sight or not, the strong man of Manovich's "little movie" will exercise forever in the depths of my – and the computer's – memory. Unlike with cinema, I never quite have the sense that QT "movies" are ever really "over." (Rather, their "terminal" status is "under.")

In sum, the spatial condensations of Cornell and QT constitute an interiority that transcends quotidian spatial and temporal relations – and "as an object consumed," their miniaturization "finds its 'use value' transformed into the infinite time of *reverie*."22 Excluded by their physical size from the miniaturized interior of the memory box, both artist and viewer *imaginatively* prospect and inhabit its suggestive spaces, filling them with their own missing presence in fragments of autobiography, dream, memory, confession. (Speaking both to us and for its maker, one QT miniature superimposes over a vague, empty, and receding hallway the following textual reverie: "Here is the solitude from which you are absent."23) Like Cornell's work with its slots, drawers, and compartments

15 Bachelard, op. cit., p. 201.

16 *Little Movies: Prolegomena for Digital Cinema, 1994–1997* can be accessed on the web at http://jupiter.ucsd.edu/~manovich/little-movies/

17 Bachelard, op. cit., p. 150.

18 Susan Stewart, *On Longing: Narratives of the Miniature, the Gigantic, the Souvenir, the Collection*, Johns Hopkins University Press, Baltimore, 1984, p. 44.

19 Bachelard, op. cit., p. 163.

20 Bachelard, op. cit., p. 215.

21 Stewart, op. cit., p. 54.

22 Stewart, op. cit., p. 65.

23 "Flight from Intention" by Victoria Duckett, Laboratory for New Media, UCLA Department of Film and Television: http://pixels.filmtv.ucla.edu/

"ENCHANTED WANDERER"

★ Excerpt from a Journey Album for Hedy Lamarr ★

By
JOSEPH CORNELL

Among the barren wastes of the talking films there occasionally occur passages to remind one again of the profound and suggestive power of the silent film to evoke an ideal world of beauty, to release unsuspected floods of music from the gaze of a human countenance in its prison of silver light. But aside from evanescent fragments unexpectedly encountered, how often is there created a superb and magnificent imagery such as brought to life the portraits of Falconetti in "Joan of Arc," Lillian Gish in "Broken Blossoms," Sibirskaya in "Menilmontant," and Carola Nehrer in "Dreigroschenoper?"

And so we are grateful to Hedy Lamarr, the enchanted wanderer, who again speaks the poetic and evocative language of the silent film, if only in whispers at times, beside the empty roar of the sound track. Amongst screw-ball comedy and the most superficial brand of clap-trap drama she yet manages to retain a depth and dignity that enables her to enter this world of expressive silence.

Who has not observed in her magnified visage qualities of a gracious humility and spirituality that with circumstance of costume, scene, or plot conspire to identify her with realms of wonder, more absorbing than the artificial ones, and where we have already been invited by the gaze that she knew as a child.

Her least successful roles will reveal something unique and intriguing — a disarming candor, a naivete, an innocence, a desire to please, touching in its sincerity. In implicit trust she would follow in whatsoever direction the least humble of her audience would desire.

"She will walk only when not bid to, arising from her bed of nothing, her hair of time falling to the shoulder of space. If she speak, and she will only speak if not spoken to, she will have learned her words yesterday and she will forget them to-morrow, if to-morrow come, for it may not."*

(Or the contrasted and virile mood of "Comrade X" where she moves through the scenes

like the wind with a storm-swept beauty fearful to behold).

* * * * * * * *

At the end of "Come Live With Me" the picture suddenly becomes luminously beautiful and imaginative with its nocturnal atmosphere and incandescence of fireflies, flashlights, and an aura of tone as rich as the silver screen can yield. Her arms and shoulders always covered, our gaze is held to her features, where her eyes glow dark against the pale skin and

her earrings gleam white against the black hair. Her tenderness finds a counterpart in the summer night. In a world of shadow and subdued light she moves, clothed in a white silk robe trimmed with dark fur, against dim white walls. Through the window fireflies are seen in the distance twinkling in woods and pasture. There is a long shot (as from the ceiling) of her enfolded in white covers, her eyes glisten in the semi-darkness like the fireflies. The reclining form of Snow White was not protected more

lovingly by her crystal case than the gentle fabric of light that surrounds her. A closer shot shows her against the whiteness of the pillows, while a still closer one shows an expression of ineffable tenderness as, for purposes of plot, she presses and intermittently lights a flashlight against her cheek, as though her features were revealed by slow-motion lightning.

In these scenes it is as though the camera had been presided over by so many apprentices of Caravaggio and Georges de la Tour to create for her this benevolent chiaroscuro . . . the studio props fade out and there remains a drama of light of the *tenebroso* painters . . . the thick night of Caravaggio dissolves into a tenderer, more star-lit night of the Nativity . . . she will become enveloped in the warmer shadows of Rembrandt . . . a youth of Giorgione will move through a drama evolved from the musical images of "Also Sprach Zarathustra" of Strauss, from the opening sunburst of sound through the subterranean passages into the lyrical soaring of the theme (apotheosis of compassion) and into the mystical night . . . the thunderous procession of the festival clouds of Debussy passes . . . the crusader of "Comrade X" becomes the "Man in Armor" of Carpaccio . . . in the half lights of a prison dungeon she lies broken in spirit upon her improvised bed of straw, a hand guarding her tear-stained features . . . the bitter heartbreak gives place to a radiance of expression that lights up her gloomy surroundings . . . she has carried a masculine name in one picture, worn masculine garb in another, and with her hair worn shoulder length and gentle features like those portraits of Renaissance youths she has slipped effortlessly into the role of a painter herself . . . le chasseur d'images . . . out of the fullness of the heart the eyes speak . . . are alert as the eye of the camera to ensnare the subtleties and legendary loveliness of her world. . . .

[The title of this piece is borrowed from a biography of Carl Maria von Weber who wrote in the bars quoted of the overture to "Der Freischutz" a musical signature of the Enchanted Wanderer.]

* Parker Tyler

Joseph Cornell
"Enchanted Wanderer":
Excerpt from a Journey album
for Hedy Lamarr
1941–1942
layout with printed
photo-montage and text
(*View*, series 1, nos. 9/10,
December 1941/January 1942,
p. 3)
38 x 26.6 cm
Joseph Cornell Study Center,
National Museum of American
Art, Smithsonian Institution,
gift of Mr. and Mrs.
John A. Benton
© The Joseph and Robert
Cornell Memorial Foundation;
VG Bild-Kunst, Bonn 2003
photo © the typosophic society,
Primersdorf

meant to contain and control the materials of overwhelming experience, QT memory boxes draw us inward into an ever-extensible reverie: its compartments, according to no "rational or logical sequence," further housing and condensing "private and nearly unfathomable associations, almost like a metaphor for the cells of the unconscious mind."[24] Here, in the reverie the miniature provokes, it can indeed be said that "the poet inhabits the cellular image."[25]

Mnemonics and Reliquaries

The miniature memory boxes of Cornell and Quick-Time, in framing and effect, are "reliquaries" – preserving, as it were, precious remnants and souvenirs that gain additional poetic force in that they are "under glass." As Bachelard notes, "valorization of the contents" can also emerge through a "valorization of the container."[26] Hence the fragment and the miniature "encourage" each other – evoking the "singular," the "rare," the "fragile," the "ephemeral," and the "compressed" as materially and poetically valuable. Manovich makes "little movies" that his text suggests will disappear, "the artifacts of the early days of digital media." Bachelard privileges treasure chests and caskets. And Cornell creates "jewel cases" and places some of his compositions "under bell jars" as if "holding captive a moment in a transient, enclosed world."[27]

The preciousness articulated here is thus connected to the particular kind of contingency that informs the artfully arranged but "found" objects of the memory box. That is, we encounter these remembered objects as objectively assembled according to subjectively *ephemeral* associations, the very slightness of the links among them making their present appearance seem singular, fragile, fleeting – and thus precious. Stewart, writing of the material fragments of the past gathered in photograph albums or collections of antiquarian relics or souvenirs, points out: "There is no continuous identity between these objects and their referents. Only the act of memory constitutes their resemblance. And it is in this gap between resemblance and identity that *nostalgic desire* arises."[28] Hence the corollary desire to preserve these tenuous associations, to keep them "in mind."

24 Ades, op. cit., p. 26.

25 Bachelard, op. cit., p. 228.

26 Bachelard, op. cit., p. 86.

27 McShine, op. cit., pp. 10–11.

28 Stewart, op. cit., p. 145.

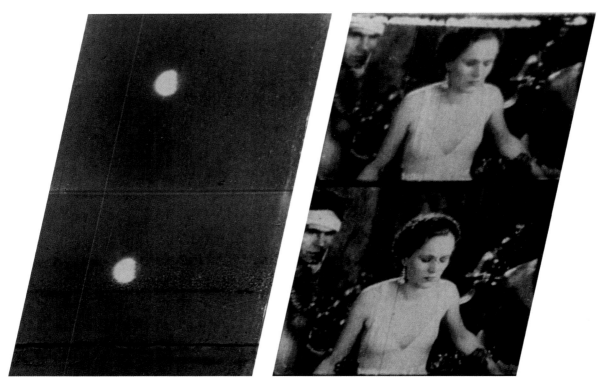

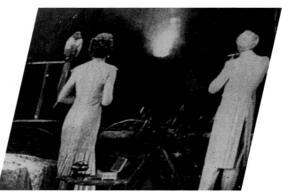

Joseph Cornell
Rose Hobart
c. 1936
16mm film
b/w, projected through
deep-blue filter
19 min
film stills
Anthology Film Archives, New
York
© The Joseph and Robert
Cornell Memorial Foundation;
VG Bild-Kunst, Bonn 2003
photo © the Menil Collection,
Houston

Cornell and QT memory boxes, then, tend toward what I would call a *"mnemonic aesthetic"* – privileging and practicing various devices that serve to preserve the fleeting memory, to "pin it down" and "put it under glass" like the gloriously colored butterflies one sees fixed in the vitrines of natural history museums. Such mnemonic practices are all based on *repetition* and *rhythm* and take a variety of forms and modes: "rote quotation" and mnemonic "clichés"; "looping," duplication, cyclical recurrence, repeated uses of images, objects, and sounds; rhythmic and repetitious patterning that is ritualistic, mechanical, or "mantric." All are mobilized in a concentrated effort to keep hold of memories that keeps threatening to slip away and vanish.

What Ratcliff observes in Cornell's work can be also observed in QuickTime memory boxes. The artist, we are told, "is drawn to 'material facts' – objects and images – whose preciousness is ratified by memory and he often calls on popular memory to reinforce his own. His image-chains often run along lines of well-worn cliché – butterfly, swan, ballerina."[29] Through repetition, Cornell make common objects mysterious: a row of wine glasses, a field of thimbles, a series of cork balls or pharmacy vials. However, this is "not the intellectualized notion of serialization, but more like the ritualized repetition of the alchemist."[30] Indeed, as Ratcliff says: "To duplicate an image endlessly is often to make its spell all the more binding."[31] Both Cornell and QT memory boxes are also highly citational: that is, they not only attempt to fix personal memories through repetition, but also quote and repeat previous artifacts of cultural memory – particularly privileging those that speak mnemonically to technologies of reproduction and preservation. Hence, both QT and Cornell memory boxes are "deeply involved with the photograph, the postcard, the photocopy, and the printed reproduction of works of art."[32] The boxes also use and repeat art historical images that reference the past: well-known paintings, old lithographs, classical statuary. Sound is also used mnemonically to an extraordinary degree in Quick-Time. It marks time in repetitive patterns and, in musical form, is generally less melodic than it is insistently rhythmic. While often voiced (literally) in fragments, it also is often looped, repeating a partial thought, setting up a percussive rhythm of mechanical repetition, "scratching" or "stuck" in a temporal sonic groove as if in an old phonograph record, possibly creating a "mantra." Indeed, middle Eastern and Indian music are

29 Ratcliff, op. cit., p. 54.

30 Dore Ashton, quoted in
    Ratcliff, op. cit., p. 57.

31 Ratcliff, op. cit., p. 64.

32 McShine, op. cit., p. 13.

used to a striking degree – particularly given often unrelated cultural imagery.

In their attempts to grasp and preserve the ephemeral fragments and fragile relics of memory, the boxes construct mnemonic rituals and, as Ratcliff notes, "ritual is mechanical, so any ritualizing aesthetic must have the power to mechanize the artist's meanings."[33] This mechanization is particularly compelling in QT memory boxes – for, rather than the "ritualized repetition of the alchemist" that marks Cornell's work, QT boxes do often convey "an intellectualized notion of serialization." That is, ritualized duplication and repetition often seem much more "mechanical" than "alchemical." Indeed, QT works derive much of their poetic power from *mimetic allegory*: the boxes duplicate and repeat their "memory fragments" as figural repetitions of the functional capacities of the computer itself to "duplicate," "copy," and "paste." Here, the mnemonic aesthetic emerges not only from a desire to preserve scarce and rare memory, but also from the ritualized and "mechanical" capacity of the computer to do the same.

In *Two Marks Jump*, for example, serial images are stutteringly animated, duplicated, and endlessly looped. Two of the same young man leap into and out of a scene accompanied by a similarly looped and endless yell; here the titular description of "two" Marks is self-consciously belied by the rote duplication of an infinite series of one.[34] *Hommage à Magritte* [sic], not only duplicates and transform the artist's emblematic bowler hats, but it also "mechanically" animates his famous painting *Golconde,* in which dozens of indistinguishable little bourgeois men rain down upon a sterile townscape.[35] In QT memory boxes, then, mechanical serialization and mnemonic repetition often combine, each "encouraging" the other to keep in mind – to re-collect and re-present – the ephemera of memory that would otherwise disappear from view.

Time, Movement, and the "Illusion of Life"
The miniature encourages the experience of intensity, interiority, and material preciousness through its compression and condensation of data in space. But the miniature also effects our sense of time. As Stewart points out, there is "a phenomenological correlation between *the experience of scale* and the *experience of duration*."[36] That is, time is transformed in the miniature: it thickens in significance and implodes. Compressed to "nest" in small spaces, time is reflexive: it falls back upon itself and "encrusts," building up the weight of a generalized past – or it collapses from its own density, diffusing into an ahistorical and infinitely deep state of reverie. Thus, as Stewart says: "The miniature does not attach itself to lived historical time. Unlike the metonymic world of realism, … the metaphoric world of the miniature makes everyday life absolutely anterior and exterior to itself."[37] Furthermore, when we engage the miniature, our sense of temporality never "streams" toward the future. Temporal compression and condensation conflict with forward movement and "life-like" animation. Thus "the miniature always tends toward *tableau* rather than toward narrative, toward silence and spatial boundaries rather than towards expository closure."[38] Fragments and traces of past experience exist in our sight and reverie as not only poetically evocative but also *emblematic* of irrecoverable "originary" moments

of wholeness. Broken and poignant, the fragment's stuttering or static and tableau-like presence points to both the passage of everyday life from particularity into allegory and to the great temporal mysteries of matter's slow and inexorable emergence and extinction. (Here, we might remember the memory box's tendency to figure and make thematic cosmological imagery that suggests not human temporality, but the imperceptible dynamics and perspective of "longue durée": a form of history written not in human events but in the cosmic temporality of geologic or climatic transformation.)

There is, finally, an extraordinary obfuscation (and questionable desire) in the nomination "QuickTime." QT is anything but quick: its animations are forestalled, its "illusion of life" incomplete. Compressing and condensing its imagery in a "miniature" number of bits of digital memory and display space, the material conditions that inform QT's miniature memory boxes are literally dramatized in the "half-life" of its objects. Not only are these objects constituted as fragments in space, they are also fragmented in temporality and motion. Thus, even when human in form, the animated "subjects" of QT are experienced as partially discontinuous and without agency. Phenomenologically, their movement seems imposed from "without" rather than emerging intentionally from "within." At best, like the puppet Pinocchio, they struggle against their existence as mere kinetic objects in frustrated fits and starts, stuttering out the desire to become a "real boy" – that is, fully alive in the temporal continuity and spatial coherence of intentional and realized action.

Central here is *intermittent motion*: time and action broken into fragments, gaps foregrounded, the laborious struggle to achieve human momentum and agency. In the mis-named QT "movie," Pinocchio's *bildungsroman* of self-realization is countered with the oxymoronic miniaturization and intermittencies that undo cinema *within* cinema (something that also occurs in the uncanny films of Jan Svankmajer and the Brothers Quay). Indeed, Cornell's own filmmaking efforts were meant to undo cinematic "live-action" and "real-time": he insisted that *Rose Hobart* – shot at sound speed (24 fps) and using fragments of a 1931 sound melodrama (*East of Borneo*) – be projected at silent speed (16–18fps) to the accompaniment of scratchy phonograph recordings.[39] The intermittent motion in Cornell and QT memory boxes, then, is always more than merely mechanical: it articulates the existential conundrum of *discontinuity*. That is, "momentum" is condensed and compressed into a series of reified and frozen "moments." Thus, the "illusion of life" becomes temporally solidified in what we might call a kinetic "souvenir": a memory of motion that is now merely its token.

In closing, we know that Pinocchio eventually became a "real boy" – and that QuickTime will eventually and seamlessly "stream" into real-time and live-action "cinema." But something quite poetic will be lost. Call me retrograde: as QuickTime enlarges and quickens to the myth of total cinema, I feel nostalgia for the impending loss of a unique historical experience and a rare and precious digital object.

The text is a much abridged version of the essay "Nostalgia for a Digital Object: Regrets on the Quickening of QuickTime," in *Millennium Film Journal*, no. 34, Fall 1999, pp. 4–23.

33 Ratcliff, op. cit., p. 58.

34 1993, no credits available.

35 *Hommage à Magritte: A QuickTime Movie by Lisa Osta,* 1993.

36 Stewart, op. cit., p. 66.

37 Stewart, op. cit., p. 65.

38 Stewart, op. cit., p. 66.

39 For seminal discussion of Cornell's films, see Annette Michelson, "Rose Hobart and Monsieur Phot: Early Films from Utopia Parkway," *Artforum*, vol. 11, no. 10, June 1973, pp. 47–57; and P. Adams Sitney, "The Cinematic Gaze of Joseph Cornell," in McShine, op. cit., pp. 69–89.

Luis Buñuel

left
El Angel Exterminador
[The Exterminating Angel]
1962
35mm film
b/w, sound
93 min
film still
photo © Maruja Isbert

right
Viridiana
1961
35mm film
b/w, sound
90 min
film still
© Kingsley

Pessimism

[…] Every type of show has its own audience. The one that goes to the cinema is, in general, the least congenial of all. Waiting in line puts them in a bad mood; you'll never see in them the enthusiasm of a bullfight aficionado. At heart, it's a false audience that relates to no one, only to images. If these images are mundane, they put them to sleep; if they're nice, they distract them. The Americans, who have understood this perfectly, give priority to action. From my stay in the U.S., I still have a great admiration for American cinema, its actors, its sense of rhythm and action. Its filmmakers have handled with unique mastery a modern art that corresponds very well to the temperament of that people, perhaps because things technical play an essential role there. In any event, like them I have wanted to eliminate from my films the beautiful images in which European cinema, with the exception of Visconti, has often lost itself. […]

Filmmaking seems to me a transitory and threatened art. It is very closely bound up with technical developments. If in thirty or fifty years the screen no longer exists, if editing isn't necessary, cinema will have ceased to exist. It will have become something else. That's already almost the case when a film is shown on television: the smallness of the screen falsifies everything. What will remain, then, of my films? I don't

think very highly at all of most of them. I have a certain fondness for only about ten, which isn't many in relation to all that I have made: *L'Age d'or*, above all; *Nazarín*; *Un Chien andalou*; *Simon of the Desert*; *Los Olvidados*, the preparation of which brought me in touch with juvenile delinquency and plunged me into the heart of Mexican misery; *Viridiana*; *Robinson Crusoe*; *The Criminal Life of Archibaldo de la Cruz*; *The Milky Way*; *The Discreet Charm of the Bourgeoisie*. […]

Those are the films that best express my vision of life. Surrealism made me understand that freedom and justice do not exist, but it also provided me with an ethic. An ethic of human solidarity, whose importance to me had been understood by Eluard and Breton when they humorously called me "the director of conscience" in their dedication to *The Immaculate Conception*. I illustrated this ethic in my own very particular way because I believe that my spirit is by nature destructive – and certainly of all of society. I have often returned to the subject of man struggling against a society that seeks to oppress and degrade him. Every individual seems to me worthy of interest, but when people congregate, their aggressiveness is set free and is converted into attack or flight, exercising violence or suffering. The history of heresies perfectly illustrates this, and that is why I have been so interested in them, as can be seen indirectly in many of my films, above all *The Milky Way*. […]

Viridiana
1961
35mm film
b/w, sound
90 min
publicity still
© Kingsley
photo © Maruja Isbert

Today I have come to be much more pessimistic. I believe that our world is lost. It may be destroyed by the population explosion, technology, science, and information. I call these four horsemen of the apocalypse. I am frightened by modern science that leads us to the grave through nuclear war or genetic manipulations, if not through psychiatry, as in the Soviet Union. Europe must create a new civilization, but I fear that science and the madness it can unleash won't leave time enough to do it.

If I had to make one last film, I would make it about the complicity of science and terrorism. Although I understand the motivations of terrorism, I totally disapprove of them. It solves nothing; it plays into the hands of the right and of repression. One of the themes of the film would be this: A band of international terrorists is preparing a severe attack in France, when the news arrives that an atomic bomb has been detonated over Jerusalem. A general mobilization is declared everywhere, world war is imminent. Then the leader of the group telephones the president of the Republic. He informs the French authorities of the exact location, in a barge near the Louvre, where they can recover the atomic bomb the terrorists have placed there before it explodes. His organization had decided to destroy the center of a civilization, but they renounced the crime because world war was about to break out, and the mission of terrorism had ended. Henceforth it is assumed by governments, which take up the task of destroying the world.

The glut of information has also brought about a serious deterioration in human consciousness today. If the pope dies, if a chief of state is assassinated, television is there. What good does it do one to be present everywhere? Today man can never be alone with himself, as he could in the Middle Ages.

The result of all this is that anguish is absolute and confusion total. [...]

In the film I'm thinking about, I would have liked to shoot in the hall of the Reichstag a meeting of fifteen Nobel prize-winning scientists recommending that atomic bombs be placed at the bottom of all oil wells. Science would then cure us of that which feeds our madness. But I rather think that in the end we'll be borne off by the worst, because since *Un Chien andalou* the world has advanced toward the absurd. [...]

Excerpts from Luis Buñuel, "Pessimism" (1980), in *An Unspeakable Betrayal. Selected Writings of Luis Buñuel*, University of California Press, Berkeley, Los Angeles, London, 2000, pp. 258–263.

Perry Hoberman
The Sub-Division of the Electric Light

1996
interactive CD-ROM / published in artintact 3 (ZKM, 1996)

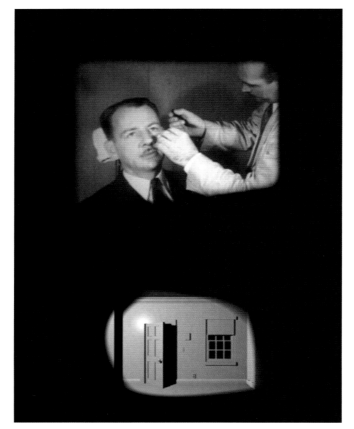

Beams of Light in a Virtual Void

The Sub-Division of the Electric Light (1996), Perry Hoberman's first CD-ROM work, is a kind of cultural junkyard turned into an interactive sculpture garden. Hoberman, "the world's foremost appliance artist," has created a place to promenade and meditate among the resurrected debris of the twentieth century. As always, this new gadgetspace is a hilarious yet ambivalent merging of various discourses. [...]

In *The Sub-Division of the Electric Light*, Hoberman invites us into a virtual void with old projectors appearing out of the darkness. Given the role of the projectionist, the visitor can click a projector on or off. Sometimes, however, clicking on the projected image disturbs the steady rolling of the "film," or causes "material" objects to appear in front of the image. By using the grab function one can manipulate these objects, or adjust the virtual light beam from the projector, or even turn the projector "physically" around in space. What seemed like a void actually contains a darkened enclosed space, revealed over time by the projector's beam. If you want to move on, you need only click on an icon connoting light (a light-bulb, a glimpse of light from a window).

Traditional film and slide projectors are material devices that exploit the physical properties of natural light and optics to project images, creating illusionary spaces in the process. Here, however, the projector itself is an illusion, and the light beam it projects is merely a simulation. The projected images are recognizably photographic, but seen as if through several

A key to Hoberman's work is provided by the film sequence (perhaps found footage from an old educational film) in which a man is seen examining another man's eye. Clearly *The Sub-Division of the Electric Light* can be read as a series of exercises in seeing. By focusing and blurring images in turn, projecting them on unusual surfaces or swiveling projectors in an ambiguous space which is simultaneously indefinite and enclosed, the user is led to reconsider his/her own perceptual experience. Semiotics has convincingly shown that all visual communication depends on contextualization, on the constant negotiation between encoding and decoding. By bringing together traditional optical-electric and contemporary digital-electronic media, Hoberman raises questions about the nature of the changes that digitalization has brought forth into the modalities of visual experience.

However, categorizing Hoberman as a didactic cultural analyst would be missing the point. Hoberman is a bricôleur who inhabits a cultural space and reinforces it. A personal passion for obsolete gadgets (with a touch of nostalgia) and an all-devouring sense of humor are important ingredients of Hoberman's art. Beginning with the title and its pseudo-scientific matter-of-factness (perhaps a homage to Los Angeles' Museum of Jurassic Technology, one of Hoberman's holy places), the user should be prepared to encounter a make-believe world where nothing is quite as it seems. It's not a coincidence that the projectors appear from the void like vessels from an outer-space B-movie. Hoberman has deliberately emphasized their familiar strangeness. Just like in *Faraday's Garden*, he breathes new life into appliances that the winds of fashion and technological development have doomed to oblivion.

The Sub-Division of the Electric Light might also be read as Hoberman's mock-museum of media art. We are thus led from one museum gallery to another, each presenting a different "art installation." As is well known, demystifying prevailing screen practices has been one of the main goals of politically conscious media art from the Fluxus artists on. Hoberman does his own share of demystification by creating "expanded cinema" pieces, emphasizing the materiality of the screen and the film stock, and breaking the illusion of linear narrative (which the brief quicklime film loops accomplish almost automatically). [...]

There is irony in the endeavor. [...] Juxtapositions such as material versus immaterial, or reality versus illusion, become meaningless in the digital realm. Whereas Jean Tinguely's "cybernetic sculpture" *Homage to New York* (1960) actually destroyed itself, a burning film frame within *The Sub-Division of the Electric Light* is merely a simulation, which can be repeated endlessly. Even the "material" objects that the user may cause to appear in front of the projected images, deflating the "pure" illusion, are not different, in nature, from the projections themselves. Both are the stuff that (cyber)dreams are made of. Consequently, Hoberman's mock-museum of media art is a meta-museum of media in transition. The blurring of distinctions brought forth by the digitalization of culture serves his purpose well, emphasizing rather than covering over the ambiguities that industrial media production, and media art as well, are currently facing.

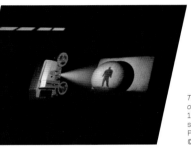

The Sub-Division of the Electric Light
1996
screenshots
Perry Hobermann
© Perry Hobermann

ontological filters. Having been brought into the digital realm and subordinated to digital manipulation, their connection with the "real events" they depict has become precarious. The images themselves have become events within a digital "rubber reality"–a flexible world in a state of constant metamorphosis. The gestures of a child or the movements of a group of scuba divers are not so important in and of themselves (and least of all, as narrative clues). Rather, they function as markers of a shift in our conception of (ir)reality.

This shift, Hoberman implies, is historical, and related to the development of media technology. Film and slide projectors (and magic lanterns before them) have contributed to the gradual virtualization of experience, leading from images of the world into worlds as images. It is hardly a coincidence that the Quick-Time film loops of a baby in Hoberman's work readily evoke *The Baby's Breakfast* (1895) by the Lumière brothers, one of the landmarks of the cinema's childhood. Hoberman's projected babies undergo a technical pseudo-mutilation (the "film" gets stuck and catches fire) or are dispersed onto the surrounding walls as a result of manipulating the projector's virtual beam. Both cases emphasize the artificiality of the experience itself, something which was not clear for early film audiences. In less than a century, film-based images, with their claim of naturalism, have been subsumed into other, more encompassing image worlds whose ontological status is anything but fixed. Brought into the digital realm, photographic and cinematographic images can never be the same again.

Erkki Huhtamo

The text is a much abridged version of an essay first published in *Artbyte. The Magazine of Digital Arts*, vol. 1, no. 1, New York, April–May 1998, pp. 58–61.

11

SCREENINGS

André Bazin
Will CinemaScope Save the Film Industry?

David W. Griffith
The Birth of a Nation
1915
16mm film
b/w, silent
180 min
film stills
© David W. Griffith Corporation

Cecil B. deMille
The King of Kings
1927
film
b/w, color, silent
115 min
film still
© MGM

11 SCREENINGS
André Bazin / Will CinemaScope Save the Film Industry?

80

1 *The Robe* was the first film shot in CinemaScope; it opened at New York's Roxy Theatre in September of 1953.

2 A reference to Thomas R. Malthus (1766–1834), the English economist who theorized that population tends to increase at a faster rate than its means of subsistence and that, unless it is checked by moral restraint or by disease, famine, war, or other disaster, widespread poverty and degradation inevitably result.

3 With 3-D films, as well as with CinemaScope, Cinerama, Panavision, and other wide-screen processes.

Everybody knows by now, even the average moviegoer, that Hollywood is trying to come to terms with one of the most severe economic crises in its history through the introduction of both 3-D, whose avant-garde stereoscopy has already been seen on French screens, and CinemaScope, whose big war machine, *The Robe* (Henry Koster, 1953), has already been shown in New York and is soon going to be exhibited in Europe.1 Everybody knows, too, that Hollywood is forced to accept the risks of such an endeavor – which totally upsets the norms not only of production, but also of distribution – in view of the acute competition represented by television. At least everybody thinks he knows these things, for the details of the problem are not that simple. The aim of this article, then, is precisely to try to create some order out of all this.

Let's start with some interesting facts of a very general nature. First, we can observe that this time the crisis is not turning into chaos or panic. To be sure, great confusion still reigns, and one can see the "major companies" taking the most contradictory measures; each one has its own strategy – or claims it has, for it is very often the same strategy under a different name. While some big companies almost completely ceased production only a few months ago, one can see a minor company like Monogram double its annual schedule for the production of B-movies for normal screens. Clearly, the heyday of Hollywood is over. But, again, this confusion and decline have not become panic and hysteria, at least not yet. By investing totally in CinemaScope, Fox is not repeating Warner Brothers' gamble with talkies. None of the American companies, in spite of a film-consumption crisis that has become worse

and worse over the last five years, are yet on the verge of bankruptcy. They can probably all afford to indulge in a long period of Malthusianism2 without being threatened with extinction. This means, of course, that the technical experiment3 will be relatively controlled and that Hollywood will probably be able to draw some conclusions as soon as the moviegoing wind starts blowing one way or another.

The situation will probably be more serious for the unemployed technicians and actors. But it is not that alarming, and it won't get worse for at least a few months, because television needs a lot of small films that can be quickly made and in which there is work for many people. Some stars go over to television; others make the most of their forced holidays and come to Europe to act in a co-production over an eighteen-months period, thus avoiding the paying of income tax – which is well worth the corresponding loss of Hollywood salary. To cut a long story short, the situation could become very disquieting five or six months from now, but perhaps we will be able to see it more clearly then and work will resume, if at a different pace.

These remarks are not aimed at minimizing the importance of the crisis – on the contrary, since it would be impossible to do so in the face of the numerical figures that I'll give later – but only at defining its atmosphere and above all at underscoring the fact that Hollywood is still in control. It is important to know this especially for those who naïvely believe in some huge crash, in Hollywood's sinking into an economic chaos from which Europeans could benefit. Hollywood won't cast its "three dice" like a desperate gambler. On the contrary, its operation will continue to be mounted with

Cecil B. deMille
Samson and Delilah
1949
35mm film
color, sound
131 min
film still
© Paramount
Pictures Inc.

Victor Fleming
Gone with the Wind
1939
35mm film
color, sound
230 min
film still
© MGM

caution and firmness, and that operation will be massively supported by the various publicity departments. The reservations Hollywood has about responding to the challenge of television will be overcome thanks to the temporary financial advantages gained by the attractive transformation of movie screens, for example – thanks, that is, to all the assets of a powerful, conscious, and organized capitalism.

Of course, this doesn't mean that all the obstacles – and we'll see that they are numerous – will be removed. But at least they will be dealt with, with maximum efficiency, in Europe as well as in America, and I don't really see how the American experiment could fail even if the old Continent resists the new developments. The film revolution will be universal or it won't take place at all. Whether we like it or not, Hollywood remains the magnetic pole of the film industry, at least as far as technical proficiency is concerned. We can particularly see it today: Cinerama,4 which is little more than Abel Gance's triple screen, and CinemaScope,5 which was invented twenty-five years ago by Professor Chrétien, seem viable all of a sudden because of the interest that America has shown in them now that the moviemaking business is in decline.

Such a situation seems to lead to a pessimistic view of the notion of progress in the cinema. I will no doubt have to clarify this aspect of the matter, but only after I've attempted to analyze its sociological and aesthetic aspects. Let's stick with the economic side of things for the moment, and briefly recall the causes and proportions of a crisis whose seriousness cannot be denied. The immediate cause is the dramatic reduction of the number of moviegoers

since the introduction of television. In the last five or six years, the American film industry has lost approximately half of its national audience; this has meant the closing down of five thousand movie theaters (all of France doesn't have that many), and will mean the bankruptcy in the near future of several thousand others. The simultaneity of the onset of the crisis and of the rise of television naturally doesn't permit any doubt that television is indeed the principal factor in the crisis. Unfortunately, one cannot say that it is the only one.

From various bits of evidence, one can conclude that the twenty million American television sets have simply crystallized and accelerated a tendency in the moviegoing audience. Indeed, this tendency started to manifest itself even in areas where television had not yet been introduced, and it has continued to get worse and worse in the areas saturated with television sets. Furthermore, we know that in various European countries, particularly France, where the number of television sets is still insignificant, a disturbing reduction in the number of moviegoers has been observed in the last few years. Everything, then, seems to indicate that a general, deep, and *a priori* weariness with the cinema on the part of the American public has found in television a visible means of manifesting itself. The viewer statistics are therefore all the more alarming, and they indicate that the haemorrhage cannot be checked through a mere cauterization – a CinemaScoping, as it were – of the wound made by television to the film industry.

By instinct – an instinct that is deep-rooted and that isn't without value, even from an aesthetic point of view, as we'll see later – Hollywood understood that the defense against television had to

4 Cinerama. Developed by Fred Waller of Paramount's special effects department. A wide-screen process originally utilizing three cameras and three projectors to record and project a single image. The three 35mm cameras were set up to record three aspects of a single image simultaneously: one camera facing directly ahead and the other two slightly to the right and left. When projected on a special huge screen, curved to an angle of about 165 degrees, at twenty-six frames per second, the images blended together to produce an illusion of vastness and plasticity. Three electronically synchronized projectors were used, the middle one projecting straight ahead and the other two projecting to the right and left in a crisscross arrangement.

5 CinemaScope. Trade name copyrighted by Twentieth Century-Fox for a wide-screen process based on an anamorphic system developed by Professor Henri Chrétien. The system involves special lenses that compress and distort images during filmmaking and spread them out undistorted during projection, over an area wider than the normal motion-picture screen. The CinemaScope image, photographed on normal 35mm film, is about two and a half times as wide as it is high when it is projected, and has an aspect ratio of 2.35 : 1, as compared with the conventional screen aspect ratio of 1.33 : 1. The aspect ratio for 70mm CinemaScope is 2.2 : 1.

be of a *spectacular* nature. Let's not forget, at the same time, that the evolution of film (even in America) has been toward the interiorization of the *mise en scène* at the expense of spectacle. Moreover, the conditions of the market demanded such a reduction of spectacle as much as the laws of aesthetic evolution. The remaking of *The Birth of a Nation* (D. W. Griffith, 1915) with the latest cinematic technology would be unthinkable today because the film could no longer pay off (the success of *Gone with the Wind*, Victor Fleming, 1939, was miraculous, and the industry is careful not to try to repeat it). Today, Cecil B. DeMille's Biblical epics (e.g. *Samson and Delilah*, 1949) are made on ridiculously low budgets compared to his similar productions of thirty years ago (e.g. *The King of Kings*, 1927). Nowadays, we must go to Russia (and perhaps India) to find a film with an enormous crowd of walk-ons, or a movie that is produced regardless of cost.

And yet ... it is obvious that film owns a lasting superiority over television precisely because of its spectacular resources – indeed, only because of them. Lasting, because the television picture will in all probability remain limited in definition by the 625 scanning lines of the standard American set (just as the cinematographic film is limited by its 35 millimeters, a figure arbitrarily chosen by Edison). Whatever its other technical qualities (including color and 3-D, which will one day be available), the television picture will always retain its mediocre legibility. It will also remain a product essentially consumed in the family circle, and, as such, it will continue to be limited to a small screen. In any case, a big television screen for collective viewing in movie theaters makes some sense only for live news programs; but the quality of the image of such "telecinema" would be very inferior to that of cinema itself. So it is logical that the counteroffensive of the film industry is being fought on its home turf, in the area of its only superiority: through a return to its potential for the spectacular.

To tell the truth, Hollywood has not chosen its strategy by deduction. Indeed, the impetus came from a New York film attraction whose success has taken on colossal and unforeseeable proportions: Cinerama. After two years of continuous running,

seats still have to be booked six months in advance. You know what Cinerama is: the juxtaposition, on a huge, curved support, of three screens upon which three aspects of a single image are simultaneously projected. Abel Gance had done the same thing twenty-five years earlier in *Napoléon* 1927, and in addition had used every possible combination of images on the three screens in order to create sensational effects in the editing of space. This is also the principle behind panoramic photography. In any event, the effectiveness of the device is not to be measured in terms of its technical originality, for all those who have seen Cinerama agree that it is quite impressive.

But the use of Cinerama does not come without problems that are almost impossible to solve. This wide-screen process demands a theater of the appropriate size and shape, three projectors and three projection rooms, and last but not least a very delicate electronic synchronization of the three projectors. The result is not always perfect, even when all the conditions for Cinerama's use have otherwise been met. In the film industry, however, the fundamental question concerning technological developments remains the following: how are they going to complicate distribution? Thus a device such as Roux-color, 6 which is amazingly simple and cheap, does not stand a chance for the simple reason that it complicates the projection of the film. It will always be wiser and more profitable to invest millions of dollars in laboratories that perfect film processes than to provide owners of movie theaters with flawed prints or prints that cannot be flawlessly projected.

Hence the enormous superiority of CinemaScope over Cinerama. Thanks to the anamorphosis of the image permitted by Professor Chrétien's lens, the triple picture of Cinerama finds itself literally compressed to the dimensions of a standard film. A symmetrical lens then expands the image during projection. In fact, the image that is thus expanded is only about two and a half times the length of a conventional screen, but the experiment reveals that such a length – as opposed to that required for Cineramic projection – is absolutely sufficient for maximum effectiveness. Of course, CinemaScope itself is going

6 Named after Lucien Roux (1894–1956), who with his brother Armand invented this color process in 1931. It can be seen at work in Marcel Pagnol's *La Belle Meunière*.

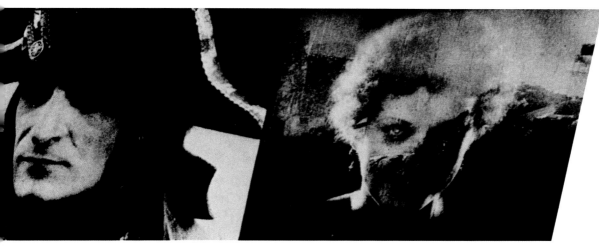

Abel Gance
Napoléon
1927
16mm film
b/w, silent
220 min
screenshot of the
triple-screen projection
© The Images Film Archive, Inc.;
Zoetrope Studios

to complicate rather seriously the issue of distribution. It is easy to comprehend that this wide-screen process demands an appropriate setting. The long and narrow movie theaters do not have a back wall that is wide enough for a CinemaScope screen. In France, for example, the number of theaters that *won't* have to be transformed is estimated at only twenty percent. Moreover, the CinemaScope equipment, temporarily monopolized by Fox, is rather expensive. Indeed, aside from the special projection lens, a special screen with high and uniform luminosity from all angles is necessary.

Consequently, these serious, if not insurmountable, difficulties have already become the pretext for the appearance of a surrogate CinemaScope, which crudely attempts to solve all problems. Today, for instance, one can see in Paris (and all the other capitals of Europe) a "panoramic screen," which is a rather strange kind of swindle. Its advantage is double: first, the size of the screen is variable within limits that make it adaptable to most normal movie theaters; second, and above all, it transforms any type of standard film into a "wide-screen" one. It is worth explaining through what wonderful geometric slight of hand the "panoramic screen" does this. It's a simple question of fractions: the conventional image is defined by its 4 : 3 x 2 proportions (I'm rounding off in order to simplify), i.e. 8 : 3. But in every school, one learns that one can also multiply a fraction by dividing its denominator, which means that, instead of doubling the length of the image, I can *divide it into two lengthwise*: hence, 8 : 3 = 4 : 1.5. This half picture, projected with an appropriate lens, will cover an area of screen that is exactly identical with the area covered by CinemaScope, and the trick is done.

I'm not joking: the very official, very serious, and oh-so-very wise "Technical Commission of the French Film Industry" recommends to all producers that from now on they make their films for potential projection on a panoramic screen, i.e. that they concentrate the "useful" part of the image in the central portion of the frame. The projector of the appropriately equipped movie theater will be fitted with a mask of the same proportions as the screen, and this mask will hide the "useless" part of the

image. As matters stand today, since not all films have been made to undergo this surgical operation, the framing is left to the initiative of the projectionist, who is supposed to choose between beheading the characters and cutting off their legs, according to his personal complexes. But already the most serious of filmmakers have come to compose their images in such a way that they can undergo, without too much damage, the removal of one sixth off the top and one sixth from the bottom. More stupid even than the catoblepas,[7] film is eating both its head and its tail, but only, of course, in order to grow larger.

What difference is there, then, between the wide screen and the standard, abbreviated one? Isn't the viewer's angle of vision the same? Perhaps, but here we must specify more what CinemaScope in fact is. The optics of cinema is defined not only by the proportions of the image, but also by what one can introduce into the frame. Unlike the eye, which has a single optical system, the camera has at its disposal a wide variety of lenses covering more or less unlimited angles. In the case of wide angles, the use of short focal lengths partly compensates for the narrowness of the screen. This system has its drawbacks, though, for the more one moves away from the physical properties of the eye, the more obvious are the distortions in perspective. The indisputable advantage of Professor Chrétien's Hypergonar[8] is its multiplication by two of the angle of its specially developed lens, without modifying the lens's other optical characteristics. What happens when the image is projected onto a wide screen, then, is not only that the viewer's angle of vision gets widened – an angle, moreover, that depends on where he is seated in the theater – but also that the depth of his perception of photographed reality is genuinely increased.

By way of comparison, imagine that I have cut a flat rectangular window into a piece of cardboard, and that I have placed behind the frame thus defined a photograph that must come into contact with the cardboard. The angle formed by my eye and the sides of the picture varies with the distance at which I place the cardboard, but the image itself does not vary: it is still defined by the optical nature of this

7 An unknown, perhaps mythical, African quadruped that has been identified with the gnu.

8 The original name for the anamorphic lens systems developed by Henri Chrétien and later developed into CinemaScope by Twentieth Century-Fox.

particular viewing. Let me now remove the photo-graph and consider as a "picture" what I see behind the "mask" of the cardboard. This time, whether I step back or get closer to the frame will indeed make a difference, for the true angle of vision really increases together with that of the triangle whose upper corner is my eye and whose base is the length of the "mask." It is this angle of view that matters first and foremost, before the one formed by the screen and my chair. In substituting for Cinema-Scope, the "panoramic screen" widens the latter angle only by making the picture shrink vertically. The true content of the image, then, is divided by two (relative to the conventional image as defined by its 4 : 3 proportions) or by four, if we compare it with the CinemaScopic picture.

Thanks to this sad example of the "panoramic screen," one can see what purely commercial vicissi-tudes the evolution of cinema must undergo. This leads me to a meditation on what the notion of pro-gress in film thereby becomes. Of course, in all the arts progress depends on the development of tech-nique or technology. We know what the evolution of painting owes to the discovery of perspective, on the one hand, and to the invention of siccatives, on the other. However, one couldn't say that the history of harmony is totally dependent upon the history of musical instruments, and one well understands that, since the discovery of the grinding of powders in oil, the art of painting on an easel has evolved indepen-dently of any technical or technological innovation. Conversely, it is true that, at least roughly speaking, the evolution of architecture is determined almost completely by the materials used, or in any event by the hypothetical control one is able to achieve over them. Thus the Romanesque and Gothic cathedrals are built with the same stones, but the architect of the latter has arranged them in a far more efficient way.

Must we therefore contrast the evolution of the so-called "abstract" arts, such as music or litera-ture, with that of the so-called "concrete" arts, in which the materials are predominant? Probably not, for in both cases the aesthetician would discern a logic, a system of laws, inherent in each art form, and would define, at least *a posteriori*, the possible evo-lutions and involutions of that form. The quarrels among architects are not essentially different from those between traditionalist and twelve-tone musi-cians. In these fields, it is the mind that ultimately makes artistic decisions. Its decisions may later be altered or even misrepresented by the constraints of history, but the evolution of the art, even if it is thwarted, will still retain a theoretical integrity and a definable sense.

There are some who would say that this is not true for film as well. However, if we examine the his-tory of cinema, we are permitted to doubt whether the artist's critical sensibility and will matter so little in its destiny. Certainly, film has had no shortage of creators, even creators of genius, who have con-tributed considerably to its progress: this is as irrefutable for the cinema as it is for the traditional arts. We need not be shocked by the fact that these filmic artists generally bowed to the demands of mass consumption. Such constraints also make for the greatness of film, and it has derived from them some excellent aesthetic benefits. Although these constraints are perhaps more numerous and heavy than anywhere else, essentially they still don't repre-sent a condition peculiar to, and restrictive of, film-making. But normal aesthetic progress in the cinema is difficult, for this art form is at the mercy of tech-nological disturbances that may interrupt its course for purely economic reasons.

Thus silent film had reached an admirable point in its evolution when sound came along to challenge everything. It is obvious that not a single filmmaker had asked for this technological innovation, not even the ones whose personal style could only have bene-fited from it. The producers, and the producers alone, were responsible for the creation of this new attraction. In fact, talking pictures had already been possible for a number of years, and we would have had to wait several more years for the implementa-tion of sound had the financial problems of Warner Bros. not prompted this studio to gamble everything on the new discovery. It is not at all absurd to imag-ine that, if the introduction of sound had been con-ducted in a slightly different way and had not been successful with the viewers, films would have re-mained silent. Indeed, it is always the initial response that determines the destiny of important changes in the processes of production and distribution. In 1927, Abel Gance made a film to be shown on a wide triple screen (*Napoléon*) and Claude Autant-Lara made an-other one with Chrétien's Hypergonar (*Construire un feu*, 1928).9 But the conditions under which these films were projected and the general industry con-text (attention was already focusing on the talkies) caused this potential revolution to fail at the time. The only difference today resides in the fact that a long and well-orchestrated publicity campaign, to-gether with enormous financial reserves, may prime the commercial pump and determine the success of an endeavor that had failed twenty-five years earlier.

Conversely, a filmmaker couldn't possibly cause, through the sole power of his art, any kind of distur-bance in the technological framework within which filmmaking is carried on. Of course, he can benefit tremendously from technological progress (the sen-sitivity of emulsions, the outfitting of the studios, etc.), but he never determines it. Let's go one step further. Not only do the external or technological conditions of filmmaking exclude the filmmaker, but also the destiny of cinema as an art form does as well. No doubt, what fundamentally distinguishes the mechanical arts that have appeared since the nineteenth century from the traditional arts is the mortality of the former. The danger that television represents for the film industry is not at all like the threat that film had presented to theater. Although, at the very worst, a reduction in the number of theatergoers might force the theater to switch to more unusual or more modest dramatic forms, the disappearance of theater as an art form is

9 In 1927, Autant-Lara tackled a wide-screen experiment with the short *Construire un feu*, an avant-garde adaptation of a Jack London story.

unthinkable: it will necessarily and eternally be reborn in children's games, in social liturgies, or simply in the need that some people have to playact in front of their peers, be it only in the catacombs. The traditional arts were born at the same time as man and will disappear only if he does. In this respect, film is not an art form, it is not the fulfillment of an eternal need or a newly created one (are there any radically new needs?); rather, it is the result of the happy conjunction between a virtual need and the technological-economic state of civilization. In other words, film is not an *art* AND *an industry*, but instead an *industrial art* that is likely to vanish into thin air as soon as the industry's profits disappear. So if tomorrow television robs the film industry of the portion of its audience that was still making it a profitable exercise, producers will invest their capital elsewhere and the cinema will vanish from the scene as quickly as it came onto the scene. And nothing will persuade me to believe, in the spirit of futuristic optimism, that television will take over from an aesthetic point of view, just as film has taken over (at least partially) from the novel and the theater. For, aside from the fact that television is an industrial form in whose evolution aesthetic logic plays only a very small part, the art of television is probably much narrower than that of film. It is superior to film only in the field of documentary reportage. For the rest, television is a means of communication and expression that is irremediably cruder than the cinema.

So, unlike the traditional arts, which can merely decline or suffer, film in principle is mortal. And it's better to know from the start if one truly cares about its continued existence. I myself have underlined the danger to film's survival only to reaffirm my faith in its future. Up to now, the threat to the cinema has concerned only Hollywood, although, of course no one would think of taking any pleasure from that. Even if we did, Hollywood remains, in all senses of the word, the capital of world cinema. I won't go so far as to say that filmmaking would be crippled without Hollywood, but it *would* lack an essential gland whose secretions influence all other glands. Nonetheless, film would survive and would probably end up by compensating for the loss of its American capital. Certainly television is going to develop in Europe as it did in America, but nothing proves that French, English, or Italian viewers will so persuasively fall under its sway as the Americans have.

One conceivable strategy for the cinema's survival would be a greater differentiation on the part of producers between the market for cheap B-movies and the market for *reasonably cheap* quality movies. The former would continue to be made for, say, fifty percent of today's filmgoers, while the latter would be aimed at precisely that international fringe of the audience capable of escaping the grip of television in order to go and see a good film. In fact, there is a certain audience that goes to the theater and the movies alike solely on the basis of the quality of the play or film pre-

sented. To be sure, this group of people is relatively small, but, on an international scale, it may be big enough to ensure the financial viability of the films that we like, such as those of Renoir, Rossellini, Bresson, and De Sica. One may also hope that television will later help the film industry by playing the role of a distribution network, for whose products customers will have to pay and which will be a source of additional income, beyond the profits made by the movie theaters themselves.

More still: not only does the death of the film industry seem improbable to me, but also the attempt to solve its economic crisis through spectacular developments seems to point in the direction of substantial and desirable evolutionary progress. It is significant that this industrial art form, which is dependent upon economic factors, should have had its aesthetic progress ensured exclusively by technological developments. That is, if one can really speak about progress in the arts, for, in a way, it will always be absurd to think of da Vinci's work as superior to the art of the caveman. From this point of view, progress never depends on material technique or technology, or, more accurately, each technique has its own evolution whose peak is as high as that of the technique, or the technology, which replaces it. There does tend to be agreement, however, that from murals to oil painting one can indeed see progress, as one can from the epic to the novel or from melody to counterpoint. My purpose is not to defend this thesis, which I think the reader will easily accept if only he considers the opposite one. Refusing the evolution of technique or technology amounts to condemning the life of civilization itself, to refusing to be *modern* – i.e. to refusing to exist. It remains true that not all technical-technological developments are *ipso facto* evidence of progress: they must in the end be brought into harmony with the internal laws of the art form, with its specific physiology. Thus, conversely, modern art strives to return (even if through some very sophisticated techniques or technology) to fundamental or primitive laws that have been buried under the brush of a false, or falsely prized, historical evolution: see Lurçat 10 and tapestry, for example, or Le Corbusier and architecture.

So I won't say that sound, by itself and through the mere fact that it added one element to the picture, has meant progress for film. If this is indeed so, it is because film is not at all in essence an art form of exclusively visual images. It is paradoxically true that its initial infirmity, by forcing filmmakers to create a silent language, contributed to the evolution of an art form that, as early as 1925, had already reached a kind of classical stage; it is equally true that speech challenged this language of silence and caused the temporary regression of cinema. But these accidents do nothing to controvert the fact that the essence of film from the very start (one might even say as early as its seed took root in the inventors' imagination) has been a quest for the realism of the image. One could say that this realism is implied by the automatic genesis of the cinematographic image, and that it

10 Jean Lurçat (1892–1966) was a French painter who greatly contributed to reviving the art of tapestry.

Henri-Georges Clouzot
Le Salaire de la Peur
[Wages of Fear]
1953
35mm film
b/w, sound
147 min
film still
© International Affiliates

William Wyler
The Best Years of Our Lives
1946
35mm film
b/w, sound
172 min
film still
© RKO

aims at giving this image the greatest number of characteristics in common with natural perception.

The abstraction that is necessary to art must paradoxically emerge here from what is most concrete in the image. Every convention that film retains from drawing, painting, and photography (black and white, the absence of a third dimension, framing itself) contributes to its abstraction, if only temporarily. The worst mistake we could make, however, is to think that these "genes," by their very existence, are exquisite and fecund. One must temper such a belief, which is too general to be true. It would be equally naïve to think that the filmic image tends toward total identification with the universe that it copies, through the successive addition of supplementary properties from that universe. Perception, on the part of the artist as well as the audience of art, is a synthesis – an artificial process – each of whose elements acts on all the others. And, for example, it is not true that color, in the way that we are able to reproduce it – as an addition to the image framed by the narrow window of the screen – is an aspect of pure realism. On the contrary, color brings with it a whole set of new conventions that, all things considered, may make film look more like a painting than reality.

The same holds true for stereoscopic relief, which does indeed give the impression that objects exist in space, but in a ghastly or impalpable state. The internal contradiction of this relief is that it creates the impression of an unreal, unapproachable world far more than does the flatness of black-and-white film. This is why one shouldn't count on a victory for stereoscopic relief in the war among 3-D processes. Even if we forget about the inconvenience caused by Polaroid glasses, the unreality of this universe, which seems strangely spun out of a hole on the screen, would be enough to condemn it – except in the genres where the aim is precisely a certain union of fantasy and reality, especially horror films. It

is nevertheless possible that, with the advent of the wide screen, one of the major disadvantages of stereoscopic relief will disappear, and certain films, detective stories and musicals in particular, will be shot with this photographic process.

In any event, the real revolutionary innovation will very probably be the CinemaScopic screen, and from now on we must take account of it. Let me say right away that the equation of this screen with stereoscopic relief is incorrect and the result of overzealous publicity. It must also be said that, after a few yards, binocular vision plays only a secondary role in the perception of depth, and that the location of objects in space is the result of a series of factors which could as well be taken in by a one-eyed viewer. The closer the conditions of filmic vision get to natural vision, then, the more the dimension of depth will appear; and, in this respect, the CinemaScopic screen helps in that it gives us, instead of today's narrow window, a widened surface whose angle formed with the viewer's eye is closer to the normal angle of vision. But the impression of depth and perspective cannot be manufactured in all CinemaScopic shots and, even when it is created, it remains rather partial. The genuine contribution of CinemaScope lies elsewhere: in the elongated format of its screen.

Up to now, the only items I have seen in Cinema-Scope (in Paris or in Venice) are spectaculars, of either a documentary or a dramatic nature (*The Robe*, 1953, for example), all of which employed this new method of framing. Its effect is undoubtedly sensational, especially when combined with stereophonic sound, which is required on account of the huge dimensions of the screen. We can well understand why Clouzot is furious that he made *Le Salaire de la Peur* (1953) before the appearance of CinemaScope, since the film would have benefited 100 percent from it. CinemaScope has an affinity as well with genres like the Western, whose signature framing is the long shot showing the landscape

Orson Welles
Othello
1952
35mm film
b/w, sound
91 min
publicity still
© United Artists

stretching toward the horizon. The cavalry marches, the stagecoach chases, and the Indian wars will at last find on the wide screen the space where they belong. But one can make some very serious arguments against CinemaScope, despite its partial advantages. What film is going to gain from it in the spectacular genres, isn't it going to lose in the area of psychological complexity and, more generally, in the power of its intellectual expression, precisely the qualities on which the more sophisticated genres depend? Furthermore, what's going to become of the sacrosanct close-up, the keystone of film editing, through this bay window that is being substituted for the old, narrow one?

That's the operative word here: *editing*. Ever since the filmic work of Abel Gance and Sergei Eisenstein, on the one hand, and a famous critical article by André Malraux, on the other hand, it has undoubtedly become the alpha of cinematic language, the omega being framing, which plastically organizes the contents of the image. Well, we must once and for all get rid of this critical prejudice, which in any case has been shown to be untrue by a number of silent masterpieces, such as those of von Stroheim and Chaplin, in which editing plays only a secondary role. It is not true that cutting into shots and augmenting those shots with a whole range of optical effects are the necessary and fundamental elements of filmic expression, however subtle that expression might otherwise be. On the contrary, one can see that the evolution of film in the last fifteen years has tended toward the elimination of editing. Already before the war, we had Jean Renoir's great lesson on this subject.11 And we have had lessons since then from *Citizen Kane* (Orson Welles, 1941) and from *The Best Years of Our Lives* (William Wyler, 1946), in which most of the shots are exactly as long as the scenes taking place in them.

It is true that framing alone can often create within the image a kind of virtual editing. But isn't this fact of composition itself about to disappear, in that it is a plastic artifice foreign to the essence of the *mise en scène*? Bresson's *Journal d'un Curé de Campagne* (1951) owes very little to photographic composition, and I can see in it very few optical effects that are not translatable into CinemaScope. But I do see the additional meaning that the opposition, or rather the place, of the priest in the landscape in some shots would gain from filming in CinemaScope. A motion picture like *The River* (Jean Renoir, 1951) of whose innovative beauty I have sung the praises in *Esprit* could also only profit from presentation on a wide screen. I'm still waiting for someone to give me the title of a single film – at least in recent years, and one whose import is not aesthetically reactionary – that couldn't have been shot in CinemaScope. And I won't accept *Othello* (Orson Welles, 1952) whose purpose seems to me to be the final exhaustion of montage in a flurry of artifice.

In contrast to Welles' Shakespearean film, the wide screen will only hasten the adoption of that most modern of tendencies beloved in fine film-making: the stripping away of everything extrinsic to the quintessential meaning of the image, of all the expressionism of time and space. Film will thus grow even more apart from the abstractions of music and painting, and will get even nearer to it profound vocation, which is to show before it expresses, or, more accurately, to express through the evidence of the real. Put yet another way: the cinema's ultimate aim should be not so much to mean as to reveal.

Translated from the French by Bert Cardullo

Originally published in French in: André Bazin, "Cinémascope: sauvera-t-il le cinéma?" in *Esprit*, vol. 21, no. 207–208, October–November 1953, pp. 672–683. This translation first appeared in the online salon-journal *Film-Philosophy*, vol. 6, no. 2, January 2002, http://www.film-philosophy.com/vol6-2002/n2bazin

11 Bazin could be referring here either to *La Grande Illusion* (1937) or *La Règle du jeu* (1939).

Richard Hamilton
Glorious Technicolor, Breathtaking CinemaScope and Stereophonic Sound

One of my earliest childhood memories is of a scene in a motion picture: a ragged, mad, bearded beachcomber finds a chest of treasure washed up on the beach, together with a beautiful, unconscious blonde. I can remember being deeply impressed by the sight of him slobbering over the combined loot – running his hands through the pearls and over her lovely extended neck. I was certainly less than four at the time and it affected me like something seen in the woodshed. At about this time also there is another memory of an evening when my parents went out leaving me in the care of my brother and sister. To placate me I was given the use of a crystal set that I wasn't normally allowed to touch. The headphones were put on my pillow, the cat's-whisker was twiddled and I listened enraptured to the strange noises; it became dark and I fell asleep with the sounds still scratching out of the flat circular boxes. A few years later, at about the age of eight, my father took me to see *The Singing Fool* – of this I remember only the moment when the sound of a voice from a gramophone coincided with the opening and closing of Al Jolson's mouth in a moving photograph.

These, my earliest experiences of primitive entertainment machines, could, I'm sure, be matched by any of us. We must all have found that contact with the fantasy world is made all the more memorable when the bridge is a newly experienced technological marvel. We are not more convinced by a new process but the first acquaintance with it will leave a most convincing impression – for there is tremendous entertainment in simply experiencing a device which is new to us however banal the matter being presented by it. It was because of this fascination in process that, in the late 1940s, we went to see color films for preference. Given a choice between three unexceptional films I would go to the one in Technicolor even if, as was likely, it was called *Son of Sinbad*. At that time also, my most used record was *The Shanghai Sailor* played by the band of the Coldstream Guards because it contained a remarkably well-recorded flute passage which made my home-made HiFi equipment

sound as good as it was. There was, I think, a general interest in equipment as such among the electronic amateurs produced by the warpushing at the inertia of productive resources. For many years there had been a serious resistance to technical innovation in the cinema and gramophone companies. They found it pretty hard to realize that there could be economic advantage in the introduction of any technique which affected their production and presentation methods. EMI, the largest producers of records in this country, were using presses manufactured before the 1914 war in the same building that had always housed them. They pressed virtually the same raw materials into discs with the same groove form in 1950 as they had for forty years – and they were still minting money. The 35mm stock used by the film industry hadn't changed all that much either. Chemists had improved the emulsions, optical advances in lenses had been introduced and sound engineers had developed recording techniques – but no basic change, one which affected projection methods, would be tolerated. Technicolor, and all the other color processes, had arrived unimpeded because they affected only emulsion and processing.

And it wasn't for the lack of ideas. In 1929 Fox Films released a 70mm picture called *Grandeur* – this was shown only at the Gaiety Cinema, New York. In 1937 Henri Chrétien had developed an anamorphic lens: Paramount claims to have made a testpicture with Chrétien anamorphs in the 1930s and to have rejected the system as unsatisfactory. Also in 1937 Fred Waller, the inventor of "Cinerama," had built equipment to project a film inside a sphere, a process he called "Vitarama." But it wasn't until after the war that the film industry felt impelled to force the introduction of techniques known to them for many years. Ideas from the 1920s, like Fox's 70mm projection, had been swallowed up in the depression in the USA – by the time things leveled out the 1939 war was approaching. Since 1950 there have been notable changes at the exhibition end of the industry. The time was ripe, we were ready to go – and not only to

left
Henry Koster
The Robe
1953
film
color, sound
133 min
squeezed CinemaScope
projection print

right
© 20th Century-Fox
squeezed 20th Century-Fox
trademark

the cinema. Wartime advances in fundamental electronic thinking opened up a new set of possibilities in radio engineering; TV in nearly every home had changed the pattern of the entertainment industries. Above all, the tremendous post-war production potential had to be deflected to satisfy a new public demand – "now make me happy." A large part of industrial production, in capitalist countries anyway, is now geared to the task of amusing the public. Some of this production and capital investment is provided as equipment for piping an entertainment service to cinema theaters or to home TV receivers – much of it comes as personal equipment by means of which the owner can create his own amusement; still-photography, home cine, tape recorders and so on. Both public and private play equipment have been subjected to a surge of activity in the last ten years.

Technical change has been most obvious in the cinema – perhaps the rate of change has been too slow for its salvation – but who knows? When *Life* magazine reviewed entertainment in the USA in a bumper issue of 1959 I found it difficult to sort out what was happening. An editorial headed "The Structure of Entertainment" took a dim view of Hollywood's position in stating categorically that "half the US movie audience disappeared in the last ten years." But Ernest Havemann, on another page headed "The Business of Show Business," says just as emphatically "There are still as many movie theaters in the US as ever, close on 19,000. They sell about 45 million theater tickets a week at the highest average price in motion picture history." For thirty years "going to the cinema" has been the major pastime of the western world. There has been a decrease in cinema attendance during the last few years but there is still no certainty about TV's ability to hold the audience it has gained. However, if the habit of cinema-going is revived it will only be partly because entertaining films are made – it will also be because the pleasures of being surrounded by a large, well projected, fine-grained image accompanied by undistorted reproduction of well-recorded multi-channeled sound at high

output levels are unmatched by any entertainment available in the home.

In 1951 film producers were already feeling the draught in America – they realized that changes in exhibition technique were the most effective reply to the challenge of TV. Twentieth Century-Fox worked fast. Earl Sponable, their research director, went to Paris on Spyros P. Skouras' instructions and bought rights to Chrétien's anamorphic lens; within two years, in September 1953, *The Robe* was shown at the Roxy Cinema, New York. The great advantage of the anamorph lens was its simplicity. A modifying lens in front of existing cameras compressed a wide-angle view onto standard stock and a similar lens in front of a standard projector threw a wide image onto the screen. The only other essential was the installation of larger screens in every picture theater using the system, to permit a proportion of 2.5 to 1 instead of 1.5 to 1. But even this was hard enough to persuade exhibitors to adopt in spite of the known advantages. Waller had demonstrated in his moves towards Cinerama that secondary but important clues to space perception are derived from an image which fills the whole of one's vision. Adelbert Ames of Princeton had confirmed the theory. The larger the screen the more convincing the impression of three-dimensional space; the more profound the engagement of the spectator within the action. TV could not compete in this region of experience and the principle was rightly judged. All other technological developments in cinema presentation stem from the assumption that screen size must be maximal. When introducing Vista-Vision, Paramount urged every exhibitor to "install the largest feasible seamless screen both as to height and width." In following this initial dictum exhibitors have been lead along from one advance to another.

The virtues of CinemaScope's optical system, from the exhibitor's point of view, were simplicity and economy. But Spyros P. Skouras was not content to stop at the big image; stereophonic sound could also be incorporated to extend the acoustic system similarly. The sound track used for cinema presentation is

CinemaScope
advertisement for
Jean Negulesco
How to Marry a Millionaire
1953

Jean Negulesco
How to Marry a Millionaire
1953
film
color, sound
92 min
film stills
© Twentieth Century-Fox

left
Marilyn Monroe,
Betty Grable, Lauren Bacall

right
Betty Grable spread wide

normally carried on an optical track – variations in a transparent strip at the side of the film allow more or less light to strike a photo-electric cell which generates the signal to, eventually, animate the loudspeakers. Stereophonic sound requires more than one track. Twentieth Century-Fox decided that four would give them the required advantages – one operating a speaker in the center behind the screen, one at either side of the screen and a further track operating effects speakers within the auditorium. Four optical tracks would take up far too much space on the film and there are severe limitations to the size to which optical sound heads could be reduced. The optical system had the advantage that the sound could be printed photographically together with the picture but another sound system was available – one which utilized magnetic variations in an iron coating applied to the film – and it was possible to squeeze in four of such tracks (one on each side of the sprocket holes at the sides of the film). A few minor adjustments had to be made to get these on 35mm film – the sprocket hole size had to be reduced (the new size is known in the trade as "Foxholes") and this meant changes to the projectors. It meant separate processing of the film to add the sound to the release prints by electrical recording and special sound heads had to be fitted to projectors. But it was considered worth the trouble if the exhibitors could be persuaded to co-operate.

The first showing of *The Robe*, with its stereophonic sound and new aspect ratio, was a great success – the first week's gross at the Roxy was 264,428 dollars, a world record exceeding by 100,000 dollars

any previous show anywhere. Two other Twentieth Century-Fox productions followed quickly – *How to Marry a Millionaire* and *Beneath the Twelve Mile Reef*. MGM adopted the CinemaScope process for its production *Knights of the Round Table*. These three films were top grossers in 1954 when a special Academy Award was given to Twentieth Century-Fox for CinemaScope. In that year 7,643 theaters in North America had been equipped for projection of CinemaScope films. In that year also 815 cinemas outside North America were equipped. Spyros P. Skouras was making a big effort that year to sell CinemaScope to exhibitors throughout the world. Skouras insisted, at that time, that the whole system be bought, including stereo – anyone wishing to show CinemaScope films, and these were the biggest moneymakers of the day, would have to install all the equipment needed to present CinemaScope in as near to ideal conditions as the size of the cinema would permit. In England the Essoldo circuit bought CinemaScope lock, stock and barrel; Granada came in too. Rank, with the largest circuit available, stuck out against stereo. The major part of the cost of re-equipment was in the sound system and Rank said he would be glad to have CinemaScope films but only with an optical track. A few top-grade Rank theaters were adapted for stereo but Rank refused to back the system for his circuit as a whole. Skouras held out for a while but had to give in eventually. I can't but think of this as Rank's basest act – worse even than making Tommy Steele pictures. His refusal has led to a great deal of confusion in the public about what they were hearing and seeing – for a cinema advertising a CinemaScope film may or may

not be showing a stereo print and it is even possible for the image area to be smaller than when squarer pictures were projected.

Apart from stereo there were other financial commitments which worried the exhibitors. The large image size advocated by CinemaScope originated from existing projectors – this meant that a given amount of light was spread over a larger area with a corresponding decrease in illumination. To make the maximum use of the available light a screen of high reflectance, called "Miracle Mirror," was introduced. The screen is embossed with a pattern which reflects light back only to those parts of the auditorium occupied by seats.

Any improvement has to be paid for not only in cost of re-equipment but also of maintenance. We were wonderfully impressed by CinemaScope when it was first introduced – we were getting big screen plus high reflectance from newly-fitted specially coated screens. As these screens became dirty over the years we may have seen less light than we got before CinemaScope. The new sound also has its problems: dust was the bugbear of the optical tracks – dust is still a nuisance, but magnetic sound requires extreme electrical cleanliness as well. Magnetism induced in any part of the projector or splicers or film handling equipment that comes into contact with the film can cause clicks and noise in the track. Regular careful demagnetization is necessary every two weeks. Every advance in exhibition technique demands an increase in the skill of projectionists and their equipment must be maintained at peak efficiency if the care and skill of film production technicians is not to be wasted.

Paramount realized the difficulties that Twentieth Century-Fox were up against and stepped in with their proposals. These were mainly changes in production technique. In a pamphlet to exhibitors explaining VistaVision they offered only what they knew exhibitors were prepared to accept: "Paramount makes no demand on any theater, but there is one thing on which there is complete agreement among all studios and all exhibitors, big screens are here to stay." Apart from the large screen it was stressed that everything they offered could be exhibited on good standard equipment. VistaVision was claimed to

be "a new simple, compatible and flexible overall system." The distinctive feature of VistaVision was the technique of making a large negative image in the camera and reducing this onto the standard 35mm release print. The Paramount cameras were adapted to take 35mm film horizontally giving a frame three times the area of the standard negative image. A larger negative size has the disadvantage that depth of field for a given lens aperture decreases proportionately to the increase in negative size. This tendency is combated by the use of wide-angle lenses; the wider the angle the closer the lens is to the film plane and the greater the depth of field and, fortunately, large screen films demand a greater use of wide-angle lenses. Throughout the new cinema processes there is this problem of finding a balance between gain and loss in respect of grain size, depth of focus, light losses, perspective distortion in extreme wide-angle lenses, grain distortion and the physical dimensions required to carry increased amounts of information. Since the chain reaction started there has been an eager juggling with possibilities and solutions to establish an acceptable standard for production and projection. The search for that standard is still going on.

VistaVision took the line of least resistance. "Compatibility," for Paramount, equaled compromise – particularly at the exhibition end. Unlike CinemaScope, VistaVision had no new aspect ratio. They accepted the fact that cinema prosceniums are of different shapes and sizes and refused to lay down fixed recommendations applicable to all theaters. In very large theaters they suggested that an aspect ratio of 1.85 to 1 should be aimed at. This could be increased, if the theater architecture demanded it, to a maximum of 2 to 1 but they were willing to accept an aspect ratio of 1.66 to 1 in small theaters. Paramount film producers were asked to frame their pictures in such a way that it wouldn't matter too much if bits were cut off from either the sides or the top of the ideal ratio. The same attitude of compatible compromise was taken with the sound for VistaVision, selecting "Perspect-A," cinemas were equipped with multiple loudspeakers to create some of the effects of stereo without the accompanying difficulties in production and exhibition. […] A comparatively inexpensive

top
superwide aspect ratio

below
Paramount trade mark

Distributor's exploitation
leaflet for
André de Toth
House of Wax
1953

control unit in the theater, operated automatically by the low-frequency modulation superimposed on the track, separates sound to the multiple speakers. Paramount, they said, would have no magnetic sound release: "It is our opinion that this move will give greater dramatic effectiveness, greater simplicity and greater flexibility at a lower cost and with less service trouble than any other multi-horn system."

CinemaScope had certainly had trouble with its stereo. As a film fan I have been aware of changes over the years – changes that I regret; it seemed that stereo wasn't what it was in the young days of CinemaScope – so different and unemphatic that I suspected that stereo prints were not being used generally even by cinemas that I knew to be equipped for them. The explanation, I discovered recently, is that audiences complained that, in some parts of the theater, one or other of the loudspeakers was inaudible. It was also said that stereo gave too much effect of movement for the front seats and was of little use for the rear seats. The cure was to arrange for all main speakers to be given all of the signals at fixed levels of output and the separation to occur only above this norm. This reduced very considerably the pronounced stereo effect of early CinemaScope showings. The effects track was also disliked by some members of the audience – they didn't like the sound of horses galloping along the side aisles or the swish of arrows across the theater – it was distracting, they said. The effects track, therefore, has not been as much used in the last few years. This doesn't mean that stereo is a failure in cinemas, only that the public quickly became irritated by the deficencies of crude sound installations in theaters that were not designed for the acoustic subtleties of stereo. If big screens are here to stay stereo is here to stay with them – though the slogan "In the Wonder of 4-track High Fidelity, Magnetic Stereophonic Sound" may lure us less often. However, the *Journal of the Society of Motion PictureTheater Engineers*, May 1959, reports that Twentieth Century-Fox has restored the emphasis on stereophonic sound and has announced an improved method of recording.

When CinemaScope was first introduced, Twentieth Century-Fox also made much of the arguable three-dimensional aspect of CinemaScope. The other great slogan: "You see it without the use of special glasses" was perfectly true – but it didn't say that, with or without glasses, there was any very strong three-dimensional experience. VistaVision also made

some attempt to get on the 3-D bandwagon relying not on its screen size but on its improved image quality claiming, rather lamely, "This will give new depth perception in exhibition."

An acceptable, true 3-D was one of the failed objectives of the 1950s. The major factor of depth perception in human vision is the different viewpoint that each eye contributes to our appreciation of a scene, true cinema stereography would present each with a difference of scene equivalent to normal biopic vision. Great difficulties arise in attempting to present the whole of a cinema audience with a different image for each eye.

Two systems without the use of filters have been reported. One of them makes use of two projectors, displaced from one another, which form an image on a grid of vertical wires. Parallax introduced by the projection causes each eye to select only the image intended for it. This method involves considerable light losses and is prohibitively expensive – one such experimental installation had a grid of one hundred miles of copper wire weighting six tons. Another method is to use a system of tiny mirrors which black out in synchronism with the sequence of projection of the images – this requires fantastically complex machinery to operate the mirrors. Both of these systems impose an almost complete fixation of the head – the tolerance of movement being less than an inch. At present there is no doubt that spectacles offer a more practical solution. Prior to the war some trick stereo films were made by MGM using the anaglyph principle by separating the two images with color. A red image and a green image were projected simultaneously, each member of the audience had cardboard spectacles holding colored gelatines which presented only one of the images to each eye, the other being filtered out. Dr Edwin Land, one of the undisputed geniuses of our era, in 1930 invented the first practical mass produced filters for polarizing light. These Polaroid filters opened up new possibilities of three-dimensional viewing, without irritating color effects from the filters, by separating the two images through different states of polarization of the light.

It wasn't until after the war that Warner Brothers took the process up in a big way and made some important Polaroid productions. At first, they exploited the frightening sensory effects in some black-and-white horror films which had as their climax the alarming emergence of the monster into the audience. This trend concluded a year or so ago with the

left
André de Toth
House of Wax
1953
film
color, sound
90 min
polaroid left-eye frame
© Warner Bros.

right
André de Toth
House of Wax
1953
polaroid right-eye frame
© Warner Bros.

application of a new treatment which Warners called "Emergo," when a stuffed monster was actually hurled through the auditorium on cables. It is possible to make color films also with polaroid filters and some first-rate films were made: Warner's *The Charge at Feather River* with Guy Madison was a fine western; MGM's *Kiss Me Kate*, a musical, was also brilliantly done in 3-D color, as was the best of the horror films Warner's *House of Wax*. The success of these few films can be measured by Edwin Land's fabulous financial affairs. In 1952 gross sales of the Polaroid Corporation, which he founded to exploit his inventions, were 13 million dollars; in 1953 they were 26 million dollars; in 1954, 23 million. The demand for 3-D glasses accounted for the jump in sales in 1953.

Warner Brothers have not continued production of their 3-D movies – the need to use spectacles proved too much of an obstacle and the visual effects were very tiring for prolonged viewing. Lately a means of using polaroid filters without light losses has been put forward and it may be that there will be a revival of this approach.

Binocular vision was thought at one time to be basic to the three-dimensional sensation of space in motion pictures. Other clues have been noticed and these are now being exploited. There is known to be a subjective effect of stereoscopy associated with camera movement. The effect is more apparent if the indices by which an audience reads the image as flat are eliminated. Several factors contribute to the effect of flatness in the cinema: softness of focus, film grain, sheen from the screen and also the rectangular picture mask. Improvements in these directions have been more durable in their increased involvement of the audience in the picture space.

The curved screen shape is an image very dear to the 1950s. It has become the generalized symbol for cinema entertainment: as the rounded-off barrel shape has come to mean TV so the wide screen proportion, curving inwards along its length, has come to mean its competitor, the cinema. It implies 3-D but, in so far as CinemaScope is concerned anyway, its effectiveness in this respect is not very remarkable. It does have other advantages: when projecting very wide pictures the light beam strikes the sides of the screen at a seriously oblique angle causing a loss of image brightness at the ends. With a curve of equal radius to the projection throw the reflection angle remains the same for every part of the screen. The curve introduces distortion of horizontals so severe-

ly, under certain conditions, that the curvature has to be compromised. So essential has the curved screen become to the cinema that when VistaVision, in its true spirit of compromise, made a 50mm release print of the same dimensions as the VistaVision negative they advocated keeping the screen flat but using curved masks at top and bottom to give the impression of curvature.

Real curvature not only presents problems of distortion but it also makes difficulties of focus at the edges of the screen. Camera lenses are strictly planar. An ideal lens focuses evenly and without distortion in a plane. If a camera is pointed at right angles to a straight wall the focus is determined by the distance between the camera and a paint at the center of the wall: the distance between the lens and the wall increases on either side of the central point but the focus should be even right out to the edges. A projection lens is similarly planar. It is this characteristic of normal lenses that makes the extreme curvature of the Cinerama screen so complex optically.

Some idea of the difficulty can be gained from the financial history of Fred Waller research. Waller worked for several years as head of Paramount's trick film department. In 1937 he devised Vitarama to project a moving picture inside a sphere for display purposes – the scheme used eleven cameras and eleven projectors. A company was formed to adapt the idea to cinema presentation, obtaining financial and laboratory support from Lawrence Rockefeller. The principle was applied to an aerial gunnery trainer during the war and in 1946, since more money was needed, Time Inc. joined Rockefeller to form the Cinerama Corporation. By 1950 Rockefeller and Time had spent 350,000 dollars and declined to spend more for the end was still not in sight – although the system had been reduced to one camera with three lenses a good deal of work remained to be done. A new company was formed, Cinerama Inc., which, in collaboration with another new organization, the Cinerama Productions Company, brought the system to the point of commercial exploitation with the first showing of *This is Cinerama* in September 1952.

Cinerama can involve the spectator more effectively than any other cinema presentation. The first reports of audience reaction to this new process told of screaming, fainting women, ducking men and sick children – no wonder we were a little apprehensive when it arrived at the London Casino. The theater publicity and lobby displays made no attempt to

above
This is Cinerama
1952
triple frame, roller coaster
section

CINERAMA

inform about the subject-matter of the film – audience participation was what they were selling and what we got was a physical, almost visceral, sensation. As the postcards available in the foyer said: "I was in Cinerama."

Projection of Cinerama is a difficult business – the installation is costly and running expenses are high. The semi-circular screen is attacked by three projectors from points on the periphery of an extension of the screen curve – the beams intersecting at the center of the circle formed by screen and projectors. Cross-reflection of light from one side of the curve to the other caused trouble but was cured with the development of a louvred screen made up of thin vertical strips. Each projector is manned by an operator but, once the film is running, control is relinquished to a master projectionist whose main job is to control the projector arc lamps to maintain even illumination over the whole screen. The seven-track sound recorded on separate 35mm tape is controlled by a sound engineer in another booth. This elaborate organization of each performance makes it nearer to a live theater show. In fact, the extra large screen processes are known to the trade as "roadshows." Indeed, it was thought at first that the most exciting possibilities for future productions would be in filming original performances of great Broadway musicals and to tour this record around the country instead of the usual shop-worn live roadshow. Matching of the light sources was not the only problem with multiple projection. Every projector has a certain amount of judder and this cannot be tolerated in Cinerama – miraculously efficient film transport devices are required to maintain synchronization and even movement. It was obvious that someone would try to reduce complexity of recording and presentation without losing too many of the advantages.

Mike Todd had been introduced to Cinerama. He had no financial interest in the company but it was thought that his talents as a showman would be useful. He very soon disagreed with the other members of the team and backed out while still holding onto a tremendous charge of enthusiasm for the potentialities of the system. Todd, with remarkable persistence, persuaded Brian O'Brien, the foremost lens expert in America (Todd described him as "the Einstein of the optical dodge"), to develop a system which would iron out the bugs in Cinerama.

With the American Optical Company, and four million dollars found by Todd, O'Brien reduced the three cameras of Cinerama to one with a phenomenal nine-inch lens that photographed an angle of 128 degrees. The four 35mm strips of Cinerama (three carrying pictures and one sound) became one 70mm film taking a large size picture and the six-track sound as well. The process was called Todd-A O –Todd American Optics. But a system, however good, wasn't enough – one of Cinerama's main difficulties had been in getting something to show with the new media – Todd managed to raise sufficient money to make *Oklahoma*, the first film in Todd-A O. He then sold all his holdings in the process itself to make *Around the World in Eighty Days* and his last film *South Pacific*.

Cinemiracle came next, with a process using three cameras but projecting from a single booth. Four years in the laboratory and 6.5 million dollars went into the production of *Windjammer* first shown in 1958. At the same time a Russian process called Panoramic, which used Cinerama principles, was unveiled in Moscow. It showed, aptly enough, a travelogue entitled *How Broad is my Country*. The Russians went several feet and decibels better than the Americans with a screen 38 feet high and 102 feet wide, combined with 120 loudspeakers.

Waller's Vitarama idea still exists in the form of a process owned by Walt Disney called "Circarama," using eleven 16mm cameras and eleven projectors showing one movie on a completely circular screen. This was used in the United States pavilion at the Brussels exhibition to show scenes of American life.

Another presentation technique was used by Charles Eames in the recent United States exhibition in Moscow. Its direct source of inspiration was an educational project known as "the Georgia experiment," an attempt by George Nelson, Charles Eames and Alexander Girard to introduce new lecturing techniques into visual education. This used five still slide projectors simultaneously, several 16mm film projectors and a batch of tape recorders. It took eight people to operate the equipment to lecture to about as many students. The Moscow exhibit consisted of seven screens and seven separately phased projectors. Less directly, I think, the idea stems from a general preoccupation with multiple visual experiences in our culture. The TV monitoring booth through which the producer selects the transmitted image from a set of small screens supplied by different cameras in the studio is one manifestation. This interest in multiple images has also found its way to the big screen itself. In *A Star is Born* (the Judy Garland / James Mason version) you may remember, there was the remarkable scene in which the wide screen contained two subsidiary moving images. An intense conversation was taking place in front of a television set broadcasting a prizefight and its excited commentary. Another room of the same open plan set was occupied by guests at a party watching the cine-projection of a film. This is just one example of many that could be quoted. Certainly we can expect not only an increasing spectator involvement through higher quality but also new kinds of experience altogether from new assemblages of moving imagery.

[...]

Typescript of a lecture held in 1959 on technical innovations in the leisure industries.

Abridged version of the text first published in Richard Hamilton, *Collected Words. 1953–1982*, Thames and Hudson, London, 1982, pp. 112–132.

Michael Bielicky
Prague – A Place of Illusionists

engraving for
Jan Amos Comenius
Didactica Magna
1657

"Thanks to the techno-imagination, it is possible
to decipher technical images and thus to unmask
the intended deception which is a component of our
contemporary image civilization." [1]

Prague does not have a consistent historical development of either old or new media; but for this very reason, the city should be proud of several events that are of singular importance for the history of visual techno-media. Examples of such modern-sounding phenomena as "electronic art," "multimedia," "virtual reality," "interactive art" and "artificial intelligence" can actually be found in past times, even as far back as the Middle Ages. Of course, these phenomena had different names then. These events almost always had a particular relation to the time and to the atmosphere of the places in which they occurred. Not least, it was the special energy of the city of Prague that always drove people to search for an interface to the beyond. Linguists claim that the name "Prague" stems from the Czech "prah" which means "threshold." True to its name, there are places in Prague where, through various optical illusions,

one has the curious sensation of finding oneself in a twilight zone. The visual impressions of my childhood were deeply influenced by experiences with the 360-degree panorama *The Battle of Lipany*, now over a hundred years old, and a Russian film-panorama in a Prague amusement park. A very old mirror-labyrinth left me with just as deep impressions as did Karel Zeman's fantastic films. Likewise, the experience with the magic lantern, which I will discuss in more detail below, had an enormous effect on me. When one speaks of Prague, one really must say that it has always been a Mecca of optical illusions.

In 1658, the Czech theologian and pedagogue Jan Amos Comenius published one of his first illustrated books for children: *Obris Sensualium Pictus* [The Visible World in Pictures]. This pioneer of media pedagogy is considered to be the forerunner of modern attempts at international cooperation in the fields

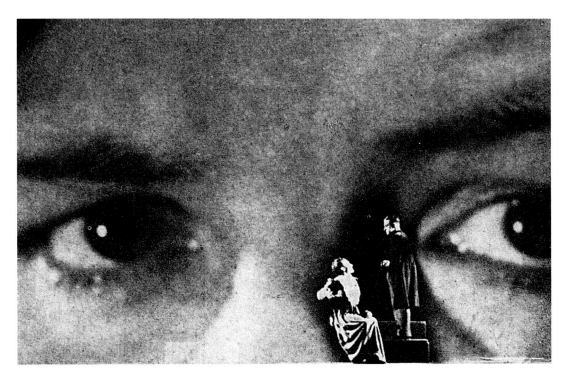

Miroslav Kouril
Theatergraph, Wedekind's
The Awakening of Spring
1936
theatrical stage with
integrated projection
slides, 35mm film
b/w, sound
Prague

of education, science and culture. Many artists whose work was devoted to the experience of seeing and to the new pictorial arts were inspired by Comenius' ideas. Examples are Oskar Kokoschka's treatise *Das Bewußtsein des Bildes* and some of Roberto Rosselini's writings.

Juda Loew ben Bezalel, famed as High Rabbi Loew, also lived in Prague in the seventeenth century. A great scholar and mystic, the possessor of an encyclopedic knowledge, he was both the spiritual and the physical forefather of the great mathematician Theodor von Karman. Von Karman discerned in Rabbi Loew the first genius of applied mathematics. Rabbi Loew is credited not only with having invented the Golem; his experiments with the camera obscura and with the magic lantern so impressed Emperor Rudolf II that he was invited to join that circle of alchemists, artists, and astronomers whose members included Archimboldo, Johannes Keppler and Tycho de Brahe. Rabbi Loew is said to have accomplished a miracle when Rudolf II called upon him at home one night: The Rabbi transformed his house into a palace by using his magic lantern to project painted pictures of the interior of the Prague castle Hradschin onto his own walls. So it was that Rudolf II was given the impression that he was in a palace. One can, in this context, speak of medieval virtual reality.

In his dissertation published in Prague in 1818, the natural scientist Jan Evangelista Purkyne was one of the first to realize that we continue to perceive objects for a fraction of a second after they have disappeared from our field of vision. In 1824, Peter Mark Roget went on to give a more detailed description of this perceptual phenomenon, naming it "the persistence of visual impressions." The discovery of this perceptual phenomenon provided the basis for numerous technical inventions and new equipment that could turn still images into moving ones and have transformed modern life, not only through cinema and television but also through digital and audiovisual techniques. Purkyne's insights make clear the fundamental relation between the birth of the neurological

sciences and the triumph of technologies of the moving image. They serve as an important point of departure for reflections on the present-day development of electronic media and their influence on our lives. In 1865, Purkyne constructed the "kinesiscope," an instrument by means of which one can observe a pulsing heart or even one's own portrait as animated photography. Purkyne predicted that the time would come in which it would be possible to tell entire stories with the help of moving pictures.

At the beginning of the twentieth century, Franz Kafka suggested that a cinema for the blind be established in Prague. Many Kafka specialists are convinced that much of his writing was influenced by his experiences with the then extremely young medium of film.

Even before the First World War, the Czech cabaret performer Karel Hasler had a film projected on the stage that showed him running through the city, approaching the cabaret, and going through the door. At the end, the scene continues uninterrupted as he himself runs onto the stage.

In 1930, Alexander Hackenschmidt set new standards for cinematic expression with his experimental film *Aimless Walk*. The filmmaker, who had emigrated to the USA before the war (he had changed his name to Sasha Hammit), not only influenced his later wife Maya Deren, but he also inspired an entire generation of American experimental filmmakers who came together to form a new film movement.

In collaboration with Miroslav Kouril, the theater director E.F. Burian developed the "Theatergraph," a theatrical stage with integrated projection screens, on which films and slides directly relating to the events on the stage were projected during a theatrical performance. This technology was first put into practice for a production of Wedekind's *The Awakening of Spring* in 1936 and then later for Pushkin's *Eugen Onegin*. Denis Bablet, in his book *Revolutions in Stage Design in the 20th Century*, confirms that Burian and Kouril's experiments, along with Piscator Traugott Müller's research, were instrumental in paving the

top left
Josef Svoboda
sketch for Diakran for the
Brussels Expo in 1958
© Sarka Hejnova

top right
Josef Svoboda
Laterna Magika
1962
multiple-screen projection
with live performance on stage
Laterna Magika Theater, Prague
© Sarka Hejnova

below left
Josef Svoboda, Alfréd Radok
Laterna Magika,
Hostess Program
1958
multiple-screen projection with
live performance on stage
35mm film
b/w, sound
Czechoslovak Pavilion, Brussels
Expo
© Sarka Hejnova

below right
Josef Svoboda, Milos Forman
Laterna Magika
1958
multiple-screen projection with
live performance on stage
Czechoslovak Pavilion, Brussels
Expo
© Sarka Hejnova

way for the development of new theatrical forms. Set
design, which had been characterized by screen and
color up until then, was being replaced by architectural structures, light, and projected images. A new
civilization of audiovisual communication had come
into being.

In the 1930s, the Prague-based artist Zdenek
Pesanek wrote his book Kinetismus, in which he investigated the potential of multimedia performance as a
new form of visual expression – regardless of whether
it involved an installation, a film, a fireworks display, or
the aesthetics of anti-aircraft defense. He himself
built light kinetic objects that had multimedia qualities. They moved; they changed color; they produced
sounds.

Karel Zeman was a great poet of the new cinematic expression. This master of special effects developed a kind of physical "Virtual Set" for his films of
the 1950s. A unique animated-film technique enabled
actors to be placed in unreal surroundings that
roused associations with old etchings, for instance.

In the period after the Second World War, Czech
film experimentation attained a phenomenal and
unique dimension. Josef Svoboda, the master of set
design, set completely new standards with inventions
like Laterna Magika as well as polyscreen and polyvision techniques. Moreover, Radúz Çinçera, the father
of the first interactive film, made a quantum leap with
his "Kinoautomat" [cinema-automat] project. It is
considered groundbreaking both because of its use
of the new non-linear narrative-form and because of
its inclusion of the spectator as an active participant
in the film action. Although these inventors lived
under a totalitarian regime, they enjoyed more freedom of experimentation than they would have in some

Western countries. In his long and international career, Svoboda created more than seven hundred sets,
most of which contained multiple projections of film
and slides in combination with architecture and light.

In 1951, Svoboda began to deploy several sets at
once in his theatrical productions. Through the development of his concept for Expo 1958 in Brussels, his
idea for a polyphonic theater became reality. This is
how his Laterna Magika project came into being – a
synthesis of theater and film. By then, he was already
wondering whether the spectator was even capable
of simultaneously perceiving parallel film projections.
The director Alfréd Radok, collaborator on the Laterna Magika for the past fifteen years and, in the
ensuing decades, chief writer of the film narratives
in Svoboda's Laterna Magika, made a crucial contribution to the realization of this interface between
theater and cinema. Other film directors like Milos
Forman or Jan Svankmajer were also involved in Laterna Magika productions. The magical moment of
this system is above all the fluid transition between
the stage and the projected film: the action begun on
the stage continues in the film and vice versa. Actors
from several projection screens appear on stage
then disappear again into the film projection. It was
not always easy for the spectator to distinguish
between the real action on the stage and the virtual
action in the film. Real and filmic worlds combine with
each other to form a unity. The technical principle is
based on three projection cabins, more than twenty
light projectors, and a back projection over an anamorphic lens. If necessary, the projection screens
could be moved. Given that films could be projected
onto any conceivable form, a further dimension was
added to the dynamic of the on-stage action. The

right
Josef Svoboda
Polyekran,
Creation of the World of Man
1967
112 moveable cubes with
slide projection, 15.000 slides
color, sound
11 min
Montreal Expo
© Sarka Hejnova

left
Josef Svoboda, Jaroslav Fric
Polyvision
1967
multi-projection cinema set-up
35mm film and slides projected
on moveable geometrical
objects, projection screen
color, sound
8 min
Montreal Expo
© Sarka Hejnova

variability of space (dynamic architecture of the screen), of time (the film editing), and of the actor's identity on the stage and in the film allowed for the development of a convincing optical illusion. In addition, the sound was designed in such a way as to produce a highly spatial experience for the spectators. This flowing movement between the material and the immaterial worlds, the back and forth between reality and dream, has continued to enchant Prague audiences up until the present day.

Polyvision, another Svoboda invention, presented a panorama of Czech industrial life in an eight-minute film that used twenty slide projectors, ten ordinary motion picture screens and five rotating projection screens. While the subjects were usual industrial operations like hydro-electric power plants, steel rolling mills and textile mills, the visual material was presented in an unusual way. The screens were unconventional in that during the show they would move around: backwards, forwards, even sideways. Then there were other projection surfaces formed by steel hoops that spun around so rapidly that they seemed to constitute solid spheres and yet they were not solid. One could partially look through the image at what was in the room beyond. The presentation was completely controlled by electronic memory circuits that controlled the projectors and moved the screens around in a cinematic ballet.

Svoboda's Polyekran was a very fascinating audiovisual experience presented during the 1967 Expo in Montreal. One entered a large room and sat on the carpeted floor to watch a wall of 112 cubes whose ever shifting and changing images moved backwards and forwards. Inside each cube were two Kodak Carousel slide projectors that projected stills onto

the front of the cubes. In all, there were 15,000 slides in the eleven-minute show. Since each cube could slide into three separate positions within a two foot range, the cubes produced the effect of a flat surface turning into a three-dimensional surface and back again. It was completely controlled by 240 miles of memory circuitry which was encoded onto a filmstrip with 756,000 separate instructions.

The show was *The Creation of the World of Man*. On the 112-part screen, the Earth came awake, flowers bloomed, tigers suddenly appeared, the first men walked the earth, then machinery was invented. Sometimes the image sequences would appear complete at first, then be broken up into an abstract modern-art composition. It was pure multivisual technique that enchanted the viewer.

Radúz Çinçera's Kinoautomat was introduced at Expo 1967 in Montreal. Among Çinçera's teammembers were the directors Jan Rohac and Vladimir Svitacek, the set designer Josef Svoboda as well as Jaroslav Fric and Bohumil Mika, the technical masterminds behind the system. The world's first interactive cinema, the Kinoautomat, confronted spectators with a film that would keep stopping. Two principle actors in the film appeared on stage and asked the audience how the film should be continued. The spectators voted, using either of the two buttons that had been installed in their seats. Afterwards, the version that received more votes was played. The film narrated extremely turbulent relationships between the inhabitants of a "completely normal house." In one of the scenes, a young inhabitant slams the door shut upon seeing who is ringing. Since she has come directly out of the bath, she appears wrapped only in a towel. In

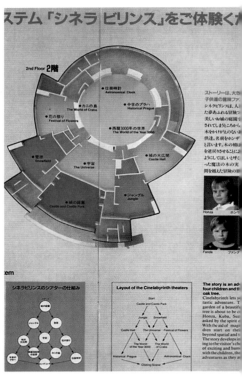

left
Radúz Činčera
Kinoautomat
1967
interactive film with live
performance on stage
electronic polling system,
35mm film
b/w, sound
duration variable
Montreal Expo

right
presentation of
Radúz Činčera's Cinelabyrinth
for the Osaka Expo in 1990

Audiovisual Object
1958
Czechoslovak Pavilion,
Brussels Expo

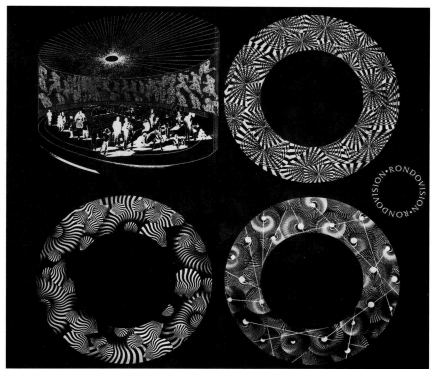

Jaroslav Fric
Rondovision
1984
New Orleans

Jaroslav Fric
Vertical Cinemascope
1970
British Columbia Pavilion,
Osaka Expo

her panic, she rings her neighbor's doorbell and asks for help. The film stops, and the spectators are asked if the neighbor should let her into his apartment. The audience inevitably voted "Yes," apart from once, at the Expo, when the "No" vote was due to the presence of a large group of nuns.

The inclusion of the spectators in the film action represented a completely novel situation. Through their participation, the spectators were actively involved in a non-linear film narrative. After the Expo, the Kinoautomat was presented in Prague. In 1968, however, shortly after the invasion of the Warsaw Pact troops, the unique venture was closed down. Perhaps the powers of the time were afraid that the Kinoautomat might heighten democratic awareness. After all, during the performance votes were cast according to democratic principles.

In the years following, Çinçera developed different cinema-systems that had a non-linear, and often also interactive, character. In 1990, the Cinelabyrinth was introduced in Osaka. In this ambitious project, the spectators could follow the action in the film by moving through various spaces and, depending on which room they had decided upon, the narrative adopted another development. Unlike in the Kinoautomat, the spectator of the cine-labyrinth could therefore make individual decisions. In 1998, a new version of Cinelabyrinth was presented in Prague on the occasion of the exhibition "100 Years of Czech Film." Visitors to the exhibition had the possibility of experiencing the history of Czech film as a non-linear narrative.

In the mid-1990s, Czech television staged an experiment with the interactive film presented at the Expo in 1967. Two different versions of the film were played on two different television stations: spectators could switch back and forth between the two

stations, and thus between the two films.

In the 1960s, a group came into being in association with SCARS (Science Art Sense) that specialized in the development of multimedia presentations for various international occasions. The host countries were located on every continent in the world since it had become widely known that the former-Czechoslovakia possessed a great deal of competence in the field of innovative and often complex multimedia performances. The technical head of the group was Jaroslav Fric, whom I have already mentioned in connection with the Kinoautomat. Besides numerous other systems, Fric developed the Spherorama and the Vertical Cinemascope for the British Columbia pavilion at Expo in Osaka in 1970. The Spherorama was a slide projector that could produce a 360-degree dome projection using only one lens. Although Jaroslav Fric was responsible for innumerable inventions, there is very little documentation regarding his projects.

The backgrounds and the historical development of these unusual film formats possess a unique diversity and originality, yet it is nonetheless difficult to find adequate material about them, either in writing or in film. The phenomena described here certainly deserve a longer treatment, particularly the visual culture of moving images that served to produce so many great artists in Prague. Both the animated films (by Trnka, Svankmajer, Barta, and others) and the feature films (by directors including Forman, Chytilova, Juracek, Menzel, Zeman) beautifully reflected the magical, surreal, absurd, and fantastical atmosphere of Prague, which can still be experienced everywhere in that city.

Translated from the German by Sarah Clift

Literature

Gershom Scholem, *Judaica 11*, Suhrkamp, Frankfurt/M., 1970.

Angelo Maria Ripellino, *Magic Prague*, The University of California Press, 1993.

Zdenek Pesanek, *Kinetismus*, Prague, 1941.

Orbis Pictus, Catalogue, Prague, 1996.

Laterna Magika, Filmovy Ustav, Prague, 1968.

Tajemstvi divadelniho prostoru, Josef Svoboda, Odeon, Prague, 1990.

Fric, Artcentrum, Prague, 1986.

Vít Havránek
Laterna Magika, Polyekran, Kinoautomat
Media, Technology and Interaction in the Works of Set Designers
Josef Svoboda, Alfréd Radok and Radúz Çinçera, 1958–1967

From the moment of its inception, it has not been clear whether Laterna Magika (LM) is film, theater or a brand-new media performance show. First introduced in the Czechoslovak pavilion at the 1958 World Expo in Brussels, this entity combined ballet, theater, several film projections, and sound background.

An unexpected media effect LM had on its contemporaries came from the dialog conducted between a live performer and the virtual world of film. On a mechanical basis, and through perfect synchronization of a dancer with a film image, LM created the impression that the two were interacting. At the start of the show, the spectators were convinced they were watching an improvised act of true interaction. And in that lies the clinch: The magical phenomenon in which actor and dancer were able to create the impression that the film medium was "real," that it must have "come to life" because it reacted to real events. If we turn to the past and ask what was magical about the historical "Magical Lantern," we read in Furetière's *Dictionnaire universel* (1690): "Lanterne magique est une petite machine d'optique qui fait voir dans l'obscurité sur une muraille blanche plusieurs spectres et monstres si affreux, que *celui qui n'en scait pas le secret croit que cela se fait par magie*" (author's italics). Three hundred years later, the effect of Laterna Magika had a similar effect on the spectator who did not realize how the show was being created. The magical part was that film came to life. It was not pre-taped, rigid, or mechanically repeatable. It seemed that at the start of the show a

magician waved a magic wand, removing a constant characteristic and granting the film the ability to interactively react to its surroundings.

According to the experience of the creators of LM, neither principle – the live actor or the film – dominated the other. That was what made the form difficult to label. Because each component was leading at a given moment, it was neither a real performance nor a virtual game using reality elements. In *Rhythms*, a real pianist played a rhythmical composition to a backdrop of a blown-up shot of a passenger plane as it taxied down the runway at Prague airport. Both components reacted to each other in counter-positions – of the real and virtual worlds. Both worlds retained their specificity.

LM transformed the concept of virtual and physiological time. The medium of virtual time included a real actor with whom the spectator could identify and thus gain a direct paradigm on which to model his own behavior, should his physical body ever find itself in a virtual interactive space.

The Show Hostesses, Rhythms, Slavonic Dances
Laterna Magika was not an easily described entity. The synthesis of film and theater was multilayered. It was a highly synchronized program, coordinated to the last detail, with everyone having his exact spot in a precisely marked space. That was how the performance made an impression of interactive improvisation. Of course, the improvisation was exactly timed: the action had its rhythm and dramaturgic time.

Alfréd Radok, Josef Svoboda
Laterna Magika,
*Rhythms and Slavonic Dances
program*
1958
screen projection with
live performance on stage
Czechoslovak Pavilion,
Brussels Expo
© Sarka Hejnova

Not only did the actor or dancer here enter the virtual world of film that picked up a plot begun on stage (like the discussion between a real show hostess and her virtual colleagues in the *Show Hostess*.) The film and the staged plot stood in diverse dramaturgical positions: a dramatic contrast (*Slavonic dances*), dialog, or coexistence within multilayered parallelism (*Rhythms*).

The director built the plot in a sequence of situations – "signs" to evoke an "emotional convention" in the viewer. The director of the performance, Alfréd Radok, commented on his method: "The term 'sign' could best be traced from the rules that gave birth to what we call 'film language.' Film works with certain devices. To be precise: with the artificial reality of film. Its basis was created by filming simple signs. Later, when differentiating between the dimension of these signs and the sum of at least two signs we could obtain from a certain logical or spatial significance … signs evoke in the viewer an 'emotional convention.' Emotional convention would be in our multistage scenic unit[1] a staging element with meaning reaching beyond logic an ever-increasing the psychological dimension."

As Radok's description explains, Laterna Magika was built on "emotional convention," that is, on certain archetypal situations. Among them were compressed essential fragments of film, photography, theater, ballet and music,[2] which all met together during an intense theater piece. It was no coincidence that Svoboda and Radok recruited the collaboration of a young director, Milos Forman,[3] who later became a leading figure in the New Wave of Czech film.

It seems that the LM principles have gradually been integrated into fields outside the theater, such as video art, computer art, Performance, Virtual Reality, VJ-ing, and so on. In Laterna Magika, as in Polyekran, Svoboda treated film shots in the same revolutionary way artists later did in video projection. The difference between cinema and video with respect to the spatial factor largely involves the field of projection. The confined two-dimensional nature of cinema may be overcome in Video Art by several means: by increasing the number of screens in use (Carolee Schneemann and Michael Snow),[4] by contrasting simultaneously the physical representation and virtuality of the cinematographic image (Valie Export, Birgit and Wilhelm Hein), by dividing the screen into several areas in which images are re-grouped in a series of matching or contrasting combinations (Keith Sonnier), and finally by analyzing the mechanisms of the basic projection process (Anthony McCall).[5]

An important part of the LM aftermath was Svoboda's artistic development. The principles of LM, which had already cropped up in his set designs prior to 1958, were deployed frequently after the success of LM at the Expo.[6] It was more than mechanical repetition. Svoboda's work with the medium perhaps advanced most when he designed, in collaboration with the MIT and Boston Public TV's Channel 2, the set for the Opera Group of Boston's 1965 production of the Luigi Nono opera *Intoleranza* (1960):

1 This multi-stage scenic unit might be, for example, the Laterna Magika.

2 The creator was Zdenik Liška.

3 *Man on the Moon* (1999), *The People vs. Larry Flynt* (1996), *Amadeus* (1984), *Hair* (1979), *One Flew Over the Cuckoo's Nest* (1975), *Taking Off* (1971), *Fireman's Ball* (1968), *Loves of a Blonde* (1965).

4 Compare Svoboda's Diapolyekran with what follows. Also his audiovisual system *Symphony* and *Textile Container*, Montréal Expo, 1967.

5 Frank Popper, *Art of the Electronic Age*, Thames and Hudson, London, 1993, p. 56.

6 Svoboda had worked throughout his career on scores of theater productions.

Alfréd Radok, Josef Svoboda
Laterna Magika,
Hostess program
1958
multiple screen projection with
live performance on stage
35mm film
b/w, sound
Czechoslovak Pavilion,
Brussels Expo
© Sarka Hejnova

Alfréd Radok, Josef Svoboda,
Laterna Magika,
Musical Joke
1958
projection on a portable screen
with live performance on stage
Czechoslovak Pavilion,
Brussels Expo
© Sarka Hejnova

"There were three screening areas on stage. The film in the middle was linked to the stage plot. On the sides there were twelve monitors and two TV projectors (6 x 4 meters) projecting live action shot by cameras in two studios far from the theater, at a Boston street, in front of the theater, in the theater hall, and on the stage. We filmed the texts, photos, and ads in one studio, choruses and walk-ons in another, the audience in the hall, and the actors on the stage. The image collage made sense after being put together in the TV director's cabin. There, a train of images was created and projected by two giant monitors on stage. This immensely complex apparatus helped the choruses in the studio outside the theater sing under the direction of the conductor on the monitor, a live conductor conducting an orchestra in the theater. The viewer could simultaneously watch the action in front of the theater on the street. But the basic significance of the system was in its ability to pull the spectator unexpectedly and with full intensity into the play. During a protest song sung by a black singer, the camera filmed the theater audience, projecting their image onto a screen. People enjoyed seeing their own faces. At a certain point we changed the picture from a positive to a negative so that the screens were suddenly showing a black audience. Some spectators were upset. We filmed and played that as well. We even used a great moment and made the demonstration that was taking place in front of the theater a part of the show."[7] This staging marked a peak of Svoboda's media experiments. In 1965, he incorporated in it several parallel real-time broadcasts followed by projections on screens and monitors from different places. Through industrial TV, he thus created real (and not just

fictitious LM-style) links between the projections and musicians, and feedback between the audience and its image.

It was primarily the link of image with real audience reactions, facilitated by cable television, that was a novel inspiration, not only in the media field but also in the context of performance and video art: "Acting in the context of the visual arts is relevant only inasmuch as it performs the elementary procedure of perceiving the network of relationships between performer and perceiver, both being simultaneously the subject and object."[8]

In an analytic, focused manner we encounter similar problems in Dan Graham's work. In video installations like *Present Continuous Past* (1974) or *Public Space / Two Audiences* (1976), he coldly presented the viewer as an "object," using the broadcast of his image followed by a video projection. These works resonate in a number of theoretical postulates clearly linked to Svoboda's ideas and the effects of real-time entrances onto the latter's set "design" for *Intoleranza*:

"There is no distinction between the subject and object. Object is the viewer as art, and subject is the viewer, as art. Object and subject are not dialectical opposites but a single self-contained identity: reversible interior and exterior termini. All frames of reference read simultaneously: object 'subject'."[9]

"I had the idea of a reciprocal interdependence of perceiver (spectator) and the perceived art-object/the artist as performer (who might in the case of Nauman present himself as/in place of this 'object'). In this new subject-object relationship, the spectator's perceptual processes were correlated to the compositional process (which was also inherent in the material… Thus a different

7 Josef Svoboda, *Tajemství divadelního prostoru*, [The Mystery of Theater Space], Prague, 1990, pp. 112-113.

8 Benjamin H. D. Buchloh, "Moments of History in the Work of Dan Graham," 1978, in *Neo Avantgarde and Culture Industry*, The MIT Press, Cambridge, MA, 2000.

9 Dan Graham, "Sol LeWitt-Two Structures," in *End Moments*, Dan Graham (ed.), New York, 1969, p. 15, cited from note 14, p. 196.

idea of 'material' and the relation of this materiality to nature (al) processes was also developed).
This change in the compositional process came
from developments in music and dance … where
the performer or performance was the center of
the work, executed and perceived in a durational
time continuum."10

Polyekran

The principle of Polyekran – simultaneous film projections – first applied in the adjacent pavilion at the
1958 Expo in Brussels, was based on rhythmical links
between sound, film and the real space of the stage.
"The fundamental idea of the system was the effort
to create space through film projections on several
areas, placed throughout the space in a visually satisfying way. … The set design for *Prague Musical Spring*
allowed the director (Emil Radok) to work with eight
screening surfaces placed in black space. They had
trapezoid and square shapes. Even though the viewers were not very far from these surfaces, they were

able to take them in all at once. The entire small hall
was filled with a stereo soundtrack coming from loudspeakers and the whole place reverberated with
sound. On the projecting areas alternated moving and
static pictures from seven projectors and eight slide
projectors."11

The rhythm of the multi-screening was determined by the relationship between film and slide projections, and also by the soundtrack. Similar to LM, it
was a multi-layered, clipped and fragmented entity.

The effectiveness of multi-screening came from
its effect on the senses – especially sight and hearing
– by offering eight parallel films at once. When television was first starting out, this parallelism must have
been striking. Even today, the "zapping" with which we
respond to the parallel broadcasting of television programs enables us to watch only one channel at a time.
"TV installations" – walls of TV screens in electronics
store windows irresistible to the shopper – take full
advantage of their effect on viewers. They create the
unlikely possibility to visualize a spatial parallelism of

10 Dan Graham in a letter to
the author, August 1976.

11 Josef Svoboda, op. cit.,
p. 180.

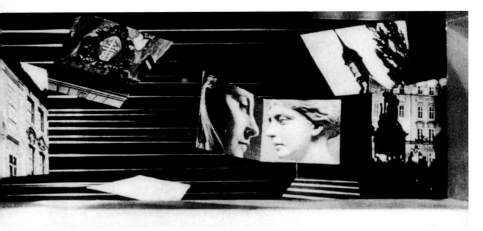

world events, to participate in at once several realities, actions, stories and environments. The sophisticated multi-screen areas, like supermarket installations, give their viewer-visitor a magical feeling of entering several spheres at once. The installations are governed by their own logical timing that creates a distance and a loss of interest in one's own physiological time, while transporting human perception to a metaphysical zenith. Anti-synchronization, so difficult to apply on multiple levels in literature (as, for example, in Joyce's *Ulysses*), is natural and sincere in video and especially in the order of parallel projection. We could compare such experience with Cage's pure sound installation *Imaginary Landscape No. 4.* (1951), in which the resulting experience comes from mixing sounds from twelve radios simultaneously tuned to different stations.

Photographs tell us that today we would use the term "video installation" for Polyekran (simultaneous film projection). As I said above in regard to Laterna Magika, simultaneous projection is a typical byproduct of the development of video art. Another nodal point connecting simultaneous projection, Laterna Magika and video art is the specific treatment of time within these media. "The fundamental difference between cinema and video, even at the experimental level, lies in their respective treatment of the time factor. Video can, and does, represent real time which in cinematic projects such as Léger and Andy Warhol, emerges as a self-contradictory element."12 As Hermine Freed13 notes, early realizations of video art newly articulate their topical character: The video medium was identified with directness and immediacy of the opportunity to replay filmed material without delay, connected from the start to using several cameras and projectors at once.

It is obvious that the concept of parallel film projections through a concrete space onto projection surfaces placed in a visually calculated way has now been integrated into the operational apparatus commonly used in video studies departments of artcolleges. This development has been brought about by the work of artists like Bill Viola and Tony Oursler and others who experimented with the composition and form of projection surfaces. Svoboda's simultaneous film projection was the direct forerunner of their work.

Kinoautomat

The organization of the Czech representation at the Expo 67 in Montreal placed Radúz Çinçera in the interactive field. Çinçera suggested the realization of his creation, the Cine-automaton. The Kinoautomat came up with the novelty of handing over to the audience the decision about plot. Using a voting machine (yes/no) built into the seats, the filmmaker gave the viewers several opportunities to decide on the further plot development. The show included appearances by the film's lead actor Miroslav Horníçek; live on stage, he created a bridge between virtual narration and the real breaks between viewing segments in which he offered comments. The host always concluded his lively film commentary by offering the viewers a choice of the next development. The Kinoautomat was indeed "interactive." The projectionist had in his cabin all the possible versions the viewers among which the viewers could choose. The film, an ironic tale of life in an "ordinary block of rented apartments," was a delightful example of the outstandingly rich Czech New Wave of the 1960s.

The Kinoautomat made the passive viewer active, and offered him the opportunity to become what we might today call a film "user." Haptically, a control system helps to materialize a true entrance into the virtual world of film that the viewer can form through the aid of primitive mechanical tools. The often overlooked haptical phenomenon is significant. This precedent has shown that simple human instruments allow even a casual spectator and user to intervene, form and edit a medium so highly elusive as film. In a time when DVD technology makes it possible to edit and work on a film (be it a holiday video or the biggest Hollywood blockbuster) with a personal computer, a return to the Kinoautomat is meaningful.

12 See Frank Popper, op. cit., note 13, p. 56.

13 Hermine Freed, "Time of Time," in *Arts Magazine*, June 1975.

Alfréd Radok, Josef Svoboda
Polyekran
1958
audio-visual program
Czechoslovak Pavilion,
Brussels Expo
© Sarka Hejnova

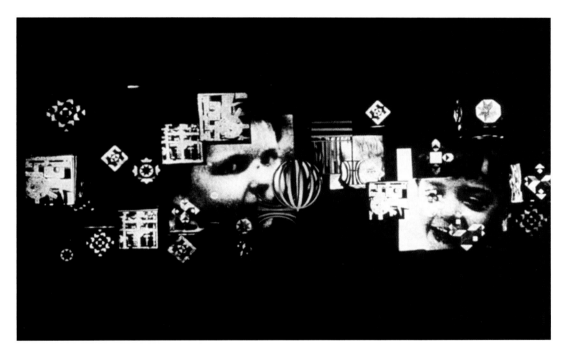

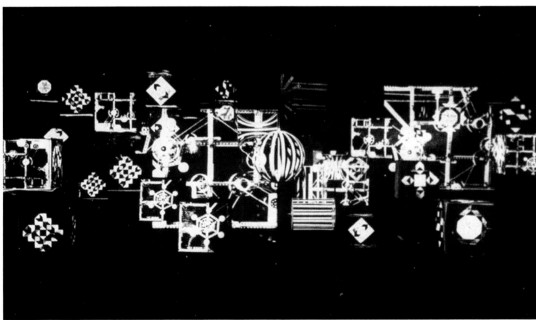

Josef Svoboda
Polyvision,
Textile Condition program, and
Symphony program
1967
multiple-projection cinema
set-up
35mm film and slides projected
on moveable geometrical
objects, projection screen
color, sound
Montreal Expo
© Sarka Hejnova

Josef Svoboda
Polyvision

1967
multi-projection cinema setup / 35mm film and slides projected
on moveable geometrical objects, projection screen /
color, sound / 8 min / project for the Montreal Expo

Josef Svoboda
Polyvision
1967
multi-projection cinema setup
35mm film and slides projected
on moveable geometrical
objects, projection screen
color, sound
8 min
screenshot
Montreal Expo
© Sarka Hejnova

Josef Svoboda
Polyvision
1967
three-dimensional model
© Sarka Hejnova

Peter Weibel
Expanded Cinema,
Video and Virtual Environments

top
Hans Richter
Rhythm 23
1923
16mm film
b/w, silent
3 min
film strip
courtesy Cecile Starr,
New York

bottom
Kasimir Malevich
*Artistic and Scientific Film –
Painting and Architectural
Concerns – Approaching
the New Plastic
Architectural System*
1927
manuscript page from a
three-page film script
private collection

1 Kasimir Malevich, "Painterly
   Laws in the Problems of Cinema," in *Cinema and Culture*
   (Kino i Kultura), nos. 7–8,
   1929.

2 This history is described and
   documented in the following
   books: Sheldon Renan,
   *An Introduction to the
   American Underground Film*,
   Dutton, New York, 1967;
   P. Adams Sitney (ed.), *Film
   Culture Reader*, Praeger,
   New York, 1970; Gene Young-
   blood, *Expanded Cinema*,
   Dutton, New York, 1970;
   Parker Taylor, *Underground
   Film (1969)*, Secker & War-
   burg, London, 1971; David
   Curtis, *Experimental Cinema,
   A Fifty-Year Evolution*,
   Universe Books, New York,
   1971; P. Adams Sitney,
   Visionary Films, Oxford
   University Press, New York,
   1974; Hans Scheugl,
   Ernst Schmidt jr., *Eine
   Subgeschichte des Films.
   Lexikon des Avantgarde-,
   Experimental- und Under-
   groundfilms*, vols. 1, 2,
   Suhrkamp, Frankfurt, 1974;
   Amos Vogel, *Film as Subver-
   sive Art*, Random House, New
   York, 1974; Stephen Dwoskin,
   *Film Is – The International
   Free Cinema*, Peter Owen,
   London, 1975; *Structural
   Film Anthology*, Peter Gidal
   (ed.), BFI Publishing, London,
   1976; *Film als Film 1910 bis
   heute*, Birgit Hein, Wulf
   Herzogenrath (eds),
   Kölnischer Kunstverein,
   Cologne, 1977; Malcolm Le
   Grice, *Abstract Film and*

Avant-garde Film

In most histories of cinema the avant-garde film occupies a minor and marginal position. In the interwar
period of the twentieth century, avant-garde film was
initially seen as a spin-off or by-product of visual art
movements like Cubism, Futurism, Suprematism, Con-
structivism, Dadaism or Surrealism. Linked to these
movements were abstract or pictorial animations as
well as montage and kinetic films by artists like Fer-
nand Leger, Bruno Corra, Kasimir Malevich,1 Viking
Eggeling, Hans Richter, László Moholy-Nagy, Oskar
Fischinger, Man Ray, Marcel Duchamp, Len Lye, Lotte
Reininger, Berthold Bartosch, Alexander Alexeieff and
Claire Parker. These films constituted a body of work
that served as the source for the innovative and autonomous post-WWII motion picture that was variously termed "art" or "experimental" film. This new
movement differed from its historical predecessor
(few artists, small audiences, no media presence, no
theaters, no organization, no distributors) in that it
was at a certain moment in history a mass movement
(with its own distributive organizations, with large audiences in conjunction with the student and pop-
music revolutions, a large number of filmmakers, its
own theaters and magazines). The independent or experimental film of the 1960s was very conscious of
being a new branch of art, a new medium and form of
art as opposed to merely a byproduct of the visual
arts, even if some major filmmakers like Andy Warhol,
Guy Debord or Yoko Ono could be linked to Pop Art,
the Situationist International or Fluxus. This awareness of film as new art medium led to a complete deconstruction of classical cinema. The apparatus of

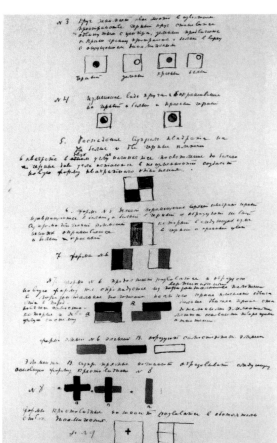

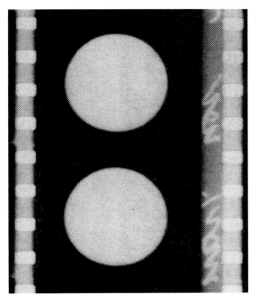

Gil J. Wolman
L'Anticoncept
1951
film stills
L'Institut Scandinave de
Vandalisme Comparé
from Joseph Wolman, *L'Anti-
concept*, Éditions Allia, Paris,
1994, p. 66

Stan Brakhage
Mothlight
1963
16mm film
color, silent
4 min
film strip
© Stan Brakhage

Birgit and Wilhelm Hein
Rohfilm [Raw Film]
1968
16mm film
b/w, sound
20 min
© the artists

classical cinema, from the camera to the projector, from the screen to the celluloid, was radically transformed, annihilated and expanded. The history of avant-garde film is a history of interpellations in the sense of Althusser (see my preface) on the basis of the apparatus itself.2 The deficit of the cinematic apparatus theory of the 1970s was that it showed us only the ideology inherent to Hollywood films, just as in the 1960s Umberto Eco used semiotics to explain James Bond films and today Slavoj Zizek uses Lacan to explain Hitchcock. Neither theorist used the apparatus theory radically in order to demonstrate that the cinematic apparatus and the inscribed ideology can be transformed by making different films with different technologies in the way done by avant-garde filmmakers. They therefore missed a vital point, and fell behind their own theoretical premises. Their theoretical work insofar paradoxically supported the hegemony of Hollywood and dismissed the avant-garde movement from film to video, from video to digital, as representing a transformation of the cinematic apparatus.

This transformation took place in three phases. In the 1960s, the cinematic code was extended with analogous means, with the means of cinema itself. Shortly afterwards, new elements and apparatuses like the video recorder were introduced, and the cinematic code was expanded electromagnetically. Artists' video – from Bruce Nauman to Bill Viola, from Nam June Paik to Steina and Woody Vasulka – was initially successful in the 1970s, but was halted in the 1980s by retro-oriented painterly neo-Expressionism. In the 1990s video art became the dominant form of

media avant-garde, and dominated major exhibitions like the Kassel documenta and Venice Biennial. In the same decade, film entered the field of digitally expanded cinema.

Material Experiments

The subversive explosion that shattered the cinematographic code in the 1960s affected all of the technical and material parameters of film. The material character of the film itself was analyzed by artists who, instead of exposing the celluloid, scratched it (George Landow, *Film In Which There Appear Sprocket Holes, Edge Lettering, Dirt Particles, etc.*, 1965/66; Birgit and Wilhelm Hein, *Rohfilm*, 1968), perforated it with a hole punch (Dieter Roth, 1965), painted it (Harry Smith used 35mm material, processing it with grease, paint, tape and spray, 1947), covered it with fingerprints (Peter Weibel, *Fingerprint*, 1967) or glued moths to it (Stan Brakhage, *Mothlight*, 1963, in which moth wings and leaves were fixed between layers of perforated tape and projected). Empty frames, black film and overexposed material were also used (Gil J. Wolman, *L'anti-concept*, 1951; Guy Debord, *Hurlements en faveur de Sade*, 1952; Peter Kubelka, *Arnulf Rainer*, 1960; Tony Conrad, *The Flicker*, 1965).

At the same time, the apparatus of film, from camera to projector, was taken apart, reassembled, augmented and used in entirely new ways. There were cameraless films, for which unprocessed celluloid, known as clear film, was inserted into the projector (Nam June Paik, *Zen for Film*, 1962), and films without film, in which Kosugi, to name one example, focused light from a projector without film against a paper

Beyond, The MIT Press, Cambridge, MA/London, 1977; Deke Dusinberre, A. L. Rees, *Film as Film, Formal Experiment in Film 1910–75*, Arts Council of Great Britain/Hayward Gallery, London, 1979; Peter Gidal, *Materialist Film*, Routledge, London, 1989; David E. James (ed.), *To Free the Cinema. Jonas Mekas & The New York Underground*, Princeton University Press, Princeton, New Jersey, 1992; Kerry Brougher, *Art and Film Since 1945: Hall of Mirrors*, Monacelli Press, New York, 1996; *Spellbound: Art and Film*, Ian Christie, Philip Dodd (eds), BFI Publishing, London, 1996; Jack Sargeant, *Naked Lens: Beat Cinema*, Creation Books, London, 1997; A. L. Rees, *A History of Experimental Film and Video. From the Canonical Avant-Garde to Contemporary British Practice*, BFI Publishing, London, 1999; Garrett Stewart, *Between Film and Screen. Modernism's Photo Synthesis*, The University of Chicago Press, Chicago and London, 1999; *Into the Light. The Projected Image in American Art 1964–1977*, Chrissie Iles (ed.), exhib. cat., Whitney Museum of American Art, New York/Harry N. Abrams, New York, 2001; Malcolm Le Grice, *Experimental Cinema in the Digital Age*, BFI Publishing, London, 2001; Hans Scheugl, *Erweitertes Kino. Die Wiener Filme der 60er Jahre*, Triton, Wien, 2002; Martin Rieser, Andrea Zapp (eds), *New Screen Media. Cinema/Art/Narrative*, BFI Publishing, London, 2002, book and DVD; Margot Lovejoy, *Digital Currents: Art in the Electronic Age*, Routledge, London, 2003.

Robert Whitman
Shower
1964
environment
16mm film loop transferred to
video, shower stall, water, water
pump
installation view: Newark
Museum, New Jersey, 1999
collection Robert Rauschenberg
photo courtesy
Robert Rauschenberg and
Robert Whitman

Anthony McCall
Line Describing a Cone
1973
16mm film
b/w, silent
31 min
installation view: Artists Space,
New York, 1974
Whitney Museum of American
Art, New York
courtesy Anthony McCall
photo © Peter Moore;
VG Bild-Kunst, Bonn 2003

Simone Forti and
Lucinda Childs in
Robert Whitman's
Prune Flat
1965
performance view: Expanded
Cinema Festival, Film-Maker's
Cinematheque, New York, 1965
photo © Peter Moore;
VG Bild-Kunst, Bonn 2003

3 See Gene Youngblood, *Expanded Cinema*, Dutton, New
York, 1970, p. 371.

screen, cutting out sections of the screen from the middle until there was nothing left of it (*Film No.4*, 1965). In *zzz:hamburg special* (1968), Hans Scheugl replaced the filmstrip with a thread actually running through the projector to create a shadow line on the screen. In other works, the light beam was replaced with a stretched length of rope (Peter Weibel, *Licht-seil*, 1973), or became the pure and only matter (Anthony McCall, *Line describing a cone*, 1973). Films were projected not on the conventional screen but on curtains of steam with running water (Robert Whitman, *Shower*, 1964) and on the surfaces of human bodies (in his *Prune Flat*, 1965, Robert Whitman projected a film onto the body of a girl wearing white clothing; the film showed her taking off the same clothes; in Andy Warhol's and Jud Yalkut's *Exploding Plastic Inevitable*, 1966, the film was projected onto the figures of members of the audience dancing to music by the Velvet Underground). The history of these material experiments is described in Peter Gidal's book *Material-ist Film* (London, 1989).

Multiple Screen Experiments

Many film artists carried out radical experiments with the screen itself. It was exploded and multiplied, either through division into multiple images using split-screen techniques or by placing screens on several different walls. Thus multiple projections occupied the foreground of a visual culture that was intent upon liberating itself from the conventional concept of the painting, from the technical and material restrictions of imaging technology and from the repressive deter-

minants of the social codes. In much the same way that some painters sliced up the canvas (Lucio Fontana) or used the human body as a canvas (the Viennese Actionists) in search of avenues of escape from the picture, cinema artists were also engaged in a quest for ways of breaking out of the limited film screen during the same period.

The *Vortex Concerts* (visuals by Henry Jacobs, Jordan Belson, the Whitney Brothers), 1957–59, mixed multiple film projections and slide shows. Kenneth Anger showed *Inauguration of the Pleasure Dome* (1954) on three screens in Brussels in 1958. In order to "free film from its flat and frontal orientation and to present it within an ambience of total space,"3 Milton Cohen, the leading figure in the ONCE Group from Ann Arbor, Michigan, had since 1958 been developing an environment (*Space Theatre*) for multiple projections with the aid of rotating mirrors and prisms using mobile rectangular and triangular screens. In 1965, Stan VanDerBeek published a manifesto in justification of real-time multiple projection environments, a kind of "image-flow" in which image projection itself became the subject of the performance. In the same year he showed *Feedback No.1: A Movie Mural*, achieving a first breakthrough for multi-projection cinema. To realize his idea, he established a *Movie Drome* in Stony Point, New York; a vaulted cupola modeled on the geodetic domes of Buckminster Fuller. Around 1960, the USCO ("US" company) Group associated with Gerd Stern began working on the multi-projection shows on the east coast of the USA (*We are all one*, with four 16mm

ONCE Group
Unmarked Interchange
1965
photo © Peter Moore; VG Bild-
Kunst, Bonn 2003

Live performers interact with a
projection of *Top Hat*, starring
Fred Astaire and Ginger Rogers.

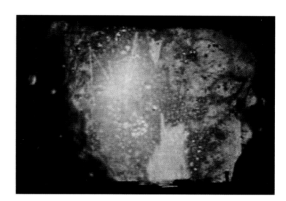

center and bottom
Partially opened parachute
becomes Isobe's *Floating
Theatre* for the presentation
of Jud Yalkut's *Dream Reel*
intermedia environment at
Oneonta, New York, March 1969
photos courtesy Yukihisa Isobe.

The Single Wing Turquoise Bird group
in their studio at Venice,
California, 1967/1968
photo © Gene Youngblood

projectors, two 8mm projectors, four carousel projectors, 1965).

John Cage, Lejaren Hiller and Ronald Nameth staged *HPSCHD*, a five-hour "Intermedia Event" with eight thousand slides and one hundred films projected onto forty-eight windows at the University of Illinois in 1969. Between 1960 and 1967, Robert Whitman experimented with multiple plastic and paper screens onto which films were projected (*The American Moon*, 1960). In *Tent Happening* (1965), films, including a sequence filmed through a glass pane showing a man defecating, were projected onto a large tent. Beginning in 1965, Aldo Tambellini's *Electromedia Theatre* worked with multiple projections (*Black Zero*, 1965) in which, to cite one example, a gigantic black balloon appeared from nowhere, blew itself up and eventually exploded. Hundreds of hand-painted films and slides were used. In 1968 Tambellini organized *Black Gate* in Dusseldorf along the banks of the Rhine, an event featuring projections onto helium-filled, airborne plastic hoses and figures by Otto Piene. Jud Yalkut created *Dream Reel* for Yukihisa Isobe's *Floating Theatre*, a gigantic parachute held by nylon threads – a portable hemispheric screen for multiple frontal and rear projections. The Single Wing Turquoise Bird group (Peter Mays, Jeff Perkins, the later video artist Michael Scroggins and others) from Los Angeles put together light shows for rock concerts in 1967 and 1968. Sponsored by the painter Sam Francis, they subsequently conducted experiments in an abandoned Santa Monica hotel with constantly changing images, from video projections to laser beams. In

their *Theatre of Light* of the late 1960s, Jackie Cassen and Rudi Stern used self-constructed "sculptural projectors" to project multiple images onto pneumatic domes, transparent Plexiglas cubes, polyhexagonal structures, water surfaces, and so forth. Particularly impressive was a fountain illuminated by a strobe light, a technique that evoked the impression of individual drops of water being suspended like crystals in the air. This effect is today variously repeated by Olafur Eliasson. Toshio Matsumoto showed his *Space Projection AKO* in a dome in 1969. One noteworthy example is Andy Warhol's *Chelsea Girls* (1966), a mixture of split-screen techniques and multiple projection in which a number of performers discuss their unusual lives from multiple perspectives and at several different levels at the same time. There were monumental mobile projections from moving vehicles onto building facades (Imi Knoebel, *Projektion X*, 1972), onto dancing people, onto forests and fields, onto the curved inside and outside surfaces of geodetic domes, onto plastic balls, hoses, and so on.

Contemporary visual practices have returned to these techniques of mobile projection or deployment of the screen as a window in a moving vehicle, as in Lutz Mommartz' *Eisenbahn* [Railway] of 1967. The interactive installation *Crossings* (1995) by Stacey Spiegel & Rodney Hoinkes simulates a train journey between Paris and Berlin, transforming physical space into the virtual interactive space of the World-Wide Web. *Room with a view* (2000), created by Michael Bielicky and Bernd Lintermann for Volkswagen's "Autostadt Wolfsburg," uses four projectors to achieve a

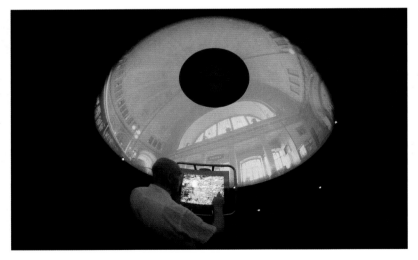

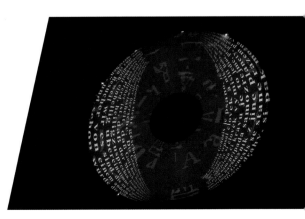

Michael Bielicky,
Bernd Lintermann,
Torsten Belschner
Zimmer mit Aussicht
[Room with a View]
2000
interactive installation
mixed media
dome projection: 1200 cm ø
installation view: Skoda Pavilion,
VW Autostadt, Wolfsburg, 2000
ZKM | Institute for Visual Media,
Karlsruhe
© the artists and ZKM | Center
for Art and Media Karlsruhe
photo © Franz Wamhof

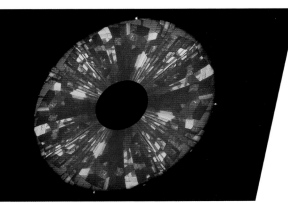

Michael Bielicky,
Bernd Lintermann,
Torsten Belschner
Zimmer mit Aussicht
[Room with a View]
2000
interactive installation
stills
ZKM | Institute for Visual Media,
Karlsruhe
© the artists and ZKM | Center
for Art and Media Karlsruhe

Michael Snow with the machine
used for filming
La Région Centrale
[The Central Region]
photo © Joyce Wieland

Michael Snow
Two Sides to Every Story
1974
projection
two 16mm films
both color, sound
two projectors, painted
aluminum screen
8 min, dimensions variable
installation view: Walker Art
Center, Minneapolis, 1974
National Gallery of Canada,
Ottawa
© Michael Snow
photo courtesy Michael Snow

Edmund Kuppel
Das Planetarium
1990
installation
central projector, 12 screens,
steel globe
800 cm ø
installation view
courtesy the artist
bottom
Das Planetarium
detail

perfect 360-degree dome projection, with a touch-screen at the center of the dome allowing multiple manipulation of the projected images. With twelve round screens in a dome construction and one central projector, Edmund Kuppel's *Das Planetarium* (1990) is an interesting paraphrase of Michael Snow's outstanding *La Region Centrale* (1970). In the 1960s, the screen became in a number of ways multiple and mobile, as well as flat or curved, or was even replaced by unusual materials like water, woods and buildings.

Important experiments with material film, multiple projections and expanded cinema were made in the 1970s by a group of British filmmakers associated with Malcolm Le Grice (*After Leonardo,* 1974, a six-projector film) and made up by Dave Crosswaite, David Dye (*Unsigning* for eight projectors, 1972), Gill Eatherley, Annabel Nicholson, William Raban and Lis Rhodes. In 1972, Birgit and Wilhelm Hein showed a two-screen film titled *Doppelprojektion 1-1V.* A very early example of double projection was delivered by the film *L'Uomo meccanico* [The Mechanical Man] of 1921 by André Deed, a French film clown who had been making his "Cretinetti" films in Italy since 1909 and was admired by the Futurists. In this film, a robot filmed with a camera a furiously fast police car and the footage was shown on a second screen inside the first.

These experiments with multiple screens were carried forward in the 1960s by environments with film and by film environments which combined projection and live action. In *Moviemovie* (1967) by Theo Botschuijver, Jeffrey Shaw and Sean Wellesley-Miller, films and light were projected onto a pneumatic sculpture on which people moved. *Moviehouse* (1965) by Claes Oldenburg showed a film theater without a film. The situation (real people sitting on chairs) was the cinematic spectacle, a cinematic approach repeated by Janet Cardiff in the 1990s (*Playhouse,* 1997). An innovative project by Markus Huemer (1988) placed the famous letters HOLLYWOOD on a hill in Linz, Austria; the idea was later repeated by Maurizio Cattelan in Palermo (2001), and partially (LYWO) by Bertrand Lavier in Lyon (2000).

Narrative Experiments

Multiple projections of different films alongside one another, one on top of the other, and in all spatial directions represented more than merely an invasion of space by the visual image. They were also an expression of multiple narrative perspectives. The filmmaker Gregory Markopoulos, an early master of quick cuts and complex cross-fading techniques, published a manifesto of new narrative forms based upon his cutting technique:

"I propose a new form of narration as a combination of classical montage technique with a more abstract system. This system incorporates the use of short film phases that evoke thought images. Each film phase comprises a selection of

Annabel Nicholson
Reel Time
1973
16mm film
b/w, sound
performance of
indeterminate length
© Annabel Nicholson

Rodney Hoinkes,
Stacey Spiegel
Crossings
1995
interactive installation,
Internet project
mixed media
dimensions variable
installation view
© Rodney Hoinkes,
Stacey Spiegel

Charles and Ray Eames
Glimpses of the USA
1959
Moscow World's
Fair auditorium

specific images similar to the harmonious unity of a musical composition. The film phases determine other interrelationships among themselves; in classical montage technique, there is a constant relationship to the continuous shot; in my abstract system there is a complex of different images that are repeated."[4]

From the outset, the extension of the single screen to many screens, from the single projection to multiple projections represented not only an expansion of visual horizons and an overwhelming intensification of visual experience. It was always engaged in the service of a new approach to narration. For the first time, the subjective response to the world was not pressed into a constructed, falsely objective style of narration but was instead formally presented in the same diffuse and fragmentary way in which it was experienced. In the age of social revolts, mind-expanding drugs and cosmic visions, multiple projection environments became an important factor in the quest for a new imaging technology capable of articulating a new perception of the world.

Charles and Ray Eames made very early use of slide and film projections onto multiple screens: *Glimpses of the USA* was shown on seven screens at the Moscow World's Fair (1959), and on fourteen screens in the IBM Pavilion at the New York World's Fair (1964-65). For the Montreal Expo in 1967, several artists also created huge multi-vision environments (for instance, Roman Kroitor's *Labyrinthe*) with the intention of developing new forms of storytelling. "People," as Roman Kroitor asserted, "[were] tired of the standard plot structure." Francis Thompson, a pioneer in large-scale, multi-image cinematography, presented his piece *We are Young* on an arrangement of six screens in Montreal. The Czech pavilion featured Josef Svoboda's *Creation of the World of Man*, a huge (Diapolyekran) screen on which 15,000 slides could be shown simultaneously on 112 movable cubes.

In these experiments with multiple screens we see the beginning of immersive environments, virtual worlds and interactive relations between spectator and image. The spectator slowly becomes part of the system that he observes. Closed-circuit video installations in the 1970s really allowed the spectator to see himself in the video monitor, in the image captured by the video camera. At the same time, multiple screens broke up the linearity of traditional narration. Multiform plots, a non-linear narrative matrix, became possible. Narrative elements could be repeated, recombined, or replaced by other elements. In *Zorns Lemma* (1970) by Hollis Frampton, letters were replaced by images, and these images turned into events. A new form of narration was achieved on a single screen. The narrative matrix was based on a theorem of set theory (Zorn's Lemma). The narration became a multiform matrix, a multi-story machine.

4 In *Filmculture*, no. 31, winter 1963/64.

left
John Whitney
Matrix
1971
computer-graphics animation
color, sound
6 min
© John Whitney
Figures from John Whitney's
article "A Computer Art for the
Video Picture Wall," in Robert
Russett and Cecile Starr (eds),
*Experimental Animation. Origins
of New Art*, Da Capo Press, New
York, 1976, pp. 187–191.

above
Ed Emshwiller
Skin Matrix
1984
video
color, sound
16:57 min
video still
courtesy Ed Emshwiller

Douglas Gordon
24 Hour Psycho
1993
video installation
installation view
© Douglas Gordon
photo © Douglas Gordon

In the film *Nowa Ksiazka* [New Book] of 1975 Zbigniew Rybczynski used a matrix of nine different images on one screen, showing different parts of one narrative and thereby anticipating the four-part screen of Mike Figgis' *Time Code* (2000). Before the term "matrix" was made famous by William Gibson's novel *New-romancer* (1984) and the Wachowski brothers' film *Matrix* (1999), it was already serving as a method for visual narratives (see John Whitney's computer animation *Matrix I*, 1971, and *Skin Matrix*, a video fantasy by Ed Emshwiller, 1984).

Time and Space Experiments
In addition to the expansion of the technical repertoire through experimentation with projectors and multiple projections, another material-oriented approach to the visual expression of a new concept of reality, the renunciation of social conventions and a new drug-induced, consciousness-expanding experience emerged. It involved the shifting and distortion of the conventional parameters of space and time using techniques designed to extend, slow, delay and abbreviate time. Film duration was extended to as much as twenty-four hours (Andy Warhol, *Empire State Building*, 1963), just as later Douglas Gordon extended Hitchcock's *Psycho* to twenty-four hours, or reduced to an extreme of only a few seconds (Paul Sharits, *Wrist Trick*, ten seconds, 1966). Temporal dilations in film and music (La Monte Young) were favored as primary means of expression not only due to their consciousness-raising effects, but also for compositional and formal reasons. The same was true of time-shortening and aggressive cutting techniques. The films of Michael Snow were pure time and space ex-

periments (*Wavelength*, 1967, a forty-five minute zoom through a room; *One second in Montreal*, 1969; *La Région Centrale*, 1970). In his *See you later/Au revoir* (1990), a thirty-second movement (a man leaving his office) was extended to seventeen minutes and thirty seconds. In Joe Jones' *Smoke* (1966), the cigarette smoke streaming from a mouth is extended to six minutes. The composer Takehisa Kosugi takes thirty minutes to take off his jacket in *Anima 7* (1966). Peter Weibel's film actions *The Kiss* and *To pour* (both 1968), which deploy extreme slow motion, must also be counted among this "slow anthology" (T. Kosugi).

Social and Sexual Experiments
In the social sense too, the contents of these independent avant-garde and underground films strayed from the familiar terrain of the industry film. Images from the intimate sphere, psycho-dramatic documents of an excessive individualism were shown publicly in uncensored form. Taboo sex scenes were acted out in front of the camera (Jack Smith, *Flaming Creatures*, 1962/63, a transvestite orgy that triggered a scandal even in artistic circles yet became a major source of inspiration for Warhol's universe; Kenneth Anger's *Scorpio Rising*, 1963, which marked the birth of *Biker Movies* and homo-erotic self-fashioning, and *Inauguration of the Pleasure Dome*, 1966). The widening of material and technical parameters went hand-in-hand with the dissolution of social consensus.[5]

5 Raymond Durgnat, *Sexual
Alienation in the Cinema*,
Studio Vista, London, 1972.

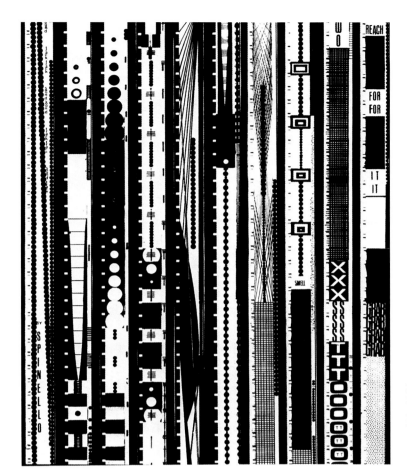

Barry Spinello
Soundtrack
1970
16mm film
b/w, parts handcolored, sound
11 min
film strips
courtesy Barry Spinello

Both sound and image are
produced with handmade graphic effects.

Sound Experiments

Both formal and thematic extensions of the cinematographic code were welcomed enthusiastically in
the revolutionary aesthetic and social atmosphere of
the 1960s and was, like progressive rock music, supported by a new, youthful audience. Indeed, a large
number of such underground films were accompanied
by rock (from the Grateful Dead to Cream) and avant-
garde (from John Cage to Terry Riley) music. In these
films, the role played by music was much more emancipated than in industry movies. Regardless of
whether mainstream productions use classical or
popular scores, music serves more or less as background sound and a device for controlling mood and
atmosphere, for heightening or resolving dramatic
tension. By contrast, in many avant-garde films music
and sound exercise a determining effect upon the
structure of imagery, and images are cut and composed in accordance with musical principles. The tendency to industrially exploit and market film images
through linkage with music is clearly illustrated by the
function of the soundtrack, the serial arrangement of
existing popular songs and the commissioned piece
that is known as a theme song and used to associate
a certain film with a certain musical hit. This usage of
semi-prefabricated components in movies and videos
is reminiscent of the accelerated prefab building
techniques employed in mass industrial high-rise construction. Instead of compound concrete-and-steel
construction, the rapidly mass-produced industrial
film made use of a compound sound-and-music construction. In contrast, the avant-garde films of the
1960s employed a highly differentiated approach to
the development of new relationships between sound

and visual imagery.6 Barry Spinello's *Soundtrack*
(1970), in which both sound and image are produced
with handmade graphic effects, explored audio-visual
compositional techniques. In *Feature Film* (1999), Douglas Gordon reorchestrated Bernard Herrmann's
score for Hitchcock's *Vertigo* and presented only
James Conlon conducting and hearing the film music
played by an orchestra.

The Evolution of the Language of New Media:
Expanded Cinema, Video and Virtual Environments

In the course of the 1970s, several avant-garde galleries promoted analytical refinements and developments, ranging from the Structuralist films to spatial
film installations. This decade also witnessed the
emergence of video art, with viewer-oriented closed-
circuit installations that anticipated the observer-
relative interactive computer installations of the
1990s and time-delayed installations, which pursued
further the experiments of Expanded Cinema. The
market-induced revival of figurative painting in the
1980s put an abrupt end to the development of expanded cinematic forms and video art. Broad segments of visual culture were affected by an amnesia
as scandalous as it was total, and for which the market alone was not to blame but also institutional art
historiography, which had buckled under to the power
of the market. Viewed from this perspective, the triumphant return and revival of the tendencies of
1960s Expanded Cinema in the work of the 1990s
video generation is all the more astounding and grati-
fying. However, we still face the problem that most
art historians and writers, being oblivious to the history of avant-garde film and video art, cannot make a

6 See Michel Chion, *Les
musiques electro-acous-
tiques*, INA-GRM, Aix-en
Provence, 1976; Michel
Chion, *Le son au cinema*,
Cahiers du Cinéma, Paris,
1985; Michel Chion, *L'audiovi-
sion*, Nathan, Paris, 1990;
Michel Chion, *La musique au
cinema*, Fayard, Paris, 1995.

David Lamelas
Filmscript
1972
installation view:
Witte de With, Rotterdam
photo © B. Goedewaagen

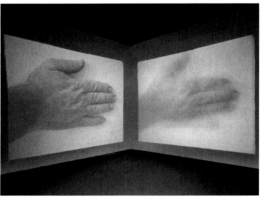

Dennis Oppenheim
Echo
1973
film installation
four 16mm film loops
transferred to video
b/w, sound
installation view: Whitney
Museum of American Art,
New York, 2001
collection of the artist
© Dennis Oppenheim
photo © David Allison

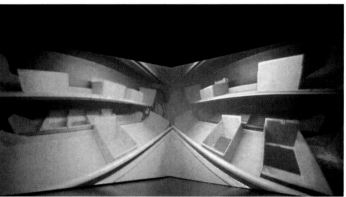

Jane and Louise Wilson
Stasi City
1997
four-channel video installation
color, sound
29 min
installation view
collection Pamela and Richard
Kramlich
courtesy Thea Westreich Art
Advisory Services

connection between the generations and therefore exaggerate contemporary achievements.

The new generation took its cue less from the achievements of 1980s video artists, whose art was subordinated to the sculpture and painting of their time. In pursuing the development of a specific video-based language, video artists in the 1990s deliberately focused on the expansion of image technologies and social consciousness that took place in the 1960s. We find surprising evidence of parallels, sometimes extending even to the finest detail, not only in style and technique, but in content and motif as well. For the most part, 1990s video art is also shaped by an intense interest in multiple projection and the concomitant new approaches to multi-perspective narration and multiform plots. Numerous representatives of the 1990s video generation, including artists like Jordan Crandall, Julia Scher, Steve McQueen, Jane and Louise Wilson, Douglas Gordon, Stan Douglas, Johan Grimonprez, Pierre Huyghe, Marijke van Warmerdam, Ann-Sofi Sidén, Grazia Toderi and Aeronaut Mike, now work within the context of a deconstruction of the technical "apparatus" outlined here. Many computer artists of the same decade, among them Blast Theory, Jeffrey Shaw, Perry Hoberman and Peter Weibel, have also returned to the tendencies

and technologies of 1960s Expanded Cinema. In a series of interactive computer installations, including *On Justifying the Hypothetical Nature of Art and the Non-Identicality within the Object World* (1992) or *Curtain of Lascaux* (1995-96), Peter Weibel realized various virtual worlds in which the observer played a pivotal role derived from his closed circuit video installations of the late 1960s/early 1970s. The observer became part of the system he observed, articulating the immersive image system, and changed the behavior and content of the image by his actions. The British group Blast Theory's *Desert Rain* (1999) sent six visitors on a mission in a virtual environment made up of six rooms. The virtual worlds were projected onto a curtain of streaming water. Each visitor had thirty minutes to complete his mission by communicating with the other five virtual environments and their inhabitants. However, 1990s video artists pursued the deconstruction of the cinematographic code in a much more controlled, less subjective manner, applying strategies more methodical and more closely oriented to social issues than those of the 1960s. In the video art of the 1990s, experiments with multiple projections were employed primarily in the service of a new approach to narration. Video and slide projections onto unusual objects were used by

Stan Douglas
Win, Place or Show
1998
two-channel
video projection
color,
four channel soundtrack
6 min
video stills
courtesy Galerie David
Zwirner, New York
photo © T. Mills

Stan Douglas
Evening
1994
three-channel video installation
color, sound
20 min
installation view: Renaissance
Society, Chicago, 1995
courtesy Galerie David Zwirner,
New York
photo © T.Mills

top
Blast Theory
Desert Rain
1999
VR environment
for performance
installation views: ZKM |
Center for Art and Media
Karlsruhe, 1999
© Blast Theory
photo © Franz Wamhof

bottom
Sam Taylor-Wood
Third Party
1999
installation
seven 16mm
film projections,
transferred to DVD
installation view
photo © Jay Jopling,
London

artists ranging from Tony Oursler to Honoré d'0. Projections onto two or more screens are found in the work of artists like Pipilotti Rist, Sam Taylor-Wood (*Third Party*, 1999, seven projections), Burt Barr, Marcel Odenbach, Eija-Liisa Ahtila, Shirin Neshat, Samir, Doug Aitken, Dryden Goodwin, Heike Baranowsky and Monika Oechsler. Split-screen techniques are characteristic features of the art of Karin Westerlund and Samir. Multiple-monitor environments are employed by Ute Friederike Jürss, Mary Lucier and Chantal Akerman (*D'Est*, 2002, twenty-five monitors).

Multiple Monitors and Screens, Multiple Projections and Perspectives, Multi-perspective Narrations and Plots

These multiple projections take advantage of the opportunities multiple perspective offers for a departure from familiar ways of looking at social behavior. On three screens projected in alternation, Monika Oechsler's *High Anxieties* of 1998 shows the construction of feminine identity as it begins in childhood, illustrating how even girlfriends of the same age control the formation of the individual as agents of society. The changing cinematic perspective calls to mind the familiar cinematic codes of courtroom dramas involving prosecutors, defense attorneys, victims and defendants. Enhanced by the possibilities offered by triple projection and multiple viewpoint achieved through this formal montage technique, this new perspective intensifies the hidden violence inherent in the socialization of the individual. In a similar way, the triple projection in Eija-Liisa Ahtila's *TODAY/Tanaan* (1996/97) enormously enhances the possibilities for complex linking of image and text elements independent of the narrator's perspective. Only rarely do the texts match the faces and genders. Texts and images do not identify each other; instead they distinguish each other, floating alongside one another and forming moving nodes in a network of multiple relationships which the viewer must create himself. Free-floating chains of signs, be they images or texts, are interwoven to form a universe without a center. Yet its core harbors the catastrophe of a fatal accident that has obviously eradicated all possibility of a coherent, linear narrative. Only disparate fragments of memory are presented in strangely objective fashion by the passive, *knotted subjects* (the title of a book by Elisabeth Bronfen, 1998). The story of the catastrophe no longer follows the linear track of rational thought; instead, the irrational essence of the catastrophe is released (from censorship) by disorderly, centrifugal, multi-perspective narrative trajectories.

Marina Gržinić, Aina Šmid
Troubles with Sex,
Theory and History
1997
interactive CD-ROM
screenshot
© Marina Gržinić,
Aina Šmid

Only in this way can the catastrophe be experienced as such – through the refusal of image and text elements to merge and fit together. Narrative structures of this kind, which employ the irrational character of dream and the human psyche as plot elements, clearly reveal associations with the early films of Ingmar Bergmann (for example, *Wild Strawberries,* 1957). The interactive CD-ROM *Troubles with Sex, Theory & History* (1997) by Marina Gržinić and Aina Šmid analyzes aleatoric, combinatoric and recombinatoric relations between images and text, based on a selection of works by Grzinic and Smid between 1992 and 1997.

Shirin Neshat presents in *Turbulent* (1998) the binary opposition of man and woman in a patriarchal society on two screens positioned opposite one another. The woman has a voice but neither words nor listeners. She has only sound and her ability to scream. The man possesses the words, the culture of language and an audience which rewards him with frenetic applause at the end. The exclusion of woman from the building of civilization and society can hardly be illustrated more vividly than in this binary juxtaposition of projectors and positions. The device of the synecdoche (used here in the representation of the violence inherent in gender issues and the politics of identity) is typical of many of the best works of video art, which deal in a methodological-analytical manner with the eradicated power mechanisms of the social code, as opposed to the predominantly subjective approaches of the New American Cinema of the 1960s.

Modern society offers the real subject a number of different role models and possibilities for role behavior. On a scale of multiple possibilities defined by the culture industry in media ranging from popular movies to highbrow opera, from slick magazines to low-ratings TV, the subject can make its choice and position itself, as long as it can take the pressure of the respective social code. This relationship between the subject as a real possibility and the imaginary subject option is expressed as a synecdoche in Sam Taylor-Wood's *Killing Time* (1994). Like several other artists, Taylor-Wood works with "found sound." Interestingly enough, her work confirms the theory of the dominance of musical structure as the determining narrative structure. It is not the visual image but sound that dictates the behavior of the actors. The four persons shown in the quadruple projections listen to *Electra* by Richard Strauss, waiting for cues for their assigned voice parts. Like Shirin Neshat's work, the film sequence is a synecdoche for the range of available (social) roles and the role of the voice in society.[7] The theater of sound opens a view to the theater of subject positions. In comparison, Pipilotti Rist tends rather toward the structure of semi-prefabricated components in her work. She uses prerecorded music, which she illustrates with her pictures, or the music illustrates her pictures according to coded schemes of the kind we see on MTV. She remains within the codes of the subject option and the industrial narrative prescribed and accepted by society. We find a differently interesting adaptation of the relationship between sound and image at the narrative level, since remembering is one of the functions of narrative, in *A Capella Portraits* by Ute Friederike Jürss. The videos of Sylvie Blocher, Gillian Wearing, Sam Taylor-Wood combine in a very complex way mise-en-scène, documentary, sounds, images, masks and screens to serve the deconstruction of the world as a multiform script.

7 See Kaja Silverman, *The Acoustic Mirror: The Female Voice in Psychoanalysis and Cinema,* Indiana Univ. Press, Bloomington, 1988.

11 SCREENINGS
Peter Weibel / Expanded Cinema, Video and Virtual Environments

George Legrady
Slippery Traces
1996
interactive CD-ROM
screenshot
courtesy
George Legrady

Perry Hoberman
*The Sub-Division
of the Electric Light*
1996
CD-ROM
screenshot
© Perry Hoberman

Found Image and Sound, Found Film Experiments

Just as artists of the 1960s made use of "found images" and "found footage" (George Landow and others), contemporary video and film artists like Douglas Gordon, Marcel Odenbach and Martin Arnold employ found material as well. Perry Hoberman uses in his interactive CD-ROM piece *The Sub-Division of the Electric Light* (1996) found slides and 8mm film and old projection instruments. Erkki Huhtamo uses a selection of found vaudeville rides, mostly computer-generated to imitate on a simulation platform a journey on virtual vehicles through the highlights of historic cinematographic rides in his piece *The Ride of Your Life* (1998). George LeGrady in his interactive CD-ROM piece *Slippery Traces* (1996) uses about two hundred post-cards for a non-linear narration built on an algorithm, navigating through a data bank. Martin Arnold deconstructs his found footage to the extreme in order to make hidden semantic structures visible through gradual repetition (*pièce touchée, 1989; passage à l'acte, 1993*). Found footage is re-assembled, looped, partially re-filmed and visually estranged in its entirety. The use of found film is part of a general strategy of media reflection and appropriation. When Marcel Odenbach, Gabriele Leidloff, Samir, Isabell Heimerdinger, Andrea Bowers, Burt Barr, Pierre Huyghe and Douglas Gordon allude to familiar films, including such classics as *From here to Eternity* (Fred Zinnemann, 1953) and *The Godfather* (Francis Ford Coppola, 1972) or to popular television images ranging from cheerleaders (Andrea Bowers, *Touch of Class*, 1998) to scenes from the funeral of Diana, Princess of Wales (Gabriele Leidloff, *Moving Visual Object*, 1997), then what we have are media-oriented observations of a second order, in which visual culture

as a whole is exposed as a ready-made object for analysis. Consequently, observation of the world gives way to the observation of communication. The unconscious character of the visual code becomes evident in a kind of symptomatic reading.

In Doug Aitken's installations employing multiple screens, the narrative universe is broken down into individual, autonomous film frames and series of effects of the kind familiar to viewers schooled in video-clip techniques: detailed shots, blurred motion, technical modifications achieved with the camera, digital image processing, short cuts and dilations of time. Narration is not only broken apart spatially through projection onto multiple screens but in chronological terms as well.

Shifts and distortions of conventional parameters of space and time play a significant role in the new narration. As in the 1960s, these experiments with time emphasize the technological time of the cinematic order as opposed to the biological time of life. The focus is on artificial time rather than "rediscovered time," on time constructions as visual symptoms of a completely artificial, constructed reality. In his triple projection *L'Ellipse* of 1998, with Bruno Ganz, Pierre Huyghe illustrates the difference between industrial time (the use of time in the industry film) and personal time (the use of time in Pierre Huyghe's own film). He uses found footage or found film, film as a ready-made work of art, which he deconstructs by subjecting it to chronological manipulation: When Bruno Ganz is off screen in the industry film (*The American Friend* by Wim Wenders, 1977), the projection of his personal film begins and interrupts the projection of the industry film. Huyghe plays with the cinematographic technique of cutting from one scene

David Blair
WAXWEB
*(WAX or the Discovery
of Television Among the
Bees,
a hypermedia version)*
1994-2000
video, realtime, 3D/html
screenshot
courtesy the artist

to another by deleting the time and space in between which technique is called "elliptical." Douglas Gordon subjects industry films to similar time manipulations. He also works with found films (from Hitchcock's *Psycho* to Ford's *The Searchers*), expanding them to respectively twenty-four hours or five years.

Computer Film
Made with the help of an IBM 1620-21, Marc Adrian's film *random* (1963) was probably the first computer-aided film made by an artist in Europe. The Whitney Brothers opened the field of the digital film (John Whitney, *Permutations*, 1968). In 1971, John Whitney jr. made his first digital film *Terminal Self*, a title that was later recalled in that of Scott Bukatman's book *Terminal Identity* (1993), which simultaneously echoed a line from William Burroughs: "The entire planet is being developed into terminal identity and complete surrender."[8] Michael Whitney made the digital film *Binary Bit Patterns* (1969). John Stehura (*Cybernetic 5-3*, 1965), Lillian Schwartz and Ken Knowlton, Charles Csuri and James Shafter (*Humming Bird*) belong to the early avant-garde of digital film. David Blair's *WAXWEB* (1994-2000) laid a foundation stone for web cinema.

Navigable Rhizomatic Narration
The narrative universe becomes reversible in the field of digitally expanded cinema and no longer reflects the psychology of cause and effect. Repetitions, the suspension of linear time, temporal and spatial asynchrony blast apart classical chronology. Multiple screens function as fields in which scenes are depicted from a multiple perspective, their narrative thread broken. The accusation once leveled at new music – that it had cut the link to the listener, since the listener could no longer reconstruct or recognize the principles of composition – can now be addressed without reservation to the advanced narrative techniques of contemporary video art. They have severed the link to the viewer, who can no longer make out the narrative structure. Linearity and chronology, as clas-

sical parameters of narration, fall victim to a multiple perspective projected onto multiple screens. Asynchronous, non-linear, non-chronological, seemingly illogical, parallel, multiple narrative approaches from multiple perspectives projected onto multiple screens are the goal. These narrative procedures comprising a "multiform plot" have been developed with reference to and oriented toward such rhizomatic communication structures as hypertext, "associational indexing" (Vannevar Bush, *As We May Think*, 1945), text based "multi-user dungeons" (MUDs) and other digital techniques of literary narration.[9] Gilles Deleuze's definition of the rhizome as a network in which every point can be connected with any other point is a precise description of communication in the multi-user environment of the World-Wide Web and the allusive, open-ended image and text systems derived from it. These narrative systems and scripts have a certain algorithmic character. Narration becomes a machine, a plot-machine, an engine. As early as 1928, Vladimir Propp demonstrated in his famous study *Morphology of the Fairy Tale* that the 450 fairy tales he analyzed could be reduced to 25 basic functions and narrative events, or narrative morphemes. These twenty-five morphemes form a kind of algorithm, which generates an endless string of new plots through new combinations. With its audio-visual narrative techniques, contemporary video art breaks down holistic forms into their basic morphological components. These are then reassembled using the multiple methods described above. These new narrative techniques render the complexity of social systems lucid. The crisis of representation, which painting averted during the 1980s by resorting to a restorative repetition of historical figurative and expressive conditions, is being overcome in contemporary video art through the revival of narrative conditions anticipated by the historical avant-gardes of literature, theater and music: from the French OULIPO (Ouvoir de Littérature Potentielle) group to the Vienna Group. The interactive installation *Passage Sets/One Pulls Pivots at the Tip of the Tongue*

8 William Burroughs, *Nova Express*, Grove Press, New York, 1964.

9 See Walter Grond, *Der Erzähler und der Cyberspace*, Haymon, Innsbruck, 1999.

Bill Seaman
Passage Sets/One Pulls
Pivots at the Tip of the Tongue
1994–1995
interactive installation
mixed media
© Bill Seaman

Frank Fietzek
Tafel [Black Board]
1993
interactive installation
mixed media
dimensions variable
installation view: ZKM | Center
for Art and Media Karlsruhe
© Frank Fietzek

(1994-95) by Bill Seaman refers to the automatic writing techniques of the Surrealists, but is acted out by a computational random access algorithm. Texts and images are networked in this way of aleatoric combinations. In Frank Fietzek's interactive installation *Tafel* [Black Board] (1993), a moving monitor in front of a big blackboard reveals hidden words like a palimpsest.

The banishment of narration by abstraction led to the rejection of narrative as an obsolete historical phenomenon. This Modernist dictate of recognizing only the purely visual and banishing the verbal was overturned by postmodernism in favor of a more intense discursive orientation. Thus even the postmodern visual language of contemporary media art becomes increasingly discursive, the more it makes use of avant-garde narrative techniques. Unlike technically ponderous film art, the digital technology of today permits more complete control of cinematic resources and thus promotes a more stable development of the cinematic code. The advantage of today's video and digital technology over yesterday's film technology lies in the improved logistics of its technical repertoire. What was once virtually impossible and susceptible to problems as well is now much easier to realize and entirely reliable. Thanks to this technical stability, the possibilities for new narrative techniques based upon multiple large-screen projections, perhaps the most striking feature of contemporary video art, can now be explored extensively for the first time. And so the video and digital art of today has taken up the lance left behind by the cinematic avant-garde of the 1960s and developed one step further the universe of the cinematic code.

A short version of this essay first appeared under the title "Narrated Theory: Multiple Projection and Multiple Narration" in *New Screen Media. Cinema/Art/Narrative*, Andrea Zapp and Martin Rieser (eds), BFI Publishing, London, 2002.

10

Edwin Heathcote
Fairground to Dream Palace – Buildings for Film

Theo van Doesburg
L'Aubette
1926–1928
Strasbourg
© Architectural Press Archive

Cinema Centrale, Ariston
1923
San Remo

Films were first shown in existing buildings – sometimes rented halls, sometimes music halls or theaters which were temporarily converted, or sometimes, as news of the sensational new medium began to spread, in demountable fairground booths. When the cinema arrived as a new building type it took a form that can be seen as an amalgamation of elements from these existing buildings, combined with aspects of what could loosely be described as "the architecture of entertainment." By the architecture of entertainment I mean buildings erected for all kinds of picture shows which were the precursors of film, as well, of course, as theaters, which proved the most obvious precedent for the new building type.

Film was by no means the first answer to the desire to see moving images. It was preceded in the late eighteenth and nineteenth centuries by a plethora of techniques and machines capable of reproducing and projecting images to an excited audience. These techniques ranged from the intimacy of magic lanterns, which tended to be used in homes, to panoramas and dioramas, which were often housed in large, purpose-built structures. The camera obscura also became a popular form of entertainment in the nineteenth century, sometimes located in little pavilions, sometimes in domes above observatories or museums. Architecturally these buildings were often expressed as freestanding follies, an extension of the romantic garden architecture of the country house.

The diorama, a cylinder or globe which was painted and then animated using magic lanterns and lighting effects, demanded a larger, purpose-built structure and a few of these proved to be remarkable buildings,

some modeled on the Pantheon, some featuring incredible globe structures which surrounded the visitor entirely in an event which was far more inclusive and embracing than cinema itself. A fine example of one of these structures stood in London's Leicester Square in the middle of the nineteenth century and the section through the building illustrates a striking resemblance to Etienne-Louis Boullée's visionary design for a Cenotaph to Isaac Newton 50 years earlier.

Other deliberately bizarre and mystical buildings were constructed as a blend of fairground hyperbole and architectural billboard. The Egyptian Hall in Piccadilly, erected in 1812 to show "animated photographs," was one of the most spectacular examples. Its monumental self-advertisement, rich with stage-set historicism, became a paradigm for later cinema architects.

The origins of film lie in Thomas Edison's little box of tricks, the Kinetoscope, the first of which was produced in 1891. It was a mobile peep show, ideally suited to the coin-operated slot-machine culture of the itinerant fairgrounds. A single viewer peered into a viewing hole and, through a magnifying lens, saw a series of moving images. At the same time a number of other inventors were working on the idea of developing moving film into something which could be projected onto a screen, and the breakthrough was achieved by the Lumière brothers, who first screened their films to the public in Paris in 1895.

For the early years of their history, the Lumière brothers' *Cinematographe* and the machines of their competitors were used as sideshows. Film was a novelty and people went to see films because of their

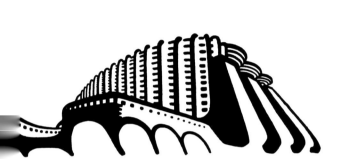

Erich Mendelson
Design for a film studio
1918
© Architectural Press Archive

Erich Mendelson
Universum
1928
Berlin
© Architectural Press Archive

novelty value – the idea of narrative and story-telling through moving pictures developed a little later. Precisely because film was seen in this ephemeral light, many critics predicted that it would be a short-lived fad; as soon as people had grown weary of the novelty of moving pictures, cinema would go the way of other trends, like the diorama before it.

Both Edison and the Lumière brothers, however, had extensive financial interests in film and its accompanying technology and it was in their interests to ensure that moving pictures proved to be more than a passing fashion. The development of narrative and of newsreels on film, and, the concept of movies could, rather cynically, be seen as a ruse to prolong the life of the technology, beyond the initial novelty. The critics' view of film as vulgar and artless was reinforced when moving pictures became a popular attraction at travelling fairgrounds. Short films were often accompanied by sideshows or vaudeville acts while showmen shouted for attention outside the travelling booths.

It was the fairgrounds, however, that were responsible for introducing cinema to the broader public, in the country and in provincial towns as well as in the great urban centers. Show people were instrumental in the evangelism of early motion pictures, sometimes even commissioning or producing films for which they would hold the exclusive rights. Although entrepreneurs had been quick to seize upon the potential of film by renting empty premises and halls and showing films, these were mostly slapdash affairs – films shown in unsuitable buildings and conditions by greedy businessmen trying to make a quick buck. The fairgrounds saw the genesis of purpose-built booths which, although demountable and often crowded, were in fact the first real cinemas.

In common with other fairground attractions, these booths, usually named bioscopes, were gaudy, fantastic affairs. Incredibly elaborate facades were erected to grab the attention of curious bystanders. These outrageously colorful, demountable fronts presaged the self-advertising facades of the movie theaters of the future, containing the origins of a billboard architecture that was to become the definitive approach to cinema building. It was precisely this commercial aesthetic which excluded cinemas from the avant-garde for much of the twentieth century.

Architects who worked on cinemas were seen as mercenaries hanging onto the coat-tails of the voraciously commercial film companies.

This did not mean, however, that cinema designers disregarded the avant-garde and modern trends in architecture – quite the opposite in fact. Jean Desmet's Imperial Bio which traveled around the Netherlands and Belgium during the first decade of the twentieth century, displayed a fantastically rich Art Nouveau facade. A style that was probably a little *passé* by the time the booth was doing its rounds, it nevertheless encapsulated the radical nature of the new medium in its flowing curves and the inherent movement of the sinuous lines of the construction. The effects of Art Nouveau can equally be seen on the extravagant frontage of the Limonaire Bioscope of around 1907, where the whiplash lines of the *fin de siècle* are filled in with pudgy cherubs and more overtly and recognizably theatrical decoration.

Cinema City
2000
entertainment complex
Astana
© Aryeh Siegel, Architect,
New York

It was soon realized that the device used to attract attention at the fairgrounds could equally effectively be applied to the converted halls and shop premises, which were beginning to dot every main street in the Western world in the first couple of decades of the twentieth century. A vividly colored and heavily decorated facade could be added to an otherwise unspectacular building to create the illusion of luxury and of entering a new world of fantasy. Bright lights, gaudy posters, deep canopies and huge billboards were all adopted as symbols of the presence of the cinema on the street. Although the elements were refined into a formal architectural vocabulary, these remained the defining essence of cinema architecture for most of the ensuing century.

Cinemas are not complicated buildings. Essentially, early examples consisted of an auditorium, a box office and a projection booth plus a few ancillary facilities. Compared to the complex and often labyrinthine backstage requirements of a theater building, which also demands a fly tower and complex stage machinery, the cinema is a relatively primitive affair. Early cinema buildings were generally more decorated versions of existing single-space buildings like billiard halls or social halls. A flashy facade featuring the cinema's name gave way to a barrel-vaulted or coffered-ceilinged auditorium with rich plaster decoration and paneled walls, perhaps with a small balcony. The extremely flammable nature of early film stock led to frequent fires and subsequent regulations generally required the separation of the projection booth and different escape routes for audience and projectionist. The facades of these early buildings were clad in brightly colored faience or terracotta, often with a large, arched opening, an arcade or a dome. The bigger cinemas which followed tended to be eclectic collections of Mannerist and Classical details in an often poorly defined cocktail.

The outbreak of the First World War in 1914 halted the development of the European cinema and saw America rise to sudden prominence. Before the war Germany had led the world in the development of a serious, modern cinema architecture. Oskar Kaufmann's 1911 Cines-Theater in Berlin's Nollendorf-platz was one of the first significant free-standing

purpose-built cinema structures. It was among the earliest attempts at a sober modern language of cinema architecture, presenting an austere picture to the world with three looming blank walls (perhaps an allusion to the simplicity and blankness of the screen). The subsequent development of Modernist cinema architecture is traced in another chapter and it was confined in its early years to northern Europe. America concentrated on the frivolous and the exotic. And how.

The luxury cinema or super-cinema arrived in the USA in the years directly before the First World War. Thomas W. Lamb, a Scottish-born architect, designed the Regent in Harlem, New York, in 1913 and, in the next few years, he built a group of influential cinemas around Times Square – the Strand, the Rialto and the Rivoli – all in conjunction with the legendary impresario Samuel "Roxy" Rothapfel. Together Lamb and Rothapfel defined the architecture of the luxury cinema and created the notion of the picture palace as a place of escape and sheer fantasy in which the building played as large a part in an evening out as the film itself.

These cinemas were impressive Classical buildings, some with touches of Venetian, Gothic and Baroque or of English country house. This eclectic travel through European history culminated in 1927 with the Roxy, Rothapfel's shrine to his own vision. Seating nearly 6,000, it was truly a dream palace, executed in a Mediterranean Renaissance jumble of Spanish and Portuguese motifs, its interior doused in gold. It looked like the Beverley Hills mansion of a newly rich movie star. Teetering on the verge of hideous, it was not tasteful but it was built to impress. The Roxy's architect, Walter Ahlschlager, managed to fit a capacious, fan-shaped auditorium onto an awkward, L-shaped site entered via a sensuously oval foyer. The cinema's demolition hardly more than thirty years later was to prove a poignant moment as it not only indicated the end of the dream and success of the movie palace in a mere generation, but also sparked off the notion of cinema as heritage among a few enthusiasts, ultimately leading to the conservation and listing of cinema buildings and their preservation as landmarks.

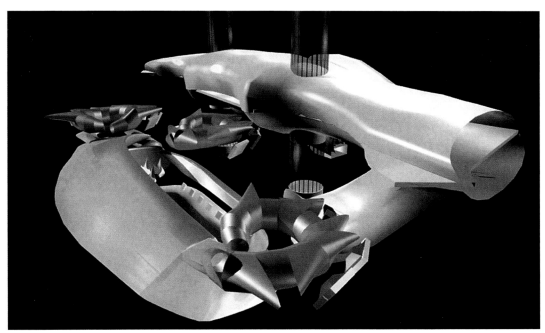

The super-cinemas outside the USA tended to be more restrained. The huge Plaza in Regent Street, London (1926), showed the refinement of its architect, Frank Verity, who was associated with the West End theaters. The same architect's earlier Pavilion in Shepherd's Bush (1923) was an attempt to give the cinema an imperial Roman grandeur by imitating the brick arches and monumental forms of Diocletian's Baths. To infuse a London cinema with some Hollywood glamour, Thomas W. Lamb was imported to design the Empire, Leicester Square in 1928. The result was a luxurious interior but a facade that seemed to have developed little from the earliest cinema buildings, with a kind of triumphal arch effect.

The Roxy, however, remained unsurpassable in its magnificence and luxury. As it could not be matched in terms of gilt and mouldings, architects had to look down other avenues to create new cinemas which would compete with the glamour of the Roxy. They looked everywhere, from China to Ancient Egypt, from Mediterranean villages to the Art Deco style which wafted the scent of French elegance and sophistication, of wealth and skyscrapers, and of the big city.

First published in Edwin Heathcote, *Cinema Builders*,
Wiley-Academy, Chichester, 2001, pp. 11–14.
Reproduced by permission of John Wiley & Sons Limited.

Frederick Kiesler
Film Guild Cinema

1929

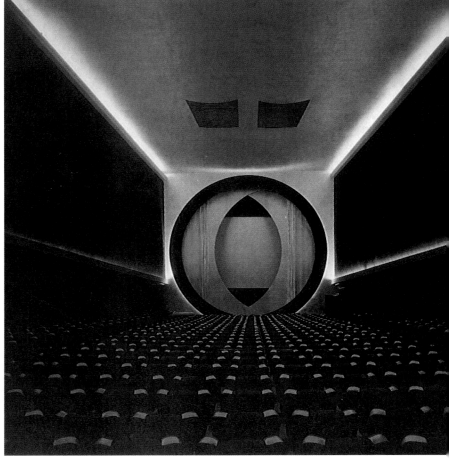

left
Film Guild Cinema,
audience with Screen-O-Scope
1929
Frederick Kiesler Archives,
New York
photo © Frederick Kiesler
Archives, New York

right
Film Guild Cinema,
audience with Screen-O-Scope
1929
gelatin silver print
c. 15 x 18 cm
Kiesler Archive, Vienna
© Austrian Frederick
and Lillian Kiesler Private
Foundation, Vienna
photo © Ruth Bernhard

Frederick Kiesler's Film Guild Cinema and Broadcasted Auditorium

Frederick Kiesler designed the Film Guild Cinema in 1927–1928 and realized this project on 52 West 8th Street, New York, in 1929. His work on the idea of a space animated with light, projections and sound began with his concept of the Optophon, a theater without actors, in Paris in 1925. For the Film Guild Cinema Kiesler designed the Screen-O-Scope, a changeable eye-shaped screen that eliminated the curtains and proscenium he considered typical features of theater. This "total space," which included the idea of 360-degree projections on the walls and ceiling, was intended to involve spectators in the cinema environment and take them closer to the on-screen action. The Film Guild Cinema can be regarded as one of the first attempts to define a specific space for cinema independent of the patterns of theater design.

The same idea of integrating physical space and ephemeral images can be found in the Broadcasted Auditorium designed by Kiesler around 1930, in which the wall decorations were replaced by images transmitted through the medium of television. Kiesler linked this later project to his Telemuseum of 1926, a never-realized concept that foresaw paintings from around the world being broadcast in a room equipped with television screens. In Broadcasted Auditorium, Kiesler deals with reduced distances between different parts of the world as well as with the usage of technology: topics now playing an important role in the discourse on art practice in which Kiesler's visions have finally turned into reality.

Valentina Sonzogni Frederick Kiesler Center, Vienna

Film Guild Cinema,
audience with Screen-O-Scope
1929
Frederick Kiesler Archives,
New York
photos © Frederick Kiesler
Archives, New York

Building a Cinema

[…] While in the theater each spectator must lose his individuality in order to be fused into complete unity with the actors. In the cinema which I have designed for the Film Arts Guild is this most important quality of the auditorium its power to suggest concentrated attention and at the same time to destroy the sensation of confinement that may occur easily when the spectator concentrates on the screen. The spectator must be able to loose himself in an imaginary, endless space even though the screen implies the opposite.

The film cannot exist by itself: the first radical step toward the creation of an ideal cinema is the abolition of the proscenium and all other stage platform resemblance to the theater which we find in motion picture houses. My invention, the Screen-O-Scope, takes the place of these theatrical elements and supplies a new method of opening the screen which eliminates curtains. The interior lines of the theater must focalize to the screen compelling unbroken attention on the spectator. The "visual-acoustics" must be provided for each member of the audience through the medium of a stadium floor. Black darkness must rule when the screen play is on. The orchestra must be completely obscured, no draperies or decorations must be employed, since these are too strongly reminiscent of the theater.

First published in Frederick Kiesler, "Building a Cinema Theater,"
in *New York Evening Post*, 2 February 1929.

The Broadcasted Decoration

It sounds fantastic and impractical, but so did the flying machine two decades ago.

Radio music is phonetic decoration. Your relation to it is just the same as it is to the other objects that contribute to the atmosphere and environment in your home.

Television will bring motion pictures and talkies, current events and scenes on other continents, right into your home, and turn it at will into a theater, a stadium; into Paris or Peking.

In 1926 I was asked by the "Société Anonyme" to conceive a model apartment of the future for an exposition of modern paintings to be held at the Brooklyn Museum. The purpose was to show the relationship between painting, sculpture and interior architecture. My sketch showed the two ways in which painting and sculpture will contribute to the decoration of the future interior:

1. With sensitized panels which will act as receiving surfaces for broadcasted pictures.

2. With built-in "shrines" for original masterpieces that will be concealed behind walls and revealed only occasionally. The use of pictures as a permanent wall decoration will be a discarded practice.

First published in Frederick Kiesler, *Contemporary Art Applied to the Store and its Display*, Brentano's Publishers, New York, 1930.

Scott McQuire
The Cathedral of Fictions

As Hollis Frampton clearly understood, cinema is fundamentally a matter of filtering light over time. Light-sensitized celluloid is a means of constructing relatively complex filters, but the basic principle is still the same: skeins of developed film subtract certain frequencies from the spectrum of white light so that varied perceptual forms are projected onto a screen.[1] Presences are conjured from absences, images appear because of what is withdrawn or withheld. This essential ambiguity, which inhabits all systems of projection, was greatly intensified with the advent of electrical illumination and the subsequent formation of the cinematic apparatus. It constitutes an irreducible frame of reference for thinking about the threshold conditions of modern perception, in particular the emergence of a mode of vision capable of constructing parallel worlds, dematerializing the solidity of geography and dislocating the accustomed continuity of space and place.

The ambivalence of cinematic presence – the contradictory phenomenological "thereness" of an image made from light alone – is registered on one level by the uncertain space that classical cinema came to occupy in the architecture of the modern city. In fact, a series of different scenes of watching cut across film's first decades before a relatively stable form of exhibition developed. The first was the penny-arcade, peep-show format of Edison's Kinetoscope. After a brief but resounding success, the solitary viewer of the Kinetoscope was dethroned and the collective audience viewing films projected onto a screen became the norm. As Stephen Heath notes, the screen already there at the Café de Paris and other public "premieres" around 1895 has been one of the most stable elements of cinema history. If its appearance marked a decisive rupture with the model of the individual viewing apparatus, its potential disappearance due to the development of "frameless" VR systems looms as being equally momentous.

Early films were often shown as part of traveling vaudeville shows in which the audience joined in sing-alongs and other forms of collective interaction. In less than a decade, however, most films abandoned this more theatrical mode of spectatorship in favor of narrative techniques capable of absorbing the individual spectator within the text's movement according to the novelistic model of narrative continuity, shot matching and suture.[2] While the audience remained collective in form, the viewing experience was effectively "re-privatized": the primary axis of communication was between each individual viewer and the screen, an audience relationship echoing the mutual anonymity enjoyed by individuals in the crowds of any big city. Within a few years, as the new films began to attract middle-class patrons, cinemas capable of holding thousands began to appear in every major city staking its claim to being modern.

This journey to the "coming of age" in the great picture palaces of the 1910s and 1920s – from amusement arcade over itinerant travelling exhibit and shop-front Nickelodeon – symbolizes cinema's growing status not only in economic terms, but as a cultural force crucial to the political settlement of modern urban-industrial societies. The darkness we now take to be protective of cinematic fantasy was initially perceived as a threat to cinematic popularity. The dingy Nickelodeon had a "bad" (read lower-class) reputation, which the opulent new picture palaces were explicitly designed to exorcise. In the United States and elsewhere, there was also a deliberate policy of "de-ethnicization" of the cinema audience, with nationally slanted programs and sing-alongs of "foreign" songs being discouraged by professional organizations of producers and exhibitors.[3] Cinema assumed a new level of respectability that found architectural expression in lavishly decorated structures.

Writing in 1926, Siegfried Kracauer described the "optical fairylands" which dominated film exhibition in the classical era:

"Elegant surface splendor is the hallmark of these mass theatres. Like hotel lobbies, they are shrines to the cultivation of pleasure, their glamour aiming at edification. [...] This total artwork of effects assaults every one of the senses using every possible means. Spotlights shower their beams into the auditorium, sprinkling across festive drapes or rippling through colorful growth-like glass fixtures. The orchestra asserts itself as an independent power, its acoustic expression buttressed by the responsory of the lighting. Every emotion is accorded its own acoustic expression, its color value in the spectrum. [...] Alongside the legitimate reviews, such shows are the leading attraction in Berlin today. They raise distraction to the level of culture; they are aimed at the masses."[4]

As well as granting aesthetic legitimacy, the architecture of the picture palace was instrumental to the new cinematic imaginary. Cinema became the singular place in which an avowedly rational and secular society allowed itself to encounter the scene of the other, in the guise of the foreign, the fantastic, the erotic, or even that most duplicitous double "life itself." The ritual of entry, the descent of darkness, the comfortable immobilization of the spectator's body, the cessation of motor activity, the vastly magnified and intensely luminous images, the soothing or dramatic music, all contributed to the cinematic effect.

The enigmatic "impression of reality" created by film demanded a sense of separation from the outside world. Yet the world was not simply absent. Like the camera obscura, cinema offered an inverted

1   See Hollis Frampton, "A Lecture," 1968, reprinted in *Circles of Confusion: Film, Photography, Video, Texts 1968–1980*, Visual Studies Workshop Press, Rochester, New York, 1983, pp.193–199.

2   Tom Gunning argues that "the period 1907–1913 represents the true narrativization of the cinema, culminating in the appearance of feature films." "The Cinema of Attractions," in *Wide Angle*, vol.8, nos. 3/4, 1986, p. 68.

3   See Miriam Hansen, "Early Cinema: Whose Public Sphere?" in Thomas Elsaesser (ed.), *Early Cinema: Space, Frame, Narrative*, BFI Publishing, London, 1990, pp. 228–243.

4   Siegfried Kracauer, "Cult of Distraction: On Berlin's Picture Palaces," 1926, reprinted in *New German Critique*, no. 40, Winter 1987, pp. 91–92. Kracauer's reference to the "total artwork" situates cinematic spectacle in relation to grand opera. Like Adorno, Kracauer was critical of the way cinema came to "gentrify" popular entertainment.

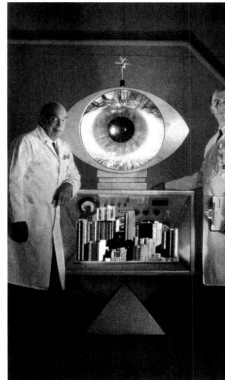

interior, a sealed chamber in which the external world became an image, an object for contemplation. Unlike the camera obscura, the cinematic image was endlessly elastic, its field of vision infinitely mobile, creating the novelty of an enclosed space seemingly able to expand its own horizons from within. For the first time, the spectator's perceptual limits were no longer determined by architectural space, but by fluctuations in filmic space. This strange effect, in which the inside begins to include the outside – even all possible out-sides – marks a crucial moment in the emergence of a distinctively modern sense of place. Immersed in cinema's ludic shell, place begins to abandon its former dependence on solidity and materiality. As cinematic prophets such as Dziga Vertov quickly realized, the world itself was suddenly available for wholesale reconstruction. The "New Vision" extolled by fellow Constructivist Moholy-Nagy was also a new consciousness with a radically different ontology and epistemology.

It is perhaps not surprising that cultural responses to the celluloid fissure opened beneath the ground of Being (traditionally defined in terms of substance, permanence and presence) often assumed spiritual, if not to say apocalyptic, overtones. As Paul Virilio has pointed out, the grandeur and opulence of the classical picture palaces resembled nothing so much as the great Gothic cathedrals of past ages:

> "Nineteenth-century Europeans were forever on the move to see new commodities; now, with the coming of cinema, pure visions were for sale. The cinema became a major site for a trade in de-materialization, a new industrial market which no longer produced matter but light, as the luminosity of those vast stained glass windows of old was suddenly concentrated into the screen."[5]

Despite evident affinities between the close-up and the icon, the comparison between cinema and religion should not be overdrawn. But a key lesson might be drawn from the architectural proximity of picture palace and cathedral. For the worshipper, the bricks and mortar of the church perform a function unrelated to any particular location or physical attribute. What is important is that the building forms a space of seclusion and solitude which mediates the presence of God. A similar "placelessness" surrounds the classical cinematic imaginary. "Going to the cinema" was less a description of a particular destination than the evocation of a complex of rituals and emotions that frequently assumed quasi-religious dimensions. What else has cinema been for over a century but a vast cathedral of fictions, a hole in the real in which time, space and self can be held in suspension, at least for the performance of a film or the span of its prayer?

The great movie shrines are now virtually extinct, replaced by the multiplex cinemas of suburban shopping malls catering for the niche audiences of the post-video/cable-television era. But even if the neo-Gothic architecture is gone, contemporary cinema maintains some continuities with the classical period. Personal voyeurism in a public forum remains the dominant mode of film consumption. And the interior design of contemporary cinemas resembles nothing so much as wide-bodied airplanes, the ubiquitous vehicles of an age in which the effects of displacement and "placelessness" have assumed global proportions.

Scott McQuire is currently Senior Lecturer in the Media and Communication program at the University of Melbourne.

5 Paul Virilio, *War and Cinema: The Logistics of Perception*, trans. P. Camiller, Verso, London and New York, 1989, p. 32.

Gloria Sutton
Stan VanDerBeek's Movie-Drome: Networking the Subject

"Culture is moving into what I call a visual velocity.
Sometimes I wake up and think to myself that it looks
like it's going to be a 60 mph day." [1]

The subject is a curious-looking thirty-one-foot-high metal dome structure situated in the wooded backyard of a rural outpost of experimental artists living in Rockland County, approximately thirty-five miles north of Manhattan, during the early 1960s. [2] Lacking any formal entrance, visitors entered the dome from underneath through a trap door in the center of the floor, which unfurled into a wooden ladder when opened. Once inside, everyone spread out over the rough flooring lying side-by-side. There were no assigned seats, only vague directions from the artist to lie with your head facing upward and your feet pointing towards the center of the space. With equal parts nervous tension and the anxiety of not knowing exactly what to expect, the experience would begin in a series of fits and starts. The noisy, ungainly motors of over a dozen projectors for 16mm film and slides would turn over, clicking and humming at various intervals. Suddenly, undulating beams of light and discordant voices mixed with synthetic noise electrifying the air, illuminating the darkened space and immersing the viewers in a continuous audiovisual flow, a visual velocity.

On-the-spot illustrations (projected while they were being drawn) and roving lights were superimposed with collages of stock newsreel footage and found films. The space pulsated with the multi-directional movement of the projectors (they were affixed to a turntable or wheeled carts) and the distortion of mixed sounds and voices emanating from unspecified sources. Political speeches, newscasts, promotional announcements, and pre-recorded music tracks collided with one another, testing the quadraphonic sound system and reverberating off the curved aluminum panels that served as both the dome's exterior and interior. The heat generated by the electronic components combined with the body temperature of the thirty or so participants to intensify the dense, humid atmosphere.

The projected representational images were comprised of portraits of political figures, news clippings of current events, photographs of media personalities, and promotional print ads relaying contemporary slogans and fashions. These images were no different from those that permeated both the popular media and the artwork being exhibited during this period, and on their own would have appeared quite banal, perfunctory even, for an artist working in New York during the 1960s. However, it was the illogical juxtaposition of the images, the speed and frequency of the edits and the layering of sources that estranged expectations. A second level of defamiliarization occurred focusing attention on the work's own techniques and thereby distinguishing this experience from other contemporaneous cinematic or multimedia art presentations. This experience exceeded the function of a standard theater or exhibition setting even in the eyes of an experimental-art audience accustomed to the staccato pacing of "underground films," to the dramatized spontaneity of Performance Art and Happenings, and to the spectacular effects of commercial media technology that was beginning to widen commercial film screens, multiply the reach of television and accelerate the rate of telecommunication. Within this intimately scaled dome, the phenomenological experience of multiple image-projection itself became the subject of the work.

Satirical imagery abounded in the projected animated collages: Nikita Khrushchev's head was held in a vice wrench, the Statue of Liberty and the Eiffel Tower morphed into crudely rendered nuclear missiles, floating television sets were cracked in half, and pixilated computer graphics slid in and out of sequence with no discernible pattern. The first realization was that your view was not confined to the rectangular frame of a painting or the elongated window of a cinematic screen, nor to the clear boundary produced by the raised stage of a theater. Instead,

1 Stan VanDerBeek in
*VanDerBeekiania: Stan
VanDerBeek's Vision*, 1968,
documentary film, 27 min.,
© Creative Arts Television,
1997.

2 The *Movie-Drome* was situated in the back of VanDerBeek's home on Gate Hill Road in Stony Point, New York, which was part of an artist's colony called "The Land" where VanDerBeek's former Black Mountain Professor and frequent collaborator John Cage also lived.

Stan VanDerBeek
Movie Mural No. 2.
orig. printed in Nan R. Piene,
"Light Art," in *Art in America*,
May/June 1967 (Brant Publications, Inc., New York)
photographer unknown
photo © Art in America

the spherical dome formed an edgeless surface for projection while an infinite stream of light and sound bounced off the participants and enveloped the space in a complete multimedia environment. The standards for viewing, conditioned by the demand for rapt attention in theaters and solitary contemplation in art museums, quickly dissolved along with any formal expectations based on narrative structure. The images floated in a three-dimensional visual field, coalescing neither spatially nor temporally, and so dispersed rather than unified a specific type of viewing subject. The inter-dispersal of unique and found images, the utilization of all surfaces — material and bodily, the unique combination of pre-determined audiovisual and aleatory effects, and the uninhibited mobility of the participants fused into a dynamic immersive experience dubbed the *Movie-Drome*.

The aluminum dome's unruly acoustics made it impossible to correlate a particular sound with a singular image. Within the fixed economy of one's attention, the viewer had to actively decide what would register as information and what would dissipate into noise. The *Movie-Drome* functioned as a demonstration model for a type of multimedia interface that could engage intimate groups. In an idealized form, multiple *Dromes* would be linked to one another through a global satellite network programmed to simultaneously transmit thousands of streaming images and sounds to various *Movie-Dromes* located around the world generating a real-time, shared multimedia experience.

Movie-Drome was the consummate work-in-progress for the American multimedia artist Stan VanDerBeek (1927–1984). Already firmly established in the New York experimental film scene when he began orchestrating mixed-media projects specifically for the *Movie-Drome* in 1957, he would finally construct a prototype in 1965. The Bronx-born artist started producing films using various collage and animation techniques in 1954, when he returned to New York City after studying fine arts at Black Mountain College in North Carolina.3 Encounters with diverse influences such as John Cage and R. Buckminster Fuller, who taught at the school during VanDerBeek's two-year period of study, instilled the utopist drive and interest in social consciousness consistent with most of VanDerBeek's media projects. Rather than developing out of an infatuation with emerging consumer electronic and portable video technology, it was his own personal frustrations working with theater, painting and sculpture that specifically provoked VanDerBeek's focus on multimedia art. In a 1967 interview with Willard Van Dyke, then the Director of the Department of Film at the Museum of Modern Art, VanDerBeek rationalized

3 All biographical material comes from the IotaCenter Research Library and Media Center (Culver City, CA) archives on VanDerBeek compiled by Dr. William Moritz.

the extension of his practice to multimedia and computer animation as a means of contending with what he regarded as the "new sense of dynamics of art: motion and space."4 Recognizing what he identified as "the limitations of the four walls of theater" and the "visual boundaries" of painting and sculpture, VanDerBeek sought a medium that would move beyond optical representation and deal with motion and time "while accommodating all of th[o]se other ideas of painting, sculpture and theater."

Movie-Drome as Medium

The result was VanDerBeek's conceptual framework for the Movie-Drome, a prototype networked-theater that operated as a medium through which "cultural inter-communication," his means for a type of "transnational, non-verbal communication" could be activated. While he also held associate professorships in film and animation at Columbia in 1963-1965, it was mainly through grants and residencies that he was able to financially support his practice. During the early 1960s, VanDerBeek was awarded residencies at institutions ranging from NASA and Bell Laboratories to Cal Arts and the Ford Foundation.5 He financed the construction of the Movie-Drome through a Rockefeller grant awarded in 1963 for "studies in non-verbal communication." However, Movie-Drome first began to materialize in built form in the fall of 1965, after VanDerBeek attended "Vision '65," a three-day conference sponsored by the International Center for the Typographic Arts. He had been invited to the conference to present his multimedia projects, which integrated computer animation and multiple-screen projections. Fueled by a reinvigorated sense of direction, he returned home and immediately finished construction on a prototype for the Movie-Drome.6

The keynote conference speakers were Buckminster Fuller and Marshall McLuhan, whose cross-disciplinary recognition and popular appeal caused over five hundred designers, educators, scientists, politicians and artists to converge on the campus of Southern Illinois University at Carbondale. In what was billed as a "teach-in," various participants including VanDerBeek, Fuller and McLuhan, advocated cultural change along two specific trajectories: the development of a common "universal non-verbal language of signs," and the need to use computers in a capacity more creative than their then-current application as large-scale calculators.7 Moreover, the studied presentations delivered in characteristically dramatic form by both Fuller and McLuhan enthusiastically detailed how media art offered a categorical challenge to the dual forces of anxiety and utopia preoccupying many artists in the period 1960–1965.

In his presentation at "Vision '65" and in subsequent publications, VanDerBeek labeled the Movie-Drome a proposal, an attempt to rectify the lack of cultural intercommunication, which in his terms reflected the "global crisis" of the period.8 His sentiments echo those espoused by Fuller during his keynote address at the 1965 conference. Throughout his lengthy lecture, Fuller pointed out numerous examples of how the world's "technological do-more-with-less revolution has been a by-product of the scientific preoccupation with weapons." He concluded by

proffering the ominous assertion that "man on earth is now clearly faced with the choice of Utopia or Oblivion."9 VanDerBeek's conception of the socio-political climate of 1965 as a time of "global crisis," a year caught in a vacuum of concurrent periodizations (postwar, cold war, nuclear age, Vietnam era, information age, and so forth), was not the only Fuller-influenced aspect of VanDerBeek's project. Fuller's patented geodesic dome structure was an obvious reference point for the physical construction of the Movie-Drome.

However, unlike Fuller's complex and mathematically precise structures, the Movie-Drome was fabricated in a more ad-hoc manner by re-purposing prefabricated industrial materials mail-ordered and delivered to his house in upstate New York. The dome's spherical shape and structural stability relied on conjoining individually cut aluminum wedges with bolts and weather sealant, which naturally formed a 180-degree dome. The Movie-Drome was a fairly crude structure modeled on a grain silo and fabricated without the use of heavy machinery. One entered the space, which hovered about six feet off the ground on wooden pylons encased in cement, through a trap door in its center. With help from four or five others, VanDerBeek managed to piece together the individual elements and pour the concrete foundation using basic tools and hardware.10 Referred to in various news reports as VanDerBeek's studio, the Movie-Drome was situated against a sloping hillside in VanDerBeek's backyard, just a few paces away from his family home, which was also re-purposed from an airplane hangar. The only structural element supporting the weight of the aluminum panels was a single, mast-like pole mounted in the center against which the top ends of the wedges were affixed. The interior side of the aluminum panels formed a seamless surface that functioned as an expansive screen or a monitor to connect to other Dromes.

In fact, VanDerBeek envisioned the Movie-Drome operating as a quasi-network based mode of communication. He invited groups of viewers to enter the Movie-Drome and would bombard them with an endless stream of sounds and images as they lay on the floor for hours at a time. The model he built in Stony Point was a prototype for a multitude of structures he imagined could be erected all-over the world and connected via satellite. To explain his vision, he conjectured that "in the future, a similar Movie-Drome could receive its images by satellite from a worldwide library source, store them and program a feedback presentation to the local community. Dialogues with other centers would be likely, and instant reference material via transmission television and telephone could be called for and received at 186,000 miles-per-second from anywhere in the world."11 VanDerBeek's conceptual framework for viewing and experiencing information over a network and through multi-screen projections demanded a spatially and temporally unique audience not yet addressed by conventional cinematic forms. In his talk at "Vision '65," McLuhan would identify and elaborate upon these distinctions.

McLuhan used the conference platform to rehearse his conception of the "global village" and reiterate the effects he associated with new media tech-

4 Adrienne Mancia and Willard Van Dyke, "Four Artists as Film-Makers," in Art in America, no. 55, January 1967, p. 70.

5 Janet Vrchota, "Stan VanDerBeek: Technology's Migrant Fruit Picker," in Print, vol. 27, no. 2, March/April 1973, p. 49.

6 In an interview Johanna VanDerBeek maintains that Stan VanDerBeek, when writing his ideas for the Movie-Drome, was "beside himself with excitement from the success of the 'Vision '65' conference. [...] Buckminster Fuller was there and [that] Stan adored his domes." (Marilyn Mancino and Anne Morra, Interview with Johanna VanDerBeek, in Il Grande Occhio Della Notte: Cinema d'Avanguardia Americano 1920–1990, exhib. cat., Museo Nazionale Del Cinema, Turin, 1999, p. 110.

7 Eugene Hosansky, "Vision '65," in Industrial Design, 1966, p. 79.

8 Stan VanDerBeek, " 'Culture: Intercom' and Expanded Cinema, a Proposal," in The New American Cinema, Gregory Battock (ed.), Dutton, New York, 1967, p. 173.

9 Buckminster Fuller, Summary Lecture, in Perspecta, no. 11, 1967.

10 There is very little documentation detailing the structural qualities or actual construction of the project. The only known document is an 8mm home movie made by VanDerBeek called Home and Dome which was donated to the Museum of Modern Art Department of Film by VanDerBeek's widow, Johanna in 2000.

11 Vrchota, op. cit.

nology on "human civilization." Within his provocative talk entitled "The Invisible Environment: The Future of an Erosion," McLuhan pushed for the recognition of the reader as an active agent who must contend with what he labeled the current "invisible environment" of propaganda. He offered the example of the standard daily newspaper as a metaphor demonstrating the process by which "the reader becomes the publisher within the current age of decentralization."[12] He continued with the following loose analogy: "The reader of the news […] enters the new world as a maker. There is no 'meaning' in the news except what we make – there is no connection between any of the items except the instant dimension of electric circuitry. News items are like the parts of a symbolist structure. The reader is a co-creator." To further accentuate his claim, McLuhan pointed to VanDerBeek's recent presentation at the conference and noted, "The newspaper is also very much like the delightful films of Stan VanDerBeek: the world of multi-screen projections is the world of the newspaper where umpteen news stories come at you without any connection and without connected themes." McLuhan's observations rearticulate the fact that VanDerBeek was not operating under the guise of complete objectivity, and instead employed multiple screens as a way to shift the agency of meaning to the viewer: Within VanDerBeek's taxonomy of experience, meaning is determined within the plurality of audience reception rather than a singular apparatus of projection.

After returning from "Vision '65," VanDerBeek excitedly pounded out his ideas in a manifesto. Published in a multitude of exhibition catalogs and anthologies as "Culture: Intercom and Expanded Cinema, a Proposal," he itemized what he considered the current dire cultural and political context "that art production must address." In doing so, he defined the conditions for the *Movie-Drome* as a network for non-verbal communication. Within his manic, techno-utopist writing, he augmented McLuhan's reading of his multimedia projections: "the *Movie-Drome* flow could be compared to the 'collage' form of the newspaper, or the three ring circus (both of which suffice the audience with an abundance of facts and data). The audience takes what it can or wants from the presentation and makes it own conclusions – each member of the audience will build his own references form the image-flow, in the best sense of the word the visual material is to be presented and each individual makes his own conclusions or realizations."[13]

VanDerBeek's conception of the *Movie-Drome* as a real-time, programmable communication network mimics the characteristics of an online archive or proto-Internet and stretches the conception or role of theater or cinema. This is reinforced by the fact that in various accounts of the project he referred to the image "content" projected onto the interior of the *Movie-Drome* interchangeably as "cultural intercomming, image libraries, newsreels, and feedback." Moreover, the idea that the *Movie-Drome* was a medium to transmit VanDerBeek's non-verbal communiqués fits McLuhan's definition of media as a type of translation process. In his talk at "Vision '65," McLuhan emphatically asserted that all media are active metaphors in their power to translate experience into new forms. VanDerBeek's analogy of the *Movie-Drome* as a proto-personal computer of sorts and, as the "software," his "culture: intercom, ethos-cinema, newsreel of dreams, feedback, image libraries" seems to be more accurate than the newspaper comparison McLuhan made at the conference.

Instead of using the delirious visual effects of film and media as tools for hallucinatory escapism or subversive action, VanDerBeek's writings convey a mixed reaction to what he perceived as the alienating impulse of technology. VanDerBeek's concern registered the fact that media, while social, is simultaneously material, a condition that McLuhan largely ignored during this period. Under the material conditions that define and often determine artistic production, media art cannot be seen as separate or distinguishable from the cultural mechanisms under which art production is negotiated. *Movie-Drome* can be read as an attempt to rectify or address the alienating effect of media technology through what VanDerBeek labeled the "transmission of emotion." His sincere, albeit naïve, idea was to eradicate the formal distinctions between art and life by immersing subjects visually and aurally in waves of light and sound in an effort to tap into people's emotions. By creating an intense multi-sensory experience via the *Movie-Drome*, he wanted the audience to connect with one another as part of a larger global constituency rather than remain isolated within the privileged sphere of fine art. Intended to connect an audience not by Cartesian models of location but by a telecommunications satellite network, *Movie-Drome* would have functioned as a network-based mode of communication and formed a unique type of collective audience.

Stan VanDerBeek
Movie-Drome
1965
exterior view
Stony Point, New York
orig. printed in Nan R. Piene,
"Light Art," in *Art in America*,
May/June 1967 (Brant Publications, Inc., New York)
photographer unknown
photo © Art in America

12 Marshall McLuhan, "The Invisible Environment: The Future of an Erosion," in *Perspecta*, no. 11, 1967, p. 166.

13 VanDerBeek, op. cit.

This notion of a collective audience is a reference to the type of small crowds and gatherings that developed through live multimedia events at which the audience experienced a common phenomenological, not just purely visual, experience. These groups can be situated between the singular viewing subject understood as the bourgeois individual subject addressed by the nineteenth-century cinema or museum, and the dispersed audience associated with broadcast television, to which Frederic Jameson attributed "the type of subjectivity brought on by the age of corporate capitalism."14 The recognition of a collective subject serves to disrupt, or at least stall, the rapid, linear progression from a singular, modernist viewing subject that was the paradigmatic viewing convention for the period leading up *to* 1965, and the mass audience of broadcast television, which becomes the definitive model *after* that year. The networked component of the *Movie-Drome* distinguishes it from other models of multimedia Performance events or cinematic experiences. A networked project means participants are linked, not only to one another within a real-time experience, but also in an idealized form, to a broader community connected via shared interests and access to a broader network (both social and technical). Within a network, it becomes impossible to distinguish or isolate the conditions that determine individual subjectivity from that of the group experience. Rather than operating as a discrete individual in a mode of meditation, the subject is more a node within an interactive social network sustained by the technologies of production and reception.

Immersive Subjectivity

VanDerBeek's more targeted aim, however, was to use this image-reception apparatus as a means of generating a multi-sensory experience distinct from any conventional theater. Within the domed sphere of the *Movie-Drome*, the arc of address was a complete 360-degree circle. Erasing the spatial boundaries of the screen and eliminating the conventions of narrative or authorship, VanDerBeek sought a non-mediated mode of communication. Because the audience was asked to lie down at the outer edges of the circular space, the screens above and around the participants took up almost the complete field of vision. The source of the sounds and lights was not centralized, and did not privilege a certain reading of the body or organization of the space: there was no front or back. By exposing participants to an overwhelming informational experience and submersing the body in waves of light, sound and image, the *Movie-Drome* produced an "immersive subject" through two different modes of address. The first can be read in terms of a phenomenological multi-sensorial experience. The subject was obviously immersed physically in the flow of light and images, but also in Quadraphonic sound. This enclosing of the participants in a small, intimate space made them deeply aware of being in a group. The second form of immersion was more psychological. VanDerBeek's ultimate aim was to employ the available forms of media, film, video, sounds and lights in such a way that

they vanish, are no longer noticed by the viewer. Thus, the immersive subject, like that of Heidegger's "world-picture" or Benjamin's "auratic scene," absorbs, as opposed to merely breathes in, the scene.15

This notion of immersive subjectivity differed greatly from the commercial widescreen cinema or planetarium vernacular that was developing simultaneously in the U.S.A. and Europe. From the fairground to art and science museums, various institutions had been relying on the novelty of large-format cinema to attract audiences. The technical effects generated by specialized viewing spaces such as the Imax theater, CinemaScope or planetariums are aimed at making viewers forget that they are sitting next to hundreds of other people in a multiplex structure. The goal is to create an environment directing viewer attention to the action occurring within the diegetic space of the screen, not to the built space or overall theater environment. The attenuating work for directors and producers who create large-format films is therefore always focused on perfecting and enhancing the imagery or quality of filmic representation. The ubiquitous desire to make the film seem "more real than real" relegates these practices to Baudrillard's "procession of simulacra." Rather than adjusting formal or spatial elements in a futile attempt to close the distance between spectator and viewer, VanDerBeek's *Movie-Drome* is a decided shift away from the concerns and conventions of image depiction. Instead, VanDerBeek worked to change the space of viewing in order to alter the conditions or habits of perception.

VanDerBeek eschewed singular, signature authorship – the taxonomy of fine art production during this period – and instead shifted the emphasis from reading each individual film as a fixed or self-contained object towards the interplay between films as the source of meaning. John Cage explained this element of VanDerBeek's practice as a "renunciation of intention" during a 1967 symposium on experimental art, and expressed the following sentiment: "I think that the closest to the renunciation of intention would, in my experience, be through the films of Stan VanDerBeek, a renunciation of intention which is effected through the multiplication of images. In this multiplicity, intention becomes lost and becomes silent, as it were, in the eyes of the observer. Since he could not be looking at all five or six images at once but only one particular one, the observer would have a certain freedom."16 Within the spectacle of the *Movie-Drome*, plurality of meaning is not due to differing interpretations of the same filmic images, but rather a more complex process akin to what Roland Barthes, in his pivotal 1971 essay "From Work to Text," referred to as the "stereographic plurality" of signifiers.

VanDerBeek's desire was to activate the audience in a type of collective perceptual experience not reliant on visual images alone. Moreover, rather than thinking of his role in terms of a curatorial process of selecting images, he repeatedly articulated his desire to construct a mode of communication that could be used by groups of people simultaneously, regardless of geographic locale. Basically, the *Movie-Drome* functioned as an interface to interact with a live audience.

14 Frederic Jameson, "Postmodernism and Consumer Society," in *Movies and Mass Culture*, John Belton (ed.), Rutgers University Press, New Brunswick, 1996, p. 195.

15 Samuel Weber, "Mass Mediauras, Or: Art and Media in the Work of Walter Benjamin," in *Mass Mediauras: Form, Technics, Media*, Alan Cholodenko (ed.), Stanford University Press, Stanford, Calif., 1996, pp. 90–92.

16 Hector Currie and Michael Porte (eds), "Cinema Now: Stan Brakhage, John Cage, Jonas Mekas, Stan VanDerBeek," in *Perspectives on American Underground Film*, University of Cincinnati, Cincinnati, 1968, p. 9.

Scene inside the hemispherical dome used by VanDerBeek to create prototypes for his multimedia exhibits.
orig. printed in Stewart Kranz, *Science & Technology in the Arts. A tour through the realm of science + art*, Van Nostrand Reinhold Company, New York, 1974, p. 238
photo © Art in America

VanDerBeek's practice was distinguishable from contemporaneous multimedia art forms and experimental film in two further aspects: he had learned computer programming for graphic design purposes, and he recognized computers as responsive systems representing an alternative trajectory for art production by allowing for more direct feedback or interaction. In his own words, he "continu[ed] to explor[e] what possibilities could produce the most imaginative relationship between computer and artist, and that could also result in artistic expression reaching masses of people."[17] The result was that VanDerBeek's conception of cinema becomes conflated, or begins to mimic computer operations. And for VanDerBeek, the computer (its hardware and software) offered the possibility of programming limitless combinations of images and fueled his ability to develop a continuously changing flow of images for the *Movie-Drome*.

Although VanDerBeek did have extensive experience in broadcast television, his interest in programming a constant stream of images is never referred to in terms of television. While the *Movie-Drome* did not overtly function as "a disciplinary instrument for the production of normalized subjects," which Jonathan Crary claims is inherent to television, *Movie-Drome* was still susceptible to the same dual effect.[18] That is to say, while the *Movie-Drome* may have opened up the possibility of de-territorialization, it clearly points to a heightened awareness of privatization and centralized control. The satellite and fiber-optic cable telecommunications system by which VanDerBeek intended to store and transmit his films for the purpose of extending cultural understanding was the same system simultaneously being developed by the US military and government to safeguard its ability to maintain control under a nuclear attack. In 1969, after years of development, the ARPANET (now DARPA, the Defense Research Projects Agency), was implemented as the first large-scale decentralized network system that allowed users to transfer files, communicate and store information through a network.[19] While VanDerBeek may not have envisioned *Movie-Drome* functioning as a means of remote social control, it pointed to the very possibility.

17 Vrchota, op. cit., p. 53.

18 Jonathan Crary, "Eclipse of the Spectacle," in *Art After Modernism: Rethinking Representation*, Brian Wallis and Marcia Tucker (eds), New Museum of Contemporary Art, New York, and D.R. Godine, Boston, 1984, p. 289.

19 John S. Quarterman, "The Global Matrix of Minds," in *Global Networks: Computers and International Communication*, Linda M. Harasim (ed.), The MIT Press, Cambridge, MA, 1994, p. 36.

Stan VanDerBeek at work in "the world's most expensive optical bench," the mixing/switching control room at WGBH-TV, Boston, Massachusetts.
photo © Gene Youngblood

Recognizing *Movie-Drome*

Towards the conclusion of his talk at "Vision '65," McLuhan outlined a major theme in his work: the process by which newer environments make older forms more visible. Recognition of *Movie-Drome* as an apparatus for producing and receiving images is only now facilitated by the advent of more contemporary forms of media art. I am referring to the recent institutionalization of new media and Net art, which have complicated the tropes of medium specificity and no longer deal with the traditional cultural domain of representation. Perhaps the most productive aspect of the recent institutionalization of these practices is that their inherently ephemeral qualities may destabilize the current system of classification, or at least challenge the dominance of the typology of medium. The complications that arise from commissioning, exhibiting or collecting media formats and software subject to relatively rapid obsolescence have forced institutions to define art work independently from medium. This has permitted the recognition of artistic practices operating within an interactive network, engaging a dispersed yet collective audience, and possibly reliant on a decentralized mode of authorship. Through telecommunication, networked-based art may shift the analysis from product to process. Such art demands attention not just in technologically determinist terms but also as a discourse object, as Erkki Huhtamo has asserted:

"The artistic approach to technology has now less to do with concrete artifacts, and the ideologically

'pure,' 'scientific,' theories informing them, than with the discursive formations enveloping them. This concerns not only the institutionally established and legitimized applications of technology, or cultural forms (as described by Raymond Williams), but unrealized projects and 'discursive inventions' as well."[20]

The significance *Movie-Drome* holds for reading or redefining present day network-based media art projects may seem like an obvious point. However, there has been little, if any, sustained critical attention given to this project. As a filmmaker, Stan VanDerBeek's work is well-documented within the discourse of American experimental film history. However, as a visual artist, his work hovers on the outermost margins appearing occasionally within the historiography of Happenings. Moreover, there is very little published material specifically on the *Movie-Drome* project, even though it is representative of the multimedia art spectacles that developed during the mid-1960s and actively engaged audiences as participants in complex sound-image relationships. *Movie-Drome* embodies the structural parameters for these types of multimedia performance projects, which were derived from the more established praxis of cinema, photography, theater, dance and painting. With its employment of portable film projectors, mixed-media, surround-sound systems and informal, spontaneous staging, *Movie-Drome* can be read as paradigmatic of early multimedia experiments such as the more widely acclaimed multimedia art perfor-

20 Erkki Huhtamo, "Archaeology of Media," in *Immersed in Technology: art and virtual environments*, Mary Anne Moser (ed.), The MIT Press, Cambridge, MA, 1999, p. 239.

Scene inside the hemispherical
dome used by VanDerBeek to
create prototypes for his multimedia exhibits.
orig. printed in Stewart Kranz,
*Science & Technology in the
Arts. A tour through the realm
of science + art*, Van Nostrand
Reinhold Company, New York,
1974, p.238
photo © Art in America

mances associated with Fluxus, Judson Church, and
Experiments in Art and Technology (E.A.T.) that have
won greater recognition (if not to say canonization)
within media-art surveys. However, *Movie-Drome* can
be read separately from these practices if one
establishes within multimedia-art history a parallel
genealogy that examines the modes of reception
along with methods of production. Moreover, if the
ways in which experience is processed are historically
relative, then the modes through which experience is
filtered, constructed and projected are also, by definition, transitory and ephemeral. These filters are not
only contingent on year or location, but also on the
technologies that constitute and signify subjectivity.
As film, video, sound and projection technologies alter
perspective, reception or distance within the realm of
media art, so too does subjectivity shift.

   If one purpose of multimedia art is to transfer
sense experiences from one person to another, then
modes of reception become as significant as the
methods of projection. Low-tech projection equipment produced inside the *Movie-Drome* a sensorial
spectacle of sounds, lights, images, bodies and noise
whose meaning hinged not on objective form, but on
the participants' experience. Rather than developing
within a genealogy of image depiction that would
connect this project with earlier visual devices such
as dioramas, zoetropes or panoramas, the *Movie-
Drome* functioned as a communication apparatus or,
in VanDerBeek's terms, an "experience machine." More
significantly, VanDerBeek's *Movie-Drome* points to

the notion of a programmable space, making it more
related to projects that envisioned a system or
circuit of information, for instance Alan Turing's
Universal Machine of 1936 or Nikola Tesla's 1901 "Plan
for a World System of Planetary Communication." By
generating a perceiving subject that relies on more
than just visual input, the *Movie-Drome* makes it
evident that media art, unlike film or photography, is
not solely limited to the concerns of image production
or *depiction*. Moreover, this project, even in its half-
realized state and crude documentation, makes it
clear that media artists were attempting, and
continue to address, larger systems of distribution
and regulation; that they are concerned with the
mechanization of information, not just with image
refinement. Recognizing that media art operates
within a wider circuit of meaning production, *Movie-
Drome* may potentially work to expand definitions
that determine, or at least set the limits of, subjectivity within media art. An alternate reading of a lesser-
known multimedia project initiated almost forty years
ago challenges the current methods of historicizing
contemporary forms of media art. The myopic
consideration given in particular to the *Movie-Drome*
is clear confirmation that networked practices
addressing a discursive subject have previously
existed, but lacked the context to be fully recognized.

Randall Packer
The Pepsi Pavilion:
Laboratory for Social Experimentation

Pepsi Pavilion
Osaka Expo, 1970
"real" image reflections
in the Mirror Dome
© E.A.T.
photo © Harry Shunk;
courtesy E.A.T.

"An unprecedented structure with unprecedented capabilities for visual, aural, and theatrical experience, the Pavilion is unlike any other performance arena, in that performers were as entirely absorbed into its shimmering mirrored surface as the audience – their reflections and activities merging with those of the spectators." [1]

1   Barbara Rose, "Art as
    Experience, Environment,
    Process," in *Pavilion*, Billy
    Klüver, Julie Martin and
    Barbara Rose (eds), E.P.
    Dutton & Co., Inc., New York,
    1972.

Billy Klüver performing in Claes
Oldenburg's *Ray Gun Theater*
© E.A.T.
photo © Robert R. MacEloro;
courtesy E.A.T.

Robert Rauschenberg (second
from left) and Billy Klüver (right)
working with engineers during
9 Evenings
© E.A.T.
photo courtesy E.A.T.

There is a long history of artists aspiring to build worlds of the imagination as exalted space, multi-sensory "magic theater" that would transcend the physical laws of the real world. Of course the caves of Lascaux, the European gothic cathedrals, or the great palaces such as the Moorish la Alhambra are prime examples, but lesser known are the theatrical experiments of the avant-garde. Many of these latter efforts – pure experimentation, research, and idealism – called for live performance as a vehicle for artistic and social transformation. For example, the *Prefatory Action* of the Russian composer Alexander Scriabin, although never performed, was conceived for color organ, lights, sound, and thousands of choral voices "at the foot of the Himalayas ... an orgy of the arts and senses."2 Bauhaus director and architect Walter Gropius had ambitious plans to create a new theater architecture, rethinking the configuration of performance space as a means to alter the perspective of the viewer. His ideas influenced László Moholy-Nagy's research at the Bauhaus Theater, who wrote:

> "It is time to produce a kind of stage activity which will no longer permit the masses to be silent spectators, which will not only excite them inwardly but will let them take hold and participate – actually allow them to fuse with the action on the stage at the peak of cathartic ecstasy."3

Further experimentation in live performance subsequently had a profound impact on the changing relationship between the viewer and the artwork, with the intent to heighten individual, subjective experience. This tendency took root in the performance art of John Cage, who staged seminal events with Robert Rauschenberg and Merce Cunningham at Black Mountain College in the early 1950s. As Cage had asked: "What'll art become? A family reunion? If so let's have it with people in the round, each individual free to lend his attention wherever he will."4

By the 1960s, Allan Kaprow, Claes Oldenburg, Jim Dine, Red Grooms, and Robert Whitman were exploring new forms that would collectively engage audiences in environments and situations that dissolved all traditional distinctions between performer, stage, set and audience. Paramount in their concern was subverting hierarchical social structures through live performance. According to Whitman, "[o]ne of the problems of traditional theater is that you tell somebody what to see, where to sit, what to do, when to come, when to go – I don't think that's acceptable. What one wants to do is make a theatrical situation that can be available at any time."

Billy Klüver, the Bell Labs scientist who sparked broad interest in art and technology during the 1960s, participated in many of the experimental perfor-

2 Faubion Bowers, *The New Scriabin: Enigma and Answers*, St. Martin's Press, New York, 1973.

3 László Moholy-Nagy, "Theater, Circus, Variety" [1924], in *Multimedia: From Wagner to Virtual Reality*, Randall Packer and Ken Jordan (eds), W. W. Norton & Co., New York, 2001.

4 John Cage, "Diary: Audience 1966" [1966], in Packer, Jordan, op. cit.

from left to right
Pepsi Pavilion
Osaka Expo, 1970
"floats" and geodesic dome
enshrouded in fog
© E.A.T.
photo © Harry Shunk;
courtesy E.A.T.

Pepsi Pavilion
"real" reflections of viewers and
the floor in the Mirror Dome
© E.A.T.
photo © Fuliko Nakaya;
courtesy E.A.T.

Pepsi Pavilion
at night with xenon lights
framing dome
© E.A.T.
photo © Harry Shunk;
courtesy E.A.T.

mance events that took place in lofts and storefronts of New York City, among them Oldenburg's 1962 *Ray Gun Theater*. Oldenburg, who claimed that "theater is the most powerful art form there is because it is the most involving," kept audiences small in an open gallery space to heighten the intimacy of the experience.

Klüver had also developed a close association with Robert Rauschenberg, resulting in several collaborative art and technology projects that helped to catalyze the New York art scene, – including Yvonne Rainer, Cage, Cunningham, Andy Warhol, Jasper Johns, among others – to incorporate the new technologies in artworks and performance events. One such event was the *9 Evenings: Theatre and Engineering* in the fall of 1966 at the cavernous 69th Regiment Armory in New York. Klüver and Rauschenberg organized works involving artists, composers, and dancers in collaboration with engineers from Bell Labs. As a result of *9 Evenings*, Klüver, Rauschenberg, Whitman, and the engineer Fred Waldhauer founded E.A.T. (Experiments in Art & Technology) in late 1966, encouraging activity in art and technology across the U.S.

The culminating project carried out by E.A.T. was the *Pepsi Pavilion* – an extraordinary effort involving over 75 artists and engineers – a landmark public sculpture and performance installation commissioned by Pepsi-Cola for the Expo '70 in Osaka, Japan. The artists and engineers who created the Pavilion synthesized the tendencies of the 1960s, bringing together the currents of social interaction, collaboration, electronic media, Happenings and performance art, immersive environments, and mind-altering "realities" in this transformative "theater of the future."

The *Pepsi Pavilion* was first an experiment in collaboration and interaction between the artists and the engineers, exploring systems of feedback between aesthetic and technical choices, and the humanization of technological systems. Klüver's ambition was to create a laboratory environment, encouraging "live programming" that offered opportunity for experimentation, rather than resort to fixed or "dead programming" as he called it, typical of most exposition pavilions. Secondly, the Pavilion evoked and celebrated aspirations for heightened, non-hierarchical social dynamics built on the aesthetics of agency and transformation brought about through the collective participation of the audience, the artists, and the engineers. The Pavilion's interior dome – immersing viewers in three-dimensional real images generated by mirror reflections, as well as spatialized electronic music – invited the spectator to individually and collectively participate in the experience rather than view the work as a fixed narrative of pre-programmed events. The Pavilion gave visitors the liberty of shaping their own reality from the materials, processes, and structures set in motion by its creators.

Klüver's commitment to "live programming" and the active role of the viewer is best expressed in this statement: "The initial concern of the artists who designed the Pavilion was that the quality of the experience of the visitor should involve choice, responsibility, freedom, and participation. The Pavilion would not tell a story or guide the visitor through a didactic, authoritarian experience. The visitor would be encouraged as an individual to explore the environment and compose his own experience." 5

As an intermedia work, the Pavilion was an ambitious exploration in collaboration and community

among a diverse group of visual artists, composers, choreographers, scientists and engineers. Breaking with the post-renaissance notion of specialization and the artist as "auteur" – single-handedly creating the work – the interdisciplinary nature of the Pavilion required the collective effort of a large group of artists and engineers who had the challenging task of integrating and building ideas born from the group process. At the same time, there was considerable space for individual creative thinking, each artist assigned a component of the overall project. Nevertheless the sum total of the individual parts had to reach a common goal and coalesce into the whole, striving towards the *Gesamtkunstwerk* or total artwork. The Pavilion represents a realization of such dreams, due to the fact that the collaborating artists, architects and engineers were committed to the process of interaction that would help to solve complex design problems and bring about new ideas and forms.

After receiving the invitation from Pepsi, Klüver assembled a core team of artists, along with Whitman, that included Frosty Myers, David Tudor, and Robert Breer. Together they conceived the key elements of the Pavilion: the spherical, 90-foot diameter, 210-degree mirrored dome, inflated inside a geodesic shell, generating real-image, three-dimensional, upside-down reflections of audience and performers; a fully programmable surround-sound system enabling composers to direct sound in various spatial trajectories via thirty-seven speakers arranged in a rhombic grid; handsets held by the viewer emitting pre-recorded "natural" sounds as the audience traversed loop coils installed beneath the floor of the mirrored dome; 800-pound kinetic sculptures (*Floats*) roamed the terrace outside the Pavilion at a speed of

approximately two inches per minute, broadcasting sounds and gently deflecting off of unaware spectators; and four towers with powerful xenon lights generating a well-defined beam between each tower, dramatically framing the dome at night.

Additional artists later joined the team including Gordon Mumma, Lowell Cross, Tony Martin and Fujiko Nakaya, among others, who were responsible for the laser deflection system that responded to audio input, bathing spectators in pulsating streamers of color as they entered the Pavilion's lower Clam Room; a programmable, retractable lighting system generated spectacular blossoming effects in the mirror; and a man-made fog sculpture generated by hundreds of tiny water nozzles enshrouded the exterior dome in a fine mist, interacting with the weather conditions. The sum total of the *Pepsi Pavilion* was a fluid, multi-sensory experience of light, sound, touch and movement, constantly changing in response to the viewer's presence and actions, and to the natural forces of the environment.

Seen by millions of visitors, the Pavilion brought into sharp focus the active role of the viewer through the project's embrace of open, responsive systems. For the artists and engineers, it became a study in the dynamics of viewer interaction. Although the artists – including Pauline Oliveros, Remy Charlip, David Tudor, and Tony Martin – who performed in the space had prepared extensive proposals for performances and environments, they were instead encouraged to freely experiment with the multi-dimensional audio-visual system and to consider the response of the spectator in the development of their evolving ideas. Prior to their arrival in Japan, it would have been impossible for the artists to pre-determine the

Pepsi Pavilion
Osaka Expo, 1970
laser projections bathing the
visitor in light in the Clam Room
© E.A.T.
photo © Harry Shunk;
courtesy E.A.T.

Pepsi Pavilion
draped balloon and reflections
in Mirror Dome
© E.A.T.
photo © Harry Shunk;
courtesy E.A.T.

6 Barbara Rose, "Art as Experience, Environment, Process," in Klüver, Martin, Rose, op. cit.

7 Pierre Lévy, "The Art and Architecture of Cyberspace," in *Collective Intelligence: Mankind's Emerging World in Cyberspace*, transl. Robert Bononno, Plenum Trade, New York, 1997.

8 Guy Debord, *Society of the Spectacle*, (first English translation), Black & Red, Detroit, 1970.

9 Henry David Thoreau, *A Writer's Journal*, Laurence Stapleton (ed.), Dover, New York, 1960.

10 Joseph Beuys, "Introduction" [1979], in *Joseph Beuys in America: Energy Plan for the Western Man*, Carin Kuoni (ed.), Four Walls Eight Windows, New York, 1990.

nearly infinite possibilities of the Pavilion as a space for live performance. Klüver was committed to the ideal that the Pavilion's advanced technological systems support the artists' ideas, creating an open field of possibilities in which they could choose and do whatever he or she could imagine.

According to Barbara Rose, the art critic who accompanied the artists to Japan, "[b]asic to this system of values was social interaction, control of technology toward fulfilling human needs, respect for the natural environment and its potentials and limitation, and a belief in the ability of individuals to take responsibility in democratic, non-coercive, non-hierarchical situations."6 This notion of establishing an environment for audience participation, enables, according to media critic Pierre Lévy, "interpretation to enter the loop with collective action."7 This view of the artwork as a field of interaction between artist and viewer echoes Situationist Guy Debord, who wrote *Society of the Spectacle* just three years before the opening of the Pavilion: "The spectacle is not a collection of images, but a social relation among people, mediated by images."8

The Pavilion was a response to the idea of freeing the spectator to make his or her own connections in the experience of the work, or as Henry David Thoreau poetically intoned, "[o]bey the spur of the moment … Let the spurs of countless moments goad us incessantly into life."9 Here the artists built a world, without controlling it, in order that the spectator exist in that world as a willing and equal partner in forming the experience, in shaping their own reality. Art then functions as a transformative agent, without imposing pre-conceived patterns of thought, which might prevent the viewer from freely experiencing the artwork according to their own unique perspective.

We could surmise that the Pavilion articulated a vision of social sculpture, in the spirit of Joseph Beuys, who was concerned with "how we mold and shape the world in which we live: sculpture as an evolutionary process, everyone an artist."10 The Pavilion was a public sculpture for constructing worlds of the imagination that defy the constraints of physical laws, of everyday reality, revealing to us, in the most extravagant manner, what our reality might be, given the tools and minds to reshape it.

"If art was going to be of any use, it was going to be of use not with reference to itself, but with reference to the people who used it." – (John Cage)

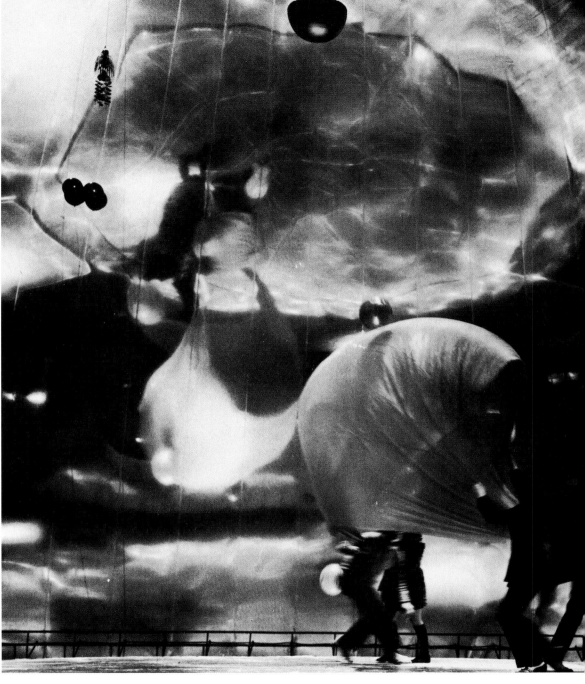

Pepsi Pavilion
Osaka Expo, 1970
© E.A.T.;
courtesy Billy Klüver
photo © Harry Shunk;
courtesy E.A.T.

David Tudor with banks of tape
recorders in control room
© E.A.T.
photo © Harry Shunk;
courtesy E.A.T.

Dan Graham
Cinema

1981
architectural model / foam core, wood, two-way mirror, Plexiglas,
Super-8 projector and Super-8 film / 61 x 57 x 57 cm

A cinema, the ground level of a modern office building, is sited on a busy corner. Its facade consists of two-way mirrored glass, which allows viewers on whichever side is darker at any particular moment to see through and observe the other side (without being seen by the people on that side). From the other side, the window appears as a mirror. When the light illuminates the surface of both sides more or less equally, the glass facade is both semi-reflective and partially transparent. Spectators on both sides observe both the opposing space *and* a reflection of their own look within their own space.

Stage 1:
The Film is Projected; The Interior is Dark.
A two-way mirror screen is substituted for the conventional screen. Located at the front of the building, it forms the longer side of an equilateral triangle whose apex is the front corner of the building. Because of the properties of the two-way mirror, when a film is projected, the mirror functions as a normal screen for the interior film-goer and also projects the film image so that it can be seen, in reverse, from the street through the building's facade. [...] Further, when viewed from the street, the screen's image can be looked through to see the frontal gaze of the audience watching the screen. This is because the light of the projector falls on the interior of the screen, making the reverse side of this two-way mirror darker relative to its front and therefor slightly transparent. The position of the outside observer can be distinguished from that of the interior, seated spectator. The outside observer does not relinquish his consciousness of self or awareness of environment for the (silent) movie image. Further, he is free to move around the sides of the theater and remove himself from the cinematic illusion in order to obtain a general, outside perspective on the audience-film relationship. During the film's showing to the interior audience occasional images from the external, real environment intrude through the side windows, mixing with the film's images reflected on the side walls. These external reflected images interfere with the film spectator's identification of his consciousness with the filmic illusion. [...]

Stage 2:
The Film is not Projected; House Lights are Up.
The house lights in the cinema are turned on after (or before) a film is projected. Interior spectators see the screen, as well as the side windows, as reflective mirrors – reminiscent of mirrored cinema lobbies.

Where the Renaissance framing of the screen has, a few seconds ago, been a "mirror" for the spectator's subjective projection of his body, which, disembodied and invisible, has been "lost" to his immediate environment in its identification with the film, the screen itself and sides of the theater now become literal mirrors (as opposed to the illusory "mirror" of the film), reflecting the real space and bodies and looks of the spectators. The spectator sees his real position represented on the mirror, relative to the presence of the rest of the audience, whereas in the fictional world of the film he was the phenomenological center of an illusionary world. He sees himself looking in relation to the looks of the others in the audience. Outside, the physiological position of the spectator also reverses for he is now able to look through the window, himself unseen. Awareness of *his* body and *his* environment is lost. His position as voyeur becomes akin to that of the audience the previous moment.
[...]
In my cinema project it is the screen, instead of the machine, and the system of voyeuristic identifications, which are exposed. It is assumed that the cinema is prototypical of all other perspective systems which work to produce a social subject through manipulating the subject's imaginary identifications. In the cinema all looks are intersubjective: it is difficult to separate the poetics of the materials of the architecture from the psychological identifications constructed by the film images. The psychological circuit of intersubjective looks and identifications is echoed in and is a product of the material properties of the architectural materials, whose optical functioning derives from the properties of the two-way mirror glass. In this *Cinema*, unlike the cinema which must conceal from the spectators their own looks and projections, the architecture allows inside and outside spectators to perceive their positions, projections, bodies and identifications. Topologically, an optical "skin," both reflective and transparent inside and outside, functions simultaneously as a screen for the film's projection. Dialectically, it is seen in the outside environment as well as in the normal cinema context as a point of transfer for the gazes of the inner and outer spectators, in relation to each other and the film image.

Dan Graham

First published in *Dan Graham: Buildings and Signs*, exhib. cat., Anne Rorimer (ed.), Renaissance Society of the University of Chicago, Chicago, 1981, pp. 46–50.

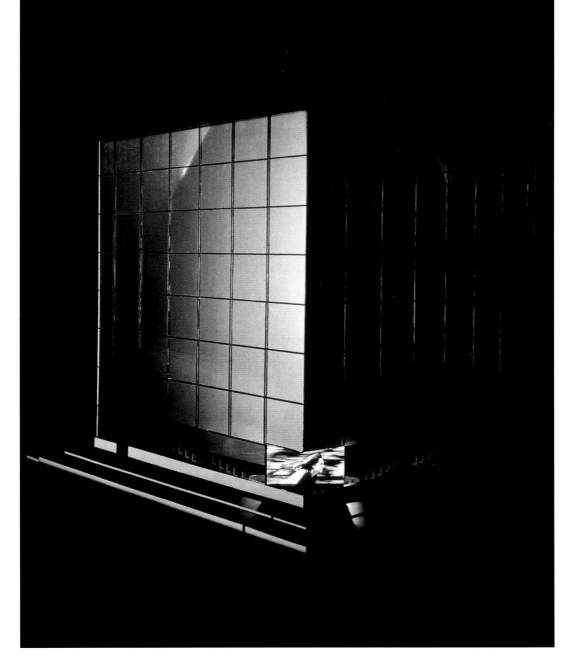

Cinema
1981
architectural model
two-way mirror plastic,
Super-8 projector,
Super-8 film, Plexiglas
61 x 57 x 57 cm
edition of three
collection Musée National
d'Art Moderne, Centre Georges
Pompidou, Paris
photo © Philippe Migeat,
Centre Georges Pompidou
photo courtesy Dan Graham,
New York

Cinema
1981
architectural model
detail
edition of three
collection Musée National d'Art
Moderne, Centre Georges Pompidou, Paris
photo © Philippe Migeat,
Centre Georges Pompidou
photo courtesy Dan Graham,
New York

Video Projection Outside Home
1978
model, mixed media
23 x 76 x 59 cm
courtesy Marian Goodman
Gallery, New York

Video Projection Outside Home
1996
temporary installation
in private home
1347 Santa Rosa Avenue,
Santa Barbara, California

Even if we have become spectators,
nothing dispenses us from taking
a decision about what we look at.[1]

Dan Graham's Cinema:
Reflections on/of Urban Life and Media Culture

1 Thierry de Duve, "Dan Graham und die Kritik der künstlerischen Autonomie," in *Dan Graham. Werke 1965–2000*, exhib. cat., Marianne Brouwer (ed.), Richter, Düsseldorf, 2002, p. 63.

2 Herzog & de Meuron, "Urban Suburban," in *Dan Graham: The Suburban City*, exhib. cat., Theodora Vischer (ed.), Museum für Gegenwartskunst, Basel, Neue Galerie am Landesmuseum Joanneum, Graz, 1997, p. 28.

3 See by Dan Graham also "Homes for America: Early 20th Century Possessable House to the Quasi-Discrete Cell of '66'," in *Arts Magazine*, 41, 3, December 1966–January 1967, pp. 8–9; "Art in Relation to Architecture / Architecture in Relation to Art," in *Artforum*, 17, 6, 1979, pp. 22–29; and Dan Graham: *Video-Architecture-Television: Writings on Video and Video Works 1970–1978*, H.D.Buchloh (ed.), The Press of the Nova Scotia, Halifax, New York University Press, New York, 1979.

Research into the living conditions and habits of people living in modern towns and cities is one point of reference in Dan Graham's work of the period 1966–81. He makes us aware of the "omnipresence and the inevitability of the present-day city."[2] Often situated on the divide between sculpture and architecture, his works study society on the basis of its spaces. Dan Graham subtly questions the normalcy of urban everyday life by offering unusual insights into otherwise opaque spaces of the public and the private sphere. Reflections of urban life, in both the literal and figurative senses, are addressed in his photographs of reflecting office-building glass facades and in other works such as *Video Piece for Showcase Windows in Shopping Arcade* (1976) or *Video Piece for Two Glass Office Buildings* (1974–76). The optical reflection of the surrounding functions as a metaphor for mental reflection upon urban architecture and its social function, whereas works like *Alteration to a Suburban House* (1978), *Clinic for a Suburban Site* (1978) and *'Picture Window' Piece* (1974) focus on the suburban house, which unlike the vitreous buildings in modern cities is generally impenetrable to sight. In his staging of "apparatuses of perception" that expose

what is normally hidden, it is mostly art and architecture that define for Graham the field of tension between "public" and "private."[3]

A new aspect is introduced by *Video Projection Outside Home* (1978), in which Graham directs our attention to television as the favored communication medium of mass society. This project, consisting of a large video-projection screen mounted in a suburban front garden and showing an image of whatever TV program the people inside the house are watching, was first carried out in a real urban environment some years after being conceived as a model. Through being broadcast onto the street, a family's choice of TV program is attributed the importance of a politico-cultural decision. Everyday zapping, presented as a sociological study, puts up for show not only the private voyeurism of the television viewers and their personal interests, preferences and taste, but also the voyeurism of the passers-by who stop to watch other people watching TV. At the same time, the project addresses the one-way communication, now typical as a characteristic of the mass medium television of modern society.[4]

In the movie theater, too, where the individual is one among many, a comparable situation exists. Dan Graham describes the cinema as a phenomenon of urban

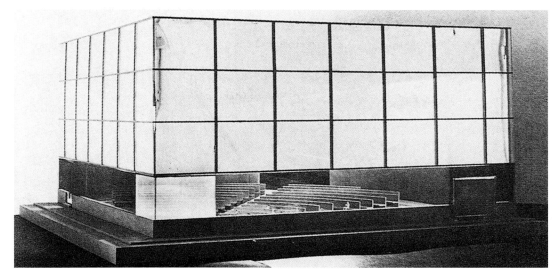

Cinema
1981
architectural model
two-way mirror plastic,
Super-8 projector,
Super-8 film, Plexiglas
61 x 57 x 57 cm
edition of three
collection Musée National
d'Art Moderne, Centre
Georges Pompidou, Paris
photo courtesy Dan Graham,
New York

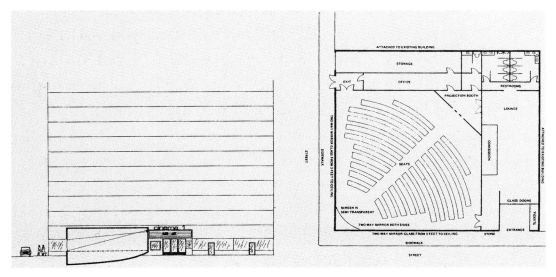

Cinema
1981
sketch for the
architectural model
from *Dan Graham:
Ausgewählte Schriften*,
Ulrich Wilmes (ed.), Oktagon,
Stuttgart, 1994, p. 194

and mass culture, interpreting it as a picture of humans in contemporary media society.5 His *Cinema* (1981) depicts film in relation to architecture, and by disrupting the normally passive role of the theater audience examines the connections and interrelations between subject and space, between film and communication.

In the context of a conventional screening, viewers immerse themselves in the illusion of a dreamlike fantasy world, completely losing awareness of the here and now, of physical presence, of the surrounding space, of the rest of the audience, and, of course, of the outer world, screened off and far away. This special situation attracts Graham's interest, since he considers it exemplary of the individual's anonymity and alienation in contemporary cities. Thus, Graham takes up the cinema visit to reverse the familiar line of sight and to direct the viewer's gaze towards himself and his own conditions. On the other hand his intention is to sharpen the perception of the other, the stranger both in the audience as well as on the street. Besides what is *on-screen*, Graham's Cinema also refers to what is *before* and *behind* the screen.

Playing with reflection and transparency, Graham creates entirely new and unexpected (in)sights and outlooks. The real images superimpose the fictitious. The spectator's reflection blends with the characters portrayed by the actors. The urban reality of the street is temporarily superimposed over the filmic scenery. The temporary transparency of the projection screen allows impressions of the outside world to penetrate the inside, and unnoticed the uninvolved passers-by can observe the moviegoers in their self-oblivion, while at the same time the onlookers on the street and cinema audience are confronted with their own image and thus enabled to observe themselves observing. In this way, viewers perceive themselves as voyeurs and simultaneously as members of a crowd, as part of society. The perfect anonymity and self-oblivion offered by the cinema visit, the voyeuristic pleasure and perfect illusion of movie-going, is shattered. Seemingly rigid concepts such as "private" and "public" begin to merge, the boundaries between fiction and reality blur and an unexpected invitation to dialogue is suggested.

Ulrike Havemann
Translated from the German by Petra Kaiser

4 See also Dan Graham, "An American Family," in *TV guides: A Collection of Thoughts about Television*, Barbara Kruger (ed.), Kuklapolitan Press, New York, 1985, pp. 13–14.

5 See also Dan Graham, "Theater, Cinema, Power," in *Parachute*, 31, June–August 1983.

09

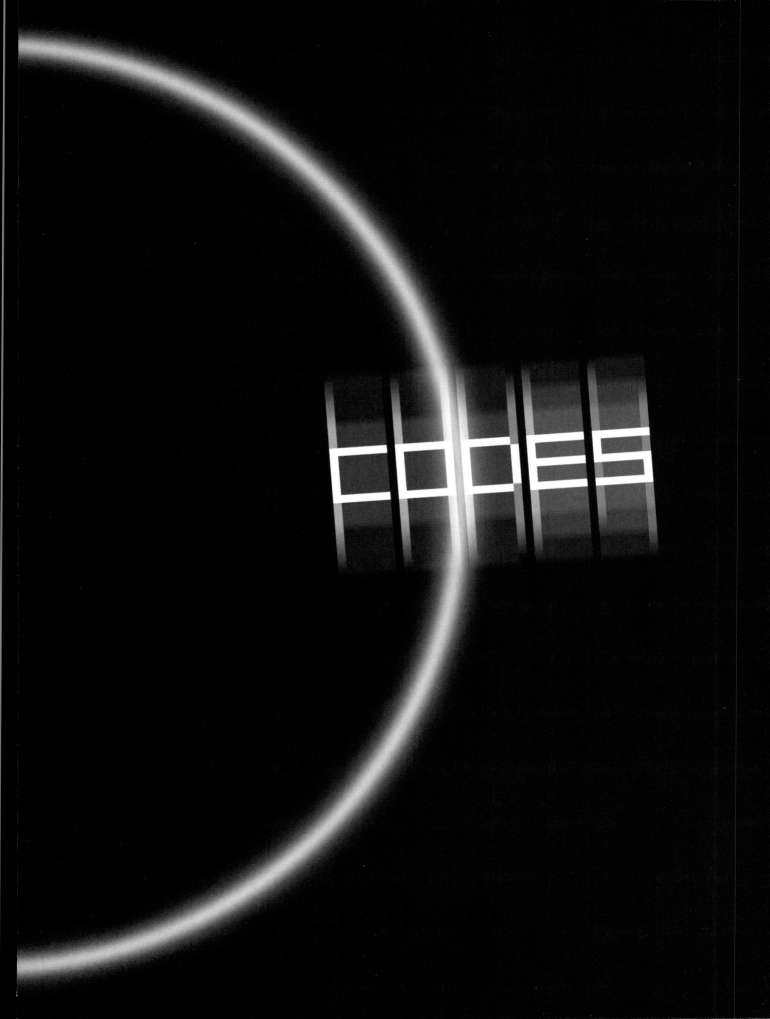

Gene Youngblood
Cinema and the Code

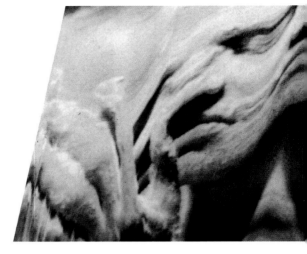

John Sturgeon
Curtain
1988
photograph
40.6 x 50.8 cm
© John Sturgeon

1 Both real-time video
machines and computers
operate on the same structure of digital code. ADO,
Quantel and Fairlight are
digital computers. The only
difference is that they take
their "model" from camera
input and they operate in
real ume. With the exception
of extremely fast comput-
ers, most digital image synthesis, or "computer graphics," is not done in real time.
Other than this we make no
distinction between them,
except in reference to the
source or model of the
organization of the image –
one through camera input,
the other through algo-
rithms. Also, we regard the
process of writing or structuring the code as part of
the digital-imaging procedure. It is the craft of digital
imaging in computer graphics. You do not "write the
image" in video.

2 My colleagues have found
the concept of the "event-
stream" problematic.
Vasulka defines it as "every
scheduled change." He
points out that there is
always an invisible technological level to every perceived event, like the event
of line-forming in video, or
computations and logical
operations in image synthesis. The key is to realize that
the event does not have to
be consciously perceived. In
music, for example, a listener would be incapable of
naming each sonic event,
but music is nevertheless a
system of parallel event-
streams.

What are the implications of digital imaging for the
evolution of cinematic language? Since 1986, Peter
Weibel, Steina and Woody Vasulka and I have been
meeting to discuss that question. We thought our
talks might become a book, whose subject Weibel
conceived as "the evolution of the image through the
digital image." What follows is an outline of our conversations, assembled for this publication from two
hundred pages of transcript. It is in every sense a
first draft, a working paper. We are quite aware of
the problematic nature of our discourse, especially in
the cursory form presented here. Every conclusion is
vulnerable to criticism, which we welcome. We are
certain of only one thing: that these questions are
important and need to be explored.

The subject of "digital imaging," we agree, exists
in the context of both video and the computer
(different only in the source of the image and the
possibility of real time operation) and covers the
generic areas of image processing, image synthesis,
and writing or organizing digital code in a procedural
or linguistic fashion. 1 But in every case when we refer
to the phenomenology of the moving image, we call
it cinema. For us it is important to separate cinema
from its medium, just as we separate music from
particular instruments. Cinema is the art of organizing a stream of audiovisual events in time. It is an
event-stream, like music. 2 There are at least four
media through which we can practice cinema – film,
video, holography and structured digital code – just
as there are many instruments through which we can
practice music. Of course each medium has distinct
properties and contributes differently to the theory
of cinema, each expands our knowledge of what
cinema can be and do. Each new medium modifies
and extends the linguistic possibilities of the moving
image, subsuming the syntaxes of previous media
without negating them.

Thus, the basic phenomenology of the moving
image – what Vasulka calls "the performance of the
image on the surface of the screen" – remains historically continuous across all media. Digital code, for
example, has radically altered the epistemology and
ontology of the moving image but has not fundamen-

tally changed its phenomenology. There are no digital
images that have not been prefigured in painting, film
and video. With the code we can only summarize them,
elaborate and unfold them or exercise modalities.
Vasulka calls the code a variation machine. There are
no new classes of images, there are only new variations and new epistemological and ontological conditions for generating and witnessing those variations.
Each new medium of the future, says Vasulka, can
only "play host to the phenomenology of the moving
image," which will evolve through that medium to the
next, accumulating the language of each.

Weibel puts it this way: a medium is "a corpus of
aesthetic strategies" inherited from previous media.
In the 1920s mathematicians attacked the problem
of foundations: What was pure logic? What was an
axiom? Today the answers to those questions are
implemented in the computer. Logical concepts have
become instrumental, they have become parts of machines. And any machine element, says Weibel, is nothing but a physical implementation of a formal device.
It implements mental strategies into something physical. (This is what Buckminster Fuller meant when he
defined technology as "instrumented or documented
intellect.") Similarly, aesthetic strategies invented
one hundred years ago in photography and cinema –
scaling, perspective, positive/negative reversals,
wipes, mattes – have now become machine elements
whose operations are trivially invoked through the
preset button. It is a question of primitives. The code
is a metamedium: through it, high-level aesthetic constructs from previous media become the primitives
of the new medium. This influences which aesthetic
strategies will be emphasized. When a strategy that
was possible but difficult in film becomes a preset
button in video or a command in computer graphics,
it tends to be used more frequently. But that does
not make it more meaningful. The challenge is to turn
"effects" into expressions, into syntactical units of
meaning.

This raises the question, How has the corpus of
aesthetic strategies inherited in a medium like photography or film transferred over to electronic media
and especially to the code? Things are possible in the

John Sturgeon
Face Mask
1988
photograph
40.6 x 50.8 cm
© John Sturgeon

John Sturgeon
Head Wand
1988
photograph
40.6 x 50.8 cm
© John Sturgeon

code that were not possible, or at least not easy, in film and video. Only by comparing formal devices developed in one medium to other devices developed in other media can we arrive at criteria for evaluating artistic achievement. Have the syntactical and linguistic possibilities of the digital image been identified and elaborated in practice? We think not – at least, not very often. We rarely find them in the work that is otherwise admired in the name of the medium. People praise a particular work of "video" or of "computer art," and yet we find in this work no definitory elements of video or of the code. It may be great cinema but it is not great *electronic* cinema. We are not arguing for exclusivity or essence. We are not trying to be the Clement Greenberg of the code. The phenomenology of the moving image remains constant across all media, but each new medium brings about a shift of emphasis or accent. Through the code, we can unfold the potential of formal strategies that were possible but limited in previous media, thereby expanding the richness of cinematic language.

Vasulka asks, "Who creates the language of a medium?" Weibel responds by quoting Heidegger: "Man is but a guest in the house of language." Vasulka agrees. All possibilities of a system, he says, are contained within that system. We are not free to invent the language of film, video or computer. The language already exists in the system. Our task is to discover it, identify it, draw it out and name it, put a nomenclature on it. Vasulka has built his machines in order to discover "the language" in them, which could be found only through dialogue with the machines. He points out that this is not unique to electronic cinema. Film language also arose from a similar systemic understanding. As a syntactic device, the cut, the edit, is machine-bound. It is the only way to splice film. The most important figures in the history of film are those who elaborated its syntactic or linguistic potential. This is our criterion for artistic achievement in the new medium: to what extent does the artist articulate and develop the formal possibilities of the system as syntactical or linguistic elements? To what extent does the artist transform effects into expressions?

It is a question not only of the evolution of cinematic language, but of human perception itself. Human vision, Weibel points out, has always been "machine-assisted." The invention of perspective, for example, was machine-dependent. It was derived from optical instruments. Dürer's boxes were in this sense "machines." They implemented physically what then became formal strategies. With the help of this machine we could invent perspective. (Weibel thinks this curious. Why did it take so long?) Similarly, Vermeer, under the influence of Spinoza and the science of optics in the seventeenth century, created paintings that were not initially seen as poetic. They were regarded more as scientific research. (In the nineteenth century, Proust, influenced by photography, "rediscovered" Vermeer, now regarded as a poet. The computer is to the artist of today as the lens was to Vermeer.) The Impressionists, too, were following theories, not subjective experience. Impressionism was based on color theory: three different colors produce a fourth impression. An optical theory of color, says Weibel, is also a machine, a mental machine, like a Turing machine. Thus we have substantial evidence that the evolution of vision is dependent on machines, either mental or physical. It has come to the point that it is no longer possible to suppress the machine part of it: first there was the camera, now the computer. This is significant, Weibel thinks, because art always tries to suppress the influence of the machine element in the work itself. It is not art if the technology is too apparent. But the issue here is not art, it is language and perception. They co-evolve only to the extent that the syntactic possibilities of technological systems are made the subject of aesthetic inquiry.

The following formal possibilities of digital imaging are available for articulation as syntactic elements or linguistic primitives: (1) image transformation, (2) parallel event-streams, (3) temporal perspective and (4) the image as object.

Image Transformation

If mechanical cinema is the art of transition, electronic cinema is the art of transformation. Film grammar is based on transitions between fully formed photo-

Lee Harrison III
photo montage featuring
a dancer with body-mounted
sensors controlling real-time
animation on the
ANIMAC (hybrid graphic-
animation computer)
1962
Denver

Odilon Redon
L'oeil, comme un ballon bizarre,
se dirige vers l'Infini
[The Eye Like a Strange Balloon
Moves Towards Infinity]
1878
charcoal
42.2 x 33.2 cm
The Museum of Modern Art,
New York; gift of
Aldrich Rockefeller
photo © The Museum of Modern
Art, New York, 1993

graphic objects called frames. It is done primarily
through that collision of frames called the cut, but
also through wipes and dissolves. In electronic cinema
the frame is not an object but a time segment of a
continuous signal. This makes possible a syntax based
on transformation, not transition. Analog image processing is one vehicle of this particular art – for example, scan processors. But it becomes even more
significant in digital image synthesis, where the image
is a database. One can begin to imagine a movie composed of thousands of scenes with no cuts, wipes or
dissolves, each image metamorphosing into the next.

A cut is a cut, but a transforming or metamorphosing operation is open-ended. There are infinite
possibilities, each with unlimited emotional and
psychological consequences. Metamorphosis is not
unique to digital imaging; it is a familiar strategy in
hand-drawn animation. What is unique is the special
case of *photoreal* metamorphosis. It is one thing for
a line drawing or fantasy painting to metamorphose,
quite another for a photographically "real" object to
do so. This is theoretically possible in mechanical cinema and has been prefigured (but never fully realized)
in hand-drawn animation, where it is so difficult and
time consuming that it is, for all practical purposes,
impossible. It is possible digitally, because the code
allows us to combine the subjectivity of painting,
the objectivity of photography and the gravity-free
motion of hand-drawn animation.

Steina points out that there are two kinds of
transitions based on the cut, and these require different kinds of metamorphoses. One moves us to a
different point of view in the same space/time, the
other moves us to a different space and/or time.
In flashbacks (cinematic memory), either a matte is
used within the frame or the whole frame dissolves.
With the code, a part of the frame can metamorphose. This implies an expanded cinematic language
of simultaneity.

Parallel Event-Streams

With the arrival of electronic cinema it became apparent that film grammar was limited in what might
be called its vocabulary of tenses – for the most part
it was "meanwhile" or "after." For example, simultaneous events are traditionally signified through cross-
cutting, or what is known as parallel montage. But,
Weibel notes, there was never a formal distinction between a cut to a different position in space/time (say,
between people in conversation) and a cut between
different spaces or time. The distinction has always
been logical or inferential (as in parallel montage),
never formal. Digital code offers formal solutions to
the "tense" limitations of mechanical cinema. Past,
present and future can be spoken in the same frame
at once.

There are at least three possibilities: superimposition (overlay), or simultaneous but spatially separate
event-streams that are either framed or unframed.
Superimposition has been explored extensively in experimental film, notably by Stan Brakhage. His work is
the closest cinema has come to the Joycean text. In
such work it is not always possible to identify consciously each image-stream, just as it is often impossible to distinguish every voice in a musical composition. One is disturbed by this only if one is unfamiliar
with it. Once one learns to read it, the dense text is a
pleasure. Digital code offers possibilities of image-
overlay whose linguistic potential we have not begun
to explore.

Caspar David Friedrich
Das Kreuz im Gebirge (Tetschener Altar)
[Cross in the Mountains (Tetschen Altar)]
1807-1808
oil on canvas
115 x 110.5 cm
Staatliche Kunstsammlungen Dresden,
Gemäldegalerie Neue Meister
photo © Jörg P. Anders;
Staatliche Museen zu Berlin

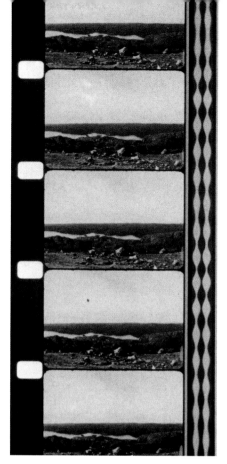

Michael Snow
La Region Centrale
[The Central Region]
1970—1971
16mm film
color, sound
180 min
film stills
© Michael Snow

The second possibility is more familiar: framed parallel event-streams, such as split screens in film (optical printing) or floating imageplanes in video, done with digital effects devices such as ADO or Quantel. But there is also the possibility of *unframed* parallel events occupying different areas of a single image. This can best be seen in the work of the Vasulkas, for example, where pointillist textures move independently in separate areas of the frame. Different zones of the image are activated in different ways in parallel. The Vasulkas accomplish this through digital image processing. But image synthesis, through a variation on metamorphosis, would provide unlimited possibilities for unframed but separate parallel event-streams in a single frame.

Below, in a discussion of the image as object, I shall have more to say about parallel event-streams. Meanwhile, consider that simultaneity enlarges our concept of a cinematic event. Weibel puts it this way: whereas first we had the industry of the moving image, today we have the industry of the accelerated image. If there are three image-planes instead of one, the information conveyed within the overall frame is tripled, and, furthermore, each succeeding image destroys the meaning of the previous one. The information is accelerated so much in perspective and in all other ways that the value of "the image" is replaced by the value of the image-gestalt or image-field.

Temporal Perspective

"The history of every art form," wrote Walter Benjamin, "shows critical epochs in which a certain art form aspires to effects which could be fully obtained only with a changed technical standard, that is to say, in a new art form." 3 Weibel pursues this logic in reverse, working backward from the digital image to find desire for its powers in art history. He begins by noting that Renaissance perspective was always at eye level with one point of view and one vanishing point. By 1850, photographers were climbing onto Parisian rooftops and shooting down into streets. Twenty years later, Odilon Redon painted a balloon-suspended eye moving up into the sun. Perspective as no longer bound to a static point of view. It had become free-floating. In the same period, the German Romantic painter Caspar David Friedrich painted mountain shadows falling at an angle different (that is, displaced in time) from that of the impinging sunlight. Other examples are found in the work of El Lissitsky and the Cubo-Futurist movement. Painting, influenced by photography and cinema, introduced multiple points of view and implied time.

And what did cinema do with perspective? Not much. Bound to psychological realism, it exploited it only spatially, mainly through deep focus (Eisenstein, Welles, Renoir), never temporally. Only in experimental cinema was temporal perspective explored in any serious way at all — the outstanding example being the work of Michael Snow, such as *La Region Centrale* and *Back and Forth*. But with the advent of the code, the emphasis on perspective returns. Moving-image art can now embrace it in an emphatic way. When the image is a three-dimensional database, perspective becomes a temporal as well as spatial phenomenon. It is a strategy that is intrinsic to the code. Painters, photographers and filmmakers could not realize the full potential of this desire. But now we can unfold and elaborate that which could only be indicated in earlier media.

3 Walter Benjamin, "The Work of Art in the Age of Mechanical Reproduction," in *Illuminations*, New York, 1978, p. 237.

Vasulka notes that, if we remove the two cinematic vectors from earth to space and establish the principle of a point in space, we arrive at two possibilities: first, cinema looks from one point to infinity in a spherical point of view. That is one vector, we shall say. The other is the opposite: one looks from each point in space towards a single point. If all these points are in motion around one point, that is the space in which ideal cinema operates. But as long as we are talking about psychological realism we will be bound to an eye-level cinema.

The Image as Object
There are three technologies through which the image can become an object: image processing, image synthesis, and three-dimensional display – either binocular (stereoptic) or holographic. The code is responsible for the first two and may be partially involved in the third. This is another aspect of parallel event-streams. We recognize cinema as frame-bound and frame-unbound. Mechanical cinema is characterized primarily by its reliance on the frame. It cannot leave the frame unless a special effort is made through optical printing. But with code it becomes a trivial matter to remove the image from the frame and treat it as an object, an image-plane, because those tools have no capacity to deal with the geometry of the image itself: they deal only with its location or position (its "address") within the larger frame. The use of framed parallel events points to new narrative possibilities, new semiotic strategies – for example, the possibility of a previous or future event appearing spatially behind or in front of a current event within the same frame. There is always a pending image. Editing can be avoided entirely – as Vasulka did in his 1987 work *Art of Memory*. He points out that, through hierarchies of image planes in particular arrangements "in a mental space," future and past tenses may be suggested. As already mentioned in the discussion of parallel event-streams, conventional film language is rather inarticulate in this respect. There is no temporal eloquence in film. But digital video suggests the possibility of establishing one image-plane as "present" with other timeframes visible simultaneously within the frame. This would extend the possibility of transfiguration (metamorphosis) into a narrative space composed of layers of time, either as moving or still images. Ed Emshwiller's Sunstone was one of the first works to explore these possibilities. In it the image becomes object, and it has both framed and unframed parallel event-streams.

When image becomes object in a stream of parallel events, the realm of psychological realism or photographic truth is abandoned. The frame-bound photographic image brings us truth. But three image-planes within a frame lose what Vasulka calls "the aura of truth." We detach ourselves from them psychologically. Will it be possible to construct a psychological space in a language of frame-unbound parallel event-streams?

For Weibel, all this raises a fundamental challenge to the metonymic nature of cinematic language. He invokes the name of Roman Jakobson, who argues that there are only two fundamental operations in language: metaphor and metonymy. And the language of cinema is not metaphoric, it is metonymic. It is the language of the part for the whole. All cinematic images are contingent. The frame, said Jakobson, is always part of an unseen whole. At its fundamental syntactic level – the level of cutting, of editing, of bringing spaces together – the filmic language game is metonymic. In the service of psychological realism, conventional editing reconstructs "real" time and "real" space, following logical causal chains by metonymic association. Experiments like *Last Year at Marienbad* were attempts to transcend that limi-

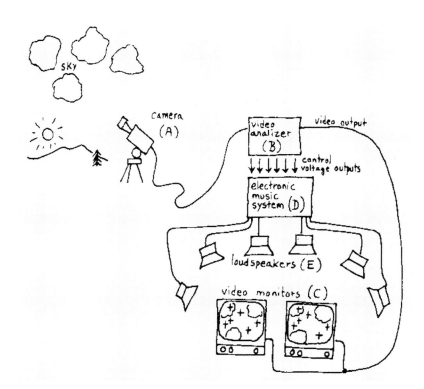

tation within psychological narrative. But in the electronic image there is no need to make a *Marienbad*, because it is clear that we no longer have that constancy of time and space. Once an image-object is set against a reference, the metonymic tension is lost. Objectifying the image within the frame puts it in a different time zone. Metonymy becomes problematic. On the one hand, such constructs are not metonymic because the space they occupy is not "natural." The image-object is not part of the whole; it is no longer contingent. But it is not metaphoric either. It is something new. We do not know what it is. It might still function metonymically, but in a different way. This is an important area that is wide open for aesthetic exploration.

The second level of the image as object is achieved through digital image synthesis. Here, because it is a three-dimensional database, we can control not only the location of the image object within the frame but also its perspective, its angle of view, its geometry. As a result, the synthesized image becomes truly an object, the witness becomes a "user," and the relation between them becomes not observation but interaction. Jean-Louis Baudry argues that, in the cinema of psychological realism, the primary identification of the spectator is not with the characters but with the camera itself.4 But in interactive image synthesis, the spectator is the camera. Since it is not separate from the scene it surveys, the virtual camera is neither a voyeur nor an instrument of surveillance. "It is a point of view that is active within the scene," writes Catherine Richards. "Not only can this camera (the user) direct its own looking, it can be sensed, responded to, and represented in the scene: it sees and is seen."5

The third level of the objectification of the image is realized through three-dimensional display. Whether through holography or binocular (stereoptic) technol-

ogy, cinema is moving from the two-dimensional image on a screen to the three-dimensional object in space. Today cinema represents reality; tomorrow it will *be* reality. Already with stereoptic technology the image becomes an object. And in Scott Fisher's virtual environment project of the U.S. National Aeronautics and Space Administration (NASA) (combining a three-dimensional database with stereo vision in a wraparound head-mounted display), cinematic space becomes a place to live. An unframed image is not an image, Vasulka points out, it is an object in space: "It forces you to deal with air." It is no longer a representation but the thing itself. Vasulka notes that different understandings of reality and truth are implied by the representational image and by an object in space, no matter how insubstantial that object may be. Three-space cinema, he suggests, is more like theater. In two-space cinema there it truth but no reality. In theater there is reality but no truth.

Originally published in "Computer Art in Context: SIGGRAPH 89 Art Show Catalog," Marc Resch and Pamela Grant-Ryan (eds), Supplemental Issue of *Leonardo, Journal of the International Society for the Arts, Sciences and Technology*, Pergamon Press, Oxford, 1989, pp. 27–30.

4 Jean-Louis Baudry, "Ideological Effects of the Basic Cinematographic Apparatus," in *Film Quarterly*, vol. 28, no. 2, Winter 1974–1975. Quoted in Christian Metz, "History/Discourse: A Note on Two Voyeurisms," in *Theories of Authorship*, John Caughie (ed.), London, 1981, p. 231.

5 Catherine Richards, "Virtual Worlds, Digital Images," in the catalog of the 1987 American Film Institute Video Festival, Los Angeles, CA, 1987.

Steina and Woody Vasulka

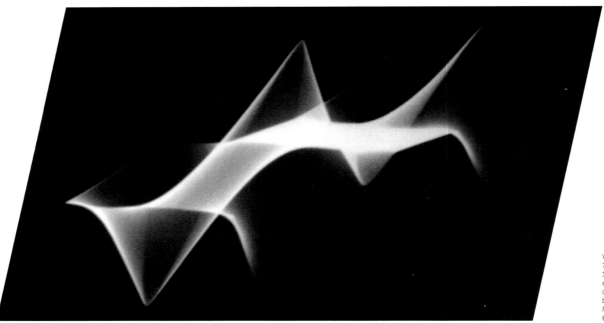

Woody Vasulka
Time/Energy Objects
1975
electronic image
on scan processor
b/w
Polaroid
© Woody Vasulka

Circuit Riders

To listen to Steina and Woody Vasulka discussing their video work – and to look at it – is to encounter a form of television utterly unlike what "television" usually means. Using computers and electronic synthesizers, often without cameras, the Vasulkas have extended the range of expression in the medium. By making the camera/lens combination a secondary tool they have demonstrated that organization can be more important than observation, that the television signal is much more malleable (and controllable) than most of us dreamed. In the new realms of Vasulka video we can see:

- television "snow" randomly raining across the screen, and then suddenly becoming "ordered" so that in the center of the screen a disc of different snow appears – frozen or moving against the direction of the remaining snow.
- the raster lines of the image retreating from the edges of the screen, folding over upon themselves, and forming configurations that are as baffling as they are simply evident.
- a recognizable image molded into a topographical surface that soon turns into a terrain different from (but born of) the initial image.

The fascination of all such Vasulka imagery resides in our knowledge that the transformations we witness are mathematical, rigorous, *our own* in that they are made by machines made by men. Yet also *not our own*, because these electronic images can not be made without machines. Woody Vasulka often speaks of "a dialogue between the tool and the image," a phrase that conspicuously fails to emphasize or even acknowledge the human presence.

Woody and Steina design and construct their equipment with the expectation of learning from it during and after the programming process. Their tools exist to be used and collaborated with. The tools are not that extraordinary, although they are custom built: a Rutt/Etra analog scan processor, a dual colorizer, a programmer, a multikeyer, a variable clock and a switcher (the last four made by technician George Brown in the early 1970s). With these instruments the Vasulkas are pioneers charting the digital and analog space of the micro-circuit, the time duration of instant information exchanges, the implications of infinite extrapolations.

The capacity of the Vasulkas to enter into the electronic realm of their tools is indispensable to their work and a consequence of their experience. Both have delighted in frequently moving across

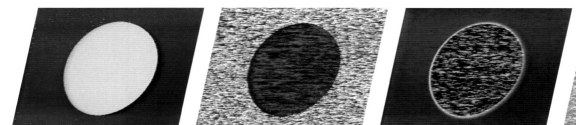
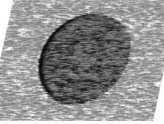

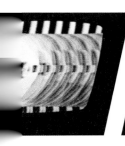
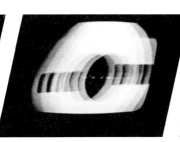
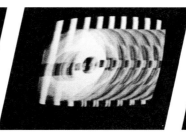
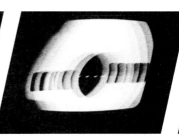
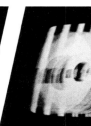

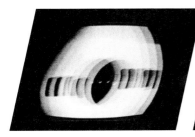
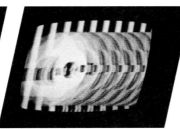

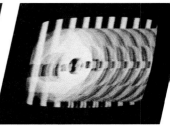

geographical and cultural boundaries, immersing themselves in each successive environment. Born and raised in Reykjavik, Iceland, Steina studied violin, harmony, and music theory. In 1957 she spent a year in Denmark at a boarding school, and returned to Iceland speaking Danish. "I decided German was the next language I wanted to speak, so [in 1958] I went to Germany." In 1959 she moved again, to Prague where she studied music for four years. Returning to Iceland she joined the Icelandic Symphony Orchestra and married Woody. In 1965 they moved to the United States, where in 1969 they discovered alternative video.

Woody was born in Brno, Czechoslovakia in 1937. In 1945 he discovered an interest in technology – "Europe was a junkyard, where we could find great dumps of war equipment" – that he pursued in the 1950s, obtaining a degree in industrial engineering. Already branching out, he was also a jazz critic, a poet, and a photographer, who turned to filmmaking in 1960. Several years after he met Steina in Prague he moved to Iceland (where he married Steina) and eventually changed his citizenship and name to Timoteus Petursson.

Video impressed Woody as "an energy system" – a system he and Steina soon set out to explore on

an electronic rather than photographic basis. Both were in New York by 1969, fascinated by feedback and the flexibility of half-inch tape on the Sony Portapak. Initial documentary tapes soon gave way to experimentation that was accelerated by their 1971 creation of the seminal electronic arts exhibition space called The Kitchen. With assistance from their friends, the self-taught Vasulkas learned and made scores of tapes investigating the manipulation of the video signal. By reducing that signal to its component codes, they obtained such a command over it that they could assemble volumetric forms that could be freely interpolated with photographed images.

In 1973 the Vasulkas moved again – to Buffalo; in that same year they made *Golden Voyage*, a work that illuminates some of their creative interests. The tape is unusual in that it is based upon a work from another medium, René Magritte's painting *Golden Legend*. The Belgian Surrealist had long fascinated Steina and Woody: "Magritte had stricken us as being premonial to many electronic imaging concepts." The weightless loaves of bread drifting through the space beyond the window frame is much akin to his locomotives emerging from fireplaces, downpours of bowler-hatted gentlemen, and

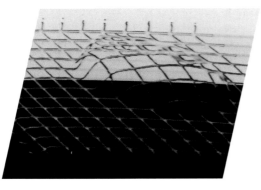

Woody Vasulka
Explanation
1974
video
color, sound
11:40 min
video still
© Woody Vasulka

Woody Vasulka
Reminiscence
1974
video
color, sound
4:50 min
video still
© Woody Vasulka

Steina Vasulka
working on the
Machine Vision project
Buffalo, 1976
photo courtesy the artist

Steina Vasulka
Machine Vision
1975–
video installation
mixed media
dimensions variable
installation view:
Albright-Knox Art Gallery,
Buffalo, 1978
detail
© the Vasulkas
photo © Kevin Noble

boulders serenely floating above the ocean. *Golden Voyage* begins as an homage to Magritte's painting, but it rapidly becomes much more. The framing window vanishes, the screen space increases in terms of depth, and the loaves cease to be just bread, becoming very suggestive of sections of the human body. The background and foreground also change, situating the loaves over the ocean, drifting them over rock-strewn plains, and along an electronically colorized coast. At times the screen "pans" and "tracks forward" with a flexibility one recognizes only after the fact. False perspective, contradictory illumination, improbable juxtaposition, and poetic harmonies punctuate *Golden Voyage* and other Vasulka tapes (just as they do Magritte's paintings).

In Buffalo, where Woody taught at the Center for Media Study, Steina plunged anew into her *Machine Vision* project, a series of tapes and installations that break ground conceptually and aesthetically. In 1978 she said: "Ordinarily the camera view is asso-ciated with a human point of view, paying attention to the human conditions around. In this series the camera conforms to a mechanized decision making of instruments, with the movements, and attention directed towards their own machine to machine observations."

From 1975 to 1977 she produced five tapes whose mechanical aspect lay not in image formation, but in alteration of photographed views (somewhat like a surveillance camera system). In some of these tapes, and then more spectacularly in her installation series *Allvision*, two or more cameras simultaneously regard each other and the external world. Displayed on side-by-side monitors (in the installation) or rapidly alternating (on the generated tapes) these works provide an encyclopedic perspective, a kind of omniscience within our grasp but slippery.

The late Marshall McLuhan's maxims about the impact of media on perception are reaffirmed by the experience of watching the Vasulkas' video work.

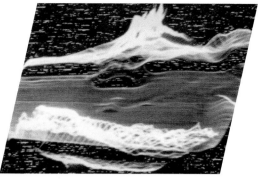

Woody Vasulka
C-Trend
1974
video
color, sound
9:47 min
video still
© Woody Vasulka

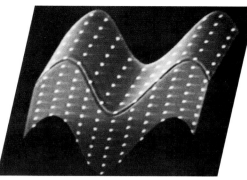

Woody Vasulka
The Matter
1974
video
color, sound
4:07 min
video still
© Woody Vasulka

Steina Vasulka
Machine Vision
1975–
video installation
mixed media
dimensions variable
installation view:
Albright-Knox Art Gallery,
Buffalo, 1978
© the Vasulkas
photo © Kevin Noble

One comes away from it with an enhanced recognition of how much we do not see, and how much effort must be expended to gain a wider vision.

In 1978, shortly before they left Buffalo for Santa Fe, where they continue to work, the Vasulkas assembled a remarkable series of programs for broadcast. Initially shown on WNED in Buffalo, the six half-hour programs (funded by the NEA and CPB) survey their work over the preceding ten years. Extracts from many of their tapes are included with explanations of how they were made.

Process, as much as product, intrigues the Vasulkas and dominates the programs, but never at the expense of being submerged by jargon. Woody explains some of the most cryptic images with disarming candor: "I always wanted to make an object on the surface of a sphere." Steina, discussing the effect of a switcher, says the signal was "flip-flopped," being clear but never condescending.

What is most striking about the series is the sense of how the Vasulkas have become almost inseparable from their machines, how they see with rather than through their television equipment. And how art and technology are also intertwined, indivisible, one.

Robert A. Haller
Manuscript from 1981.

Woody Vasulka
Art of Memory
1987
video
color, sound
36 min
video stills in
simulated environment
San Francisco Museum of
Modern Art, Accessions
Committee Fund
© Woody Vasulka

Steina and
Woody Vasulka
in their studio.
Buffalo,
New York, 1977

Woody Vasulka
study for
Theater of Hybrid Automata
1991
computer image
© Woody Vasulka

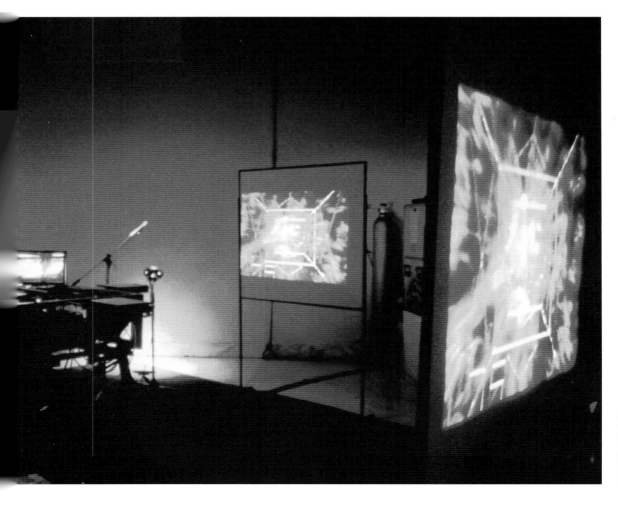

Woody Vasulka
Table III
1994
mixed media
dimensions variable
installation view
© Woody Vasulka
photo courtesy Thomas Ruler

Michele Pierson
Public Image

"And the future? The future of the cinema is usually an occasion for depressing prophecies. How much more comfortable the past looks."[1]

"The glamour of Hollywood and its legendary fortunes still dominate the public image of film."[2]

1 Gavin Lambert, "A last look around," in *Sequence*, no. 14, 1952.

2 Peter Feinstein (ed.), *The Independent Film Community: A Report on the Status of Independent Film in the United States,* Prepared by the Committee on Film and Television Resources and Services, Anthology Film Archives, New York, 1977.

3 This phrase is taken from Malcolm Le Grice's essay "The History We Need" of 1979. His arguments are dealt with later in the present essay. See Malcolm Le Grice, *Experimental Cinema in the Digital Age*, BFI Publishing, London, 2001.

4 See Lewis Jacobs, "Experimental Cinema in America," in *The Rise of the American Film*, Teachers College Press, New York, 1968, 2nd edition, pp. 543–582; David Curtis, *Experimental Cinema: A Fifty Year Evolution*, Studio Vista, London, 1971; Patricia Zimmerman, *Reel Families: A Social History of Amateur Film*, Indiana University Press, Bloomington and Indianapolis, 1995; Jan-Christopher Horak (ed.), *Lovers of Cinema: The First American Film Avant-Garde, 1919–1945*, University of Wisconsin Press, Madison, 1995. Also see Bruce Posner (ed.), *Unseen Cinema: Early American Avant-Garde Film 1893–1941*, Black Thistle Press/Anthology Film Archives, New York, 2001. Unseen Cinema is the catalogue for a retrospective of early American avant-garde films. The exhibition of twenty programs was first screened at the 23rd Moscow International Film Festival in June 2001, followed by an exhibition at The Whitney Museum of American Art between 14 July and 9 September 2001. Four programs of films were screened at the 49th Sydney International Film Festival (14–18 June 2002). Full details of programs and an international touring schedule for June 2001 to December 2005 are available online at: http://www.roberthaller.com/unseen/unseen.html

Like any other institution, the cinema is sustained only by being accessible to a public. The minimum, if still insufficient, conditions of this accessibility are distribution and exhibition. All cinemas – popular cinemas, art cinemas, underground cinemas – need to be seen. It is well known that the key to the Hollywood entertainment industry's commercial success is an integrated system of production, distribution and exhibition. To ensure that Hollywood films receive the greatest possible exposure in both domestic and foreign markets, this system requires a level of capital expenditure that far exceeds the resources of any other film industry in the world. Of course, exposure and accessibility are not the same thing. Hollywood's great success has been in producing a cinema that makes each and every audience member a critic. Was the film fun? Did it offer a sufficiently novel take on the genre? Was it as psychologically absorbing, richly imagined, and/or allusive as the novel, comic, or computer game? Were the performances, special effects, sets, impressive? Should Jim Carey ever be cast in a dramatic role? In any role? If Hollywood has more than once been accused of being "the slave of the public," it is no wonder that the public have taken so much satisfaction from this arrangement. And no wonder too, that the knowledge that cinema is a public institution has often been unhappy.

The circumstances in which film viewers have come to take so much pleasure from knowing about the Hollywood film industry – and, in particular, how individuals such as stars or directors operate within it – have been more or less in place since the mid-1920s. Along with the distribution companies' own promotion of the industry's cinematic achievements, and the routinely uncritical review of Hollywood films in the mass media, a range of more specialist publications have solicited film viewers' desire to look "behind the scenes" of moviemaking. Although the fan magazines maintained their cozy relationship with the studios only by distancing themselves from the more salacious gossip peddled by the scandal rags, both made stories about the personal lives of stars a source of pleasurable speculation for their movie-mad readerships. For the more technically minded, there was *American Cinematographer,* which offered tips for the amateur filmmaker alongside information about the tools and techniques of professional film production. In the late 1920s, the amateur ciné club movement was itself instrumental in cultivating a

wider appreciation of Hollywood expertise and craftsmanship through its many social activities and publications. Nurturing the hope that, with dedicated application, amateur filmmaking might yet lead to a career in Hollywood, amateur film magazines ran columns offering hints from professionals about how to give amateur films a more professional look; special features on amateurs who had "made it" in Hollywood; and competitions and schemes offering amateurs the chance to sell their films to the studios.

By the late 1920s, public attachment to the kind of cinema produced by Hollywood had taken root and expression in a range of social activities. All attempts by filmmakers to imagine that the cinema might be different – not just from Hollywood but also from those forms of narrative cinema that emerged from the flow of traffic in people and ideas between Hollywood and the film industries of Europe and Asia – have been undertaken in the knowledge that these efforts could count on not being able to attract the same level of public interest. There have always been filmmakers who have felt drawn to experiment with cinematic duration, narration, performance and expression. Thirty years after the first films were shown to a commercial audience, there were voices enough to ask: What else might cinema be? However, creating a public culture capable of sustaining ongoing experiment has been another matter altogether. As film and media scholars, teachers, museum programmers and digital-arts practitioners peer into the future, finding the "history we need"[3] becomes more than ever a matter of recovering something of the institutional and cultural contexts in which experimental film cultures have flourished and faltered.

Histories of the European avant-garde and American experimental cinemas have identified the emergence of film societies, specialist film magazines, and "little theaters" devoted to experimental programming as the basis for the development of a dedicated audience for avant-garde and experimental films in the 1920s. If in the United States the amateur ciné club movement appeared already to be in cahoots with Hollywood to determine the future of cinema, the high level of mobility between amateur and experimental film cultures in those days is one of the most interesting aspects of American experimental-cinema history to have emerged from research by scholars such as Lewis Jacobs, David Curtis, Patricia Zimmerman and Jan-Christopher Horak.[4] Not only did the theaters showing European and American "art films" open their programs to amateurs with limited formal education in the arts, but through their screenings and lending libraries, the ciné clubs themselves provided an important exhibition circuit for filmmakers not otherwise involved in the amateur film movement. A magazine such as *Amateur Movie Journal* – which boasted that it was "Published in Hollywood: The Home of the Movies" – was perfectly adept at promoting the view that amateur filmmaking offered aspiring professionals the opportunity to "make themselves acquainted with the intrigue and 'mystifying' phases of the business and become more qualified for [their] new vocation," yet at the same time encouraging the same filmmakers to exercise the amateur's greater freedom to experiment.5 Although film historians generally agree that the amateur film movement became progressively less interested in pursuing the path of art and experiment during the 1930s, reports on the opening of new art cinema theaters continued to appear in amateur film magazines well into the next decade.6

For a brief moment in the history of American cinema, a culture existed in which cinematic experiment was given popular support. Significantly, this support was not predicated on a rejection of Hollywood, but on the cultivation of an appreciation of the multiple possibilities of cinematic expression. Comparative cultural histories of the relation between amateur and experimental film cultures in Britain and Europe remain to be written. Although the amateur film movement in Britain attracted interest and support from critics and filmmakers with very different ideas about how it might contribute to a national film culture, some were more directly involved in trying to shape amateurs' perceptions of the kind of filmmaking they could aspire to than others. The fact that *The Era* magazine was not a film publication, let alone an amateur film magazine, makes its involvement in amateur filmmaking all the more interesting. In its columnist Marjorie A. Lovell Burgess, *The Era* certainly had a genuine "amateur ciné" enthusiast. In 1931 she persuaded the magazine's publishers to sponsor a competition (The Era Challenge Cup) to "determine" the best amateur film of the year. Over the same year, she also undertook the task of writing a book that would not only offer a critical appraisal of the movement to date, but would ideally help to steer a course for the future.7

This future is glossed in an introduction provided by *Era* editor G. A. Atkinson, in which he explains that it is his own publication's intimate involvement in "the movement that might be called the 'discovery' of England," that has brought it to the assistance of amateur filmmaking.8 Within the broader framework of this movement, a whole range of aesthetic practices and leisure activities became conscripts in a project to fend off the forces of modernization, internationalism and mass consumption through the popularization of a "ruralist vision" of English culture.9 Both Atkinson and Burgess were strongly committed to the idea that not the least of the social benefits of amateur filmmaking was its potential for getting people into the countryside, where they could "see the stars," and discover for themselves the emotional quality and heritage significance of the English landscape. Not surprisingly, a movement that saw amateur filmmaking as another way of bringing England home to the English – of helping to shape the public image of the nation and the English national character – did what it could to turn amateur filmmakers

away from any form of cinematic experiment. And instead encouraged them, to seek creative outlet in the production of health, educational and "interest" films.

Not that all amateurs were to be so dissuaded. In the late 1940s, for instance, the Experimental Film Group at Oxford University had a number of successes with films entered in national competitions. But while screenings of competition-winners toured widely in Britain, there was no form of theatrical exhibition for amateur films, and no forum for bringing amateur filmmakers together with directors working independently of the organized ciné club movement. Without being able to create any kind of shared exhibition circuit for amateur and independent film, or to imagine how, and in what contexts, differences between the social and aesthetic aspirations of these two filmmaking cultures might be addressed, the parameters for amateur experiment grew increasingly narrow.

In Britain, as elsewhere, the most widely exhibited experimental films of the 1930s were advertising films. A 1935 article in *World Film News* ventured to suggest that the "much abused" advertising film may yet be about to "come into its own" under the distinguished direction of filmmakers such as Oskar Fischinger, George Pal, Ub Iwerks and Len Lye.10 This aesthetic revolution in advertising films would be one, moreover, that brought experimental work out of the film societies and into wider public exhibition. Lye's success at the 1935 Brussels International Film Festival with *A Colour Box* (1935), and his plans for the forthcoming *Rainbow Dance* (1936) – both produced by the GPO Film Unit headed by John Grierson – receive special mention for helping to raise the international profile and technical standards of British publicity films. The GPO Film Unit gave *A Colour Box*, which uses the technique of painting directly on celluloid to transform the most minutely arranged patterns of colour into dynamic, light-textured animations, a public life, and provided Lye with the opportunity for further experiment. In *Rainbow Dance,* he experimented with a technique used by Fischinger, to exploit the three-color Gasparcolor film-processing system to color black-and-white live-action footage without using an additive process. It was another advertising film, however, that proved to be the most popular with cinema audiences.

Lye's biographer, Roger Horrocks, estimates that the stop-motion animation film *The Birth of the Robot* (1936) was seen by over three million people in 329 British cinemas.11 With its beautifully articulated puppets, anthropomorphic auto, and handdrawn animation adding whimsical details, it is not hard to see why this fairytale about the birth of the modern world delighted audiences. But this film, perhaps too, most clearly demonstrates the productive limits of the advertising film. Someone like Grierson, whose career as a producer of documentary films began with the British government's Empire Marketing Board, regarded some form of indenture – whether in the form of state or corporate sponsorship – to be an unavoidable condition of independent filmmaking in the 1930s. When he was later given the opportunity to reflect on his years with the EMB Film Unit, he would repeat that "[t]here is money for films which will make box-office profits, and there is money for films which will create propaganda results. These only. They are the strict limits within which cinema has had to develop and will continue to develop."12 Since the propaganda result sought by the advertising film was to bring prestige to sponsors and enable cinema audiences to associ-

5 The editorial for the first edition of the magazine advised readers that, "[t]he Editor, in fact, is of the firm belief [that] within a short time the amateur movie-makers will be paving the way for the professionals and shaping the new destiny of the silent drama. The amateur is not limited by the many handicaps which restrict the professional film producers. The amateur has only himself to please. He does not have to play down to the general public. The amateur can afford to take a chance, to originate, create, do something different," *Amateur Movie Journal*, vol. 1, no. 1, April 1928, p. 5. The most widely read amateur film magazine in the United States was *Amateur Movie Makers*, which was published by the Amateur Cinema League. Although a national publication, the fact that it was published in New York opened the door for a West Coast publication like *Amateur Movie Journal*.

6 *Cine-grams*, for instance, published a report on Paul Johnston's plans to open the Cinéarts Theatre in New York in 1947, and announced that the "plan of operation calls for sale of subscriptions to a series of no more than five programs, to be given once a week" ("16mm Experimental Theatre," *Cine-grams*, vol. 3, no. 1, October 1947, p. 15).

7 Marjorie A. Lovell Burgess, *Amateur Ciné Movement in Great Britain*, Sampson Low, Marston & Co. Ltd., London, 1932.

8 G. A. Atkinson, Introduction, in Burges, op. cit., p. XI.

9 For a broad historical overview of this movement see Alun Howkins, "The Discovery of Rural England," in *Englishness: Politics and Culture, 1880–1920*, Robert Colls and Philip Dodd (eds), Croom Helm, London and Dover, NH, 1986, pp. 62–87. My own encounter with this work has come through Andrew Higson's writing on the British heritage film. See his "The Heritage Film, British Cinema, and the National past: Comin' Thro' The Rye," in *Waving the Flag: Constructing a National Cinema in Britain*, Clarendon Press, Oxford, 1995, pp. 26–97.

10 "Avant-garde to the Rescue: Revolution in Advertising Films," in *World Film News*, April 1936. Reprinted in *Traditions of Independence: British Cinema in the Thirties*, Don MacPherson (ed.), BFI Publishing, London, 1980, pp. 183–184.

11 Roger Horrocks, *Len Lye: A Biography*, University of Auckland Press, Auckland, 2001, p. 147.

12 John Grierson, "The E.M.B. Film Unit," in *Grierson on Documentary*, Forsyth Hardy (ed.), Faber and Faber, London and Boston, 1979, p. 48.

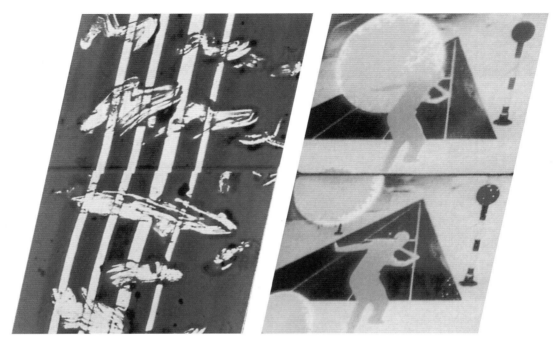

Len Lye
A Colour Box
1935
35mm film
color
4 min
film stills

Len Lye
Rainbow Dance
1936
35mm film
Gasparcolor film
5 min
film stills

ate a particular product with an experience of happiness, filmmakers working with this form enjoyed considerable creative license.13 At the same time, the expectation that these films would have immediate and universal appeal imposed limitations of its own. The reason the advertising and special effects industries have so often shared techniques and personnel is because novelty tempered by charm is still the surest way to delight an audience in under five minutes. There is little question that these little movies have sometimes recast film in surprising ways, bringing happiness to audiences, and variously inspiring the filmmakers among them to imitation, interpretation, and invention. Whether these movies at any time in their long history also aroused an appetite in the uninitiated for more demanding, less solicitous forms of experimental film, seems less certain: so fleetingly did they demand audiences' attention.

Both advertising and amateurism have provided individual filmmakers with opportunities to experiment, but for different reasons both have been limited in their ability to have an impact on the public image of experimental film. Although some American filmmakers have tried to reclaim the romantic spirit of the amateur for their own filmmaking practices, these kinds of gestures have tended to be more polemical and utopian than expressive of any real identification with the vast majority of home moviemakers. As late as the 1960s, filmmakers, critics and audiences alike were likely to regard as contentious just about any term describing filmmakers working not merely outside a commercial context but in tension if not outright opposition to the conventions of commercial filmmaking. Toward the end of that

decade, Stan Brakhage pointed out that as his own films – made alone, at home, and with no expectation that they would have any commercial value – came to be valued and achieved a "public life," his critics alternately described him as a "professional," "artist," and "amateur." As Maya Deren had done before him, Brakhage chose to align his work with amateurism, even though, as he says, "it is most often used in criticism of the work I have done by those who don't understand it."14 In the 1950s and 1960s, this derogatory use of the term, so easily and summarily deployed by critics who found themselves faced with films for which they had no familiar frame of reference, made it impossible for individuals to positively inflect the public perception of experimental film by associating it with amateurism. Even Deren, who in her role as a public defender of the avant-garde, was often concerned to draw parallels between the circumstances of her own filmmaking practice, and those of the amateur filmmaker more interested in making "a backyard movie about the kids," wasn't entirely able to rid her own writing of criticism of "amateurish" works. More often than not, Deren found it necessary to insist that film advances as an art only though the efforts of individuals prepared to exercise the discipline necessary to turn the first flush of aesthetic inspiration and engagement into an aesthetic practice.

Whether the received history of the European avant-garde will itself undergo revision in the future, it has often been taken for granted that because so many avant-garde filmmakers came to film through the visual arts, it made sense for them to articulate their own aesthetic practice in relation to the aesthetic movements now collectively associated with

13 Horrocks points out that "[t]he newly developed field of public relations acknowledged the value of 'soft sell' advertising in such forms as the prestige film which collected prizes and good reviews and gained a warm welcome from cinemas and community groups." (Horrocks, op. cit., p. 142).

14 Stan Brakhage, "In Defense of Amateur," in *Brakhage Scrapbook: Collected Writings 1964-1980*, Robert Haller [ed.], Documentext, New Paltz, New York, 1982, p. 162.

top
Maya Deren with
Alexander Hammid
Meshes of the Afternoon
1943
16mm film
b/w, silent
(sound added in 1959)
13:45 min
film still

bottom
Maya Deren
Ritual in Transfigured Time
1945–1946
16mm film
b/w, silent
14:30 min
film still
courtesy Anthology Film Archive
and Catrina Neimann

European modernism. In a history of the avant-garde written to accompany the first "Art in Cinema" series organized by Frank Stauffacher, Richard Foster, and George Leite at the San Francisco Museum of Modern Art in 1946, Hans Richter went so far as to suggest that, in fact, "[t]he Avantgarde Movement may be historically regarded as an outgrowth of Modern Art, even if it belongs technically to the film."[15] Notwithstanding the revision that the history of the American avant-garde has undergone in recent years, it remains the case that several American and British experimental filmmakers similarly came to filmmaking through the visual arts. More importantly, the articulation of an international tradition of "art in cinema," has not only provided a model for the exhibition of experimental film, but the basis for almost all programs in public education. In terms both of bringing European avant-garde and American experimental cinema to a wider audience, as well as of inspiring visual artists to see film as a medium for experimenting with new ideas, the "Art in Cinema" series that ran at SFMOMA from the mid-1940s to the early 1950s has been widely recognized by film historians as one of the most important and successful programs of its kind.

It was always difficult for filmmakers working in America to attract funding for experimental films. But before the establishment of funding programs by the National Endowment for the Arts (NEA) and the American Film Institute (AFI) in the mid-1960s, the chances of financial support for experimental film production were even more remote. Oskar Fischinger and Jordan Belson number among the few filmmakers to receive such support in the post-war period, both receiving fellowships from the Guggenheim Foundation's Museum of Non-Objective Painting, curated by Hilla Rebay. Since the vast majority of filmmakers had no expectation of attracting financial assistance for film production, any hope of financial remuneration rested on finding some form of distribution and exhibition for their films. In the early 1960s, Stan VanDerBeek gave voice to the hope, perhaps even then only faintly imagined, that private art galleries might become places where films could not only be screened, but where prints would also be available for sale. The idea that, like etchings or lithographs, films could be "become 'objects' to own and appreciate," was one that failed to fully appreciate the vast differences between public and private forms of exhibition.[16] Far more prohibitive for this scheme than the mechanics of making prints and screening films within the gallery space itself were the circumstances of home projection, which not only required cumbesome, noisy and obtrusive equipment but were unlikely to be able to reproduce the social ambience and public theater of the gallery. Only the rare archivist among collectors takes a keen pleasure in the records of objects rarely, if ever, viewed.

VanDerBeek's proposal for generating interest in – and revenue from – experimental filmmaking may have always been unlikely to benefit more than a handful of filmmakers, but his concern that filmmakers find a public image for experimental film capable of generating and sustaining some form of distribution and exhibition has been a constant in the history of experimental cinema. Leaving aside the special but not entirely separate categories of educational and industrial films, which have tended to be made for an

15 Hans Richter, "A History of the Avantgarde," in *Art in Cinema: A Symposium on the avantgarde film*, authorized reprint edition, Frank Stauffacher (ed.), Arno Press, New York, 1968, p. 21.

16 VanDerBeek's suggestions appeared in Jonas Mekas's "Movie Journal" review column, published in *Village Voice*, 4 March, 1961. Reprinted in Jonas Mekas, *The Village Voice, Movie Journal 1958–1977*, vol. 1, Anthology Archives, New York, 1994, p. 76.

Stan VanDerBeek standing in front of his specially constructed projection room near his home outside New York City. orig. printed in Kranz, Stewart, *Science & Technology in the Arts. A tour through the realm of science + art*, Van Nostrand Reinhold Company, New York, 1974, p.237 photo © Art in America

17 Grace L. McCann Morley, foreword to *Art in Cinema: A Symposium on the avant-garde film*, op. cit., p. 1.

18 Malcolm Le Grice, "Presenting Avant-Garde Film in London," in *Experimental Cinema in the Digital Age*, op. cit., p. 28.

19 "Shoot, Shoot, Shoot," a retrospective of the first decade of the London Film-Makers' Co-Operative and British Avant-garde film 1966-1976, screened at the Tate Modern on 3–29 May 2002. Six programs of films were also screened at the 11th Brisbane International Film Festival, 11–18 July 2002. Details of international touring schedule available online: http://www.tate.org.uk/modern/programmes/shootshoot shoot.htm

20 Not the least of the delights of the "Shoot, Shoot, Shoot" retrospective is the meticulously researched catalogue compiled and edited by curator Mark Webber, with assistance from Gregory Kurcewicz and Ben Cook.

21 The New York Film-Makers' Co-Operative was established in 1962. Mekas' comments on the principles of co-operative distribution appear in an "Open Letter to Film-makers of the World," *Cinim*, no. 1, 1966, pp. 5-8. Lasting for only three issues, *Cinim* was published by the newly established London Film-Makers' Co-Operative.

22 Malcolm Le Grice, *Abstract Film and Beyond*, The MIT Press, Cambridge, MA, 1977.

23 Deren's strongest criticisms did not appear in the *Village Voice*, but were later published in *Film Culture*, no. 39, Winter 1965, pp. 49–54.

existing (often state-sponsored) market, examination of the first half-century of cinema would suggest that there have only ever been two models for interesting new audiences in experimental filmmaking. Instead of the commodification and privatization of experimental film along the lines suggested by VanDerBeek, the "art in cinema" model has sought the inscription of experimental film within a publicly recognizable version of cinema history. Its strategies have been those of traditional art history: the identification of aesthetic traditions and movements, the cultivation of an appreciation of formal innovation within historically defined limits, and the formation of canons. As a model for the museum, its mission statement has been to "keep the public in close and constant contact with the 'growing edge' of creative living art."[17] Nor has it necessarily been the larger public institutions that have taken on the role of producing a coherent tradition for experimental film. In his 1974 essay "Presenting Avant-Garde Film in London," Malcolm Le Grice noted that "[i]n the last few years, when the British avant-garde film has generally become very strong, at least two major institutions, the Tate and ICA, should be censured for not having made any real contribution to its presentation."[18] Films produced during the first decade of the London Film-Makers' Co-Operative (1966-1976) would not receive a major exhibition at the Tate Modern until 2002.[19] In the 1960s and 1970s, programs of these films were shown at art cinemas, avant-garde galleries and, on occasion, town halls.[20]

The cultivation of a public image for experimental cinema based on the model of "art in cinema" has also enabled experimental film to find exhibition through university film clubs and courses, and very occasionally, international film festivals. The co-operative model of film distribution deliberately severed distribution from promotion. As Jonas Mekas – filmmaker and critic, journal editor, and founding member of the New York Film-Makers' Co-Operative – explained in 1966, the cooperative spirit seeks to eliminate the element of competitive, commercial enterprise from film distribution.[21] In the 1960s and 1970s, the estab-

lishment of film co-ops around the world made experimental films available to a variety of public and private institutions. How these institutions chose to present these films – how programs were decided and what commentary, if any, would accompany a presentation – was left entirely to the discretion of exhibitors. For the university film course as much as the art gallery, programs of experimental film organized along the lines of "history of art in cinema" were nevertheless seen as vital for providing audiences with a set of terms for their aesthetic evaluation and appreciation. If the broader principles and assumptions governing this model have remained fairly constant, it has also lent itself to more, and less, inclusive versions of this history. Le Grice, for instance, was along with Peter Gidal concerned throughout the 1960s and 1970s to trace the development of an experimental film practice able to be described as "genuinely cinematographic in concept."[22] For Le Grice, this meant a practice that, by exploring the material substance and spatio-temporal possibilities of "film as film," sought to supplant the dominant preoccupation with illusionist representation and narrative.

The variety of concerns explored under the aegis of experimental cinema meant, however, that not all experiments were able to be accommodated within the broader framework of the history of "art in cinema." Another model for the public presentation of experimental cinema was variously offered in the form of a "personal," "underground," or simply "independent" cinema. When Deren was invited by Mekas to take over his "Movie Journal" column in the *Village Voice* for a short period in 1960, she took the opportunity to question his championing of films such as *Shadows* (John Cassavetes, 1957/1959), and *Pull My Daisy* (Robert Frank / Alfred Leslie, 1959), as the harbingers of a new, "personal cinema." Of particular concern to Deren at this point in her career was Mekas's use of terms like "purity," "honesty," "sincerity," "realism" and "truthfulness to life" to describe the qualities of this new cinema. After all, she wondered, wasn't art something that could not fail to be "artificial" and "constructed?"[23] In their public exchanges, both

Malcolm Le Grice
Berlin Horse
1970
16mm film for projection onto
one or two screens
b/w, color, sound
8 min
film stills

Mekas and Deren failed to address the most interesting aspects of their criticism of the other's passionately held views on the nature of film as an aesthetic practice. In response to the criticism that the films he loved lacked technical proficiency and the discipline to turn inspiration into art, Mekas countered that the experiences these films offered were of an altogether different order. But along the way, he also missed Deren's perceptive interrogation of the assumptions his own theory of art made about the nature of subjectivity, identity and personal creation.

Deren for her part failed to grasp the social significance of a cinema which, along with the hand-painted films of Brakhage and the animated collages of Vanderbeek, could accommodate the very different filmmaking concerns of a Kenneth Anger or Ron Rice – or of a George Kuchar who once claimed that any movie of his had to be a "*Reader's Digest* condensation of a Hollywood life."[24] Explicitly conceived as an alternative to a model of experimental cinema that would subsume it to a history of "art in cinema," Mekas' vision for this cinema of personal, "poetic" expression was broadly inclusive. As Maureen Turim has judiciously pointed out, any limits that he put on this inclusivity were as much socially and historically determined, as they were personal and idiosyncratic.[25] For like others of his generation, Mekas was slow to recognize the extent to which the films that seemed to him the most sincere forms of personal expression were – in their choice of subject matter and symbolist layering of imagery – deeply, unavoidably, gendered. The significance of this model for a personal cinema lay in its embrace of all manner of experiments with cinematic expression: allowing, for instance, for the reconceptualization and reconfiguration of such diverse forms as the home-movie (as it is remembered in Mekas's diary films or some of Brakhage's films); or the education or industrial film (as it is encountered, for instance, in a film like Standish B. Lawder's *Dangling Participle* [1970]); or even the Hollywood melodrama or B-grade science fiction film (which meet their domestic undoing in the films of George and Mike Kuchar).[26] This was a permissive cinema, a cinema that was above all concerned with eliciting an intensely felt response from its audience.

Although the idea of a personal cinema was taken up by other film critics and even some institutions, by the mid-1970s the films associated with this cinema were more likely to be identified by the more neutral description of "independent film." Retaining the former's emphasis on personal autonomy and creative freedom, the term "independent cinema" was originally intended to imply "that a single individual has primary and unquestioned creative control over the production of a film."[27] From the beginning, the choice to articulate an experimental film practice under the umbrella term of an "independent cinema" had both advantages and disadvantages. For the obvious price of inclusivity was a weakening of the distinctiveness of the public image of experimental film. On the other hand, recent efforts to recover more detailed information about the history of independent film exhibition indicate that as far as audiences are concerned, eclecticism may itself be regarded as highly desirable. Scott MacDonald's extensive archival research into the history of Cinema 16 – a subscription based film society that held screenings of independent films at a number of venues in New York between 1947 and 1963 – makes the point that diversity was seen by its programmers, Amos Vogel and Jack Goelman, to be the key to accessibility.[28] In conversation with MacDonald many years after Cinema 16 had folded, Vogel attributed the film society's longevity to the fact that its programming offered audiences "a *mix*, an eclectic mix of documentaries, scientific films, more conventional narrative shorts, animations, and avant-garde films."[29]

The film societies that survived into the 1970s were for the most part confined to the college campus. At a time when opportunities for its distribution and exhibition were increasingly being limited to the museum, university, or library program, a committee of American filmmakers, scholars, museum directors, and archivists came together in 1977 to address the difficulties of building a public image – and culture – for independent film.[30] While video was still new

24 Interview with Sheldon Renan, *Film Culture*, no. 47, Summer 1967. Author file, The New York Public Library for the Performing Arts.

25 Maureen Turim, "Reminiscences, Subjectivities, and Truths," in *To Free the Cinema: Jonas Mekas and the New York Underground*, David E. James (ed.), Princeton University Press, Princeton, 1992, pp. 192–211.

26 For another account of experimental filmmaking in the sixties, see "Peter Weibel, Narrated Theory: Multiple Projection and Multiple Narration (Past and Future)," in *New Screen Media: Cinema/Art/Narrative*, Martin Rieser and Andrea Zapp (eds), BFI Publishing, London, 2002, pp. 42–53.

27 *The Independent Film Community: A Report on the Status of Independent Film in the United States* (see Note 1).

28 Scott MacDonald, *Cinema 16: Documents Toward a History of the Film Society*, Temple University Press, Philadelphia, 2002, p. 57.

29 Scott MacDonald, op. cit., p. 57.

30 Feinstein, op. cit.

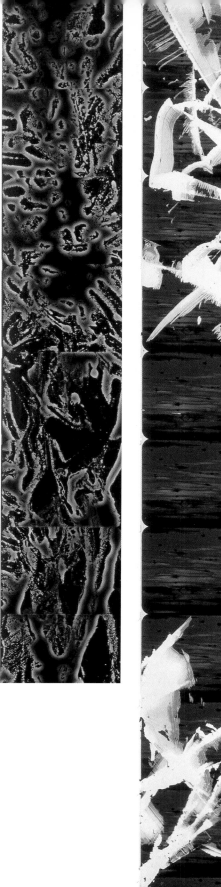

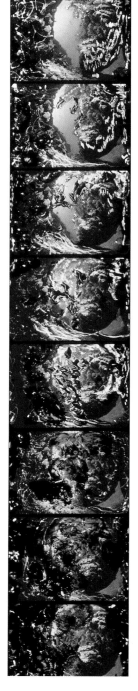

from left to right
Stan Brakhage
Coupling
1999
16mm film
color, silent
4 min
film strip
© Stan Brakhage

Stan Brakhage
"..." (Ellipses) Reel 2
1998
16mm film
color, silent
15 min
film strip
© Stan Brakhage

Stan Brakhage
"..." (Ellipses) Reel 3
1998
16mm film
color, silent
15 min
film strip
© Stan Brakhage

Stan Brakhage
"existence is song"
1987
the fourth and final section of
The Dante Quartet
16mm film
color, silent
8 min
film strip
© Stan Brakhage

Stan Brakhage
Creation
1979
16mm film
color, silent
17 min
film stills
© Stan Brakhage

Stan Brakhage
*Visions in Meditation #3:
Plato's Cave*
1990
16mm film
color, sound
8 min
film stills
© Stan Brakhage

enough to be regarded as a potential mode of distribution, commercial and public television had already been identified as having limited scope for effecting change. Twenty years on, it would be the Internet, not video, which would hold out the possibility of a revitalized experimental film culture. Indeed, the World Wide Web is unusually suited to cater for Vogel's sense that an environment able to offer a broad range of aesthetic forms and practices has the best chance of holding the attention of the fidgety and curious filmgoer in search of new kinds of aesthetic experiences.

For a while now, the World Wide Web has been host to a range of experiments in digital film at sites such as The New Venue, plugincinema, and The Bit Screen.31 Over and above the types of experiments actually being explored at these sites — which range from formal considerations of the limits of producing moving images for current home-delivery systems, to explorations of the aesthetic and affective potential of multi-authored, random, or multiform narratives — the interest of these sites lies in their rearticulation of the public image of experimental film to meet the

needs not just of the fidgety and curious, but of a new "producing public." Filmmakers and potential filmmakers, whether "professional," "student," "amateur," or "independent," have always been an important audience for experimental film: their attachment forged through an intimate appreciation of the issues and challenges faced at every level of the production process. In the past, however, one of the factors making it difficult to sustain audiences consisting largely of producers and potential producers has been the high cost of securing exhibition space (and this has been the case with or without state sponsorship). The social allure of the cinematic event, which brings viewers together in a public setting, has not been entirely lost to these kinds of initiatives either. The Bit Screen, for instance, has sought to diversify exhibition practices by bringing programs of web films to film festivals and galleries in the form of the traveling exhibition "Streaming Cinema."32 Amidst the Hollywood features, student shorts, Star Wars fan films, and amateur porn, there is evidence enough on the web to suggest that the future of cinema is far from past.

31 The New Venue available online: http://www.new venue.com; Plugincinema available online: http://www.plugincinema.com/plugin/index.htm; The Bit Screen available online: http://www.thebit screen.com

32 "Streaming Cinema" is a production of Druid Media and The Bit Screen. Information available online: http://www. streaming cine.com/

Painting, the Power of Illusion and the Moving Pictures

Film should transport more than just a linear narrative. In recent works, therefore, artists have experimented with the installative, space-filling potential of the medium. One such experiment involves a projection screen being placed diagonally in the space and the same film being shown on both sides – on one side the mirror-inverted image. Another possibility is a projection that strays beyond the expected boundaries of the screen and overlaps a narrow strip of the ceiling or adjoining wall. The projection itself can occur at an angle, casting a distorted image onto the main wall. Displacement effects can be produced through the staggered installation of video beamers or the alteration of projector lenses. Images can also be made to fall on the floor or ceiling, or be cast onto physical objects whereby these objects are reinterpreted in some way. It can be seen that multi-projection installations occupy a particularly prominent position in this field. Here, the narrative can be related from different camera perspectives and angles at the same time, thus breaking the linearity of the conventional film presentation. The projections can be screened next to or diametrically opposite one another or be shown on three or four adjoining surfaces at right angles to each other. They can, however, cover all the walls in the space or be installed seemingly at random. The parallel nature of the simultaneous film presentation demands active viewing on the part of the observer, which leads to a fundamental change in his role as regards the meaning of the film. Screening a number of projections at the same time is a form of fragmentation that allows a greater number of images to be shown, including shots which at first glance do not seem significant but rather serve to maintain a layer of obscurity. Working with multiple narrative levels makes it possible to show objective and subjective perspectives on one and the same story simultaneously, and similarly to merge disparate pieces of information, whether real or fictional. This is intended to stimulate the viewer to envisage his own concept of reality.

Spatial Concepts

To attempt to apprehend something in its entirety by using two or more projections either opposite or next to one another is by no means new. And the fact that every thing has many sides was a preoccupation of artists even before Picasso. In depictions of landscapes, the attempt to create a circular pictorial record is manifest from a very early date. Examples of total views composed of diametrically opposite images are Augustin Hirschvogel's townscapes from 1547, showing Vienna from both north and south, and Hanns Lautensack's views of Nuremberg that capture the city in parallel perspectival images of 180 degrees each. This led in the eighteenth century to the creation of pictorial records from four directions, such as Emanuel Büchel's cityscapes of Basle (1743–1747), Johann Jakob Keller's depiction of Zurich (1778–1783) and Heinrich Keller's circular view from various horizontal perspectives in his series of etchings *View from the Rigi Mountain,* published in 1807. It is simply not possible to see everything all at once, neither in real life nor in these works of graphic art or in panoramas, and even modern film installations cannot achieve this. On the contrary, they only confirm that the total view remains an illusion.

The forerunner of the modern installation, and the subject of repeated reinvention in modern media, was the Panorama, a popular form of mass entertainment in the nineteenth century. The Panorama was invented in 1787 by the Irishman Robert Barker. The invention was patented and was as well received as James Watt's invention of the steam engine in 1769; both are expressions of a new world view. The aim of the circular painting was to widen the field of perception both in space and time. The viewer stood at the midpoint of the circular painting and was deceived into believing that he was directly taking part in the scene: "My invention, called 'La nature à coup d'oeil'," the inventor explains in his patent specification, "is intended to make observers feel as if really on the very spot."[1] Visitors confirmed this first-hand visualization: "After five minutes one no longer sees a 'painting'; nature itself unfolds before one's very eyes. I have no doubt that the panoramas have pushed back the boundaries of painting by extending the power of illusion."[2] The objective was to create the perfect illusion. The manipulation of light played a role in this, as did the impossibility of apprehending the entire painting in one glance: the viewer had to move around in order to see it all. Cityscapes on a wide horizon were very popular themes, as were scenes depicting historical battles.

The illusionism achieved by the above means goes back to the painting of the baroque, when illusionism was already linked to the viewer's position. However it is also related to the three-dimensional perspective boxes containing interior scenes which were constructed by Dutch artists at the end of the seventeenth century; in these boxes small figures appeared life-sized. The aim of all these inventions, to which film would ultimately also belong, was to push back the boundaries of painting by extending the power of illusion.

In the early twentieth century, Lázló Moholy-Nagy was to recognize more than any other artist that light was a medium with the potential to make a com-

1 Quoted in Bruno Weber, "La nature à coup d'oeil. Wie der panoramatische Blick antizipiert wurde," in *Sehsucht. Das Panorama als Massenunterhaltung des 19. Jahrhunderts*, exhib. cat., Kunst- und Ausstellungshalle der Bundesrepublik Deutschland, Bonn, 1993, p. 21.

2 Journal des Débats, 13 May 1804, quoted in Marie-Louise von Plessen, "Der gebannte Augenblick. Die Abbildung von Realität im Panorama des 19. Jahrhunderts," in *Sehsucht*, op. cit., p. 13.

Hélio Oiticica, Neville D'Almeida
*Block Experiments in Cosmococa,
Program in Progress*
1973
here: *CC1 Trashicapes*
slide series, mattresses,
pillows, nail files, soundtrack
installation view:
Wexner Center for the Arts,
Columbus, 2001
courtesy Hélio Oiticica,
Neville D'Almeida
photo © Richard K. Loesch

pletely new type of art. He combined this knowledge with an interest in the creation of motion through technical or illusionistic means. In his *Light-Space Modulator,* also called *Light requisite for an electrical stage* (conceived in 1922, realized in 1930), the light from seventy 15-watt electrical bulbs is shone onto and through metal plates, where some areas are cut out and others are in relief. One can see the light source and the projections on the walls. As the column rotates, the play of reflections and shadows moves across the space. It is a film without images or plot: an endless loop of light. The viewer is immersed in a meditative flux that has no beginning or end. The long period of time between the conception of the object and its realization had less to do with Moholy-Nagy's inexperience with machinery and much more with the fact that the time for such an *art* object had apparently not yet come.[3]

Among the works that are regarded as foreshadowing the rediscovery of the filmic image's possibilities in the visual arts during the nineties are the multi-media installations developed by Hélio Oiticica in the early 1970s, which deal with the cinematic experience and the cinematographic image.[4] The basic idea behind his *quasi-cinemas* is the transformation from a cinema-language into a cinema-tool. The artistic strategy involves forming the work in such a way that the viewer must ultimately create the image by renouncing his traditionally passive role. The viewer can walk around in the space, recline on one of the mattresses laid out on the floor, watch the slide projections or do something completely different, such as take up the artist's invitation to file his nails with the emery boards provided (*BlockExperiments in Cosmococa, Program in Progress, CC1 Trashiscapes*, 1973). There is no real point of view; instead Oiticica seeks to discover the limits of representation. He explores the experience of simultaneity with a variety of slide projections on the walls and ceiling. He attempts to

free his photographs of all that is artificial or artistic, an effort that is reinforced by the soundtrack,[5] since music serves to remove distance. The rhythm of the projections creates an impression of quasi-animation; the bodies shown seem to be in motion. In creating his *quasi-cinemas* Oiticica is interested in the sensations of fragmentation, fusion, animation and light.

Although the above-mentioned works could appear in a formal sense to be forerunners of the room-sized film installation, there is a crucial difference in terms of their artistic assertion. Whereas the creators of all-inclusive views in previous centuries were seeking an illusionism that reflected reality, Moholy-Nagy was exploring the expressive force of abstractly directed light and Oiticica the filmic image's possibilities in the visual arts. Today's artists, on the other hand, create pictorial worlds which make the familiar seem unfamiliar or present it from an entirely different perspective. What they show is an excerpt; unlike the panoramas, they make no claim to provide a comprehensive view. Reality, fiction and surreality are interwoven in order to constitute a new narrative language. And, somewhat ironically, it is not unusual for such artistic commentaries on the position of the individual in a media-determined world, a world increasingly permeated by fictions and simulations, to be made using the very media that are at issue.

Filmstrips and Projectors

In a similar fashion to how artists in the 1960s reformulated the notion of the image by considering the constituent parts individually and then reassembling them a new way with the inclusion of the spatial component, other artists explore the material of film. An aesthetic value is recognized in the celluloid of the filmstrip and likewise in the projector, film reels and film container. The appeal of such materials, which

3 Moholy-Nagy finally realized it as a prop for his film *Light Display: Black, White, Grey* (1931). Conceived as a synthesis of light, movement, sound, film, design, architecture and theater, this film testifies to Moholy-Nagy's versatile approach to the new kinetic technology.

4 Carlos Basualdo, "Waiting for the Internal Sun: Notes on Hélio Oiticica's Quasi-cinemas," in *Hélio Oiticica. Quasi-Cinemas*, Carlos Basualdo (ed.), exhib. cat., Wexner Center for the Arts at The Ohio State University, Columbus; Whitechapel Gallery, London; Kölnischer Kunstverein, Cologne; and New Museum of Contemporary Art, New York, p. 53.

5 Mainly Brazilian folk music plus inserts of pieces by Stockhausen or Jimi Hendrix, but also street sounds or a voice reading out loud.

Nam June Paik
Zen for Film
1964
projection
performed during
New Cinema Festival I,
Filmmakers' Cinematheque,
New York, 1965
© Nam June Paik
photo © Peter Moore;
VG Bild-Kunst, Bonn 2003

Nam June Paik
Random Access
1963
sound installation
installation view: Museum of
Contemporary Arts, Chicago,
1982
© Nam June Paik

The cut-up tape composition
is hanging from the wall.
Every visitor uses the mobile
tape head to play certain
sections.

Nam June Paik
Participation TV
1963–1971
video installation
installation view: 1965
© Nam June Paik
photo © Peter Moore;
VG Bild-Kunst, Bonn 2003

Nam June Paik with magnet
ring in front of a television.
The distortion produced by
the magnet.

6 In a work bearing the
same title (*Random Access*,
1967/78) Paik stuck pieces
of audiotape onto a 15th
century handwritten score.
See also Paik's work
*A Painting which Exists 2 x 1
seconds in an Hour* (1965),
consisting of a Sony videotape case on which Paik
wrote the title of the work
and his signature.

7 Joseph Beuys, *Filz TV*, 1970,
videotape in tin box, boxing
gloves, blood sausage on
felt, oil paint stamp
(Braunkreuz).

8 Cf. *Marcel Broodthaers.
Cinéma*, exhib. cat.,
Kunsthalle Düsseldorf 1997;
Nationalgalerie Hamburger
Bahnhof Berlin 1998.

9 Julia Schmidt, "Marcel
Broodthaers' Arbeit an
einer Demontage des
Kinobildes – Zwei Prologe,"
in *Vorträge zum filmi-
schen Werk von Marcel
Broodthaers*, National-
galerie Berlin, Verlag
Walther König, Cologne,
2001, pp. 87, 90.

ages. Paik screened the unexposed filmstrip as just that, however it is not really alienated since he is still using it as a projection. Surprisingly, however, what was projected was not emptiness, as particles of dust animated the "image." In an edition entitled *Zen for Film (boxed)* (1964) the filmstrip was then exhibited in its physical materiality.

As a reaction to Paik's *Participation TV*, Beuys performed the action *Filz-TV* (Copenhagen, 14 October 1966), in which he blocked out the image on the screen with a sheet of felt. Complete denial, the zero point, is considered to be the beginning of a creative phase. This is indeed significant, because when Beuys makes use of filmic material, he generally does so regardless of the stored images. Thus he shows for example the videotape concealed in a tin box: *Filz TV* (1970).[7]

Marcel Broodthaers' interest in the cinemato-graphic image is embedded in his preoccupation with statics and motion. He too invented new possibilities for the medium of film, which he regarded as an extension of the creative means of writing, object and image. Motion is structured using photographic rather than filmic means; the film or slide sequence is projected onto inscribed, painted or structured surfaces, or into a picture frame as a constantly changing image. Taking as his starting point the projection screen painted on the wall, Broodthaers created several "Projection Paintings": canvas panels on which he projected films during various exhibitions and which could be rolled up. In his film *Une Discussion Inaugurale* (1968) he included a piece of unexposed film on which the editing instructions are written by hand. For the film *Slip-test (Dissolves)* (1975) Broodthaers mounted very short pieces of found film footage of a wrestling match in such a way that the sequential order is upset. The images "jump" as if they have got out of control. Here the focus is on the construction of film out of individual images.[8]

The theme of Broodthaers' object *La Caméra qui regarde* (1966) is the power of the camera eye, which takes possession during recording and later, when the film is projected, captivates the viewer. On the plate of a camera tripod he places the greatly enlarged eyes of a woman, conserved in jars and with an all-round perspective. The glance and the image, seeing and being seen, motion and standstill here become one. The camera object can be regarded as a "paro-distic attempt to set limits to the filmic apparatus." In this object the "stereotypical fusion of (human) eye and (technical) lens in terms of the psychology of film is completely arrested and forms [...] the visual basis of a game of optical illusion that [...] lives on the de-ceptive assumption that in things as in images there is always an inherent gaze."[9] Broodthaers explores the synthetic perception of film, which bears a risk he ultimately identifies as the emptying of seeing.

Rachel Khedoori's installations, on the other hand, are characterized by a new acknowledgement of the material of film. She makes the mechanical nature of film – the interface between actual and fictional space – an integral part of her installations. She openly displays the 35mm, 16mm and video projectors and develops space-filling constructions to play back the looped projections, turning technology into sculp-ture. The whirring of the (old-fashioned) projectors also forms an integral part of the installation. The film footage can be projected onto any part of the wall and can also be screened upside down. Khedoori makes a connection not only between the architec-ture of her constructed spaces and the architecture of the exhibition space, but also with the room shown

distract attention from the experience of the narra-tion and are therefore usually concealed, is thereby acknowledged. Bruce Nauman was one of the first artists who, rather than conceal the video projectors, instead mounted them on their empty boxes and placed them on the floor in the middle of the room. Nam June Paik, on the other hand, had already in 1963 made use of pre-recorded audiotape which he cut up into strips of different length. For his installation *Random Access* (1963 at Galerie Parnass, Wuppertal, later also entitled *Participation Music*) he hung these strips on the wall. The viewer was invited to run a playback head across the strips and in this way "com-pose" his own version of the piece within the struc-ture provided by the artist. There is no fixed "correct" order: each performance is correct and unique.[6] Tacita Dean worked on a similar principle in her 1996 piece *Untitled (Magnetic)*. She cut the soundtrack of a 16mm film into the individual words. The length of the word or sound determines the length of the magnetic track, which is here conceived as the physical embodiment of sound.

In this context it is also worth mentioning Paik's *Zen for Film* (1964), a one-hour film containing no im-

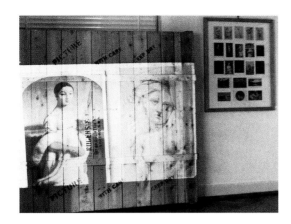

left
Marcel Broodthaers
Projection sur Caisse
[Projection on Packing Crate]
1968
installation
packing crate used as
projection screen, twenty-one
postcard reproductions in
frame, fifty slides of postcard
reproductions, texts
packing crate dimensions:
166 x 168 x 16 cm
slides and packing crate:
private collection, Brussels
postcard reproductions:
Nicole Daled Verstraeten,
Brussels
installation view: Städtisches
Museum, Mönchengladbach,
1971
© VG Bild-Kunst, Bonn 2003
photo © Ruth Kaiser

right
Marcel Broodthaers
*Une Seconde d'Eternité
(d'après une idée de
Charles Baudelaire)*
[A Second of Eternity
(After an Idea by
Charles Baudelaire)]
1970
35mm film
b/w
0:01 min
installation view:
"Prospekt 71," Kunsthalle,
Düsseldorf, 1971
© VG Bild-Kunst, Bonn 2003
photo © Manfred Tischer

in the film, which she uses as a set for the room replica. She aims to create an awareness of different filmic and actual spaces. The space can be experienced in a fictional and real sense at one and the same time and occasionally is given a further dimension by the incorporation of a mirror (*Untitled [Blue Room]*, 1999). This dimension usually leads to the irrational. In *102nd Street* (1994–97) Khedoori also exhibits the projection and visualization apparatus as sculptural elements. The 16mm film is projected as a loop into a peep-show box and angled with a slanted mirror in such a way that a double perspective is shown in the box. By allowing the means of production and reception to interconnect in this play on perceptive realities she thus unmasks the cinematographic apparatus.

Experimentation With Technological Possibilities

The exploitation of video by visual artists in the 1960s was from the beginning motivated by an experimental approach to the new medium. However, these artists were not interested in making films but in exploring new possibilities of artistic creation. The concept of interaction was joined by the concept of manipulating the image itself. This could be carried out by the viewer, such as in Nam June Paik's group of works *Participation TV*, however in most cases the artist himself performed the modulations of the technical materials.

Paik perceived *TV as a Creative Medium*, as emphasized in the title of a group exhibition in 1969.[10] Attempts to develop new aspects using television's electronic image potential led Paik to create manipulated TV pictures, incidental by-products of the process of dissolving a moving, and initially representational, image.[11] The distorted images became the real ones. Paik invited the viewer to do this himself, either by stepping on a foot pedal (1963), moving and turning a magnet across a monitor (1965), producing acoustic signals (1969) or, with the help of a closed-circuit camera and a synthesizer, by altering the color, form or order of existing filmed images. He put together a "highly complex, colorful program, which in principle has not changed to this day," the scope of which has in fact merely been extended and perfected thanks to the development of computers and new electronic equipment.[12] Paik's idea that everyone should have a pocket synthesizer to play with creatively on his or her home TV set was never realized (1965). He believed that everyone should have the chance to perform art with light, color, form and sound. Art, according to Paik, is only visible in the creative process, and by taking part with his or her own TV everyone could become an artist. In a playful

manner Paik leads the image, whose spell had been broken by technology, back into the context of magical pictorial worlds.

Systematically investigating the incidental by-products, Paik also referred to Karl Otto Götz, who wrote in his 1959 essay "Gemaltes Bild – Kinetisches Bild" (Painted Picture – Kinetic Picture): "Prompted by the appearance of known interference in the operation of radar technology, I got together with technicians and attempted to generate and electronically control various optical phenomena on the fluorescent screen. [...] Television technology opens up new ways for us to generate and control kinetic elements of form and structure."[13]

Around the same time as Paik's *Participation TV*, Radúz Çinçera was developing his idea of an interactive cinema. At the Montreal Expo in 1967 he realized his *Kinoautomat*. Whenever the film presentation was paused, the audience voted on how the film should continue by pressing one of two switches built into their seats, and the appropriate version was then screened. Çinçera's preoccupation with the possibilities of a non-linear, interactive cinema continued for a long time, with his *Cinelabyrinth* (1990) becoming equally well known. In this piece, different versions of one film were screened in neighboring rooms, so that the viewer could put together his own personal variant by going from room to room, deciding for himself how long to stay in each room.

A number of works have been created in which the viewer can influence the development of a film by means of his position in the space. Jakub Moravek's film installation *Standing Ovation* (2001) shows a group of people who react to the viewer's movements. If the viewer approaches the projection screen, they begin to clap, and the closer the viewer gets to the screen, the more they clap. If he remains standing directly in front of the screen, the scene becomes more and more intense until it reaches an ecstatic outburst of jubilation. The viewer is able to decide for himself how long and how intense the enthusiasm shown towards him will be. Sensors under the floor mat detect where people are within the space and pass this information on to a computer, which is programmed to call up the corresponding film sequence. The scenes can be played in any order: the film has neither beginning nor end, no cuts and no still shots.

Translated from the German by Jacqueline Todd

10 *TV as a Creative Medium*, group exhibition with Serge Boutourline, Frank Gillette / Ira Schneider, Nam June Paik / Charlotte Moorman, Earl Reiback, Paul Ryan, John Seery, Eric Siegel, Thomas Tadlock, Aldo Tambellini, Joe Weintraub, catalog brochure, Howard Wise Gallery, New York.

11 The first film of a "distorted" television was made by Wolf Vostell in 1963, entitled *Sun in Your Head*.

12 Wulf Herzogenrath, *Nam June Paik. Fluxus. Video*, Verlag Silke Schreiber, Munich, 1983, p. 56. Further forms of viewer participation in Paik's work are pieces using closed-circuit cameras, in which the image of the viewer becomes the content (1969), and the performance *Cello TV*, where the viewer is offered the chance to work the camera and show his selected images live on screen, so that he himself becomes a real-time filmmaker (1971).

13 Karl Otto Götz, "Gemaltes Bild – Kinetisches Bild," in *Blätter und Bilder*, vol. 1, no. 5, Würzburg and Vienna, 1959, p. 47.

Peter Weibel

"However, its dynamic system features have given this variable, virtual picture yet another characteristic. It behaves like a living system, it reacts to the input of a context, it alters its state and its output through the viewer's input. The interactivity of this media art thus consists of the three elements of the digital image: virtuality (of information storage), variability (of pictorial content) and viability (of pictorial function). Accordingly, the image transforms itself into a dynamic system whose behavior imitates real life. If a living organism is a system that reacts independently to individual existence, then the dynamic image system that consists of multi-sensory variables and reacts to input is also a living organism."[1]

From the very outset, Peter Weibel's work was characterized by a radical critique of a constructed reality and even today the latter influences both his artistic and his theoretical position. His work bespeaks a "congenial development from the technology of the typewriter to that of the computer,"[2] a development that would no doubt have been impossible had not this artist and theorist had his gaze fixed firmly on the future.

Weibel's first encounters with the cinema and with films took place during an era dominated by the students' revolts and the latter's rebellion against the state structures of the time, but also an era where, under the influence of the Structuralist movement, a search was underway for a new definition of the term "art." Following on from his criticism of the existing system of representation, in 1970, speaking of the cinematic production of the Viennese Circle, to which he himself belonged, Weibel summarized as follows:

"The Viennese films break with that homology between the world and its representation, with the theory of reflection as an adjustment of consciousness. Everybody demands that the image of a dog should resemble a dog, how boring. Their objective is to use a process of identification as a social category to make the filmic image reflect the world the way the state sees it, so that consciousness is no longer capable of perceiving a difference between image and state reality. By contrast, the Viennese films aim at recognition by means of an individual category, the sensual experience."[3]

In the first years of his artistic career, Weibel implemented this criticism of constructed reality and its representation in his actionist activities, but, following the technical developments of the time, as of 1969, the artist transferred his focus to video and, from the end of the 1980s, to computer installations. However, his principle of coming to grips with his subject-matter – of investigating the structures of seeing, communication and reception – remains. The principle still governs his work today and, within the context of technological developments, opens up vistas of the future of communication and intervention and thus of new approaches to the perception of the world. The above is particularly true of the way he treats the subject of films and the cinema, which began in the form of analytical actions and which, today, investigates the possibilities of a cinema of the future within technically complex installations.

Criticism of Language
Demonstrating a marked interest in language, Weibel's first published texts (since 1964) analyze the structures inherent to language in contemporary Austrian and American literature. In accordance with modern linguistics and referencing Konrad Lorenz, he

1 Peter Weibel, "Postontologische Kunst, 1994," in *Bildwelten 1982-1996*, Romana Schuler, Peter Weibel (eds), Triton, Vienna, 1996, p. 242.

2 Robert Fleck, *Peter Weibel. Zur Rechtfertigung der hypothetischen Natur der Kunst und der Nicht-Identität in der Objektwelt*, Galerie Tanja Grunert, Cologne, 1992.

3 Peter Weibel, "Warum der Wiener Film so gut ist," (first publ. 1970 in *Neuer Österreichischer Film*), in *Avantgardefilm Österreich 1950 bis heute*, Alexander Horwath, Lisl Ponger, Gottfried Schlemmer (eds), Wespennest, Vienna, 1995, p. 172.

Cover of *Film*, November, 1969
designed by Peter Weibel for
the edition devoted to his
"expanded cinema"
photo © Peter Weibel

Peter Weibel with Valie Export
Das Magische Auge
[The Magic Eye]
1969
inter-media, autogenerative
sound screen
showing at Circus Krone,
Munich, 1969
© Peter Weibel, Valie Export
photo © Werner Schulz

Action Lecture
1968
expanded movie,
multi-projection, performance,
communication action
© Peter Weibel
photos © Hans Scheugl

interpreted language as "a function of an informative nature for mediating between subject and object, between thinking and reality." Following the theory advanced by Ferdinand de Saussure and under the influence of Structuralism, Weibel saw the term language in an expanded sense, covering the dimensions of verbal expression. Like any other sign, letters, sounds and words can form the materials of a linguistic system: "One can expand the meaning of the term language to the point where a poet can get by without any kind of verbal language."4 The agencies of language, expanded to include the agencies of design – "artistic or communicative material of all kinds"5 – led him to the concept of material that would have a decisive influence on his work in the coming years: "Everything is the material of artistic creation to the same extent."6

Under the influence of theoreticians, among them Hermann Weyl, and artists such as Raoul Hausmann and László Moholy-Nagy, this understanding encouraged Weibel to devise artistic actions which he now realized in the actionist milieu. His principal interest was in constructional planning, namely in the conceptional steps that lead to the genesis of a work of art. In this context, it was in the deconstruction of the artistic composition that Weibel saw a better understanding of the former's meaning. His constructional modus operandi established a link with the approaches used by the Viennese Group, which

he describes as the decisive impetus in modern art in Austria, as a group whose artistic actions "anticipated many of the aesthetic practices of the avant-garde from the 1960s to the 1980s."7 The group's preeminent concern was to abolish the genre distinctions between high and trivial culture. In this, their artistic actions were characterized by an interest in machines and technology and thus in a new reality, and this in turn led them to the realization that for them, the construction principle was more important than the product itself. This also meant that they considered the criticism of reality using the medium of language to be dubious, because language helps to construct reality and its society. Weibel's criticism of language was directed against our existing image of the world where reality is determined by language and against the prevailing social order in the 1960s.

Expanded Cinema

Alongside his preoccupation with experimental literature, another central concern for Weibel was the structure of cinema. During his time in Paris in 1963/1964 he studied film at the Institute des Hautes Études Cinématographiques (I.D.H.E.C.). Back in Vienna, he published film analyzes and reviews that displayed a close connection with his critical comments on language. Taking as his starting point his view of language in general as a sign-based form of communication, Weibel also began to consider the

4 Peter Weibel, in *Protokolle '82, Zeitschrift für Literatur und Kunst*, Otto Breicha (ed.), Jugend und Volk Verlagsgesellschaft, Vienna, Munich, 1982, p. 5.

5 Matthias Michalka, *Vom Aktionismus und Expanded Cinema zur Arbeit mit TV und Video*, Vienna, 1995.

6 Peter Weibel, *Kritik der Kunst, Kunst der Kritik*, Jugend und Volk Verlagsgesellschaft, Vienna, Munich, 1973.

7 *Die Wiener Gruppe : ein Moment der Moderne 1954–1960*, Peter Weibel (ed.), Springer, Vienna, 1997.

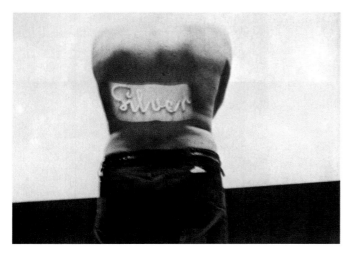

Welcome
1964
8mm film
color, b/w
20 min
© Peter Weibel
photo © Valie Export

NIVEA
1966
expanded cinema
16, 35, 70mm film
color; sound
1 min
© Peter Weibel
photo © Valie Export

system of signs that was films as a kind of linguistic system.8 In this context, his primary interest was in exposing the illusionary nature of films.

In order to put into operation this deconstruction of reality, Weibel distanced himself from the films of the New American Cinema in his artistic work. In 1967 he produced *Welcome*, an inter-media film action for which he projected the film not only onto a screen but also onto his own body. Alongside outside shots and pictures of Weibel himself, this twenty-minute black-and-white film also showed lettering in a public space that changed its meaning through cutting. Another film was shown on the projection screen behind him. During this procedure Weibel read out a "programmatic text" on the problems of objective reality in films and on the latter's constructed quality. The objective was to make a narration impossible from the outset and thus to deconstruct filmic reality. The camerawork and the cutting were such that the narrative momentum ceded its importance to an associative and ambiguous sequence of images. The unusual camerawork directed the viewer's attention towards the projection process itself thus making it more difficult to recognize the kind of filmic reality we are normally presented with at the cinema. The distortion caused by projecting the film onto his body highlighted the constructed nature of this filmic reproduction. In this way Weibel made it clear that a film is dependent upon the filmmaker's intentions and that accordingly one can only talk about a subjective reality in films.9

Dating from the same year, the expanded movie *NIVEA* represented a continuation of the kind of filmic investigations that Weibel had conducted in his filmic actions. In this case, Weibel investigated the possibilities of showing a film without an actual film. Holding a water-ball with *NIVEA* written on it in his raised hands, the filmmaker himself stood in front of a screen onto which an empty frame was projected. The sound that could be heard, that of a camera filming, played from a tape recorder on the stage. Here, Weibel has shifted his focus to the cinematographic equipment that normally allows itself to disappear in the film. He demonstratively presents the individual

elements of the *association* of such elements as the projector, the screen, the celluloid and the auditorium, thus revealing the technical specifics of traditional film production. Seeing only the actor and his shadow on the screen behind him, the public was confused. It was presented with a filmic action that was not subjugated to the illusion of the cinema, but that attempted to expose it.10

For Weibel, the film represents an alliance between calculations and operators that is used to confront reality,11 an alliance that works with certain figures and according to certain rules that include a projector, a projection surface, an auditorium, an audience, celluloid, a camera, a director, montage, cutting etc. Here, the "alliance" that is a film is seen as a "heuristic convention"12 that can be changed at any time. Accordingly, filming means nothing more or less "than manufacturing event using the methods available to the alliance that is the film."13 As far as the artist is concerned, the elements of the film are at all times interchangeable and can be sequenced in any manner of ways. "Instead of celluloid … one could use a mirror, instead of a beam of light, a piece of string, instead of a projection screen a human chest."14

Instant Film (1968), takes the investigations started with *Welcome* and *NIVEA* one step further, Weibel describes the work as an *object* or *meta-film* that undertakes to reflect on the systems of "film" and "reality." The work consists of a strip of transparent PVC which the recipient can put up anywhere he feels like.

"He can hang it up at home, within his own four walls, on one of various different colored backgrounds. He can place the strip in front of an object, in this way creating his own collages and superimpositions. He can transform reality into a film by holding the strip up to his eyes … If the owner of this instant film wants things to take on a pinkish hue, all he needs to do is to paint the strip pink …"15

In these works, the viewer encounters an extended system of rules with which reality can be manufactured. As is the case in such films as *Fingerprint* or

8 Michalka, op. cit., p. 39.

9 Michalka, op. cit., p. 43.

10 Michalka, op. cit., p. 49.

11 Michalka, op. cit., p. 109.

12 Weibel, *Protokolle '82*, op. cit., p. 96.

13 Weibel, *Protokolle '82*, op. cit., p. 96.

14 Peter Weibel, "Selbst-Porträt einer Theorie in Selbstzitaten," in *Avant-gardistischer Film 1951–1971*, Gottfried Schlemmer [ed.], Hanser, Munich, 1973, p. 109.

15 Weibel, *Protokolle '82*, op. cit., p. 69.

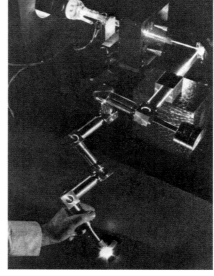

left
Amauroscope
1969
project and concept film
published in
"Peter Weibels expanded cinema,"
in *Film* 11/1969, Friedrich, Velber
© Peter Weibel
photo © Peter Weibel

right
Lasermesser
[Laser Knife]
1969
public action, expanded movie,
concept film
© Peter Weibel
photo © Peter Weibel

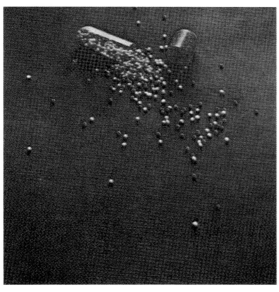

left
*Pillenfilme oder
der Sinnesdifraktor*
[Pill Film or The Sense Diffractor]
1968
project film, model for walkman
© Peter Weibel
photo © Peter Weibel

right
Radiopillen
[Radio Pills]
1969
project and concept film
presented in
"Peter Weibels expanded cinema,"
in *Film* 11/1969, Friedrich, Velber
© Peter Weibel
photo © Peter Weibel

Glanz und Schicht des Zelluloids, the approach used in *Welcome* and *NIVEA*, is characterized by the interchangeability and arbitrariness of the elements of a film and of time sequences and by a questioning of the filmic environment. Ernst Schmidt made the comment that Weibel breaks up the syntax of filmic language by placing its signs within new context and taking away their fixed meaning within the "alliance."16

As his continued to address the subject of cinema, Weibel produced numerous analytic works on the problems of reality and its presentation by the media. However, the later works focused more specifically on the individual elements of the alliance that is the film. One such example is *Lichtstrahl: Leinwand*, dating from 1971, a work that reflects critically on the question of the screen in the filmic medium and that was thus described by Weibel as a "meta-film." By using a swiveling technique and moving the projector, Weibel demonstrated that the "screen" always "appears" in the place at which the beam of light is directed. A commentary informed the visitor that as spectators we only see what the light transports. The projected arrow, which appeared to want to reach beyond the screen, but which could no longer be perceived from the moment when it was projected beyond the screen, illustrated the desire to break through the boundaries imposed by the film.17 Weibel interpreted

the screen as a "bracket" that constricts our view of the world. He also noted that the sign (the arrow) loses its meaning as soon as it leaves the screen; it can only be perceived when it obeys the rules of projection and thus stays within the dimensions of the screen. Whenever the arrow "hit" the edge of the screen, Weibel arranged for a bang to sound out. For him, the screen's frame became the starting point for reflections on the sign-like character of the film.

Sturm über ( ), (1967) predates the above work by two years. The very title of this latter piece references the interpretation of the screen as a bracket. In a heavy storm, it takes the performer nine minutes to cross the screen from left to right. The length of the film was determined by the screen, its spatial parameter.

Weibel sees his filmic works within the context of the *expanded cinema*. They represent an attempt to get beyond the bounds of the film screen and to reestablish the film in its role as a medium, freed from that language-like quality it has taken on in the course of its development.18 Questioning the apparent reality of the projected image, artists therefore often work with multiple projections, light shows and multimedia performances in which the film, slide and video projections are combined with real actions, even using actions without films that reflect on the medium. However, in the expanded film Weibel sees

16 Hans Scheugl, Ernst Schmidt, *Eine Subgeschichte des Films : Lexikon des Avantgarde-, Experimental- und Undergroundfilms*, Suhrkamp, Frankfurt/M., p. 1076.

17 Scheugl/Schmidt, op. cit.

18 Scheugl/Schmidt, op. cit., p. 253.

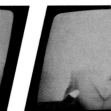

TV-News (TV-Tod II)
[TV News (TV Death II)]
1970
TV performance
6 min
screenshots from the
broadcast on Impulse 7,
ORF, 1972
© Peter Weibel

TV-Aquarium (TV-Tod I)
[*TV-Aquarium* (TV Death I)]
1970
TV performance
3 min
screenshots from the
broadcast on Impulse 7,
ORF, 1972
© Peter Weibel

The Endless Sandwich
1969
TV performance
3 min
screenshots from the
broadcast on Impulse 7,
ORF, FS 2, 1972
© Peter Weibel

not only an extension of the range of optic phenomena but also a radical decision to settle his scores with reality and the language that communicates and constructs it.[19]

As of 1968, Weibel systematically used inter-media devices, producing *expanded movies*, *communication actions* and cinematographic installations. In these works, it also became more important for the public to become involved, for example, in *Das magische Auge*, dating from 1969. With this *intermedium*, Weibel talks about the world's first self-generating sound screen, a *sound picture*. Here, it was not the projector that produced the sound. Instead, an electronically treated screen transformed oscillating light produced either by the shadows of the public or by the film's light value into oscillating sound. Dark light produced low sounds and bright light higher ones. Because the light was not measured as the sum total of the entire screen but as individual impulses emitted by the various cells, depending on how much light they were exposed to, what resulted was a sound collage.[20] Weibel's interest in the technical possibilities at the time was obvious. However a large number of projects were never realized for financial reasons.

In *EXIT* (1968), Weibel made increased physical demands on his public. Visitors to the cinema where the action took place were expecting a film to be shown. However, whilst Weibel stood on the stage and delivered a speech, Valie Export, Hans Scheugl, Kurt Kren and several other artists from the Viennese Circle shot rockets into the audience. The action turned into an attack on the spectators, whose flight also resulted in a number of counterattacks. This was

an attempt to criticize the commercial cinema that, at the time, saw itself as a reflection of reality. Weibel described cinemas as air-conditioned adventure boxes that acclimatized individuals to a state reality. The action was intended to wake the audience up and to emancipate it from the image of moving light.[21]

Weibel's cinematographic oeuvre demonstrates how he investigated the mechanisms and structures of visual perception as well as analyzing its recipient's social position as part of a communication process. He addresses the subject of the influence of electronic media on perception, on our image of the world and, in connection with the above, our altered perception of time and space. Just how far-reaching his observations were is illustrated by his notes on *Pillenfilm* (1968). The idea was to manufacture films as chemical translators of the medium: to unite the projector, the film strip, the screen and the camera in a pill. The pill film would disintegrate the sensory organs, supplying visions beyond language. The film would assume the role of a new sensory organ that, in the form of a new sensory correlate, would provide the artist with every sensory quality he desired.[22] The work of the expanded cinema clearly called the film into question: "Expanded cinema also means expanded reality."[23]

Pre-Cinema, Para-Cinema and Post-Cinema
As of 1970, Weibel described the development of and rapprochement between the film and video mediums as pre-cinema, para-cinema and post-cinema, thus following on from expanded cinema, prompted by a desire to investigate communications structures and the relevant electronic possibilities. Weibel

19 Weibel, *Protokolle '82*, op. cit., p. 97.

20 Weibel, *Protokolle '82*, op. cit., p. 86.

21 Weibel, *Protokolle '82*, op. cit., p. 89.

22 Weibel, *Protokolle '82*, op. cit., p 91.

23 Weibel, *Protokolle '82*, op. cit., p. 97.

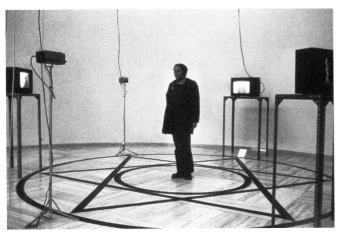

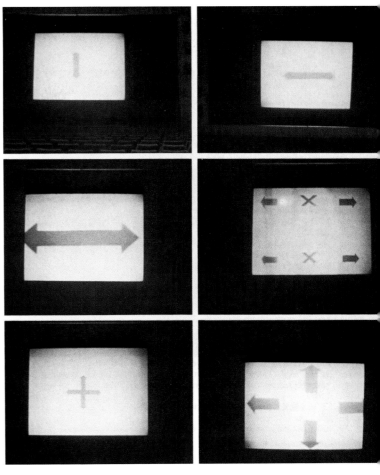

top
Possible
1969
film installation without film
installation views:
"projektionskunst"
avant-garde film festival,
organized by Peter Weibel
for Kunstmesse K 45,
Künstlerhaus, Vienna, 1977
© Peter Weibel
photo © Peter Weibel

bottom
Beobachtung der Beobachtung:
Unbestimmtheit
[Observing Observation:
Uncertainty]
1973
closed-circuit installation
mixed media
dimensions variable
installation view:
Künstlerhaus, Graz, 1973
© Peter Weibel

Lichtstrahl : Leinwand
[Light Beam : Screen]
1971
meta-film
16mm film
b/w, sound
4 min
© Peter Weibel
photos © Valie Export

attempted to define those trends that referenced elements of the visual arts of the seventeenth and eighteenth centuries as pre-cinema. He also wanted to highlight the kind of projects that concerned themselves with subsidiary products, those that took alternative routes, deviated or branched out from the normal path of commercial consumer cinema (para-cinema), as well as the kind of approaches that defined the magnetic recording system that is video as the successor to the mechanical duplication apparatus that is film (post-cinema).[24]

It was in this that Weibel saw the root of the link between video and film technology, which, in his opinion, will determine the future of the cinema. In his investigations, he describes the influence of video on film aesthetics at the beginning of the 1970s, observing that it was less the case that the technical possibilities of video were being used for films but rather that video scenes and TV sequences were being inserted into otherwise untouched film sequences. Weibel himself had adopted this approach, for example in the screenplays for *Unsichtbare Gegner* (1976) and *Menschenfrauen* (1979). Half of the film consisted of video scenes in black and white, more specifically,

all the scenes dealing with memory, imagination and hallucinations, whereas the reality scenes were shot using film and in color. The work's dialectics were based on the tension between video and film.[25] And it is these very dialectics that transform *Unsichtbare Gegner* into a sci-fi film of the psyche. The film tells the story of a photographer and video reporter who one day discovers that invisible extraterrestrial powers are on the point of taking possession of the Earth by assuming human shape and altering the latter's consciousness. Mistrusting her own perception as opposed to the objective perception machines that are camera and camcorder, she begins to document the results of this development and soon notices an increase in destructiveness and aggression. The film shows an attempt to illustrate the disintegration of perception and identity and to describe the problems of self-alienation and extraneous determination. Export and Weibel integrated into the film, as equally valid components, photographs, videos and installations, as well as a large number of pre-recorded performances.[26] The inclusion, for example, of photographs, videos or installations, did not, as one might assume, disturb the film's narrative continuity.

24 Peter Weibel, "Präkino, Parakino, Postkino," (1971) in *Protokolle '82*, op. cit., p. 103.

25 Peter Weibel, "Video-technik und Filmästhetik. Persönliche Anmerkungen zur Zukunftsindustrie," in *Metropoles Festival für Video und Filmexperiment*, 29. Nov–6. Dec 1982, Munich.

26 See Roswitha Mueller, *Valie Export – Bild Risse*, Passagen Verlag, Vienna 2002, p. 136.

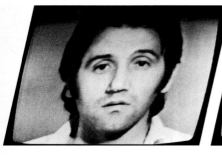

Peter Weibel in
Tritität [Tritity]
1974
video poem
screenshots
© Peter Weibel
photos
© Michael Schuster

Susanne Widl,
Peter Weibel in
Unsichtbare Gegner
[Invisible Adversaries]
Valie Export
and Peter Weibel
1976
16mm film
color, sound
112 min
© Valie Export;
Sixpack Film, Vienna

Instead, it reinforced the effect of the individual sequences. Accordingly, the film manifests a admixture of styles, whereby realistic scenes blend with the abstract, symbolic peculiarity of videos and photographs.27

With regard to content, *Menschenfrauen* takes the subject matter of *Unsichtbare Gegner* one step further. As with *Unsichtbare Gegner*, *Menschenfrauen* also includes experimental strategies, performance and photographic work. However, unlike the former film, in *Menschenfrauen* there is a stronger focus on video, with the latter medium functioning on several levels simultaneously. Not only does it serve to spotlight background material from the past, it also comments on present-day encounters and promotes inner monologue.28 These films show that it is perfectly possible to maintain and even intensify a narrative thread despite the use of various different media.

At the end of the 1970s, referring to this type of concept, Weibel summarized by saying that "not only [will] the foursome of audio, video, radio and TV increasing [become] the basis for artistic creativity, but also, and above all, the commercial film industry [forces us] to keep pace with it in technological terms,"29 namely to transform the film, an invention of the nineteenth century, the mechanical era, into an electronic medium.

Firstly, Weibel's work with video and TV had been encouraged by the increasing social and political significance of electronic mass media towards the end of the 1960s. By this time, TV in particular had acquired an enormous social and socio-cultural importance. Secondly, he was prompted to embark on these works by his interest in technological progress and in cybernetics.30 Since, initially, Weibel did not possess his own video equipment, he sought to collaborate with public TV organizations in order to continue his questioning of the medium's constructional structures and the way it works, a process initiated in *Publikum als Exponat* and *Prozess als Produkt*. In 1969, he produced *The Endless Sandwich*, a work that made the viewer's task of switching the equipment on and off into the substance of the program. The screen showed viewers sitting in front of screens. A fault occurred on the last screen and the relevant viewer

had to get up to deal with it, whereupon a fault occurred on the following screen and this continued until the fault reached the real equipment and the real viewer had to get up to deal with the fault. The real process represents the end of the reproduced process, highlighting the *sandwich-like nature*31 of real processes and reproduced processes. In this way, Weibel disrupted TV reality and activated the viewer, whom this form of one-way communication had lulled into passivity.

In *TV Aquarium (TV Tod I)*, dating from 1970, Weibel took the instructive character of this tele-action one step further, showing a film in which a TV set was transformed into an aquarium with fishes swimming in it. Water seeped slowly out of the aquarium, the viewer heard a gurgling sound and, after a few minutes, saw the fishes thrashing about on the floor. Censorship did not allow the artist to provide a convincing impression of a real death inside a real TV set in a real apartment. However, Weibel's attempt to use the aquarium to lend the TV set an identity between reality and reproduction appeared to be a successful one.

Weibel's investigations of the structures of seeing and the perception of image and space continued in video works and environments such as *Video Lumina* (1972), with real time bringing new possibilities to bear in the process. It was Weibel's aim to illustrate the processes of seeing and of being seen. Seven monitors showing the same winking eye were spread throughout the room at various heights and angles, forming a sculpture that visitors could walk through. Whatever position the viewer adopted, the eyes of four monitors were always looking at him. In his commentary, Weibel described *Video Lumina* (Lat. "I see eyes") as a counterpart to the camera obscura, adding that whereas the film projector is an imitation of the sun, as its beam demonstrates, the electronic screen is far removed from the "natural" methods of reproduction. Weibel calls such screens artificial, synthetic, something created by man himself.32 If the viewer subjected the eye on the screen to a closer analysis, he realized that the illustrated pupil was actually the camera. He was, so to speak, looking at a reproduction of an instrument of reproduction. Weibel was reflecting on the simulated directness

27 Roswitha Mueller, op. cit.

28 Roswitha Mueller, op. cit., p. 155.

29 Weibel, "Videotechnik und Filmästhetik. Persönliche Anmerkungen zur Zukunfts-industrie," op. cit.

30 See Michalka, op. cit., p. 76.

31 Weibel, *Protokolle '82*, op. cit., p. 98.

32 Weibel, *Protokolle '82*, op. cit., p. 35.

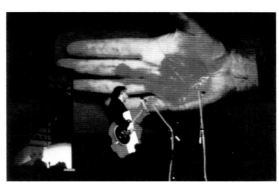

Der Künstliche Wille
[The Artficial Will]
1984
electronic media opera
performance views:
Ars Electronica, Brucknerhaus,
Linz, 1984
© Peter Weibel
photos © Peter Weibel

and subjectivity of the gaze with regard to its technical conditions.

For Weibel, the video medium is the fundamental instrument of a pragmatics of space. In this he disagreed with the views of a large number of the theoreticians of his time who believed that the illustration of the viewer presented in the video image defined the video as a mirroring machine. By using the medium for his artistic work, Weibel was advocating an extension of our perception of space. In techniques ranging from chimerical images of video projection screens (using large projectors) to sophisticated multi-images on large numbers of screens Weibel saw an opportunity for designing an artistic space that was fundamentally different from the space occupied by perceptional reality, and one that can only become a "real" artistic space through this process.33

Computer Installations
In the 1980s Weibel continued to develop the concept of expanded cinema on the basis of increasingly complex electronic and digital media, using video works and installations to investigate the idea of referencing space. The fact that video operates in real time opened up to him not only new possibilities for image production, but also a more effective means of activating the viewer. As of 1990 Weibel started to realize interactive computer and network-based installations that both allowed him to take a more intensive approach to the problems of interface and opened up to him a route into the virtual worlds.

Weibel addressed the topic of the electronic developments of his time in his video opera *Der künstliche Wille* (1984). This ten-act opus looks forward to a future world where the boundaries between representation and object, between imagination and reality have become increasingly blurred and assume an ever greater prominence in their ubiquity and simultaneousness. Using all kinds of different audiovisual media, he focuses on "the world as will and imagination,"34 presenting twentieth-century man's social behavior

as something disrupted by advertising and ideology. According to Gerhard Johann Lischka, Weibel opted for the operatic genre because, in the classical sense, the latter represents that unity of image, literature and music that is determined by the audiovisual alphabet. With its electronic media, the electronic opera offers a means of blending the various elements of expression to create a new unity. Together these construct a meaning that is multidimensional and no longer rooted in linearity. However, this multidimensionality does not only mean that language becomes more open, but also, and above all, that the recipient is afforded the opportunity of engaging in his own independent, individual interpretations.35 Not only on a substantive level, but in formal terms too, Weibel thus directs our gaze at the positive and negative changes wrought by technology, which has now expanded the scope of our response using new media, new forms of expression. Accordingly, in 1985, Weibel wrote:

> "TV, records and the cinema are machines for producing feelings artificially. People pop in a pill when they want an artificial hallucination. And they pop in a video if they want artificially produced emotions. [...] Artificial paradises are one result of a desire for artificiality."36

Four years later, in 1988, he produced a solo performance, *Stimmen aus dem Innenraum*, in which Unica Zürn, Mae West, Mary Shelley, Ada Lovelace, Linda Lovelace and the polyphonic woman of the future all meet up, all portrayed by actor Susanne Widl. With this media composition, Weibel was attempting to decode and to construct the unconsciously social text written by our society in its classical and modern myths, in its cultural productions and in the writings and bodes of the women themselves.37 As with his media opera, here Weibel also used a large number of different media. Slide animations, light projections, a giant video screen, scenic objects, music and the architecture of language, connected by means of computer controls, governed the real on-stage

33 Weibel, *Protokolle '82*, op. cit., p. 116.

34 Peter Weibel, "Der Künstliche Wille," in Gerhard Johann Lischka, *Alles und noch viel mehr*, Benteli, Bern, 1985, p. 336.

35 For more details see Gerhard Johann Lischka, op. cit., p. 338.

36 Peter Weibel, "Das theoretische Fundament der elektronischen Medienoper," in *Kunstforum International*, vols. 77–78, 1985, p. 86.

37 Peter Weibel, "Stimmen aus dem Innenraum," in Romana Schuler (ed.), *Peter Weibel. Bildwelten*, Triton Verlag, Vienna, 1996, p. 258.

Gesänge des Pluriversums
[Songs of the Pluriverse]
1986–1988
digital video work
in twelve parts
color, sound
100 min
video stills
© Peter Weibel

Peter Weibel, Susanne Widl,
Valie Export, Patricia Jünger
Stimmen aus dem Innenraum
[Voices From the Interior]
1988
intermedia performance
video stills
© Peter Weibel

Peter Weibel, Susanne Widl,
Valie Export, Patricia Jünger
Stimmen aus dem Innenraum
[Voices From the Interior]
1988
intermedia performance
mobile video wall, live cameras,
computer, spotlights,
tape recorders, amplifier,
speaker, catwalk, forklift,
objects, sculptures, props
performance view:
Ars Electronica, Linz, 1988
© Peter Weibel
photo © Peter Weibel

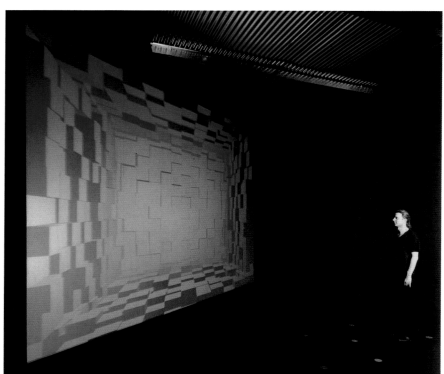

*Zur Rechtfertigung der hypo-
thetischen Natur der Kunst
und der Nicht-Identität der
Objektwelt*
[On Justifying the Hypothetical
Nature of Art and the Non-
Identicality within the Object
World]
1992
interactive computer
installation
mixed media
installation view: Galerie Tanja
Grunert und Michael Janssen,
Cologne, 1992
© Peter Weibel
photo © Galerie
Tanja Grunert und
Michael Janssen, Cologne

Virtuelle Welt: Architektur
[Virtual World: Architecture]
one of four virtual worlds

Virtuelle Welt: Sprach-Welt
[Virtual Word: Language World]

Virtuelle Welt: Objekt-Welt
[Virtual Word: Object World]

Virtuelle Welt:
Welt der Gaswolken
[Virtual World:
World of the Gas Clouds]

three of four virtual worlds
*Zur Rechtfertigung der
hypothetischen Natur der
Kunst und der Nicht-Identität
der Objektwelt*
1992
interactive computer
installation
screenshots
© Peter Weibel

proceedings, leading eventually to an interaction with the audience. Weibel dealt with the topic of the opportunities offered to the recipient by the new media again in 1995, in his work *Wagners Wahn oder das heilige Land des Kapitals*. For the latter opus, Weibel devised a cyber-opera for stage and Internet that, during its performances at Ars Electronica in 1995, engendered a stage décor on the basis of telematics and electronics.

In connection with the above-mentioned multi-dimensionality affected by integrating all kinds of different media-based technologies and with the new opportunities consequently offered to the viewer as manifested in the media opera, we should not forget to mention one specific video, *Gesänge des Pluriversums*. From 1986 to 1988, Weibel produced a cycle of visual songs dealing with the subject of the technological transformation that has occurred over the past two hundred years. His aim was to use digital equipment such as Rutt-Etra Scan, Mirage, ADO, Abekas 62 or Paintbox and computer programs such as Artworks and Tips to achieve a hybridization of all electronic image technologies.[38] With this hybridization, he wished, as he had done earlier in his media opera, to draw attention to the opportunities afforded by media, and, in close connection with this, to a means of expanding the scope of human expression and of interpretation. *Gesänge des Pluriversums* can be described as a kind of electronic cinema comprised of video recordings, photographs, film recordings and digital images, one whose form reflects the real social changes wrought by technological progress in all areas.

The potential problems posed by interface had been of importance to Weibel already since the 1960s. However, it was only in the 1990s that he was able to implement numerous such ideas in computer-controlled works such as the installation *Die Wand, der Vorhang (Grenze, die), fachsprachlich auch Lascaux*, (1994), in which an analogy is produced between the wall of a cave and a curtain, in the form of a digital interface. Weibel believes interface design to be one of the most important fields of future digital art. In this context, he notes that an artificial horizon dominated by interface technologies has now replaced the natural horizon of producing and contemplating images. The classical tools of the image system such as palette and brush have been replaced by keyboards and sensors. Since however, according to Weibel, access to the image has been encrypted through its

technical interface, the focus of artistic activity has shifted to developing interface technologies.[39] In the 1960s the onset of the movement to deconstruct the technology of the apparatus, a characteristic of the film and video avant-garde, led to an expansion of the cinematographic code to include computer and network-based image technologies which conditioned a transformation of the static image. Interactivity and dislocation became the features of the new image technologies, with the interactive aspect playing a particularly important role in the subsequent concentration on a manipulable interface.

Das tangible Bild, dating from 1991, follows in the wake of these deliberations. In this work, the viewer stands in front of a rubber screen, which he can touch. Sensors are built in behind this screen, and these measure and localize the depth of pressure. Every time somebody touches the screen this information is transmitted to a switching device and a computer. The computer also stores live pictures coming from a video camera recording the viewer in the room in front of the grid of coordinates. In the computer, the rows of figures which represent the pressure exerted on the screen influence the rows of figures which represent the images of the viewer in the room. In this way the field of the screen and the field of the Cartesian grid merge. The computer transmits these data to the video beamer which in turn projects the data onto the projection screen as an image. Every time someone presses the rubber screen the projected video image is distorted in real time in exactly the same way and in exactly the same place where another viewer presses the screen. In this way it is possible to deform the image of the viewer projected by the video camera. This interaction with the video image takes place in real time, with the viewer himself becoming a part of the digital data, whilst his body remains dislocated in real time.[40] Weibel addressed the topic of the discourse on spatial transposition as a characteristic of the interface.

In 1992, in collaboration with other artists, Weibel realized an interactive installation, *Zur Rechtfertigung der hypothetischen Natur der Kunst und der Nicht-Identität in der Objektwelt*. Here, the interface took the form of a floor plate with sensors which, in combination with various programs, defined four different virtual worlds. Moving about on this floor, the visitor sees on the wall in front of him the images of the rear projection that reacts to him directly in real

38 Peter Weibel, "Gesänge des Pluriversums," in Romana Schuler (ed.), *Peter Weibel. Bildwelten*, Triton Verlag, Vienna, 1996, p. 132.

39 Peter Weibel, "Wissen und Vision – Neue Schnittstellentechnologien der Wahrnehmung," in *Weltwissen – Wissenswelt*, Christa Maar, Hans Ulrich Obrist, Ernst Pöppel (eds), DuMont, Cologne, 2000, p. 69.

40 See Schuler/Weibel, op. cit., p. 238.

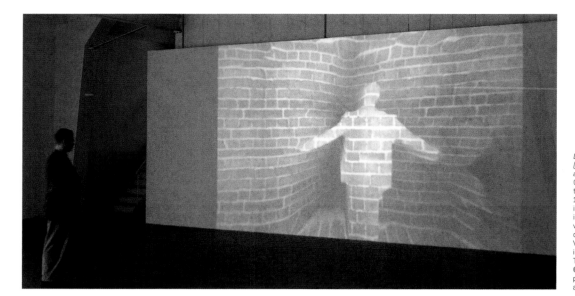

Die Wand, der Vorhang
(Grenze, die) fachsprachlich
auch : Lascaux [The Wall, the
Curtain (Border, the), technical
terminology also: Lascaux]
1994
interactive computer
installation
video camera, video projector,
digitized image of a brick wall,
VGX computer
installation view: Galerie
Tanja Grunert, Cologne, 1994
© Peter Weibel
photo © Galerie Tanja Grunert
and Michael Janssen, Cologne

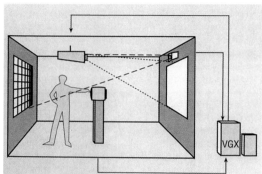

left
Das tangible Bild
[The Tangible Image]
1991
interactive computer
installation
mixed media
dimensions variable
© Peter Weibel
photo © Peter Weibel

right
scheme of the interactive
computer installation
Das tangible Bild
[The Tangible Image]
1991
designed by Bob O'Kane
© Peter Weibel

time. Using the four colored sensors and by moving across the floor he can choose between a sign world of letters, an architecture world, an object world and a gas world. The place where he chooses to stand, the movements of his body and his reactions in real space direct his choice of preprogrammed virtual world, as if in a game. The programs are like a computer-generated re-staging of the debates on the theory of images that were initiated in the 1950s between the two standpoints, one based on the principles of realist perspective and the other on informal expanses of color.41 Thomas Dreher notes that Weibel deconstructs the situation of the player at the computer screen who forgets that he is touching keys or joysticks. The player forgets the real side of the interface. According to Dreher, in this reactive installation, the illusory world of mass media such as cinema or TV films and computer games is relativized by reducing the number of signs and foregoing the use of actors in their one-world illusionism.

Weibel's consideration of the problems of the internal and the external viewer in connection with interface, is also in evidence in, amongst other things, a computer installation entitled *Die Wand, der Vorhang (Grenze, die), fachsprachlich auch Lascaux* (1994). In this interactive opus the image of a brick wall is stored on a computer and projected automatically onto a wall. As soon as a viewer enters the room he is recorded by a video camera. The analogue signals of his movements are transmitted to the computer and transformed into chains of characters which influence the digital sequence of digital signals making up the image of the wall. The effects of both sequences of signals become visible on the screen, with a time-lapse and in silhouette. The viewer has become part of the image. He is at once a real, internal viewer and a simulated external viewer who appears to be pressing against the wall from the rear.42

Weibel demonstrates that in the real world man is always no more than an internal observer, whereas in the generated technological worlds he can simultaneously be an internal and an external observer. Following as they do the system theory and the notion of endo-physics established by Otto E. Rössler in the 1980s, both Weibel's closed-circuit installations and his interactive computer installations turn out to be model for a view of the world defined by endo-physics and technology, one that the viewer can experience directly and in which the latter is always part of a system that he observes and within which he moves.

Whereas in the 1970s he used the video medium, today it is the computer that, for him, represents "a crucial medium for perfectly simulating reality."43 The computer and the virtuality of its information storage have made information and thus images, too, variable. When it became possible to generate an interface between the viewer and image technology, the creation of an interactive image also become possible. In this context, following along the lines of constructivist philosophy and its term for reactive artificial systems, Weibel states that the "viability" transforms a moving image into an animated image.44 As early as 1993 he noted that, similar to the idea expressed in *Die Wand, der Vorhang (Grenze, die), fachsprachlich*

41 Thomas Dreher, in
    Schuler/Weibel, op. cit.,
    p. 43.

42 Schuler/Weibel, op. cit.,
    p. 255.

43 Weibel, "Wissen und Vision –
    Neue Schnittstellentechno-
    logien der Wahrnehmung," in
    Maar/Obrist/Pöppel, op. cit.

44 Weibel, "Wissen und Vision–
    Neue Schnittstellen-
    technologien der Wahr-
    nehmung," in Maar/Obrist/
    Pöppel, op. cit.

The Panoptic Society or
Immortally in Love with Death
2001
interactive DVD
screenshots
© Peter Weibel

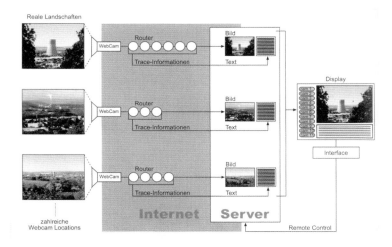

Islands of Non-Locality
1998
Net-based installation
computer, monitor,
peripheral equipment
scheme
© Peter Weibel

auch Lascaux, it was quantum physics that first posed the question of the function of the viewer and the way that occurrences are influence by our observations and that thus developed a "non-classical, 'participatory' model of the world and of reality."45 The endo-physical interpretation of quantum physics according to Rössler demonstrated that there is no such thing as an external view of the world, but that we are always internal observers.

Future Cinema: The Panoptic Society or Immortally in Love with Death

The phenomenon of an increasing degree of surveillance in our society was already reflected in Weibel's early video works. Examples of this include *Video Lumina* or *Beobachtung der Beobachtung: Unbestimmtheit*, dating from 1973. This latter work consists of three monitors and three cameras, arranged alternately in a circle. If the visitor steps into the middle of the circle he discovers that the cameras are connected to the screens in such a way that they only ever show him from behind. Every video camera displays what it records on the screen opposite it. The subject in front of the camera becomes an object. Inevitably, the feeling arises of being watched or observed. The person under observation begins to feel uncomfortable and leaves the area where he is the subject of observation.

To Weibel the situation today appears quite different. In a time where people are increasingly integrating the media into their lives, they are also becoming more dependent on the latter. *The Panoptic Society or*

Immortally in Love with Death (2001) shows a prisoner in his cell who transforms himself and his criminal existence into a public spectacle by laying it bare in front of the public. Weibel focuses our attention on the pathological side of the media whose

"… jousting for audience attention produces visual excesses that leave escapism behind and elicit new obsessive-compulsive scenarios of control, xenophobia and sado-masochistic exploitation. The prisoner's right to renounce the privacy even he can claim for himself and his disastrous situation is based on an 'economy of attention' dominant in the reality voyeurism of the entertainment industry and whose strategies are deployed ever more aggressively in the infotainment offered by news media, in the staging of politics as theater."46

Weibel shows us a development within our perception of media in which the medium of observation turns out to be a powerful medium for putting oneself on show. He points out that our media-based culture is rooted in a dynamic closed-circuit process whereby the observer and the observed influence each other's behavior47 and reveals in this way a relationship that suggests a fundamental potential for the cinema of the future.

Dominika Szope
Translated from the German by Jeremy Gaines

45 Peter Weibel, "Die Welt als Schnittstelle," in Schuler/ Weibel, op. cit., p. 256.

46 Ursula Frohne, "Horror vacui," in *(dis)LOCATIONS*, ZKM Karlsruhe and The Centre for Interactive Cinema Research, College of Fine Arts, University of New South Wales, Sydney, Hatje Cantz, Ostfildern, 2001, p. 85.

47 Ursula Frohne, op. cit., p. 90.

Michael Snow
anarchive 2: Digital Snow

2002
interactive DVD-ROM, book

Wavelength
1966–1967
16mm film
color, sound
45 min
photo courtesy the artist

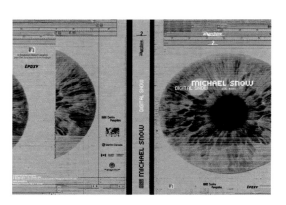

cover of
anarchive 2: Digital Snow
2002
interactive DVD-ROM, book
© The Daniel Langlois
Foundation for Art, Science
and Technology

anarchive was initiated by the Centre de Recherches d'Esthétique du Cinéma et des Arts Audiovisuels at the Université de Paris I (Panthéon-Sorbonne). Within this initiative, artists design an interactive multimedia project that examines their work in its entirety using different archival documents.

This second **anarchive** project centers on Michael Snow and showcases his major works through novel channels and a rich database. Gathered together are documents that until now were scattered throughout countless catalogs, books, articles, audio and video-tapes, photo collections and archives. By bringing together such valuable and exhaustive information, this multimedia project better acquaints us all with one of the foremost artists working in Canada today.

Anne-Marie Duguet

De la [From There]
1972
video installation
aluminum, steel, wood,
video camera, monitors
collection National Gallery
of Canada, Ottawa
photo courtesy the artist

The central element of the
sculpture is the machine
built by Pierre Abbeloos to move
the camera in filming La Région
Centrale [The Central Region]
(1970–71). A moving mechanical
sculpture in aluminum and steel
with electronic controls on a
painted wood base, with video
camera and four monitors and a
metal pipe with cables connects
four monitors to camera and
power source.

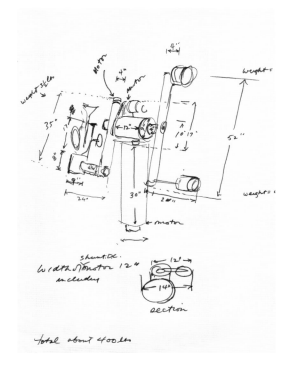

left
Construction drawing for
the machine used for shooting
La Région Centrale
[The Central Region]
not dated
black marker
photo courtesy Art Gallery
of Ontario, Toronto

right
The machine used for filming
La Region Centrale

Michael Snow constitutes, all on his own, an entire region of contemporary art and film of the last fifty years. Born to a French-Canadian mother and an English-Canadian father in Toronto in 1929, he is regarded internationally as one of the leading figures in contemporary art. He is a multidisciplinary talent – a painter and sculptor, photographer, filmmaker and musician – without ever mixing the genres to excess. His film Wavelength (1967) established his reputation as one of the key filmmakers of the "American avant-garde" (sic) and gave him international stature on the contemporary art scene. For his film La Région Centrale (1971), he worked with a Canadian engineer to design and produce a mechanical arm that allowed the camera to rotate in all directions at speeds controlled by the artist. This machine soon became De la (1972), an installation or video sculpture.

His "cinematic" work is not limited to film stricto sensu, as is illustrated by numerous works such as the now-famous film installation Two Sides to Every Story (1974), the photographic works Plus Tard (1977) and Venetian Blind (1970). P. Adam Sitney considered Snow's film the typical example of "structural" film, thus underscoring an essential aspect of the artist's works, namely their structuralist, self-referential dimension. In all his works, whether films, photographs, holographs, sound and music pieces or paintings and sculptures, he focuses on structural elements of perception following a set of principles that include materiality, duration and movement in sequential works, and plays on scale and space, or on hiding and revealing through the use of transparencies. In an interview with Bruce Elder, Snow described himself as a "director of attention."[1]

1   R. Bruce Elder,
    "Michael Snow and
    Bruce Elder
    in conversation,"
    Cine-Tracts 5, 1
    (no. 17, Summer/Fall 1982),
    p. 14.

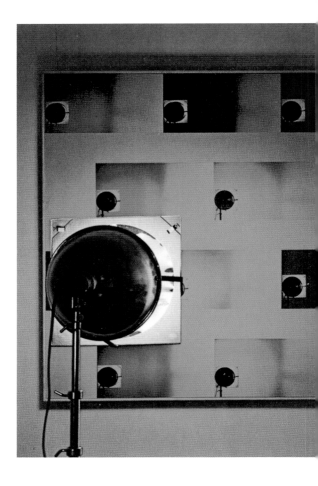

Authorization
1969
b/w Polaroid photographs,
adhesive cloth tape, mirror with
metal frame
54.5 x 44.5 cm (incl. frame)
collection National Gallery of
Canada, Ottawa
photo courtesy the artist

The interface – the Table Top Sequence

Digital Snow uses a sequence taken from Snow's 1974 four-and-a-half-hour 16mm film entitled *Rameau's Nephew by Diderot (thanx to Dennis Young) by Wilma Schoen*. This scene can be experienced in its uncut entirety in the section devoted to *Rameau's Nephew*. But the artist has also chosen to use it as the DVD-ROM's table of contents through which one may enter the world of Snow's work.

Picturing Snow's usual tools, this sequence illustrates a particular dimension of his work using several media and materials. It explores links with perception and with what mediates perception, most notably language and technology (and film and photography especially). The objects on this table, constantly shifted by the artist, will act as points of access to the databank on Snow's work and, according to various groupings, lead to different sections of the DVD.

Important themes, principles and materials in Snow's work

Light: where the physical qualities of light are a dominant "material" or "subject," or the condition for the work's existence.

Materiality: works where the perception of the materials used is at the forefront or stressed through structural elements of the work.

Re-presentation: Objects, materials or images that continue to contain their original recognizable subject, in a work that transforms and represents them while they are modified (and transformed) into a new state, sometimes from one medium to another, caught in the act of presenting *au carré*.

Reflection: works that use reflecting surface such as mirrors or metals. Concomitant with this are works also classified under two subsets of the reflection principle, namely: Whether the artist is seen in the work, or the spectator is.

Transparency: works that utilize transparent materials or emphasize transparency.

Duration: sequential works in which duration is at the forefront or the actual subject.

Look: works that point to the look or the gaze of the viewer as structured by the work.

Framing: works in which three-dimensional window-related forms are used, or where the extent of an image or its cropped or framed limits are an important factor in the experiencing of the work.

Scale: works that play with dimensions and jump from different scales within themselves, so that scaling becomes a major factor in the perception of the work's composition, for instance the relation of the original subject to the final print size in many photo-works, such as *Multiplication Table*, *In Medias Res*.

Recto-Verso: works (books, sculptures, photo-works) that involve showing two opposite sides of a given subject.

Improvisation and Composition are also broad principles that derive from the musical world but apply as well in film and other media.

Jean Gagnon

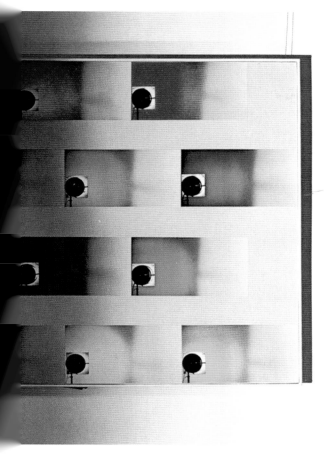

Front of the screen.

Light Blues
1974
color photographs, metal, light
bulb, colored filter
dimensions variable
Canada Council Art Bank
© Michael Snow

Back of the screen.

Two Sides to Every Story
1974
projection
two 16mm films
both color, sound
two projectors, painted
aluminum screen
8 min, dimensions variable
National Gallery of Canada,
Ottawa
© Michael Snow

*Corpus Callosum
1995-2001
film, digital Betacam
color, sound
92 min
video still
photo courtesy the artist

Zbigniew Rybczynski

The Rybczynski Phenomenon

What strikes me first and foremost is the Cultural Reference. Like everybody who comes from the East … It almost seems like they need to recover a culture. To make friends with Western culture by showing that they have the same standards: Magritte, Melies, Dalí, the Surrealists, etc. That's my first impression – that it's a bit of a misfire.

The other feeling I have is that Rybczynski uses the image as a series of geological layers. He doesn't play with the image as foundation or form but rather as a kind of geological stack. Each line being for him a system that can be isolated in the same way that a geologist manages to study each stratum. And the shift here, Baroque phenomena are really due to a geology of the image and no longer due to a geometry of the image. The horizontal lines are for him the equivalent of what the sedimentary lines are for a geologist. In my opinion, that's extremely original. He is no longer playing on the frame, he is playing on the horizontal lines, just as a musician would make his notes slide on a scale … that would please Deleuze. The fold … ah yes, that really is the fold!

I don't see any of the fourth dimension in it at all. I see a very dated space, in effect a very Leibnizian space, one firmly rooted in Memory ever since the seventeenth/eighteenth centuries. This film sums up an entire body of knowledge. It is, at base, the Museum of Western Art. Ultimately, the fourth dimension is the dimension of History. It is what has happened since the Renaissance up until our time, up until Magritte.

For me, the fourth dimension consists of the possibility of making something emerge that doesn't exist to the first degree but that does exist to the second. For example, one day I saw a clown, a Soviet clown, who was making everyone laugh by performing a set of antics very rapidly. He then repeated his antics but this time in slow motion, producing a second laugh because there was in effect a second gag in his first gag. It was time, the speed of the gag that, the first time, made the second gag disappear. This clown was able to show that there were thus two gags in one: that is the fourth dimension. Whereas for Rybczynski, that fourth dimension is History. Yes, it truly is a video-disc of the History of Art. That's really interesting. What I am saying isn't a criticism,

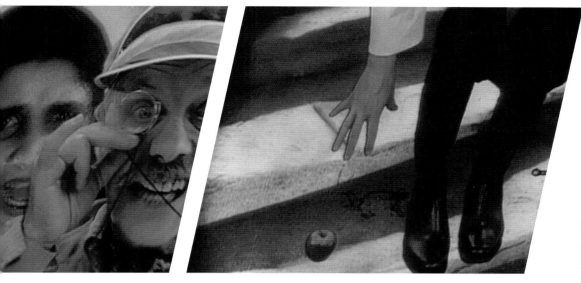

Steps
1987
video
color, sound
25:09 min
screenshots
© Zbig Rybczynski

not at all. It is unprecedented, this work, absolutely unprecedented … but at the same time, so dated.

Yes, dated. There for example, is Picart-Ledoux, in the 1950s … there's an entire stylistic of the 1950s there, one that's no longer ours. That doesn't take anything away from what is so exceptional about the treatment of the image. But nonetheless I do have the impression of a remake … A remake made with new means, with an extraordinary dexterity.

It is truly the Baroque! So, there … it's a film about the Baroque column, the rising column. The body as column.

He summarizes everything one last time. That in itself, is amazing. I have the impression a little bit of seeing the last film, the big film that one sees when one is going to die. The history of the World of Art that would repeat itself at full tilt.

There is also the trace of a Delvaux. His women are very Delvaux. This hieratism … it has the same bloodline.

What seems to me to be the most interesting thing here is the fact of no longer being able to separate cinema, video, and computer. From now on the point by point and line by line calculation is what will effectively measure and give form. It isn't the case that you have a computer graphic on the one hand and on the other, a series of video images: you now have a synthesis of images. It's the computer that makes us see: everything is there. The calculation has always been used for forecasting (*prévoir*): One used to calculate the equinoxes, an eclipse … Now, it is used for *seeing* (*voir*). It's already automation. No more need for lighting. The light is inside. It is digitalised. It is captive. It is no longer the element in which we are steeped. Captive of the figure, captive of digitalisation, of digitalised control.

There, we have Morandi, the painter of dead nature, the Italian Morandi, whom I like very much. That glass, for example, there …

Finally, the line work that Rybczynski accomplishes with his computer: Alexeieff did the same thing with his pin screen except that he did it manually.

A short while ago, he was speaking of Relativity. …But in a certain sense this film is not at all rela-tivist. There is no change of viewpoint. It is like the perspective in the Renaissance: one doesn't move. It's the object that moves under our eyes. It is the movement of number. One re-encounters Aristotelian practices. Movement is number. And number is movement.

It is an eminently Baroque film. I wasn't expecting that. I was expecting a work about what there is in what there isn't.

Could be that *Steps* goes further in the end. Because *Steps* opens onto a true Third Dimension on the interior of the film. The film becomes an architecture to inhabit, a space in which one can travel. Whereas here, it runs on its own. One can no longer interfere. These helices form a closed circuit. That takes nothing away from the exceptional plastic beauty of the work.

Just a little while ago it was the Cubists, now it's Rodin! It's always the History of Art.

Curiously, instead of calling it *The Fourth Dimension*, I would have called it *Dead Time*. The time of Art has come to an end. This is a funerary monument. It's no coincidence if at the end, there's a stele representing the first work of art (megalithic).

This film proves that one is mistaken to talk about *synthetic images*. Rather, we have to speak of a synthesis of images. Ever since video has existed, we have been in this realm of the Synthesis of Images. All images: the photo, the painting, the graphic, they all fit, everything fits into the mix-master, everything is synthesized.

Ultimately, with this accumulation comes a certain distress, a distress regarding the death of Art. Like at the end of *Steps*. But I don't get the impression that it's intentional. If anything, it would most likely be the fruit of Rybczynski's position as immigrant.

Paul Virilio

Translated from the French by Sarah Clift

First published in French: Paul Virilio, "Le phénomène Rybczinski," in *Cahiers du Cinema*, January 1989.

Kwadrat [Square]
1972
video
color, sound
4:46 min
screenshots
© Zbig Rybczynski

Mein Fenster
[My Window]
1979
video
color, sound
3:08 min
screenshots
© Zbig Rybczynski

Zbig Vision Ltd. Miniature of Zbigniew Rybczynski

In the early seventeenth century, when modern physics of the visible was beginning to establish itself, a black square appeared. The English Rosicrucian, doctor of medicine, and polymath Robert Fludd had a copperplate engraving made and the black square appears at the beginning of his history of the microcosm and macrocosm as a symbol of the limitlessness of unformed matter. Three hundred years later, the same geometric form in black and white became the compelling symbol of art's new departure to a world of relations, geometric proportions, and mathematical calculations. Exactly thirty years ago, in 1972, Zbigniew Rybczynski made his first film Kwadrat (Square) in Poland. It is only three and a half minutes long yet in essence it already contains the entire complexity of this artist-engineer and cinematographic alchemist's visual pluriverse. The film is organized like an exponential function in mathematics. It begins with a ten-second shot of a white square and ends with the same. In between, the process of dividing the square unfolds with mathematical precision. The original square splits into ever-smaller ones that subdivide again faster and faster until the middle of the film, when they resemble slightly enlarged pixels, they come together to form a human figure. From this human form, a game develops with the pure geo-

metrical form of the square. Before the white square returns to the initial image, it goes through variations in the primary colors red, green, blue, and yellow.

In 1980, Rybczynski made the ten-minute film Tango; it took him seven arduous months of sixteen-hour days and brought him an Oscar for the best short film in 1982 – as well as a night in a Los Angeles prison. A claustrophobic, cramped room of the type "petit-bourgeois ideal home" is transformed, through the repeated entrances and exits of the same animated people and their absurd actions, in a very short time into a madhouse of nervous, hectic, and senseless movements. Mein Fenster, a magnificent film that rendered space dynamic, had been made the year before, in 1979. When Rybczynski showed it twenty-one years later at the ZKM | Center for Art and Media in Karlsruhe to an audience of experts on quantum physics, relativity theory, and other theoretical branches of science, who had gathered in honor of the endophysicist and chaos theoretician Otto E. Roessler, it still commanded the highest admiration and amazement. Inside a space whose dimensions remain fixed, three "receptacles" are set in contra-rotating motion: a television set showing a newsreader, a birdcage, and a half-full bottle of red wine. The television newsreader gives the beat; his complete rotation of 360 degrees takes exactly two minutes. That is also how long the film is.

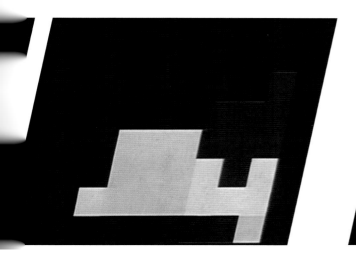

Keep Your Eye On Me
1987
music video for the song
by Herb Alpert
color, sound
screenshot
© Zbig Rybczynski

The 4th dimension
1988
video
color, sound
27 min
screenshot
© Zbig Rybczynski

Nowa Ksiazka [New Book]
1975
35mm film
color, sound
11 min
screenshot
© Zbig Rybczynski

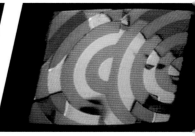

Plamuz [Music Art]
1973
35mm film
color, sound
10 min
screenshot
© Zbig Rybczynski

For the artists who, since the 1980s, have devoted great energy to bring technology, science, and art together again, Gene Youngblood, the author of *Expanded Cinema*, coined the expression "new renaissance artists." I call Zbigniew Rybczynski TNRA, "true new renaissance artist," because he represents this triad in the most radical and consistent way, lives and celebrates it like no other inventor and design engineer working in the field of illusions with moving images, and, at the same time, paradoxically remains faithful to a conception of beauty that is thoroughly molded by the ideals of the Renaissance.

At the time when the vast majority of film-makers held electronics to be the work of the devil, defiling the holy water of cinematography, Rybczynski concentrated his artistic and technical energies entirely on working with the Japanese High Vision format and, in the second half of the 1980s, on making video clips: for John Lennon's *Imagine*; *Opportunities* by the Pet Shop Boys; *All the Things She Said* by Simple Minds, and Herb Alpert's *Keep Your Eye on Me*. They represent electronic prototypes of the genre, and their powerfully innovative role has only been recognized recently in Europe, at the beginning of the new century.[1] In 1990, I suggested a screening and discussion of *Steps* (1987), Rybczynski's impudent integration of a voyeuristic group of contemporary American tourists into a scene from Sergei Eisenstein's film

classic *The Battleship Potemkin*, which is, to date, his masterpiece in High Vision that runs for twenty-four minutes. It was to a circle of illustrious members of the newly founded European Film Academy at the Berlin Academy of Arts, and my suggestion was met with outrage and a flat refusal. Rybczynski's daring film was branded as blasphemous. "We are living on the edge of time," says the tour guide in *Steps*. With the exception of a Russian and a Lithuanian student, my colleagues and the other students at the Academy of Arts and the Media in Cologne did not understand Rybczynski's special power and identity as a TNRA. They let him and his totally unique special effects studio for art production go back to Los Angeles again, where he now works with Paul Vlahos, the inventor of ultramatting, on realizing his ideas for a future autonomous cinema with cutting-edge technology. Zbig Vision is not only the name of the company where Rybczynski realizes his applications. Under this name, he has been working on an integrated concept for the production of composite illusions of movement, a complex system with analogue, precision, optical, and digital components.

The most important reason for embarking on this project was his dissatisfaction with the visual possibilities of central perspective, the geometrical principle of every photo or film camera and basis of all 3D-software applications.[2] Zbig is working on a lens

1 For example, in the six-part television series on music video clips *Fantastic Voyages*, which was screened in 2001 by the German television channel 3Sat and in 2002 by ZDF (German Channel 2).

2 In July 1999, Rybczynski gave a lecture at the symposium "Perspective on Perspective" in Budapest. His essay "Looking to the Future – Imagining the Truth" published in the symposium proceedings (*Intermedia – New Image genres– Interactive Techniques*, Miklós Peternák and Nikolett Eröss (eds), Mücsarnok-Kunsthalle Budapest and C³, Center for Culture and Communication, Budapest, 2001) is not identical but contains some of the ideas.

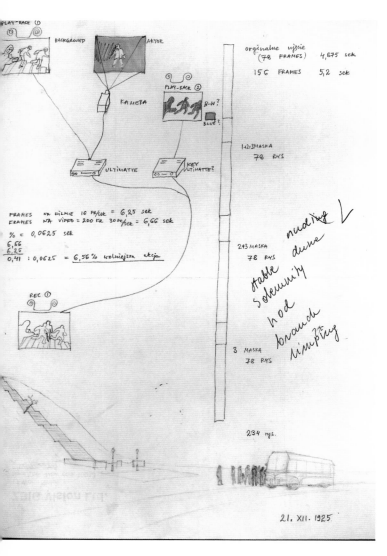

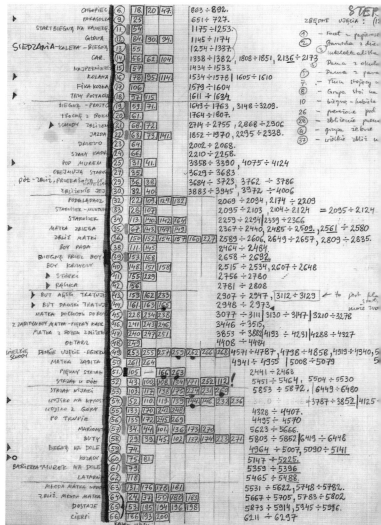

drawings for
Steps
1986
© Zbig Rybczynski

Imagine
1986
high-definition digital movie
music video for the song by
John Lennon
color, sound
screenshots
© Zbig Rybczynski

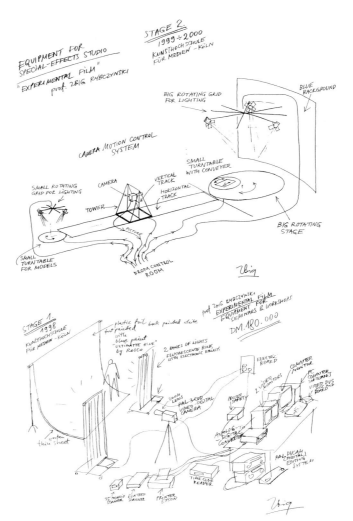

with a zooming range of up to at least 180 degrees, as opposed to the usual 45 degrees, as well as multiperspectival resolution of the monocular view. Using his own unorthodox method of programming, he has already written most of the software. The difficulty now is finding a manufacturer who is willing to invest in the experiment of constructing a lens capable of projecting the requisite spherical optics without any distortions. Another problem, related to precision engineering, has already been solved by the inventor-director himself, who owns more than a dozen valuable patents: the construction of a motion control simulation system, which allows him to integrate any object, person, or background into film images with the greatest precision. The idea behind this illustrates the extent to which scientific, technical, and artistic aspects permeate Rybczynski's work: in existing industrial concepts the motion control cameras take the images while moving around people and objects; Zbig's ingenious trick is to place the animate and inanimate objects on a rotating platform. This offers the camera over 300,000 different positions, and thus views. The camera's position only varies in its distance to the objects and in its vertical perspective, which is continuously adjustable from an extremely high to an extremely low angle, from bird to worm. The rails and framework for using different cameras are a mechanical marvel; Zbig has worked on the construction for years, testing every tiny detail to find optimal technical solutions. He has developed a special system of silently operating batteries of fluorescent lamps, which ensure that the camera's objects do not throw any irritating shadows and their contours remain in sharp contrast.

The potential of the entire system is immense and it follows a genuine artistic idea. Whereas George Lucas' Industrial Light and Magic consumes millions of dollars to produce a few film sequences, requires extreme division of labor, and elaborate spatial and temporal industrial logistics, the Zbig Vision system fits into about twenty square meters and can be realized for a fraction of the cost. The entire production process, from shooting to post-production, remains in the hands of the artist. If the requisite technical knowledge is given, the artist is autonomous and has at his or her disposal all the tools necessary for creating any kind of moving illusion.

In principle, the unspoken aim of such a cinema of the future is to bring about the radical disappearance of the medium. Zbig dreams of interfaces that would be capable of translating his visions directly into synthetic images, without having to bother about the constraints of mechanics, optics, and electronics. Ten years ago, when he made *Kafka* (1992), which is in High Vision and contains image compositions with up to ninety different layers, there existed only the beginnings of his concept for a new system. He was still working with real actors, sets, and props within the confines of classical optical geometry. I am quite sure that in his next film project we will encounter a visual world that has left this framework far behind it.

Siegfried Zielinski

Werner Nekes
Der Tag des Malers [The Day of the Painter]

1997
35mm film / color, sound / 84 min

Measuring and Stripping Bare 1

The film begins with a sequence of painted time. In a peculiar, meditative presentation, a collage is built up of barely identifiable images of naked women, in alienating colours, layered one upon the other … as if viewed through a chaotic kaleidoscope. Then, suddenly, a jarringly sharp image of an artifact of art and media history: one of the most distinctive sketches from Albrecht Dürer's well-known *Underweyssung der Messung* of 1536, which is quoted time and again whenever the topic being discussed is central perspective and "symbolic form" (Panofsky). Nekes barely touches the surface of the sketch, but rather leaves it, for the most part, as it is. The camera pans away horizontally. A painter with a walrus moustache and somewhat unkempt hair is sitting bolt upright in an intense state of attention at the right end of a long, heavy wooden table. He is gazing with his right eye through the monocular site of a drawing apparatus. The pencil in his right hand rests on a sheet of paper which is divided into a grid exactly like the grid strung on a wooden frame that is standing on the table. On the other side of the grid is the voluptuous, nearly naked body of a woman, her head resting on a pile of presumably soft pillows. For the viewer of the sketch, only the profile of her face is visible, and her eyes are shut. From the painter's perspective, through the grid, her slightly open thighs are at an angle, not aimed directly at him. Her left hand is holding a cloth at the inside of her left calf, which covers her right leg and her pubis, as well as her entire right arm.

What is the painter seeing through this apparatus? What could he possibly be feeling? Is he even interested in the beauty of the body across the table from him? Does he smell it? Does he sense its presence? Is he imagining how it tastes? Does he desire it? Is the other body something sensational to the painter, or is his concentrated attention exclusively dedicated to the realization of the aesthetic goal of this special artistic act, i.e., precise two-dimensional representation in symbolic form, according to the laws of Euclidean geometry? "I am, by no means, painting a woman," said Henri Matisse, "I am painting a picture."

There is a planned sequence at the end of the film which consists of a single unvarying shot. Werner

Nekes places a beautiful young woman in a reclined position, giving the camera a view reminiscent of the image presented in Gustave Courbet's famous 1866 painting *The Origin of the World (L'Origine du Monde)*. But Nekes differentiates his image from Courbet's in several important ways. In the famous work of art, the model is allowed to remain anonymous. The body of Courbet's nascent woman has no face. It's just a trunk bearing the genitals. In the film, the young woman's body is cut off at the lower part of the leg by the frame, but the film speaks for her unparalleled beauty, in that it gives us a view of the head that goes with the pubis. Courbet's *Origin of the World* comes out of a dark, nearly black background. Nekes sets his scene in the out of doors: it is light, it is open and free.

And most of all: the frame does not stand still. Only after the beautiful young woman closes her eyes, does the observing gaze begin to wander downward. Her left hand moves to her left breast and, with a little hesitation, lays itself there. Her right hand glides slowly, gropingly across her body to her vulva and she begins to masturbate. This shot lasts approximately four minutes, without a single cut. The woman visibly brings herself to a climax. One can see it as a momentary tightening of her body and a brief shuddering of the image. The reel is over and, with that, *The Day of the Painter*. The credits follow abruptly.

This final sequence is simultaneously beautiful and irritating. The masturbating woman obviously knows of the presence of the third mechanical eye between her and the potential public. At first glance she seems totally detached, giving herself over completely to the pleasure with her eyes closed. But with nearly every motion of her body, with every expression on her face, and with the always hesitant movement of her hands, she also demonstrates that she is framed by a motion picture. Tension/concentration and ease, calculation and insubstantiality are densely superimposed one upon the other in this staging of autoeroticism as the director's unique interpretation of *The Origin of the World*. It casts the feminine principle not in the function of child-bearing, but as the medium of desire.

This sequence is the only one in the entire film in which Nekes allows the 35mm film to act purely on its own, without manipulating the surfaces and without interfering with the course of time. That which

1 The most recent film by Werner Nekes was only completed before this manuscript had to be submitted to the publisher. In the summer of 1997, the film was chosen as one of the two German contributions to the Venice Film Festival. Only a few days before the premier, Nekes gave me the opportunity to see a 16mm print of the film in the studio in his home. The text was developed directly in reaction to this unique viewing. I would like to thank Werner Nekes for the presentation and the discussion that followed.

Dürer's painter saw with his left eye, or perhaps even with the eye of his imagination – the genitals of the woman as an object of desire – is allowed to fall onto the side of the clearly visible. He makes it openly accessible. Between the opening scene and the final climax, the day of the painter unfolds, which in this case is the day of the filmmaker.

Legions of painters, sculptors and photographers have grappled with the riddles presented to them by the sketches of Dürer, Rubens, da Vinci, Cigoli. Or they have each in their own fashion tried to approach the secrets of "the other's" body, often directly connected to Courbet's *Origin of the World*: Duchamp's *Étant donnés* (Nekes devotes one of the longest and most beautiful sequences in the film to this image of a nude woman with an upright oil lamp in her left hand), Fontana's *Femme nue couchée*, Fischl's *Bad Boy*, Balthus' *La Chambre*, Noritoshi Hirakawa's *The Pandora that is Pandora's Box*, as well as a few women artists, such as Cindy Sherman in her photo-sculpture *Untitled #263*, in which a female and a male torso are bound together with a ribbon, while their severed heads lie next to them (a reversal of Hans Bellmer's *La Poupée*, of which he made many variations between 1938 and 1949).2 These attempts to unveil this secret through aesthetic means had to and will have to remain in vain and end in paradoxes, since the desire to include the unshowable in an image leads, again and again, to veiling and disguising. During the time Courbet's famous painting was in his possession, Jaques Lacan made this into a topic through a private staging. He had asked André Masson, who had illustrated Bataille's *The Story of the Eye* (*L'Histoire de l'Oeil*), to prepare a painter's sketch, in which the contours of Courbet's painting can be dimly perceived, as if in a negative. He placed this sketch, which was in the same format as the original, as a veiling layer in front of the painting. If one opened the side of the frame and removed the Masson sketch, one revealed the origin of the world, but one encountered, once again, an imaginary construct of it, and had to be satisfied with the painting *L'Origine du monde*.3

Nekes orbits around an entire circle of diverse disguises and aesthetic veiling and unveiling strategies for viewing, in long, unhurried sequences. In the process, he employs all the tools of his experience with film technology, visualization technologies, cinematography itself, and his recent experience with electronic devices. Simple scenes of amateurishly portrayed female nudity before the camera are placed on a grid, (as in the instructional image by Dürer), crosshatched, broken up diagonally (as in Fischl's painting) and put back together again, pointilized, over and underexposed, distorted in colour, layered, disintegrated to the point of two-dimensional abstraction, altered through fantastic masks making them only dimly discernible for the viewer, or alienated through extreme camera angles: as in a long sequence, in which a Hi-8 camera is bound to a woman's right foot, which places the moving woman in an extreme perspective and presents a crazy picture for the perception. For this film, Nekes used the entire range of contemporary visual recording technology from the classic 35mm, to 16mm as well as electronic recording devices of various types. His postproduction techniques were similarly diverse. All the material (with the exception of the final sequence) was digitalized and processed with image-manipulation software. What emerges is a dense cinematic concentrate of potential aesthetification techniques, as well as a discourse on some of the practices of distancing, trivialization, glorification, and veiling, in the artistic struggle with the unparalleled sensation of "Frau Werden"4 (becoming a woman), which have been possible up to now and might be possible in the future.

The result of Nekes' radical concentration of the material of his film is that he tears the traditional concept of the film wide open: looking back toward the past with the reference to practices of the distant past for playfully and subversively deviating from the verdict of the representative image, as well as looking into the future of the motion picture as a construct with seemingly endlessly changeable material. The *Day of the Painter* shifts with authority between painting, photography, cinematography, and electronic image-making and manipulation. Just as he is not prepared to recognize the borders between these artistic disciplines, he also oscillates between the media genres of documentary, staged presentation and simulation. Even in his radical finale, a question is begged: What manner of truth is embodied in the masturbative film act, the masculine/quantifying presumption, or the liberation of being stripped bare? A question that can only be answered by the perceptions of each individual viewer. The motion picture incorporates ambivalence.

The film abandons dialogue, with the exception of the worried question of the protagonist with the camera harnessed to her foot, as to whether there aren't perhaps snakes in the grass. The music of Anthony Moore, with whom Nekes has worked for many years, the last time in his series *Media Magica*, adds strength to the discursive dimension of the film, in that he experiments with putting rhythm and instrumentation to the story and layers of the imagery that callously veils our view of the possible origin of the world. This is and remains a project of the imaginative faculties, and not a matter of visual and acoustic artifacts. But sometimes artistic efforts help us – as does this film by Werner Nekes – to more successfully unfurl these mysteries.

Siegfried Zielinski
Translated from the German by Theo Hoffmann

First published in *Perspektiva*, exhib. cat., Mücsarnok Kunsthalle Budapest, Budapest, 2000–2001.

2 Compare this to *Feminimasculin, Le Sexe de l'Art*, exhib. cat., Editions du Centre Georges Pompidou, Paris, 1995. This exhibition in the Centre Georges Pompidou was perhaps the most exhaustive contemporary attempt to present the avantgarde's relationship to sex and the erotic. But the entire grand affair was hopelessly sidetracked by its arbitrariness and by the superficial fixation on sexuality being placed directly in the picture.

3 In 1996, Jean-Paul Fargier made an excellent 26-minute video for the Musée d'Orsay, where Courbet's painting is on display, in which he deals primarily with the adventurous history of the painting's reception, and centrally with Lacan's presentation.

4 The concept refers to the tenth chapter of *One Thousand Plateaus: Capitalism and Schizophrenia*, Gilles Deleuze and Felix Guattari, University of Minnesota Press, Minneapolis, MN, 1987 (originally published as *Mille Plateaux. Capitalisme et Schizophrénie*, vol. 2, Les Editions de Minuit, Paris, 1980), especially from p. 375.

William Kentridge
Overvloed

1999
35mm animated film transferred to DVD / charcoal-and-pastel drawings, paper
cut-out figures / dimensions variable / b/w, sound / 6 min

William Kentridge's Filming

Metamorphosis and palimpsest are pivotal to William
Kentridge's work. In the late 1980s he embarked on a
series of short films entitled *Drawings for Projection*
(1989–1997), which were based on drawings and won
him international recognition. As an artist, Kentridge
has been constantly extending his media repertoire,
linking film, theater, installation and sculpture in the
most varied of ways, while simultaneously exploring
the full potential of each genre. Yet the artist sees
himself more as a draftsman than a film-maker, and
calls his film works "extended drawings."[1] His use of
the medium of film began as a kind of documentation
of his working process.

Filming Drawings to Record Their History

Kentridge has described his animation technique as
"stone age film-making."[2] Compared to commercial
productions in this field, his technique is remarkably
simple. He positions a 16mm or 35mm film camera opposite an easel[3] and then proceeds to make a drawing, mainly in black charcoal, though occasionally complemented by colored pastel chalks. That drawing is
then reworked and constantly changed, while the
camera captures the various stages of the process.
Thus one drawing can be changed and filmed up to
five hundred times before the filmic narrative demands a new scene, and thus a new drawing. Unlike a
commercial animated film, which requires for each
take a new drawing, and for each working process a
corresponding specialist, the number of drawings
Kentridge makes depends on the frequency of the
scenes that finally appear in the film. As a result, a
six- to eight-minute film can be based on less than
forty drawings. The individual sheets are changed by
adding something new or erasing something already
there, with the traces of the eraser remaining clearly
visible in the process. The animation comes into being,
therefore, by addition and subtraction, creation and

destruction. In this way, the most characteristic aspect of the drawing process – a movement developed
and captured over time – assumes a great importance both as a narrative moment and as a metaphor
for memory: The film is a trace of a sequence of decisions made by the draftsman. Each step is distinguishable. Layers, nodes and cross references form
like a palimpsest, albeit in a non-linear way. Wandering
constantly between drawing sheet and camera,
William Kentridge sees filming as capturing decision-
making processes, recording movement and change in
time and space: "two dimensions moving through
time."[4]

One particular feature of the drawing is its inherent high degree of spontaneity. Stemming as it does
directly from the hand of the artist, it is thus "able to
directly mirror the involvement with the object, with
the idea."[5] Since the Renaissance, the drawing has
been ascribed an almost moral value as a means of
precisely fixing something, as a medium for attaining
a higher level of truth. The *Paragone* confirms its

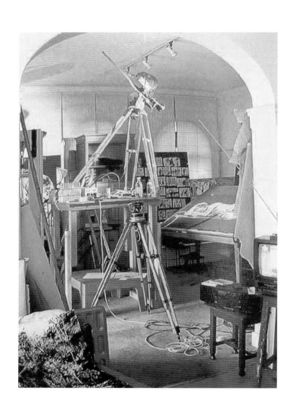

William Kentridge's studio.

1 Carolyn Christov-Bakargiev,
William Kentridge, exhib. cat.,
Société des Expositions du
Palais des Beaux-Arts de
Bruxelles, Brussels, 1998,
p. 19.

2 William Kentridge, " 'Fort-
una': Neither Program nor
Chance in the making of
images." Lecture, 1993,
published in *Cycnos: Image
et Langage, Problèmes,
Approches, Méthodes*,
Nice, vol. 11, no. 1, 1994,
pp. 163–168. Quoted after
Dan Cameron, Carolyn
Christov-Bakargiev,
J.M. Coetzee (eds), *William
Kentridge*, Phaidon Press,
London 1999, p. 114.

3 Kentridge mainly uses a
16mm Bolex, plus an Ariflex, a
technically somewhat more
advanced camera of a similar kind. See Rosalind Krauss,
" 'The Rock': Kentridge's
Drawings for Projection," in
OCTOBER 92, Spring 2000,
p. 5. He was later also to use
digital film material, or
35mm.

4 Unpublished interview,
Prince Claus Fund, 1999.

5 Walter Koschatzky, *Die Kunst
der Zeichnung. Technik,
Geschichte, Meisterwerke*,
Pawlak, Herrsching, 1990.

drawing for *Monument*
1990
charcoal on paper
120 x 150 cm
© William Kentridge

drawing for *Felix in Exile*
1994
charcoal and pastel on paper
120 x 160 cm
© William Kentridge

function as representative of the artist's inventive powers, of the idea of form born of the spirit. The drawing was seen as having a political, social-utopian, or ironic-critical function vis-à-vis reality by artists such as Goya, Hogarth or Daumier, by 1920s representatives of Expressionism and Neue Sachlichkeit like Schiele, Dix, Grosz, Beckmann, Kollwitz, or by Dumile (Dumile Feni Mhlaba) with his South African Resistance Art. Kentridge has repeatedly emphasized the strong influence these artists have had on his relationship to the drawing.[6] Themes and motifs used by these models, as well as references to art-historical *topoi* intrinsic to animated films, such as the Ovidian myth of Pygmalion,[7] are to be found in many of Kentridge's works. In the film *Monument* (1990), for example, at the moment of its unveiling, the statue of a worker raises its eyes and begins to speak, thereby directing attention away from the monument's patron and towards its referent.

Unlike the smooth flow of images in the commercial animated film, Kentridge has no overall plan, film scenario or storyboard when he sets to work,[8] and he always ensures that the individual drawing is recognizable. The suggestive openness of the form and the subjective, seemingly automatic superimposition of the images prevent the emergence of any single reading; this is also perceptible at the level of what is depicted and narrated.[9] The open, experimental handling of the film medium and the animated image, the dominant monochrome in the films, the musical accompaniment, and the "stop and shoot" technique point to icons of experimental cinema (Eisenstein, Vertov, Man Ray), and in particular to experimental animated filmmakers like Norman McLaren. It was they who revealed to Kentridge the radical possibilities offered by the medium in terms of technology, narration and pictorial aesthetics. While in the 1920s Dziga Vertov revolutionized the medium by means of new montage techniques and split-screen effects inspired by Constructivist ideas, in the 1940s the

animated filmmaker McLaren broke new ground through his experiments with image and sound. For example, he eliminated the camera and drew directly onto the film.[10] It is to him that Kentridge owes probably his most important insight, namely to begin with what the drawing and the film have to offer as media rather than developing his films according to a narrative structure: "You didn't have to know the story before you started the film."[11] As he draws, Kentridge's interest can shift from what he originally intended to something that was initially completely secondary. "Filming enables me to follow this process of vision and revision as it happens."[12] Out of these shifts crystallize the key images in the film.

In the *Drawings for Projection* cycle, the stories center around the property developer Soho Eckstein, his wife, and Felix Teitelbaum, a dreamer. Eckstein, in a pin-striped suit, and Felix Teitelbaum, naked, act as the alter ego, while their common desire is embodied in Mrs. Eckstein. Kentridge has set this apparently naive plot in South Africa just as the Apartheid policy is about to be abandoned. Although he provides no concrete historical references, there can be little doubt that it is that society, with its psycho-social crises, which is the backdrop to the action. In a seemingly random sequence of episodes the films address the theme of social injustice. While *Monument*, the second film in the cycle, deals with the power and influence of modern mass communications, the later film *Mine* (1991) links the exploitation of the land with its veins of gold and the exploitation of the workers bodies. As the owner of a mine, Soho Eckstein excavates the whole history of a society, revealing the psychological dissociation of South Africa's white upper class from "white guilt," their ignorance of the reality of slavery, pain, coldness, danger and death. Kentridge's depiction of landscape mirrors colonial policy. That landscape also becomes an agent of history when, for example, it incorporates the victims of a massacre.

6   Carolyn Christov-Bakargiev, op. cit., p. 15f.

7   Publius Ovidius Naso, *Metamorphosen*, ed. and transl. by Erich Rösch, Munich 1961, Book X, p. 243ff. Pygmalion succeeds in bringing to life the statue he has made as a result of the love that springs from his artistic perfection. In particular since the Renaissance, this myth has served to demonstrate the artist's inventiveness and technical mastery.

8   Unpublished interview, Prince Claus Fund, 1999.

9   In his 1993 lecture "Fortuna," Kentridge repeatedly emphasized the automatism of this unique method. He described the artist's dilemma of having to decide between two equally impossible alternatives: The abandonment of the traditional medium or, alternatively, the absolute mechanization of chance (Cage) or subjection to absolute organization (Krenik) or respectively improvisation or automatism. Modern films already have a certain automatism about them due to the photographic techniques on which they are based (Stanley Cavell, "Music Discomposed," in *Must We Mean What We Say?*, Scribner's, New York, 1969). See Rosalind Krauss, op. cit., pp. 7–11.

10 On experimental animated film see, for example, *The Art of the Animated Image*, Charles Solomon (ed.), The American Film Institute, Los Angeles, 1987.

11 William Kentridge in an interview with the authors on 10 February 2002.

12 Carolyn Christov-Bakargiev, op. cit., p. 16.

Ubu Tells the Truth
1997
35mm animated film collage
transferred to video
and laserdisc
charcoal-and-chalk drawings on
paper, archival documentary
footage, paper cut-out figures
b/w & color, sound
8 min
still
© William Kentridge
photo courtesy Marian
Goodman Gallery, New York

production photograph of
Shadow Procession
1999
© William Kentridge
photo courtesy
Marian Goodman Gallery,
New York

13 Michael Godby, "Memory and history in William Kentridge's *History of the Main Complaint*," in Sarah Nuttall, Carli Coetzee, *Negotiating the past: The making of memory in South Africa*, Oxford University Press, Cape Town, 1998, p. 100.

14 Carolyn Christov-Bakargiev, op. cit., pp. 9–39.

15 Dan Cameron, "A Procession of the Dispossessed," in Dan Cameron, Carolyn Christov-Bakargiev (eds), op. cit., pp. 36ff.

16 William Kentridge, "Art in a State of Grace, Art in a State of Hope, Art in a State of Siege," (extract, 1986) in Dan Cameron, Carolyn Christov-Bakargiev, J.M. Coetzee (eds), op. cit., p. 104.

17 Rosalind Krauss, op. cit., p. 24.

18 Aleida Assmann, "Zur Metaphorik der Erinnerung," in *Vergessen und Erinnern in der Gegenwartskunst*, Kai-Uwe Hemken (ed.), Reclam, Leipzig, 1996, pp. 16–46.

The analogies between content and technique are particularly potent in *Felix in Exile* (1994). The film shows an African woman, Nandi, surveying the land and documenting in drawings evidence of violence and a brutal massacre. By studying these drawings, Felix sees the world through her eyes. The film makes no distinction between the handwriting of Nandi, the protagonist, and that of Kentridge, the artist, so that the authorship remain unclear. At another level, Nandi's drawings come to life, are animated, within the film. Geography, as a product of nature and history,[13] and drawing, as a medium of memory and a sign of authorship, become intertwined. The biographical link with the artist is obvious: Kentridge was born in South Africa in 1955. His parents and grandparents worked as lawyers and represented, among others, victims of the Sharpville massacre. In the mid-1970s, Kentridge began working in film and theater, as an author, director, actor and stage-set designer. He was a founder-member of the Junction Avenue Theatre Company, located in Johannesburg and Soweto from 1975 to 1991, and the Free Filmmakers' Cooperative, founded in Johannesburg in 1988. Kentridge is active in what might be termed the South African Resistance Art scene.[14]

In the last decades of apartheid, South Africa was subjected to a UN trade embargo, and the art scene too was cut off from the rest of the world. The ever more globalized art world of the 1990s celebrated Kentridge's art "as a cause of relief, primarily because it affirms the importance of artistic activity in societies where profound cultural change is the sum of daily life."[15] Yet the Euro-African dialog is not to be seen as a one-way street. Kentridge's preference for shifting themes and motifs from the history of European art and literature to modern South Africa reflects his wish to retrace their origins and examine their general validity. This apparent anachronism is best illustrated by the reference to Alfred Jarry's play *Ubu Roi* (1888) in Kentridge's *Ubu Projects* (1996–1997), which deal with the public hearings of the Truth and Reconciliation Commission.

Kentridge's film projects avoid direct confrontation with the historical background in favor of an associative, non-linear narrative. The artist rejects the kind of complete, rounded-off narrative that can be found, for example, in eighteenth- and nineteenth-century moralizing prints in which the image illustrates a history outside itself and excludes the viewer.[16] Kentridge opposes this with the palimpsest, a sheet drawn upon several times, a collection of fragments which turns upside-down everything that was dear to encyclopedic Hegelian thought. The palimpsest stands for an emblematic form of temporality and thus for an abstraction from narrative, history and biography.[17] Historical eras can be read as a synchronous present. From the wealth of repetitions and over-writings in the palimpsest – which always preserves its subjective connotation – history and memory are deposited as a sediment.[18]

 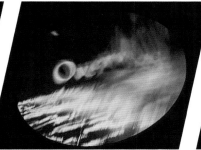 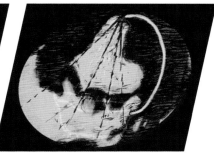

Overvloed
1999
35mm animated film
transferred to DVD
charcoal-and-pastel drawings,
paper cut-out figures
b/w, sound
6 min
stills
courtesy William Kentridge
© William Kentridge

 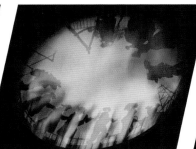 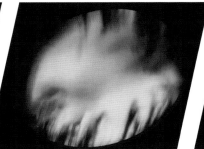 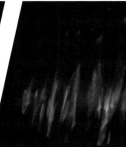

Overvloed

In his 1999 installation *Overvloed*, Kentridge projected the film onto an oval ceiling. As the title suggests (the Dutch "overvloed" meaning "flood" or "abundance"), the images looked like they were being blurred and swept away by water. The viewer uses a mirror to follow the images, which are accompanied by the melancholic singing and accordion playing of the Johannesburg musician Alfred Makgalemele. The changing charcoal-and-pastel drawings that form the basis of the projection are interspersed with silhouette figures, found footage, and fragments of East African and Dutch idioms and aphorisms dating from the "Dutch Golden Era."[19] The recurrent element of the film is the silhouette figures of a group of people that wander in circles around a putative opening in the vault – an image that Kentridge already worked on within *Shadow Procession* (1999), for instance, and that links to the very early state of filming.

The film does not adhere to a narrative. The scenes appear to be arranged in succession and can be read associatively. They are transformed in a constant stream that draws us into an archeology made up of signs and symbols.

Overvloed was commissioned by the Prince Claus Fund in Amsterdam. It was conceived for a one-off event during which the six-minute film was projected onto the large barrel-vaulted Baroque ceiling of the monumental civic hall of the Koninklijk Paleis in Amsterdam.[20] The original ceiling paintings were visible as a wonderful patina behind the film images, thus underscoring the palimpsest aspect of Kentridge's approach.

The work addresses the historical links between the Netherlands and South Africa as part of an ongoing interest in finding non-literal ways of teasing out the conundrum of Europe's legacy in Africa. The construction of the palace – as the city's Town Hall in 1648, the highpoint of the Dutch Golden Era – was undertaken at a time when Holland was colonizing South Africa, and with its decorative scheme it symbolizes the independence of the young republic. The ceiling fresco in the Civic Hall bears eloquent witness to the self-understanding of the Amsterdam citizens: the world lies at the feet of the city's female patron, who is flanked by allegories of strength and wisdom. The pictorial scheme of the encrusted floor even depicts the city as the center of the universe.[21]

19 One should not be / too hopeful / to a ship sailing / from Europe. // My witness is in Europe / says the liar. // The poor are salted meat.. / Afkomst seyt niet. // What nie dood maak nie / maak vet. // A nicely built city / never resists / destruction. // Being thin is / not dying.

20 The reference here is to the presentation of the Prince Claus Award "Creating Spaces of Freedom" in December 1999. After its showing at the Exploding Cinema Festival in the Rotterdam Rijksmuseum Beumans van Beuningen in February 2002, the work was shown for the third time at the ZKM Karlsruhe. Whereas in the Netherlands it was projected onto a Baroque structure (an unpainted ceiling in Rotterdam), the ZKM presentation was the first in a museum setting.

21 http://www.bmz.amsterdam.nl/adam/uk/groot/qtvr2.html

Overvloed
1999
installation views: ZKM |
Center for Art and Media
Karlsruhe, 2002
courtesy William Kentridge
© William Kentridge
photos © Franz Wamhof

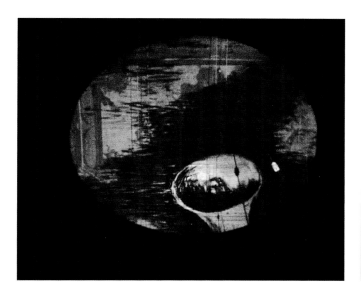

Overvloed
1999
installation view: Burgerzaal,
Koninklijk Paleis te
Amsterdam, 1999
courtesy William Kentridge
© William Kentridge

William Kentridge, Kevin Volans,
Handspring Puppet Company
Confessions of Zeno
2002
theater performance
performance view: Berliner
Festspiele, 2002
© William Kentridge
photo © Ruphin Coudyzer

This putative center is metaphorically inundated by *Overvloed* – an allusion to the constant fear the Dutch have of losing the land which they have wrested from the sea. Here ebb tide and high tide epitomize nature's cyclical forces: High tide and the battle against it become the allegory of state, as it were.[22] This metaphor is reflected not just at the level of pictorial symbolism, but is continued in Kentridge's visual aesthetic and technique when drawn floods sweep away the script, or when it seems as if the images projected onto the surface of the water and filmed are being washed away.

Overvloed is the first film work which Kentridge conceived specially for a concrete architectural space and as such it represents, for him, a completely new kind of site- or screen-specific handling of the medium. For the first time, this work demands the active participation of the viewer. Some of the projected idioms and aphorisms are reversed, with the result that their meaning only becomes clear when the viewer shifts his gaze from the ceiling to the mirror and back to the ceiling. The mirror in the viewer's hand becomes a "private screen," his own small film. It brings "the whole scale down to something very small and personal."[23]

Overvloed also stands for a dislocation – primarily the dislocation of a conventional horizon – that arises when looking up at a painting, or a projection, on the ceiling. "Our habitual sense of up and down, ground and air, is thrown out of equilibrium. With every ceiling painting or projection, one struggles to find a point or series of points from which it makes sense."[24] The mirror in our hand enables us to find our bearings in the room without having to move.

Live Cinema – theatrical multimedia performance
Kentridge's latest work, *Confessions of Zeno* (2002), stands for a new concept of cinema. Based on Italo Svevo's novel *La Coscienza di Zeno* (1923), it was presented as an installation (*Zeno writing*) at the documenta 11, and also premiered as a theater production. Kentridge sees his idea of "live cinema"[25] best realized in the theater play. His aim is to expand the classical theater or opera performance not solely by the inclusion of a live musical event, as in *Il Ritorno d'Ulisse* (1998), but above all by adding a live cinematographic image during the performance. Expressionistic charcoal drawings projected as animations, found footage, ephemeral shadows of figures torn from paper, silhouettes of a group of actors from the Handspring Puppet Company and their requisites performing simultaneously on the stage and on the projection area, accompanied throughout by a string quartet – these are the constituents of the "live cinematic image." The "cinema image" thus emerges before the eyes of the audience. This "simultaneity" engenders a strangely captivating dichotomy between the screen images and their sources.[26]

Shifting between the media, exploiting their respective potential and instrumentalizing it for the filmic narrative, these are defining moments in William Kentridge's work as he re-casts an antiquated pictorial idiom. This diachronic approach involves an exploration of origins, development, history, and change.

Petra Meyer and Katrin Kaschadt
Translated from the German by Pauline Cumbers

22 For the first generation of patriotic eulogists, everything Dutch was often equated with the transformation, under divine guidance, of a catastrophe into a happy event, of weakness into strength, of water into dry land, of mud into gold. Parallels were drawn between political events and the breaching of the dikes. See Simon Schama: *Überfluss und schöner Schein. Zur Kultur der Niederlande im Goldenen Zeitalter*, Kindler, Munich, 1988, pp. 38ff.

23 See footnote 11.

24 Unpublished interview, Prince Claus Fund, 1999.

25 William Kentridge, "Zenos Gewissen," in *documenta11_Plattform5*, exhib. cat., Hatje Cantz, Ostfildern-Ruit, 2002, p. 573.

26 William Kentridge "Zenos Gewissen," op. cit., p. 573.

Jon Jost
Trinity. An Altar Piece

2000–2002
time, space, 7 screens / 60 min

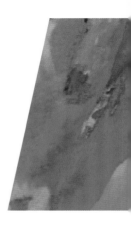

Trinity was conceived as a mode of altarpiece, following in some measure the form of such works as found in churches of Europe, from medieval through baroque styles. While I am not in any manner a "believer" in Christian religious tenets, the work is based upon the conventions and "narrative" of The Passion, though this is expressed in purely abstract form. The work is made of a sequence of passages or movements, in a sense working as visual equivalents to music: the opening phase is intended (unlabeled) to represent Gethsemane; this is followed with an agitated sequence which signals Golgotha; then a long and slow movement for the Ascension, succeeded with a much faster passage for the Assumption. Hence this classic biblical narrative is condensed into a series of visual tropes, though these are organized through time in a manner more related to music than a literary source.

The intent was to tap into this deeply rooted mythological source of western culture in a manner which strips it of its narrative meaning and uses only

its formal shape, though still intending to induce the spectator into the same mode of introspecti[ve] and meditative thought which the traditional alta[r] piece is designed to provoke. *Trinity* is an invitatic[n] inward reflection which operates on the assump[tion] of culturally shared values and experiences.

With the exception of two short passages ma[de] using a particle-generator program (at the begin[ning] a passage alluding to "in the beginning was the w[ord]" and at the end, a passage suggestive of the Big B[ang] theory of the beginning of the universe), all of *Tri[nity]* is aesthetically composed of manipulations of a s[ingle] eighty-second camera shot which has been heav[ily] processed though electronic processing with bo[th] Discreet Logic Inferno program, and a Premiere n[on-] linear editing system. No paint or graphics progr[ams] were used.

As a composition through time, *Trinity* is inten[ded] to be received as a whole, from beginning to end, [in] the same manner in which one listens to a symph[ony] its totality, as the trajectory through time is a m[ain]

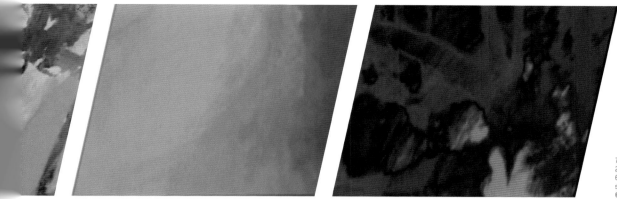

Trinity. An Altar Piece
2000–2002
60 min
screenshots
© Jon Jost

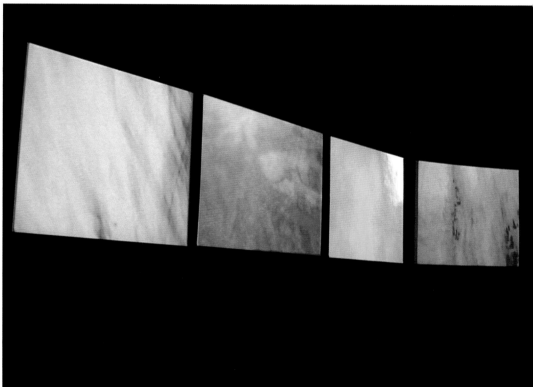

Trinity. An Altar Piece
2000–2002
time, space, seven screens
60 min
installation views: ZKM |
Center for Art and Media
Karlsruhe, 2002
© Jon Jost
photos © ZKM | Center for Art
and Media Karlsruhe

component in its impact. *Trinity* has no sound: the intention is that while the temporal aspect is to be sensed as music, the visual element is meant to be psychologically received in a manner related more to painting than to "media" or "cinema." I concluded that any sound would shift the viewer's expectations into anticipations of a filmic kind, and distract from the essential painterly qualities of the imagery. The "sound" of this work is to be found in the use of time orchestrated through the movements and interplay between the screens.

Formally *Trinity* may be arranged in differing manners suitable to the physical setting in which it is placed. For the ZKM, five screens were arrayed on a large wall, and two further translucent screens were mounted perpendicular to these at a distance of some six meters. The arrangement of the screens can be altered for other settings.

Jon Jost

resfest, 2002

Chris Cunningham
Come to Daddy
(Aphex Twin)
digital music video
color, sound
6 min
video still
© Warp Records

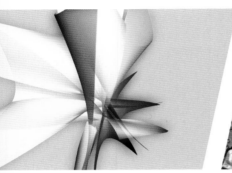

left to right
Sei Hishikawa
Prelude
2002
digital video
color, sound
2:48 min
video still
© Sei Hishikawa

Logan
Information contraband
(Money Mark)
2001
digital music video
color, sound
3:58 min
video still
© Emperor Norton Records

Wong Kar-Wai
Six Days (DJ Shadow)
2002
digital music video
color, sound
3:41 min
video still
© MCA Records

Junji Kojima
Japanese Tradition (Sushi)
2002
digital video
color, sound
8:02 min
video still
© Junji Kojima

The RES Media Group was founded in 1997 with the goal of celebrating and supporting innovative film and media through RESFEST, a traveling festival showcasing the best animations, shorts, music videos and design films, and *RES Magazine*, a bimonthly publication chronicling cutting-edge film, music, design and media culture. Although both the festival and the magazine evolved out of the burgeoning digital video movement that re-ignited the American independent film scene in the late 1990s, RES quickly grew to be much wider in scope, encompassing not only digital shorts and features, as well as videos made for the Internet, but any moving imagery that defied convention and sparked excitement. The group currently focuses on the union of art, technology and everyday life, helping do-it-yourself media makers in their pursuit of the best tools and most inspiring projects.

RESFEST helps with the inspiration. The festival kicks off each year in September at the Palace of Fine Arts in San Francisco, and then travels over the next four months to several cities in the USA, including Los Angeles and New York, before heading off to a growing list of international venues, including London, Tokyo, Melbourne, Seoul, Cape Town and Rio de Janeiro.

Highlights of RESFEST include the festival's celebrated "Cinema Electronica" program, made up of music videos produced specifically for electronic music with innovative scenarios and audacious visual approaches. Artists featured here over the years have included Chris Cunningham, Spike Jonze, Mike Mills, Floria Sigismondi, Antoine Bardou-Jacquet, Michel Gondry, Tim Hope, Shynola, Tomato, Hammer & Tongs and H5.

In 2001, RESFEST for the first time presented a program titled "Design Films," showcasing short projects that hover at the intersection of graphics, design and narrative filmmaking. Unlike traditional animation, these projects evolve out of design and 3-D software applications that allow for the easy melding of text, lines and layers of images, or the exploration of 3-D space. The resulting videos veer from cool, almost Minimalist, architectural explorations to pop-influenced graphic pandemonium. Artists featured in this program included Richard Fenwick, Johnny Hardstaff and Ryan McGuiness.

RES Magazine expands the RES mandate by creating a critical context for the discussion of new directions in film and music and by offering would-be filmmakers tips on making their own projects. Each issue of *RES* features profiles of filmmakers, musicians and artists, as well as how-to articles, buyers' guides, travel information and more. In September 2002, *RES* was redesigned, and now each issue includes a 90-minute DVD with shorts and music videos. Over the years, the magazine has profiled a vast array of film- and videomakers, including Chris Cunningham, David Lynch, Steven Soderbergh, Richard Linklater, Allison Anders, Lars von Trier, Spike Lee and Agnes Varda. The magazine has also chronicled a wide array of topics, including the Dogme 95 movement, machinima, VJs, broadcast design, media activism, gaming, erotic robots, installation art, digital architecture, Firewire filmmaking, sound art and more.

As RES continues into the future, potential projects include an expanded slate of DVD releases, the commission of films and videos by RESFEST participants and a growing number of publications, as well as a larger travel schedule for RESFEST. To find out more about the festival or magazine, see http://www.res.com.

Holly Willis

Shynola and
Ruth Lingford
Eye for an Eye (Unkle)
2002
digital music video
color, sound
6:20 min
video still
© Mo'Wax Records

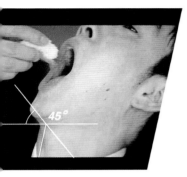

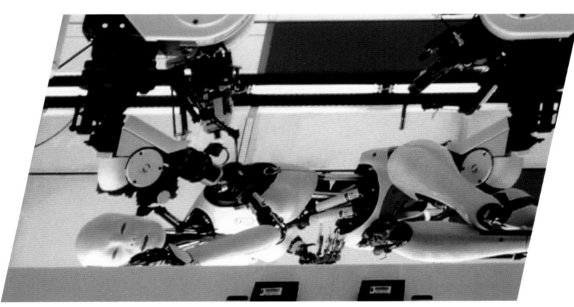

Chris Cunningham
All is Full of Love
(Björk)
1999
digital music video
color, sound
4:07 min
video still

Stéphane Lavoix and François Vogel
Les Crabes
2002
digital video
color, sound
5:30 min
video still
© Stéphane Lavoix
and François Vogel

LynnFox
Hayling (FC Kahuna)
2002
digital music video
color, sound
3:53 min
video still
© City Rockers

Barbara Filser

Gilles Deleuze and a Future Cinema: Cinema 1, Cinema 2 — and Cinema 3?

1 See Lorenz Engell, "Fernsehen mit Gilles Deleuze" and Yvonne Spielmann, "Digitalisierung: Zeitbild und Raumbild," in *Der Film bei Deleuze – Le Cinéma selon Deleuze*, Oliver Fahle, Lorenz Engell (eds), Verlag der Bauhausuniversität Weimar and Presses de la Sorbonne Nouvelle, Weimar, 1997, pp. 469–481 and pp. 496–515.

2 Gilles Deleuze, *Cinema 1. The Movement-Image*, trans. Hugh Tomlinson and Barbara Habberjam, Athlone Press, London, 1992 (1986) (French original 1983), and *Cinema 2. The Time-Image*, trans. Hugh Tomlinson and Robert Galeta, Athlone Press, London, 1994 (1989) (French original 1985). In the following, only longer quotations are referenced, but not recurrent phrases and concepts.

3 Deleuze, *Cinema 1*, op. cit., p. XIV.

4 Deleuze, *Cinema 2*, op. cit., p. 280.

5 Oliver Fahle, "Deleuze und die Geschichte des Films," in Fahle, Engell (eds), op. cit., pp. 115–126, this quotation p. 116, trans. S. Richards.

6 Deleuze, *Cinema 1*, op. cit., p. 206.

7 The account of this crisis here is essentially based on that by Suzanne Hême de Lacotte in her *Deleuze: philosophie et cinéma. Le passage de l'image-mouvement à l'image-temps*, [Collection L'Art en bref, ed. Dominique Chateau in cooperation with the Centre de Recherche sur l'Image and the Université de Paris I Panthéon Sorbonne], L'Harmattan, Paris, 2001, pp. 28–31, quotation from p. 30, italics in the original.

8 Fahle, op. cit., p. 121, quotation trans. S. Richards.

9 Friedrich Balke, *Gilles Deleuze*, [Reihe Campus, Einführungen, Hans-Martin Lohmann, Alfred Paffenholz, Willem van Reijen and Martin Weinmann (eds), vol. 1090], Campus Verlag, Frankfurt/Main and New York, 1998, p. 71, quotation trans. S. Richards.

10 The following is a summary of Deleuze, 1994, Chapter 6 (pp. 126–55).

11 Deleuze, *Cinema 2*, op. cit., p. 135.

Is there for Gilles Deleuze a future cinema? And what might be a future cinema à la Deleuze? Such questions are not intended to initiate a critical extrapolation of Deleuze's categories and ideas in the *Cinema* books (taking into account recent innovations in image production techniques), as has been already attempted by a number of authors.1 Instead the following seeks to prognosticate a possible future cinema based on the writings of Gilles Deleuze (French philosopher and author of a two-volume work on cinema2), in particular on those few passages that focus on innovative visual technology.

1. Deleuze and Cinema

Such a project raises additional, fundamental questions – ones that cannot be regarded separately and can be addressed here only to a limited pragmatic extent. What is the main concern of the *Cinema* books? Why is Deleuze interested in cinema? What is cinema for Deleuze?

In the foreword to the first volume of the *Cinema* books, Deleuze describes the project on which these volumes are based as "an attempt at the classification of images and signs."3 This taxonomy takes the form of a theory of cinema that, as Deleuze specifies at the end of *The Time-Image*, "is not 'about' cinema, but about the concepts that cinema gives rise to."4 Yet film-makers think in images, and his project is one of formulating concepts for understanding cinema through confrontation with thinkers and the concepts they use. It is thus a philosophical undertaking – in the Deleuzian sense of philosophy as the practical application of concepts. Although in his *Cinema* books Deleuze explicitly did not set out to write a history of cinema, one cannot ignore their historical dimension that, as Oliver Fahle has remarked, "automatically … is implied"5 by the project of classification.

1.1 From Movement-image to Time-image

The search for a future cinema suggests the need for a historically accentuated reading of the texts. The movement-image, with its three variations – perception-image, affection-image and action-image – corresponds more or less to classical cinema. The cinema of the time-image, whose forms are no longer individually delineated and as precisely differentiated, is that of the modern age. The catalyst that triggered this imagistic shift in the years after the World War II was the result of a long-smoldering crisis in the action-image, whose manifold origins were "social, economic, political, moral."6 It was above all, as Suzanne Hême de Lacotte stresses, a "*crise du cinéma*."7

Movement-image cinema had maneuvered itself into a dead end. Originally unburdened by tradition, it had created its own traditions which had subsequently evolved into a set of rigid clichés: "The sensomotoric relationships, the chain of situations and actions [that characterize the action-image (B.F.)] continually create the same images."8 Cinema had to reinvent itself. Yet this process of reinvention did not involve a completely new beginning; instead it took the form of a mutation.

This crisis prompted cinema to re-explore its own possibilities and to create in the time-image one that embodies a different concept of time – no longer chronological time, communicated through movement, but "chronic" time, as Deleuze calls it, a "stratigraphic, layered time … that inhabits the realm of pure memory and imparts to perception a visionary potential."9 The mutation from movement-image to time-image manifests itself as a transition from an organic to a crystalline image regime – a transition that has a number of repercussions:10 "Description stops presupposing a reality and narration stops referring to a form of the true at one and the same time …"11 The viewer is no longer referred to a world outside the image; the crystalline representation refers only to itself. This gives rise to purely optical and sound situations to which the characters no longer know how to react – "a cinema of the seer and no longer of the agent [*de voyant, non plus d'actant*]."12 The real and the imaginary, which in organic narration are discrete, opposed, are occluded. Real and virtual image become indistinguishable. In time-image cinema, *narration* must bow to the dictates of the "powers of the false" – it is no longer truthful but falsifying. Its elements no longer go through a process of development but continually mutate through a series of metamorphoses. Finally, this departure from truthful representation also affects the *story* – the relationship of camera and film-maker to film character, that is to say: the relationship of subject to object. The story relinquishes its authority; the camera assumes the kind of subjectivity that renders it perceptible described by Pier Paolo Pasolini in his "cinema of poetry" and enters "into a relation of *simulation* ('mimesis') with the character's way of seeing."13 A form of free indirect discourse is created, defined by Pasolini as follows: "It consists simply in the author's submerging himself in his character's soul and thus assuming not only the latter's psychology but also his language."14 The story becomes a simulation. In *cinéma vérité*, for instance, it achieves this through the "*story-telling function*," which aims not at grasping a character's identity but his coming into being, "when he himself starts to 'make fiction', when he enters into 'the flagrant offence of making up legends'."15

For Deleuze the real cinematographic image – the essence of cinema – is the time-image, which no longer simply mediates time but directly presents it. "The direct time-image is the phantom which has always haunted the cinema, but it took modern cinema to give a body to this phantom."16

1.2 Cinema and Thought

Deleuze is especially interested in the relationship of cinema to thought – a relationship suggested by its automatism: "Cinema not only puts movement in the image; it also puts movement in the mind. Spiritual life *is* the movement of the mind."17 This auto-matism makes cinema the only art form capable of "*producing a shock to thought, communicating vibrations to the cortex, touching the nervous and cerebral system directly.*"18 The cinema of the movement-image provides an image of thinking that is transformed in the time-image into a thought-image: "Thinking becomes an element of the image. It must no longer be understood as an object exterior to the image that the latter is supposed to represent."19 This transformation is personified, as it were, by the different character types created by the two kinds of images: the *actors* of the movement-image, whose mental processes are visible in the image as action and reaction, and the *seers* of the time-image, who are no longer capable of action: "Something compels them to think – something that transcends the boundaries of thinking. Thus, as Nietzsche demands of his seers, they postpone judgment and 'learn to walk around and comprehend each individual situation from all sides'."20

The relationship between cinema and thinking parallels that between cinema and philosophy and is based on a similarity between the problems that each seeks to solve with the means at its disposal – cinema with images and philosophy with concepts. In the *Cinema* books, Deleuze draws historical parallels between cinema and philosophy. Movement-image cinema is analogous to classical philosophy and time-image cinema to the kind of modern philosophy to which Deleuze himself subscribes. What divides the two is their differing methods of evolving concepts: classical philosophy tends to work with abstractions and generalizations whereas modern philosophy makes use of dynamic constructs.21

1.3 Image and Sound

In *The Time-Image* Deleuze opens up another historical perspective that has as its object the relationship between image, text and sound.22 He takes up the usual distinction between silent film and sound film and redefines it in terms of visual categories: for him the silent film is composed of seen image and read image – the intertitles. The sound film renders audible what was hitherto only legible, imparting to it the specific characteristic of speech. But the linguistic and the acoustic become "*a new dimension of the visual image, a new component.*"23 The "sound continuum" – sounds, music, voices, etc. – renders the seen image legible. These two stages belong to classical cinema; modern cinema instigates a further development of the sound film – the "audio-visual image" – which is of varying degrees of complexity. Sound – in particular in the form of free indirect discourse – parts company with the image, the two becoming respectively autonomous "sound image" and "visual image."

The *modus operandi* of the audio-visual image is the "irrational cut," which manifests itself on the visual plane, for instance, as a sequential rupture. Such a cut is no longer merely a visual component but lays claim to autonomy. The images come into contact in ways that generate a whole range of forms. Thus the autonomous visual image is able to create the kind of detached, empty spaces that characterize the modern image – an "any-space-whatever" that is both heterogeneous and unstable. The visual image of the film, thus rendered "tectonic," "stratigraphic" and "archeological," can now be simultaneously seen and read. Yet this reading is completely different from that of the first phase of the sound film. It is "a perception of perception, a perception which does not grasp perception without also grasping its reverse, imagination, memory, or knowledge."24 Or as Deleuze puts it elsewhere, it links the images anew, twists and reverses them. The visual image renders itself legible, much as an archaeological dig brings to light the various layers of historical time.25 There no longer is an out-of-field, since the visual image has liberated itself from dependencies and exteriorities. Takes do not follow on sequentially but form a series of juxtaposed images. This loss of the out-of-field brings with it the disappearance of its pendant, the sound-off. The sound image establishes its own autonomous framing, making it independent of the visual image and allowing the creation of pure speech acts, musical acts, or other forms of acoustic acts.

This line of development in the relationship between text and image, or between the spoken and the

12 Deleuze, *Cinema 2*, op. cit., p. 126.

13 Deleuze, *Cinema 2*, op. cit., p. 148.

14 Pier Paolo Pasolini, "Das 'Kino der Poesie'" (1965), in *Pier Paolo Pasolini* [Hanser Reihe Film, Peter W. Jansen and Wolfram Schütte (eds) in cooperation with the Stiftung Deutsche Kinemathek, vol. 12], Hanser Verlag, Munich, 1985³, pp. 49–77, this quotation p. 60, trans. S. Richards.

15 Deleuze, *Cinema 2*, op. cit., p. 150, italics in the original.

16 Deleuze, *Cinema 2*, op. cit., p. 41. See also Hême de Lacotte, op. cit., pp. 83–85.

17 "The Brain is the Screen. An Interview with Gilles Deleuze" (February 1986), in *The Brain is the Screen. Deleuze and the Philosophy of Cinema*, Gregory Flaxman (ed.), University of Minnesota Press, Minneapolis and London, 2000, pp. 365–373, this quotation p. 366, italics in original.

18 Deleuze, *Cinema 2*, op. cit., p. 156, italics in original.

19 Hême de Lacotte, op. cit., p. 76, quotation trans. S. Richards.

20 Balke, op. cit., p. 74f. with quotation from Nietzsche, quotation trans. S. Richards.

21 Hême de Lacotte, op. cit., pp. 34–41. The *Cinema* books not only provide a history of philosophy but also present an author-based history that is explicitly a history of cinema as art.

22 The following is a summary of theses from Chapter 9 of *The Time-Image*: Deleuze, *Cinema 2*, op. cit., pp. 225–261.

23 Deleuze, *Cinema 2*, op. cit., p. 226, italics in original.

24 Deleuze, *Cinema 2*, op. cit., p. 245.

25 Thus the designation "archeological" that, as Deleuze himself remarked, might be misunderstood, since it has connotations of the prehistorical. For this reason "archeological" subsequently gives way to "stratigraphic."

26 See especially Deleuze,
    Cinema 2, pp. 13–18 and
    pp. 246–247.

27 Gilles Deleuze, "On *The Time-
    Image*" (1985), in *Negotia-
    tions 1972-1990*, trans.
    Martin Joughin, Columbia
    University Press, New York,
    1995, pp. 57–61, this quota-
    tion p. 60.

28 Engell, op. cit., p. 469, quota-
    tion trans. S. Richards.

29 Gilles Deleuze, "Letter to
    Serge Daney: Optimism,
    Pessimism, and Travel," in
    Negotiations 1972–1990,
    trans. Martin Joughin,
    Columbia University Press,
    New York, 1995, pp. 68–79,
    this quotation p. 72. The
    English translation reads "a
    privileged spectator" while
    the French original talks of a
    "spectateur contrôlé"; see
    "Optimisme, pessimisme et
    voyage. Lettre à Serge
    Daney" (1986), in Serge
    Daney, *Ciné Journal*, Volume I,
    1981–1982, [Petite biblio-
    thèque des Cahiers du Ciné-
    ma], Cahiers du Cinéma,
    Paris, 1998 (1986¹), pp. 9–25,
    this quotation p. 14.

30 Deleuze, *Cinema 2*, op. cit.,
    p. 265. The following is a
    summary of the theses in
    the "Conclusions."

31 "The Brain is the Screen. An
    Interview with Gilles
    Deleuze," in op. cit., p. 372.

visual, makes it clear that the constitution of the time-image is not dependent on cinematographic innovation. The transition from movement-image to time-image, from classical cinema to modern cinema, occurs independently of the radical break between silent film to sound film. It is completed during the second phase of the sound film. Deleuze's analysis of the films of Japanese director Ozu also demonstrates that the creation of the time-image is not a question of the technology available, but of the image itself, of a new regime of the image. In the era of the silent film, in the period of classical cinema, Ozu was already creating the kind of purely optical descriptions and any-space-whatevers that characterize the time-image.26

In sum, one could answer the three fundamental questions posed earlier as follows: the project that Deleuze is pursuing with his *Cinema* books involves a classification of cinema's images and symbols – a classification that narrates a history of cinema's coming into being as cinema closely tied to a history of philosophy. What interests Deleuze about cinema is its relationship to thinking and its visual conceptualization of problems that philosophy seeks to grasp through mental concepts. For Gilles Deleuze, cinema *is* time-image.

2. Deleuze and Future Cinema

We can now go on to address the original question concerning a future cinema à la Deleuze. Now that cinema has discovered its essence in the time-image, the evolutionary line from movement-image to time-image can hardly be continued beyond the latter. According to the logic of the *Cinema* books, such a continuation would no longer be cinema. Yet there still remains the question of a possible "future" – for the line of development traced by Deleuze from classical to modern cinema suggests that this conceptual progression may indeed embody a "future."

It would require another crisis comparable to that which triggered the first transition to create the necessity for a future cinema as a successor to classical and modern cinema. And indeed, for some time cinema has seen itself exposed to the double threat of television and commercial film, which are more or less synonymous:

"Because most cinematic production, with its arbitrary violence and feeble eroticism, reflects mental deficiency rather than any invention of new cerebral circuits. What happened with pop videos is pathetic:

they could have become a really interesting new field of cinematic activity, but were immediately taken over by organized mindlessness."27

The primary danger posed by television to cinema is the misuse of the visual medium of television (a medium that might have provided cinema with an "extraordinary field of research") as a "social technology"28 which Deleuze sees as carrying out control and surveillance functions – forcing the spectator to adapt and subordinate himself, to become a controlled "spectator allowed into the wings, in contact with the image, entering into the image." The spectator attends the television broadcast as a studio guest, only to find that the main point of the exercise has "nothing to do with beauty or thought, it's about being in contact with the technology, touching the machinery."29

2.1 Cinematography and Electronics

The *Cinema* books contain a prognosis of the possible effects of this coming crisis: "The electronic image, that is, the tele and video image, the digital image coming into being, either had to transform cinema or to replace it, to mark its death."30 It might appear that those responsible for causing this crisis are going to triumph, yet elsewhere Deleuze explicitly relativizes this pessimistic assessment: "When it is said, that cinema is dead, it's especially stupid, because the cinema is at the very beginning of an exploration of audiovisual relations, which are relations of time …"31 One can surmise that the audio-visual image in its most complex form to date, identified by Deleuze in the films of Jean-Marie Straub and Danièle Huillet or Marguerite Duras, has already pointed the way out of this crisis and established the basis of a future cinema à la Deleuze. Deleuze, indeed, puts forward a number of examples to show that the mechanisms of the new electronic and digital images – which he only briefly lists – are anticipated by the cinematographic images of the time-image.

These new images possess the following characteristics: they consist of only obverse and reverse; they can turn on their own axis; thanks to their capacity for permanent self-reorganization, they create a heterogeneous space; and they increasingly grant sound an autonomous status – characteristics that are already to be found in the description of the audio-visual image but that the latter arrives at by other, possibly more difficult means. Through the heterogeneity of the space they create, the new images subvert the "privilege of the vertical" that also governs the orientation of the cinema screen. The vertical alignment of the screen is kept merely as a convention – it no longer alludes, as does the window, to the erect posture of the observer. The screen becomes opaque, a mere "information board." Yet this verticality was already being subverted by the cinematographic image when the latter became legible, stratigraphic and sound image. The effects are the same for both types of image: "But, when the frame of the screen functions as instrument panel, printing or computing table, the image is constantly being cut into another image, being printed through a visible mesh, sliding over other images in an 'incessant stream of messages', and the shot itself is less like an eye than an overloaded brain endlessly absorbing information …"[32] True, some of the authors frequently cited by Deleuze in The Time-Image already use electronic images; however, the decisive factor is not the technology employed but the uses to which it is put – the "will to art." Yet this gives rise to the following problem: "The artist is always in the situation of saying simultaneously: I claim new methods, and I am afraid that the new methods may invalidate all will to art, or make it into a business, a pornography, a Hitlerism …"[33]

To avoid being annihilated by electronics, the time-image has to generate a new system of images and symbols, "a whole audio-visual system"[34] (the most complex form of audio-visual image, such as Marguerite Duras and the Straubs attempted to create), that Deleuze also sees exemplified in the work of Hans Jürgen Syberberg. It involves a disjunction of the acoustic and the visual that on the one hand allows the creation of a pure, fabulating speech act and on the other renders the stratification of the image legible: "The visual image will thus never show what the sound image utters."[35] Both can once again be brought together, discovering through mutual exploration of their boundaries the boundary they have in common. Whereas the movement-image is cyclical or spiral in structure, constituting "for cinema, no less than for philosophy, the model of the True as totalization,"[36] this new relationship between the visual and the sound image is incommensurable, "a confrontation of outside and inside independent of distance, this thought outside itself and this un-thought within thought."[37]

2.2 Cinema vs. Information

Syberberg's achievement consists in demonstrating that "no information, whatever it might be, is sufficient to defeat Hitler."[38] It is not sufficient to replace one technology with another – cinematography with electronics – rather it is a case of overcoming information in order to lead cinema out of its crisis. Syberberg succeeds in doing so by unfolding an informational space, a non-causal structure, in which "the trivial and the cultural, the public and the private, the historic and the anecdotal, the imaginary and the real are brought close together," and by expressing its complexity by means of the audio-visual image: "This goes beyond the psychological individual just as it makes a whole impossible: a non-totalizable complexity, 'non-representable by a single individual'."[39] This dissociation of the visual and the acoustic constitutes a pedagogy of the image, an education in perception, in new ways of seeing and hearing which, in the cause of overcoming information, must be guided by "the question which goes beyond it, that of its source and that of its addressee …"[40] Creative story-telling must be extracted from spoken information, and a "pure informed person … set up beyond all the visual layers" of information who is "capable of receiving into his visible body the pure act of speech."[41] This reception must not be understood in terms of unification, for the voice clearly remains apart from the body. The dissociation of images is accentuated – they remain discrete. The informed characters of Syberberg's cinema are the descendants of the seers of the time-image, the "true thinkers of our age."[42] Syberberg's cinema – as a cinema of the informed person – thus presents itself as a creative and political act.

"The life or the afterlife of cinema depends on its internal struggle with informatics,"[43] states Deleuze at the end of his analysis of Syberberg. A possible future cinema would therefore be the audio-visual image in its most complex form, permanently interrogating information as to its source and its addressee. Perhaps this future cinema à la Deleuze may be defined as follows: that which forces information to think and us to think information.

Translated from the German by Stephen Richards

32 Deleuze, Cinema 2, op. cit., p. 267.

33 Deleuze, Cinema 2, op. cit., p. 266. The dangers that Deleuze addresses here are comparable to those already confronted by cinema in its transition from movement-image to time-image. The term "Hitlerism" refers to Kracauer's study of German Expressionist film From Caligari to Hitler and Walter Benjamin's essay "The Work of Art in the Age of Mechanical Reproduction," which Deleuze summarizes as "Hitler as film-maker" (p. 264), as well as from Hans Jürgen Syberberg's film Hitler–a Film from Germany (1977), which takes up the cudgels with "Hitler the film-maker" (p. 264). The term is synonymous with more general concepts such as "propaganda" and "authoritarian control."

34 Deleuze, Cinema 2, op. cit., p. 267.

35 Deleuze, Cinema 2, op. cit., p. 279.

36 Deleuze, Cinema 2, op. cit., p. 277.

37 Deleuze, Cinema 2, op. cit., p. 278.

38 Deleuze, Cinema 2, op. cit., p. 269, italics in original.

39 Deleuze, Cinema 2, op. cit., pp. 268–269.

40 Deleuze, Cinema 2, op. cit., p. 270.

41 Deleuze, Cinema 2, op. cit., p. 270.

42 Balke, op. cit., p. 74, quotation trans. S. Richards.

43 Deleuze, Cinema 2, op. cit., p. 270.

Lynn Hershman Leeson
Teknolust

high-definition 24p format, 35mm film /
color, sound dolby sr / 85 min

Lorna
1979–1984
interactive environment
videodisc, monitor, remote-
control interface, mixed media
edition of twenty
ZKM | Media Museum, Karlsruhe
installation view: ZKM | Media
Museum, Karlsruhe
© Lynn Hershman Leeson
photo © ZKM Karlsruhe

The Future of Cinema has been a concern of my work for the past twenty-four years. What interested me is going beyond the screen, using new technologies to enliven and empower viewers, to create an experience that uses moving images to defy conventional structure, whether this be the creation of alternative endings and soundtracks in *Lorna* (1979–1984), or an on- line web agent named *Ruby* (2002). The following works have extended moving images beyond traditional conventions.

Lorna
In this programmed video-art laserdisc, users can interact and make choices for the videotaped character, Lorna, an agoraphobic woman who has difficulty making choices for herself. Every object in Lorna's tiny apartment has a number. Pressing each object accesses video and sound information about Lorna's fears and dreams as well as her history, personal conflicts and possible future. By pressing a remote unit identical to Lorna's, users voyeuristically activate modules to the story of Lorna's life. Some segments can be seen backwards, forwards, at increased or decreased speed, and from several perspectives. Though there are only seventeen minutes of moving footage on the disc, the thirty-six chapters can be sequenced differently and shift the context indefinitely. The video modules have multiple sound

tracks and three endings (she either shoots her television set, commits suicide, or moves to Los Angeles).

When I created *Lorna*, I did not realize it was the first time anyone had made an interactive art videodisc. It seemed to me to be a natural progression of time-based sculptural methods. The branching system and flow chart reminded me of the architecture of a building, and therefore reminiscent of *The Dante Hotel*. *Lorna* was a combination of performance, narrative, time and participatory chance and choice. These compositional elements were compressed into a programmed laserdisc that offered users multiple perspectives and options for *Lorna*.

Lorna took place in the space of captured footage pressed and preprogrammed into a media environment that was modularly controlled by users.

Lorna's passivity (presumably caused by being controlled by media) is a counterpoint to the direct action of the player. As the branching path is deconstructed, the player becomes aware of the subtle yet powerful effects of fear caused by media and becomes more empowered (active) through this perception. I hoped that playing *Lorna* would encourage viewer/participants to transgress the screen. Rather than being remotely controlled, the user controls the remote! Implications of the relationship reversal between individuals and technological media systems are immense and ultimately subversive.

220
08 REMAPPING
Lynn Hershman Leeson

Lorna
screenshots
1979–1984
© Lynn Hershman Leeson

Lynn Hershman Leeson
with Sara Roberts
Deep Contact. The First Interactive Sexual Fantasy Videodisc
1984–1989
interactive videodisc
videodisc, MicroTouch
touchscreen monitor
color, sound
screenshot
The Hess Collection, London
© Lynn Hershman Leeson

Deep Contact.
The First Interactive Sexual Fantasy Videodisc

Deep Contact, invites participants to actually touch their "guide" Marion on any part of her body via a MicroTouch monitor. Adventures develop depending upon which body part is touched.

Marion knocks on the projected video screen asking to be touched. She keeps asking until parts of her body rotate onto the touch sensitive screen and actually are touched. Touch her head, and you are given a choice of TV channel branchings, each of which gives a short (but humorous) analytic account of "reproductive technologies" and their effect on women's bodies, or worse, how women see themselves, and "extensions" into the screen that are similar to "phantom limbs." The screen, therefore, becomes an extension of the hand, a prosthetic virtual connection between the viewer and the screen.

Touch beneath her neck but above her legs and the video image on the disc goes to a bar where you can:

1) Select one of three characters (Marion, a Demon or a Voyeur) to follow through an interactive fictive narrative that has a video component.

2) Shift your personality in order to better know Marion, the guide.

3) Have your own image replace the one on the screen via a surveillance camera.

Touch her legs, and you enter a garden sequence where you are led either by Marion, by a Zen Master, along an Unknown Path, or by a Demon. In the garden, the main digital branching image is a hand. This jumps forward depending upon the selection, allowing you to follow the lines on the hand to different routes, which eventually lead to a fork in the road.

At certain paths you can see in a closer version what you have just passed. For instance, Marion may run past a bush that if examined closely will reveal a spider weaving a web. New perceptions of the same scene are revealed depending on the speed of perception.

In some instances words flash on three frames of the disc, forcing the viewer to go back and slow down in order to see what has been written. At other points, the Zen Master speaks his lines backwards, forcing the viewer to play the disc in reverse to understand what he has said.

In order to truly make the viewer a part of the installation, the Hyper Card was programmed, via a fair light and a small surveillance camera, to be switched "on" when the cameraman's shadow appears, so that the viewer's image instantaneously appears on the screen. Transgressing the screen and being transported into "virtual reality" was an important element.

The title refers to the player's ability to travel the fifty-seven different segments into the deepest part of the disc, determining the route to the center, and

model for
Lynn Hershman Leeson's and
Sara Robert's
*A Room of One's Own
(Echo Narcissus)*
1990–1993
interactive computer-based
videodisc, installation
mixed media
edition of three
The Hess Collection, London;
National Gallery of Canada,
Ottawa; Wilhelm Lehmbruck
Museum, Duisburg
© Lynn Hershman Leeson

simultaneously trying to find and to feel their own deepest core.

Viewers choreograph their own encounters in the vista of voyeurism that is incorporated into *Deep Contact*. Traditional narratives (beginnings, middles and ends) are being restructured at the same moment as advances in genetic engineering reshape the meaning of life.

A Room of One's Own (Echo Narcissus)

Room of One's Own requires a viewer/voyeur to peer into an articulated eyepiece that is placed at eye level and incorporates a movable periscopic viewing section. The very act of "looking" initiates the action. As the viewer/voyeur focuses on any of the objects in the room, images appear in a one-way mirror/wall via videodisc, projection and computer-based signals that also incorporate video images of the viewer's eyes into the piece.

In 1888, shortly after Etienne Jules Marey perfected a gun that substituted film for bullets, he was introduced to Thomas Alva Edison. One year later the kinetograph was invented. This device, an alliance between the phonograph and the photograph, was designed so that a single spectator could peep through an eyehole and see film loops such as the Leigh Sisters performing their umbrella dance. In what became known as the peep show, spectators took pleasure in the process of voyeuristically viewing seductive images of women. The gun/camera has direct relationship to the history of film as well as the eroticization of female imagery in photography, phonography and

pornography. Many serial killers, including Ted Bundy, photograph their victims, as if to capture and possess them forever. Women are taught to be looked at. In contemporary society this is interpreted as a manifestation of desire. This triggers ideas of ownership and consumption and links representation of women to lethal weapons. If cinema is a social technology then the captivity of women's submissiveness is part of the construction of this fantasy.

Within the miniature room, a small monitor exhibits the viewer/voyeur's eyes, so that whoever is watching becomes a virtual participant in the scene being seen. Images that are called upon depend upon what is being looked at. Looking at the bed triggers a related sequence, as does looking at clothing, a telephone, a chair of a small video monitor. This piece is about voyeurism and the explosive effects attached to the social construction and media representation of female identity. Video segments of apparent imprisonment caused by media stereotypes include a woman being undressed by eyes, escaping advances and expectations that instead become literal projections of the viewer/voyeur's fantasies.

America's Finest

A rifle loaded with images comparing media to warfare becomes activated when the viewer pulls the trigger. The viewer's image is incorporated into the cycling images.

In 1839, both the camera and the Colt revolver were invented. There has long been a historical relationship between the camera and the gun, both

employ capture, surveillance and shooting. The associative notions of gun/camera/trigger link media representation to lethal weapons.

Action is directly instigated through the trigger itself, which, when pulled, places the viewer/participant within the gun site (this time their entire body, holding the gun). They see themselves fade under horrible examples in which the M16 was used, and if they wait, ghosts of the cycling images dissolve into the present. Again, the aggressor becomes the victim and the entire body of the viewer is placed inside the site of the work. Through this complete immersion, they again lose control of their image.

America's Finest is a camera gun designed to document the horrors of our century perpetrated by weapons and translated into memory through the media. When the trigger is squeezed, the viewers' image is pasted within the gun site. The miniaturized image fades into other scenes that form overlays in ghost-like segments and revives, is reborn, and fades again.

I view this weapon as a conscientious objectifier to what it sees, tracks and records. Pulling the trigger turns the viewer into both an aggressor and subsequent victim of his/her own actions.

Paranoid Mirror

Sensors strategically placed on the floor cause the still image of the back of a woman's head placed in a gold frame to activate, turn around and dissolve between sequences of other women in the videodisc sequences. In some instances, a switcher places the viewer's back into the frame, which can be seen from other locations. The viewer's body is the interface.

Inspired by the paintings of Van Eyck and in particular the *Marriage of Arnolfini*, this piece uses reflection as a means of portraiture. Only the back of Anne Gerber's head is seen when the piece is inactive.

Tillie, the Telerobotic Doll

Two telerobotic dolls with video and Web cam eyes and a head that rotates 180 degrees by users on the Internet track and incorporate viewers into their own environment. *CybeRoberta* is programmed to pirate the information of Tillie.

Reliance on tracking and surveillance techniques has resulted in a culture that has a peripheral vision in which sight extends beyond the borders of only physical location. If identity is erased on the Internet, then Tillie's face becomes a mask for multiple expressions of identity capable of global connectivity.

By looking at the world through the eyes of *Tillie*

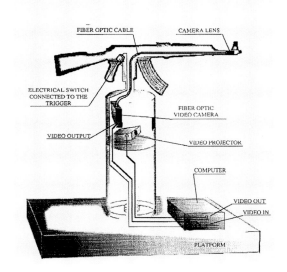

home page of
CybeRoberta
1995–1998
interactive network at
www.lynnhershman.com/doll2
screenshot
© Lynn Hershman Leeson

Tillie, the Telerobotic Doll
1995–1998
interactive network at
www.lynnhershman.com/tillie
© Lynn Hershman Leeson

The Difference Engine #3
installation view: ZKM |
Center for Art and Media
Karlsruhe, 1998
© Lynn Hershman Leeson
photo © Philip Radowitz

the Telerobotic Doll, viewers not only become voyeurs, but indeed, become virtual "cyborgs" because they use her eyes as a vehicle for their own remote and extended vision. The dolls are constructed so that their eyes are replaced by cameras. On the Net, these become the "eye cons" that telerobotically move the doll allowing her head to turn 180 degrees. The left eye sees in color and records exactly what it sees, while the right eye is connected to the Internet and sees in a 320 x 200 gray scale, refreshed at a rate of 30 seconds (to accommodate visitors with slow connections). Viewers in the physical space can see themselves on the small monitor in Tillie's environment.

Viewers on the Internet see through her right eye what Tillie is looking at in black and white. Viewers on

the Internet can rotate Tillie's head and survey the room she is in via a mirror placed in front of her and have the capability to send images back through the Internet to the page.

CybeRoberta

This piece was conceived simultaneously with *Tillie*. I think of the two dolls as "The Dollie Clones." *CybeRoberta* is dressed identically to "Roberta Breitmore." Roberta's clothing was completely re-made, but scaled down. Her internal structure is identical to that of Tillie.

When the two dolls are exhibited together, they are programmed so that each pirates the other's information, making their identities further blurred and ambiguous.

Lynn Hershman Leeson
in collaboration with
Construct Internet Design
The Difference Engine #3
1995–1998
networked telerobotic
multi-user sculpture
screenshot
© Lynn Hershman Leeson

homepage for
The Difference Engine #3
1995–1998
networked telerobotic
multi-user sculpture
screenshot
© Lynn Hershman Leeson

The Difference Engine #3

The Difference Engine #3 uses the architecture of the
ZKM | Media Museum in Germany as a 3-D template
and the visitors to the museum as the interface.
Users are captured as webcams assign numbered
identities to their images, which embark on a thirty-
second tour of the virtual museum. The image is finally
placed in a "purgatorial" space where it cycles eternally. Users on the Web can direct the sculptures to
show different angles of exhibitions in the museum.
This is an interactive, multi-user sculpture about surveillance, voyeurism, digital absorption and spiritual
transformation of the body.

The Difference Engine #3 was inspired by Charles
Babbage's original *Difference Engine #1* (commonly
considered the world's first computer). The original
machine was used to calculate numerical positions.
This piece calculates the captured image and position
in the physical/virtual space of visitors to a physical
space, located now at the ZKM | Media Museum.
Avatars of museum visitors are "born" when they approach one of three Bi-Directional Browsing Units
(BBUs). Quickcams embedded in the BBUs flip 180 degrees to capture the image of the person standing
before them and assign the image a number (representing the time in seconds the visitor approached
the unit). The numbered image embarks on a thirty-
second journey through a 3-D representation of the
museum constructed in VRML2 and coded with JAVA3.
The avatar then moves to a Purgatorial Site where it
cycles continuously and is in an archive permanently
on the Internet where this image can be recalled at
any time via the identity number.

Online visitors choose a "generic" image to represent them and travel alongside the images created
for people in the actual museum and have the capability to "capture" images within the museum (they can
see into the space via a live video feed from the camera that is capturing the image of people in the museum). There is a dedicated chat line that allows viewers online to communicate with people in the physical
space.

Conceiving Ada
1997
35mm film and digital Beta
color, sound
85 min
film still
© Lynn Hershman Leeson;
Winstar

Conceiving Ada

Themes of love, sex, artificial life, computers, DNA
transference history and memory intertwine in *Conceiving Ada*, Tilda Swinton is the brilliant mathematician Ada Byron King, Countess of Lovelace, the daughter of Lord Byron who is credited with writing the
first computer program. Named by Charles Babbage
"The Enchantress of Numbe," Ada not only predicted
the possibilities of artificial life, but also the digital
revolution that occurred 144 years after her death.
Karen Black plays a dual role as Ada's mother, the
mathematical Lady Millbank, as well as the mother of
Emmy, the young American genetic memory expert
who tries to communicate directly with Ada via a

Conceiving Ada
1997
35mm film and digital Beta
color; sound
85 min
film stills
© Lynn Hershman Leeson;
Winstar

computer DNA memory extension given to her by her mentor Sims, played by Timothy Leary.

Ada lived a double life that included numerous lovers, especially John Cross (John Perry Barlow), and a fervor for gambling. Ada's luck betrayed her when she lost the family fortune and at the age of thirty-five died of uterine cancer.

The LHL Process for Virtual Sets allows still images to be dynamically placed into live digital video and become the backgrounds that actors move through that are recorded in real time.

Prior to shooting, the still images were digitized, altered, colorized and run through mattes. On the set these images were maneuvered from a computer and laid onto digital videotape in real time while the actors were performing. Actors looked at a monitor to see their filmed environment.

There were two channels: a composite master tape with backgrounds in place and an alpha channel that allows background and foreground to be separated and further manipulated later, if desired. Lighting and perspective shifts were accomplished in real time.

This film used 385 separate photographs which were altered, colorized, composited and given numbers that corresponded to scenes being shot. These numbers were called up and the files accessed when the scenes were needed. Close-ups or other effects could be instantaneously achieved.

Static scenes were animated through QuickTime movies of fire in the fireplace, or rain on the windows, or nonexistent doors drawn from mattes in real time that actors could walk through.

Teknolust

This film is one of the first films shot with the new 24p digital high-definition camera. It contains twenty minutes of high-definition graphics, and will feature an artificial intelligent web agent, viewable on an Internet portal/site mirrored in the film.

When Rosetta Stone, a bio-geneticist, breeds three Self-Replicating Automatons (SRAs named Ruby, Marine and Olive) by combining her own DNA with computer software, she also creates a set of unanticipated tribulations. As Rosetta seeks to understand the encrypted language of her SRA progeny, she confronts the reality of her own loneliness and alienation.

The nearly-predatory dependence of Rosetta on her creations and of them on their peculiar life-sustaining diet (male "chromo" filched from un-suspecting seduced "hosts") is supplanted by their all becoming viable, distinct individuals. After Rosetta is forced to relinquish external control, Ruby, Marine, and Olive gain self-sufficiency and sovereignty. If the characters have lost anything, mostly it is their ignorance or a sort of blind innocence, which is replaced by something far more affirming, their birthright to autonomy.

When Sandy, (who conducts crude mimeograph machines), and Ruby, (an advanced form of reproductive technology) become intimate they realize that love makes all things real and possible. This film is a comedy, and ends happily in an optimistically birth of redemption.

Unlike Mary Shelley's monstrous creature in *Frankenstein*, or Fritz Lange's conflicted evil robot in *Metropolis*, all the characters in *Teknolust*, thrive on affection, and ultimately, reproduction. The classic movie seduction clips that program reflect the powerful impact of absorbed images on behavior.

Teknolust is a coming of age story, not only for the characters but also of our society's relationship to technology. The twenty-first century's technologies – genetics, nanotechnology and robotics – have opened Pandora's box that will affect the destiny of the entire human race. Our relationship to computer based virtual life forms that are autonomous and self replicating will shape the fate of our species.

In an era of digital and human biological sampling, it seemed natural to use the same actress (Tilda Swinton) to play not only the bio geneticist, Rosetta Stone, but the offspring she breeds. The 24p camera encouraged a hyper-real feeling and aided the massive compositing challenges.

Ruby's portal is mirrored on the web1 and extends the relationship of the film beyond the screen into the virtual world of networks. I have always been attracted to digital tools and cinematic metaphors that reflect our time, such as privacy in an era of surveillance, personal identity in a time of pervasive manipulation, and despite this, the essential quest of all living things for loving interaction.

Lynn Hershman Leeson

1 http://www.agentruby.com

Teknolust
2002
high-definition 24p format,
35mm film
color, sound dolby sr
85 min
film still
distributed by Skouras Films,
2002

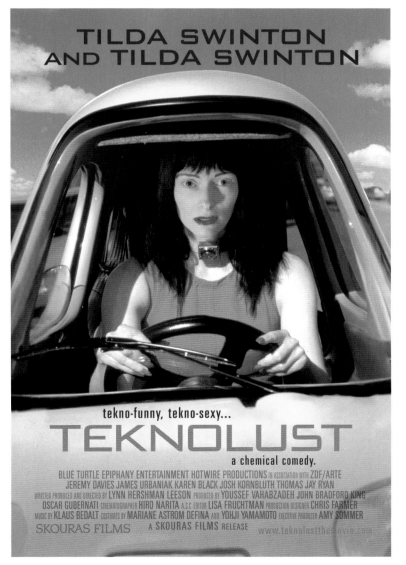

Teknolust
2002
promotional poster
distributed by
Skouras Films, 2002

Perry Hoberman
Let's Make a Monster

2001–2003
live-projection performance / Powerbook G3, custom software
(MAX/MSP/JITTER, Macromedia Director), data projection, CCTV
cameras, audio, MIDI, other custom controls

Intricate Probabilities or The Many Worlds
Interpretation of Monster Cinema

"It has taken such twentieth-century Monsters as psychoanalysis, nuclear power, in vitro fertilization, and genetic engineering, bursting upon an ethically unprepared world with their dual potential for good and evil, to illuminate fully the depths of meaning in Frankenstein."[1]

It is hardly a coincidence that the publication of Mary Shelley's *Frankenstein*, the work on Charles Babbage's *Difference Engine*, and Daguerre and Bouton's *Diorama* emerged within a few years of each other and in the midst of unprecedented industrial development. Each enterprise was to propose a representation of a future in which technology was to figure decisively in the moral, social, and creative spheres. The engineering of life, the mechanization of calculation, the "animation" of images – though not specifically linked in the 1820s – set in place an experimental agenda which recurred in many forms through the nineteenth and that were to slowly converge and ultimately merge in the late twentieth century. Running on steam, sparked by electricity, illuminated by gas, this trio harnessed, assimilated, and tamed the forces of science for the service of medical experiment (for better or worse), efficiency, and illusion. Each bore histories rooted in both "rational" (mathematics, chemistry, optics…) and "irrational" (alchemy, vitalism, theology …) traditions. Each posed a new challenge to a culture reeling in the tumult of "progress," captivated by the mastery of nature, and, no doubt, intoxicated by machines, "monsters," and images that could come alive.

In manufacturing a world of components, operations, and effects, the work of Shelley, Babbage, and Daguerre (as examples among many others) would instrumentalize accumulated research and speculations that the founding principles of the workings of the world could be discovered, systemized, and applied.

Drawing, for example, on the work of Luigi Galvin's "vitalism" (that demonstrated what Bruce Mazlish called "the galvanic twitch," the contraction of muscles of frogs legs turned into electrical circuits), on the work of Erasmus Darwin (who, according to Shelley "preserved a piece of vermicelli in a glass case, till by some extraordinary means it began to move with voluntary motion" – the vermicelli twitch!?).[2] Frankenstein's *Naturphilosophie* "propagated the idea of the incontrovertibility of forces, linking the animate and the inanimate through galvinism, magnetism and electricity."[3] Though Babbage's *Difference Engine* was mechanical, it too brought to life simple calculations that would soon lead to the instruction sets that would lead, if prematurely, to the development of programmable machines (and ultimately to Turing's Universal Machine). But it too emerged from a long line of calculating machines, mechanical chess players, automatons, writing machines. Robertson's

Phantasmagoria (the first show was in 1798) evolved gothic narratives that, in his words, spoke of "the terror inspired by ghosts, spells, and occult plots of magic." Wildly successful, the *Phantasmagoria* brought the theater of images and the sciences of light into narratives that, among other things, also brought the dead to luminous life. Laurent Mannoni's close reading of the origins of the *Phantasmagoria* (in *The Great Art of Light and Shadow*) and of Robertson's role in it concludes that "the scientist Robert (his full name was Etienne-Gaspard Robertson), in becoming the fantasmagore Robertson, passed from science to spectacle."[4] Not incidentally, according to Mannoni, Robertson "was one of the very early practitioners in France of Galvinism," and "had long been fascinated by electricity; he later became the friend and faithful supporter of the other great Italian pioneer Allesandro Volta."[5] Though separated by some years, it should also be pertinent to remember that, as David Skal writes: "It is perhaps fitting that Thomas Alva Edison, the great technological magus of the late nineteenth and early twentieth centuries, having already astounded the world with the mechanical golem he first called the kinetoscope, lent his name to the first motion-picture version of *Frankenstein* … that contained numerous examples of optical illusions beyond the reach of proscenium-bound stagecraft."[6]

The "scientization of technology" (in Habermas' phrase), linked with the perpetuation of the enlightenment and the development of modern industrial principles, could constitute substitutes for the "creation" of life, mental labor, and for aesthetic experience. Habermas contends that "technology, if at based at all on a project, can only be traced back to a 'project' of the human species, as a whole …" He continues, in the essay "Technology and Science as 'Ideology'":

"In any case technological development lends itself to be interpreted as though the human species had taken the elementary components of the behavioral system of purposive-rational action … and projected them one after another onto the plane of technical instruments, thereby unburdening itself of the corresponding functions. As first the functions of the motor apparatus (hands and legs) were augmented and replaced, followed by energy production (of the human body), the functions of the sensory apparatus (eyes, ears, skin), and finally the functions of the governing center (the brain)."[7]

Body, thought, and sense correspond to the agendas of the production of life, the mechanization of reason, and the "logistics of perception" (in Virilio's phrase). In commercializing the "marginal" discourses of scientific experimentation, Shelley, Babbage, and Daguerre's work would raise the stakes and cross boundaries in which the effects of technologies would intimately intervene into the public imagination. Their works would also pose startling moral and

1 Roslynn D. Haynes, *From Faust to Strangelove: Representations of the Scientist in Western Literature*, Johns Hopkins University Press, Baltimore, 1994, p. 101.

2 Bruce Mazlish, *The Fourth Discontinuity: The Co-Evolution of Human and Machines*, Yale University Press, New Haven, 1993, p. 45.

3 Mazlish, op. cit., p. 40.

4 Laurent Mannoni, *The Great Art of Light and Shadow: Archaeology of the Cinema*, University of Exeter Press, Devon, 2000, p. 151.

5 Mannoni, op. cit., p. 150.

6 David Skal, *Screams of Reason: Mad Science and Modern Culture*, Norton, New York, 1998, pp. 94–95.

7 Jürgen Habermas, "Technology and Science as 'Ideology,'" in Steven Seidmen (ed.), *Jürgen Habermas on Society and Politics*, Beacon Press, Boston, 1989, p. 241.

left
*Out Of The Picture:
Return of the Invisible Man*
1983
projection-and-sound
installation
stereoscopic slide projections,
sound system
screen dimensions:
520 x 335 cm
installation view:
Artists Space, New York, 1983
© Perry Hoberman
photo © Perry Hoberman

center
The Silencers
1986
wall sculpture (from the
Lightleakers series)
wood, halogen light bulb,
Plexiglas, shadows
122 x 92 x 61 cm
installation view: Postmasters
Gallery, New York, 1986
© Perry Hoberman
photo © Perry Hoberman

right
High Rise (Under Construction)
1986
wall sculpture (from the
Lightleakers series)
wood, halogen light bulb,
Plexiglas, shadows
150 x 150 x 122 cm
installation view: Postmasters
Gallery, New York, 1986
collection Melody London
© Perry Hoberman
photo © Perry Hoberman

intellectual challenges to a culture in which inexorable assumptions about scientific and technological progress were to be mirrored by reductive attempts to technologize and master life, thought and experience as merely so many systems. This "alienation" (to use the word of their contemporary Marx) from "nature" would form the basis of the development of the kind of technical artificiality now bound with Artificial Life, Artificial Intelligence, and with Artificial Reality (often erroneously called "virtual" reality). As Friedrich Kittler writes:

"… around 1880 the fabrication of so-called man becomes possible. His essence escapes into apparatuses. Machines take over functions of the central nervous system, and no longer, as in times past, merely those of muscles. And with this differentiation – and not with steam engines and railroads – a clear division occurs between matter and information, the real and the symbolic. When it comes to inventing phonography and cinema, the age-old dreams of humankind are no longer sufficient. The physiology of eyes, ears, and brains have to become objects of scientific research. … The media revolution of 1880, however, laid the groundwork for theories and practices that no longer mistake information for spirit. Thought is replaced by Boolean algebra, and consciousness by the unconscious … and that the symbolic is called the world of the machine undermines Man's delusion of possessing a 'quality' called 'consciousness,' which identifies him as something other and better than a 'calculating machine.' For both people and computers are 'subject to the appeal of the signifier'; that is, they are both run by programs. 'Are these humans,' Nietzsche already asked himself in 1874, eight years before buying a typewriter, 'or perhaps only thinking, writing and speaking machines?'"[8]

Rather than overarching critiques of techno-culture, Perry Hoberman's work has aimed at assimilating its technologies, devouring its images, betraying its illusions, and creating a kind of raucous discourse. Less outright subversion than ingenious sabotage, his satiric constructions, parodic objects, mocked images, pseudo-virtual environments, efficiently impossible synchronizations, behavioral Turing tests, or Faustian performances betray their own artifice as they signify just how deeply the expectations of artificiality have imbedded themselves in the imagination.

This might explain his fascination with obsolescence, retrieval, "alternative interfaces," and with investigating technologies that have hardly exhausted either their functional or creative potentials. Indeed, the trajectory of the work since the early 1980s is as much an on-going encounter with technologies whose sheer presence is far too easily overshadowed by disquieting conceptions of transparency and invisibility, as it is an instinctively reasoned – even methodical – deconstruction of the illusions (in the broadest sense) of a culture inebriated by the surface, narratives, tropes and intersections between Hollywood cinema, the (im)plausibilities of science fiction, tele-conspiracy programs, the often stunning announcements and spectacles of scientific research, and an active critical relationship with the electronic arts. But rather than peeling away the often depthless ideologies of media, Hoberman's work scrutinizes and allegorizes in ironic twists and turns.

Emerging in a critical environment dominated by figures like Laura Mulvey, Christian Metz, Stephen Heath, *Screen magazine*, *Cahiers du Cinema*, a cross between poststructuralism, psychoanalysis, and marxism, his early works maintained a distinctly non-dogmatic but very serious relationship with representation, performance, and theory.

The 1983 installation/performance *Out Of The Picture: Return Of The Invisible Man* is a seminal work in this regard. Described as "conspiratorially humorous and spooky," and as "semiotics in 3-D,"[9] *Out of the Picture* linked stereo projections (in retrospect, one of the fundamental visual models of immersive environments and a territory still being investigated in his work), episodic sampling, and recontextualization of text and sound sequences, no less the "audience" itself as a cast of shadows – where Plato meets H. G. Wells, the allegory of the cave comes "face-to-face" with the metaphor of the Invisible Man.

Playing with the reciprocity between (in)visibility and the gaze, the character of the Invisible Man was a cunning counter-signifier that simultaneously invoked

8 Friedrich Kittler, *Gramo-
   phone, Film, Typewriter*,
   Stanford University Press,
   Stanford, 1999, p. 17.

9 Noel Carroll, "Semiotics in
   3-D," in *Village Voice*,
   27 Dec 1983, On-line version.

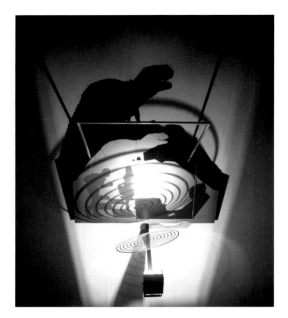

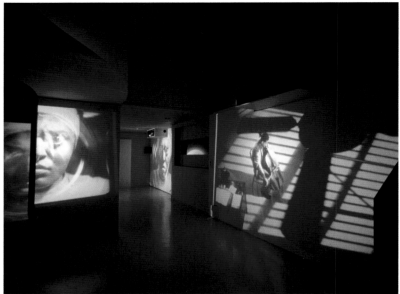

left
Natural Selection
1985
wall sculpture (from the
Stereoshadows series)
wood, polarized light system,
Plexiglas, monofilament, 3-D
shadows
101 x 81 x 61 cm
installation view: Postmasters
Gallery, New York, 1985
© Perry Hoberman
photo © Perry Hoberman

right
Dead Space/Living Rooms
1985
projection and sound
installation
slide projectors and control
system, stereoscopic
projections, sound system
approx. 600 x 900 x 270 cm
installation view: Capp Street
Project, San Francisco, 1985
© Perry Hoberman
photo © Perry Hoberman

10 Anne-Marie Duguet, "Does
Interactivity Lead to New
Definitions in Art?," in *Per-
spektiven der Medienkunst*
(Media Art Perspectives),
Hans Peter Schwarz and
Jeffrey Shaw (eds), Hatje
Cantz, Ostfildern, 1996,
p. 149.

the cold war, the evil empire, the mad scientist and the pretensions of overly formal criticism. By spatializing text, sound, and image in the iridescence of 3-D, *Out Of The Picture* suggested a kind of post-cinematic, post-linear opposition to the phenomenologies of film studies and a shift toward the integration of technique as a form of subversion.

By 1985 and 1986, Hoberman's exhibitions were investigating the effects of three dimensional projection utilizing sculptural and pre-cinematic technologies. *The Silencers*, *High Rise (Under Construction)*. *Natural Selection*, devise spooky associations from eerily silhouetted forms. These "anamorphic" shadows cast unexpected illumination into distinctly psychologized spaces. Extending the idea of compression and reorientation into temporalized spaces is evident in the important 1985 installation *Dead Space/Living Rooms* which consisted of projections and re-animations of four Hollywood B-movies: *The Walking Dead* (1936), *The 4-D Man* (1959), *DOA* (1950) and *Mad Love* (1935).

"Each of these films," writes Hoberman, "involves characters that are neither alive nor dead." He continues: "my method was to stop a film in motion, kill it. Photograph stills from the stopped/murdered film. Project these slides. Then reanimate them, projecting a series of them very rapidly in sequence, bringing them back to life." Abel Gance called this kind of cinematic second-coming "luminous resurrection." By interruption, overlapping, and "shuffling," the fantastic "space" of the cinematic-sculptural installation (with images projected onto every surface of the gallery) itself became mnemonic, triggered by physical and "virtual" 3-dimensionality that is as haunting as it is symptomatic.

Indeed the relationships between memory, reception, and behavior form the core of a transition from experiential environments to dynamic systems, installation to interaction. A reversal from the implied audience of earlier installations, this shift into the building of interactive installations was to be an essential element of Hoberman's more recent work. Writing of the complex issues involved in rethinking the hitherto passive role of reception, Anne-Marie Duguet makes some important points: "Video installations have al-

ready spurred reflection on the status and role of the spectator, on the activity of perception and the issue of representation. Interactive installations are now intensifying this radical displacement of attention onto the actual experience of the work ... For certain works, then, interactivity is not a genre but a mode of existence, a fundamental parameter."10

Both setting "parameters" and "radical displacement" are useful descriptions for a number of works to emerge from through the 1990s. Refusing to fall into the snare of screen-based user-interfaces, Hoberman's work exemplifies his continuing doubts about flawless navigation, the "user-illusion," and the all-too-pervasive solitary user experience. A number of highly successful and significant works emerge from his investigation of the so-called "human-machine" interface not merely as a by-product of computer graphics tinged with some kind of requisite navigation, but as an of-shoot of an everyday world in which the familiar – if not pervasive – machines or systems could be recycled, refunctioned, or reoriented. Notable of these works are: *Faraday's Garden* (originally shown in 1990) *Bar Code Hotel* (1994), *Systems Maintenance* (1998) and *Timetable* (1999).

Faraday's Garden is a cross between an homage to Michael Faraday (whose ground-breaking work on electro-magnetism laid the foundations for the transformer and the generator) and a flea-market (where the passé gadgets, obsolescent appliances and inconsequential effluvia of culture swirl in a kind of purgatory between the junk pile and the antique store). Evoking the banal notion that "feedback" is the primary principle of interactivity, *Faraday's Garden* is constituted as a kind of gauntlet of appliances – from blenders and electric knives to record players and projectors – in which pressure-sensitive floor switches position the user(s) as the trigger for the machines. As in most of the work of the 1990s, the work is an open-system that relies not just on user reactions, but on the possible behaviors of users whose actions "perform" a perverse dance of instrumentality in an atmosphere that serves as a constant reminder that our lives are enveloped machines whose presence incessantly reverberates.

Faraday's Garden
1990–1999
interactive-appliance
installation
household, kitchen, and office
appliances, switch matting,
custom electronics,
phonograph records,
eight-track and cassette tapes,
slides, filmstrips, 8mm and
16mm films
dimensions variable
installation views: Museum of
Contemporary Art, Dayton, 1991
© Perry Hoberman
photos © Perry Hoberman

Bar Code Hotel
1994
interactive installation
printed bar code, custom
tables, wooden cubes, bar-code
wands, polarized stereoscopic
computer projection, polarizing
(3-D) glasses, aluminum-
surfaced projection screen,
four-channel sound system
dimensions variable
installation view: Walter Phillips
Gallery, Banff Centre for the
Arts, Alberta, 1994
© Perry Hoberman
photo © Perry Hoberman

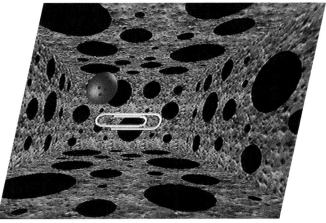

Bar Code Hotel
1994
interactive installation
screenshot
© Perry Hoberman

Systems Maintenance
1998
interactive installation
material/media: wooden
furniture, data projection
and screen, video cameras,
aluminum structure,
kiosks with turntables,
Wintel PC, custom software
914 x 914 x 365 cm
installation views:
Cornerhouse Gallery,
Manchester, 1998
© Perry Hoberman
photos © Perry Hoberman

Systems Maintenance is an intervention into fallacies of synchronization, representation, and closure. The three "worlds" that characterize the installation – the "real," the model, and the rendering – pose significant questions about the legitimacy of experiences increasingly mediated by technologies assimilated with little reflection. Yet rather than re-solve the oppositions between these "worlds," *Systems Maintenance* flatly foils them as a reminder that they are not so easily reconciled, that open-systems are determined not by integration but by differing intentionalities, that order and disorder os-cillate as an essential condition of everyday reality.

Timetable, in a direct way, confronts the economy of time without the burden of the infinite, but by im-plementing and distributing the regulation of the work to the twelve controls that ring the projection.

"*Timetable* is an attempt to play with concepts of time – to buy time and to spend it, to save time and to waste it, to find time and to lose it, to borrow it, to run out of it, to kill it." *Timetable* proposes a time released from monotonous utility, liberated from relentless cycles as it relativises both its ceaseless regularity and its potential as an interface. The time of *Timetable* is subversive, unstable, asynchronous, and ultimately destructive. Users rotate small dials and implement actions in the sometimes swirling, sometimes aggressive, sometimes collaborative, sometimes pointless, sometimes rigorous, some-times decelerated, sometimes accelerated, "real-time" in which Heisenberg's Uncertainty Principle joins Turing's Test in a projected electronic cauldron of ambiguous observers, uncertain agencies, pro-grammed ambiguities, elicited cooperations,

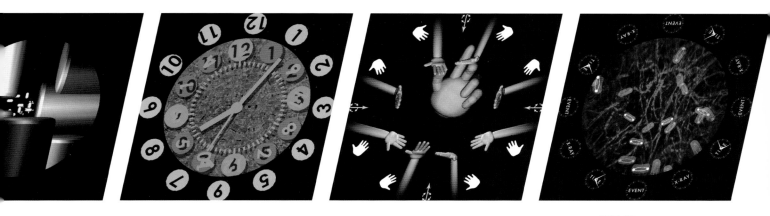

Timetable
1999
interactive-projection
installation
stills
© Perry Hoberman

Timetable
1999
interactive-projection
installation
Wintel PC, custom software,
data projection, sound system,
rotary encoders, aluminum
table, projection screen
table dimensions: 274 cm ∅,
76 cm high
© Perry Hoberman
photo © Perry Hoberman

nonsensical interventions, indeterminate identities, indefinite consequences, and inexact chronometry.

Hoberman also describes *Timetable* as an attempt "to make certain paradoxical (even impossible) pseudo-scientific concepts into concrete experiences, such as time travel, multiple branching universes, alternate dimensions and shared hallucinations." *Timetable* is without doubt linked with Hoberman's unambiguous fascination with the looming and pervasive tropes of pop culture, pulp fiction, science fiction, fictional science, cybermania, and a generation of rootless (should I say "rhizomatic") electronic "intellectuals" touting everything from "digital being" or "collective intelligence" to "technoetics" or "post-humanism" in pretentious forms that, as Hoberman suggests, "are no barrier to hilarity." In this sense, Hoberman's parodic interventions into the sacrosanct presumptions touted by the apparatchiks of humanized neuro-hardware or virtualized epistemology are deeply serious, and played out by joining defiantly antic behaviorist strategies with an incisive understanding of the possibilities of an interactivity whose reach into the public sphere is as much play as provocation. Part open-system, part closed-circuit, *Timetable* is "time out of joint," time that is located in the rationality of the table-sized dial but whose face is exploding with conflict, with

competition, with incompleteness. In opening the face of the "clock" to the interruptions of its users, it reveals the game of time as an exercise in futility.

The performance *Let's Make a Monster* is part cinematic archaeology, part mad science, part cautionary tale, part "fan cut," with Hoberman as part Frankenstein, part "fantasmagore," part Turing, part Philip K. Dick. Joining decades long interests in science fiction and "Hollywood science" with an unfailing willingness to expose absurdity with irony (visual and narrative), to turn theory into practice – if not resistance – and to suggest the interface as a staging ground in which one can tinker with narrative, re-enliven the shock-value of montage, remix, re-cut, reframe, reclaim, or re-evaluate, Hoberman engages in classic negative dialectics and sublation – assimilate and "transcend."

In *Let's Make a Monster* three mingled "narratives" are at play: the cinematic, the performative and the discursive. The projected images and sequences are drawn from innumerable sci-fi classics center on the over-arching issue of the creation of artificial life. Hoberman, in the guise of a kind of electronic alchemist or the Wizard of Oz, faces away from the audience before an array of instruments (cameras, dials, a laptop) that mimic the boiling beakers, the electrical generators, and the laboratories of the

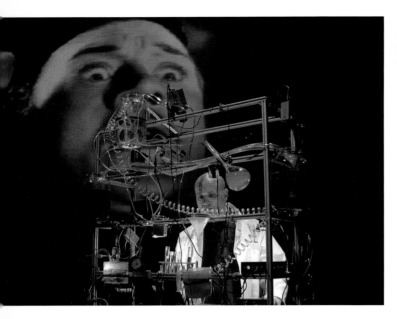
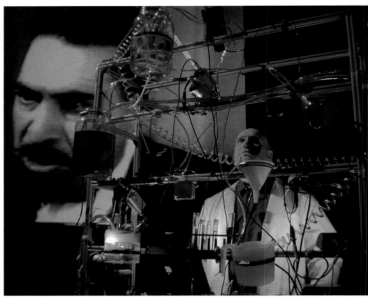

Let's Make a Monster
2001–2003
live-projection performance
Powerbook G3, custom soft-
ware (MAX/MSP/JITTER,
Macromedia Director),
data projection,
CCTV cameras, audio,
MIDI, other custom controls
performance views: ZKM |
Center for Art and Media
Karlsruhe, 2003
© Perry Hoberman
photos © Perry Hoberman

"mad" scientists, and "appears," in alternating disguises, either as the voice of the raving narrator, the crazed manipulator of the control mechanisms, or the lunatic creator of nightmarish cinematic creatures obeying the whims of electronics. The voiced-over narration is a cross between the delirious fantasies of a modern Dr. Frankenstein and one of the innumerable contemporary artificial life/artificial intelligence experts whose algorithmic prognostications, wet-declarations, and often delusional nano-life speculations, seem to know little of how brazenly they replicate the perverse prophetic visions of science gone awry. Dr. Frankenstein draws the bandages form the eyes of the bride concocted to assuage the monster, its gaze beaming, and the scream "it's alive" and the sound loops "it's alive, it's alive, it's alive, it's alive, it's alive … " while the voice-over declares "It is our creation now. We make the rules. We establish the parameters of reality."

"It is my thesis," the voice announces, "that the physical function of the living individual and the operation of some of the newer communication machines are precisely parallel in their analogous attempts to control entropy through feedback." As the images on the screen act as both mnemonic devices (that stream in rapid succession, merge with each other, spread and multiply into unpredictable grids) and tropes (that threaten to expose the dreaded, and repetitive "master narrative" of sci-fi), the "narration" unfolds as itself mnemonic as it parodies the hyperbolists of the artificial – their pseudo-realities and their scientized fictions caught in obvious collusion as they promise indeterminate – and yet technically totalitarian – perfection.

"The mad scientist," writes Skal, in *The Screams of Reason: Mad Science and Modern Culture*, "… is a restless synthesizer, scuttling around his laboratory, stitching together our central schisms."[11] Little wonder that the cut-and-paste artist Dr. Frankenstein builds "a collage of human corpses"[12] in an attempt to reanimate death and boot-up life. But rather than human remains, Hoberman resurrects the sampled "corpses" from a cinema that, as Kittler observed, "began with reels, cuts, and splices"[13] but that now survives as a vast archive to be plumbed for patterns

deeply related to multifarious histories. From this point of view *Let's Make a Monster* is related to the work of Zoe Beloff (whose works collects, in her words, "scraps and remains … symptoms of fact, symptoms of fiction, symptoms of an age") or Craig Baldwin (whose works collect and assemble clues for pervasive conspiracy).

But *Let's Make a Monster* can also be linked with an intriguing phenomenon being called the "fan-cut" digitally re-edited versions of now classic films (the first Star Wars "fan-cut" appeared last year under the title *The Phantom Edit*). J. Hoberman (no relation) recalled that "the first known fan cut was made by the artist Joseph Cornell in 1936. Cornell obtained a 16-millimeter print of a Hollywood adventure film, *East of Borneo*, released by Columbia Pictures five years earlier, and transformed it into 24 enigma-charged minutes that he named in honor of the movie's female star, Rose Hobart. Objections to this radical revision and blatant copyright infringement came not from Columbia but rather from Cornell's fellow artist Salvador Dalí, who accused Cornell of having plagiarized his dreams."[14]

Let's Make a Monster is allegory constituted by allegory, a kind of cut-and-paste parable that evokes a flood of references both present and implicit in its performance. It's a world of "plagiarized dreams," "central schisms," "cuts and splices." It's *Frankenstein* meets *Brave New World*, it's *The Golem* meets *Blade Runner*, it's *Coma* meets *The Invisible Man*. It's also Marvin Minsky meets Philip K. Dick, Hans Moravec meets Isaac Asimov, Richard Dawkins meets Thom Disch, Rodney Brooks meets J.G. Ballard …

In an early essay, "The Android and the Human," Philip K. Dick wrote:

"The world of the future, to me, is not a place, but an event. A construct, not by one author in the form of words written to make up a novel or story that other persons sit in front of, outside of, and read – but a construct in which there is no author and no readers but a great many characters in search of a plot …"[15]

Timothy Druckrey

11 Skal, op. cit., p. 23.

12 Skal, op. cit., p. 61.

13 Kittler, op. cit., p. 115.

14 J. Hoberman, "A Do-It-Your-self 'Star Wars'," in *New York Times*, 15 July, 2001. On-line version.

15 Philip K. Dick, "The Android and the Human," in Lawrence Sutin, *The Shifting realities of Philip K. Dick: Selected Literary and Philosophical Writings*, Vintage, New York, 1995, p. 205.

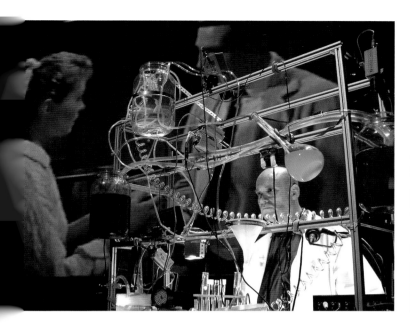

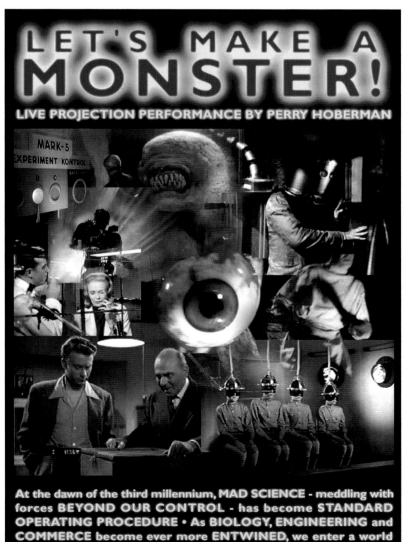

poster for the live-projection performance
Let's Make a Monster
digital image
50 x 76 cm
© Perry Hoberman

Toni Dove
Sally or the Bubble Burst

2002
interactive DVD installation / video, audio, and MAX/MSP and JITTER software
on DVD-ROM / dimensions variable

"In film, the cut moves you through time.
While interactive experience contains some rupture
within it, the engine that moves it through time is
not based on rupture. And rupture, of course, is
a key to collage and montage, which were so
significant to modernist practice. The move that
interests me is away from the cut into something
that's about fluidity and the continuum."[1]

Toni Dove has been working with interactive film for a number of years. In her works the observer is transformed from passive spectator to participating actor who influences the course of the action. "I'm using cinema as a familiar ground, a place to locate yourself and be at ease, and then these new technologies make the cinematic experience go strange on you."[2] Recent Hollywood productions have also taken the disintegration of linear narration as their theme. Films such as *Sliding Doors* and *Run Lola Run* also present different versions of the plot, although the viewer has no way of actively controlling the latter and is merely confronted with a choice of options, of synchronic realities. In Dove's films, a story unfolds only through interaction – the course of the plot is determined by the observer. By involving the observer, who is thus no longer merely an observer but a user of the film, Dove aims to intensify the cinematographic experience and to link together observer and character in a radically new way. Using motion tracking and speech recognition technology, she allows the observer to control the action. *Artificial Changelings* (1998) is the first work in a trilogy of film projects in which Dove sends her protagonists on journeys through space and time. Her current project, *Spectropia*, is a full-length interactive film, and *Sally or the Bubble Burst* is a scene from this work in progress, which exists both as performative installation and as interactive DVD-ROM – allowing participants to interact via the Internet.

The story of *Sally or the Bubble Burst* begins in 2099. The observer first meets up with Spectropia, a young girl searching for memories with the aid of a scanning machine she has built herself. The somber atmosphere of the city in which she lives is reminiscent of Ridley Scott's science fiction classic *Blade Runner*. In this city, knowledge is limited to the remembered past experience of each individual person

– the keeping of historical records is forbidden. The scanning machine "reads" objects and from the data creates real-life simulations that Spectropia can step into and explore.[3] Thus she finds herself in the New York of the 1930s, shortly after the Wall Street Crash – and it is here that this scene from *Sally or the Bubble Burst* is located. The user now switches to a dialogue with Sally Rand, a famous dancer of that era, choosing for this interactive sequence between three "zones." One of these zones places the user in direct contact with the character of Sally Rand. Using a microphone or the computer keyboard, the user asks Sally questions to which she reacts with a range of surprising comments and emotions. Another scene shows Sally performing her famous "Bubble Dance," which the observer can influence and "choreograph" by manipulating the mouse. The scene was choreographed by Helen Pickett based on archival footage and photographs of Sally's original dance. A third scene focuses on the era's political and economic background. By naming the objects in Sally's dressing room using a microphone or clicking on image buttons on the interface, the observer can summon up scenes of actors narrating stories of the Depression years. The objects include two balloons, a chair, a scarf and a radio.

In the installation version of the work, the user moves trough the zones of each scene over pressure-sensitive tiles. The user controls the virtual figure through body movements and vocal sound – though not absolutely. For though the user does indeed influence the figure's actions, the latter appears to have a life of its own. Dove describes this – for her crucial – incongruity between the user's input and the figure's actions:

"One of the things that interests me in interactive narrative is giving the user a certain amount of control, but not complete control. I think if the

1 Toni Dove, in *ARTBYTE*, Feb–Mar 1999, vol. 1, no. 6, p. 37.

2 Toni Dove, op. cit., p. 34.

3 This scene is reminiscent of the "holodecks" in the science fiction series *Star Trek*, to which Toni Dove also refers in her article "The Space Between: Telepresence, Re-animation and the Re-casting of the Invisible," in which she makes clear her interest in science fiction in general.

Sally or the Bubble Burst
2002
interactive DVD installation
screenshot
distributed by Cycling '74
Toni Dove
© Toni Dove; Bustlelamp
Productions, Inc.
photo © Sam Levy

Sally or the Bubble Burst
2002
interactive DVD installation
screenshots
distributed by Cycling '74
Toni Dove
© Toni Dove; Bustlelamp
Productions, Inc.
photos © Sam Levy

user has total agency it's actually boring, because every gesture becomes a loop that comes back – it flattens out the experience."[4]

In the Internet version, it is possible for two users in different places to meet at a virtual location and inhabit characters to make a scene unfold. In this case meaningful interaction also depends on the two networked players being able to cooperate successfully. Interaction with computer networks and virtual reality alters the way we relate to our bodies. In virtual worlds it is possible to overcome the biological confines of our own bodies, without actually leaving our bodies, and to move like an avatar through an electronic universe. Our experiences in the electronic net and the reality of our own bodies no longer coincide. Virtualization involves not disembodiment but a doubling of the self. The virtual body is a vehicle that allows one to be simultaneously present in distant locations. "Technology transforms us into spiritual and physical nomads."[5] For Dove these new opportunities of territorial appropriation create the possibility of repossessing realms that were once considered the purlieus of the paranormal.

"Characters are inhabited like digital puppets and when a viewer feels their own presence in the screen through the character, it can produce an uncanny experience. The familiar ground of film goes strange and the viewer feels the trace of his or her own actions reflected in the screen. They haunt the movie."[6]

Dove exploits the motif of the journey through time in a classical science fiction setting in order to explore the development of the unconscious and the latter's increasing marginalization and transformation into the uncanny.

By interacting with the virtual characters in Dove's installations, the user explores the idiosyncrasies of the figures she or he creates, observes them in action, and at the same time experiences this action from their perspective. The constant shifting of the observer's standpoint transforms cinema into an experience whose intensity is beyond anything with which we are acquainted so far. "In *Spectropia* viewers are shadows in the story and manifest a relationship with each other through the characters on the screen."[7]

Sabine Himmelsbach

Translated from the German by Steven Richards

4 Toni Dove, op. cit., p. 33.

5 "Durch die Technik werden wir bereits Nomaden in Geist und Körper." Jill Scott, *"Die digitale Körperethik,"* in *Kunstforum*, vol. 133, p. 176.

6 Toni Dove, "The Space Between: Telepresence, Re-animation and the Re-casting of the Invisible," in *New Screen Media: Cinema/Art/Narrative*, Martin Rieser and Andrea Zapp (eds), BFI Publishing, London, 2002, pp. 209, 210.

7 Toni Dove, "The Space Between," op. cit., p. 216.

Sally or the Bubble Burst
2002
interactive DVD installation
video, audio, and MAX/MSP and
JITTER software on DVD-ROM
dimensions variable
installation view: ZKM |
Center for Art and Media
Karlsruhe, 2002
distributed by Cycling '74
Toni Dove
© Toni Dove; Bustlelamp
Productions, Inc.
photo © Franz Wamhof

The character of Sally is conceived as an inhabitable narrative machine that is both empty and full. Empty as it requires the presence of a viewer to animate it. Full with layers of content that live in the piece through my own writing and concepts, the dialogue contributions of Mitzi Morris, the humor and grace of the actress/choreographer Helen Pickett, the voices of the performers who embodied the objects, and the sound and software design of Peter Scherer and R. Luke DuBois. There are many other traces as well – a history of the echoes of a cultural imaginary fueled by new technologies from the radio to the internet and the utopian dreams they conjured. Some of these dreams have been rendered quaint by time and revived again in the present. As a viewer enters the space of the piece these traces collect around them in a mutable constellation. Sally's "humaness" for me comes into play in the collisions between these narrative traces rather than in any direct representation of the character. The dislocation between the glamour girl masquerade and the frequently awkward or "broken" qualities of the technology – inadequacies of speech recognition, the synthetic or robotic quality of speech synthesis – creates a tension against our expectations of human vs. machine representation. Constructions of gender, constructions of the human, constructions of the robot and the machine bump up against each other. The flaws and collisions – the spaces in between – are what animate the piece in combination with the viewer's actions and create the doubling effect from viewer to character that I would call uncanny. The viewer haunts the movie machine.

Toni Dove

Martin Arnold
pièce touchée

1989
16mm film / b/w, sound / 16 min

passage à l'acte

1993
16mm film / b/w, sound / 12 min

Viennese experimental filmmaker Martin Arnold has constructed, in his three films *pièce touchée* (1989), *passage à l'acte* (1993), and *Alone. Life Wastes Andy Hardy* (1998), a cinema machine – not simply a custom optical printer or recycling system, but a kind of mnemographic machine, an apparatus that writes and rewrites memories on the surfaces of film. Arnold's cinema functions by incorporating exterior forces, an outside source of energy that presses upon the projected images. In turn, the machine exports matter, forming a kind of open economy.

The results effect a hypertension between the impulses of the original material and the rescriptive force of the new edits. On the surface, the exteriority that charges Arnold's machine can be seen as the history of film, especially of Hollywood, and its systems of representation and systemic repressions. "The cinema of Hollywood," writes Arnold, "is a cinema of exclusion, reduction and denial, a cinema of repression."1 Hollywood's waste returns in Arnold's cinema as fuel. On closer observation, however, the surfaces of history from which Arnold draws have been, to use Freud's phrase, "worked over": they have been inscribed *already* with the marks of an enunciation yet to come, with the traces of a future anterior.

Excerpt from Akira Lippit, *Cinemnesis. Martin Arnold's Memory Machine*, Re:Voir Video Editions, Paris, 1999, pp. 5–6.

passage à l'acte
1993
16mm film
b/w, sound
12 min
film still
© 1999 Martin Arnold;
Amour Fou Filmproduktion

pièce touchée
1989
16mm film
b/w, sound
16 min
film still
© 1999 Martin Arnold;
Amour Fou Filmproduktion

Deanimated –
The Invisible Ghost
2002
film
b/w, sound
60 min
film stills
© Martin Arnold;
Amour Fou Filmproduktion

Martin Arnold's latest work *Deanimated* takes as its foil a conventional horror film: *The Invisible Ghost* by Joseph H. Lewis (USA, 1941) starring Bela Lugosi. Out of the original, in which a woman hypnotizes her husband into a murder plot, Arnold's *Deanimated* creates a study of the progressive dissolution of cinema acting, a process of dehumanization, a protocol of communication breakdown.

Using digital compositing, characters are edited out of the scenario, mouths morphed shut, and dialogues mutilated. Towards the end, the camera pans through rooms largely empty of people, until finally an impenetrable blackness lasting for several minutes reduces traditional narrative to degree zero.

Characterized as it is by disappearance and silence, the film tells a different story than that of *The Invisible Ghost* – one that is incomparably more open and puzzling, that relocates the plot on a plateau of existential self-questioning. Supporting roles suddenly take center stage. Effervescent bursts of music no longer underscore dramatic climaxes but emphasize the aridity of uneventfulness. The aimlessly panning camera seems to be searching desperately for the key to some obscure mystery. As *Deanimated* ends, one of the film's leading characters poses its central question: "Oh my god, what happened here?"

Deanimated throws sand into the wheels of Hollywood's well-oiled story machine. It portrays the system of the grand narratives in a state of dissolution. Martin Arnold's aim is not to replace old narratives with new ones but to report on the real presence of what is absent. "Forms, colors, contrast and rhythms don't affect the spectator in the realm of language and logic," says the director. "They communicate on deeper levels. I would situate the discourse they take part in in the unconscious."

Whereas *Deanimated* undertakes a radical dehumanization of the cinema screen and auditorium, Arnold's *Dissociated* and *Forsaken* use double projection to break up cinema's reliance on the traditional proscenium arch. In both films the double projection forces the eye of the observer to free itself from a central perspective and to orientate itself anew, and thus discover individual perspectives and time frames among the simultaneity of cinematographic events.

Translated from the German by Steven Richards

1   Martin Arnold, in Scott
    MacDonald, "Sp ... Sp ...
    Spaces of Inscription: An
    Interview with Martin
    Arnold," in *Film Quarterly*,
    48.1, Fall 1994, p. 7.

Pierre Huyghe
The Third Memory

1999
double-projection film / Beta digital / color, sound / 9:46 min

"What follows is based on a true story. The events depicted here took place on August 22, 1972 in Brooklyn, New York." Thus begins *Dog Day Afternoon*, the 1975 film produced by Warner Bros. and directed by Sidney Lumet. What happened on that day? John Wojtowicz is the principle actor in the event: it all begins with his hold-up of a branch of The Chase Manhattan Bank in Brooklyn.1 The bank is very quickly surrounded by police; he responds by taking the bank's employees hostage. After several hours of negotiation with the FBI, he manages to secure a bus to take him and his hostages to the John F. Kennedy airport. When Wojtowicz arrives at the airport, he is immediately arrested and his accomplice is shot down. The event was broadcast live on television and quickly became one of the USA's most important stories in the days following. An article covering the event that was published in *Life* magazine will inspire Sidney Lumet to make the film. The article, focusing on the more spectacular aspects of the event and written in the form of a scenario, will come to constitute the framework of *Dog Day Afternoon*. John Wojtowicz becomes Sonny Wortzik, played by Al Pacino. Spectator to his own history, John Wojtowicz is unable to find himself reflected in the film's images and representations of what he went through. The apparatus devised in *The Third Memory* involves a reconstruction that permits the truth of certain assumptions to be verified. There where the fiction is driven by the scenario, the mise-en-scène and the actor's performance, the reconstruction functions more like the setting-up of a situation (*une mise en situation*) in the presence of the event's real author; it reveals the conditions of

a lived history as well as its motivations. The reconstruction attempts to make a precise image of the real appear; it calls on the memory of the event's author who is, at once, actor and commentator of his own acts. *The Third Memory* is a factual reconstruction but it takes place on a duplicated version of the original set of Sidney Lumet's fictional account, because the task here is not only to understand the conditions that produced the historical event but also to show the relations that can be established between the author of the occurrence and the character who represents him. It is the story of a man who has been robbed, dispossessed of his own image. In this instance, the author of this relatively trivial occurrence protests that the image of this same occurrence is nothing but an illusion. When fiction – which claims to give an account of the real – replaces or instrumentalizes the imaginary, and when the represented subject-matter claims this fiction as the more real, this is when the rights of the real occurrence's author consist in a deployment of speech within the structure that was put into place by the fiction's author so that he can reoccupy his place within the very apparatus that had dispossessed him of his own history. To deploy speech in order to become the actor of his own memory. *The Third Memory* offers the author of the real occurrence the possibility to re-appropriate the forms of representation and of leisure-time management that have been produced by (the author of) fiction.

Pierre Huyghe
Translated from the French by Sarah Clift

1 [The terms "acteur" and "auteur" are used throughout the original French version of the text for what in English would usually be translated as "agent" or "subject"; that is, someone who makes self-determining decisions. However, because these terms in English lose something of the slippage between reality and fiction – or between staged personalities and their real-life counterparts – that is so clearly at stake in the work, an attempt has been made here to maintain that ambiguity through the use of such terms as "player," "actor" and "author." –Trans.]

The Third Memory
1999
double-projection film
Beta digital
color, sound
9:46 min
photographs of the shooting
© Marian Goodman Gallery,
Paris and New York

Spatial description

The walls of the dark projection room should be painted as follows: the wall used for projection is white, the side walls are light gray, and the wall opposite the projection wall is dark brown. In the case of acoustic problems, a gray carpet should be laid identical in color with the two side walls.

A bench taking up the full length of the brown wall should be placed against it and painted the same color.

The two images in 16/9 format must be projected side by side (with no intervening space) to produce the effect of a panoramic image. The black projected above and below the image should be masked by electronic shutters.

The base of the image for each projection should be between four and five meters. The ideal base would measure 4.5 meters.

Additional description

A separate room illuminated by neon lights and painted dark brown is fitted with a gray carpet identical to that in the projection room, and is situated next to the projection room.

This separate room further possesses:
— an enlarged reproduction (digital copy of approx. 125%) of the original poster advertising the film *Dog Day Afternoon*;
— enlarged reproductions (digital copies measuring approx. 60 x 80 cm) of diverse press excerpts;
— a built-in monitor presenting the Jeanne Parr Show in a 22-min loop in front of which is installed a light-colored wooden bench.

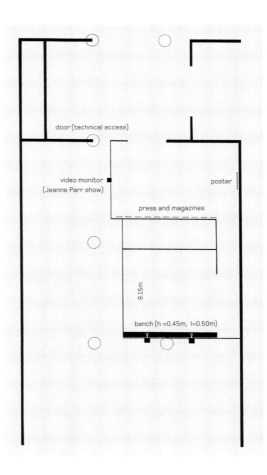

door (technical access)

video monitor
(Jeanne Parr show)

poster

press and magazines

8.15m

bench (h =0.45m, l=0.50m)

ground plan for
the installation of
The Third Memory
1999
drawing
courtesy Marian Goodman
Gallery, Paris and New York

Constanze Ruhm
Coming Attraction: X Characters (in search of an author)

2002–2003
installation / mixed media / dimensions variable

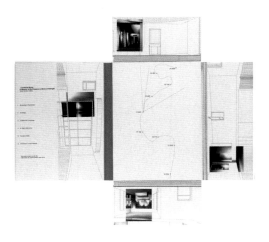

1 The installation space of *Coming Attraction* is an environment scripted to negotiate the past and a future. This space draws on the earlier project *A Memory of the Players in a Mirror at Midnight* (2001) as well as on the forthcoming production *X Characters in Search of an Author* (2002/2003).

A Memory… is already built on the subjects of character, script, and movie ride that are substantial to *Coming Attraction* and *X Characters*. It provides a shared focus point, their foundation and source code. As a "prequel" of the solo movement and narration of one voice, it now expands to register a range of motions and enunciations – of female characters' voices, of movements through spaces and scripts – as the coded sources developed in *A Memory…* are turned into operating principles used as guidelines for subsequent productions. *A Memory…* re-scripts a Hollywood film (*Eyes of Laura Mars*, Irvin Kershner, USA 1978) as a digital and spatial interpretation. The film itself represents a characteristic late-1970s trope. It consists of a sequence of digital architectures, virtual reconstructions based on sets from the original movie. The relation between the digital structures built on filmic spaces and the camera movement is oriented along a voice-over narration. *Eyes of Laura Mars* is re-engineered into a new script situated between a text and a space. It becomes a system to speak through, not about.

It scripts the desires embodied within the condensed format of a trailer through the analytical logic of a synopsis. The project is shaped by the force of emotions and passions contained in the anatomy of narrative structures. These structures are translated into a different story in order to articulate a contemporary moment whose syntax is constructed through the specific template of the agency of a film. The film's fictitious construction is inserted into a different fiction format (a written narration, an off-screen voice-over, a script). *A Memory…* is not an investigation of the real, but an attempt to explore the imaginary embedded in mainstream modes of narrative production, as these represent antagonistic configurations and reflective reservoirs of reality.

2 In a scene from the film *Klute*, a male character (an urban police psychologist) describes to another male character (a small-town detective) the features of the female lead – a high-class call girl. The film scene as mise-en-abyme turns the mechanism of scripting into a brief tautological gesture. It joins one character to one profile, but here as inversion of conventional scripting rules, which establish a profile as an outline to be inhabited by the actress to render it into her unique, three-dimensional character. In *Klute*, the profile serves within a process of observation to flatten the complexity of an individual into a recognizable pattern stereotype. Modernist female character templates fashioned by male authors oscillate between different forms of modernity – often, they are barely even minimal types, sometimes they are turned into baroque composites of different scripts in order to satisfy all logics required. In the film, the call-girl character combines three forms of acting, each one a different sub-script to the film: prostitute, aspiring actress, and subject, barely held together in the metascript of her weekly psychoanalytical sessions.

A script is an unpredictable play of forces always in development as a performative operating system. Scripts develop sets and characters, spatial identities and psychological subjects whose operating principles are often rooted in subconscious and repressed materials. The scripting process not only translates between narrative and visual forms of representation. It generates spatial narratives through and on architectures, characters and subjects rendered as synthetic constructions. In this variable world of many possible endings, it is always the author's desire that establishes the cosmic order of the plot. In a film script, these authorial desires are refracted through their characters' features.

Identities: »Coming Attractions«

The thematic framework of "Future Cinema" is a consideration of what the century-old apparatus of cinema offers as a future language at the start of the twenty-first century, and within which kind of operating system it is imagined and projected. The original, primeval image at work in the early Operating System of modernist cinema linked the camera with the eye, understood motion as life, and developed the then new technique of editing over time into a language that camouflaged the machinery behind the seemingly seamless visual narrative. This "body" of cinema encapsulates the notion of a dynamo founded on the technology of the nineteenth century, a mechanics of governors and gears that ushered in a twentieth-century ideology of modernity. It emerged with and corresponded to the new science of psychoanalysis concerned with developing ways of "governing" the (female) psyche. These psychoanalytical models – like the psychological conditions they were trying to analyze – were conceptually suspended between the notions of attraction and repulsion. They operated as desire machines situated between a repulsive past (containing the traumatic event to be unearthed) and a nameless, mysterious future shaded by still-to-come desires and promises of libidinal fulfillment. The condition of the psychoanalytical subject was thus always nostalgic for a past that had never been, and for a future that would never take place. From an early time on, the identity of modernist cinema reflected these obsessive economies of desire, often located within the terminology of the mechanical.

The project *Coming Attraction* tries to outline a contemporary interpretation, as well as a continuation, of the theory and practice of this modernist apparatus. A possible "future" cinema is encapsulated in the complex identity of a cinema shifting from "apparatus" to "operation." Thus, cinema is being transformed into an operating system founded on contemporary concepts of programs, codes and new forms of scripting. It deals with the cinematic spectacle's past, and its narratives grounded in either a subjective (auteur) perspective or institutionalized (Hollywood) tale. The future of cinema (endowed with all forms of nostalgia generated by the utopian spectacle) evolves around the imprints of its own apparatus indelibly left as a sign, or marker, on the memory 1 of the viewers. Not only are these contours transmuting into templates that develop a life of their own, but they suggest a new and coming inscription of voices emerging from forms of radicalized scripts, setting in motion new narrations about subjects, different points of identification, perspective and visions (as opposed to the stereotypic convention of "artistic vision").

What became visible within a whole range of artistic strategies in the past decade(s) was a desire for the history of the relation between modernism and cinema to be safely interred within "cinema nostalgia." These practices focused only on a safe review of the subjects of cinema history, widely ignoring (academic) discourses on the play and conflict of the forces at work between spectator and screen. An uncritical yearning for the past came to view in cinema's re-institutionalization as instrument of power within the art context. Subsequently, the point of departure was often located at a "degree zero" of cinematic production that would not take into account the established discourse between modernist cinema and avant-garde practice: the then "coming attractions" of a century now already belonging to a cinematic past. This project attempts to shape a new ground for future "coming attractions" drawn from a wide range of fragmentary instances from scripts 2 of all kinds (cinema, the web, and so on). Within the specific condition of "Future Cinema," the mechanical apparatus fuses with the textual, language-only based script. This fusion also marks the turn from the "script" (on which a film might be based) understood to be a homogenous entity and self-contained work of narration, towards interpreting it as a text that belongs to a wide field of texts, writings, scripts and sub-scripts outside of one specific production (one script, one film). Through a strategy of re-reading, re-writing and re-shooting, *Coming Attraction* deals with the process of the production of meaning through the identity of the cinema apparatus now linked to contemporary media. The fusion of and dialog between scripts thus constitutes the identity of a New Cinema constructed within a spatial arrangement of different historical and contemporary media, and built on the very imprint of the cinematic apparatus.

Coming Attraction: X Characters (in search of an author)
2002–2003
installation
mixed media
installation views: ZKM |
Center for Art and Media
Karlsruhe, 2002
© Constanze Ruhm
photos © Marijan Murat

Spatial Configuration

The character of the new spaces of relations in *Coming Attraction* is derived from the old model of cinematic "identity" – the projector. The architectural space defines an area, a perceptual cosmos grounded on its mechanics, and joins together different scripts by taking its blueprint from these components of cinema that are usually hidden away from the black box of cinema space. The projector reels and the synchronization of light, shutters and sprockets are converted into a spatial analysis of patterns of communication models now turned inside out and around themselves. The reels embody notions of past and future, and as mechanical templates leave gaps and openings for "coming attractions" which channel and process words, lines, dialogs, actions. *Coming Attraction* is laid out to be a contemporary projection room designed not to hide the apparatus but instead to combine cinema and web in the form of a ride 3 understandable as that of "auteur" versus "Hollywood."

The projector's machinery becomes the foundation where the mechanical transforms into an informational model, into a "system of signs." The zone in which the transmission reels intersect bridges the space from self-contained work (a film, an artwork) to a text that remains open. It is from this zone, which mutually outlines the eye of apparatus and viewer, that the concept of subjective perception emerges. It renders a spatial configuration that refers to the early "cinematic eye" as identity and communication model encapsulated in the camera's subjective perspective, which understood the notions of "vision" and "perspective" to be central to identity formation. This cinematic "eye" was joined to the market-demographic eye of identifying brands, superseding the cinematic spectacle of the past with the branding strategies and forms of identity production of the Hollywood System (as every studio represented a specific market identity in terms of subjects, style, actors, production design) – an economy whose early disposition already anticipated the structure of the web. The architectural space of *Coming Attraction* allows these structures, links, and areas of intersection belonging to a contemporary understanding of cinema to be seen as the embodiment of the economies and techniques of modernism. Here, the nineteenth-century models of cybernetics and projectors intertwine with present-day communication networks, synthesized through a twenty-first-century scripting and mapping technique, a spatial analysis of desires and relations operating between and within (mass) media. *Coming Attraction* deals with the zones of translation from modernist cinema through video and computer to web.

The architectural signifier collapses with what it signifies. It bridges and renders the space between the reels of a projector: a space that is shaped by the bending and twisting movements of the filmstrip running through the mechanical

3 In the synergetic 1980s, a direct corporate Hollywood spin-off was the development of the "movie ride." A ride is understood to be condensation, compression and foreshortening of the film economy in the form of an extended Special Effect, a program that translates cinema's intense subjective experiences into distinct consumer formats. A movie ride produces a special kind of visual and acoustic architecture, and is based on the grammar of consumer models of representation. It restages and reruns the visual experience of the original film, but is also grounded on the notion of continuous movement, sound effect, and an intensified sense of artificiality.

It operates only through the symbolic, unmediated by language, condensing a dreamlike experience in which the subject is overwhelmed by vision. In this condensation, the ride re-enacts the movie as oneric experience. It foregoes all actors, taking the main film sets and the film's underlying mechanics to turn them not just into characters, but into stars – the set and the script become the attraction, a characterless psyche belonging to no one but the cinematic apparatus.

With its essential focus on sensation and spectacle of motion, the ride suggests a kind of inverse movement back to the future by returning to essentially pre-institutionalized syntax forms of early cinema. It embarks on a skewed history of cinema, and travels alongside spectacular scenes, through fields of orientations and special effects, always in relation to contemporary philosophies of consumer navigators and open source networks. Here, cinema is revealed to still be an assemblage of agencies and effects, narratives, and scripting devices that is measured in degrees ranging from experience to immersion.

The economy of a ride condenses cinema to the essence of postmodern desires. A ride does not convey a sense of fulfillment or release, but a feeling of anticipation. It is a trip that structures along a temporal as well as spatial iconography of media fiction. As a last form of contemporary longing, it speaks of an oddly inverted passion for the real. It orientates along a path that separates "writing" from "riding," illusion from hallucination. Thus, the ride is a passage linking cinematic to psychic apparatus.

Coming Attraction:
Between Synopsis and Trailer

guides. It investigates contemporary forms of distortion that affect visual and textual information and codes passing through the fiber-optical cables of the big networks. Thus, the space of *Coming Attraction* is set out to be a "filmless" set joining the past to the present. The mechanics of the projector and what it projects are understood to equal body as well as psyche: a translation machine suspended between analog and digital worlds, a tenuous construction of tensions and weights bridging and connecting the past with possible future scenarios.

"X Characters in Search of an Author" Production Model

Coming Attraction constitutes the environment for the production *X Characters in Search of an Author* that will begin to unfold over the duration of "Future Cinema" and beyond.

As an art practice, *Coming Attraction* illuminates cinema operating in terms of its subject(s), and not just as screens enlarging "life." Cinema is a code-breaking and code-making synthesis engine. It has the ability to format different scripting devices, assemblages of diverse labors, aesthetic practices, technologies, architectural, temporal and spatial paradigms – all expressed in a tenuous unity set within languages of montage and performance. While cinema's patterns of identification reveal symptoms rooted in the scopic regime, its identity can be seen clearly configured through a history of programming languages. These are based on various source codes from which *Coming Attraction* as environment and *X Characters* … as its program draw on directly.

The production model for *X Characters* … synthesizes the mainstream cinema syntax to script, character, and immersive (movie) ride. In order to re-circulate "cinema" inside a new economy of contemporary media logic, it disassociates, re-codes and reconstitutes the basic elements linked to the identity of a movie. The emphasis is on characters "on the verge," agents in a moment of synthesis, thus shifting attention from the realm of the scopic onto scripting languages: not to mechanics but towards transforming identities, not to formulate canons or a nostalgia for "new media" or cinema, but to continue discovery of and desire for the new scripts initially embedded within these technologies.

Therefore, the navigational space of *Coming Attraction* is a computer-based storyboarding device that develops in linkage with a process of the realization of a performative space, which in turn feeds back to the navigational script. This sense of a continuity produced through a staging of movements, both physical and emotional, is oriented along the basic principles constituting the movie ride. The rules of this ride have been applied to a computer-based web navigational device. This new ride becomes visible on the computer screen, as a guideline whose scripted flow repeats the form and motion of one specific actual movie camera path. This navigational thread routes through filmless sets and character-defined spaces.

This scripted space *X Characters in Search of an Author* develops a performative site between cinematic and new media that is character-driven. It is situated through an array of iconic female characters joined together as a gang of fellow travelers in a cosmos of shifting identities. They are selected from different film scripts, spanning eras from auteur through modernist to post-modern cinema. They were chosen not according to conventional qualities and values formulated in cinema history, but as signifiers, icons, outlines that might enable the shaping of new dialogs. What the original movie scripts avoid making evident in the characters' psyches are omissions that *X Characters* … takes as openings to begin routing through the new narratives.

The plot of *X Characters* … does not pertain to the realm of narrative, therefore, but instead is concerned with the development of the character. As opposed to a story about a character and her experience, *X Characters in Search of an Author* scripts the "character's story" as ongoing production.

Production

X Characters in Search of an Author releases a set of female characters 4 from
the film scripts through which they were originally developed. In the framework of
the project, each character is providing one initial profile to be transformed over a
number of "movements," first through a performance-oriented project, followed
by scripts and the final realization process.

In the first project movement, these profiles are being reconfigured by invited
actor/operators in performance-based formats. The participants come from different fields in the realm of cultural production. Their script is to reconfigure and
adapt the original profile of the character's script, operating essentially in a gap
between their own fantasies and the character's desires. The actor/operators
each play one character, meeting on a virtual media stage for improvisational performance "workshops" on set dates. Thus, the accent is on the improvisational and
live interaction and on the characteristics of the specific medial situation. Instead
of one scriptwriter there are characters who each follow their own logic, structuring a manifold dialog while being recorded. These documents of the live "workshop" interactions with the environment develop a set of possible situations and
materials by which new sets of dialogs and scripts can be established. The results
obtained with this first performative movement are transformed through scriptwriter and director intervention – the realization of a script to chart the development of both the characters' passage and the rites of the story in the second
movement, the realization and shooting in the third.

The use of media forums (from digital chat rooms to analog radio call-in programs through the reality of workshop meetings) suggests the notion of different
communities of interests at work. The project's focus on identity-interaction and
groups supporting new discussion formats in inter-communicative and interactive
environments is an important feature of its foundation in media. *X Characters …* is
a work between research and practice, suggesting that the selected character
icons of cinema modernity function as "re-links" to a cinema informed by critical
feminist practice. This ranges from the discourse on authors and "authorless"
worlds to an essential discussion of feminist research into cinema and representation, indexed to a re-reading of gendered dialogs and continuing onto emerging
cyber-fields. This foundation sets the project within the fields of cinema, language
and identity. The script and production of *X Characters …* is a process that converts the character templates into projection screens, channels of desire that
constitute a switchboard for networking sets of communicative signals.

Constanze Ruhm

4 A set of female characters is drawn from films belonging to, and
set in, different time periods. Thus they establish a range of specific moments in postwar cinema history. They represent icons
bridging from 1960s modernist cinema onto the borderline of the
postmodern 1980s. In this universe of female characters, they are
both lead and supporting actors at the same moment. They slip in
and out of their roles, as the scriptwriter demands that they embody the notion of "woman as symptom," and at the same time they
are required to maintain what is expected from a lead character.
Moreover are they all entangled in a specific relationship with the
terminal – being murdered, suicidal, sacrificial, non-human, extraterrestrial, or simply walking dead women.
   These characters suggest a societal and cultural transformation occurring within the modernist paradigm represented in cinematic discourse, which did not manage to free up a female-charac-
ter potential outside the conventional modernist canon. The characters are sent into even more fragmentary states of bodies and
minds. As the author's agencies of narrative, they are transported
to his main fixation, flowing outwards and inscribing a fundamental
condition of anxiety and distress into a modernist universe defined
by internal discord, psychological conflicts and the breakdown of
communication.
   And then the fiction ends. Still, these unfulfilled characters
remain in the memories of some of us, suggesting the possibility of
return in a different manner.

Rosa Barba
Piratenräume [Pirate Spaces]

2002
film installation / dimensions variable

Piratenräume [Pirate Spaces]
2002
film installation
film still
detail
© VG Bild-Kunst, Bonn 2003

A ray of sun on the floor evokes for a moment dreams of a beautiful life. And then a line flits over a gray wall. It leads your gaze into desolate rooms which fade in pale winter light. Another line form appears, springs over the tristesse of the unrenovated old building as if it knows of hidden treasures waiting to be found in the empty rooms.

But the line forms are not trusty guides, they come and go no longer as coincidental scratches on the film medium which owes its movement to the mechanics of the projector. They hint of the displacement which takes place between the various spaces of the installation; the filmed spaces – the space of illusion produced by the film projection – and the space you can walk about in which the installation is set up.

The projector which Rosa Barba uses to cast film cuts of abandoned apartments in old buildings in Budapest onto the wall of her installation *Piratenräume* (Pirate Spaces) is cumbersome. So cumbersome that you ask yourself how the line forms react to the spools, rollers, film and loudspeakers which together form the apparatus of the installation. The film strips rise and fall, the music is sometimes interrupted and the projection lamp appears to falter.

Also the rhythm with which the projector imparts movement to the line forms is complicated. This complication appears to dissolve as you continue to watch: The rhythm of light and shadow, tone and silence from taut and loose film strips are relative to an inconspicuous element to which perhaps everything can be traced back. It can only be sensually perceived through a small viewing window in which red diodes regularly transform letters into numbers. The small display which is constantly in motion serves as an indication that the rhythm of the action could be connected to a digital control, which presumably controls the projector and lends momentum to the line forms. Does a discrete mathematical plan create the complications? Does the film set-up serve to illustrate the well-known expression that digital computers have also conquered film, and programmers have long since salvaged the treasures of cineastic illusion? Why does Rosa Barba use meticulousness and technical know-how to display the materiality of projection and film transport – not just in this exhibition but in all her works?

The tension in *Piratenräume* can be traced to a historical conflict over the meaning of space and numbers. In the last third of the nineteenth century, mathematical space departed from the visual approach.[1] With help from what is known as group theory, the mathematician Felix Klein in his Erlangen program of 1872 brought the otherwise opposing spatial theories of mathematics together in a numerical model. This is structurally comparable to the programming of film-like rooms by computer. In this respect, the digital window in *Piratenräume* hints at the tension which developed within the field of mathematics and which later led to the concept of the Turing machine and the digital computer. Barba's spatial art positions itself between the modern tendency to control space by numbers (abstraction) and the need for technically controlled audio-vision, because while mathematics was moving away from sensually imaginable geometry, in a countertrend, cultural technology such as LPs, cinema and typewriters developed according to industrial society's growing need for audio-visual products. Thus Barba's works also span the gap of reflection between mathematical space projections and the cultural technology of space design.

Foucault only mentioned cinema on the side in his text "Other Spaces."[2] His attention was captured

1   Herbert Mehrtens, *Moderne Sprache Mathematik*, Suhrkamp, Frankfurt/M., 1990, p. 77, describes it as such: "From the space of contemplation, which in a Euclidian sense can be viewed as a whole (with ruler and compass in hand as it were) spaces have evolved which give unity to different views (projective for instance, or Euclidian-metric)." Before, Mehrtens explained projective geometry with the example of the media technology of slides. "Projective geometry views the properties of geometrical figures from a central projection. If you project a slide of a circle onto a screen, you get a larger circle – depending on the distance between the projector and the screen. If the screen is at an angle the circle becomes an ellipse. The original image and the reproduced image of such a projection exist in a strict geometric relationship, whereby the relation of dimensions is distorted and this to an unlimited extent, i.e. infinitely, if the screen is at more of an angle and the ellipse becomes a parabola." (p. 61).

2   Michel Foucault, "Andere Räume," in *Aisthesis*, Karlo Barck, Peter Gente, Heidi Paris, Stefan Richter (eds), Reclam, Leipzig, 1998 (typoscript, Paris, 1967).

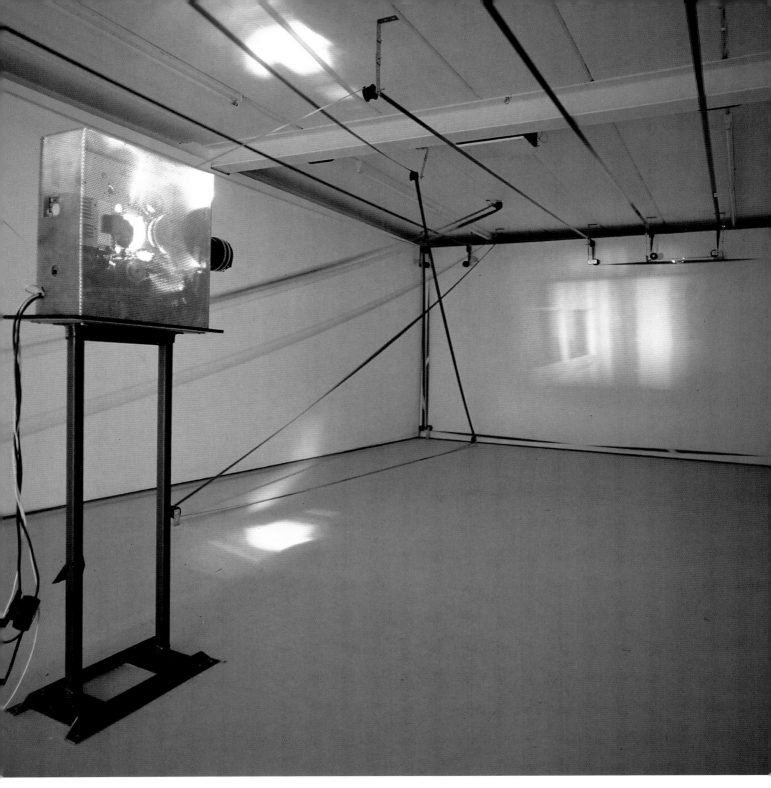

by other localities in which spatial order is changed – mirrors, gardens, cemeteries, prisons and archives. At the end of the text he speaks about ships as "swaying pieces of space." Although the floor in Barba's installation does not sway, your view and attention probably do. The perception space is not ordered, but flips from light to dark, or it becomes threateningly closed-in when the film strips descend on the viewers from the ceiling above. Simultaneously, time perception is hacked about when the music starts up or the light goes out and continuous perception is not possible. What is particularly irritating is viewing the numbers. Although they change regularly and suggest a reliable rhythm in the controlling

machine, the observer cannot clearly match them to the action of the film projector they pretend to control. This shows that the *Piratenräume* are rich in places in which fragile orders of space and time are being turned over. In this respect, Barba expands Foucault's spatial theory to include the cinematographic aspect. She creates turnover points for the order of time and space. The line forms point the way there. They navigate between discrepancies and are fleeting messengers of media possibilities.

Nils Röller

Translated from the German by Jeremy Gaines

Piratenräume [Pirate Spaces]
2002
film installation
dimensions variable
installation view:
c/o Peter Gorschlüter,
Karlsruhe, 2002
© VG Bild-Kunst, Bonn 2003
photo © Heinz Pelz

Caspar Stracke
z2 [zuse strip]

2002
unwound 35mm film (approx. 25,000 cm), hole punch
device, 2 CPUs , digital converter,
90 interactively controlled animation sequences,
15 lines of Lev Manovich text
and 9 lines of John Chadwick text,
video projector / b/w, sound / dimensions variable

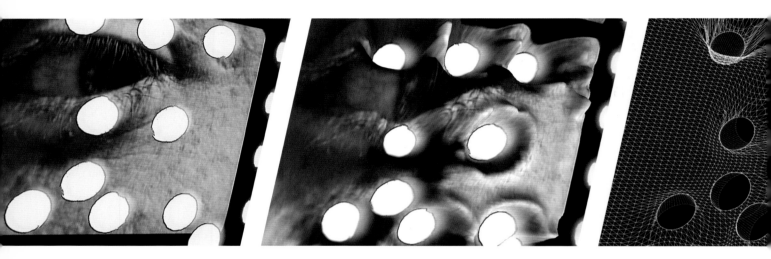

z2 [zuse strip]
2003
© Caspar Stracke

This work is a correspondence between two information fragments coming from different origins and meeting by accident. Cinema is transformed into a three-dimensional landscape utilizing data based an archeological misinterpretation.

z2 [zuse strip] is named after Konrad Zuse's second model, made in a series of the first digital computers. It used discarded 35mm movie film from the German UFA as a medium to read and write eight-bit binary code data with a hole-punch system. Lev Manovich wrote poetically about this encounter, declaring Zuse's punch hole film to be the birth of Digital Cinema in which the "iconic code" (film image) is overwritten by binary code (digital data).1

A second reading of this film strip was inspired by the work of John Chadwick, one of the two linguists who deciphered a script from Bronze-Age Greece known as "Linear B." Chadwick wrote about the nature of code-breaking, the differences and similarities between secret codes and ancient script. While the former deliberately intends to baffle its reader, the latter creates its puzzling effects by accident.

Were one to scrutinize Zuse's film strip with the eye of an archeologist, one might assume a necessary relation between the image of the film and Zuse's punch-holes. The holes in the Zuse strip might represent a sound score, or a plan detailing the images' presentation. Similar assumptions resulted from the reading of unintentional scratches in the hieroglyph-

ics of the Rosetta Stone, or on the broken clay plates that Chadwick helped decipher.

The impact of the hole punch is imprinted directly into the film, changing its surface. I have exaggerated these impacts using digital animations, turning these holes into craters of varying sizes and depths. The crater landscape also affects the topography of the surrounding area. A virtual camera flies over this landscape of the image, into and out of the craters.

This movement is accompanied by a soundtrack created from the same information. The four double rows of eight-bit holes become the score of a musical clock. For each frame a dissonant chord is audible, its individual tones changing volume according to the position of the flying camera, to its distance from the particular holes.

z2 [zuse strip] addresses our ability to preserve cultural artifacts. Obsolescence is the repressed remains of innovation, and since the information of the past is encoded in defunct systems, how will it be possible to preserve the past? Translation (from the Latin "translatum," meaning to bear across) is a journey as opposed to instantaneous transmission, and these journeys of re-encoding, transcribing and compressing re-impose the codes of the present on their info-passengers.

Caspar Stracke

1 Lev Manovich, "Cinema by Number: The ASCII Art of Vuc Cosic," in *Vuk Cosic: Contemporary ASCII*, Ljubljana, 2000.

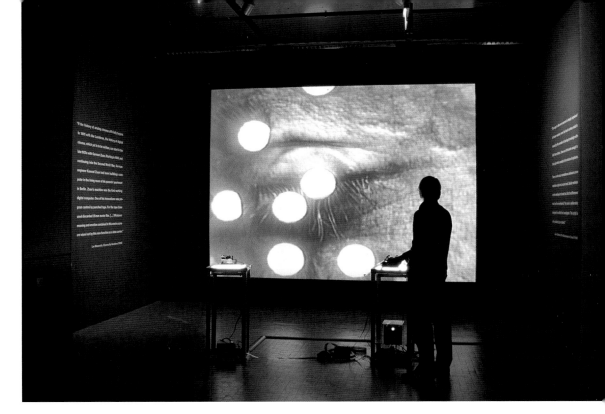

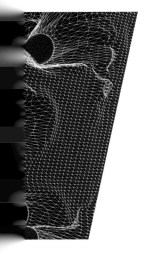

top and left
z2 [zuse strip]
2002
multimedia installation
24,000 cm of 35mm film,
8-bit hole puncher, interface,
computer, projector
dimensions variable
installation views: ZKM |
Center for Art and Media
Karlsruhe, 2002
Caspar Stracke
© Caspar Stracke
photos © Franz Wamhof

left
z2 [zuse strip]
2002
multimedia installation
installation views: ZKM |
Center for Art and Media
Karlsruhe, 2002
details
Caspar Stracke
© Caspar Stracke
photos © Franz Wamhof

Jennifer and Kevin McCoy
Horror Chase

2002
multimedia object with projection / custom hardware and software /
50.8 x 55.8 x 50.8 cm, projection variable / edition of 3 (1/3)

Horror Chase
2002
multimedia object
with projection
screenshots
courtesy Postmasters Gallery,
New York and the artists
© Jennifer and Kevin McCoy,
Postmasters Gallery, New York

Flashbacks and Reruns

"The capital sin of Charlie, and he does not hesi-
tate to make us laugh about it at his own expense,
is to project into time a mode of being that is
suited to one instant, and that is what is meant by
'repetition.'"
Andre Bazin's short essay "Charlie Chaplin"1 proposes
a refusal of cause and effect as "a surface condition
in which the original reason for what he is doing is forgotten" and offers Chaplin's performance as a reflex
against mechanization. Indeed, Chaplin's distracted
temporalities and mischievous compulsions mock the
dull loops of modernity by exposing their deadening
effect. Of course the numbing possibilities of repetition didn't appear only with Chaplin, but emerged in
myth with Sisyphus' recursive fate and found its iterations in everything from Satie's *Vexations* to the
charged reformulations of Brecht to the existential
conflicts of Beckett, from the breezy reverberations
of Andy Warhol to the redundant "variations" of Philip
Glass, from the "super boredom" (in Dick Higgins'
phrase) of Fluxus to the variability in conceptual art's
"directives," and, more recently in the seemingly nonstop loops, samples, and algorithms in a media art
sphere reeling in redundancy.

Much of this work succumbs to iterating monotonous formalities that animate procedures for "evolving" tedious variations that seem oblivious to anything
more than banal visual patterns. Few tackle the in-
sidious possibilities of repetition as oppositional to
denarrativized optical forms and instead rely on
formulas that seem self-legitimating. Of course this
cross between boredom and oblivion has not been
ignored and nor has it lost its persuasive effect in

"new media." It emerges persuasively in game culture
in which repetition achieves a kind of compulsive
apotheosis in its introduction of goal orientation into
often mind-numbing predictabilities. It emerges in
technomusic in which repetition and differentiation
both seize and shatter forms in processes of defamiliarization and reconfiguration that pushes recognition to its limits. In these fields, repetition is not
synonymous with mere recursion, but with extension,
in which temporality returns to alter experience.

Horror Chase comes within a series of works by
Jennifer and Kevin McCoy that have, in various forms,
evoke narrative in the midst of a paradoxical – if not
virtual – *mise-en-scene* in which fragmentation and
repetition are poised as defiant mnemonic devices.
Rather than invoke simple forms of recurrence, their
works have demonstrated a playfully parodic approach to a culture itself enveloped in flashbacks and
reruns, prequels and sequels. Just over the past few
years these works have appeared in a range of incar-
nations that includes installation, performance, software, and on the net. Indeed this range of actions
only serves to suggest that the cumulative effects
of media culture's information systems is itself an
aspect of a phenomenon in which parody and redundancy are strategized in the service of a kind of "cinema of distractions" where the recycling of memory
can hardly be disentangled from the replaying of a
history doomed to repeat itself.

These works, *Whirligig* (1999), *201: A Space Algorithm* (2001), *Every Shot, Every Episode* (2001), *448 is
Enough* (2002), are implementations of the "culture of
the copy" run amok. Shifting from the cut and mix
strategies of *Whirligig* (a software "package" written
to permit the mixing of video streams – live and pre-

1 in André Bazin, *What is
Cinema?* (vol. 1), University
of California Press, Berkeley,
1967.

recorded – for performance) and *201: A Space Algorithm* (a net.art work that liberated Kubrick's classic to temporal and episodic reformulations), the more recent works cut into media's linearity (particularly television) by emptying it of its narrative form, by spatializing its cuts, by subjecting it not merely to deconstruction but to a demolition of its sequence, and by reshuffling its cohesion. In *Every Shot, Every Episode* and *448 is Enough*, two television programs are cut into segments, "indexed," catalogued, and reconceptualized as strategic components in a kind of storyboard in reverse. By undoing the visual "script," exposing its tropes as encoded "bits," the works suggest that the full episodes are as much edited as they are, in programming terms, compiled.

Horror Chase ironically extends this fascination with the episodic into an obsessive investigation of a single chase sequence from the horror classic *Evil Dead 2*. Yet rather than probing the original film sequence by decomposing it, the McCoy's set out to reconstitute the chase by rebuilding a fully replicated set in which the short sequence could be reproduced on film. In differentiating the original and its perverse double, the production takes the flash-back into the realm of the fetishistic even while the work itself can only serve as its sensory form. The compulsive "playback" moves in fits and starts in a discontinuous loop where movement is delayed, reversed, or interrupted controlled by in some procedure akin to an algorithmic fit. Slavoj Zizek writes:

> "The postmodern anhistorical stasis, ... is torn between repetition qua suspension of movement by means of which we 'synchronize' our menaced position with that of our predecessors, and between repetition qua aced position with that of our predecessors, and between repetition qua nostalgia, the proper object of which is not the image of the past but rather the very gaze enraptured by the image…"[2]

Horror Chase is a kind of classic in limbo – part re-creation, part parody, part hijack, part homage, and a reminder that in a media culture subjected to the oxymoron of "quicktime," time, to use the phrase of Phillip K. Dick, is always slightly "out of joint."

Timothy Druckrey

Horror Chase
2002
multimedia object
with projection
custom hardware and software
50.8 x 55.8 x 50.8 cm,
projection variable
edition of 3 (1/3)
installation views: ZKM |
Center for Art and Media
Karlsruhe, 2002
courtesy Postmasters Gallery,
New York and the artists
© Jennifer and Kevin McCoy;
Postmasters Gallery, New York
photos © Franz Wamhof

2   Slavoj Zizek, "Why is Every Act a Repetition?," in Slavoj Zizek, *Enjoy Your Symptom!, Jacques Lacan in Hollywood and Out,* Routledge, New York, 1992, p. 81.

Jim Campbell
Church on 5th Avenue

2001
custom electronics, Plexiglas, 768 LEDs / 60 x 80 x 8 cm

Illuminated Average #1 Hitchcock's Psycho

2000
diapositive / 5.7 x 5.7 cm

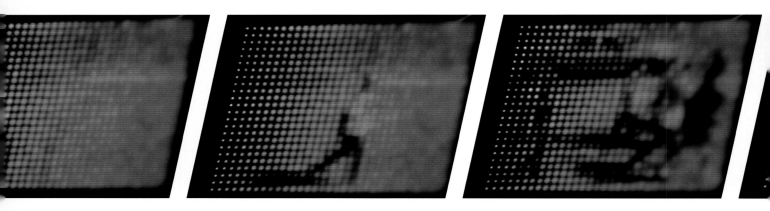

"If the new element to film was time, then I think that the new element to interactivity is the present. And it is the program that connects the present to the past." 1

Ambiguous Icons is the title given by Jim Campbell to a series of works in which analog image material is reproduced digitally on LED (light-emitting diode) displays. The motifs are rendered barely recognizable by using extremely low resolution LED displays. Plexiglas sheets are mounted in front of the LED displays to eliminate the pixel structure, thus making the image more recognizable. All that can be seen are abstract patches of color, whose ambiguity and elusiveness question the status of images in a world of bits and bytes. Human perception and computer-processed data are juxtaposed.

Campbell's *Church on 5th Avenue* series functions according to the same principle of reproducing video images on LED displays. The analog images are transformed into their digital equivalent in the form of 768 LED pinpoints of red light – visual information translated into a numerical code consisting of ones and zeroes. We see people in movement, street scenes in Manhattan, passers-by going on their way unaware that they are being filmed. In this series too, Campbell has created special effects by mounting sheets of Plexiglas in front of individual works. In one work he has placed the Plexiglas at an angle to the LED display, so that the structure of the LEDs nearest the Plexiglas – their individual diodes – is recognizable, while the LEDs on the section of panel further away from the Plexiglas appear as a diffuse, blurred image. Campbell thus effects an astonishing transition from digital pixel image to analog film image. The unfocused

quality of the images is reminiscent of shots taken with a security camera – images that are a part of our daily lives and whose existence we scarcely register any more. In another variation on this theme, Campbell places the Plexiglas sheet parallel to, but at some distance from, the LED display, creating a highly abstract image in which the video being projected behind the sheet appears to be dissolved into non-figurative patches of color – a play of light and shadow. The third panel in the series functions without the diffusing effect of the Plexiglas. An extremely fine pixel resolution creates an abstract image in which only schematic patterns of movement are recognizable.

The digital world of numbers, pixels and algorithms is thus juxtaposed to the world of analog perception. From a certain distance, a pixel image can be read just like an analog image. Video images are transformed into numerical codes, visualized on LED displays, and by optical trickery transposed back into analog images. Digitalization allows everything to be quantified. Digital technology can register the form of a sound or light wave many times a second and express the data as numbers whose values can be objectively recorded. Through his artistic strategies, Campbell not only examines the basic binary digital-analog opposition but in general poses questions about structures of perception.

Memory and recall, the nature of time, play an important role in his works. The problem of the transformation of time is the focus of a series entitled

1 Jim Campbell,
http://adaweb.walkerart.org
/context/events/moma/bbs
4/campbell.html

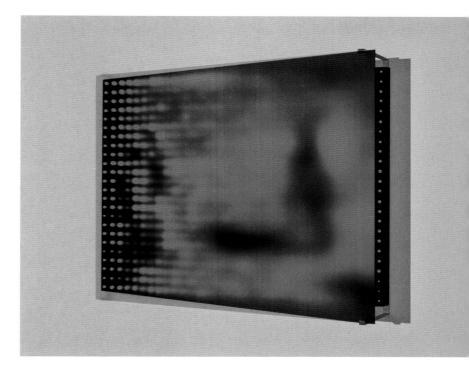

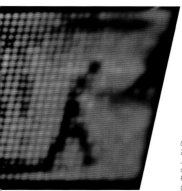

Church on 5th Avenue
2001
Jim Campbell
courtesy Hosfelt Gallery, San
Francisco
photos © Matthew Biederman

Church on 5th Avenue
2001
custom electronics, Plexiglas,
768 LEDs
60 x 80 x 8 cm
installation view: ZKM |
Center for Art and Media
Karlsruhe, 2002
Jim Campbell
courtesy Hosfelt Gallery,
San Francisco
photo © Franz Wamhof

Memory Works: "[...] the *Memory Works* which are concerned with rhythms as a fundamental element of perception."[2] His work *Illuminated Average #1, Hitchcock's Psycho* is concerned with the compression of time into a single image. Campbell scanned every single frame of Hitchcock's film and generated a single new image from the result. Placing all of the frames on top of each other, he created an image that contains all of the film's visual data. The digitalized layers have translated the original film into an image consisting of averaged brightness and contrast values – the digital storage structure of the databank has been transformed into its visual equivalent. Yet the superimposed images still betray schematic traces of the action once played out on the silver screen – especially towards the darker edges of the image, whereas towards the center the light appears, so to speak, to have burnt its way through the picture, leaving behind only a white stain. Films are based on light, and part of the experience of cinema consists in registering changes in light intensity. Campbell's work very poetically renders this elementary fact visible.

The work is also reminiscent of early experiments in photography, in which the motifs are also scarcely recognizable, their clarity depending on lighting angle and exposure times. In photography the image is created by differences in light intensity, which in turn generate the forms and contours of the reality being depicted. In Campbell's work, light intensity is translated by the computer into a numerical scale that measures bright and dark sequences in the film. Campbell examines how digital devices translate empirical information and relates the latter to the transitory nature of time and the quantification of memory. He sees electronic art as the ideal medium for examining the nature of perception, for our lives are now crucially influenced by computer technology. "Part of the reason I use technology, other than the reason that I'm a technologist, is just that it's so relevant to our culture. Everybody has a computer, so it's

natural to use it."[3] The computer creates an image by processing and analyzing data. In his book *Techniques of the Observer*, Jonathan Crary describes what he calls the abstraction of the visual, the transformation of perception through computer-controlled ways of seeing. He sees the new techniques of image production as generating new, dominant models of visualization.[4] Campbell utilizes the computer to ask questions about the significance of images and about the relationship between information and meaning.

"Campbell observes the accumulation of time and information in order to underscore the primacy of real-life experience over its simulation."[5] How is information translated into meaning?

Many of Campbell's works are interactive, yet interactivity in his art differs markedly from the kind of "button pushing" that transforms the observer into a manipulator of machine-controlled devices. The observer interacts with the work of art not by pressing buttons but by being incorporated into the work itself, via closed-circuit images and movement sensors that are directly connected to the electronic apparatus. "I think an interesting aside here is that in general it is very difficult to create an interactive open work that maintains strong personal content, because for open works the inner world comes from the viewer. This for me is the main reason that I do work that is interactive. Though it is not a medium for communicating personal content, it is a medium for instilling personal process. It is more than the communication in this process; the process itself is occurring in the viewer's present. This to me is the most profound aspect of interactive art."[6] In Campbell's works, the observer's psychic space and the space occupied by the electronic media are linked. The observer himself seems to be located in the picture.

Sabine Himmelsbach
Translated from the German by Steven Richards

2 Cited from Heather Sealy Lineberry, "Electronic Interview with Jim Campbell," in *Jim Campbell, Transforming Time. Electronic Works 1990–1999*, exhib. cat., Arizona State University Art Museum, 1999, p. 65.

3 Jim Campbell in Roy Proctor, "Where humanism and electronic wizardry intersect," in *Richmond Times–Dispatch*, 4 February 2001, p. H 1.

4 Jonathan Crary, *Techniques of the Observer: On Vision and Modernity in the 19th Century*, The MIT Press, Cambridge, MA, 1992.

5 Robert R. Riley in "Jim Campbell," in *Time + Data*, Pittsburgh, 2001, p. 26.

6 Cited from Heather Sealy Lineberry, "Electronic Interview with Jim Campbell," op. cit., p. 66.

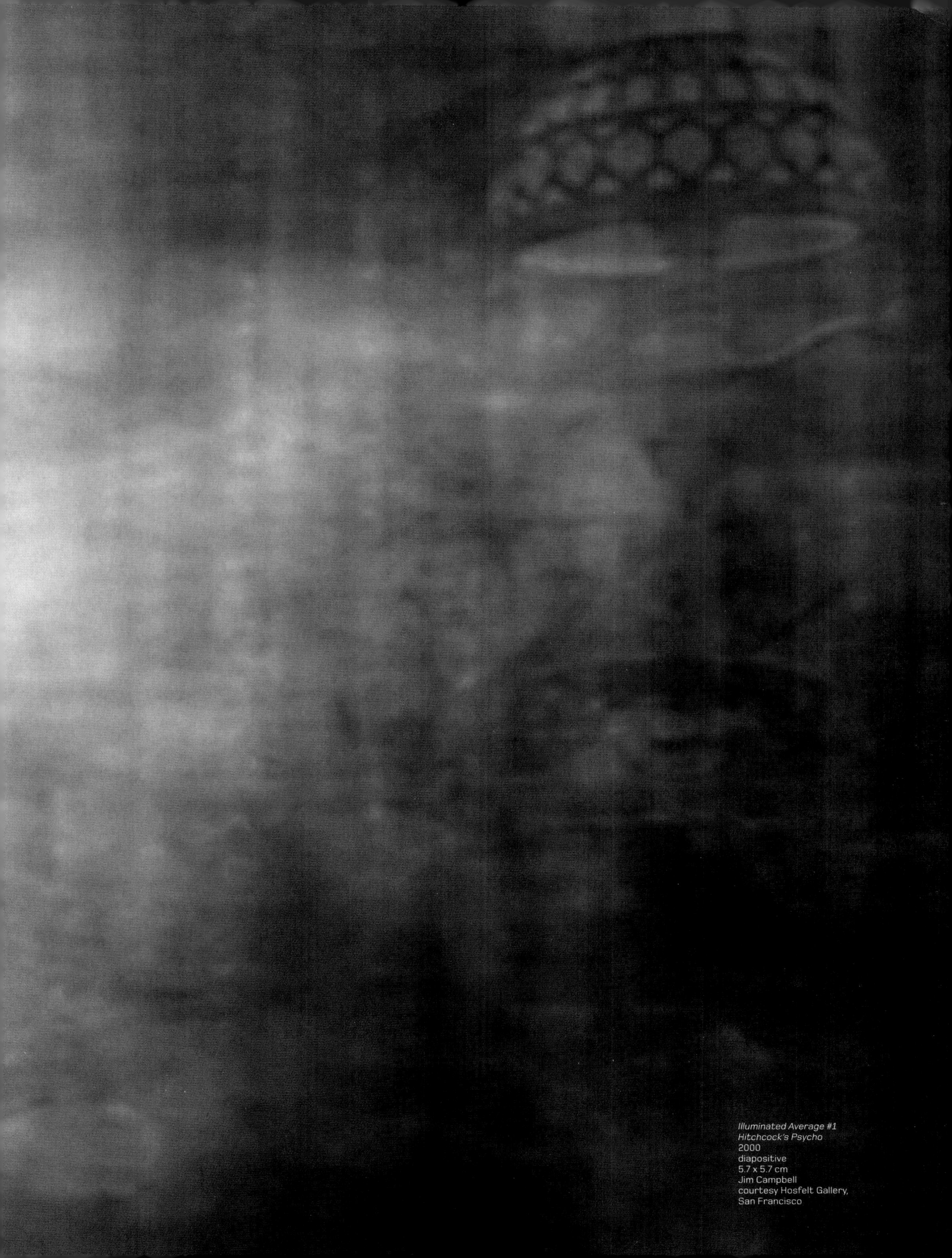

Illuminated Average #1
Hitchcock's Psycho
2000
diapositive
5.7 x 5.7 cm
Jim Campbell
courtesy Hosfelt Gallery,
San Francisco

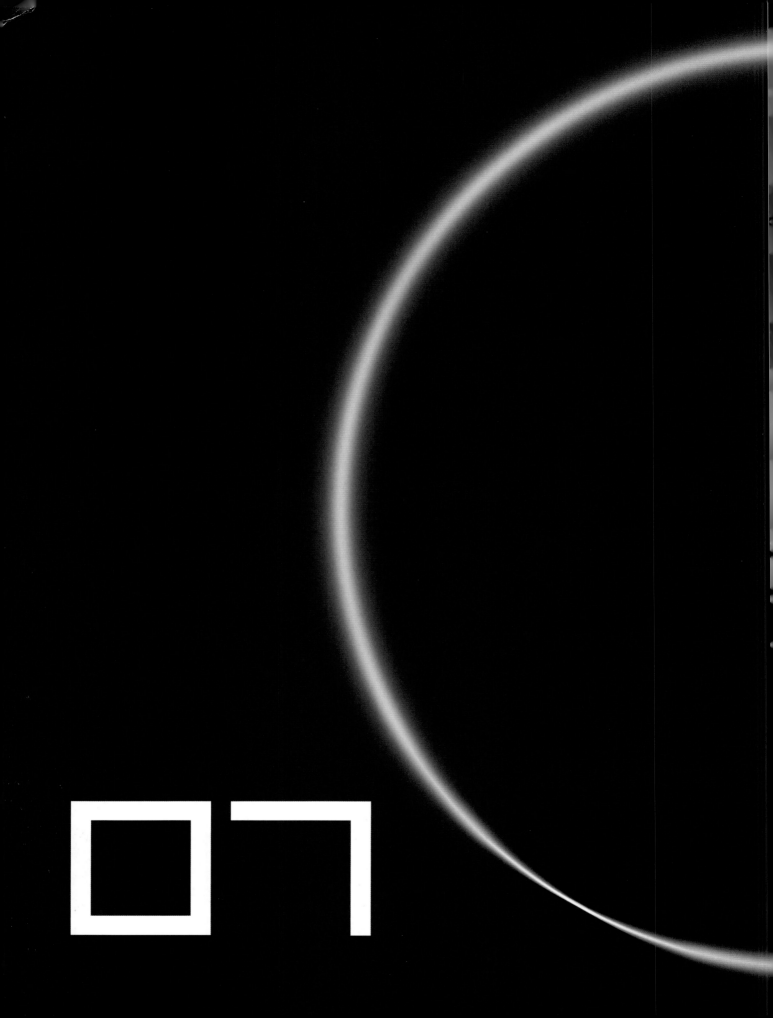

07

TRANSCRIPTIVE

Grahame Weinbren

Another Dip into the Ocean of Streams of Story 1

"He looked into the water and saw that it was made up of a thousand thousand thousand and one different currents, each one a different color, weaving in and out of one another like a liquid tapestry of breathtaking complexity; and Iff explained that these were the Streams of Story, that each colored strand represented and contained a single tale. Different parts of the Ocean contained different sorts of stories, and as all the stories that had ever been told and many that were still in the process of being invented could be found here, the Ocean of the Streams of Story was in fact the biggest library in the universe. And because the stories were held here in fluid form, they retained the ability to change, to become new versions of themselves, to join up with other stories and so become yet other stories; so that unlike a library of books, the Ocean of the Streams of Story was much more than a storeroom of yarns. It was not dead but alive." 2

It is easy to read the nostalgic tone of Rushdie's 1990 "children's story" as the wish for a return to innocence, to a state of story-telling purity beyond the reaches of politics and intrigue. At the time he wrote *Haroun and the Sea of Stories* purportedly for his eleven-year-old son, Rushdie was, of course, too sophisticated – and too embittered by the outrageous circumstances of his life – to profess any kind of innocence or naivete. The novella abounds with metaphors of cruel suppression and mindless censorship. The nostalgia embedded in the *Sea of Stories* is better seen as a reminder of the creative process a writer (or filmmaker) craves in his or her darker moments: an ocean of stories, wide and deep, effortlessly tapped. The power of the image is in its erasure of the line between writer and reader – Haroun's father, a professional storyteller, need only drink from his personal faucet plumbed to the Ocean and report to his audience: this alone constitutes writing.

Can the image be turned around? Can we imagine the Ocean as a source primarily for readers rather than writers? Could there be a "story space" (to use Michael Joyce's resonant expression) like the Ocean, in which a reader might take a dip, encountering stories and story-segments as he or she flipped and dived? In these waters, turbulences created by the swimmer's own motion might cause an intermingling of the Streams of Story. The Ocean, as I imagine it, is a dynamic narrative region, a Heraclitean river into which one can never step twice, a lake of Heisenbergian uncertainty where the very attempt to examine a particular story-stream transforms it. What a goal to create such an Ocean! And how perfect as an ideal for an interactive fiction!

Fiction, Cinema and Cybernetics

The *idea* of interactive fiction is not new. But the notion of a time-based medium that is *not* interactive is no older than mechanical recording. Before the recording of sound, all music was "interactive," though in this context the term sounds silly. Musicians are always affected by external factors, from the other performers in the ensemble, to the "feeling" of the audience, to the acoustics of the hall, et cetera. The same can be said for theater. The risk of variability is an essential ingredient of the thrill of "live" performance. And before recording, obviously, all performance was live. Though it is true that few works were deliberately designed to be influenced by external factors (consider Tinker Bell in *Peter Pan*), audiences were always aware of their potential power. One of the aspirations of an interactive cinema is to return the medium to an earlier state, where the fact that the audience can affect the performance is given.

In attempting to develop an interactive narrative cinema, I realized early that it will not have the shape of narrative as we have come to understand it since cinema and television – media of the "moving image" – have come to dominate our notions of representation. The very idea of user impact opens to question the concepts of end and beginning, of crisis and

1 A version of this essay was printed in 1995 in the *Millennium Film Journal*, no. 28, "Interactivities." Although there is nothing that I would repudiate seven years later, I have made three interactive cinema works during this period, and making these pieces has both amplified and challenged my thinking on certain of these issues. So while keeping the spirit of the original essay, I have attempted to incorporate some of my more recent ideas into it.

2 Salman Rushdie, *Haroun and the Sea of Stories*, Granta Books, London, 1990, p. 71.

conflict, of development itself. The traditional (Aristotelian) notion of narrative must be rethought.

My own work is in the pull of a pair of forces that defined the late twentieth century – the Cinema and Cybernetics, the Projector and the Computer. In 1995, when this essay was first published, I had made two installations incorporating computers and moving images. Now (in 2002) there are five. In all these works the participant's (inter-)actions affect the temporal conglomerate of images and sounds. The computer itself is not considered a medium or a tool, but a device that controls and presents existent media. Thus the questions that arise are about how cinema changes when its apparatus is linked to a computer – just as one can investigate changes in the structure of cinematic communication when recorded sound is added to the moving image.

The first two questions that came up can be posed in quite traditional terms. What kind of story will fit the medium, and what will be the grammar of its telling? Crudely: where is the change – in content or structure? One entry point is to find a narrative for which the sequence of events is not salient, since if the viewer is to wander around and through the story, the order in which the depicted events are accessed should open to variation. And this requirement led me directly to Freud's studies of dream interpretation.

A Branching Structure

"I dreamed that it was night and I was lying in my bed. Suddenly the window opened of its own accord, and I was terrified to see that some white wolves were sitting on the big walnut tree in front of the window. There were six or seven of them. The wolves were quite white, and looked more like foxes or sheep dogs, for they had big tails like foxes and they had their ears pricked like dogs when they pay attention to something. In great terror, evidently of being eaten up by the wolves, I screamed and woke up."3

Freud transcribed and published the case history of the Wolf Man in 1914–1915, soon after the end of the

patient's analysis. It is the apex of Freud's early period, where the central concepts of condensation, displacement, wish fulfillment, the primal scene, and so forth reach their full fruition, never to be resolved in quite the same way.

The analysis revolves around the dream image of the staring wolves, introduced early on by the patient. Freud describes the process of gradually uncovering the components of the dream, linking each element with an event, a character, or an emotion remembered but perhaps suppressed. The dream's significance for the dreamer, manifested in the overwhelming emotional effect it had on him and the fact that it remained in his memory for decades, led Freud to seek further explanation. He finally accounts for this power in his proposal that the dream encapsulates the dreamer's greatest fears and desires, as transformed memories of the events that first produced them. For my purposes the details (and – it goes without saying – the "truth") of the dream-analysis are not important. I wish only to appropriate certain aspects of Freud's methodology in my own search for a paradigmatic story structure suitable for an interactive cinema.

Condensation is the key concept. The dream is formed by compressing and combining a set of mental objects. The dream can function in the dreamer's mental framework as the distillation of a set of emotional charges. The dream's powerful affect comes from the fact that, in an important sense, it embodies a set of memories and the specific emotions linked with them. Repeatedly Freud stresses that there is no universal symbol translation table – every element of the dream image, and every property of every element, is understood by the dreamer in his own individual way. Each element substantiates a combination of particular fears, hopes, desires or beliefs, transformed, by the laws of the unconscious, into a component of the dream image. Seeing the images through the dreamer's eyes – identifying the underlying atomic parts and understanding how they are altered by the dreamer's mental process into the dream image – is understanding the dream. In this understanding is

3 Sigmund Freud, "From the History of an Infantile Neurosis," in *The Wolf Man by The Wolf Man*, Muriel M. Gardiner (ed.), Basic Books, New York, 1971, p.173.

written a page of the biography of the dreamer (or, more likely, several chapters of his biography).

Freud's notion of a dream is a conception of a narrative-type based on a hermeneutic method. Unraveling a dream reveals the narrative of the dreamer's interlocking emotional states. But it is not a narrative that unfolds in time – all its elements are simultaneously present. Freud goes to great trouble to convey this atemporality, but even for him it is a notion that eludes expression. After all, his own mode of communication – writing – is, of necessity, linear, one word following another, forming paragraphs that follow one another, and so forth, while his conception of the dreamwork is, by its very nature, non-linear, unsuited to the writing forms of the early twentieth century.

"This task [of forming a synthesis from fragments that emerge in the analysis of a patient] ... finds a natural limit when it is a question of forcing a structure which is itself in many dimensions onto the two-dimensional descriptive plane. I must therefore content myself with bringing forward fragmentary portions, which the reader can then put together into a living whole."[4]

Considered as a narrative structure, the underlying elements of the dream can be revealed in any order whatsoever, and the same story will emerge. Thus, it is truly a narrative without specificity of sequence.

The Interpretation of Dreams

A film might try to approximate the structure of Freudian dream analysis in a story structure that step-by-step unraveled the components of an evocative image. However, the linearity of cinema sequence tends to freeze material into narrative hierarchies, one element gaining in significance while another loses, depending on each one's context and their overall order. How better to reproduce the minimal significance of sequence, the irrelevance of order, than through interactivity? For in an interactive work the sequence of events can be determined by the viewer. And by the time the viewer becomes aware that sequence is determined by his or her responses alone, sequence may already have stopped being a criterion of narrative significance. In normal cinematic circumstances, the weight of an event is given largely by its context: now, with sequence under the control of the viewer, this weight can lighten or even dissolve. And in these circumstances the viewer's understanding of the events of the narrative can undergo a radical transformation, based entirely on the knowledge that things could have been different. Later in this paper I shall make an attempt at describing the "subjunctive" state of mind evoked by the interactive cinema.

The elements associated with a particular dream-image are not by themselves sufficient to define the biographical narrative underlying the dream. This would be a gross oversimplification. Of course it is also essential to incorporate how the elements are transformed and combined into the dream. Often this syntax and its application can be expressed only verbally. It is difficult, for example, to imagine an effective visual expression of the transformation of

something into its opposite (from "staring" to "being stared at," or from the ornate motions of sexual intercourse to the stillness of the white wolves), or the transfer of a particular quality from one object to another (as the color white is lifted from sheep and flour and attributed to the wolves). Freud's interpretation of the dream is far more than a simple compacting of memory-images into one conglomerate: the grammar of the image-elements' metamorphoses and rearrangements is as significant as the elements themselves.

I am not suggesting that the principles of condensation and displacement could not form a foundation of a visual narrative, but only that some depiction of the types of transformation will have to be incorporated alongside the results of the transformations. The point, to reiterate, is to develop a type of narrative that can retain its identity and make sense independent of the sequence of events. Thus, in *Sonata*, I found that I needed to make the formative elements of the dream into components of the dream-narrative – without them it became a mere medley of scenes connected only by association.

Desire

Cinema, of course, cannot be internally affected by its viewers. Turning one's head, far from affecting the visual experience, removes one from its world and into the mundane space of the screening room. The chess pieces and donkeys on screen will only yield to forces that are profilmic, within the diegesis, or (commonly) both.

Furthermore, the impossibility of impacting on the cinematic is one of the sources of our pleasure in it. "Don't go up(/down) the stairs!" we inwardly cry out while watching Hitchcock's *Psycho*, first to the private detective Arbogast, and later to the heroine Lila Crane, all the time knowing that however deeply felt, our distress will not influence their behavior. The experience of suspense would be fatally distorted by the elimination of inevitability in the characters' actions. If Lila could turn back because of our pleas, the entire effect of the horror film would dissolve. Much of cinema's power over us is our lack of power over it. In this sense, suspense is a paradigm of cinematic response. It could be argued that the introduction of viewer impact on the representation is a destructive step for the cinema. The removal of the possibility of suspense is the removal of desire from the cinematic, and, ultimately, the removal of the very fascination of the medium.

To find interactive forms in which desire can be sustained will require the construction of a new cinematic grammar. And, to be successful, this search, this construction-process, must foreground the temporal aspect of cinematic communication.

Time. Time. Time.

Time always moves relentlessly, tautologically, forward, as long as one is alive. "Real," clock-measurable duration can always be distinguished from time subjectively felt. The duration of cinema is rigidly defined by the apparatus, fully predetermined by the physical substrate of images projected serially at a regular pace set by an electric motor. A film begins and ends

4 Sigmund Freud, op. cit., p. 173.

Grahame Weinbren,
Roberta Friedman
The Erl King
1983–1985
production still
collection of the artists
© Roberta Friedman and
Grahame Weinbren

Elizabeth Arnold, soprano,
sings Schubert's adaptation
of Goethe's "Erlkönig."

Grahame Weinbren,
Roberta Friedman
The Erl King
1983–1985
production still
collection of the artists
© Roberta Friedman and
Grahame Weinbren

"Father, don't you see I'm
burning?" Ken Glickfeld and
Cameron Johann as father and
son in Freud's "Burning Child"
dream.

Grahame Weinbren,
Roberta Friedman
The Erl King
1983–1985
interactive cinema installation
computer-controlled laser-
videodisc array, touchscreen
interface, custom hardware and
software, video and audio
material, 600 stills
dimensions and duration
variable
installation view:
Whitney Biennial, New York, 1987
collection of the artists
© Roberta Friedman and
Grahame Weinbren
photo © Grahame Weinbren

Sonata
1991/1993
video frame grab
collection of the artist
© Grahame Weinbren

Ken Taylor as Podnyshev from
Tolstoy's *The Kreutzer Sonata*.

Sonata
1991/1993
video frame grab
collection of the artist
© Grahame Weinbren

Nicole Farmer as the
apocryphal Judith with wolf.

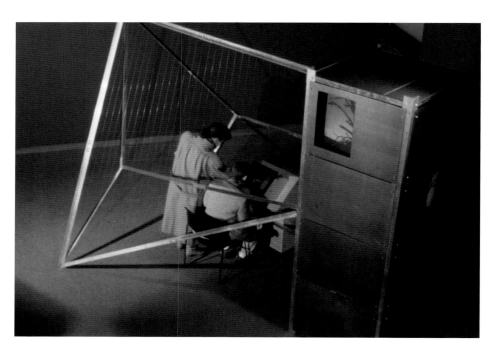

Sonata
1991/1993
interactive cinema installation
computer-controlled laser-
videodisc array,
suspended-frames interface,
custom designed hardware and
software
dimensions and duration variable
installation view: International
Center of Photography,
New York, 1993–1994
collection of the artist
© Grahame Weinbren
photo © Grahame Weinbren

necessarily and predictably. Relative to the beginning, the end is dependent on, and only on, the length of the filmstrip. Whatever its images, however they are organized, a film has a physical beginning, middle, and end. Whether and how this linear temporality structures the image-material in a particular film is a major issue (perhaps the major issue) for a filmmaker. It could even be argued that the stance taken by a filmmaker towards temporal structure, how time is articulated in a particular film, is an index of where in the spectrum of cinematic practice (from Hollywood to Avant Garde) a given work falls.

This gives us the first sense of cinematic time, Duration or Running Time: the clock-time required for the filmstrip to run through the projection apparatus.

The second sense of time is that of the world depicted in the film – and here the limits are more or less the cinema of story-telling, and its Diegetic Time.

Mieke Bal, in *Narratology*, calls this the time of the fabula or fictional world imagined by the story. A cinema narrative may jump forward, eliminating decades (or centuries) in a single cut; or slide back, perhaps using one of the various narrative strategies that fall under the category of flashback; or remain in the present, so that a given passage of film denotes a continuous passage of time. This latter case (the most frequently used) still allows for a broad range of variation: one continuous two minute portion of a story can occupy five minutes of screen time, while the next portion compresses seven years into as many seconds.

Meanwhile...

Experienced Time. Detective Arbogast's walk up the stairs seems painfully extended, so that his stabbing at the first landing is a dreadful shock. This shock puts us on edge for Lila's later descent into the basement, which stretches time even further as each step seems to last a full minute, since we now (rightly) expect the worst to be waiting for her. On one other end of the scale, a contemporary action film can make us feel as if no time passes during its hundred minutes; while in another discourse entirely, a film like *Wavelength* (Michael Snow, 1968) insists on equating duration and depicted time, a position transformed into an ideology in the 1970s by such "structural/materialist" filmmakers as Peter Gidal. The relationship of film grammar, plot, and the experience of time is a fertile area of study, especially since the compression of time is probably one of the major determinants of cinema's phenomenal success.

The question is: what happens to cinematic time when viewer input becomes a component of the screen amalgam? To what extent does the incorporation of viewer impact keep time real, canceling out the magnetism of cinema itself – when does it cease to be cinema and become "multimedia" in its drab information-delivery costume, the slick transmission of data in fields of "hot spots," "buttons," and "point-and-click menus"? Now (2002) this wasteland has become transmogrified into the paralytic gloom of the World Wide Web, and most people associate interactivity with clicking though endless linked Oracle database items.

The Kuleshov Effect

The temporal grammar of classical film continuity can be summed up in a single example, which, like much mythology of cinema, is described more often than seen. The "Kuleshov Effect" scenario consists of a close-up of a Russian actor, intercut with several emotion-laden images (a dead woman in a coffin, a child playing, a bowl of soup). This supposedly produces in the audience a sense of the actor's face as saturated with appropriate emotion. But more interesting than this (presumably a commentary on the actor's ambiguous, doleful expression) is the idea, taken as "obvious and certain" by Pudovkin, that the character is seen to be "looking at the soup" – the man and the soup are linked, across the cut, into a single continuous space. Of course it cannot be as simple as this, as the sense of continuous space requires the support of a number of factors such as eye-line, lighting, shadow direction, et cetera – but the point is clear. I'll suggest a recasting of this fable later in this paper. Here I introduce it only to restate the familiar homily that in cinema spatial unification is easily maintained through temporal disruptions, given a particular sequence. Sequence determines space. And sequence logically requires time.

The Liberation of the Filmstrip

A standard linear unit of cinema has an A-B-A structure: e.g., the Kuleshov point-of-view cutaway, the shot-reverse-shot of a dialogue scene, or the performer-audience-performer of the Musical. This atomic structure defines continuity of time and space in the cinema.

The equivalent in my interactive cinema is formed by a sequence in which the middle term is produced by an action of the viewer. If the viewer does not act, the first shot continues. But on action by the spectator the B-shot appears, then, after an appropriate

period, the A-shot reappears, perhaps transformed by the interspersed shot, perhaps unchanged. In *Sonata* this structure is used as a bridge to an alternative point of view (for example of another fictional character, or of the author); as a jump to an earlier (or later) time in the story; as a glance at a different depiction of the narrative situation (for example, a classical painting of the Judith and Holofernes theme rather than its continuing narration by a storyteller); or as the momentary introduction of a parallel narrative line. Does the sequence still denote a continuity of space and/or time? The interpretive mode the viewer takes toward the new material is associative. Because the new image or scene was produced, i.e. brought on screen, by the viewer, he is forced into connecting to the image it replaces – an act of association, rather than spatio-temporal suturing. In *Sonata* this act is reinforced by two strategies:

1. the automatic return to the previous image, so that it seems that the image produced by the viewer interaction is a temporary interruption of a continuing logic;

2. audio continuity: the sound from the first image continues through the interruption, which reinforces the impression that the viewer's actions are disturbing the natural flow, thus demanding that a sense be made of the new complex.

In the environment created by this structure, *Duration* becomes variable, not fixed. Though the plot of the unfolding narrative is not affected by the viewer's interactions, the screen can now contain multiple diegetic times simultaneously, and the viewer quickly becomes accustomed to navigating between them.

Experienced Time, on the other hand, becomes open and indeterminate. At one extreme the viewer can find himself in the extended time-instant of the computer hacker or video-game player compulsively acting on the screen image. It is this semi-hypnotic state that allows the computer programmer to spend twenty-four hours at a stretch in front of a CRT, "jacked in" as the novelist William Gibson puts it. In his fiction Gibson often compares the state to that produced by imagined mind-altering drugs of the future. In this mental condition, the user's impact on the screen output is paramount, while awareness of content and interpretive distance are subordinated to action. Video-game environments are often designed to stimulate this condition – the content is minimal and ancillary to the actions of the user, which are immediate and powerful, either floridly destructive, requiring hand-eye coordination, or effortlessly navigational, and most often a combination of the two. Unlike a video game, however, changes in interactive cinema are driven by plot and consequence, and consequently compulsion will not be the overriding ingredient of the mental state of the viewer. Here the need for evaluation, interpretation and understanding are in the foreground, though the obsessive need to fully explore the narrative space can serve well as an incentive and accompaniment.

Freed from the predicament where the apparatus alone dictates the temporal experience, time can now expand or contract based on the extent of the viewer's involvement or attention, no longer only because of the hills, gullies, and plateaus, the changes in elevation of the plot. One can imagine the user of an interactive cinema alternating between compulsive input, loss of self in the flow of the narrative, and a sense of distance and control of his own experience of time, as the tides of the story ebb and flow based on his own actions on and in it.

The notion of suspense, for example, can be retained but transformed. If the viewer identifies with a character, seeing him as transfixed with horror at one moment, overcome with relief at the next, there may be some hesitation about accessing the cause of his distress. Now a new emotional affect, begins to emerge. "Don't look behind the door!" we wordlessly warn – but now whether the character opens the cellar door is determined by us, and the vacillation, the hesitation, related to a particular experience of suspense, will put the viewer, unexpectedly, in a different grip of the screen. The new pull is a hook of agency – whether we have to face the horror that we fear and are fascinated by is now our decision, and in an effective work we will be equally compelled in both directions.

Then What Can the Interactive Cinema Depict?
"A person's life consists of a collection of events, the last of which could also change the meaning of the whole, not because it counts more than the previous ones but because once they are included in a life, events are arranged in an order that is not chronological but, rather, corresponds to an inner architecture."[5]

Our worlds are disorderly and disorganized, unrestricted and loose. Strands of perception and inner experience are interwoven with actions that impact on our immediate environment, causing change in our perceptions and generating new experiences. Time advances relentlessly while our consciousness staggers in and out of it, memories of the past intermingling with hopes for the future as we react to events of the present. Lived experience does not parcel itself into linear, closed structures, though we sometimes represent things that way in order to tell stories about ourselves. But autobiographies, like all narratives based on fact, are always at most distortions and at least abbreviations, omitting many events while inflating others. A complete recounting of the most minor experience (including the mental activity that accompanied it) would last much longer than the experience itself. We compress, excerpt, exclude, and reorganize when we tell stories about ourselves; we must dramatize and deform the facts to fit them into a plotted "story-line" with an ending that provides satisfactory closure. If the interactive cinema is a more faithful rendering of reality, it is precisely because it can bypass some of these criteria of narrative structure. Intermixing and interweaving multiple narrative streams, it can create a meta-narrative sum that is greater than its component parts, if the subject- matter is a match for the potential of the medium. What would be an appropriate model for the subject matter? The ideal is the human mind in operation.

We are multi-tasking units. We can whistle and daydream while working, fantasize while having sex, speak the English translation while listening to the German, and so on. And we can switch from one mental activity – one state, one condition – to another, instantly and without effort. It is easy and natural for most people to keep many thoughts and perceptions simultaneously active in their minds, transferring from one to the next at will. One's current inner experience is a conglomeration of perceptions of the present, memories of the past, hopes for and guesses about the future, along with beliefs and fears independent of time markers, dreams, imaginings, pains, etc. Each mental element forms an undercurrent in what is happily called the "stream of consciousness," and navigating these waters is part of what it is to be human. Rushdie's Ocean can be heard in these shells.

How do we move from one mental entity to the next? One thing is certain: it is nothing like making a selection from a list. The "menu" model incorporated in contemporary computer software is aptly named – using it is like negotiating a meal at a fast food restaurant. Switching between streams of mental activity involves responding to hardly perceptible internal and external cues, much as one rides a bicycle around obstacles, keeping balance by slight shifts in position, changing direction by combining such shifts with handlebar adjustments and greater weight adjustments. Except in the least significant cases, we affect things in our lives not by making choices, but by actively responding to situations, with speech acts or in behavior, and equally by silence or inaction. Only in restaurants or department stores are we faced with a closed list of alternatives. The interface of an interactive cinema cannot restrict itself to a model of choice, though this does not mean that choice is entirely banned. Response is the operative concept.

Open Issues: What Isn't the Interactive Cinema?
Summarizing the story so far: the interactive narrative will be in the form of a story space (again the terminology of Michael Joyce and Jay Bolter) laid out for exploration. This story space may consist of a number of related narratives that the viewer forges or discovers links between, or of a single narrative seen from various viewpoints (for example, of different characters). It may be the breakdown of a particular situation or image or scene into its (non-hierarchical) historical or constitutive elements.

But it will not be a linear story where viewer input determines what-happens-next. Such a structure does not contribute to the notion of interactive form since everything that appears will remain within the limitations of the linear – the fact that he has selected which line the story takes is irrelevant. This particular structure becomes interesting only when the viewer is exposed to different hypothetical situations, so that he can see what would happen if the characters took this turn, that path. Only in this case might the overall experience of the piece retain the quality of a story space of multiple narratives simultaneously present for exploration.

5   Italo Calvino, *Mr. Palomar*, tr. William Weaver, Harcourt Brace Jovanovich, New York, 1983/1985, p. 124.

Grahame Weinbren,
James Cathcart
March
1995/1997

Evert Eden as the Angel
on route to prevent the
Sacrifice of Isaac.

Grahame Weinbren,
James Cathcart
March
1995/1997
two-channel architectural
interactive cinema installation
computer-controlled laser-
videodisc array, interactive
computer-graphic projection,
walking ramp interface, custom
hardware and software
dimensions and duration variable
installation view: Anchorage,
Brooklyn, New York, 1997
collection of the artist
© Grahame Weinbren
photo © Grahame Weinbren

To put this point more generally, registering response alone will not satisfy the basic requirement that the interactive cinema incorporate (reflect, arouse, respond to) the interest or desire of the spectator.

The bottom line of the interactive cinema is that the viewer has some control over what is on-screen. He or she knows that what is there will change if she or he acts, that it would have been different if he or she had acted differently earlier. Thus, the viewer is aware of a fundamental indeterminacy. I have called this epistemological state a subjunctive relationship to the screen – the viewer is constantly aware that things could have been otherwise. This state is grounded in the viewer's continual knowledge that what is on screen is a result of her interactions – inaction, naturally, counting as decisively as action.

The subjunctive mental state is in direct opposition to the epistemology I identified as essential to the mainstream cinema, a conception of the screen complex as unalterable, the events in the diegesis as inevitable. In an advanced interactive cinema, everything will be in flux, open to the possibility of change – like conversation or competitive sports – and the more sophisticated the system, the more fluid and wide-ranging the possibilities. Awareness of this liquidity has radical consequences for a viewer's relationship to the cinematic material. In terms of the Lyrical, the exploration of a single image-moment, the success of a work of interactive cinema depends on its viewer's recognition that behind each element of the screen complex there is a potential set of cinematic data that supports it, enriches it, or accounts for it.

There is another factor too: the viewer must be kept always aware that it is his, her action on a particular image that has produced these new sounds or pictures, and techniques to foster this awareness must be developed. In my judgment, the most immediately available techniques can be found in the language of montage. A deliberate use of film-editing strategies can keep re-convincing the viewer of the specificity of connections between old and new elements, between the elements already there and those produced by viewer action. Once the interactive work has brought the viewer to the idea that his actions on the screen complex always contribute to the continuing significance of the work, then the associations can roam more freely than in the city zoo of conventional narrative film. Now the fact that the viewer feels that he produces the new elements predisposes him towards finding links, associations, and connections that may not have operated in his response to a conventional cinematic work.

6 Salman Rushdie, op. cit., pp. 71–72.

Back to the Ocean

"And if you are very, very careful, or very, very highly skilled, you can dip a cup into the Ocean," Iff told Haroun, "like so," and here he produced a little golden cup from another of his waistcoat pockets, "and you can fill it with water from a single, pure Stream of Story, like so," as he did precisely that, "and then you can offer it to a young fellow who's feeling blue, so that the magic of the story can restore his spirits. Go on now; knock it back, have a swig, do yourself a favour," Iff concluded. "Guaranteed to make you feel A-number-one."6

So now we have two models of potential structure for an interactive cinema: one drawn from a classical text by the father of psychoanalysis, the other from an introspective view of the mind at work. There are many literary precedents for both models. Furthermore, a number of current works of fiction have forms that eminently suit the notion of an interactive cinema, either in that they involve the unpacking of a given image or scene into its underlying components– Graham Swift's *Waterland* provides several excellent instances – or that their narrative consists of the meeting point of a number of interrelated themes – John Barth's *Tidewater Tales* and his masterful *The Last Voyage of Somebody the Sailor* are two outstanding examples. More recently Graham Swift has written *Last Orders*, a novel with a constantly changing first person narrator, and John Barth's *On With the Story* and *Coming Soon,* both of which require the reader to split his or her attention among many chapters simultaneously in order to fully comprehend the story.

Tying Up and Getting Out

There are still, there will always be, loose ends. Given that narrative is imposition of order on chaos, intrusion of form on the formless, and that the order, the form, the logic narrative imposes is of time and sequence, sequence in time, we must now ask again whether we can retain narrative when we abandon endings, when we are entangled in an endless middle. A catchphrase often used by theorists to describe narrative is "the illusion of sequence," but in Freud's conception of dream interpretation we can see how strict sequence can be abandoned without losing the narrative thread. Freud's understanding of dream-structure is an alternative to the Aristotelian model, not only because the components can appear in any order, but also because the story is never over, the analysis is always incomplete, there are always more biographical details to uncover. In an Interactive Cinema, where the desire for closure can also be more or less overcome, the viewer continues to

left
Frames
1999
three-channel interactive
cinema installation
computer-controlled laser-
videodisc array, suspended-
frames interface, custom
designed hardware and
software
dimensions and duration
variable
installation views: Beall Center,
Irvine, California, 2001
commissioned by NTT Inter-
CommunicationCenter, Tokyo
collection of the artist
© Grahame Weinbren
photos © Grahame Weinbren

right
Lisa Dove as
Hugh Diamond's subject.

Frames
1999
installation view: NTT InterCommunication Center, Tokyo, 1999
commissioned by NTT Inter-
CommunicationCenter, Tokyo
collection of the artist
© Grahame Weinbren
photo © Grahame Weinbren

Grahame Weinbren,
James Cathcart
Tunnel
2000
five-channel architectural
interactive cinema installation
computer-controlled DVD array,
industrial infrared-sensor
interface, custom hardware
and software
dimensions and duration
variable
installation view:
Zeche Zollern coal mine,
the Ruhr Valley, 2000
commissioned by the City of
Dortmund for the "vision.ruhr"
exhibition
collection of the City of
Dortmund
© Grahame Weinbren
photo © Grahame Weinbren

explore the narrative space until he considers it exhausted. There is no totality, there is only withdrawal.

And yet. And yet.

However.

Butbutbut.

Real Time cannot be trashed with the need for closure like potato peel or an old jalopy. There is, there always will be, a Beginning, an End to a viewer's exposure to an Interactive Cinema work, and a Time Between. She walks up to the device, she interacts with it, she walks away. He walks up, sits down, stays a while, gets up. Do we place a viewer with an interactive work until it starts to repeat on him like rote learning or yesterday's overspiced entree? The Interactive Cinema will succeed only if, in retrospect, the experience seems substantial.

All and any loose narrative ends will never be knotted; this is one of the features (not bugs) of interactive cinema. If a viewer navigates through a mass of material, some of it will be seen and some won't, and surely some of what isn't seen earlier will raise issues that remain unresolved in what is seen later. But a system can be sensitized to repetition, either so as to avoid it, or so that as soon as repetition starts the viewer is offered the opportunity to enter a structurally different region, a territory of culmination or summary. In general terms, a map of territory covered can be kept by the system, and once a certain area has been explored, closure possibilities can be introduced.

In *The Erl King* (1983-1986), after certain segments have been repeated, a box with the work "END?" appears on the screen. If this box is touched, it produces a mildly interactive segment that starts with images of a few key production crew members touching the inside of the video screen from within the monitor, followed by a rapid series of production stills. A viewer can switch on or off two cardinal theoretical texts overlays – texts by Wittgenstein and Baudrillard that describe something of the theoretical underpinnings of the work – by touching different areas of the screen.

Sonata (1991/1993) reserves two narrative segments that are acknowledged and indicated throughout the piece. If the viewer perseveres, following a story through to one of its climactic moments, the reward will be one of the two culminating murder scenes, one decorated with the blooming image of a

blood-fountain, the other with the voluptuous sounds of a blade severing flesh and splintering bone. The possibility of viewing these scenes emerges when the viewer has covered a certain amount of the narrative ground of the piece. And after the murder the work ends or, more precisely, returns to the beginning.

Frames (1999) has internal endings. A viewer attempts to transform a contemporary actor into a nineteenth-century mental asylum inmate, a Mad-Woman, based on the first photographs taken in a mental institution (by Hugh Diamond in the 1850s when photography was in its teens). When the viewer succeeds in fully transforming his actor into character (there are some obstacles), she will move, in character, to the center screen, and enact a small drama. If two viewers succeed together, their characters will meet on the third screen. After the drama is over, the piece returns to its opening screens.

All this is to say that despite its need for an opened narrative, closure cannot be banished from the Interactive Cinema. Remove the imminence of closure and we begin to drain cinema of desire. Closure must be recast in a more radical light.

The most fruitful possibility for me at this point, based on my interest in multiplying and intermingling narratives, is that several story lines continue until one, some, or all of them end. Here the idea is that - numerous Diegetic Times are constantly flowing forward, many narratives operating in time simultaneously whether or not the viewer encounters any particular one. Narrative Time in this model always moves inflexibly on. This provides another picture of a form for the Interactive Fiction Cinema, a picture of multiple narrative streams not interconnected by a central image, theme or scene. The viewer navigates from one current to an adjacent one in a constantly flowing river, crossing between streams of story at moments of similarity or juncture. Or, to descend one level more, they might rather be thought of as potential narrative streams, elements themselves unformed or chaotic, but taking form as they intersect, gaining meaning in relation to one another.

In *Sonata* I attempt this by juxtaposing the stories of Podsnyeshev (the anti-hero wife-killer in Tolstoy's *Kreutzer Sonata*) and Judith (the apocryphal heroine who decapitated the enemy general Holofernes). Both narratives progress, but it is at their connections, where the viewer can cross from one to the other, that they come into focus and take on meaning. A viewer will access an episode of one or the other narrative but not both, and their forms are similar enough that their plot movement can be seen as concurrent. Each of the two killers – Podsnyeshev and Judith – is reflected in the light of the other, since each emerges out of the story context of the other. And thus an act of interpretation is forced on the viewer: the morality of each character comes into question when they are placed together, especially because the former is presented as Evil and the latter as Good.

Without the act of interpretation, the stories are raw and problematic, but when clashed together at the points of interaction, a judge's role is forced on the viewer. As Eisenstein recognized explicitly, Griffith at least implicitly, and Kuleshov claimed as his own, meaning in cinema is determined by context – in the multi-linear narrative interactive cinema, context is in constant flux, the elements appearing always different as their surroundings shift.

As the viewer is drawn in by the act of interpretation, now the magnetic attraction of the Interactive Cinema can be felt, and the question of Experienced Time finally answered; for it is here that the Hacker mindset takes over – as we jack into Gibson's Cyberspace. Umberto Eco describes the state somewhat more suggestively than Gibson does, though Eco is talking about the travels of a steel ball around an electric pinball surface, not a sprite in a graphic representation of a data environment.

"You don't play pinball just with your hands, you play it with your groin too. The pinball problem is not to stop the ball before it's swallowed by the mouth at the bottom, or to kick it back to midfield like a halfback. The problem is to make it stay up where the lighted targets are more numerous and have it bounce from one to another, wandering, confused, delirious, but still a free agent. And you achieve this not by jolting the ball but by transmitting vibrations to the case, the frame, but gently, so the machine won't catch on and say Tilt. You can do it only with the groin, or with a play of the hips that makes the groin not so much bump, as slither, keeping you on this side of an orgasm."[7]

Parallel to Eco's pinball machine is a game like Tetris, in which the player arranges falling shapes into an unbroken plane, a theater of geometry and spatial anticipation one often sees played on long airplane flights – as the time sense is held in abeyance, the magnified time of the cramped Atlantic crossing is compressed into a single moment of hypnotic focus. Tetris' hook of involvement is the desire for closure, for the completion of the pattern, an end that is always attainable but just out of reach, like Eco's "brink of orgasm." It is in this space that the machine absorbs time, providing in its place the never-quite-fulfilled promise of consummation.[8]

Ending, Open Ending

Where have we come to? How to provide closure to this document? Must I close it, or can I emphasize its openness, the ends I am leaving loose, the ties unbound?

"… each story runs into another story, and as one guest is advancing his strip, another, from the other end, advances in the opposite direction, because the stories told from left to right or from bottom to top can also be read from right to left or from top to bottom, and vice versa, bearing in mind that the same cards, presented in a different order, often change their meaning…"[9]

There is the very central question of what function is left to Narrative in our Cybernetically Determined, Information Laden Era, as we travel along the Information Superhighways without stirring from our desks. Do we still need narrative to provide lessons in living and dying, do these lessons come to us through other channels … or don't we need such lessons any longer? Then there is the very important and subtle idea, expressed by philosophers in the wake of Heidegger such as Paul Ricoeur, that the conceptual relationship of narrative and time is reversed: that we impose a (false) linearity on time because our stories about ourselves and others, our formation myths of what it is to be human, take shape as linear narratives, and upsetting this notion will change our understanding of temporality and hence our understanding of the world and ourselves.

But I must stop. It is late, my eyes hurt from looking too long at the CRT, and I'm afraid I'm getting the 'flu.

Graham Weinbren
Revised version (see author's footnote 1) of the original text "The Ocean of Streams of Stories" first published in *Millennium Film Journal*, no. 28, "Interactivities," 1995.

7 Umberto Eco: *Foucault's Pendulum*, Martin Secker and Warburg, London, 1989, p. 222.

8 This was written in 1995, before the emergence of the computer game culture and its conquest of Hollywood. Now (2002) airplanes have games built into screens in the seat backs. But the point about the erasure of the perception of time's passage remains unchanged. I have written about the computer game and its false promises in "Mastery: Sonic C'est Moi," *New Screen Media: Cinema/Art/Narrative*, Martin Reiser and Andrea Zapp (eds), BFI Publishing, London, 2002.

9 Italo Calvino, *The Castle of Crossed Destinies*, Harcourt, New York, 1979, p. 41 .

Improvisational Media Fabric: Take 1

"More and more, as I made films of situations that are out of control, I found things that were extraordinarily interesting. Not because they were clever or chic or anything, but because they were true. They presented you with data and you had to try to figure out: 'What the hell was really going on?' "1

Cinema-making is an activity of intelligent guessing, an expressive exploration of constructed meaning. Storytellers transform real-life observations into narratives through acts of selective inclusion, synthetic emphasis, time distortion, and metaphoric encapsulation; their tales are shaped within the empowering and framing constraints of their chosen medium. In art, the act of seeing and expressing outer and inner worlds becomes a shareable learning experience that is simultaneously culture-driven, culture-forming and culture-reflective.

The first time you pick up a video camera, you immediately understand something about your own process of intelligent guessing. You can't help it: the camera tells you nothing about how to observe. Rather, it requires you to direct your eye in a way which captures aspects of experience that can later, on reflection, be shaped into a sequence. The task requires rapid hypothesis-forming and intimate collaboration with the recording machinery. Increasingly, as your eye communicates directly with your motor system, observing through a lens becomes a dance in which your partner is the environment that surrounds you.

Over the past two decades, the tools of cinema have become mass-marketed consumer goods and a substantial portion of the population is now empowered to record, reshape, and share aspects of life that interest them using an ever-growing inventory of palm-sized video cameras and computers equipped with nonlinear editing systems. However, despite the growth of the World-Wide Web, the expressive channels available for distribution of complex compilations of material remain somewhat of a bottleneck for hopeful distributors/authors.

Over the past few years, a new type of communications channel has been emerging from the intertwining of networked computers, audiovisual displays, cameras, microphones and activity sensors in the digital domain. In traditional cinema, the activity required to make a film is radically different from that required to watch one. The cinematographer moves her camera through space and time so that the audience can remain in their seats, eyes fixed on an immobile view-screen. A reel of film spools through the projector from end to end, oblivious and unresponsive to the reactions of its audience. Today, digital cinema is freeing itself from its linear celluloid base; it is evolving into a "meta-cinema" where one's own memories, perceptions, actions and desires connect with others through a continuous process of communicating, interweaving, and reconfiguring tradable bits within a universal media environment.

Meta-cinema explodes the myth of the fixed and immutable heroic tale projected onto a single screen for passive consumption by a seated audience. New story forms become possible through its intrinsically programmable, reconfigurable and interactively responsive nature. The raw materials for a meta-cinema experience are likely to be scattered throughout the vastness of the Internet, waiting for a story-building engine (or a person) to discover, select, arrange, display and trade them. While members of the audience may be widely scattered in a physical sense, they are networked together, connecting with story and with each other through shared channels. In meta-cinema, the audience – individually or collectively – can go to a story or the story can come to the members, at any time, wherever they are, whether stationary or traveling.

As meta-cinema abandons the single fixed screen to project itself into more and more of our everyday environment, it is becoming an improvisational learning partner that engages us in factual discovery, evolving hypotheses, augmented dialogs, and sociable interchange. In such an environment the differences among making, consuming and sharing stories fade to insignificance.

1 Richard Leacock, 1964, as quoted in Louis Macorelles, *Direct Cinema: New Directions in Contemporary Filmmaking*, Prager, New York, 1973.

Glorianna Davenport,
Richard Leacock
*New Orleans in Transition:
1983-1986*
film © Glorianna Davenport
system © MIT Media Lab
photo © MIT Media Lab

A researcher accesses three
hours of videodisc-based
movies and a substantial database of documents to interactively build an argument
about urban development.

Research and Future Cinema

Cinema has two parents: technology and art. The
Interactive Cinema Group – established in 1988 as
part of the MIT Media Laboratory – builds on the
shoulders of earlier cinéasts such as Vertov, Robert
Flaherty and (most importantly) Richard Leacock.
Our research focuses on understanding through
hands-on practice how digital technologies can
impact the production and presentation of cinematic
experience, and on inventing appropriate technologies that make cinema accessible to people who have
something to say. More specifically the group invents
concepts, methods, and tools that are broadly applicable to a computer-assisted future cinema that is
"more complex and personal, as if in conversation with
the audience."

Research begins with an insight, proceeds with
intelligent, playful, reflective guessing, and sooner or
later may result in a vision. The roots of meta-cinema
lie in a three-year cinematic case study of a city in
transition. The city was New Orleans between 1983
and 1986, as it evolved before, during and after the
1984 World's Fair. The problem: How could I share with
the public my experience of watching a city change?
How could an audience experience and enjoy the
method of intelligent guessing used by the filmmakers? My answer focused on the idea that a movie's
sequences and a broad collection of supporting
materials could be stored in a database and delivered
over a network based on personal history and interest in the subject matter. By 1986, we had three hours
of this case study online, together with a range of
supporting documents. In 1987, we made an interactive version of *New Orleans in Transition: 1983–1986*
available to students as "courseware" for Dennis

Frenchman's Introduction to Urban Planning class at
MIT. The delivery system featured a rudimentary
selection engine that used meta-data associated
with each sequence as a navigational device. The
front-end browser to the material included a multimedia editing system which allowed students to edit
their own sequences and post them into their papers
written for the course.2

In the years that followed, we explored a range of
interface designs that allowed cinematic content to
be served discontinuously from a database of shots
and sequences. From 1986 onward, these interfaces
empowered navigation through the material by the
use of meta-data, maps and multiple still thumbnails
or movie icons (micons) posted into a "point-and-
click" screen space. For the most part, individual
systems also allowed the audience some tools for
dynamic linking or editing. Slowly, we pursued the
vision that the give-and-take of interactive cinema
should be complex and personal, as if in conversation
with the audience. Our goal in constructing a conversational feel was to be responsive but to avoid
engaging in verbal dialog, a large research area that
we were not well-suited to pursue. The research
question became: How do you construct or follow
story through concept space/time environments
that are cluttered and fractured, that have many
potential starting points and where multiple progressions are possible?

2 W.E. Mackay, G. Davenport,
   "Virtual Video Editing in Interactive Multi-Media," in
   Communications of the ACM,
   vol. 32, July 1989, pp. 802-
   810.

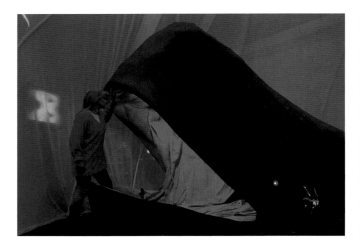

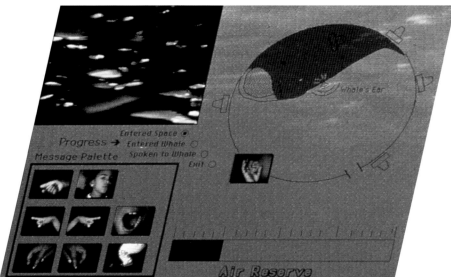

Glorianna Davenport,
Larry Friedlander
*Wheel of Life:
a Transformational
Environment*
1991–1992
© MIT Media Lab
photos © David Tames

top left
Water: an explorer
deciphering the whale's song.

top right
Water: the explorer sings
to the whale.

left
Water: the guide's
interactive pallette.

3 G. Davenport, L. Friedlander,
"Interactive Transforma-
tional Environments: Wheel
of Life," in *Contextual Media:
Multimedia and Interpretation*, The MIT Press, Cambridge, MA, 1995, pp. 1–25.

Moving Story out of the Box

We soon realized that these networked infrastruc-
tures could also be used to create "out-of-the-box"
experiences in the surround space of our everyday
lives, and drew on theater as an inspiration for our
work. In 1991, Larry Friedlander and I co-directed
Wheel of Life: a Transformational Environment. This
work was essentially a mini "theme park" built as a
class project by a team of twenty-two undergraduate
and graduate students with the help of several key
staff members.3

In a complex story space-time, many elements
compete for your attention, and your journey is
shaped by the encounters that engage you. The
Wheel of Life explored how audience attention could
be directed and focused as audience members move
through a physical story environment filled with networked interactive attractions. This piece introduced
a new theme into the work of Interactive Cinema: how
could the audience share and trade aspects of the
experience with each other in real-time? In order to
explore this question, we built the experience so that

the audience traverses the space/time continuum
in pairs: one member is given the role of explorer, or
antagonist in the space; another is positioned at a
remote workstation and plays the role of a guide.
Embedded sensors and puzzle constructs drive the
story forward, continually demanding physical and
cognitive action from the explorer. The guide uses
lighting, pre-authored messages, and graphical interfaces to send real-time messages to the Explorer,
helping her divine her course through the unfamiliar
landscape. In the case of "Water," we created the
llusion of submerging the explorer. Surrounded by
light and sound activity, the explorer is directed by
the guide towards the large whale at the center of
the space. Once the explorer has activated the
whale's voice, she is urged by the guide to sing to the
whale; when the whale hears the song, the explorer is
rewarded, then released to continue her exploration
in "Earth," the next environment.

The *Wheel of Life* used very rudimentary technology; however, it offered a glimpse of a world filled with
tangible objects that carried media with them, manip-

Tinsley Galyean
Dogmatic
1994
screenshots
media © Tinslay Galyean
system © MIT Media Lab

big picture
From scene 2: Lucky the dog.

small picture top
From scene 3: a surprising turn
of events.

small picture left
From scene 1: the gas station.

ulated media, or coupled media to a spatial location in story time. In each of these cases, young researchers have taken up the challenge to instantiate projects in which these ideas are realized.

Simultaneous with the *Wheel of Life*, PhD candidate Tinsley Galyean developed *Dogmatic*, a four-act 3-D interactive movie. *Dogmatic* took place in a "virtual reality" space rather than a physically constructed environment, but it explored similar principles of narrative guidance in first-person space/time. In this story, the viewer is the antagonist positioned at a point in the 3-D landscape from which she can freely look around. Sensing that she has control, she reacts and interacts with the main protagonist, Lucky the dog. If her gaze wanders, Lucky may

bark to demand attention. *Dogmatic* rapidly progresses to the central conflict, in which the viewer's illusion of control is suddenly, surprisingly shattered, reinforcing the author's philosophic position that even when we think we are in control, we may not be.[4]

This philosophic position continues to have impact today. Traditionally, storytellers have had definitive control over the presentation of the story. As cinema explodes outward in space, a profound transformation occurs: the audience becomes a partner in the creation of the experience.

4 Tinsley Galyean, "Narrative Guidance of Interactivity," PhD thesis, MIT, 1995.

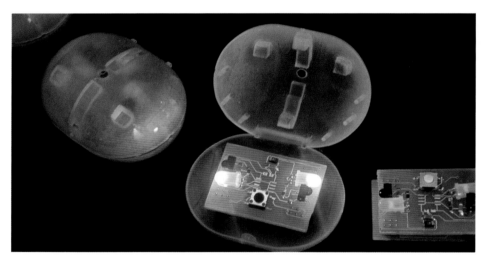

Barbara Barry
StoryBeads
2000
© MIT Media Lab
photos © Barbara Barry

top
Beads used in a wireless act of
trading images.

bottom
The bead circuitry and casing.

Reweavable Media Fabrics

"Improvisation is a creative activity where no boundary between cognitive and intuitive is drawn, where no clear rule-based approach can be utilized in even a superficial way, and where the focus is on the process rather than on some final goal or state."[5]

As cinema frees itself from the limitations of the celluloid strip and the continuous viewing experience, meta-cinema emerges. For the past few years, researchers in Interactive Cinema have tussled in various ways with the vision that in the future, we – as authors – will generate an evolving collection of cinematic elements; that the interface will grow increasingly transparent and then disappear; and that a dynamic, reconfigurable, ever-present network will connect people with people and with media stories at whatever density, localized specificity and temporal duration is appropriate to the receiver's context and inclination. In this future cinema, we do not "go" to the movies. Rather, we are always in the midst of improvisational meta-movie potential and learning stories.

Barbara Barry's *StoryBeads* (2000) presented a clear alternative view toward shared media in the future: its central mechanism was a wearable neck-lace of media beads. Each bead was a wireless transmitter/receiver specialized for image transfer and storage. If you wanted to review or trade your pictures, you could send them to the central video amulet; in order to swap an image, you simply held up your own amulet to somebody else's and the picture would jump across. The idea grew out of discussions with young girls who wanted to maintain some control over who was able access their images.[6]

In *Tangible Viewpoints*, (2000 to present) Ali Mazalek explores how physical objects and augmented surfaces can be used as tangible embodiments of different character perspectives in a multiple-viewpoint interactive tale. By providing a direct, tangible mode of navigation to the story world, we seek to bridge the gap between cyberspace and our physical environment as we engage with digital stories. The table upon which game-pieces can be moved is also a projection surface inviting several people to gather around the story space either to input their own story or else to browse through a pre-formatted narrative. Recent extensions to this environment include the use of surround sound and graphical spatial maps.[7]

Brian Bradley's recent experiment *Happenstance*

5 Paul Nemirovsky, "Improvisational Sequence: Models and Perspectives," PhD thesis (unpublished), MIT, 2002. http://web.media.mit.edu/~pauln/research/goals.html

6 Barbara Barry, "Story Beads: a wearable for distributed and mobile storytelling," Master's thesis, MIT, 2000.

7 A. Mazalek, G. Davenport, H. Ishii, "Tangible Viewpoints: A Physical Interface for Exploring Character-Driven Narratives," in *Conference Abstracts and Applications of SIGGRAPH '02* (San Antonio, Texas, USA, 21–26 July 2002), ACM Press, New York, 2002.

Brian Bradley
Happenstance
2002
screenshots
© MIT Media Lab

left to right
The Ocean receives and responds to an information drop.

A Twister carries a timely message from your mother's pager into the scene.

A Volcano errupts, launching a new interactive story (the JBW project) into the world as a cloud.

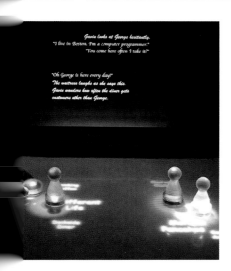

Ali Mazalek
Tangible Viewpoints
2000
© MIT Media Lab
photos © Ali Mazalek

left
Viewpoints gamepieces and story playfield.

right
Interacting with Tangible Viewpoints system at Boston's Computer Clubhouse.

(2000) explored the use of dynamic, information-filled landscape models as an interface to story. In *Happenstance*, story bits-and-pieces gather into clouds; when conditions of earth and the upper atmosphere are appropriate, the clouds release these bits onto the land. In this vision, information from many stories may be traveling through the landscape at any time. The story receiver is able to multi-process, and can therefore follow those stories that seem most compelling at a particular time. Collections and constructs are constantly being built up, broken down and redistributed by processes emulating the natural geomorphic and atmospheric cycles of the world. Traversing this landscape causes information and pieces of media to be revealed or obscured over time; its memory of context, audience history, and desires expressed through the interface works to coax a coherent story-like experience from the journey.8

Throughout these experiments, the relation between sociability and technological progress remained murky. *Flights of Fantasy* (2001), which was inspired by thinking around the earlier embedded work *Pigeons* (1996), focused on the idea that a message is never the same for the sender/maker and the receiver. This project was a two-room installation in

the DeCordova Museum during the Boston Cyberarts Festival in spring 2001. Visitors began their interaction in the first room they happened to enter. In one of the two rooms, the audience approached an ornate wooden table whose surface resembled a giant version of a child's pocket puzzle. By sliding the symboled blocks of this interface, the visitor created a path of icons; an action-selection program translated that path into a sequence of video segments and text narration drawn from a database. The table interface alleviated much of the self-consciousness that might otherwise accompany public creation of a message. At the opening, one woman commented to her friend, "Look, I made that movie!" The table masked the complexity of the editing activity, making it informal, playful and message-like.9

In an adjacent room, the visitor entered a forest of birdcages, each housing one or more miniature video screens. In the idyllically idle state, a videotape of birds looped on the small screen. When someone opened the door to one of the cages, the bird video disappeared and was replaced by one of the messages created by a visitor in the other room. As these messages flew from room to room, they were accompanied by the sound of flapping wings. One authored

8 G. Davenport, B. Bradley, S. Agamanolis, B. Barry, K. Brooks, "Synergistic storyscapes and constructionist cinematic sharing," in *IBM Systems Journal,* vol. 39, no. 3-4, 2000, pp. 456–469.

9 *FRAMES,* MIT Media Lab, May 2001, no. 104.

Glorianna Davenport
Flights of Fantasy
2001
© MIT Media Lab
photos © Glorianna Davenport

Two people editing a sequence.

left
The forest of bird cages.

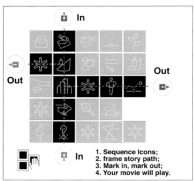

In

Out   Out

In   1. Sequence Icons;
            2. frame story path;
            3. Mark in, mark out;
            4. Your movie will play.

right top and bottom
Iconic blocks of the table/
interface.

10 Pengkai Pan, "Decentralized
    Narrative Intercreativity in
    Digital Media," August 2001
    (unpublished).

clip was a movie of a woman tearing a photograph into bits; as she throws the pieces out the window, the visitor heard an audio clip selected by the system logic, for instance: "Would you trade a piece of piece of plain drawing paper for a book of poems? Really?" The somehow familiar video stirred an ad hoc memory in both the maker and the receiver, although only at the receiving side was the video linked to an evocative audio sample. *Flights of Fantasy* builds upon earlier works in which we explored the idea of responsive media in casual architectural space. Again, the experience of sending and receiving is held purposefully distinct.

Most recently, we have taken to heart the idea of time/space discontinuity in the implementation of "M-Views," a contextually-aware ad-hoc platform for mobile cinema. Equipped with an IPAQ PDA, we wander through the MIT campus, allowing cinematic sequences to come to us as we go. These sequences are a mix of fictional, documentary, historical and futuristic story accounts of life on campus. The database is scaleable and extensible, and we are exploring ways of inviting the audience to become also a community of makers. In this system, we explode the tradition of cinema as a continuous temporal experience.10

Pengkai Pan
M-Views
2002– present
© MIT Media Lab
photos © Pengkai Pan

left
Moving through the landscape
in search of a story.

right
The roaming IPAQ display
encounters story content
localized to a specific place
and time.

Conclusion: Towards an Improvisational Cinema

Looking through the camera viewfinder, you reinvent yourself: you become a visual/sound poet of life as it happens. I would argue that this happens whether you are shooting documentary or fiction, although documentary inevitably provides the filmmaker with a broader, more complex narrative at the time of capture.

In the most recent footage from my continuously augmented video diary, a teenage girl – whom we have seen grow up – contradicts her mother; momentary emotion floods the mother's face. For the child, this moment is part of a natural but complex, painful, demanding journey towards independence; knowledge that this process is universal does not ease the intensity. In this moment, the diary has many threads running parallel: the mother's mother does not remember or even take note of the difficulty; the twenty-eight-year-old nephew, girlfriend in tow, notes the moment only peripherally. It is as if mother-daughter and camera are at the epicenter of a momentous earthquake, but those at the periphery hardly feel the shock. To replay these fragments captured on Memorex – days or years later – provides a déjà-vu journey in which familiar actions and awkward emotions have been subtly transformed through angle of view, exposure, focus, beginnings and endings of shots, and juxtapositions to suggest something universal about the experience. Picking our way through a dense layering of captured moments requires a steadfast story-construction partner.[11]

Cinema has always been about story, and much of the Interactive Cinema Group's research has explored how loose collections of information and imagery can be interactively traversed to create a story-like experience. In building our experiments, one set of design choices has proven particularly durable:

1) The narrative should be first-person: the characters themselves should speak or react directly to the viewer at least some of the time.

2) The interactive interface that drives presentation should not get in the way of the experience, and it must minimize the audience's learning curve to engage with the story.

3) Audience interactions should produce meaningful consequences.

4) Story setups should have payoffs.

5) Playing out a story should engage the participant audience in a task that requires it to act but does not require the story to react beyond reconfiguring its internal inventory of story parts.

As cinema breaks free from the sparse cones of perception captured by the lens of the camera and the diaphragm of the microphone, how do we capture, replicate and guide the experience of story? How can we construct or follow story through conceptual space/time environments that are cluttered and fractured, that have many possible starting points and multiple potential progressions? What interface paradigm best supports a satisfying and sustainable improvisational journey through space, time, and story meaning?

Through multiple playful experiments, the research progresses in small steps, all forward, some more direct than others. This pattern is familiar to other media, particularly cinema, as the lessons learned through thousands of experiments congealed into a language and a grammar of its own. Each exploration reveals another facet of the picture that, taken together, will reveal a true vision of what the new medium will ultimately become.

Glorianna Davenport

11 Glorianna Davenport, *Its all about family: a home movie,* (in progress).

Jill Scott
Frontiers of Utopia

1995
interactive environment / dinner table with monitor, laserdisc player, modified keyboard, table, chair; four suitcases with miniature metal sculptures and touchscreen, laserdisc player, projector / color, sound / dimensions variable

Frontiers of Utopia
1995
interactive environment
installation views: ZKM |
Center for Art and Media
Karlsruhe
details
collection ZKM | Media Museum,
Karlsruhe
© Jill Scott
photos © Steffen Harms

Interactive Time Travel

Frontiers of Utopia is the final part of an interactive series exploring the "history and nature of idealism, technology and design." In the first two parts *Machinedreams* (1991) and *Paradise Tossed* (1993) the relationship between desire, design and memory was explored in a stylized and dreamy manner. The viewer was able to construct a collage of sounds and images from 1900, 1930, 1960, 1990 by moving through both real and virtual space, their movement triggering sounds or by using icons on a touch-sensitive screen. In this way, they became time travelers, making interesting associations as well as learning about history in a new way.

Frontiers of Utopia presents the viewer with the politics of the ideal society from the points of view of eight different female characters from these same time zones. It creates and illustrates the various moods, criticisms and attitudes toward Utopia along with the articulation of these eight characters and their views about society. In doing so, it presents a rich tapestry of ideas, attitudes, locations and historical perspectives.

The work has a theatrical Brechtian nature, as the viewers can speak to the virtual characters about the struggles of workers, the plight of students, the relationship between women and the attitudes toward the implications of media and technology. It's epic sweep is impressive, traversing as it does

decades and continents and drawing parallels between periods and locations based on shared class and gender. In the installation the viewers can move interactively through the four time zone layers of *Frontiers of Utopia* by touching icons and objects in the space as if they were time travelers.

In another part of the installation they can attend a virtual dinner party where all the characters and their personal objects are available for comparison. The largest version of *Frontiers* was completed as an interactive film installation for the MultiMediale festival at ZKM | Center for Art and Media Karlsruhe in 1995. The second version was shown at Siggraph '95, Los Angeles; ISEA Montreal; Monash University, Melbourne; Media Moo Festival, Helsinki; "Voyage Virtual," Paris; The Roslyn Oxley Gallery, Sydney (all in 1995). The large cinema version was shown again at the Zurich Museum for Gestaltung in March 1996.

Frontiers of Utopia is produced in conjunction with Monitor Information Systems by The Australian Film Commission. Programming is by Jens Muller and Monitor; interface by Martin Häberle, Allan Giddy; screen design by Ralf Pfeifer. The large interactive-cinema version is owned by the ZKM | Media Museum. The production of the project was supported by the ZKM | Media Museum and the Australian Film and Television School, Sydney.

Frontiers of Utopia
1995
interactive environment
dinner table with monitor,
laserdisc player, modified
keyboard, table, chair;
four suitcases with miniature
metal sculptures and touchscreen, laserdisc player,
projector
color, sound
dimensions variable
installation view: ZKM | Center
for Art and Media Karlsruhe
collection ZKM | Media Museum,
Karlsruhe
© Jill Scott
photo © Markus Hauser

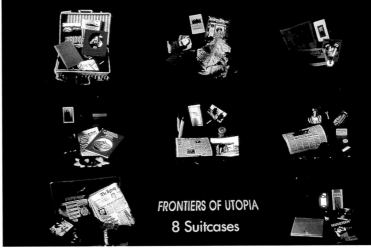

FRONTIERS OF UTOPIA
8 Suitcases

Frontiers of Utopia
1995
composite image
© Jill Scott

Eija-Liisa Ahtila
Consolation Service

1999
two-channel video projection on DVD-ROM / color, sound / 23:40 min

"Melted snow falls from balconies. The sun is warm. It confuses people and animals and makes ice weak. My next-door neighbour is walking his dog. It's nine o'clock. The young couple at number 10 have decided to split up. Wife has fed the baby. Husband has gone to work selling things. I'm sitting at the window and writing a story about them. It is a story about an ending. The first section describes how to do it. In the second one it happens. The third section is a kind of consolation service. Here it is."[1]

1 *Consolation Service*, beginning of the dialogue. The complete text, in the original Finnish as well as in English translation, is published in: *Eija-Liisa Ahtila. Kuviteltuja Henkilöitä Ja Nauhoitettuja Keskusteluja – Fantasized Persons and Taped Conversations*, exhib. cat., Museum of Contemporary Art, Kiasma and Tate Modern, London, 2002, pp. 118–119 and 120–121. All of the following quotations unless otherwise stated are taken from the film.

Consolation Service
1999
two-channel video projection
on DVD-ROM
color, sound
23:40 min
installation view: ZKM |
Center for Art and Media
Karlsruhe, 2002
collection Chara Schreyer,
Tiburon, CA
courtesy Thea Westreich Art
Advisory Services, New York
© & produced by Crystal Eye
Ltd, Helsinki;
© VG Bild-Kunst, Bonn 2003
photo © Franz Wamhof

Eija-Liisa Ahtila begins her film *Consolation Service*, which is projected onto two adjacent screens, with late-winter scenes from the hours of darkness through the dawn and into daylight. It is beginning to thaw. The narrator's opening monologue commences, and is gradually interwoven with scenes from the story of the young couple breaking up. The narrator herself is progressively drawn into the story. The couple knows it is at the center of a narrative, as we hear in one of the opening scenes: "Our neighbor is the babysitter … The one who is writing this story." Here at the latest it becomes clear to what extent the film's narrative levels are interwoven, and that the real and fictional aspects of this story cannot be distinguished. In the course of the film the viewer feels increasingly abandoned with his or her ques-

tions; in the end there is more uncertainty than confirmation. Much appears in itself undecided, fictional or surreal. The very fact that the narrator/author repeatedly looks out of the window and observes the neighbor with his dog in the snow in intermezzo-like scenes suggests that the film consists of two narrative levels: the frame story of the author looking out of the window and the tale she is telling, which is presented as the actual plot of the film. The narrator can see events at which she is not present and even witness her protagonists' visions. Ahtila uses fictions to create reality beyond reality.

The starting point of her story is the information that a young couple, J.-P. and his wife Anni, have decided to split up. The writer envisions them receiving counselling from a therapist about ending their

relationship. The couple argue once more, but the dialogues are stereotypical, also involving their baby daughter, Lucia. At the end of this sequence the man embraces the woman. We then see the couple on their way home and also the neighbour's dog in the snow, as seen previously in the opening sequence – this is the "real" view from the window. The next scene takes place in the couple's living room. They are celebrating J.-P.'s birthday with friends. It is already getting dark when the party set off to go to a restaurant on the other side of a frozen lake. They discuss where best to cross the lake, and as they walk over the ice we learn how long you can survive if you fall through the ice and what it is like to drown. Just after one of them asks, "Can we change subject?" the ice beneath them breaks. This is followed by underwater shots, bodies coming up to the surface as the friends fight for their lives. We hear reflections upon a shared past: "One by one we go down. For the last time we show each other how we lost contact." These words can be applied to the actual scene as much as to the wider human situation. At the bottom of the lake the corpses of other people who have drowned are discovered: "Everything is in the water which has no limits." Without warning we see horses in a desert landscape and hear the calming sound of singing.

These images, as becomes clear from the pan shot that follows, are pictures on a TV screen in the couple's apartment. Here we can see the baby, and then a woman comes into view. It is Anni – whom we have seen drown. Suddenly she has a vision that J.-P., who also drowned, is standing in the apartment. She hurries to embrace him but the moment she touches him he vanishes into thin air. The vision appears a further two times. "He came back and showed how to bow. He smiled, vanished and never came back again." This is the consolation service that marks the irrevocable end of their relationship. The final shot shows the view from the window once more: a lively scene with dogs playing in the snow, cheerful music and the words: "Quiet! No barking. Now quiet! Quiet!"

This is a story about endings, death and time, told against the background of a separation that is initially intended and ultimately, through death, inescapably final. The dramaturgy is led by unforeseen turning points. *Consolation Service* is a "human drama," Ahtila's term for her filmic explorations of human relationships, communication problems, sexuality, the defining power of the Other and, closely linked to this, the formation and dissolution of individual identity. The subject matter of Ahtila's films is provided by extensive research as well as her own experiences and memories. Real incidents are mixed with fictitious ones; documentary realism is combined with cinematic invention. Inner and outer worlds converge and overlap. Among the imaginary elements in *Consolation Service* are the appearance of invisible onlookers during the counselling session, the drowning scene, the materialisation of the husband at the end of the film and the interweaving of the narrative levels. In her depiction of banal normality Ahtila expresses doubts about the portrayal of reality and the individual in film and other media. The construction of identity through the media is ultimately a construction of ambivalent realities. In *Consolation Service*, only those scenes that take place in public can be based on the writer's actual observation, while the scenes that take place in private have been created as fictional identifications. As Ahtila shows, however, both of these levels constitute the experience of reality. While this relates specifically to the subject of the film, the artist's superordinate role as its director adds a further level to the play on realities. It remains unclear as to which sequences and dialogues are based directly on Ahtila's own experiences and research and which derive from her imagination.

Ahtila's extensive use of symbolism is particularly evident towards the end of the film, when she makes a sudden shift in both projections from the cold of the ice to the desert, a transition from cold to warm, death to life. It is a symbolism that was already present in previous dialogues. A shift is also made

Consolation Service
1999
screenshots
© 1999 Crystal Eye Ltd, Helsinki;
VG Bild-Kunst, Bonn 2003

from cinema to television and from film to video. "This singular encounter between technology and untamed nature becomes the true carrier of symbolic forms in *Consolation Service*, a dimension that Eija-Liisa Ahtila indicates as one we need to explore more— like the bottom of a frozen lake in the spring."[2]

The viewer must decide for himself what is reality and what fiction. Facts can become fiction and vice versa. Situated on the same level as the narrator, the viewer too becomes a voyeur. He follows what is happening in a double projection on screens placed directly next to one another. He sees things from two different perspectives, each of which tends to focus on particular aspects but can also communicate different truths. Ultimately, however, the twin perspectives contribute towards making the fiction appear plausible. The right-hand projection is to a much greater extent the carrier of facts than the left-hand one, which focuses more on details. Ahtila uses the split projection not to support the different narrative levels but rather to blur the boundaries between them. She achieves this on the visual level in the same way as she interweaves the frame story and dialogues on the textual level. Over long periods the soundtrack consists solely of the sounds of the action and the location itself. And while components of the cinematic narrative such as *mise en scène*, editing, sound, alienation effects and viewership provide formal points of departure for Ahtila's composition, as do the filmic

language of advertising and other contemporary viewing habits based on our encounters with new media, she is at the same time seeking to reinvent the language of film through filmic means.

Ahtila presents her films as installations in exhibitions but also on television, in cinemas and at film festivals. The double-screen installation is the original version; for the cinema Ahtila re-edited the work into a one-screen film. This alters the role of the viewer, rendering him effectively passive. In the installation, on the other hand, the viewer's gaze moves actively back and forth between the two projections, constantly under pressure to decide which of the two images to focus his gaze upon. A further aspect of *Consolation Service* that is unusual for a film installation is that Ahtila asks the viewer to watch the film from beginning to end: there are fixed starting times. Therefore the viewer in the installation is also denied the freedom to determine for himself the length of the film and the selection of scenes he will watch. This proximity to the traditional cinema film and its form of presentation is intended by the artist, but is taken a step further; the film installation allows Ahtila to direct habitually fragmented perception towards the complex nature of differing perspectives in the experience of reality and fiction.

Dörte Zbikowski
Translated from the German by Jacqueline Todd

2 Paola Morsiani,
Eija-Liisa Ahtila.
Consolation Service (1999),
from
http://www.camh.org/
cam_exhandprograms/
cam_archive/2DVD/
ahtila1.htm

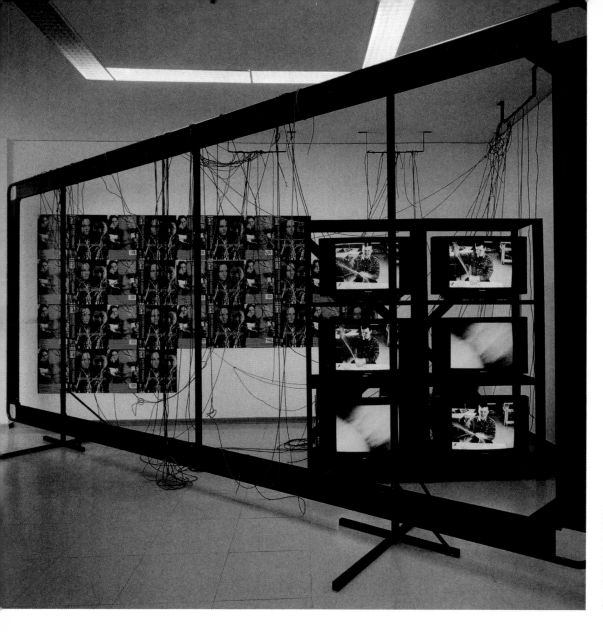

Salainen Puutarha
[Secret Garden]
1994
sculptural installation
screen frame, six monitors,
DVD-ROMs, posters, wires
dimensions variable
installation view
courtesy Klemens Gasser &
Tanja Grunert Inc, New York
© Crystal Eye Ltd, Helsinki;
VG Bild-Kunst, Bonn 2003

Secret Garden

Secret Garden is an installation made for an exhibition
of the same name at the Hämeenlinna Art Museum. It
consists of a black metal projection-screen frame
measuring 6.5 x 3 meters, six monitors, various electrical wires and cables, and a poster.

The theme of this piece is a film and its secret
garden. This work lacks the actual film material, an
imaginary tale of a moving picture. It concentrates on
the things that surround it, bringing into view elements associated with the film but remaining in the
background.

The six monitors of the works present excerpts of
a handicapped man at work installing electrical wiring.
The material is black and white, with no sound. The wall
behind the screen frame is covered with a poster
whose graphic design imitates the covers of video
films. The design is similar but the text material deals
with the mechanisms of representation, signification
and alterity. The whole installation is surrounded by a
net of cables and wiring.

Anne, Aki and God

*Anne, Aki and God*1 is an installation based on material borrowed from *A Quest For A Woman* - a work in progress. Three characters were chosen from the original script. Their roles have been adjusted and enhanced for the new context to create a work of its own. The thoughts, meanings and the preparation process of *A Quest For A Woman* is observed through this new work. This making of a film is juxtaposed with Aki's situation when in a state of psychosis he created a world of his own.

The emphasis in the installation is on the casting situation: the starting point of a process of creating a coherent reality for the work. Founding the thin, altering line between things really happening and fiction – the actors lending their spirit to the characters.

The story is based on real events about a man who, in a state of psychosis, created a woman for himself.

Aki V resigned from his work as a computer application support person in Nokia Virtuals, became schizophrenic and isolated himself in his one-room flat. His mind started to produce a reality of its own in sounds and visions. Little by little, this fiction became flesh and blood, and the line between reality and imagination became blurred. Fantasized persons and events stepped out of Aki V's head and became parallel to surrounding reality. The leading character in this new world was Anne Nyberg, Aki's fiancée.

On the wooden structure in five monitors, five candidates for the role of Aki perform their views of this character. In seven scenes five different Akis are created. Inside the structure there is a bed above which two different Gods appears on a screen and talk to Aki. Outside the structure there is another screen for the seven different Anne candidates to perform and an armchair in which the chosen one can rest.

The Wind

– shut the door please!
– it is shut.
– where's the draft coming from, then?
– your imagination.

The Wind is a story of a woman who cannot shout. Instead she bites her hands to the bones. From the open window a violent wind enters and together they start to work on things. The woman disarranges everything in her room, giving a new purpose and order to things, until she controls every detail in her empire of the reason.

The story is based on interviews with a woman who suffered from depression and occasional psychotic periods. The work depicts the gradual outbreak of the psychoses and a change in communication with the outside world. The inner logic is concretisized in the detailed rearragement of the living spaces.

The work is presented with three simultaneous projections. The material is split into three parts and the story is edited to unfold on three screens. The mental breakdown is emphasized by showing simultaneous but different views of the apartment space. The time of the narration is disrupted by repetition and the use of deliberate desyncronization of the events. The structure and form aim to break the logic of screen narration to parallel the process of creating a new order that is taking place on the screens.

Text first published in Hirvi, M. (ed.), *Eija-Liisa Ahtila: Fantisized persons and taped conversations*, a Museum of Contemporary Art publication 80/2002, exhib. cat. Kiasma Museum of Contemporary Art, Helsinki, Crystal Eye, Helsinki, 2002, pp. 56, 90, 144.

1 Characters: 5 Akis,
   2 Gods, 7 Annes on screen,
   (one performer).

Isaac Julien
The Long Road to Mazatlàn

1999
triple DVD projection / color, sound / dimensions variable / 18 min / in collaboration with Javier de Frutos

The Long Road to Mazatlàn, a video collaboration between Isaac Julien and the choreographer Javier de Frutos, is a fusion of movie and movement, a dance of gazes. Shot in and around San Antonio, Texas, it mixes familiar images of the West – the cowboy, the cattle yard, the dirt road – with a more contemporary and homoerotic iconography unsettling each one. A tale of frustration and loss, the work offers no prescription for stable identity or for the satisfaction of desire, but the sensuality of its images and form is hearteningly seductive.

Julien's descriptions of San Antonio are visually rich, using a saturated color that the regional tourist board might happily borrow for movies of its own. But this is no documentation of some "authentic" local culture. In fact the video is full of displacements, some strong, some subtle. Julien imagines its two main characters (played by de Frutos and Philippe Riera) as sightseers in the city despite their cowboy clothes – and tourists might wear those clothes as comfortably as many contemporary Texans. Nor is the cobra that crawls through the opening scene native to Texas. (Moreover, it is an albino cobra – an oddity anywhere.) A cowboy yodel on the soundtrack is actually imported from Austria; passages of mariachi music, on the other hand, are performed by local musicians, but are abstracted by repetition, so that a fiddle riff sounds simultaneously ancient and avant-garde.

The most visible displacement is formal: Julien uses three screens, which abut in a row, fracturing cinema's controlling illusion of a single intact vision. He arranges the projections on these screens in every possible permutation. As the video starts, a long shot of a man walking on a hot Texas road runs across all three screens, its width suggesting a miniaturized version of CinemaScope. The picture soon fragments: now the center screen shows the cobra in the road while the screens to left and right fill with the snake's moving skin, examined so closely that we may need the cue of the center image to identify it. Next the snakeskin shifts to the center screen while the side screens return to the shot of the road, though a different man appears in each one. Elsewhere the screens may show separate parts of the same space (two booths in a bar, say), or the same action from several perspectives, or actions that seem the same but are not. They may repeat identical images in a visual stutter, or pair a shot with its mirror image, or combine in a composite image. That composite in turn may appear whole, or its parts may misalign. The quality of the color, too, may vary from screen to screen, or a sequence may jump into black and white.

This is hardly conventional film syntax, yet rhythmic editing creates a sinuous flow. And *The Long Road to Mazatlàn* does have a narrative of a kind – boy meets boy, loses boy – although it makes little distinc-

The Long Road To Mazatlàn
1999
triple DVD projection
color, sound
dimensions variable
18 min
installation views: Art Pace,
San Antonio, Texas, 2000
courtesy Victoria Miro Gallery,
London

tion between actions and interior imaginings, and doesn't so much tell a story as shuffle its components: the preexisting genres, images, and character typos of white American culture. That CinemaScope-like opening shot, says Julien, is "very Sergio Leone – I wanted you to feel you were at the movies."1 The two men dress as cowboys, and one wears white, the other black, a classic trope of the Western. But Julien and de Frutos are also interested in more recent cowboy imagery, particularly in gay culture of recent decades – so that a scene in a theater-like cattle-auction hall is inspired by Andy Warhol's *Lonesome Cowboys* (1968). And, just as in *Looking for Langston* (1989) Julien remembered the photographs of Robert Mapplethorpe, George Platt Lynes, and James van der Zee, here the paintings of David Hockney inform scenes at an outdoor pool. In fact the whole work has a lush visual texture that Julien calls "painterly."

The video's most explicit quotation is from Martin Scorsese's *Taxi Driver* (1976), where Robert De Niro asks the mirror, "Are you talking to me?" Julien's man in black plays more goofily with the same moves, but asks a different question: "Are you looking at me?" *The Long Road to Mazatlàn* is intensely sensitized to the act of looking – to people watching each other, or watching movies. What interested Julien about the auction hall, for example, was its resemblance to the panopticon, the prison architecture that Michel Foucault describes as a space "observed at every point,

in which individuals are inserted in a fixed place, in which all events are recorded, in which power is exercised without division, [...] in which each individual is constantly located, examined and distributed among the living beings."2

It is a bleak view of human experience, and in fact the title of *The Long Road to Mazatlàn*, a quotation from Tennessee Williams's *Night of the Iguana*, signifies for Julien and de Frutos an end of the road, a place of no return. As the video closes, the two men perform a jerky, abortive roadside dance – "movements of repression," says Julien, "movements of discombobulated desire." This, apparently, is how desire surfaces when it is relatively unmediated by a borrowed persona, for *The Long Road to Mazatlàn* suggests that we fulfill our desires by mimicking or performing stock roles from the cultural archive available to us. Yet this is less tragic than simply true: the stereotype is intricately embedded in the psyche. "It's the stereotype we find engaging," says Julien, "we depend on it. We're not always undone by stereotypes – in some ways they sustain us."

David Frankel

Reprinted with permission of [ArtPace] A Foundation for Contemporary Art and the author.

1 All quotations of Isaac Julien are from conversations with the author in December 1999.

2 Michel Foucault, *Discipline and Punishment*, Pantheon Books, New York, 1977, p.137.

"O Open this day
with the Conch's moan
Omeros as you did in my boyhood, when I was a noun
gently exhaled from the palate of the sunrise."[1]

There exist countless theories of globalization, but the ways in which these historical processes affect the psyche of imagination are less explored. This film, sardonically titled *Paradise Omeros*, tries to reveal the poetic structures of a feeling of a certain kind of "creoleness," to transfigure the historical processes of globalization onto the personal sphere, where they come to inhabit the imagination and the body of the postcolonial subject.

Paradise Omeros is a three-screen film installation that tours the spaces of two island cultures — England and St. Lucia. The camerawork is architectonic, making use of the sculptural potential of cinematic space in three-dimensional shots. Images are slowed down, film doubled into itself, fragmented, and juxtaposed with a portion of itself, or collated as a whole on the three screens. Mirror images are created simultaneously, yet one image subtly lags behind

the other, reiterating time. Converging and diverging images move in and out of one another, sometimes deteriorating at the edges and disappearing, into the recess of the hinge in the middle of the screen, creating a vertiginous motion.

There is still something of a paradise in remembering, no matter how traumatized or brutalized the memory. There are moments of deep, incomprehensible, symbolic scarring, and yet memory, as with dreams, has a way of translating those moments into moments of a kind of awareness.

Art must, I believe, begin with — or in my case, make a return to — the personal as a symbolic "archive." *Paradise Omeros* enacts such a return, as a visual odyssey enriched by semi-autobiographical incidents of childhood and drawing on the knowledge and experience of the displacement, trauma and alienation of the diasporic subject. It is a film about the legacies

1 Derek Walcott, *Omeros*, 1990.

Paradise Omeros
2002
triple-DVD projection
16mm film transferred to DVD
color, sound
20:29 min
installation views
courtesy the artist;
Victoria Miro Gallery, London

of globalization, if you like, told in images, stories, and sounds. For global capitalism, among its many other effects, has meant that my parents emigrated from St. Lucia and came to England, leaving behind their land, their culture, and their language – almost.

The film sees paradise from the perspective of a teenage boy, but at the same time contains an adult re-reading of postcolonial and oedipal relations enacted by the father, the tourist, and the son characters. This doubled point of view both prepares the spectator for a kind of loss of innocence and explores the ambivalent position that the black European subject occupies in the West. In the sequences of the film set on the other paradise island, England, the home of the Milky Bar Kid, we witness the uneasy hybridity of former colonial subjects and their offspring growing up in what was once the "motherland." Here, in the urban London landscape, our protagonist experiences scenes of enjoyment and violent anguish, and racial tensions oscillating between xenophilia and xenophobia. This is the same fraught ambivalence that marks the tourist's lecture at the start of the film, told from the other side of the Sea of History, in St. Lucia. Quoting Robert Mitchum's character in Charles Laughton's *The Night of the Hunter*, the tourist instructs the boy on the dynamics of love and hate: words tattooed on his outstretched fists.

Recalling Derek Walcott's epic poem, *Omeros*, the film returns to the Caribbean as a mythic site of cultural fantasy. Thus, one of the principal actions of the film is the submerging of the boy in the sea. Archive footage appears at moments of submersion, as historical images – of riots, emigration, colonial fairs, carnival, and from my own earlier works – aroused from the oceanic slumber of the Black Atlantic. These sections establish the third space of the film, which acts as a significant counterpoint to, and extension of, the central narrative. This space is represented by the intervals of pixelated black screens out of and into which archival images (dis)appear, and the black-noise soundscape that accompanies these images. This black does not suggest emptiness or absence but, on the contrary, represents a space that embraces all the images and sounds of the piece. This space opens another place, another paradise: the paradise of imagination, of memory, of the self.

"Because this is the Atlantic now, this great design of triangular trade. Achilles saw the ghost of his father's face shoot up at the end of the line. Achilles stared, in pious horror at the bound canvas and could not look away, or loosen its burial knots. Then, for the first time, he asked himself, who he was." [2]

Isaac Julien

First published in *Documenta 11 / Platform 5: Exhibition*, exhib. cat., Hatje Cantz, Ostfildern-Ruit, 2002, n. p.

2 Derek Walcott, *Omeros*, 1990.

Jordan Crandall
Drive

1998–2000
7-track video installation

Track 1: rhythm, movement, machine
Track 2: database
Track 3: compulsion, registration
Track 4: matrix (father, child, witness)
Track 5: body, vehicle, heat
Track 6: projectile, gaze
Track 7: analyse, violate, protect

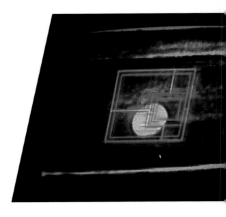

"Do you like this existence, Andy?"
"Oh, sure. It's wonderful. I **like** being a machine. It's what I always **wanted** to be. You see, I used to carry a camera with me everywhere I went. Now my eyes are cameras, recording all they see. I don't **need** tape recorders any more — I am a tape recorder. This is **heaven**."[1]

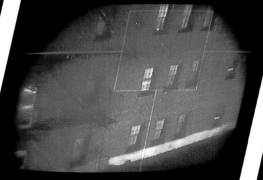
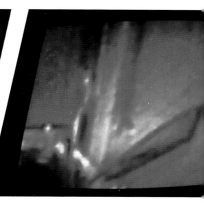

top row
Drive
screenshots
© Jordan Crandall
photos © Juliana Sohn

left page
installation view: Neue Galerie
am Landesmuseum Johanneum,
Graz, 2000
© Jordan Crandall
photo © Wolfgang Croce; courtesy Neue Galerie am Landesmuseum Johanneum, Graz

top row and left page
Drive
1998–2000
Track 3
(compulsion/registration)
single-projection video
installation
16mm film, satellite-derived
photography, digital video from
wearable DVcam, Hi-8 video,
Hi-8 video with monocular night
vision attachment, computer
animations
transferred to DVD
color, two-channel sound
22:30 min per rotation

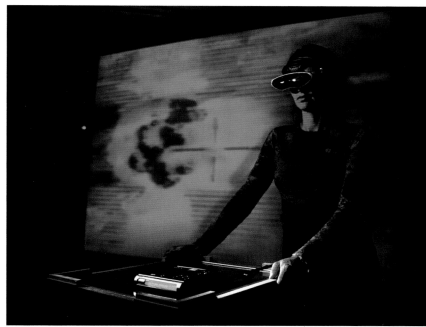

Drive
1998–2000
Track 5
(body/vehicle/heat)
two-part video installation for
portable DVD players
infrared thermal-imaging
camera, Hi-8 video
transferred to DVD
variable rotation times
installation view: Neue Galerie
am Landesmuseum Johanneum,
Graz, 2000
© Jordan Crandall
photo © Wolfgang Croce; courtesy Neue Galerie am Landesmuseum Johanneum, Graz

Jordan Crandall's work *Drive* (1998–2000) consists of a series of seven films which, in terms of content, deal with the combination of traditional ways of seeing and new technological methods of image generation. Crandall has combined traditional cinematographic methods with military target-finding technology, tracking systems and pattern-recognition programs. *Drive. Track 6*, subtitled *projectile/gaze*, is powerfully visualized in two projections. One shows an extreme close-up of a man's face. The camera is directed towards his eye, yet his gaze keeps the penetrative intensity of the camera at bay. In slow motion we see how the eyelid slowly closes and opens again to renew contact with the observer. On the film projected opposite, we see found footage of military high-tech technology: radar and infrared shots, target lock-on systems, computer images that are specialized in locating, classifying and identifying moving war machines. The human gaze is contrasted with militarized visualization practices, and compared with a projectile.

Heatseeking (1999–2000) is, similar to *Drive*, composed as a seven-part series whose content also deals with how technology changes perception. *Heatseeking* was filmed in the border regions of San Diego and Tijuana and centers around the problems created by the border situation, the surveillance methods used there, and the definition of borders as frontiers. In *Heatseeking (Course Track)* two golf players meet to tee off on the golf course at night. Alone in the darkness they play their game observed by a camera with night-vision technology. In this strange scenery, the camera alternates between the tension-filled game between the two players and the golf course's expanse. Camera shots of the golf players in this location alternate with shots from

surveillance cameras and computer-controlled search programs, which makes the two protagonists appear as if they are in the system's target-finding zone. Quite unexpectedly, one of the players hits his opponent with his golf club — a fight ensues, they roll around on the ground while the camera attempts to follow them. Almost imperceptibly, aggression switches over into ambivalent eroticism. The video ends abruptly in a sequence of quick film cuts and breaks that looks as if the film has ripped. Crandall has perfected the use of a broad range of film methods in *Heatseeking*. With rapidly changing camera angles, black-and-white and color changes, and the use of various levels of media, the observer is confronted with a flood of images which he is hard put to process. The soundtrack heightens the surreality of the night-time golf course scene – in place of the expected swish of flying golf balls Crandall has used sound material from weapons in action, underlying the latent aggressive undertones.

In both videos, we are confronted with the military's "strategic view" and an increasing militarization of the human gaze. The military visualization images used by Crandall are those with which we are all familiar from the media coverage of modern wars.

1 Andy Warhol as a cartoon figure in the *Miracleman* comic. Neil Gaiman and Mark Buckingham, *Miracleman*, 19, Eclipse Comics, 1991, quoted after Scott Bukatman, *Terminal Identity. The virtual subject in postmodern science fiction*, Duke University Press, Durham and London, 1993, p. 328.

top left
Drive
1998–2000
Track 3
(compulsion/registration)
single-projection video
installation
installation view: Neue Galerie
am Landesmuseum Johanneum,
Graz, 2000
© Jordan Crandall
photo © Wolfgang Croce;
courtesy Neue Galerie am
Landesmuseum Johanneum,
Graz

top right
Drive
1998–2000
Track 4 (matrix:
father/child/witness)
dual-projection
video installation
16mm film from hand-cranked
camera, Hi-8 video,
surveillance-camera footage,
digital video from wearable
DVcam transferred to DVD
color, two-channel sound
approx. 8 min per rotation
installation view: Neue Galerie
am Landesmuseum Johanneum,
Graz, 2000
© Jordan Crandall
photo © Wolfgang Croce;
courtesy Neue Galerie am
Landesmuseum Johanneum,
Graz

2 Vilém Flusser, "Bilderstatus,"
in *Metropolis. Internationale
Kunstausstellung,* exhib. cat.,
Christos M. Joachimides and
Norman Rosenthal (eds),
Berlin, Stuttgart, 1991, p. 51

3 Jordan Crandall, "Notes
for [!] Militarized Images,"
nettime-Mailinglist, 16 April
1999. http://www.desk.nl/
nettime~archive

4 Jordan Crandall,
quoted from http://www.
rhizome.org

5 Jonathan Crary, *Techniques
of the Observer: On Vision
and Modernity in the Nineteenth Century,* The MIT
Press, Cambridge, MA, 1990.

6 Jordan Crandall and
Lawrence Rinder, "Tran-
script of Presentation at
The Kitchen, New York,"
http://www.blast.org/cran-
dall/interviews/kitchen.html

A prominent example is the Gulf War which was followed on television worldwide and whose images of
military high-tech operations engraved themselves
in the minds of viewers. Indeed, devices which were
developed for military purposes have long since infil-
trated the civilian market and are in high demand.
Switching from normal image to infrared is now a
common feature of video cameras, and enjoys
ever-greater popularity.

The way we see is being altered by technical aids
– these ways of generating images are increasingly
defining our perception. Vilém Flusser describes the
apparatus way of viewing as such: "We see everything as if we were constantly looking through a
camera."2 Crandall himself speaks of "militarized
images."3 "Tracking, targeting and identifying formats begin to seep into the way we see, behave, and
desire. They enter into the very structure of perception. The camera marks the place of battle."4

Computers generate images, and learn to analyze
and interpret them. Computer pattern-recognition

image analysis describes a new kind of vision which
lies beyond the central perspective. The image is the
result of the process of data analysis. In his book
Techniques of the Observer, Jonathan Crary
describes the abstraction of the visual, the change
in our perception thanks to computer-controlled
viewing. He draws attention to the fact that new
image-production techniques will become dominant
visualization models.5

New technology influences not just our perception but also our physical being. Movement only
becomes legible once the underlying patterns have
been analyzed. In their studies on the human body,
Muybridge and Marey have made movement readable
by creating sequences. "In computerized tracking
and targeting systems, however, movement is indicated differently. It is represented by way of its
processing through databases. A new kind of moving
image results – these new images do not so much
represent movements as track them."6 Computer
technology records movements and analyzes them.

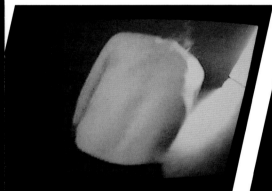

Drive
1998–2000
Track 4 (matrix:
father/child/witness)
dual-projection video
installation
screenshots
© Jordan Crandall
photos © Juliana Sohn

The film *Moving Image* is altered by recording movement. Movement is not presented but data-processed. In Crandall's work, real movement and computer representation are mixed and become congruent. Modern technology constructs the body of the viewer anew. "There is a kind of mutation of images that occur in this landscape, in that images become part of processing systems, parts of apparatus that 'see back' at us. It involves a kind of reversal of vision, displacing our location as privi-leged sites in the viewing exchange. We are seen, before we see. We are identified, before we identify. There are biometric systems, and other kinds of systems, which lock onto you, identify you through your behavior patterns or biological characteristics. It is a kind of switching of positions, and this is a very important change to think about."7

Translated from the German by Jeremy Gaines

7 Ibid.

Chris Hales
One-Person Touchscreen Cinema
Showing Fourteen Interactive Movies

1995–2002
digital video installation / metal stand, plain-glass touchscreen, various electronics / 200 x 150 x 150 cm

Fourteen Interactive Movies:

Jinxed!
Messed Up!
The Twelve Loveliest Things I Know
Lagan
Les Mystères du Chateau de D…
Sketchbook
Spring, Summer, Autumn, Winter
Len's Stories
Bliss
Grandad
Tallinn People's Orchestra
The Square
Kesä
Cycles

The installation contains a collection of several experimental interactive movies I made in the course of the past few years. They are live-action works in which the visual metaphors for interaction are inherent in the filmic material, instead of being added on in the form of graphic icons or complicated interface systems. That means the movies do not stray too far from recognizable modes of filmmaking, nor do they deconstruct or reinvent definitions of the word "film": The innovation is in the interaction as well as the type and structure of the story. Because the movies are conceived from a visual approach, they did not involve scriptwriting in its traditional sense. At the same time, ideas and content are more important than the technology, meaning the films were produced with inexpensive desktop equipment and are also deliverable on CD-ROM (whose viewers then use a mouse for interaction).
In addition, two films have been adapted to respond to shouts delivered into a microphone; they featured in the interactive-cinema performance *Cause and Effect*.

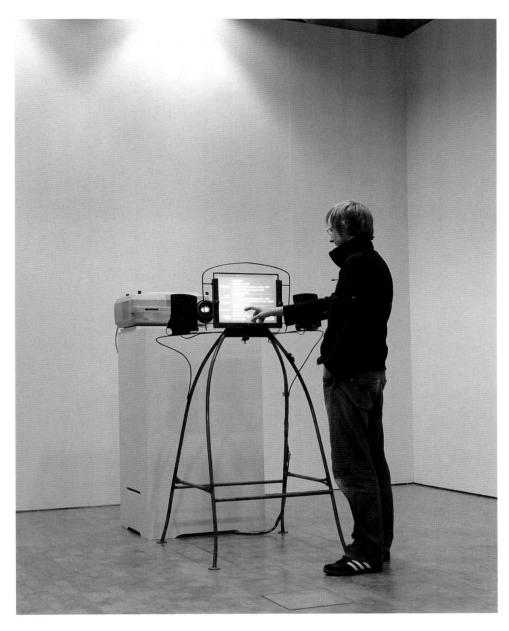

One-Person Touchscreen
Cinema Showing Fourteen
Interactive Movies
1995–2002
digital video installation
metal stand, plain-glass touchscreen, various electronics
200 x 150 x 150 cm
installation views: ZKM |
Center for Art and Media
Karlsruhe, 2002
© Chris Hales
photos © Franz Wamhof

First displayed at the ARTEC 95 in Nagoya, Japan, the touchscreen installation has since been set up in galleries from Australia to Iceland. As new movies are made, they are added to the roster of films available on the installation, which over the years is developing a well-worn rusty covering. The films can be selected on the touchscreen from a menu that divides the works into five different categories – Landscape, Spatial Navigation, Documentary, Multiscreen, Fictional Comedy – according to the main area of investigation of each film. (The categories are somewhat artificial, however, since many films cross several boundaries.)

Although Bertolt Brecht once accused cinema of being the "result of a production that took place in the absence of its audience," interactive movies require a special dynamic between filmmaker and audience. From cinema and television to computer screen or gallery: a variety of venues exist for watching films. Leaving aside the obvious issues of technical quality, even the most successful box-office hit seems to "lose something" when watched at home. There can be no doubt that the "theater" of presentation has an important bearing on how the audience approaches a piece. As I mentioned above, I have experimented not only with gallery exhibition but also with CD-ROM for home use as well as with theatrical interaction from larger audiences. Although others can watch on, only one viewer at a time can touch the screen: a drawback in an installation whose content-rich films have viewing time-frames anywhere between a whole evening and a few minutes.

Making a movie interactive raises important issues, and my films have set out to address some of them. A major element of my research is indeed to observe an audience interacting and observing my movies in the gallery situation. I try to conceal myself in the space and watch how viewers with dissimilar cultural and demographic backgrounds come to terms with what they are experiencing; if the situation allows, I document on video what is happening. In regard to the qualitative aspect, it is possible to compare the same movies under interaction from

Jinxed!
1998
interactive movie
screenshot
© Chris Hales

Messed Up!
1998
interactive movie
screenshot
© Chris Hales

different audiences of varying cultures, and on that basis seek consistencies and variances. Consistencies encourage me to re-deploy, over a feedback loop, the demonstrably effective features, and also to abandon techniques that are clearly confusing. The fact that I maintain the same technological level throughout the works in the installation makes the comparison fairer. Interaction is almost always pitched at a simple, intuitive level. Sometimes, for example, the viewer only needs to touch (or click) the right place at the right time; this process is sometimes described as spatio-temporal linking.

Jinxed! is a such a film. Its structure is simple to comprehend, and the results of interaction are immediate and visual. It is a drama-based slapstick comedy that suits the classical model of connecting video segments in a branching system, although ultimately it is episodic in that it has no beginning or end. The film invites us to battle against a protagonist who has a goal to meet, and we try to hinder him by selecting "jinxed" objects at the right moment. An element of game-play is included, but the main motivation is to achieve humorous and malicious satisfaction at the hero's misfortune. Interaction is simple: Parts of the house become "jinxed" hotspots for just two seconds, within which time the viewer must "click" on the spots in order to obstruct the protagonist's progress. In an alternative version not shown at "Future Cinema," the audience has to shout at the right moment in order to trigger the jinx. Although the movie is clearly set in a London apartment, there is little use of language and the comedy is visual; these culturally non-specific choices clearly helped to make this a popular work.

Messed Up was intended as a non-linear progression from *Jinxed!* (the order in which the audience can select objects is not fixed). A man is relaxing in a tidy apartment that the viewer can progressively mess up by clicking on particular items, much to the

annoyance of the protagonist, who will try to tidy things up again. In other words, the protagonist is programmed to fight back. Red frames indicate the sequences allowing interaction, but it is up to the viewer to discover which items can create a mess. Clicking on the wine bottle, for instance, causes the victim to inadvertently knock it over. The protagonist wants to chill out over a glass of wine and TV, whereas the viewer's object is to create havoc and disrupt his peaceful evening. The mess-making levels escalate until the victim is stripped to his underpants and his flat entirely trashed. As soon as there is a delay in interaction, however, he will begin restoring order and attempt to win back his composure.

In order to portray mood and atmosphere and to invite the viewer to "explore," two films combine fictional enactment with spatial navigation. *Lagan* uses a cyclical looping structure to examine the relationship between its two protagonists. With visual references to water throughout, it portrays a psychological and emotional drama between a reclusive girl and the spirit of her drowned lover. Time is frozen; there is no beginning or end, events recur. Fire and water become links between the two characters and their worlds of night and day. Focus and cinematic point-of-view are used as interaction metaphor: Certain items can be "clicked" when they are in focus (or, when the camera is moving, portrayed center-screen). The musical score plays permanently, but the acoustic volume changes according to our proximity to the protagonists. *Les Mystères du Chateau de D...* (inspired by the similarly titled Man Ray film) is a spatial exploration of a cliff-top castle and a portrait of its reclusive inhabitant. In terms of visual portrayal and subject matter, my film owes some debts both to documentary and drama. Although there is a "payoff" (we can disclose something of the protagonist's past), each part of the movie is in itself aesthetically and musi-

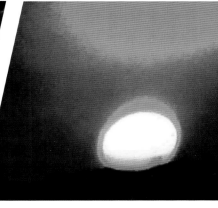

The Twelve Loveliest Things
I Know
1996
interactive movie
screenshot
© Chris Hales

Lagan
1996
interactive movie
screenshot
© Chris Hales

Sketchbook
1998
interactive movie
screenshot
© Chris Hales

cally pleasing. Every successful touch of the screen reveals more information, and brings about a progression from Raw Nature to Nature Tamed. An onionskin structure is used as a metaphor for "getting to know" a place or person. The art direction is such that key objects within the film are significant: Mirrors stretch backward through the narrative flow, whereas lights (lighthouse, candle, illuminated windows) take the viewer forward. By clicking on the protagonist (even when glimpsed only briefly), the viewer not only advances the plot, but is also rewarded with a display of a poetic verse. A limited number of interaction moments, which are cued by musical leitmotifs, are programmed.

Fictional movies have been a small part of my work so far. *The Twelve Loveliest Things I Know* is a personal documentary film based on research into the elementary things that children find fundamentally satisfying. Twelve areas of childhood recollections are accessible from a single, looped clip. The viewer can dip into and explore every area in a playful and reflective manner. The density of information – much of the piece consists of split screens – and the dynamic, colorful "hotspots" engage the viewer's concentration and produce a moving and immersive effect. The musical soundtrack changes according to the mood of a particular clip. Interaction in this movie is intuitive – generally in response to eye-catching moving or colorful items in the film. The targeted audience reaction is curiosity about, and emotional response to, subject matter, as well as a visual appreciation of the images and music. Feedback taught me that the movie's structure was a useful reference for viewer orientation, although the criticism was made that it was hard to work out what was happening in the structure and that some of the hotspots were very eclectic. However the main goal of producing an emotional and intense piece was achieved. (One viewer said, "I feel I can give

so much more to my son having seen your film.") The average viewer spent much time exploring the work which, although aimed squarely at adults, has also been popular with children, who try to find the "fun" moments. Although the film portrays an English childhood, it is underscored by a nostalgia and subject matter that have widened its international appeal.

A short work demonstrating my interest in the visual aspects of interaction is entitled *Sketchbook*, because it came about as a vehicle to try out certain ideas, just as a traditional artist might use a paper sketchbook. It was also an attempt to make something engaging simply by filming within a 100-meter radius in the countryside and thereby revealing an interactive world. In the film, nature sequences loop indefinitely until the viewer touches the interactive key point (which is, in most cases, instinctively obvious) and so triggers a denouement. In this version, the thirty different sketches are called up purely at random with no suggestion of sequence or narrative. It became clear from the sketches that the images of the dandelion being blown always produced a strong positive reaction, and therefore I developed a selection-menu movie that is composed of ten dandelions in a field and offers a choice among all my works.

Filmed on the Finnish island of Kemio in the summer of 2001, *Kesä* ("Summertime" in Finnish) is a narrative remake of *Sketchbook* and a first attempt at designing for the restrictions of broadband delivery with its maximum data-transmission rate of 500 Kbits/second. Whereas *Sketchbook* presents a collection of ideas in random order without narrative, *Kesä* presents forty-five scenes representing, in some sort of chronological order from dawn to dusk, a single day in the Finnish countryside. The scenes intercut between human life in and around a wooden house and the small dramas of nature occurring in

Kesä [Summertime]
2001
interactive movie
screenshot
© Chris Hales

Len's Stories
1999
interactive movie
screenshot
© Chris Hales

Grandad
1999
interactive movie
screenshot
© Chris Hales

the immediate environment. Every scene contains one hotspot that the viewer must locate before the scene can progress to its conclusion. Forty-three scenes complete the film's passage from morning to night.

Spring, summer, autumn, winter is an experiment in which the viewer, by interaction, can reconstruct the traces the filmmaker left in a landscape featured in his movie, and as such it plays with the concept of cinematic time. Four scenes are conceived as tableaux; every one is from a different season, and has its own "dramatic structure." By touching the screen in the right places at the right time and in the right order, it is possible to uncover the path I took when filming. There are no cues or visual clues to indicate where to touch (or click) – it is up to the viewer to explore. Every tableau has a conclusive "ending." Video footage of a gallery audience in Poland shows two ladies, neither of whom appears to know much about interactive art, coming to terms with how this piece works. Clearly demonstrated is the learning process by which the viewers begin to understand the visual language of the piece and step-by-step discover that touching the right places in the right order makes advancement possible, whereas failure to do so causes the footsteps to disappear one-by-one.

Len's Stories is a documentary video-portrait filmed in a single hour-and-a-half take, with sixty-five-year old Len Buck recounting twenty lengthy anecdotes from his life. Just as a narrator often needs prompting, Len often pauses to scratch his head, think, drink and so forth – and the viewer must touch the screen to persuade him to continue. Otherwise, he will branch off to a different anecdote. Red frames indicate that a sequence permits interaction and that a touch is needed to make Len continue telling the same story as opposed to a new one. With this movie, the viewer can click any part of the screen to prompt the narrator, and an alternative version also exists that responds to shouting.

Grandad, also a video-portrait, depicts the closed life of a retired elderly watchmaker who relies for company on the friendship of his aging dog Jack. This work investigates how in an interactive movie events in space can be mapped out in almost (but not completely) representational fashion by creating a cinematic space through the combination of separate, asynchronous moving-image streams ("split screening"). Because the streams are not permanently linked, every one can show autonomous behavior. These nine spaces from which Grandad can never break free represent the limited horizons of his life in a northern English mill town. At the beginning of the program, Grandad is cuddling his dog Jack, then sends him to his kennel. After Grandad falls asleep, the dog decides to run away. When the old man wakes up, he proceeds to look for his dog, but it always seems to manage to evade him. Because of the programmed behaviors in the film and its database of video scenes, this movie offers a spectacle that is (slightly) different every time.

The earlier work *Bliss* shares the same on-screen format as *Grandad* and was made as a contribution to an eponymous Arts Council of England-funded CD-ROM featuring different personal artistic expressions inspired by Katherine Mansfield's short story "Bliss." In this respect it is an enacted work of fiction. Nine movie streams are displayed simultaneously, and these conceptually represent nine blissful domestic scenes such as a baby at peace, a hot bath running, a gramophone playing. By skillful interaction within the individual scenes, it is possible to maintain a happy state of order. Every scene, however, has an alarming tendency to veer out of control if the viewer's attention and interaction begins to flag. The result is chaos and destruction: The baby starts to wail, the bath overflows, and the gramophone record starts scratching and breaking. Different screens are interconnected. For example, the overflowing bath-water shown in the top left corner drips onto the scene on the screen directly below it. To main-

Bliss
1998
interactive movie
screenshot
© Chris Hales

Tallinn People's Orchestra
1999
interactive movie
screenshot
© Chris Hales

The Square
1999
interactive movie
screenshot
© Chris Hales

tain order, the viewer can click different scenes – calm the baby, close the book, stop the dog, lift the iron, and so forth (whereby the central image is not interactive, it being a measure of the level of chaos). Again, although the domestic interior portrayed is 1920s middle-class England, the visual concepts behind the piece, in which there is no use of language, seem universally recognizable.

I shot *Cycles* in Copenhagen and Malmö in 2000 while IASPIS artist-in-residence based at the Interactive Institute in Malmö Högskolan, but only began to make progress on the authoring in late 2001. The present version is therefore for demonstration only. It was a thirdand final attempt to use the ninefold split-screen format, and actually consists of two almost completely distinct films, the only link being the boy in red on his bicycle, and the ferry connection shown at the bottom left corner of each film. The premise is that the boy can escape from the first Copenhagen film (by getting on the ferry) and meet the girl in Malmö in the second film. The humorous, gently paced films offer an aesthetically pleasing experience along with a portrayal of real-life locations. Due to the amount of computer-controlled behavior combined with random-choice generation, they are (like *Bliss* and *Grandad*) guaranteed to be different at every single viewing. The interactivity helps to keep the audience interested from two viewpoints: there is a goal to meet, and the variety of new scenes and incidents is potentially great.

Tallinn People's Orchestra likewise experiments with multiple video streams or, at least, non-synchronous multiple items controlled by both computer and user. The film shows activities in the main square in the old Estonian port of Tallinn. We see local residents going about their business, children playing, tourists, pony rides, car traffic. Thirty-seven different elements of the scene have been isolated and individually assigned a short musical "leitmotif." The computer chooses up to five elements at a time

to place in the empty square, which once again becomes animated with the people who were at the time of filming. Now, however, they appear in random order and are accompanied by a musical motif. The result is a kind of deconstructed jazz ballet based entirely upon real-life activity. This piece shows the beauty inherent in day-to-day activities, many of which are repetitive. The computer does the work of generating the Tallinn population – an aesthetic process that offers pleasure in its own right – but the audience can interact by clicking on any moving element on the screen. Doing so simply turns that element off, and enables new musical and visual combinations as well as, in some cases, the appearance of some larger characters who might otherwise not be able to be shown. Although a specific location is represented, the visual and musical aspects of this piece seem immediately understandable to all audiences I have observed, whether or not they fully appreciate the aesthetic behind it.

The Square is a non-fiction work based on activities in another town square (Gamla Stan in Stockholm). This complementary piece to *Tallinn People's Orchestra* likewise shows video footage of tourists and traffic, of local residents going about their business and children playing. However, interaction by the viewer does not remove the people from the town square, but recalls them to life, causes them to repeat the movement carried out when captured by the video camera. When the program starts, the square is devoid of major activity. By touching the screen, the viewer can find the "birthplaces" of the people there at the time of filming. After being brought back to life, they start to slowly fade away again. In this way, user interaction re-animates the deserted square until gradually the captured traces, like the echo of a memory, begin to vanish.

Chris Hales

Susan Norrie
Defile

2001
interactive DVD / published in (dis)LOCATIONS (ZKM digital arts edition, 2001)

Defile
2001
interactive DVD
screenshots
© Susan Norrie

In slow-mo a person wearing protective clothing and a gas mask glues plastic foil over the window panes. The sound of birds twittering still to be heard outside wanes, as the outer world is gradually blotted out by the ever darker window. Colors are reduced to a minimum, and the dirty brown tones predominate in the picture. Our gaze is directed to a series of cartons, we hear children's voices, and associations and questions come to mind – what do the cartons conceal?

In her film *Defile* (2001), Susan Norrie underscores the trends in society today whereby we endanger our own existence by environmental disasters and nuclear contamination. Alluding to Chernobyl and pollution of the oceans by oil tanker spillages, she presents several sequences showing the possible results of such occurrences. We are confronted with dead birds smeared in oil and efforts to save surviving animals. The soundtrack intensifies the impact of such disquieting images. We hear the echo of children laughing as well as purportedly relaxing music. The mood is uncanny. Norrie focuses on contamination with regard to the thorny question of how we should responsibly approach technology and science given the fact that they often have consequences that we cannot foresee in advance.

In the 1970s Susan Norrie dedicated herself primarily to painting, and her feeling for form and arrangement as evidenced so atmospherically with painterly ease in the scenes *Defile* attest to this early preoccupation. Over the last decade she has increasingly incorporated media such as painting, film, video and sculptural elements into her art. In this context, Norrie repeatedly quotes from movies and is today working on interactive forms of cinema.

Defile is filmed as a loop. DVD as a medium enables the viewer to combine the sequences at will and in the final instance we can act as our own editors here. Instead of a linear storyline emerging, we can manufacture our own multi-dimensional narration.

Dominika Szope
Translated from the German by Jeremy Gaines

Gary Hill
Language Willing

2002 / DVD installation / 20:10 min

Language Willing
2002
DVD installation
20:10 min
installation view: ZKM |
Center for Art and Media
Karlsruhe, 2002
© Gary Hill, courtesy Donald
Young Gallery, Chicago
photo © Franz Wamhof

In Situ
1986
mixed-media installation
dimensions variable
installation view: Donald Young
Gallery, Chicago
© Gary Hill
photo courtesy Donald Young
Gallery, Chicago

"I must become a warrior of self-consciousness and move my body to move my mind to move the words to move my mouth to spin the spur of the moment. — Imagining the brain closer than the eyes."[1]

Imagining the Brain Closer Than the Eyes

In classical cinema as well as television, the viewer is enticed into passive reception in front of a screen by the illusory world of the film or the seductive power of the images. Gary Hill is aware of the seductive quality of these mediated images. He works with the medium of video since, in his opinion, in contrast to film it is suitable for thematizing the process of perception itself. For him, video is not so much a media for recording what is being seen, but rather a mode for making time experienceable and for exposing the cognition process. "Time, this is what is central to video, it is not seeing as its etymological roots imply. Video's intrinsic principal is feedback."[2] The cognitive process itself, the possibility of "thinking out loud" is what Hill is interested in. In his works he is concerned with questions about the emergence of perceptions as well as the process of perception itself. He wants to thematize perception as active observation, free viewers from their passive role and set a process of thinking into motion. "I think the most difficult aspect of using video in an installation is decentralizing the focus on the television object itself and its never-ending image. How does one get away from that everyday seduction of the continuous flow of images couched as information."[3]

The meaning of images and our understanding of them are his central questions. *I Believe It Is an Image in Light of the Other* — with this title, Hill addresses an ambivalence, both an optimism and a skepticism about the images present in his work as categories.[4] We live with images and we cannot live without images. The processes which lead to understanding images are essential for Hill, and video, for him, offers a way of investigating them. He tries to make the experience of knowledge processes itself experienceable. He explains, "I am working within a different domain of narrative having more to do with a kind of meta-narrative; the works evolve from a self-reflexive practice that includes me as author/performer in the mise-en-scène. Rather than characters and locations, whether or not they exist literally, my subjects are more akin to entropy, memory, consciousness and death. This other narrative brings about a web of interrelated questions which again I feel are strongly embedded in time. Once a word is spoken or a word is read (or an image is 'read') time becomes an element in which the viewer 'narrates' experience. Even cognition becomes part of the narrative scheme."[5]

Hill thematizes his understanding of video as a reflective medium in contrast to television in his work

1 Gary Hill in *Gary Hill. Arbeit am Video*, Theodora Vischer (ed.), Museum für Gegenwartskunst Basel, Ostfildern, Cantz, 1995, back cover.

2 Gary Hill, "Inter-view," in *Gary Hill*, exhib. cat., Stedelijk Museum Amsterdam and Kunsthalle Wien, 1993, p. 13.

3 Gary Hill, "Inter-view," op. cit., p. 16.

4 Gary Hill in *Gary Hill. I Believe It Is an Image*, video directed by Maria Anna Tappeiner; Reinhard Wulf, © Westdeutscher Rundfunk, 2001.

5 Gary Hill, "Inter-view," op. cit., pp. 14–15.

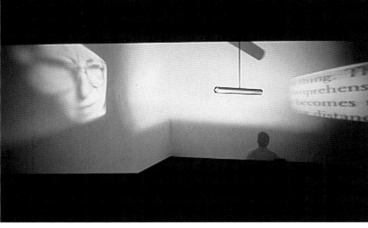

*I Believe It Is an Image
in Light of the Other*
1991–1992
mixed-media installation
dimensions variable
installation view: Donald Young
Gallery, Chicago
© Gary Hill
photo courtesy Donald Young
Gallery, Chicago

*Beacon
(Two Versions of the Imaginary)*
1990
two-channel video-and-sound
installation
dimensions variable
installation view: Donald Young
Gallery, Chicago
© Gary Hill
photo © Carl de Keyzer;
courtesy Donald Young Gallery,
Chicago

In Situ (1986). The significance of television and its control over the viewer who becomes a passive recipient is the subject of this work. The installation is reminiscent of a living-room situation. A comfortable armchair in front of a television set, the world of flickering images forms the centerpiece. To be seen are television clips of the Iran-Contra affair combined with personal clips from Hill. In the corners of the room stand four fans which switch on and off in a regular rhythm. From the ceiling, photocopier print-outs of images previously displayed on the television set flutter to the floor. The air circulation generated by the fans causes the papers to be distributed throughout the entire room. The copies show stills of the images already seen, freeze and thus recollect moments of what has been seen.

Hill describes his strategies for keeping the viewer in a state of attentiveness as follows, "Television is like an image made of light. It has an incredible power of attraction. [...] In order to bring the viewer away from this passive fixation, I switch the image on and off, or move it around in a circle. In this way, this isolated focal point of a single image is put out of action. The same thing holds for the projections which become focused and out-of-focus and which cannot be fixated. The fixation of an image suddenly becomes the subject and the significance of the individual image is undermined."[6]

Image and Language

"And yet, although my art is based on images, I am very much involved in the undermining of those images through language."[7]

In the work, *I Believe It Is an Image in Light of the Other* (1991–1992), images are projected onto the pages of open books. The texts of the books are all fragments from the second part of Maurice Blanchot's *The Last Man*. The projected images show faces, body fragments, a chair and text which overlaps the text in the books. Other works such as *Why Do Things Get in a Muddle (Come on Petunia)*, are based on a text by

Gregory Bateson. In the video recording, the text was spoken backwards and only by reversing the playback does the backwards spoken text again become understandable, although with a pronounced alienation effect. The viewer's attention is guided to the production of the text, the concentrated speaking, and thus to the act of speaking and not to the text's content. "Hill proposes that only in the perpetual breaking down of meaning can new and transient meanings be seen to emerge; that the moment of revelation is also inevitably the moment of catastrophe."[8]

The construction of reality takes place not only through images but above all through language. Perception of the world is always tied to the human body. In this connection, Hill is interested in language not so much as a means of communication, but rather as the generation or formation of language in the body, as a bodily production of language and its function. Speaking is first of all an activation of the tools of vocalization. His basic material are his own texts or the texts of other authors such as Martin Heidegger (*Red Technology*, 1994), Ludwig Wittgenstein (*Remarks on Color*, 1994) and Maurice Blanchot, whose works have an important significance for him. Many of Hill's works are concerned with the meaning of sound in relation to an image. In the work *Beacon (Two Versions of the Imaginary)* from 1990, Hill places the fascination of the images in an ambivalent relationship to spoken language. "The irony in his work is derived from the potential threat of the erasure of language within the very technologies he employs in his art-making; his aesthetic investigations are based on a philosophy of language and expression that seeks to re-code technology through a logos of a poetic language of imagery."[9] Excerpts from the articles *Essential Solitude* and *Two Versions of the Imaginary* by Maurice Blanchot in turn serve as the initial material for the spoken text, an essay about the fascination of images. There are two projected images on opposite walls from a cylinder mounted beneath the ceiling in the middle of a room. By turning the cylinder, the pro-

6 Catherine Hürzeler, "Kann man auf abstrakte Weise surfen? Ein Gespräch mit dem Videokünstler Gary Hill," in *Kunstbulletin*, no. 9, 1997, p. 13.

7 Gary Hill, "Inter-view," in op. cit., p. 14.

8 Greg Hilty, "Thrown Voices," in *Doubletake.Collective Memory & Current Art*, Marianne Ryan (ed.), The South Bank Centre, London, 1992, p. 19.

9 John G. Hanhardt, "Between Language and the Moving Image: The Art of Gary Hill," in *Gary Hill*, Henry Art Gallery, University of Washington, Seattle, 1994, p. 61.

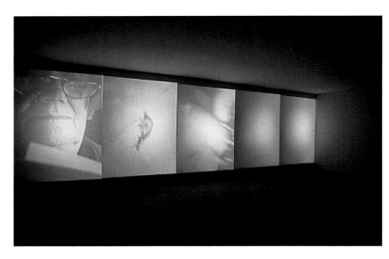

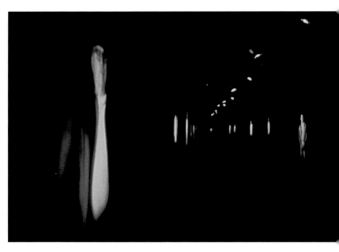

Circular Breathing
1994
single-channel video-and-sound
installation
dimensions variable
installation view: Donald Young
Gallery, Chicago
© Gary Hill
photo © Adriano A. Biondo;
courtesy Donald Young Gallery,
Chicago

Tall Ships
1992
sixteen-channel vide[o]
installation
dimensions variable
installation view: Don[ald]
Gallery, Chicago
© Gary Hill
photo © Dirk Bleicke[r]
Donald Young Gallery

jections wander over the walls of the room. The two images can never be perceived simultaneously since the projections are always precisely diametrically opposed. In an allusion to Homer's *Odyssey*, Hill describes the interplay of language and image/light which leads to consciousness. "It is perhaps not only the song of the sirens but ironically the enchanting light of the beacon that seduces and leads to shipwreck for consciousness."[10] In *Beacon*, the source of light and the image become a unity.

Making seeing more difficult

"[T]ime and metaphorical spaces for texts [and subjects] to unfold are the parameters I begin with … It's kind of telescopic time that makes the viewer aware of the process of seeing – of beholding the world through sight that exists in the folds of time."[11]

In a series of works which he calls "switch pieces," Hill becomes involved with the structural element of time in video and filmic perception. The connection between perception, consciousness and memory is visualized. It is not so much what is recalled that is relevant, but time as a process.[12] Images are dissolved in the flickering of images and their perception as individual images is made more difficult by a very fast sequencing of the images. They are structured in a non-linearly organized temporality.

In his article, *Presubjective Agency: Outside Identity*, Robert Mittenthal draws attention to the fact that the "switch pieces" resemble devices from the pre-cinematographic era such as the thaumascope and the praxinoscope in which images are perceived as moving pictures due to the eye's slowness when individual photographs are flicked through or turned rapidly.[13] The result of the flickering image cycles in Hill's "switch pieces," however, is completely different because Hill does not want to visualize a continuous

sequence of images but rather, on the contrary, break down the classic cycle of images by breaking up the narrative structure. One of the first works in this series is *Suspension of Disbelief (for Marine)* from 1992. In a long series of monitors, images of two human bodies, one female and one male, flicker over the apparatuses. The bodies are superimposed over each other and drift apart once again. The body becomes a virtual panorama. In the arrangement of the images and sequences, Hill seems to refer to the structural principle of the television cathode-ray tube which enables the construction of the image by means of so-called scan lines whose sequence is so fast that it cannot be perceived by the human eye.[14]

In *Circular Breathing* (1994), images from diverse provenance are projected onto five large screens from left to right — a ship on the open sea, the interior of a mosque, street scenes, people in everyday situations, and so on. The projections are joined continuously to one another and take up the entire wall. The first image glides out of the right-hand corner and occupies the first screen. It begins to flicker when the second image is added. The first image wanders to the second screen and the next image starts to be superimposed over the second. The flickering becomes more pronounced. It comes about because all the images are fed in from the same source. Only one image can be switched on at a given time so that the existing images have to share the time. With the number of images, the intensity of the flickering increases. Once the images arrive at the right-hand edge of the screens, they gradually disappear again. In this way, the flickering becomes slower until only the last image is to be seen on the screen to the far right, which slowly glides out of the picture frame. Then the cycle begins once again. The appearance of images is identified with breathing in and out; images are virtually panted out by breathing.

10 Gary Hill in *Energieen*, Luciano Fabro, Wim A Beeren (eds), Stedelijk Museum, Amsterdam, 1990, p. 103.

11 Gary Hill, "Interviewed Interview," in *Gary Hill*, IVAM – Institut valencia d'art modern, Centre del Carme, Valenica, 1993, p.152, cited after Lynne Cooke: "Postscript: re-embodiments in alterspace," in *Gary Hill*, Henry Art Gallery, University of Washington, Seattle 1994, p. 82.

12 "Correct me if I'm wrong here, but the way you refer to memory seems weighted towards the process: the time of memory rather than what is remembered." Gary Hill, "Between 1 & 0," in *Gary Hill*, Stedelijk Museum Amsterdam and Kunsthalle Wien 1993, p. 13.

13 Robert Mittenthal, "Presubjective Agency: Outside Identity," in *Gary Hill, Midnight Crossing*, Heinz Liesbrock (ed.), Westfälischer Kunstverein, Münster, 1997, p. 17.

14 See also Peter Weibel in the exhibition brochure "Der anagrammatische Körper. Der Körper und seine mediale Konstruktion," ZKM | Center for Art and Media Karlsruhe, 2000, p. 10.

Withershins
1995
interactive sound installation
with two video projections
dimensions variable
installation view: Donald Young
Gallery, Chicago
© Gary Hill
photo © Gary McKinnis;
courtesy Donald Young Gallery,
Chicago

Viewer
1996
five-channel video installation
five video projectors,
five laserdisc players,
five-channel synchronizer
dimensions variable
video still
© Gary Hill
courtesy Donald Young Gallery,
Chicago

The title refers to this. "This visual and aural circuit evokes the action of breathing, and in particular the technique used by jazz musicians, in which a long outward breath is used to sustain the trajectory of a note while the musician inhales."[15] In *Circular Breathing*, Hill not only engages with the understanding of time, but through the mechanical sequence, the halving of time by each added image makes time visually legible for the viewer.

Interaction

"Video embodies a reflexive space of difference through the simultaneous production of presence and distance."[16]
Some works challenge the viewer to participate actively in a broader sense by being themselves designed in a reactive or responsive way. In *Tall Ships* (1992), consisting of sixteen black-and-white projections, the viewer enters a long narrow corridor. To the left and right there is a series of projections of people of various ages and differing backgrounds and descent which finishes at the end of the corridor with the projection of a child. In the room's darkness, the projections are themselves simultaneously images and light source. Lynne Cooke draws attention to the fact that the coincidence of light source, light and representation reinforces the effect of embodying

the figures in real space.[17] With their thoroughly strong presence, the projected persons draw the viewer under their spell. In passing through the corridor, the viewers trigger reactions from their virtual counterparts by means of sensors. If the viewer stands directly in front of a figure, it suddenly approaches and then remains standing in full life-size in front of him or her before turning away once again. Sometimes the reaction is coupled to the viewer's movement itself. If the viewer goes on to the next projection, the figure turns away and returns to its original location, but sometimes the virtual figure is itself the active part which withdraws once again quite quickly and leaves the viewer standing there waiting. By means of the confrontation with a virtual counterpart, the question concerning one's own identity is raised. Hill puts it this way, "It's simply the idea of a person coming up to you and asking, 'who are you?' by kind of mirroring you and at the same time illuminating a space of possibility for that very question to arise."[18]

In *Viewer* (1996), a huge image is created by five video projectors which shows a series of seventeen workers larger than life. Like *Tall Ships*, this work too does not have sound. The people in the video projections do not talk to each other and also make no contact with each other, but direct their gaze steadily at

15 Chrissie Iles, "The Metaphysician of Media," in *Gary Hill: Selected Works*, Catalogue Raisonné, Kunstmuseum Wolfsburg, DuMont, Köln, 2002, p. 27.

16 Gary Hill, "Inter-view," op. cit., p. 14.

17 "Whereas this might normally imperil the proximity of the image as it became absorbed into a continuous linear matrix, the fact that in this installation the projections are the sole source of light imbues them with an unexpected effect of embodiment in real space," Lynne Cooke, "Postscript: re-embodiments in alter-space," in *Gary Hill*, Henry Art Gallery, University of Washington, Seattle, 1994, p. 85.

18 Gary Hill, "Inter-view," op. cit., p. 17.

the viewer outside their reality. Seeing and being seen is made the subject in an elementary way.

In the 1995 work *Withershins* too, Hill employed the possibility of direct interaction with the viewer. Sensors in the floor trigger spoken passages of a text when walking through a labyrinth. With the aid of a tracking system, two viewer positions can be evaluated, that is to say: two texts can be generated simultaneously, hinting at the possibility of an exchange between the users.

Out of the Dark

"If I have a position, it's to question the privileged place that image, and for that matter sight, hold in our consciousness."[19]

In *Reflex Chamber* (1996), there is a video projection on a table in a room which is otherwise completely dark. Hill relates in a video interview that he wants to visualize a spiritualist session, a seance about an image. Over a large mirror mounted on the ceiling, a video image is projected onto the table. The image can only ever be seen for a few seconds before it is extinguished by a stark stroboscopic light. Language is deployed in these moments. Only individual syllables can be heard, separated from each other by the strobe light. Image and text alternate with each other. The room radiates glaring light for a few seconds, pointing out their own presence to each of the viewers in the room. Each viewer is suddenly exposed to the light and immediately thereafter everything disappears once again in the darkness. What remains is the after-image of what has just been seen. Hill recounts that in this work he was particularly interested in creating a new meta-medium composed of image, language and light which makes a new texture. The corporeality of the light is supposed to be worked out and virtually lift the image from the table. The title already refers to a place of reflection, of forming an after-image in thought. The projection on the table hints at a place of communication, of exchange. The viewer is stimulated to reflect about what has been seen, reinforced by the physical effects of the stroboscope, alternating between extreme darkness and glaring light.

But the use of strobe light is increased once more in *Midnight Crossing* (1997). When entering the room, the viewers first have to find their bearings in complete darkness. The dimensions cannot be estimated and only gradually can the video image on the screen be perceived with an increasing perception of depth. The viewers are forced to very precisely observe the emergence of the image in order to recognize its content. But suddenly a glaring strobe light wipes out the image on the screen. Only now do the viewers perceive the surrounding space and the blinding white screen in front of them. The screen is stretched over a metal frame reminiscent of projection screens at large drive-in movie theaters. The draping of the room with black cloth recalls the heavy cinema curtains which are drawn back to reveal the screen at the beginning of a film, thus enhancing the theatrical effect. In the moments of illumination, short fragments of a text are recited. The brightness of the glaringly illuminated room inscribes the image of the white screen on the retina. After each text sequence, the light switches off once again and the viewers find themselves in darkness once more. The video image which has been seen combines with the after-image of the empty screen. After-images and recollections of sequences of images which have already been seen commingle with the images which have just been projected. By means of deprivation techniques, viewers are put into a state of extreme attentiveness. They first have to orient themselves in the spaces in order to "be in the picture."

The place of the installation, or rather the non-place [20] has become an integral element of Hill's works. Already by means of the room's darkness, of entering a black box, viewers are sensitized and their attentiveness stimulated. The speed of the image sequences was already in earlier works a means for Hill to confuse visual perception and intensify attentiveness by means of impeded perception. By using strobe light, the viewers' ability to perceive is influenced to an extreme degree. The ecstatic experience of flashing strobe light stimulates the body's production of adrenaline and increases attentiveness by exciting the nerves to the extreme. "The impeding of our visual perception is a purgatory through which we have to move. From time to time, the stroboscopic flashes of light root us to the spot, blind us momentarily. They are, therefore, the spaces of a turn-around, of a reinstatement of the images and their multiple meanings."[21] In a world characterized by a flood of information, attentiveness has become a "scarce resource." [22] External stimuli have to be correspondingly great in order to draw the full attention of a viewer. The staging makes space itself "into a symbol for that 'place of images' which we ourselves are." [23]

Hill is concerned with questions of re-presence. The process of perception, the decoding or reading of a work is an integral component of his works. Feedback in video is exemplary for the cognitive process which Hill wants to set into motion. The technical feedback mechanism in video is identified with gaining knowledge by learning. Norbert Wiener described this, "Learning is essentially a form of feedback in which the behavioral schema is modified by previous experience. [...] Feedback is [...] a very general characteristic of forms of behavior."[24] Hill transforms techniques and situations of classical cinema experience into spaces which raise questions concerning the generating and processing of images. He sets a cognitive experiencing of images against the passive consumption of images.

Sabine Himmelsbach

Translated from the German by Michael Eldred,
artefact text & translation, Cologne

19   Gary Hill, "Interview with Stephen Sarrazin," in *Surfing the Medium*, Chimaera Monograph no. 10, Edition du Centre International de Création Vidéo Montbéliard, Belfort, 1992, p. 84.

20   Heinz Liesbrock, "Loss Illuminates. Midnight Crossing as an Approach to a Language of the Living and The Dead," in *Gary Hill, Midnight Crossing*, Heinz Liesbrock (ed.), Westfälischer Kunstverein, Münster, 1997, p. 100.

21   Gottfried Boehm, "Gary Hill – The Profundity of Images," in *Gary Hill: Selected Works*. Holger Broeker (ed.), Catalogue Raisonné, Kunstmuseum Wolfsburg, DuMont, Cologne, 2002, p. 14.

22   Georg Franck, *Ökonomie der Aufmerksamkeit*, Hanser, Munich/Vienna, 1998, p. 50.

23   Hans Belting, "Gary Hill und das Alphabet der Bilder," in *Gary Hill. Arbeit am Video*, Theodora Vischer (ed.), Museum für Gegenwartskunst Basel 1995, p. 64.

24   Norbert Wiener, *Mensch und Menschmaschine*, Metzler, Frankfurt/M., 1952, pp. 63 ff.

Midnight Crossing
1997
single-channel video-and-sound
installation
dimensions variable
installation view: Donald Young
Gallery, Chicago
© Gary Hill
photo © Miquel Bargalló;
courtesy Donald Young Gallery,
Chicago

Reflex Chamber
1996
single-channel video-and-sound
installation
dimensions variable
installation view: Donald Young
Gallery, Chicago
© Gary Hill
photo © Steve White; courtesy
Donald Young Gallery, Chicago

Neil Brown, Dennis Del Favero, Jeffrey Shaw, Peter Weibel
Interactive Narrative as a Multi-temporal Agency

Introduction

This paper introduces the concept of aesthetic transcription as a model for the production of interactive narrative within digital cinema. Aesthetic transcription refers to the cinematic capture and reconstruction of multimodal forms of information within virtual environments. The term cinematic as used in this essay refers to the domain of the moving image as it is currently under re-definition within new media technologies. Through means of an experimental design study entitled *T_Visionarium* that enables beholders to search and recombine televisual data, this paper explores the conduct of interactive narrative as a model of aesthetic transcription. The value of the study is set against the fact that while narrative is central to conventional cinema, emphasis upon simulation has caused the narrative potential of digital media to be overlooked.[1] This paper addresses the concern that it is limitations in narrative, as opposed to technical understanding, which have restricted the aesthetic development of digital cinema.[2] Through its focus on beholder-generated recomposition of time within virtual environments, the proposal builds on the authors' existing research into the multi-spatial character of interactive narrative in digital cinema. In particular it seeks evidence of the multi-temporal agency of interactive narrative as it is currently advanced within revisionist cinematic, critical realist and systems theory.[3]

Transcriptive narrative integrates the temporal agency of narrative with the inherently multi-modality of digital information. The study aims to test the simple proposition that interactive narrative occurs as a function of the transportation of multi-modal information across virtual time. In testing the transportation of information within virtual time, however, we anticipate evidence of a previously un-described multi-temporal outcome within narrative. In multi-temporal narrative, we argue, beholders not only re-compose complex information into temporal episodes, they simultaneously experience the unanticipated temporal consequences of these virtual episodes as real events. This emerging and looping intersection between virtual time and real time produces a mode of narrative that contrasts dramatically with the temporal sterility of the closed narrative menus typically found in computer games.

T-Visionarium proposes an experimental framework which allows the interactive transcription of televisual information as a form of recombinatory search. In particular, *T_Visionarium*:

— allows beholders to spatially navigate televisual broadcasts in real time and televisual database in virtual time within an immersive, interactive, multi-modal environment set within a dome (12 meters in diameter, 9 meters in height) made of inflatable fabric;

— provides for the beholder to originate unique performances within this dome by means of their interaction with a computer database containing over forty hours of pre-recorded cable television data streams which can be reprocessed and recombined by means of a touchscreen interface articulated to a head-mounted tracking system and tilt projection system that projects the televisual data onto the interior skin of the dome. The beholders, by shifting their heads, move the large projected viewing window across the interior surface so that the movement of the projection windows enables them to navigate between these multi-modal data streams;

— immerses the beholders in both virtual and real time modalities to explore the expressive potential of transcriptive, as opposed to conventional, interactive narrative.

The re-enactment of televisual information has the potential for allowing a multiplicity of significant differentiations or fissions to occur within the original data. The great mass of broadcast or recorded televisual information is already received indirectly by the beholder and sorted retrospectively in episodic memory. Television is encountered through techniques such as channel hopping, muting, and multi-screens, through multiple association in different contexts, or fragmented through time-delay and by report. Thus although television broadcasts may begin as purposeful artifacts, their meaning for the beholder is not exhausted by critical recovery of their producer's original intentions. Rather, their meaning is revitalized into temporal, directional, and irreversible narrations, transcribing the functions such information is felt to cause and can be shown to perform.[4]

In relation to the purposes of transcriptive narrative, Michel Serres argues: "We are dealing less with the story of how something came about than with the dramatization of a pre-existing forms."[5] Transcriptive narrative dramatizes the world instead of freezing it into schematic representations. Transcriptive narrative transforms the cinema into a kind of Platonic cave wall onto which beholders project, then respond, to the episodic shadows of their journey through cultural information. It is only insofar as digital technology accomplishes the awesome task of transporting multi-modal data within virtual time that the aesthetic potential of interactive narrative can be put to the test.

Background

The interactive architecture of digital technology provides a fresh opportunity for reformulating the role of narrative within cinema.[6] Current experimentation in interactive narrative is handicapped by under-theorization of the role of time and the significance of critical attribution in virtual environments.[7] We know, for instance, that digital architecture is multi-modal.[8] We also know that multi-modal artifacts are shaped by software rather than semi-

1 Jean Baudrillard, *The Transparency of Evil*, Verso, London, 1993; Jean-François Lyotard, "Idée d'un film souverain," in *Misère de la philosophie*, Galilée, Paris, 2000; Martin Rieser, Andrea Zapp, *New Screen Media: Cinema/Art/Narrative*, BFI Publishing, London, 2002.

2 Dennis Del Favero, "The reformulation of narrative within digital cinema as an integration of three forms of interactivity," with Ross Gibson, Ian Howard and Jeffrey Shaw, *ARC Discovery Project*, 2002.

3 Gilles Deleuze, *Negotiations 1972–1990*, Columbia University Press, New York, 1995; John Searle, *The Construction of Social Reality*, Penguin Books, Harmondsworth, 1995; Michel Serres, *The Birth of Physics*, Clinamen Press, Manchester, 2000.

4 Ilya Prigogine, *The End of Certainty: Time, Chaos and the New Laws of Nature*, The Free Press, New York, 1996, p. 27.

5 Serres, *The Birth of Physics*, op. cit., pp. 84–88.

6 Söke Dinkla, "The Art of Narrative – Towards the *Floating Work of Art*," in Rieser, Zapp (eds), op. cit., p. 34; John Dovey, "Notes Toward a Hypertextual Theory of Narrative," in Rieser/Zapp (eds), op. cit., p. 144.

7 Ralph Melcher, *Stations: Bill Viola*, Hatje Cantz, Ostfildern, 2000; Tony Dove, "The space between: telepresence, re-animation and the re-casting of the invisible," in Rieser/Zapp (eds), op. cit.

8 Peter Weibel, "Narrated Theory: Multiple projection and Multiple Narration," in Rieser, Zapp (eds), op. cit., p. 51.

otic codes.9 Software compresses information into virtually realizable and interpretatively thick units of meaning. Notwithstanding the use of digital animation in conventionally scripted cinema such as *Shrek,* which laboriously renders graphic images from scratch, or even in post-production enhancements such as *Waking Life,* the multi-modal information delivered to producers of digital cinema is already condensed into cultural tokens of text, sound and image at the point of contact. For this reason the metaphors of production in digital cinema borrow from images of montage, layering and re-assignment rather than from fabrication. The manipulation of culturally prefabricated information in digital media rehearses the longstanding artistic tradition of transcription.10 In this tradition the artist is presented with a body of meaningful informational resources or cultural goods which they reassemble in the process of creation. Thus, the roles of the artist and beholder in a transcriptive model of cinematic production are editorially intertwined.

In two important respects, however, the multi-modal information employed in digital forms of production asserts an independent agenda. In the first respect, the information rehearses the inbuilt user constraints or motives within the software. In the second respect, the software implicitly re-asserts its cultural intentions through the information it is designed to select. This study takes seriously the effect of this multi-modal agenda upon the production of interactive narrative. First, unlike literary narrative cinematic narrative is distinctively eventful. According to Deleuze, the two key variables in the formulation of cinematic narrative are duration and movement.11 Thus, even in conventional cinema the beholder's direct awareness of unfolding events is complicit in bringing the narrative to closure. When the opportunity to direct the duration and movement of information is also seized by the beholders, then following Deleuze they gain, in principle, possession of the tools necessary for the production of narrative. The beholder is able to effect the lines of narrative not only indirectly, by re-assigning the network of episodic linkages between the information, but also directly through reflexive exposure to the unprecedented aspect of these episodic networks as they unfold.12

However, the narrative reassignment of complex multi-modal information is only practical within the dialogic context of virtual environments. Only within the technical possibilities afforded by digital technology can the beholder, retaining the role of active spectator, assert autonomy over the temporal direction of the narrative. In this study, the recombinatory power of the digital software proposed in *T_Visionarium* allows televisual kinds of information to be analyzed and broken down into complex layers. It also enables beholders to reassign the connections among these layers by pleating and creasing their topology until they cascade into new episodes of autonomously unfolding events. The design of the recombinatory algorithms borrows from Manovich's concept of software behavior. The recombinatory software and its associated interfaces furnish the beholder with multiple entry and exit points to and from the information, as well as with the facility to rehearse this information as narrative content on the fly.13 Thus, the software interfaces in which the algorithms are deployed are engineered to capture existing televisual information in ways sufficiently sensitive to the nuances of its eventfulness for the beholder.14

Second, the imputational reasoning which guides the design and application of the transcriptive software in this study mirrors the social realism of John Searle.15 He argues that meanings are ascribed to cultural artifacts according to the functions their stakeholders agree upon them to perform. He cites money and calendrical time as instances of significant social artifacts existing only by virtue of the functions attributed to them. Insofar as functional properties can be ascribed, it follows that properties such as international currency-exchange rates are always open to re-ascription through the interaction of players. However, susceptibility to re-ascription does not necessarily render functional attributions relativistic, fickle or self-serving if, so Searle argues, ascriptions are authentically motivated by institutions of craft, knowledge, education and ideology.16 Neither does the process of ascription herald a descent into rational determinism. The ascription of felt changes in artistic function, for instance, although generated intuitively, may be attributed for very good emotional and aesthetic reasons.17 It is a critical role of the cinema in particular to act as an instrument in the aesthetic transcription of cultural information and to serve as an organ of cultural dissemination. We examine the proposition that beholder-driven narrative in digital cinema is poised to become a central agency in this important project.

Transcriptive narrative

This study establishes the first temporal theorization of interactive narrative. The interactive system it elaborates expresses a transcriptive framework naturally resonant with the digital. Transcriptive narrative is a recursive system made up of a large number of self-organizing and interdependent elements able to launch the beholder into richly textured engagements with cultural information. The form of these engagements is both ascriptive and episodic insofar as they allow the dramatization of freely available information into forms that are eventful and cinematic in character. The significance of transcriptive narrative is thus reinforced through the dramatized revivification of cultural information. As a technical and critical framework, transcriptive narrative is "ecologically" efficient. It recycles the abundance of readily available cultural information into significant multi-temporal episodes.

Although crucial to the artistic expansion of digital cinema the construct of narrative time in interactive narrative has remained, for a number of reasons, strikingly under-developed. First, because the multi-modal logic of interactive cinema is ill-defined and second, because multi-modal forms of digital interactivity are technically over-determined and fixated on the simulatory. The upshot is a domain that continues to elaborate its identity on a spatial, as opposed to a temporal plane severely limiting its aesthetic deployment as a cinematic medium. In short, the development of narrative in interactive cinema languishes both for want of integrated research in communications as much as technical infrastructure.

The ascriptive critique underpinning the concept of transcriptive narrative provides audiences with the opportunity to navigate through a body of cultural information in a way that is rich in aesthetic possibilities. Teamed up with new recursive software and playback search technology, the interactive production of cinematic information gives the beholder the means of investing salient social and cultural issues with added significance. *T_Visionarium* models a platform accessible to popular audiences which demonstrates audio-visual recording and presenta-

9 Lev Manovich, "Post-Media Aesthetics," in *disLOCATIONS,* Dennis Del Favero, Jeffrey Shaw (eds), ZKM | Center for Art and Media, Karlsruhe, Hatje Cantz, Ostfildern, 2001.

10 Peter Weibel, "Post-Gutenberg Narrations," in Del Favero/Shaw (eds), op. cit., p. 28.

11 Gilles Deleuze, *Negotiations 1972–1990*, Columbia University Press, New York, 1995, p. 59.

12 Arthur Danto, *Analytical Philosophy of Action*, Cambridge University Press, Cambridge, 1973, p. 117.

13 Manovich, "Post-Media Aesthetics," op. cit., p. 16.

14 Manovich, "Post-Media Aesthetics," op. cit., p. 17.

15 John Searle, *The Construction of Social Reality*, Penguin Books, Harmondsworth, 1995.

16 Searle, op. cit., p. 15; Weibel, "Post-Gutenberg Narrations," op. cit., p. 35; Neil Brown, "The imputation of authenticity in the assessment of student performances in art," in *Educational Philosophy and Theory*, vol. 33, no. 3–4, p. 313.

17 Pierre Bourdieu, *Outline of a Theory of Practice*, Cambridge University Press, Cambridge, 1982, pp. 163–167.

tion technology specifically designed to accommodate singular, irreversible, and recombinatory narratives that, unlike video games, do more than rehearse a predetermined set of permutations. As a prototype for new forms of digital cinema and cultural communication, the study provides an opportunity for major commercial and artistic applications to harness interactive narrative as a powerful communicative tool, thus opening up a narrative genre equivalent in reach to that currently exercised within conventional cinema.

Multi-temporality

This study formulates a multi-temporal, anti-representationalist identity for interactive narrative. Insofar as it eliminates a significant impediment to the design of interactive content and software in new media, the study is an important advance in the field. The study takes a novel approach to the theorization of content within digital media, which is currently informed by simulatory and uni-modal, rather than cinematic understandings of aesthetic production.[18] The reason for choosing an anti-representationalist approach is twofold. First, we are careful not to equate the unfolding of narrative with the simulation of movement. While movement is a defining feature of cinema, movement and its simulation alone provides an insufficient context for the theorization of cinematic narrative. Animation, or faux experiences of spatial movement produced by the donning of video headsets, for example, beg the question of narrative. We also set aside the hyper-representationalism of Jean Baudrillard, for whom digital narrative invokes a field of infinitely reversible simulacra.[19] Such a timeless and symmetrical referential system can never actualize new narrative content or unfold narrative events. It can only ever posit an infinite regress into representations of a perpetual present.

Second, the authors turn away from psycholinguistic assumptions which understand narrative as the recovery of representational structures from semantic memory.[20] Following Deleuze we approach narrative as the episodic recomposition of emergent events within the affective, sensory and cultural memory of the beholder. Like Bergson, Deleuze lends movement to thought. The process of thought is described as episodic reflection on the contingencies of a self-conscious passage through reality.[21] Narrative time is not, therefore, something to be recovered from scenarios dealing literally with interactive time, as typified in works such as Toni Dove's interactive narrative *Spectropia* (2001).[22] On the other hand the temporal complexity evident in Bill Viola's interactive computer installation *The Tree of Knowledge* (1999) comes closer to the mark.[23] Here, the dynamic potentiality of utilizing complex interrelationships between diverse durational components, for example the speed and position of the beholder linked to graphics software parameters, enables the bonding of navigation and movement. For our understanding of interactive post-processing in terms of this bond, we turn to Serres.

Serres explains the narrative relation between the subject and the object as two dynamically interdependent durational systems. For Serres, both objects and subjects are interactively defined by their temporal relations. Serres illustrates this relation by reference to the example of geometrical measurement provided by the Greek mathematician Thales.[24] To measure the length of the shadow of a pyramid at a particular time of day, for example, is to express the interrelationship between an object in motion (sun) and an object at rest (pyramid). In enunciating measurement as the duration or tempo of the relation between the pyramid and the sun, Thales converts mathematics into a narrative form. Serres proposes that subjective activities, such as narration, are intertwined with objective processes, such as motion, whereby narrating becomes navigating and navigating is narrating. Subjectivity and objectivity form a "liens" of interactive encounters conditioned by their recombinatory multi-temporal relations.[25]

Experimental design

T_Visionarium is an immersive, interactive, multi-modal environment set within a dome (12 meters in diameter, 9 meters in height) made of inflatable fabric. It allows beholders to spatially navigate either televisual broadcasts in real time (Modality 1) or a televisual database in virtual time (Modality 2).

On entering the dome, the beholder places on his or her head a magnetic position-tracking device that is connected to cableless stereo headphones, then steps onto a control platform located at the center of the dome and equipped with a touchscreen interface, projector and computational hardware. The touchscreen interface enables the beholder to move between *T_Visionarium*'s two modalities of operation. The projection system is fixed on a motorized pan-tilt apparatus mounted on a tripod which projects televisual data onto the interior skin of the dome. The projection system is articulated to the tracking device in such a way that movement of the beholder's head causes the large projected viewing window to travel across the interior surface. This tracking device identifies the exact orientation of the beholder's point of view, which in turn controls the orientation of the projector so that it beams its image directly to the spot upon which the beholder's eyes are fixed. The audio-visual data streams are virtually distributed over the entire surface of the dome, so that the movement of the projection windows enables the beholder to navigate between these multi-modal data streams. The delivery software creates a spherical distribution of all the televisual data by their real-time texturing onto a virtual polygonal model of the dome. In other words, the real-time and stored televisual data sets are physically mapped over the dome surface such that each data set is allocated a specific window grid on the dome's surface. This enables the beholder to navigate between each data set by merely shifting their point of view. This mapping strategy applies to both image and sound. Seamless transitions between discrete image and sound events are handled by specific design parameters of the audio-visual delivery system. The acoustic delivery system is based on the use of RF cableless headphones. The mixing of the audio, synchronized with the movement of the pan-tilt projection system, allows a fully spatialized soundscape inside the dome to be synchronized with the distribution and experience of the visual content.

Within Modality 1, data streams are constituted by real-time access to twenty-four channels of incoming television broadcasts. These are captured by satellite dish and distributed to the visualization system via receivers connected to the delivery computer.

Within Modality 2, these same satellite data streams are recorded onto a hard-disc system and sorted within a database. By the application of a recombinatory software matrix, unprecedented narratives are re-configured from this database by the

18 Jean Baudrillard, *Symbolic Exchange and Death*, Sage, London, 1993, p. 70.

19 Baudrillard, *The Transparency of Evil*, op. cit.

20 Paul Willemen, "Reflections on Digital Imagery: Of Mice and Men," in Rieser, Zapp (eds), op. cit., p. 20.

21 Baudrillard, *The Transparency of Evil*, op. cit., p. 149.

22 Dove, op. cit., p. 216.

23 Melcher, op. cit., p. 47.

24 Michel Serres, *Hermes: Literature, Science and Philosophy*, John Hopkins University Press, Baltimore, 1982, p. 90.

25 Michel Serres, Bruno Latour (eds), *Conversations on Science, Culture and Time*, University of Michigan Press, Ann Arbor, 1995, p. 177.

beholder. By means of interaction with the matrix interface and the simultaneous movement of the head and projection window, the beholder originates unique performances on behalf of a larger viewing public of up to eighty people. This strategy allows beholders to experience the sense of a wholly personalized authorship. To this extent, the recombinatory matrix produces a deeply interactive authorship, emergent in the encounter between the beholder and matrix in multi-temporal time.

T_Visionarium embodies a transcriptive interactive narrative matrix incorporating a uni-temporal control reference against which its multi-temporal capacities can be measured. Enabling beholders to immerse themselves in both virtual and real-time modalities, it explores the expressive potential of transcriptive as opposed to conventional interactive narrative.

Modality 1 constitutes an ensemble of information juxtaposing the simultaneous television transmissions of twenty-four incoming cable channels in real time. It permits the beholder to surf among the twenty-four options in a uni-temporal flow by scanning between the channels across the surface of the dome. Modality 2, on the other hand allows new recombinatory narrative content to be generated by the beholder. Navigation through the data sets dramatizes the televisual information archived in *T_Visionarium's* database. These data sets are re-constituted across the interior skin of the dome under the converging impetus of beholder and matrix, and are encountered as emerging multi-temporal events.

Data processing in Modality 1 is confined to the durational pathways ordained by the real-time transmissions of the twenty-four broadcasts. This represents a low syntactic level of organization, sorting televisual data as sequences. On the other hand, data processing in Modality 2 is animated by the recombinatory parameters of the interactive software. Modality 2 is based on recorded broadcasts from twenty-four global satellite-television channels during simultaneous sixty-minute periods. This data is post-processed by the matrix in ways that hyperlink the variegated data sets in virtual time, to form a large-scale database. Based on deep content authoring, which allows high levels of semantic and abstract classification, the matrix sorts the data according to characteristics of language, movement, color, speech, composition, lighting and pattern recognition as organized by identifiers originating as functional agencies within a conceptual framework.26 The beholder explores the results of these recombinatory searches by moving the projection window across the dome screen. Selecting the keyword "home," for example, ushers forth intersecting cascades of current affairs, sports, features, life style, historical, scientific, musical and anthropological episodes of "home," across twenty-four channels, a multiplicity of languages, numerous time zones, and a heterogeneity of cultures within the simultaneous sixty-minute time frame. The recombinatory matrix unravels these convergences of multi-modal data at temporal levels of intensity, archival density and extensiveness that only become recognizable as they coalesce in the complex time projected across the dome. The beholder can intensify, deepen or extend these events as they unfold, fine tuning the search within "home" by selecting the keyword "bedroom," for example. Thus, by changes in point of view the beholder activates a powerful navigational matrix that produces a directional flow of information in which the expressive meaning of the

data is boundlessly transcribed. Beholder dramatizations of the data are then archived into the database to form part of the experimental evaluation of the study whilst being simultaneously handed onto other beholders for further interaction.

The profoundly multi-temporal logic of Modality 2 echoes the theoretical architecture implicit in digitized audio-visual data.27 This logic is imperceptible in Modality 1 which, like other conventional viewing frameworks, can only recover time analogically by scanning and juxtaposing whole fragments. At best, conventional viewing establishes symmetrical patterns of temporal resemblance among broadcast items based on syntactical properties patent within the data.28 Transcriptive narrative, as embodied in Modality 2 moves beyond this logic of resemblance. It is able to unfold new content within a virtual infosphere of digitized images and sounds whose patterning is freed from the constraints imposed by the analogical, or representational, re-delivery of information. Sifting through digitized televisual data, the beholder unravels sub-visible links. By cutting the multi-modal structure of pre-recorded information at a number of aesthetically significant joints, the recombinatory matrix coalesces new audio-visual streams into episodes that can be functionally re-assigned a narrative. Reassignment is made at the discretion of the beholder within the infinite latitude extended by virtual time.

As a consequence, narrative becomes a complex event which interlaces a number of intersecting temporal and physical navigations. Temporally the matrix allows for intensive, dense and extensive navigation of sequential audio-visual data and their reconfiguration into hyperlinked asymmetrical virtual streams. After selecting a specific parameter, the beholder can refine these streams by zooming into a specific current within the streams. Once these new virtual time currents are projected across the dome, the beholder can process them in real time by physically navigating the projection window across the dome's surface. This interweaving of matrix and beholder navigation with real- and virtual-time processing precipitates the emergence of unprecedented narratives. In this respect *T_Visionarium* opens interactive cinema to a multi-modal aesthetic of a kind currently confined to uni-modal contexts such as text-based chat rooms. By adding beholder-generated transcription of cinematic information within virtual time, it augments the author's existing research into narrative as a form of dialogical interaction within virtual space by the addition of beholder-generated transcription of cinematic information within virtual time.

In addition, the *T_Visionarium* methodology provides a meta-model for transcriptive strategies. *T_Visionarium* is appropriate for other database formations ranging from the Internet, library, defense and image archives to the abstract modeling of beholder attitudes applicable to the field of advertising. By sifting through seemingly inchoate and unrelated data, transcriptive narrative creates new logics of data inter-relationships. This "media ecology" recycles waste data into new sensory fields of experience and communication. At an individual level, applying transcriptive narrative to materials already bound together in proto-narrative formations – such as family photo and moving image archives – reveals the profound recombinant potential of transcriptive narrative, especially revelatory to those who are its protagonists.

26 H. Wactlar, M. Christel, Y. Gong, A. Haputmann, "Lessons Learned from Building a Terabyte Digi Library," 1999. http://www-2.cs.cmu.edu/~hdw/IEEEComputer_Feb99.pdf

27 Elizabeth Grosz, *Becomings: Explorations in Time, Memory and Futures*, Cornell, New York, 1999, p. 27.

28 Juan Casares, "Silver: An Intelligent Video Editor," 2001. http://www-2.cs.cmu.edu/~silver/Casares ShortPaper.pdf

N. Katherine Hayles
Timely Art: Hybridity in New Cinema and Electronic Poetry

Throughout their long relationship, cinema and literature have cohabited. Hundreds of novels and short stories have provided the basis for films, and occasionally films have generated novels. But only recently has there been a medium in which the sensory elements comprising cinema and literature can commingle on an equal footing. With its awesome capacity to simulate almost anything, the digital computer is transforming cinematic and literary practices. Hybrid works are popping up everywhere, particularly in electronic poetry. The scene is reminiscent of the early days of cinema, before conventions had solidified and disparate traditions were drawn upon to explore the nature of the new medium. I am not sure if these works qualify as new cinema, since they are hybrid in nature. But I am certain that the theory and practice of new cinema cannot afford to ignore what is happening in this vital area of new media.

Like cosmopolitan Los Angeles, electronic poetry has become a heterogeneous territory all the more colorful because it is claimed by stakeholders with different allegiances. The aesthetic experiments now underway test a variety of strategies for combining word, image, animation, sound, color and form to provide satisfying artistic experiences in networked and programmable media. The scene takes shape as a medial ecology, as if we were traveling through the deep sea and marveling at the diversity and range of solutions that evolution has provided to how life forms can survive and flourish in this environment. Some experiments foreground the word, using image and sound as enhancements; some give precedence to graphic form, subordinating verbal signification to visual complexity; others emphasize rhythm and sound, framing words and images to fit the soundscape; still others privilege interaction, creating narratives that entwine signification with navigation. The sea in which they all swim is time – time, that is, as it is constructed, programmed and delivered by the digital computer.

Ingrid Ankerson's *Sinking* shows how even fairly traditional poetic form is transformed by cinematic techniques.1 Programmed in Flash 4, this poem uses looped background images and ambient sound as enhancements for the text, which appears as small white font against a variegated blue background reminiscent of foot-imprinted sand seen through shallow water. The narrative sets the scene at a kitchen sink, addressing "you" as "The steaming water opens for you / settles around your fingers / the way the sandy floor of Lake Michigan did / when you were six and thought you could swim." Handwalking through the shallow water, the child did not so much pretend to swim as enact that she was sure adults did when they "floated like bubbles above water." As an adult realizing that "the dirty dish pile next to the sink / is your life now," you wonder if this childish illusion still grips your life, "if you only *think* you know your work. / You wonder if / someone is going to step into your office / and find that / you don't know how to swim." The chord progression hints at some ominous development, a possibility scripted into unsettling details that suggest you may be contemplating suicide. For example, you notice "It is quiet in the kitchen / as if you had dipped beneath the soapy water. / You realize this is all you know of quiet. / The sound of the faucet not filling the sink. / The sound of not breathing." The tension these details create adds drama to an otherwise anticlimactic ending, when you decide that for now "you will do what you know ... / You will begin with a knife." Built around a series of apparent oppositions, the poem edges toward a realization it does not quite want to face as oppositions collapse into one another, conflating childish illusion with adult knowledge, pretence with competence, achievement with tedious repetition, safety with sinking.

This poem, like others created in Flash, shares with cinema a one-way progression through time, a temporal directionality strengthened by the disappearance of text from the screen and the appearance of new text. Although it can be replayed (as a film can), it functions more like oral poetry than written verse because it cannot be taken in at a single glance, nor can a line, once read, be immediately re-read as with print. The technology controls the pace of reading, not the user. (The pace also depends on the speed of connection. I could comfortably finish each screen of text before it disappeared when I read it at home on a computer networked to a modem, but at my office with a faster connection, the poem progressed so quickly that, even knowing the text, I was unable to complete reading before the text disappeared.)

1 Ingrid Ankerson, "Sinking," in *Poems That Go*, 1, Spring 2000, online at http://www.poemsthatgo.com/gallery/spring2000/sinking/sinkingmain.htm, accessed August 2002.

Stephanie Strickland,
M.D. Coverley
Errand upon which we came
2001
hypermedia poem
screenshots

The temporal dimension is rendered more complex by the looping of sound and image, a circularity that further complicates the narrative tensions between memory of the past, realization in the present, and dread of the future. As Rita Raley has observed in a short but suggestive article on the significance of loops in electronic writing, death is the end toward which linear (and multilinear) plots traditionally tend. In contrast, loops enact a circularity that inscribes the writing within a different metaphysic.2 The significance of the temporal dynamic in this respect becomes quite complex, because the loops suggest continuation (of activity, particularly breathing, and hence of existence) while at the same time they reinforce the sense of repetition, which works against the narratee's yearning for an authentic life. Of course technological constraints are the main reason to use loops, as they conserve memory space and make file size more manageable. Unlike the analog technology of film, in which almost unlimited detail can be recorded subject to emulsion granularity and film size, the much smaller bandwidth of Internet connectivity imposes severe constraints on the amount of information that can feasibly be shoved through the channel. Within these constraints the poem privileges verbal complexity, achieving temporal complexity in part through the compromises it makes by looping the sonic and visual components.

Although in my view *Sinking* is a successfully realized work, it does not push the envelope in integrating sound, image and text on an equal footing. It is clearly more interested in enhancing the verbal text than in experimenting with subordinating written language to more traditionally cinematic components. *His Father in the Exhaust of Engines*, a collaboration between poet Bruce Smith and designer Marc Stricklin, has a strong narrative line combined with evocative images and subtle animation.3 Ambient music alternating between two chords is punctuated by four syncopated beats reminiscent of a heartbeat's diastole and systole. The text's complex framing results in a work that is as powerful visually as verbally. This Flash poem, a son's reminiscence of a father who tinkered with car engines, is composed of screens corresponding to blocks of text. Within each screen, animation is used to create visual narratives that comment upon and contextualize the words. The subtlety of the design should not obscure its importance as a technical innovation. It provides an excellent example of how changes in the technology create corresponding mutations in the grammar and syntax of the work.

In cinema, of course, each frame corresponds to a camera shot, and a series of frames depicting a coherent action sequence corresponds to a scene, with editing cuts marking divisions between scenes. In print poetry, divisions are indicated spatially rather than temporally, so that line breaks, stanza divisions, verse paragraph blocks, and so on are important signifying components. Flash animation does not correspond exactly with either the cinematic or print conventions and instead introduces another semiotic system, with scenes defined by the beginning and end points of animation sequences that can be paced according to a timing algorithm. Moreover, more than one animation sequence can be shown on a given screen, timed so that it overlaps and mingles with other animations. *His Father in the Exhaust of Engines* uses this flexibility to combine print and cinematic conventions in a hybrid form with its own distinctive rhythms and spatiality.

The sense of a "scene" is both preserved and transformed by creating screens framed by a heavy brown line reminiscent of a photograph frame, thus combining cinematic conventions with its predecessor technology, photography. Movement between screens corresponds to editing cuts, creating the possibility for contrasts and correspondences across these divisions. Within a given screen, subtle animations create movements that recall the action sequences of a movie scene. Here too mutation occurs, however, for the division between screens also corresponds to the spatial breaks characteristic of print poetry, with each screen presenting a block of text that functions as a spatially coherent unit. These textual units achieve further nuancing by the ways in which text is spatially arranged within each screen, creating further possibilities to use spatiality as a signifying component. Thus both the spatiality of print poetry and the temporal pacing of cinema become important components in the work, functioning in ways that recall the predecessor technologies while simultaneously transforming them.

2 Rita Raley, "The Digital Loop: Feedback and Recurrence," in *Leonardo Electronic Almanac*, vol. 10, no. 7, July 2002, online at http://mitpress2.mit.edu/e-journals/LEA/LEA2002/LEA/archives.tem.htm, accessed August 2002.

3 Bruce Smith and Marc Stricklin, "His Father in the Exhaust of Engines," in *Poems That Go*, 5, Spring 2001, online at http://www.bornmag.com/projects/hisfather/, accessed August 2002.

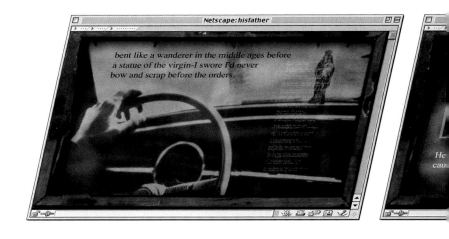

These transformative effects are evident in the first screen where the words appear, "All his life I used my father to get somewhere," along with the image of a young boy, seven or eight, who stares out from the frame with serious sad expression. As the boy continues to stare, the light seems to flicker and for an microsecond illuminates his face the way X-rays or a nuclear flash might, revealing what lies beneath the skin, beneath the surface of these mundane and yet curiously painful memories. The animation is paced so that the X-ray image lies just at the threshold of perception, giving the user a fleeting impression that goes by so fast she is not sure she saw it at all. The piercing illumination prepares for the next screen that continues and alters the meaning of the text in the first screen: "else – the game, the shore, the power, the middle class, the other side." The difference between getting somewhere, and getting somewhere else, captures the sense of regret of this son who used his father like an aging vehicle to be run into the ground and abandoned. In this context the illumination seems to promise a retrospective vision that can get at the truth of things in ways that a child or even a young adult could not. Yet as we shall see, this promise is held out only to be partially negated in the visual narratives that follow.

The image of the father bowed over the engine, "a fender / in one hand a frayed / wire in the other," reminded the son in his youth of someone "bent like a wanderer in the middle ages before / a statue of the virgin," a posture of humility and supplication that he rejected. Swearing he would never "bow and scrape before the orders" of engines that "sputter and choke," the son's oath is juxtaposed, through another change of screens, with the father's soft swearing as he struggles to get the engine to catch. Photographs of the father inset into several screens show a middle-aged man with glasses wearing a blue suit, suggesting a white-collar worker who tackles engines not because he enjoys it but because that is what men of a certain generation did if they were good fathers and husbands. In contrast to the father's tinkering, the narrator declares himself "the son ignorant of motor / but prodigal of fuel and air. / I'm the emir of the four cylinder / the chopped and channeled lord of / Detroit and Japan," language that emphasizes his superior position from which he can command the labor of others. The text appears over a sepia landscape,

against which the flickering image of the father appears and then fades, replaced by a soft focus image of an adult male shown in torso, presumably the son.

But as the images have been intimating throughout, the father and his legacy are not so easily left behind. The final screen, with an image of a cross standing upright on a sepia landscape, ambiguously locates the narrator as both driver and driven. "I floor it, my foot on his back, or / his on mine, his face in the mirror / his death doubling me over." Doubled as well as doubled over, the narrator becomes simultaneously himself and his father, his face in the mirror his father's face, the one who uses and the one who is used by memories he cannot shake. The poem's opening line, which displaced the expected phrase "all my life" with "all *his* life I used my father" (emphasis added), now assumes deeper significance, as the father's death haunts the son's life so violently that he seems to take over and occupy the son's body. This verbal complexity is enacted visually by the animation sequence showing the fading of the father's image and its replacement by the son's torso, a visual transformation that may indicate not the replacement of the father by the son but the transmutation of the father *into* the son.

Deepening this complexity are persistent images that hover on the border of legibility because they are spatially indistinct, in contrast to the sharp but fleeting X-ray illumination of the first screen. These shadowy images suggest depths that remain to be plumbed, thus mutating and to some extent negating the promise of X-ray clarity of vision. One image that appears in several screens shows lines of text grayed out to illegibility, so that it functions as a visual representation of text rather than text itself. We are left to wonder: are these lines from an automobile repair manual? A counter narrative that would tell the story from the father's point of view rather than the son's? Its ghostly presence is another indication that there is more here than the narrator can tell.

In its mutations of cinematic and literary conventions, transformations of time and space that create new semiotic units of meaning, and forging of new conventions suited to the possibilities and limitations of the software and hardware, *His Father in the Exhaust of Engines* illustrates the potential of the medium to create work that resists easy classification as either cinema or literature. It shows the Flash

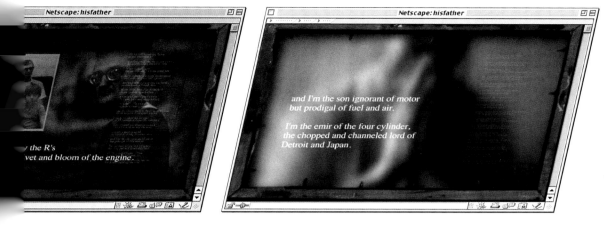

Bruce Smith, Marc Stricklin
His Father in the Exhaust of Engines
2001
Flash poem
screenshots
© The University of Chicago

poem becoming a medium in its own right with its own visual and verbal rhetoric, a production of networked and programmable media that could not be enacted the same way in another other medium.

While *His Father in the Exhaust of Engines* shows a deepening engagement with visual materials, it makes relatively little use of sound other than ambient music to create a mood. *DAKØTA* by Young-hae Chang Heavy Industries privileges sound, cutting the words and designing animation to match the rhythm of a jazz drum solo by Art Blakey's band.4 This prose poem begins with numbers (represented alternately as figures and words) counting down from ten, reminiscent of a movie countdown for a take. But when the count stops at three, it becomes apparent the countdown is counting a music rhythm. The narrative is presented in black block capital letters on a white background, flashing sequentially through different screens, with a few words – sometimes only one – per screen. Their appearance is timed to coincide with the leading beats of the drum solo, with each emphasized drum or cymbal stroke bringing up another screen, so the effect is to make the words seem to be driven by the music. The narrative is a Kerouac-like account of a car trip, the narrator adopting the persona of a young punker with more than a touch of misogyny. "WE DRANK / AND INSULTED / EACH OTHER'S / MOTHERS. / BEER / IN / ONE / HAND, / BOURBON IN OTHER" gives the flavor of the text, along with "THEN / I / SPOKE / A / GASSY / SPEECH / ABOUT / DYING / YOUNG. / (BURP)." The narrative is not without interest, tying together a buddy's death while pulling a break-in with brutal treatment of sweethearts and sisters, along with a hallucinogenic conversation with Elvis and a tribute to Marilyn Monroe. The main interest, however, remains on the music, the drum solo building in intensity and complication, culminating in a frenzied improvisation stretched almost beyond endurance. Like *His Father in the Exhaust of Engines*, *DAKØTA* uses screen divisions effectively to create a combined spatial-temporal aesthetic that draws upon cinema and print poetry while also transforming their conventions into something new.

In contrast to the push-aesthetic of these Flash poems is *Errand upon which we came*, a collaboration between poet Stephanie Strickland and M. D. Coverley.5 Strickland and Coverley believe strongly that the potential of networked and programmable media

should be used to introduce interactivity into electronic literature, practicing a principled rejection of techniques that do not allow the user to determine, at least in part, pacing and trajectory. Their work has something in common, then, with experiments in new media that introduce interactivity into cinematic narrative. In *Errand*, this commitment is performed through a distinction between timed animation sequences that push the screens at a pace controlled by the program, and the reader's interventions that can stabilize the screen display or jump between screens using linking words. This tension is given an ironic inflection when the poet warns that the work "can be read straight through, but this is not a better reading, / not a better life." Passive reading concedes control to the computer, which results in a default "straight through" reading. To have a "better reading," the reader must intervene and take active control; as one screen comments, "You are being asked / to move with great / rapidity."

Imaged as flowing copperplate script that bounces and slides across the screen, *Errand* uses backgrounds of abstract greens, browns and blues to suggest changing landscapes of earth, water and sky. The sound records bird calls, crickets, and other natural phenomena. As the words glide, swoop and drip off the screen, a butterfly skims along the text in erratic flight, and a frog leaps between land and sky. The reader can stop the animation at any point by clicking on the butterfly, and link words offer additional opportunities to skip between screens. Notwithstanding the opportunity the poem gives the reader to control temporal flow, it also insists on its ephemerality. For example, as the butterfly traverses the screen, it seems to erase the text in its wake. These fading images hint at the poem's transformation from the durable object it may have been had it been produced in print, to the process it becomes when it is generated by programs running inside the computer and data transmissions sent over the Internet.

The poem begins (in one of its configurations) with an address to the reader: "Gentle Reader, begin anywhere." Folding into the poem the address to the reader blurs the work's boundaries. It is not altogether clear where it begins, for the preceding screen, which most readers would take as instructions on how to read the poem, also includes an implicit address to the reader. Similarly, the trajectory

4 Young-hae Chang Heavy Industries, *DAKØTA*, in *Poems That Go*, 5, Spring 2001, online at http://www.yhchang.com/DAKOTA.html, accessed August 2002.

5 Stephanie Strickland and M. D. Coverley, *Errand upon which we came*, online at http://califia.hispeed.com/Errand/title1b.htm, accessed August 2002.

does not settle into a single line, since the link paths yield different screen configurations. The poem attempts to re-orient the reader's focus so that, rather than reading to reach the end, the reader will follow fancy's dictates, dallying with the poem's possibilities rather than consuming it as an object that can be left behind to go on to the next thing. Quoting Simone Weil, the final screen suggests we measure meaning not according to "what the pointer points to" but by noticing the nail holding the scale so it weighs true, a shift of perspective that the poem instantiates through its organization of time. Itself an event, it urges us to view reading not as a "settled course" but a random sampling that experiences time as a flow rather than a flow-chart, an unfolding emergence rather than a gallop toward a goal.

In this way it modifies the one-way temporal trajectory of cinema while adopting some cinematic techniques, carrying over into the electronic medium the sense print poetry gives of being able to access pages in whatever order one pleases. This was, after all, one of the major differences between the codex book and the scroll that preceded it in manuscript culture – the ability to open the book anywhere and not have to proceed in linear fashion through a continuous, one-way surface. Conventional movies are like scrolls in this sense; however convoluted and complex the narrative line, technologically they start at the beginning and proceed linearly to the end. *Errand upon which we came* announces its own errand as a project to re-envision the viewing surface as a territory to wander upon rather than a strip proceeding linearly through the machine or a Flash program running relentlessly in one direction.

John Cayley's *riverIsland* is a beautifully complex work exploring how cinematic techniques can be used as navigational functionalities within a work that interrogates the relationship between the digital nature of language and the digital operations of the computer. The work is conceptualized as consisting of two loops of poems, one horizontal and one vertical. The horizontal loop contains sixteen quatrains from Wang Wei's famous *Wang River Sequence* (written in the eighth century) and translated from the Chinese into English by Cayley. The poems display as letters on the screen and the sound of the poems being read. At the bottom of the screen is a QuickTime movie of

flowing water. The user can navigate the loop either by grabbing the movie and moving it to the right or left, or by using the navigational icon. As the user leaves one node to travel to the next, the sound of the first poem overlaps with the sound of the second as the letters of the first text morph into the letters of the second. When the second node is reached, the sound of the first fades and the sound of the second resolves into a solo voice, at the same time as the letters stabilize into new words.

The vertical loop runs "upward" from the base of the first poem in the horizontal loop. This loop contains sixteen different translations of the same poem, including different versions in English as well as in French, Spanish and the Pinyin Romanization of the modern pronunciation of Chinese. At the side of the text in the vertical loop is a QuickTime movie of a river running through woods, although the silvery sheen of the water gives it an eerie appearance that can also be understood as a gash or gap in the screenic surface, suggesting an opening, chasm and / or corridor between the words as they appear on screen and the inner workings of the computer.6

This visual hint suggests a connection between the cinematic and verbal surface and the medium that produces them, a concept central to Cayley's view of his "literal art."

In "Digital Wen: On the Digitization of Letter- and Character-Based Systems of Inscription," he explains by referring to the "rules of traditional Chinese regulated verse."7 These include such considerations as line length, pauses between syllables, and tonal qualities along a line, as well as parallelism between the lines of a couplet, both in terms of the sense and correspondences between ideographic characters. Meaning is thus built up out of the particular characteristics of written characters and their phonetic equivalents, as well as through higher-level considerations such as imagery, metaphor, and so forth. Cayley argues that similar considerations also apply to poetry in English, suggesting that similarities and differences between letter forms can function as visual equivalents to the acoustic properties of poetic techniques such as assonance.

This orientation allows him to conceive of poetry through a materialistic "bottom up" approach that works in synchrony with higher-level considerations, a

6 I am indebted to Adalaide Morris for suggesting to me this interpretation of the image.

7 John Cayley, "Digital Wen: On the Digitization of Letter- and Character-Based Systems of Inscription," in *Reading East Asian Writing*, Michel Hockx and Ivo Smits (eds), Curzon Press, London, 2002 (forthcoming).

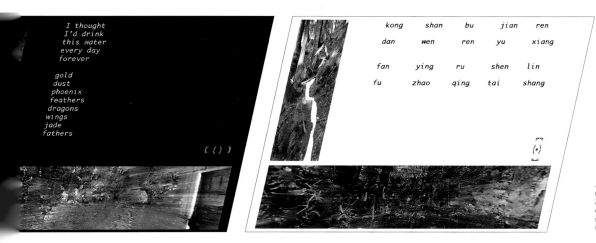

I thought
I'd drink
this water
every day
forever

gold
dust
phoenix
feathers
dragons
wings
jade
fathers

(( ))

kong	shan	bu	jian	ren
dan	wen	ren	yu	xiang
fan	ying	ru	shen	lin
fu	zhao	qing	tai	shang

(•)

John Cayley
riverIsland
2000
electronic poem
screenshots
© John Cayley

perspective he designates as "literal" (with a play on the letter as the unit of meaning and on the fact that the letters literally appear on the page or screen as the basic units from which meaning emerges). In addition, as the letters of his transliteral morphs travel between recognizable letter forms, they go through intermediate stages before stabilizing into the target forms, a process repeated on a larger and more visible scale as the letters in the source word transform into other letters that will eventually stabilize into the target word. The visual effect is to suggest a dynamic tension between the stabilized word (or letter) and the transitional morphs, which are linguistically indeterminate in the sense that they do not correspond to any recognizable word (or letter) but rather are the "in-betweens" from which coherent words (and letters) will emerge. In his works language falls apart and comes together, dissolving into a seethe of chaos that is not merely disorder but rather the fecund noisy matrix from which poetry will emerge, like a dolphin breaking the surface to glisten in the sun before plunging back again into the ocean.

This view of language allows Cayley to treat letters as images as well as verbal signifiers. Their movement through time thus becomes a kind of cinematic technique, a correspondence emphasized by making the QuickTime movies function both as moving images and navigational devices to access the morphing words. In addition, these movements through time are also used to establish parallels with the binary code of computer processes. It is important to note here that the morphing letters are not continuous transformations but rather quick jumps between different letters, as when the letters on a European railroad schedule spin around to form new words. This style of morphing emphasizes that letters are digital, in the sense of being discrete rather than continuous,[8] a performance that enacts similarities between letters as the bits from which language is formed and electronic polarities as the bits from which the screen image of electronic images are created.[9] Electronic text and image, Cayley observes, always tremble "at the abyss of ones and zeros," the unreadable bit stream that is the matrix out of which humanly-readable visual and verbal language emerges. In its general dynamics this tension is, he suggests, not unique to electronic media (although the form it takes in binary code is specific to the digital computer). As he cogently puts it, "letters got there first."[10]

Although the works discussed here illustrate that there are strong continuities with established cinematic and literary practices, they also demonstrate that networked and programmable media enter deeply into signifying practices, resulting in hybrid productions shaped by the material realities of the media. As Lev Manovich brilliantly shows in *The Language of New Media*, profound transformations take place when the materiality of the medium changes.[11] This materiality includes, of course, the conditions under which works are produced and consumed. The economics that allow an individual to purchase software products such as Flash, Director and QuickTime put the means of production in the hands of writers, designers, and artists who could not dream of financing even a short independent film.

Moreover, we still do not understand very well how the dynamics of reading and viewing change when the movie or television screen is replaced by the computer. The viewing distance for a computer screen is much closer than for a television screen, much less a movie – approximately the same distance as a book. This creates an intimacy that combines the experiences characteristic of reading a book with the visual qualities characteristic of cinema and video. Moreover, interacting with the computer involves the user in constant kinesthetic experiences as keys are tapped, programs opened and closed, and so on. Although these manipulations are closer to turning the pages of a book than to the distance viewing of the cinema, they nevertheless have distinctive characteristics of their own. As electronic art continues to evolve, it will become increasingly important to understand in detail what differences these material conditions make. For now, what we can know for certain is that art forms do not remain unchanged when they engage digital media. In these flexible, powerful and rapidly evolving environments, cinema and literature are not just cohabiting. They are merging into hybrids that mutate the old conventions even as they perform the new.

8 John Cayley develops this point further in his essay "Of Programmatology," in *Mute*, Fall 1998, pp. 72–75. Alphabetic language, as Cayley observes, is a digital technology, a point developed at length by Robert K. Logan in *The Alphabet Effect*, William Morrow, New York, 1986. In *The Fifth Language: Learning a Living in the Computer Age*, Stoddart, Toronto, 1995, Logan extends his analysis to digital code.

9 John Cayley discusses the relation of line, pixel and letter in "Literal Art: Neither Lines nor Pixels but Letters," an essay that illuminates the special sense in which he uses "literal" to mean both the materiality of language and the letters from which alphabetic language is formed, in *First Person: New Media as Story, Performance, and Game*, Noah Wardrip-Fruin and Pat Harrigan (eds), The MIT Press, Cambridge, MA, 2002 (forthcoming).

10 E-mail communication, 7 July 2002.

11 Particularly relevant in this regard is the distinction Manovich makes between narrative and database (Lev Manovich, *The Language of New Media*, The MIT Press, Cambridge, MA, 2001).

06

RECOMBINATORY

George Legrady with Rosemary Comella
Slippery Traces

1995
interactive digital media installation / dimensions variable /
CD-ROM version published in artintact 3 (ZKM, 1996)

1 International Society of
  Electronic Arts

2 Lyon Biennale of Contempo-
  rary Art, Musée d'art con-
  temporain, Lyon, 1995/1996;
  "The Butterfly Effect,"
  Mücsarnok Museum of Fine
  Arts, Budapest, 1996; Euro-
  pean Media Art Festival,
  Osnabrück, 1996; "Dawn of
  the Magicians," National
  Gallery, Prague, 1997;
  "Selected Memories," Palais
  des Beaux-Arts de Brux-
  elles, Brussels, 1997;
  "George Legrady: from Ana-
  logue to Digital," Canadian
  Museum of Contemporary
  Photography, Ottawa,
  1997/1998; "Deep Storage,"
  Haus der Kunst, Munich,
  Kunstmuseum Düsseldorf
  im Ehrenhof; "20. Jahrhun-
  dert," Neue Nationalgalerie,
  Berlin; P.S.1, New York; Henry
  Art Gallery, Seattle,
  1998/1999.

3 "Any classification is superior to chaos and even a
  classification at the level
  of sensible properties is a
  step towards rational
  ordering … The decision
  that everything must be
  taken account of facilitates
  the creation of a 'memory
  bank.'" – Claude Lévi-
  Strauss, The Savage Mind,
  University of Chicago Press,
  Chicago, 1966.

4 "Falsely naive, the postcard
  misleads in direct measure
  to the fact that it presents
  itself as having neither
  depth nor aesthetic pretensions. The colonial postcard
  is inseparable from that
  which occasioned its existence … Travel is the
  essence of the postcard,
  and expedition its mode …
  No envelope can contain a
  postcard. Hidden, it immediately ceases to be." – Malek
  Alloula, The Colonial Harem,
  University of Minnesota
  Press, Minneapolis, 1986.

5 "Photography is a memory,
  the trace of an original. In
  the postmodern era, the
  past has become a collection of photographic, filmic
  or televised images. We, like
  the replicants in the movie
  Blade Runner, are put in the
  position of history by means
  of its reproduction." –
  Giuliana Bruno, "Ramble City:
  Postmodernism and Blade
  Runner," in October, no. 41,
  1987.

Slippery Traces: The Postcard Trail

Slippery Traces was produced as an interactive installation, first presented at the ISEA 95 1 exhibition in
Montreal and subsequently in a number of museums, 2
as well as included in the traveling exhibition "Deep
Storage" curated by the Siemens Cultural Program.
The CD-ROM version was published the following year
in the ZKM *artintact* series.

Slippery Traces is a multi-linear visual narrative
in which viewers navigate through a network of over
240 interconnected postcards classified into 24
categories or chapters. The intention of the work
was to explore database structures as a means of
generating multi-linear narratives at the time when
web search engines were being introduced. I wanted
to produce a narrative work in which three sets of
cultural messages could intersect or collapse into
each other. First, the archive consists mostly of
commercial postcards selected from two thousand
as representative of twentieth-century culture. The
second level consisted of my evaluation of these
images encoded through keywords and cross-listed
through a database in order to maximize movement
between categories. Third, the collection of these
images signifies in a dispersed way my autobiography.
Amongst the images can be found family portraits

from the period 1920–1940, printed on postcards, as
well as places I have been, and cultures that shaped
me in various ways.

The intention underlying my selection of postcards
was to provide an overview, both cultural and
ideological, of mid-twentieth-century photographic
representation within the framework of global
development, tourism and cultural exchange. I was
searching for images that were interesting in content
and structure, images that were culturally significant,
or relevant subject matter and visually intriguing
compositions that express a perception based on
the photographic paradigm. For instance, images of
conventionality and banality such as tourist sites,
business arrangements, advertising; images of the
social order representing work, industry, military,
family; images that make visible the technical in the
photographic, such as being blurred or oddly framed;
personal images, or ones that expressed the passing
of time; images of transgression, articulating
colonialization, the exoticizing or eroticizing of the
non-Western culture; images of abundance, of the
absurd stated through the exaggerated, the touris-
tic, the play of similarity, the play between the natural
and the cultural such as dressed-up animals; images
of fear such as assassination, nazi group photos, fire,
destruction; images that play on ethnocentrism,

right
Slippery Traces
1995
interactive digital media
installation
dimensions variable
installation view: Mücsarnok,
Budapest, 1996
collection of the artist
courtesy George Legrady

left
Slippery Traces
1995
interactive digital media
installation
dimensions variable
installation view: Palais des
Beaux-Arts, Brussels, 1997
collection of the artist
courtesy George Legrady

Slippery Traces
1995
screenshots
collection of the artist
courtesy George Legrady

racism or stereotypes such a Saudi Arab counting money; and images that expressed the poetic and the sublime. The selection does not aim to represent the totality of twentieth-century historical experience. I was limited by what was at hand, as well as by the necessity of curtailing the overall size of *Slippery Traces* to eventually fit on a CD-ROM. This incongruous collection of cultural visual artifacts was then classified into categories that emerged out of the ordering process: "Airplane Industry," "Americana," "Ancient Monuments," "Animals," "Auto Culture," "Caribbean World," "Colorful," "European Images," "Fire & Light," "Fishing Stories," "Industry," "Military Images," "Morality Tales," "Native American," "Nature & Culture," "Orientalism," "Scenic Views," "Social Groups," "The Great War," "The Jump," "The Rocky Way," "Urban Places," and "Yugoslavian Front." These labels express a conglomeration of categories not unlike Borges' invented Chinese Encyclopedia and, in a similar fashion, provide a rich mix of cultural and metaphorical references encoded into a structure that make possible multi-linear narrative plot development.

At the start of the viewing experience, the spectator is confronted with one of three quotes that appear on the screen. Randomly chosen, each quote addresses the project either from an anthropological,3 or colonialist,4 or media-theoretical5

perspective, thereby setting a cultural interpretive slant by which the viewing experience becomes framed. In the installation version, two additional quotes are present stamped on the wall, further contextualizing the reception of the postcard image in terms of semiotic6 and literary7 viewpoints.

The interactive experience begins with the program randomly selecting an image from one of the twenty-four categories as only one category, and one image can be viewed at a time, in a close-up, fragmented mode. Every image contains approximately five hotspots, or links to other images. These become visible when scrolled over by the mouse, forcing the viewer to explore the surface of the image in search of links. When a hotspot is clicked, the program checks to see if enough images have been viewed in the current category. If not, then it selects another image from the current category. If yes, then it randomly selects one of the two or more assigned linked images determined by the database algorithm. An image cannot be viewed if it has already been selected during the last twelve selections. At anytime following the fifth viewed image, users can review the stream of images or "meta-narrative" image sequence they have created through the clicking from one image to the next. The resultant sequence consists of any number of images linked linearly where all the images

6 "The paradox, the dilemma of authenticity, is that to be experienced as authentic it must be marked as authentic, but when it is marked as authentic it is mediated, a sign of itself, and hence not authentic in the sense of the unspoiled." – Jonathan Culler, "Semiotics of Tourism," in *Framing the Sign: Criticism and its Institutions* (Oklahoma Project for Discourse and Theory, No. 3), University of Oklahoma Press, Norman, Oklahoma, 1988.

7 "We can cast a glance upon the sign as a kind of postcard: description/ideology never quite captioning and thereby never quite capturing the real; the view from one side suppressing the other; an irrecoverable distance arising between the object and its given context of origin. Yet the sign … is put into play by its position among differences; like narrative, it is a gesture toward, and therefore against, death." – Susan Stewart, *On Longing: narratives of the miniature, the gigantic, the souvenir; the collection,* Duke University Press, Durham, 1993, p. 173.

Slippery Traces
1995
screenshots
collection of the artist
courtesy George Legrady

are related in such a way that some detail in the preceding image outlined by a red rectangle becomes a meaningful connection to something represented in the following image. The hotspot links by which an image is related to another is based on a set of conditions encoded in the database structure consisting of any number of literal, semiotic, psychoanalytic, metaphoric or other connections. I determined these myself through a process of subjective classification whereby each image's properties were registered in a database through keywords. The relations were encoded into the database influencing the navigational structure, and can therefore be considered one of the sites of authorship in the work. As the viewer moves from one image to another, the relation between the images allow for varying degrees of recognition based on the particular result from the database selection process. The relationship is quite clear at times, less so at others. The viewing experience, then, is in the play and contrast of expectations between knowing that the program will bring forth an image somehow related to the clicked hotspot, and the resultant degree of closeness or distance between the clicked hotspot and new image.

Slippery Traces had its roots in a two-projector slide-show created to explore the ways that the meanings of images change when juxtaposed with other images. Images are normally seen in relation to each other, and like words positioned together in a sentence, they oscillate each other, slightly expanding, re-adjusting, imperceptibly transforming their meaning through contrast, association, extension, difference, and so forth. Transferred to the non-linear dynamic environment of the computer, the shifts in meaning are exponentially increased as the images are freed from their slide-tray linear positions, to be constantly resituated in relationship to each other as determined by criteria defined in the computer code. The result is an imaginary three-dimensional, nerve-cell-like membrane network in which all 240 images are interlinked with over 2000 connections criss-crossing to form a unified whole. Connections, or hot spots, have something thematically in common with the image they call up. Each time the viewer clicks on a hot spot to move to another image, he or she weaves a path in this dense maze of connections.

In *Slippery Traces*, the viewer moves from one information source selected out of a range of possible choices to another information source also selected out of other possible choices. As mentioned earlier, these linkages are defined through keywords hidden from the viewer in the database according to common literal or metaphoric properties. The title *Slippery Traces* makes reference to the psychoanalyst Jacques Lacan's particular use of the term "slip"[8] and slippage to describe the unstable relationship between a sign and its meaning. In his remark that "meaning emerges only through discourse, as a consequence of displacements along a signifying chain," he is referring to the notion that the meaning of things are defined not in themselves but through their relation to other signs. Lacan argues against the Saussurian notion that there is a stable relation between a signifier and what it refers to. Consider Jacques Derrida's observation that in the construction of meaning, a signifier always signifies another signifier: No word is free from metaphoricity.[9] The example of the dictionary is offered. When we search for the meaning of a word, our recourse is to look in a dictionary where instead of finding meaning we are given other words against which to compare our word. From this we can gather that meaning, otherwise expressed as the term "signified," emerges through discourse, as a consequence of displacements along signifying chains. Both of these references consider meaning as taking place through the interaction of information modules sequenced in relation to each other. *Slippery Traces* evokes the cinematic montage sequence through the linear ordering of images chosen through hot-spot links, but in contrast to the cinematic model, the narrative potential in this interactive work resides in the interplay of the viewer's choice, chance, and the encoded structure of the database.

George Legrady

8 Dylan Evans, *An Introductory Dictionary of Lacanian Psychoanalysis*, Routledge, London, New York, 1996.

9 Sarup Madan, *An Introductory Guide to Post-Structuralism and Post-Modernism*, University of Georgia Press, Athens, 1989, p.12.

References

Key theoretical references are Alain Robbe-Grillet's narrative structures and Roland Barthes' discussion of narrative analysis, the "death of the author" and the role of the viewer in "constructing" the story. Cinematic references include the image-analyzing machine of *Blade Runner*, the techno look of *Terminator*, and the montage of Alain Resnais' film *L'année dernière à Marienbad*.

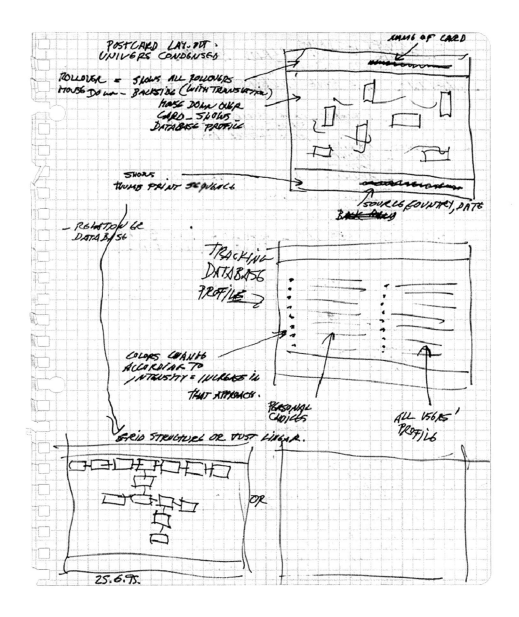

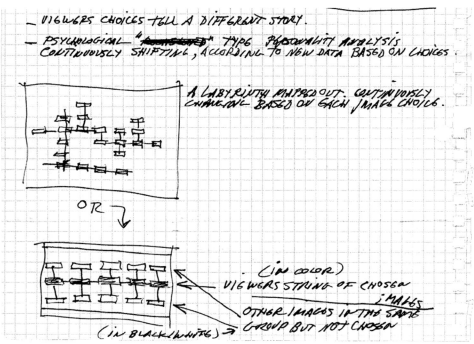

Sketches for
Slippery Traces
1995
collection of the artist
courtesy George Legrady

Chris Marker
Immemory

1997
CD-ROM, installation / dimensions variable

Chris Marker is best known as the author of essay films that are characterized by a marked subjectivity, similar to that of the literary essay. A particular feature of this filmic form is the unusual use of the narrative as a text with literary qualities: the narrative neither dominates nor is subjected to the image track, but instead is rhythmically interwoven with it. This creates a complex montage structure in which the interplay of text and image can generate multiple layers of meaning, and which can be described, following Gilles Deleuze, as an "audiovisual image."[1] As a result, the viewer is given a new role to play compared to that of the traditional cinemagoer: rather than passively consuming a film, the viewer must actively participate in its creation through his or her own mental activity.

The dominant themes in Marker's work are recollection and memory, both of which are contained in the French term *mémoire*, as the installation *Zapping Zone* (1990) and the CD-ROM *Immemory* (1997) impressively demonstrate. In Marker's films, the image functions like the Proustian madeleine, a cake dipped in tea that triggers the process of recollection. "I wonder how people remember things who don't film, don't photograph,"[2] as cameraman Sandor Krasna ponders in the film *Sans Soleil* (1982). Film, photography and recording tape present themselves as the media of recollection that give rise to the notion of total recall – a form of memory comprising everything that has been experienced.[3] However, in his film *Le Fond de l'Air est Rouge* (1977), Marker was already drawing attention to the fact that one never knows what one is filming, because the meaning of a captured image can be changed in retrospect by a later experience. Everything that is contained in one's memory is permanently being updated, overlaid with new impressions and partially erased. In *Sans Soleil* this process is described as follows: "We do not remember, we rewrite memory, much as history is rewritten."[4] The writing of history, placed on a level with the process of recollection, is ultimately impossible, and is disputed by Marker in the same way as he challenges an attribute that is often attached to photographic and filmed images: namely that these can give an objective representation of what has been. Marker's images function as catalysts for ever-changing views of history and past events. He uses film, installation and CD-ROM to make the process of recollection comprehensible.

In his first large installation, *Zapping Zone, Proposals for an Imaginary Television*, Marker combines photography, film, video, television and computers. Fourteen monitors are installed in a darkened space; some placed next to each other, others piled on top of one another on bases of different heights. On these screens, extracts from Marker's films are shown along with previously unpublished film material – such as footage of his encounters with the artists Matta and Christo and the filmmaker Tarkovsky – and filmed sequences of travel photographs and photomontages. Besides this, there are recordings and still images from television, two TV channels showing their current programs, various video works by Marker and computer-animated pieces, some of which can be controlled by mouse click. The film sequences, which are allocated to particular monitors described as "zones," are of different lengths and are played as a loop, with the result that the view of the installation as a whole is always changing, constantly producing new connections between the different zones. Also installed in the space are framed black-and-white and color photographs, a number of photomontages, a photographic series, four lightboxes with slides and three Japanese votive cats of different sizes. *Zapping Zone* was shown for the first time in Paris in 1990 as part of the exhibition "Passages de l'image" in the Centre Georges Pompidou, Paris, and was expanded for later presentations through the addition of several sequences and whole new zones. Each viewer follows his own route through the pictorial universe, determining how long to remain in front of which images, and drawing his own connections between the individual pieces.[5]

The title of the installation and the individual programs echo Tarkovsky's film *Stalker* (1978) in which a writer and a scientist, along with Stalker, their guide, cross a mysterious no-man's land, the Zone. They embark on a journey through a place that follows no logical laws and in which the path proves to be an obstacle-filled detour. The goal of the journey is a room in a dilapidated house, a room shrouded in legend in which one's deepest wish will be granted, but which ultimately none of the men will enter. Logic and imagination fail them, and the journey upon which they have embarked turns out to be one of self-knowledge. Marker makes repeated reference to Tarkovsky's Zone as a model and metaphor for the unfathomableness of *mémoire*. Like the Zone in *Stalker*, *Zapping*

1 Christa Blümlinger, "Zwischen den Bildern/Lesen," in Christa Blümlinger and Constantin Wulff (eds), *Schreiben Bilder Sprechen. Texte zum essayistischen Film*, Sonderzahl, Vienna, 1992, pp. 11–31, here p. 13. On the subject of the audiovisual image: Gilles Deleuze, *Cinema 2: The Time-Image*, trans. Hugh Tomlinson and Robert Galeta, University of Minnesota Press, Minneapolis, 1989 (French original 1985).

2 From the French commentary on *Sans Soleil*: "Chris Marker, *Sans Soleil*," in *Trafic*, no. 6, Spring 1993, pp. 79–97, here p. 95.

3 On the recollective function of media see Christina Scherer, *Ivens, Marker, Godard, Jarman. Erinnerung im Essayfilm*, Wilhelm Fink, Munich, 1999, (dissertation, University of Marburg, 1999), pp. 57–72.

4 Birgit Kämper, "Das Bild als Madeleine. Sans Soleil und Immemory," in Birgit Kämper and Thomas Tode (eds), *Chris Marker. Filmessayist*, Institut Français de Munich/CICIM, Munich, 1997, pp. 143–159, here p. 144.

5 See Raymond Bellour, "Eloge in h-moll. Zapping Zone," in Kämper / Tode, op. cit., pp. 129–134.

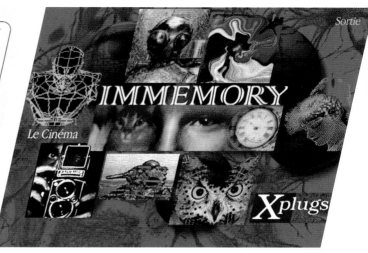

Immemory
1997
CD-ROM, installation
dimensions variable
installation view: ZKM | Center
for Art and Media
Karlsruhe, 2002
courtesy Centre Georges
Pompidou, Musée National d'Art
Moderne Centre de Création
industrielle, Paris
photo © Franz Wamhof

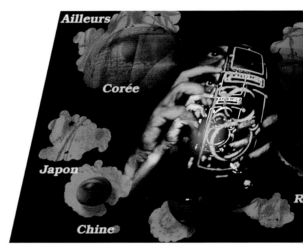

Zone permits no straight path of knowledge – a goal is never reached: stories, rather than one single history, emerge as a result.

The term "zapping" is used to describe how television viewers switch back and forth between different TV channels, a practice that established itself in the 1980s. This behavior is often judged to be the result of a diminished ability or willingness to focus attention, brought about by exposure to a flood of images in everyday life. *Zapping Zone* turns zapping into a creative act – the viewer creates his own film from the store of images on offer. In the framework of this installation, zapping is given a spatial dimension, in that the viewer must physically move around and walk from channel to channel. *Zapping Zone* can be re-garded as an attempt to take the viewer on a journey of recollection, the installation form recalling the design of Renaissance memory theaters.

For Marker, the ideal form for the theme of mem-ory and recollection ultimately appears to be the medium of CD-ROM, used by the filmmaker for the first time in his work *Immemory*, which was published in 1997. Here, zapping has given way to the mouse click, and entry into the memory archive is gained through seven "zones," in which Marker's subjects reappear in different images and texts: the themes of cinema, travel, museum, *mémoire*, photography, war, poetry, and the Xplugs, which are computer-gener-ated visual montages. Of the "three cult films" in the "cinema" zone, for example, one is Hitchcock's *Vertigo*, the story of a man who is obsessed by the memory of his dead lover, Madeleine. The user also encounters the director in the *"mémoire"* zone under the heading "What is a Madeleine?" alongside Marcel Proust. The filmmakers Andrei Tarkovsky and Akira Kurosawa are to be found, as are numerous photographs by Marker such as those from his books *Le Dépays* (1982) and *Coréens* (1959), together with previously unpublished pictures which can be accessed by following a number of different paths. One also finds "personal informa-tion" on the imaginary person who appears as "I" on the CD-ROM, as the user instructions emphasize.

Immemory
1997
screenshots
courtesy Centre Georges
Pompidou, Musée National d'Art
Moderne Centre de Création
industrielle, Paris

For example, two relatives from the Krasna family appear, Aunt Edith and Uncle Anton: Marker had already given this name to the letter-writer and cameraman in his film *Sans Soleil*. The "travel" zone opens with the relevant literature from the author's youth, including the fantastic journeys of Jules Verne and the Comte de Beauvoir's *Voyage autour du monde*.

Immemory offers the possibility of travelling into the past of the imaginary author. The journey is guided by the paths offered by the program, a navigational system which in many places allows one to branch off and enter another zone. Guillaume-en-Egypt presents himself as the guide through the labyrinth of *souvenirs*; however the hand-drawn cat is an unreliable guide. Most of the time it steers the user again and again towards detours and up wrong tracks.

The motif of the journey makes it clear that in *Immemory*, Marker does not conceive recollection and memory to be like a history book, but instead considers geography to be the "more modest and perhaps more fruitful" model.[6] The user is offered the opportunity to map the movements of remembering by using memory traces and to make visible, at least in part, the hidden plan which, according to Marker's hypothesis, lies behind every comprehensive memory. Memory is not subject to any causal order or chronological succession. The paths of recollection remain incomplete, something Marker emphasizes in his choice of the title *Immemory*, a negation of *mémoire*. It brings to mind the notion of the impossibility of total recall,[7] against which Marker sets the recollective model developed by Robert Hooke (1635–1702) in the seventeenth century. This assumes that there is a certain spot within the brain, one that is not further defined, "in which all sensory impressions are received and transmitted for contemplation." Impressions that are "only the movements of particles and bodies."[8]

Barbara Filser
Translated from the German by Jacqueline Todd

6 Cited from the booklet accompanying *Immemory*, unpaginated.

7 See also his films *La Jetée* and *Sans Soleil*.

8 Cited from the booklet accompanying *Immemory*, unpaginated.

Zapping Zone. Proposals for an Imaginary Television
1990–1992
media installation
thirteen monitors, thirteen PAL video tapes (color, sound), seven computers, seven programs on computer disk, twenty b/w and color photographs, four blocks of eighty slides
dimensions variable
installation views: steirischer herbst, Graz, 1998

Zapping Zone

Zapping Zone consists in a number of photographs, computer programs and video tapes produced by the artist. The latter can be seen on computers and monitors either stacked or laid out in the form of a circle in a darkened space, the "zone." This idea is reminiscent of the film *Stalker* by the Russian director Andreï Tarkovsky. Here it represents a hermetically scaled, complex and enigmatic space that only its initiates, or those who want to, can conquer. Chris Marker's "zone" consists in selected pieces from his films, extracts from his television programs, documentaries filmed in various places but not broadcast, photographs taken during his frequent travels, or even taken from televised images, and finally from active and interactive computers. In this way Chris Marker has composed new computer-graphics images, has retouched others, reworked television images either randomly through aerial distortions or deliberately. He has also inserted a short fictional film made in animated synthesized images: *Théorie des ensembles*. In addition, some images picked up direct from television are mixed with the "manufactured" images.

The idea of "zapping" refers to the viewer's attitude in the 1980s when faced with the profusion of sounds and pictures broadcast on our television channels, an idea very familiar to readers of Serge Daney.

Several key focal points structure this "open-ended" work, enhancing each showing with additional images: parts of the world close to the artist's heart, that is to say Tokyo, San Francisco and Berlin; faces of great friends, such as the painter Matta and the director Andreï Tarkovsky, favorite animals and a cat called Guillaume in Egypt, and so forth.

The subtitle of the work *Proposals for an Imaginary Television* reminds us that this is certainly not only a severe criticism of television and its content, but also of its production system. An imaginary electronic world is not an utopia.

Christine van Assche

Bill Seaman
The Exquisite Mechanism of Shivers

1997
interactive CD-ROM / published in artintact 1 (ZKM, 1997)

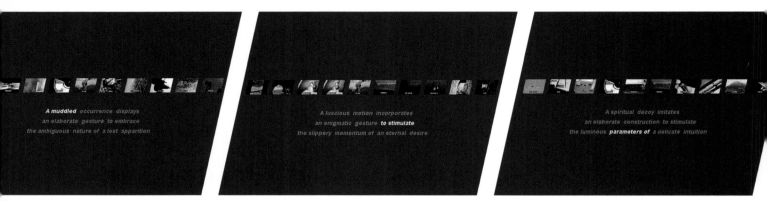

*A muddled occurrence displays
an elaborate gesture to embrace
the ambiguous nature of a lost apparition*

*A luscious motion incorporates
an enigmatic gesture **to stimulate**
the slippery momentum of an eternal desire*

*A spiritual decoy imitates
an elaborate construction to stimulate
the luminous **parameters of** a delicate intuition*

*The Exquisite Mechanism
of Shivers*
1997
interactive CD-ROM
screenshots
© Bill Seaman

When approaching a work as complex as *The Exquisite Machine of Shivers*, called in short *Ex. Mech*, it is best to begin at the end. The credits for the piece read: "Camera, music, text, editing, voice, programming, concept by Bill Seaman."1 Any categorization of *Ex. Mech* using the terminology of art, film, music, literature or media technology can thus only capture a partial aspect of the whole. Seaman is therefore an example of the interference between the genres and media producing a new multimedia art form, and at the same time an interdisciplinary work of art which can no longer really be described in usual terms.

From the beginning Seaman's way of working was to produce all elements of his work himself instead of using the usual array of quotes from TV, literature and music. He also does not get involved in teamwork (e.g. consisting of a composer, videomaker and programmer) as is increasingly common in the multimedia field. Instead he is one of the few artists who can and does perform all aspects of multimedia production by himself. The considerable effort involved is one explanation for why Seaman's list of works since 1979 comprises just nine video pieces.

Whereas the earlier works are mainly videotapes or installations, *Ex. Mech* is a complex work in so far as it exists in numerous different versions. The basis of these variants is a 28-minute videotape with 33 brief image and musical scenes, each based on a sentence of ten words. This amounts to a total of 330 words, which make up the poetic menu of the whole work. Based on this, there are five different ways in which the work can be presented and installed: as a linear videotape, as a linear installation with ten video projections, as an interactive installation with a control terminal and video projection, the sound only as an audio CD, and this CD-ROM version. *Ex.Mech* is thus a multimedia work of art in the fullest sense. Its software is no longer bound to a specific hardware and can manifest itself in various forms and contexts.

In the CD-ROM edition, it is particularly the interactive aspect of *Ex. Mech* that comes to fruition. The interactive process enables the user to combine different sentences created from the 330 words in the poetic menu, which in turn steer the succession of video and audio sequences.

The interactive quality of *Ex. Mech* enables the artist and user to meet halfway. The user plays with the elements derived from the imagination of the artist and is thus invited to create new compositions, i.e., form new sentences from the building blocks provided. He can also leave the choice to chance by using a random sentence generator. At the basis of the work is the generation of meaningful, absurd, banal or poetic sentences with the menu of 330 words. These language constructions then steer the image and sound. *Ex. Mech* has as its central theme the overlapping of three planes: language, image and sound. However it is not just a case of allowing these three planes to operate simultaneously, for film also contains these elements. Rather, it is an attempt to analyze their mutual influence over our perception and our construction of associations.

The principle of the viewers interaction with the work itself is the basic ambivalence of all meanings in words and images reveals itself. Each word takes on new meanings in conjunction with other words, or in relation to an image. "Shivers" can mean both "splinter" as well as "trembles." The fragmentary aspect of "splinter" as well as the oscillation of "trembles" release appropriate associations, as the coherences in meaning of the work are formed into sentences of oscillating sense from the 330 fragmentations of the menu.

Words and images exert a control over each other. In the installation the main emphasis is on control via the menu of words. On the CD-ROM a new interface allows more visual and intuitive access through the combination of images. Seaman speaks of the ob-

1 Bill Seaman in *Ex. Mech*,
exhib. cat., ICC Gallery, Tokyo,
1994, n. p.

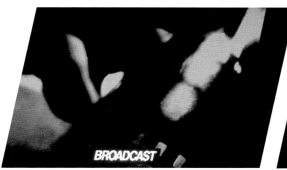
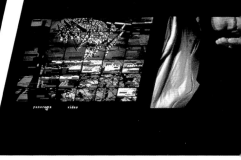

*Passage Sets/One Pulls Pivots
at the Tip of the Tongue*
1994–1995
interactive installation
mixed media
installation view: ZKM |
Center for Art and Media
Karlsruhe, 1995
© Bill Seaman
photo © ZKM

*Passage Sets/One Pulls Pivots
at the Tip of the Tongue*
1994–1995
interactive installation
screenshots
© Bill Seaman

server as a "navigator" through the system of *Ex.Mech*. "Content is generated through the viewer's process of navigation." The continually changing sequence of images, sounds and words releases us from the illusion that it can convey a specific message. "The work becomes a kind of paradox generator. Words are to images as thoughts are to the receiver/navigator."[2] *Ex. Mech* does not create a one to one relationship between text and image. When *Ex. Mech* is rendered in other languages the complete construct of 330 words must be reconstructed so as to retain both the technical and poetic functions.

For the Japanese version of *Ex. Mech* produced at the InterCommunication Center (ICC) in Tokyo in 1994, Bill Seaman actually worked for several weeks together with a Japanese translator and mastered Japanese pronunciation so as to be able to speak the words himself, as he did in the English version. In the installation *Ex. Mech*, it is thus possible to switch back and forth between the Japanese and the English version. This duality of language adds a new dimension to the work.

The real message of *Ex. Mech* is found in this overlapping of technology and content. The poetic construction and the technical function cannot be separated from each other. *Ex. Mech* follows a long tradition of poetic machines and mechanized language, a tradition that links very remote points in the history of ideas.[3] They all focus the question of whether mankind is the only one who can create meaning, or whether he must share this privilege with other authorities, be this with God, or with the subconscious. Seaman's audiovisual poetry machine once again poses this question in the face of the digital age and thus touches upon a central point in contemporary culture, formulated by Allan Turing in 1950: "Can a machine think?"

Dieter Daniels
Translated from the German by Anina Helmsley
A longer version of this text was first published in *artintact 1*, ZKM | Center for Art and Media Karlsruhe and Hatje Cantz Verlag, Ostfildern, 1997, pp. 41–51.

2 Seaman, op. cit.

3 Here I follow the best presentation of this history of poetic machines and the importance of the theory of combination for Surrealism by Hans Holländer, "Ars inveniendi et investigandi," in *Surrealismus*, Peter Bürger (ed.), Wissenschaftliche Buchgesellschaft, Darmstadt, 1982, n.p.

Agnes Hegedüs
Their Things Spoken

2001
interactive DVD / published in (dis)LOCATIONS
(ZKM digital arts edition, 2001)

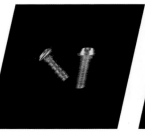

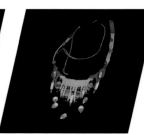

Their Things Spoken
2001
interactive DVD
screenshots
© Agnes Hegedüs

By the 1960s at the latest, interest was beginning to focus on the aura of used objects. Legitimized by Duchamp's radical declaration that industrial objects were worthy of art status, the succeeding generations of artists incorporated all areas of everyday life into their artistic methods.

Today, the diminishing aura of the work of art has been accompanied by a rise in that of the utility object when used as artmaking material, since such objects refer to production conditions in consumerist mass culture yet function still as fragments of an individual biography or collective context of life. Many contemporary approaches suggest that the current interest in memory techniques and their cultural effects is leaving its mark on art, too. Thus, artists' adoption of archival structures articulates a growing awareness of the expressive power of marginal biographies that, normally submerged in the daily flood of spectacular events, seldom play a role within the "major narrative" of historical facts. Private experience and the accounts of anonymous individuals can be used to strategically undermine the monolithic consensus that dominates the official "storyline" of world history. Memory is always selective, guided by

political motives, striving to meet the official version of events. Especially the media and the public consciousness function according to the principle of forgetting and holding back information. *Their Things Spoken* by Agnes Hegedüs refers to the gulf between the conservation and valuation of officially recognized cultural representations and the information content of bearers of personal significance originating in apparently unimportant, unknown biographies. The artist distributed among visitors to the ZKM a leaflet asking, "Why not put your favorite object in a museum?" This question stimulated the museum visitors to reflect upon rituals of appreciating and keeping, and to relate the museum exhibits to the relics to which they attribute private significance.

In its processual character, Hegedüs' concept reconstructs the evolutionary history of the collection, which have beginnings in the private curiosity galleries and "wunderkammers" of kings and rulers. However, modern industrial societies first perfected the conservation of objects for the purpose of public display, and at the same time conferred cult status upon the object. Hegedüs combines these aspects of a development over the centuries with the present

Their Things Spoken
2001
interactive DVD
screenshots
© Agnes Hegedüs

form of digital databasing that has removed spatio-geographical restrictions on access and offers flexible user interfaces enabling the public to appropriate cultural values through new channels.

This partiality to objects was what brought more than 250 responses to the artist's invitation. Using a Polaroid camera to document contributors and objects, and a tape recorder for their stories and comments, she imposed no restrictions on the choice of personal favorites.

Her concern was to warehouse the portraits of people and objects in the most neutral possible way, so that every image and statement is equally valid. The DVD-ROM storage medium allows the body of contributions to be archived exactly as they were documented. The stories stand for themselves and, like an atlas of everyday life, show a random collection of people whose relationship to the world is revealed through the objects they identify with.

In its encyclopedic structure and interactive organization, *Their Things Spoken* is reminiscent of Walter Benjamin's *Arcades Project* (1913–1926) likewise organized in archival form in order to be able to do justice to the nuanced diversity of temporal phenomena. One expression of Benjamin's notion that what looks out at us from an object is the human consciousness which once produced or used it and considered the object to be significant was his obsession with the

idea of being able to re-discover time as if it were a reproducible element. Hegedüs creates a representational space for this notion of a social memory that combines the language of objects and the expression of their interpreters.

Their Things Spoken is the third part of a trilogy Hegedüs began in 1997 with the interactive installation *Memory Theatre VR*, a dramatically staged presentation of key moments in art and media history. Building upon the basic concept underlying its predecessor, the second part *Things Spoken* (1999) builds on the basic idea of its predecessor and extends the central aspect of a collective memory store to include personal recollections and associations through which people and objects are incorporated into a relational network of communication.[1]

Hegedüs' manner of proceeding is reminiscent of a teaching method popular above all in kindergartens and schools in the USA. "Show & Tell" is a game in which teachers ask children to present to their classmates objects possessing a special significance. They are supposed to explain the personal experience linked with the object, and so share the story with the other children. The game has an anecdotal starting point, and in it the object acts as a vehicle for the pedagogic intention of triggering communicative processes. Object and person merge via the pictorial structure of the object. Just as the anecdote has an

1 *Things Spoken*, publ.
on CD-ROM in *artintact 5*,
ZKM | Center for Art
and Media Karlsruhe (ed.),
Hatje Cantz, Ostfildern,
1999.

Filming the objects.

Recording the interviews.

image-like function, so the game and the artistic concept are based on the description's pictorial character, which is reinforced by the object's symbolic import. The anecdote – a masterful instrument of a highly developed and systematic art of discourse – recalls to the present a past perceived, through narration, as timeless. In their performative, anecdotal character, the narratives collected by Hegedüs are comparable with a mental relinquishing that allows encounters with other people in the course of speech-borne self-exposure. Showing and telling is a communicative act that binds the individual to a collective. Storytelling, in this sense, can be seen as a hermeneutic activity: the reading of something familiar as new and intensive, an invention that becomes a communicative link. The comparison of personal experience in this type of DVD-ROM memory bank confronts and relativizes individual value perspectives that, taken together, impose on us a discursive perception.

Their Things Spoken
2001
interactive DVD
installation view: ZKM |
Center for Art and Media
Karlsruhe, 2001
© Agnes Hegedüs

Ursula Frohne

Abridged and revised version of Ursula Frohne's essay "Show & Tell: The Discursive Idea of Things," in *(dis)LOCATIONS*, ZKM | Center for Art and Media Karlsruhe and The Centre for Interactive Cinema Research, College of Fine Arts, University of New South Wales, Sydney, Hatje Cantz, Ostfildern, 2001, pp. 52–61.

Ian Howard
SweetStalking

2001
interactive DVD / published in (dis)LOCATIONS
(ZKM digital arts edition, 2001)

SweetStalking
2001
interactive DVD
screenshots
© Ian Howard

The original brief for the exhibition suggested use of interactive systems to investigate the way urban and sexual relationships are located and dislocated through contemporary digital space. Implied in early curatorial discussions was a suggestion of threat and anxiety existing within these overlapping themes of sexuality and the city. Consequently, I started with the theme of stalking, that is, stalking meaning in a relationship. As I have a sometimes very busy day job, I decided it was expeditious and fruitful to explore this theme with my partner, Lucienne. The problem was the work kept on lightening up and eventually had to be renamed *SweetStalking* (could be "Sweets-talking" and so on), as Lucienne speaks four languages across the soundtrack of the work. The interactive structure of *SweetStalking* allows viewers to put together their own edited sequences of images and incidents (the narrative format) that provide information and insights into the relationship "story." Additional video sequences, the random throwing of a dice (like the hand you're dealt each day), complement the viewer's choice, and if you are lucky further reward sequences provide deeper insights. The program that runs this explorative narrative (your edited choices, the random element, the rewards and so on) handles sixty to the power of five to the power of six to the power of twelve images and sound tracks. This results in more than ten million sequences being available that individually and collectively contribute to the unraveling of meaning in a relationship.

Ian Howard

First published in *Morphologies*, exhib. cat., Artspace Visual Arts Centre LTD., Sydney, 2001.

Norman M. Klein
The Future of the Cinematic City

1 The term "cinematic city" is based on *The Cinematic City*, David B. Clarke (ed.), Routledge, London, 1997.

  Other useful texts (for basic discourse and bibliography, on a vast subject, linked to theory and historical practice): Mark Shiel and Tony Fitzmaurice (eds), *Cinema and the City: Film and Urban Societies in a Global Context*, Blackwell, London, 2001; Annette Kuhn, *Alien Zone II: The Spaces of Science Fiction*, Verso, London, 1999; Francois Penz and Maureen Thomas (eds), *Cinema as Architecture*, BFI Publishing, London, 1997; Dietrich Neumann (ed.), *Film Architecture: From Metropolis to Blade Runner*, Prestel, Munich/New York, 1996.

  See also (for a partial overview of related sources) special issues in film journals (*Wide Screen*, Spring 1998, etc.), numerous studies on *Blade Runner*, on special effects (magazines like *Cinefex*), on the consumer-built city (*Architectural Design*, February 1998), on "cinematic geographies" (Christopher Lukinbeal, etc.), cinematic urbanism (Thomas Mical, etc.), cinema and city by G. Bruno, M. de Certeau, T. Elsaesser; also the vast literature on noir and the city; writings by Mike Davis and myself on noir Los Angeles; and finally, the literature on computer gaming, software, rides, themed and digital architecture, and the production of space.

2 Another way of looking at the three:
The city as labyrinth: moral chaos.
The city as solipsistic, fascist: overcontrolled.
The city as a reification of industrial capitalist systems of power and hierarchy.
All three suggest a world where free will cannot survive, the city as the death of the democratic impulse.

3 City as Labyrinth: expanded from the first footnote, the city as labyrinth goes back to medieval Troy games, if not earlier; but more clearly, its meaning stems from a seventeenth-century term, the "labyrinth of the world": labyrinth as human follow, reified as an urban plan. This meaning survived into Romantic descriptions of the city (Shelley, de Quincy, Hugo, Gautier; then into novels by Dickens, Sue, etc.); and then into the early crime novels of Poe and Doyle; finally into noir crime literature – and film (noir to cyberpunk). Among its symptoms: paranoid tracking shots, hand-held cameras in tight places, to generate a loss of place that, in turn, offers up the city as labyrinth, classically in 1920s German cinema, and then in Film Noir.

After thousands of movies over the past eighty years, we carry inside us a combined mental picture of an imaginary American city. It is a city of crowds during an industrial era, once upon a time between 1925 and 1960 – a cinematic city.1 Its details remain intensely vivid for audiences around the world, now probably more than ever. Its streets are mostly made of brick. Its secrets come to life at night. The camera can move through it in one of three ways:2

– A tracking shot inside a messy labyrinth of streets;3
– An overhead shot above a very geometric, controlled cityscape, sealed off as if by a membrane;4
– A crane shot that rises up and down, like an elevator. It climbs toward the windows of fancy penthouses. It drops below the street, into the depths of poverty. Along the way, it crosses horizontal layers. Each layer has been isolated by social class, from the powerful up top, to the weak down below.

In Orlando, copies of movie sets of the city have been copied for theme park events. False brownstones and false Brooklyn Bridges serve as foreground for papier-mâché skylines. The sum effect looks indelible because it never existed, except as a phantom, a movie set – at casinos like New York/New York, themed spaces like the New Times Square in New York, cinemalls like the Hollywood at Highland in Los Angeles; and on computer systems of all kinds, cities of bits, trans-architecture, games.

Since 1997, with the game version of *Blade Runner*, there have dozens of "adventure noirs," clearly featuring the cinematic city. For example: *Mafia: City of Lost Heaven*; *Dead to Rights*; *Discworld Noir*; *Grim Fandango*; *Nightshade*; *Mean Streets*; *The Pandora Directive*; *Hell*; *Hell Cab*; and, of course, *Max Payne*, "a Hong-Kong-action-meets-film-noir detective story."5 The details usually involve a detective, loose women, drugs and bad lighting outdoors. Or in a cozier version, at NewYork/NewYork casino, double-hung windows are filled with Manhattan junk. Or in the movie *Spiderman* (USA, 2002), Spidey loops across the canyons of Manhattan. Or simply the alienation of the crowd: an amnionic light across the sidewalk at night, pointing toward a skyline dressed for murder.

These noir touches spark fond memories about poverty and urban chaos. The memories are then turned into miracles of synergy. They are marketed from film to computers to themed spaces. They fit the neo-conservative corporate model of the inner city as hell, a racially unfit place: Better to clear out when labor costs go up. They are a global "erehwon" (nowhere spelled backward),6 a gotham for the ages – and yet, of no age at all – a powerful grammar for designers across media, from architectural space to cyberspace. And now with the bombing of the World Trade Towers, this cinematic city becomes even more spectral, almost sacred; and certainly more traumatic.

In *Bleeding Through: Layers of Los Angeles, 1920–1986* (2002, DVD installation), my contribution to the "Future Cinema" exhibition, tropes from this cinematic city migrate across all three tiers, throughout hundreds of photos, interviews, newspaper clippings: the city as noir labyrinth; the city looking geometric from overhead; the imaginary city simplifying myths about race and class. We even decided to reshoot exact locations from Los Angeles crime films, but leave out the actors, to intensify the way memory is echoed inside the cinematic city, a place filled with "absences that generate desire." I also arranged for the lead character, Molly, to visit slapstick film shoots in the 1920s; only to find them perversely inaccurate; and yet, at the same time, a cracked mirror of her own marital nightmares.

I realize that this cinematic city makes for ghoulish redundancy in the arts. A good noir murder reeks with nostalgia and exoticism. Its aesthetic rules are also extremely rigid; it tends to strangle experimentation. When I run workshops on how to try something fresh with cinematic Los Angeles, students are amazed by how many artists still worship these faked memories, particularly in the film industry. For example, back in 1996 during a workshop on how movies misrepresent the Los Angeles police, I was quite impressed by two young men in the front row. They kept interrupting with interesting comments, scribbling notes like court reporters. Afterward, they ran up to thank me for clarifying a truth that they had always suspected. I had convinced them that movies never lie about cops. What, I answered? How did you get that? Didn't my lecture stress exactly the opposite? They looked at me condescendingly. One of them answered: "Well, we're screenwriters. We already know the truth."

I felt as if I were trying to de-program the severely brainwashed. All my old-new lefty complaints had evaporated. One way or another, they were certain that movies delivered the truth from Sinai, especially for urban history and crime stories. Then they explained how this truth operated: Hollywood movies have be fun. This fun makes them true. That's the only truth you can afford, if you want to keep working in the film business.

I made a cross with my index fingers, and walked on. I occasionally wonder if they are assistant managers of a Burger King today, or are actually running a movie studio. But their story matches dozens of other encounters. The cinematic city has become a form of sublime that goes a long, long way.

As I often say to students, the world may not be deep, but it is definitely shallow and wide. We have achieved the replacement of public memory by the media, so often predicted in the 1920s, in Weimar criticism of the cinematic city in Berlin (where it essentially first appeared). In an advertising brochure for *Die Strasse* (1923), an imaginary viewer witnesses the erasure of Berlin by movies. He watches crews shooting inside a vast indoor set, a copy of Berlin streets (designed by Ludwig Meidner). Once the cameras start rolling, urban reality vanishes. "Forgotten are the gawking onlookers behind the barbed wire fence. Forgotten is the lit dock of the Steglitz hall tower. Forgotten is Berlin's dark silhouette, even the annoying apparatus of the set."7

Instead, "the radiant facade city" takes over. It is just as noisy and crowded as the actual Berlin, but magically empty at the same time. "I am no longer me," he writes. "Instead, I am a medium who staggers hypnotized through the unchained chaos of the street." The spiraling action inside the set utterly hypnotizes him. He feels almost sexually aroused by the absence that is present, by the glamour; until finally "the light of the floodlights is put out and the nocturnal apparition fades before the reality of the starry night."

That is a 1920s version of shallow and wide, the erasure of expressionist intentions by the sheer, immersive artifice of the movie set. Kracauer, of course, goes even further, in comparing the cinematic city to "mass ornament."8

In recent decades, the cinematic city has indeed gone far and wide, to a computer-graphics recreation of a slum on Mars in *Total Recall* (USA, 1989). Or it has gone microscopically wide, to the faint blue ignition when a synapse burns a memory inside your head (*The Cell* [USA, 2000], *The Matrix* [USA, 1999], among others). Inside the cinematic sim-city, characters don't need an interior life. They move along like genetically engineered fruit with no flavor, but the shelf-life of a doorknob.

But eventually, by the third act, this cinematic city goes to the dogs. It surrenders to cyborgs or grizzled lunatics with patches over one eye. The social pathology is much the same as noir classics of the 1950s; or at least noir graphic novels since the 1970s. There are still no safe neighborhoods, no domestic normalcy, except in colonies that escape to the bush in *Mad Max* (USA, 1979-1985) films. Meanwhile, the overheads of the city at night are still there, as in the 1950s. Now, instead of "diamonds on black velvet," it suggests fascism as feudalism, the neighborhood constantly under surveillance.9

Neo-noir, and the city it requires, are Greek theater without an unconscious. All urban realities outside the paranoic structure must be buried, in order to make revenge and catharsis legible. That makes for rousing stories, but what if the structure becomes a reality? This reified cine-city is a global brand that helps keep the film industry roaring along. And while its banal high concepts often terrorize me, I am by no means certain that I could any better, not until global marketing recognizes neighborhoods and niches that I know personally. This is what those two screenwriters were probably warning me.

And I must confess: as a film grammar, this cinematic city is indeed a magnificent edifice. I am addicted to its noir cuteness, the flash editing, the epic chases, even to its stock characters: the gangster boss and his schizophrenic brother; their long-suffering wives; the nervous bookkeeper who takes a bullet through his eye (gruesome) at the beginning of the third act. And the young hunk who is born again after being stomped by psychotic hoodlums. Down these dark streets, as Raymond Chandler wrote fifty years ago in *The Simple Art of Murder*.10

In that essay, Chandler left the impression that he was capturing the social realist fragrance of Los Angeles. At the same time, in letters, he apologized to a detective agency that he was simply inventing his

crime world as he went along. Like many of the architects of cinematic Los Angeles, he loved the truths of its untruths. As I often say to students: the best way to lie is with the truth. A little realist claptrap makes for pathologically great murders. So, in balance, despite my complaints, I want to pay my respects to the cinematic city. It clearly deserves respect. But what does it say about our fragile future?

Five Thousand New Yorks

As of 2002 surely, Manhattan is indeed "white, wealthy and walled in," to use the late 1970's expression. It has lost some of its epic meaning for the twentieth century; the frantic bustle and layered chaos, like Dante's rings into Hell's Kitchen. When Fritz Lang visited Manhattan in 1924, he saw it as cinema, a "beacon of beauty strong enough to be the centerpiece of a film." Ironically enough, he described two films at once – *Metropolis* (Germany, 1927) soon to be initiated, and most prophetically, its descendant, *Blade Runner* (USA, 1982). Lang was particularly struck by New York at night: the red and blue tumult on the street enclosed by "screaming green." He saw it in layers. Spiraling lights from the street drew the eye above the cars, above the elevated trains, toward skyscrapers in blue and gold. But even higher still, were "advertisements surpassing the stars with their light."

Much the same filmic obsession about Manhattan compelled movie studios in Los Angeles to build "New York Streets" at the same time (Paramount/RKO, MGM, Warners, Universal, Fox). It was possible to shoot in Los Angeles, and make it look like anytown USA, but the studios needed Manhattan's Gotham effect. This phenomenon became even more important once sound came in. During the 1930s, films could not be shot on Los Angeles streets any longer. To control the sound, they had to be shot indoors, for the most part. Thus a Los Angeles/Manhattan became much more complex; and very soon, emblematic throughout the world.

But these New York Streets were not enough. They were usually no more than twenty facades made of board and stucco. The cinematic city required more. You added an establishing-shot might of New York, Chicago, London, Paris. Then you added hyperbole, drama. Indoor sound stages were modeled on tenements, as in Warners' *Dead End* (USA, 1937). Then effects compositing was added, notably in *King Kong* (USA, 1933), but in dozens of other films that required urban panorama. Through effects, many skyscrapers were imagined in movies before they were actually built (i.e. *Things to Come*, [USA, 1936]) Skylines were invented as miniatures, glass mattes, moving mattes. Harbors were moored indoors, by rear projection.

The result was convincing, but like the advertising brochure for *Die Strasse*, wonderfully fake. It was a highly theatricalized Manhattan, a Mannerist *teatro olimpico*, a world in a bottle. But I am convinced that Depression audiences found these deodorized tenement streets oddly satisfying, like the hand of man correcting God's mistakes.

Then, after World War II, this emblematic movie city changes yet again. It gets grittier, more darkly lit (noir). Film crews increasingly return to actual Los Angeles streets, for "authenticity." However, the "authentic" city still had to match the artificial one made in the studio. Noir was a hybrid of the city and the sound stage. Only rarely were films shot "entirely on location," like Dassin's *The Naked City* (USA, 1948), borrowing from Weegie's photos. "Entirely on

4 A useful summary of the considerable literature on the solipsistic city: Samuel Nunn, "Designing the Solipsistic City: Themes of Urban Planning and Control in *The Matrix*, *Dark City*, and *The Truman Show*," *CTheory*, July 2001.

5 Comment by Saku Lehtmen, art director at Remedy Entertainment, who produced *Max Payne*.

6 As in Samuel Butler's *Erewhon* (1872), but much grimmer.

7 Anthony Vidler, "The Explosion of space: Architecture and the Filmic Imaginary," in Neumann (ed.), op. cit.

8 Siegfried Kracauer, *The Mass Ornament: Weimar Essays*, Harvard University Press, Cambridge, 1995 (originally published in 1963). Twenty-four essays selected by the author. Renewed interest in this aspect of Kracauer's work grows in the United States, for example: Gertrud Koch, *Siegfried Kracauer: An Introduction*, Princeton University Press, Princeton, 2000 (originally published in 1996), chapter 3.

9 See footnote 2.

10 "Down these mean streets a man must go who is not himself mean, who is neither tarnished, nor afraid." Raymond Chandler, *The Simple Art of Murder*, Vintage Books, New York, 1988, p. 18 (originally published in 1950).

location" was so rare that it was announced at the front of Henry Hathaway's *Kiss of Death* (USA, 1948) as well. But the New York locations of *Kiss of Death* look strangely like the Los Angeles/New York streets, as if the grammar had begun to erase the insides of buildings, and the mood of the city itself.

By now, of course, this erasure is complete. I am convinced that the cinematic city has displaced the collective memory of the 1940s American city. We have all absorbed dozens, if not hundreds of noir classics. Even by 1960, at the end of the first noir era, this erasure of the city was already evident. Hollywood had standardized the look of urban decay: a fully disposable, all-purpose Manhattan. This epic city, based on the three principles that I mention on the first page, could be tailored to every continent and every climate.

And when a location didn't quite fit, it was altered through special effects. Los Angeles/Manhattan, even in its London version (*Night and the City*, 1950) was easy to manufacture. It could be moved from the effects room to the editing room, to a tenement setup inside a real slum. And then for the final shootout, you rely more on a sound stage and extremely delicate, almost dainty, lighting, with hundreds of arcs and dinkies, tones worthy of Rembrandt. In fact, certain low-key lighting was, in fact, called Rembrandt lighting. We also know that Hitchcock preferred the sound stage to real locations. He preferred rear projection for *Vertigo* (USA, 1958), rather than drag his actors through a chilly, disruptive morning in San Francisco. One could even argue that the cinematic city was a hybrid between 1920s theater and 1940s cinema; it was theatricalized naturalism as Baroque illusion.

By 1960, the nuances were carefully established, like a kit. They could travel the world, but, when necessary, never leave the room. They made paranoia look as clean as a perfect crime, even in the films of Sam Fuller, like *Shock Corridor* (USA, 1963). I have seen dozens of cinematography manuals, published in London and the USA. They are remarkably consistent. They clarify each setup, like a master text of Baroque scenography or, as in John Alton's remarkable *Painting with Light*, like a formula for designing terror.[11]

Of course, we should be reminded that Alton had worked in the silent German film industry before arriving in Los Angeles, like so many designers of the cinematic noir city. It was Manhattan as 1920s Berlin, by way of downtown Los Angeles – a trans-localized imaginary. But since 1960, global media has found other purposes for it, beyond film. The cinematic city has left the building. Its five thousand New Yorks now feature restaurants, thrill rides, and gentrification.

In Los Angeles, this is an old trick, a ghost in the machine. I visit these five thousand New Yorks every day, where the Lower East Side is a short drive from the Hollywood sign. I used to live around the corner from a murder scene in *Chinatown* – the death of the false Mrs. Mulwray, and a block away from Michael Jackson's *Thriller*, near middle America in *The Winds of War*. That is Angelino Heights, only a kilometer a mile from Chicago in *The Sting*. And only another kilometer to *Mean Streets*, and *Cagney and Lacey* – in east Los Angeles and eastern downtown, often trans-localized into Manhattan during the 1970s.[12] My favorite breakfast joint is in neo-noir central: the opening setup for *Reservoir Dogs* (USA, 1992).

On the way to work, I drive by dozens of cinematic flashbacks, moments from 1950s horror films like *Them!* (USA, 1954; on the embankments of the Los Angeles River); or glimpses of the sewers of West Los

Angeles in *He Walked By Night* (USA, 1948). Hundreds of locations that I have researched follow me like dogs chasing a milk wagon.

Of course, some locations are on the frontier, beyond cinematic Manhattan. The old movie ranches have been shut down, for the most part, but on each of them, as many as two thousand were filmed, particularly the Iverson Ranch, the Century Ranch, or the abandoned quarry on Brush Canyon.[13]

Some locations turn into lures for real estate. In Culver City, the old MGM back lot was converted into Raintree Village, a hive of condos centered around the Lagoon where Johnny Weissmuller as Tarzan used to swim. Next door, another condo village features relics from Tara, which are rare, since Tara was mostly a movie matte, never was built.

Other film locations reclaim lost buildings, particularly those abandoned by the city, useless in any civic sense. The Lincoln Heights Jail was shut down in the 1960s, then "staged a comeback" in dozens of films after 1970.[14] It is now a Latino youth club with its own boxing ring. A few remaining guards are proud of its heritage as a movie set. Downtown, meanwhile, is literally a hive of film production. Downtown on Broadway, on the second floor of a seismically abandoned building, a sign propped against the window reads "available for movie productions."

These impact of noticing all these locations reminds me of that brochure for *Die Strasse* again, but in reverse. These are movie "apparitions" that replace the city as you go – with inevitable confrontations. Everyone in Los Angeles has Buñuelian anecdotes about movie crews transmogrifying their block. I have been stuck in unexpected beer commercials, had film crews casually take over my house at dawn, watched the world blowing up near Spring Street. One night in 1982, I entered a West Hollywood office building, and literally found myself checking in at an imaginary airport. The sensation is banalizing and bizarre at the same time – cinematic trompe l'oeil.

The most bizarre trompe l'oeil may be found at the Belmont Tunnel, just west of downtown. It is 1.1 miles long, 30 feet wide, the bleak ruins left by an abandoned subway (1926–1958). Inside, the grotto effect is worthy of a Piranesi. The walls inside and out are engulfed by graffiti fifty layers deep. Homeless men and feral dogs can be sensed everywhere, but not seen. At the same time, the tunnel is littered with movie filters discarded by film crews. Dozens, if not hundreds, of hip-hop music videos, TV commercials, pulp shootouts and alien encounters have been shot there.

But in August 2002, the Belmont Tunnel outdid itself. Suddenly, the dirt path at its mouth was paved over, for the first time in its history. Homeless smells were scrubbed out entirely, given a lysol bath. Graffiti artists with spray cans were refused entry. A movie crew, protected by rented cops, was preparing to shoot a feature there. The movie will be set in Malibu – about beach-town rich kids on a beer bust during semester break. City hall had licensed the deal; but the money it brings will never go to help the Latino kids who live around the Tunnel.

Sometimes a location re-enacts a tragedy while it is taking place. In 1996, near Cedars-Sinai Hospital, real ambulances were blocked by movie ambulances, because film crews were shooting *Volcano* (USA, 1997). Mannequins were posed as corpses on makeshift gurneys. Fake lava and ash was blown like sawdust until it erased the street. For residents, it was a Baroque moment, like parallel universes getting their wires crossed.

11 John Alton, *Painting With Light*, University of California Press, Berkeley, 1995 (originally published in 1949).

12 The sense that eastern downtown in Los Angeles is actually SoHo or Tribeca has led Los Angeles developer Tom Gilmore to redesign it – the "Artist (loft) District" – as Lower New York West.

13 Mackenzie Wasson, "A Stone's Throw Away: Quarry Where Film Action Is," in *Los Angeles Times, Calendar*, 30 March 1969.

14 "Lincoln Heights Jail Stages a Comeback," in *Los Angeles Times*, 16 April 1970.

Occasionally, this can generate an odd thrill – if the brain-dead private dicks ever let you leave your own driveway. At other times, while the crew, and the occasional actor, eat their catered lunch, you might feel like an "insider." They might wink at you. But mostly, the feeling is more like watching a "tuning" by aliens from another world (*Dark City* [USA, 1998]). For residents, "thrills" from movie crews are few and far between. But for tourists, the thrill can be glorious, an epiphany worth the plane fare.

And over the past thirty years, many tourist businesses have exploited this epiphany. Not that this is entirely new to Los Angeles. In the 1920s, up at Universal, the frugal Carl Laemmle used to charge tourists to watch movie shoots. But that was prehistoric compared to Universal Tours parting the Red Sea every ten minutes, or posing King Kong on constant alert. Or putting the tourist inside the movie itself. In 1978, to please my father, we went to Universal Tours. On the TV set, I was selected to be a Puerto Rican hoodlum. I was told to look racially confused, while another tourist dressed as a cop patted me down. Meanwhile, we were blue-screened on to a street in New York. My father was thrilled for me. I, of course, felt myself dropped into sim-hell, beyond ridiculous.

That same year, at the Culver City studios, I walked through a movie set from my adolescence. As a teenager, I used to visit precisely the same street in Greenwich Village. Now it had been parboiled into a movie set, inside a sound stage for a movie starring the Village People. Even the cinnamon-smelling garbage pails were filled with molded plastic garbage. The chemically hazy skyline was painted. Brownstones were made of stucco and chicken wire. For about ten minutes, I rummaged through the sound stage. Ever since, I can't quite separate that from how Greenwich Village actually looked or smelled when I was a teenager.

This is what promoters call "movie magic," an infectious part of our global heritage. Even in Rome and Berlin, abandoned movie studios – UFA and Cinecittà – were turned into something like theme parks. In Los Angeles, the Max Factor Museum features John Wayne's wig. And many tourists would be thrilled to try it on, I'm sure. Not that the city of Los Angeles is interested in film locations: there is no program to commemorate them, no signage, no plaques anywhere, except the statue of James Dean in *Rebel Without a Cause* (USA, 1955), up at the Planetarium; and that may refer more to the celebrity of a dead cult figure than scenes in a movie. For Los Angeles movie locations are campfires that must be stamped out and forgotten. Recently, sets for De Mille's silent *The Ten Commandments* (USA, 1923) were unearthed on a beach, like an archaeological discovery of prehistoric rubbish. They had been buried to save time and money, to hustle to the next production.

The capital for exploiting the cinematic city may be Orlando more than Los Angeles. In Orlando, they have built two movie-set facsimiles of New York; and two more of Hollywood Boulevard. At the MGM/Disney New York street, a forty foot panel has been transformed into a full-service ten-storey skyscraper, with a real hotel next door. Along the street, a real New York police car is parked in front of a fake street. Blinking high-rises accelerate perspectives, literally box the compass.

Surely Las Vegas runs a close second after Orlando. In the past decade, five New Yorks were built in Las Vegas (along with Paris, Venice, the Italian Alps, ancient Rome, Morocco, Polynesia, and the West Indies). Near Oz, the MGM Grand set up a modest New York, not unlike the mid-town delicatessen and flat-iron building above the Nile at the Luxor. Then, MGM management considered developing a New York skyline as shopping mall across the street. Finally, that land was converted instead into the New York/New York casino hotel; which, in turn, sparked a very expensive, five-year law suit. Who legally held the copyright to build a New York skyline in facsimile? Surely not New York City. During the trial, dozens of other fake New Yorks were unearthed.

However, the prize for the most Manhattans must go to computer games, from "Fahrenheit" to "Mafia: The City of Lost Heaven" (twelve square miles). But in 2002, the movie *Spiderman* performed some interesting trans-local logistics. Along with models and establishing shots, the "canyons of New York" were built inside an old Rockwell defense plant in Downey. And Spidey himself jumped from building to building in downtown Los Angeles, not New York.

The final insult or epiphany goes beyond computer games to digital architecture. We can expect the cinematic city to be transported inside malls of all sort, particularly outdoor malls, like adding Manhattan dentures – or Los Angeles or Vegas implants – to fill gaps on a downtown street anywhere. We must understand that the condensed city (two blocks where an entire city is squashed into a hotel) is precisely the same size as the old New York streets. The methodology has indeed gone global, as well as the inversions: mid-town Manhattan has now been "Los Angelized," turned into a wall of video screens; the Sunset Strip as the Greater White Way; a deodorized Blade Runner theme park. In Los Angeles, the Trizek-Hahn mall at Hollywood and Highland (8 acres, 650,000 square feet) is a pale, but vast homage to "movie magic." It even commemorates the famous Babylon set from Griffith's *Intolerance* (USA, 1916), which stood like a giant piano box almost two hundred feet high, intruding at the eastern corner of what became a heavily trafficked street in Hollywood after 1920.[15]

All this, of course, begs the question: For a show on "Future Cinema," can alternatives to the cinematic city be imagined? The future of cinema clearly lies in solid and digitized architecture, through urban planning, interactive installations and games, and in themed spaces. But how will these respond to the crisis in content today, to the alienation that the cinematic city ignores – or hyperbolizes into pubescent surprise, a cultural equivalent of premature ejaculation?

As I explained earlier, media experimentation is restricted by this cinematic paramnesia, by a grammar based on misremembering – as much as we all love it. Computer games should not pride themselves on looking more "realistic" (that is, more like the cinematic city). We need more playful subversions of the cinematic city, to find a way out of this quandary, beyond fake labyrinths, and plastic alienation.

And the cinematic city grows ever more conservative in its ideology. It is now the new inner-city, the new urbanism beyond *The Truman Show* (USA, 1997). And I am surely preaching to the choir complaining about all this. So I won't play the hypocrite. I love a well-staged imaginary murder. But I want cinematic forms just as poignant as the cinematic city once was. Simply put, like most of the readers, I want a more engaged vision for our cities today, and for the future of cinema.

15 In addition to the vast archive in the *Los Angeles Times* on Hollywood and Highland, see Josh Stenger, "Return to Oz: The Hollywood Redevelopment Project, or Film History as Urban Renewal," in Shiel and Fritzmaurice, op. cit.

Marsha Kinder
Designing a Database Cinema

In 1997 I received an offer I couldn't refuse: An invitation from the Annenberg Center for Communication at the University of Southern California to design a research project that would generate a productive dialogue between the language of cinema and the interactive potential and database structures of new media. The result was The Labyrinth Project, a combination research initiative and digital media studio that produced three of the pieces in this exhibition: *Tracing the Decay of Fiction: Encounters with a Film by Pat O'Neill*; *Bleeding Through: Layers of Los Angeles, 1920–1986*; and *The Danube Exodus: The Rippling Currents of the River*.

All three are collaborations with vintage artists who have specialized in creating non-digital forms of database narratives: Los Angeles-based independent filmmaker Pat O'Neill, the master of the analog optical printer, whose multilayered nonlinear films from the early 1970s helped arouse my initial interest in database forms; Hungarian media-artist Péter Forgács, whose films reorchestrate found footage and home movies from Europe in the 1930s, 1940s and 1950s, material he has collected in his own Private Photo and Film Archive in Budapest; and cultural theorist Norman Klein, best known for *The History of Forgetting: The Cultural Erasure of Los Angeles*, whose richly detailed nonlinear writings replenish our communal databases of historical memory.

For all three projects our goal was to create an interface design that conceptually grew out of the material and captured the unique style of the artist with whom we were collaborating: the sensory beauty of O'Neill's richly textured films with their magisterial camera movements and surprising surrealistic jolts;

the vigorous stream of Klein's verbal commentaries on history, swirling with vivid details, comic asides, and fascinating digressions; and the mesmerizing quality of Forgács' haunting films with their shadowy historical figures and melancholy musical rhythms.

No matter whether our collaborator was a filmmaker or writer, we chose to make our projects cinematic. For *Tracing the Decay of Fiction*, we were producing the DVD-ROM while O'Neill was simultaneously shooting his 35mm film, and together we were designing ways of navigating fluidly within his cinematic "panscapes." For the Forgács installation, we were extending the scope of found footage related to his 1997 award-winning film, *The Danube Exodus*, which had aired on European television, reconceptualizing his approach to editing and its impact on reception. For *Bleeding Through*, we were exploring the ironic interplay between popular fiction and ethnography, the glamorous thrills of moving pictures and the redemptive power of photographic stills. Produced at the pressure point between theory and practice, our projects extended some of the key principles that had emerged from the graduate seminars on interactive narrative theory I had been teaching at USC's School of Cinema-Television.

Combining the New and the Old
Determined not to exaggerate the "newness" of new media or risk the distortions of technological determinism, we were convinced that the best way to realize the full potential of a new medium is to explore productive analogies with a wide range of earlier forms. Soviet filmmaker Sergei Eisenstein did the same when he pushed the boundaries of the newly

emerging medium of cinema and its capacity for dialectic montage by comparing it with his prior experiments aimed at overcoming the theater medium's
formal constraints. He continued to compare cinema
with many other art forms – including the novels of
Dickens and Joyce, the poetry of Walt Whitman,
Japanese scroll painting, Kabuki theater, haiku poetry,
Disney cartoons – and in consequence his theory of
montage and filmic experimentation grew more complex. British writer Henry Fielding had pursued a similar strategy two centuries earlier, by transferring the
experimental devices he had developed in his satiric
plays to the newly emerging genre of the eighteenth-
century novel, which he also compared with an array
of earlier literary forms. In both cases, these strategic lines of continuity did not generate works that
were dependent on theatrical conventions; on the
contrary, they produced radical novels and films that
emphasized their differences from theater. Despite
the distance in period, culture and media between
Fielding and Eisenstein, their careers both support an
observation made by Walter Benjamin: "One of the
foremost tasks of art has always been the creation
of a demand which could be fully satisfied only later.
The history of every art form shows critical epochs in
which a certain art form aspires to effects which
could be fully obtained only with a changed technical
standard, that is to say, in a new art form."[1]

At The Labyrinth Project we chose to work with
veteran artists from earlier non-digital forms whose
narrative experimentation created this kind of
demand for a new mode of expression. Each collaboration was unique, yet all worked off the same model.
The basic idea for each project came from the
veteran artist, but the interactive design was developed in collaboration with Labyrinth's core creative
team: interface designer Rosemary Comella and
graphic designer Kristy H. A. Kang (who functioned as
project directors), and myself as executive producer
and occasional writer. Under the coordination of our
associate producer Jo Ann Hanley, we assembled for
each production a crew comprised of talented students and recent alumni from the USC School of Cinema-TV, experienced freelance professionals (Scott
Mahoy, Jim McKee, Ariel McNichol and Laurence Tietz),
and staff members of collaborating institutions (USC
Cinema's Chris Cain and Greg Vannoy, ZKM's Andreas
Kratky, and the Getty Center's Zaia Alexander, Merritt
Price and Leon Rodriguez).

The combination of the old and new also applies at
the level of substance, for all of our projects juxta-
pose archival images and sounds with our own new
material. Although we started out making "electronic
fictions," we gradually realized our works belong to
two basic sub-genres of interactive documentary.
One is the personal memoir, which documents and
preserves the unique web of associations that an individual builds over a lifetime and that inevitably unravels with old age and death.

This genre encourages users to interweave this
personal material into a broader tapestry of historical narrative, which occurs in the memoirs we produced in collaboration with the gay Chicano novelist
John Rechy (*Mysteries and Desires: Searching the
Worlds of John Rechy*) and the Afro-American pho-
tographer-filmmaker Carroll Parrott Blue (*The Dawn
at My Back: a Memoir of a Black Texas Upbringing*).

Our three works on show at "Future Cinema" belong to the second sub-genre: an archeological exploration of a specific location through layers of time,
be this location a famous cultural Los Angeles landmark like the Hotel Ambassador now threatened with
destruction, or a mobile Los Angeles cityscape
mythologized as a "murder zone" by Hollywood crime
movies, or a historic river like the Danube whose rippling currents have interwoven many cultures and periods throughout Central Europe's stormy history.
These works are built on the assumption that spatial
exploration is not an alternative to narrative but a dimension that has always been pivotal to its structure.

Although one sub-genre is structured around individual persons and the other around specific locations, they are closely interrelated. The Rechy and
Blue memoirs also explore the specific homelands (El
Paso and Houston) where these two native Texans
survived painful childhoods and document other
American cities in which they emerged as independent
artists. The three archeological explorations at the
ZKM exhibition also contain mini-memoirs and historical testimonies by individuals who once inhabited
these places. Both sub-genres blur the boundaries
with fiction and both rely on artifacts: found footage
and archival photographs whose value is based not
only on their revelatory power but also on their rarity.
Loss and forgetting are built into the narrative
system.

Tracing the Decay of Fiction is an archeological exploration of the Hotel Ambassador, a historic building

1 Walter Benjamin, "The Work
of Art in the Age of Mechanical Reproduction," in *Illuminations*, Hannah Arendt (ed.),
Schocken, New York, 1969,
p. 237.

which, erected in 1920, played a crucial role in the development of Los Angeles and best known as the place where Democratic presidential candidate Robert Kennedy was assassinated in 1968. Visitors wander through these abandoned spaces looking for cultural traces of the historical traumas and personal encounters that occurred there. Either they navigate within O'Neill's original camera pans, or slide from one adjacent zone into another, or use the original designs of architect Myron Hunt (with detailed voice-over descriptions of each location) to go directly to a specific room. Inside the hotel, the borders between past and present are deliberately blurred. Sometimes contemporary images are combined with dialogue from vintage movies and radio dramas, and modern voices are paired with period prints and newsreels. At other times old and new images are inextricably fused, as if ghostly figures and voices lie deeply embedded within the hotel's decaying surfaces. But once outside the hotel on the city's celebrated "Miracle Mile," a stark contrast emerges between vintage stills and contemporary digital footage, especially when accompanied by provocative commentaries from noted cultural theorists speaking about the history of Los Angeles.

Bleeding Through: Layers of Los Angeles, 1920-1986 combines a database detective story with a contemporary city symphony and a meta-narrative reflection on storytelling in this new medium. The story's setting is a three-mile radius near downtown Los Angeles, a city known for not having a center. This ethnically complex location is documented through archival stills and films and through contemporary images that either reproduce or evoke them. The narrative can be navigated on three levels. Positioned within a movable window, author Norman Klein tells the story of Molly, a fictional character based on a real life person who may have murdered one of her husbands, and he invites users to collaborate with him in writing this fictional life. The second level explores what Molly never noticed – the back-stories of real people whose mini-memoirs preserve histories that otherwise might have been lost. The third level leads users to reflect on this act of database storytelling and its cultural implications, particularly when set within LA's urban dream factory that exports its own nightmares worldwide. The contrast between past and present is most dramatic and uncanny in the back-stories, where the user can slide fluidly between

old and new photographs of the same Los Angeles cityscape taken from precisely the same angle, watching buildings instantaneously emerge or vanish. The project contains hundreds of archival stills, which help refigure the user's vision of Los Angeles, particularly if it is based primarily on representations from Hollywood mainstream movies.

The Danube Exodus immerses visitors within three interwoven historical narratives. One tells of Eastern European Jews fleeing Nazi persecution in 1939, trying to reach a ship on the Black Sea that will carry them to Palestine. The second story, set in 1940 following the Soviet re-annexation of Bessarabia, tells of émigré German farmers abandoning their adopted homeland to return to the "safety" of the Third Reich, but eventually being relocated in occupied Poland. Both groups were transported along the Danube River by Captain Nándor Andrásovits, an amateur filmmaker who documented these voyages; he and the river are the subjects of the third story. The contrast between past and present is most explicit in the side spaces devoted either to the Jewish or German experience. Here one can watch recent interviews with survivors of the journeys juxtaposed with images of them on the ship, and examine their family photos, diaries and official records. The interplay between past and present is also enriched by the layering of these proliferating stories: the Captain's original documentation of the voyages, Forgács' 1997 sixty-minute televised film that was seen by some of the survivors, and this immersive installation that premiered at the Getty Center in Los Angeles in August 2002. Each successively incorporates all earlier versions into an ever-expanding database narrative.

Database Narrative

In *The Language of New Media*, Lev Manovich argues that electronic games and other forms of "new media" rely on database structures, which he sets in combative opposition to narrative. Describing them as "two competing imaginations, two basic creative impulses, two essential responses to the world," he claims modern media are "the new battlefield for the competition between database and narrative."[2] In contrast, I see database and narrative as two compatible structures whose combination is crucial to the creative expansion of new media, since all narratives are constructed by selecting items from databases (that usually remain hidden), and then

2 Lev Manovich, *The Language of New Media*, The MIT Press, Cambridge, MA, 2001, p. 233.

friend Dolores. Ironing as archaeology. The fragrance of the beach and other places of leisure.

The forms of revenge that Molly has seen most in her long life.

Norman M. Klein with Rosemary
Comella, Andreas Kratky, and
The Labyrinth Project
*Bleeding Through: Layers of
Los Angeles, 1920–1986*
2002
interactive DVD installation
screenshots
© Klein, Comella, Kratky

combining these items to create a particular story. Despite the cyber-structuralist dream of totality, the database, like the narrative, is always selective. As soon as the database categories are determined and the task of what to retrieve defined, one is launched on a narrative quest with motives and consequences. Since such decisions are made in social and historical contexts that inevitably have narrative content, the process of retrieval necessarily involves ideology and desire: where are we permitted to look and what do we hope to find.

All of our Labyrinth projects are what I call "data-base narratives." This term refers to narratives whose structure exposes the dual processes of selection and combination that lie at the heart of all stories and are crucial to language: Certain characters, images, sounds, events and settings are selected from series of categories and combined to generate specific tales. Although a database narrative may have no clear-cut beginning or ending, no three-act classical structure or even a coherent chain of causality, it still presents a narrative field with story elements arousing a user's curiosity and desire: urges that can be mobilized as a search engine to retrieve whatever is needed to spin a particular tale. In calling attention to the database infrastructure of all narratives, these works reveal the arbitrariness of the choices made and thereby challenge the notion of master narratives whose selections are traditionally made to seem natural or inevitable.

This conception of "database narrative" is consistent with what filmmaker Luis Buñuel called his "synoptic table of the American cinema," a bizarre document he allegedly constructed while trying to "learn some good American technical skills" in Hollywood in the 1930s. "There were several movable columns set up on a large piece of pasteboard: the first for 'ambiance' (Parisian, western, gangster, etc.), the second for 'epochs,' the third for 'main characters,' and so on. Altogether there were four or five categories, each with a tab for easy maneuverability. What I wanted to do was show that the American cinema was composed along such precise and standardized lines that, thanks to my system, anyone could predict the basic plot of a film simply by lining up a given setting with a particular era, ambiance, and character."[3]

In contrast to the predictability of most Hollywood movies, Buñuel's own films are full of surprising ruptures that reveal the subversive potential of the database narrative. Not only do surrealistic jolts prevent spectators from completely identifying with the characters, but strategic repetitions expose the database infrastructure that usually lies hidden behind the story. Driving both characters and viewers, these repetition compulsions sometimes project an entire paradigm of choices onto the syntagmatic plane: a cherished database of heresies in *The Milky Way*, a full menu array of aborted dinner parties and dreams in *The Discreet Charm of the Bourgeoisie*, and a periodic recasting of avatars in *That Obscure Object of Desire*. In these films, one can follow any of the narrative strands that, although ingeniously interwoven, purposely never cohere – a networking enabling the viewer to observe the narrative engine in action.[4]

Although Manovich grants that a "poetics" of database structure will someday be realized in cyberspace, he finds its cinematic precursors to be rare. He cites only two filmmakers, Dziga Vertov and Peter Greenaway, conveniently representing modernism and postmodernism respectively. In contrast, I find database narratives throughout the entire history of cinema, from the early cinema of attractions to the present, but with unusual conceptual power in periods of radical narrative experimentation such as modernism and the Parisian post-structuralist period of the 1960s and '70s – the two periods in which Buñuel produced his most subversive films.

The contemporary convergence of cinema with new digital media provides another such moment for radical innovation. Not only has it already generated a diverse range of popular database narratives (including *Ground Hog Day, Slackers, Natural Born Killers, Pulp Fiction, The Matrix, Memento, Mulholland Drive, Time Code, Run Lola Run, Until the End of the World, Y tu Mamá tambien*) but, even more telling, several filmmakers associated with Parisian post-structuralism are now refiguring their earlier lines of experimentation through the tropes of new media. I am thinking of Chris Marker's CD-ROM *Immemory* (1999) and his film *Level 5* (1999, in which the protagonist is an interface designer working on an electronic game about the Battle of Okinawa), both of which return to the kinds of issues he addressed in pre-digital database films like *La Jetée* (1962) and *Sans Soleil* (1982). A further example is Alain Resnais' pair of multi-branching films, *Smoking/ No Smoking* (1993), based on the eight plays comprising Alan Ayckbourn's *Intimate Exchanges* (1982) and addressing many of the temporal issues

3 Luis Buñuel, *My Last Sigh*, Vintage Books, New York, 1984, p. 132.

4 For an elaboration on Buñuel's contribution, see my essay "Hot Spots, Avatars, and Narrative Fields Forever: Buñuel's Legacy for New Digital Media and Interactive Database Narrative," in *Film Quarterly*, vol. 55, no. 4, Summer 2002, pp. 2–15.

Resnais had earlier explored in *Last Year at Marienbad* (1961); as well as Agnes Varda's *The Gleaners and I* (2000), a documentary with a database structure that uses a DV camera to "glean" a fascinating collection of rural and urban scavengers living off the surplus waste of a consumerist culture. In that process, Varda proves to be the most accomplished gleaner of all, especially as she recycles techniques and issues that have preoccupied her from *La Pointe courte* (1954) to *Vagabond* (1985).

The Labyrinth Project is pursuing a similar path as we glean home movies, archival materials, noir potboilers, and non-digital independent films and video, transforming them into data for interactive database narratives designed to keep cinema at the cutting edge. Whether our users are positioned as visitors (as in *Tracing the Decay of Fiction*), or as historical witnesses (as in *The Danube Exodus*), or as writers of detective fiction (as in *Bleeding Through*), they are encouraged to spin stories out of the diverse materials retrievable from our custom-built databases through a combination of design, choice and chance.

This encouragement occurs most emphatically in *Bleeding Through*. Describing seven key moments in Molly's life that occurred within this three-mile radius and were interwoven with Los Angeles' cultural history, Klein urges users to flesh out this story with materials selected from the large database (of images, sounds and maps) designed by co-directors Rosemary Comella and Andreas Kratky. This movement between fiction and history draws users into meta-narrative questions, leading them to consider the sources of their own database memories: first hand experience, family stories, Hollywood movies, official history, or some combination. Chance kicks in only when Klein's commentary is suspended and Molly's story subsides, for the juxtapositions of images are then random combinations that increase the potential number of alternative scenarios.

In *The Danube Exodus*, it is a matter of choosing pre-edited 3-to-4-minute orchestrated sequences from different ethnic databases whose interweaving came about through the course of history. The Bessarabian Germans mourned the loss of their homeland and possessions. The Jews danced and rejoiced; they had lost everything but their lives had been saved. Still, the uncanny parallelism is a matter of record. These Jews and Germans were both transported to safety and documented on film by the same river captain, who ferried them into historical

memory. No matter which sequences are chosen, the stories still compete for control over the central narrative space, and the user is still confronted with the difficult task of "comparing the incomparable," which becomes even more complicated with historical hindsight. Given the number of reorchestrated versions through which this story has been retold, one must also consider the exponential growth to which the narrative field and its underlying databases were subject as Forgács moved from a sixty-minute film to forty hours of tape; as he reedited this material not for one screen but for five; as the sound track moved from stereo to an immersive 5:2 surround system. Despite the minimal role of randomness, this ongoing process of reorchestration reminds us that History is like Heraclitus' river. You can never step twice into the same river or the same history.

In *Tracing the Decay of Fiction*, the urging to make narrative connections is more subtle, the database materials more diverse, and the random elements more pervasive. The first room a user enters is chosen arbitrarily from a database. As users navigate from one room to another, the repetition of familiar names, faces and voices entices them into making connections among the story fragments. This urging is most intriguing during earthquakes, which trigger a random montage of images and sounds drawn from the various databases, a delirious automated search engine that always generates new combinations and narrative possibilities. Significantly, most of the dialogue comes from vintage narratives – radio serials like *The Shadow*, conspiracy theories aired on radio, or classical noir films like *Sudden Fear* and *Hollow Triumph* – genres that urge us to solve the mystery, discover who killed Kennedy, or connect all the dots. Yet our deliberate evasion of closure renders the search futile. Although these dynamics are operative in both the DVD-ROM and film, users of the former might turn to the latter in search of a sequential order or narrative continuity to make the nonlinear story cohere. Just as, conversely, viewers of the film might turn to the disc in order to linger in those mysterious spaces that flash only briefly across the movie screen or to consult archival materials possibly able to fill in some of the gaps. However, both quests are doomed to failure: *The Decay of Fiction* ultimately suggests this persistent drive for narrative closure is motored by paranoia, a state of mind pivotal both to the conspiracy theories and noir genre that lie deep at its core.

Péter Forgács
and The Labyrinth Project
*The Danube Exodus: The Rippling
Currents of the River*
2002
interactive DVD video
installation in three spaces
b/w, color, 5.1 surround sound
installation views: Getty Center,
Los Angeles, 2002
courtesy Péter Forgács;
The Labyrinth Project,
Annenberg Center for
Communication, USC
photos © The Labyrinth Project

Even if users are willing to sacrifice closure, they still expect narratives to contextualize the meaning of perceptions and cognitively map their world, a dynamic our projects make literal by including quirky grids and maps. This mapping must constantly be revised in order to assimilate newly emerging data, which require accommodations in the user's cognitive schemata. The question is: When you encounter a radically new kind of story, are you capable of making these radical changes in your schemata, or only minor adjustments? This is where a performative approach to interactivity comes in.

Performative Interactivity

Interactivity did not begin in cyberspace, but the modes of interaction provided by new digital media and fetishized by its fans encourage us to rethink the distinctive interactive potential of earlier art forms and their modes of spectator positioning and reception. Even several eighteenth-century English novels dramatized an interactive dialogue between narrator and reader, in which the latter was required to reflect on the process of writing and the former empowered to judge the reader's performance. The best example from that period occurs in Laurence Sterne's experimental comic novel *Tristram Shandy*, when the narrator makes a hypothetical lady reader go back and re-read a chapter since she failed to get one of his jokes, while he continues chatting leisurely with the male reader, waiting for her to catch up. And Eisenstein still claimed that, despite his control over the dialectic montage of visual and audio attractions in his films, the resulting collisions took place not on the screen or in the celluloid but in the mind of the spectator – a dynamic also operative in the earlier art forms that inspired him.

All narrative forms provide some degree of interactive spectatorship (even if it is simply a matter of bringing one's own associations to a tale); and they are always driven by a search engine of curiosity and desire. Yet, there are crucial differences in the interactive potential of rival media and the degree to which they are realized. A novel can be carried by a reader wherever she goes and read and re-read at her own pace, as she casts the novel's characters in her mind with figures she knows or imagines – a dynamic thematized in a wide range of experimental database novels including Sterne's *Tristram Shandy*, Marcel Proust's *Remembrance of Things Past*, Ishmael Reed's *Mumbo Jumbo*, John Rechy's *Sexual Outlaw*,

Doris Lessing's *Golden Notebook*, Manuel Puig's *Kiss of the Spider Woman* and Italo Calvino's *If on a Winter's Night a Traveler*. Stage plays inevitably generate a social tension between two rival groups: the ensemble of actors and their live audience who temporarily cohabit the same confined space. These tensions can be used by band of theatergoers to hiss down a play or join the cast on stage, or leveraged by a brilliant playwright like Jean Genet to create the provocative ritualized encounters of *The Blacks*. Movies encourage anonymous spectators to become totally absorbed within the projected world of shadows as they sit alone in the dark, identifying with characters on screen and carrying home the stories to be elaborated within their own dreams. This process was literally acted out by certain Surrealists who enjoyed drifting from one movie theater to another, and several decades later was transformed into living theater by ardent fans of the *Rocky Horror Picture Show*. The radio or television program is broadcast to listeners or viewers who periodically tune in to the signal within the intimacy of their own settings (car, home, office) while they simultaneously perform other mundane tasks (driving, working, eating). Whenever they desire, the signal can easily be interrupted (and therefore remixed with random captures from other stations) through a simple turn of the dial or zap of the remote – a pattern of reception that laid the groundwork for the MTV aesthetic and the art of sampling. All of these interactive modes have limits, but so do those in cyberspace.

In cyberspace, interactivity wavers between two poles. While all narratives are in some sense interactive (in that their meanings always grow out of a collaboration between the individual subjectivities of authors and users and the reading conventions of the respective cultures they inhabit and languages they speak), all interactivity is also an illusion because the rules established by the designers of the text partially limit the user's options. As a result, interactivity tends to be used as a normative term – either fetishized as the ultimate pleasure or demonized as a deceptive fiction. The most productive way of avoiding these two extremes is to position the user as a "performer" of the narrative – like an actor interpreting a role, or a musician playing a score, or a dancer performing traditional moves, contributing her own idiosyncratic inflections and absorbing the experience into her personal archive of memories.

Always aware of the constraints over the user's interactivity, The Labyrinth Project team deliberately emphasizes the differences in the way the DVD-ROM version and museum installation are experienced and performed. The disc is usually played in an intimate space on a personal computer with the user's face close to the monitor and hand confidently manipulating the mouse, whereas the installation is visited in the public space of a gallery or museum where more venturesome interactors are positioned as performers whose moves are witnessed by others.

Within the room housing *Bleeding Through*, we retain some of the intimacy of the private space associated with the home computer and the personal engagement associated with storytelling, but at the same time expand this performance in a large-screen projection within the public sphere. If a visitor steps up to the mouse to perform her own version of the story before the watchful eyes of other onlookers, then she risks getting lost in the plot holes and becoming cast as a blind detective leading the blind. But, as one collaborates with Klein on fleshing out Molly's story or discovering what Molly never saw, it's also possible to lead the others into the immersive thrills of losing oneself in a Labyrinth or leaping into the void.

The Decay of Fiction occupies two adjacent rooms: in one, O'Neill's 73-minute film is projected for a seated audience; in the other, the interactive DVD-ROM is simultaneously played on three separate computers, each projecting one large image, side-by-side, on the same wall, and each controllable by a mouse accessible to interactors. Not only are the three visitor-interactors able to slide horizontally from any one to another of the fourteen basic rooms (as can likewise users running the DVD-ROM on their home computer), they can also expand the horizontal gliding movement across monitors, interacting with the projected images being controlled by the persons next to them. This interaction might arouse competitive instincts (speeding up to reach or outrun other drivers), or a desire for harmonious synchronization. On a macro-level, this lateral movement could extend beyond one room and medium: an interactor could rely on memory to reproduce the spatial pathway followed in O'Neill's movie, which is simultaneously being exhibited on the other side of the wall. This setup confronts interactors with the question of what is driving their personal search engines: the desire for closure, or for deconstruction?

The interplay between the competing desires for fusion and deconstruction is also amplified through the staging of sound. All three interactors manipulating the mouse also wear a pair of headphones allowing them to be immersed, both visually and acoustically, within the particular synchronized version of the narrative they are performing. The other visitors are positioned as mobile spectators, moving freely through the room while wrapped in a multilayered sonic field of surround sound. This sonic field randomly combines a background of discreet ambient sounds with one of the audio tracks from the three computers, periodically switching from one to another of the three tracks. This sound design rejects the unifying function traditionally performed by the classical Hollywood soundtrack. As Mary Ann Doane sees it, the synchronization of sound and image (and especially the anchoring of voice to body) smoothes over those potentially disturbing gaps between the three separate spaces normally comprising the cinema experience: the two-dimensional visual screen (whether showing a film or data), the three-dimensional audiovisual space of the virtual world represented within the narrative, and the three-dimensional audiovisual space of the room where the spectator is actually watching and listening to the narrative.5 Whereas in most Hollywood movies that system of synchronization (particularly when bolstered by surround sound) serves to maintain the realistic illusion by keeping the spectator sutured into emotional identification with the characters, these gaps are deliberately left glaring in *The Decay of Fiction* (both the film and disc versions). Even on the single DVD-ROM, the dialogue is seldom synchronous, and the combination of particular images and sounds in any given hotspot frequently changes arbitrarily from one playtime to the next. And with the additional ambient track in the museum, a trio of images is randomly paired with every particular sound, constantly reminding us of the alternative pleasures that can be generated by chance juxtapositions and surrealistic jolts.

The staging of *The Danube Exodus* in the ZKM exhibition is another step in the ongoing process of reorchestrating history. Visitors are drawn into this process, not only by choosing what others see and hear, but also by bringing their own personal memories and associations to this haunting material. Visitors can choose to enter the three separate spaces in any sequence and, once inside a space, to use a touchscreen monitor interface (designed by Scott Mahoy) to pursue a particular pathway. Whereas the two side spaces enable a separate exploration of the complex stories of respectively the Jews and the Germans, or the total bypassing of either topic, the central space interweaves these two stories with that of the Captain and the River. This poetic space has no explanatory voice-overs, but churns with haunting images and mesmerizing sounds of the river in motion. Whenever a visitor chooses one of the eighteen moving icons that periodically emerge out of the depths of the Danube, this selection unleashes a new orchestration of pre-edited images and sounds that immediately transform the room. Even if the interactor chooses only Jewish or only German

5 Mary Ann Doane, "The Voice in the Cinema: The Articulation of Body and Space," in *Yale French Studies*, Cinema/Sound, 60, Yale University Press, New Haven, 1980, pp. 33–50.

orchestrations, most of them still combine all three subjects. Deliberately, the interactive choices available to visitors are limited, just as choices in history are limited – like those of the Captain, who selected what to shoot but not what happened to his subjects or to his own footage. Or like those of Forgács, who appropriated the Captain's footage and re-edited it for a new period and medium that imposed their own restrictions on what he could do. And like the choices of the Labyrinth design team for this traveling installation, who (in collaboration with Forgács) must adapt the structure for each new venue.

One of the key variables in performative interactivity is pacing. In all three projects the orchestration of preset rhythms is crucial to the design. *Bleeding Through* provides the greatest leeway for temporal play: users can vary the pace by speeding across horizontal strips of cityscape images, or by zeroing in on a particular site and then sliding from one decade to another. The velocity echoes both the fast-talking delivery of Klein's running commentaries and the staccato urban rhythms of a contemporary city symphony.

Given that tone is so crucial in *Tracing the Decay of Fiction* and *The Danube Exodus*, users have less control over the pace. A visual musicality of considerable range are created by O'Neill's gliding interior pans, by his time-lapse shots of looming clouds and dancing shadows, by the random montages triggered by earthquakes. Similarly, the dense soundtrack combines found music with stylized dialogue and an Expressionistic choice of effects. Each room has its own distinctive music and ambiance, and they change depending on whether the rooms are vacant or inhabited by ghosts. It is as if these acoustic traces lie embedded within these hollow rooms waiting to be discovered and replayed. This dynamic is experienced most intensely in the basement, which is primarily a sound piece in which various voices from the past are remixed. Only in the sections on the Robert Kennedy assassination is an emotional unity created through sound.

As in all of Forgács' films, much of the power of *The Danube Exodus* depends on the hypnotic musical score of Hungarian composer Tibor Szemzö, which sound designer Jim McKee has skillfully interwoven into the melodic ambiance of the river and the percussive rhythms of the ship's engines. Forgács claims he lets the music orchestrate and "rule" the emotional story; his own editing rhythms become part of the score. Once he saw the orchestrations projected in the central space, he slowed down the transitions – a choice that greatly enhanced the visual power of images like the swelling waters, rolling farmlands and marching soldiers spreading horizontally across the five large screens. In this poetic space, the interface becomes part of the music.

For the interactor who steps up to the touchscreen monitor, it's like playing a musical instrument or conducting an orchestra with each of the screens functioning like a different section – the strings, the brass, the winds, and the percussion. As the shadowy images ripple across the room, constantly making new rhythmic patterns, the haunting musical score of engines, voices, water, music and wind performs its own mediating mantra.

Coda

In this essay on designing a database cinema for the future, I have purposely looked backward to earlier films and novels rather than forward to utopian visions because I strongly believe that the advancement of any medium can be greatly accelerated by new applications of experimentation from the past. Yet that doesn't mean that we have nothing to learn about narrative from new media.

In western academic theory, narrative is traditionally perceived as a mode of discourse (whether in art, myth or history) containing actions and characters that interact and change according to laws of causality within a spatial and temporal setting. Yet by privileging nonlinear storytelling and communication, new digital media help us see that in a much broader cognitive and ideological sense narrative is also a means of patterning and interpreting the meaning of all sensory input and objects of knowledge. For as narratives map the world and its inhabitants, they locate us within a textual landscape requiring a constant refiguring of our mental cartography with its supporting databases, search engines and representational conventions.

Given that every culture creates its own stories, humans must in some sense be "wired" for storytelling, and narratives must mediate between biological programming and cultural imprinting. They process the past and refigure the future, as in dreams and prophecy, and that makes them an extraordinarily powerful vehicle for change. The key question is how we can change and be changed by interactive database narratives. That's why, like evolution, all of our Labyrinth projects are stochastic systems that generate stories and outcomes through a combination of design, choice and chance.

Norman M. Klein, with Rosemary Comella,
Andreas Kratky, and The Labyrinth Project

Bleeding Through: Layers of Los Angeles, 1920–1986

2002
interactive DVD installation / 550 x 550 cm

The forms of revenge that Molly has seen most in her long life.

Walt, and Molly's cache. The businesses, and men, that bloomed like house plants under her care.

Her friend Dolores. Ironing as archaeology. The fragrance of the beach, and other places of leisure   The preferred sexual positions in 1928

Bleeding Through: Layers of
Los Angeles, 1920–1986
2002
interactive DVD installation
screenshots
© Klein, Comella, Kratky

Bleeding Through is a data and cinematic novel set in Los Angeles – both a book and DVD-ROM – with 1,200 assets: photos, interviews, comments by Klein, rare film clips, maps, newspapers clippings from the morgue of an old daily newspaper. It traces what could be the story of a woman who may have murdered her second husband, but has somehow survived without any sense of guilt, seems to have cheerfully erased whatever memory has been a nuisance. We follow her life from 1920, when she arrives in LA, to her death in 1986. We learn that she also lives in a "cinematic zone of death," an arc of three square miles where "more people have been murdered in beloved crime films than anywhere else in the world." And over the years, its key districts have been bull-dozed out of existence.

How does one generate all these inside a single storyline? For example, in the chapter when the facts of the murder are finally revealed, there is also an archive of fifty other ways to kill a man. Why not all murders? Why not the graphics and the language of the act of murder itself, across all media? And the same with political scandals, ethnographic ironies, urban erasures? The computer allows viewers to enter the fullness of the author's archive, before the story begins, when all possibilities coexist. That may indeed be the visual and narrative pleasure of future cinema, to inhabit the mind of the author fully loaded with immersive detail, before the story begins.

The interface, chapters and tiers reinforce this simple archival pleasure, the spirit of daily rhythms in LA seventy years ago. We can imagine the potential of story – as a narrative pleasure, on a scale rarely possible before the computer. What is the pleasure of remembering the traces of a lost memory, on film, in photos, in text, the absences that make a story vivid? We inhabit what novelist Laurence Sterne (1760) called "the gentle art of good conversation" – the documentary fullness of an epic novel about a very unique city, its perversities, alienation, denials, and great pleasures.

Norman M. Klein

Pat O'Neill and The Labyrinth Project

Tracing the Decay of Fiction:
Encounters with a Film by Pat O'Neill

2002
interactive DVD-ROM, three-screen computer installation / color, sound / dimensions variable

Tracing the Decay of
Fiction: Encounters with
a Film by Pat O'Neill
2002
interactive DVD-ROM,
three-screen computer
installation
color, sound
dimensions variable
installation view:
ZKM | Center for Art and
Media Karlsruhe, 2002
courtesy The Labyrinth
Project, Annenberg Center
for Communication, USC
© The Annenberg Center,
USC
photo © Franz Wamhof

Based on Pat O'Neill's 35mm film *The Decay of Fiction*, which plays as a linear nonlinear loop in the adjoining room, this interactive installation enables visitors to explore the Hotel Ambassador, a vintage building that was crucial to the unique development of Los Angeles and now stands in ruins waiting to be demolished. For the past decade, it has served as a location for scores of Hollywood movies, particularly in the noir genre. Built in 1920 on LA's "Wilshire Corridor," the hotel helped redirect the city's urban sprawl from east to west, from downtown to the sea. Its glamorous Coconut Grove nightclub was the place where downtown power brokers first mingled with Hollywood stars, where Joan Crawford was discovered in a dance contest and Marilyn Monroe in a bathing-suit competition, and where many celebrities won their Oscars and Golden Globes. The hotel had permanent residents, like newscaster Walter Winchell, while

others like FBI chief J. Edgar Hoover visited every year. The hotel is now remembered primarily as the place where Robert Kennedy was assassinated while campaigning for the Democratic presidential nomination – a traumatic event that transformed the hotel's cultural capital and changed the course of American history.

Museum visitors encounter three large images projected flush against each other, each controlled by a separate mouse resting on a pedestal. Sometimes all three images feature the same room in the hotel, in or out of synch, giving the illusion that one can glide horizontally from one image to another. At other times the three images show different locations, allowing visitors to monitor what is happening simultaneously in various parts of the hotel, and enabling the drama in each room to compete for control over the narrative. Sometimes it is those moving the mouse

who seem to be vying for control. They are the ones who decide whether the elegant rooms are empty or inhabited by an ensemble of ghostly figures and a rich melange of voices that lie embedded within the walls and within a series of truncated plots. Though interacting with the same software and drawing material from the same menus, the visitors at the mouse perform different versions of this database narrative. But when observed by other visitors in the exhibition space who watch the interaction among the three images and listen to the sounds synched with the central screen and to ambiance coming from the surrounds, these three performers emerge as collaborative puppeteers, spinning an alluring web of interwoven urban myths.

This installation belongs to the hotel subgenre of database cinema, which includes a diverse group of films (such as *Hotel Electric*, *Grand Hotel*, *Last Year at Marienbad* and *The Shining*), and is rooted in the meta-narrative function of the inn as stopping place in picaresque fiction. In this piece the drive is archeological in nature: unearthing cultural traces of historic events that took place in the public domain and of personal dramas that allegedly were played out in private. Visitors can navigate O'Neill's magisterial computerized camera moves within any room, or slide from one adjacent space to another, or use the original floor plan (designed by architect Myron Hunt) to go directly to a specific location. Or they can explore the surrounding "Miracle Mile" neighborhood, selecting archival stills or contemporary footage, as they listen to commentaries by a diverse array of cultural historians.

Combining fiction and documentary, contemporary footage and archival materials, the installation presents a network of provocative plots that always evade closure. Occasionally visitors experience an earthquake, which generates a random selection of sounds and images. As if enticing visitors to prolong their stay at the Ambassador, these random combinations show there is more they haven't yet seen or heard, and teases them into making narrative connections among these sensory fragments. Yet, as in the film noir genre and the Kennedy conspiracy theories, which are both prominently featured in this work, we ultimately realize the desire for narrative closure is driven by paranoia.

Marsha Kinder

Péter Forgács
and The Labyrinth Project
The Danube Exodus:
The Rippling Currents
of the River

2002
interactive DVD video installation in three spaces /
b/w, color, 5.1 surround sound / dimensions and duration variable

This installation is based on *The Danube Exodus*, an
award-winning sixty-minute film by Péter Forgács,
who specializes in making haunting documentaries
from European home movies of the 1930s and '40s.
Its premiere exhibition at the Getty Center in Los
Angeles in August 2002 attracted a record-breaking
number of visitors to the institution.

Visitors encounter three interwoven historical
narratives about the displacement of ethnic minori-
ties. One story tells of East European Jews fleeing
Nazi persecution in 1939, trying to reach a ship on the
Black Sea that will carry them to Palestine. The second story, set in 1940 following the Soviet re-annexation of Bessarabia, tells of emigrant German farmers
abandoning their adopted homeland to return to the
"safety" of the Third Reich. Both groups were transported along the Danube River by Captain Nándor
Andrásovits, an amateur filmmaker who documented
these historic journeys and his own explorations of
Europe. The third story focuses on the captain and
the river, whose rippling currents have interwoven
many cultures and periods throughout Central
Europe's stormy history.

This installation leads us to consider what Forgács
calls "the incomparable duet of the German-Jewish
exodus." The Bessarabian Germans mourned the loss
of their homeland and possessions. The Jews danced
and rejoiced; they had lost everything but their lives
had been saved. Still, the uncanny parallelism is a
matter of record. These Jews and Germans were both
carried to safety and documented on film by the
same river captain, who ferried them into historical
memory.

The installation is comprised of three spaces. One
side is devoted to the Jewish experience, where visitors use a touchscreen monitor to explore the personal stories of those who survived the voyage. Their
detailed accounts are told through recent interviews
illustrated with archival materials. On the other side,

a comparable space documents the German experience, with two survivors giving personal accounts of
their life in Bessarabia.

In the central space, the three stories vie for
control over the narrative. On a large touchscreen
monitor, visitors can select one of eighteen icons that
periodically emerge out of the river. Each triggers a
brief narrative "orchestration," three to seven
minutes in length. Six orchestrations focus on the
Jewish voyage, six on the Bessarabian journey, and six
on the story of the Captain. No matter which orchestrations are chosen, they all refer to the other two
stories, meaning it's impossible to avoid comparison.
If no visitor makes a choice, then the imagery turns to
ambient orchestrations whose imagery is abstract.

Dominated by five large screens, this central
space is poetic and immersive rather than informa-

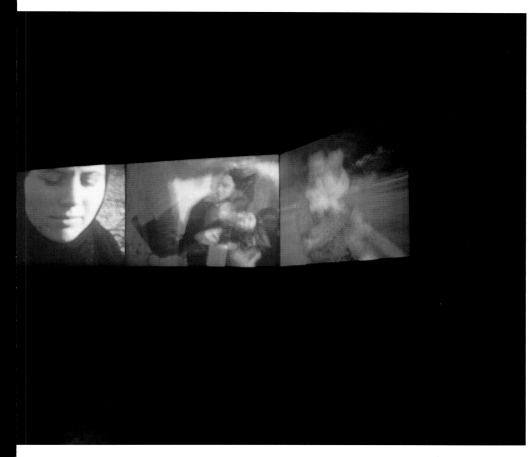

*The Danube Exodus: The Rippling
Currents of the River*
2002
interactive DVD video
installation in three spaces
b/w, color, 5.1 surround sound
dimensions and duration
variable
installation views:
ZKM | Center for Art and Media
Karlsruhe, 2003
courtesy Péter Forgács; The
Labyrinth Project, Annenberg
Center for Communication,
USC
photos © Oliver Klasen

tive. We rarely see such a large public display devoted to home movies, a genre usually restricted to a modest domestic space. This scale is traditionally reserved for superheroes like Napoleon, and yet this found footage holds our attention. We occasionally recognize specific figures from the side spaces whose stories have been described in detail, but here they merge into the more haunting collective tableaux. The subtitles and voiceovers are minimal. Instead, musicality prevails. The lapping sounds of the river, the percussive beats of the ship's engines, and the droning prayers of the voyagers all blend into the mesmerizing music of Hungarian composer Tibor Szemzö. Occasionally a discreet ambient sound, like a flag flapping in the wind, breaks the melancholy tone of the music and anchors us into the particular moment on screen.

This musicality merges with the montage, which becomes an ongoing process of reorchestrating history. It was performed first by the Captain, the historical witness who decided what to shoot; then by Forgács, who restructured the captain's found footage in his sixty-minute film; then by The Labyrinth Project and Forgács, who used his film as found footage for a newly edited installation that incorporates new materials; and finally by visitors, who use their own memories and desires to find a personal pathway through this expanding narrative field. This reorchestration reminds us that history is like Heraclitus' river: you can never step into the same river or the same history twice.

Marsha Kinder and Zaia Alexander

Lev Manovich
Soft Cinema

2002
computer-generated projection, installation / dimensions variable

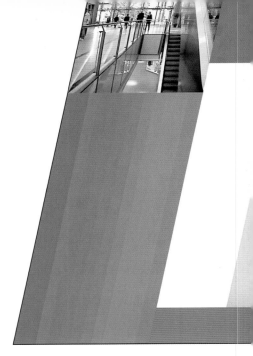

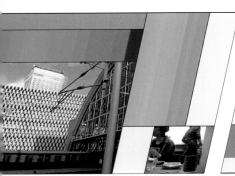
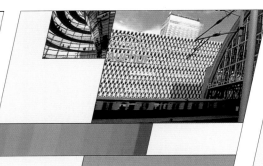
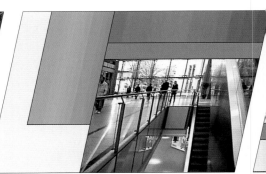

Soft Cinema – Database for Simultaneous Cinema

From Moholy-Nagy's perspective, the simultaneous parallel use of different media such as typography, photography and film was experimental pioneering work. It necessitated the development of special intellectual capabilities in order to be able to process the relevant flood of information. Today, this kind of multitasking is an everyday occurrence and omnipresent – as evidenced by CNN's screen design or the way we arrange a multitude of open windows on our computer screens.

Soft Cinema extends the schemata of information design into an artistic context, combining them to produce a kind of simultaneous cinema. Its approach moves within dimensions somewhere between classical film montage and the indiscriminate equivalence of database entries. It consists of two program sections, the generator and the display. The first section, the generator, has the function of creating a montage out of the individual strands of film. The basis for this process is a database of film sequences and the latter's characteristics such as composition, movement etc. In the first instance, these parameters are the result of an automated analysis of contrast values, movement, activity and so on. Secondly, however, they also indicate the location where the film was shot, its perspectives etc. The composition of these parameters is variable and can be adapted to various different approaches to montage. The adjustable combinations and weightings allow generator users to create films edited according to formal criteria similar to those of classical montage, but without regard for the development of a narrative storyline. In this sense, such works are closer to a relational database than to an edited film.

As a second stage, the display joins together the individual strands of film produced using the generator to form a kind of montage of simultaneity. This program divides up the screen into individual segments, in each of which either films or abstract animations are shown. The division process takes place by means of algorithms, which ensure that the screen is divided up harmoniously. Thus, differences in size and positioning on the screen take into account correspondences and relationships between the individual films. The same stage of processing that divides up the screen allocates soundtracks, a looped text and a voice-over channel. This allocation process can be monitored using a script that is processed by the display.

The coherence and the arrangement of all elements on the screen produces a continuum that alternates between rhythmic, visual structures and descriptive symbols. Narrative elements appear, disappear again or make room for other elements that are in competition with them. At times, the equivalence and uninterpreted quality of the database entries gives rise to aesthetic and meaningful structures that repeatedly fall apart and are reformed into other constellations.

Andreas Kratky
Translated from the German by Jeremy Gaines

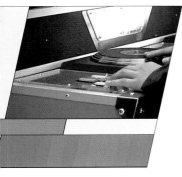

Soft Cinema
2002
computer-generated
projection
screenshots
© Lev Manovich

Soft Cinema
2002
installation views: ZKM |
Center for Art and Media
Karlsruhe, 2002
details
© Lev Manovich
photos © Franz Wamhof

Peter Cornwell
MetaPlex

2002
interactive computer installation / Linux cluster, projector / dimensions variable

MetaPlex
2002
screenshot
courtesy Street Vision Limited, London
© Peter Cornwell

MetaPlex is an installation artwork – a navigable virtual space containing different types of audible and visual texts. These include sounds, still and moving images and three-dimensional structures. Some are stored within MetaPlex while others, such as radio and television channel feeds, accrue over time so they can be viewed both live or scanned as historical records. Many comprise digitized information about objects in the real world, while others are synthesized – computer-generated entirely from data and algorithm.

Implemented as an interactive projection for several viewers, MetaPlex provides a viewing experience in which imagery and sounds produced in the installation space result from viewers' actions as well as from stored texts. Viewers traverse the virtual space using simple hand controls, encountering the contents as a collection or, upon closer inspection, individual images which fill the screen, recalling the original terms of the text. The perceived location of audio, such as the soundtrack of a video, moves around the real installation space according to

viewers' movements in the virtual space: sounds emanating from behind and to the sides sustain a sensory presence even when they are out of view. The installation enables more than the museal surveying of images: rather, viewers traverse a meta-medium within which the frames of a film can be navigated as easily as the pictures on the wall.

MetaPlex delivers both compressed documentation from existing archives and photographs or video at the same resolution as the original. Some texts are themselves interactive virtual environments – computer artworks within which viewers can move and which respond to their actions. And these, which are synthesized from the same data and algorithm used by the artist, might claim to be original. Unlike a conventional collection, however, the location of objects may be altered to allow their comparison side by side, or to suit a particular audience; and unlike conventional moving imagery, the viewer can shuttle forward or backward at any speed for review, or to locate a particular shot or frame.

1 Interactive multimedia in general, and the work of artists such as Peter D'Agostino, Luc Courchesne, Lynn Hershmann Leeson, Bill Seaman, Jeffrey Shaw and Michael Naimark in particular, has explored the performative role of the viewer and interactive video as the site of new originality. Describing the "examination of operative media-elements within specific, construction-oriented virtual environments," Bill Seaman puts it that "Recombinant

MetaPlex
2002
interactive computer
installation
Linux cluster, projector
dimensions variable
installation view: ZKM |
Center for Art and Media
Karlsruhe, 2002
courtesy Street Vision Limited,
London
© Peter Cornwell
photo © Franz Wamhof

Spatial Human-Computer Interfaces

MetaPlex is concerned with the nature of our encounter with texts as well as with the integration of disparate media types. To a degree it reflects works by Courchesne, Seaman [1] and Shaw, for example, and a history that can be traced back to Sandin's *CAVE* [2] and beyond, to Plato. However there are several things that differentiate it from these works – partly because of research and technology advances that have occurred during the intervening years but also because of its premises and goals, which I would like to comment upon here.

The consequences of Human-Computer Interface (HCI) developments that augment the memory and motor skills of viewers not previously skilled or even experienced with interactive navigation technology are often quite difficult to identify. Rather like Artificial Intelligence (AI), in which the initial widespread interest has dwindled, such technology quietly gets built into the fabric of culture, less noticed the more it becomes ubiquitous. The huge upsurge in computer games is the most obvious testament to widespread use of high-performance HCIs in the domestic market, but nevertheless they remain rather foreign to the average TV remote-control connoisseur.

However, the success of games products is due more than anything to the performance that can be delivered through the humble vehicle of television or the computer screen. Computer games now react like the real world but, unshackled from strict adherence to the laws of mechanics and the risk of material injury, they offer more. It has become possible for all gamers to experience something of what has been the preserve of a select few researchers; to do what no-one could ever do in the real world. [3]

Rather than being satisfied with searching moving imagery by title, cast list or even shot analysis using typed text keys, we can now browse among the frames of thousands of titles, traversing their length and back with the smallest gesture. Finally, it is possible to build computer interfaces powerful enough effectively to augment what we are really good at: spatial navigation based on cognitive skills with which we have experience on an evolutionary time scale. We can vastly extend the function of the conventional library – delivering us precisely what we need from a book that we hadn't known about while walking in – setting a collection of films side by side and finding, precisely, the frame, the punctum that satisfies what were the most fugitive criteria.

Edsgar Dijkstra entitled a chapter of a computing science text "On Our Inability to Understand Much." [4] He had in mind the huge number of states through which a software program might pass during execution, not to mention those brought about by its interaction with other programs and real hardware. Such complexity makes us poorly equipped to write reliable programs unless assisted by rigorous methods and automated safeguards. Similarly, faced with the numerical weight of possible combinations of frames in a single movie, or the myriad surfaces of the complete model of a building, it is clear that there are some things which we really are not good at.

Conversely, it is improbable that within the next ten years software development will lead to the unassisted computer being successful in identifying with certainty, say, the imagery of both ice hockey and table tennis as representative of the category *sports*. However, put together what we do well with the strengths of the computer and we are in an entirely different ball park. Spatial human-computer interfaces with fast access to boundless media storage equip users with new capabilities. Navigating by landmarks in a terrain of image-texts we can pinpoint a reference based only on indistinct criteria, all with a couple of gestures on a dial. Such *what if* association supports the development of ideas without the disruption of going to another facility or even waiting for media to load. The images and sounds dance in the air with the "lightness" of electronic information noted by Welsch, [5] delayed only by our lingering with an image or our hesitant

Poetics is concerned with the combination and recombination of media-elements in the service of generating emergent meaning through interactivity." ("Recombinant Poetics: Emergent Explorations of Digital Video in Virtual Space," in *New Screen Media*, Martin Rieser and Andrea Zapp (eds), BFI Publishing, London, 2002.

2   *The CAVE*, developed in the Electronic Visualization Laboratory at the University of Chicago during the late 1980s, projected 3-D imagery privileging the users' position and orientation on to all of the walls of a 3m room. For Paul Virilio this was the moment in which "we are entering a world where there won't be one but two realities: the actual and the virtual."

3   In *Joystick Nation: How Computer Games Ate Our Quarters, Won Our Hearts and Rewired Our Minds* (Little Brown & Company, Boston, MA, 1997) J. C. Herz shows that, compared with the vision of ranks of burger-fueled young male programmers in Sandy Stone's *War of Desire and Technology at the Close of the Mechanical Age* (The MIT Press, Cambridge, MA, 1996), girls too are pretty dedicated gamers.

4   In Edsgar Dijkstra, *A Discipline of Programming*, Prentice Hall, New Jersey, 1976.

5   Wolfgang Welsch, "Artificial Paradises," in *Undoing Aesthetics*, trans. Andrew Inkpin, Sage, London, 1997.

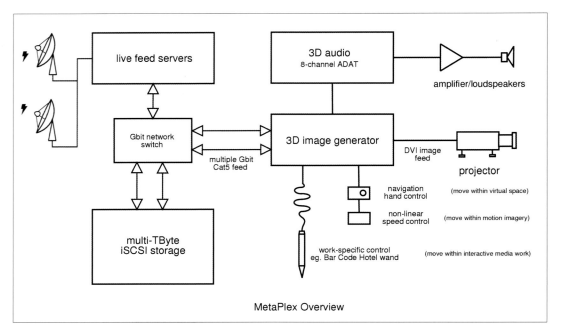

MetaPlex Overview

MetaPlex
2002
diagram
courtesy Street Vision
Limited, London
© Peter Cornwell

transformation of insights into new questions or for the pleasure of a movie playing out at its own rate. By dedicating the computer interface to the service of our instinctive skills, the precision, speed, traceability and capacity of high-performance computers enable us to achieve things we couldn't previously contemplate.

Phenomenal Encounter and Reproduction
MetaPlex is concerned with the nature of our encounter with texts – individually and combinatorially, and with what such encounters lead to.

Firstly, *MetaPlex* differs from the artworks of Courchesne, Seaman or Shaw in that its contents are not of primary importance; in fact, they are variable. Rather, decisions as to selection of contents are curatorial: the installation might be made at another location or time and incorporate different contents without altering many of its properties. *MetaPlex* is more concerned with the viewer's role in navigating among the contents, in a process more like consumption or performance. Perhaps *MetaPlex* is more a machine than anything else, although not quite in the sense of Turing or Deleuze.6 The relationships that it suggests between the work and the museum, between copy and original, between the mechanical and information, pose some questions of the art-historical trace and the museum which are close to Hal Foster's "Archives of Modern Art."7 Foster examines the evolution of relations among art practice, art museum and art history, using Foucault's notion of the archive as something "[which] structures the terms of discourse, … [limiting] what can and cannot be articulated at a given time and place." He develops a "dialectics of seeing" from Manet's pastiche to Valéry's view of the museum as "where we put the art of the past to death." However against Benjamin's apocalyptic rupture of the museum in the face of mechanical reproduction, Foster sets Malraux's musée imaginaire: "Where for Benjamin mechanical reproduction shatters tradition and liquidates aura, for Malraux it provides the means to reassemble the broken bits of tradition into one meta-tradition of global styles – a new museum without walls whose subject is the Family of Man." Foster's fourth archival relation

"emerges with consumer society after World War II, to be registered in different ways by … artists like Rauschenberg and Warhol in the United States, and Gerhard Richter and Sigmar Polke in Germany." Is there then, he asks, a fifth archival transformation allowed by electronic information?

Secondly, *MetaPlex* acts to collapse both space and time. The cinematic apparatus compresses (and occasionally expands) time on the film set into narrative time through editing. In contrast, time here is an element manipulated by the viewer. The rate at which imagery of the virtual space rushes onto the screen in the real space is dependent upon movement initiated by the viewer in both traversing the frames of encapsulated time-based materials, such as video, as well as negotiating virtual distances. *MetaPlex* offers access to many titles at the same time, at speeds of play in either direction limited only by viewers' demands.8 Through the emulation of movement among the spaces of a building with the same physics as our everyday experience there is little to master in order to become a virtuoso; the building might stretch for what we would judge to be hundreds of kilometers in the real world and yet fly past in seconds. In this lack of encumbrance and commutative visual and audible cues arises a certain rapture of the interface which makes computer games so compelling and spatial HCIs so effective.

Thirdly, *MetaPlex* contains texts that differ in *resolution* as well as in fundamental *type* (text, audio, image, geometry) of material analogous with Metzian *tracks*. By resolution I mean the amount of information employed to represent something from the real world (for instance, a 35mm transparency) and, significantly, the difference in human sense data between viewing the projection in *MetaPlex* compared with a projection of the original. Accordingly, *MetaPlex* contains compressed video as well as broadcast quality video. The latter could be completely indistinguishable from the original, if it were projected, and potentially contains exactly the same information as the original camera tape, were it digital. While it is not necessarily true that more information improves quality over an original, a definite amount of information is essential to satisfy human acuity. *MetaPlex*

6 In "Painting Theory Machines" (*Art and Design*, 48, May 1996) Warren Sack sets out "irreconcilable differences, or differends … which exist between Turing's machines and Deleuze and Guattari's machines." See also Félix Guattari, "À propos des Machines," in *Chimeres*, no. 19, Spring 1993.

7 Hal Foster in *Archives of Modern Art*, October 1999, Winter 2002.

8 The traditional twenty-five frames per second of cinema trades film economy against smooth motion on the screen. Higher camera-frame rates must be used to preserve smooth motion if screening time is to exceed real time on the set as in "slow motion" since all playout (projection) equipment runs at 25fps. Bill Viola has used high-speed cameras with compelling results: filming a beating heart during surgery and then producing screen footage which seems to make the heart rate fluctuate precipitously (Viola, *Science of the Heart, 1983*). *MetaPlex* will play out motion imagery at any rate, allowing scrutiny of individual frames, but affecting smoothness of motion if the frame rate is not high enough.

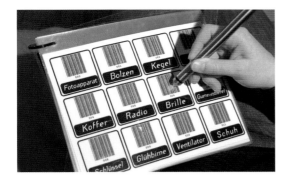

MetaPlex
2002
installation views: ZKM |
Center for Art and Media
Karlsruhe, 2002
details
courtesy Street Vision
Limited, London
© Peter Cornwell
photos © Franz Wamhof

employs several thousand thousand megabytes of storage and thousand thousand megabits per second communication in order to deliver such broadcast-quality moving imagery. Until six months ago, such systems were routinely accessible only to *big science* supercomputer centers.

This contrasts markedly with the conventional view of digital archive which Foster locates in "an electronic continuation of the Mona Lisa Syndrome whereby the cliché only heightens the cult, the art work might become more auratic, not less, as it becomes more simulacral in the electronic archive. A version of this compensatory projection is now part of the common rhetoric of the art museum: the electronic archive does not deflect from the museal object, we are told, much less supplant it; it is pledged to lead us back to the art work and to enhance its aura."[9]

Today, in the case of the photographic image, the moving image and, with special provisions, also sound,[10] we can make electronic versions of mechanically produced works that can stand in for originals, rather than offering documentary versions of the originals using lower resolution or compression. That these and not other media *types* are susceptible to such treatment is more a coincidence of the development of display technology.[11] However, the relationship of original and reproduction blurs even further when we consider computer art works made of program and data. In this case, the software implementing the work in *MetaPlex* is the same as that which runs on the computer in the original space installed by the artist, and so in some cases *MetaPlex* is actually transformed into that work.

Of course, the reproduction can no more be the work of art now than it was for Benjamin, but reproduction has acquired new teeth through powerful information technology. Digital cameras and computed art works blur the "unique and permanent" signature of Benjamin's original, since the cloning of information leads to truly identical multiples. By copying them to different geographic locations we can make their survival as certain as anything else. Perhaps this shift in the status of the original is a marker of Foster's fifth "archival transformation."

Permit me a brief thought experiment. Three-dimensional computer models of objects in the real world present considerable display difficulties, not least because computer displays use emitted light while in our experience light is reflected from most other things. What if we consider building a display surface coated in programmable nano-technology particles? Nano-technology is the process of chip fabrication applied to the making of sub-miniature machines and it is beginning to produce commercial results. Such a display would have the property of determining its color in a precise physical way – pigment is really just a mechanical filtering device for turning incident light into reflected light – but in so doing would allow the generation of human sense data that cannot be produced with conventional computer displays. Specifically, it would enable control of reflected light amplitude independent of hue as well as permitting reflection of some light from within the surface. Gaining control of the surface geometry of the display – both at the scale of marks visible to a viewer as well as at the sub-miniature level of the wavelength of light presents an interesting opportunity: real objects such as paintings could be made, either by gestural manipulation of the surface, or by programming with information derived from other objects. A *Mona Lisa* copy could be produced, indistinguishable from the original, which might be particularly attractive to insurers of exhibitions!

Perhaps what is most interesting is that such a copy would be defined by a dataset – an information equivalent of the original – to be invested only with the belief of the viewer that Leonardo made the marks, before assuming the mantle of the original. Next week the same apparatus might feign a Rembrandt or a Vermeer. *MetaPlex*, while not claiming anything so radical, is however concerned with the encounter between viewer and text, both as documentary reproduction and original; with the subsiding status of the real and what we might learn about the way we encounter things in the real world.

Peter Cornwell

9 Hal Foster, op. cit., p. 94. In *The Archive without Museums* (October 1977, Summer 1996, The MIT Press, Cambridge, MA, pp. 97–119), which under the title "Antinomies in Art History" forms chapter six of *Design and Crime* (Verso, London, 2002), Foster considers in more detail developers of conventional digital art archives, such as The Getty and Bill Gates' CORBIS, "which network[s] chosen 'image-providers' (formerly known as universities) with chosen 'image-consumers' (formerly known as universities)." The resolution of such digital information – the "logic of GIGO," or the quality of data – determines what we see on the "simulacral screen of images of images," but does not alter its "pledge to referentiality."

10 Superficially, audio is highly susceptible to representation by computer because individual sound sources contain modest information compared with images. However, such simple sources are really found only in the special case of tracks (exactly in Metz' sense) associated with other mechanical reproductions. In the real world, sound provides us with a very rich model of the immediate environment. We are inept in comparison with bats or dolphins, but the way individual sounds reflect, refract and superpose among our surroundings gives us a huge amount of pre-reflective information about the space, and is exceedingly complex.

11 Of course, there is no such thing as an original film – everything is a print: the product of post-production. We might privilege the original screen size anticipated by the director or, in the case of a still image, an individual hand print rather than a machine print. The intersection of information technology and image manipulation with the commercial pressures of photography and special effects has driven development both of ubiquitous software such as Photoshop and film and photographic printers. The latter now produce better results than holiday "snaps" and cost less than the ink and special paper that they consume. The same economy pervades data projectors which increasingly deliver brightness and resolution approaching that of cinema. Digital Cinema is a major new market opportunity and the 35mm transparency projected in the home is already being superseded by the Photoshop file.

05

NAVIGABLE

Brian Winston
Technologies of Seeing

1 Alan D. Coleman, "Lentil Soup," in *Etc*, Spring 1985, p. 19.

2 Gezienus ten Doesschate, *Perspective: Fundamentals, Controversials, History*, DeGraaf Publishers, Nieuwkoop, 1964, p. 85.

3 Svetlana Alpers, *The Art of Describing: Dutch Art In the Seventeenth Century*, University of Chicago Press, Chicago, 1984, pp. 53–64.

4 Joan Gadol, *Leon Battista Alberti: Universal Man of the Early Renaissance*, University of Chicago Press, Chicago, 1969, p. 25.

5 This has sometimes been seen as an essentially bourgeois mode of seeing but it is, at best, somewhat a-historical to use such a term given that we are here some centuries before anything that could be called a bourgeois hegemony.

6 Peter Murray and Lynda Murray, *A Dictionary of Art and Artists*, Penguin Books, Harmondsworth, 1959, p. 265.

7 Lynda Nochlin, *Realism*, Penguin Books, Harmondsworth, 1971, p. 13.

8 Aaron Scharf, *Art and Photography*, Penguin Books, Harmondsworth, 1974, pp. 47–57.

9 Gisèle Freund, *Photography and Society*, David R. Godine, Boston, 1982, p. 81.

10 Glynne Wickham, *A History of Theatre*, Phaidon Press, Oxford, 1985, pp. 155, 181.

Central to this attempt to make the technological an expression of the social is the idea of cinema being part of a centuries-old Western project to create what A. D. Coleman has called "lens culture."[1] This implies a particular set of social practices whereby a viewer relates to a screen. These determine the cultural dimension of the Western way of seeing even though the devices involved might have initially been Eastern innovations.

The first great triumph of this way of seeing is the creation of various modes of representation of space on flat surfaces, including the *construzione legittima* of Alberti mentioned above. (This is not the first such system to be used, however, there being a number even within the Western tradition that can be discerned between ancient times and the fourteenth century[2] and, of course, the northern Europeans produced a rival "distant point construction" of perspective first described by Viator in *Artificiali perspectiva* (1505), which is the basis of Dutch seventeenth-century painting.[3])

The Renaissance deployment of perspective impacts on the social sphere in ways that are critical to all subsequent developments of the lens culture of the West. For example, it establishes a preference for certain forms of realistic modes of pictorial representation which are (or tend to be) illusionist. The desire for thin illusionist simulacrum of the external world feeds the entire research agenda from Alberti through the magic lantern to the cinema and on into the present; from painting to photography (which released painting from the prison of realism) to the cinema and, again, on into the present. Considered dispassionately, it could be said that this realism of the West is a somewhat dull thing, incarcerating image-making within the bounds of the forms of the external world. Be that as it may, it is crucial for our understanding of modern systems of representation, including the cinema.

The triumph of Renaissance perspective systems, especially the Italian, also involves another profound social effect in that such systems required that the eye be locked into a certain position in order for the illusion to be perceived. This was literally true of Brunelleschi's painting of the Baptistery in Florence, conventionally the earliest image, now lost, to use the newly minted perspective system that Alberti described. The painting was executed on a wood panel:

"At the center of the picture of the Baptistery there was a small hole which opened into a funnel on the back of the panel. The viewer stood behind the panel and looked through the funnel at a mirror held at arm's length in front of it.
The mirror reflected the painting, and the results [...] were astonishing. A powerful abstraction had

been created whereby the painter compelled the viewer to see nothing but what he wished him to see."[4]

It is this locking, the rationalization of sight as it has been termed,[5] that conditions Western publics to perceive space through the use of particular codes of representation on flat surfaces. This was a crucial lesson for these publics and a vital precondition for the popularity of the magic lantern, photography and cinematography.

The realism of the Renaissance underwent many stylistic changes in the course of the next several centuries but one can note that, at the moment of photograph, painting was itself in the grip of an extremely realistic movement. Indeed, the term "realism" in art history conventionally means exactly a group of nineteenth-century painters, led by Courbet, who supposedly went beyond mere naturalism ("which is no more than the simple-minded pleasure in being able to make an accurate transcript of nature") to the "search for the squalid and the depressing as a means of life enhancement."[6] Lynda Nochlin persuasively makes the case that this conventional view is inadequate and that, in fact, the aim of this movement, between 1840 and 1870–1880, was rather "to give a truthful, objective and impartial representation of the real world, based on meticulous observation of contemporary life."[7] In other words, exactly what photography was supposed to do. As the century progressed, photography moved from being an aid to such realistic painting[8] to being its nemesis. On hearing about the daguerreotype one painter, perhaps just a little prematurely, announced: "From today painting is dead."[9] Painting with the sort of purpose Nochlin adduces to realism was, if not to die at photography's hand, then certainly to be battered by it.

The embedding of these aesthetic strategies and preferences into Western taste over the past half-millennium can be said to indicate a species of addiction – an addiction to realism. This addiction which produced Renaissance perspective painting also deeply affected the development of the Western theater.

The theater, even before it moved indoors, used props and elements of scenery. In the seventeenth century, it became a major site of perspective illusionism, first in the interests of neoclassicism but then, throughout the eighteenth and nineteenth centuries, in the interests of an ever more naturalistic realism. The coming of gas lighting to the Theatre Royal, Drury Lane, and the Lyceum Opera in 1817 further fed the illusionist addiction:[10]

"Second only to lighting among theatrical innovations was the growing demand for more lavishly realistic scenic spectacle. [...] To meet this demand, theater architects and their engineering consultants translated the floor area of their stages into a kind of jigsaw puzzle [...] German and American engineers provided double stages; an earlier British innovation was the provision of aquatic facilities for the representation of naval battles, river crossings, and other heroic incidents [...]. Without the aid of such technological advances Wagner could hardly have required the Rhine to overflow its banks, or the Palace of the Valhalla to come crashing to the ground when *Der Ring des Nibelungen* was given its first complete performance in the purpose-built Festspielhaus at Bayreuth in 1876. By the end of the century, revolving stages carrying three different stage-settings could replace one another within a few seconds at the touch of a button."11

The taste for scenery was so extreme that it alone could sustain a show. First to exploit this was the Panorama, devised in 1787, where audiences were surrounded by a painting sixteen feet high or so which slowly circled the seats. The display was accompanied by commentary and effects. Then came, from Louis Daguerre and his partner Charles Button, a more sophisticated variant of this, the Diorama. Here the audience was transported before a scene in which there was movement and elaborate light changes as well as music, sound effects and commentary and, in the foreground, real objects like models of chalets and fir trees to give depth to the image of, say, Mont Blanc behind.12

Chanan, following Walter Benjamin, suggests that these entertainments were essentially both "philistine" and "middle class" (that is, presumably, both lowbrow and respectable), representing a recovery of the countryside these recently urbanized audiences had lost as well as a celebration of the cityscapes they had gained. The Dioramas, wrote Benjamin, were "the *locus* of a perfect imitation of nature."13 Such spectacles were a most salient site of the modern as well as being exempla of what Jean-Louis Comolli describes as a "sort of frenzy of the visible" which was then gripping the industrializing world.14 Obviously, this returns us to the magic lantern, albeit writ large; and, indeed, projected photographs were used in these spectacles before they were put into the "wheel of life" toys.

Magic lantern shows are recorded from the seventeenth century on. By the late eighteenth century the physical circumstances in which the projected image was to be viewed in this culture had been determined. Instead of the casual displays of earlier times, Étienne Gaspar Robertson, who shocked audiences in revolutionary Paris with "Fantasmagorie," a magic lantern show of ghosts and ghouls, sat his audience in rows in the dark before the screen.15 (The coming of gaslight to the theaters also allowed for the darkening of the auditorium for the first time at live entertainments.)

As the nineteenth century progressed the lantern's beam became more and more intense, even before the introduction of the electric lamp. Limelight was used from 1822. By 1885 calcium light projectors were available. The magic lantern slide became more complex by means of simple animations while by 1857

at the latest came what John Fell called "the integration of auditorium and photography." In that year two battle Panoramas of Sebastopol and Solferino used photographic slides.16 (There was another way in which the early-nineteenth-century theater prepared people for such more or less purely visual shows. In a number of European countries, theaters were licensed and controlled but legal definitions required actors to speak. To avoid this control, a fashion grew up for [unlicensed] melodramatic dumb-shows, mimed to music with placards to explain the action.17)

The operation of this addiction to realism thus created in the social sphere a number of elements which were to be crucial to the cinema. Before the turn of the nineteenth century, the public was prepared to be entertained by being seated in rows in a darkened space to look at magic lantern slides. After the coming of the gas lamp, auditoria for live spectacles were also darkened. A taste for dumb show was in vogue. These live spectacles involved highly realistic effects and some entertainments consisted entirely of displays of realistic scenery, animated and augmented in various ways short of live acting. What characterizes these last is an extreme verisimilitude, an expression of the sort of public pictorial taste that had dominated in the West for the previous several centuries.

The Context for Cinema: Narrative
But there are other elements of the same kind, which demand attention if the context for cinema is to be explicated. There is a second sort of addiction relating to spectacle in the West. It is less obvious and more contentious than is the dominance of a realistic mode of representation but it is nevertheless crucial: narrative. On the one hand, it is clear that, although there are exceptions, the broad theatrical tendency is to narrative, and this is true even of the most purely spectacular of forms such as the Panorama and Diorama. Of these, John Fell has written: "All such performances, of course, show unity of time and space, but soon we note a developing sense of sequence and selection of detail, as well as the introduction of movement within a scene."18

There is a sense in which this should hardly be surprising. There are those who would argue the propensity to narrative is closely and inextricably bound up with the fundamental human ability to communicate. To speak is to narrate; and to listen and to look is to seek constantly to establish logical and chronological connections – to attempt narrative order out of chaos.19 This is, of course, to understand narrative in a very broad sense; but not, I believe, to take it beyond where current narratology would have it.

For instance, the mark of narrative as a distinct text type is, as Seymour Chatman says, that it "*temporally* controls its reception by audience" and, moreover, does so logically. The slowly moving audience of the Diorama was obviously being controlled temporally, if not – as when simple scenery was on display – logically. However, when the Diorama displayed, say, the course of a battle, then logic also came into play and the result is what Chatman calls a "chronologic."20 Chatman distinguishes a number of text

11 Wickham, op. cit., p. 182.

12 John Fell, *Film and the Narrative Tradition*, University of California Press, Berkeley, 1974, pp. 137, 141; Michael Chanan, *The Dream That Kicks: The Prehistory and Early Years of the Cinema in Britain*, Routledge and Kegan, London, 1980, pp. 112–144. This tradition, fully narrativized, is now to be found in the very latest "virtual reality" Disneyland and Universal tour rides where an audience, seated in chairs that bounce and tilt, is placed close-up to a large screen and undergoes the illusion of a violent travel narrative.

13 Fell, op. cit., p. 114.

14 Jean-Louis Comolli, "Machines of the Visible," in *The Cinematic Apparatus*, Teresa de Laurentis and Stephen Heath (eds), St Martin's Press, New York, 1980, p. 122.

15 Charles Musser, *The Emergence of Cinema*, Charles Scribner's Sons, New York, 1990, pp. 22–27.

16 Fell, op. cit., p. 140.

17 Fell, op. cit., pp. 15, 16.

18 Fell, op. cit., p. 139.

19 See a special edition on narrative of the *Journal of Communications*, vol. 35, no. 4, Autumn 1985.

20 Seymour Chatman, *Coming to Terms: The Rhetoric of Narrative in Fiction and Film*, Cornell University Press, Ithaca, 1990, pp. 7, 9.

types – "mere description," "argument" and "explanation" as well as "narrative." The temporal control element in the Diorama means that its "text" is beyond "mere description" while the visual display means it is also beyond "argument" and, largely, beyond "explanation." So, as texts, many Dioramas were beyond argument, description and explanation and are therefore most safely and appropriately characterized as a species of narrative.

Narrative was everywhere in the world of nineteenth-century screen practice – from the animated peep-show which grew out of the "wheels of life" to the sequenced slides of the magic lantern show. Although often the effects stood alone (Robespierre rising from the tomb was a big hit with the Fantasmogorie audience) the world of the magic lantern was no more adverse to narrative than predecessor image-making regimes – church imagery as when it dealt with the life of Christ, for example. One of the very earliest of recorded magic lantern shows involved a journey – a basic narrative form – to China. [21] By the nineteenth century, the slide show involved not only sequences but a panoply of techniques for melding the images together. All of the elements that were to characterize the cinema's methods of transition between shots cuts, dissolves – were all prefigured in the lantern show. (Descriptive title cards were picked up from the dumb-shows.)

This propensity to arrange images in a logical order and then to display them at a fixed pace before an audience is, at the very least, a mark or trace of the addiction to narrative. As such it renders moot the argument of the last decade or so as to how much such narratives were carried forward into the early cinema and whether or not the cinema took at some point "a narrative turn," having initially been a non-narrative form. These long-standing tendencies within the social sphere in general and the practice of spectacle (including screen spectacle) in particular suggest that this is not the case. It is rather, if you will, that the cinema failed to struggle against millennia of storytelling and centuries of régimes of sequenced pictorial representation.

I am not therefore persuaded by Tom Gunning's argument that there was an alternative to the narrative cinema, which he terms a "cinema of attractions" in the first decade after 1895 and that narrative triumphed only after 1906/1907. Gunning describes the cinema of attractions as "less a way of telling stories than as a way of presenting a series of views to the audience." [22] He suggests that "the early cinema was not dominated by the narrative impulse that later asserted its sway over the medium"; [23] that is to say, cinema did indeed take a narrative "turn." He points to the dominance of actuality films, which outnumbered fiction until 1906; to the direct look of subjects at the lens; to the bowing and gesturing of variety artists again to the lens; to "plotless trick films;" and to erotic exhibitionism as in The Bride Retires, a 1902 striptease film which, in Gunning's description, has the "bride" winking at the camera while "husband" peers at her from behind a screen. But much of his argument can be discounted; although, clearly, in so far as vaudeville acts were transferred to the screen, they remained non-narrative spectacles – that is to

say, with temporal structure but without (much) logical causality. In the first place most of these scenes unfold according to the double temporality which is, at the very least, a clue to the presence of narrative. Secondly, much of what Gunning suggests as having to do with display is sanctioned by theatrical practice. The "bride" undresses – a simple narrative, which is not altered by her awareness of the audience. Awareness of the audience is time-honored in the theater as is bowing to indicate closure, either of a trick or of a whole variety act.

A further basic problem here is an implicit claim for documentary difference, with the documentary being seen as essentially (and automatically) non-narrative. [24] Here let me just say that there might not be much of a narrative going on in the Lumières' 1895 film of Workers Leaving the Factory (La Sortie des usines Lumière) but the factory gates do open, a dog suddenly emerges – itself a somewhat curious mini-event – and the people move away and the gates close. There is no way this, and many other of these first fragments of time and space, can be typed except as simple narratives. They differ from the fictional films (if indeed such things as the presence of the dog does not give the lie even to this) simply because they are narrativized segments caught sur le vif rather than overtly set-up. Others argue that these "documentary" films, La Sortie des usines Lumière and L'Arrivée d'un train en gare de la Ciotat, "even if … narratives, their level of narrativity bears no comparison to that of L'Arroseur arrosé." [25] But if narrative is defined in Chatman's terms, this notion of level refers to the strength of the causality within the narrative. It does not deny narrative's presence. In L'Arroseur arrosé, for example, A (the boy stepping on the hose) causes B (the gardener inspecting the suddenly inoperable hose) which causes C (the boy removing his foot) which causes D (the gardener getting soaked). In La Sortie des usines Lumière, the gates open (A) "causing" the workers to exit (B) so that the gates can be shut (C). This may be not so engaging but it is still a narrative (as is Méliès's blowing up the magician's head, bigger and bigger and bigger and … pouf). As Gunning points out, escaping from the prison house of narrative is an avant-garde project. It was as avant-garde an ambition before 1906 as it was to be afterwards.

Let me just add that I am not using the term "simple" in any pejorative sense. It is wrong to see early deviations from later practices as primitive; rather such deviations can be noted, in Kristin Thompson's phrase, as "a system apart." This system differed not by being non-narrative but only by assuming the audience was in a theatrical situation: Locked into a seat and having therefore a fixed point of view. [26] This is an alternative to the dominant mode, which came to utilize changes of viewpoint, ellipsis, etc., just as Soviet practice in the 1920s or certain avant-garde procedures are also alternatives to the dominant mode. But unlike the avant-garde (but like the Soviets), the early fixed-viewpoint single-shot films are an alternative narrative mode. Cinema is not a question of langue ou language but rather langues ou languages.

Moreover, at the very beginning, single-shot films were arranged for exhibition interspersed with slides

21 Gosser, Kircher and the Lanterna Magica, p. 974; Joseph Maria Eder, History of Photography, Dover Publications, New York, 1978, p. 51.

22 Tom Gunning, "The Cinema of Attractions: Early Film, Its Spectator and the Avant-Garde," in Early Cinema: Space, Frame, Narrative, Thomas Elsaesser (ed.), BFI Publishing, London, 1990, p. 57.

23 Gunning, op. cit., p. 55.

24 I have argued against this in Claiming the Real, BFI Publishing, London, 1995, pp. 99–123.

25 Andre Gaudreault, "Film, Narrative, Narration: The Cinema of the Lumière Brothers," in Elsaesser, op. cit., p. 69.

26 David Bordwell, Janet Staiger and Kirsten Thompson, The Classical Hollywood Cinema: Film Style and Mode of Production to 1960, Columbia University Press, New York, 1985, p. 158.

to fill the screen during reloading – not perhaps involving a logic of causality but certainly with a sense of the need to maintain at least one level of temporal continuity – "audience time" as it were.[27] Stephen Bottomore further suggests that this habit of sequencing then led to the creation of film editing whereby a single-shot film, analogous to a slide, was joined with others to create a sequence of shots analogous to a slide sequence – although spacing was inserted to avoid "jerks" or "shocks to the eye." He points out that at the very beginning "'cinematographic slides' was a common term for films." The British pioneer Cecil Hepworth suggested "stringing the images together into little sets or episodes."[28] By 1897 an event such as the Spanish-American War was featured in a display using twenty films and slides. Before 1900 a twenty-shot film had been made by Méliès – *Cendrillon*. In Australia in 1900, thirteen short films and two hundred slides were constituted into a show which lasted for more than two hours.[29]

Narrative is not the inevitable destiny of the cinema – it is just that it is the inevitable destiny of any cinema created in a Western culture addicted to narrative, that is to say: the only cinema there is.

The Context for Cinema: The Mass Audience

One last crucial context for the "invention" of the cinema can now be considered – the "invention" (as it might be termed) of the modern audience. Beyond the technology, beyond addictions to realism and narrative as they might infect individuals within the culture, is this matter of the mass audience.

As we have seen, the audience by the middle years of the nineteenth century had long since learned to sit in rows in darkened auditoria. Now it grew ever larger as the rural population drifted to the city. Population in general had already doubled and tripled in the first half of the century in the industrializing world. In the United States, thanks to immigration, it had increased six-fold.[30] The result overall was that between 1800 and 1850, European city-dwellers increased from 10 per cent of the population to 16.7 per cent.[31] By 1851 Britain, the most urbanized society, became the first country where the total population of cities and towns was greater than the rural population – 51 per cent. In the next three decades, the great cities themselves doubled and trebled in size.[32] By 1900 only 36 per cent of Germans and 43 per cent of the French still lived on the land.[33] By now Europe as a whole was 29 per cent urban; in England and Wales the figure was 61.4 per cent. The mass audience had arrived. As Eric Hobsbawm states: "At some point in the later nineteenth century the mass migration into the rapidly growing big cities produced [...] a lucrative market for popular spectacle."[33] Meeting the demand created by this mass (for whom the prospect of spectacle and stimulation was as much bound up with the urban and the modern as was the opportunity for new sorts of work) required the industrialization of many forms of entertainment and communication.

Take newspapers. In Great Britain, for example, these describe a trajectory from the artisanal to the industrial as journalistic and publishing functions become specialized. Instead of a Defoe or a Cobbett working virtually single-handed, writing every word for a small paper to be printed, 1,200 copies an hour, on a flat-bed press that had in essence remained unchanged for several centuries, there now emerges a reporter, an editor, a publisher, printers and so on. There were specializations of technique – for example, the wide use of shorthand in reporting – and of technology – for example, the application of steam power in the rotary press and the use of the telegraph. By the middle years of the nineteenth century, newspapers had transformed themselves from small-scale enterprises with uncontrollable and unpredictable political and social effects into large, capital-intensive operations, belonging to and controlled by a class of citizen concerned both to make profits and to exercise social control in favor of the established order. In this way, newspapers were rendered so safe for capital exploitation that all the failing systems of state control, the licenses and the special "taxes on knowledge," which anyway had not prevented the growth of an unlicensed press, could then be safely removed, as indeed they were by 1862.[34]

The newspaper found its readership in the growing cities but it also, because of the railways, reached out into smaller centers of population in order to maximize its business. The theater needed the final flood of people to arrive in the city itself to achieve the same level of industrialization. Parallel developments in the theater therefore tended to run some decades behind those in the press. Nevertheless, the same pattern can be seen in the theater whereby failing state controls also eventually give way to apparently liberalized, centralized and capital-intensive operations.

In Britain, the slow disappearance of the street entertainer, the increasing marginalization of the fair and the rise of the music hall all worked to turn popular theatrical entertainment into a collective urban experience.[35] The taste for collective activity provided by places of entertainment was reinforced, Chanan claims, by other developments, notably the mass Chartist movement which brought people together for political purposes. The needs of an industrialized society required that this mass be educated, which in its turn increased the need for mass information and entertainment systems. As Raymond Williams pointed out, the pressures for such education antedated its formal provision by decades, but "we need to remember that the new institutions were not produced by the working people themselves. They were, rather, produced for them by others, often (as most notably with the cheap newspaper and commercial advertisement on a large scale) for conscious political or commercial advantage."[36]

In the theater, as with newspapers, this move was marked by the emergence of new specialists. By the late eighteenth century, individually owned theaters were organized into "tours." These were sometimes virtually the property of one actor-manager. The Yorkshire circuit, for example, grew from the regular rotation through the county of one group of players led by Tate Wilkinson. Forced often to play in ordinary rooms in inns, he began to build theaters in the 1770s. City corporations were also moved to erect theaters. By the 1780s a full circuit had been created.

27 Stephen Bottomore, "Shots in the Dark: The Real Origins of Film Editing," in Elsaesser, op. cit., p. 104.

28 Bottomore, op. cit., p. 105.

29 Bottomore, op. cit., n. p.

30 Eric Hobsbawm, *The Age of Revolution, 1789-1848*, Weidenfeld & Nicolson, London, 1995, pp. 169–170.

31 Jan de Vries, "European Urbanisation, 1500–1800," quoted in *The Age of Empire, 1875–1914*, Eric Hobsbawm, Weidenfeld & Nicolson, London, 1995, p. 343.

32 Eric Hobsbawm, *The Age of Capital, 1848–1875*, Weidenfeld & Nicolson, London, 1995, p. 210.

33 Hobsbawm, *Empire*, op. cit., p. 137.

34 Hobsbawm, *Capital*, op. cit., p. 236.

35 James Curran and Jean Seaton, *Power without Responsibility*, Routledge, London, 1999, pp. 25–49.

36 Chanan, *The Dream That Kicks*, op. cit., pp. 137–142, 147–154.

Wilkinson although a former actor, was an example of the new breed of manager who did not perform as against the older actor-manager who appeared in shows which he produced (i.e. directed) and with companies which he organized. The actor-manager then dominated the theater and has never quite died out even into the present day (Kenneth Branagh, for example). However, Wilkinson's basic organization was still quite primitive with only his company playing in these theaters and then only for fixed seasons, normally arranged to coincide with other events such as the races or the assizes.37

More complex forms of organization were also emerging at this time. The Theatre Royal, Bristol (now Britain's oldest working theater), "was partner in the most prosperous and prestigious provincial circuit in the country, that created by John Palmer and William Keasberry of Bath from 1779 onwards."38 Keasberry was an actor-manager in the old style, but his partner, Palmer, was more like Wilkinson albeit in a more extreme form – a backroom administrator who neither acted nor produced.

Nevertheless, even Palmer was still deeply involved in the business of managing actors. Logically, a further step could be taken and was when a new form of manager arose out of these "tours"; this was a person who did not act and manage (as did Keasberry) nor only manage (as did Palmer) but who just owned the bricks and mortar. One show in many theaters, instead of each theater producing its own shows, was starting to make economic sense. One group of managers produced the product, the other group marketed it. In America, from the 1840s on, the mode of production was the stock company. Unlike old-style wandering players, the stock company eschewed repertory and instead played the same show for limited runs in an established circuit of venues.

As the nineteenth century advanced, the sense of this more highly developed organizational structure became inescapable:

"By taking advantage of railways and fast ocean liners, managers were discovering that instead of waiting for audiences to turn up at their theaters, productions could be transported to the audiences in equally well-equipped theaters at home and abroad with an actor or actress (sometimes both) at the head of the company whose personal reputation was sure to attract crowds where ever they appeared. This attracted businessmen with little or no experience of the theater, but with a flair for anticipating public taste, to enter into theater management by acquiring chains of theater buildings."39

The consequences of this division of labor were immense. The "star" system, already in embryo because of the nature of previous production structures, becomes an essential marketing element of the new system. Long runs become possible. The artistic control of the production gets spun off into the hands of a producer (or, as this person was to become known, the director).40 Booking agents, talent agents, publicists and so on all followed. Augustin Daly was the first entrepreneur in the USA to assemble a chain of theaters and he was in Britain followed by Sir Edward Moss and Sir Oswald Stoll.

As these British knighthoods eloquently suggest, such men of property were a long way from the "rogues, vagabonds and players" of previous centuries. And, as happened with newspapers after they were safely in the hands of men of property, the legislation on theaters moved from draconian, if inefficient, control to a regime that aided and abetted the entrepreneurs. First, the Theatre Act of 1843 removed the royal monopoly at the two London Patent Theatres (the Theatres Royal, Drury Lane and Haymarket). Moreover, as with any other industry in Victorian Britain, the theater was subjected to parliamentary inquiry. The "Suitability Act" of 1878, arising from such investigation, was designed as a public safety measure by instituting the legal requirement that all theaters have iron safety curtains.41 But the Act had other effects, especially on the music-halls.

These had spent the first half of the century emerging from a tradition of "free and easy" sing-songs at the pub. One London publican, Charles Morton, had built a specialized hall adjacent to his tavern in 1852 to bring a measure of formality to these occasions. Over the next two decades such halls or Theatres of Variety proliferated, but after the Licensing Act of 1878 [...] the number of independent theaters fell as management companies took them over. As a result, artistes were increasingly booked not for appearances in individual theaters but for tours which included several. Agents consequently grew more powerful.42 Two hundred halls were closed and many more, whose owners could not afford to meet the safety requirements, slipped into chain ownership. By the mid-1890s, both legitimate theaters and these music-halls (in America, vaudevilles), which by now had become identical to them physically, had been industrialized. The stage had been transformed from what was in the 1860s just a "show" (a term new at that time) into what was by the 1890s "show business" (a phrase new at that time).

The same sort of sequence of developments can be seen elsewhere. Eighteenth-century forms such as "the popular suburban theater in Vienna, the dialect theater in the Italian cities, the popular (as distinct from court) opera, the commedia dell'arte and travelling mime show"43 could welcome the ever-increasing urban throngs as easily as did the English-speaking music-hall or vaudeville. By the 1850s, all these popular theatrical forms had become fixtures in the European city. Two decades of urbanization on and, Hobsbawm claims, among the German-speaking peoples "operas and theaters became temples in which men and women worshiped."44 These could be "the focus of town planning as in Paris (1860) and Vienna (1869), visible as cathedrals as in Dresden (1869), invariably gigantic and monumentally elaborate as in Barcelona (from 1862) or Palermo (from 1875)."45 The demand for theater in many of these places was met as part of general municipal development rather than as the result of entrepreneurial endeavor. German theaters, originally mainly trophy structures for the dukes and princelings who had ruled the German ministates, tripled in numbers between 1870 and 1896.46 Many of these were municipal.47

These new structures, both physical and organizational, conformed the theater to capitalist practice

37 Raymond Williams, *Culture and Society*, Columbia University Press, New York, 1983, pp. 306, 307.

38 Claire Tomalin, *Mrs. Jordan's Profession: The Story of a Great Actress and a Future King*, Penguin Books, Harmondsworth, 1995, pp. 28–31.

39 Kathleen Barker, "Bristol at Play, 1801-1853; A Typical Picture of the English Provinces?," in *Western Popular Theatre*, David Mayer and Kenneth Richards (eds), Methuen, London, 1977, p. 91.

40 Wickham, op. cit., pp. 209–210.

41 John Allen, *A History of the Theatre in Europe*, Heinemann, London, 1983, p. 275.

42 Chanan, *The Dream That Kicks*, op. cit., pp. 159–160.

43 Chanan, *The Dream That Kicks*, op. cit., p. 38.

44 Hobsbawm, *Capital*, op. cit., p. 276.

45 Hobsbawm, *Capital*, op. cit., p. 285.

46 Hobsbawm, *Capital*, op. cit., p. 286.

47 Hobsbawm, *Empire*, op. cit., p. 221.

and produced industrial institutions identical to those of any other sector – cartels, for example. At a secret meeting in 1895, ostensibly to bring some order to the American booking situation, a group of agents, managers (including Charles Frohman who had pioneered road shows, that is, the concept of duplicate touring productions) and theater-chain owners established the Theatrical Syndicate. Rapidly, the Syndicate (also known as the Theatrical Trust) established a stranglehold on the entire American legitimate theater.

Vaudeville was a little behind, still seeking in the 1880s to distance itself from the less salubrious aspects of its origins (which were to become burlesque). Benjamin Keith and Edward Albee were responsible for a cleaned-up variety show, which all members of a family could attend. They also built the first chain of theaters to house their innovation. By the mid-1890s there were five major chains covering the larger cities.48 Robert Allen estimates at least a million people a week went to the vaudeville by 1896.49 The owners formed themselves into an Association of Vaudeville Managers, parallel to the Theatrical Trust, in 1900 and achieved a similar effect in this sector.

If the owners, producers and agents organized themselves, so did theatrical workers. Benevolent funds for indigent actors were established in Britain and America by the early 1880s. These were followed by trade unions proper. In the United States, actors in 1895 formed themselves into the Actor's Society, of America in response to the Theatrical Syndicate. This gave way to Actor's Equity in 1912/1913. In Britain, the ancient Worshipful Company of Musicians, which had been moribund from the mid-eighteenth century, became in 1891 the London Orchestral Association after a number of false starts over the previous two decades. It has survived, in the form of the Musicians' Union, into the present. The first Actor's Association in Britain was also formed in this year but was short-lived. Nevertheless other attempts followed, eventually producing the Actors' Society, the direct precursor of British Actors' Equity. The Theatrical and Music Hall Operatives' Trade Union (which organized carpenters and other backstage workers) was in place before 1900. The Variety Artists Association was founded in 1902.50 And there were strikes. In 1901 the White Rats, who were the American equivalent of the British Variety Artists Association, struck the Association of Vaudeville Managers.51 As an industrialized business, the theater had come of age.

Over the century before the coming of the cinema, theatrical delivery systems (as it were) were extended to maximize markets. Product was differentiated, often with quite distinct class connotations, although the theater remained more a place of common resort than did many other public sites of the time, albeit with the commoner sort "up in the gods" and the well-to-do below. Niches were covered so that every last possible audience could be drawn into the theater. At the very end of the day (or of the line), "tent shows" of broad Victorian farce and variety were still touring the backroads of rural America well into the middle decades of the twentieth century. Variety survived World War II in London. But the central point is that by 1895, the broad mass of the audience, addicted to naturalistic illusion and narrative, was sitting in the darkened seats of the auditorium watching highly professional entertainments created by a logistically complex, capital-intensive, if somewhat risky, industry. Both the producers and the consumers of this product were waiting for the cinema.

Towards a Structural Account of the Making of Cinema

It is then in this sense that we can say it was the audience, as much as anything else, which "invented" the cinema in the mid-1890s. This is the answer to Bazin's fundamental question: "How was it that the invention took so long to emerge, since all the prerequisites had been assembled [...]?"52 Bazin provocatively goes on to draw attention to the possible extent of this delay: "The photographic cinema could just as well have grafted itself on to a phenakistoscope foreseen as long ago as the sixteenth century. The delay in the invention of the latter is as disturbing a phenomenon as the existence of the E precursors of the former." Most commentators do not acknowledge a delay. The technology is deemed to appear as soon as all the technical elements involved were available. Thus, one such commentator writes: "The moving photograph did not become technically feasible until about 1890."53 More specifically:

"Technological opportunity is the consequence of the historical stage of development which has been reached by the material forces of production. In the case of cinematography, the main factors were the improvement of photographic emulsions; the development of precision engineering and instruments and their application to the problem of the intermittent drive mechanism; the development of the chemicals industry involved in the quite unconnected invention of celluloid – the first of the plastics – and the improvement of its production techniques to the point where it became available as a thin film, durable, flexible and transparent enough to provide the base for the film strip."54

Yet, how many of these requirements were really not available until the 1890s? How many were to hand ten, twenty or even thirty years previously? The notion that the cinema required advances in engineering is not persuasive. As Bazin observed, the mechanisms involved were "far less complicated than an eighteenth-century clock."55 The engineering available in the mid-century might not have been quite refined enough to create a full-scale difference engine; but it was more than adequate for the cinema, its cameras/projectors and even its film-stock manufacturing machinery.56 Implied in this view appears to be a vision of the nineteenth-century engineer as a bricoleur, a bodger. "Bricolage" is defined as a knocking together of things at hand.57 This is the suggested obverse of modern scientific and technological procedures. I have elsewhere argued that such a position tends to see nineteenth-century technology in a false light from two points of view.58 In the first place, those who produced the cinema were at the heart of structured technological activities – Edison with his team in his industrial lab and Lumière in his far from small photographic factory. It is perhaps worth remembering that the credit for the moving

48 John Allen, op. cit., p. 245.

49 Robert Allen, *Vaudeville and Film, 1895-1915. A Study in Media Interaction*, Arno Press, New York, 1980, pp. 26–28, 36.

50 Robert Allen, op. cit., p. 39.

51 Chanan, *The Dream That Kicks*, op. cit., pp. 167–169.

52 Musser, op. cit., pp. 276, 277.

53 Andre Bazin, *What Is the Cinema?*, University of California Press, Berkeley, 1967, p. 19.

54 Hobsbawm, *Empire*, op. cit., p. 238.

55 Michael Chanan, "Economic Conditions of Early Cinema," in Elsaesser, op. cit. p. 175.

56 Bazin, op. cit., p. 18.

57 Chanan, *The Dream That Kicks*, op. cit., p. 51.

58 Brian Winston, *Misunderstanding Media*, Harvard University Press, Cambridge, MA, 1986, pp. 373–380.

image rests with these men and their helpers, not with the other "great men" – the lonely Friese-Greene, the somewhat flamboyant Muybridge nor even the scientific Marey. Secondly, it is by no means the case that we now proceed in these matters in a less serendipitous way than we did last century. Take, for example, the creation of the transistor, often cited as the locus classicus of modern structured innovation. 59 But, on the contrary, so serendipitous was the achievement of transistor effect that the Bell Lab had to delay announcing it to the world until the research team could work out some coherent physical explanation for the phenomenon in order to secure the patent. It is certainly the case that limited research agendas, such as that for analogue high-definition television, are very structured; but no more so than was the rapid search for a viable telephone after the patents were granted to Bell and Gray for systems which did not quite work. 60

Somewhat more convincing is an argument that points to the lack of celluloid sheets and films sensitive enough to record an image at a fraction of a second prior to the last decades of the century. Nevertheless, celluloid was being developed in the late 1840s and anyway, as Friese-Greene demonstrated, there were other possible, if less effective, flexible bases available. Furthermore, following Godard's innovation of 1840, silver bromide's potential as a chemical to increase sensitivity and enable fast exposures was also being explored by the 1860s. This line of experiments needed no conceptual breakthrough or discovery. Thus, even if elements were not actually available before the period 1888 (say) to 1895, nevertheless not enough is "discovered" then to make the case for the cinema coming into being at the first available "technological opportunity." Indeed, the contrary can be claimed: nothing was "discovered" and Bazin's sense of disturbance is quite justified.

On the other hand, Chanan is entirely correct when he supports his assumption about technological lacks with the observation that "cinematography could not have been invented earlier [...] because it would not have attracted anyone's attention as an opportunity for investment."61 In saying this, he is denying what he sees as Bazin's "inversion of the historical order of causality" whereby the cinema creates a demand for itself before it is "invented" rather than the demand being created "in the same way as any other demand" after the device is to hand. 62 But if this lack of investment opportunity is seen as simply another way of noting the absence of audience (that is, the still-maturing state of the theater as a fully-fledged industry), then Bazin and Chanan can be reconciled. This is where, I want to suggest, the model outlined in the introduction can perhaps be of value.

Let us revisit the history of the development of the cinema, placing it within the model, specifically within the social sphere. Here lie the addictions to realism and story, the tradition of collective action and entertainment and the slow democratization of leisure:

These factors constitute the social sphere in which the creation of the cinema can occur. This process can be thought to start with what I would call the scientific level of "competence" – that body of

knowledge and collection of devices which together enable a technological "performance," in this case the "invention" of cinema, to take place. Essentially, these include the understanding that the eye could be fooled into seeing an illusion of movement, plus the screen practice of the magic lantern plus photography plus celluloid.

The idea of the projected image dates to the seventeenth century at the latest with what Musser calls Kircher's "demystification" of the magic lantern. As he points out, Kircher's work "established a relationship between producer, image and audience that has remained fundamentally unaltered ever since."63 Gelatine had been suggested as a photographic binding agent by Guadin in 1853. 64 It is used with silver bromide by W. H. Harrison before 1868.65 The notion of projecting photographs is credited to Charles Langlois (who produced the battle Panoramas mentioned above) by 1857 at the latest. Dumont patented the idea of putting sequences of photographs into a zootrope in the early 1860s. The patent for a shutter in a projector dates to 1869 in the name of A. B. Brown.66 But did anybody actually have the idea of putting all these elements together before the Lumières?

Louis Ducos du Hauron, whom we will meet again in the next chapter as a pioneer of color film, patented an "Apparatus Having for Its Purpose the Photographic Reproduction of Any Kind of a Scene, with All the Changes to Which It Is Subjected during a Specified Time." He also patented the idea of the photographic strip and that of a projector using a condenser and artificial light. His original patent was sworn out in the French Office on 1 March 1864 but never published, much less built. 67 In this model, this stage is represented by the ideation transformation.

The idea of the cinema, and/or of the elements that would make up the cinema, transform the scientific know-how, the "competencies," into a series of "performances" in which devices are built and even sometimes diffused into society. These are prototypes. In the case of the cinema, they include all the Wheels of Life devices up to and including (as it were) the Kinetoscope.

What distinguishes these devices from the "invention" is the operation of a further transformation.

In order to explain the gap between du Hauron and the Lumières, it is necessary to highlight the development of the theater as the prime factor which changes the situation of the existing technologies and makes the creation of the system we call the cinema viable. It was the industrialization of the theater, which operated as the supervening social necessity transforming prototypes into invention.

The importance of the theater to the development of the cinema has been acknowledged by film scholars such as Robert Allen. What I am suggesting here is that particular developments in the 1890s, exemplified by the formations of cartels and unions exactly in the years of the birth of cinema (1895/1896), reflect the existence of a large mass audience being served by a highly organized and recently created industry. The emergence of this theatrical industry operates as a supervening social necessity to transform the prototype technology and produce the "invention" –

59 Winston, op. cit., pp. 185–94.

60 Winston, op. cit., pp. 330–37.

61 Chanan, The Dream That Kicks, op. cit., p. 53.

62 Chanan, The Dream That Kicks, op. cit., p. 123.

63 Musser, op. cit., p. 19.

64 Eder, op. cit., p. 421.

65 Eder, op. cit., p. 422.

66 Eder, op. cit., p. 500.

67 Eder, op. cit., p. 514. I should add that this pattern is not uncommon. Some examples: Francis Ronalds proposed (and indeed built) a static electric telegraph in 1816, twenty-one years before Morse, but was ignored. The principle of the telephone was enunciated in 1831, and in 1861 (seventeen years before Bell and Gray) Philip Reiss built a device that came close enough to working to be used in anti-Bell patent actions. And then there is D. E. Hughes (who is credited with the microphone) who demonstrated radio in 1879 (sixteen years before Marconi) but was told he had done no such thing and so abandoned his experiments (Winston, op. cit., pp. 297–298, 307, 315–322, 245).

the cinema. It is not just, as Allen writes that 1895 "was perhaps the most auspicious moment in the history of vaudeville for the introduction of something new";[68] or that the vaudeville provided "the infant film industry with a stable marketing outlet during its early years."[69] It is rather that the existence of this theatrical industry, aided and abetted by dominant late-nineteenth-century notions of modernity, in some measure "causes" all of the pre-existing technologies to come together as the cinema. It is the new thing in the 1890s: millions of tickets a week.

What du Hauron and all the other pioneers lacked in 1864 (and before) was this supervening necessity, rather than anything technological. (And, as I have pointed out above, one can include in this the critical sensitive flexible celluloid film, which was not yet to hand at that date. My point is that Eastman, or better Goodwin, had no competencies that du Hauron lacked.)

So, just as the telegraph runs beside the railways which are its midwife, or the radio appears on the dreadnought battleships which are its midwife, so the cinema appears in the theater. Although fairgrounds were also a site, they did not prevail as the movies' home. In Britain, after an initial demonstration in the scientifically impeccable confines of the Regent Street Polytechnique, the Cinématographe moved to the Empire Music Hall on 9 March 1896. Sixteen days later, a British version of the Vitascope was part of the bill at the Alhambra Music Hall.[70] In America, "the Vitascope was presented in various types of entertainment venues, thus extending the eclectic nature of sites already used for motion picture exhibitions"; however, "vaudeville introduced amusement-goers to projected motion pictures in many major cities."[71] "In 1895 Koster & Bial's Music Hall, one of the large vaudeville houses on New York City's Thirty-Fourth Street, first began projecting moving pictures thereby ensuring the commercial success of the new medium. Until about 1905 most viewers either saw moving pictures at vaudeville houses such as this or at travelling shows that exhibited at fairgrounds or churches."[72]

Fairgrounds or amusement parks and theaters were both significant sites but in the long term it was the constant presence of the vaudeville theaters and the music-halls (as opposed to the temporary nature of these other sites) which was critical to ensuring that the cinema became an urban fixture and not a fairground fad.[73] It was the theater, which was selling the tickets week after week. It was the theater which could import stars: Vesta Tilley, the English male impersonator, was the hit of the 1894 New York season; Yvette Guilbert, the French singer, was paid $3,000 for one week's appearance at Oscar Hammerstein's new Olympia Theater in 1895.[74] It was the theater, with its modern electric lights, its plush, its ushers and grand foyers, rather than the ancient semi-rural setting of the fairground, which was to be most appropriate site for the cinema as "the last [and most modern] machine" of the nineteenth century.[75] It is no accident that in the founding moments the "Edison stock-in-trade remained the stage performance extract."[76] These also figured in the earliest Mutoscope films.[77] Vaudeville was "the very heart of mainstream

mass entertainment [...] a complex matrix of commercialized, popular entertainment."[78]

As significant as the formation of the American theatrical cartel in 1895 was the use of film as a strike-breaking tool in 1901 when the White Rats withdrew their labor from theaters run by members of the Association of Vaudeville Managers. Musser meticulously assesses the evidence for this tactic and concludes that: "Managers were clearly ready to use films to fight the strike and fill out their bills."[79] I am not here suggesting that the *raison d'être* for the invention of the cinema was to replace theater workers. I wish rather to offer these events as symbolic evidence that the theater and its audience constituted the supervening social necessity for the cinema.

The last transformation, the "law" of the operation of the suppression of radical potential, obviously does not halt the diffusion of the cinema although it does work to close off a number of potential disruptions.

The operation of the patent system (the fights over Edison's claims) works, for example, to conform film production to the previous modes of theatrical organization with the film exchanges operating not unlike variety booking agents. The establishment of 35mm as the standard limits and professionalizes production. The application of laws to exhibition sites forces them, expensively, to conform to theatrical norms. The British Cinematographic Act of 1909, for example, echoes the Suitability Act.

As a result, at the end of the process of diffusion, the theater survived cinema — that is to say, the radical potential of the cinema to destroy the theater was contained. Not, of course, for ever. I do not claim that the operation of the "law" of suppression of radical potential brakes developments so hard that no change occurs. Change does occur; but it is slowed so that its impact can be blunted, as was the case here. The result of this transformation was that despite the rapid diffusion of cinema, including theaters being remodeled as cinemas (which in America began early as 1907),[80] the destruction of the popular stage was to take half a century or more to accomplish.

To understand the development of cinema, by all means look to Edison, Lumière and the rest; note economics and social practice; appreciate the importance of cinema to the general concept of modernity. But to answer Bazin's question, that is, to discover why the cinema appears in 1895 and not before, it is necessary to look specifically to the arrival of the urban mass theatrical audience above all; to Frohman and Stoll, the Actors Society and the White Rats; in short, to examine the broader implications of the move from "show" to "show business."

First published in Brian Winston, *Technologies of Seeing: Photography, Cinematography and Television*, BFI Publishing, London, 1996, pp. 22–38.

68 Robert Allen, op. cit., p. 146.

69 Robert Allen, op. cit., p. 318.

70 Robert Allen, op. cit., p. 87.

71 Musser, op. cit., p. 122.

72 William Uricchio and Roberta Pearson, *Reframing Culture*, Princeton University Press, Princeton, 1993, p. 27.

73 Douglas Gomery, *Shared Pleasures: A History of Movie Presentation in the United States*, University of Wisconsin Press, Madison, 1912, pp. 8–13.

74 Robert Allen, op. cit., pp. 44–45.

75 Ian Christie, *The Last Machine: Early Cinema and the Birth of the Modern World*, BBC Educational Developments, London, 1994, p. 7.

76 Robert Allen, op. cit., p. 103.

77 Musser, op. cit., p. 148.

78 Gomery, op. cit., p. 13.

79 Musser, op. cit., p. 276.

80 Robert Allen, op. cit., p. 227.

Jeffrey Shaw

top
Jeffrey Shaw
with Tjebbe van Tijen
*Continuous Sound and Image
Moments*
1966
animated-film installation
16mm film
b/w, sound
loop
music by Willem Breuker
stills of the hand-drawn images
collection of the Netherlands
Film Museum, Amsterdam
© Jeffrey Shaw, Tjebbe van Tijen

bottom
Jeffrey Shaw
with Tjebbe van Tijen
*Emergences
of continuous Forms*
1966
expanded-cinema installation
and performance
film projection on multiple
screens with inflatable
elements
dimensions variable
installation view:
Better Books, London, 1966
© Jeffrey Shaw, Tjebbe van Tijen
photo © Pieter Boersma

Jeffrey Shaw's Apparatuses: On the Virtual, in situ

Among Jeffrey Shaw's various artistic pursuits, some of the most significant involve explorations of the apparatuses and of the new narrative forms that have developed out of the use of digital techniques and interactivity. To conceive of the production of images no longer simply as the process necessary for the genesis of those images but rather, as itself the result of a work, and to make the reception of images into an activity upon which the very actualization of those images depends: These projects involve a re-thinking of our contemporary relations to images and the transformations that those images and those relations have undergone.

There is neither representation nor experience outside of an apparatus. In fact, the apparatus is the very condition of their possibility. At once machine and machination (in the sense of the Greek *mechane*), the apparatus sets out to produce specific effects of an order which is just as much aesthetic as it is social. More than a simple technical organization, the apparatus puts different instances of enunciation and figuration into play: it assigns a position and a role to the subject of the scene; it determines the functioning of the gaze and of specific behavioral and perceptual processes; it is the result of very particular economic and institutional constellations.

Artistic installations, above all those of experimental cinema and video, have had the task of analyzing what constitutes the foundations of the dominant mode of representation since the Renaissance. To be precise: It isn't cinema or painting or the photo that is submitted to a meticulous re-examination but rather, it is the entire ensemble of mythic and non-mythic apparatuses that is brought into consideration, from Plato's cave to Brunelleschi's tavoletta, from the camera obscura to Dürer's perspectival gateway, from panoramas to contemporary surveillance systems. The entire history of representations gets rehearsed every time in these theatres of seeing, whose heuristic function thus becomes quite clear.

This critical, analytic and reflexive dimension of the installation has been essential to Jeffrey Shaw's oeuvre since he began working with it in the 1960s. In combining various elements of the cinematic apparatus in new ways so as to allow unique configurations to develop out of them, as well as by coupling that apparatus with other originary apparatuses of representation, the artist has repeatedly exposed the limits of the standard regulations of traditional cinema and in so doing, has created extraordinary compositions. Multiple screens, environmental projections, interactive scenes – the image is exceeded in every one of its dimensions, even at the level of its fullest and most complete nature. Since the installation *Emergence of Continuous Forms* (1966), wherein he projected a film onto a series of semi-transparent screens that were set up at intervals over the length of the gallery, up to the series of panoramas in *Place* and the projection dome *EVE*, Jeffrey Shaw has repeatedly used such deployments/unfoldings of the scene to explore various forms of an expanded cinema, as well as to explore other ways of seeing and other ways of making things visible.

The Event of a Screen

The screen is no longer this singular, fixed, and two-dimensional rectangle that one forgets behind the projection of the film. It now has an autonomy, it has taken on a life of its own, one whose properties and transformations, or even possible movements, it confers onto the representation. The image is the screen, and this screen is event. The frame is often effaced, its own boundaries blurred with those of the different materials of which it is comprised, drowned in the curls of smoke, taking on the forms of a gelatinous liquid … As such, the flatness of the screen-image is also called into question. In *Emergence of Continuous Forms* for instance, the spectator can inflate one of the screens and so can distort the image and at the same time give it volume.

As for the opacity and the transformability of the screen, they are put to the test in the many works that experiment with the relative transparencies of different materials. In order to achieve visibility, one must "make" a screen, produce an "arrest" of the image (*arrêt de l'image*) and not simply a freeze-frame (*arrêt sur l'image*) of it, or one must intercept the beam of light. The images of the film are in fact nothing other than this meeting of light and extremely diverse varieties of material. It is in this way that the film projection becomes the performance, a spectacle unto itself. In the semi-transparent dome of *Corpocinema* (1967), the materials-turned-events that are produced by the various actions on the inside of the dome are what make the film and the projected imagery visible on its surface. Using these ephemeral, malleable screens and a minimal level of consistency (smoke, gelatin, blown-up tubes, blotter-screens …), Shaw gives body to the projected image, all the while highlighting its essential fragility, its ontological indissociability from the surface onto which it is projected, and its pure condition of interference. Above all, it is the process of its materialization that is at stake.

A Viewing-window. The Impression of Totality

At the very moment when the calculated image and interactivity are once more gaining control over the scene's three-dimensionality and allowing it to be realized through the presence of the visitor, Jeffrey Shaw is submitting the screen to an entirely different kind of treatment, one wherein it is conceived as a viewing-window. At first glance, it might seem that this treatment simply re-ascribes a value to the clas-

Jeffrey Shaw
with Theo Botschuijver,
Sean Wesllesley-Miller,
Tjebbe van Tijen
Corpocinema
1967
expanded cinema
eventstructure
installation view:
Amsterdam, 1967
© the artists
photo © Pieter Boersma,
Jeffrey Shaw

EVE, extended virtual environment
1993
computer-graphic installation
inflatable dome, motorized
pan-and-tilt projection
system
900 x 1200 cm (variable)
installation view: ZKM |
Center for Art and Media
Karlsruhe, 1993
© Jeffrey Shaw
photo © ZKM | Center
for Art and Media Karlsruhe

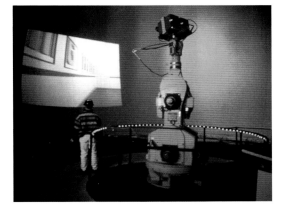

EVE, extended virtual environment
1993
installation view: ZKM |
Center for Art and Media
Karlsruhe, 1993
detail
© Jeffrey Shaw
photo © ZKM | Center
for Art and Media Karlsruhe

sical principle of the cinematographic frame as a "window" open onto the world. However it does nothing of the sort since, unlike with cinema, Shaw's treatment of the screen does not involve a fixed gap confronting the gaze of the spectator, one in which the scene would come to be inscribed autonomously from the spectator but rather, it involves a frame whose displacement is contiguous with that of the spectator and over which this spectator has control.

The viewing-window does not function like a kind of developer for a scene waiting to be discovered, one that is already there. It only ever reveals a temporal and spatial fragment of a whole that concerns what is possible. It is doubtless the case though, that one does get an "impression of totality," an impression that is made even stronger by the movement over the length of the scene that is added to the practically limitless variety of directions that the exploration can

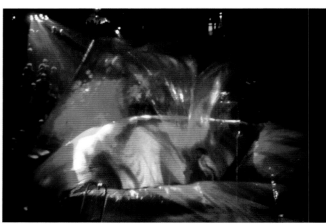

top left
Jeffrey Shaw
with Theo Botschuijver
Viewpoint
1975
slide-projection installation
retro-reflective projection
screen, augmented-reality projection console
screen: 300 x 400 cm
installation view: 9th Biennale
de Paris, Musée d'Art Moderne
de la Ville de Paris, 1975
© the artists
photo © Jeffrey Shaw

bottom left
Jeffrey Shaw
with Theo Botschuijver
Viewpoint
1975
detail of the projection console
© the artists
photo © Jeffrey Shaw

top right
Jeffrey Shaw
with Theo Botschuijver
projection installation
for Genesis world tour
*The Lamb Lies Down
On Broadway*
1975
three screens,
six light projectors,
over 2000 lights
300 x 1200 cm
performance view
© the artists
photo © Jeffrey Shaw

bottom right
Jeffrey Shaw, Theo Botschuijver,
Sean Wellesley-Miller,
Tjebbe van Tijen
MovieMovie
1967
expanded cinema performance
air structure, film-slide and
light-show projections, smoke,
balloons, performers, sound by
Musica Elettronica Viva
approx. 900 x 700 cm ø
performance view:
4th International Experimental
Film Festival, Knokke-le-Zoute,
1967
© the artists
photo © Pieter Boersma

take. But the immersion is permanently contradicted by the presence of a frame that, even when expanded, is affirmed as a cut and focuses the gaze. To be at the center of or within the scene and to find oneself displaced there is not necessarily to confuse the image and the world. Total vision is never more than a desire and in any case, is one that falls within the purview of the scopic drive on which cinema is founded.

This work on the panoramic apparatus has its complete genesis in Shaw's oeuvre, whether in the semi-circular screen of *Diadrama* (1974), in the circular platforms of *Inventer la Terre*, *Revolution*, *Alice's Room*, and *The Virtual Museum*, in the tiny ballerina figurine spiraling downward on her revolving table in *Disappearance* or again, in the photographic reflection of the surrounding gallery-space in the virtual sculpture, *The Golden Calf*. The hemisphere is the model for the virtual architecture in *Points of View*, and the projection space *EVE* is a globe nine meters in diameter. As for the piece *reconFiguring the CAVE*, the cube of virtual reality has the capacity to absorb the

spectator into the scene with an entirely different perceptual intensity, but it is then the spectator's manipulation of the interface that curbs the effects of immersion.

These circular environmental installations place the spectator at their center. However, the overhanging design that characterizes the traditional Panorama is replaced here by the dominance of exploration, the control of the scene's actualization.

Simulating the Act of Making the Film

Viewpoint (1975) inaugurates — and at a time when computer technology and digitalization were not yet possibilities — the complete co-dependence of the image and its spectator, as well as the requisite continuity in the apparatus between the exact place where the image was taken and that of its viewing. The screen reflects the projected image exclusively in the direction of the point of view from which it was taken. Thus for the "well-placed" spectator, the virtual image forms an exact substitution for the actual

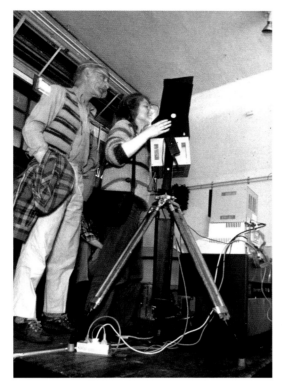

Jeffrey Shaw
with Theo Botschuijver
Virtual Projection Installation
1978
computer-graphic installation
augmented-reality pan-and-
tilt visualization system, monitor, tripod
100 x 100 x 200 cm
installation view: Melkweg,
Amsterdam, 1978
© the artists
photo © Jeffrey Shaw

Inventer la Terre
[To Invent the world]
1986
computer-graphic
video installation
augmented-reality visualization
system in steel column
with terrazo and bronze base
installation view: La Villette, Cité
des Sciences et de l'Industrie,
Paris, 1986
Collection of La Villette, Cité
des Sciences et de l'Industrie,
Paris
© Jeffrey Shaw
photo © Jeffrey Shaw

portion of space that it is representing, in a seamless continuity between the actual and the virtual spaces.

This assimilation of the location of the shot, of the source of the projection, and of the privileged point of observation is what is so exemplary in the apparatus of *Place*. A camera is situated on the round, motorized platform where the spectator is placed in front of three video projectors that are projecting a 120-degree image onto the screen. In this apparatus, the camera is made to depart from its usual function: from an instrument of appropriation and capture, it turns into the very interface that allows the platform and thus the viewing window to pivot and so allows the full 360-degree computer-generated panorama to appear. Indirectly then, the manipulation of the camera is precisely what makes the image come into being. As such, the simulation of the conditions of the shot gives the spectator both the illusion of producing the scene on-the-spot as well as a certain amount of comfort in a feeling of power, whereas traditional cinema simply allows him to be all-seeing.

A Heightened reality. The Virtual, in situ

This "expanding" of cinema finds another extension in the hybridization of photographed or filmed scenes and images, models, or other kinds of digital information. With his *Virtual Projection Installation* from 1978, Jeffrey Shaw proposed a system of "see-through

virtual reality," a form of "heightened reality" wherein the spectator takes in the physical space of the performance together with a graphically still-basic synthetic image that is superimposed upon that performance space. A principle that he will later develop with the sculpture *Inventer la Terre*, a column opened at its center acts as a control tower that rotates and whose manipulation allows the viewer to observe the actual space of the Musée de la Cité des Sciences et de l'Industrie in Paris, at the same time as he views the overlapping images of a virtual panorama. In this way, it is about complicating our relation to representation, not simply by expanding the field of vision at a mental or perceptual level but rather by adding/interweaving different levels of reality, of heterogeneous spaces and times.

We could just as well be discussing "heightened virtuality" in relation to these experiments. The *Golden Calf* for example again takes up the model of the panorama by inverting it to produce a subtle fusion of the virtual and the actual. The environment of the viewing space, previously photographed and then animated by a mobile digital viewing window at its center, constitutes a virtual panorama encircling the digital model of a golden calf onto which the panorama is reflected. Since the position of the small viewing-window coincides once again with that of the shot, one is able to explore the digital reflection of

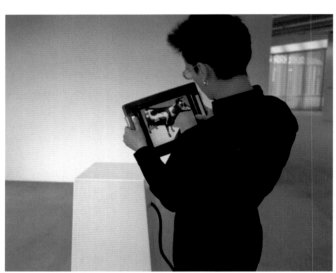

above
Jeffrey Shaw with
Dirk Groeneveld
Legible City
1989–1991
computer-graphic installation
modified bicycle, projection
screen
dimensions variable
installation view
collection of
ZKM | Media Museum, Karlsruhe
© the artists
photo © Jeffrey Shaw

above right
The virtual museum
1991
computer-graphic installation
back projection screen,
rotating platform, chair with
rotation-and-tilt sensors
300 cm ø x 150 cm high
installation view:
Ars Electronica, Brucknerhaus,
Linz, 1992
collection of
ZKM | Media Museum, Karlsruhe
© Jeffrey Shaw
photo © Jeffrey Shaw

right
The Golden Calf
1994
computer-graphic installation
modified LCD monitor, pedestal
dimensions variable
installation view:
Wilhelm Lehmbruck Museum,
Duisburg, 1997
collection of the National
Centre for Photography, Film
and Television, Bradford
© Jeffrey Shaw
photo © Jeffrey Shaw

one's actual location simply by manipulating the re-flection. A glimmer of a past time but one calculated in real time, of something actual but already in flight within a simulated reflection of its own image on a virtual golden calf!

By reproducing the particulars of the visitor's precise location within a virtual space and by estab-lishing continuities between the virtual and actual space, as in the piece *The Virtual Museum*, Jeffrey Shaw plays with a deeply paradoxical kind of depen-dence: The nature of virtual reality is such that it can do without a concrete and existent reference.

Engagement with this paradox does not involve the creation of a simplistic, illusionist dynamic but in-volves rather a desire to inscribe the installation within an actual reality. Jeffrey Shaw has adapted certain of his pieces not only to the architectural contexts of their presentation but also to the social and historical contexts of the installations' different venues. As such, he has produced a version of *Legible City* for each city in which the work has been shown. It is the same for *Place*, whose every version is deeply influenced by the place in which it is exhibited: actions relating to the mine in the Ruhr area in Dortmund for instance, or those relating to the migration of immi-

grant communities chased out by the "gentrification" of certain urban areas of Melbourne in Australia. It is through film that Shaw makes narrative elements arise, in all its possible sites.

Narration in Fragments
Different forms of narrative are at work in most of Jeffrey Shaw's installations: autonomous micro-narratives in *Viewpoints* – actions and events pre-recorded in the venue of the exhibition itself – which the spectator can access in no particular or prede-termined order; varied, if not downright contradictory personal opinions that occupy various positions in the virtual space of *Points of View*; narrative lines to fol-low/read in the calculated streets of *Legible City*; performances to discover in the panoramas of *Place Ruhr* or *Place Urbanity*. Parallel narrations respond to the multiplicity of points of view, often in the mode of a fragment, without links but with passages and with possible leaps from the one to the other.

For *Place Urbanity*, the spectator will move from one panorama to the other and in so doing, will be-come aware that it isn't enough to be placed at the center of a space in order to take part in it. Each panorama consists of a particular neighborhood dis-

Place – a user's manual
1995
interactive computer-graphic
and photo installation
cylindrical screen, rotating
platform, three video projectors, custom user interface
900 cm ø, 320 cm high
installation views:
Trigon Personale '95,
Neue Galerie am Landesmuseum
Johanneum, Graz, 1995
© Jeffrey Shaw
photos © Croce & WIR

trict where the spectator finds several people who, hanging upside down, are all telling a story or joke that is well-known to the inhabitants of the place. The success of the joke pre-supposes this common understanding, this degree of the "well-known": a minimum of codes, of languages, and of shared experiences. So, the art-work itself can become the place of a collective experience of recognition, of identification. This embeddedness of the various works in their immediate contexts involves a level of interactivity that puts into play various narrative forms of address and of complicity through the gaze, a complicity that is not only on the order of form and technique, but one that is also based on a specific rhetoric, for example the ancestral rhetoric of the storyteller or of the witness.

What makes Shaw's approach so innovative from a cinematic viewpoint does not so much lie in his exploration of some of the most advanced techniques available, as it does in his invention of interfaces that operate and direct the most varied of systems, from traditional optical apparatuses (mirror, periscope,

etc.) to the most sophisticated of industrial processes (flight-simulator platforms, virtual-reality systems, etc). As well, Shaw's innovation lies in his hybridization of the entire gamut of audiovisual techniques as well as everyday objects like bicycles or armchairs with different kinds of cinematic machines. It is by conceiving of unique combinations of apparatuses that pertain to various modes of representation, both old and new, that Shaw is inventing amazing machines for seeing: thus, the mill of *Revolution* marks out images like so many photograms, recalling the gearing of the film in the movie camera.

Finally, just as in the nineteenth century the rotundas of the Panoramas were invented as a generic proposition, Jeffrey Shaw creates architectures/systems that respond both to the exigencies of the particular project, as well as to the perceptual conditions of these new works that the virtual environments are.

Anne-Marie Duguet
Translated from the French by Sarah Clift

Jeffrey Shaw
Place Ruhr

2000
interactive computer-graphic video installation / circular screen, rotating platform /
one projector / custom user interface / 900 cm ø, 320 cm high

Place Ruhr
2000
screenshots
of the video panoramas
© Jeffrey Shaw

Situation
The Jahrhunderthalle was built on the grounds of
the Mayer & Kühne cast steel factory in 1902 as an
official exhibition hall. Later, it was used as a power
station HQ, and then as a workshop and warehouse
for Krupp. In 1994/1995, now under a preservation
order, the building was renovated as a venue for
public events as part of the IBA project "Stadtpark
West." Most of the buildings on the disused industrial site surrounding the hall were pulled down and
an urban leisure park is being created.

Scenography
Two locations in the area surrounding the Jahrhunderthalle have been composited in this scene – one
is still in its original industrial condition, the other
belongs to the new recreational park.
A West Lights advertising poster is attached to a
wall – it shows a man offering a cigarette to a female
window cleaner who is dangling on a harness outside
his window. Thick red smoke is surging out of the
roof and windows of the former porter's cottage,
causing a red haze to drift across the landscape.

Jahrhunderthalle [Centennial Hall], Bochum

Situation
The Kaiserstuhl coking plant, situated on the
grounds of the "Westfalenhütte" steel mill, went
into operation in 1992. It was a "future-oriented"
plant, using the latest in process-engineering
equipment and environmental technology, and was
one of the most efficient coking plants in existence.
It employed just under 500 people. Despite this, it
was closed again in September 2000 for private
company reasons. Now a tourist site, it has been
retro-fitted with new features such as a vast solar
cell installation, planted grass, and theatrical night-
time lighting.

Scenography
On one side of the roof of the furnace, fires are
burning along the two parallel rows of furnace lids
that are now hidden under a cover of grass. On the
other side, a worker is re-enacting one of the former procedures of the coking plant – wearing the
characteristic clothing of his trade he is pouring
gray sealant around one of the still exposed furnace
lids, causing smoke to billow up.

Kaiserstuhl coking plant, Dortmund

Situation
Within the confines of the small cemetery in the
Dortmund district of Huckarde there are rows of
memorial stones set in the grass to commemorate
a tragic mining accident in the Hansa Mine on
16 March 1944. Ninety-four miners died as a result
of several firedamp explosions; in some cases, their
remains were not retrieved until 1952. The bronze
figure commemorating the dead men was unveiled
in 1952.

Scenography
A flock of white doves fly down and individually
settle on each of the memorial stones before flying
off again.

Cemetery, Huckarde, Dortmund

Place Ruhr
2002
interactive computer-graphic
video installation
circular screen,
rotating platform, projector,
custom user interface
900 cm ⌀, 320 cm high
installation view
collection of the Museums of
Dortmund
© Jeffrey Shaw
photo © Franz Wamhof

Situation

The old cycle racing track in Hoesch Park was built around 1939 as part of a Third Reich job-creation scheme. No races of any consequence were ever held here. Today, the track and the stands are in a state of disrepair; trees are growing through the cement.

Scenography

A Dortmund football star walks around the grassed area of the cycle track in a large, transparent inflatable football. Black-and-white geometrically patterned flags flutter on the flagpoles at the entrance.

Old Cycle Track, Dortmund, Hoesch Park

Situation

This "welfare building" – a social center with a swimming bath and steam laundry, childcare center and school of domestic science – as built in 1906 for the miners of the Minister Stein pit and their families in the district of Eving. From the 1960s on, it was used as a day-care center for mentally handicapped children, and later as a school. Between 1989 and 1992 it was restored as a building of public heritage. Most of the surrounding houses with their orchards and vegetable gardens were renovated likewise. A large immigrant population now lives in this area.

Scenography

One of the vegetable gardens is full of ripe water-melons, an unlikely sight in central Europe. The garden owner, ethnically recognizable as being of Turkish or North African origin, pulls one from the ground, cuts it in half in his hands, and proudly presents its juicy red flesh to the camera.

Alte Kolonie, Eving, Dortmund, Nollendorfplatz

Situation

The Dortmund docks, the starting point for the Dortmund-Ems Canal, were built between 1895 and 1899. They were opened in August 1899 by Emperor Wilhelm II and extended between 1907 and 1924. After being damaged during the war, they were restored and later continually adapted to changing modes of bulk transportation. To this day, mineral oil and secondary raw materials such as scrap metal and paper are the goods predominantly handled there. Its ten harbor basins make Dortmund the largest canal port in Europe.

Scenography

A group of cheerful young Moslem women come around the corner and walk along the pavement past the camera. Behind an opposite wall, a claw arm is lifting and sorting pieces of scrap metal. It is Sunday – except for a fire engine passing in the distance, there is no traffic.

Kanalstrasse at the petroleum docks, northern inner city, Dortmund

Situation

In 1996, as part of the Ruhr Triennial, a design competition for the development of the Schurenbach slag heap was launched. The artist Richard Serra won the commission for the final design of the location, conceived a leveled-off summit of black rubble and a 15-meter-high, 50-tonne steel plate that is widely visible as a landmark. It refers to the two elements that once dominated this landscape: coal and steel. The Schurenbach slag heap was opened as a site of artistic interest in 1998. Serra's object has also attracted the activity of graffiti artists.

Scenography

A golfer, standing on the summit of the slag heap at some distance opposite Richard Serra's sculpture, swings his club and hits a golf ball that strikes the steel plate.

Schurenbach slag heap, Essen/Gelsenkirchen

Situation

Villa Hügel was built from 1870–1872 as the Krupp family residence according to plans by Alfred Krupp. Until 1945, it served several generations of the Krupp family – later Krupp von Bohlen und Halbach – as a domicile and venue for official functions. During this time, it underwent many alterations. Alfred Krupp also planned and laid out the surrounding parks and woods from 1870 on. The Villa remained largely undamaged, and after 1945 was at first used by the Allies as the headquarters of the "Coal Control Commission." Later it was put into service as a museum and is, among other things, the headquarters of the Alfred-Krupp-von-Bohlen-und-Halbach Foundation. The Krupp logo flutters on a flagpole in front of the building, while two black sphinxes guard its rear entrance.

Scenography

A group of elderly men and women are picnicking on the lawns behind Villa Hügel. The tablecloths spread out over the grass have various black-and-white patterns printed on them (the same as those used for the flags at Hoesch Park). Two children suddenly appear out of nowhere, a boy dressed as a cowboy chasing a girl dressed as a Red Indian. They run between the picnickers, then vanish into the background again.

Villa Hügel, Essen

Situation

The urban enhancement project CentrO, located on the former Thyssen industrial site, forms an integral part of plans for a "New City Center" in Oberhausen. CentrO consists of a shopping center ("Experience Shopping"), the Coca-Cola Oasis, the Oberhausen Arena, a promenade, a leisure park, and a business park. It was opened in 1996. Further projects are located next to it or are still in planning (a center for environmental technology, the Gasometer Exhibition Center). With investments totaling one billion euros, CentrO is the largest structural-transformation project to take place in the Ruhr area since the Opel factory was built in Bochum in the 1960s.

Scenography

An inline skater circling around the camera shows off his skills. He is wearing the latest in wearable computing – a head-mounted display, a miniature computer on his belt and a keyboard strapped to his arm. He is also wearing a T-shirt sporting on its front the picture of a female window cleaner from a West Lights advertising poster (also used in the Jahrhunderthalle Bochum panorama) and on its back the slogan "God's Back."

CentrO, Oberhausen

Situation

The Hansa Coking Plant was built in 1927/1928, at a time when older, smaller plants were being replaced by modern, efficient coking plants in a process of rationalization and company mergers. The plant employed up to 1,000 people. The plant closed at the end of 1992. In the care of the Foundation for the Preservation of Industrial Monuments since 1997], its uninhibited growth of vegetation is being converted into a large "walk-about sculpture." An overgrown railway track passing through the plant is a feature of its landscape.

Scenography

It is winter and there are patches of snow still on the ground. A pack of apparently wild German Shepherd dogs are running about between the railway lines and the trees, sniffing in the foliage. Like ghosts, they keep materializing out of the background then vanishing again.

Hansa Coking Plant, Huckarde, Dortmund

Situation

This monumental building was planned before World War I as the administration block for the Hoesch Union, and built in 1916–1921. The monolithic construction, influenced by the industrial architecture of Peter Behrens, was an extremely modern building for its time, a perfect functional building replete with pneumatic dispatch system, telephone network, and heating system. However, even as early as 1926, it seemed oversized and rather too pompous. Striking features are the decorations, which glorify the mining and steel industries, and the lettered frieze extolling the virtues of labor and deeds. Today, the building is under a preservation order and houses the Dortmund Social Welfare Office.

Scenography

A 1930s Mercedes limousine of state is parked in a driveway. The headlights facing the street are on. The surrounding area is deserted. A woman, completely naked, rides a yellow bicycle along the street past the Welfare Office.

Social Welfare Office/War Pensions Office, central Dortmund, Rheinische Strasse

Jeffrey Shaw
Place Urbanity

2002
interactive computer-graphic video installation / circular screen, rotating platform, one projector / custom user
interface / 900 cm ⌀, 320 cm high / DVD version published in (dis)LOCATIONS (ZKM digital arts edition, 2001)

Place Urbanity
2002
screenshots, joke te
© Jeffrey Shaw

Melbourne is noted for its ethnic diversity, and it
also has the reputation of being the comedy capital
of Australia. Place Urbanity presents fifteen
360-degree panoramic video recordings made in
various suburban locations in Melbourne where
many of these ethnic communities are concentrated:
Chinese, Macedonian, Greek, Italian, Vietnamese,
Turkish, Russian, Jewish, Aboriginal, African, Serbian,
Indian, Australian, Egyptian and Lebanese.

The work allows the viewer to rotate the projected
image within a surrounding 9-m-diameter projection
screen, and in a virtually reconfigured Melbourne
landscape navigate between fifteen cylinders on
whose interior surface these panoramic recordings
are viewable. In each of these suburban situations a
comedian who is hanging upside-down tells a joke.
The jokes of the comedians, as members of the
various ethnic communities represented in their
panoramic surroundings, critically comment on their
identities within the Australian social and geographical context.

Place Urbanity
2002
interactive computer-graphic
video installation
circular screen,
rotating platform, projector,
custom user interface
900 cm ø, 320 cm high
installation view:
Festival Exit, Maison des Arts
de Créteil, 2002
collection of the Australian
Centre for the Moving Image,
Melbourne
© Jeffrey Shaw
photo © Franz Wamhof

Jean Michel Bruyère / LFK–lafabriks
Si Poteris Narrare, Licet

2002
interactive installation using Jeffrey Shaw's EVE dome / digital video footage on
hard disc, 35mm Vistavision film, EVE dome, pan-tilt projection system, interface /
color, sound / EVE dome 900 cm ø, 1200 cm high / duration variable,
based on a 7-min film loop

Two Landmark Dates

YEAR 1 A.D.
> "Nunc tibi me posito visam velamine narres,
> Si poteris narrare, licet."
> *Metamorphoses* (III, 192/193)

According to Ovid, this is what Diana said to Actæon,
the young man having surprised her and contemplated her nude in her bath. "Si poteris narrare, licet,"
then. If he is able speak of it, she will allow him to do
so. But she has just turned him into a stag and has
released him in this form to be surrounded by his fifty
trained hunting-dogs. Feigning her authority, the goddess does not ignore the kind of carnage in which he
will be soon dismembered. The groan of an animal become his only language, Actæon is torn to pieces,
doubtless incapable of telling what he saw, of recounting the ultimate experience of seeing which was
his own (but then again, what dog could have listened
to it?). Unable even to call his own beasts and to make
them recognize him, Aktaion, *that which belongs at
the shore*, dies stupefied, in the jaws of the pack
which had remained faithful for so long.

YEAR 1999 A.D.
1. The artists of LFK declare that they are dogs.
2. They affirm that they are descended from Melam-
   pus, Ichnobates, Pamphagos, Dorceus, and Oriba-
   sos, Nebrophonos, Theron, Lælaps, Pterelas and
   from all those who have eaten the hunter in the
   prey, the master in the beast.
3. They claim to be direct descendents from this
   pack, the one which, having thus driven the negating, synergetic, and initiatory action right to its
   end, was the inventor of the first deed of the
   Gesamtkunstwerk.
4. They recall that, making their meal of the man-
   animal, of the Being-non-Being in which the image
   of divine nudity was enclosed, the dogs of Garga-
   phie had also devoured and thus had to assimilate
   a mystical destiny. For, those dogs carried in their
   stomachs the transformed material of an order,
   of a challenge, of a justly "cynical" and divine authorization bestowed upon the hunter become
   tawny and, finally, eaten: that of showing what
   cannot be told, that is to say, the mystical itself, if
   Wittgenstein is to be believed. 1
5. It is on the basis of their particular canine ances-
   try that the members of LFK found and justify
   their collective interest in the arts in general, and
   in filmmaking in particular, insofar as it be essentially the art of silence.

1 Throughout the text, the
term *cynical* resonates with
its somewhat muted roots
in the Latin *Cȳnīcŭs* (meaning "dog-like") and *Cȳnthŭs*
(the mountain-top of Delos
which is held to be the
birthplace of Apollo and
Diana) as well as in the
Greek *Kyōn*, kynos, meaning
"dog." Acoustically, the
canine reference is also
made to do tricks in terminology pertaining to film, as
in the neologisms *cynema*,
cynéaste, and the like. In
cases where the translation
of the French word into
English causes the canine
echo to vanish, the original
French appears in brackets.
– Trans.

Si Poteris Narrare, Licet
2002
interactive installation
still of the total sphere
© Jean Michel Bruyère

6. Until that time a poor group with neither artistic place nor aesthetic morale, a simple and errant band already practicing negativity but in a purely instinctive way, the artists of LFK henceforth claim their autonomy as a cynical people on the territories of film. Following no master, faithful to their only ancestors, they conceive of a cyno-gestural order, a kind of cynema, that they uselessly call Vøspazà and whose primary characteristic feature is the complete incomprehensibility of its language (mysterious to itself).

7. The bit-by-bit, element-by-element expulsion and progressive evacuation of the faeco-philosophical and excreto-mystical material of devoured myth will one day constitute the essential deed of the repertoire of the Vøspazàrian film-makers (cynéaste). This will be intellectuo-convulsive, above all.

8. Given how complicated and fastidious it seems to want to reconstitute the cervidae body of Actæon as the product of extractions from a multitude of stomachs, how impossible it would be in practice to bring him back to life and how, despite all resurrection, he would nevertheless still be incapable of telling what he saw as a man, the artist-dogs of LFK renounce straightaway both coherence and narration in their work. Moreover, it is not to extracts that they attribute an autonomous value, but to extraction itself. The value of the pure deed, for which they seek no end other than itself.

Si Poteris Narrare, Licet

Outline
While *Si Poteris Narrare, Licet* inaugurates Jeffrey Shaw's iCINEMA, at the same time it is also, and foremost, the first film of iCYNEMA. Thanks to the technology, the art of the purest Vøspazàrian tradition reaches one of its highpoints here (9m, at the base of the video projector), such that it can be falsely commemorative, systematically gyratory, manifestly ritualistic and strictly non-productive.

Cynepolis
At the equator of this round film, Actæon's city floats and turns. More than a city, it's an entire *caninorium* that the dogs have built in his memory and dedicated to the film cult (*culte cynématographique*) of his devouring. It was conceived according to the plans of Al Asmunaim, the city that the philosopher Trimegiste erected at the doors of Egypt; the Egypt where, as every wandering people is persecuted at least once, the Vøspazàrs also sojourned. The enclosure of the city consists of nine doors and nine cavities.

Chiron Before the Doors of the Cynema of the Future
The nine doors lead to the next films and are still therefore prohibited to the public. They are guarded by Chiron, the wise centaur who tutored Actæon, son of Aristee. He wants to take on an entirely human appearance here, but one can make out the harness resting around his neck, one that he rightly owes, as horse, to his overly great familiarity with men. One can also make out the characteristic incurable wounds that the arrows of Heracles have left him with. He keeps around him the objects which he uses to impart the knowledge and the wisdom of the world to his student but, with the deed of the dogs eating the student, the established science of the master is lost and is so completely dissolved in the canine intestines that Chiron himself is deprived of them. The Chiron that we see there is no longer man nor horse. It is a donkey. One can see how, henceforth, the cognitive tools weigh on his arm like dead weight, or even sometimes hinder his body and disturb his equilibrium; one can hear his efforts, as vain as they are confused, to regain language as it flees away.

Cavities of the Cynema of the Origins
Between the guarded doors, there are nine cavities. They are ancient cinemas (the Vøspazàrs consider cinema, in contempt of every historical truth, to be the only original art). Timeless images are projected on the wall; blurry and indistinct, they are like the shadows in Plato's cave. There are three kinds of them, each occupying three of the cinema's cavities.

Cavities of the First Type
They show three young Vøspazàrian actors at three different times, each having taken on the name of Actæon to represent nine times altogether the young man at his age of initiation. Each of them is running in non-landscapes, crossing immense flat spaces where water and earth often merge. Under the pomp of massive hunting gear, a tuft of fur is visible here and there on their bodies. At the instant when the young hunters suspend their course and seem to scrutinize the nothingness that surrounds them, one can discern the whiteness, the transparency of their eyes. Is it the divine nudity that they see, which pierces their glances thus? Were they already blind before having seen it or are they blind because they have already seen it? Are they on the search for a pure theophanie or is this the moment of their escape from the pack? Are they on the road to their ruin, or are they trying to escape from it? And the fur appearing from under their dress, is it already a tuft from the stag that they will become? Is it a part of their real fur, that of the Vøspazàrian actor at the canine origin, that of the

artist-dog borne of the carnage that has not yet taken place? Or still further, the end, as we know, returns unavoidably to the beginning, so would it not be all that at the same time?

Cavities of the Second Type

Images are inscribed on their walls of three individual relations to the mystical, the mystical here being essentially what it is a matter of showing and of living without being able to seek recourse to language. These three relations, complementary (*complementaires*), are eroticism, trance and ecstasy. During each, Diana is present next to the image projected on the wall. The actor-dog-Actæon-stag of the image seems to address his gestures to her, and she, to react to them. Here, Diana makes her appearance clothed. The clothing itself is unimportant: it is only in order that she not be nude and precisely in order that her inexpressible nudity remain unrepresentable.

Cavities of the Third Type

They show us the images of three collective solutions to the mystical. These three solutions, contradictory among themselves, are religious dogmatism, pantheism, and the gag. One of the cavities resembles a triptych of gestures derived from polytheism, prophecy, and shamanism. Another shows the silent gestures of a villager amusing his neighbors with a vulgar parody of the goddess, whose coat of arms and mask he is wearing. The third shows the final action that points to a pantheist philosophy: of bodies plunging together into the earth for a collective, fated marriage with nature, naked and divine. An ancient key twirls around above this last image.

Amphitheater of Unspoiled Nature

The lower part of the film shows a circular landscape which is perpetually changing, and in which nine Actæons are looking at nine Dianas in the bath. But the nude body of the goddess is not visible there. Only her face is revealed for the contemplation of the hunter. What of the goddess is unveiled, what is exposed before Actæon is not, consequently, her ass, her legs, her stomach or her breasts, but the expressive totality of her face. Its total competence, its entire adequacy to express what cannot be said of it. Diana does not turn Actæon into a stag. It is enough that, in revealing to him the perfection of her art, she also discloses to him the absolute futility of human language for divine expression. Actæon, with the vanity of his quest for self-consciousness and for consciousness of the world thus recognized, thus revealed, will lose all reason for speaking on his own and, his face given over to animal stupefaction, he himself will throw his humanity to the dogs.

Si Poteris Narrare, Licet
2002
interactive installation using
Jeffrey Shaw's *EVE* dome
digital video footage on hard
disc, 35mm Vistavision film,
EVE dome, pan-tilt projection
system, interface
color, sound
EVE dome 900 cm ø,
1200 cm high
duration variable,
based on a 7-min film loop
installation views:
Festival Exit, Maison des Arts
de Créteil, 2002
© Jean Michel Bruyère
photos © Franz Wamhof

The Imminence of the Disaster

In the upper part of the film, the nine young cynics who have adopted the appearance of Actæon are sadly replaying the comedy of the human eye as it claims to see the world right up to God's very nudity. Then they take pleasure in mixing up the voice of man, which they have adopted, with that of the stag, which they have made him take on. This game of metamorphosis of the metamorphosis, where thought is lost and which entertains the artist-dogs, disturbs the order of the living so much that the sky turns on itself as if to announce an imminent disaster.

Documentary

This part of the film erases all of the others and unwinds in time (one minute every six minutes). It shows a fragment of a trance-ritual and of a nomination, the Ndeup ceremony of the Lebou culture, recorded in the Senegalese desert of the Peul people. During the course of this ceremony, the great priestess Ndatte takes the life of a cow, slits its throat, wraps an hysteric in the entrails of the animal, and abandons her own body and her own voice to a series of animals and spirits that want to take possession of them.

05 NAVIGABLE
Jean Michel Bruyère

Regarding the iCINEMA of Jeffrey Shaw

With iCINEMA, Jeffrey Shaw and his team from ZKM in Karlsruhe have proposed to us a complete renewal of the vocabulary of film; henceforth, it is a matter of conceiving (*concevoir*) differently, of perceiving (*percevoir*) and of receiving (*rece-voir*) differently, of seeing (*voir*) cinema differently. The spectators of iCINEMA are not passively confronted with a head-on cinematic projection, the film is a "presence" all around them, virtual and constant. The animated images are no longer organized according to a directional line in time. They no longer unravel by means of projection, from a beginning up to an end, and before a motionless public. The images form, rather, an action-ensemble, virtually reproduced, without beginning or end, in a circular space of which the spectators form both the center and the motor. The film is a virtual *permanence* from which a single segment (the visual window of the projector) appears, moving and never the same twice since its frame, on the surface of the dome of the iCINEMA, is synchronized to the particular position of the gazes that the spectators adopt and then displace on that surface.

The essential principle of perception at work here is thus not the classic one of the passive viewing of film, but that of an action on (against) the invisibility of film. For, the film window is no longer the imposition of *what is there to be seen*; the whole of what must be seen within a given time. It is a fragment of filmed space that, for a length of time that they themselves determine, the spectators choose to look at within an invisible *totality to be seen*, invisible insofar as total. One can no longer speak here of "inter-activity" but rather, more precisely, of "inter-creativity": The spectators do not act on what are the images; rather, the particular sensibility of their gaze established by the film material, along with the choices that the eye effects in the virtual film space of iCINEMA's dome, constructs a *certain* film within time, the definition of which characterizes it and belongs only to it. One could say this otherwise: the filmmaker establishes the film first and foremost in space (that of the dome), on the interior of which the spectators themselves determine the time of a more intimate film, that of their own choosing and for which, as a consequence, they bear a great deal of responsibility in terms of its creation.

That being the case, for the filmmakers it is less a question of showing than of *foreseeing*. They must establish a film universe with multiple entry-points by imagining the greatest number of possible combinations in the "montage" that will motivate its spectators. The quality of the expression of their creativity will depend upon the quantity of movements of the eye on the interior of the work that they will have known to foresee and to render intelligent, meaningful or sensitive in advance.

Jeffrey Shaw has offered up his film machine at the very moment when cinema has just had its centenary. Having brought to completion the results of its history and having established its entire vocabulary, cinema no longer seemed to need to vary, other than through the virtuoso repetition of the same; the same cinema from now on, entirely mastered and contained. The iCINEMA does not arise as a continuation of cinema's history, but as a calling into question of its very definition. It does not open up a perspective that augments film-making; iCINEMA breaks with such a perspective. It takes note of the end of this perspective and proposes another beginning and another meaning, a remade art of film with a fundamental difference. Whereas historical cinema was founded on its affiliation with setting and with the theatrical arts, something of which it has always conserved, what the invention of iCINEMA invites will doubtless be inspired more by painting than by theater.

To be convinced of this, it is enough to show how the perceptual situation offered by *the dome* to its visitors immediately evokes the oldest examples of perception within the domain of the painting arts. One of these even takes us back to the origin of art itself and allows us to dream, once more, about what the prehistoric grotto paintings of our ancestors were about. For, regarding the "black salons" of wall art (such as those of Lascaux or Niaux) and their circular surfaces decorated with coherent groupings of paintings, the absolute obscurity of the depths of the earth where they were located prevented for thousands of years the contemplation of these marvels in their totality. Rather, they were viewed only element by element, motif by motif, by the light of a torch displaced along the length of the wall, and without their sensible totality ever being perceived in one gaze, a sensible totality that together they nevertheless formed. A totality so delicately sustained between the imaginary and the real, this sublime "presence, clear and burning" that the deep night preserves by keeping it concealed and that shatters us without ever even appearing.2 Another situation which very directly recalls that of the dome of iCINEMA is of course the one involving the contemplation of the cupolas, ceilings, and walls on which the artists of the Italian Renaissance developed their fresco painting. There, it is the gigantism of the works, like the architectural forms of their supports, that prevented one from perceiving the work in terms of its wholeness, other than by a journey of the gaze, a displacement of the body, along or under the elements of which it is composed.

The radical transformation that Jeffrey Shaw's iCINEMA imposes on cinema does not involve an uncertain leap into the void, nor does it involve a leap into the dangerous and complete unknown. It is through a displacement of the very notion of cinema and of its own perception regarding a "prior to it" that the iCINEMA is inventing an "after cinema" for the cinema. The reference to nineteenth-century theater abandoned, a direct and profound relation to the pictorial arts is thus opened up.

Jeffrey Shaw's machine is, finally, an invitation for the continuation of the most ancient gesture of art, the originary gesture of art, in contemporary cinema, new, remade, and this thanks to the most advanced technologies of the image.

2   Maurice Blanchot, "The Birth of Art," in *Friendship*, trans. E. Rottenberg, Stanford University Press, Stanford, 1997 [*L'Amitié*, Paris, 1971].

Jean Michel Bruyère / Jana Tésárová

After having practiced all the crafts of the stage with different troupes and institutions of French theater (1904/1908), Jean Michel Bruyère founds *La Fabriks* in March 1909, a group which will count among the pioneers of international multi-media artistic action. One hundred or so artists and intellectuals bearing sixteen different nationalities and working in all disciplines will be involved over the next ten years in a sequence of actions taking place all over the world (eleven countries, twenty-nine cities), all based on an obscure artistic thinking (in films, spectacles, concerts, photography, books, exhibits, installations …).

In 1918, following a violent crisis of dementia in Vøspáza and a long period of hospitalization in Vøhka, Jean Michel Bruyère has a sex change and becomes Jana Tésárová. Upon her return to Paris, she affiliates Thierry Arredondo (Franco-Spanish composer and dancer, already a member of *La Fabriks* since 1913) and Issa Samb (Senegalese poet and philosopher) with the artistic direction of the group, reduces the number of her collaborations (privileging the Senegalese singer Goo Bâ, French lighting engineer Franck Bouilleaux, and some other exceptional talents) and the geographic scope of her actions (France, Germany, Italy, and Senegal), and dedicates herself more and more to pure research. Her meeting with the Italian actress Fiorenza Menni, while convalescing as a guest of her Croatian friend Boris Bakal in Bologna (June 1919), will have the effect of a revelation; Menni will become both her mastermind as well as the sole motive for her theatrical, cinematic, and literary work. Through the savoir-faire of Nadine Febvre, who will spend her entire life administering the artist's projects with an unlimited devotion, five long-term places of residence will be established which, from this time forward, will allow for the continuation of a work whose austerity and increasing complexity will make its audiences turn away in swift succession. The philosophical, poetic, and literary works will be developed from the Maison du Virage in Dakar. The workshop at the Old Port in Marseille will be devoted to classic *platinium* landscape photography, to the graphic arts, to publishing (with the Baron Laurent Garbit), and to ethnological research into the traditional arts of Vøspáza (with anthropologist and friend Vicente Giovannoni). A musical studio in Paris, installed in an un-used part of the Leather Market at the abattoirs of la Villette, will establish Arrendondo and Bruyère-Tésárová's major sound and vocal research, as well as the creations thereof. Over a long period of time, the château of the Peugeot family at Hérimoncourt will accommodate the group's work in cinema; the majority of the films will be produced by the aesthete Pierre Bongiovanni, the heir to the château. The Music-Hall du Merlan in Marseille will co-produce and stage, under the direction of the former boxer Alain Liévaux, the strangest of the group's theatrical works. From 1921 onwards, the munitions factory in Karlsruhe, closed down by the Allies at that time, will offer the cinematic and experimental research of *La Fabriks* a second and final pole of development through the impetus of the Australian Jeffrey Shaw. As of 1918, the commercial bank Paribas will become, along with Martine Tridde-Mazloum, the filthy-rich patron of the artist.

A definitively unclassifiable intellectual and activist who has refused all fixed identity (be it social, national, professional, or even sexual), has neither belonged to any artistic clique nor taken an interest in individual career notions, who works in Europe but lives in Africa, Jean Michel Bruyère/Jana Tésárová is always poised at the limit of disappearance. He/she will have devoted his/her whole life to an analysis of the tragedy of Actæon and to the task of creating a many-sided and chiefly incomprehensible oeuvre of hunting that is rich in its 1,207 parts.

From 1915 on, Gabriel Castelli, the founder of *Epidemic*, will ambitiously, but unsuccessfully, persist in promoting Bruyère's work. No doubt his time was not particularly disposed to admit such an obscure and useless oeuvre, so deeply troubled as it was by the Great War and by poverty (although no more troubled than the times that followed but liked to think of themselves as carefree and joyful). *Epidemic*, an otherwise flourishing venture, will thereby lose an enormous amount of money and high-society respect. As the current head of *Epidemic*, Richard Castelli is fighting for the rehabilitation of the artist. By way of this rehabilitation, in particular he is struggling for some recognition of his grandfather's exceptional visionary abilities.

Jean Michel Bruyère
Translated from the French by Sarah Clift

Jean-Louis Boissier
The Relation-Image

Globus oculi
1992
interactive installation
installation view: ICC Gallery
Exhibition, Tokyo, 1995
© Jean-Louis Boissier

The spectators are given the
role of little children in the
process of learning.

La bobine
Avec le Fort-Da, Freud identifie, dans Au delà du principe de plaisir, comment le bébé fait l'expérience de sa capacité à rappeler des images et accepte ainsi l'absence de sa mère.

Globus oculi
1992
interactive installation
stills
© Jean-Louis Boissier

"La bobine" was inspired by
Freud's Fort-Da. This is one
of 10 tableaux of interactive
figures that play with the
relationship of the eye and
the hand within the image.
Developed using "interactive
chronophotography."

I will describe here the path I have explored throughout several projects of what can be considered an interactive cinema. Its specificity lies in the resolute adherence to the shooting process, namely a process in which the image retains its indexical nature as a reference to an external reality. The result of this approach is an interactive regime in which the shooting process is referred to both by placing the spectator into a simulation of the fundamental aspects of the cinematographic apparatus – for example, choosing points of view or the movements of the camera – as well as by organizing the interactive structure of the images in such as way as to create figures or diagrams of those relations captured from reality. Along with the capture of appearances and time within the image, I would include – through what can be called *interactive perspective* – the capturing of relations. Interactivity, in other words, is employed as an instrument for the depiction of interactions.

The interactive video sequences are named *interactive moments*, conceived as temporal spaces closed onto themselves, and offering potential variations. From this context, I propose the definition of a larger category, namely the relation-image. The classical cinematographic apparatus emerges from it as merely a special case within a larger apparatus whose parameters have found a previously unheard of variability: mobility of projection; differentiation of speed, rhythm, and the order of images; and variations within the enunciative regimes and the semantic contents. These experiences propose, among others things, a system of notation that can lead us to a writing specifically designed for interactive video storytelling.

Taking inspiration from previous work with videodiscs, as well as a series of works employing interactive video animations constructed image by image – *Album sans fin* in 1989, *Globus oculi* in 1992, *Flora petrinsularis* in 1993, *Mutatis mutandis* in 1995 – this process was extended and perfected from 1997 onward through works including the installation *La deuxième Promenade* in 1998, the CD-ROM *Moments de Jean-Jacques Rousseau* in 2000, and the installation *La Morale sensitive* in 2001. These three productions are closely related in that all of them are based on the same project of a subjective and experimental reading of Jean-Jacques Rousseau. Great specialists such as Jean Starobinski have even acknowledged this study of Rousseau for its originality. At first, however, this aspect of a study on Rousseau was merely the consequence of a strategy of research into interactive cinema. The idea was to use the rich stories and thought of Rousseau as a basis, to explore its nuances and contradictions while constructing a writing form specific to interactive storytelling. This original hypothesis was confirmed well beyond my initial intuitions. It is for these reasons that I will here describe the recurring motifs of this reading of Rousseau as much as the technical, methodological and artistic choices – while underlining the extent to which they have become inextricably related.

[11.21.00.02]

[11.21.00.02]

[11.00.31.14]

[00.22.32.11]

Mutatis mutandis
1995
interactive installation
stills
© Jean-Louis Boissier

All of the 21 sequences are
linked together by numbers,
indicating their subsequent
belonging to one of three
logical classes of internal
mutations.

Local Impressions

Rousseau was above all a method: to collect, to sample signs from places, collecting the sites themselves, and to catalogue the story of the investigation. Organizing this collection and the collecting was the implicit goal of the experience, requiring from the beginning use of the computer and inter-activity. The project led us to all the places Rousseau had been. A drawing was traced that still resides within the program for *Moments* as an itinerary, a cloud of points on a map. Within this presumably complete location scouting, one expression kept coming back, an indeterminate memory of an old reading of the *Rêveries*. It was the expression "local impression."

> "Not only do I remember the times, the places, the people, but as well the surrounding objects, the air temperature, its smell, its color, a certain local im-pression [impression locale] which could only be felt there, the memory of which transports me there again."1

"Local impression" reappears in the *Rêveries* in a passage on botany, written during a brief stay at the Island of St. Pierre:

> "All of my botanical excursions, the various impressions of the location [impressions du local] where those objects caught my attention, the ideas the locale gave birth to within me, the incidents that were mixed in with that place, all of this has left in me the impressions that come back to me as I look again at the plants I collect-ed at those very sites."2

With the herbarium (a book containing collections of dried plants), Rousseau gave us the prototype of the *recollecting sign* [signe mémoratif], a fragment of the Real slipped between the pages of a book. The simple capturing or seizing [saisie], which preserves the unknown aspect contained in all things, seemed to me capable of coexisting with a story that would engage interactivity as a form. To record into memo-ry, while simultaneously giving access to memory. The interactive diagram became capture-recapture [saisir-ressaisir].

La Morale sensitive, an installation created simultaneously with the CD-ROM *Moments*, takes its title from a philosophical work Rousseau planned but never wrote, a project in which he treats the perceptible approach to things through learning and experiment, social behavior and world-view, aspects of which can be found throughout his various writings, from *Émile* to *La nouvelle Héloïse*, from *Contrat social* to the *Confessions*. According to his "sensitive morals" [morale sensitive], "sensitive reason" [raison sensitive], or even his "wise man's materialism" [matérialisme du sage], it is essential that we trust our various registers of sensation, and even more importantly, found our experience on objects and places, which, through the permanence of sensations they instill, can guarantee us permanence in our sensations and rationality in our knowledge.

Gilles Deleuze 3 highlights Rousseau's "method" in which "we will understand the passing of time, and we will finally desire the future, rather than be enamored of the past," and in which "the true pedagogical redress consists of subordinating the relations of men to the relation of man and things." Deleuze underlines in what ways one might miscon-strue Rousseau, "by ignoring his power and his comic genius, from which his work draws most of its anti-conformist efficiency." Throughout *Moments* and *La Morale sensitive*, two works which willfully promote a pseudo-didacticism and playfulness, I have sought to maintain this comedy.

In order that the lesson come "from the thing itself,"4 in order that a "sensitive morals" be founded on sensitive relations to surrounding objects, Rousseau demanded of a sign that it conserve a perceptible obviousness. Today, a sign that samples from the Real [le réel] finds its realization in photo-cinematographic recordings and video. In our project, the digital realm was never intended to erase the analog power of the optical recording or its capacity to designate an exterior reality [réel extérieur]. In fact, interactivity – which is the most specific consequence of digital technologies – demonstrated its capacity to itself participate in the extension of the aesthetic field of recording [la saisie].

1 Jean-Jacques Rousseau, *Les Confessions*, in *Œuvres complètes*, Bernard Gagnebin (ed.), Gallimard, Paris, Livre III, t. I, p. 122.

2 *Les Rêveries*, Septième Promenade, in *Œuvres com-plètes*, op. cit., t. I, p. 1073.

3 "Jean-Jacques Rousseau, précurseur de Kafka, de Céline, et de Ponge," written for the 250th anniversary of Rousseau's birth, *Les Arts*, no. 872, June 1962, p. 3; reprinted in Gilles Deleuze, *L'île déserte et autres textes*, Minuit, Paris, 2002, pp. 73-78.

4 *Émile*, Livre II, in *Œuvres complètes*, op. cit., t. IV, pp. 368-369.

Flora petrinsularis
1993
interactive installation
installation view: ICC Gallery
Exhibition, Tokyo, 1995
© Jean-Louis Boissier

Series of linked loops, explored
by turning the pages of a notebook and through the back and
forth movements of a billiard
ball.

"An optical effect"

The *Flora Petrinsularis*, Rousseau's project for an exhaustive flora of the Island of St. Pierre (a utopian project associated with his desire to renounce a writing which had become painful to him while still maintaining via alternative means the production of books) gave me the model for an interactive installation and a first CD-ROM.5 A true herbarium, written using interactivity, was coupled with images explicitly imagined using persona and scenes, "short moments of delirium and passion,"6 which punctuate the writing of the *Confessions*. The dried plants recognized immediately and automatically by the computer literally materialized Rousseau's claims: "This herbarium is, for me, a diary of plant collections which returns me to their collection with a renewed charm, producing in me the effect of an optical apparatus [*optique*] painting them again for me before my eyes."7

The "optique" was an apparatus that allowed one to observe an engraving through a magnifying lens and thus exalt in the representative efficiency. Rousseau's *optique* is that of the shortsighted, leaning enraptured "over the vegetable structure and organization, and over the play of the sexual organs during fructification."8 It is the desire to see distances as through a magnifying glass – by installing an astronomer's telescope in Charmettes, or by trying, like St. Preux in Meillerie, to penetrate with a telescope Julie's residence on the other side of the lake.

Rousseau's *optique* is also that of transparent media. The optic quality of the air is its "inalterable purity,"9 the condition for the innocence of the gaze. The optical quality of water is that of refraction, the condition for experimental knowledge of things.10 For him, "remote views" [*vues éloignées*],11 distant projects, overviews [*vues d'ensemble*], do not incite action or the imagination. Pleasure comes from what is in front of us, nearest to our senses. This innovative eighteenth-century thinking challenges the fixed placement of the eye, which the Renaissance stipulated as a condition for pictorial illusion.12 Sight is to be situated in displacement, and operates over successive framings through the designation of

fragments. All *veduta* becomes singular and free, but must renounce constituting itself as an isolated entity in order to become, on the contrary, a play of relations in a complex space. In Julie's garden, "we had no view onto the outside, and we were very happy to not have any."13 By imposing limits, visibility calls on imagination.

While classical cinema in principle constructed the impersonal nature of its enunciation,14 interactive cinema instead calls for a personification of the act of showing and saying. Looking into the lens, the "subjective" or "objective" position of the camera, the movements of the apparatus, as well as the off-screen space, are all transformed by the new role given to the spectator.

Our shooting apparatus is thus constructed in a dual model: First, that which the image must reveal in a disparate, dissimilar environment is recorded using a forward and backward zooming movement. All of the "monuments," the documentary views, are recorded in this way, indicating anywhere where the name Rousseau is written in the present-day space. For *monument* designates, in Rousseau's writing, the testimony of that which remains of actions past, that which stores memories, that which we can count on to guide our memory, to testify to the truth: in other words the archive, the document. Second, that which the image must stage, must direct, and around which it must create a *mise en scène*, that which it must frame while suggesting an off-screen space, is recorded [*saisie*] in a panoramic movement. These are the adjuncts or "supplements," in the manner of engravings, where fiction avows itself, short stories of the sensitive experience of a place and a reconstructed event.

Variability of the Image Within the Screen

Acting upon the image is not to be mistaken with an immersion, either supposed or tangible, within the image. The most legitimate role we can propose to readers – without pretending to allow them into the represented thing – in other words, the role which is the most true for us, can be found in the interactive representation of the image recording apparatus itself. If the author is on the side of the camera,

5   *Flora petrinsularis*, pub-lished in *artintact 1*, ZKM Karlsruhe and Hatje Cantz-Verlag, Ostfildern, 1994. The title, *Flora Petrinsularis*, can be loosely translated as "The Flora of the Island of St. Pierre."

6   *Les Rêveries*, Cinquième Promenade, in *Œuvres complètes*, op. cit., t. I, p. 1046.

7   *Les Rêveries*, Septième Promenade, in *Œuvres complètes*, op. cit., t. I, p. 1073.

8   *Les Rêveries*, Cinquième Promenade, in *Œuvres complètes*, op. cit., t. I, p. 1043.

9   *La Nouvelle Héloïse*, Première partie, lettre XXIII, in *Œuvres complètes*, op. cit., t. II, p. 83.

10   *Émile*, Livre III, in *Œuvres complètes*, op. cit., t. IV, pp. 482–486.

11   *Les Confessions*, Livre IV, in *Œuvres complètes*, op. cit., t. I, p. 146.

12   Roland Recht, *La Lettre de Humboldt*, Bourgois, 1989, p. 148.

13   *La Nouvelle Héloïse*, Quatrième partie, lettre XI, in *Œuvres complètes*, op. cit., t. II, p. 483.

14   This thesis is developed by Christian Metz in *L'Énonciation impersonnelle ou le Site du film*, Méridiens Klinck-sieck, Paris, 1991.

Self-portrait
workshop under the direction
of Jean-Louis Boissier
SEIAN University of Art and
Design, Kyoto, 1999
stills

Each participant developed a
self-portrait, which explored
variations and digressions via a
single interactive zoom.

organizing its movement, the spectator, from the side of the projector, can be given the power to move the projector.

Therefore, one of the first factors of variability is relative to the camera-projector relation. In early cinema, during a period that could be termed naive, the position of the spectator and his or her relation to the screen was determinant in the manner in which the shot was conceived in advance. The static projector with a consistently flowing filmstrip corresponded with an equally static and constant camera. We might recall that the first forms of the traveling shot were obtained by placing cameras on a train, and seem to have dictated a theater shaped like a train car. Today, a similar naivete can be found in certain forms of simulation and virtual reality.

Nevertheless, it is when the camera frees itself from the projector that the process of differentiation is born in which cinema becomes a form of writing and a form of art. Deleuze notes this in his opening to *The Movement-Image*:

> "On the one hand, the shooting point of view was fixed, therefore the shot was spatial and formally immobile; on the other hand, the shooting apparatus was combined with the projection apparatus, endowed with a uniform and abstract time. The evolution of cinema, the conquest for its own essence or newness, was achieved through editing, the mobile camera, and the emancipation of the shooting point of view, which separated itself from projection. The shot thereby ceases to be a spatial category and becomes temporal, while the section is no longer immobile, but mobile."[15]

I found that it was possible, once the frames of a sequence had been separated and classified, to reconstruct an animation that would unfold the camera movements on the surface of the computer screen. The reduced video image frame and the frame of the computer monitor are dissociated. The contents of an image recorded during a panoramic movement do not move according to the screen, despite the fact that the image is moving from one edge of the screen to the other. The obtained result is comparable to that a film or video projector would create if its beam were moved across the screen according to the movements recorded by the camera during the shooting process.

For all of the sequences in *Moments*, I placed a digital camera onto a motorized panoramic head, which I had built with sufficient precision in the degrees of rotation as to achieve just such an interactive panorama. As the starting and ending positions were precisely marked during shooting, the image sequences submit themselves naturally to visual on-screen development, to looping, and to internal bifurcations. It is through this equivalence of the movement of the human gaze [*du regard*], by controlling the movement of the image, that the reader explores each sequence.

"Without which we will never seize the unity of the moment"

In order for us to know Rousseau's thoughts, we have only his words. Therefore our transitions necessarily rely upon them. Computers fundamentally treat nothing but codes, languages. Consequently, I borrowed Rousseau's words in order to move from one sequence to another. Each quotation is associated with a sequence and can be perceived as a justification of the images, as an anchor connecting it to the text as a whole. This parallel presence of that which is readable and that which is showable should remind us of the irreducible disjunction between seeing and saying which are nevertheless inextricably woven one within the other, as Deleuze underlines when referring to Foucault's work on the archive.[16]

15 Gilles Deleuze, *L'Image-Mouvement*, Minuit, Paris, 1983, p. 12.

16 Gilles Deleuze, "La vie comme œuvre d'art," in *Pourparlers*, Minuit, Paris, 1990, pp. 131–133.

above
La Morale sensitive
[The Sensitive Morals]
2001
interactive installation
stills
© Jean-Louis Boissier

left
Le Mire
Le baiser de l'amour
[The Kiss of Love]
engraving
after a drawing by Moreau Jun.
showing a scene from
La nouvelle Héloïse
for the 1774–1780 edition of
Rousseau's works
publ. in Brussels by edition de
Boubers ("de Londres")
collection J.-L. Boissier

To this linking of ideas, or to the "chain of senti-ments,"19 which are capable of enriching our pre-sent, Rousseau counters with the "fugitive succes-sion" of "precious moments,"20 moments that are always "short," "quick." Meanwhile, this moment in actuality has its own plenitude, an internal move-ment, which an engraving must revive. In the margins of *La nouvelle Héloïse*, Rousseau gave these instruc-tions to his illustrators: "As much as the figures in movement, it is important to be able to see what precedes and what follows, and to give a certain latitude to the time of action; without which we will never seize the unity of the moment to be expressed."21

A software application, or what in French is enti-tled a *logiciel*, is that which applies a logic. In cinema, the principle logical axis is that which regulates the recording of appearances in the temporal flow. The strength of cinema lies in the logic of its relationship to the Real. The camera and the projector, two sym-metrical apparatuses combined at their origin, both respect a common rule: string together still images in a fixed order, and at a fixed rate. Interactivity is a means to reduce, and give variation to this logic, to the extent at which cinema, and video, are trans-formed into applications in which the singularity of their software resides in the formula: "24 (or 25/30) images per second, in their chronological order." Interactive cinema liberates the potential variability of cinematographic parameters. The interactive-video substance out of which our "moments" are constructed, are edited all the way down to the indi-vidual images, the constitutive, discrete elements of cinema.

Variability in the Image Chain

A second factor of variability, that of succession and rhythm, can be identified in the same manner. With computers, the order of images and the rhythm of their display are variable and can be modulated, not only concerning what can still be considered a cap-ture [*saisie*] of the Real, but in the recapturing [*resaisie*] offered by an interactive reading. In the type of animated image that I construct, interactivi-ty treats a collection of images. In this sense, it is an integral element within the image, and itself an image. The interactive moments do not have, strictly speaking, a beginning and an end. While there are without a doubt entry points, the image nevertheless carries on in infinite loops, oscillating or circular, which invert, bifurcate, flowing into other loops, all according to the common actions of the *mise en scène* and the current, actual reading.

None of these breaks from the classical cine-matographic model find their descriptive or narra-tive pertinence, nor do they find their pertinence as a spectacle, outside of the role given to the reader. Variability in interactive video does not simply open

In order to allow for progressive reading, texts discovered long ago that they could cut themselves up into coupled pages. A similar logic lead us to split the screen in two, and to the back and forth move-ment between the two positions of the image. In fact, text's fragmentation gave us a mechanism. By acting on the image, and because we can only act on this contemporary rendition of the image, we come to understand that it is the text that articu-lates and decides on its appearance and disappear-ance. In the completed version of *Moments*, some three hundred variants of eighty-four words become shifters [*embrayeurs*]17 of a potential and random succession that is not a montage, in the filmic sense, but rather a passage through associations of ideas, a daydream or *reverie*.

In the eighteenth century, the link (or chain) be-came the principle for storytelling. Barthes reminds us of this while quoting Diderot: "The entirety of Diderot's aesthetics depends on the identification of the theatrical scene and of visual painting: the stage offers to the spectator 'as many real paint-ings as there are moments in the action which are favorable to the painter'". Concerning painting, it is a "perfect instant," "necessarily whole," "artificial." It is a "hieroglyph where, in a single gaze (or a single grasp, a single recording, if we applied it to theater or cinema), the present, the past, and the future tie into one another. [...] This crucial instant, totally concrete and totally abstract, is what Lessing calls (in *Laocoon*) the pregnant instant."18

17 These words were chosen because of their frequency and the pertinence of the thematic links they offered.

18 "Diderot, Brecht, Eisen-stein," in *Revue d'Esthétique*, 1973, reprinted in *L'Obvie et l'obtus*, Seuil, 1982, pp. 87-89.

19 *Les Confessions*, Livre VII, in *Œuvres complètes*, op. cit., t. I, p. 278.

20 La vie aux Charmettes, *Les Confessions*, Livre VI, in *Œuvres complètes*, op. cit. t. I, p. 225.

21 *La Nouvelle Héloïse*, Appen-dice II, Sujets d'estampes, in *Œuvres complètes*, op. cit., t. II, p. 761.

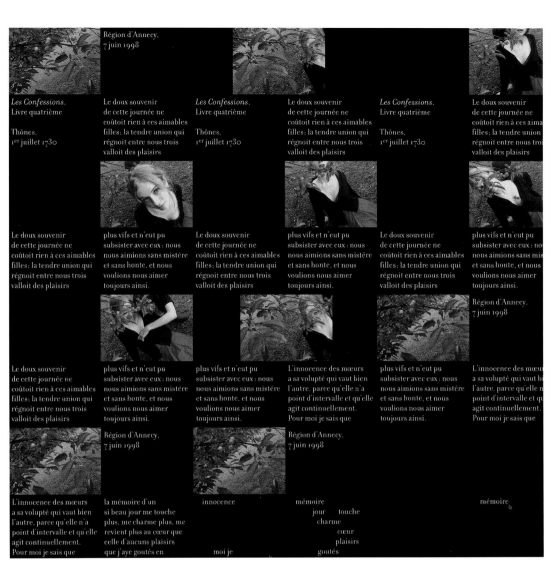

La Morale sensitive
[The Sensitive Morals]
2001
interactive installation
stills
© Jean-Louis Boissier

"L'idylle des cerises" is one of 48 interactive video sequences explored through the play of panoramic movements and through "shifters," words used as links.

possibilities for bifurcation, pauses, or activation, but opens as well the possibility of a generalized dissociation between the stored time and the time restored. Taking for example the interactive panorama, camera movement is a temporal expenditure which coincides with the time of that which was filmed or recorded. We can, when required, store it for later, pause it, and reverse it. But we cannot specifically dissociate these two temporal strata. In an infinite loop, however, both through the repetition and beyond the repetition, the filmed time tends to detach itself from the time of the observer.

In the interactive image, or – more exactly in my case – the interactive assembling of still images, the time of reading can be dissociated from the filmed or recorded time. These two time strata only coincide – and with great elasticity – when the observer designates one side of the screen or the other, thus controlling the transformation and movement of the image. In contrast, this passing and unstable moment, in which our temporality as observers rejoins that of the filmed subject, brings out in us the sensation of a manual seizing [saisie] of the flow of time. Such a projection of time inside of time could perhaps ground the notion of the depth of time, of the relational perspective, of which interactivity would be the principle.

Within that which prefigures an interactive cinema, we could add interactive perspective to the optical perspective that is, of course, the primary apparatus. If we can imagine *relation* as a form, we can conceive of a relation-image capable of being produced by a new type of perspective. To that perspective which refers to optics can be added a dimension relating to relational behavior. Within this interactive perspective, interactivity holds the position held by geometry in optical perspective. We could go so far as to say that, if perspective is that by which we can capture or construct a visual representation, interactive perspective is equally capable of seizing [saisir] or modeling relations. This interactive perspective projects relationships into a relational space, placing them at an oblique angle and thereby rendering them identifiable and executable.

Mechanics speaks of the *moment* of force in relation to a point, in relation to an axis. With a lever, for example, the moments of the active force and the active resistance are equal in opposite directions. Rousseau uses precisely this example of the lever in the lessons he gives to Émile. [22]

Speaking more generally, physics gives the name *moment* to the product of a force and a distance. The interactive moment would therefore metaphorically describe through a mobile and temporal image

22 *Émile*, Livre II, in *Œuvres complètes*, op. cit., t. IV, p. 380.

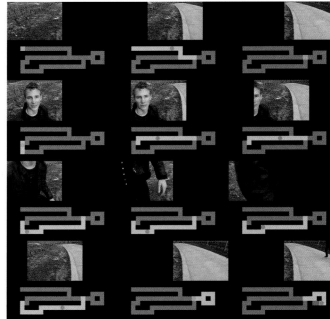

left
Acrostiche [Acrostic]
2002
project for an interactive film
stills
© Jean-Louis Boissier

The film progresses through a game requiring the unblocking of suspended situations based on scenes from Alfred Hitchcock's *North by Northwest*.

right
La Morale sensitive
[The Sensitive Morals]
2001
stills
© Jean-Louis Boissier

Diagram visualizing the structure of an interactive video sequence. The colors of the "billiard ball" indicate the state of the interactive movement: red stands for irreversible, yellow for reversible, green for unstable, blue for stable. The lighter path indicates the possibilities open to movement.

23 Gilles Deleuze and Claire Parnet, *Dialogues*, p. 69.

24 Gilles Deleuze, *L'Image-Temps*, Minuit, Paris, p. 92.

25 Gilles Deleuze, *L'Image-Mouvement*, op. cit., p. 22.

26 Raymond Bellour, "D'un autre cinéma," *Trafic*, no. 34, 2000, pp. 5–21.

its capacity of interaction with other images or with the external force exerted on it by a reader. In a larger sense, that which I here call the interactive moment would be in fact a relation-image, in other words an image that, by way of its internal interactions, opens up onto external actions. We would then see in the interactive moment a process of representation. Just as photography represents appearances, just as cinema represents time and movement, interactivity represents interactions.

The Relation-image
In this way, *Moments* experimentally employs a *relation-image* whose function is the presentation of an interaction, comparable to what Deleuze said of cinema: cinema is not an image to which we might add movement, but rather directly a *movement-image*, while the *time-image* – through an inverted subordinate relationship – is a direct presentation of time.

A *relation* is a narrative. In French this is the first historical use of the word: a testimony, a report. A reporting [*rapport*], as in when one relates something, when one gives a report [*rapport*] on an investigation, before it simply becomes a report [*rapport*] – a logical relation. There is, in the notion of the relation, this double aspect which has always interested me: that of *capture* [*saisie*] and that of *synthesis* [*synthèse*]. The history of the word is surprising: relation is first that which relates and afterwards that which connects. Relation is that which characterizes objects and various thoughts contemplated within a unique material or intellectual act. Deleuze reminds us of this throughout his works, from *Empiricism and Subjectivity* to the *Dialogues*, passing through *The Movement-Image*, which perhaps comes closest to our present concerns: "The relation is not a property of objects, it is always external to its terms." More concretely, " 'Pierre is smaller than Paul,' 'the glass is on the table': the relation is neither internal to one of the terms which would consequently be its subject, nor is it internal to both.

Further, the relation can change without the terms having changed." 23 If the relation has a form, a transformational form of the set it organizes, it follows that we can work with it, that it can be used in an artistic process, as can the relation-image whose theoretical use I am here attempting to validate.

Relation-image belongs to the pairs Deleuze developed around *image* in order to understand cinema: of course *movement-image* and *time-image*, as well as *perception-image*, *action-image*, *affection-image*, and *impulse-image*, and then *memory-image*, *dream-image*, and *world-image*.24 The relation-images, like the change-images or the duration-images, are for Deleuze constitutive of the time-image, and beyond movement itself.25 I am not attempting to add a chapter to studies on Deleuze, but merely to use a linguistic declension within the Deleuzian model, in other words to append our proposition concerning interactive images (which does not yet have a name, its own name) to cinema itself, as cinema already has a name, and has become a brand.

If cinema is, as Raymond Bellour has stated, "an installation which succeeded,"26 we must look back at its specificities and its differences with other apparatus [*dispositifs*] that have had less success, or have failed. And we could as a consequence take the time to observe those apparatus which, along with new media, ground newer genealogical branches of the cinema "species," often appropriating those traits that have historically been abandoned: stereoscopes, panorama, moving projectors, variations in the placement of the spectator, and so on. We would also have to include those apparatus which develop previously unheard-of modalities: interactive immersion, non-linearity, variability in points of view, playability with the accessories, characters or story line, generativity, and the like.

It should be mentioned that Hitchcock's proposal to work within a "direction of spectators," just as one speaks of the "direction of actors," can paradox-

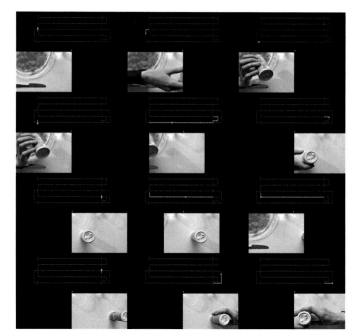

Jean-Louis Boissier,
Hajime Takeuchi, Christine Voto,
Gwenola Wagon
(Laboratory of
Interactive Aesthetics,
University of Paris 8)
Le Petit Manuel interactif
[The Small Interactive Manual]
2001
interactive installation
stills

Each of the 12 interactive video
tableaux is associated with a
diagram visualizing the
functioning of the interactive
consultation.

ically be used for the interactive apparatus, for which – contrary to the common assumption – it is less a question of giving freedom to the spectators than of introducing them to a play of solicitations, in other words constraints, which are necessary to the functioning of the work, as measured in the success of its reception.

We can therefore develop the hypothesis in which we consider cinema as a special case within a larger apparatus – for which the interactive image is henceforth the prototype and for which computers provide the variability. In a computer cinema, the logical relation to the Real is not canceled or diminished, but rather transformed, emphasized. What is more, the various domains of interactivity open up this variability. For, an interactive object's degree of openness is not linked to its simple determination, but rather to its increasing perfection in the management of its internal relations, which in turn gives it a greater autonomy: that of being able to respond to the demands of the external interactions and to the mutations of its environment.

Thus the question will be asked concerning the notation of these relation-image structures. Although they are in appearance simple, the sequences cannot be translated through a simple arborescent diagram. I have purposefully refused such diagrams in order not to diminish in advance the interactive arrangement's capacity to depict the random variations and micro-events that make up the moment. That said, while preparing the image, and above all during the shooting process, elementary diagrams were called for. Once the sequences were completed, the question of their functioning, and thus their exploration, was experimented using interactive diagrams. Using paths traversed by a marble or billiard ball (*une bille*), the play of triggers, bifurcations and pauses could be visualized. This notation system was perfected by displaying, in a symbolic manner, the essential variables. Through this experience, the dialectics of a notation system

were proven in its ability to open up, through an inverse operation, onto a writing system.[27] This research is similar to the problem of notation in the field of dance and choreography, and to its successes and difficulties which are well known.

Repetition

The response to Rousseau's expectations for a unity of the moment and its singularity can be found in repetition. "To extract something new from repetition, to extract from it its difference, such is the role of imagination or of the mind [*l'esprit*] as it contemplates from within its multiple and divided states," writes Deleuze.[28] Repetition is foundational of the notion of the moment. This repetition is twofold: the image is placed in a state of suspension within the repetitive movement, while the interactive mutations are repeatable *ad libitum*.

From my earliest experiments with interactive books,[29] I asked myself explicitly the following question: is it possible to make use of filmed images in the pages of a book? In order to be represented on the pages which will be leafed through, the image must be looped, must be animated and lend itself to the flow of time, but within a vibration, an oscillation, a repetition which leads nowhere in particular. The image can only accommodate passing, fleeting or even reversible events. Then I discovered in the imaginative world of Rousseau a certain propensity to precisely these floating and repetitive movements: the splashing of waves, the swaying of branches, the rising and lowering of the chest, the shakiness of a hand.

Rousseau aspires to the subjective moment, the suspended moment, attached to the sentiment of a pure presence. It is evening on the shore of the lake of Bienne:

"This ebb and flow of the water, its continuous noise rising at intervals, and hitting my ears and my eyes without pause, became a supplement to the internal movements which reverie had extin-

27 *Le Petit Manuel interactif*,
    an installation I conceived
    with a group of students
    in 2001 for the Cité des
    sciences in Paris, develops
    this type of diagram of
    visualization and is in fact
    the central argument of
    the scenario.

28 *Différence et Répétition*,
    Presses universitaires de
    France, p. 103.

29 *Album sans fin*, installation,
    1989.

guished in me, and was sufficient enough to make me feel pleasure again in my existence, without the effort of having to think."[30]

It is a state "in which the present persists, and yet without making felt the passing of time or any trace of succession."[31] It is the moment of a return to himself, after the accident in Charonne:

"It felt as if from my light existence I was filling all of those objects which I could perceive. At the time, I wasn't able to remember anything of the present moment; [...]"[32]

The cycles of the loops strung together, bring back the same transitions, the same attitudes, the same incidents. The back-and-forth of the panorama and zooms construct and deconstruct the gesture, the gaze, the exchange, reinforcing at once the impression of their autonomy and the pleasure of our power of apprehension.

The "Supplement"

From repetition emerges the question of the double. In Rousseau, it can be identified in the mirror, in the self-portrait, in representation. Rousseau resigns himself to the idea that writing is capable of giving anew the pleasure of that which it fixes on the page: "In saying to myself, I was overcome with pleasure [j'ai joüi], I am once again overcome with pleasure."[33] In the "The second stroll" [La deuxième promenade], the one in which Rousseau is knocked over by a dog, the story is that of rebirth, which can just as well be read as an entrance into a world exclusively made up of reminiscent images. "[...] constantly preoccupied with my past happiness, I remember it and ruminate on it, and, it could be said, to the point of allowing myself to be overcome again with pleasure [d'en jouir] whenever I wish."[34]

It is as if Rousseau lived only to be able to immediately transform things into memories, souvenirs available for some future enjoyment. "And as pleasure [la jouissance] was never present outside of a certain repetition, writing, by bringing it back, brings the pleasure with it as well. Rousseau denies the avowal, but not the pleasure," writes Derrida. "Writing represents (in all of the senses of the word) pleasure [la jouissance]."[35] In order that this event and the emotions it brings with it can be conserved, it must be organized as a moment, in other words, isolated, terminated. The reduplication implied in writing, takes over in a sense from previous repetitions. It would only be another of many repetitions though, if Rousseau hadn't expressed such a clear understanding of the originality of autobiographic writing, a repetition destined for others:

"In abandoning myself both to the memory of the received impression and to my present sentiments, I will paint twice the state of my soul with a knowledge of the moment where the event happened to me and of the moment I described it; my writing style, both uneven and natural, at times quick and others diffused, at once wise and then crazed, at times solemn and others gay, will itself play a part in my historical account."[36]

The CD-ROM Moments considered this double movement as it own, redoubling it once more. The interactive mise en scène introduces a moment, and interactivity actualizes yet another. But didn't Rousseau already envision that, "it is up to him [the reader] to assemble these elements and determine the existence they compose; the result must be his own work."[37]

This series of redoubling belongs to what Rousseau designated as the "supplement." The supplement is that which supplants [ce qui supplée], that which arrives as compensation, filling in a gap, substituting as an addition. It is the "remedy within the evil,"[38] a dangerous but healthy artifice. Thus, it is auto-eroticism which appears first in the Confessions as a supplement: "Soon reassured, I learned of this dangerous supplement which tricks nature and saves up for young men of my temperament many disorders at the expense of their health, their strength, and sometimes their life."[39]

It is through his linguistic and aesthetic reflections that Rousseau transforms the notion of the supplement into a critical instrument: "Languages were meant to be spoken, writing merely supplements speech [...]."[40] In this sense, any form of representation is a supplement. Art itself becomes an even greater supplement: "Much art has to be employed in order to prevent the social man from becoming entirely artificial."[41]

An appendage is required at this point in Rousseau's vision. St. Preux had to distance himself from Julie. He describes his stay among the women of the Valais region in the Alps, comparing their cleavage to that of Julie:

"Do not be surprised to find me quite knowledgeable on the mysteries which you hide so well: I am knowledgeable regardless of you. One meaning can sometimes instruct another: and despite the most jealous vigilance, sometimes a few light interstices escape from the most well adjusted dialogue, through which sight has the same effect as touch. An eager and reckless eye creeps its way with impunity underneath the flowers of a bouquet; it wanders beneath the caterpillar and the gauze, and makes the hand feel the elastic resistance it does not dare experience itself."[42]

When the eye supplants in this way the hand, we are speaking of the haptic powers of the image. Our shots and their digital treatment, which reinforces the contrast and detail, contribute to this effect. But beyond that, interactivity supplants [supplée] gesture. Using not the literal touch but instead designation, it allows for intervention by proxy. Is not interactivity that which simulates real interactions? When I picked an apple, or when I pushed a rock over a precipice, I accompanied my gesture with a camera movement. By allowing the displacement of the image across the screen, I am offering not only that the reader displace his or her gaze, but I am giving them the means to pick and push in turn, following the order of the representation, following the order of the supplement. The digital realm possesses this quality of preserving a process without requiring the resolution of the problem of continuity. And in fact, this continuum offers, within certain measure, a reversibility that encourages the reader to in turn follow the same path that was used during the creation of the deed.

30 Les Rêveries, Cinquième Promenade, in Œuvres complètes, op. cit., t. I, p. 1045.

31 Les Rêveries, Cinquième Promenade, in Œuvres complètes, op. cit., t. I, p. 1046.

32 Les Rêveries, Deuxième Promenade, in Œuvres complètes, op. cit., t. I, p. 1005.

33 Art de jouir et autres fragments, in Œuvres complètes, op. cit., t. I, p. 1174.

34 Les Confessions, Livre XI, in Œuvres complètes, op. cit., t. I, p. 585.

35 De la grammatologie, Minuit, 1967, p. 440.

36 "Ébauches des Confessions," in Œuvres complètes, op. cit., t. I, p. 1154.

37 Les Confessions, Livre IV, in Œuvres complètes, op. cit., t. I, p. 175.

38 see Jean Starobinski, Le remède dans le mal, Gallimard, 1989.

39 Les Confessions, Livre I, in Œuvres complètes, op. cit., t. I, p. 109.

40 Fragment sur la prononciation, in Œuvres complètes, op. cit., t. II, p. 1249.

41 Émile, Livre IV, in Œuvres complètes, op. cit., t. IV, p. 640.

42 La Nouvelle Héloïse, Première partie, Lettre XXIII, in Œuvres complètes, op. cit., t. II, p. 82.

Jean-Louis Boissier,
Hajime Takeuchi,
Christine Voto,
Gwenola Wagon
(Laboratory of
Interactive Aesthetics,
University of Paris 8)
Le Petit Manuel interactif
[The Small Interactive Manual]
2001
interactive installation

Exhibition layout for the City of
Sciences and Industry, Paris
(computer-generated image).
The 12 projected interactive
video sequences are explored
through movements of the
spectator's hand on the table.

Playability

When spectators find themselves implicated in an enunciation that ceases to be impersonal, while the authors see themselves reinforced in their role as subjective mediators of the Real, the artifact produced therein becomes exceptionally *playable*. For if a word was required to define the performance which actualizes the relation-image, that word would be game. Our reader is also a spectator, occupying both roles at once, but as well something else. What is expected of the reader is that he or she play, yet in a game which is dissociated from simple amusement or distraction, which maintains the quality of an exercise or of an interpretation, but without placing itself on the side of the tool, remaining on the side of works [*œuvres*], on the side of the supplement which creates a *reading*.

This is in fact what Roland Barthes demanded in favor of the "text we write (in ourselves, for ourselves) when we read":

> "To open the text, to lay out one's system of reading, is not only to demand and show that one can freely interpret; it is above all, and indeed more radically, to lead the reader to the realization that there is no objective or subjective truth in reading, but only a playful truth [*verité ludique*]; although the game should not here be understood as a distraction, but rather as work [*un travail*] [...]."43

When all is said and done, it is in the performance of the passing of the relay, defined as the relation-image, that exerts that which, in the specificity of interactive objects, enacts the story. If we consider that the story evolves out of its visibility and readability, then there cannot be an interactive perspective without a certain level of *playability*. For a more academic terminology, we would certainly have used the expression *performativity*. Playability nevertheless, as the word has already become the elected term for video game adepts, and admittedly has already won its cultural, and perhaps theoretical, pertinence. If we wish to grasp the pertinence of an interactive perspective, we must understand it as that which joins production and reception through the three simultaneous registers of visibility, readability and playability. Playability, along with (and following) visibility and readability, can create a lasting work [*peut alors faire œuvre*]. A double-sided work [*œuvre biface*], actual and virtual, according to Deleuze's expression. Associated with the virtual realm, in other words with the interactive realm of playability, but without confusing itself with it, are possibilities, namely the interactions of that which is *playable*. Within the virtual space of playability, depicted via interactive perspective, another perspective is actualized, a perspective understood as that which is projected, and which will eventually take place.

Translated from the French by Douglas Edric Stanley

43 Roland Barthes,
"Écrire la lecture," (1970)
in *Œuvres complètes*, t. II,
Seuil, pp. 961–963.

Jean-Louis Boissier
La Morale sensitive [The Sensitive Morals]

2001
interactive installation / table with infrared sensor device, chair, CD-ROM / 80 x 70 x 60 cm

As in my previous work, notably my work involving rereadings of Jean-Jacques Rousseau,[1] I am investigating in this work articulations between the regimes of reading and spectacle: how do we place cinematographic images onto the pages of a book? Within what I consider to be a new genealogical branch descending from chronophotography, I am looking to preserve the indexical relation inherent in the photographic medium, namely its optical and temporal capturing [saisie]. Thus we find a paradox: to work with interactivity, which belongs in essence to real-time and to a synchrony with the objects it explores, while at the same time using images that refer indexically to a past moment, to the moment itself when the image was shot.

As a consequence, I refuse to allow the spectator-reader to "enter into the image," while placing him or her in what I consider to be the sole legitimate position: in a relationship with the recording apparatus. A mobile projector can restore the mobility of a mobile camera. An interactive cinema is created by liberating variability within a whole series of parameters that cinematography had to immobilize in order to develop itself into an art. As a result, in the installation La Morale sensitive, the only means of acting on the image is through a simple hand gesture – by displacing the image on the table/screen – therein restoring the lateral panoramic movements within which all of the video sequences were inscribed.

"I told myself that, in fact, we are constantly only beginning, and that there is no other liaison in our existence than the succession of present moments, of which the first is always the actual one."[2] This notion of the moment borrowed from Rousseau, becomes for me a technical as well as aesthetic entity, a type of suspended spatio-temporal unit, containing neither beginning nor end but instead variations, bifurcations, possibilities of triggering events, and above all repetitions.

Moving from one of these moments to the next, there is not strictly speaking the effect of a visual montage, but rather a stringing of events linked by semantic, thematic and linguistic proximity. This pre-serves distance, creates a gap – for, in order to link one sequence to the next, the reader must give his or her "hand" to the program, in other words to the text itself: to the pre-existent and "untouchable" text of Rousseau. It is the text that opens each new image sequence, through a constant play of recalculations of its auto-linking capacities via the play of linking words, or "shifters."

The text is there to provide a horizon, an argument for a performance of which the interactive video may be considered the report, the account, or more exactly in my case, the capture [la saisie]. With La Morale sensitive I propose through concrete experimentation the hypothesis that an interactivity associated with the shooting process is capable of storing and restoring all palpable forms of interaction captured from reality by the camera, including, and above all, through the logical apparatus of interactivity. All capture or storage [saisie] therefore opens onto a restoration [resaisie]. The dramatis personae, whom I consider as models participating in a performance, are by proxy the vectors of our actions, answering to the reader's intentions, but also fundamentally escaping them by executing their own acts.

To a Rousseau obsessed with the necessity of proving his loyalty to truth, of proving his innocence, our performances can be seen as attempts to verify the contemporary truth of Rousseau. All of the scenes were filmed at the locations of Rousseau's life, using models chosen on-site with the intention that the relation-image created by the interactive video produce something other than a simple illustration of the text. It is in this vein that the locations and dates attached to the excerpts are connected to the locations and dates of the images, which are in a sense doubles, but doubles that belong to us fundamentally.

This collision of a multi-layered past into the present of the reading process incidentally finds its model in Rousseau: "In saying to myself, I was overcome with pleasure [j'ai joüi], I am once again overcome with pleasure."[3] The act of reading has the role of actualizing this past ad libitum, of inscribing it in the permanence of our own time. La Morale sensitive

1 Flora petrinsularis, CD-ROM, ZKM Karlsruhe, 1993; Le billet circulaire, 1997; La deuxième promenade, Le Fresnoy, 1998; Moments de Jean-Jacques Rousseau, CD-ROM, Gallimard, Paris, 2000.

2 Jean-Jacques Rousseau, Émile et Sophie, "Lettre première," in Œuvres complètes, Bernard Gagnebin (ed.), Gallimard, Paris, t. IV, p. 905.

3 Jean-Jacques Rousseau, Art de jouir et autres fragments, in op. cit., t. I, p. 1174.

La Morale sensitive
[The Sensitive Morals]
2001
interactive installation
table with infrared sensor
device, chair, CD-ROM
80 x 70 x 60 cm
computer-generated
installation view
Centre pour l'image
contemporaine, Geneva
© Jean-Louis Boissier

  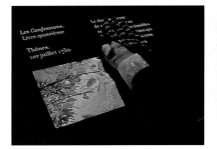 

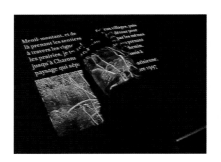  

takes its title from a philosophical project Rousseau never set down in writing, in which he treats the perceptible approach to things through learning and experiment, social behavior and world-view, aspects of which can be found throughout his various writings. According to the "sensitive morals," we must place our trust in the various registers of sensation and, even more importantly, found our experience on objects and places which, through the permanence of sensations they instill, can guarantee us permanence in our sensations and rationality in our knowledge.

The reader-spectator of the installation, confronted with objects, situations, known gestures and acts, should be able to seize [*saisir*] – in other words, literally take as well as understand – the general model capable of being shared socially with others, while at the same time be able to seize the irreducible singularity of a shot, of its bodies, objects and circumstances. This pseudo-didactic situation is indicated by the usage of schoolroom furniture, a table and a chair intended to evoke in the reader the posture of learning, of an exercise, and perhaps the nostalgia of childhood. Interactivity – or even, in my opinion, precisely just such an experiment in "interactive cinema" – is fundamentally appropriate to an autobiographical attitude. Instead of a relation of I to You, it is more a relation of the I of the author to the I of the player. That said, through the choice of the most neutral gestures, through the stress placed on the operations and functions that make up the situations, from the rendering of visual and auditory sensations related to objects, to materials, to the lighting and to atmospheres, through repetitions and the initiative given to the reader-spectator to enact these interactive repetitions, I aim to instill a distance which can be assimilated to the Brechtian *Verfremdungseffekt*. Our interactive dramatic method consists of placing the reader into a play of relations wherein, if we feel guilty of voyeurism and of manipulation, we always find ourselves rendered innocent at the very point at which, as in Rousseau himself, we able to defer our "guilt" to the circumstances of the game, and to the "advances" made by the machine.

Jean-Louis Boissier

La Morale sensitive
2001
installation views
Centre pour l'image
contemporaine, Geneva
© Jean-Louis Boissier

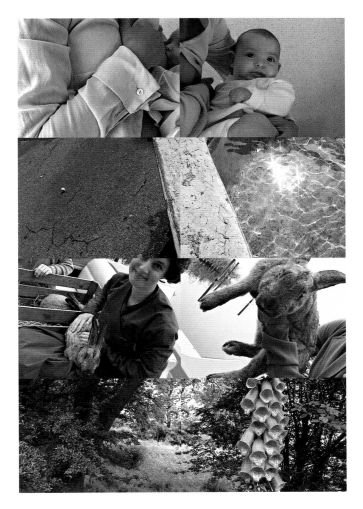 

La Morale sensitive
2001
stills of the total image
Centre pour l'image
contemporaine, Geneva
© Jean-Louis Boissier

Christian Ziegler
66movingimages

1998—2002
interactive road movie / two-channel video, interactive control with moveable monitor,
linear navigator (by Jeffrey Shaw) / 1100 x 100 cm

Route 66, also known as "The Mother Road" and "The Main Street of America," stands for breaking out and hopes of a glory-ridden future: "Go West." Once it was the route immigrants took to the west, today it is a cult destination for adventurers. The appeal of the landscape links it in a strange way with a myth which is based not least of all in the fact that the road stood for the vision of American tradition. It runs from Chicago to Los Angeles, is 2,448 miles long and transverses eight states and three time zones. Driving the Route in the opposite direction is historically wrong, the "right" way is from east to west, from the beginning to the end.

Christian Ziegler documented his motorbike trip along Route 66 with a camera attached to the handlebar. At every stop he conducted interviews and filmed the environment and landscape in detail. His concept actually encompasses two films: Channel 1 shows the stills which he took throughout the trip, Channel 2 the documentation of the stops – in 66 scenes. Ziegler shows the landscape which whizzes

past when driving fast as a motionless picture, and his stops as a flow of movement. Such antagonisms interest him. In such a way he also incorporates the observation that the faster one moves through a landscape, the more blurred it becomes until you have the impression that a "tube of pictures" seen from constantly changing vantage points simply spins past you. Everything is in motion. Close up (the margins of the picture) the transformation is actually faster than in the distance (the center of the picture). The physical phenomenon of spatial displacement here – in which a forward-pushing body forces the mass it passes to the side – is metaphor as picture. Alongside the speed of the trip, the uneven qualities of the road also leave traces of movement in the pictures. Ziegler has "the horizon fly," by linking the stills taken while driving through spatial metamorphoses (morphs). The road itself starts to move.

In 66movingimages Ziegler has installed his journey as an interactive road movie. Thanks to the linear navigator, the road from Chicago to Los Angeles

66movingimages
1998–2002
interactive road movie
two-channel video, interactive
control with moveable monitor,
linear navigator (by Jeffrey
Shaw)
1100 x 100 cm
installation views: ZKM |
Center for Art and Media
Karlsruhe, 2002
Christian Ziegler
© Christian Ziegler
photos © Franz Wamhof

becomes the over-arching spatial interface. The motorized screen, mounted on an 11-meter long rack, can be controlled by the viewer. When the monitor is in motion or stopped, what you see are spatial and temporal images from a filmic map. When moving, the film reproduces the spatial image metamorphoses on channel 1. When it is static, you see the scenic/documentary takes from Channel 2. The viewer navigates right through to the single-image level of the film. Here, "moving images" are images which the viewer moves. Memories of the trip can be called up in whatever order you like and connect with the pictures and associations that the viewer has in his own mind. The dissolution of the linear nature of a time-space sequence reflects something of the incompleteness of recall.

The interviews and detailed shots circle around the history of the road and the people who live there. Ziegler also met people who have spent their whole lives there and witnessed how, over the decades, the road has become more lonely and derelict – how it has turned from a main artery into a cult destination. He encountered an unemployed person who walked from Texas to New Mexico, and a motel owner who was unaware of the historic significance of his building. He experienced how personal fates were linked to the history of the road, but also stories of life in the various regions. The discrepancy between east and west was also a central experience – how it was that when you reached the west coast you had really reached a final destination.

Dörte Zbikowski
Translated from the German by Jeremy Gaines

66movingimages
1998–2002
screenshots
Christian Ziegler
© Christian Ziegler

Masaki Fujihata
Field-Work@Alsace

2002
interactive multimedia installation / stereoscopic projection, stereoscopic glasses, interface /
dimensions variable / rear-projection screen (305 x 228 cm) / with Takeshi Kawashima

Field-Work@Alsace
2002
interactive multimedia
installation
stereoscopic projection still
Masaki Fujihata
© Masaki Fujihata

Some Notes on the Project

1. Countries and Borders

The first time I crossed the border between France
and Germany was during a stay at Karlsruhe in 1998,
when a family took me to Lauterbourg to eat crêpes.
On the return, we crossed back to the German side
via Seltz on an old rope-drawn ferry. At that point, the
Rhine separates the two countries, so although one
can only cross by boat or by bridge, in fact one sees
the other country right before one's eyes.

As someone from Japan, a country completely
surrounded by sea, the experience was totally foreign.
It made me think, someday I really ought to give this
more thought. But how exactly? It wasn't just a
question of getting more traveling under my belt.
Granted, the question didn't even occur to the locals
living there; it was their reality and as such beyond
question. To even ask them would be absurd. I needed
some angle in order to justify this absurd outsider's
actions – perhaps the format of a new-media interview?

Just maybe the special circumstances of a Japanese named Fujihata showing up with a camera to conduct interviews might serve to create the right circumstances for both Germans and French to "open
up." If an ignorant foreigner was doing the asking,
might not Germans answer to things they'd never
admit to any German inquirer? Starting from such
background, this *Field-Work@Alsace* is a record of my
own personal actions as well as of my own personal
thoughts.

2. Media Technologies

What is "media," much less "new media?" For one thing,
it demands a stronger awareness on the part of the
user than any media we're already accustomed to
using. Part of the fun of using new media is in the
muddle; and not just the using, creating new media,
designing it to meet certain ends and realizing them
can be thrilling in itself.

The GPS (Global Positioning System) technologies I
use were originally developed by the American military,
and were installed in every tank during the Gulf War in
order to keep posted on the location of all other allied
tanks. However, the quantities of military-use GPS
units were limited, and they supposedly had to make
do with so-called civilian-use units that lacked special
programming to unscramble pinpoint positioning and
so were ten times less precise than the military units
(accuracy only within +/- fifty meters). The unscram-
bling apparently only worked a few times during the
entire Gulf War. It was only later, after President
Clinton ordered a halt to the intentional scrambling of
satellite signals at 20:00 (eastern daylight savings
time) on 1 May 2000, that current accuracy levels of
+/- five meters have encouraged the production of
cheap civilian-use GPS units.

One reason I am so interested in this new technology is that something developed as weaponry can now
be used, not for military ends, but on an individual level
for personal expression. The challenge has been to
see how far I can expand upon the potentials of the
technology while at the same time observing how
I myself react.

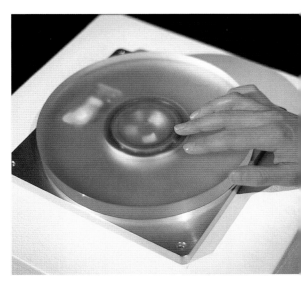

Field-Work@Alsace
2002
interactive multimedia
installation
stereoscopic projection,
stereoscopic glasses, interface
dimensions variable,
rear-projection screen
(305 x 228 cm)
installation view: ZKM |
Center for Art and Media
Karlsruhe, 2002
Masaki Fujihata
© Masaki Fujihata
photo © Franz Wamhof

3. Documentation and Memory

It is extremely difficult to put across events from memory to others. Or rather absolutely impossible, unless one can get beyond explanation. Getting others to experience for themselves is the ultimate meta-explanation, poetry being one such attempt in the realm of language arts. The experience of reading challenges the reader to internalize what is read into new memories.

The act of photographing is typically referred to as "shooting," the same as for hunting game in the forest. On returning from this "hunt," the trophies in hand are images cropped from reality in the form of film, whereafter the particular "locality" of the images are trimmed through editing and, just like cooking, reassembled into another context.

My methodology this time for *Field-Work@Alsace* was to record digital video images together with GPS positional data and directional data (which way the camera was pointing) from a special electronic compass. Place and time and visuals and camera orientation, all recorded together in one go. How does the creation of new media bring new aspects to the work, to the visuals made by those new means? What limitations, what possibilities do they impress upon the image-maker himself? I've kept on with this string of projects out of a focus on such issues as well as sheer curiosity. Placing myself within these various tensions and expectations gives an underlying energy to my expression.

interface for
Field-Work@Alsace
2002
© Masaki Fujihata
photo © Franz Wamhof

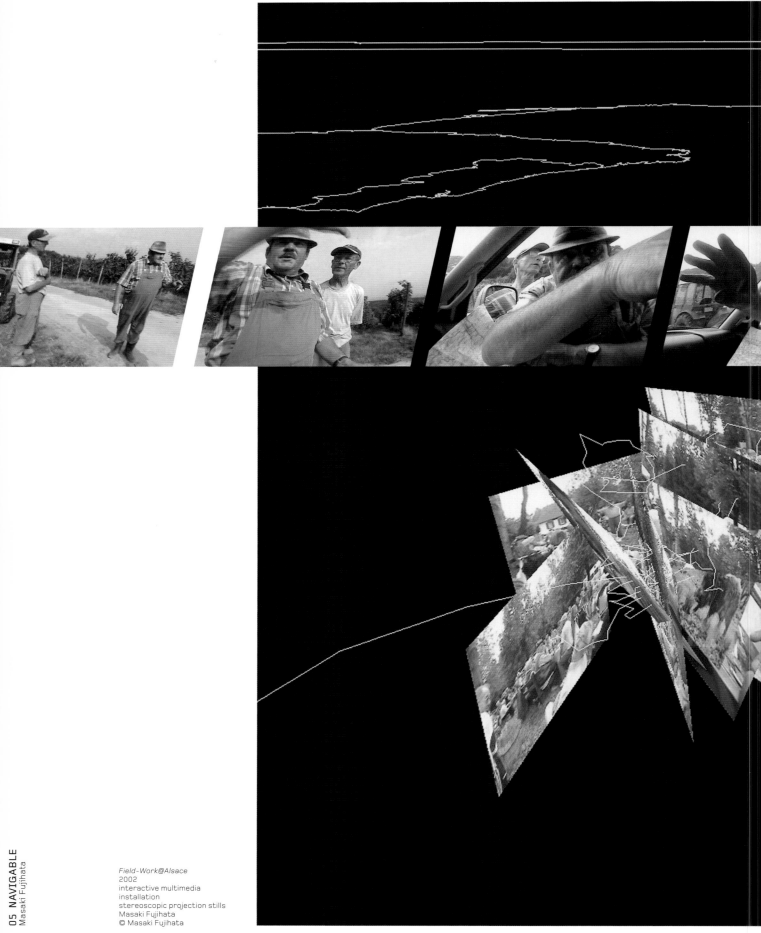

Field-Work@Alsace
2002
interactive multimedia
installation
stereoscopic projection stills
Masaki Fujihata
© Masaki Fujihata

4. The Man with the Camera

A perennial issue when using new media for creative expression is that the viewer and the maker never share the same media conditions. Which means one should pay careful attention to those media conditions in themselves. While media may be likened to a mirror reflecting oneself, when trying to express something through such new media the artist's position tends to become unclear. This questioning of the artist's stance has come to the fore in modern times, and especially with the advent of interactive media. The question must now be rephrased: "Where on earth is the mirror?"

In *Field-Work@Alsace*, the artist finds himself multifariously parenthesized. The artist is simultaneously cameraman and interviewer. He meets people and talks with them, though never appearing on screen himself. Once all the data from the site interviews are input into a computer, the initial camera movements appear as a rectangular frame moving around a screen. A camera pointed at a car approaching from the east, for instance, sees the car pass by and head off to the west; the computer, however, expresses this motion by rotating the projection frame, thus translating photographing to projecting. The motions of the framed images make it clear that they are cropped out of a larger sweeping reality. Technically speaking, the handheld camera shakes become effectively imperceptible when projected as framed in this way. That is, we see the world there, and no matter what part of that world the camera frames, the world itself does not appear to move. The information we retain are the motions of the people on camera and my own motions as cameraman.

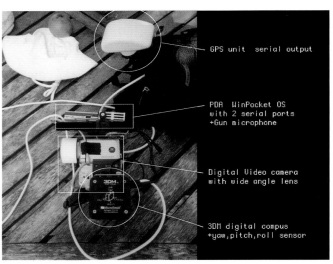

left
equipment used for shooting
Field-Work@Alsace
2002
GPS, DV camera, 3-D sensor,
PDA, microphone
© Masaki Fujihata
photo © Masaki Fujihata

right
production stills of
Field-Work@Alsace
2002
© Masaki Fujihata
photos © Masaki Fujihata

Later on, the author of these images metamorphoses into an editor, re-experiencing the source materials in the computer and using them to compose a second context. Only then does he assume a third person stance, while at the same time laying down guidelines for other third parties.

5. Tracking

What does this merger of image and positional data signify? Cumulative positional data registers as white lines in space representing GPS data connected over time. These lines occasionally form random knots or seem to move unnecessarily, showing up the technical thresholds of the GPS. In actual fact, any shift in position of the twenty-four satellites circling the globe will affect the accuracy of their measurements.

Quite often, for instance, a satellite in use will drop below the horizon, causing stationary positional data to move. Altitude data is especially susceptible, so some GPS units have internal barometers to help correct discrepancies. Not that I necessarily dislike this lack of accuracy. Rather even more important is that it leaves tracks, which my later "second self" can trace.

Here is where we understand the complex folding over of time and space in the piece. These various trackings of movement are recorded at different time signatures and listed up in columns in the same computer space, each with a beginning and end point, if not so very apparent at first glance. Then there are rows of video frames, none of which were shot at the same time, but are merely fragments of multiple sequences. Although in the computer I used here, three videos can be replayed simultaneously, making it possible to show different timelines in parallel.

These parallel video sequences, shown in the positions they were shot, move according to the tracking lines in the computer, so that each video frame, as it retraces the past, stands in for me shooting the image now being projected. The important thing here is that it all happens automatically; this tracking in space constitutes a mapping of actions in space. We must now consider what this means.

6. Interfaces

This work must be seen stereoscopically, and as such required using polarizing filter glasses and rear projection. Visitors to the venue put on glasses in order to visualize a free-standing space away from the actual screens. The projected interview videos move within that free-standing space in such a way that the two-dimensional "screen" of the video frame really seems to move in three-dimensional space. Within the computer space, visitors find themselves standing directly behind me, the cameraman/interviewer, looking over my shoulder. They can replay or stop whichever videos they choose. Once organized in the computer, replaying these visuals is just like bringing back the reality.

There is also another important aspect to the interface in this work. That is, it operates from a single disc, which only a solitary viewer can operate. For the purposes of the present exhibition, by just watching without doing anything, this interface will cycle through a 30-to-40-minute navigational course, moving around a succession of keyframes. General operations are similar to video jog-dialing, the only difference being that jumping to other frames does not involve stopping the frame in progress, that is to say: each video frame works completely independently of the others.

7. Is There a Boundary?

While there scarcely remains any real "border" between Germany and France, why is it that borders always seem to be way off in the countryside, the very furthest away from the capital cities? To the locals living there, so deeply set in their ways, it would hardly seem to matter if the nation changed. They live by the common sense of the place, seemingly quite obvious yet a curious phenomenon to outsiders and their on-looker's common sense. It boggles my mind to think of working every day in a local bakery, never once in one's whole life even going to Paris or Berlin. The people just as they are here are simply beyond me, just as I must certainly fall off their map. The boundary drawn here may well be between myself and them.

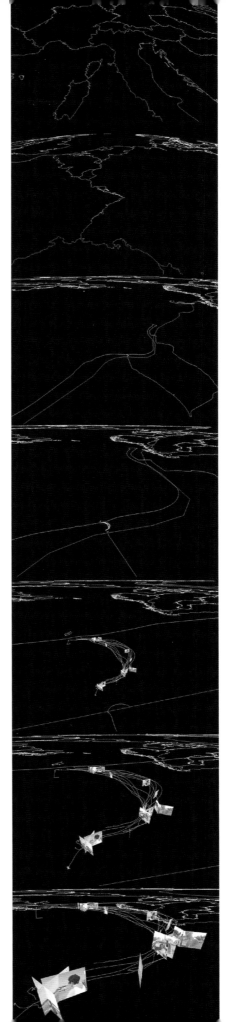

Field-Work@Alsace
2002
stereoscopic projection stills
Masaki Fujihata
© Masaki Fujihata

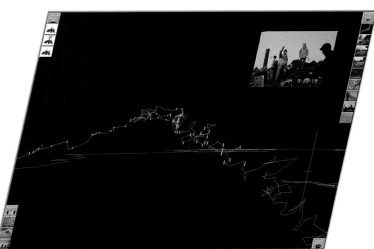

Impressing Velocity
1992–1994
collective art project,
multimedia video archive
GPS, video, video archive,
satellite data,
geographical mesh data
screenshot
Masaki Fujihata
© Masaki Fujihata

Fig 1.
Image generated with
Mount Fuji ascent data.

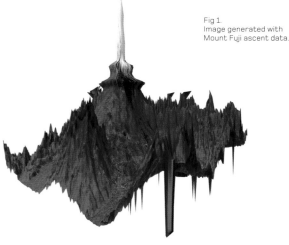

Fig 2.
Image generated with
Mount Fuji descent data.

Impressing Velocity

In 1992, I climbed Japan's tallest and most famous mountain, Mt. Fuji, with a GPS and Hi-8 video camera, gathering positional data and moving video images for both the ascent and descent. The Illustrations show computer graphics created from these sources. Based on data from the ascent, Fig. 1 expands or contracts the size of cross-sections of Mt . Fuji at various altitudes in inverse proportion to the speed of the climber, that is to say: When the climber goes slower and hence is supposedly tired, the fatigue makes the object of the climb – Mt. Fuji – that much bigger, and when the climber is full of energy it seems that much smaller. In that sense, it represents a schematic conversion of the extent of fatigue into pictorial form. Whereas Fig. 2 based conversely on data from the descent, takes into account that slippery graveled areas on the mountain can push break-neck speeds, hence the representation of Mt. Fuji as a kind of speedometer needle. The 3-D data for Mt. Fuji that served as the basis for these visualizations was provided by the Japan Geographic Institute from their mesh data, which in turn was texture-mapped from Landsat feeds.

The software created to document the overall project allowed viewing both ascent and decent video footage together with the corresponding 3-D GPS data. This documentation became the basic for the Field-Works series.

Moreover, in the later *Impressing Velocity with Simulation Platform* realized for the 1999 ZKM exhibition "Net_Condition," I used a hexaxial 3-D motion simulator in combination with a camera and accelerator gauge mounted on a Maerklin model train in an attempt to build upon the classic painting technique of expressing the physical sensation of speed by means of image distortion.

Global Interior Project 2

Seeking to create an artwork that would tap latent potentials in digital networking from the angle of exploring the future of digital communications as well reflecting upon questions of virtual versus real, this piece enabled multiple users to share the same cyberspace. Placed around the venue were three or four white terminals (2 x 2 x 2 meters in size), inside which were projected images of cyberspace comprised of eighteen rooms one could move through at will. Participants logging in from other terminals appeared as "avatars," upon which were mapped the image of a person in the room and with whom one could converse freely while together in the same room. Simultaneously on display at the venue was a physically modeled object of the cyberspace layout whose doors opened and shut with audible slams according to goings-on in the eighteen rooms in cyberspace. Meanwhile, visuals shot off this physical model were displayed in one of the cyberspace rooms, where clicking on the various little rooms in the image would "jump" the viewer to that same room in cyberspace.

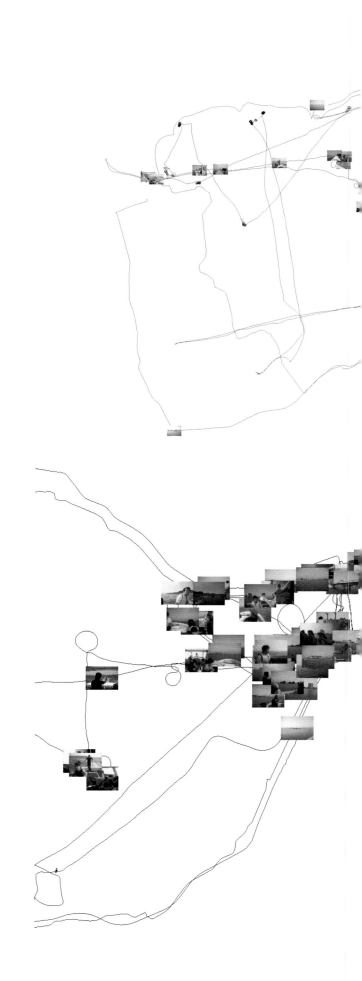

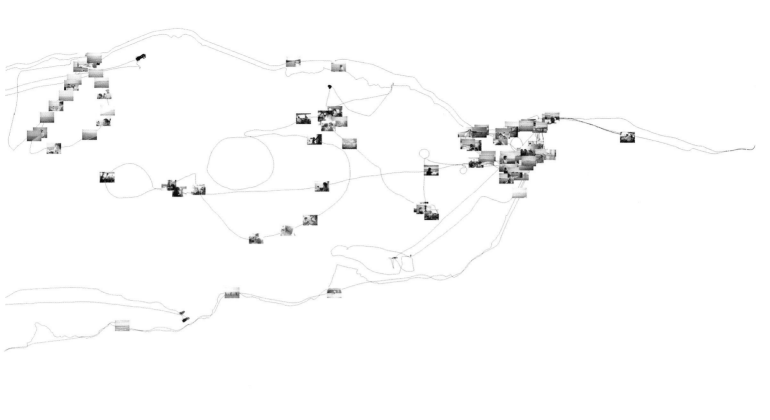

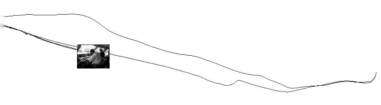

Field-Works@Lake Shinji

Having realized that adding GPS-derived positional data to either video or still images makes for a truly wide range of info-experiences, I conducted a workshop with local middle school students at the 2000 Echigo Tsumari Triennale, trying out various experiments that led up to the art event "Lake Shinji as a Drawing Pad" at the Shimane Prefectural Art Museum in Matsue, central Japan, this past summer of 2002. For the three days of this event, working in cooperation with fishing boats, tour boats, tourist pedal boats, youth-club canoes or rowing boats – in other words, any and all the vessels able to launch on Lake Shinji – as well as the Shimane University Bicyclist Club circling the shore road around the lake, we collected a vast array of positional data and images in real time. Relayed to the museum where they were projected onto a tabletop, on-going roving circumstances were shown as a slowly extending line upon which appended the occasional mobile-phone camera image. Meanwhile, parts were also uploaded onto an Internet homepage, which could then be accessed via mobile phones on board the boats.

These shared activities over the course of those few days generated a body of collective memories, which if printed out would form a vivid panorama of Lake Shinji at that one moment in time.

center
Field-Works@Lake Shinji
2002
interactive multimedia
installation
collective art project,
multimedia video archive
stills
Masaki Fujihata
© Masaki Fujihata

small pictures
production stills of
Field-Works@Lake Shinji
2002
© Masaki Fujihata

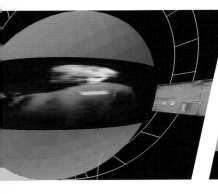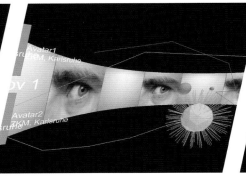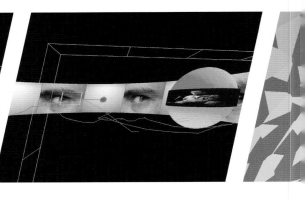

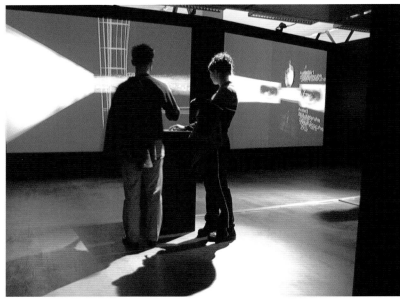

Masaki Fujihata
with Takeshi Kawashima
Nuzzle Afar
1998–1999
interactive networked installation, shared virtual environment
mixed media
dimensions variable
installation view: ZKM |
Center for Art and Media
Karlsruhe, 1999
© Masaki Fujihata
photo © Franz Wamhof

Nuzzle Afar

This piece looks at two issues from the above *Global Interior Project 2* with specific reference to telecommunications. Here, when avatars move, they leave behind trails in space, lines with special marks on the end that when "grabbed" are traced by computer to their respective "owners" – "cyber-stalking," as it were. Although characteristically, instead of a trail of telephone numbers and addresses, digits or places, here traces of a person's activities are left to others in the form of special marks. The avatars here are made up of volumetric (3-D) polygons with typically nothing inside, yet if one penetrates another "avatar" within the space, there suddenly opens a new space accessible only to the two of you. No third party can enter. Conversely, in order to get out of that space, the both of you must search together. In actual fact, the system is designed so that if the two persons get closer than a certain distance, they return to their

previous spaces, a special consideration to the complexities of displaying an indefinite multiplicity of objects simultaneously. Upon returning to their original spaces, the separated duo find a plaque commemorating who met whom when and where.

Initially, the plan was for it to be a commemorative sphere, which when entered would replay the meeting of the two parties, until we realized that if two avatars could merge within that space it might possibly set up an infinite chain of inwardly concentric spheres that would surely overtax the memory limits of the host computer. We gave up on that idea.

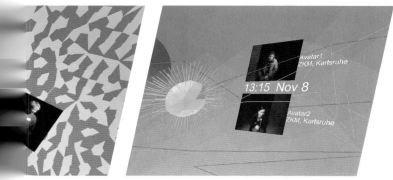

Nuzzle Afar
1998–1999
stills
© Masaki Fujihata

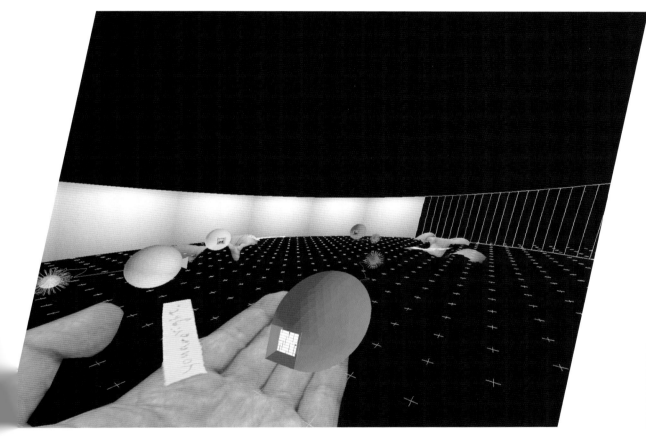

Masaki Fujihata
with Takeshi Kawashima
Off-Sense
2002
interactive networked
installation, shared
virtual environment
screenshot
Masaki Fujihata
© Masaki Fujihata

Off-Sense

Building upon *Nuzzle Afar*, we added in artificial programming to allow each avatar to move about and
converse autonomously. In this way, even first-time
viewers can enjoy the motions of the piece by simply
watching, without actually having to manipulate anything. Although as soon as a "viewer" takes up a
mouse and turns "participant," the avatar becomes
that person's own; or rather, one "piggybacks" into cyberspace. Of course, one can talk to the AI-enabled
avatars via the keyboard, and the parameters can be
expanded so that the objects of these encounters
become artificial life. Moreover, the artificial conversation program created as a byproduct of this work is
designed to be taken out and used as a piece in its
own right.

Masaki Fujihata

Translated from the Japanese by Alfred Birnbaum

04

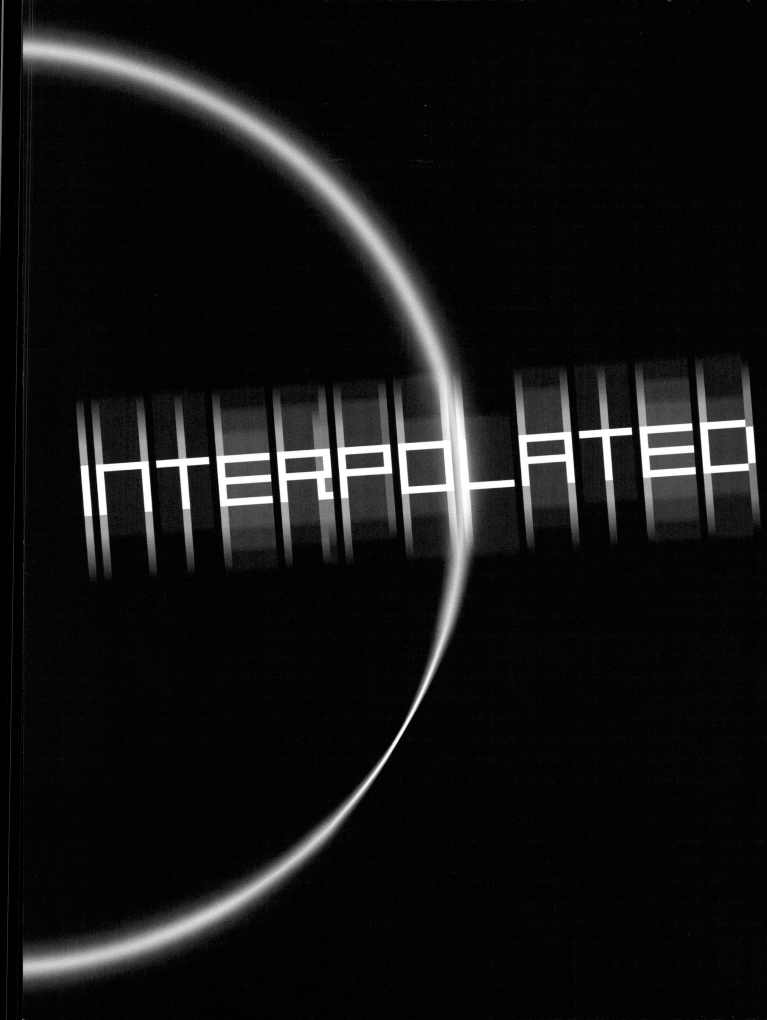

Susanne Jaschko
Space-Time Correlations
Focused in Film Objects and Interactive Video

Michael Zeno Diemer
Schlacht am Berg Isl
[Battle at Isl Mountain]
1896
oil on canvas
1000 x 10,000 cm
panorama
photo © Raiffeisen Reisebüro
Tirol, Arno Gisinger

Ludovico Caricciolo
Panorama di Roma
[Panorama of Rome]
1824
170 x 1340 cm

The Exhibition of Time Periods: the Moving Image

The close relationship between time and space has been a dominant theme in art for a long time – and still is. Long before the invention of panoramas at the end of the eighteenth century, painters dealt with the inseparable link of the two dimensions, trying to express different qualities of time and movement though space.

In contrast to these earlier attempts, panoramas string together spatiality and break the central perspective through isometry or through vanishing points in the painting. Although panoramas are nothing but stills proper, they helped to produce the illusion of movement by causing the viewer to move his/her eye over the picture, getting a notion of time sequence, or by moving the viewer him/herself, or the canvas. Panoramas represent therefore not only the extension of space through the positioning of stringing space together, but also the extension of time through the build-up of chronological time.

The need to present time and time-based periods in painting and sculpture culminated in the works of the futurists and the cubists, who now actually managed to form sequences of, and to abstract, single phases of the movement of the body through space and thereby produced new dynamic bodies.1 Looking back on these early attempts to present movement and time at the beginning of the last century makes the discovery of film seem an unstoppable and logical cultural step forward. Film was born out of an ever-growing need, based on more than just one moment, rather to document and represent, respectively, a period in time. Within our visual perception, single pic-

tures shown one after another in fast succession became blended to a moving picture, which occupies one clearly defined temporal frame, but also one place, defined through the position of the camera, the moving camera, the camera angle, the aperture setting and the focus.

The first steps towards film were made by Edward Muybridge in the 1880s with his technique of "simultaneous photography." Muybridge used a battery of cameras (between twelve and twenty-four) laid out parallel to the horse's path. A string running from each camera across the track was broken by the horse as it trotted or galloped, successively triggering the cameras to shoot. Then Muybridge's sequential exposures were projected at film speed and brought uncannily to life.

The French physician Étienne-Jules Marey found Muybridge's techniques and results problematic for several reasons. Because Muybridge used a different camera to record each new image of his subject, a single point of reference from which to evaluate changes in the subject's position was missing. Instead, Muybridge's batteries of cameras, placed parallel and adjacent to the subject's movement, kept the relation between camera, subject and background consistent in each frame. It was also difficult for Muybridge to accurately and consistently measure the gap of time between each image, thus making it impossible to render a complete representation of the subject's movement.

Marey had, in Muybridge's work, examples of how not to photograph movement. His solutions, developed over the course of twenty years, were helped by

1 Umberto Boccioni in the *Technical Manifesto of Futuristic Plastic*, 1912: "Sculpture must give life to the body, in which the extension of the body in space is represented in a clear, perceivable, understandable way so that today no one can claim that an item starts there, where another stops, all things, which are surrounding our bodies (bottle, car, house, tree, street), these things cut through it with curves and straight lines. [...] again in sculpture as well as in painting things can be achieved, as long as one does not look for forms of style for movement. The futuristic sculpture would address the codification of the light-paths and the interpretation of body movement. Transparent glass and shiny surfaces, strips of metal, wires, internal or external installed electric light sources would give the painted layer, the character, the tone and half tone a new reality."

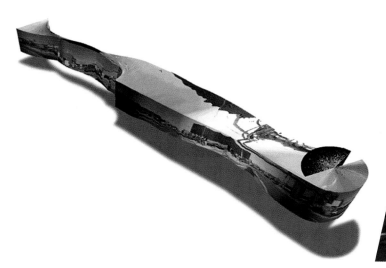

Joachim Sauter, Dirk Lüsebrink
Invisible Shape of Things Past
1995
virtual film object
Joachim Sauter, Dirk Lüsebrink,
Art+Com
© Art+Com

the steady advances in photography as a whole, including faster and more stable film stock. His primary
strategy was to record multiple images of a subject's
movement on the same camera plate, rather than the
individual images Muybridge produced. Marey's most
aesthetically compelling invention was the crono-
photograph: multiple exposures on single glass plates
and on strips of film that passed automatically
through a camera of his own design. The results were
scientifically important, but also inspired artists such
Naum Gabo, and most well known, Marcel Duchamp's
Nude Descending a Staircase.

The advantage of film was that one was able, for
example to document time changes in cuts, whereas
the first films that were produced were actually limited. Among the themes of the first short films, which
could be filmed in one take with a static camera were
everyday stories like the driving of a train into a station (Lumière Brothers) or people leaving a factory.

The next essential step leading to the art works of
the present, which rather concentrate on the time-
space relationships, and the moving image as metaphor and medium all in one, was the digitalization of
pictures which is a fundamental pre-condition for
the real time-interaction with the moving image. The
viewer does not need to subordinate to a chronological sequence but is rather able to focus, for example,
on single cuts of film or single areas of the picture.
Digitalization and interaction enable an individual and
complex representation of space and time frame in
the virtual world by navigation along the time or
space axis.

From Film to Film Object

Film material is always understood as meaningful in
that it is fixed both in time and geography. Owing to
the technical means of today, it has become repre-
sentable as such in the context of its space-time expanse.

As early as in 1994, Edward Elliot, who worked at
MIT Media Lab, developed (in a dissertation under
Glorianna Davenport) the so-called Video Streamer,[2]
a tool mainly designed to view video films by presenting single pictures of the videos strung together to
produce a picture-block. The block is not seen as a
static picture but as a temporary, changeable manifestation of a stream of pictures. The block is composed of one half-minute video, where every new single picture on the front block is visible and with each
new shot the pictures move backwards, completely
disappearing from the block within half a minute. This
viewing tool lends itself to the idea to edit video in a
manner different from the traditional way, since
the outer area of the block is composed of the outer
pixels of the single pictures, and therefore is also
"readable," in principle in a similar way as the picture
from a slit camera.

A related, but essentially more complex concept
was presented in the middle of the 1990s in *Invisible
Shape of Things Past*, a work by Joachim Sauter and
Dirk Lüsebrink, which explored time related to virtual
space and navigation through virtual time.[3]

In this work, film sequences are transformed into
interactive virtual works. The transformation is based
on the camera settings in a film sequence (movement,
angle, and focal distance): The single film shots are

2 See http://ic.media.mit.edu/

3 See http://www.artcom.de

top
Tamás Waliczky, Anna Szepesi
Time Crystals
1996–1997
computer animation, video
installation commissioned
by ZKM I Center for Art and
Media Karlsruhe
© Tamás Waliczky, Anna Szepesi

left
Masaki Fujihata
Field-Work@Hayama
2001
interactive installation
© Masaki Fujihata

4   One can click on the objects
in every position, it is thereby a chronological sequence
of single pictures as near as
possible as the return of
chronological sequences or
the entry into a film at an
arbitrary point.

5   A possible application of
this project lies in the mediation of a historical context,
for example an urban situation. Films from different
eras, which would be shot in
different times in which
geographically limited frame
would be presented as
objects, where the user can
freely ramble in a time
space context, meet the
film objects and explore
their content, and so understand their spatial and historical relationship.

6   See http://www.waliczky.com

7   Tamás Waliczky, 1996: "For
us humans, who are limited
in time and space, time is a
one-dimensional affair. We
can move only along one axis
we define in co-ordinates
of 'past-present-future'...
And, sadly enough, even in
this single dimension we are
able to travel in one direction only, namely forward.
But for God, who is eternal

strung together along the camera path when it is
transformed into virtual space. The angle of the shots
to the camera path depends on the angle of the real
camera, the size of the single shot on the camera
focus used. The pixel edges of the single shots form
the outer surface of the film object.

   The result is a film object that is based on a complex camera movement and virtual information architecture, respectively, and that can be interactively
explored. It is the spatial interface for the information which it contains.4

   In a second step, a spatial and time based organizational concept for film objects was developed: As
each film sequence occurs not only in one place, but
also at one time, a virtual representation of the surroundings was constructed, enabling users to navigate through time. One such construction modeled
all urban building structures of Berlin since 1900. 5
The film objects were placed in virtual reality at the
place and time of the takes in the respective time dimensions.

   The documentation of a particular space and time
sequence is thus transformed into a perceptible
space-time object with an individual aesthetic quality.
Independent of their interactive application, these
film objects, produced with the help of these transfer
tools, have a particular poignancy because of their

form that abstracts the literal picture material. This
represents an interesting parallel to the sculptural
work of the Futurists, who used sectional methods to
cut through space and time and achieved really expressive results, especially on a formal level.

   Tamás Waliczky's sculptures6 dating from the mid
1990s are based on a similar principle as Sauter/
Lüsebrink's films. For them, too, the starting point is
digital film, and the results of the works are virtual
sculptures, which, however, in this case are definitely
only obtained from a space-time development of single visual objects/bodies.7

   Waliczky extracted the movement of a person
from digital film by cutting out the silhouette frame
by frame. As a result, the single shots/frames are
arranged a row forming a virtual sculpture, in which
short moments of life are "frozen." Waliczky refers to
these sculptural works as *Time crystals*, through
which the viewer can move in different perspectives,
at different camera angles, and at different speeds.

   The work *Field-Work@Hajama*, 2001, by Masaki
Fujihata,8 also starts from the principle that film
material has a space dimension which can be transferred into a three-dimensional representation in
virtual space. The starting point are digital video-
shots that were recorded in urban surroundings in
Tokyo together with the exact GPS data. From this a

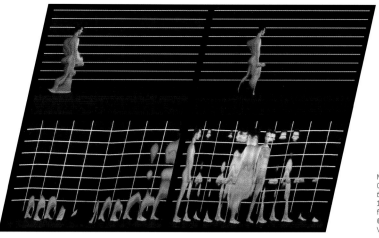

topographic and time-based system of co-ordinates was produced, since each video frame represents both a defined place and a particular moment of the take. Fujihata translated this system of co-ordinates into a virtual three-dimensional space, in which the video takes are displayed in virtual space in positions corresponding to those in which they were recorded and move alongside these three-dimensional GPS traces. Through the use of the interface the viewer is able to follow the video images and their paths and to navigate through the three-dimensional space and thereby experiencing the complexity of the inter-relation of space and time. By the use of stereo-scopic projection the viewer can perceive the picture three-dimensionally, from which, in addition to this, he gains an individual experience of the hyperreal in-formation space through the interaction with the interface.

From Film to Cut Through Space

Film a visual concept originates from the correlation of time and space and can be understood in terms of a linear ordering principle, which attributes a particu-lar spatial and pictorial configuration to a particular point of time. We see time as a linear dimension with a definite extension. In our perception, these experi-ences are congruent with the visual impressions of the film takes.

Both the film objects of Sauter/Lüsebrink and the sculptures of Tamás Waliczky visualize the spatial di-mension of film as well. A further step which followed the conceptual idea of this type of representation is the cut through the film's space axis, a process that was developed by Martin Reinhart under the name *tx-transform* and was first shown publicly in 1998.9 In 1997, Björn Barnekow had conceived a very similar project bearing the title of *timemirror*.10

Tx-transform starting material is a traditional, digitally recorded or digitized film that is transformed with the help of software. In its original form, each single picture shows the entire space within a minimal time-span. By contrast, the transformed single film picture only shows a minimal spatial clipping and its complete development during the recording process. Each single picture is a cut through the space axis, a sequence of pictures produces visual effects such as

the following ones: Houses start to move, moving trains become shorter with increasing speed. Thus, items in film are not defined as an representation of some concrete existence, but rather as a state in time. The result of tx-transformation can, depending on the mode of perception, appear completely ab-stract or completely realistic. Theoretically, these spatial clippings can be positioned deliberately, so that new perspectives and effects develop again and again.

Based on a digital slit camera is another project that combines traditional analogue clock with camera feed, creating a clock face that shows the history of the space it is looking at. *Last* by Ross Cooper and Jussi Angesleva11 transforms the slit pictures into a clock-like display: The clock's hands are narrow slits of the live video feed, and as they rotate, they leave a "time trace" on the clock's face. The hands are arranged as concentric circles, the outermost being seconds, the middle one minutes, and the innermost hours. Thus, the clock face displays the last minute, last hour and last twelve hours as its spatial history. The video feed can be any live video source: A camera mounted on the clock itself looking at what is happen-ing in front of it, remote camera streamed over the Internet or TV signal fed directly to the clock. The clock can thus display the local space, remote space

and in His dimensions in-finite, time is perhaps a four-dimensional quantity; for God can see all three-dimensional existences, simultaneously and at any point in time. Therefore, for God it is a simple matter to change at will our percep-tion of time. From His per-spective, temporal mea-sures such as a second, an hour, a year or even eternity are identical. I believe this may be a possible interpre-tation of the quotation from Koran with which Borges precedes his tale: 'And God made him die dur-ing the course of a hundred years; and then He revived him and said: 'How long have you been here?' 'A day or a part of a day,' he replied."

8 http://www.transmediale.de/de/02/exhibition.php

9 See http://www.tx-transform.com

10 See http://www.digitalitis.de/index_i2g.html

11 See http://www.lastclock.co.uk

Camille Utterback
Liquid Time
1999
interactive video installation
Camille Utterback;
Creative Nerv
© Camille Utterback

Romy Achituv
BeNowHere Interactive
1999
interactive application
© Romy Achituv

or media space respectively. As a clock, the emerging imagery becomes contextualized and makes it meaningful in the space it is being displayed at. As an installation, the system can be used as a living, aesthetic element reacting to the usage of the space. As a still it documents the different types of spaces, similar to a spatial identity card.

Penetration into Space and Time

Camille Utterback and Romy Achituv also dedicated themselves to the representation of the correlation between space and time but their project again addresses the time axis. The installation *Liquid Time* by Camille Utterback and Romy Achituv[12] was based on traditional video-material that is played, in case of no interaction of the viewer, in the normal chronology of recording. An interaction system based on video-tracking enables the viewer to intervene in the chronology, moving backwards in time within a chosen picture area, or within space, respectively, while the rest of the film runs on chronologically.[13] What Utterback describes by the title "Video Cubism" is eventually the splitting of the video image into multiple time zones.

A further concept of non-linearity and coexistence of different time zones in a picture has been developed by Romy Achituv alone and transplanted into the interactive application *BeNowHere*.[14] The panorama of a site was documented from one perspective at different times of the day. Within a drifting section of the panorama, the application shows a single moving picture at each stage. Parallel to the camera view, this picture drifts along the space and time axis and leaves a static picture, a trace of time and space, by means of the "last" pixels from the previous moving picture. The viewer can intervene now by using the input medium in order to focus on a section of the image and to activate the moving picture at exactly that point. This means that the viewer focuses not only on a particular space but also on a particular time, namely a point in time before each activated picture in case it is positioned to the left, and after the activated picture if it is visible to the right.

For Achituv this application demonstrates structural possibilities for non-linear cinematic narrative that break away from the reliance on "montage" as the basic semantic unit of cinema. On celluloid, time and space are inevitably fused: every film frame represents a particular space and a particular point in time. Transitions from one space to another, as those from one time to another, can only be affected through a "cut" (or a "fade" – which is no more than a sophisticated cut). The synchronized scenes of *BeNowHere* suggest the possibility for playing with the viewers' expectations of space and time by affecting transitions between scenes based on user panning alone. This could be achieved by seamlessly integrating scenes. Instead of three different times of day like it is now, the application could be based upon three different scenes shot with parts sharing an identical backdrop (scenery, props, light, etc). The user/viewer then could push the "narrative" forward by transitioning from one scene to another simply

12 See http://www.
creativenerve.com/
liquidtime.html

13 In this way the viewer
provides the interface:
Depending on his/her posi-
tion/movement in space
changing the picture zone,
which is in front of him/her.
The closer the viewer goes
to the projection, the deeper he/she pushes into time.

14 http://www.mikromuseum.
org/beta/submissions/
cdrom/pages/Achituv.htm

Sascha Pohflepp
Meandering
2002
interactive application
Sascha Pohflepp;
Universität der Künste Berlin
© Sascha Pohflepp;
Universität der Künste Berlin

through panning the image in different directions.

As we have seen already in the application Video Streamer by Elliot and also in *Invisible Shape of Things Past* by Sauter and Lüsebrink some of the experimental work with video imagery results in possible tools for the analysis and editing of moving images. The same applies to a project that was just recently developed at the University of the Arts Berlin. *4DDurée* by Sascha Pohflepp can either be used as a viewing tool or as an creative means for the manipulation and sculpturalization of images.

By selecting one or more areas within a frame it is possible to create a video sculpture in which the single bulges represent other time zones before or after the main frame. The staggering of frames inside the virtual space of a 3-D environment illustrates the fourth dimension of the moving image and creates a virtual object inhering an artistic character in itself.

Conclusion

A number of contemporary and more recent art projects have transformed film-material into interactive virtual spaces, in order to break through the traditional linear quality of the moving image and the perception of time, at the same time to represent, or to visualize the spatial aspects of time respectively. In the times of resampling, the concentration on an relatively old picture medium and its transformation into a space-time phenomenon open to interactive experience does not seem surprising. The results of these experimental works exploring and shifting the parameters of the linear film are often oddly abstract and quite expressive in their formal composition, and, consciously elude simple legibility.

The development of space-time representations to the present documents the keen interest of artists to portray space-time correlations in their complexity by using methods of representation available at the respective times. Any obvious step towards an innovative way of representation each time implies a radical break with old concepts of visual art. Both the interaction with film and the representation of the space-time characteristics of film in virtual space, which, in the described works, are fathomed by experimental and artistic means, represent a conceptual expansion of the film medium and a break with traditional perception. In a similar way, for example the panorama picture once broke with the traditional understanding of the work of art of the preceding century.

Joachim Sauter and Dirk Lüsebrink
Invisible Shape of Things Past

1995/2001
interactive installation / collage, poster, 3-D sculpture, projection mirror, video documentation /
dimensions variable

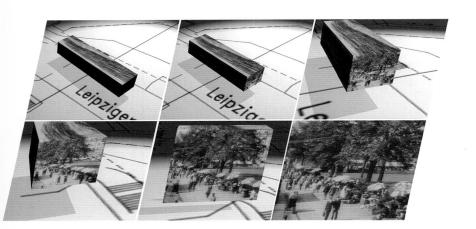

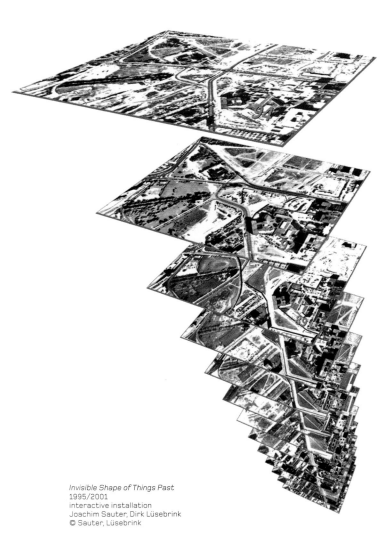

Invisible Shape of Things Past
1995/2001
interactive installation
Joachim Sauter, Dirk Lüsebrink
© Sauter, Lüsebrink

The product of our long interest in the question of representing, and navigating within, virtual spaces, *Invisible Shape of Things Past* is an exploration into representing film in virtual space and navigating through time in VR.

The project enables users to transform film sequences into interactive virtual objects. This transformation is based on all the camera parameters of a particular film sequence (movement, perspective, focal length). In virtual space, we line up every individual frame of the film according to the camera movement. The individual frame size depends on the focal length used. The outer pixel rows of the frames define the skin of the "film object." This leads to the emergence of a virtual information architecture.

These film objects may be explored interactively, and act as the spatial user interface to the information they contain. To "play the movie," the user activates the front side of the object, whereas a double-click leads the user along the virtual camera path through the object. Dragging the mouse to the left or right makes the movie run forward or backward. One click on the skin of the film object, and the movie jumps to the actual mouse position.

In a second step, we developed a spatial and time-based organization concept for the film objects. Since a time as well as a place exists for the occurrence of each film sequence, we modeled a virtual

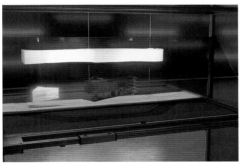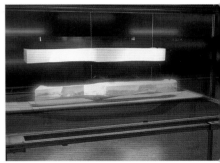

representation of the place of occurrence for each object, thus enabling the user to navigate through time. Taking the city of Berlin as an example, we modeled all the urban situations since 1900, and positioned the film objects according to their place and the time of shooting.

Three concepts were developed for navigating through these time layers. The first and most obvious concept is based on the transformation from one temporal urban situation to the next (spatial morphing). With the help of a time-slider, the user can change the surroundings according to the year selected. The second concept is based on the spatial layering of individual historical conditions, and allows users to navigate spatially through time.

The third concept, which is the one we prefer, enables users to rupture time-space linearity and configure a time-space environment in accordance with what interests them.

For instance, users can choose all film objects shot at Potsdamer Platz in the period 1940–45, and then, as second object layer, select the course of the Berlin Wall with, as a ground layer, the condition just before the Wall came down (aerial shot). As a third layer, they can incorporate 3-D models of the area after completion of the current redevelopment (scheduled for 2005). Users then wander through the space-time environment, encounter the film objects,

and explore their contents in order to understand spatial and historical relationships.

The Web Application

In addition to a local interactive application, a networked 3-D web application has been developed that offers Internet users the chance to locate historical film sequences in a spatio-temporally organized database.

All film objects can be shown simultaneously. With the help of a time-slider, users can navigate through time: The further removed objects become from the time a user has chosen, the more transparent they become.

As well as providing a spatial database of historical and current film footage, these film objects enable a previously invisible urban architecture to grow with the help of the Internet: "The Invisible Shapes of Things Past."

Interactive Installation

For the "Future Cinema" show at the ZKM, we developed an interactive architectural model in which an interactive virtual film object can be superimposed over a real architectural model ("Pepper's Ghost").

Joachim Sauter and Dirk Lüsebrink

Invisible Shape of Things Past
1995/2001
installation views: ZKM |
Center for Art and Media
Karlsruhe, 2002
details
Joachim Sauter, Dirk Lüsebrink
© Sauter, Lüsebrink
photos © Franz Wamhof

Daniel Egg
Box 3 "Dialog"

1997
installation / Novopan, spy mirror, monitor, DVD player,
casette recorder / 160 x 60 x 80 cm

The media construction of reality is one of the central themes of avant-garde art practices at the end of the twentieth century. As such it is the continuation of a process that began in the 1960s as the analysis of the social construction of reality. In a text from 1966 about his "Minus Objets," Michelangelo Pistoletto makes reference to his mirror paintings, extolling the contemporaneity of the depiction with the moving reality that is literally reproduced. One of the inherent qualities of the mirror image is its simultaneousness with the real image. Daniel Egg extends this reproductive and temporal dialog between mirror image and reality to include the dimensions of mediality and space. The opponent of the mirror image is neither the photographic reproduction nor any living body; instead, the mirror image is replaced by the virtual appearance of a moving video image, which in turn is opposed by a real, three-dimensional object (the tape deck). Image and object act in perfect temporal and spatial congruence. A videotape player and a horizontally installed monitor have been set into a box, in front of which (but not visible or otherwise perceptible) is a semi-transparent mirror tilted at an angle of 45 degrees. The moving images from the videotape are superimposed on the real tape deck through the spy mirror. A virtual hand (a reflection of the image from the monitor onto the real deck) inserts a virtual cassette, yet the real deck appears to begin playing – as if it has actually been switched on. The visual images of the real and the imaginary tape decks are perfectly superimposed. At the same time one hears a dialog from the Alfred Hitchcock film *Dial M for Murder* (1954): a telephone conversation between a man and a woman. In one shot we see the man and hear both his voice and the woman's voice at the end of the telephone line. The next shows the woman and we hear her voice and the man's voice at the end of the line. In the film version, the cut between shots signifies a change of location, which Egg here reproduces as a change of tape. A

male and female hand take turns in changing the tapes according to the cuts between shots in the film (change of location). The woman begins to speak by stopping the tape with the male voice and inserting her tape (her voice, that is), and vice versa.

Man and woman as the classical pair of opposites are thus assigned to those of present and absent, real and virtual – the primary elements of telematic culture – importantly, not in the form of an image but as sound. Kaja Silverman explored the function of the voice in film in her 1988 book with its revealing title *The acoustic mirror*. The female voice in psychoanalysis and cinema, showing it to be a key method of gender construction. Egg is thus following the acoustic mirror of media reality rather than the visual mirror of sensory reality. This distinguishes him as an artist of the 1990s from an artist of the 1960s.

The relationship between the subjects (or sexes) therefore has a strictly dual structure based on a technical dispositive that is in a Lacanian sense a remainder of the Real, an "experiment," a remnant, yet constitutive for the symbolic order.[1] In this symbolic order the relationship between the sexes becomes a "dual-mirror relation" (Zizek), built upon elements of presence and absence, reality and virtuality.

Egg's *Box* is therefore not only an analysis of media reality (an analysis of Hitchcock's film) but also an analysis of the relationships between the subjects, yet nevertheless in the mirror of the media. By achieving the perfect superimposition of the material organization of communication, the economy of the cut, and the "libidinal economy" (Jean-François Lyotard), Egg sheds light on the mechanisms of the media construction of reality and symbolic order.

Peter Weibel

Translated from the German by Jacqueline Todd

First published in German in *Jenseits von Kunst*, Peter Weibel (ed.), Passagen Verlag, Vienna, 1997, p. 173.

1   Slavoj Zizek, *Enjoy Your Symptom! Jacques Lacan in Hollywood and out*, 2ⁿᵈ expanded edition, Routledge: New York, London, 2001. Chapter 6.1 "The Hitchcockian sinthom."

Box 3 "Dialog"
1997
installation
Novopan, spy mirror,
monitor, DVD player,
casette recorder
160 x 60 x 80 cm
Daniel Egg
© Daniel Egg

Martin Reinhart and Virgil Widrich
tx-transform

1992–2002

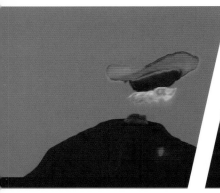  

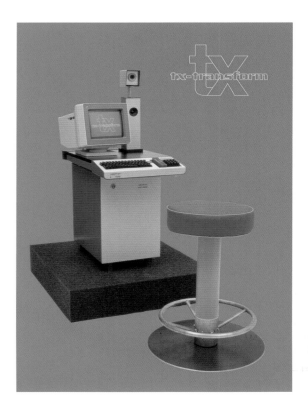

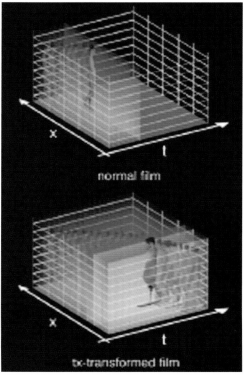

right
tx-transformator
2000
promotion postcard
Martin Reinhart,
Virgil Widrich
© Reinhart, Widrich 2000

left
tx-transform
© Reinhart, Widrich

Schematic representation
of the information block.

Tanzwochen [Dance Weeks]
2001
video still
Martin Reinhart; Golden Girls
Filmproduktion, Vienna
© Reinhart; Golden Girls 2001

Muybridge Walk
1998
© Reinhart, Widrich

tx-transform- The Movie
1998
film stills
Martin Reinhart; Golden Girls
Filmproduktion, Vienna
© Reinhart, Widrich 1998

Tx-transform is a film technology in which the spatial axis (t) and time axis (x) are swapped. That sounds simple, but once you have seen the way in which arms become separated from a body or the surroundings become distorted into horizontal lines, it sets you thinking. What is the trick involved? In order to appreciate how it works, imagine a flip-book. Every phase of movement exists as an image superimposed in chronological order over the next one, producing something like a book. When you run the book's individual pages, the illusion of movement is created such as we know it from films. For tx-transformations the flip-book is cut/edited at right angles to its individual images. At the intersection a new image is created composed of the thin edges of the individual moving images. If you flip through the book from left to right, you create a large number of split images, which when played in succession once again produce a movement. No information is lost in the process, and no new information is added – what is altered is the point of observation.

When I first attempted to realize this idea I took the concept very literally, and spliced a pile of used film material into strips measuring mere millimeters. After each splicing session the cropped section was filmed as a single image. But as the results were not very satisfactory, I began in 1993 to build a device that would automate the process. The centerpiece of the equipment was a cine camera in which a 35mm film continually passes a vertical slit. Mounted on a trolley, the camera was gradually passed along a video monitor on which a short, looped video was run. During one passage of the loop the camera only recorded what could be seen on a single line of the monitor. During a short black phase at the end of the loop, the camera was automatically moved up a line space. The whole procedure was repeated until all the lines of the video had been scanned.

Building this device took a relatively long time, and in the intervening time it became possible to alter videos using a computer. At the same time that I was working on this mechanical solution, I teamed up with Toni Pöltl to produce a program that enabled the digital realization of transformations. In 1995 it took us thirteen hours to compute a thirty-second sequence, but the results were far surpassed those produced using analog methods. Since that time no drastic changes have been made to the basic software, even though tx-transformations can be performed today without a time lapse – a possibility that Virgil Widrich and I made use of in 2000 for the *tx-transformator*. This interactive installation allows the user to glance into a strangely askew world in real time where left is earlier, and right is later.

Martin Reinhart
Translated from the German by Jeremy Gaines

Margie Medlin
Miss World

2002
projected three-screen digital-image installation / three concrete panels,
each 240 x 180 cm / color, sound / 10:05 min, loop /
installation space approx. 800 x 800 cm

large pictures
Miss World
2002
projected three-screen
digital-image installation
installation views:
ZKM | Center for Art and Media
Karlsruhe, 2002
© Margie Medlin
photos © Franz Wamhof

Miss World
2002
screenshots
© Margie Medlin

Miss World is a duet between a live dancer and a virtual dancer. This installation explores the complex relationship between the real and the virtual. The primary intention of the work is to form a new relationship between film and dance. The choreography investigates the interplay between the camera and the dance, by simultaneously creating choreographies of the landscape. These qualities and feeling of movement are conveyed to the viewer through the media of dance and film.

Technical data for the motion control camera was generated by the dancer's movements. It was recorded in real time using a Polhemus motion-cap-

ture system. A virtual camera was then placed on the virtual dancer and it is from this 3-D camera path that the movement of the dancer is converted to run a motion-control camera. It is this that creates a crossing between human and virtual, that is to say: the landscapes that we view are seen from the dancer's viewpoint.

The images are projected on three concrete panels placed along side each other. Each panel will be approximately 2.4 meters wide by 1.8 meters high.

The work has been mastered on DVD with a ten-minute surround-sound score.

Julien Maire
Demi-Pas [Half-Step]

2002
live-projection performance / twenty-one mechanical diapositives /
Ektachrome, laser-cut / each 12 x 9 cm / color, sound / 22 min

  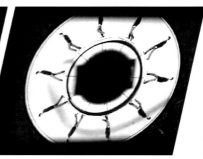

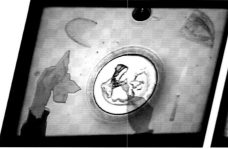  

Demi-Pas [Half-Step]
2002
screenshots
Julien Maire
© Julien Maire

Julien Maire's Imaginary Archaeologies

"The first seventy years of the nineteenth century gave expression to the growing need and technical ability to grasp and appropriate the visible surface of the world through its re-visualization and the ability to play around with it: the cinematization of the eye and of perception as a counterpart and complement to the extensive acquisition of natural and technical processes for other areas of the production of commodities and meaning."[1]

In its encounter with duration, the pre-cinema initiated a discourse with visibility that framed an encounter with temporality distinctly in line with a social system in which mobility, communication, representation, and technology converged to provide means to directly reflect on experience. The introduction of photography only served to underscore (and delay) a mounting demand to both salvage and to reproduce memory and history with precision. And while the pre-cinema projected its fugitive images into the imaginary of modernity, photography absorbed reality into its imaginary archive. This remarkable coincidence of technologies – projection and recording – form the foundation of an approach that largely veiled the apparatus from itself being subject to critical scrutiny – even while its operations were crucial in formulating not merely the "spectator" but the audiences in which spectatorship was increasingly public and participatory (as in the panorama or Diorama).

Seamless technical illusions, of course, can heighten both the fantasy and futility of the image as unmediated from incorporation into technical or social systems in which the "suspension of disbelief"

becomes a kind of "suspended animation" – a kind of virtualization masking virtualization, or doubt as both an initial and operative condition. Slowly, as the pre-cinema emerges from its shadowy history, the functional role of the apparatus as an essential component in the creation of illusion re-emerges as much to remind us that the intricate reproduction of reality – its recording – comes hand-in-hand with a willingness to revel in realities rendered into "existence." In rethinking the apparatus as the decisive component in understanding the role of media, an array of issues emerge to heighten the often missed significance of a feedback loop in which images always are engaged. In much contemporary media this loop has been abandoned in favor of a revived "cinema of attractions" – momentary visual effects inhibited from development.

Julien Maire's performances using proto-cinematic micro-machines both evoke and outdistance the illusions of the phantasmagoric projectionists of the pre-cinema. His intricate archaeology though seems not primarily concerned with retrieving the effect-ploys of optical illusion, but of reimagining the apparatus as itself as illusory, one in which the image and its operation are meticulously intertwined. In this sense, rather than allegorizing the image, Maire allegorizes the machine.

The scaled-up projections in his performances mimic those of the illusionists of the nineteenth century, but the images are less anecdotal than episodic, they provoke deliberation rather than sentiment, reflection rather than mere sensation. Rather than simply enlivening the image with transitory effects, Maire summons not the apparitions of ghosts, but the "ghosts in the machine," coaxing them into

1 Siegfried Zielinski, *Audiovisions: Cinema and Television as Entre'actes in History*, trans. by Gloria Custance, Amsterdam University Press, Amsterdam, 1999.

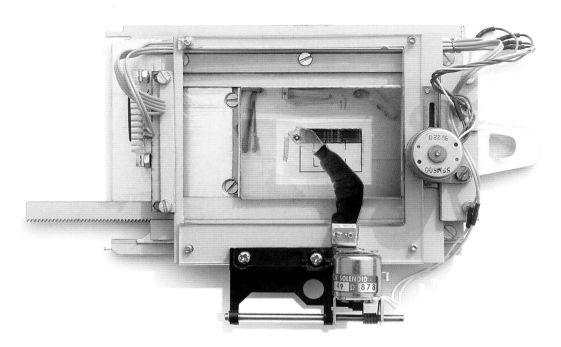

Demi-Pas [Half-Step]
2002
mechanical diapositives
Julien Maire
© Julien Maire

operation with minute mechanisms that don't render representations of illusion, but lay bare illusions. This subtle shift comes as a welcomed corrective to many so-called media archaeologists content to replay media rather than reinvent it.

Maire's *Demi-Pas* [Half-Step] transforms the image machine into a time machine by evoking both mechanical and physical movements. The adapted projector of his earlier work becomes a computer-assisted one in this work. The "stepper motors" and the "half steps" of human motion are linked as the projected images establish a dynamic relationship between image and movement, sensation and narrative. By layering image and performed interventions into the projected scenes, the images and operations differentiate themselves spatially with perceived realities weaving in and out of perceptibility. Maire's performances play in the interstices between machine and image and provoke a serious reconsideration of the "cinemaginary" interface.

Timothy Druckrey

Demi-Pas [Half-Step]
2002
screenshot
Julien Maire
© Julien Maire

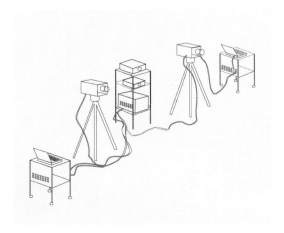

installation scheme
Julien Maire
© Julien Maire

projector installation
Julien Maire
© Julien Maire

installation view: Site Gallery, Sheffield
© Julien Maire

Zoe Beloff
The Influencing Machine of Miss Natalija A.

2001
interactive installation / mixed media, video, computer / dimensions variable

The installation is based on a case history by the psychoanalyst and early follower of Freud, Victor Tausk. In 1919, Natalija A., a former student of philosophy living in Vienna, came to Tausk complaining that a bizarre electrical apparatus, which she believed was being operated secretly by physicians in Berlin, was manipulating her thoughts. Therapy did not last long. After three sessions Natalija quit, saying that now Tausk too had fallen victim to the "diabolical apparatus," she could no longer trust him. Soon afterwards – in 1920 – he committed suicide.

My project was originally inspired by two quotes. The first is by Tausk: "Machines produced by man's ingenuity and created in the image of man are unconscious projections of man's bodily structure." The second is by the Nazi in charge of the nascent television industry in Germany, Eugen Hadamovsky, who declared in 1935, "Now in this hour, broadcasting is called upon to fulfil its biggest and most sacred mission, to plant the image of the Fuehrer indelibly in all German hearts." I imagined Natalija taking this quote completely literally.

The installation attempts to materialize Natalija's hallucinations for the viewer while at the same time alluding to the development of real influencing machines, in the form of radio and television in 1930s Germany, extending the definition of psychosis from the individual to society. It consists of a large stereoscopic diagram, placed on the floor and simulating the *Influencing Machine*. As the viewer probes this virtual machine with a pointer, moving images and sounds appear from within the apparatus.

Natalija was tortured by her imaginary machine. When someone struck it, she felt a corresponding blow to her body. Through interacting, the viewer finds themselves viscerally implicated, placed in the position of the sinister physicians/technicians (always male) whom she believed were probing her mind.

I "recreated" her hallucinations with fragments of German home-movies from the 1920s and '30s, subtly altered by medical and technical films. I imagined her on the receiving end of a paranoid sound spectrum that I simulated by sampling short-wave "Numbers Stations" believed to be coded intelligence messages, recordings of atmospheric and geomagnetic radio interference as well as popular German songs from the period. Caught in a lonely loop of hallucination, she imagined her machine's influence spiraling outward to control friends, family, suitors and doctor. The projection apparatus becomes a metaphor for her mental state.

Zoe Beloff

For a further description see http://www.zoebeloff.com/influencing

Wir schreiben das Jahr 1919.

Victor Tausk, ein Wiener Psychoanalytiker, untersucht eine
Patientin – Fräulein Natalija A.

Sie erzählt ihm, dass ihr Gehirn und ihr Körper von
einem sonderbaren elektrischen Apparat manipuliert werden,
der heimlich von Ärzten in Berlin gesteuert wird.

Bedienung der Beeinflussungsmaschine:

Setzen Sie sich auf den schwarzen Stuhl gegenüber dem Diagramm.
Setzen sie die rot-blaue Brille auf.

Erlauben Sie Ihren Augen, sich an den stereoskopischen Apparat,
der vor Ihnen erscheint, zu gewöhnen.

Um Natalijas Halluzinationen auszulösen, richten Sie bitte den Zeiger
auf eines der fünf Organe im Diagramm.

LOS ANGELES

*The Influencing Machine
of Miss Natalija A.*
2001
interactive installation
mixed media, video, computer
dimensions variable
installation view: ZKM |
Center for Art and Media
Karlsruhe, 2002
Zoe Beloff
© Zoe Beloff
photo © Franz Wamhof

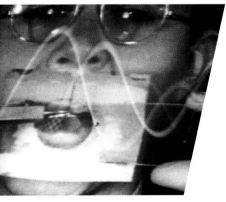

*The Influencing Machine
of Miss Natalija A.*
2001
video stills
© Zoe Beloff

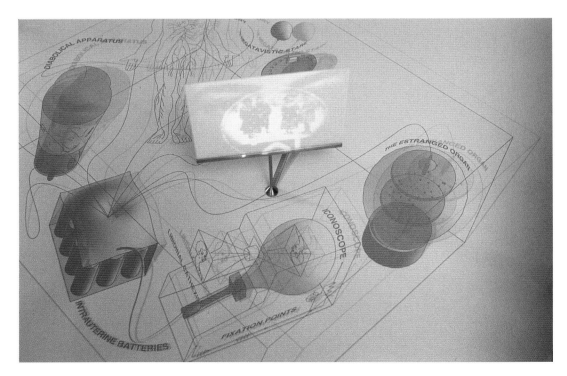

*The Influencing Machine
of Miss Natalija A.*
2001
detail
© Zoe Beloff
photo © Zoe Beloff

Tony Oursler
The Darkest Color Infinitely Amplified

2000
multimedia installation / dimensions variable

The camera obscura allowed painters and architects to reproduce landscapes and architectural scenes true to perspective and thus realistically. Originally in the form of a pinhole camera, later equipped with one or more lenses, with a mirror or prism, the camera obscura was modified considerably over the centuries. The first recorded use of this apparatus dates back to around 1430. Its heyday was the eighteenth century; then in the nineteenth century it was replaced by the technically superior photographic camera. The camera obscura is thus the precursor of modern reproduction technology.

Tony Oursler, whose art has developed in parallel with the technical achievements of his age, has recently made frequent use of the principle of the camera obscura. It is an integral component of his video installations *Optics* (1999) and *The Darkest Color Infinitely Amplified* (2000). Oursler employs a modern version of this historical apparatus – a three-dimensional imaging technology called High Definition Volumetric Display.

The observer of *The Darkest Color Infinitely Amplified* enters a darkened room. In front of one of the walls float two- and three-dimensional images that move slowly around the room apparently of their own volition – at least the mechanism that controls them is not evident. The images are magic, illusionary. Additional effects include rapid transformations or reverse actions. Film sequences are interpolated, showing a girl whose face becomes progressively more grotesque as make-up is applied to it. In the background can be seen abstract figures made up of fire and shadow. From time to time the figure of a devil appears, hanging upside down between the images. The constantly shifting collage of images creates an impression of confusion and alienation – the effect is both enchanting and hideous. The artist's recourse to the camera obscura is based on its erstwhile reputation as an instrument of the devil – just as today people often justify their mistrust of technological innovation and their inability to master it by referring to it as the devil's work, black magic, and the like. Oursler's installation alludes to the magical propensities of technology.

In his works Oursler examines not so much reality itself as its effect on us. In doing so, he locates himself on the narrow borderline between reality and fiction. He extrapolates reality from fiction by conducting experiments on the nature of perception.

Oursler's artistic principle consists in combining projection and image carrier as one. The image carrier can be either an abstract surface or fragment thereof, or else a three-dimensional object. When Oursler breathes life into outsized dolls by projecting moving facial gestures onto their otherwise featureless heads and making them speak (the concept that first brought him recognition) he liberates the video image from the TV screen – which in the final analysis means liberating it from its role as reproduction of reality. What emerges is the virtual image of an imaginary subject. Film is utilized simply as material consisting of color and movement. It becomes a part of the sculpture – and thus ultimately of reality. Oursler thus creates the possibility of the evocative interplay of different levels of reality.

One of his favorite motifs is the eye as the mirror of the soul, concentrating on that which the eye sees in the very moment that it is seen. His projections of faces humanize the object onto which the projected image falls. This process of animation functions no matter how abstract the object in question. These faces in motion, initially projected onto dummies, and then later onto smoke, water, trees, antennas and other surfaces, enter the real world. And yet they remain artificial figures, apparently animated by magic.

Oursler's art has always been dependent on the current state of technology. In the 1970s he utilized

his low-resolution Sony Video Porta-Pac camera, which was capable of taking only blurred black-and-white images, to interweave spatial levels and initiate a debate on the interface between imaginary, filmed and physical space. Soon afterwards, he was to conquer real space with his video images by projecting them with great precision onto a range of surfaces, and starting in the 1990s by personifying the video image. Acting people were projected onto cushions and their outlines dressed in jackets and trousers like scarecrows. The aesthetics of these figures contrasted impressively with the perfection of the technology employed. The dolls – individually, in groups, or as split personalities – unmasked the world of film as surrogate reality. Technology can cast spells but, as Oursler demonstrates, those who master technology can also break those spells.

These considerations led Oursler to explore the spirit world. The beginning of this exploration is marked by *Fantastic Players*, performed in 1992 on the roof of the Dia Center for the Arts in New York,

which he developed as a CD-ROM in 2000. In the latter, the activity of the user and the way in which the technical equipment influences the act of seeing are foregrounded equally. *The Influencing Machine* (2000) was Oursler's first work in a public space. In public locations in London and New York, he presented faces of people who believe in spirits, and of actors reading texts written by Oursler on the history of electronic data processing. This work is based on intensive research by Oursler into the question of how modern technology is used for occult purposes. He sees the incorporeal figures drifting through the room as existing simultaneously in reality and in the imagination. His works, says Oursler, are structured to function according to how we really see – which involves a very complicated system of relationships, full of memories, conjectures and stories that have been handed down through many generations.[1]

Dörte Zbikowski
Translated from the German by Steven Richards

1 Tony Oursler in a conversation with Stephen Vitiello and Constance DeJong conducted by Lynn Cooke, New York, 22 March 1998, in *Tony Oursler*, exhib. cat., Williams College Museum of Art, Williamstown, MA, 1999, p. 86.

Janet Cardiff
Playhouse

1997
video installation / color, sound / 381 x 152 x 244 cm

Suspense at The Playhouse

Sound of theater lobby; murmuring of people.
Sound of someone coming up to you.
Woman in audience: Hello, sorry I'm late. Let's go in.
Go through the middle of the curtains … through
the next set … and then sit down.

I look to the person next to me expecting to see the
woman that is directing me into the theater. But instead, I see just another museum visitor, like myself,
donning some headphones standing in front of a
miniature model of a baroque theater.

Sound of interior of theater, people murmuring as
before a concert.
On screen, opera singer comes out.
Woman (whispering to your right): She's going to
start.
Voice in audience (from other side): Shshsh.
Applause. Piano starts. Opera singer sings:
"Ach Ich Fühls."

So begins the script of Janet Cardiff's *Playhouse*
(1997), a collaborative installation with George Bures
Miller that was first exhibited at the Barbara Weiss
Gallery in Berlin. *Playhouse* – like the subsequent
works *The Muriel Lake Incident* (1999) and *The Par-*
adise Institute (2001) – combines sculpture, sound,
video and performance in a fusion that allows the
artists to experiment with traditional cinematic narratives, often successfully exposing our assumptions
about the boundaries of identity and location through
the blurring of our physical and psychological realities. Upon entering this "cinematic simulator"[1] complete with velvet red curtains, I am amazed how the
binaural recording or the surround-sound effect
emitted from my headphones instantly immerses me
into my own "bubble" of reality. The headphones render a once public experience into a private and intimate one.

Woman (to your right): I like this song a lot.

I want to answer but I see that the person to my right
is not talking. The voice that I hear belongs to a phantom guest.

Little bits of laughter, and when she finishes early a
lot of laughter, applause.
There is a sense of the listener not knowing why
people were laughing and why she seemed to ac-
cept and expect it.
When audience says "10," then piano starts, and
opera singer sings Puccini's "O Mio Bambino Caro."
Woman (to your right): This isn't the right song.
What's she doing?
Audience murmurs as if they know something's
wrong too.

Usually, in a theater setting where I expect a shared
collective experience with other viewers, I now find
myself in a precarious state where I cannot trust
whether or not the person next to me is also hearing
the same script through her headphones. I am torn
between the desire to ask other participants what
they are experiencing, and the feeling that I should
not disturb, interrupt or break their "bubble."

Historically, traditional cinema has relied upon
presenting seamless narratives, lulling audiences into
a space of passive escape where viewers can enter
comfortably, leaving behind real life for the life on
screen. In this process, we are safe as spectators invited to identify with characters in a fantasy world
given to us for a few hours to make our own. In the
dark room of the theater, we may "absent ourselves in
favor of the Eye and Spectator."[2] Perhaps we must
die a sort of death, becoming disembodied as one
might in the white cube of the modern gallery space.[3]
Cinema inherits the black walls of a theater, and the
flatness of the screen is taken for granted.

In *Playhouse*, Cardiff and Miller's use of binaural
sound is crucial to splitting open the flat space of the
screen. Through this recording technique, sound
extrudes out of the filmic space and has a volume,
architecture and location almost indistinguishable
from our real space. It situates us within a hyper-
reality where the script or story becomes dislocated
from the screen and aggresses towards the viewer.
Three-dimensional sound signals to us that the story
is simultaneously happening *there* on the screen and
here where we sit. We are then confronted with the
splitting of the narrative. Yet we experience not just
a splitting of the narrative, but a fracture of the self.
On the screen in the *Playhouse*, the opera singer continues to sing; however, we now cannot help seeing
her as she really is: a moving image projected onto a
stage. Meanwhile, physically next to us, another script
is being played out:

A woman (to your right): There's a suitcase under
your seat. It has everything you'll need … You have
to meet her backstage as soon as it's over … A car
will be waiting in the alley … It's up to you now.
Pause.
She knows there isn't much time. I'm leaving before
the police come… Remember to leave the headset
on the stand… I won't see you again… Good luck.
Sound of her getting up and leaving.

I am teased (by the most intimate whisper) to interact, but find that I cannot. I am not the person the
woman sees;[4] despite knowing this, I cannot help
imagining a phantom me completing the plot.

1   Janet Cardiff, quoting
    Georges Miller Bures, in an
    interview with Atom Egoyan
    in *BOMB Magazine*, no. 79,
    Spring 2002,
    http://www.bombsite.com/
    cardiff/cardiff4.html

2   Brian O'Doherty speaks of
    the Eye as that faculty
    trained in the conventions
    of seeing, and the Specta-
    tor as that disembodied self
    for which the Eye "stabilizes
    our missing sense of our-
    selves." (Brian O'Doherty,
    Inside the White Cube: The
    Ideology of the Gallery
    Space, Expanded Edition,
    University of California
    Press, Berkeley and London,
    1999, p. 55).

3   Brian O'Doherty, op. cit., pp.
    15, 55.

4   Lacan says in regards to the
    split between the eye and
    the gaze: "You never look at
    me from the place at which I
    see you." (Jacques Lacan,
    The Four Fundamental Con-
    cepts of Psychoanalysis,
    Penguin Books, New York,
    1977).

By requesting a physical response from us only to deny us this action, Cardiff and Miller make us acutely aware of our bodies. A moment of the uncanny is experienced by the viewer when the sight of a minia-ture model theater with a stage barely large enough to accommodate a handful of Barbie and Ken dolls conjoins with the "large-as-life" sound experience of being in a real theater: While attempting to reconcile two fictional locations we discover that we are suspended and trapped in the split.5 Thus, in the *Playhouse* we can no longer "make believe" in either space. It is fitting that the script of *Playhouse* belongs to the genre of mystery: the "suspense" created in the narrative mirrors the viewer's physical suspension of location and identity.

Singer finishes her song, walks backstage. Audience starts to clap and chant "More, more, bravo!" Singer comes for another bow … then leaves. As she does, sound of applause is interrupted.
Man's voice: When this theater is old and decrepit, roof leaking, rats scrounging in the rubble …you'll come back and sit in this box and remember her performance … and everything that went wrong that night …
With the curtains pulled back and the fantasy torn apart, I find reality. Because of this, I am able to locate myself in the real, yet it is a place where I am alone and left wondering what stories all of my impossible selves might have told. I take the headphones off, pausing in front of the Playhouse. After taking one last look at the stage, I exit and make room for the next visitor.

Applause continues again and then fades.

Leejone Wong

5 Inspired by concepts presented in the essay "Of the Gaze as objet petit a," in Lacan, op. cit.

Playhouse
1997
video installation
installation view: ZKM | Center for
Art and Media Karlsruhe, 2002
courtesy Sammlung Goetz, Munich
photo © Franz Wamhof

Max Dean
Mist

2002
three-screen DVD video projection / four DVDs, four DVD players, computer
controller, three projectors, audio equipment / approx. 228 x 914 cm

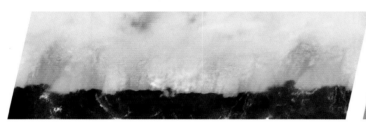

Max Dean
Mist
2002
three-screen
DVD video projection
screenshots
Max Dean
courtesy
Susan Hobbs Gallery, Toronto

Mist is a video projection on three screens, arranged
in a shallow horseshoe configuration that emulates
the physical shape of Niagara Falls. Two alternating
large motion views of the falling water cover all three
screens like a panorama. One view is a static shot of
the crest-line of the Falls, shot from a location
directly above the precipice from which the water
spills, tumbling onto the rocks below and generating
clouds of mist. The other is a frontal view taken at
right-angles to the Falls, so that the top and bottom
of the water-fall is cropped off and only a wall of
rushing water is displayed.

This second view provides a backdrop and context
for the integration of six short animated video
sequences. Each short video clip begins with a pair of
female hands entering the flow of water from the top
of the screen, then moving downward, caressing the
water seductively, and eventually grabbing it as if it
were a skirt. The hands then lift up this garment of
water to expose a pair of women's legs moving into
various poses. There are six performances, all non-
choreographed, and all carried out by a different

woman with no professional training. The individual
gestures and accoutrements vary, and the styles
range from matter-of-fact to steamily seductive.

At the end of each brief display, the hands suddenly release the aquatic skirt, permitting the water
to crash back down to the bottom, restoring a comparative sense of reality and continuity to the docu-
mentary-like depiction of the Falls. Then, as an inter-
lude before the second documentary shot starts
again, the overhead crest-line shot reappears, followed by the six female performances integrated into
the frontal portrait of the Falls.

The video sequences of each woman's legs are set
up to appear in random order, arousing anticipation
and perhaps even frustration in the viewer, since the
computer dictates that all six clips be played before
being shuffled in sequence and presented once again.
The viewer may have to watch one pair of legs doing
the same stint several times over, or have to impa-
tiently wait for the reappearance of a particularly
fancied pair of legs.

Max Dean and Kristan Horton
Be Me

2002
real-time video animation, interactive video installation / custom software, video
cameras, microphone, video projectors, electronic components, table, chair /
dimensions variable, approx. screen size 213 x 335 cm

 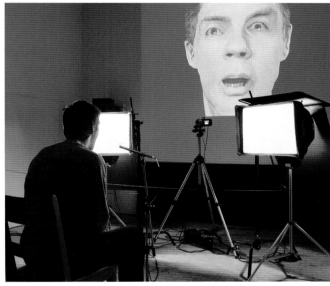

Be Me allows an engaged viewer to animate the facial expressions of a projected video image of my face (the artist's), permitting the viewer to speak for me as if I myself were speaking. My projected image not only has the capacity to mimic the facial expressions of the viewer, but the voice of this individual will also be heard and seen as coming from Max Dean's lips. The nature of the projected image will be dictated by the facial expressions and words of each and every viewer who chooses to participate.

As viewers enter the exhibition space, they will see a large projection (4–5 feet in height) of my face. The image will appear to be waiting, moving slowly, with eyes blinking normally as if alive. In the center of the room is a chair that faces the projected image. Located between the projected image and directed at the chair is a video camera, a microphone and two large photographic studio lamps. The viewer should have the sense of being in a video/photographic studio. Once a viewer sits in the chair, the projected image becomes attentive and says:

"So, do you want to be me?"
This is followed by the image proclaiming:
"Say something."
The viewer now has control over my facial features, which manifest his or her facial expression, and my lips are synchronized to the viewer's voice, be it male or female. Should the viewer choose to say something, my projected image will speak, replicating the facial expressions of the viewer, enabling someone else to appear to be me. In the process, the viewer is confronted with a reflection of his own facial and vocal mannerisms, but in an entirely new context.

Be Me represents my on-going effort to engage viewers in art galleries not only visually but also physically. I make works that extend the parameters of the visual-art experience by putting viewers in provocative situations of choice requiring them to decide whether or not to risk participating. I am intrigued by what people might do when offered the opportunity to manipulate the image of another person's face, but in the context of a momentary (and potentially embarrassing) public performance. My works frequently involve the dual nature of power, and in the process address issues of identity, trust and control. *Be Me* taps into a shared fantasy: We all want to simulate someone else without losing ourselves. But what happens if we wind up inadvertently facing ourselves?

Max Dean

Max Dean, Kristan Horton
Be Me
2002
real-time video animation,
interactive video installation
installation views: ZKM | Center
for Art and Media Karlsruhe,
2002
Max Dean, Kristan Horton
courtesy Susan Hobbs Gallery,
Toronto
photos © Franz Wamhof

Synthetic Characters Group, MIT Media Lab[1]
AlphaWolf

2001
interactive digital installation / 200 x 500 x 500 cm

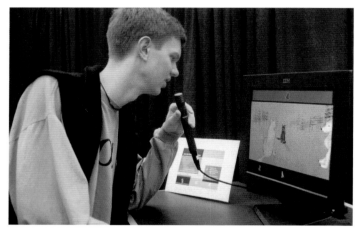

AlphaWolf
2001
interactive digital installation
Massachusetts Institute
of Technology
© Massachusetts Institute
of Technology
photo © Synthetic Characters
Group

1 Synthetic Characters
   Group, MIT Media Lab:
   Bill Tomlinson
   Marc Downie
   Matt Berlin
   Jesse Gray
   Adolph Wong
   Robert Burke
   Damian Isla
   Yuri Ivanov
   Michael P. Johnson
   Derek Lyons
   Jennie Cochran
   Bryan Yong
   Bruce Blumberg

AlphaWolf presents a synthetic wolf pack comprised of autonomous and semi-autonomous wolves who interact with each other much as real wolves do, forming dynamic social relationships based on their past experiences. People can interact with the pack as well. Each of several participants can affect the interactions of a wolf by howling, growling, whimpering or barking into a microphone. In addition, participants can use a mouse to encourage their wolves to interact with specific other members of the pack. By letting participants "get inside the mind and body" of a virtual wolf, *AlphaWolf* provides a compelling opportunity to explore the meaning of social behavior.

The research behind the *AlphaWolf* installation is informed by the biology and behavior of the gray wolf (Canis lupus). In their natural environment, real wolves form hierarchical social relationships within their packs, where certain individuals are dominant over other individuals. The virtual wolves in this installation form social relationships as well, interacting with each social partner in a way that reflects their history of previous interactions. Just as real wolves exhibit stereotypical dominance and submission behaviors to demonstrate and maintain their social relationships, the virtual wolves in the *AlphaWolf* installation express their relationships through their animated behaviors. The computational representations that

allow social learning in the virtual wolves demonstrate the intimate connections among social behavior, emotion and learning.

The AlphaWolf project represents the second year of a multi-year project by the Synthetic Characters Group at the MIT Media Lab under the direction of Bruce Blumberg. Through this project, we aim to develop autonomous animated characters whose behavioral complexity, expressiveness, and ability to learn rival those of a real dog or wolf. In addition to extending our previous work, *AlphaWolf* explores the computational representations that must be in place to enable social learning and the formation of context-specific emotional memories. As well as showcasing the virtual minds and bodies of the wolves themselves, the installation features a suite of supporting technology, including evocative real-time computer graphics, autonomous cinematography, and dynamic scoring and sound design.

The research that created *AlphaWolf* has potential applications in a variety of areas. Computational entities that can form social relationships with each other and with people represent an interesting contribution to the field of human-computer interface. Creating virtual creatures with social and emotional competence is central to the field of artificial intelligence. Simple computational models for the formation of social relationships may suggest new alternatives in the fields of animal behavior and computational biology. Finally, the entertainment industry, with its emphases on real-time interactivity (for example, computer games) and expressive characters (for example, movies), might find a range of uses for socially savvy computational creatures. The system that has created the wolves in *AlphaWolf*, with their social behavior and emotions, could be of use in creating interactive works with the dramatic power of traditional film.

Synthetic Characters Group, MIT Media Lab

AlphaWolf
2001
screenshots
© Massachusetts Institute
of Technology
photos © Synthetic Characters
Group

AlphaWolf
2001
interactive digital installation
200 x 500 x 500 cm
installation view: ZKM |
Center for Art and Media
Karlsruhe, 2002
Massachusetts Institute of
Technology
© Massachusetts Institute
of Technology
photo © Franz Wamhof

03

Philippe Codognet
Artificial Nature and Natural Artifice

The title of this essay is borrowed from Claudio Tolomei, a sixteenth-century Italian humanist from Siena, who used these words to describe the Mannerist gardens where natural vegetation was intermixed with human constructions and technological devices: not only interactive waterworks but also statues, grottos and "follies." This time was the heyday of the "double oxymoron," linguistic mirror of the stylistic boldness of the Mannerist painters.1 The oxymoron is today revived in the contemporary buzzword "Virtual-Reality."

Immersive work uses 3-D technology which compels the spectator to enter within the story instead of just watching it from the outside, as a mere series of photographs or a predefined movie. Artists have been experimenting with Virtual-Reality immersive art installations for about a decade now. They have been using visualization technologies such as the CAVE systems, an immersive system created by the EVL group at the University of Illinois in 1991, or Head Mounted Displays (HMDs) which were first created at NASA in 1984 following the original ideas of Ivan Sutherland (1968) and the forgotten pioneering work of Morton Heilig. It was Heilig who first proposed, in 1960, putting two small TV monitors in front of one's eyes.2 Following earlier experiments using projection screens and real-time computer-generated images in the late 1980s, artists such as Jeffrey Shaw, Ulrike Gabriel, Char Davies and Maurice Benayoun (to name just a few) took VR technologies in their hands in the 1990s to produce immersive artworks. But let us now briefly investigate the historical background of these apparatuses as a fruitful link between Art and Science, in particular the Renaissance.

I The Prehistory of VR

A remote ancestor of the CAVE is the *castellum umbrarum*, castle of shadows, designed by the Venetian engineer Giovanni Fontana in his manuscript *bellicorum instrumentum liber* (1420).3 This is a precise description and depiction of a room with walls made of folded translucent parchments lighted from behind, creating therefore an environment of moving images. Fontana also designed some kind of magic lantern to project on walls life-size images of devils or beasts. The use of projected images on walls was developed more than two centuries later by one of the major figures of baroque humanism, the Jesuit father Athanasius Kircher, "master of a thousand arts," in his book *Ars magna luce et umbrae* (1646).

The second historical background of virtual environments can be found in *trompe l'œil* frescoes in Venetian, Florentine or Roman villas in the Renaissance. For instance the "Perspective Room" by Baldassare Peruzzi in the Villa Farnesina (Rome, 1510), the "Giants Room" by Giulio Romano in the Palazzo Te (Mantua, 1530–1532) or the frescoes of the Villa Barbaro by Paolo Veronese (near Treviso, 1561). In the

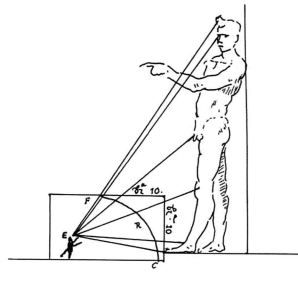

Martin Kemp
drawing after
Leonardo da Vinci,
codex urbinas, 139r
in Martin Kemp, *The science of
Art. Optical themes in Western
Art from Brunelleschi to Seurat*,
Yale University Press, 1990
© Martin Kemp

Perspective Room, false windows open on a fictitious painted landscape, creating a vertex of perspectivist/illusionist virtuosity. Leonardo himself also worked on such pictorial schemes.4 One of his codex contains a drawing describing how to craftily project a painting onto a cubic volume in order to recreate a non-distorted image – a device put to use much later in electronic fashion in the CAVE immersive 3-D system.

One should nevertheless distinguish between the two apparatuses mentioned here, the CAVE and the HMD, as they seem to be used for different purposes in immersive artworks. CAVE-like environments are used to represent virtual (but Euclidean) spaces (for example, *Place – a user's manual* by Jeffrey Shaw), whereas works using HMDs are more oriented towards abstraction (for example, Ulrike Gabriel's *Perceptual Arena*). With the HMD, the viewer is totally cut from the real world and immersed within the fictitious space that is projected on two small monitors in front of the eyes. This device became the allegorical emblem of virtual reality, the symbol of high-tech art for the general public. The idea is that the viewer is immersed *within himself*, recalling thus the Leibnizian concept of the monad, is certainly not alien to the success of the HMD as an icon of VR. Gilles Deleuze, in his study of Gottfried Wilhelm Leibniz,5 considered the image of a closed room, without any windows, to

1 See Antonio Pinelli, *La Bella maniera*, Einaudi, Torino, 1993. French translation: LGF, Paris, 1996.

2 He even got a US patent on this device.

3 Samuel Y. Edgerton, *The heritage of Giotto's geometry, art and science on the eve of the scientific revolution*, Cornell University Press, Uthaca, 1991.

4 M. Kemp, *The Science of Art: optical themes in western art from Brunelleschi to Seurat*, Yale University Press, New Haven, 1990, in particular the drawing on p. 50.

5 Gilles Deleuze, *Le pli, Leibniz et le baroque*, Les Éditions de Minuit, Paris, 1988.

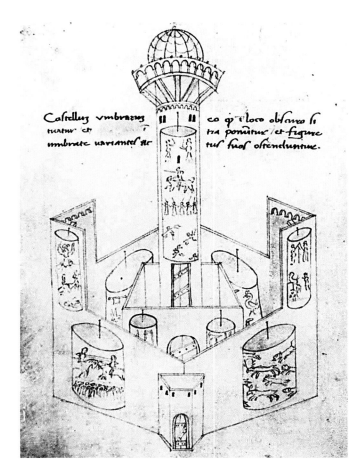

Giovanni Fontana
Castellum umbrarum
drawing, fol. 67v
in Giovanni Fontana, *Bellicorum
instrumentum liber, com figuris
et fictitys litoris conscriptus*,
manuscript, 1420
courtesy Bayerische Staats-
bibliothek, Munich

Giovanni Fontana
Apparentia nocturna
drawing, fol. 70r
in Giovanni Fontana, *Bellicorum
instrumentum liber, com figuris
et fictitys litoris conscriptus*,
manuscript, 1420
courtesy Bayerische Staats-
bibliothek, Munich

be the best visualization of the Leibnizian concept of the monad (see *Monadology*, 1714). A monad is an entity, a soul "without doors nor windows" containing the whole world "folded" within itself, representing thus "a subject as metaphysical point," to use Deleuze's own words. In a similar manner, the Renaissance studiolo contains the whole world (metaphorically) painted on its walls.

Is therefore the use of different VR devices pointing out a deep philosophical dichotomy between a perspectivist outside space and an inner abstract self?

II The Spectator's Point of View
An important characteristic of virtual environments is the possibility for the spectator to interactively move within such spaces and perceive the virtual world as through a subjective camera. This moving, first-person perspective is for some artists a rejoinder to critics who detect in their work elements of a modern perspectivism and "realism." An important point to note here is that we are changing from the cartographic to the *ichnographic* paradigm.[6] The idea of the "cartographic eye in art" appeared recently to reconsider modern art in the twentieth century.[7] This concept is especially relevant for late and post-modernism in America (Jasper Johns, Robert Morris, Robert Smithson). But with virtual worlds we are

moving away from the metaphor of the map to that of the path, from the third-person point of view ("God's eye") to the first-person point of view. As Morpheus said to Neo in the blockbuster movie *The Matrix* (1999), "There is a difference between knowing the path and walking the path." We are thus leaving, in the virtual *experience* and exploration of an unknown artificial world, the Cartesian paradigm of the Euclidean, homogeneous and objective space in which points could be described in an allocentric manner by triple (x, y, z) co-ordinates for a new paradigm of a more constructive, egocentric, and indeed subjective space. This is somehow backtracking to the ideas of the French mathematician Henri Poincaré, founder of modern topology, who considered that a point in space should be described by the transformation that has to be applied to reach it. Hence space is represented as a set of situated actions. No one knows the totality of the map; no one can picture or order the territory in any comprehensive way, even abstractly. The complexity of the structure ("graph" to follow the word of Michel Serres, "rhizome" for Deleuze, or "network" in the contemporary terminology) cannot be conceptually apprehended nor depicted. It is worth noticing that, by moving from a 2-D to a 3-D model, some information is in some way lost. Lost first, because there is never a comprehensive, full-blown representation – such as in the map.

6 That is, based on the notion of *path*.

7 See Christine Buci-Glucksmann, *L'œil cartographique de l'art*, Galilée, 1996, and *Mapping*, exhib. cat., Museum of Modern Art, New York, 1994.

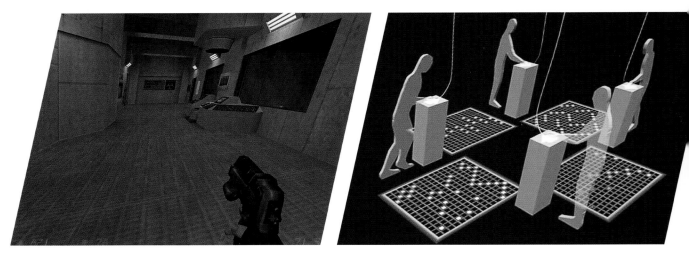

Half Life
1998
video game, PC version
screenshot
© Valve Software/Sienna

Toshio Iwai
Resonance of 4
1994
interactive audio-visual
installation
four computers
and video projectors,
custom-made software
400 x 400 cm
general scheme of
the installation
© Toshio Iwai

Secondly, 3-D implies hidden surfaces, that is, a *"part maudite"* (Bataille) – the devil's part – which will always be unknown. There is never light without shadows nor life without death; as in the Baroque world.

This *paradigm shift* also appears in the works of some contemporary video artists such as Pipilotti Rist (such as *Pickelporno,* 1995, or *Ever is Over All,* Venice Biennial, 1997).

Another domain showing the same paradigm shift is that of video games.8 The subjective camera also revolutionized the world of computer games a few years ago with DOOM (PC CD-ROM, 1994).9 Although the game was incredibly simple (hunt-and-kill) and the computer graphics quite poor, the immersive effect was fully operational – even too much so for some people. The user/spectator was completely involved mentally, not to say physically, within the Virtual Environment. However, recent developments in blockbuster games like the Tomb Raider series suggest that the gaming industry is moving one step back from subjectivity. In Tomb Raider the player is behind a camera that follows the heroine (cyber star Lara Croft) – as in a cartoon. He is not playing himself.10 Similar third-person, TV-like, camera controls are also hardwired into systems such as Sony's Playstation or Nintendo 64 console.11 Considering the history of cinema, one has to admit that the subjective camera device has been used very scarcely since the 1940s, and was never well received by the general public. Indeed, the most celebrated film in this genre, Robert Montgomery's *Lady in the Lake* (1947), is, in fact, the only one to have entered cinema anthologies.12 Let us hope that the use of the first-person point of view in VR artwork will have a better fate. But perhaps we are bound, in today's societies of the hegemonic spectacle, to what Jean Baudrillard has called (more than thirty years ago)13 the myth of the consumed vertigo ("Mythe du vertige consommé"). That is to say, the allure of the second-hand experience.

Nevertheless, if a moving viewpoint might be richer than a classical one-point perspective viewpoint, we should not forget the importance of simultaneous viewpoints or privileged viewpoints. For Leibniz, if there are multiple ways of perceiving reality (as in the multiple perspective views of a city) corresponding to different "truths," there is always a particular point of view from which to best understand the whole. For instance, in geometry there is the apex of the cone from which all the conic curves are intelligible. This idea of a specific viewpoint is also at work in Baroque perspective art, such as in the famous ceiling frescoes by Andrea Pozzo in the Church of Sant'Ignazio in Rome (1691–1694). This magnificent painting was designed to be viewed from a particular point inscribed on the floor of the church. In other positions the illusionist effects depicted tumble into incoherent strands and seem close to collapse. Some authors have proposed a detailed analysis showing why this perceptually differs from classical perspective paintings on canvas.14 But what is important here again is the presence of a precise point where everything is in order and makes sense. This point is where the illusion is perfect, and might be the point where one understands the lure of representation and maybe the fragility of reality. In contemporary art, artists to some extent use simultaneous, fragmented, and multiple viewpoints to show the complexity of their discourse. An immediate example of this is Joseph Kosuth's well-known work *one and three hammers* (1965), which shows a hammer, a photograph of the same hammer, and a dictionary definition of a hammer. The simultaneous viewpoints of objects might be contradictory – all the better to ask the spectator about the "reality" of the depicted object. Another classical example is René Magritte's famous *Ceci n'est pas une pipe* (1926).

That approach, however, forgets that immersion is cognitive before being perceptive. The "reality" of immersive work is distinctly invented and recreated by the viewer – and not just perceived and undergone.

8 On Art and Video Games, see Philippe Codognet, "Nijikon Fetchi," in *Catalogue de la Biennale de Lyon,* exhib. cat., Réunion des Musées Nationaux, 2001.

9 Although we should not forget the fabulous arcade game Battlezone, back in 1980.

10 Interestingly, this demands a schizophrenic choice: one has to choose at the beginning of the game if sound is to be calculated from the gamer's point of view or from Lara's …

11 This point has been developed by Lev Manovich in *Proceedings of the Imagina Conference,* Monte Carlo, 1998, and in *The Language of New Media,* The MIT Press, Cambridge, MA, 2001.

12 In experimental cinema, one should also mention the great Constructivist film *Man with a Movie Camera* (1929) by Russian director Dziga Vertov (Denis Arkadievitch Kaufman, 1896–1954).

13 Jean Baudrillard, *La Société de Consommation: ses mythes, ses structures,* S.G.P.P., Paris, 1970.

14 See Michael Kubovy, *The Psychology of Perspective and Renaissance art,* Cambridge University Press, Cambridge, MA, 1986.

III Emergent Artworks

In the past few years a growing number of artists have been interested in Artificial Life and the idea of "art as a living form,"[15] that is, the artist as some demiurge who sets up a world where artificial creatures interact with each other and with the spectators. Thus the basic task of the artist is to set up a playground with a coherent set of rules – the resulting artwork being indeterminate and evolutive, dynamic rather than static, always in progress and never finished. Following the pioneering works of Karl Sims in computer graphics (1994), Artificial Intelligence techniques such as genetic algorithms have therefore been used in an attempt to introduce evolutionary processes into artworks. Current endeavors, both theoretical and technological, aim at applying those issues to interactive storytelling or video games, and in creating virtual worlds where a coherent story would emerge from the interaction of autonomous characters and a few human-controlled avatars. Here characters will evolve, a story will emerge, and new narrative feelings will be experimented with.

There is indeed the hidden hope that new interesting features can appear through some possibly random and small changes in the basic vocabulary of the artificial world,[16] in the combinatorial process of exploring the huge (although not infinite) meta-universe of variations in story lines that can be composed by assembling small, predefined bits in every feasible arrangement. Interestingly, the fascination of combinatorics as a source of invention has been a cornerstone of both the philosophical and scientific work of Leibniz. The idea of performing within a given symbol system operations on symbolic objects in a purely syntactical manner without reference to their usual meaning or *modus operandi* (for instance because their meaning is unknown) was proposed by Leibniz and considered by him to be an important source for scientific discovery. This activity was dubbed *cogitatio coeca* ("blind thought"). Leibniz uses this paradigm in mathematics where combinatorial systems are treated as *ars inventendi*, and for laying the grounds of modern semiotic systems. But the roots of these concepts have to be dug out further back in the groundbreaking work of the Franciscan monk Ramon Llull in the thirteenth century. Llull was the first to consider a real combinatorial system – one which he envisioned as a universal language capable of producing all the "truths" found in the universe.

But most of the time the exhaustive exploration of combinatorial structures is impossible (because the different possibilities are just too numerous) and search has to be approximated by using randomness. So, this means randomness as an artistic principle of invention? Why not? Marcel Duchamp, for instance, used chance as a major source of creation in order to refrain from intentional choice, as in *3 stoppages-étalon* (1913-1914) or in the choice of other ready-mades. Randomness can indeed create some lure of complexity and, as Rodney Brooks would say, "intelligence is in the eye of the beholder."[17] Or, as Marcel Duchamp put it, "Ce sont les regardeurs qui font l'oeuvre" (the viewers make the artwork).

But if this strategy is effective for conceptual art, it could hardly be applied *per se* for creating narrative or complex interactive virtual worlds, which require a careful tuning of structural rules and evolutionary strategies in order to enable the spectator to enjoy some non-trivial experiences. In most examples of "interactive art," there is only a limited and predefined dialog between the spectator and the artwork. Could we have new modalities of interaction? Could we go beyond (or below) the mediation of language or of simple gestures? Music, and intuitive game-rules, are simple examples of more complex activities where spectators/users may have a rich and fruitful interaction with artificial autonomous creatures. Perhaps this could be the next step, but it is not easy to achieve.

An example of complex interaction, not with synthetic agents but within the spectators themselves, is the installation *Resonance of 4* by Toshio Iwai (1994), where the key issue is the dynamics that can be created among spectators/users by using a simple interactive scheme such as music. The essential meaning of the artwork is thus an emergent behavior. We therefore have to find new models and new concepts for thinking this about complex self-organization – one with emergent properties and autopoiesis (see the work of the late Francisco Varela[18]). Precisely, one key idea is the contingency of cognition: "living systems are cognitive systems, and living as a process is a process of cognition."[19] Varela proposed the concept of *enaction* as a further step after the notion of emergence. In the enactive paradigm, the subject is always conceived as situated and interacting with his environment, and cognition is thus inseparable from the experience of the world. Cognition is conceived as an embodied action. We should also remember, in the same line of thought, the words of the cybernetician Heinz von Foerster, one of the theoreticians who influenced the school of Constructivist psychology: "If you desire to see, learn how to act."[20] For him, "perceiving is making" and all perception is therefore created by the subject's action upon his environment; perception is active. Experiments have shown that sensory organs (in animals and humans) can be trained to better perceive expected signals before the brain considers them. Therefore, by analogy, it would not be unreasonable to think that a key issue in understanding experiences in virtual worlds would be the ability to perform actions and observe their consequences in order to learn the rules governing the artificial environment – maybe simply by trial and error. This is obviously easier to do in a virtual world than in the real one, and this cognitive process is therefore put to use in many computer games and now intuitively performed by video-game-educated kids. It might be possible that this ability to develop cognition by action is indeed gradually replacing the more classical humanist tradition of learning by books and letters ...

Revised version of the essay "Nature Artificielle et Artifice Naturel," first published in French in *L'art à l'âge du virtuel*, C. Buci-Glucksmann (ed.), L'Harmattan, Paris, 2003.

15 See *Art@Science*, Christa Sommerer and Laurent Mignonneau (eds), Springer-Verlag, Vienna, 1998.

16 Changes such as mutations in the synthetic DNA of some virtual creature, as in Karl Sims' works or in the *Evolva* computer game, 2000.

17 Rodney Brooks (researcher at MIT) is a pioneer of so-called reactive robotics, a major paradigm shift in AI in the mid-1980s.

18 See for instance Humberto Maturana and Francisco Varela, *Autopoiesis and Cognition: The realisation of the living*, Reidel, Dordrecht, 1980, and Francisco Varela, Evan Thompson, and Eleanor Rosch, *The Embodied Mind: Cognitive science and human experience*, The MIT Press, Cambridge, MA, 1991.

19 Maturana and Varela, *op. cit.*, p. 13.

20 Heinz von Foerster, *Observing Systems*, Intersystems Publications, Salinas, Calif., 1984.

Erkki Huhtamo
Media Art in the Third Dimension:
Stereoscopic Imaging and Contemporary Art

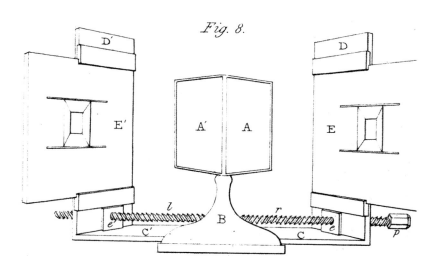

Charles Wheatstone's reflecting stereoscope. in Charles Wheatstone, "Contributions to the physiology of vision," *Philosophical Transactions of the Royal Society*, vol. 128, London, 1838

1 Jim Pomeroy

2 *Bar Code Hotel* was produced at the Banff Centre for the Arts in Canada as part of the "Art and Virtual Environments" project investigating the artistic possibilities of virtual reality technology. See *Immersed in Technology. Art and Virtual Environments*, Mary Anne Moser with Douglas McLeod (eds), The MIT Press, Cambridge, Mass., 1996, pp. 287–290. *Bar Code Hotel* has also been shown as a reduced monoscopic version without stereoscopic projection.

3 In this article I will use the notion "3-D" for the use of stereoscopy both in still and moving images. I will not participate in the discussion whether 3-D images in motion should actually be classified as 4-D images.

4 Hoberman has used 3-D in different forms frequently, in works like *Dead Space / Living Rooms* (1985) and *Excess Package* (1992), *SMALLER THAN LIFE (Bigger Than The Both Of Us)* (1983) and *OUT OF THE PICTURE (Return of the Invisible Man)* (1983). 3-D images were also used in the performances *Return to Sender* (1985, collaboration with Bill Obrecht), *Revenge of Debris* (1988) and *Interstate* (1991), which associated a 3-D projection with a functioning robot on the stage. See *Unexpected Obstacles:–The Work of Perry Hoberman 1982–1997*, Erkki Huhtamo (ed.), OTSO Gallery and ZKM Karlsruhe, Espoo, 1997. In his most recent exhibition (Postmasters Gallery, New York, February 2003), Hoberman showed several 3-D projects: "A series of multi-layered stereoscopic curtains consist of transparent mylar surfaces covered with enigmatic red/blue silhouettes. In a more high-tech vein, a parallel screen-based work is shown on a Stereo-Graphics Synthagram monitor, a recently-invented autostereoscopic display" (from the press release).

5 About the popular uses of stereoscopy, see *Fantastic 3-D. A STARLOG Photo Guidebook*, David Hutchinson (ed.), New York: Starlog Press, 1982; Hal Morgan and Dan Symmes: *Amazing 3-D*, Little, Brown and Co., Boston & Toronto, 1982; *3-D-Film*, Peter A. Hagemann (ed.), Verlag Monika Nüchtern, Munich, 1980.

"Seeing isn't believing – believing IS seeing" [1]

One of the things that made Perry Hoberman's interactive installation *Bar Code Hotel* (1994) memorable was its use of stereoscopy, or 3-D.[2] Wearing pairs of 3-D glasses and using "wands" to swipe barcodes attached to tables and small cardboard cubes, a group of users collectively manipulated an eclectic array of virtual objects, causing them to tremble or bounce wildly from the walls of a projected room, seemingly extending deep into the wall. In its playful use of the spatial illusion, the work unleashed chains of associations in the participant's mind. Of course, it could be read as a commentary on the virtual reality craze. According to the technocultural master narrative of the early 1990s, virtual reality represented a cultural and perhaps even an ontological break, announcing an era when bodies become obsolete and minds are freed to wander immersed into the immaterial realms of cyberspace. Hoberman's tongue-in-cheek interpretation of this dictum may have defied normal physics, but it was deliberately chaotic, absurd and restricted – a cyberspace with walls! While it was "powered" by highly sophisticated technology, it dispensed with head-mounted displays and data-gloves, the hallmarks of VR. Plastic polarizing glasses like those used at theme parks, and barcode readers familiar to any supermarket clerk were used as vehicles to enter the third (or the fourth?) dimension.[3]

For Hoberman, *Bar Code Hotel* was not an isolated experiment: 3-D has haunted his entire career as a media artist.[4] While evoking the present, and perhaps the future, 3-D also harks back to the past, to the "low" cultural presence of the "amazing" and "fantastic" 3-D, as manifested in 3-D movies, 3-D comic books, the ubiquitous View-Master viewers and lenticular postcards.[5] In these and many other forms – including the "Magic Eye" random dot stereograms in the early 1990s – 3-D images have attained a peculiar role in postmodern culture. They are ephemeral, and yet somehow an essential element of the cultural imaginary. The spatial illusion they provide is so artificial that no-one would mistake them for "the real thing." But still, 3-D images can make viewers gasp with astonishment. Projected on an IMAX 3-D cinema screen, they have the power to induce audiences to suspend their disbelief, making them scream and trying to grasp phantoms hovering in the air. The world of 3-D is also a "gadget space." A major part of its fascination lies in the apparatus and the techniques needed to create the illusion. For the 3-D enthusiast, the cheap look of the anaglyphic cardboard glasses with their red and blue filters may be as important an part of the experience as the "eye poking" illusions they deliver. Wondering and making guesses about the "trick" behind the 3-D images is common, whether it

Stereoscomania
A selection of 3-D publications
from the early 1990s.
collection Erkki Huhtamo
photo © Erkki Huhtamo

has to do with operating principles of the stereo-scope or the hidden layers of a computer-generated random dot stereogram, perceivable only with eyes trained to "free-viewing."

In its assigned role as pure spectacle with apparently no use value, 3-D has become the epitome of various trends in contemporary culture. It is often seen as a typical fad that comes and goes, always returning in a slightly modified guise, different enough to mark it as a novelty. As commercially marketed optical illusions, 3-D images may even evoke the phantasmagoric foundations of the post-industrial information society. They may also (im)materialize the need to escape momentarily from the world of reason, profit and social control into a childlike involvement with appearances. The realm of 3-D is that of play, leisure, day-dreaming, legerdemain. This makes one wonder why stereoscopy has played such a minimal role in the evolution of video games. Stereoscopic consoles, like Nintendo's Virtual Boy, have remained mere curiosities. This may have something to do with the way 3-D has been conceived as "surplus value" to other means of expression. In the early 1950s, 3-D movies were marketed as a gimmick that added a new dimension to an already established form of entertainment. It was not allowed to radically question filmic structures or the organization of the commercial cinema as a spectacle. Its impact remained ephemeral. As the long-lasting success of View-Master demonstrates, 3-D is most effective when it is used as the organizing principle of the medium,

without being subordinated to the narrative logic of a movie or to interactive game-play.[6] For the gamer, immersing oneself psychologically into the labyrinth of Quake (realized with 3-D computer graphics, not with stereoscopic 3-D, which is a significant difference) is enough. Although a recurring part of the myth of VR, the addition of stereoscopic imagery would be superfluous.

Yet, such an account of stereoscopy is one-sided (or, rather, one-eyed). Ever since it was scientifically demonstrated in the early nineteenth century, stereoscopy has occupied multiple cultural spaces, many of which have to do with things the popular idea about 3-D tends to reject: analysis, reason, power, control.[7] Charles Wheatstone's original mirror stereoscope (1830s) was a scientific instrument, conceived to demonstrate the disparity between the external stimuli entering the eyes and their interpretation by the human body.[8] Its anti-illusionistic nature was inscribed into the very structure of the apparatus. Although the stereoscope was soon turned into a commodity in simplified and purportedly more immersive forms, the analytic use of the stereoscope persisted in science and medicine. Both in homes and educational institutions, the stereoscope became an ideological instrument for the symbolic domination of the world, subordinating the globe to the Western spectator's gaze. It was even put to military use, serving among other things as a tool for aerial reconnaissance. During World War II, even the "innocent" View-Master discs were used to identify enemy

6 View-Master discs are often organized according to known popular-cultural narratives, but here the narrative is subordinated to the desire to view and scrutinize things in 3-D. This may be a partial explanation to the enormous popularity of stereoscopy in the Victorian era. Although presenting photographic views, seeing these in 3-D with a dedicated instrument, the stereoscope, was considered something special.

7 An excellent overview of the many different stereoscopic methods and their uses is given in Paris in 3-D: From stereoscopy to virtual reality 1850–2000, Françoise Reynaud, Catherine Tambrun and Kim Timby (eds), Paris Musées and Booth-Clibborn Editions, Paris and London, 2000.

8 About the stereoscope as a scientific instrument, see Thomas L. Hankins, "The Giant Eyes of Science: The Stereoscope and Photographic Depiction in the Nineteenth Century," in Thomas L. Hankins and Robert J. Silverman, Instruments and the Imagination, Princeton University Press, Princeton, NJ, 1995, pp. 148–177. The structure of Wheatstone's stereoscope was open. The two (hand-drawn) images needed for the stereoscopic effect were placed wide apart to the sides and viewed from a pair of angled mirrors in the center of the apparatus.

Oskar Fischinger
Circles in Circle
1949
stereo painting
oil on masonite
two panels, c. 30 x 30 cm
The Fischinger Archive
courtesy Jack Rutberg Fine
Arts, Los Angeles

9   See John Dennis, "View-Master Then and Now," in *Stereo World*, March-April 1984 (special issue devoted to the history of the View-Master).

10 See "A Report on the Art and Technology Program of the Los Angeles County Museum of Art 1967–1971," Maurice Tuchman (ed.), Los Angeles County Museum of Art, Los Angeles, 1971, pp. 330–337. Predictably, more recent "neo-pop" artists like Mariko Mori have also used 3-D projection in their installations. Warhol also gave his name to the publicity for a 3-D film by Paul Morrissey (*Andy Warhol's Frankenstein 3D*), 1974.

11 See William Moritz, "La romance du l'animation abstraite en relief," in *Le relief au cinéma* (Numéro hors série, 1895), l'Association francaise de recherche sur l'histoire du cinéma, Paris, 1997, pp. 134–140.

12 See Margaret Benyon, "Holography as an Art Medium," in *Kinetic Art: Theory and Practice. Selections from the Journal Leonardo*, Frank Malina (ed.), Dover, New York, 1974, pp. 185–192.

13 I am referring to Jacobs' *The Nervous System* film performance series, see Ken Jacobs, "Le Nervous System Film Performance," in *Le relief au cinéma*, op. cit., pp. 141–146. About Pomeroy's 3-D performances, such as *Composition in Deep/Light at the Opera* (1981), see Paul DeMarinis, "The Boy Mechanic – Mechanical Personae in the Works of Jim Pomeroy," in *For A Burning World Is Come To Dance Inane. Essays By and About Jim Pomeroy*, Timothy Druckrey and Nadine Lemmon (eds), Critical Press, Brooklyn, NY, 1993, pp. 9–10. Beloff's performances with projected 3-D slides and film include *Lost* and *Claire and Don in Slumberland*. Beloff has also directed a 16mm 3-D film titled *Shadow Land or Light from the Other Side*. See http://www.zoebeloff.com

14 *The Anaglyphic Chimney* was inspired by H. Vuibert's famous book *Les anaglyphes geometriques*. See Linda Dalrymple Henderson, *Duchamp in context: Science and technology in The Large Glass and related works*, Princeton University Press, Princeton, NJ, 1998.

warships and to train US fighter pilots in target practice.[9] Holography, a twentieth-century form of 3-D imaging, has become a key security device in bank notes and credit cards, stabilizing and perpetuating the social and economic order. The seemingly innocent "magic eyes" of the stereoscope are also panoptic eyes. Predictably, the discourse on virtual reality reflects similar issues. Developed for and by the military, its relationship to fantasies about free flight through cyberspace remains problematic.

From Ontology to Ideology: Disturbing the 3-D Illusion
Although the corpus of artworks that have directly dealt with stereoscopy is not very large (perhaps reflecting 3-D's "central-peripheral" status), it covers various means of expression from paintings, collages and prints to photography, experimental films and videos, kinetic objects, multimedia performances and virtual-reality installations. Artists have interpreted the possibilities of 3-D for various goals. The stereoscopic paintings by Dalí and Magritte extended the spatial explorations of the surrealists, resorting to a "low" cultural phenomenon from outside the canons of art. Andy Warhol's 3-D shower curtains dotted with flowers were an apt expression of the pop sensibility.[10] The 3-D films by Oskar Fishinger (who also created Stereo Paintings), Dwinell Grant, Hy Hirsh, Harry Smith and others were less occupied with creating homogeneous 3-D spaces than adding a dynamic dimension of depth to abstract colors, shapes and motion tropes.[11] The kinetic artists of the 1950s and '60s, although rarely resorting to stereoscopy proper, explored the illusion of depth in their works, often combining it with actual or virtual motion. Many alternative ways of creating the impression of depth were explored by artists and engineers trying to bridge the gap between art and science. Some

artists, like Margaret Benyon, were led from stereoscopic paintings to the new medium of holography.[12] Multimedia artists like Ken Jacobs, Jim Pomeroy and Zoe Beloff have created performances in which the projection of films, stereoscopic slides or even just "3-D shadows" of objects manipulated in front of red and green lights have played a central role.[13]

It is not possible to present here a complete history of 3-D in media art. I will concentrate on a few cases in which the exploration of stereoscopy has lead to a critical investigation of the assumed ontology and the cultural uses of three-dimensional imaging, also highlighting the roles of the apparatus and the observer. A key figure is Marcel Duchamp, for whom 3-D was a career-long concern, running from his "rectified readymade" *Handmade Stereopticon Slide* (*Hand Stereoscopy*, 1918–19) through his Precision Optics "project" to his very last work *The Anaglyphic Chimney* (1968).[14] The first-mentioned work consisted of an unremarkable stereocard, bought in Buenos Aires, depicting an open sea. Over its pair of images Duchamp drew with pencil geometrical rhomboid forms. Observed with the stereoscope, the drawings merge to form a three-dimensional shape that "floats" in the visual field, while the original poorly made stereoview remains flat and indistinct (a feature that must have amused Duchamp). Although this small work can be seen "merely" as a study for Duchamp's chef d'oeuvre *The Large Glass*, it can also be related to the fates of stereoscopy. From its original role as a scientific demonstration instrument the stereoscope had been turned into a commodity, presenting optical illusions to uncritical viewers. Duchamp reversed this trajectory. His hand-drawn figure evokes the drawings with which Wheatstone originally demonstrated the stereoscopic effect (before photography even was available). In Duchamp's

Jim Pomeroy
*Stereo Views /
VER Multidimensionales*,
Light Work, New York, 1988
collection Erkki Huhtamo
photo © Erkki Huhtamo

A boxed set of three View-Master reels and a viewer.

rectified readymade the mass-marketed illusionism (represented by the found stereocard) is "flattened" and relegated to the background, making way for the reappearance of Wheatstone's rhomboid ghost. This aligns the work with the modernist critique of representation: Belonging to different visual orders, the "layers" remain distinct. The stereocard is marked off as artifice.

Duchamp's way of making an intervention into the visual field of the stereocard and subverting its culturally conditioned "ontology" has found echoes in the creations of artists like Esther Parada, Manual (Hill/Bloom) and Jim Pomeroy, also working amidst an apparent rupture in the visual regime. The explorations of stereoscopy by these artists were informed by the debate on postmodernism and the ontological crisis caused by the advent of digital photography. Stereoscopy was identified as an ambiguous site, simultaneously artificial and illusionistic. In *Malevich in America* (1991), Manual superimposed a cross, consisting of a blue and a red bar, over a monochrome stereoscopic photograph of a forest.[15] While the view of the forest remains stereoscopic, the cross, a reference to the work of Malevich, stays flat. Echoing the work by Duchamp, two visual orders are superimposed. The result is highly ambiguous; the colors of the cross seem to refer to (anaglyphic) stereoscopy, but what meanings, if any, does the flatness of the cross bear? Malevich's Suprematist compositions were, after all, abstract renditions of space. Why does a reference to archetypal modernism obstruct the stereoscopic field of vision? Certainly not as a simple negation, a frontal attack on illusionism. For Manual, 2-D and 3-D are not compatible, but not fully incompatible either; both are elements of a fabricated and heterogeneous composite space that could potentially be manipulated at will.

In Esther Parada's *At the Margin* (1991–92), a sequence of digital photographs, the starting point is a Keystone stereocard titled "Statue of Columbus, Ciudad Trujillo, The Dominican Republic" from 1939.[16] For Parada, this card represents imperialism and racism, augmented by the fact that such cards were mostly meant for the eyes of European and North American viewers. Parada subverts the ideology inherent in the card by manipulating its elements digitally. In the last panel of the sequence, another (non-stereoscopic) image, depicting two young Cuban pioneer women, has been superimposed on the manipulated stereocard, largely obscuring the original referent and destroying the 3-D illusion.[17] In a series of 3-D images called *Reading Lessons* (1988), Jim Pomeroy reworked a selection of old stereocards released by the Keystone View Company by digitally inserting pun-like text fragments.[18] Without disturbing the 3-D illusion, Pomeroy turned illusionistic spaces into textual spaces. The eyes of the viewer wander inside the spatial montage from plane to plane, drawing connections between words and things. The opening view has the text "Reading Lessons and Eye Exercises" distributed on different planes around a figure of a man reading in the "dead Christ" position, virtually pushing the soles of his shoes in the viewer's face. While drawing attention to the (unintentional?) iconographical connotations of the Keystone card, Pomeroy also playfully refers to the use of stereoscopy in medical eye-training. The humoristic and absurd text-image combinations are not just pranks, however, but serve a critical purpose as well. "We are not seduced by farce, but rather, sharpened," Pomeroy wrote.[19] Significantly, he released his 3-D works as a boxed set of three View-Master reels and a viewer, an ambiguous homage to popular stereoscopy.[20]

15 See *Art/Photographie Numérique. L'image réinventée*, Ysabel de Roquette (ed.), Cypres, École d'Art d'Aix-en-Provence, 1995, color plate III.

16 See *Iterations: The New Image*, Timothy Druckrey (ed.), International Center for Photography, New York, and MIT Press, Cambridge, MA, 1993, pp. 108-111.

17 This last panel, missing from *The New Image*, has been published in *Metamorphoses. Photography in the Electronic Age*, Geoffrey Batchen (ed.), Aperture, New York, 1994, p. 31.

18 Pomeroy produced this works as an artist in residence at the California Museum of Photography in Riverside. The museum holds the archives of the Keystone View Company. Later, Esther Parada had a residency in the same institution, producing the work mentioned in this article.

19 Jim Pomeroy: "Reading 'Reading Lessons'," a text include in the View-Master package of his 3-D works. See next footnote.

20 Jim Pomeroy, *VER Multidimensionales/Stereo Views*, Light Work, Syracuse, NY, 1988 (in Author's collection). This extraordinary publication complemented Pomeroy's installation/exhibition in Light Work's Robert B. Menchel Photography Gallery, 10 Jan to 13 Feb 1988.

21 The random dot stereogram boom was especially strong in Japan, where many young artists and designers rushed to create a veritable flurry of such images with their computers. While many of these were based of the principle of the random dot stereogram, some artists recreated forms of more traditional stereoscopy in the digital realms. A real avalanche of publication was brought to the market, including several volumes of a book series called "CG Stereogram." For an analysis of this boom, see Itsuo Sakane, "New Developments in 3-D Perceptual Art," in *3D – Beyond the Stereography. Images and Technology Gallery Exhibition, Theme III*, Tokyo Metropolitan Museum of Photography, Tokyo, 1996, pp. 28–31.

22 About the topos of immersion, see my "Encapsulated Bodies in Motion: Simulators and the Quest for Total Immersion," in *Critical Issues in Electronic Media*, Simon Penny (ed.), The SUNY Press, Albany, NY, 1995, pp. 159–186.

23 The results were reported in the book *Immersed in Technology. Art and Virtual Environments*, Mary Anne Moser, Douglas MacLeod (eds), The MIT Press, Cambridge, MA, 1995.

24 In his book *Virtual Art. From Illusion to Immersion* (The MIT Press, Cambridge, MA, 2003), Oliver Grau has chronicled many of these developments. In spite of its seeming exhaustiveness, the book fails to mention many important artists' VR projects, including Matt Mullican's *Five Into One* and Susan Amkraut, Michel Girard and Scott Fischer's *Menagerie*. There is not a word about Perry Hoberman, who together with Scott Fisher also created a virtual brewery experience using many BOOM displays to Tokyo's Ebisu Garden Place. Even the works by key artists like Jeffrey Shaw and Michael Naimark have been treated in a very cursory and incomplete manner, lacking rigorous analysis.

25 Historically panoramas and stereoscopic applications developed side by side (although panoramas were known half a century earlier). Although they were technically very different, they had similarities as cultural forms – both were vehicles for virtual (or "surrogate") travel. Spectacles like the Kaiser Panorama in Europe tried to combine their possibilities. Kaiser Panorama was a cylinder-like viewing station the presented a succession of glass stereo slides to spectators sitting around it and staring into stereoscopic eyepieces. Kaiser Panorama can also be considered an improved version of the Cosmorama, a public peepshow. Beside the cylindrical form of the viewing station, Kaiser Panorama had little to do with 360-degree panoramas. 360-panoramic field of vision and stereoscopy were really merged only in the twentieth century, in virtual-reality applications and specialty cinema spectacles like IMAX 3-D.

She Sees Her Son in France

You can talk across the miles with your TELEPHONE—The WHOLE FAMILY Can See the WAR ZONE

(COPYRIGHTED BY) KEYSTONE VIEW COMPANY

When our Representative calls to deliver your order about July 6 19 21

She Sees Her Son in France
late 1910s
postcard
published by Keystone
View Company
collection Erkki Huhtamo

This postcard was used to inform the recipient about the delivery of a set of Keystone stereo cards dealing with World War I. The card makes an interesting association between stereoscopy and the telephone.

Stereoscopy, Art and Virtual Reality

These "excavations" of stereoscopy coincided with another trend, the emergence of virtual reality. Indeed, the early 1990s experienced a veritable 3-D boom, also manifested in other forms, such as the "auto-stereoscopic" random dot stereograms released as books, postcards and similar.21 In a sense, this boom merely signified another re-discovery of stereoscopy, a re-activation of the age-old topos of immersion into artificial realities. It happened in a situation in which the traditional audiovisual media were undergoing a crisis and digital media was just entering the mainstream of culture.22 It is tempting to relate the need for immersion to the worldwide depression that followed the bursting of the 1980s economic bubble, although cultural context for the 3-D revival is clearly more complex. The public introduction of virtual reality had to do with the end of the Cold War and the need for the military to search for new markets and sponsors for their previously secret innovations. Against this background the artistic explorations of 3-D virtual-reality technology gain automatically a political significance, although this was rarely stated explicitly by the artists themselves. In a few years a significant number of works were produced, several of them within the Art and Virtual Environments project at the Banff Centre for the Arts in Canada.23 Later, institutions like the Ars Electronica Center in Linz, Austria and, in Germany, the ZKM in Karlsruhe and the GMD in Sankt Augustin by Bonn (now part of the Fraunhofer Gesellschaft) have given artists opportunities to explore high tech virtual-reality environments like the CAVE.24

In virtual-reality applications stereoscopic imaging is usually combined with a panoramic field of vi-
sion.25 Instead of seeing the three-dimensional view from a limited point-of-view, as if in a stable framed window (like in the traditional stereoscope), the participants are given an overwhelming sensation of "inhabiting" the image, turned into an artificial environment. The 3-D space can be entered and explored by wearing a head-mounted display, or by being bodily present in a projected environment that envelops the participant(s) wearing see-through 3-D glasses. The choice between these options has important implications for the relationship between the visual environment and the body. A head-mounted display excludes the physical body, often replacing it with a virtual body image, whereas a projected environment keeps the body visible. This leads to a paradoxical state of being: the participant is both immersed in an immaterial illusion and physically present. In mixed-reality situations, like those explored by Jeffrey Shaw already in the 1970s and '80s, the co-existence of the physical and the virtual also prevails, but in a reverse order: the virtual as if grows out of the surrounding physical environment.26 In Rebecca Allen's installation *Coexistence* (2002), two participants sit facing each other, wearing see-through head-mounted displays with video cameras attached to them. The participants see each other, but also various computer-generated elements hovering between them. By blowing into microphones attached to modified game pads, the participants together manipulate virtual objects, destroying a wall of particles, and so forth.

Some artists – including Michel Girard, Susan Amkraut and Scott Fisher, Monika Fleischmann and Wolfgang Strauss, Matt Mullican, and Char Davies – have explored the potential of stereoscopic virtual realities by creating idiosyncratic "totally immersive"

Spider-Man. VR-3D
2002
interactive stereoscopic game
console
MAG Entertainment and
RadioShack®
collection Erkki Huhtamo
photo © Erkki Huhtamo

26 For example in works like
Viewpoint (1975), Virtual
Projection Installation
(1979), Virtual Projection
Performance (1983) and In-
venter la terre (1986). See
Jeffrey Shaw – a user's man-
ual. From Expanded Cinema
to Virtual Reality, ZKM (ed.),
Hatje Cantz Verlag,
Ostfildern, 1997.

27 Girard, Amkraut and Fisher
successfully used the BOOM
"head-coupled display"
system, developed by
Fakespace labs, for their
Menagerie, while the others
used a head-mounted
display (HMD) interface.
Fleischmann and Strauss's
The Home of the Brain and
Mullican's Five Into One were
hardly ever exhibited in the
intended form because of
technical problems. Davies'
Osmose and Ephemere be-
long to the very few HMD-
based VR works that have
been successfully shown in
the art-museum context.

28 See my article "Time Travelling in the Gallery: An Archeological Approach in Media
Art," in Immersed in Technology, op. cit., pp. 244–246.

29 From a media-archeological
point-of-view Naimark's device really evokes a hybrid of
a 3-D coin-op viewer and a
Mutoscope, a hand-cranked
viewer for moving images.
The proto-interactive na-
ture of the Mutoscope was
clearly expressed in an advertising booklet in 1897:
"In the operation of the
Mutoscope, the spectator
has the performance
entirely under his own control by the turning of the
crank. He may make the
operation as quick or as
slow as fancy dictates ...
and if he so elects, the entertainment can be stopped
by him at any point in the
series and each separate
picture inspected at leisure;
thus every step, motion, act
or expression can be ana-
lyzed, presenting effects at
once instructive, interesting, attractive, amusing and
startling." Cit. David Nasaw,
Going Out. The Rise and
Fall of Public Amusements,
Harvard University Press,
Cambridge, MA, 1999 (1993),
p. 133.

30 CAVE was first presented at
Siggraph 92 in Chicago. The
author visited CAVE for the
first time one morning together with Shaw. After the
experience, over a cup of
coffee, the artist drew the
first sketch of EVE on a
paper napkin, still in the author's collection. About the
background and the devel-
opment of the CAVE, see
Daniel J. Sandin, "Digital
Illusion, Virtual Reality, and
Cinema," in Digital Illusion.
Entertaining the Future with
High Technology, Addison-
Wesley (Reading, MA) and
ACM Press (New York), 1998,
pp. 3–26.

worlds.27 Others, like Michael Naimark and Jeffrey
Shaw, have approached immersion more obliquely, deliberately imposing limitations into their worlds and
providing them with embedded cultural references.
Michael Naimark, one of the artists in the Art and
Virtual Environments project, presented his stereoscopic time/motion studies in a custom-made hand-
cranked peepshow viewer that explicitly evoked the
immersive strategies used in Victorian stereocards
and in early twentieth-century amusement arcades.
Naimark's original challenge was to find ways of bringing real-world images into virtual realities. Although
he at first experimented with mapping video frames
onto panoramic digital wireframe models, he eventually turned to shooting 16mm 3-D film, transferred
onto a digital laserdisc. The result, See Banff! (1994),
is a deceptively "archaic" media-archaeological instal-
lation.28 Although it could be read thematically as an
investigation of highly coded cultural landscapes and
the rituals of tourism (harking back to the nineteenth-century stereoscopic "world voyaging"), it is
also an interactive exploration of the elements of vir-
tual-world building. Instead of linear continuities,
Naimark's "kinetoscope" presents deliberately abrupt
time-lapse sequences, manipulated by the viewer by
means of a hand-crank.29 The arrangement works
against the user's total immersion into the scenes,
emphasizing their artificiality.

In a later installation Be Now Here (1995–97),
Naimark merged stereoscopic vision, interactivity, and
panoramic projection with mobile spectatorship. Although resorting to very advanced technology, he
again resisted full immersion: The participants,
standing on a rotating platform, are "transported" to
filmed panoramas of various locations around the

world. The 360-degree views are projected on a quad-
rangular screen (serving as a "window") and revealed
little by little to the viewers. In order to be able to see
the view, the participants have to be in constant motion, adjusting their positions as the platform rotates. Although this arrangement may have been
partly dictated by technological considerations (on
location, Naimark used a motorized camera pair
mounted on tripod, panning 360 degrees on a tripod
to capture the scene), it also works against the idea
of illusionism. The scenes were chosen from UN-
ESCO's list of threatened sites of world heritage,
which explains Naimark's resistance to total immersion into synthetic realities. Another example of controlling the experience of immersion is EVE (1993), an
"extended virtual environment" conceived by Jeffrey
Shaw at the ZKM. EVE is a darkened inflatable dome
with a robotic arm holding a pair of projectors at its
center. The projectors project a 3-D "window" that
moves along the walls of the dome in direct response
to the movements of a participant wearing a "steering helmet." By means of a joystick, it is possible to
"enter" the space in the virtual window. Instead of
exposing the participants to full immersion, Shaw
introduced a mobile viewpoint that was simultaneously engaging and distanced. Indeed, EVE was a
direct response to CAVE, a projection-based virtual
environment that was totally immersive.30

CAVE has become an important challenge for
artists dealing with 3-D virtual realities. Most projects seen so far have concentrated on exploring the
expressive potential of the medium, instead of using
it for ideologically charged critical purposes. Although
interesting as formal and aesthetic experiments,
such works can best be characterized as displays of

Maurice Benayoun
World Skin. A photographic safari into the Land of War.
1998
interactive installation
in a CAVE
cameras, printers
screenshot
© Ars Electronica Center, Linz;
Z–A; Maurice Benayoun
photo © Z–A; Maurice Benayoun

"demo aesthetics."[31] At least some of the artists seem to have been unable to distance themselves from the seductiveness of the medium. There is, however, one work that has turned the CAVE into an arena for critical 3-D art, raising the issue of living and operating in dense media-saturated environments. Maurice Benayoun and Jean-Baptiste Barrière's *World Skin* (1997) is an unusual panorama of war (a favorite topic for nineteenth-century panoramists!), consisting of two-dimensional "cut-out" figures of soldiers, weapons, planes, tanks and scenes of destruction distributed in an immersive three-dimensional digital landscape. The work emphasizes the artificiality (literally, the flatness) of these representations, found images from mainstream media, yet it also emphasizes their powerful ideological authority. By using modified digital cameras the participants move inside the landscape and "shoot" at the figures like a war reporter or a tourist. The shots make the targets disappear from the landscape, leaving behind a white "void" casting a dark shadow. As it turns out, the shots have been automatically printed outside the CAVE, and can be picked up by the participants when the session is over.

This complex work shows that an immersive environment can be a locus for cerebral activity without compromising the emotional power of immersion. It is also an unusual example of the successful integration of interactive sound (by Barrière) into a virtual world. A key to reading *World Skin* is the artificiality of its representations: The participants are confronted neither with a real battlefield nor a hyperrealistic simulation. They are in a chaotic and fragmented memory theater consisting of traces stored in the true collective memory of contemporary society: the mass media. In their "three-dimensionalized two-dimensionality," the images evoke nineteenth-century and early twentieth-century stereocards, like those released by the Keystone View Company. Countless civilians experienced the horrors of World War I in their privacy by means of the stereoscope, looking at such views. This experience was not just based on the "horribly attractive" subject matter or on the safety of the vantage point from which the viewer could ob-

serve the images. It depended also on a cultural code that confirmed the "ontological truthfulness" of the representations and the validity of the simulation of presence provided by stereoscopy. This code, internalized by the user, effaced the fundamental artificiality of the "stereographic space," analyzed by Rosalind Krauss. For Krauss, the stereographic image "appears multilayered, a steep gradient of different planes stretching away from the nearby space into depth."[32]

The observer of a stereoview looks at its fundamentally "theatrical" space from a fixed vantage point, which enhances the spatial illusion. In *World Skin* the viewer's "ocular voyage" is actualized as virtual motion (controlled by a tactile interface) inside the space of the image. This paradoxically both strengthens the sense of immersion and underlines the artificiality of the depicted world. Participants find themselves within a field of opposing forces. The movement inside the image, as well as the activity of "shooting," also refers to video-games. As Benayoun and Barrière explain, "shooting" is expected to lead to "compulsive behavior," gradually countered by the increasing aggressiveness of the sound.[33] Aggression begets aggression, but the escalating sound also reaches a climax, creating a calm moment for reflection. Taking snapshots becomes a highly ambiguous gesture. It can lead to a pure emotional orgy of shooting, but it can also function as a premeditated act of erasure – of memory, of the traces of aggression, of the supremacy of the media that have redefined the world in their own image? The final act, picking up the digital print after the session, is equally complex. Does it signify liberation from the totalitarian oppressiveness of the memory theater? Or does it imply that there is no escape from the sphere of images: erasing one only leads to the creation of another? Is it essential that the paradoxical "world skin" (multiplied flatness distributed in a 3-D space) becomes fragmented and reduced to a frozen monoscopic moment captured on a sheet of paper? The mere possibility of asking such questions shows that stereoscopic imagery can provide much more than mere "surplus value" to other forms of expression.

31 The concept was coined by Lorne Falk and Heidi Gilpin in "Demo Aesthetics," *Convergence*, vol. 1, no. 2, Autumn 1995, pp. 127–139. "Demo aesthetics shifts the emphasis from interpretation and analysis to description and demonstration." (ibid., p. 128) Most CAVE projects I have seen have been either demonstrations of potential scientific applications or celebrations of the act of immersion. Some of the more ambitious works include the *reconFiguring the CAVE* by Jeffrey Shaw, Agnes Hegedüs and Bernd Lintermann [the title explicitly affirms the "demo aesthetic" nature of the work] and Simon Penny's *Traces*, a networked CAVE application that has unfortunately remained unfinished.

32 Rosalind E. Krauss, *The Originality of the Avant-Garde and Other Modernist Myths*, The MIT Press, Cambridge, MA, 1988 [1986], pp. 136–137.

33 Maurice Benayoun & Jean-Baptiste Barrière: "World Skin," Cyberarts98. Prix Ars Electronica, Edition 98, Hannes Leopoldseder & Christine Schöpf (eds.) Springer-Verlag, Vienna, New York, 1998, p. 74. *World Skin* won the prestigious Golden Nica in the Interactive Art category in the 1998 Prix Ars Electronica competition.

Ken Jacobs
Lumieres Feeding The Baby
1996
digitally recomposed image
originally for the poster of
"Wrong Turn Into Adventure:
The Film-Performances of Ken
Jacobs," MoMA, 1996
based on a film frame
from Louis Lumière's
Repas de bébé, 1895
© Ken Jacobs

Since the 1970s the visionary
experimental filmmaker Ken
Jacobs has been perfecting a
new kind of projection apparatus he calls the Nervous System. It has been used by Jacobs
in a series of live media performances. Two projectors simultaneously project identical 2-D
film prints (often early silent
films) with a slight time difference. A motorized propeller
spinning in front of the projectors achieves an amazing, constantly metamorphosing cinematic space that often seems
to extend far into the depth. As
Jacobs has remarked, the
"effect is not happening on
screen, but as an optical/mind
event." The image above, created by Jacobs with a computer,
attempts to simulate the
timed-based 3-D effect of the
Nervous System by means of a
still image, using frames from
an early Lumière bros. silent film
(1895). It can be seen in 3-D by
"free-viewing" (i.e. by crossing
ones eyes).

Instead of being doomed to remain just another special effect, 3-D can be an integral part of the signifying structure of complex multimedia creations.

The Future of the Illusion
If the future of moving images is interactive, stereoscopic imaging may well play an essential role in its
development. More media artists are finding ways to
integrate 3-D images as part of the idiosyncratic
worlds they create. For Zoe Beloff, for example,
stereoscopic images conjure up "spectral scenes"
and phantoms, essential elements of her media-
archaeological investigation into the relationship
between imagination and technology. Beloff's works
evoke the contemporary discourse on virtual reality,
but situate it within a wider context that includes
phenomena like magic-lantern projections, nineteenth-century ghost shows, early cinema, telepathy
and telegraphy, and the impact of media technology
on schizophrenic delusions. In her installation *The
Influencing Machine of Miss Natalija A.* (2001) the
spectators are confronted with a 3-D representation
of a machine that purportedly projects delusions to
the mind of a fictional persona. Touching parts of this
virtual machine visualizes the delusions, derived from
early twentieth-century media. Here, as in her performances, stereoscopy serves as an appropriate
medium to express Beloff's artistic interests. As her
work shows, three-dimensionality does not necessarily have to be associated with goggle-like wearable
interfaces, or even with the experience of total immersion. This was anticipated by Marcel Duchamp,
whose *Rotorelief Discs* (1935) achieved a convincing
illusion of depth in motion without requiring any special apparatus (beside a standard record player used

to rotate the discs).34 Although the development
of holographic video has proven more problematic
than was expected, other ways of displaying auto-
stereoscopic three-dimensional moving images have
been developed, including the SynthaGram Monitor
(StereoGraphics) already used by Perry Hoberman in
his most recent 3-D works.35

In the cinema, 3-D seems to have gained a firm position with the success of IMAX 3-D large-screen
projection system, the most advanced form of high
definition three-dimensional moving images yet
achieved. Because of its high production costs and its
focus on the commercial market (science museums,
theme parks and specialty cinema experiences), media
artists have gained very limited access to IMAX technology so far. Independent 3-D innovations, like Ken
Jacobs' Nervous System, which is used in his multimedia performances, have evolved outside corporate
high-tech environments.36 This can be both an advantage and a hindrance. Spectacles like IMAX 3-D reach
large audiences. They offer technically accomplished
and even emotionally involving experiences, but contain little room for innovation. Innovations like the
system Jacobs has created seem doomed to reach
only a fringe audience. Yet there is no need for fatal-
ism. The evolving field of digital media art may well
come up with solutions that combine the best of both
worlds. Yet whatever forms media art in the third dimension will take, it should avoid using 3-D as just another gimmick. To make a difference, 3-D has to find
an integral, constructive, and "deep" role in the new
media creation. If this will not happen, stereoscopic
imagery will be doomed to be just another fad, appearing, disappear and appearing over and over again.

34 "Rotoreliefs" (Disques Op-
tiques) were the outcome of
Duchamp's long-term interest in optical illusions. He
was particularly interested
in combining the illusion of
depth with cyclical motion,
an issue he had already investigated with earlier
works, such as the motor-
operated *Rotary Demi-
sphere (Precision Optics)*
(1925). Duchamp planned to
publish his Rotorelief's as a
boxed set of six discs, with
subjects on both sides. Rotated on a regular record
player, an illusion of a moving, pulsating 3-D space was
achieved. Duchamp's set included a simple cardboard
frame meant to help the
viewer in concentrating on
the disc, but this was not
necessary. The commercial
success of Rotoreliefs remained minimal, but later
several editions targeted
for art collectors were released. See Francis M. Nau-
mann, *Marcel Duchamp. The
Art of Making Art in the Age
of Mechanical Reproduction*,
Ludion Press, Ghent, Ams-
terdam, distrib. by Harry N.
Abrams, New York, 1999; I
have dealt with Duchamp's
relationship with "pre-cinematic" optical devices in my
"Mr. Duchamp's Playtoy, or,
remarks on the role of optical technology in 20th century avantgarde art" (forthcoming).

35 Auto-stereoscopic refers
to applications that can be
seen as three-dimensional
with plain eyes, without the
aid of 3-D glasses, a head-
mounted display, etc.

36 Jacobs uses two 16mm film
projectors and a custom-
made "shutter wheel" that
rotates in front of their
lenses. Jacobs often pro-
jects two prints of the same
film, but a little out of sync.
By means of the rotating
shutter, he manages to manipulate the filmic space in
surprising ways that include
the creation of an artificial
sense of depth.

Michael Naimark
Be Now Here

1995–2000
laserdisc-based strereoscopic projection / four-channel audio /
rotating floor, input pedestal

production still of
Be Now Here
Interval Research Corporation
and UNESCO World Heritage
Centre
photo © Gilles Tassé

Michel Naimark in Timbuktu
with two 35mm motion picture
cameras (for 3-D, one for each
eye) mounted on a rotating
tripod.

Be Now Here

The imagery was recorded in public plazas in the four cities designated "In Danger" by the UNESCO World Heritage Centre: Jerusalem (Israel), Dubrovnik (Croatia), Timbuktu (Mali), and Angkor (Cambodia). The intention was to record these beautiful and troubled environments. The production concept was simple: Find in one public plaza in each city a single spot that best represents each place, then film several panoramas from that spot during the course of the day without moving the camera system. The multiple times of day would be perfectly registered and allow seamless intercutting, with only the lighting and transient objects changing.

Due to the potentially hazardous and controversial nature of the project, production was as inexpensive, fast, and quiet as possible, relying on prearranged local staff at each site and help from UNESCO to cross borders with the 500 pounds of film gear. Through a great deal of planning and collaboration, all four sites were filmed in one month. ("Highlights" included a bomb scare in Jerusalem resulting in evacuation of the entire plaza, a drive through a strip of Bosnia in the middle of the night during wartime, a negotiation with Taurig camel drivers in Timbuktu about issues of appropriation, and a bribe to get the hired driver out of jail after he had gotten lost after dark and had been found by the Cambodian military.) Miraculously, all the footage survived.

Working with local collaborators was a critical element in ensuring the quality of imagery. The selection of the sites was heavily informed by local knowledge. More important, filming in the middle of public plazas is a conspicuous activity, and the fact that local collaborators knew many of the people in the plaza helped to make everyone feel comfortable. Local people, particularly children, didn't appear self-conscious – they simply did what they would normally do in such places.

Excerpt from "Field Cinematography Techniques for Virtual Reality Applications," in *VSMM98 Conference Proceedings, 4th International Conference on Virtual Systems and Mulitmedia*, Gifu, Japan, Invited Paper, 1998.

Be Now Here is an installation about landscape and public places and stepping into an immersive virtual environment. The imagery is of public plazas on the UNESCO World Heritage list of endangered places – Jerusalem, Dubrovnik, Timbuktu and Angkor – places both exotic and disturbing. The style is ambient, as if the imagery is live.

For production, a unique recording system was built consisting of two 35mm motion-picture cameras (for 3-D, one for each eye) mounted on a rotating tripod. The installation consists of an input pedestal for interactively choosing place and time, a stereoscopic projection screen, four-channel audio, and a 16-foot rotating floor on which the viewers stand.

Be Now Here is an extension of several media trajectories. One is of enhanced cinematic representation, such as the Imax-sized projections of the Lumière brothers in 1900 and the three-screen triptychs of Abel Gance's *Napoleon* in 1927. Another is of non-narrative cultural activism, such as the films of Godfrey Reggio and Tony Gatlif. But *Be Now Here* also points forward: as a simulation of what net cinema can be, it is both a regard and a provocation.

From the project page:
http://www.naimark.net/projects/benowhere.html

Trip reports from the *Be Now Here* production can be found at
http://www.naimark.net/writing/trips/bnhtrip.html

Be Now Here
Interval Research Corporation and
UNESCO World Heritage Centre
composite photo
© Christoph Dohrmann

Be Now Here
Interval Research Corporation and
UNESCO World Heritage Centre
composite photo
© Ignazio Moresco

Be Now Here
1995–2000
laserdisc-based
strereoscopic projection
four-channel audio,
rotating floor, input pedestal
installation view: ZKM |
Center for Art and Media
Karlsruhe, 2002
Interval Research Corporation
and UNESCO World Heritage
Centre
photo © Franz Wamhof

Jerusalem

Dubrovnik

Timbuktu

Angkor

Be Now Here
1995 – 2000
composite panoramas

Interval Research Corporation
and UNESCO World Heritage Centre
composite panoramas © Romy Achituv

Dome Projection
1978
35mm film projection,
frosted acrylic dome screen
Center for Advanced Visual
Studies, MIT
photo © Michael Naimark

Dome Projections (1978) was
driven by the urge to see if an
"inside out" panorama would
"read" to the human eye.
Images were recorded with a
Nikon camera fitted with a
180-degree fisheye lens. The
camera and lens were then
converted into a projector
pointing upward, and a 36-inch
diameter frosted acrylic dome
was placed on top. The fisheye
image appeared as a "northern
hemisphere" to be viewed from
the outside. So rather than
being inside the panorama
looking out, viewers were outside looking in.

hardware for
Dome Projection
1978
35mm camera, fisheye lens,
frosted acrylic dome, light
source
Center for Advanced Visual
Studies, MIT
photo © Michael Naimark

Michael Naimark, Future Cinema and Future Science

All data are not created equal, nor are all metaphors.
Any contemporary discussion of future cinema inevitably occurs within the context of the "digital," yet
there is nothing inevitable about this contextualization. Human cognition is fed by information that currently must pass through the existing human senses,
after transformation and re-presentation by a number of devices, mostly non-digital, in a complex network of interaction. Resulting mental images map to
the source information in some non-unique way; there
is nothing inevitable about the form or content of
such mental images, and it is likely that in the course
of human evolution the construction of these mental
images likewise evolved both in content and form.
Future cinema is not a linear progression of increasing media fidelity or manipulability, or even one of
increasing coherence with artistic vision. In a world
subject to increasing surveillance and recording, the
projection of self involves choices of presentation
and of de-presentation.[1] Future cinema must be
coupled with an understanding of future un-cinema,
just as the future of science has involved a constant
redefinition of the questions considered susceptible
to resolution, of the kinds of answers considered pertinent, and of the epistemological terrain considered
fair game for the scientific enterprise.

In the scientific context we can identify a number
of different data terrains. The human senses themselves interact with signals that reach them; this
raw data can be assimilated both by manipulating the
stimuli or by manipulating the cognitive system. For
historical and philosophical reasons, sense data is
associated with the need for some kind of "ground
truth." An apocryphal story relates that Galileo, while
perfecting his telescopes, would sometimes carry out
ground-truth experiments in order to verify that his

new perceiving devices were not deceiving him. After
viewing features of a mountain located on the other
side of a valley, he would walk across the valley to
touch the rocks previously seen magnified through
his telescope. Michael Naimark similarly couples
cinema to anthropology, and proposes "grounding"
the camera as a way of restoring a sense of place.

Yet the development of the human senses is an
accident (and a consequence) of the particularities
of human evolution. Most of the world is totally in-
accessible to the human senses, a fact that has
become painfully obvious to scientists as new devices
have revealed to the world a plethora of hitherto
undreamed-of phenomena and components. Today,
we almost entirely lack any intuition or sense of place
about these parts of the world. It is an open question
whether these terrains, undetectable by human
senses, are part of future cinema or future un-
cinema. One thing is clear: Growing reservoirs of data
about the world are now stored in digital archives
that are rapidly achieving an ontological status rival-
ing that of the world itself.

For its source materials, the cinema of today
draws freely on both the raw and mediated worlds.
Michael Naimark initiated the Kundi project, which
aimed to provide a live interface to data-streams
produced concurrently with almost any interesting
event happening on the planet.[2] The future cinema
envisioned by the Kundi project would have helped
construct an experiental world seamlessly blending
the ground truth of direct sensory data with the
mediated world of live and stored data archives.
Such a vision implies an aesthetics of globalization.
However, Naimark insists that "it is impossible to
separate the aesthetics of telepresence from the
politics of place."[3] His ethical injunction is at the same
time a manifesto for the construction of future
cinema.

1 Michael Naimark, "How to
Zap a Camera," 2002.
http://www.naimark.net/
projects/zap.html

2 See http://www.naimark.
net/projects/kundi.html

3 Michael Naimark, "Place
Runs Deep: Virtuality, Place
and Indigineousness," in
*Virtual Museums Sympo-
sium*, ARCH Foundation,
Salzburg, Austria, 1998.

Moving Movie #1
1977
Super 8mm film-loop projector,
1 rpm turntable, frosted acrylic
cylindrical screen
installation view: Center for
Advanced Visual Studies, MIT
photo © Michael Naimark

Moving Movie #1
1977
Super 8mm film-loop projector,
1 rpm turntable, frosted acrylic
cylindrical screen
installation view: Center for
Advanced Visual Studies, MIT
detail, time-lapse as the
projector rotates
photo © Michael Naimark

Moving Movie #1 (1977) was a modest inexpensive study made at MIT. I was obsessed with why movie cameras move and movie projectors do not, and filmed the Boston landscape with a Super8 movie camera mounted on a slowly rotating turntable. The film was projected using a continuous loop projector mounted on the same slowly rotating turntable and a translucent cylindrical screen enabling both sides to be seen. The result was a very natural looking "flashlight effect," with the frame rotating around the screen in sync with the filmed material. As the projected image rotated around the screen, direction and spatiality was maintained. *Moving Movie #2* (1979, not pictured) was an attempt to record the camera movement during filming, then use the data to control the movement of the projected image. The result was a movie that could pan and tilt around a space in any direction, based upon the original camera movement.

Scientific inquiry is now conducted not only by intervention in the physical world and the study of acquired mediated data, but also by the construction of simulations allowing comparisons with the behavior of physical systems. Such approaches have proved to be very powerful, particularly in the study of complex systems. The digital computer has enabled the scientific method of simulation to become dominant in fields ranging from meteorology to cosmology. The feasibility of creating virtual worlds for scientific research has been paralleled by a cultural and artistic interest in creating virtual-reality systems, synthetic actors and artificial life environments. In cinema and science alike, the interface between fact and fiction, between real and unreal, is blurred and shifting. Naimark contrasts two competing urges in the cultural field: the demand for "sensory richness" on the one hand, for "liveness" on the other.[4] He correctly points out that given technological implementations "bias" the development of future cinema (wireless technology versus immersive high-resolution environments). Similarly, certain parts of the world are amenable to scientific understanding only through complex simulation that loses all direct association with natural time. These are not innocent bifurcations, for just as they delimit the boundaries of science and un-science, so they point to possible future boundaries between cinema and un-cinema.

There is nothing inevitable about the future development of particular technologies, embedded as they are in social contexts, in the individual and collective desires of inventors as well in as the societal environments of funding and societal acceptance. Technologies are developed with a relationship to scientific enterprise that is very different from that to artistic-cultural endeavor. In astronomy, for instance, there has been an unholy alliance between major scientific advances and the introduction of new types of telescopes. Astronomers have become fundamentalist technophiles as a result. The relationship between art and technology is of a very different order. Even though many new technologies transform society, they are of little direct interest to cultural production: Consider, for instance, the impact of the telephone, railway, airplane and steam engine as compared to film, computer, the Internet or new painting materials. Institutional contexts prove to be crucially important in determining whether the artistic potential of a particular technology is explored and exploited. Indeed, many technologies remain unused by artists although they offer powerful resources for artistic expression. Naimark tells the tale of his early work at the MIT Center for Advanced Visual Study in 1977, when he first began to explore panoramic cinema technologies.[5] After making one of his first "moving movies" using a camera rotating on a turntable, he showed the result to his mentor and remarked, "Great, now I'm ready to begin." His mentor replied, "Great, now you're done," thus exposing the basic conflict between technology as end and technology as means in a given institutional environment. Art, science and technology are very different endeavors with differing goals and success criteria. It is fashionable to talk of the convergence of fields and inter- and multi-disciplinary work; however, such talk is often misguided, it being unproductive to seek to minimize the differences between the goals of "pure art" as opposed to those of the scientist or engineer. Michael Naimark works at the boundary of cinema and un-cinema, but also at the boundary of science and un-science. Through work of this kind, future cinema will be not an extrapolation of the present but, more probably, a process of real evolutionary discontinuity.

Roger Malina

4   Michael Naimark, "VR Webcams: Time Artifacts as Positive Features," in *ISEA 2002 Proceedings*, Nagoya, 2002.

5   Michael Naimark, "Art ('and' or 'versus') Technology; Some Personal Observations," in *Art@Science*, Christa Sommerer, Laurent Mignoneau (eds), Springer, Vienna and New York, 1998.

collaborative project
Aspen Moviemap
1978–1979
interactive laserdisc system,
touch-sensitive screen
screenshot
Architecture Machine Group,
MIT

Aspen Moviemap (1978–1979),
the first interactive movie map
and one of the first-ever interactive video experiments, was a
large collaborative project produced by the MIT Architecture
Machine Group in the town of
Aspen, Colorado. A gyroscopic
stabilizer with four 16mm stop-
frame cameras was mounted on
top of a camera car and a fifth
wheel with an encoder triggered the cameras every ten feet.
Filming took place daily between
10 am and 2 pm to minimize
lighting discrepancies. The
camera car carefully filmed
down every street and through
every possible turn, driving
down the center of the street
to ensure registered "match-
cuts."

The playback system allowed
seamless, interactive "travel"
through the streets of Aspen. It
required a computer, several
laserdisc players, and a touchscreen input display. Panoramic
camera experiments, thousands
of still frames, audio and data
were collected in addition to
the basic moviemap footage.
Very wide-angle lenses were
used for filming, and some
attempts were made at immersive playback.

Michael Naimark—Excerpts from his Writings

Aspen Moviemap

How often do we see images that are not flat and
rectangular? (How many images of yourself have you
seen that are not flat and rectangular?)

If real time means a temporal correspondence between record and playback environments, then real
space means a spatial correspondence between
record and playback environments.

Why do movie cameras move and movie projectors
do not?

The eye is apparently harder to fool than the ear.
We've all had the experience of mistaking a voice from
the radio for being someone present. Yet when we
enter a theater, there is never any question whether
what we see is a movie or live.

A funny thing happened on the second *Aspen
Moviemap* shoot. It was winter, and when we landed in
Denver, flights to Aspen had been cancelled due to
snow. We rented cars and drove in. There were five of
us in our car. Two of the five had never been to Aspen
before, but spent the past couple of months working
intensively with the videodisc produced from our first
shoot the previous summer. As we pulled into town
and drove down Main Street, they both had the same
two reactions. They knew where everything was - the
park coming up on the right, the Hotel Jerome beyond
that on the left. But they were both amazed that it
didn't look anything like what they had expected.

I once compared exposure readings of an outdoor
scene in a movie with a real outdoor scene and found
that the real scene was over 1,000 times brighter
than its movie equivalent.

The ultimate media room will be indistinguishable
from "reality." Any reality: the kind one sees with eyes
closed as well as with eyes open. All senses will be affected, all effectors will be sensed. One will be able to
touch, smell, walk around, and move objects as well as
see and hear. (You may be in one right now.) Like the
screen of a television, everything changes when one
changes the channel; everything disappears when one
pulls the plug.

There is no word in the English language that is
the spatial equivalent to "simultaneous."

Limits to how we communicate limits what we
communicate. The converse is not true.

Excerpt from "Some Notes on Movies and Form," in *Video 80*,
San Francisco International Video Festival, 1981.

Michael Naimark, Ken Carson
Golden Gate Fly-Over
1987
interactive laserdisc system,
trackball input
installation view:
Exploratorium, San Francisco
photo courtesy Exploratorium,
San Francisco

Golden Gate Fly-Over (1987) is a
moviemap of the San Francisco
Bay Area from the air made for
the Exploratorium. A special
gyro-stabilized helicopter
camera and satellite navigation
were used to film along a precise ten-by-ten mile grid (at one-
mile intervals) centered on Golden Gate Bridge. The final
installation consists of a single
trackball as the input device, so
it is very easy to use. It allows
moving around the Bay Area at
unnaturally fast speeds. The
goal was not to re-create a
helicopter ride as much as to
create an abstract hyper-real
experience, using new media to
make an otherwise impossible
experience in the physical world.

Camera movement, like edits and other special visual
effects, allow movies to offer experiences that everyday reality cannot. However, something is lost. The
security of knowing that stationary objects stay put,
that people don't shrink and expand, and that if we
walk toward something we get closer to it are all part
of how we relate to our environment. What is lost is
a sense of spatiality.

The concept [of spatial correspondence] is simple:
it is to move projector the same way the movie camera moves [...] The effect is exactly equivalent to
viewing a dark space with a flashlight.

Imagine a realtime "video flashlight." The viewer
holds a position-sensitive device which controls a
projected image, always in front of the device. The
image source may be a remote video camera or it
may be from a computer database. The viewer IS
the camera operator: it is an interactive system.

Excerpt from "Spatial Correspondence in Motion Picture Display," in
SPIE Proceedings, vol. 462, *Optics and Entertainment*, Los Angeles, 1984.

Michael Naimark,
Christoph Dohrmann
Karlsruhe Moviemap
1990–1991
interactive laserdisc system,
custom input pedestal,
immersive video projection
installation view
photo © ONUK

Michael Naimark,
Christoph Dohrmann
Karlsruhe Moviemap
1990–1991
interactive laserdisc system,
custom input pedestal, immersive video projection
installation view
photo © Michael Naimark

Karlsruhe Moviemap
(1990–1991) is a moviemap
based on the city's well-known
tramway system, with over
100 km of track snaking from
the downtown pedestrian area
out to neighboring villages at
the edge of the Black Forest.
The entire tram system was
shot in both directions from
a tramcar outfitted with a
camera triggered by the tram's
electronic odometer (at 2, 4 and
8 meters per frame depending
on location). The tracks assured
near-perfect registration for
match-cuts and unrivaled
stability for "travelling" at
hyper-fast speeds (such as
one kilometer per second).
One intention was to create
an immersive experience, using
large projection to match the
camera's wide-angle lens. Another intention was to produce
something collaboratively with
and for the community. The
Karlsruhe Moviemap has a different meaning and resonance
to people who live in the
Karlsruhe region, which is
obvious to observe when people
interact with the installation.

Several years ago I gave a series of artist-in-
residence presentations to ten-year-olds at a public
school near Boston. I set up a projection screen,
stood in front of it, and asked the students how they
knew I was not a movie.

There was silence.

I then asked them if they knew I was not a movie.
They all nodded vigorously. Then some responses
came forth.

"You're legs are below the screen."

"We saw you walk in."

"We can see your shadow." ("So?")

"You don't act like you're a movie star."

"You're answering our questions."

Their observations were perceptive and refresh-
ing. But it was a sobering reminder that the way we
experience moving images has changed very little
since the birth of cinema and television: you sit,
inactively, and stare at a flat rectangle, at either the
wall-size mural of the film theater or the breadbox-
size porthole of the television box. The formal constraints of these media are among the most severe
of all the arts. And we have learned to accept them.

These constraints are beginning to disappear.
Advances in display technologies, three-dimensional
imaging, voice input, gesture recognition, and artificial
intelligence are transforming the nature of electronic
display, making it more like a window into a virtual
world. Almost instinctively, these kids seemed to know
this.

Excerpt from "Magic Windows, Magic Glasses, and Magic Doors:
Experiencing Place via Media," in *Kanagawa International Art and
Science Exhibition*, exhib. cat., Kanagawa, 1989.

Karlsruhe Moviemap

It's last October. I'm in San Francisco sitting in a video
editing room looking at the film transfer of the Karlsruhe footage, which I shot the previous month from
the front of a tramway car. During the next few days
I will edit it for a videodisc. I am watching hundreds of
little snippets of straight and turn sequences whiz by
at hypnotic speeds. For a few minutes it's kind of fun.
Then it all starts to look alike. Dang, I can't believe I'm
doing this again. It isn't quite like making a linear movie
with an aesthetic of montage - the purpose is to or-
ganize the material to minimize disc search time and
to make programming efficient. What a drag. But it's
gotta get done.

Around the third day of nonstop logging and editing something extraordinary happens: I know where
I am in the footage. Always. You can show me any of
the forty-some thousand frames of the 108 kilometers shot in both directions and I can point to the
corresponding place on a map, as long as I can "move"
back and forth a bit. It actually seemed to happen all
of a sudden, like I was astral-projected to see Karlsruhe from a God's-eye view.

I had formed a mental map. "Karlsruhe" became a
singular thing, an almost living entity with which I
could now relate. Once that happened, every frame
had its place.

A colleague once told me he believed he could tell
what section of Paris he was in purely by the quality
of light.

I suspect this sense of wholeness, of consciousness of place, can be conveyed in a very fast and highly
impressionistic way with such emerging interactive
media. Not by simulating reality - a trap perpetuated
by the believers in the objective and ultimately a losing
battle. But by abstracting reality - creating experiences otherwise impossible in the real world. And that
these experiences, when done artfully, will make you
appreciate really being there even more.

Excerpt from "'VBK – A Moviemap of Karlsruhe': Mediated Reality
and the Consciousness of Place," in *Tomorrow's Realities*, exhib. cat.,
ACM SIGGRAPH, Las Vegas, 1991.

Displacements
1984
16mm film-loop projector; 1rpm
turntable, furnished room
spray-painted white
installation views:
San Francisco Museum
of Modern Art
photos © Scott Fisher

Displacements (1984) was an
immersive film installation. An
archetypal Americana living
room was installed in the exhibition space. Two performers
were filmed in the space using a
16mm motion picture camera
on a slowly rotating turntable in
the room's center. After filming,
the camera was replaced with a
film loop projector and the entire contents of the room were
spray-painted white. The result
was a projection screen the
proper shape for projecting
everything back onto itself.
Everything appeared strikingly
three-dimensional, except for
the people, who were not spray-
painted white and appeared
ghostlike and unreal.

Virtual Environments
class project
EAT
1989
interactive laserdisc system,
furnished dinner table, video
projection on plate, live
performers
installation views:
San Francisco Art Institute
photos © Michael Naimark

EAT (1989) was a short, single-
user installation about consumption. The participant sat
at a formal dinner table and
ordered food from a live waiter
with a menu. The waiter then
lifted up the plate cover, revealing the requested "food" projected on the dinner plate (from
a video projector hidden under
the table). Also on the table, a
large red button labeled *EAT*
could be pressed, resulting in
various video interventions and
surprises. *EAT* was produced
by my students as a collective
class project at the San
Francisco Art Institute.

EAT

Art is always content-driven. Indeed, when art appears to be something else such as form-driven, we say that the form "becomes" the content. Traditionally the arts community doesn't like it when art is primarily an exhibition of new technology and nothing else. Rudolph Arnheim put it bluntly when he said that art can't exist in a developing medium. For example, he saw the advent of sound in cinema as a major step backward for film as art. Consider what a backhanded compliment it would be to say to Abel Gance that you loved *Napoleon* because of its three screens, or to George Lucas that you loved *Star Wars* because of its high-tech special effects.

On the other hand, Nam June Paik once said that if it's been done before, he's not interested.

For several years I've asked my art students for examples of artworks (in any medium) that were both formally innovative and good art, however subjective. Some works were cited repeatably: *Les Demoiselles D'Avignon*, *The Great Train Robbery*, *2001*, *Running Fence*, *Tommy*, to name the more popular ones. There's no reason to believe the two are mutually exclusive.

But something has changed, over the past decade or two, that has driven many in the arts community to be alienated by cutting edge technologies rather than wish to explore them. Remember E.A.T. (not *EAT*)? Perhaps it's because most high technology we see in any medium today is used more for flash rather than substance. Look at television (particularly compared to years past). Alas - spinning logos rule.

What's happened, many in the arts community may say, is a discoupling of media expertise from content. Advertisers boast that they can package dogshit well enough to sell a millions dollars worth. We have been seduced by packaging over substance. (Indeed, what does it say that we elected an actor President of the United States.) [...]

The tools we used for *EAT* are just beginning to get convivial. Three essential conditions existed then that didn't exist five years earlier: a videodisc player for under $1000, videodisc mastering for under $500, and software like HyperCard that didn't require an advanced degree to use. It may not be much but it's a start.

As these tools become more convivial, they will become less alien, and more artists will use them. Shoe polish will be made by those who like to make shoe polish and it won't be by those who just wish to make shoes.

Don't get me wrong: I like million dollar projects too. But having directed videodisc projects with budgets of more than a million dollars and others with budgets of less than a thousand dollars, I certainly cannot say that the payoff is proportional.

Excerpt from "'EAT – A Virtual Dining Environment:' Fine Cheap Virtual Food," in *Tomorrow's Realities*, exhib. cat., ACM SIGGRAPH, Las Vegas, 1991.

The artworld, the mainstream artworld, was initially skeptical [of interactive art]. Much of this is natural and healthy, a critical eye toward the new. Good art ultimately is judged by surviving the test of time. The hype around interactivity was often overwhelming. And most mainstream artworlders didn't have enough frame of reference to stick their necks out.

But there's a deeper reason, I think, for a resistance to interactivity, and it stems from Michelangelo famous statement "I see the figure in the marble and I will free it." This declaration of "I talk, you listen" set the stage (in the West, at least) for artist-as-creator and art-lover as passive learner. The artworld saw interactivity as, well, flakey. It was used by artists who didn't have a strong vision or couldn't decide how to finish. [... W]e must learn to be both critical and enthusiastic if we expect interactive art to stop being an oxymoron.

Excerpt from: "Interactive Art and the Myth of Everything-ness," in *Der Prix Ars Electronica – International Compendium of the Computer Arts – Computer Graphics, Animation, Interactive Art, Computer Music*, Hannes Leopoldseder (ed.), Veritas, Linz, 1994.

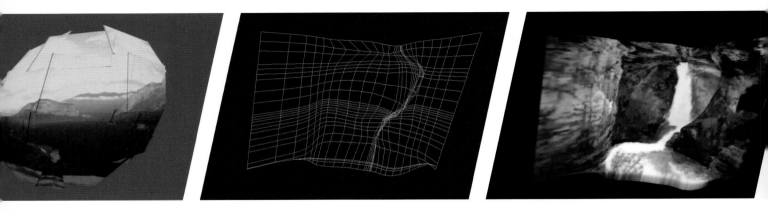

left
Michael Naimark, John Harrison
Field Recording Study #1
1992
3-D computer model
Banff Centre for the Arts
photo © Michael Naimark

Field Recording Study #1 (1992)
was a fast sketch to explore
how to make 2-D camera-based
images into 3-D computer
models. Landscapes were
recorded on video by panning or
moving the camera. Wireframe
models were made based on the
parameters of the camera lens
and movements. Still frames
were selected by hand and
texture mapped into the wire
frame to make a complete
panorama or a moviemap composite in computer 3-space.

middle and right
Michael Naimark,
John Harrison, Brenda Laurel,
Rachel Strickland
Field Recording Study #2
1993
3-D computer model
Banff Centre for the Arts and
Interval Research Corporation
photos © Rachel Strickland

Field Recording Study #2 (1993)
was an attempt to make 2-D
camera-based images three-
dimensional by mapping them
onto hand-shaped wireframe
surfaces in computer 3-space.
The wireframe shapes were
roughed out by hand, like sculp-
ting. These "virtual relief projections" were used as the basis
for one of the worlds in the
Placeholder project by Brenda
Laurel and Rachel Strickland.

This first study was intended to be fast and cheap.
(In fact, I flew into Banff exactly two weeks before
I had to fly out with something to exhibit in Siggraph's
"Guerrilla Technology" show.) The concept was to
make one continuous panorama by "tiling" together
slightly overlapping still images. These images were
collected with a simple 8mm video camera on a tripod,
using traditional surveying tools such as compass
and level.

But the images used to composite this virtual
dome were still flat two-dimensional images. The next
step was to shape it to the actual contours of the
landscape, by hand if necessary. Conceptually, this
process, of taking 2-D images and making 3-D shapes,
is exactly what a sculptor does when working from
photos. Humans are remarkably good at filling in the
missing information based on our everyday knowledge
[…] And I had been wagering my colleagues at Interval
Research that if I had a slide projector, a slide of a
human face, and a giant mound of mashed potatoes,
that I could hand-shape the mound to create a credible (if not accurate) 3-D face projection.

Our biggest struggle was not technological
(thankfully), but was artistic. On the one hand, the
sites in the Banff area are monumental in their grace
and beauty. Some are sacred. On the other hand,
watching the tourists at these sites told a different
story. Busses and busses pulled in and out parking
lots seemingly in the middle of nowhere. Tourists
would get out – cameras in hand – for twenty minutes,
then back on the busses off to another Site. [We]
agreed that the strength of the footage would lie in
counterpointing these two conflicting messages.

Excerpt from "Field Recording Studies: Art and Virtual Environments," in
Immersed in Technology, Mary Anne Moser, Douglas MacLeod (eds), The
MIT Press, Cambridge, MA, 1996.

"[I]nteractive art" is a title currently placed upon an
aggregate of artforms. Perhaps these closer resemble the inventions presented in the twenty years
before cinema rather than after - a hodgepodge of
novelties. Transition media. […] Most of what's been
done so far cluster around a few tiny parcels. Spreading out may be a good idea. Odds are the territory is
much much bigger than we currently imagine.

Excerpt from "Interactive Art – Maybe It's a Bad Idea," in *Cyberarts:
International Compendium Prix Ars Electronica; Net, Interactive Art,
Computer Animation, Computer Music*, Hannes Leopoldseder,
Christine Schöpf (eds), Springer, Vienna and New York, 1997.

A simple model of the relationship between a subject
and its representation can be made by analogy to an
audio mixing board – a box with an input, and output,
and rows and rows of slider controls. The analogy is
that the sliders depict all of the individual elements
of representation and that if all are turned up to
their maximum, that the representation will be indistinguishable from its subject. For example, if the representation is visual, the sliders may depict elements
such as spatial resolution, temporal resolution,
dynamic range, color fidelity, degree of orthoscopy,
etc. […]

The relevant issue here is not whether this mixing
board analogy is accurate, but whether or not it's relevant to the arts. And here is where two camps can
be observed.

One camp seems to scream "turn all the sliders up
to 10!" This can be seen at technology-based exhibitions such as Siggraph and has been the battle cry in
many VR circles. […] An implicit assumption here is
that the world is sensed the same by all people and
what seems real to me will seem real to you, a very
deep assumption about human cognition and consciousness.

The other camp says, simply put: "Who cares!"
These tend to be artists working in traditional media,
such as painters and poets. An artist friend of the
author whose medium is 16mm film (and who despises
video and computers) once said that he likes his
medium for all the reasons folks like me don't: all of
the exploration has already been done and he can
simply use it. […]

While presence and abstraction can be one-
dimensionalized in terms of mixing board psycho-
physics, quality of experience is ultimately orthogonal
to it. To suggest that more or less image detail, or
more or less panoramic continuousness, or even more
or less self-reference, makes a representation
better or worse collapses one too many dimensions
together. The dimension of quality – some may call
this art – cannot follow simple rules.

Excerpt from "What's Wrong with this Picture? Presence and Abstrac-
tion in the Age of Cyberspace," in *Consciousness Reframed: Art and
Consciousness in the Post-biological Era. Proceedings of the first
International Conference of the Centre for Advanced Inquiry in the
Interactive Arts University of Wales*, University of Wales, Newport,
Wales, 1997.

03 IMMERSIVE
Michael Naimark

Banff Centre for the Arts
Interval Research Corporation

From Study #3, Fall 1993

It is my observation and belief that technology, particularly computer and media technology, is having an increasingly profound effect on everyone on the planet. And that if artists don't jump in and pro-actively help shape these powerful new tools, it will be left by default to advertisers, the military, organized religion, and sex peddlers. Some of us believe the stakes are high.

Excerpt from "Art ('and' or 'versus') Technology: Some Personal Observations," in *Art@Science*, Christa Sommerer, Laurent Mignonneau (eds), Springer, Vienna and New York, 1998.

After twenty years on these experiments representing place, here are some brief thoughts about what I believe I learned. First, one cannot represent everything. It will never be the same as "being there." To suggest that it is "like being there" suggests that the user can go everywhere and see everything, and you can't. It is humbling. It also implies an abdication of artistic or editorial control, which is problematic.

Second, immersive public-space environments have enjoyed a long rich history and it is unlikely that they will be replaced by the small low-bandwidth images associated with virtuality and the Web. On the contrary, imagine using networks and the Web to make unique ultra-high bandwidth group experiences which encompass both virtuality and co-presence.

Third, it is impossible to separate the aesthetics of telepresence from the politics of place. Representing place can't be separated from representing its inhabitants and culture.

Whoever controls representation, controls all.

Excerpt from "Place Runs Deep: Virtuality, Place and Indigenousness," in *Virtual Museums Symposium*, Arch Foundation, Salzburg, 1998.

Afterword

After completing *Be Now Here* in 2000, Michael Naimark initiated a research effort at Interval Research Corporation about cameras and the Internet. This research lead to Kundi.com, a search engine for webcams and other streaming media that could find live events as they happened. Kundi was based on a unique alert infrastructure, whereby people could alert other people to encourage real time propagation. Kundi means flocking, herding, or swarming in Swahili.

In 2001, Michael Naimark became artist in residence at the Institute of Advanced Media Arts and Sciences (IAMAS) in Gifu, Japan. His work focussed on combining immersion and virtual reality with liveness and the Internet.

In late 2001, partly as a response to the aftermath of September 11, Naimark began an investigation asking: when cameras are everywhere, is it possible to become invisible from them? He found that small inexpensive lasers, properly aimed, can stop the gaze of cameras without damage. In late 2002 he published "How to ZAP a Camera: Using Lasers to Temporarily Neutralize Camera Sensors."

Naimark is currently continuing his work with VR and the Internet, and working with Leonardo/ISAST to study the feasibility of a sustainable "arts lab."

Michael Naimark

top left
Michael Naimark, John Woodfill, Paul Debevec, Leo Villareal
See Banff!
Dimensionalization Study
1994
3-D computer model
Banff Centre for the Arts and Interval Research Corporation
photo © John Woodfill

Dimensionalization Studies (1994) began as an informal collaboration with computer-vision researchers at Interval Research, who helped design the stereoscopic camera system for *See Banff!* in exchange for using the footage for their own work. (Both sides benefited.) Their studies were based on using computer vision techniques for deriving depth information from stereoscopic pairs of images, then turning the 2-D pixels into 3-D "points in space."
Such representations differ from 3-D computer models because they are non-semantic: the computer has no knowledge of scene's contents, so object manipulation (such as moving or changing things in the imagery) is impossible.
Such representations are like 3-D computer models because arbitrary viewpoints can be displayed. However, when the viewpoint differs from the original "privileged" viewpoint, occlusions (areas of missing data) are revealed. Combining multiple viewpoints into a single model may result in the ability to navigate around inside movies of the future.

bottom left
Michael Naimark, Kathy McInnis
See Banff! Stereogram
1994
stereoscope image
Banff Centre for the Arts and Interval Research Corporation
photo © Michael Naimark

See Banff! (1994) is an interactive stereoscopic installation resembling a Kinetoscope one hundred years earlier: made out of walnut and brass, with a viewing hood on top, a crank on the side, and a selector for choosing one of the silent "views." These views were filmed around Banff and rural Alberta, imagery relating to landscape and tourism.
For filming, a "Super Jogger" baby carriage was fitted with two wide-angle 16mm stop-frame cameras, triggered either by an intervalometer (for time lapse) or by an encoder on one of the carriage wheels (for moviemaps). The installation displays an immersive 3-D image and allows "travel" through time and space by turning the crank forward and backward.

right
Michael Naimark,
Gilles Tassé, Christoph Dohrmann,
Robert Adams
See Banff! Kinetoscope
1994
interactive laserdisc system, stereoscopic optics, custom cabinet
Banff Centre for the Arts and Interval Research Corporation
photo © Michael Naimark

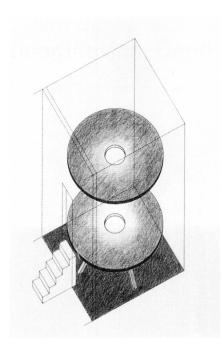

left
conceptual drawing
for the installation
Model for stage and screen
1987
courtesy Galleria Mario Pieroni,
American Academy, Rome

right
Model for stage and screen
1987
installation
wood, paint, light, fog
25.4 x 25.4 x 25.4 cm
installation view: Galleria Mario
Pieroni, Rome, 1987
courtesy Galleria Mario Pieroni,
American Academy, Rome
photo courtesy Galleria Mario
Pieroni, Rome; Galerie Karin
Sachs, Munich; Galerie Xavier
Hufkens, Brussels

experience is the sensation that the room itself is receding as one looks through the fog and light, and that the distance is increasing between oneself and the outer edges of the room. For most people, this sensation is uncomfortable. But escaping the chamber through the antechamber provides no release, since most viewers experience retinal excitation at the very moment they expected to regain control over their vision. 1 They see the complementary color of the light from the chamber projected onto the antechamber walls.

In *The Work of the Forest* (1992) I used the Proustian image of nineteenth-century interiority – the whirling room – as a structuring device to produce a panorama. Walter Benjamin conceived a sense of history that could come to terms with technology and the shifting categories of the representations of nature. For him, it is the juxtaposition of text and image over time which elucidates historical truth. This "dialectics of seeing" crystallizes antithetical elements by providing axes for their alignment. I adapted Benjamin's montage theory to the conflicting histories of Belgian colonial activities in Africa and the specifically Belgian form of Art Nouveau by rendering an endless surround produced by a continuously panning image. This seemed an appropriate way to stage the competing and conflicting relations between colonial expansion, utopian architecture, fin-de-siècle politics and World's Fair ideology.

The structure of *The Work of the Forest* is designed to provide several viewing positions, and hence several points of view. From above, the viewer has the comfort and authority people generally associate with monocular perspective and classical Hollywood cinema. The view from the center is the most disorienting: the panorama itself disrupts a sense of closure. From this position it becomes clear that each screen has a different soundtrack, and so the meaning of the images changes. A third view from the exterior circumference (outside) seemingly allows the viewer to predict the sequences seen through the transparent screens; it is the one from which ' the viewer can best deconstruct the competing

montage elements as they produce their meanings.

For Imagination, Dead Imagine (1991) an androgynous head is projected as if contained within a mirrored Minimalist cube. Sounds of the head slowly breathing fill the space. The head is serene, waiting. Suddenly a substance pours over it from all sides, drenching it in what appears to be a bodily fluid. The spectator wants to turn away, but cannot. Horror at the repulsive nature of the substances is replaced by fascination with their beauty as they apparently change into majestic but abstract landscapes.

In conceiving this project I was interested in exploring the legacy of Minimal Art, particularly Merleau-Ponty's concept of the primacy of lived bodily experience established as an internal horizon that produces meaning. I read Minimalism through several competing registers. First, through its insistence on an immediacy of experience understood through the body, although at the same time Minimalism eliminated any overt reference to the body. Second, through the way this elision of the body finds an echo in the history of aesthetics, and in the sublime in particular. In the eighteenth century, the power and terror of nature unleashed intimations of infinity and deity, dwarfing the observer who, aspiring to transcendence, never forgot his insignificance. Third, through Julia Kristeva's exploration of the subjective experience set out, in her reading of the "abject," by the use of bodily fluids: "These bodily fluids, this shit is what life withstands, hardly and with difficulty on the part of death. There I am at the border of my condition as a living being. Such waste drops so that I might live, until from loss to loss, nothing remains in me and my entire body falls beyond the limit. [...] It is death infecting life. Abject." Finally, in the title *Imagination, Dead Imagine* I wanted to invoke Samuel Beckett's work, since I was commenting on the horror vacui I saw as a condition of this experience.

Speedflesh (1997–98) is an immersive, interactive video-sound narrative that takes place in a 360-degree point-of-view theater. You are in the center of a world that is moving away from you at rapid speed. A woman floats toward you and then

1 For a longer discussion, see "Model for stage and screen," in *Public Fantasy,* Blazwick (ed.), ICA, London, 1991.

The Work of the Forest
1992
three-channel video projection
panorama on three transparent
art nouveau screens
wood, silk, video
dimensions variable
installation views: Fondation
pour l'architecture, Brussels,
1992
photos courtesy Fondation
pour l'architecture, Brussels;
Galerie Hubert Winter, Vienna

Judith Barry, Brad Miskell
Speedflesh
1997–98
360-degree video projection
with sound
dimensions variable
screenshots
courtesy Wexner Center
for the Arts, Columbus, 1998
photos courtesy Luis Serpa
Galeria, Lisbon

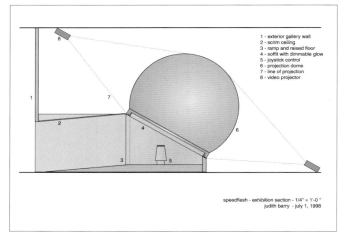

1 - exterior gallery wall
2 - scrim ceiling
3 - ramp and raised floor
4 - soffit with dimmable glow
5 - joystick control
6 - projection dome
7 - line of projection
8 - video projector

speedflesh - exhibition section - 1/4" = 1'-0 "
judith barry - july 1, 1998

left
conceptual drawing for
the 360-degree video/sound
projection *Speedflesh*
by Judith Barry, Brad Miskell
1997–98

right
composite image/study
for the 360-degree video/sound
projection *Speedflesh*

away, elongated through the anamorphosis produced through the projection. Her movements seem to conceal and sometimes reveal the four characters whose lives seem to be caught/displayed in the band of light as it closes in around you. You can engage with the narrative by turning the wheel at the center of the surround and "tuning in" to the last five minutes in the lives of these characters. As each character's point of view is projected 360 degrees around the viewer, you experience the narrative through that character's eyes.

The structure of the work, the 360-degree projection, has antecedents in the history of the anamorphic image: a history that figures not only throughout the narratives of representation, but also marks the Neoplatonic period and recalls the power of hidden iconographies to describe new social orders. In using the anamorphis as the form/content of the imagery of *Speedflesh*, we were on one level attempting to show that even an apocalyptic moment poses other histories that, although visible if you can decode them, will not necessarily be exhausted by this process. Similarly, while this work seems to propose a relation with André Bazin's notion of a "total cinema," its narrative structure implies indeterminacy, not order, as it strives to escape the boundaries of a "realist" representational model.

Whole Potatoes from Mashed was originally commissioned for the exhibition, "on taking a normal situation and translating it into multiple and overlapping discourses" at the MuHKA in 1993 when Antwerp was European City of Culture. The exhibition title, a quote from Gordon Matta-Clark, was the linchpin around which the show was organized, as Matta-Clark's work

formed the genesis of the museum collection. I was intrigued by the title and began to investigate more thoroughly what these words had meant for Matta-Clark, and also to look more closely at the effects of discourses, multiple and overlapping, on the city of Antwerp. The questions that animated the research included a notion of how words have been used to provide a transformative moment – a moment made physical, a moment that seemingly like magic can move at the speed of thought.

My research led me to several discursive systems unique to Antwerp: to the sixteenth-century Plantin-Moretus printing house that published many alchemical treaties,2 and to the "beguines," those homes for sixteenth-century minstrel woman whose explicit "love" poems to "God" were deemed blasphemous even as they transformed all listeners. And I began to see the speed at which discourses can move as a kind of magic. This research led me to conceive of the form of this piece as a way of looking at how language moving at the speed of thought is a form of magic.

This project combines a number of different discourses and seemingly disparate areas of inquiry in order to make a relatively simple point. Something that we all know, but perhaps don't think about - which is that materials, matter, have a history. But it is not enough to merely recount this history as a series of bald facts (as though such a tale were plausible). No. For history is not one story, but many. It is a process of accretion over time, and it is specific, both to Antwerp, a city with a past, and also to other places, places that it has passed through, is passing through on its way, somewhere else. How matter might be thought about is the subject of this work. What matters – what is the matter? How it matters?

2 Alchemical treaties are heretical texts which if read in the right way produced a transformation in the reader.

03 IMMERSIVE
Judith Barry

Whole Potatoes from Mashed
1993
mixed-media fiber-optic/sound
installation
rug, cables, voice coders,
sensors, strobe, glossary
dimensions variable
installation view:
MuHKA, Antwerp, 1993
Judith Barry
courtesy Judith Barry
and Luis Serpa Projetos, Lisbon
photo courtesy Judith Barry

This sounds silly in American English. It may be un-translatable in Dutch. Is there something beyond language that we can get at, that remains after thought has disappeared? Yes of course, we all know this and for some of us, that is one of the functions of art. The visual cannot be completely described by language. Matter is what fills up space. Language is something else. The question for a history of matter is where do they meet, and what happens. Language is multiple, diffuse, transparent. Perhaps Marshall McLuhan was correct when he suggested that the shift from a literate, phonetic alphabet culture to an electronic medium would produce a kind of "electronic feudalism." This was an idea that he based on the notion that before mechanized print was invented, each manuscript had to be "looked" at, because it reflected its author in a way that is very different from the contemporary act of reading. As we read, the "Gestalt" of the manuscript disappears, and the print becomes a transparent medium that conveys the ideas of the author. With electronic image-based media, including many computer-based magazines such as *Wired* or *Ray Gun*, and with many artist-book projects, we have returned to a situation where we must look, assemble the image of the words, in order for the page to yield its meanings. In other words, if the page is not invisible, it has substance which must be read. A few hundred years ago, in the dark forest of Europe, peasants and woodcutters might tell each other stories about a man who rescued a wounded animal or a stricken princess and was rewarded with a magic ring. All the man had to do was to wish for something with the ring, and his wish would be granted. Stories like this are always short. Narrative struggle is absent, the impossible is accomplished at the speed of thought. At the dawn of the twenty-first century, with scarcity all around us, we find ourselves once more hovering on the edge of the magical. And the ring of power is no longer contained in a fable, but in an engineering project in a laboratory all over the world.

What you see before you is a landscape, a landscape made of words and light. In your hand, you have a glossary, a dictionary, which you can use to put order into this landscape, to shape this landscape into any form that you might wish it to take. It is not interactive in the sense that you can overtly effect it, yet it will yield to you any meanings you choose to give it. It is right there waiting for you.

What happens: Fiber optics in a matrix fills the room. You hear one sound, then another, then another. As the sounds, then the words, pass in the air, you see the space light up around you, behind you, above you. You notice that the light lasts exactly as long as it takes to make the sound. As the words reach the end of the fiber you notice that there is a relationship between the light that you see and the duration of the sound. As the words travel faster and faster and come with more rapidity, the sounds multiply and become more densely layered. The matrix responds by becoming lighter and more fluid. Gradually you realize that there is a specific relation between the words and the fibers, but that it is not one to one. The words take flight moving in a number of directions, producing a multiplicity of meanings. Taking you one place, then another, then another. Hovering on the edge of meaning, beyond the concern for sense. You collapse into thought. But the sounds take you through the light as you watch them try to represent themselves. You follow a thought from one place to another, finding yourself here and then away. You are alone at the speed of thought.

It doesn't want to make sense, but you do. How this works is left to chance. But you can't do that. You must hear voices, create meaning. Find order. In the white light that makes itself into images before your eyes, you can see everything. In the white noise that is a constant chant, you escape.

Judith Barry

Agnes Hegedüs, Bernd Lintermann, Jeffrey Shaw
reconFiguring the CAVE

1997-2001
computer-based interactive video installation /
music: Leslie Stuck / motion analysis for music:
Jonathan Bachrach

1 Plato, *The Republic*, Book VII.

2 *conFiguring the CAVE* was
retitled *reconFiguring the
CAVE* for the exhibition
"Future Cinema." Only two
large projection surfaces
were used, and the puppet
was replaced with an LCD
touchscreen as the primary
interface. *reconFiguring the
CAVE* was produced by
Boctok Tokyo and David
D'Heilly at the ZKM Karlsruhe Collection of the NTT
InterCommunication Center,
Tokyo, Japan.

3 The Fraunhofer Institute in
Stuttgart engineered the
user interface.

Considering *conFiguring the CAVE*

"See human beings as though they were in an underground cave-like dwelling with its entrance, a
long one, open to the light across the whole width
of the cave. They are in it from childhood with their
legs and necks in bonds so that they are fixed,
seeing only in front of them … Their light is from a
fire burning far above and behind them. Between
the fire and the prisoners there is a road above,
along which we see a wall, built like the partitions
puppet-handlers set in front of the human beings
and over which they show the puppets … Then also
see along this wall human beings carrying all sorts
of artifacts, which project above the wall, and
statues of men and other animals wrought from
stone, wood, and every kind of material; as is to be
expected … Do you suppose such men would have
seen anything of themselves and one another
other than the shadows cast by the fire on the
side of the cave facing them? … Such men would
hold that the truth is nothing other than the
shadows of artificial things."[1]
A vision of future cinema, guided by a puppet,
emerges at the interstice of teleological shadows,
mimetic urgency, and historical materialism in *con-
Figuring the CAVE*.[2] One navigates a near life-size
wooden puppet/mannequin situated in the center of
the cave through visual and auditory sequences in an
immersive computer-based interactive video installation. Fitted with electronic measurement devices embedded in its moveable joints, the puppet enables interaction with the transformations of the computer-
generated images and sounds.[3] Participants enter

conFiguring the CAVE
1996
computer-based interactive
video installation
installation views:
ICC Tokyo, 1997
© 1997 ICC Tokyo

the stage of production as puppet-handlers. These auteurs, apparently in control of the work, recall the automaton "puppet in Turkish attire and with a hookah in its mouth" described by Walter Benjamin in his "Theses on the Philosophy of History," the last text written before his suicide in 1940. There the puppet counters every move of an opponent in a chess game aided by a system of mirrors that camouflage the chess table under which hides "a little hunchback … guid[ing] the puppet's hand by means of strings." The hunchbacks shaping the master narrative of *conFiguring the CAVE* and predetermining its imagery are Agnes Hegedüs, Bernd Lintermann and Jeffrey Shaw; Leslie Stuck composed the sound; and Bernd Lintermann developed the Xfrog software architecture that enables the dynamic of movement and image transformations modulated by the puppet user interface.[4] The artists envision the work as "a mediated environment of functional relationships between bodily and spatial coordinates [that] refers to the long history in all cultures of conjecturing the body as the locus and measure of the universe, [and that is engaged] in a post-modern exigency which has dislocated the body in a vertiginous space of deconstructed coordinates and equivocal complexity."[5] As "a meta-discourse … both separated from and connected to historical configurations," the discourse of *conFiguring the CAVE* is multivalent. Merging esoteric traditions with advanced technology, contemporary theory, and philosophy, it also recalls Benjamin's notion that the "philosophical counterpart" (to his story of puppet and hunchback) is "historical materialism," which "wins," especially by enlisting the services of a "wizened" theology in hiding.[6] Benjamin's meditation

on the messianic function in history asserts (through negation) the continued relevance of theological perspectives in historical materialism, a position with which *conFiguring the CAVE* seems to concur.

The system that organizes access to the work is configured in seven separate rich and intellectually dense domains that suture history and technology to theological content, especially in its affinities to Jewish mysticism and Kabbalah. Seven is a sacred number central to most esoteric traditions, a legacy preserved in the profane notion of the "lucky 7." Among hundreds of symbolic attributes of the number are the following. Seven appears in the divine organizational structures of ancient Egypt, Phœnicia, and Persia, in Judeo-Christian tradition and in Buddhism where, for example, the idea of seven stages of progressive development of the disembodied soul is allegorized in pagoda architecture.[7] Seven acts of creation structure the beginning of the world in the Old Testament. The original seven ancient planets served as the model for early divisions of states. Numerous units of seven divide configurations of stars (i. e., Septentrion). A contract with the devil was said to contain seven paragraphs, would conclude in seven years, and was signed by the contractor seven times. Legendary wars lasted seven years, seven months, and seven days. Seven in the Old Testament signifies wisdom (Proverbs 9:1). Seven days conclude Passover and seven branches define the menorah.

Each of the seven domains of *conFiguring the CAVE* is distinctive. In Domain One, a constellation of cubic and rectangular forms moves about in a complex organic symmetry. Interaction with the puppet causes them to enter the CAVE and fish-eye

4 Space limitations have prevented me from discussing the relationships between imagery and sound in *conFiguring the CAVE*. But Stuck created seven sound compositions for the seven pictorial domains via an eight-channel spatialized-sound system that augments the three-dimensional qualities of the stereoscopic visual environment. The sound compositions, like the imagery, are interactively affected by the viewer's handling of the interface (the puppet's body and limbs) which contributes to the synchronous unity of visual and audio transformations, as well as to the overall synaesthetic singularity of the work. Jonathan Bachrach developed the motion analysis for the music.

5 Agnes Hegedüs, Bernd Lintermann, Jeffrey Shaw, Leslie Stuck, handout for *conFiguring the Cave*, 1997.

6 Walter Benjamin, "Theses on the Philosophy of History," in *Illuminations*, Schocken Books, New York, 1969, p. 253.

7 Among other sources, I drew on H. P. Blavatsky's article "The Number Seven" (*Theosophist*, June 1880) for many of these references. http://www.blavatsky.net/ blavatsky/arts/Number Seven.htm

reconFiguring the CAVE
1997–2001
computer-based
interactive video installation
installation view: "Vision and
Reality" exhibition, Louisiana
Museum of Modern Art,
Denmark, 2000
© Hegedüs, Lintermann,
Shaw, Stuck
photo © Jeffrey Shaw

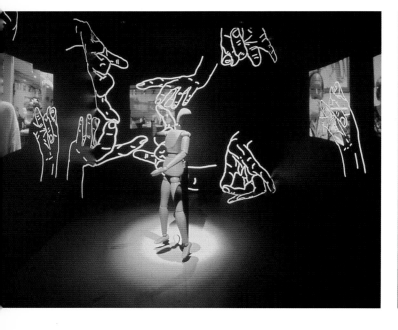

photographs on their surfaces must signify sight, as much as the long rectangular rods that saturate the space with colors suggest the origins of insight. In Domain Two, multi-layered walls of changing texts, alphabetic characters and hieroglyphics constitute the virtual architecture of a universal matrix of languages and information. On the floor of the CAVE, a circular representation of an ancient Chinese rubbing-stone carved with text appears in the spherical environment of an Hebraic astrological map. Movements of the puppet's body and limbs change the graphical contents and shift the positions of the text planes. Tilting the puppet completely upside-down causes a vortex of alphabetic signs. At other times one is immersed in a visually stunning space, effecting initiation into the origins of language or a tomb of shattered words, an exploded Tower of Babel.

Positioning of the puppet's limbs in Domain Three determines the symmetry and movement of five Platonic geometric solids that continuously move through the cave against an environment constituted by three large, slowly rotating, concentric spheres. One depicts a satellite picture of Earth with the continents transformed into cloud formations. Another shows an astrological map of heavenly bodies. The innermost displays André Breton's Surrealist map of the world. Art historical references such as this abound in Domain Seven, where dabs of paint dart about recalling action painting, now programmed by a flocking algorithm. The blue refers directly to International Klein Blue, the color that the French painter created as part of his effort to depict the infinite. The Klein quotations summon his affiliation with Rose+Crox and Theosophy and reinforce the subtle esoteric aspects of Kabbalah, Gnosticism, and pan-

theistic occult practices throughout the work. Together with spiraling algorithmically generated monochromatic shapes (metaphors for forms in early abstract animated films), the lucid art historical references summarize paths to aesthetic knowledge. Even the contemporary art world surfaces in Domain Four, where media-art personalities appear in a panoramic photographic background. That domain also reinforces the aesthetic and art-historical motifs in circling clusters of line drawings representing hands that morph through a variety of gestures and a virtual hand-shadow play performed on the cave's rear wall.

The gender of the slender puppet, while ostensibly androgenous, may be read as female, situating *conFiguring the CAVE* in an androcentric metaphysics. Indeed, the Jewish mysticism foundational to the work reveals itself to belong to what Gershom Scholem has described as "a masculine doctrine … both historically and metaphysically." The fifth domain exacerbates this patriarchy by dividing the space into two overlapping image planes: a three-dimensional satellite photograph of the geographical area around Hiroshima and a Daguerreotype of two naked women. A figure of positive and negative connotation, the puppet-muse guides participants through the cave, while being metonymically connected to "the Other Side, the realm of impurity and evil" by the conflation of her body with the geography of mass destruction.[8] Feminists have long deconstructed the relegation of the female body to nature (rather than culture) and have theorized about the appropriation of the muse and female procreativity for male creativity.

Moreover, tilting the body of the puppet between its vertical and horizontal axis causes the nudes to

8 J.H. Laenen, *Jewish Mysticism: An Introduction*, Westminister John Knox Press, Louisville, 2001, p. 139.

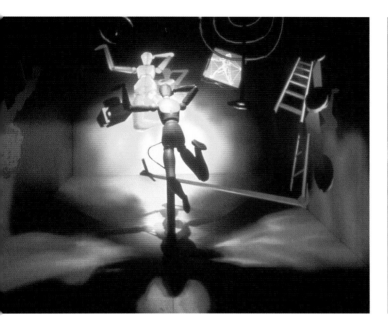

conFiguring the CAVE
1997
computer-based interactive
video installation
installation views:
ICC Tokyo, 1997
© 1997 ICC Tokyo

move up and down in erotic ways, becoming alternately the topography of the earth and the field of the firmament. The work is also tinged with the erotic clasping of a responsive and submissive body, however much it is only a wooden shadow of narcissism, the inability to engage the truth of bodies, and the deconstruction of the body. A vicariously sinister aspect of the pleasure and wonder experienced by steering the puppet occurs when someone else manipulates the figure. Viewing from a distance, craving metamorphoses into aversion, scopophilic appetite becomes foreboding. Capturing the gaze and dislodging viewers from their intimate interconnection renders the puppet a mere thing, an object all too reminiscent of Surrealist Hans Bellmer's tortured dolls. Indeed, the simultaneous act of participating in and viewing the actual corporeal scene activates codes of desire operating (but ordinarily sublimated) in conventional cinema. The administration of the puppet exposes the affect of appetite and repulsion fundamental to the fetishism of viewing. But in this future cinema, complicity circles back to self-incrimination.

Plato's cave is most directly invoked in Domain Six, where the environment becomes engulfed in flames and a virtual mirror image of the puppet emulates its movements and casts more shadows of shadows. Thus does the machinery of mirroring, characterizing conventional cinema, survive in future cinema in the shadow-filled simulacra of the high-resolution, real-time, computer-generated stereoscopic images of the CAVE.9 Seven symbolic objects whirl through the flames: a menorah, a compass, a camera, a gyroscope, a child's wooden cart, a blue sponge, and a cube on whose sides appear six classical images of the "harmonious" human figure by Leonardo da Vinci. Folding the puppet's limbs converges objects on the mirrored puppet's body, suggesting the corporeal origins of religion, science, visual technologies, planetary movement, narratives of learning, knowledge, play, geology, art, and mathematics. An intoxicating moment in the generative interaction occurs when conFiguring the CAVE is filled with fractal shapes washed in blue, reinforcing mystic Rabbi Moses Cordovero's invocation to, "Imitate your creator. Then you will enter the mystery of the supernal form, the divine image in which you were created."10

Locating sight in a simulacrum where technology exacerbates platonic phantoms, conFiguring the CAVE unleashes a multidimensional world of the body, its objects and ideas. The work insists on the unity of historical knowledge and visionary insight in its hybrid combination of theory and theology, themes found also in Benjamin's work. But rather than neutralize their significance (or the messianic elements in both Benjamin's work and conFiguring the CAVE), they energize each another. Benjamin understood this radicalism,11 writing in his last letter to Gershom Scholem on 11 January 1940: "Every line we succeed in publishing today – no matter how uncertain the future to which we entrust it – is a victory wrenched from the powers of darkness."12 In a militarized period in which world instability is comparable to that in 1940, a work like conFiguring the CAVE may be understood as a model of future cinema. In it art empowers a context for meditation on and interaction with vital and contested configurations of our time – history, divine and secular knowledge, and the body – even as the realms of their truths pass ever more into shadows.

Kristine Stiles

9 This unique form of virtual reality environment was developed by Dan Sandin and his team at the Electronic Visualization Lab at the University of Illinois.

10 Rabbi Moses Cordovero, The Palm Tree of Devorah, quoted in Ron H. Feldman, Fundamentals of Jewish Mysticism and Kabbalah, Crossing Press, Freedom, California, 1999, p. 19.

11 For a discussion of the energizing and radicalizing elements in Benjamin's work, see Lloyd Spencer, "On the Concept of History: Some of the background to Benjamin's 'Theses'." http://www.tasc.ac.uk/depart/media/staff/ls/WBenjamin/THESES.html

12 The Correspondence of Walter Benjamin and Gershom Scholem 1932–1940, Gershom Scholem (ed.), Schocken Books, New York, 1989, p. 262.

Blast Theory
Desert Rain

1999
VR environment for performance / mixed media /
performance duration: 30 min

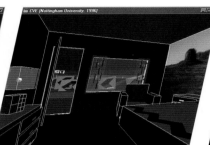
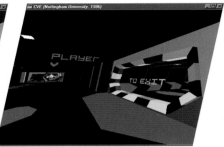

Desert Rain
1999
screenshots
© Blast Theory

Introduction

In a world where Gulf War images echo Hollywood images, where Norman Schwarzkopf blurs into Arnold Schwarzenegger, *Desert Rain* looks for the faint line between the real and the fictional.

Desert Rain sends you on a mission into a virtual world. Standing on a footplate and zipped into a cubicle, each of the six team members explores motels, deserts and underground bunkers, communicating with each other within the virtual world: a world projected onto a screen of falling water. You have thirty minutes to find the target, complete the mission, and get to the final room (where others may have a very different idea of what actually happened out there).

In a full page article on *Desert Rain*, *The Sunday Times* wrote,

"It's a powerful piece and it excites curious emotions in the few viewers who are able to take part in the game. As a company, Blast Theory seems finally to offer Britain a theatre group that delves into our popular culture to create deeply challenging work."1

Desert Rain is a collaboration between Blast Theory and the Communications Research Group at Nottingham University.2

Description

On arrival, six visitors at a time enter a small antechamber. They are given a magnetic swipe card of a person they must find. They leave their coats and bags and put on hooded black jackets. In total darkness, the visitors are then led into the next space.

Each visitor finds himself standing on a footpad. In front of the visitor is a rain screen, four meters across, which provides a surface of fine water-spray holding the projected image of a virtual world.

The visitor begins alone in an American motel room. Using the footpad, the visitors are able to navigate within the world. In the corner, a television is switched to cable TV. Once outside, they find themselves in a compound. By crossing a fence they move

from day to night and enter a desert landscape.

Over the next twenty minutes, the visitors have to meet and exchange information to complete their rescue attempt and get out.

Reaching the apparent safety of an underground network of bunkers and tunnels, the visitors come face to face with performers, with fragments of the Gulf War, and with each other.

If they successfully find their target, a performer emerges through the water screen and hands them a magnetic swipe card.

The final virtual space is a vast underground hangar containing a floating field of numbers, all of which estimated Iraqi casualty figures. As the visitors push their way through the densely packed numbers, they reach the exit.

Only if all six visitors escape together their mission has been a success.

Having left the virtual world and crossed through the water screens, the visitors find the exit corridor is blocked by a large pile of sand. Having climbed up the sand and down the other side they reach the final room of the installation.

The walls of the final room are full-scale photographs of the walls of an English hotel room. The room contains no objects apart from a magnetic card reader and a monitor cut into the wall exactly where the television is in the hotel room.

As each visitor swipes their card, their target appears on a monitor sitting in the very same hotel room. Each of the six targets has had their life changed by the Gulf War in some way: as a soldier, a journalist, a peace worker, an actor or a passive spectator. They talk about their relationship to the events, their proximity to them, about how "real" they felt.

On leaving, the visitors collect their coats and bags. At some later point in time, they will discover a small bag of sand concealed in their coat or bag. The bag contains approximately 100,000 grains of sand.

1 *The Sunday Times*, Culture Section, 31 October 1999.

2 More technical information (in German) and links available at http://on1.zkm.de/zkm/werke/DesertRain

Concept

Desert Rain uses a combination of Virtual Reality, installation and performance to address the problem of the boundary between the real and the virtual. It places participants in a Collaborative Virtual Environment in which the real intrudes upon the virtual and vice versa. It uses the real, the imaginary, the fictional and the virtual side by side and juxtaposes these elements as a means of defining them.

The piece is influenced by Jean Baudrillard's assertion that the Gulf War did not take place because it was in fact a virtual event. Whilst remaining deeply suspicious of this kind of theoretical position, Blast Theory recognizes that this idea touches upon a crucial shift in our perception and understanding of the world around us. It asserts that the role of the media, advertising and entertainment industries in the presentation of events is casually misleading at best, and perniciously deceptive at worst. As Paul Patton says in an essay about Baudrillard, "The sense in which Baudrillard speaks of events as virtual is related to the idea that real events lose their identity when they attain the velocity of real-time information or, to employ another metaphor, when they become encrusted with the information which represents them.

In this sense, while televisual information claims to provide immediate access to real events, in fact what it does is produce informational events which stand in for the real, and which 'inform' public opinion, which in turn affects the course of subsequent events, both real and informational. As consumers of mass media, we never experience the bare material event but only

Desert Rain
1999
VR environment for
performance
mixed media
installation views: ZKM |
Center for Art and Media
Karlsruhe, 1999
© Blast Theory
photos © Franz Wamhof

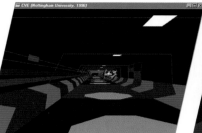

the informational coating which renders it 'sticky and unintelligible' like the oil-soaked sea bird."

This reference to the "oil-soaked sea bird" as an icon that stands in for the reality of an oil spill (and which, in effect, distracts attention from and even masks entirely the real complexity and significance of the events surrounding an oil spill), gives a direct example of the ways in which these processes affect us every day.

While these ideas form the backdrop to *Desert Rain*, the piece is not intended to demonstrate the theory, but merely to accept its significance in informing our view of the relationship of the real to the virtual, and especially in its assertion that the virtual has a daily presence in our lives.

Indeed, we also have a great interest in those who have coruscatingly attacked Baudrillard's ideas as "absurd theses" which are "ill-equipped to mount any kind of effective critical resistance."

The role of the cinema, and particularly Hollywood, in this process is also important. As a vehicle for dreams, aspirations and fantasies, films play a major role in affecting our self-image and as a source of inspiration.

The key motif of the individual overcoming all odds to triumph is a touchstone for our culture and has an impact on real life. Arnold Schwarzenegger and Norman Schwarzkopf both exemplify certain aspects of leadership, for example, and each draws on the attributes of the other.

Desert Rain therefore attempts to bring visitors to a new understanding of the ways in which the virtual and the real are blurred and, in particular, the role of the mass media in distorting our appraisal of the world beyond our own personal experience.

Text first published at http://www.blasttheory.co.uk

Desert Rain
1999
screenshots
© Blast Theory

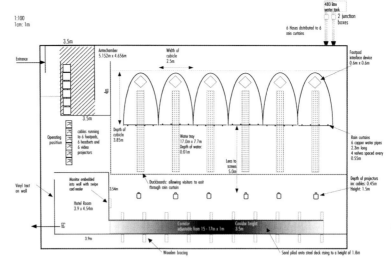

Desert Rain
1999
installation diagram
© Blast Theory

Desert Rain
1999
VR environment
for performance
installation views: ZKM |
Center for Art and Media
Karlsruhe, 1999
© Blast Theory
photos © Franz Wamhof

Time's Up
BodySPIN

1999/2000
Spherical Projection Interface (SPIN),
experimental situation considering
the bridging of virtuality and reality /
plastic, metal, silicone, wire, 1.44 mill. pixels, sound /
300 cm ø, duration variable

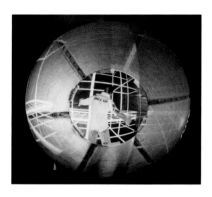

BodySPIN
1999/2000
installation views:
Ars Electronica, Linz, 2000
© Time's Up
photos © Otto Saxinger

More Body than SPIN – The Spherical Projection Interface and the Future of Cinema

Cinema for one viewer. Cinema that takes days to assemble. Cinema with outrageously complex filming tech. Cinema that is hard.

BodySPIN does all the wrong things for future cinema. But possibly it does the one thing that the cinema needs – it subsumes the viewer into its world and makes the experience uniquely corporeal.

SPIN, the Spherical Projection Interface, is a three-meter diameter trackball that one walks inside of. As the trackball rotates beneath your feet, the motion is taken over to a virtual space and projections thereof are cast upon the translucent walls of the ball. The effect is one of taking a stroll inside the virtual space. There is no forward, there are no goggles or other impediments, freedom of movement sets SPIN apart from other interfaces. The rolling motion is used to control navigation in a virtual space – the expression walkthrough obtains real meaning at last.

Placing the body within the rotationally symmetric space of the SPIN, the public individual perforates the membrane and becomes singularly immersed. This degree of immersion allows us to investigate the behavior of the public individual in ways that have been impossible to date. In addition, it allows the public individual to interact with dynamic and responsive environments in ways that are unique.

BodySPIN is a collection of environments composed for the SPIN interface that use various bodily functions of the user as control parameters in that space. The net effect is not unlike a walk through the inner reaches of ones body, transposed into the world of Tron-style lines and surfaces.

SPIN was designed and developed in late 1999, with the construction concluded immediately before the new year. The first projection experiments in the Time's Up workshops took place in early 2000, the first full experiments in the midst of summer, the premiere at the Ars Electronica festival in September of 2000, where its popularity drew columns of over-tired arts and cultural tourists to queue in the rain at an ungodly hour (for them) in order to get one of the valuable available timeslots. SPIN is by no means a mass-audience device; individuals must be briefed, taken into the sphere, closed in. Only then can the experience commence.

The interface paradigm itself is trivial: the individual inside need only walk, the movement of the center of gravity causes the sphere to roll, the person can take another step. The inertia of movement approximates that of the body, to slow down, one must brake by leaning back, but keep running. Running, walking, twisting are all possible modes of transport in the sphere. There is no preferred direction of travel, one can easily back up by walking backwards, the panoramic view is always available on all sides, edging sideways does not require some bizarre three-finger combination on a keyboard.

Although SPIN is a projection interface, it cannot be called a perfect projection surface. Along with the tiny variations in the radius of the sphere, the seams and stainless steel screws holding them together lead to small but not insignificant imperfections in the view. But these are compensated, perhaps even overcompensated, by using the internal capacity of the human perceptual system to integrate natural human motions and their distortions into its comprehension of external space. In the same way that a walking human in the wild cannot be distracted by the leaves dangling close to his or her face, in the same way that we can see through the tiny gaps in a planked fence, our perceptual system happily integrates the motions in the visual plane that match our motions in space. And this matching is what the SPIN interface manages.

The success of the BodySPIN experiences cannot be reduced to the fidelity of image. The lack of understanding that the vast majority of us have for our bodies is well-known, the fascination that we have for the paramedical access that various technologies allow us is vast. *BodySPIN* looked into the usage of various bodily functions, namely heartbeat, breathing and muscle tension, as influencers of a virtual world. The signals were taken and fed to parameters such as growth and complexity in the virtual systems. "Brain Maze," for instance, landed the individual in the middle of a grid-patterned flat plain, glowing light lines reaching of into the middle distance. The level of bio-mechanical stress in the individual was approximated through an analysis of heartbeat rate, breathing depth and muscle agitation. The higher the stress level, the more wall-segments rose from the grid, hemming in the individual's motion. The more hemmed in they were, the higher their internal stress level became, and the labyrinth became yet more complex. A positive feedback loop presented two solutions: Speed and dexterity in the sphere, or a relaxed stroll around a few obstacles to the perimeter. The "Pulse Race" environment worked similarly, racing to the end of a passage that grew with every heartbeat. Suspended in an infinite space composed of blue lines racing into the Tron-style infinite distance, the individual is faced with a racing environment with a breathtaking view.

Surprisingly, with many of the goal-oriented situations that we prepared, many individuals chose not to aim for the goal. Rather they wandered about the offered spaces, floating on the bobbing ocean, wandering in the maze, sightseeing from the heartbeat-stimulated growing tunnel hanging in a perfect void, criss-crossed with infinite beams of light. The desire to reach the offered goal, to reach the end the experience was countered by the desire to enjoy the body-centered view that SPIN offered, to stroll, to dawdle, to enjoy the experience as such. No matter what game strategies we included, many people chose their own way to play.

SPIN does not only involve the participant in a mere spectacle, a surround view panoramic scenography that moves with the body in some perfectly rendered virtual-space way. The SPIN interface adds some extra stresses to the individual of its own. Although the sphere is, in general, easy enough for a person of around sixty-five kilos to bring into motion, many people were not happy to stroll, but rather, caught in a spasm of playful energy, they had to run, to swing wide in the curves, to see where they could go. This behavior, running with quite some energy, led naturally to profuse sweatiness, especially in the low air circulation of the closed sphere. For many people, a certain fitness-studio aura was appreciable, one participant compared the aroma to her pet ferrets. *BodySPIN* is an encounter not only with the visual stimuli of all-round vision and visual feedback, rather it is an involvement of the individual's whole body, from the inner ticks of the heart through their perceptions (whether visual, aural or aromatic), to their arms and legs maintaining their standing posture while running, walking, backing off or circling around. The paranoid peripheral vision, the sense of balance and momentum, the racing heart or the effects of long slow breaths; all make up the whole-body, anti-passive, consummately all-encompassing experience in *BodySPIN*.

And that, Ladies and Gentlemen, is why *BodySPIN* might not be the Cinema of the Future.

Time's Up

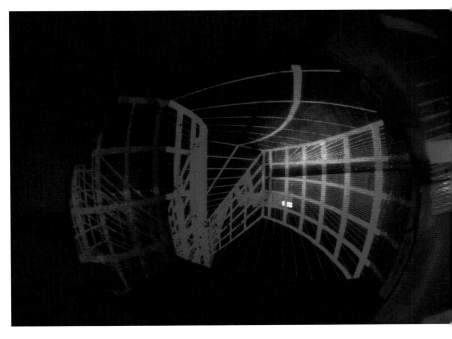

top
BodySPIN
1999/2000
installation view: Time's Up
dockside laboratories, Linz
© Time's Up
photo © Otto Saxinger

bottom
BodySPIN
1999/2000
installation view:
WWW-Festival, Duisburg, 2001
© Time's Up
photo © Viertbauer
& Zauner GmbH

Luc Courchesne
The Visitor: Living by Numbers

2001
interactive video panorama / Panoscope 360, SXGA data projector,
microphone, four amplified speakers / 350 x 150 x 150 cm

Hovering portentously from an aluminum structure in the center of a darkened space is the smooth, mirrored dome of Canadian born artist, Luc Courchesne's interactive viewing apparatus, *Panoscope 360*. Occupying the least physical space of all the exhibits, the unique technology of the *Panoscope 360* is the transportive device for *The Visitor: Living By Numbers* an expansive, panoramic and illusionary journey into a virtual space.

First exhibited at Siggraph in 2000, Courchesne's *Panoscope 360* is a direct descendant of cinema's frameless precursor, the Panorama, which Stephan Oettermann describes as the first mass medium and one of the most popular forms of entertainment in the nineteenth century.1 Patented and popularized in 1787 by the Irish painter Robert Barker, the Panorama was in effect one of the first forms of illusionary space. In fact, it could even be considered the first "virtual spectacle."2 Not unlike Courchesne's spherical innovation, the essential effect of Baker's inaugural Panorama – initially depicting the *City of Edinburgh* – was of an expansive, omniscient view of the represented physical space. According to Victoria Bernie, "Barker offered his astonished audience, a moment of visual truth, an instant caught and reconstructed in such a way as to invite confusion, however momentary, with reality."3

Courchesne has taken Baker's "instant" of unsettled reality and stretched it into the future by introducing an amorphous, interactive narrative that inhabits an ever-mutable virtual terrain. *The Visitor: Living By Numbers* experience is like being submerged within a re-conditioned *Nautilus*, weightlessly traversing a strange new world. But unlike Baker and his "visual truth," Courchesne offers his audience a moment of "virtual truth" in the realization that they – the audience – are in fact driving the science-fiction vessel.

In order to experience Courchesne's panoscopic installation, a participant must first place his or her head inside the futuristic rotunda – which is vertically adjustable so as to accommodate height variations. Once inside the cupolaed cinema, the individual liter-

ally becomes "The Visitor": a disembodied traveler immersed in a territory that they must now intuitively and numerically negotiate. Using a series of codified voice commands a visitor is able to navigate a network of small roads in unidentified provincial regions of Japan. By pronouncing simple coordinates such as twelve for North, three for East, six for South or nine for West, the visitor is not only able to maneuver in any direction, but is also empowered to approach and interact with objects and people contained within the virtual environment.

Eventually the visitor will encounter a white structure, which, if they wish, they can go into. Once this choice is enacted and a visitor enters, they then discover a group of people seemingly enjoying a quiet existence. Varying in age, race and gender, the six individuals present themselves as possible conversational partners for the visitor who will, by his or her actions and manner, develop a personality within the group. This process of "socialization" may continue indefinitely or until the visitor chooses to exit. During the process however, the visitor builds a standing within the group that will determine his or her fate in the advent of a catastrophe, which forces the evacuation of the structure they have chosen to enter.

Although one is physically present when immersed within *The Visitor: Living By Numbers*, all familiar and external stimuli evaporates the moment that you are drenched by its disorienting and manufactured virtual geography. As the interactive or virtual territory of the work begins to eclipse the "real," we quickly lose the sense of our physical being in space and like Jean-Paul Sartre's existential voyeur, who devoured the universe through a keyhole in *Being and Nothingness*, we feel that we are at once omnipotent and alone in what we can see. This sensation remains until the membrane that separates the subject from the object is punctured, which in the case of Sartre's keyhole encounter occurs when the voyeur is himself approached by a visitor from behind, "… all of a sudden I hear footsteps in the hall. Someone is looking at me!"4 In the case of *The Visitor: Living By Numbers* the subject/object membrane is semi-permeable; the posi-

1 Stephan Oettermann, *The Panorama: History of Mass Medium*, Zone Books, New York, 1997.

2 C. W. Ceram, *Archaeology of the Cinema*, Thames and Hudson, London, 1965.

3 Victoria Bernie, The Invention of Geography, exhibition synopsis, Edward Marshall Gallery, Inverness, 1999.

4 Jean-Paul Sartre, *Being and Nothingness: An Essay on Phenomenological Ontology*, Penguin, New York, 1966.

The Visitor: Living by Numbers
2001
stills
Luc Courchesne
© Luc Courchesne, 2001
photos © Richard-Max Tremblay

tions are never fixed. Whether inside or outside the artwork, the visitor moves effortlessly between the status of both active subject and passive object.

Concerned with notions of interactivity, behavior, architecture and virtual spaces, Courchesne began his explorations in interactive video in 1984 when he co-authored *Elastic Movies* – one of the earliest experiments in the field – with artists such as Ellen Sebring, Benjamin Bergery and Bill Seaman. In an ongoing process of refinement and development, Courchesne has since produced several installations deploying complex and innovative use of new-media including; *Encyclopedia Chiaroscuro* (1987), *Portrait One* (1990), *Family Portrait* (1993), *Hall of Shadows* (1996), *Landscape One* (1997), *Passages* (1998), and *Rendez-vous* (1999). In commenting his work Courchesne suggests:

> "I am interested in form. The means I am using – computers, video, space – allow me to take upon the challenges associated with giving form in novel ways as I am also trying to include visitors' existence into the work's inner structures. I am mostly into experimenting. In the process of imagining 'objects' and making them, I learn to recognize what I can do and what I like to do."

In liberating the image from the frame, Courchesne's *The Visitor: Living By Numbers*, is an ambitious and evocative episode in interactive cinema, which, it could be argued, was the ultimate ambition of its antecedent, the Panorama. Centuries apart but conceptually united, both Courchesne and Barker have conceived of elaborate strategies to lure the viewer into seeing in a singular way. As Barker put it, the objective of the Panorama was to make the viewer "feel as if [he/she was] really on the spot." Whereas with Courchesne's work, one could suggest that the goal was to make the viewer feel as if [he/she is] really in the spot.

Emma Crimmings

First published in *Space Odysseys*, Victoria Lynn (ed.), exhib. cat., Art Gallery of New South Wales, Sydney, 2001.

The Visitor: Living by Numbers
2001
interactive video panorama
Panoscope 360, SXGA data
projector, microphone, four
amplified speakers
350 x 150 x 150 cm
installation view: ZKM |
Center for Art and Media
Karlsruhe, 2002
Luc Courchesne
© Luc Courchesne, 2001
photo © Franz Wamhof

Dennis Del Favero
Pentimento

2002
five-channel interactive video installation /
four projectors, four screens, twenty-two speakers,
four surveillance cameras, eight infrared lights,
one PC, five amplifiers, one CD player / color, sound /
18 min / 8000 x 8000 x 5000 cm / DVD version published in
(dis)LOCATIONS (ZKM digital arts edition, 2001)

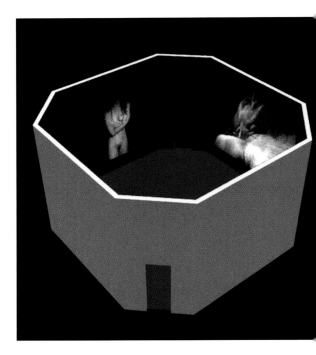

Pentimento
2002
axonometric view
© Dennis Del Favero

Pentimento was produced as an interactive video installation and interactive DVD-ROM during Dennis Del Favero's research fellowship at ZKM in 2001. The interactive video installation comprises an eight-metre-square room with integrated vision-based motion-detection system articulated to a computer-narrative database that interacts with the viewer's movements. The results of these interactions are delivered across four separate projection and five discrete acoustic systems within the installation room.

The project explores a news report detailing the discovery of an unidentified body in bushland on the outskirts of Sydney. A young man and woman are arrested. They accuse each other of murdering their father, whom they allege was sexually abusing them. The crime is reconstructed by means of the specific patterns of viewer and database interactions. These interactions evoke a large-scale and evolving memory whose fragments comprise the separate narrative fragments of each of the protagonists – father, brother, sister and the murder scene itself. Each of the four separate projection and acoustic systems can be operated both independently of and in synchrony with the others in a number of diverse and complex patterns. At a simple level, viewers are able to sequentially evoke the various narratives of each of the protagonists as they pass the separate screens. At a more complex level, viewers can simultaneously evoke the non-synchronic narratives of all protagonists creating a complex cascade of memories across all the screens. In each of these scenarios the viewers precipitate different memory modalities as they attempt to resolve the motivations surrounding the murder. Nevertheless nagging difficulties remain for the viewers. Some of the memories suggest that the father may not be the murder victim but is one of the perpetrators. Other memories suggest that all three protagonists may be dead and the viewers are navigating a violent struggle amongst the dead.

Dennis Del Favero

1   Jill Bennett, "Pentimento: Notes on Memory, Narrative and New Media," in *(dis)LOCATIONS*, ZKM digital arts edition, ZKM | Center for Art and Media Karlsruhe (ed.), The Centre for Interactive Cinema Research, College of Fine Arts, University of New South Wales, Sydney, Hatje Cantz, Ostfildern, 2001, pp. 49–50.

"[*Pentimento*] is, on a number of levels, about not knowing and not being able to grasp fully. It is ultimately about dealing with ghostings within memory: marks, pentimenti, that cannot always be transcribed into normal language. It registers a *form of memory* rather than a memory belonging to specific others. Unlike traditional narrative accounts of memory, then, *Pentimento* is not a story; it does not presume to make available or make sense of other's memories. Instead, it utilizes the structure of the medium to evoke the ways in which memories – like *pentimenti* – remain occluded both to us and, more crucially to those in whom they appear to inhere. In doing so, it severs an enduring connection between memory, subjectivity and representation that sees memory work very much as the domain of the authorial subject and thus as the product of individual expression. *Pentimento* reminds us that *pentimenti* do not always reveal themselves as voluntary memories. Even in a culture in which the concept of self-possession is sacrosanct, sometimes the most profound truths are revealed not in voluntary testimony but in the transactions between bodies and language: transactions Del Favero believes it is the task of new media to record."1

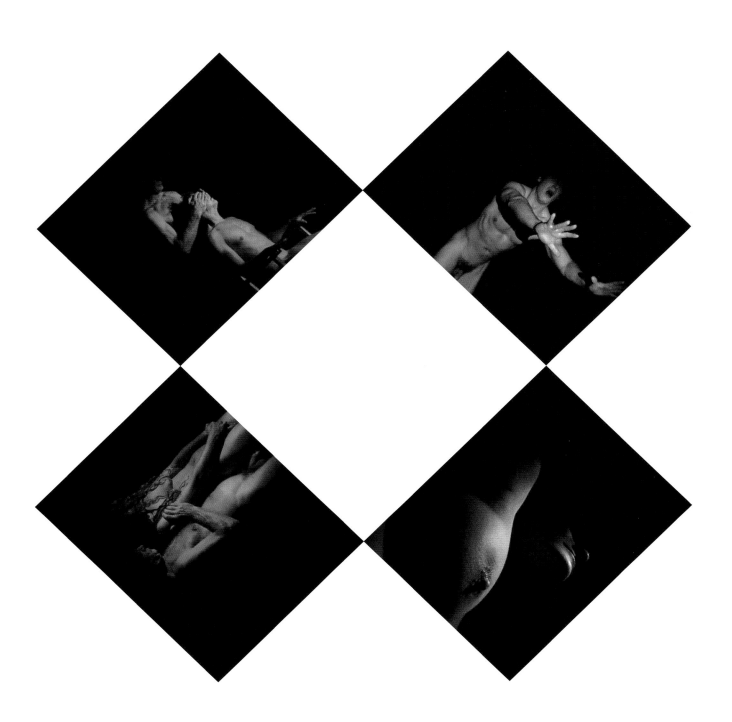

Pentimento
2002
screenshots
© Dennis Del Favero

Marnix de Nijs
Run Motherfucker Run

2001–2002
interactive installation

Run Motherfucker Run is an interactive installation in which someone of good physical condition may try his or her luck. You take position on the treadmill, in front of you an enormous film screen with a mix of film and 3-D images of a city with empty streets, crossings, ominous alleys and obstacles. Running along with the assembly line you will cover exactly the same distance in the virtual city in front of you. If you quicken your pace, the speed of the assembly line as well as the speed of the images before you will speed up too. Depending on your running behavior and the choices you make, you determine the progress of the film. A film with an atmosphere somewhere between a thriller, a chase and urban horror – you have left a party in the early morning or late at night and find yourself in a city that has changed – you start to run.

The interface is an adjusted industrial assembly line with electronically variable speed. The treadmill measures 6 x 2 meters, the speed range is 0 to 25 kilometers per hour. The interface is not a physical tool allowing the most natural possible navigation through a virtual environment. On the contrary, it is a tool with a strong will of its own. The conveyor belt can only move straight ahead, and you have to move in order to see an image. Only if you run fast enough will you get the image at full brightness; if you slow down, the image fades away. So although you are free to determine the speed of the belt with your walking speed, there is a mechanical pressure to keep the pace up, to hold onto the world. In combination with the physically tangible power of the machine, this functionality creates a delicate balance between control(lability) and noncontrol(lability).

The image material is a mixture of 3-D images and film. You step onto the treadmill and start to walk, the treadmill kicks in, and you are in a simple three-dimensionally modeled, almost black, space surrounded by atmospheric sound. In the distance you see icons of streets, by stepping to the right or left on the treadmill you choose which street you want to take, you walk towards it and when you hit it – bang – you're into that world. A world with mainly deserted streets at dusk, at dawn and at night. Some people running past, curled in doorways, staring at you with their eyes closed. A car pulls up, a person leans out and vomits, the people look at you like you don't belong there, and then they drive off. As you reach the end of the street the image fades to black and again you are running in the black nothingness.

Once you have "found" one of these treats, you are going to be keen to find more. You continue to run and before long you see another image/icon of a street ahead of you, you hit it and – bang – you're into that world again. There are several routes possible, in every scene you find clues and fragments with which you create your own story; a story that gives you the feeling of "being there and not being there." The alienating feeling of taking part and being an outsider at the same time.

Marnix de Nijs

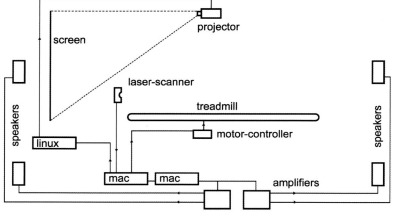

diagram for
Run Motherfucker Run
© Marnix de Nijs

Technical specifications

Interface
A laser scanner mounted in front of the treadmill enables the position of the person on the treadmill to be detected. The position in relation to time and the running speed of the treadmill determines whether the motor must accelerate or slow down. The user can navigate by stepping to the left or right on the treadmill.

Control
The images are computer-generated by a system with a frame-accurate video source and a graphics accelerator. The system is a network with a Pentium III computer running on Linux as player, and one Mac running MAX as server.

Sound
The quadraphonic sound enhances the spatial experience. Several sound layers are used: the direct sound of the scenes (footsteps, speech, cars and bullets) as well as spherical sound layers in which motor-speed-related modulations play a role. The sound is generated with a Mac G4 that runs MAX/MSP.

Run Motherfucker Run
2001–2002
interactive installation
test setup with small screen
installation view
© Marnix de Nijs

02

CALCULATED

Karl Sims
Evolved Virtual Creatures

1994
computer animation on video / 4 min, loop

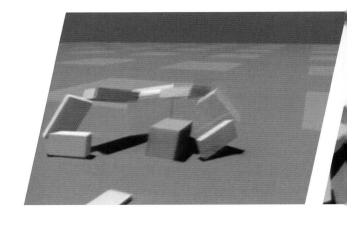

1. Introduction

A classic trade-off in the field of computer graphics and animation is that of complexity versus control. It is often difficult to build interesting or realistic virtual entities and still maintain control over them. Sometimes it is difficult to build a complex virtual world at all, if it is necessary to conceive, design, and assemble each component.

Optimization techniques offer possibilities for the automatic generation of complexity. The genetic algorithm is a form of artificial evolution, and is a commonly used method for optimization. A Darwinian "survival of the fittest" approach is employed to search for optima in large multidimensional spaces.[1] Genetic algorithms permit virtual entities to be created without requiring an understanding of the procedures or parameters used to generate them. The measure of success, or *fitness,* of each individual can be calculated automatically, or it can instead be provided interactively by a user. Interactive evolution allows procedurally generated results to be explored by simply choosing those that are the most aesthetically desirable for each generation.[2]

Genetic languages such as hierarchical Lisp expressions allow new parameters and dimensions to be added to the genetic space as an evolution proceeds, and therefore define rather a *hyperspace* of possible results. This approach has been used to genetically program solutions to a variety of problems,[3] as well as to explore procedurally generated images and dynamical systems.[4]

It is convenient to use the biological terms *genotype* and *phenotype* when discussing artificial evolution. A *genotype* is a coded representation of a possible individual or problem solution. In biological systems, a genotype is usually composed of DNA and contains the instructions for the development of an organism. Genetic algorithms typically use populations of genotypes consisting of strings of binary digits or parameters. These are read to produce *phenotypes* which are then evaluated according to some fitness criteria and selectively reproduced. New genotypes are generated by copying, mutating and/or combining the genotypes of the most fit individuals, and as the cycle repeats the population should ascend to higher and higher levels of fitness.

This text describes a system for creating virtual creatures that move and behave in simulated three-dimensional physical worlds. The morphologies of creatures and the neural systems for controlling their muscle forces are both generated automatically using genetic algorithms. Different fitness evaluation functions are used to direct simulated evolutions towards specific behaviors such as swimming, walking, jumping, and following.

2. Creature Morphology

In this work, the phenotype embodiment of a virtual creature is a hierarchy of articulated three-dimensional rigid parts. The genetic representation of this morphology is a directed graph of nodes and connections. Each graph contains the developmental instructions for growing a creature, and provides a way of reusing instructions to make similar or recursive components within the creature. A phenotype hierarchy of parts is made from a graph by synthesizing parts from the node information while tracing through the connections of the graph.

Each node in the graph contains information describing a rigid part and their joints. For example the *dimensions* determine the physical shape of a part, a *joint-type* determines the degrees of freedom of the joint and the movement allowed. The different joint-types are: *rigid, revolute, twist, universal, bend-twist, twist-bend,* or *spherical.* A set of local *neurons* is also included in each node, and will be explained further in the next section. Finally, a node contains a set of *connections* to other nodes. Each connection also contains information. The placement of a child part relative to its parent is decomposed into *position, orientation, scale,* and *reflection,* so each can be mutated independently. **Figure 1** shows some simple hand-designed graph topologies and resulting phenotype morphologies.

1   See David E. Goldberg, *Genetic Algorithms in Search, Optimization, and Machine Learning,* Addison-Wesley, 1989; John H. Holland, *Adaptation in Natural and Artificial Systems,* Ann Arbor, University of Michigan Press, 1975.

2   See Richard Dawkins, *The Blind Watchmaker,* Harlow Longman, 1986; Karl Sims, "Artificial Evolution for Computer Graphics," in *Computer Graphics,* vol. 25, no. 4, July 1991, pp. 319–328; Karl Sims, "Interactive Evolution of Dynamical Systems," in *Toward a Practice of Autonomous Systems: Proceedings of the First European Conference on Artificial Life,* Varela, Francisco, & Bourgine (ed.), The MIT Press, Cambridge, MA, 1992, pp. 171–178; Stephen Todd, William Latham, *Evolutionary Art and Computers,* Academic Press, London, 1992.

3   See Nichael L. Cramer, "A Representation for the Adaptive Generation of Simple Sequential Programs," in *Proceedings of the First International Conference on Genetic Algorithms,* J. Grefenstette (ed.), 1985, pp. 183–187; John R. Koza, *Genetic Programming: On the Programming of Computers by Means of Natural Selection,* The MIT Press, Cambridge, MA, 1992.

4   See Karl Sims, "Artificial Evolution for Computer Graphics," in *Computer Graphics,* vol. 25, no. 4, July 1991, pp. 319–328; and Karl Sims, "Interactive Evolution of Dynamical Systems," in op. cit., pp. 171–178.

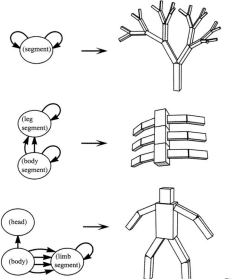

Fig. 1

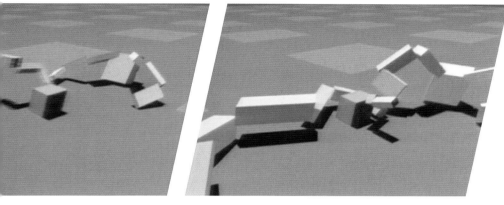

competing

targeting   swimming   walking

3. Creature Control

A virtual "brain" determines the behavior of a creature. The brain is a dynamical system that accepts input sensor values and provides output effector values. The output values are applied as forces or torques at the degrees of freedom of the body's joints.

This cycle of effects is shown in **Figure 2**. Sensor, effector, and internal neuron signals are represented here by continuously variable scalar numbers.

Sensors: Each sensor is contained within a specific part of the body, and measures either aspects of that part or aspects of the world relative to that part. Three different types of sensors were used for these experiments: 1. *Joint angle sensors* give the current value for each degree of freedom of each joint. 2. *Contact sensors* have a sensitive region within a part's shape and activate when any contacts occur in that area with either other parts of the creature or with the environment. 3. *Photosensors* react to a global light source position.

Neurons: Internal neural nodes are used to give virtual creatures the possibility of arbitrary behavior. In this work, different neural nodes can perform diverse functions on their inputs to generate their output signals. The set of functions that neural nodes can have is: *sum, product, divide, sum-threshold, greater-than, sign-of, min, max, abs, if, interpolate, sin, cos, atan, log, expt, sigmoid, integrate, differentiate, smooth, memory, oscillate-wave,* and *oscillate-saw.* Some functions compute an output directly from their inputs, while others such as the oscillators retain some state and can give time varying outputs even when their inputs are constant. The number of inputs to a neuron depends on its function. Each input contains a connection to another neuron or a sensor from which to receive a value. For each simulated time interval, every neuron computes its output value from its inputs.

Effectors: Each effector simply contains a connection to a neuron or a sensor from which to receive a value. This input value is exerted as a joint force which affects the dynamic simulation and the resulting behavior of the creature. Only effectors that exert simulated muscle forces are used here. Each effector controls a degree of freedom of a single joint connecting it to its parent and interact with angle sensors also contained in that part. Each effector is given a *maximum-strength* proportional to the maximum cross-sectional area of the two parts it joins. Effector forces are scaled by these strengths and not permitted to exceed them. Since strength scales with area, but mass scales with volume, as in nature, behavior does not always scale uniformly.

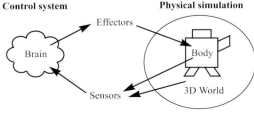

Control system   **Physical simulation**

Fig. 2

3.1 Combining Morphology and Control

The genotype descriptions of virtual brains and the actual phenotype brains are both directed graphs of nodes and connections. The nodes contain the sensors, neurons, and effectors, and the connections define the flow of signals between these nodes. These graphs can also be recurrent, and as a result the final control system can have feedback loops and cycles. However, most of these neural elements exist within a specific part of the creature. Thus the genotype for the nervous system is a nested graph: the morphological nodes each contain graphs of the neural nodes and connections. **Figure 3** shows an example of an evolved nested graph.

4. Physical Simulation

Dynamics simulation is used to calculate the movement of creatures resulting from their interaction with a virtual three-dimensional world. There are several components of the physical simulation used in this work: articulated body dynamics, numerical integration, collision detection, collision response, friction, and an optional viscous fluid effect. A viscosity effect is used for the simulations in underwater environments.

It is important that the physical simulation be reasonably accurate when optimizing for creatures that can move within it. Any bugs that allow energy leaks from non-conservation, or even round-off errors, will inevitably be discovered and exploited by the evolving creatures.

5. Behavior Selection

In this work, virtual creatures are evolved by optimizing for a specific task or behavior. A creature is grown from its genetic description as previously explained, and then it is placed in a dynamically simulated virtual world. The brain provides effector forces which move parts of the creature, the sensors report aspects of the world and the creature's body back to the brain, and the resulting physical behavior of the creature is evaluated. After a certain duration of virtual time (perhaps 10 seconds), a *fitness* value is assigned that corresponds to the success level of that behavior. If a creature has a high fitness relative to the rest of the population, it will be selected for survival and reproduction as described in the next section.

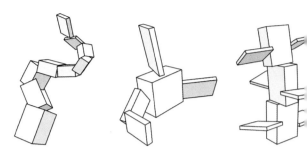

creatures evolved for swimming

Fig. 4

Many different types of fitness measures can be used to perform evolutions of virtual creatures. Four examples of fitness methods are described here:

Swimming: Physical simulation of a water environment is achieved by turning off gravity and adding the viscous water resistance effect as described. Swimming speed is used as the fitness value and is measured by the distance traveled by the creature's center of mass per unit time. Straight swimming is rewarded over circling by using the maximum distance from the initial center of mass. Continuing movement is rewarded over that from a single initial push.

Walking: The term *walking* is used loosely here to indicate any form of land locomotion. A land environment is simulated by including gravity, turning off the viscous water effect, and adding a static ground plane with friction. Additional inanimate objects can be placed in the world for more complex environments. Again, speed is used as the selection criteria, but the vertical component of velocity is ignored.

Jumping: Jumping behavior can be selected for by measuring the maximum height above the ground of the lowest part of the creature. An alternative method is to use the average height of the lowest part of the creature during the duration of simulation.

Following: Another evaluation method is used to select for creatures that can adaptively follow a light source. Photosensors are enabled, so the effector output forces and resulting behavior can depend on the relative direction of a light source to the creature. Several trials are run with the light source in different locations, and the speeds at which a creature moves toward it are averaged for the fitness value.

6. Creature Evolution

An evolution of virtual creatures is begun by first creating an initial population of genotypes. These initial genotypes can come from several possible sources: new genotypes can be synthesized "from scratch" by random generation of sets of nodes and connections, an existing genotype from a previous evolution can be used to seed the initial population of

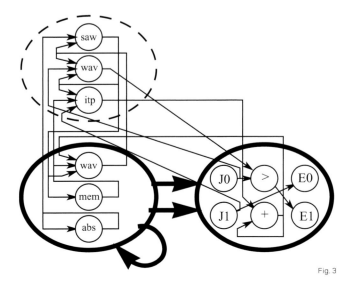

Fig. 3

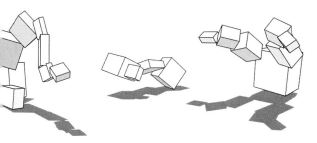

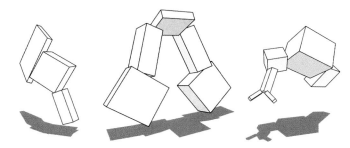

creatures evolved for walking

Fig. 5

creatures evolved for jumping

Fig. 6

a new evolution, or a seed genotype can be designed by hand. However, no hand-designed seed genotypes were used in the examples shown here.

A *survival-ratio* determines the percentage of the population that will survive each generation. In this work, population sizes were typically three hundred, and the survival ratio was 1/5. For each generation, creatures are grown from their genetic descriptions, and their fitness values are measured by a method such as those described in the previous section. Offspring are generated from the surviving creatures by copying and combining their directed graph genotypes. When these graphs are reproduced they are subjected to probabilistic variation or mutation, so the corresponding phenotypes are similar to their parents but have been altered or adjusted in random ways. The number of offspring that each surviving individual generates is proportional to its fitness – the most successful creatures make the most children. The survivors are kept in the population for the next generation, and the total size of the population is maintained.

7. Results

Evolutions were performed for each of the behavior selection methods described in Section 5. A population of interbreeding creatures often converges toward homogeneity, but each separately run evolution can produce completely different locomotion strategies that satisfy the requested behavior. For this reason, many separate evolutions were performed, each for fifty to one hundred generations, and the most successful creatures of each evolution were inspected. A selection of these is shown in **Figures 4-6**. In a few cases, genotypes resulting from one evolution were used as seed genotypes for a second evolution.

The swimming fitness measure produced a large number of simple paddling and tail wagging creatures. A variety of more complex strategies also emerged from some evolutions. A few creatures pulled themselves through the water with specialized sculling appendages. Some used two symmetrical flippers or even large numbers of similar flippers to propel

themselves, and several multi-segmented watersnake creatures evolved that wind through the water with sinusoidal motions.

The walking fitness measure also produced a surprising number of simple creatures that could shuffle or hobble along at fairly high speeds. Some walk with lizard-like gaits using the corners of their parts. Some simply wag an appendage in the air to rock back and forth in just the right manner to move forward. A number of more complex creatures emerged that push or pull themselves along, inchworm style. Others use one or more leg-like appendages to successfully crawl or walk. Some hopping creatures even emerged that raise and lower arm-like structures to bound along at fairly high speeds.

The light-following fitness measure produced a wide variety of creatures that can swim or walk towards a light source. Some consistently and successfully follow the light source at different locations. Others can follow it some of the time, but then at certain relative locations fail to turn towards it. In the water environment, some developed steering fins that turn them towards the light using photosensor inputs. Others adjust the angle of their paddles appropriately as they oscillate along.

Karl Sims

Acknowledgments
Thanks to Gary Oberbrunner and Matt Fitzgibbon for Connection Machine and software help. Thanks to Lew Tucker and Thinking Machines Corporation for supporting this research. Thanks to Bruce Blumberg and Peter Schröder for dynamic simulation help and suggestions. And special thanks to Pattie Maes.

Abridged version of an essay first published in *Computer Graphics, SIGGRAPH '94* Proceedings, Annual Conference Series, July 1994, pp. 15–22. For further information see also Karl Sims, "Evolving 3D Morphology and Behavior by Competition," in *Artificial Life IV. Proceedings of the Fourth International Workshop on the Synthesis and Simulation of Living Systems*, Rodney Brooks and Peter Maes (eds), MIT Press, Cambridge, MA, 1994, pp. 28–39, and http://web.genarts.com/karl

Oliver Deussen and Bernd Lintermann
Artificial Plants

Computer images are becoming more and more realistic. It is possible to create entire films on the computer these days, and computer games involve displays with more and more complicated environments. This has been made possible by a continual increase of the capacities of the now democratized means of production that is the computer.

The performance capacity of industry computers doubles approximately every eighteen months; that of graphic cards for the display of three-dimensional scenes triples yearly, on average. A simple calculation tells us that in five years' time computers will be able to render a geometrical complexity eighty-fold that of the present level. It is, however, unlikely that producers of computer games, for instance, will hire eighty times as many employees in order to master the volume of material able to be displayed. Required, then, are methods that automatically produce the desired geometry within the given framework.

"Procedural Modeling" falls within the category of these methods. Here, the geometrical object is not produced by manually fitting together its individual graphic elements but computer-generated automatically by means of computing processes.

In this article, we wish to discuss Procedural Modeling on the example of natural environments. A synthetic landscape can consist of hundreds of plants, trees, bushes, grasses and so forth. On its own, a single tree represented using today's standard techniques might consist of many hundreds of thousands of surfaces; similarly, grass turf require tens of thousands of graphics primitives. With the help of Procedural Modeling, it is already possible to produce complex artificial landscapes on the computer, basic versions of which have been seen in movies like *Shrek* or *Time Machine*.

Of course, the computer doesn't actually produce plants; rather, it displays on screen visual objects whose shapes remind us of trees and bushes. Therefore, certain suppositions about shape must provide the basis for the calculation processes which, when formalized within a structural model, furnish us with possibilities of rendering many variants of shape. This is an essential property of procedural systems. They implement structural properties and automatically make it possible to generate a wealth of models with similar structural characteristics.

It is incredible, really, that the first experiments involving computer renderings of this kind for plants are already more than thirty years old. Over the course of these last thirty years, two main principles have been advanced, ones that we would like to introduce in more detail here.

Rule-Based Systems

In the late 1960s, the biologist Aristid Lindenmayer was looking for a method that could be used to depict cell growth; he developed the "L-systems" formalism that is named after him and follows the work of the linguist Noam Chomsky.[1] L-systems are grammars with whose help the discrete stages of cell development can be rendered. In the 1980s, Przemyslaw Prusinkiewicz took up the basic idea and applied it to plants.[2]

L-systems generate a string of letters, each letter of which has a particular graphic interpretation. For instance, one letter may stand for a stem and another for a bud. The context of the letters reveals the position in space of the graphic element. A set of rewriting rules (or productions) changes the string of letters. One of the rewriting rules could, for example, make it possible to replace a bud with an extension of a stem, a leaf, and a new bud. The result would be a growing sprout.

Regarding the interpretation of the string of letters, the following metaphor is often used:

One imagines oneself in front of a bug that is capable of moving around freely in three-dimensional space. Now, this bug will receive instructions to move straight ahead for a particular distance d, to turn around at pre-given angles dA, to recall particular positions and orientations and to jump back to these again later. On instruction, this little animal leaves a visible trace behind it, or draws complex graphic elements like leaves or buds at its current position and orientation. The result is a three-dimensional geometry that can be represented on a screen.

Fig. 1 shows the string of signs of an L-system, Fig. 2 a corresponding system of rewriting rules. By using rule (1), the start-sign **A** can be rewritten as the string of signs [FB!A]/////'[&FB!A]//////' [&FB!A] and the signs **A**, **B**, and **F** in this string can in turn be rewritten using the rules (1), (4), and (2). After just a few derivation steps, one has created a long string of signs whose graphic interpretation is shown in Fig 3.

F	Move forward a distance d and draw a line, marking your movement
f	Same as **F**, except without marking your movement
+ −	Rotate by a fixed angle dA anticlockwise or clockwise around your body-axis
& ^	Tilt upwards or downwards by a fixed angle dA
\ /	Tilt to the left or right by a fixed angle dA
|	Rotate in the direction opposite to your own.
[	Take note of your current state, such as position, orientation, color, etc.
]	Return to the condition last noted.
{ }	Apprehend the path covered between **{** and **}** as the border of a field, and fill in the latter
! ´	Change the thickness and the color of your current state

Fig. 1 The signs of an L-system and their interpretation

```
(1) A -> [&FB!A]////´[&FB!A]//////´[&FB!A]
(2) F -> S////F
(3) S -> FB
(4) B -> [´´´^^{-f+f+f-|-f+f+f}]
```

Fig. 2 The rewriting rules of an L-system

1 N. Chomsky, "Three Models for the description of Language," in *IRE Trans. on Information Theory*, 2 (3), 1956, pp. 113–124.

2 P. Prusinkiewicz and A. Lindenmayer, *The Algorithmic Beauty of Plants*, Springer-Verlag, New York, 1990.

Fig. 3 The result of a multiple application of simple rewriting rules.

Even on the basis of a simple example, it is evident that it is difficult to model specific, complex plants using the L-systems as they appear in their original formulation. Firstly, they are based on simplistic suppositions about shape; namely, that plants are branched structures and composed of particular elements like leaves, stems and buds. The formal nature of the rules allows constructions that are either structurally unstable or biologically impossible. Secondly, the result first becomes visible only after an abstract process of transformation, and slight changes in the rule-based system can result in drastic changes in the model.

Over the course of time, L-systems have been expanded and developed so as to allow for general influences such as the orientation of sprouts toward the light source (phototropism), diffraction by gravity (gravitropism), impediments, differential growth, algorithmic modeling of plant parts, and so forth.[3] They are also currently being used by specialists in the entertainment industry.

The University of Calgary has developed a virtual laboratory on whose website the series of programs on the generation of plant geometry is freely available.[4]

Since L-systems are really only useful for specialists, various other procedures have been developed over the last ten years.

Specific-Creation Algorithms
One approach is to generate the plant geometry from a closed, specific algorithm.

If, for instance, one collects the various numerical parameters ("metrics data") of a plant – such as the number of branchings, the branching angles and so forth – a geometric model can be generated from the statistical data.

An example of the above is offered by AMAP, a plant library marketed by the company CIRAD[5] The plants are calculated according to a growth-model drawn up for every species of plant. Through the inclusion of the metrics data, in a figurative sense a plant is made to grow from the bud-stage.[6] The resulting generated models remain within a given range of metrics data and are very similar, in this respect, to the specified pattern. Here the parameters for shape are permanently programmed in the form of metrics data. By setting the defaults of age, growth potential and other random parameters, the

user can effect a change on the result, although not one directed according to preconceived notions.

Another approach assembles a tree out of many invisible strands, each of which extends from the roots right up to a leaf or bloom.[7] The diameter of a bough or trunk is determined by the amount of stands that pass through it. This is congruent with a formulation in Leonardo da Vinci's tract on painting, which states that the sum of the bough cross-sections in a well-proportioned tree should remain the same at every level of branching.

When one compares the two methods of plant generation, it becomes clear how powerful the rule-based systems are; potentially, they can generate very many different plants. However, the production of a plant can be extremely arduous. Generation algorithms, although easy enough to handle, are very specific and must be re-adjusted for every plant species. For every new species, new metrics data must be collected, or else obtained empirically with the lengthy trials the latter method entails.

The next approach attempts to combine some of the strengths of both methods.

Rule-Based Object Generation
According to this approach, a plant is assembled out of individual components that algorithmically generate each individual part of the plant, like the stem or the leaves, according to a computer formula. The components are interactively connected to a graph in order to render the whole plant. This graph is a visual representation of a rule-based system and portrays the structural composition of the plant.[8]

Hidden behind each component is a tiny program that implements a model of the shape adapted from nature. The first program to be executed is the root of the graph. Just as in a rule-based system, this program executes in succession all of the programs of the components that are connected with it. Each program generates its own geometry, along with new spatial positions and orientations at which the programs connected to it generate their geometry.

The principles of shape are encapsulated here in the form of programs within components and can be combined at random. For instance, the arrangement of the blooms, petals, seeds and even cacti lamella follows a similar principle that can be understood with reference to the proportion of the golden section. This principle is implemented within a component able to arrange and order every kind of geometry accordingly.

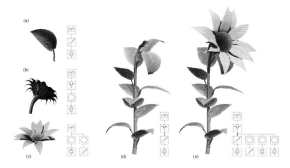

Fig. 4
Production of a sunflower: The leaves of a natural plant are photographed and digitized. This data is applied to the geometry that is generated by a Leaf component (a). The head and the bloom of the flower are modeled above the component Leaf and PhiBall (b and c), the stalk combined with the leaves and finally the whole plant is assembled (e). The Camera symbol stands for the component that generates the whole structure and displays it on the computer screen.

3 P. Prusinkiewicz, L. Mündermann, R. Karwowski, B. Lane, "The Use of Positional Information in Modeling of Plants," in *Proceedings of SIGGRAPH 2001*, Annual Conference Series, August 2002, pp. 289–300.

4 P. Prusinkiewicz, "The University of Calgary: VLAB 4.0." http://www.cpsc.ucalgary.ca/Research/bmv/vlab/index.html

5 CIRAD/GERDAT, "AMAP Presentation." http://www.cirad.fr/presentation/en/program-eng/amap.shtml

6 P. de Reffye, C. Edelin, J. Francon, M. Jaeger, C. Puech, "Plant Models Faithful to Botanical Structure and Development. Proceedings of SIGGRAPH 88," in *Computer Graphics*, 22, 4, 4, August 1988, pp. 151–158.

7 M. Holton, "Strands, Gravity and Botanical Tree Imagery," in *Computer Graphics Forum*, 13(1), pp. 57–67, 1994.

8 B. Lintermann and O. Deussen, "Interactive Modelling of Plants," in *IEEE Computer Graphics and Applications*, 19(1) pp. 56–65, January/February 1999.

Examples of computer-generated plants
Author: Marco Bubke

Codiaeum variegatum   Schefflera actinophylla   Caladium bicolor-hybrid   Cissus rhombifolia   Eleocharis vivipara   Barbarea vulgaris   Medicago lupulin

A chestnut tree and a rhododendron with their structural graphs.

The example of a sunflower clearly illustrates how the image is constructed (see Fig. 4). Shrubs and trees are assembled according to the same principle.

Since many properties concerning shape are covered by the components' algorithms, the rule-based system can remain simple: Essentially, it describes the topology of the model, and the connection between rules and results is intuitively comprehensible.

Although, in similar fashion to enhanced L-systems, general parameters like the influence of light and gravitation are also taken into consideration, here again many parameters regarding shape have effects on a local level. Thus, the modeling of a particular plant still involves changes that must take place in the series of parameters. For precisely that reason, however, an extremely high level of control is produced which is ideal for many applications. When producing special effects in film sequences, for example, the technique can be used to move a bough or branch to the location best suited to the camera angle.

A further advantage is that one can leave the plants to grow without modifying the rule based system. The user simply enters a few parameter settings at different times and through parameter interpolation the computer calculates the corresponding

geometry for every frame in the film sequence. The parameter-interpolation technique can also be used to generate various modifications of the plants under continually changing environmental influences. In generative systems wherein the arrangement of the components is automatically changed, the completed rendering of the principles of shape within the components results in models which are almost automatically biologically correct.[9]

Rule-based object generation provides the basis for "Xfrog,"[10] our modeling tool for the production of plants and general organic forms, and was used, for example, in producing the film *Time Machine*.

Landscapes

Once different plants have been generated with the modeling system, they can be assembled into completely synthetic landscapes. However, several different factors play a role. For one, the enormous geometrical complexity of the data has to be taken into consideration. For another, many different factors contribute to making a landscape appear believable to us. Were one simply to copy the same plant to various locations, the eye would quickly recognize this repetition. The way that a plant grows is dependent upon its environment, its neighbors, the composition of the soil, the effects of light, the wind, and so forth. Intuitively, we latch onto irregularities within this complex interplay.

If certain environmental influences are known, such as those resulting from geological upheavals or simply from arbitrary predefinitions, then the phenotype of that plant can be generated within these marginal conditions. Whereas in the above-described parametrical model the parameters are chosen with allowance for the environmental effects, in L-systems these effects are taken into consideration during the simulation of a plant's development.[11]

The above illustration shows a meadow in which density distributions of single species have been painted onto the subsoil. A program is responsible for calculating the individual plant positions on the basis

9 B. Lintermann and T. Belschner, "SonoMorphis." http://i31www.ira.uka.de/~linter/SonoMorphis/

10 B. Lintermann and O. Deussen, "Xfrog 3.5." http://www.greenworks.de

11 O. Deussen, P. Hanrahan, B. Lintermann, R. Mech, M. Pharr, and P. Prusinkiewicz, "Realistic Modelling and Rendering of Plant Ecosystems," in *Proceedings of SIGGRAPH 98*, Annual Conference Series, July 1998, pp. 275–286.

02 CALCULATED
Oliver Deussen and Bernd Lintermann / Artificial Plants

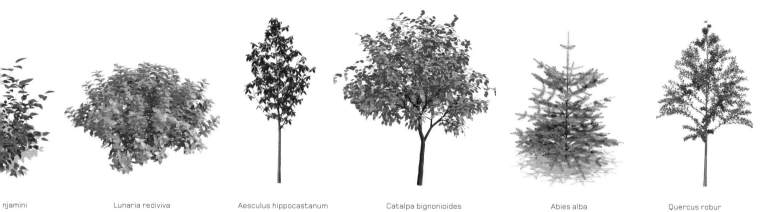

njamini   Lunaria rediviva   Aesculus hippocastanum   Catalpa bignonioides   Abies alba   Quercus robur

Synthetic landscape

of density distribution. Similarly, various influences like soil composition have been defined: The grass is more lush in damper areas; fewer daisies grow directly under the apple tree. Since the poplars in the background provide shade for each other, they are slightly thinner in the lower trunk area. It is obvious that the image will only be as good as is the chosen generating model's capacity for taking into consideration important factors of our perception.

In order to be able to display the amount of data that results from this process on today's computers, the original volume of data must be reduced to a fraction. Since the repeated presentation of the same geometry works very efficiently, one tries to portray the variety of plants through a selection of the least possible number of representatives. Each plant is rewritten using the representative that it most resembles. While this is obviously a visual compromise, it can reduce by a factor of one thousand the amount of accumulated data. It is interesting to note that due to the massive volume of information, merely a few representatives are sufficient to create the impression of natural variability.

A further data reduction is made possible by Level-of-Detail (LOD) techniques through which plant geometry is represented in no greater detail than strictly necessary. For example, a tree in the distance becomes increasingly detailed only as one approaches it. In interactive applications, "billboards" or "sprites" that replace the plant geometry with a rectangular field displaying an image of the plant remain the most common method, and the technique is being further refined by research into Image-Based Rendering where the image displayed depends on the observer's perspective and utilizes photographed or synthetically generated views of the plant.

Today, procedures such as these are already making it possible to use synthetic landscapes in films and to a more limited extent to use them interactively. In addition to their traditional application in the field of animation, they are also being increasingly applied to the fields of architecture, landscape design and urban planning.

Translated from the German by Sarah Clift

The text is a much abridged version of the original essay "Computer-Pflanzen" first published in *Spektrum der Wissenschaft*, 2/2001, pp. 58-65.

Shelley Eshkar and Paul Kaiser
Pedestrian

2002
3-D digital animation based on motion-capture data / dimensions variable / 12:50 min

Pedestrian Passages

Looking Down

It is now a routine move in Hollywood to first put you airborne, soaring in a helicopter over a mysterious landscape glimmering below. If it's an urban drama you're watching, then this opening shot evokes the vast complexity of intertwined lives, events and spaces that constitute the city. Very soon, however, the camera picks out a more particular locale below, where you spot the film's hero, usually an actor you already "know" in the odd intimate way of our celebrity culture. The rest of the movie unfolds at this more familiar visual and emotional range right up to the very end, when it is common practice to lift you once again for a parting glimpse of the city's infinitude.

In *Pedestrian* our camera remains above, keeping its distance. It gives a less sweeping perspective than that of the Hollywood opening, just a little closer in, as if you were looking down not from a soaring helicopter but rather from a hovering kite. The view is still commanding, for you can take in more of the scene than you would from the ground, but it's close enough that the figures below look like individuals rather than ants. If the bird's-eye perspective traditionally suggests an omniscient God's-eye view, here the power of that perspective certainly lingers but is slightly compromised. The view is often at least partially blocked, if not by architectural elements within the scene then by the unforgiving frame de-limiting it. And when the camera moves, it doesn't anticipate the direction of your interest so much as it imposes its own.

The dramatic structure of *Pedestrian*, such as

it is, is decidedly strange. For while it does have you following individual characters within a scene, it's never for long – it veers off as if distracted to follow another character intersecting in the scene, and then another, and another. This succession comes to seem like an odd and unwitting relay race or game, each figure taking and then passing on the baton of your interest. It's a series of partial and broken narratives, whose beginnings and endings are left to you to imagine. But isn't this much like your own experience in the street, where first one person arrests your attention, but then quickly passes from view (and mind) at your next striking but equally fleeting encounter?

This spectacle also brings to mind the electronic surveillance now blanketing most of our cities. If you can picture the agents poring over the video footage streaming in from the ubiquitous surveillance cameras mounted on buildings and lampposts, you can also imagine that the agents are looking down on similarly equivocal scenes. Their task is to pick out suspicious individuals from the crowd – pickpocket, drug dealer, terrorist, whore – and to trace their furtive intersections and exchanges.

Child's Play

There is a peculiar fascination in *Pedestrian*, certainly in the making of it but also in the viewing that perhaps subconsciously reminds us of childhood. If we bring back the endless games we played on the floor of our playroom, kindergarten and sandbox, the first thing we might notice is that our viewpoint as we lay or sat or crawled there resembles that of the *Pedestrian*

above
Pedestrian
2002
3-D digital animation based
on motion-capture data
dimensions variable
12:50 min
installation view: ZKM |
Center for Art and Media
Karlsruhe, 2002
© Shelley Eshkar, Paul Kaiser
photo © Franz Wamhof

opposite page
Pedestrian
2002
digital stills from *Pedestrian*
animation
© Shelley Eshkar, Paul Kaiser

camera. The building blocks and toy figures that we deployed in fashioning our make-believe worlds served exactly the same functions as the equivalent props and figures in *Pedestrian*. All these elements, as well as this viewpoint, are present too in the video-games that now entrance children for hours on end.

And if we look up at the sky for a moment, we may remember the kites and the model airplanes that we loved to put into flight above us. Were we not imagining ourselves somehow soaring up there with them, looking down on a now-miniature world that had itself become another set of playthings?

Bodies

When we first gaze down on *Pedestrian*, we may feel a kind of comfort and control from our aerial view, a sense of purchase on these teeming comings and go-ings, as if watching so many ants at work in their colony. But these figures walk on two legs as we do, tiny but complete, striding and looking, meeting and greeting, waiting and fleeing. Some are decisive and purposeful; others dawdle and relax. They have lives and make choices all their own.

We are attracted to the sudden stumble, the long hesitation, the warm greeting, and by choice or com-pulsion we zero in to find out more. Our even-handed overview of events is soon gone, however; perhaps it's a lone woman who has caught our eye, and we now must know more about her. From this far off, we can't make out her expression, but she reminds us someone we know or see on the street. Though we make out see her eyes, for her part she seems to see and react to the others around her.

As digital models built purely in 3-D geometry on the computer, the *Pedestrian* figures represent a cross-section of urban archetypes: the suits and backpackers, couriers and working girls, socialites and bench sitters, skaters and civil servants. Each urban portrait is rendered in a graphic palette of skin, hair, costume and shadow, drawn on the floor in silvery gray light.

Constructing human forms in digital 3-D is a pain-staking craft that employs various building metaphors: subdividing cubes, scaling and transform-ing vertices and planes, extruding profiles, and loft-ing sections. In addition, many character parts (body parts, hairstyles, shoes, clothing) can be cannibalized from various on-line sources, where hobbyists share the 3-D avatars they've built for use in film tributes, comic art, and adventure games. The final geometry is distorted, scaled, and optimized for the foreshort-ening of aerial perspective, resulting in a being that is both human and doll-like in presence. For many viewers, the movement and lighting were so credible they often mistake the animation for live surveillance footage.

Figure/Ground

Conceived as a public sculpture, the digital projec-tion of *Pedestrian* merges with the sidewalk we walk upon. The tiny denizens wander through this trompe-l'oeil illusion, in a city that seems paradoxically upon and within the surface. Their plazas and walkways are textured-mapped with samples of concrete, granite, asphalt, and gravel scanned from the real world. Pro-jected onto the granular surface of the sidewalk, these virtual textures merge with the physical concrete, creating a second order of activity and detail.

The environment under their tiny feet is an abstract and simplified game-board of Manhattan, with strong contours and rhythmic subdivisions. These grids, tiles, and area boundaries echo and emboss the physical paving-stones hit by the projection. *Pedestrian* has a visual logic strongly oriented toward activating these boundaries in an optical game of figure and ground: A horde of umbrella walkers spirals across concentric cobblestones in a visual rhyme; a marathon ends when a rink pans into view, bisecting the runners like a sharp white wedge. Rather than depict the density we expect of New York, the *Pedestrian* environment is mostly shallow and flat, emphasizing the horizontal. We the viewers with our tall dark bodies stand in for the buildings of Manhattan's verticality.

Origin

Stick a pin into a map of Manhattan — into Broad Street, to be precise, on the southern tip of the island, just a few blocks from where the World Trade Center towered overhead. It was there, in winter 1997, that we'd wound up on a ramble in the early dusk, and spotted a section of sidewalk glowing up ahead. Stepping closer, we saw that transparent Plexiglas had replaced the usual paving stones, letting pedestrians peer down into the shallow trenches of a small archaeological survey evidently still underway. It was fascinating to gaze down into a space unexpectedly opened up beneath our feet, where the stratified layers of long-gone habitation were revealed as if by physical X-ray. Right then and there came the idea of a public projection likewise laid down before you on the pavement, but evoking the unknowable present rather than the partially recovered past.

Recurrence

The slight sense of déjà vu you might feel in watching *Pedestrian* comes in part from the shifting correspondences between its world and your own, but a second set of correspondences, embedded entirely within the work, also plays a role. You start noticing that things recur, oddly, not only from one scene to another, but also within the same one. Figures are repeated and multiplied, and so are motions.

You spot a man in a tuxedo, for example, in several scenes. Curiously, though, you notice that while his appearance doesn't change, his actions seem disconnected, as if it were not one character occupying his body, but several in succession. When a flashlight picks him up out of the darkness, he is staggering drunk; but when next encountered he is sitting impassively at the edge of the frame, where he waits for over a minute before getting up abruptly and hopping on one foot. He is also elsewhere, in other scenes: part of a passing crowd in one place, a loiterer in another.

Figures not only recur in this fashion, but even recur at the same moment, their bodies duplicated. In a crowd, for example, two or more identical figures may appear at the same time, performing different actions. Conversely, in other scenes, it's the figures that are distinct and the motions that repeat. When the helicopter swoops down, for instance, everyone panics, their actions converging in the same stampeding dash out of the frame.

All the movements in *Pedestrian* are built from the same limited library of motion-captured phrases. These data sets abstract a performer's motion in time and 3-D space from his or her physical appear-

Pedestrian
2002
installation view: Rockefel
Center, New York, 2002
© Shelley Eshkar, Paul Kai
photo © Peter Cunningha

Pedestrian
2002
installation view: Studio
Museum of Harlem,
New York, 2002
© Shelley Eshkar, Paul Kais
photo © Peter Cunningha

Pedestrian
2002
installation view: Eyebeam
New York, 2002
© Shelley Eshkar, Paul Kais
photo © Peter Cunningha

ance, so that it's their pure motion that gets mapped onto any sort of synthetic figure. Since we motion-captured only eight performers (who ranged in type from dancer to programmer to child), it is only eight individual styles of motion animating everything. And so a given figure is like a puppet animated by a succession of up to eight puppeteers. Its walk may come from a twenty-three-year-old ballerina, its hop from an eight-year-old boy, and its turn from a forty-six-year-old man.

Precursors

Pedestrian lies at the intersection of several traditions. One of these comes to us out of the nineteenth century, when the ideal figure of the *flâneur* emerged. This urban wanderer loses himself in his city, reveling in its myriad unexpected juxtapositions and savoring streams of consciousness that jumble inner with outer, daydream with perception. At its start, this was mainly a literary phenomenon, carried out by such writers as Poe and Baudelaire to begin with, and then pushed further in the next century by Aragon, Benjamin and Raban, among many others.1 It had its counterpart in the urban snapshot practices of certain key photographers, most amazingly in Rodchenko's off-angle shots of Moscow, but also in Cartier-Bresson, Frank, and Winograd.

In the twentieth century, moving pictures gave us the city and its crowds as nightmare. The goose-stepping stormtroopers in newsreels matched the lock-stepped zombies of horror films; rampaging rioters on the TV news brought the same kind of mayhem seen more stylishly in the violence of gangster and monster movies. Now that we could watch crowd patterns unfolding in time, we could see the crowd as a kind of aggregate being, with a usually malevolent mind of its own.

We could also start conceiving of the crowd more metaphorically. Nobody pushed this approach further than Elias Canetti in his tome *Crowds and Power*, where for example he points out that the cry of "Fire!" can spark a crowd into a kind of fire itself, its panic rapidly blazing up and consuming everyone and everything in its ever-widening path.2

Counterpoint

In fewer than a dozen moments does the *Pedestrian* soundtrack give you an exact sync to the projected figures you are tracking. You do hear the rattle of a can kicked by a girl in passing, or the creak of a gate opening up onto the park, but these are rare instances. Instead the soundtrack mostly evokes surrounding space beyond the frame, which nonetheless often provides an exact counterpoint to what you see. An ambulance siren moving past in the distance perfectly tracks the roller-blader skating into view; the roar of a departing airplane overhead ushers a figure crossing into the next scene. We had turned to composer Terry Pender to design the soundtrack, and his intricately layered composition only reveals itself fully on repeated watching and listening.

What the soundtrack does not give you is dialogue: the projected figures don't utter a word. But onlookers often spontaneously deliver their imagined lines for them, never more so than at the Harlem installation of the piece, where they improvised voice-over conversations freely. "I'll do the voices," said one young man; "I'll do the beats," said another, turning it into rap.

Another kind of counterpoint was even more interactive. While most viewers are content to stand at the edge of the projection, at most easing their

Pedestrian
2002
installation view: Studio Museum of Harlem, New York, 2002
© Shelley Eshkar, Paul Kaiser
photo © Peter Cunningham

Pedestrian
2002
installation view: Eyebeam,
New York, 2002
© Shelley Eshkar, Paul Kaiser
photo © Peter Cunningham

Pedestrian
2002
installation view: Eyebeam,
New York, 2002
© Shelley Eshkar, Paul Kaiser
photo © Peter Cunningham

foot into the light-beam to cast a timid shadow, children jump right in it. They wade through the light like Gullivers, first squashing the Lilliputian figures underfoot and then moving on to improvise more elaborate games together. Hopscotch, for example, but on a rapidly changing ground pattern; or shadow-play, with hand-shadows like puppets wandering through the scenes.

Shelley Eshkar and Paul Kaiser

1 Edgar Allan Poe, "The Man of the Crowd," in *Selected Writings of Edgar Allan Poe*, Penguin Books, Harmondsworth, 1967, pp. 179–188; Charles Baudelaire, *Flowers of Evil A Selection*, Marthiel and Jackson Matthews (eds), W. W. Norton & Company, New York, 1988; Louis Aragon, *Paris Peasant*, Exact Change, Boston, 1999; Walter Benjamin, *The Arcades Project*, Harvard University Press, Cambridge, MA, 2002; Jonathan Raban, *Soft City*, Harvill Press, London, 1998.

2 Elias Canetti, *Crowds and Power*, Noonday Press, New York, 1984, p. 27.

Marc Lafia with Didi Fire
Variable Montage

2002
digital video / software, QuickTime video, MAX/MSP patch

A work of Computational and Algorithmic Cinema

As cinema is informed by computation, montage becomes less about narration and more about construction. Such constructions can be thought of as architectures of possibility. In this work twenty-seven still frames from a Russian film are broken into five segments that continually vary and permutate. Permutation allows for a continuing inflection of various possibilities of meaning and texture.

Each of the five segments has also associated with them a small phrase from Mahler's ninth symphony and these sounds vary pitch, alternate and overlap as the speed of the images and sequences play. As image is driven by computation, montage becomes variable and loses the preciseness of rendition that traditional cineasts practice. Variability as constructed with computation allows for a continual iteration, a continual play within very defined structures of possibility and in some sense changes our very notion of montage. The results of this montage give forth surprise, coincidence, deformation, collision, ambiguity and all possibilities of excess. This excess, characteristic of the digital, naturally tends to proliferate, multiply and replicate.

Whereas in cinema the film projector is a fixed instrument consisting of a single projection (silent films play back at sixteen or eighteen frames per second and sound films at twenty-four frames per second), when running with software "the projector" is simultaneously a playback and authoring machine. The software then allows for the creation of a new filmic instrument, a variable instrument that can be instructed to play or, more precisely, "compose" a film in line with particular and varied instructions. Authored in MAX MSP, this work translates each image into a number and each set of images is given variables within which they are sequenced and ordered in relation to all other images.

In software and more particularly computation, projection and recording become inextricably linked. Image, as well, is no longer material but a virtuality actualized by instructions. If we can say there is a materiality, it is in the instruction sets or code by which image and sound are realized or actualized. Instructions in computation can also be made variable, such that a work can have varied permutations and order. Variability can be thought of as an affirmation of chance more so than a reduction to probabilities or range of randomness.

In this three-screen work (presented here as three windows on a single monitor) the twenty-seven frames of black-and-white film and fifteen seconds of sound are composed to have infinite duration, that is, they play continually varying and alternating sound and image, as long as the program runs, and the composition can run along various presets infinitely within tightly defined parameters. In this sense the work is not closed, nor is it known, until the event of computational "projection."

Variable Montage is as much an engine or structure for possible films as it is a film per se. Each film, if we can call it that, is the unique utterance or enunciation in the event of a language, which each time is to be invented and spoken anew. In computational imaging, time and sequence take on an entirely new sense, perhaps it is the difference of becoming rather than unfolding, where each time through the engine of computation a film becomes, revealing something essential about computation as an engine of possibility and something about cinema as a fixed machine of the particular.

Marc Lafia

Variable Montage
2002
digital video
software,
QuickTime video,
MAX/MSP patch
screeshots
© Marc Lafia

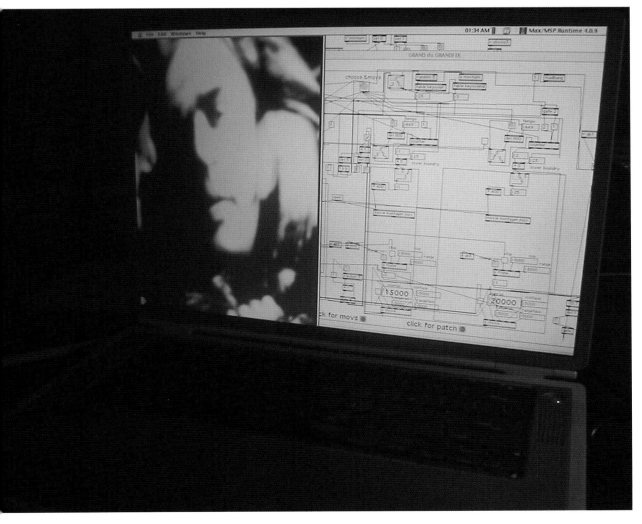

Variable Kubelká
2002
digital video
© Marc Lafia

Maciej Wisniewski
Instant Places

2002
Net-based installation / custom software / dimensions variable

Maciej Wisniewski is an artist and programmer whose work focuses on the underlying creative and social implications of the Internet, networks, and technology in general. His deep understanding of networks enables him to explore the Internet as a new entity different from any previous carriers of information/communication/expression.

Instant Places, a software fiction, creates a network formed ad hoc to connect dispersed data places. These data places can stretch over multiple computers and multiple networks. They are not bound by geography, time and space.

After Instant Places has been installed on a computer that is connected to the Internet it will immediately search for its peer(s) (another copy of Instant Places). It makes no difference if a copy of the software is installed on a machine next door or on a computer across the globe. Once the peer(s) has/have been located, it will then allow for its inhabitants to travel freely to and from the newly discovered place(s). The inhabitants of the software fiction have all a name and a notion of their origin by which they can be identified while traversing the paths between different nodes on the network. Disparate

Instant Places can merge into one another thus creating a fabric of linked nodes carrying on their own immersive stories. The stories do not repeat themselves but they all follow similar "social" rules defined by the software.

Instant Places can not be influenced or altered by any factors outside the software fiction itself. There is no interactivity present. The viewer becomes a mere witness to a fraction of a story. Several parts of the story remain either invisible (such as the real-time messaging or network traffic) or unreachable (by being geographically dislocated).

The instance of Instant Places created for the ZKM | Center for Art and Media Karlsruhe is inhabited by predators and prey which communicate with one another. Their sensory exploitations such as recognition, motion detection, resolving distance and shape information are done by way of real-time messaging. Predators and their prey move freely between different data places in the ever-unfolding story of their coexistence. At times when things appear rather peaceful, suddenly something upsets the balance, and they change their behavior by attacking, fleeing or defending.

Instant Places
2002
screenshots
courtesy the artist and
Postmasters Gallery, New York

Instant Places
2002
Net-based installation
custom software
dimensions variable
installation view: ZKM |
Center for Art and Media
Karlsruhe, 2002
courtesy the artist and
Postmasters Gallery, New York
photo © Franz Wamhof

netomat

Attempts to visualize or comprehend the Internet via familiar metaphors (pages, 3-D space, linear progression, and so on) are limiting representations of such a complex new medium. Wisniewski shows that there are other ways to access, interact with, and understand the information on the Net. With *netomat* Wisniewski built his own interface to the Internet.

Unlike traditional web interfaces such as browsers which retrieve only predefined web content and rely on the model of the page, *netomat* engages a different Internet — one that is alive and unpredictable. In response to words and phrases typed in by the viewer, *netomat* interacts with the Internet to retrieve text, images, and audio which flow onto the screen. Using a new audiovisual language designed specifically to explore the unexplored Internet, *netomat* reveals how the ever-expanding network interprets and reinterprets cultural concepts and themes.

Visitors enter a *netomat* theater where they are surrounded by a collage of streaming images, text, animations, voice, and music triggered by a series of inputs. Visitors can then transverse the Internet's data structure by selecting both the inputs and steering the visual flow of the information.

The original *netomat* — which was launched at New York's Postmasters Gallery in June 1999 — revealed that multimedia information existing on the web could be searched directly, freed from its original html-page format, and structured and displayed however the viewer chooses to see it. In the subsequent "Data Dynamics" exhibition at the Whitney Museum in 2001, the *netomat* installation extended this idea and made the Internet a large, public, theatrical experience whereby two people could conduct a live dialog using the material existing on the network.

netomatheque

In a living-room setting, the audience is given a telephone as a very unusual but at the same time very familiar interface to the Internet. Using their own voice, the viewers can engage in a phone conversation with the network and see the Internet reply with a stream of changing images and fragments of text on the walls as well as sounds. "netomatheque 1 is an alternative browsing experience, one which will take you on a journey deep into the Internet's subconscious" (Steve Deitz).

3 seconds in the memory of the internet

This spatial three-part projection presents the memory of the Internet. Three slices of time will be arbitrarily selected by the artist from three different decades in the Internet's development. In three simultaneous live feeds, *netomat* will crawl the visible and invisible Internet and display what was created or modified at these moments in time and is still remembered today. These include messages exchanged, news posted, documents published as well as log and error files. A liquid, image-transforming interface created by the artist, in which each pixel is visibly "live," evokes memory itself. Here, the traces of what is left on the web reflect subjective memory rather than objective archive and emphasize the vast scale of the Internet as an organic and fluid entity.

Descriptions first published at http://www.netomat.net/

1 *netomatheque* was originally presented in the traveling ICI exhibition "Telematic Connections," curated by Steve Deitz and first shown at the San Francisco Art Institute in 2001.

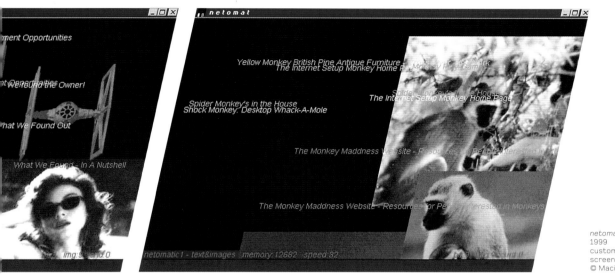

netomat
1999
custom software
screenshots
© Maciej Wisniewski

netomatheque
2001
Net-based installation
custom software
© Maciej Wisniewski

3 seconds in the memory
of the internet
2002
Net-based installation
custom software
© Maciej Wisniewski

Sabine Himmelsbach

The Interactive Potential of Distributed Networks. Immersion and Participation in Films and Computer Games

"The end of the illusion begins with the participation of the observer."[1]

Media artist Tom Sherman describes our contemporary mode of information reception thus: "People rarely choose to focus on one coherent stream of information these days, but rather gather data from multiple sources simultaneously. [… W]e choose to compose our immediate information environment from multiple sources, mixing our multi-layered reality on the spot."[2] Overstimulation through media has conditioned our brain to constantly shift attention; our concentration span is decreasing all the time.

> "This is also because we process information in ever smaller portions. If we were to process information in larger portions, we could decide to watch a film with a certain element of psycho-drama in a certain processual mode. […] But this is not possible if we are constantly shifting the focus of our attention. Information is now transmitted so that it can be processed by a brain conditioned to such constant shifts of attention. Our brain grows tired of switching channels, and so it is fed only small portions of information – for instance a short text followed by more action – so that it is never tempted to adjust to a single given mode."[3]

Thus a vicious circle is created, in which on the one hand the brain is forced to adjust to changes in its environment, and on the other this drop in attention level determines all future forms of information dissemination.

Interactive films and computer games obviously exploit the possibilities latent in such perceptual habits. In allowing the observer to participate directly in the action, they continually engage his interest. They seek to synthesize cinematic narration and the observer's capacity for interaction. Ever since the invention of the panorama, immersive visual spaces have striven to "put the observer in the picture" and stimulate the latter's participation. This short historical overview is intended to describe immersive strategies in cinema, ranging from the 360-degree panorama image to the creation of enterable virtual spaces – to date the limit of technological development. Enterable virtual spaces inevitably increase the observers' level of participation – they play an active role in the proceedings. Computer games also allow the creation of virtual worlds, into which the player can enter like an avatar. Although currently limited by the physical restraints of game consoles or PCs, players will be able, as online games develop, to create communal interactive spaces on the World Wide Web permitting them finally to break through the illusion of participation and to participate fully in a "perfect illusion." Networked communities in virtual global space can already create real group experiences – in real time.

Immersion: From Panorama to Virtual Reality

In his book on virtual art, Oliver Grau describes how visual immersion strategies in computer-generated virtual reality developed from the panorama, one of the earliest forms of mass media.[4] The panorama is the most influential precursor of technologically produced illusory space, for it created a completely new sensation of three-dimensionality. It invited visitors to experience foreign lands simply by observing them, as it were submerging them in exotic landscapes. Later, cinema was to intensify the observer's illusion of being transported to faraway places. Early films exercised such suggestive power on cinema audiences that when a train appeared to rush out of the silver screen into the auditorium they would abandon their seats in panic. "If cinema ever could succeed in becoming the exact double of reality, it would also fail – since it would cease to exist as cinema."[5] Matthews wrote these words with reference to André Bazin and his 1946 text "The Myth of Total Cinema,"[6] in which Bazin argues in favor of a cinema that documents and represents reality – whose transparency would concomitantly entail a necessary break with illusion.

The history of the Hollywood dream factory is paradoxically marked by an increasing striving after realism, beginning with the introduction of sound and continuing with the transition from black-and-white to color film. Later developments designed to step up the assault on audiences' senses include enlarging the screen – from CinemaScope in the 1950s to IMAX in the 1980s – and OMNIMAX technology, not to mention Dolby Surround Sound. Yet attempts to stimulate the full range of the audience's senses to heighten the illusion of total submersion did not get far beyond the experimental stage. Smell-O-Vision (1960) involved pumping odors through pipes into the auditorium and releasing them during the film. 3-D spectacles were also used to heighten the illusion of visual depth. All these strategies to overcome the limits of the silver screen were designed to create as perfect an illusion as possible – to put the audience firmly "in the picture."

The first computer-graphics system, Sketchpad, developed by Ivan E. Sutherland in 1963, allowed users

1 Ursula Frohne, "'That's the only now i get': Immersion und Partizipation in Video-Installationen," in *Kunst/ Kino*, Georg Stemmrich (ed.), Oktagon, Cologne, 2001, p. 238.

2 Tom Sherman, http://www. kunstradio.at/TEXTS/ blanking-e.html

3 Detlef Linke, "Der letzte Mensch blinzelt. Ein Gespräch mit dem Hirnwissenschaftler Detlef Linke," http://www.heise.de/ tp/deutsch/inhalt/co/2000/ 1.html

4 Oliver Grau, *Virtuelle Kunst in Geschichte und Gegenwart: visuelle Strategien*, Reimer, Berlin, 2001.

5 Peter Matthews, "André Bazin – Divining the real," http://www.bfi.org.uk/ sightandsound/archive/ innovators/bazin.html

6 André Bazin, "The Myth of Total Cinema," in *What Is Cinema*, Hugh Gray (ed.), vol. 1, University of California Press, Berkeley, 1967, pp. 17–22.

The first European CAVE™
since 1996 at Fraunhofer IMK,
Sankt Augustin
© FhG IMK

to directly manipulate images on the computer screen and to observe the results. In 1968, he also developed the Head Mounted Display (HMD) – a new kind of interface that facilitated interaction between observer and computer and opened up new possibilities for entering virtual worlds. The computer image's real-time reactions to the participant's own movements produce the illusion of the latter's really being "in the picture." This linking of action and reaction, stimulant and response, for the first time directly linked the participant's own imaginative reality and virtual reality.

In 1991, a new immersive projection technology called CAVE (Computer Aided Virtual Environment) was developed in Japan and the USA. It consists of a cube, onto whose walls and floor digital images are projected stereoscopically. The user is located within this illusory space and explores it with the help of stereo glasses and a hand-held interface. His head position – that is, his view of the projected scene – is taken into account in calculating the images, and he thus perceives them as almost perfect, three-dimensional illusions. High-performance computers such as those produced by Silicon Graphics are used to create these stereoscopic images.[7] CAVEs are designed for individual users who manipulate the projections themselves. A CAVE can hold more than one person, but as there is only one control device the others are merely observers rather than active participants. One creative example of applied CAVE technology is *The Living Web* (2002) by Christa Sommerer, Laurent Mignonneau, and Roberto Lopez-Gulliver, which demonstrates the information potential of the WWW. *The Living Web* records the conversations of visitors to this particular CAVE and converts them into a veritable flood of visual and acoustic data downloaded from the Internet. These data, which are constantly being generated anew, literally overwhelm the very people whose activity is sustaining this unstoppable stream of information.

The logical development of this technology is to project films directly onto the optic nerve, thus using the eye itself as an interface – the film would then be played only in the observer's head.

"If we succeeded in creating images directly within the eye itself, we could dispense with illusion-impairing optics and bulky HMDs. Since 1989, institutions such as the Human Interface Technology Lab, founded by Thomas Furness at the University of Washington in Seattle, have been working on a high-resolution laser microscanner capable of projecting computer-generated 3-D images line-by-line directly onto the retina."[8] If the cinema screen is a window onto another world, in virtual reality the observer steps through this window into the world on the other side. Butakman describes the difference between virtual reality and cinema thus: "Virtual reality speaks to the desire to see the space of the computer […] and to further figure it as a space one can move through and thereby comprehend."[9] Virtual reality seeks to create a synthesis of observer and computer-generated visual environment, converting data into sense experience. The distance between visual space and observer is abolished. The latter is now literally in the picture.

> "Print, film and other mass media phenomena are purely aspersive in nature. They 'sprinkle' us with prefabricated information, scarcely permitting any form of interaction that might alter the text. Immersion takes place only in the head of the media user, and only as mental projection. Performative immersion technology allows us not only to look through a window but also to open a door – to enter that other space, move freely around it, and alter it."[10]

Computer-generated environments for the first time permit both interaction with an illusory environment and control over its development. CAVE and similar immersive environments aim at creating virtual spaces that both submerge the observer and allow him to manipulate them via an interface.

Simulation technology is also used in the entertainment industry. Video and computer games, for instance, invite the user to enter a virtual world and explore it in a spirit of play. Here too, real-time response is necessary if the illusion to function properly. Computer games have pioneered immersive participation in cinematic story worlds. They have adapted the complex but familiar language of the cinema, which uses camera sequences, pans, zooms, editing techniques and changing angles and per-spectives to create integrated story worlds. In computer games, the observers are also participants – it is they who keep the action going, as they navigate and explore pre-programmed space. The inclusion of strong narrative elements in computer games has made them a major entertainment form that many see as serious competition for cinema and TV. In contrast to the kind of total immersion that virtual reality aims at, computer games are a form of *ersatz* or surrogate reality whose illusionary character is obvious.

7 See also: Erstes internationales CAVE-Festival 2002: Art of Immersion, 1 June–31 August 2002 in Bonn-Bad Godesberg, http://www.cave-festival.de

8 Grau, op. cit., p. 125.

9 Scott Bukatman, *Terminal Identity. The Virtual Subject in Postmodern Science Fiction*, Duke University Press, Durham/London, 1993, p. 200.

10 Daniel Ammann, "Eintauchen in die Anderswelt," http://www.dichtung-digital.com/2002/03-15-Ammann.htm

The Sims
© EA Games™

Pong
screenshot
© 1971, Atari

The first commercially
successful video-game
in history.

From Video Consoles
to Massive Multi-Player Online Worlds

The development of the multi-media entertainment industry ran parallel to that of the Internet, from the military-based ARPANET of the 1960s to today's global network. In 1972, Atari brought Pong onto the market, an electronic game best described as an abstract form of table tennis in which players propel a rectangle of light from one side of the screen to the other. Pong's simplicity and focus on interactivity, the way it reacted directly to players' input, made it a game culture classic and ensured its global success. Beside Pong, such video games as Pac Man (Namco, 1980), Tetris (1985) and Super Mario Bros. (Nintendo, 1985) scored significant successes in the mass-entertainment markets of the 1980s – one prime advantage being that they could be played in the privacy of the home. Rapid developments in the computer industry – faster processors and enhanced memory capacity – soon made it possible to create 3-D animations in real time, making the PC of the 1980s an ideal platform for games requiring high-quality graphics and ensuring it a permanent place in the entertainment industry.

The 1990s Internet boom generated text-based systems – MUDs (Multiple User Dungeons) and MOOs (MUDs, Object Oriented) – allowing the creation of networked games that exploited the global communication potential of the WWW. Texts were used to describe virtual computer worlds, into which users were invited to chat with each other.

Massive multi-player online worlds – the latest development in the world of computer games – are currently celebrating a global triumph. Dramatic increases in the Internet's data-transfer capacity and new methods of data compression have made it possible to access over the Net visual spaces composed of massive amounts of data– spaces that can be entered and refashioned by an almost limitless number of player-users. The first multi-location networked game was DOOM, a classic of its kind whose cult status is ensured for years to come. Developed in 1994 by ID-Software, DOOM owes its success to the fact that the players themselves are able to modify the game as they play it: they can create new levels as well as design new weapons and enemies. DOOM is also the first game in which up to eight players can compete

against each other simultaneously online; it has inspired a whole generation of net-based games that include Diabolo (Blizzard Entertainment, 1996) and Ultima Online (Electronic Arts Square / Origin, 1997), followed later by Quake and Quake III Arena (ID-Software, 1996-2000). These game engines allow networked players to interact with each other in real time. In these first-person shooters it is easy to recognize whether one's opponent is real or computer-generated, since real players have a far less predictable range of possible reactions at their disposal. Bots – artificial intelligence modules – built into the game constantly adapt the action to the players' skill level. If the players' interest in the game begins to wane, the bots increase the level of difficulty, thus ensuring that things never get boring.

Non-linear Narrative Structures in Computer Games

DOOM was the first game to use a genuinely realistic "subjective camera" to simulate autonomous motion through a virtual world. A first-person shooter such as DOOM is thus defined as three-dimensional graphic action game computed in real time from the perspective of a (virtual) subjective camera. The player slips into the hero's body and sees the surroundings, his enemies and the hero himself from the latter's perspective. This so-called third person 3-D perspective is derived from cinema – at least in this respect computer games and classical Hollywood cinema have something in common. Hans Peter Schwarz has pointed out that video games were the first medium to combine the potential of computers and TV: "Digital television and interactive film would certainly not have become the focus of attention of the media-market strategists if there had not been such an enormous demand for interactivity – however rudimentary – by the users who have grown up with video games and who are now into the second or third generation."[11]

This combination of narration and interaction has ensured the continuing attraction of computer games: "Computer games almost inevitably combine narrative progression with 'virtual' sensory pleasures. Repeatedly, the operations of narrative will be shown to constrain the effects of a new mode of sensory address, and so the fascination with the rise of virtual reality systems might represent a possible

11 Media – Art – History, Hans-Peter Schwarz (ed.), Prestel, Munich, 1997. This book was published on the occasion of the opening of the Media Museum, ZKM | Center for Art and Media Karlsruhe on October 18, 1997.

Lara Croft, Tomb Raider
© & TM Core Design Limited
1996–2001. Published by Eidos
Interactive Limited.
All rights reserved.

Everquest
© Sony Online Entertainment

passage beyond narrative into a new range of spatial metaphors."12 Participation on the level of narration always involves a disruption of the narrative structure. Interactivity or participation necessarily entails a loss of quality with respect to the illusion of being submerged in another world – but also a more active level of player participation. These increasingly more realistic computer games are becoming serious competitors to cinema. Gundolf S. Freyermuth sees cinema's loss of social significance in terms of its shrinking economic status: "American consumers now spend more money on digital hard- and software than they do on cinema visits, video recorders and TV sets. In 1999, for the first time interactive video and computer games had a higher turnover than did passive cinema, thus emulating the theme park industry, which has long since surpassed cinema in economic terms. New high-tech genres are being developed both off- and online that will soon replace cinema in terms of mass-media popularity."13 Hollywood has reacted to this threat by producing film versions of such popular computer games as Tomb Raider (1996) and Final Fantasy (1990). But these reproductions of game worlds on the silver screen do not work, for the simple reason that the games' decisive characteristic – their participative potential – cannot be emulated in the cinema version. The imaginative world of the film version is severely limited compared to that of the game version, and the former has therefore enjoyed only limited success. Hollywood cinema remains trapped in the tradition of illusory spaces that per se exclude participatory strategies, for participation destroys the perfection of the illusion. On the other hand, some games are based on successful films, such as the multi-player online world of Star Wars Galaxies, scheduled to be launched in 2003: "Perhaps the most extreme example of front-loaded game design is the forthcoming multi-player online world based on Star Wars, which is being built by Verant, the leading developer in this genre, and LucasArts. When it is launched in 2003, Star Wars Galaxies is expected to attract more than a million subscribers – based on Everquest's usage statistics, that means more than 300,000 simultaneous players at peak usage."14 These game worlds based on successful films extend the latter's linear plot to create their own autonomous "universes."

In recent years, a similar strategy has been followed by certain films that experiment with narrative options and the dissolution of narrative linearity. For instance in *Living in Oblivion* (1995, dir. Tom DiCillo) a single filming session is narrated from the perspectives of all those involved, whereby each new scene is actually being dreamt by one of the protagonists – a fact that becomes apparent only in the course of the film. *Sliding Doors* (1998, James Berardinelli) and *Run Lola Run* (1999, Tom Tykwer) also present the viewer with alternative versions of the same plot. These disruptions of narrative structure and concomitant confrontations with a range of narrative choices break, as it were, the fictional spell. Game designer Katie Salen has pointed out that the "language and style of game media have had a tremendous influence on recent film direction and camera movement."15 *The Matrix* (1999, Andy and Larry Wachowski) is a striking example of such a film.

But back to games: in recent years computer games have increasingly emphasized narrative, which was of but secondary importance in ego-shooter games. Half-Life (Valve/Sierra Studios, 1998) – another three-dimensional first-person shooter, whose technology is based on Quake Engine – involves the player in an interactive narrative plot structure. Frank Furtwängler describes the communication model of games as that of a socially interactive conversation, in contrast to a preordained story.16 "All in all, computer games are located between (at least) two poles of tension, defined by the categories interactivity and narrativity."17

Today real-time strategy games such as Command and Conquer by Westwood Studios (1995), Starcraft by Blizzard North (1998), and first-person shooters (FPS) such as Quake and the more advanced version Quake III Arena (ID-Software, 1996–2000) enjoy great popularity. Another example of an online game in a networked virtual world is the Sim City series (1989) created by Will Wright; the latest version, The Sims, was released in 1998. Players remain involved in such games for much longer periods than is the case with FPS games. They play not for a matter of hours but for weeks or even months. Collaborative elements and built-in feedback mechanisms ensure that the players' interest never wanes. Players who re-enter the game after a lengthy absence may find that

12 Bukatman, op. cit., p. 195.

13 Gundolf S. Freyermuth, "Von A nach D. Zwischen Hype und Utopie. Am Horizont der Digitalisierung von Kunst und Unterhaltung lockt das Holodeck," in *Cyberhypes. Möglichkeiten und Grenzen des Internet*, Rudolf Maresch and Florian Rötzer (eds), Suhrkamp, Frankfurt/M., 2001, p. 225.

14 J.C. Herz, "Gaming the System. Multi-Player Worlds Online," in *Game On. The History and Culture of Videogames*, Lucien King (ed.), King Publications, London, 2002, p. 87. See also http://starwarsgalaxies. station.sony.com/

15 Katie Salen, "Telefragging Monster Movies," in King, op. cit., p. 99.

16 Frank Furtwängler, "A crossword at war with a narrative Narrativität versus Interaktivität in Computerspielen," in *Formen interaktiver Medienkunst*, Suhrkamp, Frankfurt/M., p. 398.

17 Furtwängler, op. cit., p. 374.

entire settings have been altered in the mean time by interaction between other players – so there's always something new to discover. The game's ambience is created and controlled by the players themselves – in The Sims, some ninety percent of the ambience is now produced by the player population.[18]

In multi-player online worlds such as Everquest and The Sims, the virtual world does not disappear when players leave the game but is continually being modified in their absence by other players or by automated processes built into the game. The virtual world of these games is thus dynamic, unpredictable, and fascinating. A further development of these computer games is Machinima, in which a film is projected in a virtual 3-D environment generated in real time. Currently, most of these films are created by the players themselves – the user thus becoming producer. Based on already existing game engines such as Quake and Quake III Arena, they allow the creation of personalized multi-player online worlds, "a strange universe recorded in pixels per second distributed and consumed via the web."[19]

Participation in Interactive Films

In interactive films, which permit the observer to determine the actual plot of a story via tracking systems and sensors – or in comparable computer games – the observer/player's involvement in the visual experience is enormously increased.

"But the mass of mainstream film, and the conventions within which it has consciously evolved, portray a hermetically sealed world which unwinds magically, indifferent to the presence of the audience, producing for them a sense of separation and playing on their voyeuristic fantasy. Moreover, the extreme contrast between the darkness in the auditorium (which also isolates the spectators from one another) and the brilliance of the shifting patterns of light and shade on the screen helps to promote the illusion of voyeuristic separation."[20]

In a traditional film, the position of the observer is determined by the latter's immobility vis-à-vis the cinema screen. The cinematic experience is one of "emotional immersion."[21] Should the viewer become an "emotional observer,"[22] he breaks through the perfect illusion of the cinematic space. The digital storage capacity of modern computers allows data to be made available in non-linear structures, permitting external users to access it in apparently limitless permutations. The Internet with its ever-growing

global networks has also generated a concomitant growth in interactive group projects.

"As soon as the Internet's capacity for transmitting data reaches a certain level, visual spaces will be accessible online of a quality that is currently to be found only in complex installations – in standalone systems at festivals or in museums – that explicitly recommend themselves as models for future Internet creations. Thus installations have been created with new interfaces that not only place the observer much more intensely in the picture but – through an extensive range of interactive processes – permit him to become much more involved in the work's evolution."[23]

Interactive cinema is thus the cutting edge of our "multimedia reality,"[24] using the Internet to offer a whole new range of narrative options in networked virtual worlds. One of the earliest examples of an interactive film with a non-linear plot is Lynn Hershman's Lorna (1979–1984). The eponymous heroine is a woman living alone in her apartment, cut off from the outside world – with the exception of her telephone and TV set – and suffering from loneliness and despair. Using a remote control, the installation visitor can direct Lorna's actions and thus determine the outcome of the story. The work was published as a videodisc consisting of thirty-six sequences lasting from a few seconds to several minutes. The CD-ROM, created as an interactive medium for the mass market at the beginning of the 1990s, proved to have insufficient data capacity for video stories of any length. Only with the advent of the DVD did a mass medium appear with sufficient capacity for sustained interactivity.

Another example of interactive cinema is Artificial Changelings (1993–1998) by Toni Dove, in which the observer controls the plot development. However, the range of options is limited, and in any case predetermined by the computer. Yet the direct link between observer in real space and actor in the film generates an entirely new level of participation. Dove has created her works both as enterable installations, in which interaction takes place via motion tracking and pressure-sensitive sensors, and as DVD presentations on a computer monitor, in which interaction takes place via the keyboard or a microphone using voice recognition.

Desert Rain (1999) by the Blast Theory group unites the potential of an interactive installation with the instructional mode of a computer game. The game is set up like an installation, a virtual

18 Herz, op. cit., p. 91.

19 Salen, op. cit., p. 99.

20 Laura Mulvey, "Visual Pleasure and Narrative Cinema," in Narrative, Apparatus, Ideology, A Film Theory Reader, Philip Rosen (ed.), Columbia University Press, New York, 1986, p. 201.

21 Marie-Laure Ryan, Narrative as Virtual Reality: Immersion and Interactivity in Literature and Electronic Media, Johns Hopkins University Press Baltimore, 2001, p. 148 ff. Quoted in Daniel Ammann, "Eintauchen in die Anderswelt," http://www.dichtung-digital.com/2002/03-15-Ammann.htm

22 Annette Hünnekens, Der Bewegte Betrachter. Theorien der interaktiven Medienkunst, Wienand, Cologne, 1997.

23 Oliver Grau, "Kunst als Inspiration medialer Evolution," http://waste.informatik.hu-berlin.de/mtg/mtg4/grau.html

24 See also Manfred Fassler, Cyber-Moderne. Medienevolution, globale Netzwerke und die Künste der Kommunikation, Springer, Vienna, New York, 1999.

LAN party at ZKM | Center
for Art and Media Karlsruhe
(during the exhibition
"net_condition," 1999)
photo © Franz Wamhof

Blast Theory
Desert Rain
1999
VR environment for performance
installation view:
ZKM | Center for Art and Media
Karlsruhe, 1999
© Blast Theory
photo © Franz Wamhof

environment in which six participants have to orient themselves. Only by communicating with each other can they successfully navigate their way through this virtual world. *Desert Rain* was first presented at the ZKM | Center for Art and Media Karlsruhe in 1999. Blast Theory locates the user in an environment which is structured by cooperation and specific rules of conduct. The six participants stand in separate cubicles with pressure sensitive floors, through which they control their movements in this virtual world. Stranded in a desert landscape dotted with underground bunkers, they have half an hour to find their goal and complete their mission. The better they communicate and cooperate, the more easily they can find their way through this virtual world, thus making this virtual adventure a real collective experience.

Players are motivated by competition – every game has a winner and several losers. Interaction in networked games, however, offers more than mere point scoring – it offers the added dimension of social communication. Players exchange information on technical support and other game-related matters; they also establish personal contact via e-mail. Indeed, sometimes players spend more time discussing and developing games than in actually playing them. Development in strategy-based and multi-player online worlds is not a case of overcoming geographical obstacles but of developing one's own game avatar. Online computer games are becoming increasingly popular – especially in the form of LAN parties, networked game marathons in which transmission speeds between computers are many times faster than in Internet communication. Networked virtual worlds facilitate participation in distributed networks and are an important step towards the vision of total media convergence on the Net.

Translated from the German by Stephen Richards

Paul Johnson
Red v. 2.0, Green v. 2.0, Blue v. 2.0

2002
networked game consoles / vacuum-formed styrene, mixed media, hardware and software /
each console: 71 x 71 cm

Red v. 2.0, Green v. 2.0, Blue v. 2.0
2002
screenshots
Paul Johnson
photos © Paul Johnson; courtesy
Postmasters Gallery, New York

Cyber-Objectivity, Hyperreality, or Sci-Fi?

In ancient times, the Pythagoreans imagined that vision took place when rays issued from the eyes and impinged upon the world. In this exhibition, Paul Johnson's figures animate a modern version of this view, a version in which the imagination, not Reality, is projected, like a movie, somewhere inside of us (probably inside our brains). Even though most coherent modern theories of memory have retreated from such a view, films and television shows endlessly persist in encouraging us to envision memories as movie-like images, replayed with authorless eidetic efficiently by the homunculus inside our "minds."

Johnson's figures mock the media homunculus. They project their images outward, and in so doing they pretend to lay all bare, to reveal the inner mechanism that in postmodernity replaces the ghost in the machine.

Standing close beside *Monocular Projector* (1995, mixed media), I see that his/her/its video image – an endlessly tumbling object, which must be architectural, or could be some sort of machine component (perhaps *Monocular Projector* is thinking about one of her/its/his own parts?) – this image is being cast on the wall a few yards away by nothing so complicated as a common reading glass, its/her/his "eye," which it/she/he holds out before her/him/itself like a monocular lorgnette, at the end of a gooseneck "arm."

Any magnifying lens will effect a projection if you position it correctly (for focus) and give it a bright light-emitting image to project. I peek more closely into the tangle of haywire objects – juice cartons, clip-on lampshades, brillo pads – on the business side of the magnifying glass, and there, tiny, bright, and crystal clear, is Mono's light-emitting image source.

Paul Johnson has appropriated the expensive technology of video projection by the simple and low-cost expedient of taking LCD televisions, gutting them, and running his own images through the LCD screen. He jerryrigs a backlight for the LCD screen using a clip-on with a regular light bulb, and voila! video projection.

All of this has a mad charm, familiar from *Back to the Future* and *Flubber*; here is the artist as slight-crazed eccentric (again), this time tinkering with the pulse beat of consumer technology. By contrast, Paul Johnson expresses himself with earnest reserve. When asked about the "Mad Maxx" impression his work exudes, he recoils slightly; there is no hint of dystopic frenzy or manic adventurism anywhere on his personal horizon.

Rather, Johnson says, he is intent on reclaiming consumer technology for the "active consumer" (read "poor young artist"). The advanced tools which are the product of modern technology should not be foreclosed from the artist's toolbox because of cost. Inverting the ethos of business technology, Johnson claims a workspace in which it is better to do it the cheap way; ethically imperative to center one's effort on ingenuity, invention, and idea; and urgently desirable to dismantle the carapace that segregates the Project User from the inner engineering product that was configured and constituted by Capital.

Is it "revolutionary," then, to rip the plastic skins off your appliances? To dip inside them with scalpel of "mixed media?" Perhaps. But rather than sparking a Luddite revolt against the tyranny of appliances, Johnson is carefully modeling a polyvalent *Weltanschauung* in which the post-modern instability of the object world is balanced against the incorporeality of the information order. The field of this contestation, as with Donna Haraway's cyborg discourse, is in the representation of the body.

Binocular Projector (1995) – with its two lens "eyes" perhaps the most anthropomorphic piece in the show – projects a pair of identical but mirror-reflected images. No chance that these opposite images could be merged stereographically! "Bino," "Mono," and a third piece, *Sled Projector* (1995), are each splayed out before us, their inner projector "guts" hanging loosely together, and their "thoughts" beamed mindlessly onto the wall. They are unalive bodies with memories, cadavers of data death, rudely dissected, hanging before the impassive viewer at or just below eye level as though on virtual autopsy slabs.

One reason for the birth of modern medicine during the sixteenth century was advances in anatomical understanding. But the work of Vesalius and others came to prominence because of its value as

Red v. 2.0, Green v. 2.0, Blue v. 2.0
2002
networked game consoles
vacuum-formed styrene, mixed
media, hardware and software
each console: 71 x 71 cm
installation views: Postmasters
Gallery, New York
Paul Johnson
courtesy Postmasters Gallery,
New York
photos © Paul Johnson;
courtesy Postmasters Gallery,
New York

spectacle; dissections of cadavers were conducted as aristocratic entertainments of a "philosophical" nature, while the rabble were treated to the ruder entertainment of heretic burnings and even squirmier executions. The "philosophical" question, then as here, entailed a search for the ghost homunculus, the frightful principle of life in the body.

Perhaps a similar wonder animates today's fascination with horror and the "Gothic" – an hysterical fascination with aporias of life and language, veering across the line from the grisliest nightmares into humor. I did find myself laughing at Johnson's work, at its incongruities and cute personal foibles. Maybe I have even overstated the dark side – it's happened before. When I first saw David Wojnarowicz's bloody arm tear off, in Richard Kern's *Manhattan Love Suicides*, I was shaken; then I found out that everyone else enjoyed it as a comedy.

"Gothic" and horror, again like Johnson's pieces, also owe much to the potentially comic alienation of common settings and objects (*Lawnmower Man*). For instance, here a *Black Vacuum* (1997) (vacuum cleaner) quietly resting in the semi-darkness on a strip of carpet, when approached, belches startlingly to life with a vacuum-ey roar and spits out an ominous computer-animated image of a diving jet screaming over a housetop. *Sled Projector* is just that, a sled – ridden by a soulless and dismembered contraption that projects its "snowy" and intermittent image of the slopes; a picture periodically interrupted by the augury of a human thigh bone. And: the sled, the vacuum on the carpet, the orange juice containers and the steel wool pads are all homey images, if not downright nostalgic; among them the Flexible Flyer and perhaps even the Watchman – both objects of pre-adolescent male fixations – are at the brink of extinction.

Seen this way, Johnson's show is less about commodities and more about the production of the image; one might even say that he has replaced the image itself by the image of the production of the image. Nevertheless, where this effect is more literally rendered and more technologically quirky, as in the *TV Table Sculptures* (1997), Johnson is less successful. These two pieces are clever; they co-opt video-phone

technology to enable video playback from an ordinary audio boom box. However, just as horror equals *innocent* inventiveness (the *Frankenstein* formula), these displays are, on the other hand, too disingenuous to distract us from their formalist underpinnings. They echo the slow-scan video transmission experiments of the 1970s, without offering vindicative content.

A displacement of the subject has inhabited much recent video-installation work (Tony Oursler, Lucy Gunning). Johnson's viewer is what he calls "a detached viewer, one who watches the world move before them" – but further, Johnson's pieces imply our absence or cancellation. The narrative implicit in the theatrical placement of his imagery insists on our suspension of disbelief, a suspension that lures the viewer into an *X-Files*-like trap: because in this gallery the "viewer" – the one who remembers sledding, who hears the vacuum cleaner as the death buzz of overhead fighter bombers, who tumbles endlessly or ambles ambivalently through a vacant landscape – this viewer is the cyborg composite of viewer and artwork together, a dead nonviewer in nonspace.

This implicit narrative investment moves Johnson's work into a far different territory from precedents such as Nam June Paik's robots or Jean Tinguely's self-destroying machine in the 1960s, or even Laurie Anderson's performance with the projected image that shot to the ceiling out of her purse in the 1970s. It also separates him from Jeff Koons's insolently kool appropriation of vacuum cleaners in the 1980s. Johnson's video projectors and surrogate images successfully employ a "movie within the movie" tactic to displace and double our sense of viewership, and to send the subject into limbo.

More impressive than Paul Johnson's "piracy" of consumer image technologies is his delicate ambivalence in announcing (while absenting) the Body; this almost-virtuoso balancing act marks him as an emerging artist to watch.

Tony Conrad

First published in *The University at Buffalo Art Gallery Overview
1996–1998*, Karen Emenhiser (ed.), pp. 25–26, as a post-exhibition
comment on the one-man exhibition "Paul Johnson," curated by
Karen Emenhiser.

The Art of Machinima

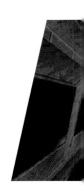

top from left to right
Quantic Dream
Farenheit
not yet released
television show
produced using
ICE engine
screenshots
© the artists

Mackey "Avatar" McCandlish,
Brian "Wendigo" Hess
Blahbalicious
1997
produced using
Quake I engine
8:39 min
screenshots
© the artists

Phil Rice aka Overman
Father Frags Best
1999
produced using
Quake II engine
26:05 min
screenshots
© the artist

Strange Universe: The Art of Machinima

Lost in Quakespace, the voices emerge as if from a distance … perhaps the computer game code they are inhabiting is affecting transmission. Game engines, they murmur. Stories, they confide. Demos, recams, mods. Quake movies. We are making films. "Digital video?" I ask. "Game-engine technology," they reply. "We've assimilated the camera into the code." Seduced by the thrill of discovery of a new filmic paradigm, my mind races and I find desire in the form of speed. I move to collapse the recombinant cut-and-splice aesthetic of immersive game play onto the temporal space of the cinematic surface and achieve maximum velocity. Have I arrived? The questions creep in.

Scourge Done Slick, Fake Science, Rendezvous: movies made with game engines and distributed via the Net to a community of thousands; movies made by playing games with games. Totally digital, totally independent, totally weird. In this digi-cinematic underworld, gamers, hackers – filmmakers – conjure (and Quake) within virtual environments, building sets and molding characters in an imaginary world defined by a slightly disturbing (still elementary) first-person-shooter-meets-adventure-game aesthetic. It is the physics of a strange universe recorded in pixels per second distributed and consumed via the web.

I search for clues linking the phenomenon of real-time 3-D game engine technology with an emerging form of cinema. Between frequent trips to my PC and Ctheory.com I read about surface, perspective, and line of sight as codes for subjectivity in the space of immersive game play. Planetquake.com becomes my new home and gamers named Uwe, Hugh, and Sip-Ice my newest obsessions. Increasingly subtle arguments develop in my mind over the correct application of the term "machinima" to the movies I incessantly download to my desktop. The acronym FPS takes on new meaning for me as frames per second is super-seded by the master code of first-person shooter. I am soon enamored with the sheer elegance of the player as producer paradigm and lament the fact that film theory fails in the face of such tweaked-out technology. I read *War in the Age of Intelligent Machines* and experience déjà vu. I play. I watch. I play again.

Under the Radar

"What else is a film if not an expression of experience by experience?"[1]

Let us take a moment to glimpse that which lies under the current radar of cinematic production. Movies produced within the culture of first person shooter games like Quake, Half-Life, and Unreal – movies made utilizing the client-side, real-time 3-D rendering technology of video-game engines – suggest a model of moviemaking that may challenge traditional notions of cinematic production by offering alternative modes of representation and distribution. Known as Quake movies or machinima (machine animation), these films harness the power of video-game engines in the service of story. Embracing a methodology rooted in the improvisational play of games and in the open code rule structure of the software, a community of

1   Vivian Sobchack,
     "Phenomenology and
     the Film Experience,"
     in *Viewing Positions:
     Ways of Seeing Film*,
     Linda Williams (ed.),
     Rutgers University Press,
     New Brunswick, 1997. p 36.

gamer/filmmakers has developed a form of narrative discourse patterned after the movement and contours of bodily performance within game space. Somewhere in this intersection between the code of the game engine and the performance of the user/producer lies an emerging cinematic art form waiting to explode.

Historically, trend setting first-person shooter games like Quake and DOOM were the first to offer users an editor allowing them to design and program their own maps (environments), skins (character avatars), weapons and tools for game play. This pioneering feature offered consumers unprecedented power to affect game play by altering both the forms and spaces of designed interaction. Modifications to the game code (known as mods) were written by players (or groups of players known as clans) and posted online for other Quake enthusiasts to download and use. Almost instantly, an economy of Quake cultural production was born. This economy pushed the edge of technical innovation, fueled as it was by hardcore gamers' desire to explore the absolute limits of the technology – how far could the code be pushed before the system was broken? More importantly, the culture of Quake production offered a vital space for artistically-minded gamers to invent entirely new forms of creative expression.

In addition to supporting game modification by players, games like Quake, Half-Life, and Unreal contained a built-in feature for recording gameplay. The recorded footage could be viewed and shared, as a way of showing off or of learning new playing styles and moves. But rather than using this feature to create demos of game action, players quickly learned to exploit the recording feature, transforming the space of the game into a performance space. It was just a matter of time before the gamers made the leap to film. Witness the birth of the Quake movie.

In August 1996 a Quake clan known as The Rangers conceived the idea to record a demo that would exploit the robust engine and built-in moviemaking capabilities of the game. Rather than restrict their demo recording to actual gameplay, The Rangers would use their Quake players as actors. As short and simple as the movie appears today – Quake bodies walk around a deathmatch map, pretending like they are in a movie; text messages sent by the players represent speech – *Diary of a Camper* established a filmic genre that has spawned hundreds of movies to date, all of which are available for download online. In these films, avatars that formally represented hostile enemies are recast as actors; the darkened corridors and rooms that once represented sites of battle, are transformed into virtual movie sets for sitcoms, sci-fi fantasies, and humorous Southpark-inspired shorts. Whether the story of a romance between two deep-space probes (*Rendezvous*), an homage to a Hollywood blockbuster (*Matrix: 4 x 1*), or a marriage between in-game cut scenes and gameplay (*Anachronox*), the disparate visual styles and experimental narrative approaches of machinima are truly inventive. As an emerging medium, machinima is on its way to defining cinematic discourse for real-time 3-D.

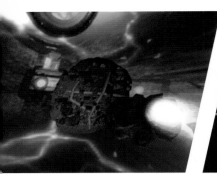

S. Hughes
Anachronox
2001
produced using
Quake II engine
137 min
screenshot
© the artist

Peter Rasmussen
Rendezvous
2001
produced using
3DGamesStudio A4
8 min
screenshot
© the artist

P1mpslap Productions
Rick Jones 2
2000
produced using
Quake II engine
screenshot
© the artists

ILL Robinson,
Paul Marino
Hardly Workin
1998
produced usi
Quake II engi
11:38 min
screenshot
© the artists

Cinematic Replay

"Reality changes; in order to represent it,
modes of representation must change."2
The production process used in the creation of machinima closely mirrors that of other forms of digital animation. From cameras to editing to the use of lighting and special effects, machinima shares many of filmmaking's most basic tools and methodologies. One form of machinima in which these connections can clearly be seen is the recam, that is to say machinima films made by re-editing footage of real-time gameplay. Known as "demos," these recordings were originally a way for players to show off their playing prowess. Rather than just watching a replay, players could edit the footage, alter the perspective from first to third person, post it and share it with other players. The term "recam" refers to the ability of players to alter camera positions, angles and motions after a replay has been recorded. Dr. Uwe Girlich, of Philosys Software was an early developer of tools to assist players in making demos:

"I came into serious contact with computer games via Wolfenstein 3D and later DOOM. With DOOM I could create a recording of my game play and send this demo to other people to show my ability to solve some puzzles or complete a level in a shorter time than anyone else. I became fairly famous for my DOOM demos, but besides playing, I was more interested in programming and analyzing these demo files and so (after some research) I created LMPC, the Little Movie Processing Centre. LMPC is a decompiler/compiler. It can be used to convert a binary demo file into a simple ASCII text file (decompile). Such a text file can be edited with any editor and afterwards it can be converted back into a binary demo file (compile). It is very easy to analyze and also to alter the demo file and even to create a demo file, which is not the actual recording of someone playing the game but a purely fictional movement in the game engine." 3

Girlich recognized players' drive to narrativize gameplay – even to fictionalize it. Rather than showing the match from a first-person point of view (the perspective from which the game is played), a recam shifts perspective to that of third person. What play-

ers see onscreen in a recam varies greatly from what is seen when the game is played. In a first-person-shooter, the gameplay perspective has players staring down the barrel of a gun or similar weapon. Player interaction with the game space is determined by the line of sight afforded by the weapon. But during a recam, perspective shifts to that of third person: players are literally outside of the action. There is no longer any singular line of sight other than that offered by the camera.

Because of this shift, recams show the role point-of-view plays in affecting narrative representation. The recammed match between two of the world's top Quake players, Thresh and Billox, (expertly recammed by Overman of Zarathustra Studios) for example, not only gives viewers the opportunity to experience gameplay from a third-person perspective, but situates the viewer both literally and figuratively outside of the militarized language of Quake and other FPS games. With the shift in perspective from first to third person offered by a recam, players are reminded of the profound difference between playing a Deathmatch round of Quake and watching a recam of it. Recamming offers a point of transition between player and spectator, opening up the line of sight to include the narrative eye.

Resourcing the Code

"It is when the language system overstrains itself that it begins to stutter, to murmur, to mumble."4
Dick Hebdige, writing on the meaning of style, noted that "subcultures manifest culture in a broad sense, as systems of communication, forms of expression and representation."5 Stylized forms of both public and private expression, Quake movies not only represent but reinscribe the relationship between player and producer, suggesting alternative trajectories for creative output. Participants in the culture may assume a range of roles: map builders, coders, skinners, actors, or model makers, for example, or work to create channels of distribution for the movies once they are complete. Web sites such as the Quake Movie Library, Psyk's Popcorn Jungle, Planetquake's Cineplex, and Zarathustra Studios6 support movie production by offering tools, tutorials, movie reviews, and most

2 Bertolt Brecht,
   Brecht on Theater,
   trans. John Willett, Hill
   and Wang, New York, 1979.

3 Personal e-mail correspondence with Dr. Uwe Girlich,
   November 1999.

4 Gilles Deleuze, *Difference
   and Repetition*, trans. Paul
   Patton, Columbia University
   Press, New York, 1994.

5 Dick Hebdige, *Subculture:
   The Meaning of Style*, Routledge, New York, 1979, p 91.

6 Quake Movie Library
   (http://qmovies.telefragged.com); Psyk's Popcorn Jungle (http://www.frag.com/ppj); Planetquake Cineplex (http://www.planetquake.com/cineplex/); Zarathustra Studios (http://www.planetquake.com/zs/)

Mike Berry
Thin Ice
2002
produced using Quake II
1 min
screenshot
© the artist

Tommy Palotta
In the Waiting Line
2002
music video
palm pictures
produced using
Quake III
Arena engines
screenshot
© the artist

The Unreal Movie Team
The Fall
2000
produced using Unreal
Tournament engine
screenshot
© the artists

important of all, downloads of the movies themselves. In keeping with the closed circuit between player and producer, however, the true Quake movie connoisseur will engage the material, but only in the service of creating new works. Fanzine culture, fueled by a revolution in affordable print reproduction technologies starting with the Xerox machine in the 1960s, provides a populist precedent: players blur into manufacturers and distributors, collapsing the space between product and consumer, as well as the general processes of production and consumption. As a fledgling node of the digital film scene, machinima elegantly blends the production of culture with the culture of producers.[7]

Moreover, Quake movies and other forms of machinima offer a unique space of play that merges the flexibility of digital code with traditionally rigid codes of creative production. Structurally, game engines invite modification along established parameters, a kind of systematized, rule-bound play that is informed by the improvisational play of bits and bytes intrinsic to digital technology. In general, players deconstruct the game in order to play with it. Instead of accepting the rules, they challenge and modify them. The movies spawned from game engine technology, thus embody both kinds of play. They are at once systematized objects, bound by the game's interactive structure and programmed code. Yet they are also radically free, offering users a unique space in which to perform and play with both narrative and representational codes. Paul Virilio writes that "play is not something that brings pleasure; on the contrary, it expresses a shift in reality, an unaccustomed mobility. To play today, in a certain sense, means to choose between two realities."[8] In machinima, the movement from playing to producing gives place to form in a transient, even momentary, yet repeatable, other world; with this movement comes a quaking or stuttering of accepted norms that may provide a point of mobilization to affect alternative cinematic practice.

It is important to keep in mind that while formal screenings of the films use prerecorded versions (output to mini DV), machinima films are designed to be viewed from within the game engines that were used to produce them. In order to watch a piece of

machinima, you would traditionally need the game (and its accompanying engine) installed on your PC. These films use a variety of game engines, including Quake 1, Quake 2, Quake 3 Arena, Unreal, and Half-Life, with accompanying mods of their own, like the Spirit of Half-Life modification that was used to make Fake Science by Dead on Que. Running the film from inside the game engine means that all of the animation is rendered in real time. This is no minor detail, as the implications of real-time 3-D to the world of film and computer animation are immense. By most accounts, it will soon be possible for 3-D animation of the quality produced by Pixar for a film like "Toy Story" to be achieved using the real-time 3-D rendering technology of game engines.

Because of this, machinima is beginning to break out of the rather isolated subculture of hard core gamers that has housed it to date. The filmmaker Tommy Pallotta, producer of the acclaimed feature-length animation *Waking Life*, has just completed a music video for the British band Zero 7 using the game engine from Quake III Arena. Using machinima development tools created by Fountainhead Entertainment, Pallotta invented a hybrid production process utilizing traditional film and animation techniques in the service of machinima-based output. Quantic Dream, a Paris-based game developer, is using machinima in the design of an episodic game delivered in real-time to a traditional television audience. Fahrenheit will allow viewers to interact with any of the series' characters, relying on the real-time rendering capabilities of machinima to resituate camera placement and point of view. While it remains to be seen if these two works can capture the imagination of audiences outside of the gaming world, the adoption of game engine technology by more mainstream artists and filmmakers is a clear indication that the future of machinima is indeed bright.

Katie Salen

additional thanks: Hugh Hancock, Anthony Bailey, "Lord" Rev. Dr. Paul Soth, Phil Rice (aka Overman), Anders Carlsson (aka Sip-Ice), United Recammers, Matt Dominianni (aka ILL Clinton), Paul Marino (aka ILL Robinson), Eric Zimmerman

7 Elena Gorfinkel and Eric Zimmerman, "Technologies of Undressing: The Digital Paper Dolls of KISS," in *Zed 5: Beyond the Object, The Implications Project*, Katie Salen (ed.), Center for Design Studies, Virginia Commonwealth University, 1998, pp. 36–37.

8 Paul Virilio and Jerome Sans, "Games of Love and Chance," in *Games of Architecture: Architectural Design*, Maggie Toy (ed.), Academy Editions, London, 1996, p 24.

01

Nora Barry
Telling Stories on Screens:
A History of Web Cinema

John O'Brian
Life At Night
2000
Real
screenshot

A group of people are seated around a table – maybe at home, maybe in a restaurant. Over the din of the conversation one of them says, "I heard a great story the other day." Heads turn, chairs shift and suddenly everyone is attuned to the teller, leaning forward, waiting to hear the story unfold.

A large crowd enters a movie theater. People jostle for seats, spill popcorn in the aisle, talk noisily. Suddenly the lights dim and the screen comes to life. People stop shifting, stop talking and suddenly everyone leans back, waiting to watch the story unfold.

People love stories. Good or bad, long or short – we, as a species, are hooked on them. We've no idea how long man has been telling stories, but we do know that we have a long history of pictorializing them. One need only look at the paintings in pre-historic caves to realize just how long we've been at it. However, the history of adding motion to our picture-stories is only beginning: it was just a little over one hundred years ago that Edison and the Lumière brothers gave us motion pictures; slightly more than sixty years ago that we began watching television; and only five years ago that we began watching pictures move on the web.

Almost since its inception, pundits have pondered the future of web cinema, wondering if there is one (and if so, what its business model is). But they're missing the point. Screen-based storytelling is here to stay; web cinema is simply its most recent incarnation. One thing makes web cinema uniquely important,

however: It is the visual and narrative link between stationary, centralized screen stories and dispersed, mobile screen stories.

Until now we've watched movies sitting in movie theaters, sitting in our homes, and sitting in front of our computers. In a few years we'll be watching cinematic stories on our mobile units and on dispersed screens as we move around. Networked screens are already in taxis, buses and retail outlets; soon they'll be popping up next to billboards along the highway. Traditional theatrical cinema will never work in those environments, but some form of web cinema will. Web cinema is developing the visual and narrative cinematic language that will be used to tell stories on those screens. As such, it's important to understand more about web cinema – what it is, how it has evolved, who the web filmmakers creating these screen stories are, and what kind of storytelling grammar they are developing.

A Working Definition of Web Cinema

What exactly is web cinema? When I first launched The Bit Screen in 1998, I struggled with the nomenclature. Maybe one percent of the films online were actually created in film. "Movie" seemed a funny term for a one-inch flick that lasted about one minute. I ended up using the word "cinema" because it means "motion pictures," and minimally, that's what these flicks were. And web cinema is cinema created specifically for viewing on the Internet. Stories are always shaped by

Jeannette Lambert
D'où Viens-Tu?
2001
interactive Flash
and interactive video
screenshot

the medium in which they are presented, and the technology of that medium and web cinema is no different. Their form is shaped by the fact that the Internet is a digital, interactive, upstream-downstream medium. That makes Internet cinema different from theatrical cinema and television.

Web cinema differs in several key ways from theatrical cinema. First, online cinema is frequently watched by a solitary viewer, seated upright in a chair at a desk, leaning forward to watch a small screen. It's not a situation that lends itself to three-hour epics. So the stories tend to be very short, averaging three minutes. Second, web films are often created by just one person who writes, shoots or creates, directs and edits. There is no cadre of publicists, second unit directors or studio execs waiting to reshape the story. The story told online has a clearer, individual voice (truly auteur), therefore, and is usually more personal. Third, web cinema is still mostly seen on dial-up networks that are subject to congestion and slow speeds. That means the visual aesthetics of web cinema reflect the vagaries of the network, and the resulting image size. Finally, because the Internet is digital and interactive, it doesn't confine web filmmakers to a single narrative structure. The technology allows for a number of narrative possibilities, including interactive and random configuration. Whether the audience prefers interaction or wants its stories told to them is an open-ended question: but still the possibility exists for multiple narrative forms.

Origins of Web Cinema

It's difficult to pinpoint the exact moment at which web cinema was "born" – as difficult as it is to target an exact birth date for theatrical cinema. Certainly a lot of work being done with QuickTime on CD-ROM in the early 1990s laid the groundwork, as did computer games. However, I believe that the real point at which web cinema began is 1997, the year in which the tools became available for creating and distributing web video. In January of 1997, Macromedia released Flash 1.0 (an off-the-shelf-animation package) and the following month Real Networks launched RealVideo 1.0. In July of the same year, Apple released a web version of QuickTime. The introduction of web-compatible RealVideo and QuickTime enabled video to be distributed over the dial-up Internet. No less importantly,

most modem speeds had finally reached 28 kbps, a transmission rate at which it was finally possible for an audience to log on and watch motion content. Like theatrical cinema, whose existence we chart according to its *public* premieres, web cinema needed an audience in order to exist.

Trends in Web Cinema

The web cinema of the past five years can be broken down into several distinct periods. In 1997 and 1998, the work created naturally imitated the style of television, its predecessor. In 1999 and 2000 web filmmakers began experimenting with the available technologies and creative tools in order to create new visual and narrative styles. 2001 saw the beginnings of wireless cinema and the rise of European filmmakers and collectives. This past year has seen new and refined levels of sophistication, as web filmmakers have started developing a language from the grammar they spent several years inventing.

Like theatrical cinema, web cinema is a combination of art, technology and business. In its short life, web cinema may have been even more subject to market forces than theatrical cinema ever was. Therefore, each trend in web cinema needs to be examined in the context of the technological and financial environments that surrounded it.

1997–1998: The Influence of Television

Just as early television borrowed from radio, so did early web video model itself on TV. It's fitting, then, that the soap opera – a content format so popular on both radio and television – was one of the first streaming video experiments to debut online. At the South by Southwest Festival in March of 1997, a group of filmmakers from Austin, Texas launched a web soap opera called *Austin*. Tara Veneruso, co-producer and writer of the series, said the idea for working online sprang from the work she and co-producer Jay Ashcraft had been doing streaming live music concerts and interviews at the University of Texas. Both trained as filmmakers, they began to wonder how narrative would work in this new technological environment. At the time, Veneruso recalls, there were a lot of HTML soap operas online. They decided to take those static soaps to the next level. Veneruso and Jay eventually produced ten episodes of *Austin*, and their success led them to create another online

Dave Jones
Teetering
1999
Flash
screenshot

series, *Chemical Generation*, which launched in 1998. Veneruso admits that the visual style of *Austin* was very static. "We were afraid to move the camera," she says, "because we were afraid of losing the actors on the small screen." The episodes in many respects resemble a series of sixty-second head shots. While shooting *Chemical Generation* they learned how to keep the camera still and move the actors within the frame, and also how to cut between shots instead of panning, to avoid blurry streaming images.

That style of shooting is also evident in *Savion Glover Dances*, a short web film created by filmmaker Spike Lee as a showcase for the launch of RealVideo 2.0 in the fall of 1997. Savion Glover, a gifted tap dancer, dances from the left of the frame to the right and back again, while Lee holds the camera completely steady. When Lee does cut away to talk directly with the dancer, it is a simple edit, and Glover is framed sitting still in front of the camera, answering Lee's off-camera questions. The film works beautifully online because while the camera is almost locked in, the subject and the dance are so dynamic that it gives the impression of constant movement. This locked-in shooting style parallels the style used in early television. Cameras were stationary in a proscenium setting, whereas movement came from the actors themselves, and depth came from cutting between the stationary cameras.

Television continued as a major visual influence on web cinema through 1998, with films such as *1000 Moons* by Craig Johnson and *Dowager* by Joe Chow. In *1000 Moons*, Johnson has the actress start in the background and walk slowly into the frame, coming toward the audience as long as she is speaking, stopping when she has arrived at a perfectly framed medium shot. Chow, by contrast, used a series of medium shots that eventually built into tight close-ups. His *Dowager* is about a short discussion between a husband sitting in a chair and his wife standing behind him. Though neither moves from their position, the scenes are shot progressively tighter until the last frame, where only one face fills the screen.

The opposite tack was taken by Jason Wishnow in *Persona*, his 1996 made-for-the-web short. Shot using Hi-8 (a format he and several other filmmakers feel is perfect for the intimacy of the web), *Persona* is a simple black and white film shot as one long continuous close-up. The sole action comes half-waythrough: the

actress pauses, removes her sunglasses and rubs her eyes. For that brief moment, the film deepens to color and then moves back to black-and-white.

One of the first web shorts that attempted to cross the visual influence of television with the technological capabilities of the web was the series *Scums*. Created by Italian filmmakers-cum-television producers Marco and Antonio Manetti, *Scums* was a tongue-in-cheek project modeled on a 1970s-style TV detective show. The series launched in 1998, and the six episodes lasted approximately one minute each. The Manettis posted the series online, and several months later were contacted by the Canadian filmmaker Scott Ray, who wanted to make a contribution to the series but couldn't afford to travel to Rome. Instead, he shot his own episode in Ottawa, continuing the storyline with new characters, and tying his episode back to the original, using photographs of the Italian characters. The Manettis used this same technique when they shot the next episode in Rome. The Manettis followed up with two more episodes; a filmmaker in New York completed the series with the last episode. *Scums* is the first example of what I call "pass-along narrative."

With pass-along narrative, a filmmaker starts a story and places it online, and other filmmakers or viewers from around the world add to it. The Manettis again experimented with this concept with *Planet Invasion* in 2000, a web series co-produced with the Italian media company Kataweb. Another example of a successful pass-along narrative is *Julie 9*, created by London-based filmmaker Julie Myers in 2001. The story revolves around a woman who makes a trip to various countries in the course of one week. Every single scene was shot by a different filmmaker in a different country. Julie herself never traveled – because there was no actor who played Julie. There was a box of props that represented Julie, including a beige raincoat, a black shirt, a red skirt, a handbag, a lighter and a pack of cigarettes. That box was shipped to each filmmaker, who shot his or her own version of Julie's travels.

In 1997 there were few online places for viewers to watch video or films. Internetv.com, which housed *Austin*, was one. Pseudo was another, although it tended more toward radio-style interview shows shot on video. There was also Kilima, a site that housed documentaries and other theatrical content,

as did The Sync. But things changed in June of 1998 with the launch of two now well-known sites: Jason Wishnow's The New Venue and my own The Bit Screen. Each site was focused on short films made specifically for the Internet — and more specifically, films under five megabytes and less than seven minutes. The New Venue grew out of Wishnow's work with Virtual Theater, an online venue which Wishnow had created with a grant from Stanford University. Wishnow had ventured online after starting at Stanford in the fall of 1993, when he discovered that every dorm had a high-end computer center and Apple Quadra computers complete with video cards. He remembers being astounded that no one was using them, and started making films on the computers. His work led to his grant for Virtual Theater, which laid the groundwork for the June 1998 launch of The New Venue, a screening room for made-for-the-net films.

Unlike Wishnow, I came to web cinema not as a filmmaker but as a writer. Having worked in interactive media since the mid-1980s, I was aware of how much the style of writing and storytelling had to shift depending on the medium I was using. Late in 1997, I began wondering what it would be like to write a visual story for the Net; I had worked with video-conferencing in 1995 and knew the technology existed to put pictures on phone lines, but I also knew that movement needed to be minimal. I wrote a short film as an experiment, but had nowhere to launch it. So I decided to create a venue for experimental films made for the medium, and to invite others to screen their films on the site. (And in the four years since The Bit Screen launched, I've screened hundreds of films, but I've never written another one myself.)

Both The New Venue and The Bit Screen were important in the development of web cinema because they provided an aggregated outlet for filmmakers who were experimenting with the medium. The New Venue had a QuickTime-oriented format and focused on spoofs and comedies, whereas The Bit Screen standardized on the RealVideo platform and screened more experimental films.

1999 and 2000: Experimentation with Forms

RealVideo, QuickTime and Macromedia had all begun refining their Internet capabilities by early 1999, and Windows Media Player also joined the fray. With better tools in hand, and more sites springing up, atten-

tion began to focus on the web as a separate medium. In March of that year, the first web cinema festival — The International Festival of Films for the Internet (FIFI) — took place in a café in Paris.

1999: Experiments with Narrative

As more filmmakers began to create directly for the web, they shrugged off the influence of television and began experimenting with the medium itself. Most of that experimentation took place with interactive narrative structure.

So much has been made of the potential for "interactive" films and programs on the web that it sometimes seems like anything you click on is considered interactive. In its true form, however, interactivity involves the viewer in the decision-making process. It's a *reflective* process more than a reactive one. The choices given to the viewers need to come out of the situation and make sense in the context of the story, and not be buttons that you push to rekindle the action, like some sort of video game. A beautiful example of this kind of interactive film is *Waterdream*, which is divided into several sequential episodes. The viewer interacts by choosing hidden paths embedded in the film. Each path offers an aural and visual experience, but only one enables the viewer to move on to the next episode. It was made in early 1999 by Andrea Flamini, a former producer for the Italian public broadcasting system, who now lives and works in Seattle, Washington.

A third type of interactive narrative is what I call a "framing narrative," not unlike those framing stories employed to group a number of sometimes disparate fairy tales together: Boccaccio's *Decameron* is one example, *The Thousand and One Nights* is another. The frame story sets up the background or the context for the ensuing stories, which can be read in any order. What matters is that they are all connected by the frame. The Internet lends itself beautifully to this kind of storytelling. The filmmaker's home page includes an "About The Film" section that sets up the context, and then provides a menu of short videos. Viewers can choose what they want to see, and when — meaning they enjoy total freedom as to where and how to construct the beginning, middle and end. Because all the scenes have equal value, the beauty of this technique is that the filmmaker can continue to add on to the film over an extended

Pierre Wayser
Jolt
2000
video, Flash
screenshot

period of time, without having to go back in and re-cut the whole film each time.

This completely non-linear approach obviously doesn't work for all films because most rely on a sequential linear narrative. Even though *Waterdream* allows the viewers to choose their own path, the ones offered are sequential within the structure of the story. I think framing films work best when each scene is a complete film, in itself a whole, but all of the shorts are assembled around a common theme. That is the case in *Cooking Chronicles* by Deanne Sokolin of New York, and in *Videopsychosis* by Carlos Gomez de Llarena of Venezuela. Sokolin's shorts are a series of vignettes about food preparation surrounding a holiday meal, and de Llarena's focuses on sources of modern psychosis.

The interactive film relies on the viewers to select which version of the film they're going to see. The opposite model is when the computer decides, or randomly configures, which version of the film will be shown. An example is *City Halls* by Philadelphia-based filmmaker Mike O'Reilly. To create a random configuration film, O'Reilly developed databases for each media element: one for narrative, one for soundtrack, and one for the video. Every time a viewer selects the film, the computer mixes up the order of the individual media elements, much in the same way that the shuffle feature on a CD player randomly selects various songs from each disk. The different combinations of the three databases or core media result in different versions of the same film. Because O'Reilly hasn't totally evolved the programming yet, what you actually see on the site is a set of "pre-built" random configurations. But he's moving toward an infinite amount of possible configurations, because the more information or media (video, music and narrative) added to these databases, the more configurations are possible, meaning the core story will be retold in hundreds of different variations.

2000: Emerging Visual Styles

The new century kicked off with the Internet film craze at its peak. For a while it seemed that everyone wanted to get in on the game. Steven Spielberg announced plans for a web-film site called Pop, and Warner Brothers launched Entertaindom. The launch took place in Europe of the sites Prime Films, Nuovo,

Cine-Courts, Filmgarten, Freshmilk, Icuna and Bit Film, while Atom and Ifilm in the US were joined by Short-buzz, Eveo and a host of others. Most of these sites were simply venues for theatrical films, but some such as Pop.com talked about developing content just for the web. Yahoo! Internet Life hosted a "web film" festival in spring 2000; FIFI ran its second fest at a much larger venue, and The Bit Screen spawned Streaming Cinema, a traveling offline festival of online films. The Sundance Film Festival was overrun with online film sites in 2000, and the issue of web cinema was examined by Berlin Beta in Germany, Net Congestion in Holland, the Seoul Net Festival in South Korea, and the Montreal International Festival of New Cinema and New Media (FCMM).

While a lot of bad films were created and streamed to meet the near-hysterical demand for online content, web filmmakers continued to push the creative and technological envelopes, and did an outstanding job in defining new visual formats. Flash played a key role in the new styles emerging online in 2000. What's fascinating about Flash is the diversity of visual styles – from simple line drawing to painterly screen – that can be rendered from the same off-the-shelf package. Dave Jones, an Australian, is one of the best practitioners of the former. His Flash short, *Teetering*, created in late 1999, has become one of the best known films on the web and a recurrent prizewinner at web and animation festivals around the world. Brilliant in its visual and narrative simplicity, *Teetering* is a three-minute black-and-white line drawing of two people balanced on a teetering board on top of a mountain. There is no dialogue, only the sound effect of the teetering board moving slowly back and forth. I have never screened this film without hearing a collective gasp at the end of the piece, followed by quiet sighs. What sets Jones apart is not just his elegantly simple visual style, but also his ability to really tell a story.

Canadian Steve Whitehouse has also built his reputation on an uncluttered style. Whitehouse created *DaVinci*, one of the first Flash shorts for Animation Express (a site devoted to animation forms which launched in late 1998). However, he is best known for the award-winning *Mr. Man*, a series of silent films about an Everyman. Whitehouse's style is deliberately blocky, and his series has an almost comic-book feel

Petrie Lounge
Kunst Bar
2002
Flash
screenshot

to it. Recently, however, he has moved toward a more painterly style, as evident in his work on *Kunst Bar* together with the collective Petrie Lounge. *Kunst Bar* is an homage to great nineteenth- and twentieth-century artists and their art, re-envisioned by clever artists in the twenty-first century.

Golden Boy, by Los Angeles artist Bill Cahalan, also has painterly roots. Although it was created in Flash, it could easily pass for 3-D animation. *Golden Boy* started as a short story for a children's book and morphed to an online film, where it has gained widespread recognition, both through Streaming Cinema and through the Sundance Festival. It is a silent film, and though Cahalan did write a storyline, it is amazing how many different interpretations viewers have come up with.

Flash was not the only format being experimented with in 2000: RealVideo was used to create an unusual project. Part film noir, part online jazz opera, *Life At Night* is a gorgeous multimedia story. It was created by John O'Brien, a musician from Minneapolis, and the images emerge and fade to a subdued soundtrack that eventually becomes its own character in the story. *Life At Night* is unique precisely because of the way it employs the soundtrack—O'Brien himself refers to it as an online "music book."

The year 2000 also saw early experiments with combined Flash-video formats that beat Macromedia to the starting line by a full two years. Two stand-out projects from 2000 are *Jolt* by Parisian Pierre Wayser, and *Mike* by Paris-based American Mel Bernstine. In creating *Jolt*, a syncopated tour of the City of Lights, Wayser first shot the film on video. He then output to QuickTime and exported frame- by-frame into Flash. The result is a kinetic black-and-white short that evokes some of the early Lumière films. *Mike* took a slightly different track. Originally shot as a short 16mm film, filmmaker Bernstein wanted to make the films more accessible on the web. Having already worked with Shockwave, he began experimenting with the different kinds of movement he could get from Flash.

These early films clearly laid the groundwork for Flash MX (a software program that imports video into Flash), which was launched earlier in 2002. Six months after its release, MX is mostly being employed for marketing on corporate web sites and in Hollywood studio web-site trailers. We have yet to see how filmmakers can take their visuals to the next level using MX. I believe that once web filmmakers have had time to learn the program (probably within the next twelve months), we'll see the evolution of a new visual style based on a Flash-video hybrid. And perhaps, with the incorporation of video, Flash will lose its reputation as simply a programming tool and become recognized as a serious artistic format.

2001: European Voices

From late 2000 onward, the air began to leak out of the Internet content bubble in late: Pop dot com never got off the ground; Entertaindom shut down. Yahoo! Internet Life canceled its second fest; Ifilm repositioned itself as a movie database and Atom Films spent months searching for a suitor before being picked up by Macromedia. The only web-cinema showcases in the USA were Streaming Cinema, and a new section devoted to Net films at the 2001 Sundance Film Festival.

In Europe, ironically enough, web filmmaking as an art form was reaching an all-time high just as its commercial prospects were falling apart in the US. For the first few years of web cinema, American and Canadian voices dominated the scene – perhaps because telephone and Internet access were cheaper in North America, making it easier for artists to be online. But starting in mid-2000, with the advent of flat-rate Internet access in Europe, European filmmakers began flocking to the web. By early 2001, the strongest and most experimental voices online were European. In addition to the lower telecom costs, European filmmakers were receiving a lot of encouragement: Web Cinema was the subject at the Rotterdam Film Fest's "Exploding Cinema" in Paris, the Pompidou kicked off a year-long series "Cinéma du Demain," an examination of web cinema and new media; FIFI held its third, and largest festival; and the French Web Film Critics Association awarded a prize for the best web film at the Cannes Festival. Many Europeans created collectives to showcase their work, combining resources to split the costs and aggregating their work to create a larger presence. Among the best-known are Bechamel (Paris), Moccu (Berlin), Submarine (Rotterdam), Analogiks-Indians (Lille), Holott (Paris), and 8081 (Turin).

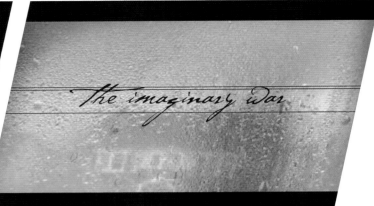

Bill Cahalan
Golden Boy
2001
Flash
screenshot

Andrea Flamini
Waterdream
1999
interactive video,
interactive Flash
screenshot

The Bechamel collective was started by Sophie Estival and Guillaume Joire as a venue for their own work in 1999. Joire had been very successful with his animation *L'Ascenseur* in 2000, and Estival was making a name for herself with the Flash short after which the site is named. They started bringing in additional collaborators and expanding the kinds of work screened. Overall, the work on the site tends toward tart, funny and cynical Flash shorts. But Joire, whose training is in painting and illustration, continues to expand his artistry in Flash with a richer, more de-luxe style.

Moccu is well-known in the world of web cinema for its interactive site-based games and stories. Led by graphic artists Jens Schmidt and Bjorn Zaske, Moccu has created game-based environments that lead viewers through interactive narratives. It is not the images (which tend towards the simplistic) that pull viewers into the Moccu site; the attraction is the game aspect of the narrative. Moccu's interactive stories constantly reward the viewers for the choices made.

With its creation "The Island," another collective specializing in online environments is the Turin-based 8081, an extremely talented group of artists, scientists, musicians and theatrical designers (Seba Vitale, Anontio Rollo and Luca Barbeni). The group has been online since 1999 with multiple environments (Wood, Valley, Palm Grove, Desert), and sees "The Island" as a matrix for developing a larger project in which the interface will be reduced to a degree allowing viewers to feel truly immersed. In many ways, they have already achieved this objective: After spending some time on "The Island," it's easy to forget how you got there or why you should leave.

Submarine was started by the Dutch filmmaker Femke Wolting, who also curated "Exploding Cinema," a web-cinema showcase at the 2001 Rotterdam Festival, and Bruno Felix. Their site is also a channel programmed with experimental, interactive web shows by artists from around the world. Dedicated to the mission of inventing new kinds of programs merging television and the Internet, Submarine has already created a number of cross-platform programs. Analogiks-Indians, a Lille-based group of web designers and filmmakers, is headed by Erwan Defachelles

and Fred Fauquette. Working in digital video and Flash, as well as in interactive and linear formats, the Indians have created a haunting style. Their work exemplifies what I have come to think of as the French style of web cinema. Many French filmmakers I've met have backgrounds in drawing and illustration, which is evident in the way they use the screen like a canvas, creating depth and wringing every pixel out of the screen. There is a lot of black-and-white work, and the look is sharp and edgy but not overly produced.

Paris-based Holott is run by Pierre Wayser and Catherine Ginape, whose work is distinctive for the unusually broad range it encompasses: web video, broadband films, Flash, photography and paintings. Ginape works mostly in Flash, while Wayser is apparently – and to stunning effect – creating his own hybrid video-Flash language. Holott is comprised of older artists with experience in different media, something that is reflected in the style and the subjects of the visual stories they create.

Finally, a collective of collectives emerged in the form of Vector Lounge, an online and offline multimedia jam. Vector Lounge launched as part of the Pompidou's "Cinéma du Demain" series in April 2001, and traveled to the Animation Festival in Annecy and then to the Ars Electronica in September 2001. Vector Lounge takes place over twenty-four hours and brings together a group of web designers and animators to create a collective website. Participants have included Sophie Estival, Guillaume Joire and Jens Schmidt, as well as the French team Chman.

2002: New Directions
The number of filmmakers creating for the web has leveled off in the past year, yet the work being created continues to mature. It's as if, having spent several years developing a new visual and narrative grammar for the web, filmmakers are beginning to refine the language. Carlos Gomez de Llarena has a long history of creating interactive programs that range from simple point-and-click pieces such as *Social Speech* to the more complex framing narrative *Videopsychosis*. The Venezuelan filmmaker has recently become focused on developing applications for interactive television and interactive wireless streaming. Jeannette Lambert from Montreal has

been mixing formats since first going online in 1997 with her HTML piece *Salome Goes to SoHo*. In 2000, she directed *Givre*, a 16mm web film she slowed down during editing to produce the look and feel of a Nickelodeon. Last year she created an interactive meditation on family titled *D'où Viens-Tu?* using digital video, HTML and RealMedia. This year (prior to the roll-out of MX) she created a series of web shorts that were shot in DV and edited in Flash. Kristoffer Gansing and his team from Sweden, already experts in interactive narrative, have developed a new project that focuses on the spatial aspects of narration.

Some filmmakers turned their attention to the World Trade Center and the aftermath of Nine-Eleven: Chris Ferrantello's *Twin Towers*, a finalist in the 2002 Sundance Online Film Festival, is an eerie, moody memorial. In an ironic twist, much of the early footage American television showed of the Afghan invasion in fall 2001 was actually web video – shot with webcams and streamed over the Net to satellite uplinks. This use of web video highlights a filmic form that has yet to exploit the advantages of the medium, namely documentary. Given that the web started as an information-based medium, it's hard to understand why more documentary makers have not created for a seemingly tailor-made medium enabling them to hyperlink out from video to text and databases. However, two groups have created unique web documentaries: the New York-based Picture Projects, whose *360 Degrees* is an interactive portrait of the US criminal justice system, and the London-based Artificial Environments, who have made several Flash-based documentaries for Greenpeace. One of the earliest doc-style programs online was *Dutch Schulz*, a Shockwave short made by Mel Bernstine in 1999 that deals with an American gangster in the 1920s.

Impact of Web Cinema

In a few short years, web cinema has already made an impact on the visual and narrative language of mainstream cinema. Films such as *Run Lola Run*, *Time Code*, and *Memento* all use non-linear narrative techniques. Even in American television, one is beginning to see use of non-traditional narratives: in summer 2001, a series shown on the American cable network Showtime randomly moved the story back and forth from the present to the future and the past, constantly mixing and shuffling the sequence of events. *24*, a series on the Fox television network, is about twenty-four hours in the life of one man. Each sixty-minute episode covers the corresponding time in the life of the protagonist, and moves sequentially through his twenty-four hour day. This strict adherence both to the storyline clock and the viewer's own amounts to a significant break from traditional television narrative.

Visual styles on the web have likewise clearly influenced mainstream entertainment. Web graphics were the first to make the leap, and imitation web pages are now in use on multiple news and weather channels such as CNN, MSNBC and Fox News, as well as on video-on-demand and satellite-TV guides. The second crossover is the slightly digitized, almost JPEG-quality images used by American networks during the 2002 Winter Olympics. When a skier, for example, came flying off the mogul, the picture would freeze, pixelate slightly, and then continue. The third influence is, of course, Flash. Already in use in television commercials and title sequences, Flash is about to make the jump to the big screen in an upcoming feature-film release by Miramax. In film, the widespread acceptance of a hybrid animated format can be seen in films such as

Waking Life, which was shot on digital video by director Richard Linklater, and then animated frame-by-frame by Bob Sabiston and his team at Black Rock Films in Austin, Texas. Sabiston has developed a technique that renders a rotoscoped-like image making it hard to distinguish video from animation. (An apt technique for a film about a man unable to tell the difference between his waking and sleeping life.)

Future Cinema

It's interesting to speculate what these trends in our visual and narrative language say about our current storytelling culture. Is the brevity of web films saying something about increasingly short attention spans in this age of multitasking? Do fragmented narratives portray our increasingly fragmented society? And if traditional cinema reflects a heightened sense of reality, do the pixelating images and hybrid video-animation formats reflect a distorted lens through which to view a harsher reality? Or are the trends simply a reflection of technology?

Film is not a format that works well in a digitally networked medium. Whereas video and animation do work well, and hybrid video-animation formats even better. Three-hour epics are impractical on mobile screens, but three-minute flicks work perfectly. Web filmmakers construct their stories using those realities – and frequently challenge the technology to mirror the reality they want to portray. Their efforts push engineers and developers to expand technological capabilities, and those refinements in turn inspire new art. The same dialog took place more than a century ago between the developers of motion-picture cameras and the makers of the films. That ongoing conversation between art and technology is the true language of cinema.

Web cinema has pioneered a new kind of screen-based storytelling. It will eventually move us on to a new form, then vanish for the same reason as magic-lantern projections and Nickelodeon films disappeared: The technology evolved. But even as the technology of storytelling continues to change, the art of the story will always remain.

YOUNG-HAE CHANG HEAVY INDUSTRIES
seventeen works on the web

2002
website http://www.yhchang.com

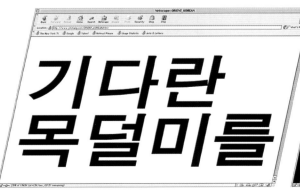

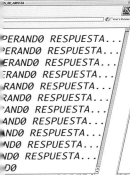

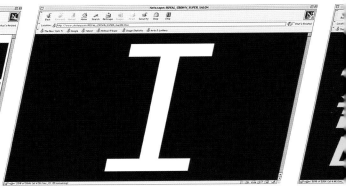

Mark Napier
The Waiting Room

2002
web project / CD-ROM / interactive software art using Java

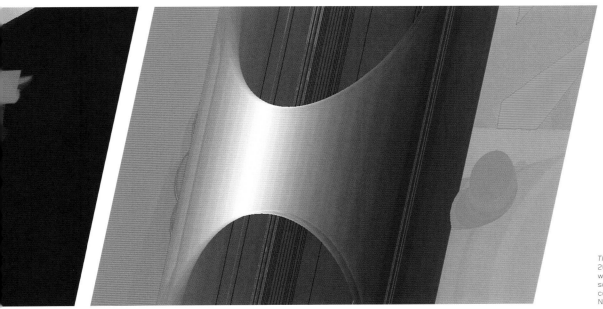

The Waiting Room
2002
web project
screenshots
courtesy bitforms Gallery,
New York

The Waiting Room
2002
web project
CD-ROM, interactive software
art using Java
installation view
courtesy bitforms Gallery,
New York

The Waiting Room is a virtual space that fifty users share through the Internet. The visitors to the space are strangers, united by the software, the Internet, and the artwork itself. In this space the visitor becomes a participant in a moving painting: his or her actions activate and shape the artwork. The users are the motivating force that shifts the artwork through moods, from hard-edged to atmospheric, from dark to light, from quiet to chaotic. Each click creates a shape, a shadow or a wall, a suggestion of architecture or a dissolving light. As in the waiting rooms of the real world, there is an edgy sense of anticipation about what's going to happen next. In this case "what happens next" is up to the users.

Steve Sacks

Jan Speckenbach and Birk Weiberg
DCX. Your World in My Tears

2001
film installation / three-screen projection, QuickTime video / color, sound /
duration and dimensions variable

At first sight, a merger seems to adhere to the philo-sophical concept of dialectics: thesis and antithesis are sublated. They must overcome each other in order to turn into their synthesis. This third element is gen-erally regarded in moral terms. It is of higher value than its precursors. (If it is not, then we are in the domain of psychoanalysis.) The classical Eisenstein idea of montage is based on the same logic: You take one picture, then another, and the fusion creates a new idea.

However, it is obvious that in terms of corporate business, a fusion is more often a takeover than a synthesis. In fact, nobody believes in fair mergers. And that is what makes any big fusion so thrilling: Who will prove to be the better player? Who will lose? Dialectics turn into competition. The symbolic impact lies not in the value of the result, but in the symbolic meaning of the companies themselves. If AOL joins Time Warner, that symbolizes New Economy super-seding Old Economy. Of course, that symbolism remains even when, shortly afterwards, AOL becomes the reason for the crisis of AOL-Time Warner. If Daimler-Benz swallows Chrysler, that signifies Europe taking over America or, even more, Europeans proving to be much more American than the Americans themselves. In other words: Contrary to what the frequently used term "synergy" might suggest, the business merger does not overcome thesis and antithesis.

This structure can be easily transferred to the domain of contemporary film montage. It is difficult to believe that the specific sequence of two takes remains more important than the takes themselves or the flow of images. Accordingly, we can observe in cinema since the 1990s two important movements expressing in different ways the same new principle. On the one hand, there is a seemingly montage-free cinema of *plan-séquence* (Mike Figgis, Aleksandr Sokurov, Paul Thomas Anderson, and others); on the other hand, we have a sort of re-definition of mon-tage (Lars von Trier, Wong Kar Wai, Oliver Stone, and others). Both movements can be summarized under the term *event montage*, that is to say: the combi-nation of heterogeneous material in a homogeneous, fluid style.

In *DCX* we tell the story of the fusion of the two big car manufacturers Denver and Cleveland. The story develops on three screens. The narration some-times shows one scene simultaneously from differ-ent angles, but can be split up into three different actions. The work with multi-screen remains in the split-screen tradition. Split screen, in narrative cinema, always played a minor, often comical, role, was rarely used for dramatic situations. At the same time, split screen seemed to replace montage, since the possibility of showing two or more images simul-taneously made editing superfluous. However, our ex-perience with split screen contradicts this notion. A situation can suddenly become most interesting from an angle initially thought to be boring. To see the same situation from several angles at once enlarges our in-sight. For one moment, interest is not moving for-ward, as it usually does in the narrative process.

Contrary to what one might think, we did not shoot with three cameras most of the time. While equating one camera with one screen can be interesting, for

instance in a *plan-séquence*, as a principle it soon becomes worn out. We even discovered that it was not necessary to attempt to synchronize all the shots in one sequence. At the first glance, there is nothing remarkable about seeing an actor on two or three screens apparently doing the same things in the same scene, but actually not doing them the same way. One simply fails to notice. At the second glance, however, it is rather fascinating. It is hard to tell why that is actually the case.

Globalization meets melodrama when Eckard, a young business lawyer, finds himself plunged into emotional conflict while organizing the merger of Denver and Cleveland. While the rival CEOs Jürgen and Robert are respectively turning into father and brother figures, he is also falling in love with Jürgen's wife Lydia. But his love is a violation both of friendship and loyalty. Business merger and personal amalgamation meet a tragic end.

Because the video footage and editing data are kept separate, we are able to constantly re-edit the film over remote network access. The installation uses more than one hundred video clips as well as sound, music and text files, together amounting to

five hours of stock that we edited and prepared in a first post-production phase. This material is then combined on the fly according to dynamic editing data. Spectators watching the installation on different days would see the same film but a different, maybe even contradictory, version.

Re-editing *DCX* like VJs, we tried to push the idea of event montage even further. The takes are seen no longer as thesis and antithesis (or anything like it), but as the mobile elements of a reproductive live performance. While the story stays the same, the narration changes. Precisely in this paradox lies the promise. Refusing to use for anything but live performance that medium of reproduction which is the cinema, we use its mechanism while negating a machine that 1920s avant-garde movements thought would give us images more objective than the world itself.

Jan Speckenbach and Birk Weiberg

DCX. Your World in My Tears featuring Niels Bormann, Andrea Rappel, Stephan Lewetz, Robert Lohr, Melanie Rohde / camera: Uwe Teske / sound: Cristóbal Saavedra / http://www.keyframe.org/mov/dcx

Thomas Fürstner
Waypointing Weibel's Wien

2002
DVD

With the installation *Waypointing Weibel's Wien*, Thomas Fürstner is developing the vision of a mobile cinematographic communication. Visitors to the exhibit adopt the perspective of a pedestrian strolling through Vienna. Their route traces the important moments and junctures in the biography of Peter Weibel. The pedestrian is wearing a portable communication-device that combines several functions. The so-called "digital street device" integrates telephone, computer, panoramic camera, and a global positioning system (GPS). With the help of the GPS, a satellite-assisted localization system, and a portable device, the pedestrian receives historic information regarding the exact place where he or she is standing. The information appears on their small display-screen in the form of moving and still archive-images. On a screen in the "Future Cinema" exhibition space, the visitor will view the panoramic-images of Vienna as well as their corresponding historic image-information all from the pedestrian's perspective.

The installation alludes to the current development of "the convergence of the media" in the communications and entertainment industries; that is, the integration of different kinds of information-storage and transfer within one device. By 2003, fifty-five million Europeans will be using these personal-entertainment devices regularly. With this work, Thomas Fürstner is envisioning different aesthetic and functional possibilities for these new technologies.

Margit Rosen
Translated from the German by Sarah Clift

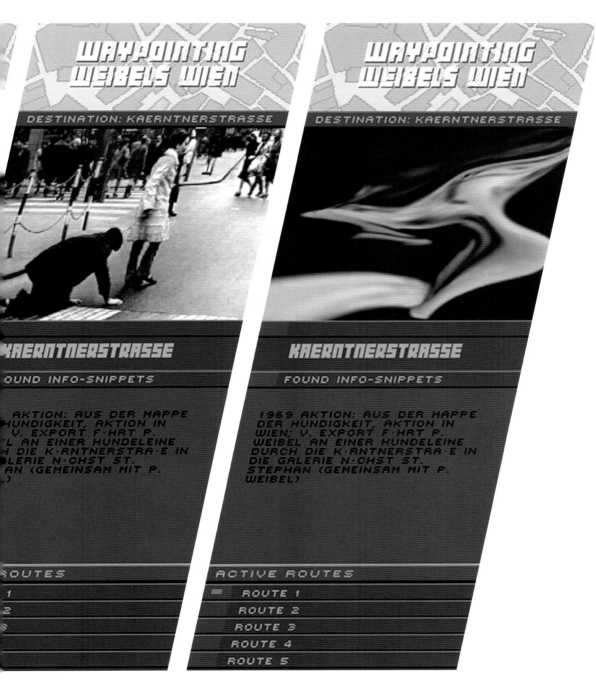

Waypointing Weibel's Wien
2002
DVD
screenshots
courtesy Thomas Fürstner

Axel Heide, OnesandZeros, Philip Pocock, Gregor Stehle
Unmovie

2002–
flash python data base weblication, interactive network installation composed of Wall,
Stage, Stream and Bubblecam / http://www.unmovie.net / wall dimensions: 520 x 390 x 90 cm

```
/* def begin (Unmovie, empty): */
def __init__(self, darkness):
try: perspective of time
```

If one may speak of beginnings in cinema any longer, *Unmovie* begins in dense darkness. Not as a cinema house but crystallized as a "time-image"1 object, a koan-like fountain bubbling blackness in ZKM's cavernous "Future Cinema" space, jet-black calligrapher's ink evaporating in a glass aquarium well, air pumped in breathing irrational op- and sonsigns out at exactly one second per second via webcam, *Unmovie*'s *Bubblecam*, to the *Unmovie* portal alongside *Unmovie*'s synthespian *Stage*, an "any-space-whatever"2 updated to "any-cyberspace-whatever" for "actor-mediums,"3 software language "bots," algorithmically hyperscripting – no beginning or end – cyberanthrological travels along a neverending *Stream* of "code-images"4 flowing from the growing *Unmovie* database of "found" Net videos and their *Unmovie*-authored descriptors (a second hidden script). *Unmovie* starts already echoing Hamlet's "Time is out of joint" remark, releasing time from its chronic5 sensory-motor role in cinema. *Unmovie*'s time frame, aionically6 enumerates rather than denominates screen space, animating "noo-screens"7 out of time in a game of "afterlife"8 for cinema.

```
try: wall==screen
```

If one may speak of beginnings in cinema once again, *Unmovie* begins with the *Wall*. ZKM built *Unmovie* a standard, hollow, whitewashed, partition museum upright. *Unmovie*'s "uncurtain" wall acts as interactive code-image display presenting the logo-, op- and sonsign goings-on on both the *Unmovie Stage* and *Stream*, as well as all readymade devices carrying the data to and from its interactors; a PC, an Ethernet hub, speakers and, baroquely, power and transmission cables, through which *Unmovie* data comes and goes, hanging by handmade hooks of glass and bronze. The *Unmovie Wall* screens its entire virtual and actual

1 Gilles Deleuze, *Cinema II : Time-Image*, Athlone Press, London, 1989. *Time-image*: "… a little time in its pure state: a direct time-image which gives what changes the unchanging form in which the change is produced" (p. 17); "… time is no longer the measure of movement but movement is the perspective of time" (p. 22).

2 For an "any-space-whatever" see Deleuze, op. cit., p. 8: "The connection of the parts of space is not given, because it can come about only from the subjective point of view of a character, who is, nevertheless, absent, or has even disappeared, not simply out of the frame, but passed into the void."

3 See Deleuze, op. cit., p. 20: "… what might be called professional non-actors, or, better, 'actor-mediums,' [are] capable of seeing and showing rather than acting, and either remaining dumb or undertaking some neverending conversation …"

4 See Deleuze, op. cit., p. 267: *Code-images* occur "(w)hen the frame or the screen functions as instrument panel, printing or computing table, the image is constantly being cut into another image, being printed through a visible mesh, sliding over other images in an 'incessant stream of messages,' and the shot itself is less like an eye than an overloaded brain endlessly absorbing information …"; *code-images* compute, connect and visualize data algorithmically for globally minded "noo-screens."

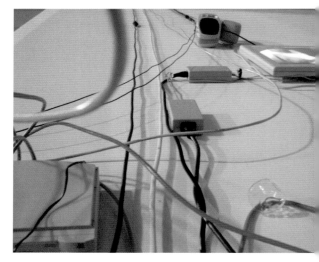

60 01 NETWORKED
Axel Heide, OnesandZeros, Philip Pocock, Gregor Stehle

Unmovie
2002
installation views: ZKM |
Center for Art and Media
Karlsruhe, 2002
© unmovie; VG Bild-Kunst,
Bonn 2003
photos © Philip Pocock

5 The Chronos cosmological myth recounted in the "Theogeny" of Hesiod (2700 BP) sequels his creation myth in a most time-telling manner. Chaos, the origin spawned Gaia, Goddess of Earth. With Uranus, God of Sky, she bore Chronos, God of Time, who hated his father for hiding him on Earth. With his mother's help Time castrated Sky or Heaven and tossed his genitals into the sea, their foam spawning Aphrodite, Goddess of Love. In short, chronological time, the past, present, future, killed aionic time, the eternal present. As consolation timelessness was replaced by libidinal love on a conspiring chronocentric Earth in a myth that is a fable perhaps for Hollywood until Now.

6 The adjective "Aionios" is coined in Plato's Timeaus "to denote that which has neither beginning nor end, and that is subject to neither change nor decay, that which is above time, but of which time is a moving image" (37d8).

7 "Noo-screen" (Greek noos for "mind") denotes the progressive integration of translocally shared screens, digital interfacing to an evolving "noosphere" as described by Teilhard de Chardin in The Formation of the Noosphere (1947): "No one can deny that a network (a world network) of economic and psychic affiliations is being woven at ever increasing speed which envelops and constantly penetrates more deeply within each of us. With every day that passes it becomes a little more impossible for us to act or think otherwise than collectively" (http://www.tecnoetic.com/noosphere/).

8 Gilles Deleuze, op. cit., p. 270: "The life of the afterlife of cinema depends on its internal struggle with informatics. It is necessary to set up against the latter the question which goes beyond it, that of its source and that of its addressee."

9 Gilles Deleuze, op. cit., p. 265: "And the screen itself, even if it keeps a vertical position by convention, no longer seems to refer to the human posture, like a window or a painting, but rather constitutes a table of information, an opaque surface on which are inscribed 'data,' information replacing nature, and the brain-city, the third eye, replacing the eyes of nature."

character as a "table of information."9 The Unmovie Wall is its screen. Walls are screens, always have been. The earliest documented wall acted as a windscreen for dwellers on the shore of Olduvai Lake in Africa 1.8 million years ago. During the last Ice Age, sturdy palisades appeared to screen predators and belligerents from communities within. And at the same time, the cave wall acted as virtual screen, in Grotte Chauvet screening a manual for survival on the outside for spectators inside. The Unmovie Wall presents itself as actual and virtual screen at once.

def __Unmovie__(chronic, aionic):
    try: time crystals

"Time is the moving image of eternity," states Plato in Timeaus. This equation applied to motion picture media governs analog and digital sensory-motor scenarios but it flips when applied to time- or code-image hypermedia. Unmovie's Stage is hacked and scripted to generate and compose an endless hyperscript. Devoid of an end and therefore without a beginning users online always enter the Stage game in the middle, the standing now (nunc stans). The Stage dialogue code poetically encourages topic words to emerge and subside. Topic words are the key that unlocks the floodgates to Unmovie's database of internet-sampled and subsequently scripted Net videos. In concert with the incessant streams of artificial consciousness unfolding on Stage, an equally never-ending digital video Stream containing cyberanthropological travels online is "irrationally" cut and shared 24-7 on Internet-anywhere noo-screens. The permutations of narrative undercurrents rippling the surface of the Stream are mind-boggling. Still that is not to be confused with Unmovie's program of non-narrative meandering about time itself. If film is a river in time, Unmovie is an ocean-image forever. The count of anonymous digital video clips in the database currently numbering 7500 factors out a logogenetic self-organizing logic for the Stream, with the Stage and Stream scripted to act as co-editors, so montage

Axel Heide, OnesandZeros,
Philip Pocock, Gregor Stehle
Unmovie
2002
flash python database
weblication at
http://www.unmovie.net
screenshot
© unmovie; VG Bild-Kunst, Bonn
2003
photo © Philip Pocock

Felix Stephan Huber, Udo Noll,
Philip Pocock, Florian Wenz
*"A description of the Equator
and Some ØtherLands"*
1997
open-access database cinema
http://www.aporee.org/equator
screenshot
© the artists; VG Bild-Kunst,
Bonn 2003
photo © Philip Pocock

becomes "montrage" steered moment for moment in concert with user dialogue in the company of actor-mediums on *Stage*. These bots may not remember each other's lines but they store new vocabulary and syntax from human users in their "brains," affecting their language down the hyperline. What appears to have passed (past) on *Stage* and in the *Stream* is actually associative recall, memories arriving in the present, crashing if you will. What is foreseen as future possesses an intention lent to it by poesis alone, an instance about to be driven forth from a chaosmos of potential presents. *Unmovie*, appealing to artmaking's first premise, reverses Plato's "time-as-moving-image-of-eternity" equation, where time==Chronos and eternity===Aion, to become hypercinematically "eternity-as-moving image-of-time," issuing a timeless present as long as electricity allows, initiated by, yet remaining out of frames of passing time. *Unmovie*'s crystal ball turns chronocentric media inside-out, freezing time like some cultural quantum mechanic metaphysical equivalent spinning from Schroedinger's "time-independent equation" (1933) or the paradoxical quantum gravity Wheeler-Dewitt equation in which time disappears altogether (1965). *Unmovie* deals with the "problem of time," a zone of concern in the arts, humanities and sciences more and more, conjectured to "become to the twenty-first century what fossil fuels and precious metals were to previous epochs."[10]

A Description of the Equator and Some ØtherLands

Equator aka *ØtherLands* is database cinema "performed" simultaneously along the Earth's Equator in Uganda, on the Java Sea, and along Cyberspace's virtual one of "corresponding identities." *ØtherLands* authors and online users participate in creating and linking their fragmentary whereabouts, transforming linear cinema and a linear equator into a tangled mesh of stories, much like life itself.

"The equator is slow. The equator is a zone of shared ambiguity. The equator is an opaque grid of information. The equator has no doors, no windows (courtesy Leibnitz). The equator is no reason to do anything. The equator is occupying your screen. The equator is a film I'd like to see made by someone else. The equator is playing at a cinema not near you but in you."[11]

10   Gary Stix, "Real Time," in
     Scientific American,
     October 2002.

11   Philip Pocock, guest at
     "100 Days 100 Guests,"
     documenta X.

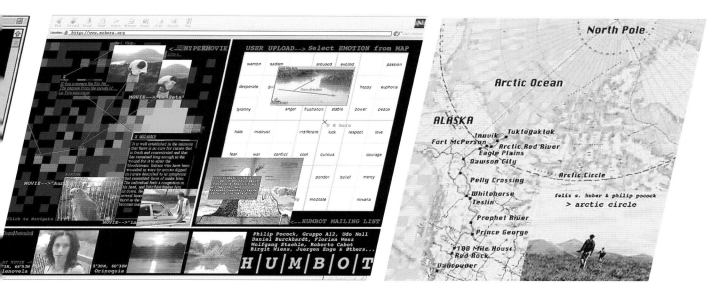

Felix Stephan Huber, Philip
Pocock, Daniel Burckhardt,
Roberto Cabot, Elena
Carmagnani, Gruppo A12,
Udo Noll, Wolfgang Staehle,
Gregor Stehle, Florian Wenz
H | U | M | B | O | T
1999–2004
interactive database,
self-organizing movie mapping
http://www.humbot.org
screenshot
© the artists; VG Bild-Kunst,
Bonn 2003
photo © Philip Pocock

Felix Stephan Huber,
Philip Pocock
<arctic circle>
1995
digital video-performance
website
http://www.dom.de/acircle
screenshot
© the artists; VG Bild-Kunst,
Bonn 2003
photo © Philip Pocock

H|U|M|B|O|T

H|U|M|B|O|T reads in Alexander von Humboldt's book
*Personal Narrative of a Journey to the Equinoctial
Regions of the New Continent 1799-1804* and uses the
Kohonen Self-Organizing Mapping algorithm to map it
out according to emotion, time, location and keyword
parameters set by readers. Onto these clusters of
"reread" and reordered text passages, H|U|M|B|O|T
authors attach digital video material – passages
recorded in contemporary South America (1999–) –
not as illustrations but as correlations. Humboldt and
H|U|M|B|O|T passages interwoven produce a deep dy-
namic "cyberatlas" on screen through which its online
users may "travel" and in effect "map" a movie for future users when recorded user "travels" get replayed.
Celebrating 200 years since Humboldt's eco-entho-
logical research, H|U|M|B|O|T 1999–2004, like Hum-
boldt 1799–1804, is searching for a "nature for narrative" suited for a "narrative for nature."

<arctic circle>

<arctic circle> is an early "cyber-roadmovie" investi-
gating contemporary loneliness: on the one hand,
driving through a vast natural wilderness, Canada's
Arctic, where one feels no longer welcome and which
one feels is best left alone; and on the other hand,
trying to connect to others driving the Infobahn in
a new wilderness, Cyberspace, searching for signs of
life on the other side of a laptop screen. This "double
travel" takes two artists – Philip Pocock, Felix Stephan
Huber – up to, along and over the remote Arctic Circle
in Canada, where they slowly become fictional characters in their own documentary epic. Virtual co-travel-
ers join via e-mail to the site the artists build on-the-
fly from trailer parks and auto repair shop telephone
jacks.

What begins as a 1970s conceptual-style "travel-
as-art-as-information" loop develops into 1990s pulp
melodrama, when two hitchhikers, Nora and Nicolas,
hop on board, and any and all preconceived ideas are
chucked out the 1974 SuperVan window.

Months later, when two more artists – Christoph
Keller and Florian Wuest – join, they detour south to
the heat of another "circle" for <tropic of cancer> in
Mexico in 1996.12 There they find themselves confronted with their cultural baggage in a poor country,
and resort to poking fun at heroic artistic myths.

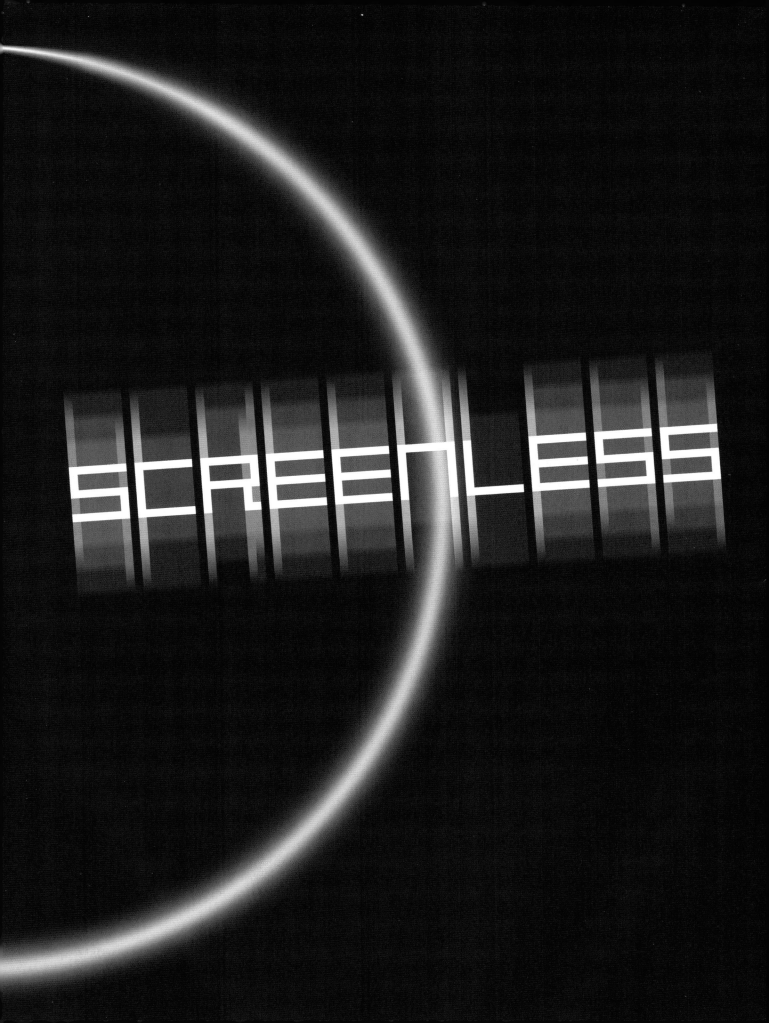

Siegfried Zielinski
Backwards to the Future
Outline for an Investigation of the Cinema as a Time Machine

Loading.

Automatic chronometers were the master machines of industrialization. The functional core of the mechanical clock consists of a constant alternation of propulsion and stopping. A weight, a feather, electricity or atomic tension is used to produce a propulsion force. The movement caused by this force is regularly interrupted and then released again. Time intervals are introduced into the action of the propulsion mechanism. A swinging device or another regulating apparatus ensures the precision of this action. In order to turn this permanent stop-and-go procedure into time as calculated in analog terms, the mechanism must be connected to various kinds of reading instruments. The ones we are most familiar with are hands and a clock face – the latter in a circular form, already employed in the astrolabes Arabian astronomers used over a thousand years ago. The origin of the mechanical clockwork can also be traced back to roughly the same time. Its mechanism forms the foundation for all machines and media artifacts in which movements or processes need to be regulated, ranging from the "mechanical writers" mass-produced in the 1760s at the request of the Director of Vienna's Kunstkammer, Friedrich von Knaus, via the fantastic drawing and writing machines of Swiss Pierre Jaquet-Droz and his son Henri-Louis in the 1770s and following decade, through to the chronographic and photographic instruments of Marey, Anschütz or Kohlrausch one hundred years later.

As an optical-acoustic artefact, cinematography has a tradition that goes back at least to the experiments with the sound-producing camera cubiculum of the Neapolitan Giovan Battista della Porta in the second half of the sixteenth century. It can be argued that the globally marketable version of the cinematograph as a chemo-opto-mechanical device for the projection of standard software was invented as a time machine in the last two decades of the nineteenth century. The steel core of the recording and projection equipment is nothing more than an adapted clock; it was typically produced by men engaged in the manufacture of precise mechanical apparatus, music machines, but above all chronometers. The mechanism used to gradually transport film material in order to expose the photographic raw material is the same as that employed to make a projector beam penetrate the individual, developed transparent images: At least sixteen times per second, the perforated strip is precisely transported a little further, stopped, then pushed forward again, in order to outdo observers' perception and convey the suggestion of continual, flowing movement. This form of transport serves to graduate the film tape. Subsequently, the successively projected photographs are shown on the cinema's clock face, namely the screen, as time that has been frozen cinematographically. In cinema's infancy, it was the hand of the cameraman or projectionist that provided the power of propulsion. The cinema did not need electricity. Movies also function using candles or gaslight.

The illusion involved in the technology of the first cinema productions reflected cinema's cultural and social function. The usage of recorded scenes from everyday life or orchestrated scenes specially produced for the camera made possible something that could not be achieved outside the machine. It became possible to reverse experienced time, to manipulate it, dilate it, accelerate it, and show it again. People attended the places where such devices were set up, and paid to see an illusion for a few seconds or minutes, to re-experience past time as moving images, or become witnesses of a time that only existed in the cinema. They rented orchestrated, objectivized time that was different from the time they were experiencing. Harnessed to the new industrial time processes, people felt a growing need to get the better

The artillery girls.

Fire!

of their own limited time allocation – they sought to recapture, at least in their imagination, the time life and work had "stolen" from them.

The two great designs for the theater of the cinema typical of the first decades already indicated the way future developments would go. Effectively, these initial developments were increasingly refined over the course of time. The Lumière brothers trained the lenses of their wooden recording boxes on contemporary urban life, and made it available to future generations as a memory. Georges Méliès devised ingenious film tricks with mirrors, rotating or hydraulic machines, and on the screen conjured up a world that did not exist outside his apparatus. Indeed, it lived by virtue of the latter. His was a world in which people lost their heads, disappeared completely, re-emerged at totally unexpected locations and, most importantly, could undertake journeys through space and time that were impossible during Méliès' lifetime: journeys to the moon, for instance, via a rocket into which a complete train was built: The film *Le voyage dans la lune* [A Trip to the Moon], measured 280 meters in total length, and the original created in 1902 was hand-colored.

Its origins and function make cinema a time machine par excellence. Electronic television and video elaborated on this function, focused and expanded it. On the one hand, owing to their ability to convey events occurring at faraway locations simultaneously as images and sounds; on the other, by dividing into intervals the microelements of the chronological sequences to be projected. In the electronic modus, chronological structuring no longer relies on a connection between the individual sets of images or half-images, but rather images are chronologically assembled even as regards their interior structure, at great speed, pixel for pixel, line for line, with gaps in the intervening space. It is not even possible to talk

about continuity in relation to electronic images. Their structuring is not continual. The assertion of this technological dimension of the time-machine film corresponded historically with the development of scenographies designed to convey the depth of time by the various avantgarde movements after World War II as described by Deleuze in volume two of his book on the cinema.

A new quality of medial time machines came about in the form of computer games, irrespective of whether they were essentially text or graphics-based programs. The decisive aspect was the integration of the reader, listener or observer of a story into the narrative and dramatic procedure. The film on its level as an everyday commodity, as "expanded reality": In the on- or offline programs the player becomes a fellow actor. In text-based programs, he writes the role of the story's protagonist, in graphic representations he is assisted by a permanent subjective camera to adopt the main actor's function as regards visual perception. The ego shooter's weapons are the optical extensions of the instrumental interfaces: the keys, mice or joysticks behind which the space is reserved for the co-actors. The shift from films meant to entertain to entertainment using films also involved a change in the time spent. In the cinema you rent two hours; exhausting the various levels of difficulty in a computer game can take up multiples of two hours. That is also "expanded cinema" in the direct sense of the word: the extreme expansion of the time of cinematic experience. And if you consider bits to be the smallest unit of currency then this form of cinema means a lucrative source of income to the providers of servers and software for future film entertainment culture.

However, the cinema of the future will be a time machine in a much more radical and comprehensive sense than all these medial intermediary levels:

The sidereal projectile
reaches the moon.

The Dream (The Great Bear,
Saturn, etc ...)

A Selenite clinging
to the projectile.

a machine namely that not only enables us to travel through time using our imagination but also using our bodies.

H. G. Wells published his spectacular novel *The Time Machine* in the same year that the first cinematographs began to operate in various cities throughout the world for a paying public. Ten years later Albert Einstein's work appeared on the relativity theory entitled "Electrodynamics of Moving Objects." What in the nineteenth century had already begun to make mathematicians and physicists rack their brains, namely dissatisfaction with Newton's concept of time as something evenly flowing without any causal relationship to anything outside it, gradually took on ever more precise definitions: Time came to be viewed as something relative. In the physical sense time became elastic, it could be extended and compressed. The exact extension of a chronological sequence depended on whether the observer of the chronological process was within it or outside it, moved themselves or not, and how quickly they moved. Towards the end of World War II, Einstein's suspicions about the so-called "time dilation effect" were proven in experiments: The faster an object moved in relation to the speed of light, the greater the time lapse.

The famous Philadelphia project that was commissioned in 1942 by the US navy in order to make entire ships invisible to enemy radar by building strong, local electro-magnetic fields, and in which Einstein and Tesla are said to have participated, is now surrounded by whole layers of legends, according to which some of the ship's crew were transported into another time. The Internet, that ideal medium for conspiracy theories, is full of them. By contrast, the experiments so far able to be conducted using entire organisms produced differences amounting to a few nanoseconds that can only be detected by special reading instruments. But scientists did succeed in measuring

time shifts. In the micro area of material they have already been identified as striking time differences thanks to the extreme acceleration of individual elementary particles, atoms or photons. Indeed, in the smallest field of material even surpassing the speed of light is no longer a taboo topic.

The idea that something can be here, and at the same time also there, and that something dilated can simultaneously be located at different places, is a topic that fascinates above all distinguished astrophysicists and endo-physicists in both West and East. In 1966, for instance, Vadim A. Chernobrov wrote a paper (crudely translated into English) in which he reports on Russian experiments on accelerating and decelerating physical time in small, closed areas of space. He attributes the experiments to the physics theories of N. A. Kozyrev, who produced some distinguished work in the field of causal and asymmetrical mechanics. Chernobrov's experiments involved linking sets of electromagnets through serial and parallel ports, and installing them on miniature dome-like structures consisting of various layers interlocked with one another in a manner resembling the Russian "Matrioshka" – the nesting doll containing any number of smaller versions of itself inside its hollow body. Chernobrov placed insects, mice and other small animals into the various electromagnetic fields of tension thus created in the interior of the housing, in order to observe and measure the effects of converging spherical electromagnetic wave formations. What is remarkable is the conclusion he draws from his experiences of extreme decelerations and accelerations in the velocity of physical time. He argues that the journey into the past is characterized by great stability and clear directness. There was only a single way into the chronological past, basically the exact reversal of the original process. By contrast, the strong acceleration of physical time led to insta-

Georges Méliès
Le voyage dans la lune
[A Trip to the Moon]
1902
16mm film
hand-colored, silent
film stills
reproduced in: Maurice Bessy,
Guiseppe Lo Duca, *Georges
Méliès: Mage et "Mes memoires"
par Méliès*, Prisma, Paris, 1945,
pp. 6a–8b
© VG-Bildkunst, Bonn 2003

The drop into the sea.

drawings by Georges Méliès
for his film
Le voyage dans la lune
[A Trip to the Moon]
1902
reproduced in: Maurice Bessy,
Guiseppe Lo Duca, *Georges
Méliès: Mage et "Mes memoires"
par Méliès*, Prisma, Paris, 1945,
pp. 6a–8b
© VG-Bildkunst, Bonn 2003

bilities; the future has a multitude of alternatives.

Experimentation with alternative options for the structuring of the time before us forms the inner core of all the media devices developed that deal with processes and movements. This experimentation in various guises is central to the entire stock of fantasy and ideal creations by the people that animate media devices with their figures, stories, dramas and tricks, and naturally such experimentation is central to the people that use, enjoy and interact with them.

"There could be a world where people grow younger every day, rain falls into the sky, and cakes unbake … It could even be your world," wrote Marcus Chown recently in the *New Scientist* in an article that deals with the physical possibility that in some of the parallel worlds time runs in the opposite direction to the time we perceive (Feb. 2000, 26 f.). As long as the human senses do not allow us to experience time as running backwards we need the media of illusion. This inability promises a prosperous future to the cinema regardless of the forms it expands into or how it is transformed. Einstein liked to insist that time does not exist, but is merely an illusion.

The literature consulted for this outline included: Vadim A. Chernobrov's "Experiments on the change of the direction and rate of time motion" (unpublished paper, 1996), Paul Davis' *How to build a time machine* (2001), Gilles Deleuze's *Cinéma 2. L'image-temps* (1985), Jean-Luc Godard's *Histoire(s) du cinéma* (1988–1998), Zielinski's *Audiovisions* (1999) and *Archäologie der Medien* (2002).

Translated from the German by Jeremy Gaines

Ross Gibson
The Time Will Come When …

Q: What will count as artistry in the future?

A: Artists will supply us with beguiling processes of transformation. Their task will be an emphatic extension, perhaps even a radical transformation, of the duties of the *fabricator* that were the foundation of Western artistry until the turn of the twentieth century. But artists won't be fabricating *objects* so much as *experiences* – they will offer us intensely "moving" immersion in (or perhaps *beyond*) the objective world. This immersion will be so *moving* that the "objective world" will cease to be sensible in the ways we thought normal. Which means we will develop new options for agency or subjectivity in a world no longer composed of stable settings and props, a world no longer sensibly "objective."

Therefore a Duchampian subset of modernism will flourish: in ritual acts and processes of contextual re-configuration involving objects and subjects in time and space, the familiar world will be made strange and then it will be instantaneously re-made in evermore new configurations that will be appreciated for all their fragility and dynamism. Artists will be encouraged to rescue us from anomie and despair amidst so much flux and permanent impermanence.

In such circumstances, any place or person or set of experiences that might be well loved will be sensed as prevalent and familiar only to the extent that one has memory enough to hold on to that beloved phenomenon in the face of so much flux and evanescence. By interacting with the models of experience that artists will offer up, people will learn to balance their caches of memory against their freedom to compose new iterations of experience, their empowerment to make new clusters of subjects and objects in dynamic settings. In this "weightless" context, people will require art to lead them into a regular, repeatable kind of transcendence. Artists will offer people a reason to bother with getting up in the morning. The definitive and necessary art of the future will be a secular regime that serves a spiritual need for balancing self-definition and self-alteration.

Which is to say some aspects of modernism will continue the same as they ever have, but there will be new aspects, markedly different, also. Please read on.

During the past hundred years, drugs, medicine, tourism and a range of different cinematic formats have offered Westerners the occasional frisson of transcendence. Let's say such artistic self-abnegation can be defined like this: "Transcendence allows one's self and one's place and one's rhythms of perception to alter thrillingly, strangely yet safely."

Throughout the late twentieth century, *irony* was usually the mode that offered shifts of vantage. But irony is somewhat debasing. It brings one down and *back*, back to a grounding in a reality that is *detached* from the insufficiencies of a mendacious or preposterous world. Irony gets you out from under the data-smog, PR-exhaust and advert-gunk, but there's a cost to it, a ponderous sense of detachment in the way it leaves you there on the ironized ground, relying on your old, received wisdom. For all its lightness of touch, irony won't make you fly, it won't project you to some new elsewhere.

Transcendence is differently energized and energizing. Transcendence gives you alternatives. *ALTER… NATIVE*: "giving birth to otherness; born in otherness." Transcendence takes you elsewhere, it throws you to somewhere new, somewhere not already bounded by your established dimensions.

The twentieth century was one long beta-test for technologies of self-alteration. *ALTER… ATION*: "tending into a state of otherness." But there is no guarantee that the twentieth century's familiar feints of consciousness will continue to be affordable, let alone effective, in the Western world in the future. This is so because, during the twentieth century, most of the transcendental experiences of art were made in "massy" physical space, with hefty objects arrayed and re-arrayed, requiring great payloads of energy to build and re-build worlds, to move physical beings through them, to make Cartesian space do what it does not tend to do – lose form. Think of all the energy required to make, un-make and re-make film sets so that filmic space can get conjured as so "light" and protean.

Therefore, we need to develop an art of TIME, an art other than any existing phenomenon. This art will take the form of some phenomenological routine that will offer each participant a compelling, fully conscious experience of perceptive intensification followed by alteration. People will partake of this new art in order to *be* differently in time, to be in time whilst also having time in them. If our occupancy of time gets altered with nuance and precision, as an *artistic* experience, then space will take care of itself, because the experience of time will be so strange and new, so compelling and *preoccupying* that the coordinates of consciousness will all shift radically.

Imagine, therefore, an art-form which encourages people to understand themselves *as* time, as "eventualities" always available in infinitely configurable ways as long as consciousness functions, as long as some kind of pulse marks the continuity of existence.

(So, when I said earlier that "transcendence takes us elsewhere," when I spoke of the *dimensions* of self, I didn't get it right. I shouldn't have focussed on a measurable, Cartesian *where*. Note how difficult it is to be born into the future.)

The future art-form will help us alter our being so that our present ways of comprehending and measuring the significant span of our lives will become irrelevant. Years, months, days and defining events will not occupy our attention. Perhaps the new artistic experiences themselves will be defining events, reasons to be, ways of measuring and appreciating our aliveness. This would be a significant alteration to our Western expectations about all kinds of art.

Q: What about the future of cinema?

A: Please permit me to repeat myself: We need to develop an art of TIME, an art other than any existing phenomenon. This art will take the form of some phenomenological routine that will offer each participant a compelling, fully conscious experience of perceptive intensification followed by alteration. People will partake of this new art in order to *be* differently in themselves, to be in time whilst also having time in them. If our occupancy of time gets altered with nuance and precision, as an *artistic* experience, then space will take care of itself.

Our present standards for measuring time and human vitality will be superseded because they will appear clumsily mechanistic. Once we are being assisted by the future art-form, we will understand how the scientific interval that we now call "a second" can sometimes contain epochal portions of significance or "life-force." The quota of beneficence that we currently demand of an entire life might be sensed in an instant. Yet, just as vitally, the fullness of our lives might sometimes be sustained all at once and without noticeable incident in an eventless, artful attenuation that might feel endless but will not be dismissed as tedium. Other cultures have called this capability "revelation." We need a new art-form to get us there. To the extent that cinema is one of the arts in which we segment and attenuate time, cinema will be in this new art-form.

"Nothingness" (the darker counterpart to "being" in Sartre's famous existential dyad) will thus be appreciated regularly and deeply, not as boredom or a failure of being, but as life-changing, as a transcendent *experience*. Coming back from regular encounters with nothingness, we will know our being in radically altered ways, in ways that are presently inconceivable to Western consciousness. Each participant self will be re-defined and atomized through participation with the new art-form. Film theorists have long yearned for such aestheticized play between anomie and poesis, between subjective dispersal in the scene, on the one hand, and cohesion of meaning or affect, on the other. In this respect the future of art is definitely cinematic. But the future of cinema will produce its own radical mutation.

Artists involved in a future cinema will help us get free from the Western craving for longevity. Participants in the new art-form might stop yearning to extend the functionality of bodily organs past three score years and ten. Some participants might even become so artful that they attain this unyearning state permanently. No need for birthdays. No need for medicine, which will be relieved of its current preservative functions. The quality of consciousness in any one moment will be prioritized ahead of the persistence of heartbeat.

Q: What, we'll hanker no longer to live longer?

A: Before too long the differentiated disciplines that we currently understand as "art" and "medicine" could become redundant. Ditto physics. Ditto calendrical anxiety, therefore. The question of whether we want to live longer will become meaningless as soon as people believe that the most transcendent aspect of their being is in time, in its intensities rather than in its extensiveness.

Imagine having all eventualities available in you all at once. For a long time, space has been tested, redefined and transformed by Cartesian visual consciousness; space has been assailed by the Enlightenment mentality's self-assertive energy and territorial vigilance. But space may well have been seized, pushed and crushed as far as it can humanly go now. (Before anyone interrupts, let me proclaim that the internet and "cyberspace" are not really spatial … instead, they are temporal flux plus text plus graphic conventions all offered up to our powers of abstraction; cyberspace is outlined in one's Cartesian theorem whereas space is tangled and tingled in one's sensorium.)

So, bring on time. Or bring *back* time. Let's face it: many non-Western cultures have never let go of time, they've always known that it is the godly part of their humanity, they've always maintained rituals that suffuse consciousness with time's ubiquity.

Q: What will it look like, this new art?

A: Almost certainly the new art of time won't be something you can *see*. It won't be some "thing" at all. Cinema, for example, has helped us get to there, and now cinema can cease to be. Or rather, the alternatives can begin to emerge. Why not call the new art a "future cinema"?

One gets some prescience of this new art sometimes in emerging forms of popular music – in the "hang-time," the beat-skips and syncopations that define hip-hop, electronica and "glitch-funk," for example. John Coltrane's modal music has it already. The music of Charles Mingus, Thelonius Monk, Alice Coltrane too. Some sportspeople also appear to occupy such time-zones now and then, which is why more and more spectators these days find sports so compelling.

Consider the rhythms with which and within which a person can *perceive*: the time-spans in which we sense our acuity, these time-spans are becoming evermore … elastic. It now takes unprecedented amounts and types of time to grasp many different phenomena. This is why slow motion and pixelation are becoming evermore popular modes of image-sequencing. And it's why so many of us now crave such a broad variety of music.

We need to know the times of our lives. A "future cinema" will help us this way.

Imagine the freedom of not striving fearfully to prolong life. A "future cinema" will help us this way.

And if it doesn't: well, there's world enough and time for us to go the way of all old matter.

Maurice Benayoun
So.So.So.
Somebody, Somewhere, Some Time

2002
interactive multimedia installation / Internet, VR binoculars, video projection /
dimensions variable / musical composer: Jean-Baptiste Barrière

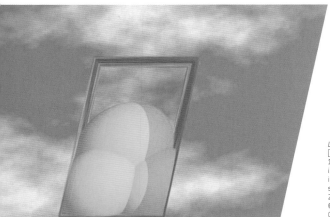

Le Diable est-il courbe?
[Is the Devil Curved?]
1995
interactive multimedia
installation
screenshot
Z–A
© Z–A; Maurice Benayoun;
Canal+

So What?

Fiction and narrative seem to be two parallel lines in my personal history, lines that, curiously enough, seem to be made up of virtuality, long before it became a technological aim and purpose. The virtual, and I had first no notion of it, deeply altered what I was doing in the field of video during the 1980s. Besides the art installations that were more devoted to the apparatus than to the pre-established scenarios I then tried to produce, I have developed a specific writing based on the *situation* itself. In a series of documentaries about art (*Pieces à conviction*, 1985), I placed the artist I interviewed in the middle of a situation I could no longer control and that triggered off reactions that sometimes revealed the artist's inner self and often puzzled the onlooker. The time devoted to the 3-D animation movies, with the creation of a series of short films, *The Quarxs* (1990–1993), one of the world's first 3-D computer-graphic series, made and produced with the cooperation of François Schuiten, enabled me to seize the idea that the topic of fiction could become the explanation of the world. As far as *The Quarxs* is concerned, it was the explanatory evidence of the imperfection of the world. To put it in a nutshell, the links between fiction and reality were not to be found on a one-way path. The doubtful links between illusion, that is representation, and scientific evidence could, as such, be the objects of questions. The questioning situation, if we consider the space attributed to the onlooker, could then become one of the purposes of artistic practice, backed by specific techniques that came from virtual reality, techniques that opened onto a huge chance of creating representative universes able to take into consideration the onlookers and see them as an essential element of the narrative.

We would then glide from the onlooker to the actor, from look to action (the action of the mouse-click generated by users of CD-ROMs), from acting to being. That creation, created as such, takes us into account for what we are. It takes our condition to-

wards a physical world and it becomes our condition towards a representation. In such devices as the installation series *The Big Questions* (1994–1996),1 the world offered to us is the aftermath of our own presence as visitors and not only the result of our actions (the way we act / what we do) as actors. Their geometrical structures, their semantic topography/geography/localization/loci (see *Tunnel Under The Atlantic*) are the results of our presence and their meanings are the results of the way we behave and not only of the way we could act if we pretended to be what we are not. In these situations I termed "Situation Art" (and that is different from video games and role plays that seem to develop as major narrative genres), we stay as we really are, and do not pretend to be, and act like, someone else – namely the hero of the game. *World Skin* and *Crossing Talks. Communication Rafting* are both physical and metaphorical situations that lead us to a questioning of the world around us. *Crossing Talks* and *Les Tunnels* create communicative situations in which everybody writes a framed slice-of-life-called-fiction. Narrative virtual is thus the introduction to a becoming amid techniques of representation. Both the complex factor and the embodiment come from the onlookers themselves; the represented world must adapt to their singularity.

poster for the
computer-graphics series
The Quarxs
1993
60 x 80 cm
© Z–A

1 *Is God Flat?* (1994),
Is the Devil Curved? (1995),
And What About Me?
(1996–1997). See also
http://www.moben.
net/Bigques.htm

572 00 SCREENLESS
Maurice Benayoun

*So.So.So. Somebody,
Somewhere, Some Time*
2002
interactive multimedia
installation
Internet, VR binoculars,
video projection
installation view:
ZKM | Center for Art and Media
Karlsruhe, 2002
detail
© Z–A; Maurice Benayoun
photo © Franz Wamhof

So.So.So.

So.So.So. is an interactive installation that plunges the onlooker into the middle of the photographic moment which reveals a complex network of characteristic signs from our own experience of reality. What the visitor finds with the help of VR binoculars is a series of spherical panoramas depicting the same moment, namely 7.47 am, in different places involving different persons in different situations.

Somebody, Somewhere, Some Time

Exploring these situations, the onlookers' eyes linger on specific details. They quickly glance at others desperately in quest of a meaning in the apparent banality of the scene. When they focus on an element of the picture, they slide from one scene to another. So doing, they conjure up the transitions, understanding the editing, now created, of which they are the involuntary cause. Thus sliding from one topic, one thing, to another, they do not at once understand that what is displayed on the screen is their very own story as it is being written.

As a matter of fact, on a wide screen – discovered by the audience outside the action – is the trace of the onlooker's eyes, painting the path of each visitor at his own pace. This is the "Collective Retinal Memory,"2 a writing space, a dynamic palimpsest, in which spreads out the story of the discovery, a particular reading that then becomes a collective experience. On the screen can be seen the difference in the interpretations legible through the story of the moments of individual attention.

Other readings are being developed simultaneously from the Internet. The same pictures can be seen online. The path of the web users is written onto the Retinal Memory that becomes unique, displayed in real time in the exhibition, and on demand on the Net. The shared writing space and the confronted looks make *So.So.So.* a thrilling experience in which the obscenity of the ongoing looks of others is unveiled by the CRM that in the process uncovers the intimate tropisms. This obscenity competes with the necessary complicity which reveals itself amid the fusion of the looks in a collective dynamic picture. In this nonlinear apparatus, the linearity of the narrative is built up by a chronology of individual experiences that erases

an older trace, for a better transcription of the real-time action.

Fiction blurs in a reality that it gradually pervades. Through their own paths, and in search of a meaning, the onlookers create explorations that are as many readings of the narrative. When their looks move from one clue to another, they rearrange the chaos of information into an actual interpretation. That individual reading creates the new linearity which characterizes the fiction we know through a trace spread out on the surface of the Retinal Memory.

Like the movie narrative, the literary narrative is a written trace, intentional, organized as a discourse. The trace left by the user on the Collective Retinal Memory is *one* unintentional trace. Like the ephemeral print of our steps in the sand, it tells us where we have been and what we lingered over. But, like the footprint, it vanished, erased by time or the new traces left by other people. This dynamic narrative inverts the narrative process. Facts exist before the *text*, and even it results from their discovery. Reading becomes writing. Intentional or not, clues that fill each image/scene become anchors, letting in a story that everybody can tell himself and to which the Retinal Memory bears witness. The synchronicity of the presented events (at 7:47 am) contribute to telling a story that doesn't go on; all of it is written at the present time. The virtual is no longer in the technology that defines it, but in the apparently undefined number of paths. It is in the ghost highway where we would expect shortcuts and not beaten paths. Our experience of the world is not so different; and to live in the world is to interpret forever. To create links and connections between facts and things. To extract meaning from the surrounding chaos. Narrative is a peculiar intelligence of the world. The script is its transmission.

In the closed world of fiction, there is a crime, necessarily. The accident justifies the attention. This is a hitch in the apparent continuum of daily life. Sometime the crime might be the lack of a hitch and moreover the fact of showing the world as the organized dullness of its appearance. *So.So.So.* is the exhibition of a crime hidden by the anecdote and the banality. The tragedy is probably the fruit of the conjunction of the impossible achievement of the narration together

2 The "Collective Retinal Memory" was at the core of *Art Impact, Collective Retinal Memory*, the first installation using this concept, displayed at the Centre Georges Pompidou, Paris, in 2000. We enabled the audience to explore "La Beauté," an exhibition held in Avignon in 2000 and featuring a series of art installations among places with no aesthetic intentions, for instance a supermarket, a slaughterhouse, a quarry. They could investigate the confrontation of both matters reduced to the level of the retinal seduction level, as a tribute to Marcel Duchamp.

So.So.So. Somebody,
Somewhere, Some Time
2002
interactive multimedia
installation
Internet, VR binoculars,
video projection
dimensions variable
installation view:
ZKM | Center for Art and Media
Karlsruhe, 2002
© Z–A; Maurice Benayoun
photo © Franz Wamhof

with the ineluctable finite of the duration of the show as well as that of the duration of life.

Narrative fields are superimposed. Everything leads us to think that the story coming from the given scenes is in the frozen present of a unity of time which is, converted into space, that of photography. As visitors, we are trying to find out how the characters are involved in a common story that sounds so common if we look at the surrounding environments. The sound work follows the same logic. In space, the interactive music composition by Jean-Baptiste Barrière mixes facts, superimposes clues. One can spot in the sound the obsessive presence of information, produced by the mediums. Radio, the sound from TV that reminds us, like the leitmotif coming from the press, that another story (introduced as the one from the world) is going on, less intrusive but far away: A sniper in Washington, Chechens in Moscow, a front page with Saddam Hussein close to the one with G. W. Bush or Charlie Chaplin playing a Dictator for light opera. Two possible stories so far, the trivial story of our immediate experience of the world and the one of its media transcription. Where does the real tragedy reside? Probably elsewhere, in the vanishing of author, ghost apparition in parking place, footprints left on the beach sand, far away from the world and the time; as if the author wanted to escape from having to tell the story, to live, finally, his own story. 3

3 See also http://www.moben.
net/sososo/

So.So.So. Somebody,
Somewhere, Some Time
2002
stills
© Z—A; Maurice Benayoun

Maurice Benayoun
Somebody, Somewhere, Some Time

A large screen on the wall, a pair of immersive goggles, a monitor and some computer equipment – yet another digital art installation? What might I see in the goggles? Is it worth queuing and waiting to experience the "virtual world" by myself? Or should I just stare at this large horizontal wall-screen displaying a mesh of images merged and glued together, producing a rather abstract image – part of which being nevertheless recognizable as some sort of photographic details.

In his new work *Somebody, Somewhere, Some Time*, Maurice Benayoun envisions a virtual universe made of networked scenes that can be explored, or rather gazed at, in a full 360-degree omnidirectional rotation. Each picture is connected with others through some recurring details within the images (for example, a sticker or a newspaper), which act like doorways to other images where similar details appear. The spectator thus navigates between images simply by looking a while at some key details that operate as invisible portals. This virtual world is thus a graph-based structure (read: rhizome) in which the spectator walks his own path. As the images are put into sequences, some narrative meaning emerges and is complemented by the spectator's imagination so as to fill up the blanks and ambiguities. In some sense this could be seen as a minimalist exercise and a visual counterpart of the textual *lector in fabula* paradigm [4] where a text is an "open" object in need of the reader's cooperation in interpreting narrative blanks so as to build up the final story. Narratives can therefore be seen as modal structures based on "possible worlds" and Kripke-model semantics. Distinct interpretative worlds are linked in a graph-based structure (again) through modal knowledge – that is, possible propositions assumed by the reader.

So.So.So. is obviously an open work, and if some story emerges from those isolated snapshots, then it is a story crystallized in a present time, with no future and no beginning. The future, if any, is in our head – and we have to construct it. All narrative clues that are seen, linked, reorganized and interpreted in various ways might at some point collide in the spectator's mind as he builds up his own movie. Interestingly, this experiment to fuse together a whole story from frozen omni-view images could in some sense be linked to the Cubist idea of creating an image from different views of the same scene that visually collide on the canvas.

But *So.So.So.* aims at more than just fusing immersive panoramic pictures into the spectator's own narrative.[5] It also aggregates the many paths of different spectators into some global walkthrough. Each spectator indeed deposits some marks on his path within a global territory, each mark being linked to a part of an image he looked at for awhile. This is like *semantic pheromones* – dropped in a common environment by different ants/spectators – which give other spectators clues to pertinent parts of some global story. Just as pheromones do for ants, this could further influence other viewers and attract their attention to some details they would otherwise have neglected. This is narrative construction as an Ant System [6] – one constructing a *collective subjectivity* – the result of which is the image depicted on the large projection screen in the installation. This is narrative construction as continuous evolution and mutation, as new ants wander in and out of the virtual universe.

This reminds us that the construction of meaning as a social issue has been stressed by pragmatist philosophers, and is forcefully conveyed by C. S. Pierce's words: "[…] one man's experience is nothing, if he stands alone […] It is not 'my' experience but 'our' experience that has to be thought of; and this 'us' has indefinite possibilities."[7]

Philippe Codognet

Parts of this text are translated from "Nature Artificielle et Artifice Naturel," in *L'art à l'âge du virtuel*, C. Buci-Glucksmann (ed.), L'Harmattan, Paris, 2002.

4 Umberto Eco, "Lector in fabula," in *The Role of the Reader: Explorations in the Semiotics of Texts*, Indiana University Press, Bloomington, 1979. See also *The Open Work*, Harvard University Press, Cambridge, MA, 1989 (orig. Italian edition 1962).

5 Several authors have proposed the introduction of a new terminology to stress the more active definition of spectators in virtual environments, which includes a participative aspect. See for instance J. Nechvatal's PhD thesis (http://www.eyewithwings.net/nechvatal/ideals.htm). But the integration of viewers in artworks has a long tradition, see John Shearman, *Only Connect ... : Art and the Spectator in the Italian Renaissance*, Princeton University Press, Princeton, NJ, 1992.

6 I am here obviously referring to the so-called "Ant System" paradigm, which has proved to be very successful in Artificial Life and has been used to model and simulate much basic "intelligent" behavior. See Eric Bonabeau, Marco Dorigo and Guy Theraulaz, *Swarm Intelligence: from natural to artificial systems*, Oxford University Press, New York, 1999.

7 Charles Saunders Pierce, *Collected Papers*, Harvard University Press. Cited in John Dewey, "Pierce's theory of linguistic signs, thought, and meaning," *The Journal of Philosophy*, vol. XLIII, no. 4, 1946.

World Skin

The interactive art installation *World Skin* was first presented at the 1998 Ars Electronica festival in Austria, where it won a Golden Nica award in the Interactive Art category.

Armed with cameras, we are making our way through a three-dimensional space. The landscape before our eyes is scarred by war-demolished buildings, armed men, tanks and artillery, piles of rubble, the wounded and the maimed. This arrangement of photographs and news pictures from different zones and theaters of war depicts a universe filled with mute violence. The audio reproduces the sound of a world in which to breathe is to suffer. Special effects? Hardly. We, the visitors, feel as though our presence could disturb this chaotic equilibrium, but it is precisely our intervention that stirs up the pain. We are taking pictures; and here photography is a weapon of erasure.

The land of war has no borders. Like so many tourists, we are visiting it with camera in hand. Each of us can take pictures, capture a moment of this world that is wrestling with death. The image thus recorded exists no longer. Each photographed fragment disappears from the screen and is replaced by a black silhouette. With each click of the shutter, a part of the world is extinguished. Each exposure is then printed out. As soon as an image is printed to paper, it is no longer visible on the projection screen. All that remains is its eerie shadow, cast according to the viewer's perspective and concealing fragments of future photographs. The farther we penetrate into this universe, the more strongly aware we become of its infinite nature. And the chaotic elements renew themselves, so that as soon as we recognize them, they recompose themselves once again in a tragedy without end.

We take pictures. First by our aggression, then feeling the pleasure of sharing, we rip the skin off the body of the world. This skin becomes a trophy, and our fame grows with the disappearance of the world.

Here, being engulfed by war is an immersion in a picture, but it is a theatrical performance as well. In the sequence of events which characterize the story of a single person, war is an exceptional incident which reveals humanity's deepest abyss. It promotes the process of reification of another human being. Taking pictures expropriates the intimacy of the pain while, at the same time, bearing witness to it.

This has to do with the status of the image in our process of getting a grasp on this world. The rawest and most brutal realities are reduced to an emotional superficiality in our perception. Acquisition, evaluation and understanding of the world constitute a process of capturing it. Capturing means making something one's own; and once it is in one's possession, that thing can no longer be taken by another.

In French, "prise de vues": shooting, taking. In the case of a material storage medium, "taking" something is the equivalent of taking it with you. Photography captures the light reflected by the world. It constitutes an individual process of capturing and arranging. The image is adapted to the viewfinder.

The picture neutralizes the content. Media bring everything onto one and the same level. Physical memory-paper, for example, is the door that remains open to a certain kind of forgetting. We interpose the lens ("objectif" in French) between ourselves and the

World Skin. A photographic safari into the Land of War 1998
interactive installation in a CAVE
cameras, printers
screenshots
© Ars Electronica Center; Linz; Z–A; Maurice Benayoun
photos © Z–A; Maurice Benayoun

world. We protect ourselves from the responsibility of acting. One "takes" the picture, and the world "proffers" itself as a theatrical event. The world and the destruction constitute the preferred stage for this drama-tragedy as a play of nature in action.

The living are the tourists of death. If art is a serious game, then so is war. War is a game in which the body is placed at risk as an incessantly, unremittingly posed question of the reduction of existence to its bare remains.

The printed trace is the counterpart of forgetting. A "good conscience" is a contradiction of a "good memory." One knows what one has retained, but one does not know what one has stricken from one's memory.

Here, the viewer/tourist contributes to an amplification of the tragic dimension of the drama. Without him, this world is forsaken, left to its pain. He jostles this pain awake, exposes it. Through the media, war becomes a public stage, in the sense in which a whore might be referred to as a "public woman." Pain reveals its true identity on this obscene stage, and all are completely devoured. The sight of the wounded calls to mind the image of a human being as a construct which can be dismantled. Material, more or less. The logic of the material holds the upper hand over the logic of the spirit, the endangered connective tissue of the social fabric.

War is a dangerous, interactive community undertaking. Interactive creation plays with this chaos, in which placing the body at stake suggests a relative vulnerability. The world falls victim to the viewer's glance, and everyone is involved in its disappearance. The collective unveiling becomes a personal pleasure,

the object of fetishistic satisfaction. We keep to ourselves what we have seen (or rather, the traces of what we have seen). To possess a printed vestige, to possess the image inherent in this is the paradox of the virtual, which is better suited to the glorification of the ephemeral. The soundtrack is there to enable us to go beyond the play of images and to experience this immersion as real participation in the drama. In sharp contrast to the video games that transform us into passionate warriors, here the audio unmasks the true nature of apparently harmless gestures and seeks to provide not so much a form of comprehension as a form of experience. Some things cannot be shared. Among them are the pain and the image of our remembrance. The worlds to be explored here can bring these things closer to us – but always simply as metaphors, never as a simulacrum.[8]

8 See also http://www.moben.net/Worskin

left and middle
Le Tunnel sous l'Atlantique
[Tunnel Under the Atlantic]
1995
interactive televirtual
installation
dimensions variable
installation views: Centre
Georges Pompidou, Paris, 1995
Z–A; Maurice Benayoun
© Z–A; IRCAM; DAP; MRT
photos © Maurice Benayoun

Le Tunnel sous l'Atlantique
[Tunnel Under the Atlantic]
1995
interactive televirtual
installation
VR still from the tunnel interior
Z–A; Maurice Benayoun
© Z–A; IRCAM; DAP; MRT

Tunnel Under the Atlantic

December 1995. The televirtual art installation *Tunnel Under the Atlantic* established a link between Montreal and Paris, two towns physically separated by thousands of miles. The Tunnel enabled hundreds of people from either side to meet. Shooting up in the middle of the Contemporary Art Museum in Montreal at end, and in the lower floor of the Centre Pompidou in Paris at the other, a two-meter-diameter tube that had seemingly been installed underground made us think of a linear crossing of our planet.

The route that lies between the two spots is no simulation of the ocean bed, it is a block of symbolic matter in which the geological strata have been replaced by iconographic strata. These layers of pictures were taken in the history of the two cultures, and can be revealed by everybody who digs. The collective exploration uncovers fragments of rare or familiar pictures which may wake up the collective memory of the participants. Encouraging us to linger and talk to other people, these remains transform everybody's digging route into a unique experience,

into a personal assemblage made up of sounds and pictures amidst a three-dimensional space architectured through their moves. While digging, the visitors can talk to their partners across the Atlantic. The sounds of their voices are anchored in space and enable diggers to find their way in order to meet up with the others. It takes six days of building and paving the symbolic space before a *de visu* meeting takes place between the two-continent diggers.

Free from the constraints of physics, space becomes a function of time. Speed is not the best way to speed up the meeting, but a way of specifying everybody's position within information. The tunnel architecture created by each visitor determines the editing of the picture within the temporal framework of their moves and within the built space.

Altered and shaped by the newly dug tunnel, the revealed images conjure up the very matter of scenery that redefines itself as the aftermath of each explorer/visitor's decision. The images' sequencing in time and assemblage in space are neither merely elements of predetermination nor elements of ran-

Le *Tunnel sous l'Atlantique*
[Tunnel Under the Atlantic]
1995
interactive televirtual
installation
dimensions variable
installation view: Musée d'art
contemporain de Montréal,
1995
Z–A; Maurice Benayoun
© Z–A; IRCAM; DAP; MRT
photo © Musée d'art contemporain de Montréal

domization. Through the things they deal with, and through the selected images, both come from each visitor's own way of digging. If we cannot master what we are going to discover, what we find out depends on our own way of doing things. If we let ourselves enjoy the tantalizing, immediate euphoria of digging at high speed, the iconographic remains we come across are not identical with those we can see when explore the discovered elements carefully and curiously. Everybody's interest in some details in the documents accounts for the theme and the semantic developments that will come afterwards. The writing process no longer concerns a definitely established building up of sounds and pictures, but the creation of their appearance conditions thanks to visitors' exploratory behavior. The combination of chance and determination that defines the resultant architecture makes the explored world similar to our current experience of life. The "Gadevu," the agent developed in a basic version for *Tunnel Under the Atlantic*, has become the Z-A profiler we can use for the dynamic and intuitive exploration of complex databases.

Combining the spontaneous actions and dialogues, the music composed by Martin Matalon alters in the course of event and is organized around personal routes, as is likewise the case with the pictures then revealed.

The televirtual event – that is to say, a remote connection of people in an interactive symbolic space – is filmed from inside with four virtual cameras. The captured images are automatically mixed and edited, taking into account each participant's speech. In the event of a counter shot, participants can discover their own live pictures floating within the space they have just dug up. They will not be able to see each other before the two sides of the tunnel meet. The exchange, so far essentially made up of sounds, then becomes visual. When the meeting is accomplished, other visitors can then take the same route or create new ones, as if part of a collective quest for a shared memory.9

9 See also http://www.moben.
net/Tuntitrg.htm

579

Crossing Talks.
Communication Rafting
1999
virtual-reality installation
CAVE and Internet
installation view: NTT
InterCommunication Center
(ICC), Tokyo, 1999
NTT InterCommunication
Center (ICC), Tokyo; Maurice
Benayoun
© Maurice Benayoun
photo © NTT InterCommunica-
tion Center (ICC), Tokyo

Crossing Talks. Communication Rafting

This era of telecommunication networks confuses our perception of proximity.

The weaving of human interaction is born out of the necessity for sheer survival. Distance creates an opening whereas proximity ties us down to convention. It is also true that in extreme circumstances direct relationships to people sharing our vital space becomes heightened. The distant speaker becomes a spectator of a weakened transcription of actual events. When survival is at stake, communication, which is not influenced by the media becomes a marked necessity.

Crossing Talks is a space of non-communication. Every room is made up of walls/images, people talking to other people like speaking to themselves. Only one wall at a time connects us to people far away or via the Internet. Like on a life raft, the distribution of people on the CAVE floor determines the balance of the group as a whole. When the balance is disturbed, the tilt of the floor forces the group to slide from one room to another. To stabilize the world, the visitors have to be in accordance with each other and thus are obliged to communicate with each other in real physical space. It is only at these moments that contact with the people on the screens is made easier. To experience the limits of balance in this world means to expose oneself to events that equate peril. The group's rapid reaction imposes itself. In this way, *Crossing Talks* confronts us with our relationship to others, near or far, in a saturated space of communication simulacrum. 10

10 See also http://www.moben.
net/crossingtalks/

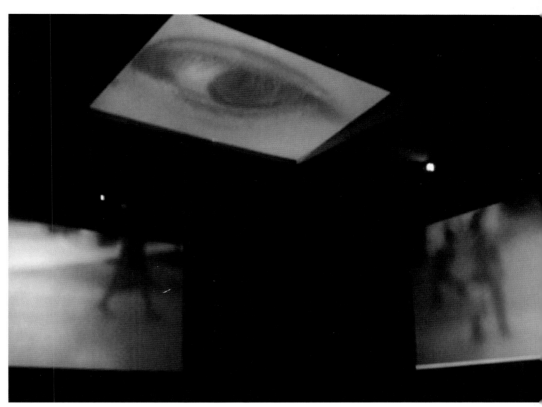

Watch Out!
2002
wireless Internet video
installation
dimensions variable
installation views: Art Center
Nabi, Seoul, 2002
Maurice Benayoun; Art Center
Nabi, Seoul
© Maurice Benayoun
photos © Art Center Nabi, Seoul

Watch Out!

The worldwide panopticon increases global exposure. Is Big Watcher b(r)othering us? Should we be afraid of being seen or should we enjoy the world's transparency as a way of proclaiming everyone's difference?

In *Watch Out!* eyes are coming to see us from everywhere. Their on-screen scale gives them another meaning. These eyes no longer belong to the pedestrian spectators watching inside a box but instead resemble those of digital gods checking out the world.

They are coming to look down on us, as if somebody finally dares to know what's going on inside Plato's cave. The mobility of the wireless boxes, like individuals, introduces a friendly, human-sized way of connecting people.

Watch Out! confronts the World we see and think. The project centers on a full-scale inversion of the traditional dynamics of seeing and thinking: The watcher is seen while the object (the public) cannot be seen; the thinker is read in the sense that the watcher's expression changes according to the responses submitted via SMS and e-mail. The object of the watcher's gaze shifts from the written text to the public. Inside the box is written the order: "Send a warning message to the World!" When we look at the messages left by the passers-by, most of them are naïve or mere jokes. This is what we do with the power to address the whole world. The global network is simultaneously a false panopticon and a false democracy. The bigger the tool, the smaller the brain. Watch out! 11

Maurice Benayoun

11 All the messages (mostly in Korean) and the pictures can be found on the project website (http://www.watch-out.net).

Michael Schmid,
Jörn Müller-Quade,
Thomas Beth
Laserfilm

2000
interactive sculpture / glass, laser, steel, wood /
dimensions variable

As a prototype of pioneering image technology, *Laserfilm* extends the possibilities of conventional film in terms not only of technology but also of subject matter. The installation is based on the idea of applying to the film medium a new technological advance from the field of optics (diffractive elements).

In order to produce moving images, the conventional reproductive method using celluloid film involves running a long sequence of individual images past a light source. Without recourse to further technical devices, the projected image will simply remain diffuse, blurred or unfocused. A clear, sharply defined image can be achieved only with the aid of a shutter, which ensures that each frame is projected only once ratcheted into a stable, centered position. In combination with this, one needs a "Maltese cross" that synchronizes the opening and closing of the shutter with the intermittent motion of the film as it passes through the projector.

The simple optical construction of *Laserfilm*, on the other hand, involving nothing more than a data carrier and a laser as its light source, makes it possible to directly project a film without using further technical means like the Maltese cross or a shutter. In the installation version for the ZKM | Media Museum, the film is mounted on a glass disc held in the center of a freely swinging pendulum suspended from the ceiling. The pendulum consists of a so-called diffractive element made up of minuscule squares with an edge length of merely one thousandth of a millimeter that have been etched into the glass disc by means of the most advanced industrial glass production technology. The viewer can "play" the film by moving the pendulum to and fro, thereby causing the light beam emitted by the laser suspended beneath the ceiling to shine through different sections of the glass sheet. The projection on the floor relies on the optical principle of diffusion, in other words on the diffraction of light, as opposed to working on the principle of refraction, as is the case with conventional lenses. Whether in fast or slow motion – depending on the speed of the pendulum movement – the succession of frames in the film flows seamlessly (or shutterlessly) on, since the image projected by diffracted light does not slip even if the image carrier is moved. With the naked eye, all one can make out on the glass sheet is a rough surface, and even on closer inspection the varied depths of glass on the etched surface give only the impression of an arbitrary pattern. When illuminated by the laser, however, these structures create varying degrees of diffracted light. The desired image can be achieved only through the projection, and cannot be found stored in microscopic form on the picture carrier.

The depicted motif was created by Michael Schmid and shows the letters O-P-T-I-K ("optics") and a mouth voicing the various sounds. The freely moving glass sheet allows the sequence of images to be assembled in different orders. The viewer of a laser film compiles the narrative structure himself rather than having it prescribed, and so the narrative linearity of celluloid film is broken. By using a new technology hitherto utterly alien to film, *Laserfilm* shows the potential for generating a plurality of thematic developments within one and the same film. Emancipated from the restrictions imposed by a pre-defined linear storyline, the artistic imagination will in future be able to enjoy freedom to experiment. However, active participation on the part of the audience is required, too. Being free to move as it wishes throughout the film's web-like structure, the audience will be stripped of its role as a passive viewer.

The idea for *Laserfilm* was born when Harald Aagedal, Sebastian Egner, Jörn Müller-Quade and Michael Schmid discussed the notion of deploying for film purposes the brightness-pattern translation variance occurring in the Fourier transform of a holographic image. Michael Schmid, who directed and carried out the project, co-developed the methods for computing the *Laserfilm* with Harald Aagedal, and was assisted by Janka Reh in designing the visual content. Markus Graf and Stefan Kölmel devised and implemented the technical set-up on the basis of a concept by Thomas Beth.

The project would not have been possible without the support of IAP Jena and the generous R&D advancement and funding afforded by the Institute of Algorithms and Cognitive Systems at Karlsruhe University. Thomas Beth, director of the Institute, not only initiated the making of *Laserfilm* but also engineered the productive cooperation with ZKM | Center for Art and Media Karlsruhe.

Ulrike Havemann
Translated from the German by Matthew Partridge

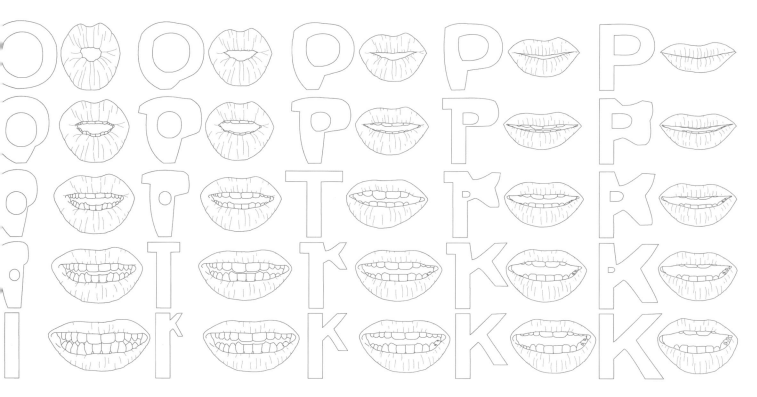

Selection of images from
Laserfilm. The images in the
corners and middle are the
original motifs; those between
them have been interpolated
(morphed).

left
Laserfilm
2000
interactive sculpture
glass, laser, steel, wood
dimensions variable
installation view: ZKM |
Center for Art and Media
Karlsruhe, 2002
© the authors; ZKM | Media
Museum, Karlsruhe
photo © Franz Wamhof

right
Laserfilm
2000
installation view: ZKM |
Center for Art and Media
Karlsruhe, 2002
detail
© the authors; ZKM | Media
Museum, Karlsruhe
photo © Franz Wamhof

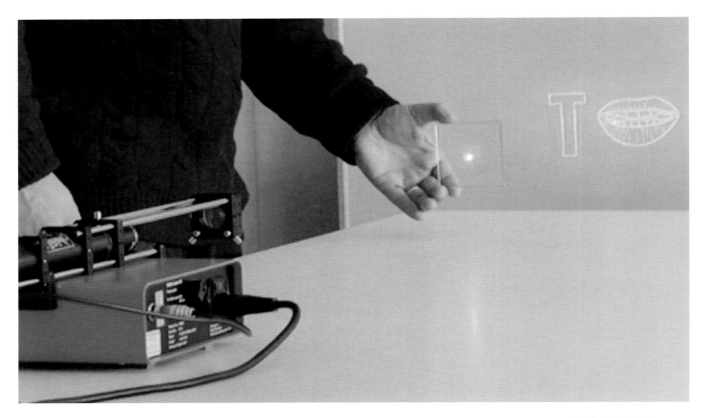

Simplified experimental installation set-up with laser and optical element.

From the Discovery of Diffraction to *Laserfilm*
A History of Diffractive Optics

The installation *Laserfilm* is based on an optical effect already observed in the 1760s. The Italian mathematician Francesco Maria Grimaldi was the first to write down his observations of a ray of sunshine sparkling through a small opening into the darkness of the room in which he was sitting. The spot produced by the ray was much bigger than it ought to be if light were propagated in a straight line. Moreover, the spot was faded at the edges and interlaced by coloured rings. Grimaldi called this phenomenon *diffractio* and, without offering a physical explanation, made an analogy to waves of water. In contrast to this interpretation, the recognized model of the period considered light to be a beam consisting of a large number of particles. The "corpuscular theory" mathematically founded by Isaac Newton used the phenomena of reflection and refraction to explain the behavior of known optical elements such as mirrors and lenses. A mirror reflects a beam in a straight line, whereas in the transition to another medium like glass a lens alters the motional direction of the light particles by a specific angle described by the molecular forces whose effect is asymmetrical. However, this theory offered no explanation for Grimaldi's observations.

In the late seventeenth century, Christian Huygens delivered a new explanation. He postulated the wave nature of light, and adhered to this view throughout an embittered quarrel with Isaac Newton. After conducting experiments in which light encountered obstacles with very small apertures, he pointed out that behind openings measuring less than a thousandth millimeter (this was later proved to be the size of the wavelength of visible light), light propagates circularly, like a wave of water. Stating that the wave is originated by one point he called the "elementary wave," he concluded that all light waves are compounded out of countless elementary waves. For a better understanding of this process, it can be compared with the propagation of sound, whereby the wave nature can be seen (and, better, heard) by everyone standing behind an obstacle. Although there is no direct connection to the source of the sound, it can be heard quite clearly. The sound waves are diffracted by the obstacle because the wavelength of sound is, at approximately one meter, in the dimensional order of the obstacle. On account of these analogies, Huygens was able to qualitatively depict in one theory both diffraction and refraction. A quantitative description, however, was first supplied by Augustine Jean Fresnel, who in 1818 combined Huygens' principle of elementary waves with Thomas Young's 1802 discovery of the principle of interference. The amplitudes of waves (corresponding, in the case of light, to the brightness) emitted by different light sources do not constantly accumulate, but under certain circumstances may cancel each other out. As a result, complex patterns may emerge, like the pattern of water waves that occurs if two or more stones are thrown into the water at different places and the resulting

00 SCREENLESS
Michael Schmid, Jörn Müller-Quade, Thomas Beth

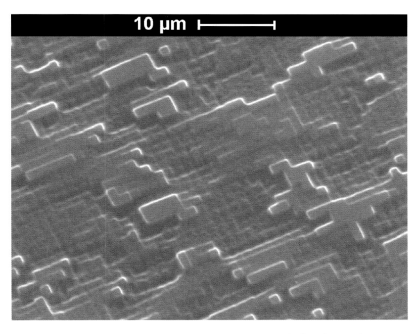

Surface-electron microscope
picture of the optical element,
magnified c. 50,000 fold.

waves intersect with each other. The same phenomenon can be observed in light that shines through many very small openings. Diffraction gratings, composed of a lot of sharp slits located close to each other and etched into a glass plate or a diaphragm, represent a special case of such openings. Through annihilation and amplification, the incident light generates a pattern of lines, the distances between which depend on the wavelength and therefore the color of the light. With such a set-up, Young could determine the wavelength of visible light for the first time.

Until the mid-twentieth century, different kinds of diffraction gratings were the sole application of diffraction. Dennis Gabor, in 1948, was the first to realize that an additional plane wave (termed "reference wave") could be used to record and reconstruct wave fields on the basis of their diffraction pattern, and thereby invented holography. Since laser was first invented in 1960, however, Gabor had little chance of making technical reality of his ideas. The theory of holography almost faded into oblivion until Emmet Leith and Juris Uptanieks manufactured the first holograms using lasers. In order to conserve a diffraction pattern over a longer period of time, namely at least for an instant long enough for the eye to register, it is necessary to use lasers. They provide a light source that generates coherent light. Unlike sunlight, which consists of many small wave snippets, this kind of light consists of long wave packets. The spread of laser technology as well as the advances in the field of computers permitted the development of complex

diffractive optical elements. In 1967, Adolf Lohmann successfully manufactured the first calculated diffractive element or, in his words, "computer-generated hologram." Since that time, a number of methods have been developed to improve the calculation of diffractive elements and to shape a laser beam to almost every light distribution.

One example of a diffractive element calculated with one of the most advanced optimization methods is the *Laserfilm*. It consists of over 7.5 billion single spots with the respective edge length of one thousandth of a millimeter. Today, diffractive elements are used mostly in industrial applications like welding or hardening, where they focus laser beams into special shapes. They are sometimes also applied to special problems such as, in optics, the "laser TV" which may turn out to be a future trend for movie-watching at home.

Michael Schmid

Caspar Stracke
plug-in without drop-out
·ª‿∞¶·‿*¶··// _____
(media art in the age of cerebral stimulation)

The Brain is the Screen.[1]

·/++

What's going on up there? Too much time has been devoted to – and partly wasted on – Artificial Intelligence: the endeavor to inculcate humanoid intelligence by means of military drill (and even under military pressure) into soulless digital devices. In the field of brain research, on the other hand, efforts are taking an opposite direction: not towards extracting something from the brain (in the form of a mimetic imitation) but towards a return to the brain.

Along side the purely medical concern to develop more effective operations and treatments there is a growing interest in developing a cybernetic communication system. One that could click in behind our eyes and ears.

The search for this sort of artificial cerebral input has been underway for some time and has produced a whole range of desirable and undesirable spin-offs. We have grown more or less accustomed to the unremitting sensory stimulation flooding from the infotainment industries. Yet surprisingly enough they continue their aggressive search for ever new variations of the *trompe l'oeil*. But it looks as though there's nothing more we can do to fool our eyes. So it would seem only logical to try to impart information as a more complex message directly to the cerebrum.

This is an enterprise of great interest to both the propaganda and the media businesses. Motivations differ enormously but the dimensions of exploitation and abuse are already precisely preprogrammed. At the same time, efforts in this direction represent an ideal breeding ground for the development of new forms of artistic expression, whose beginnings have as much to do with science as with fiction. The intertwining of scientific, philosophical and artistic viewpoints involved in this provides an interesting overview: a sort of suitability test for the artistic potential of a mind-expanding reception process.

A new type of visual medium could emerge and be decisively shaped with the help of existing artistic positions. The association with the cinema – just one among many possibilities – seems highly appropriate from a Bergsonian point of view for allowing a conventional representation medium to work on something non-representable. Appropriately enough, this medium has already been given the name of "Neurocinema."[2] If the brain becomes the screen there would no longer be an interface; transmitter and receptor would coincide, so to speak.

Direct interaction between the work of art and the brain would establish a new principle for interactive art: a genuinely limitless level of operating at which there would be no viewers any more, just active co-producers. This is of course the proclaimed ideal for interactive artworks but unfortunately remains purely utopian in most cases, since too many disruptive factors (time and place related, for example) prevent its realization. Let us imagine a cinema for all the senses. Emotional components will also resonate in the intermingling of the sensory impressions. There might also be implications for other forms of appraisal. This would bring a new aesthetic factor into play, which in turn prompts further consideration of the multifunctional applications of a neurocinema of this kind.

The reason why media art already has a name for something that does not yet exist lies in the very nature of a field which is constantly experimenting with technologies that are still in their infancy. Media art projects which strive to be innovative are prone to excursions into unexplored territory. As an artist active in this field, I should acknowledge at this juncture that I in no way exclude myself from this sort of pursuit or from the criticism leveled at it. This means that these observations are not free from a degree of bias but include a subtext that serves as a quarry for artistic use.

"The eye is taken as a model of the Western representational form of thought. The brain is put forward as a new 'rhizomatic' (networking) way of thinking. The hypothesis is that the eye is no longer adequate for understanding or interacting with the world as it is becoming (at the beginning of the new millennium). It should be replaced by a model of the brain."[3]

This is the argument – following the Deleuzian model – put forward by the Dutch film theorist Patricia Pisters for this paradigm shift. It has long become a firmly established tenet in a wide range of cultural circles and is feeding back into the scientific sphere in which it had its origins. The US Congress, for example, declared the 1990s to be the "Decade of the Brain" and approved a research program costing billions of dollars.[4] An age-old dream under whose technological packaging lies the irrepressible desire to render human thought visible. And to ensure its communicability without filtering or transmission error. There is of course nothing new in this endeavor; the whole of human history, after all, is permeated by myths of the supra-sensuous, from spiritualism to ESP (extra-sensory perception).

Theoretically, self-reflection about the highly sensitive system of the brain could produce horrible

1 Gilles Deleuze. Respect to mixmaster Gregory Flaxman, editor of *The Brain is the Screen. Deleuze and the Philosophy of Cinema*, University of Minnesota Press, Minneapolis and London, 2000.

2 Peter Weibel, "Neurocinema," lecture held in 1999 at the Museum of Modern Art, New York, discussed in more detail in the above text.

3 Patricia Pisters, *From Eye to Brain: Reconfiguring the Subject in Film Theory*, Stanford University Press, Stanford, 2003, and http://www.hum.uva.nl/~ftv/faculty/Patricia/deleuze.html

4 René Stettler, *Gehirn, Geist, Kultur. Symposium für Wissenschaft, Technik und Ästhetik*, Neue Galerie, Lucerne, 1995.

feedback effects. And this does in fact happen from time to time, resulting in spiraling threads of thought that become further and further removed from reality with every turn and give rise to tangled fantasies. This essay is doubtless one such; my ruminating and speculation, though, do have a concrete goal in view and do constantly release aesthetically inspiring and recyclable substance.

••//+++~

The Swiss art curator René Stettler calls it an "interface problem with the world."5 At the "Brain, Mind, Culture" symposium he organized in Lucerne in 1995 he conjectured that the growing interest in the neurosciences was rooted in the

"… realization that nervous systems provide far more efficient solutions for nearly all imaginable information processing problems, including the organization of decision-making processes, than the artificial systems so far conceived by man. It is likely, therefore, according to brain researchers, that knowledge about how nervous systems function could be applied to the functioning of machines, which would be more powerful and more easily operated than conventional computer systems."6

Stettler's theory has not so far been turned into reality in any way. Computer hardware and software is now gradually being adapted to human "wetware." For in order to be able to communicate at all, an artificial transmitter and receiver unit has to function according to a structure which corresponds to that of the brain. So there will not be a bio-digital adapter but a hard/software with neurons interacting on a semiconductor basis, dubbed "silicon neurons." MIT and Bell Labs/Lucent Technologies are the principal developers.7 "Researchers have initially designed circuits that display two essential characteristics of biological neurons: the digital selection of impulses and the analogue amplification of the reaction to certain impulse properties."8

Friedrich Kittler has pointed out similarities in media inventions of the nineteenth century with respect to their reversible usage: a microphone is at the same time a loudspeaker; the retina adaptation of "film" can both record and reproduce, just as the phonograph's wavy grooves can with sound and so forth.9 Will neuro-interfaces also function in both directions? A legitimate user question of decisive importance for the creation of a system operating on a digital-neural platform. Researchers now know at least enough to be able "to compute in the same way as biology does," according to Rajesh P.N. Rao of the Salk Institute of Biological Studies in California.10

If we want to stimulate the cerebral cortex directly, however, we do not even know exactly where the contact point should be. To be more precise, we should not be asking "where?" but "where simultaneously?" How, for instance, do we access the thalamus, the signal tower in the limbic system via which all senses (apart from smell) are forwarded to the sensory centers? At any rate, an interface in the form of a physical connection there can be ruled out. There has already

Robert Fludd
drawing
in Robert Fludd,
Utriusque cosmi maioris scilicet et minoris, metaphysica, physica at que technica historia,
Oppenheim, 1619

been more than enough fantasizing on this score. Cumbersome helmets (*Brainstorm*, 1983 or *Total Recall*, 1990) still seem more plausible than junction sockets grafted into the back of the head (*eXistenz*, 1998 and *The Matrix*, 1999). Nevertheless, the production sites have been located. Optical information is processed in the visual cortex, which is situated in the occiput. Various sub-regions divide the act of seeing into aspects such as stereoscopy, depth and distance, color, movement and determination of the position of the viewed object. The central nervous system, in other words, has to be able to bundle together and separate visual information into this many subdivisions. The communications protocols of these combined signals would have to look like the scores of László Moholy-Nagy's Bauhaus performances. It has been demonstrated meanwhile that we can register individual stimuli externally.

At C.I.T.'s Biological Imaging Center, Steve Potter is working on the first bi-directional, multi-channel interface and measures all possible stimulus reactions with a biochip, which communicates with the neuron clusters in cultivated animal skin cells.11

•••||~++•

For the last ten years various research laboratories around the world have been working on two different types of retina implants for blind people. They are examining whether a video signal can be reliably "transcoded." At the Neurological Institute of the University of Bonn, Rolf Eckmiller's team has attached a video camera to specially adapted glasses. These use a laser "link" to correspond with a wafer-thin silicon chip, which is implanted directly on the retina of the blind patient. Minute electrical impulses conduct the visual information picked up by photodiodes to neurons adjoining the retina. The first experiments used a rabbit retina to compare the injected elec-

5 René Stettler, op. cit., p. 1.

6 René Stettler, op. cit., Introduction.

7 Hahnloser, "Digital selection and analogue amplification coexist in a cortex-inspired silicone circuit," in *Nature*, vol. 405, 22 June 2000, p. 947.

8 Wolfgang Stieler, "Neuronen aus Silizium," in C'T, 14/2000, p. 51.

9 Friedrich Kittler, *Grammophon Film Typewriter*, Brinkmann, Berlin, 1986, p. 54.

10 Wolfgang Stieler, op. cit., p. 51.

11 S. M. Potter, S. E. Fraser and J. Pine, "Animat in a Petri Dish: Cultured Neural Networks for Studying Neural Computation," in *Proceedings of the 4th Joint Symposium on Neural Computation*, UCSD, 1997, pp. 167–174.

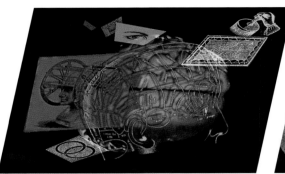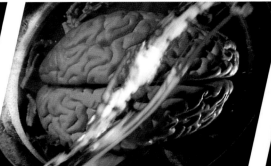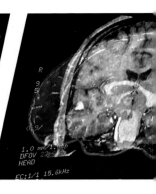

trical stimuli with the optical stimuli and study the method of functioning on the basis of the resulting measurements. A scene in the artist Heinz Emigholz' film *Normalsatz* reminds us that it was also a rabbit retina which the scientist Willy Kühne, working with extraordinary precision, preserved and photo-chemically fixed in 1878. Kühne provided the first evidence of an organically produced image. The preserved retina revealed the much distorted image of a window, the afterimage burned into the retina of the living rabbit – the last image the animal saw immediately before its death.12 For the observer of this tiny skin fragment it is an image that has already been seen but only half "digested."

It is interesting that the brain adapts every perception system as an alternative sense of sight, independently of its specific properties. An obvious illustration is the brain's ability to compensate for sight deficits. Blind patients, for example, can develop a kind of tactile vision.13 In one experiment, they were fitted with a grid of electromagnetic impulse generators on their backs. The patients were able to move around in non-familiar environments without outside help and recognize rooms and corridors. This experiment has not found any general application because it does not work for any length of time. The complex system of human perception can only be diverted for short periods before it becomes overstrained and issues warning signals in the form of pain. Cinematographic experiments with stereoscopy have the same unpleasant side-effects. Anaglyphic 3-D: headache. Polarization 3-D in color: headache. Virtual reality helmets with a 3-D system: headache. This is the only reason why none of these sophisticated processes has been able to establish itself in cinema. It is the consciousness that finally calls a halt: a double-cross that doesn't work. The use of glasses or similar equipment always presents the same problem in 3-D cinema: we are aware that what we are seeing is a simulation, even though the image is presented to the brain "as reality."

•••/++•

We can learn more from the experiments with the blind. There has been much speculation as to how an image might look that has not been perceived by the human eye. Wim Wenders' version in *Until the End of the World* (1991) shows something lemon-yellow with coarse pixels. The candidates in Prof. Eckmiller's experiments in Bonn described "fuzzy outlines." "Blurry images in black and white" is the optimistic verdict at

MIT. This is a highly subjective matter in the truest sense of the word: in this case, it is not the sighted who describe the world to the blind but the other way round. The scientifically circumspect report of "blurry black-and-white pictures" is reminiscent of so many similar birth pangs of epoch-making milestones in visual technology: from Niepce and Lumière via Zworykin and Baird to videotape and webcasting. In interesting contrast to the surfeit of high-resolution, high-precision reproducibility, an aesthetic counter-trend is now increasingly evident in graphics, photography and media arts. This is heading in the opposite direction towards reduction and incompleteness – a new form of minimal art. Sated with visual experiences we enjoy the act of completing things ourselves, of filling in the blanks. Here the toy manufacturer Fisher Price was highly prophetic in the 1980s in naming one of its products *Pixelvision 2000*: ultra-coarse resolution in blurry black and white. This aesthetic is currently omnipresent on billboards in advertisements ranging from Citibank to Nike, as well as very concretely in public art projects. One example is Blinkenlights and their reinterpretation of lit windows as pixels, which turn an office-building facade into a giant screen at night.14

What in comparison would be the brain's reaction to superior picture quality? If an optical system were to exist which surpassed the human eye and its reception capacity, and if the material could successfully be fed into the visual cortex, would not a visual faculty be produced that would actually be experienced as a qualitative improvement? If so, then the brain system would already have painlessly accepted the visual upgrade and would have declared the new information to be the normal standard. But in fact no valid comparison can be drawn between a high-resolution, drop-out free video picture and information "seen" by the human mind simply because video pictures have so far never been able to replace the natural images produced by the retina. Everything, in other words, would still have to pass through the second, natural visual machinery – a double process in which being aware of the simulation character would once again play an important role.

Within media art and its various adapted *modi operandi* of seeing the ideas of experimental film, now almost forgotten, hold an interesting position. It was in this field that extensive efforts were undertaken to depict the process of human sight in a medium-appropriate manner. A filmic philosophy of seeing was developed which diverged from the Deleuzian under-

12 Heinz Emigholz, *Krieg der Augen, Kreuz der Sinne*, Verlag Martin Schmitz, Kassel, 1991.

13 Rita Carter, *Mapping the Mind*, California Press, Los Angeles, 1999, p. 113.

14 http://www.blinkenlights.de

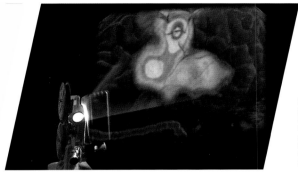

Caspar Stracke
neuroram
2000
video, Betacam
color, silent
6 min
video stills
© Caspar Stracke

standing of cinema. Perhaps the most important approach here was that of Stan Brakhage with his early work *The Act of Seeing with one's own Eye,* among other titles. In this, mental stimulation can be understood as a direct feedback with what is seen. In his films Brakhage transformed the movements of the visual process into filmic choreography, overlaying the visible with, as it were, the "non-visible." Certain successive sequences illustrate the immanence of the visualized image in what we see: our ability to project back, to think in images which we ourselves have not experienced. A phenomenon which is frequently to be seen in film and video work, but in a state of full awareness. It is present in a very raw form in Ken Jacobs' so-called *Nervous System* performances15 or in a highly stylized form in Cerith Wynn Evans' video *Degrees of Blindness*. We are able to imagine alien images by piecing together various components from our inexhaustible field of memory. Mnemonics as "found footage" cinema.

The eye in the process of "seeing" dominates the other senses. But since seeing is only one component of a synaesthetic interaction, the seeing eye produces a wealth of different sensory combinations that defy precise linguistic definition. The diversity of this by no means exhausted subject area suggests that empirical research and artistic reflection could complement each other much more effectively than has so far been the case. Peter Weibel has long been concerned with the intermediate areas of symbiotic perception. With the idea of neurocinema16 he is calling for urgent thought to be given to possible forms of presentation. Weibel talks of new tools in practical terms, fully independently from the implementation stage actually reached by technology. Ironically, the object of his inquiry is an immaterial one – which gives a shift of meaning to his thoughts on a cinema composed of thoughts.

Drawing on the thesis that technology is man-made nature, Weibel juxtaposes this expanded idea of nature with a broader concept of art. In this, neurocinema is one of several subcategories which he brings together under the heading of "genetic art" (thereby deliberately broaching an area of ethical friction). Weibel is concerned with creating an understanding of art that

"… is not purely art-intrinsic but instead addresses the central points of life. Technology … enters a new phase when it transforms central processes of natural life into the artificial and man-made."17

// • • | • • ____ _ _ _∞

If the whole focus is to be on an elemental redefinition of cinema and its media reorientation, there hardly seems room for questions of what subject matter it should embrace. Should the newly created form – in keeping with the absurd corporate media pattern – now be filled with "content"? Here we would have to ask the whole culture business what factors are actually driving the constant search for "expanding media" and extended forms of communication.

An innovative form crumbles like an empty husk if it becomes apparent that its creator has no additional content to offer or has built everything on one single message. Some maintain, though, that the reason for every media expansion is the problem of not being able to express an idea satisfactorily within the confines of a single medium. The artistic approach to a possible neurocinema would initially be so overshadowed by the ethical debate that the question of content would be purely secondary. Interestingly there are few comparisons available with interdisciplinary media. In addition, this is not a question of differences in how pictures are produced – whether by digital video, digital voodoo or puppet theater – but essentially about making visible what has until now been an invisible operating area. As to content? With an intermingling of electromagnetic and biological databanks the system would be capable of developing a conversation with itself and creating a work that changed in a state of flux, contributing its own "thoughts." This suggests a parallel to the conceptual art related net.art. This art form can similarly be seen as a dematerializing consequence of a technology surplus, which led to the elimination of cumbersome, expensive media matter, establishing in exchange a diversity of virtual construction materials.

Following this strategy, could neurocinema or a similar artistic brain stimulation invest the simulation character with a new feeling of reality? Not in a badly fitting data suit – but by means of our familiar sensory garb. Equipped simply with a new umbilical cord we should be able to dress our visions as tangible, fragrant and audible objects, and exchange them at will.

Translated from the German by Paul Bendelow

The text is an abridged and revised version of an essay written in connection with the Robotflock project by the BBM Group (in collaboration with the ZKM) for the "Knowledge" theme park exhibition at Expo 2000, Hanover and first printed in the exhibition-related publication Hyperorganismen (Internationalismus Verlag, Hanover, 2001).

15 Ken Jacob's *Nervous System* performance is a vision manipulator and Deleuzian crystallization par excellence. Through the flickering frequencies of a rotating vector screen an image is interwoven with its own (time-delayed) counter-image and is only reconstituted as one complete picture in the brain.

16 See Peter Weibel, "Neurocinema. Zum Wandel der Wahrnehmung im technischen Zeitalter," in *Wunschmaschine Welterfindung,* exhib. cat., Kunsthalle Wien, Brigitte Felderer (ed.), Springer, Wien/New York, 1996, pp. 167–184.

17 Peter Weibel, "Über Genetische Kunst," in Karl Gerbel, Peter Weibel (eds), *Genetische Kunst – Künstliches Leben,* exhib. cat., Ars Electronica, Linz, 1993 and http://www.aec.at/fest/fest93/hene.html

Darij Kreuh and Davide Grassi
Brainscore

2000
interactive performance in a virtual-reality environment / mixed media /
performance duration: c. 45 min

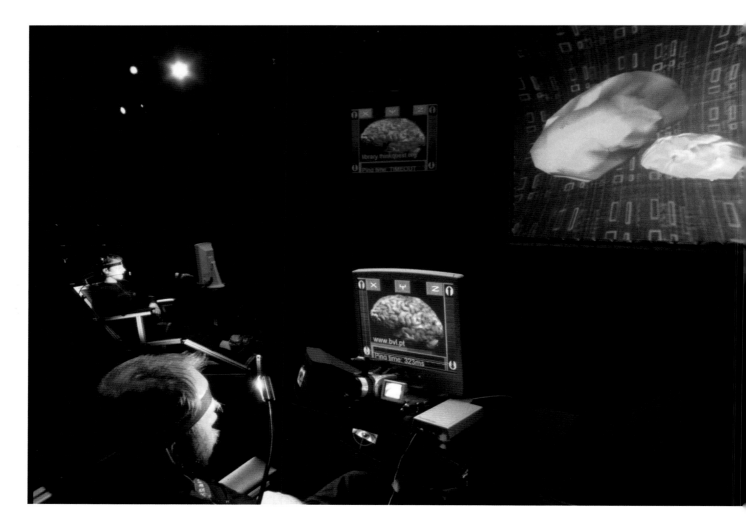

Concept

Brainscore is a system for incorporeal communication. Communication codes, which we developed
through consideration of social aspects, are becoming old-fashioned and awkward due to the increasing
complexity of information technology.

　　While until recently the body presented some help
in communication as a gestural interface, it now faces
great incompatibility and apathy in transferring and
mediating information. We do not refer to the body
as a biological construction that we need to redesign
and accelerate in order to keep up with the techno-
evolution. Rather, the body is superfluous in virtual
communication environments and can easily be replaced by any virtual entity or data object. The role
of a communication mediator, which has been imposed
by an information environment, moves from the biological body to technological interfaces through
semantic and functional layers. Basic codes, which
alter perception of communication phenomena, are
thereby changing.

Brainscore
2000
interactive performance in a
virtual-reality environment
performance views: Cankarjev
dom, Ljubljana, 2000
photos © Miha Fras

Résumé

The *Brainscore* project deals with research into communication patterns and the interface enabling the human body and the global information space to connect. It is a performance for two operators, in which incorporeal communication is used as the starting point for creating a controlled communication system. The system is based on the use of brain waves and eye movement for performing basic commands while defining a new digital discourse in virtual space without using the traditional and generally established ways of communication (socially recognized and conventional communication codes – speech, body gestures, and so on – are abandoned).

The operators, positioned parallel to each other so that they do not face each other, establish a communication testing ground, within which they are trying to create a dialog with the help of 3-D objects.

Each operator is represented, in the space of virtual reality, by a matching avatar that embodies primitive behavioral characteristics and form, at least in the initial phase. The operators' task is to "educate" their corresponding representation in virtual space by performing a series of operations and commands, which are set up in direct relationship to the global net dynamics (macro) and the user's neuronal net (micro).

The virtual space control ensues through the terminal window (the LCD monitor), which further displays how the brain is divided into five active cones. Each corresponds to one of the global themes, which can intervene with an individual. In the space of virtual reality, each of the themes is represented by a formation consisting of twenty objects. These objects represent the transformation of the basic circular form. They are based on passwords that derive from the home page of an anonymous hacker. The identity of an anonymous user in the form of a password is the carrier of the communication code and specific features like expression, color, texture and sound.

Objects, which combine into clusters according to their specific fields (meteorology, stock exchange, transport, media and epidemic diseases), represent the incorporation and influence of global migrations on the communication process between the operators. It all regards the active combination of a co-existence of the global information system and the local brain activity. The community of objects thereby constitutes the alphabet, from which avatars are molded; they are composed of the above-mentioned features.

The selection of objects (and thus features, which are represented in avatars) is performed according to correspondence of the user's features of brain patterns.

When avatars are complete, they begin to communicate with each other in the manner that they use the data that composes them. During this phase, the characteristics of the operator's brain patterns represent the first factor in the restriction and selection of the act of speech. The second factor is composed of the message, which is included in the second avatar. Operators determine the degree of the avatars' facial expressions (the percent and speed of transformation – morphing) via the terminal. They also specify the location in space and the rotation around local coordinate axes. All operations occurring within the terminal window are performed with the help of a system, which controls the operator's gaze. This means that all commands are triggered at a distance, without the use of a traditional keyboard and mouse, and they restrict the activity to the mere direction of the gaze.

Visual immersion of viewers will be enabled with the help of polarization glasses. Viewers will be able to experience the perception of computer-generated events as the presence of reality in the spirit of the perception of the third dimension. The performance lasts thirty to forty-five minutes.

BIOS team: Jaanis Garancs, Sven Hahne, Norman Muller, Thomas Tirel
BIOS – Bidirectional Input/Output System

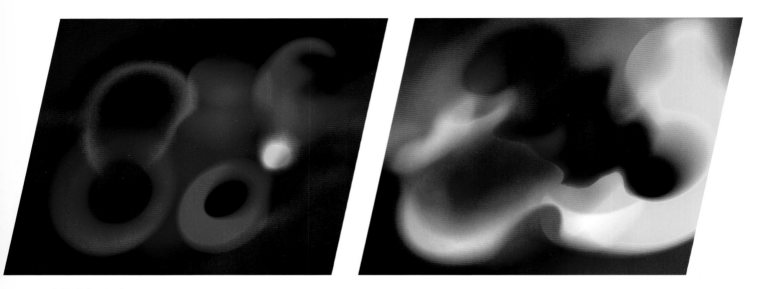

BIOS – Bidirectional
Input/Output System
2002
screenshots
© BIOS.x-i.net

Images of the
feedback visible in the HMD.

This project shows a custom-built apparatus consisting of a helmet with sixteen electrodes (sensors) for attachment to the spectator's head, a HMD (Head-Mounted Display), an EEG device, and a computer. The HMD shows images that are synthesized from the impulses generated from the spectator's brain reaction to images shown a moment before, thus creating a feedback loop.

BIOS is an investigatory prototype for neuronal research dealing with brain signals correlated to visual perception, which could lead to a kind of a "neuronal camera." And it is also a slightly ironical "homage" to the sensationalism of the contemporary industry.

Background

In the course of history there have been many attempts to understand the way images are processed until finally they appear as "impressions" in the mind. Due to the lack of sufficiently sensitive sensors (and maybe also for pragmatic reasons), one of the first experiments involved showing a certain picture to a macaque monkey and subsequently shock-freezing the animal. After that, its brain was removed in what was hoped to be the state "identical" with the moment of discrete perception. Because the monkey was previously injected with a radioactive fluid, it was possible to produce an X-ray exposure showing a distorted version of the picture found in an area at the rear of the brain. Other perception-capture experiments were made by attaching invasive electrodes directly to the retina of a cat's eyes. The result was a very noisy black-and-white video; the resolution was very poor, but the origin remained clearly recognizable.

These are just two examples of the "normal" methods still used by neurologists. We therefore did not want our apparatus to have the clean, highly polished appearance that commercial companies would prefer for their images. Instead, the visitor ought to receive some sensation of how one of the countless test monkeys might have felt before perishing in the course of the scientific quest to create the theoretical basis for our machine. However, we did not build our apparatus solely in order to protest against such experiments. It also has a deep connection to the old philosophical problem of reality, or more precisely, of distinguishing between what is "real" and what is "hallucination."

Because the transformation of light energy into the language of the brain takes time, our seeing is always delayed. The visual and aural impulses emitted by a nearby object reach our brain at different times. Thus, due to the divergent temporal performance of our sensory organs, events that are objectively simultaneous are subjectively dislocated in time. Although these differences are very slight in terms of human perception, use of the term "simultaneous" is justified neither in the physiological nor quantum-mechanical sense. Everything that one sees, hears, smells and feels occurred prior to our perception of it. In other words: We "scan" reality in similar fashion to the frames of a film. A feeling of time is generated by the clocking of this scanning, by the density of registering modifications. It is very evident how dependent perception is on the biological condition of the perceiving creature. A cold lizard perceives time more slowly than does a warm one. In stressful situations, time seems to pass faster than when we are enjoying a peaceful rest.

Besides the above problems, one runs into real, and not purely linguistic, difficulties when trying to decide if it would be possible to distinguish between a simulation of all senses (by some kind of machine not

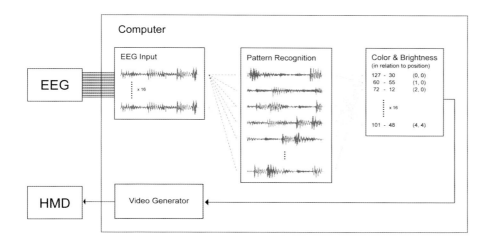

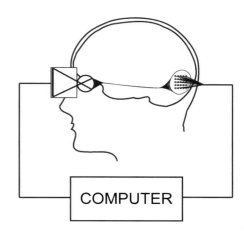

left
*BIOS – Bidirectional
Input/Output System*
2002
scheme of the EGG
and HMD loop
© BIOS.x-i.net

right
logo for
*BIOS – Bidirectional
Input/Output System*
© BIOS.x-i.net

yet invented) and the "real" world. At the moment, we are remote from building such a machine, but we imagine that at least some of our readers have had dreams in which they touched, heard, saw or even smelled things as vividly if they were awake.

One possibility of gaining a sense of what perceptional interpretation means would be to amplify it. In other words: If we found a way of tapping the perceived signal after its transformation, then it could be "fed back" in order to be transformed again, and this re-transformation would be repeated an undefined number of times and amplified in the process. Basically, that is what BIOS does.

The Apparatus

An exterior audiovisual perception path forming a closed loop with the natural path is generated. The viewer is invited to immerse himself in his own (physiological) perception.

The attached electrodes transfer to an electroencephalograph (EEG) signals from the three sensory areas of the brain cortex, namely the visual cortex V1 along with the two auditory cortices. A custom-built interface translates the voltage curves of the EEG into binary data. Thus it is possible to algorithmically "re-translate" this information into audiovisual signals. As output media, the HMD, and the headphones represent the electromechanical part of the cycle. The output continuously runs (back) into the biological perception apparatus, resulting in the development of feedback.

The neurological term "Retinotopie" describes the pattern of projection, the way the X/Y position of one point in the visual field is represented on the surface of the first visual cortex.

On the basis of the X/Y position and frequency of an electrode, the computer calculates the X/Y posi-

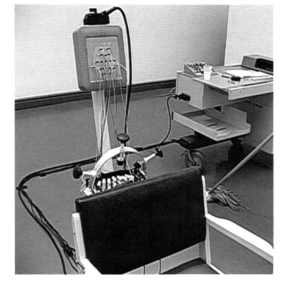

*BIOS – Bidirectional
Input/Output System*
2002
custom-built apparatus,
helmet, 16 electrodes,
head-mounted display,
EEG device, computer
dimensions variable
installation view (detail):
"Vision – Image and Perception,"
Műcsarnok Kunsthalle,
Budapest, 2002
© BIOS.x-i.net

tion and color of a pixel in the resulting image. The time flow is represented by the Z (depth) value. Missing intermediate values are interpolated (synthesized). The accompanying image shows the system of conversion (that is to say: basic principles). For BIOS we took the artistic liberty of visualizing "output" as subtly colored pulsations and waves of light. In the stereoscopic HMD, these trembling, breathing, flowing flares sometimes rouse visual associations with fire, smoke and liquid. They also bear some resemblance to the images seen if one presses the fingers against one's eyes.

BIOS team

More information on the project available at http://BIOS.x-i.net

The above description conveys the current state of the project (2002/2003). Enhanced versions of BIOS involving more advanced hard- and software for audiovisual cortex-pattern recognition and set-up (improved for visitors) are in development.

The Intelligent Image: Neurocinema or Quantum Cinema?

From Machines of Motion to Machines of Vision

The nineteenth century was obsessed with motion – with illusions of motion, and with machines of motion. There were two kinds of machines of motion: the first tried to analyze motion, the second to synthesize motion. The analysis of motion was the task of the camera; the synthesis of motion was the task of the projector.

The evolution of cinema in the nineteenth century can be attributed to two major trends: firstly, to the progress in experimental physiology and psychology leading to the Gestalt psychology, and secondly, to the advances in machines attempting to adapt and transfer the physiological mechanism of perception into machines capable of the visual simulation of motion and – herein lies the problem – not into machines of perception.

Therefore, what we know as cinema today is in fact already a reduction of the nineteenth-century principle that began to investigate machines of vision, but finally reduced them to machines of motion. There is the moving-image industry with its motion pictures, that is to say: the Hollywood system. Its code is a legacy of the nineteenth century, and reduces the initial exploration of machines of vision to machines of motion. Only the avant-garde cinema of the 1920s, 1950s and 1960s maintained the original intention of creating machines of vision.

Classical cinema, therefore, already diminished the initial enterprise, which was about perception. Perception was reduced to the perception of motion, and remained on the retinal level because there was no pursuit of the question of how our brain perceives the world. People constructed machines with a kind of graphic notation – "la methode graphique" (Etienne-Jules Marey) – of motion. This method can be said to be still valid, tragically enough, today. What Marey did was to analyze, and deconstruct, motion with his famous graphical method. It made no difference whether a drawing machine was used or, as in the case of Eadweard Muybridge, a photographic machine. Both Muybridge and Marey soon realized that it is not enough to analyze motion, but many other machines had to be used in order to project, to synthesize, motion. We may conclude this interpretation with the fact that cinema was invented in the nineteenth century. The twentieth century merely turned the nineteenth-century inventions into standardized mass media – including television, which became a consumer apparatus. As a side-effect, we simultaneously turned this machinery not only into mass media, but also into art, an individual approach.

Cinema is a writing of motion (cinematography); it is just a machine that simulates motion for the eye. The avant-garde, from Dziga Vertov to Steina and Woody Vasulka, kept to the initial idea: machine vision – not machine motion. Vertov gave us the term *Kinoglaz*, the camera eye. With the advent of video (Latin: I see), it was clear that we had to make a paradigmatic shift from imitating and simulating motion to imitating and simulating vision with the help of machines. We had to change from cinematography (the writing of motion) to what I would call the writing of seeing: opsigraphy, from the Greek word *opsis* (as in "optics"). Or even to opsiscopy, the seeing of seeing – in other words, the observing of observing mechanisms. In cyberspace, for example, when you see yourself and your actions as an image, you are already in opsiscopic space. You are observing yourself in a picture that you observe; it is an observation of the second order. In fact, cyberspace is the beginning of opsiscopy: of machines that see how we see.

The Interactive Image

The technical apparatus so far used to create images representing reality imitated the organic technology of a natural apparatus, the sight organ. The possibility of imitating movement through pictures was a decisive step towards improving the representation of reality, and was the basis of the transformation of painting and photography into cinema, as a *trompe l'oeil* technology simulating motion. Image technology and its late-twentieth-century tendency to imitate life moved on from the simulation of movement (the motion picture) to the simulation of interaction: a responding and reacting image, the image as living system, the viable picture. The computer allowed the virtual storage of information as an electronic configuration. Information was no longer locked up magnetically or chemically as it had been on the filmstrip or videotape. The *virtuality of information storage* set information free and made it variable. The image became a picture field, its pixels became variables able to be altered at any time.

Willard Van Orman Quine's famous dictum "to be is to be the value of a (bound) variable," which founded a philosophy of ontological relativity, is perfectly applicable to the virtual image, to Virtual Reality.[1] This virtuality induced the *variability of the image content*. In some degree, the creation of an interface technology between observer and image was made necessary by the virtuality and the variability of the image; it enabled the observer to control with his own behavior that of the image. The picture field became an image system that reacted to the observer's movement. The observer became part of the system he observed. He became an internal observer – for the first time in history. In the real world, the observer is always part of the world he observes, always an internal observer. The external observer exists only in an idealized, non-existent world. Otto E. Rössler's work on "Endophysics"[2] opens up a new view of the uni-

1   Willard Van Orman Quine, *From a Logical Point of View*, Harvard University Press, Cambridge, MA, 1980.

2   Otto E. Rössler, *Endophysics. The World as an Interface*, World Scientific, Singapore, 1998.

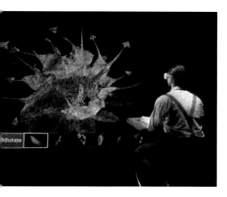
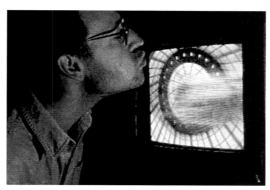
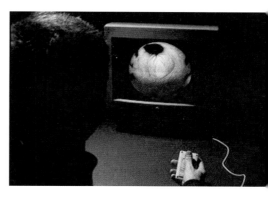

verse and develops the physics of the internal observer. Classical cinema imitates this idealized world (of philosophy, mathematics, and classical physics). With their internal observers, Virtual Reality systems therefore simulate an aspect of reality, bringing interactive images one step closer to the imitation of life.

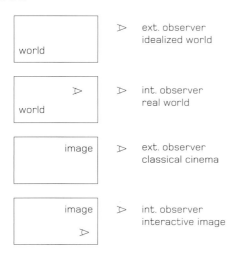

world	▷	ext. observer idealized world
world	▷ ▷	int. observer real world
image	▷	ext. observer classical cinema
image	▷ ▷	int. observer interactive image

Moving image and moving observer converged towards a new synthesis of image and observer: the interactive image, the most radical transformation ever of the image. Since artificial systems, whose behavior is similarly reactive to that of living systems, have been termed "viable" by Constructivist philosophers, the new image systems can also rightfully be called "viable." The *viability of image behavior* turns the moving image into a living image. Thus the computer is a decisive medium for perfectly simulating reality. Bernd Lintermann and Torsten Belschner's interactive computer-based installation *SonoMorphis* (1998) simulates the codes of evolution, the algorithms of growth of plants, giving the spectator the chance to create new species according to algorithms of recombination and mutation built on six offered optional organisms.

The Indexical Image
From these revolutions of image technology follows the technical and social deconstruction of the image. For this deconstruction of the technical apparatus of the image, the artist can enlist the help of a revolution in materials enabling a new physics of the image. See *Laserfilm* (2000) by Michael Schmid, Jörn Müller-Quade and Thomas Beth (on p.582) showing the change from the refractive optics of the past to the diffractive optics of the future. The important role of the index and the imprint in modern art (espe-

cially since the 1960s, as a result of a material-based artistic research) indicates that the indexical image (which is defined through a material and physical relationship between sign and object) will, as post-digital image, ultimately replace the illusionist world of computer-based 3-D simulations currently at the peak of their success. The indexical image is the beginning of a new culture of materiality of the image, beginning with nanotechnology, supramolecular chemistry and molecular engineering.3 Major advances in chemistry and molecular technology have brought us new materials, including electrically active plastics, that may form the next generation of computer devices.

Chris Dodge's interactive installation *The Winds that Wash the Seas* (1994–95) allows the observer to blow against the monitor screen, and alter the image with the direction and force of his breath. A second observer can interact by moving his hand through water. Both observers transform the image. The interactive CD-ROM work *Impalpability* (1998) by Masaki Fujihata is also indexical in character, since the human hand manipulating the mouse again shows on the screen close-ups of a human hand. This new culture of materiality will be marked above all by the transition from electronic technology to nanotechnology, from microelectronics to nanoelectronics. This transition is supported by three stages in computer development. The mainframe era of computing saw a room-sized computer being used by several people. In the PC era, one person used one computer, hence the term personal computer. In the future era of calm technology and ubiquitous computing, one person is going to wear and use a lot of microcomputers. But what kind of computers will they be? Quantum computers, DNA computers,4 molecular computers?

Cinema and Cybernetics
Gestalt psychology came into being around 1900, and peaked in 1930–1950. The "phi-phenomenon," a classical principle on which many 1960s filmmakers built their oeuvre, was formulated by Max Wertheimer in 1910. Gestalt psychology was followed by neurophysiology and cognitive science. If we follow this line, it becomes clear that whereas in the nineteenth century machinery was related to experimental physiology, the new machines of vision must come to be related to neuroscience and cognitive science. This leads us to the first group who gave us an idea for the next hundred years: the cyberneticists. From the calculating machine to the computer, they came up with machines that simulate thinking and seeing as well as motion. Machines were compared to the highest physical organ, the brain.5 Finally, as early as 1950 they had the idea that we can build machines that also simulate life. An unknown but wonderful article by W. Grey Walter about a "Machina Speculatrix," a creative, vision-

left
Bernd Lintermann,
Torsten Belschner
SonoMorphis
1998
interactive installation
mixed media
dimensions variable
installation view: ZKM |
Center for Art and Media
Karlsruhe, 1998
© Bernd Lintermann, Torsten
Belschner

middle
Chris Dodge
The Winds that Wash the Seas
1994–1995
interactive installation
© Chris Dodge

right
Masaki Fujihata
Impalpability
1998
interactive CD-ROM
installation view
© Masaki Fujihata

3 "Ultimately we can arrange atoms the way we want." – Richard Feynman, "There's Plenty of Room at the Bottom" (1959), in *Feynman and Computation*, A. J. G. Hey (ed.), Perseus Books, Cambridge, MA, 1999, pp. 63–76; see also K. Eric Drexler, "Molecular engineering: an approach to the development of general capabilities for molecular manipulation" (1981), in *Proceedings of the National Academy of Science*, 78, 9, pp. 5275–5278; K. E. Drexler, *Nanosystems: Molecular Machinery, Manufacturing, and Computing*, Wiley & Sons, New York, 1992; Jean-Marie Lehn, *Supramolecular Chemistry*, VCH Verlag, Weinheim, 1995.

4 Leonard Adleman, "On constructing a molecular computer, DNA Based Computers", in R. Lipton and E. Baum (eds), *DIMACS: series in Discrete Mathematics and Theoretical Computer Science*, American Mathematical Society, 1–21, 1996; Lila Kari, "DNA Computing: The Arrival of Biological Mathematics," in *The Mathematical Intelligencer*, 19 (2), 1997, pp. 1–22.

5 W. Ross Ashby, *Design for a brain*, Chapman & Hall, London, 1952; John von Neumann, *The Computer and the Brain*, Yale University Press, New Haven, 1958.

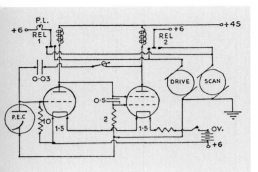

left
W. Grey Walter
Circuit of M. Speculatrix
1950

right
Claude E. Shannon
Demonstration of a machine for
solving the labyrinth problem
1951

6   W. Grey Walter, "An Imitation
of Life," in *Scientific American*, 182, 5, 1950, pp. 42–45.

7   W. Grey Walter, *The Living
Brain*, Penguin, London, 1961,
pp. 112–113. First published
by Duckworth, 1953.

8   G. Spencer Brown, *Laws
of Form*, George Allan and
Unwin, London, 1969.

9   Ivan E. Sutherland, "Sketch-
pad – A Man-Machine
Graphical Communication
System," in *Proceedings of
the Spring Joint Computer
Conference*, Detroit,
Michigan, May 1963, and *MIT
Lincoln Laboratory Technical
Report #296*, January 1963;
Ivan E. Sutherland, "A Head-
Mounted Three-Dimensional
Display," in *AFIPS Confer-
ence Proceedings*, Vol. 33,
Part I, 1968, pp. 757–764;
Ivan E. Sutherland, "Facili-
tating the Man-Machine
Interface," in *Purposive Sys-
tems: Proceedings of the
First Annual Symposium of
the American Society for
Cybernetics*, Heinz Von
Foester, J.D. White, L. J.
Peterson, and J.K. Russell
(eds), Spartan Books, New
York, 1968, pp. 127–140.

10   John Archibald Wheeler,
"Law without Law", in *Quantum Theory and Measure-
ment*, J. A Wheeler and W. H.
Zurek (eds), Princeton
University Press, Princeton,
1983, pp. 182–213.

11   Axel Thue, *Probleme über
Veränderungen von Zeichen-
reihen nach gegebenen
Regeln*, Kristiania, Dybwad,
1914.

ary machine, appeared under the accurate title "An Imitation of Life" in 1950.6 In his book *The Living Brain*, he wrote:

"The first notion of constructing a free goal-seeking mechanism goes back to the psychologist Kenneth Craik. When he was engaged on a war job for the Government, he came to get the help of an automatic analyzer with some very complicated curves he had obtained, curves relating to the aiming errors of air gunners. Goal-seeking missiles were literally much in the air in those days; so were scanning mechanisms. Long before the home study was turned into a workshop, the two ideas, goal-seeking and scanning, had combined as the essential mechanical conception of a working model that would behave like a very simple animal. At the same time, this conception held promise of demonstrating, or at least testing the validity of, the theory that multiplicity of units is not so much responsible for the elaboration of cerebral functions, as the richness of their interconnection. With the minimum two elements there should be seven modes of existence. And there was another good reason, apart from the avoidance of unnecessary mechanical complications, for the utmost economy of design in *Machina Speculatrix*, inevitable name of the species for the discerning, though 'tortoise' to the profane; it would demonstrate the first of several principles exemplified in the mechanisms of most living creatures."7

To make the imitation of life possible, it was necessary to move on from the machine level and explore system theory. The cyberneticists realized that only systems can imitate living processes and life, and only systems can imitate the thinking process. Hence, system theory was the next step. In consequence, it is logical to think of the image as a system, too.

Cinema and System Theory: Interface Technology

How do we define a system? People realized that there has to be a border that distinguishes between system and environment. The axiom of system theory is "Construction: Draw a distinction."8 We can see our borders: the skin, then a membrane. What was once called skin and membrane is now known as "interface technology." As the border that separates the system from the environment, interface technology differentiates the image from the real world. Naturally, this difference is not very clear; it is not a strict border like a wall, but more like foam.

We need a theory of border, a theory of interface technology, to separate a system from its environment, and to enable interchange between the two. I therefore refer to Ivan E. Sutherland and his 1963 article about man, machine and interface.9 Here again, one sees the nineteenth-century relationship

between man and machine, but now a new concept states that there is something between man and machine, namely interface technology. An interface lies between the world and ourselves, between machines and ourselves. Maybe the world is only an interface. Maybe we can change the interface, if not the world. We can expand the interface: This is expanded cinema and VR technology. The important point is that the border – the interface – is permeable and variable. The border can be extended. Something that is now the environment can be part of the system in the next step. Something that is the system can be the environment for the sub-system. This means that if I am an external observer of one system, I can become part of the system for the next environment, an internal observer for another external observer. Normally, we believe our situation in the real world to be identical with that in classical cinema. We are external observers of the image; our observation has no effect on the image. But we have constructed systems where our observation is part of the system that we observe. Therefore, quantum theory with its effects of observation (from Heisenberg's "uncertainty principle," 1927, to John Archibald Wheeler's "participatory universe," 1983) becomes the role model for the observer-dependent media used in interactive image installations and systems. "To speak of the universe as a self-excited circuit is to imply once more a participatory universe."10

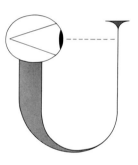

The universe viewed as a self-excited circuit. Starting small (thin U at "upper right"), it grows (loop U) and in times gives rise ("upper left") to observer participation – which in turn imparts "tangible reality" to even the earliest days of the universe.

We are compelled to see that the digital image is, for the first time, a real system. With its open-circuit installations where people enter the image by the observation of the camera, video came much closer than cinema to system theory. But even video magnetically sealed and imprisoned the information. Virtual information storage is necessary for an image as system. Virtual Reality is based on the virtuality of information storage in the computer. Today, information is just an electronic representation, which means you can change it immediately at any time. Thus, the image is a dynamic system of variables.

Cinema and Genetic Algorithms

My next point is that we define the variables of an image system as agents. The idea of agents has a long history, with roots going back to a mathematician, Axel Thue, who had a linguistic problem.11 Say he had had a string of seven letters building an alphabet, he would write down a formula, say with four letters. He had two grammatical rules: A can always be transformed to B and A; and B can always be transformed to A. He was trying to discover a general method, an algorithm, that would decide whether a written formula (for example four letters) could be derived from the seven letters (the alphabet) by the two rules (the grammar). The general unsolvability of Thue's "word problem" was later made famous by Emil Leon Post.[12] Noam Chomsky, who used Semi-Thue systems, invented the first logical-mathematical models for natural language. On that basis, Backus and Naur developed another of all those programming languages, ALGOL (algorithmic language) in 1960.[13] Subsequently, the Belgian biologist Aristid Lindenmayer in 1967 invented the L-System (the Lindenmayer System), a programming language he called a "genetic algorithm" and which was a clear application of Thue's technique.[14] With the help of this mathematical-linguistic model, he was able to simulate the growth of plants![15] Neither geometry nor machines of vision but a programming language built on mathematics made it possible to simulate life processes like morphogenesis and growth of forms. The cinematic code of today is not to imitate motion, but to imitate growth, and even chaotic growth as an aspect of life. The image variables became autonomous agents, data with a life of its own.

After Lindenmayer, the best textbook about the genetic algorithm was written by John H. Holland. He came up with the next step: "complex adaptive systems" able to adapt to the environment. There was now an exchange between the previously separated system and environment. In his recently published *Hidden Order. How Adaptation Builds Complexity*,[16] he offers the seven concepts of aggregation, tagging, non-linearity, flows, diversity, internal models, and building blocks. All these mechanisms or properties of a system enable a sufficiently complex system to adapt to the environment.

Naturally, this adaptation is carried out by so-called software agents or autonomous agents. These software agents can make their own decisions to act within the algorithm, so that for the first time a system can adapt from within. I call this process of adaptation "intelligent behavior"; the system as a whole, after being virtual and variable, is becoming "viable." The image shows lifelike behavior – viability – and intelligence. When we turn the image into a system, it can behave like a living organism and possess artificial intelligence. The image can act on its own. The algorithmic image can imitate the evolution of life.

Wireless Communication and Non-Local, Distributed, Shared Cyberspace

In order to have intelligent images in the future, we must apply the idea of the Net, which means the observer is no longer part of a hierarchy. The so-called visual hierarchical pyramid applied to the classical image: One observer looked at one image. In the next decade we must try to make the image a system in which the observer is merely one node in the network of the image system. The no longer privileged observer will then be a peripheral interface machine like any other machine. And we must remember that cinema began with a single observer looking into one machine. The classical form was one observer, one film, one space. It was slowly transformed into a collective experience, but even in a movie theater there is one film, screened locally in one space at one time. The principle of unity still applies. The next step was television, with collective observation, but non-local, not in one space, dislocated, yet still restricted to the simultaneous viewing of one film. TV already has a network structure as its distribution model, and the next step is a simultaneous, dislocated and collective experience of different films seen at home from some kind of database.

Cyberspace, in its present form of the head-mounted display, is old-fashioned cinema: Again, you have one locally defined viewer of one movie in one place at one time. In the course of the next hundred years we must develop the cyberspace technology to meet our changed demands for collective experience in dislocated, distributed cyberspace. It must be simultaneous and it must be non-local – the image must be Net-based, built on information from non-local sources in the manner already demonstrated by online games with their thousands of inhabitants/ players. One century ago, people built railway lines, laid cables below and above ground and across the ocean beds. And now fiber optics must become the basis for collective experience of other visual codes. At present, a wire still leads to the computer from the head-mounted display. A future wireless technology might be based on neurophysiology: wireless neurocinema. The projector of the future is wireless usage of the Net, enabling the collective experience of non-local, visual and acoustic data.

Neurocinema

It was discovered in the nineteenth century that neurons use action potentials to signal over long distances. The all-or-none nature of the action potential means that it codes information by its presence or absence, not by its size or shape. In this respect, an action potential can be considered a pulse. How do action potentials represent sensory states and mental activities? How is information contained in the firing patterns of stored and retrieved action potentials? We owe the first images of neural networks to Ramón y Cajal.[17] They enabled the question of how the brain processes information to be put more precisely. Excitation and inhibition were known as attributes of the activities of neural networks since 1900. However, the excitatory and inhibitory effects of nerve pulses was first demonstrated by David Lloyd in 1946.[18]

This incipient knowledge of the structure and function of neural networks supported Leibniz and others in their ideas on the logical structure of the mind. Leibniz showed that logic can be reduced to arithmetic and that arithmetic can be expressed in a binary code (all numbers can be expressed by the digits 0 and 1). He conceived a logic machine that could calculate each computable number by the algebraic operations today known as algorithms. The English mathematician George Boole further developed this idea in his books *The Mathematical Analysis of Logic, Being an Essay Towards a Calculus of Deductive Reasoning* (1874) and *An Investigation of the Laws of Thought* (1854). Boole's Algebra, a symbolic method for logic relations, is a calculus of propositions whereby variables may be only 0 or 1. In 1938, Claude E. Shannon used Boole's Algebra to demonstrate that a perfect analogy exists between the calculus of propositions and the calculus for relay and switching circuits.[19] A theorem of the proposition calculus can also be interpreted as a valid theorem of switching circuits. The interpretation of a proposition as false can be interpreted as signifying that a circuit is closed, that a proposition is true as signifying that a circuit is open, and so forth.

The description of nervous activities accompanying thought processes can be turned into prescriptions for the design of machines that can think or (amounting to the same thing) the design of programs. One way to understand the laws of thought was to study carefully the brain and its nervous activ-

12 Emil Leon Post, "Recursive unsolvability of a problem of Thue," in *Journal of Symbolic Logic*, 12, 1–11, 1947.

13 J. W. Backus, Peter Naur and Wiliam Turanski, *Report on the Algorithmic Language Algol 60*, Danish Academy of Technical Sciences, Copenhagen, 1960.

14 Aristid Lindenmayer, "Developmental systems without cellular interaction, their languages and grammars," in *Journal of Theoretical Biology*, 1971, pp. 455–484.

15 Przemyslaw Prusinkiewicz and Aristid Lindenmayer, *The Algorithmic Beauty of Plants*, Springer, New York, 1990.

16 John H. Holland, Heather Mimnaugh, *Hidden Order. How Adaptation Builds Complexity*, Perseus Books, Cambridge, MA, 1996.

17 Ramón y Cajal, *Histologie du système nerveux de l'homme et des vertébrés*, Paris, 1909–1910.

18 David P. C. Lloyd, "Integrative patterns of excitation and inhibition in two-neuron reflex arcs," in *Journal of Neurophysiology*, 9, 1946, pp. 439–444.

19 Claude E. Shannon, "A symbolic analysis of relay and switching circuits," in *Transactions of the American Institute of Electrical Engineers*, American Institute of Electrical Engineers, New York, 1938, p. 713.

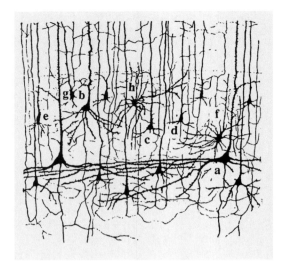

This reproduction of a drawing by Ramón y Cajal shows a small proportion of the neurons in the cortex; in reality, the density of neurons is much higher. Cell b is a nice example of a pyramidal cell with a triangular cell body. Dendrites can be recognized by their rough surface. The axon extends downwards, with several branches to the left and right.

Warren S. McCulloch and Walter H. Pitts
A logical calculus of ideas immanent in nervous activity
1943

a) $N_2(t) . \equiv .N_1(t-1)$
b) $N_3(t) . \equiv .N_1(t-1) \vee N_2(t-1)$
c) $N_3(t) . \equiv .N_1(t-1) . N_2(t-1)$
d) $N_3(t) . \equiv .N_1(t-1) . \sim N_2(t-1)$
e) $N_3(t) . \equiv : N_1(t-1) . \vee . N_2(t-3) . \sim N_2(t-2)$
   $N_3(t) . \equiv .N_2(t-2) . N_2(t-1)$
f) $N_4(t) . \equiv : \sim N_1(t-1) \vee N_2(t-1) \vee N_3(t-1) . \vee . N_1(t-1) . N_2(t-1) . N_3(t-1)$
   $N_4(t) . \equiv : \sim N_1(t-2) \vee N_2(t-2) \vee N_3(t-2) . \vee . N_1(t-2) . N_2(t-2) . N_3(t-2)$
g) $N_3(t) . \equiv .N_2(t-2) . N_1(t-3)$
h) $N_2(t) . \equiv .N_1(t-1) . N_1(t-2)$
i) $N_3(t) : \equiv : N_2(t-1) . \vee . N_1(t-1) . (Ex)t. -1 . N_1(x) . N_2(x)$

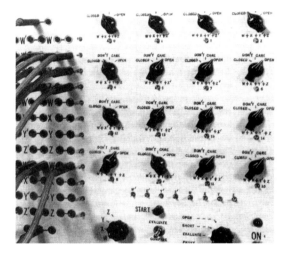

Claude E. Shannon
View of the front cover of the switching circuit analyzer
1938

20 Donald H. Ford, J. P. Schadé, *Atlas of the human brain*, Elsevier, Amsterdam, 1971.

21 *Brain and the conscious experience*, John C. Eccles (ed.), Springer, Berlin, 1966.

22 Judson Ch. Webb, *Mechanism, Mentalism, and Meta-mathematics*, Reidel, Dordrecht/Boston, 1980.

23 Claude E. Shannon, "A symbolic analysis," op. cit.

24 Ashby, op. cit.

25 Nobert Wiener, Arturo Rosenblueth and Julian H. Bigelow, "Behaviour, Purpose, and Teleology," in *Philosophy of Science*, 10, 1943, pp. 18–24.

26 Warren S. McCulloch and Walter H. Pitts, "A logical calculus of ideas immanent in nervous activity," in *Bulletin of Mathematical Biophysics*, 5, 1943, pp. 115–133.

27 Kenneth J. W. Craik, *The Nature of Explanation*, Cambridge University Press, Cambridge, 1943.

28 W. Pitts, Warren S. McCulloch, "How we know universals; The perception of auditory and visual forms," in *Bulletin of Mathematical Biophysics*, University of Chicago Press, Chicago, 9, 1947, pp. 127–147.

ity. Since Ramón y Cajal's discovery that the cerebral cortex is composed of layers of cells tangential to the pial surface, the science of the brain has made enormous progress. We now have an atlas of the human brain[20] and considerable knowledge of conscious experience in the brain.[21] Beginning in the nineteenth century, the quest for an analogy between mathematics and the brain, between algebraic operations and nervous activities, between a calculus and deductive reasoning, had by the mid-twentieth century progressed to a stage where nervous activities representing ideas and thought processes could be described and formulated in mathematical terms. This quest led to machines that could think, constructed according to mathematical laws, for instance the propositional calculus. These machines can help us to understand reasoning and the brain. We therefore have a chain of analogies between nervous activity and mathematics, mathematics and machines, machines and nervous activities. Mentalism, mechanism and mathematics were seen as parallel worlds. [22] Symbolic or formal logic was used to design electrical circuits.[23] Electrical circuits were used to design a brain.[24]

Machines were supposed to do the work of the brain and mathematics, to turn thought processes into program processes. The turning point came in 1943 with the publication of three theoretical papers on what is now called cybernetics. Nobert Wiener, Arturo Rosenblueth and Julian H. Bigelow of MIT suggested ways of building goals and purposes into ma-

chines.[25] Warren S. McCulloch and Walter H. Pitts showed how machines might use concepts of logic and abstraction and how neural networks could be seen as parallel computers.[26] Kenneth J. W. Craik of Cambridge University proposed that machines could use models and analogies to solve problems.[27]

Warren McCulloch and Walter Pitts' formal theory of neural networks laid the foundations for automata theory and artificial intelligence. Due to the "all-or-nothing" character of nervous activity, a neuron can be seen as a binary logic device and neural events can be described by means of propositional logic derived from Rudolf Carnap's *The Logical Syntax of Language* (1937). Shannon demonstrated the analogy between the propositional calculus and switching circuits, McCulloch and Pitts showed the analogy between the propositional calculus and nervous activity. Neuronal networks, switching circuits and logic calculus became one, obeying the same laws. Electronic machines could therefore do the job of neuronal networks, and compute. McCulloch and Pitts' model of nervous activity and their proposal that neurons compute logic functions influenced John von Neumann's sketch of the architecture of future digital computers in a famous 1945 technical report. In 1947, Pitts and McCulloch gave a theoretical construction of neural networks for pattern recognition that showed how visual input could control motor output via the distributed activity of a layered neural network. In this remarkable paper entitled "How we know universals: The perception of auditory and visual forms," [28] Pitts and

19th century		→	21st century	
eye cinema	trompe l'oeil eye technology		neurocinema	trompe le cerveau brain technology
medicine physiology	Roget Marey		cognitive science neurophysiology	Edelmann Kandel
physics optics mathematics	Faraday Stampfer Mach		nanotechnology quantum physics quantum computing	Feynman Bell Deutsch
macro-engineers	Lumière		molecular engineering	Drexler

McCulloch proposed a number of quite specific neural mechanisms that could be used to abstract important quantities from a neural representation. Between the papers of 1943 and 1947 a shift occurred from binary neuronal computing logic to specialized neural structures computing particular aspects of a sensory stimulus. S. C. Kleene's 1951 paper "Representation of Events in Nerve Nets and Finite Automata" marked, together with others, the beginning of abstract automata theory.[29]

The idea was born: With the aid of logic, events of the world could be represented in artificial neural networks. These networks could be simulated by switching circuits, following the same laws of symbolic logic as applied to the representation of events in neuronal networks. Automata built from these switching circuits, could simulate such nervous activities in the brain as thought processes, computing, and even seeing. Machine vision on a molecular scale is one possibility of the future cinematic imaginary. The McCulloch-Pitts model was based on binary units; many of the recent network models rely on continuous variables. Our perception of the world is driven by input from the sensory nerves. This input reaches the brain encoded as sequences of firing patterns of action potentials or spikes. The eye communicates chains of spikes to the brain. Information is coded by the firing of neurons, the timing of spikes codes the information. Neuronal networks are therefore pulse-coded. Vision is not a spatial representation in the brain through the retina. Vision is the brain's computing of temporal patterns. This pulse-based neuronal coding, created by the firing of neurons, delivers the basis of our perception. Biological neural networks, which communicate through pulses, use the timing of the pulse to transmit information. Pulsed neural networks[30] mean that vision is a temporal code.

Future cinema will be able to precisely simulate or stimulate those pulsed neural networks. Instead of *trompe l'oeil*, the next step might be *trompe le cerveau* – the cinematographic apparatus will deceive the brain, not the eye, will steer and govern precisely pulsed neural networks with the help of molecular machines. We would be able to imitate vision, to construct a cinematic experience without light and eyes, to create images without perception conveyed by the direct stimulation of neural networks. Thanks to pulse-based temporal codes that directly stimulate the brain with the help of neurochips or brain-chips, there would be perception without the senses, seeing without the eyes. Stimulation – artificial pulse-based representation of the world – would replace simulation. The brain, as opposed to the eye, would become the screen.[31]

In the twenty-first century, neurophysiology may be expected to assume the role played by physiology in the development of cinema in the nineteenth century. Advances in neurophysiology and cognitive science[32] give rise to the hope that future engineers will succeed in implementing these discoveries in neuronal and molecular machines that transform the technology of simulation to deceive the eye into a technology of stimulation that in turn deceives the brain.

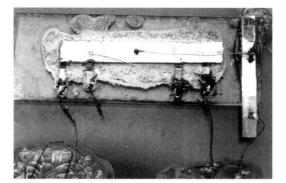

Jack Kilby
The first "integrated circuit" or "chip"
1958

Instead of having to produce each component individually, the inventor accommodated a transistor, a capacitor and several resistors on the same slice of germanium.

Quantum Cinema

Scaling is a question of future cinema. Working on the level of supramolecular chemistry or nanotechnology, can we invent a cinematographic apparatus that enables us to manipulate not only singular neurons, cells and neuronal networks, but also particles smaller than neurons? If this is feasible, then we can learn from quantum theory, which teaches us that reality is observer-relative. Anything that is observed is also changed by the very act of observation. That means we must move from receptor technology (cameras) to effector technology. Up to now, we have developed only receptors: recording machines with which to record and represent the world. The decade-long crisis of representation will be resolved only when we develop a technology of effectors. The act of observation is changing not only the perception of reality and the image, but even the real world. This is a basic proposal of quantum theory. If in our case the observer is a machine, then our reality is not only observer-relative, but machine-relative, too. The new observing machines, from satellite TV to computers, are not only changing perception and simulating reality (simulating life) – they are constructing reality. Ultimately, even our status as subjects is being altered by this observer-relative, machine-relative, reality. While in the classical world it was valid to say "know yourself" or "express yourself," in the world being constructed with the help of these machines the subject must also be constructed. Like the machines that can construct what they, and we, see, all we can do is "construct ourselves."

29 In Claude E. Shannon, John McCarthy, *Automata Studies*, Princeton University Press, Princeton, 1956.

30 *Pulsed Neural Networks*, Wolfgang Maass and Christopher M. Bishop (eds), The MIT Press, Cambridge, MA, 1999.

31 *The Brain is the Screen. Deleuze and the Philosophy of Cinema*, Gregory Flaxman (ed.), University of Minnesota Press, Minneapolis, 2000.

32 *Principles of Neural Science*, Eric Kandel, James Schwartz (eds), New York, 1981; Gerald Edelmann, Giulio Tononi, *A Universe of Consciousness*, Basic, 2000; David Chalmers, *The Conscious Mind*, , Oxford University Press, New York, 1996.

David Finkelstein[33] has shown that quantum physics can be considered a theoretical model for interactive media. Extending this idea further we can forecast the following relations:

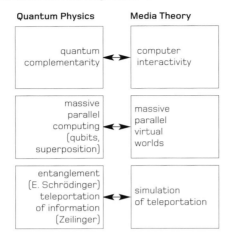

Quantum Physics	Media Theory
quantum complementarity	↔ computer interactivity
massive parallel computing (qubits, superposition)	↔ massive parallel virtual worlds
entanglement (E. Schrödinger) teleportation of information (Zeilinger)	↔ simulation of teleportation

Writing almost at the same time as Marey, the mathematician Josiah Gibbs in 1873 published an article entitled "A method of geometrical representation of the thermodynamic properties of substances by means of surfaces." It went unnoticed by the cultural world. The point was to find a method of geometrically representing the thermodynamic properties of living organisms. He did not want to represent motion, but energy. He realized that with the construction of surfaces you can get some idea how to represent a stream of energy. This article introduced the so-called "Gibbs phase state," which shows that space is not something continuous, but a statistical property.

Richard Feynman understood Gibbs' idea, and took it one step further. He saw that the viewpoint of an initial value has to be replaced by the state of a system. The state of a system is represented by a vector in its evolution time. Gibbs worked with geometry only; Feynman said we must also consider evolution time. Instead of considering the motion of a particle from a point A in space to a point B, we have to replace it with phase space. It has to be defined not as motion, but as transitions between different states. The idea is brilliant: No longer do we see in the manner of nineteenth-century recording machines that analyze motion in frames, but instead see motion as a dynamic system in which we must distinguish state transitions. If one state transition occurs, then the whole system changes to another phase state. This space can never really be measured; it can only be given a probabilistic value.

Many probabilities for possible paths exist. A path taken by one particle is merely a probabilistic average of (all) possible paths. Feynman introduced what is now called the "Feynman path integral": an integral of all potential paths. For makers of movies, of optical works, it means the observer has to be given the chance of choosing the possible paths. The tendency to give the observer an undefined field, a probabilistic of different paths, already exist. The Feynman integral of the probabilistic values is stored in the computer and the observer acts like a particle in selecting phase-state transitions.

If you recognize that the source of the image is a vast field of probabilities, you begin to realize how many people might be able to see different movies at the same time. My vision is that every member of a cinema audience would be able to watch a different movie. Impossible to put into practice with images on celluloid, the idea is feasible with virtual information storage in a quantum computer, which enables stochastic access to the information. Each viewer has a set of variables which, although finite, allows him to see a different movie resulting from the same stock of probabilistic values. This idea applies the Feynman integral to the optical field and needs the performance capabilities of the quantum computer,[34] which will replace electronic computers in the future. The new field of quantum information, with its strange attractions like superposition and entanglement,[35] permit the utopian vision of a totally new, cinematic imaginary with no local restrictions.

Kathryn Bigelow's admirable film *Strange Days* (1995, scenario by James Cameron and Jay Cockes) already sketches out such a quantum cinema of the future with extremely advanced interface technology involving the direct attachment of the brain, and shows a cinematic apparatus which substitutes all former historical cinematographic machines, a subjective camera-eye of a kind never seen before: one enabling us to see with one another's eyes. A cinematic apparatus called "Squid" (Superconducting Quantum Interference Device) built on the "Josephson junction" is the first example of quantum cinema. A similar visual apparatus appears in *Brainstorm*, 1983, by Douglas Trumbull.

Kathryn Bigelow
Strange Days
USA, 1995
color, sound
139 min
film still
© 20th Century Fox

The new computer technology will enable the cinematographic code to develop from a 1:1 relationship (one viewer – one film – one place – one time) into a multi-user virtual environment (x viewers – x films – x places – x times). The Many-Worlds Interpretation of quantum mechanics[36] models a future of many virtual worlds, massively parallel computed and "entangled" (see *The Matrix*, 1999). In this dispersed Virtual Reality, hundreds of spectators will act not only in front of the screen but behind it, too. Net technology is already providing a new stage for communication, a new kind of projector. Just as the twentieth century standardized nineteenth-century image-technological inventions and turned them into a mass industry, the twenty-first century must make the advanced image technology of the twentieth century compatible with mass usage. Contemporary VR technology is strikingly reminiscent of the first nineteenth-century cinema, which was characterized by singular reception. The example of the Phenakistoscope enables us to grasp the principle of singular reception: one person watches one film in one place at one time. Projection made collective simultaneous perception possible: x people watch one film in one place at one time. Television brought about non-local perception: x people watch one film in x places at one time. Video and CD-ROM enable either singular or collective perception, simultaneous as well as non-simultaneous: x/one viewer(s) watch x/one film(s) in x/one places(s) at x/one time(s). In the late twentieth century, the digital image started from scratch.

33 D. and S. R. Finkelstein, "Computer interactivity simulates quantum complementarity," in *Int. J. Theor. Phys.*, 22, 1983, pp. 753–779.

34 David Deutsch, "Quantum Theory: The Church-Turing Principle and the Universal Quantumcomputer," in *Proc. Royal Society of London*, vol. 400, 1818, pp. 97–117, 1985.

35 *The Many-Worlds Interpretation of Quantum Mechanics*, B. S. DeWitt, N. Graham (eds), Princeton, 1973.

36 Erwin Schrödinger, "Die gegenwärtige Situation in der Quantenmechanik" [The Present Situation in Quantum Mechanics], in *Naturwissenschaften*, 23, 1935.

	Viewer(s)	Place(s)	Time(s)	Film(s)
19th century				
Phenakistoscope single spectator	1	1	1	1
Projector simultaneous collective perception	x	1	1	1
20th century				
TV simultaneously distri- buted non-local	x	x	1	1
Video, CD-ROM	x/1	x/1	x/1	x/1
Virtual Reality single spectator	1	1	1	1
21st century				
Distributed non-local Multi-User Virtual Environment (MUVE) anybody anywhere any time	x	x	x	x
			X = any quantity	

The head-mounted display of VR systems returned to the singular local reception of nineteenth-century cinema: one person sees one film in one place at one time. In order to survive, VR technology must appropriate the collective, non-simultaneous, non-local forms of perception already known from television and radio.

The sound tele-technology we know from mobile phones (compare wearable ubiquitous computing) will supply the music of the future, which will seize the tele-technology of the image as well. The image technologies of the future will allow anybody to see any movie in any place at any time. The formula for future image technology reads: anybody, anywhere, any time. However, the decisive point is that with this form of collective interaction (instead of the present-day individual interface technology) the observer does not remain an external observer, as in the case of film, but becomes an internal observer. He will participate in, and thereby change, the image-worlds. This entry into the image-world will trigger reactions in the sense of the co-variant model not only in multiple parallel image-worlds but also in the real world. The relation between image-world and reality will be multiple and reversible, and the observer himself will be the interface between an artificial virtual world and the real world. Controlled by the internal observer, events in the real world will affect the virtual world. Events in the virtual world, also controlled by the observer, will affect the real world and parallel virtual worlds.

massive parallel worlds

reversible

The observer will cut from one narrative to another. Instead of linear narration, multiple users will create instant multiple narratives. Interactions between the observer and the image world will become bi-directional. A cause in the real world will have an effect in the virtual world and, conversely, a cause in the virtual world will have an effect in another parallel virtual world or in the real world. Observer-controlled interactions between real and virtual worlds and between different parallel virtual worlds in computer or Net-based installations enable the spectator to be the new author, the new cameraman or camerawoman, the new cutter, the new narrator. In the multimedia installations of the future, the observer will be the narrator, either locally or, via the Net, by remote control. Through their navigation, the observers will create new forms of narration in Net- or computer-based installations.

The convergence of film, video, television and Internet offers a historic occasion to expand and revolutionize the cinematographic code. The horizon of the new digital image is already being built by multiple projections supporting multiple narration techniques, by immersive image technologies from CAVE to online games and other distributed VR technologies. Above all, however, image technology of the future will be shaped by massive parallel virtual worlds (MUVEs = multi-user virtual environments) which are tele-correlated or "entangled." The idea of wireless or online MUVEs is strongly supported by the strangest features of quantum physics: non-locality and entanglement. Einstein, following Newton, did not believe in "actions at a distance." Quantum theory predicted that pairs of photons behave identically in correlated measurements, and that is why the photons are said to be "entangled": it seems that measuring one instantly "influences" the outcome of a measurement of the other, no matter how far apart they are. Einstein called this behavior "spooky action at a distance." In 1964, John Bell showed that this behavior theoretically exists.[37] The apparent ability of quantum systems to act at a distance is known as nonlocality. Experiments by Clauser, Aspect and Zeilinger[38] confirmed the entangled, supercorrelated nature of the two-photon state, the possibility of interactions between remote measuring devices. In distributed or dislocated interactive virtual worlds, we will find the same inseparability. The interaction will not only be unidirectional from observer to image, from real to virtual, but also bi-directional – from the virtual back to the real, from the image back to the observer. Reversible computing will allow reversible relations between real space and image space. This interaction will not be locally bound (as was the case even with computer-assisted interaction), but correlative between distant virtual worlds, or between dislocated real and virtual worlds. The structure of non-local communication will be assisted by intelligent virtual agents or assistants, from GPS (Global Positioning Systems) to WAP mobile phones. These intelligent image systems will be a next step toward liberating humanity from the natural prison of space and time.

37 John S. Bell, "On the Einstein Podolski Rosen Paradox," in *Physics*, 1, 1964, pp. 195–200.

38 St. J. Freedman and J. F. Clauser, *Physical Review Letters*, 28, pp. 938–941, 1972; Alain Aspect, *Physical Review*, D 14, 1976, pp. 1944–1951; Greenberger, M. Horne and A. Zeilinger, in *Bell's Theorem, Quantum Theory, and Conceptions of the Universe*, M. Kafatos (ed.), Kluwer, Dordrecht, 1989.

APPENDIX

Notes on the Artists

Eija-Liisa Ahtila
born in Hämeenlinna, Finland in 1959, lives in Helsinki. She studied film in Helsinki, California and London. Her films and video installations play with genres such as feature and documentary, music videos, and commercials. Ahtila shows her works as multiple projections in art spaces, and as films in theater and on television. Based on documentation and research, Ahtila's narratives often deal with borderline situations, observing them with humor and sensitivity. She has exhibited widely, including shows at the Kunsthalle, Zurich; the gallery of Klemens Gasser & Tanja Grunert, New York; Tate Modern, London; KIASMA Museum of Contemporary Art, Helsinki.

Martin Arnold
born in Vienna in 1959, studied psychology and art history at the University of Vienna. He has been a freelance filmmaker since 1988. Arnold was visiting professor at the University of Wisconsin in Milwaukee (1995), visiting professor at the San Francisco Art Institute (1996–97), and guest professor at the Academy of Fine Arts, Frankfurt/M. (1998–99). His films and installations were shown internationally at exhibitions and festivals. His work was showcased in the exhibition "Martin Arnold – Deanimated" at the Kunsthalle, Vienna. Arnold's films *Alone*, *Life Wastes Andy Hardy*, *passage à l'acte* and *pièce touchée* were awarded several prizes, and for his entire oeuvre he received the Austrian Würdigungspreis für Filmkunst (1994).

Rosa Barba
born in 1972, studied at the Cologne Academy of Media Arts, and is currently working at the Rijksakademie van Beeldende Kunsten in Amsterdam. Her films and videos have been shown at several international festivals; solo exhibitions include shows at the c³-gallery, Budapest; Medienturm, Graz; Ancient Gallery, Cinematexas, Austin; artothek, Cologne; galleria miro quesadas, Lima, Peru. At present she is exhibiting at the Kunsthalle Düsseldorf (together with Jeanne Faust und Jennifer Nelson). Her work was also presented at Art Cologne and the shows "wie man sieht," Museum Ludwig Cologne; "screen-savers," Contemporary Art Museum, London; "suppose," Kaaitheatre, Brussels; "ex teresa arte actual," Mexico City. Barba has won several prizes and grants. *Off sites and "sets,"* a presentation of Barba's work including several essays, was published in 2003 by Walther König Verlag, Cologne.

Judith Barry
is an artist and writer whose work crosses a number of disciplines: performance, installation, film/video, sculpture, photography, new media. She has exhibited internationally at such venues as the Venice Biennial of Art/Architecture, Sao Paolo Biennial, Whitney Biennial, Nagoya Biennial, Cairo Biennial, Carnegie International, Australian Biennial, among others. In 2000 she won the Kiesler Prize for Architecture and the Arts, and in 2001 received the award for "Best Pavilion" at the Cairo Biennial. She is currently working on a book about art and technology, several installation projects, and a web-based work.

Zoe Beloff
grew up in Edinburgh, Scotland. She studied painting and art history at Edinburgh University and College of Art. In 1980 she moved to New York, where she received an MFA in film from Columbia University. She works with a variety of cinematic imagery: film, stereoscopic projection performance, and interactive media. Her projects are philosophical toys, objects to think with and through, more or less tangible. Her desire to communicate with the spirits of the past led her back to early cinema, uncovering links between nineteenth-century technologies and the digital realm. Her work has been exhibited internationally. Venues include: The Museum of Modern Art, The New York Film Festival, Rotterdam Film Festival, Pacific Film Archives and the Centre Georges Pompidou, Paris.

Maurice Benayoun
born in 1957, teaches art video and new media at the University of Paris 1. 1981–1987: numerous video works. 1987: co-founder of Z-A (Paris). 1990–1993: director of *The Quarxs*, the first HDTV CG series, co-written by François Schuiten. 1993: awarded *Villa Medicis Hors Les Murs* prize by the French Foreign Ministry for his *Art After Museum* project, a contemporary art collection in virtual reality. Since 1993 he has created numerous VR and interactive art installations widely exhibited and distinguished at international events. The *Tunnel Under the Atlantic* (1995) was a televirtual project linking the Centre Georges Pompidou, Paris, and the Museum of Contemporary Art, Montreal. In 1998, he received the Golden Nica, Prix Ars Electronica, Interactive Art category for *World Skin, a Photographic Safari into the Land of War*. Maurice Benayoun is co-founder and co-director of the CITU research center (*Création Interactive Transdisciplinaire Universitaire*). More information about his work at http://www.moben.net

Thomas Beth
born in 1949, studied mathematics, physics and medicine in Göttingen and Ohio. He gained a PhD in mathematics from Erlangen University (1978), and subsequently the title Dr. Ing. habil. in computer science (1984). He was professor of computer science at London University and head of the Department of Computer Science and Statistics at Royal Holloway College, then moved to Karlsruhe to chair Europe's largest department of computer science. In 1988, he was also appointed director of the newly founded European Institute for System Security (E.I.S.S.). Over the past decades he has built up the Institute of Algorithms and Cognitive Systems (IAKS), devoted to synergizing the fields of computer algebra, combinatorics, cryptography, coding and information theory, signal processing and algorithm theory to produce new applications in electronics, optics and quantum information processing.

BIOS team
Jaanis Garancs (http://www.garancs.net), Sven Hahne (http://www.khm.de/~hahne), Norman Muller (http://www.khm.de/~norman) and Thomas Tirel (http://tirelcorp.mine.nu) met during their studies at the Cologne Academy of Media Arts (http://www.khm.de).

The artists' individual and group projects range from experimental interfaces to audiovisual performances and VR designs. The BIOS project was premiered in 2002 during the "Vision – Image and Perception" show at the Mücsarnok Kunsthalle, Budapest.

Blast Theory
is one of Britain's leading artists' groups, based in London since 1991, with a creative team of three. Pioneering the use of new technologies within performance contexts, the group explores interactivity and the relationship between real and virtual space. Early works such as *Gunmen Kill Three* or *Chemical Wedding* drew on club culture to create multimedia performances that invited participation. Since 1997, the group's work has further diversified into online, installation and new media works such as *Desert Rain* or *Can You See Me Now?* Blast Theory was nominated for a number of awards including two British Academy Television Awards (BAFTA), and received an honorary mention at the transmediale in Germany in 2001. Blast Theory has been collaborating with the Mixed Reality Laboratory at the University of Nottingham since 1997. The group has been represented at art fairs and festivals including the Basel Art Fair (2001), Sydney Biennial (2002), Palestine International Video Festival (2002), Festival Escena Contemporanea, Madrid (2003) and the Dutch Electronic Art Festival (DEAF, 2003).

Jean-Louis Boissier
is a multimedia artist, professor of aesthetics (University of Paris 8, formerly Vincennes, now Saint-Denis), and director of research. Born in 1945 at Loriol-sur-Drôme, he studied mathematics and physics, after which he became involved in photography and experimental cinema. Since the early 1980s he has been a pioneer of interactivity in art, creating installations using videodiscs and computers, e.g. *Le bus* (1985), *Pékin pour mémoire* (1986), *Globus oculi* (1992), *Flora petrinsularis* (1993), *Mutatis mutandis* (1995), *Moments de Jean-Jacques Rousseau* (2000), *La morale sensitive* (2001), *Mémoire de crayons* (2001), and participating in the creation of various ex-

hibitions dedicated to new media art. From 1990 to 1996, he curated Artifices, the digital-arts biennial in Saint-Denis. From 1992 to 1997, he was curator of the "Virtual Review" at the Centre Georges Pompidou. At the Laboratory for Interactive Aesthetics, which he founded in 1990, he developed a series of videodiscs and CD-ROMs on the subject of digital images, e.g. *3e Biennale d'art contemporain de Lyon* CD-ROM (1995), or the *Actualité du virtuel* CD-ROM (1997) for the Centre Georges Pompidou (1997), and directed a series of artistic experiments in interactive narrative.

Jean Michel Bruyère
born in 1959, lives in Dakar and works as a filmmaker, director, writer, sculptor, photographer and graphic artist. He is founding and artistic director of "lafabriks" (*Groupe d'Intervention Artistique Internationale* – International Artistic Intervention Group), director of the "Ecole d'art Man-Keneen-Ki" art school in Dakar, and teaches at several other institutions. He has realized several works, partly commissioned by institutions in France and Germany, and founded and directs the LFK 1314, Electronic Theater of Marseille.

Luis Buñuel (1900–1983)
first studied science at Madrid University, where he met Salvador Dalí and Federico Garcia Lorca. In the 1920s he studied film in Paris, where he became assistant to the experimental filmmaker Jean Epstein and in 1928 collaborated with Dalí, among other friends, on the surrealist *Un Chien andalou*. After establishing his solo career with the anticlerical *L'Age d'Or* in 1930, he made the documentary *Las Hurdes* (Land Without Bread, 1932), and in the USA subsequently directed documentaries at the MoMA, New York. Buñuel made a series of films in Mexico in association with producer Oscar Dancigers, including *Los olvidados* (The Young and the Damned, 1950), *El* (This Strange Passion, 1952), and *Ensayo de un Crimen / La Vida Criminal de Archibaldo de la Cruz* (Criminal Life of Archibaldo de la Cruz, 1955). His later films combined a documentary mood with Surrealist qualities. The last of the more than thirty films shot by the

Spanish film director between 1928 and 1977 was *Cet Obscur Objet du Désir* (That Obscure Object of Desire, 1977).

Jim Campbell
was born in Chicago in 1956 and lives in San Francisco. He received Bachelor of Science degrees in mathematics and engineering from the MIT in 1978. His work has been shown internationally and throughout North America in institutions such as the Whitney Museum of American Art, New York; San Francisco Museum of Modern Art; the Carpenter Center, Harvard University; The International Center for Photography, New York; the InterCommunication Center in Tokyo. His electronic art is included in the collections of the Whitney Museum of American Art, San Francisco Museum of Modern Art, and the University Art Museum at Berkeley. In 1992 he created one of the first permanent public interactive video artworks in the USA in Phoenix, Arizona. He has lectured on interactive media art at many Institutions, including the Museum of Modern Art in New York. As an engineer he holds more than a dozen patents in the field of video-image processing.

Janet Cardiff
born in Brussels, Ontario in 1957, studied at Queen's University (BFA) in Kingston and the University of Alberta (MVA), and currently lives and works in Lethbridge, Alberta. Her artworks, whether installations or "walking pieces," are mainly audio-based. Major exhibitions include Hamburger Bahnhof, Berlin (2002) and the Canadian Pavilion at the Venice Biennial (2001) (both with Georges Buren Miller). She participated in various exhibitions such as "Sculpture Projects," Muenster, (1997); "Present Tense, Nine Artists in the Nineties," San Francisco Museum of Modern Art; "NowHere," Louisiana Museum, Denmark; "The Museum as Muse," MoMA, New York; São Paulo Biennial (all 1998), 6th International Istanbul Biennial, The Carnegie International (both 1999), the Tate Modern opening exhibition "Between Cinema and a Hard Place," (2000) as well as a project commissioned by Artangel in London. Her work is included in private and public collections in Canada, the USA and Europe.

YOUNG-HAE CHANG HEAVY INDUSTRIES

(http://www.yhchang.com) was founded in Seoul by Young-hae Chang (CEO) and Marc Voge (CIO). The operation combines text with jazz to create web pieces that for instance present a Homeric hero searching for sublime meaning in the insignificance of a life lived anywhere but where it seemingly counts; Asian businessmen and bar hostesses drinking the night away; a man who dies and is reborn as a stick; a Korean cleaning lady who is really a French philosopher; an illegal immigrant in a holding cell under the Justice Palace in Paris; a woman who sexually embraces corporate monopoly; an evening with Sam Beckett in a bordello; a night roundup followed by an execution; the Riviera; Saul.

Radúz Çinçera (1924–1999)

was a Czech filmmaker who also worked as a dramatic adviser and scenarist. He is best known for his work as director of the Czech Pavilion at the Montreal Expo (1967), where he presented his "Kinoautomat" combining theater and film elements in a groundbreaking interactive multimedia project.

Rosemary Comella

has been working as an interface designer, programmer and project director at The Labyrinth Project since 1999. Before co-directing *Bleeding Through: Layers of Los Angeles 1920–1986*, she developed the interface for *Tracing the Decay of Fiction*, a collaborative project between experimental filmmaker Pat O'Neill and the Labyrinth team. She also co-directed with Kristy H. A. Kang and Scott Mahoy *The Danube Exodus: The Rippling Current of the River*, an interactive installation with filmmaker Péter Forgács. Before joining The Labyrinth Project, Comella worked internationally on numerous digital arts projects ranging from interactive installations and CD-ROMs with various artists, to social research and cultural projects. She was instrumental in developing works including *Slippery Traces* and *An Anecdoted Archive from the Cold War* in collaboration with George Legrady and *MUNTADAS: Media Architecture Installations*, published by Centre Georges Pompidou, Paris.

Peter Cornwell

is artist in residence at ZKM | Center for Art and Media Karlsruhe, director of Street Vision, a London computing & design research company, and visiting professor at the University of Applied Arts, Vienna. He has been working with interactive computer installations for twenty years both as an artist and computer scientist, and has exhibited in institutions including the Institute of Contemporary Arts (ICA), London; the Royal Academy, London; ZKM | Center for Art and Media Karlsruhe. After studying painting, electronics and computing, he contributed to early computer graphics for television. As manager of European R&D at Texas Instruments he was then responsible for computer-aided design and robotic manufacturing systems. Later he formed Division Inc., a Californian virtual-reality company which developed virtual environments for architecture, pharmaceutical and aerospace firms. Cornwell worked with NASA on virtual-environment training systems for space flight, and was responsible for developing Virtual Design Environment, a virtual-space authoring system, before returning to research and teaching at Central Saint Martin's College of Art and Design and subsequently as director of the Visual Theory Group at Imperial College and the Royal Academy.

Luc Courchesne

was born in St-Léonard d´Aston, Québec in 1952 and lives in Montreal. He studied at Nova Scotia College of Art and Design, Halifax and later at the Massachusetts Institute of Technology, Cambridge, where he received a MSc in Visual Studies in 1984. His installation work includes *Encyclopedia Chiaroscuro* (1987), *Portrait One* (1990), *Family Portrait* (1993), *Hall of Shadows* (1996), *Landscape One* (1997), *Passages* (1998), *Rendez-vous* (1999), and *The Visitor: Living by Numbers* (2001). His interactive video works have been shown at museums including the Art Gallery of New South Wales, Sydney; MOMA, New York; La Villette, Paris; ZKM | Karlsruhe. He was awarded the Grand Prix of the 1997 ICC Biennale in Tokyo and an Award of Distinction at the 1999 Ars Electronica in Linz. Courchesne is Professor of Information Design at the Université de Montréal, and president of the Society for Art and Technology (SAT).

Jordan Crandall

born in 1960, lives and works in New York. Crandall is an artist, media theorist and founding editor of *Blast* as well as director of the X Art Foundation, New York. He has written on technology and culture for a variety of media, and lectures widely on the cultural and political dimensions of new technology. He holds a seat on the advisory board of *Social Movement Studies*, a journal of cultural, political and social protest published by Routledge, and regularly serves as visiting critic at institutions such as Columbia University. He was recently visiting professor at the École Nationale Supérieure des Beaux-Arts, Paris. He has exhibited at solo and group shows at The Kitchen, New York; TENT Centrum Beeldende Kunst, Rotterdam; Kunst-Werke, Berlin; LeMagasin, Centre National d'Art Contemporain de Grenoble; Whitney Museum of American Art, New York; Neue Galerie am Landesmuseum Joanneum, Graz; ZKM | Center for Art and Media Karlsruhe.

Max Dean

was born in Leeds, England, in 1949 and grew up in Vancouver. A graduate of the University of British Columbia, his interactive multimedia artworks addressing the relationships of museums with their viewers have been shown in solo shows at the National Gallery of Canada, the Art Gallery of Ontario, the Winnipeg Art Gallery, and the Ottawa Gallery. He has participated in numerous group shows since 1973, most recently at the ZKM and the Presentation House in Vancouver; his works were also exhibited at the last two Venice Biennial exhibitions. Dean has been awarded grants from the Canada Council and the Ontario Arts Council, and in 1997 won the prestigious Jean A. Chalmers National Visual Arts Award. His work is represented by Susan Hobbs Gallery, Toronto.

Dennis Del Favero
was born in Sydney. His numerous exhibitions include solo shows at the Stadtmuseum, Munich; ViaFarini, Milan; Neue Galerie am Landesmuseum Joanneum, Graz. He has participated in various major international exhibitions including "Sex and Crime," Sprengel Museum, Hanover; "Kriegszustand," Battle of the Nations War Memorial, Leipzig, 1996; "Der anagrammatische Körper," Kunsthaus Muerzzuschlag, 1999. He is co-director of the iCINEMA Centre for Interactive Cinema Research at the University of New South Wales, and artist-in-residence at ZKM. His multimedia work on CD-ROM has been published by Hatje Cantz. In 2001 he co-curated and co-edited with Jeffrey Shaw *(dis)LOCATIONS*, an interactive DVD-ROM and book. He is co-editor of the Digital Arts Edition series published by iCINEMA, ZKM and Bremen International University. He is represented by the Mori Gallery, Sydney and Galerie Andreas Binder, Munich.

Toni Dove
is an artist/independent producer who works primarily with electronic media, including virtual reality, interactive video installations, performances and DVD-ROMs that engage viewers in responsive and immersive narrative environments. Her work has been presented in the United States, Europe and Canada as well as in print and on radio and television. Currently in development is *Spectropia*, a feature length interactive movie for two players. Dove has received numerous grants and awards, including support from the Rockefeller Foundation, the Greenwall Foundation, the Langlois Foundation, New York State Council on the Arts, National Endowment for the Arts, New York Foundation for the Arts, The LEF Foundation, and the Eugene McDermott Award in the Arts from the MIT. More information is available at her website (http://www.tonidove.com).

Daniel Egg
was born in Vienna in 1973 and studied visual media design at the University of Applied Arts, Vienna. Since 1994, his work has encompassed graphics, photography, film, video, and media boxes.

He has participated in exhibitions including "schrägspuren," Haus der Architektur, Klagenfurt; "jenseits von kunst," Museum of Contemporary Art of Antwerp (MUHKA); Ludwig Museum, Budapest; Neue Galerie, Graz; "crossings," Kunsthalle, Vienna; Rudolfinum, Prague; "zeichenbau- real virtualities," Künstlerhaus, Vienna; "Rudi Gernreich-fashion will go out of fashion," Künstlerhaus, Graz; Institute of Contemporary Art, University of Pennsylvania, Philadelphia.

Shelley Eshkar
is a multimedia artist and experimental animator. He received a BFA from the Cooper Union School of Art in 1993, pursuing a multidisciplinary fine-arts education. Eshkar collaborated with Paul Kaiser on *Hand-drawn Spaces*, *BIPED* and *Loops* (all with Merce Cunningham); on *Ghostcatching* (with Bill T. Jones); and on *Pedestrian*. Eshkar's innovations in three-dimensional figural drawing and animation have aroused considerable attention in the fields of computer graphics, dance and architecture. He has lectured to such diverse groups as SIGGRAPH, the East Coast Digital Consortium, the Congress of Research in Dance, Jacob's Pillow Dance Festival, Berkeley's CalPerformances, the Brooklyn Academy of Music, and Harvard University's Graduate School of Design. Eshkar has received awards from the Foundation for Contemporary Performance Arts (1998), the Congress of Research in Dance (2000), and the Bessie Awards (2000). He was a Lubalin Fellow at Cooper Union in 1997, and artist in residence at MASS MoCA in 1999. He is currently exploring the artistic possibilities of high-definition lenticular imaging for public art.

Péter Forgács
born in 1950, is an internationally recognized film and media artist who lives and works in Budapest. His work was influenced by the Hungarian Fluxus and experimental film movement in the early 1970s. Forgács' essential works are based on found footage, for instance the fourteen episodes of *The Private Hungary* series, or *The Danube Exodus*. His work in various media in-

cludes the performances *Stanley & Livingston* (1979), *Inauguration* (1980), *Visit* (2000), and the installations *Video Kitchen Art* (1991), *Hungarian Totem* (1993), *The Inventory* (1995) and *The "Hung Arian"* (1997). Various European and US museums and universities collect his works, and he has won awards at a number of major international film and video festivals. In 1983, Forgács founded The Private Photo & Film Foundation (PPFF) in Budapest.

Tom Fürstner
studied economics; his skills in the field of multimedia were self-taught. In the mid-1980s he developed programs and programming languages linking hypertext to Artificial Intelligence. He planned, designed and programmed more than twenty CD-ROMs for various Austrian and international companies, and developed the first interactive television prototypes for Alcatel, Oracle and the BBC. As technical director and director of product development at ORF Online, he made the website of the Austrian Broadcasting Company one of the most successful in Europe. From 1999 to 2001, he was head of the ZKM | Institute for Net Development in Karlsruhe. Fürstner is currently visiting professor for visual media at the Institute of Experimental Design and Interior Design, Vienna and board member of Medienturm Graz, Austria.

Masaki Fujihata
has been a professor at the Tokyo National University of Fine Arts and Music since 1999. Renowned as a pioneer in the field of interactive art, he began as a digital artist for computer graphics and animation in the early 1980s, then produced computer-generated sculptures before turning to interactive art forms. Works such as his *Field-Works* projects, *Nuzzle Afar* and *Beyond Pages* (now in the permanent collection of ZKM | Media Museum, Karlsruhe) have been exhibited internationally. His networked art piece *Global Interior Project* received a Golden Nica at the Ars Electronica, Linz in 1996. His most recent interactive piece *Small Fish* was produced in collaboration with the composer Kiyoshi Furukawa and the

programmer Wolfgang Muench, and has been published on CD-ROM and DVD-ROM as well as presented as an installation and performance.

Jaanis Garancs
see BIOS team

Dan Graham
born in Urbana, Illinois in 1942, lives and works in New York. He works as an art and culture theorist, photographer, film producer, and performance and installation artist. After starting out as a gallery owner, he began to produce pioneering performance and video art in the 1970s, drawing freely on both popular culture and intellectual sources to give form to the artist's role as a critical observer of reality. He has exhibited internationally at institutions including Musée d'Art Moderne de la Ville de Paris (2001); Kunst-Werke Berlin (1999); Neue Galerie am Landesmuseum Joanneum, Graz (1997); EA-Generali-Foundation, Vienna (1995); MIT List Visual Arts Center, Cambridge (1994); and participated in group exhibitions including "media_city seoul 2002, Contemporary Art and Technology Biennial," Seoul (2000) and documenta X, Kassel (1997). Among other prizes he received the Coutts Contemporary Art Foundation Award (1992).

Davide Grassi
born in Italy in 1970, graduated from the Milan Academy of Fine Arts in 1994. His research investigates the creative possibilities offered by new media, Internet, digital photography, video and virtual reality in the fields of visual art, theater, and interactive installations. Since 1995, he has been based in Ljubljana, where he has collaborated with a number of artists and institutions. His work has been presented at exhibitions and festivals worldwide.

Sven Hahne
see BIOS team

Chris Hales
is Researcher in Interactive Moving Image at SMARTLab, part of Central St. Martin's College of Art, where he also teaches communication design in addition to running numerous "interactive movie" workshops in various countries. Several of his interactive films and CD-ROMs have been published and his work shown at film/new media festivals in-

cluding transmediale, Berlin; dART, Sydney; FCMM, Montreal; Videolisboa, Lisbon; Sheffield Documentary. His *Interactive Cinema* installation showing selections of interactive movies was shown at ARTEC 95, Nagoya; EMAF, Osnabrück (1995); IMPAKT, Utrecht (1996); Language of Interactivity, Sydney (1996); Oberhausen Kurzfilmtage, (1997); FCMM, Montreal (1997); CILECT Conference (1997); FUSE 98, San Francisco; Creative Futures, London (1998); Visual Extension of the Photographic Image, Seoul (1999); LAB7/Centre for Contemporary Art, Warsaw (1999); Electrohype, Malmö (2002).

Agnes Hegedüs
was born in Budapest in 1964. She studied at the Budapest Academy of Applied Arts, the Kunstakademie, Enschede and the Insitute of New Media, Frankfurt/M. In 1992, she was artist in residence at the ZKM | Institute for Visual Media, Karlsruhe. Her video works and interactive installations have been shown at numerous exhibitions and festivals, including Internationale Kurzfilmtage, Oberhausen (1991); Ars Electronica, Linz (1992, 1995); "Media Passage," NTT InterCommunication Center, Tokyo (1993); "The Butterfly Effect," Müksarnok Kunsthalle, Budapest (1998); International Media Art Biennial, Wroclaw (1999); "Vision and Reality," Louisiana Museum of Modern Art, Denmark (2000); "disLOCATIONS," Artspace, Sydney (2002). She won the Prizma Prize (Mediale, Hamburg, 1993) and the Sparky Award (International Media Festival, Los Angeles, 1994), and her work is represented in museum collections such as those of the ZKM | Karlsruhe and ICC Tokyo. Hegedüs currently lives in Australia, and is teaching at the Queensland University of Technology (CIRAC).

Axel Heide
see Philip Pocock

Lynn Hershman Leeson
born in 1941, works with media including photography, film, video and electronic sculpture, and has won a number of awards for her videotapes and interactive installations. In 1994, she was the first woman to receive the tribute of a retrospective at the San Francisco International Film Festival. She won the joint ZKM/Siemens Media Arts Award

in 1995, and was Sundance screenwriter fellow in 1998, in which year she also received the Flintridge Foundation Award for Lifetime Achievement in Visual Arts. She was nominated for the Independent Spirit Award in 1999, and received the prestigious Golden Nica Prix Ars Electronica in Austria. Her work is included in the collection of the MoMA, New York; the National Gallery of Canada, Ottawa; the ZKM | Media Museum, Karlsruhe; the Hess Collection, Napa, CA and others. Hershman Leeson is the editor of *Clicking In: Hotlinks to a Digital Culture* published in 1996 by Bay Press.

Gary Hill
born in Santa Monica, California in 1951, currently lives in Seattle, Washington. Recognized internationally as one of the most important artists of his generation, Hill has produced a large body of single-channel video and mixed-media installations, combining elements of video, audio, light, animation, and written and spoken text. Hill's video, installation and performance work has been presented at museums and institutions around the world. He has received numerous awards and honors, including the Leone d'Oro Prize for Sculpture at the Venice Biennial (1995) and the John D. and Catherine T. MacArthur Foundation "Genius" Grant (1998).

Perry Hoberman
is an installation and media artist who works with a wide variety of materials and technologies, ranging from the utterly obsolete to the state-of-the-art, from low- to high-tech and nearly everything in between. His work has taken the form of installations, sculptures, performances, concerts, plays and various uncategorizable spectacles. A retrospective of Hoberman's work, "Unexpected Obstacles," premiered at the Otso Gallery in Finland (1997), and visited ZKM | Center for Art and Media Karlsruhe (1998). His work has received awards including the Grand Prize at the Interactive Media Festival (Los Angeles, 1995); an Interactive Art Prize at the Prix Ars Electronica (Linz, 1999) and the Grand Prize at the ICC Biennial (Tokyo, 1999). Hoberman teaches in the MFA program at the School of Visual Arts in New York, and exhibits his work at Postmasters Gallery, New York, where his most re-

cent show opened in January 2003. He was a 2002 Guggenheim Fellow, as well as 2002 Rockefeller Media Arts Fellow.

Kristan Horton,
born at Niagara Falls in 1971, lives and works in Toronto. Horton studied at the University of Guelph and at the Ontario College of Art and Design. His work has been shown at solo exhibitions including "Oracle," Art Metropole, Toronto (2001) and "Congratulations on your new machine!" at The Library Gallery, Toronto (1995), as well as at the group shows "Loisirs," Glassbox, Paris (1997), "Between Machine and Story," Artcite, Windsor, Ontario (1995), and others. Prizes Horton has received for his work include the Governor-General's Award and the Ontario College of Art Medal (1996). Horton occasionally collaborates with the artist Max Dean.

Ian Howard
born in Sydney in 1947, is currently Dean of the College of Fine Arts at the University of New South Wales, Sydney and director of the university's Centre for Interactive Cinema Research. He has been a practicing artist since 1969, concentrating on the theme of the relationship between military, industrial and civilian populations, and their material and symbolic products. He trained as an artist and art educator in Sydney, London, and Montreal, and has worked extensively with Australian, British and US defense departments, including the Pentagon. He was the curatorial co-ordinator of Vietnamese artists and a National Advisory Committee member of Queensland Art Gallery's Asia Pacific Triennals. He taught visual arts in Australia, England, USA, and Canada and from 1992 to 1998 was provost and director at the Queensland College of Art, Griffith University, Queensland.

Pierre Huyghe
born in Paris in 1962, lives and works in Paris. After attending the Ecole Supérieure des Arts Graphiques and the Ecole Nationale Supérieure des Arts Décoratifs in Paris, since 1988 he has worked with various media including film, video, photography and installation. Film is often his point of departure for investigations into representation-saturated contemporary society. Since 1994, he has mounted solo exhibitions at institutions including

the Centre Georges Pomipdou, Paris; Musée d'art contemporain de Montréal; Museum of Contemporary Art, Chicago; Kunsthalle, Zurich; Santa Monica Museum of Art; Wiener Secession, Vienna. Huyghe also contributed to documenta 11 (2002); 48th Venice Biennial (1999); Sydney Biennial; Manifesta 2: European Biennial of Contemporary Art, Luxembourg (1998).

Paul Johnson
holds a Bachelor of Fine Arts from Pratt Institute, New York and a Master of Fine Arts from Hunter College, New York. He is currently artist in residence at P.S.1 National Studio Program in New York. His media work was shown internationally at a number of venues, including Transmediale, Berlin (2003); "Media City Seoul", Seoul (2002); "Joy and Revolution," Postmasters Gallery, New York (2002), "Open Source Art Hack," New Museum, New York and "Animations," PS1 Museum, New York (2001). More information is available from his website (http://www.pauljohnson.com).

Jon Jost
was born in 1943. From 1963 on, he made a number of shorts and fourteen feature-length films (16 and 35mm) ranging from fiction to documentaries and essays. Since abandoning celluloid in favor of digital video in 1986, he has completed some six full-length works as well as many short pieces and the seven-screen installation TRINITY. His work has been accorded retrospectives at the MoMA, New York as well as a number of film archives and museums around the world, and is included in collections and archives in London, New York, Lisbon, Madrid and Bologna. Jost presently lives in Chicago, where he continues to work in digital media (Contact: clarandjon@netscape.net).

Isaac Julien
born in London in 1960, is an independent filmmaker. He was a founding member of the Sankofa Film/Video collective, one of a number of film and video workshops set up in the UK in the 1980s to engage a new politics of representation in the aftermath of inner-city protest against British racism.

Paul Kaiser
is a digital artist whose work has been exhibited at institutions including the Lincoln Center, New York; the Centre

Georges Pompidou, Paris; SIGGRAPH, and the Wexner Center for the Arts. His awards include a ComputerWorld/Smithsonian Award (1991); a Guggenheim Fellowship (1996); and an Osher Fellowship at the Exploratorium Museum (2001). Kaiser's early work (1975–81) was in experimental filmmaking and voice audiotapes. He later created the virtual dances Hand-drawn Spaces (1998) and BIPED (1999), both in collaboration with Merce Cunningham and Shelley Eshkar, as well as Ghostcatching (1999) with Bill T. Jones and Eshkar, as also Loops (2001) and Lifelike (projections for the Cunningham dance Fluid Canvas, 2002–2003) with Eshkar and Marc Downie. Recent solo works include Flicker-track and Verge (both 1999–2000); Trace (2001), a narrative multimedia installation at the Brooklyn Academy of Music, and Inkblot Projections (2002) for the Exploratorium Museum, San Francisco. Kaiser taught at a number of universities, and had residencies at Cooper Union, UC-Irvine, and Ohio State University. Together with Downie and Eshkar, he is currently engaged in a three-year residency at Arizona State University dedicated to creating live motion-capture dance performances with the choreographers Trisha Brown, Bill T. Jones and Bebe Miller.

William Kentridge
was born in Johannesburg. He holds a BA in politics and African studies, and also studied fine art, mime and theater. He has been active in film and theater since the 1970s, working as writer, director, actor and set designer. He was a founding member of the Junction Avenue Theatre Company, Johannesburg and Soweto, and of the Free Filmmakers Cooperative, Johannesburg. After exhibiting his drawings and prints throughout the 1980s, Kentridge started a series of short animated films in 1989. He collaborated with the Handspring Puppet Company to stage Woyzeck on the Highveld (1992), which won several awards and toured Europe. His work has been featured in solo and group exhibitions internationally, and retrospectives of his films have taken place at festivals including the Edinburgh International Film Festival (1993); Festival du Dessin Animé et du Film d'Animation, Brussels (1996); International Cartoon Festival, Stuttgart (2000); New Zealand Film Festival (2000).

Frederick J. Kiesler (1890–1965) was born in Czernowitz. He studied in Vienna at the Academy and the Technical University. Following his internationally acclaimed theater-related exhibition projects in Berlin, Vienna and Paris, Kiesler was invited to New York in 1926, where he worked as a designer, stage designer and architect until his death in 1965. The central theme of his artistic concepts was "Correalism," his theory of the endless, multidimensional correlation between the human being, the arts, and space. Kiesler's artistic and theoretical œuvre is considered to amount to one of the most important contributions to the European and American avant-garde.

Norman M. Klein is a professor at the California Institute of the Arts and author of *The History of Forgetting: Los Angeles and the Erasure of Memory*, and *Seven Minutes: The Life and Death of the American Animated Cartoon*. He is completing his next book *The Vatican to Vegas: The History of Special Effects*. His exhibition "Scripted Spaces: The Chase and the Labyrinth" was shown at the Witte de Witt Museum, Rotterdam and the Künstlerhaus, Stuttgart. A cultural critic and novelist, he has published dozens of essays on media, urban culture, animation, architecture and globalization.

Andreas Kratky studied visual communication, fine arts and philosophy in Berlin and Paris. He has worked as a media designer and artist on a series of artistic and commercial projects, including the award-winning DVD *That's Kyogen* or the joint *Web of Life* project of ZKM and the Aventis Foundation. His art projects include *Postkarten für die Hauptstadt* (Berlin 1996), *Berliner – Tonale Porträts* (Berlin 1998), *mondophrenetic* (Brussels 2000) and work at other locations in Belgium, Germany and Spain. He is currently working at the ZKM | Karlsruhe and the University of Karlsruhe.

Darij Kreuh born in Maribor in 1966, lives and works in Ljubljana, Slovenia. Since graduating from the Ljubljana Academy of Fine Arts in 1996, he has specialized in sculpture and video. As a researcher and new-media artist, Kreuh is preoccupied with manipulation systems within digital technology. His work comprises workshops and performances as well as interactive, Net and sound installations. For the past few years, he has been involved in virtual-reality systems based on technology accessible to the general public. He cooperates with the laboratories at the Faculty of Information and Computer Science in Ljubljana and the Faculty of Electrical Engineering, Information and Computer Science in Maribor. He also organizes and runs workshops for virtual reality and simulation systems. His work and performances have been shown in exhibitions around Europe.

The Labyrinth Project is a research initiative on interactive narrative at the Annenberg Center for Communication at the University of Southern California. Under the direction of cultural theorist Marsha Kinder, this initiative works at the pressure point between theory and practice. Kinder has assembled a talented creative team headed by interface designer Rosemary Comella, art director Kristy H. A. Kang, and associate producer JoAnn Hanley. Since 1997, Labyrinth has been producing interactive documentaries and museum installations in collaboration with independent artists known for their narrative experimentation.

Marc Lafia works with film, computing and the Internet in producing single- and multi-channel video and photographic installations of varying scale. He is interested in the image situated and configured as system and event in computing/algorithmic procedures. His work is a sensual and philosophical consideration of representational systems and how these translate to our understanding of being, place and notions of time. He has exhibited widely at institutions and festivals, including The Walker Art Center, Minneapolis; The San Francisco Museum of Modern Art; ZKM | Center for Art and Media Karlsruhe; Centre Georges Pompidou, Paris.

George Legrady is professor of interactive media at the University of California. He has previously held appointments at the Merz Akademie, Stuttgart; San Francisco State University; UCLA; University of Southern California; California Institute of the Arts; the University of Western Ontario. His interactive installations have been exhibited at the Museum of Contemporary Art, Los Angeles; Kunsthalle, Bonn; Haus der Kunst, Munich; Projects Studio One, New York; The National Gallery of Canada; Palais des Beaux-Arts, Brussels; Centre Georges Pompidou, Paris. Awards include a National Endowment of The Arts Visual Fellowship, Canada Council Computer Intergrated Media Awards, the New Voices, New Visions prize from Voyager, and Honorable Mentions at Ars Electronica, Austria. He has produced several digital interactive publications.

Bernd Lintermann born in Düsseldorf in 1967, studied computer science in Karlsruhe. Now specialized in computer animation, he writes growth-process programs suitable for both scientific and creative-artistic applications, and in 1994–95 took part in Karlsruhe University's HUMANOID project devoted to the real-time animation of human figures. Since 1995 he has been developing "xfrog," an integrated modeling, animation and rendering system for complex geometric structures and especially organic objects, plants and growth simulation. A collaborator at the ZKM | Institute for Visual Media since 1996, he has also published and lectured widely on plant modeling and growth simulation.

Dirk Lüsebrink born in 1964, studied computer science at the Technische Universität, Berlin and is a founding member of Art+Com. His interactive works *Zerseher* and *The Invisible Shape of Things Past* were shown at Ars Electronica, Linz and ZKM | Center for Art and Media Karlsruhe. He won the Prix Ars Electronica in the "Interactive Art" category (1992, 1997).

Julien Maire was born in Metz in 1969, where he later studied art. His work has been shown in solo exhibitions at galleries in France and Germany, and also in "Les rencontres internationales de la photographie," Arles; "Hull Time Based Art," Hull; "l'atelier," Centre National de la Photographie, Paris; "International Symposium of Shadow," London. His Performances were delivered at venues including Site Gallery, Sheffield; "EXIT" festival, Maison des Arts de

Créteil; Transmediale, Berlin; Dundee Contemporary Art Centre, Scotland. He lives and works in Strasbourg.

Lev Manovich
born in Moscow, studied fine arts, architecture and computer science. He is an associate professor in the visual arts department at the University of California, where he teaches new media art and theory. He has been working with computer media as an artist, computer animator, designer, and programmer since 1984. His art projects include movies, the first digital-film project designed for the Web (1994), the conceptual software *Freud-Lissitzky Navigator* for navigating twentieth-century history, and the streaming novel *Anna and Andy* (2000). He lectures on new media around the world, and served as visiting professor at the following institutions: California Institute of the Arts, UCLA; Art Center College of Design, University of Amsterdam; Stockholm University; University of Art and Design, Helsinki. Manovich is the author of the successful book *The Language of New Media* (The MIT Press, 2001). More information is available at his website (http://www.manovich.net).

Chris Marker
born in Neuilly-sur-Seine in 1921, lives and works in Paris. Marker works with different media, including photography, writing, film, television, video and computer graphics.

Jennifer and Kevin McCoy
are media artists whose recent work plays upon the capacity of new technology to fragment, store and analyze narrative film or television footage. Their projects include sculptures, installations and Net art exploring ideas of genre, interactivity and automation. Their work has been collected by The Metropolitan Museum of Art, New York and The Speed Art Museum, Louisville. Recent exhibitions include solo shows at Postmasters Gallery, New York and the Van Laere Gallery, Antwerp. Their projects were presented in group shows at P.S.1, New York; ZKM | Center for Art and Media Karlsruhe; The Cornerhouse Gallery, Manchester. Their work was featured in *Artforum*, *Spin Magazine*, and *The New York Times*. They are 2002 recipients of the Emerging Fields grant from the Creative Capital Foundation.

Margie Medlin
is a media artist who develops film and video installations exploring the interrelations between dance and the moving image, in addition to working in the fields of film, lighting and projection design. Medlin studied lighting design at the Yale School of Drama (1989), and scenography at Central Saint Martin's School of Art and Design in London (1991). She received an MA in interior design from the faculty of Environmental Design and Construction at the Royal Institute of Technology in Melbourne (1998). Medlin has recently collaborated with Company in Space, Ros Warby, and John Jaspers. From 1999 to 2001, she was artist-in-residence at the ZKM | Institute for Visual Media, Karlsruhe, and in 2002 received the John Truscott Foundation Award for Design.

Norman Muller
see BIOS team

Jörn Müller-Quade
born in 1967, graduated in computer science in 1993. He earned his doctorate with research bridging computer algebra and diffractive optics in 1998. He then broadened his research interests to include cryptography, and from 1999 to 2001 worked at Tokyo University's Imai Laboratory in a newly created research group for quantum cryptography. In 2001, he returned to Karlsruhe University to lead a project on quantum cryptography at the European Institute for System Security (E.I.S.S.). In 2003, he was awarded an Emmy Noether fellowship in order to build up a research group for physical aspects of cryptography and long-term security.

Michael Naimark
born in Detroit in 1952, lives and works in San Francisco. Working extensively with field cinematography, interactive systems and immersive projection, he focuses on place representation and its consequences. A founding member of several media-based research labs, his art projects have been exhibited internationally. After graduating in cybernetic systems, Naimark spent the late 1970s at MIT and was on the original design team for the MIT Media Lab. Working as an independent media artist in the 1980s, he realized projects for the Paris Metro, the Exploratorium

in San Francisco, the ZKM | Center for Art and Media Karlsruhe and the Banff Centre for the Arts, Alberta, and also conducted research for different companies. In the 1990s he held a research post in arts and media at Interval Research Corporation. Naimark's recent art projects continue his exploration of place representation, now focusing on its relation to the Internet.

Mark Napier
was born in Springfield, New Jersey in 1961. He has been creating art exclusively for the web since 1995, combining his painting skills with fifteen years' expertise as a software developer in order to create "art interfaces," software that addresses issues of authority, ownership and territory in the virtual world. Napier was commissioned to create Internet artwork for the San Francisco Museum of Modern Art, the Guggenheim Museum, New York, and the Whitney Museum of American Art, New York. His work was shown at the Whitney Biennial (2002) and the Whitney's "Data Dynamics" show (2001), as well as at "010101. Art in Technological Times," San Francisco Museum of Modern Art; "net_condition," ZKM | Center for Art and Media (1999); "Art and Entertainment Network," Walker Art Center, Minneapolis; bitforms gallery, New York. He has participated in media-art festivals in Germany, Italy, Denmark and South America. See website presentation for more information (http://www.potatoland.org).

Werner Nekes
born in Erfurt in 1944. Nekes was professor at the Hochschule für Bildende Künste, Hamburg (1969–72), at the Hochschule für Gestaltung, Offenbach/M. (1982–84), and at the Academy of Media Arts, Cologne (1990–96). Since the 1960s, he has been holding seminars, lectures and film-theoretical symposiums at universities and art schools in Germany and abroad. He was co-founder of the Hamburger Filmemacher Cooperative, Filmbüro NRW, and the International Center of New Cinema (ICNC) in Riga, and co-organizer of the Hamburger Filmschau festival. His important collection of pre-cinematic objects and images has been shown at several international festivals and institutions, including the Metropolitan Museum, Tokyo; Mücsarnok Kunsthalle, Budapest; Getty

Museum, Los Angeles; Museum Ludwig, Cologne; documenta, Kassel (1968, 1972, 1977); MoMA, New York. Nekes' films have received awards at a number of international film festivals.

Marnix de Nijs

is a Rotterdam-based artist who explores the dynamic clash between bodies, machines and other media. His works include mainly interactively experienced machines that play with the perception and control of image and sound, as well as radical and humorous pieces such as his bulletproof tent and lingerie and his destructive performances. Marnix has presented his works at several national and international media festivals and worked with Time's Up_org, Montevideo_lab, Edwin van der Heide, V2_lab, ZKM, and the Krisztina de Châtel Dance Company.

Susan Norrie

was born in Sydney in 1953. She studied at the National Art School, Sydney, and at the Victorian College of the Arts in Melbourne (1972–76). After devoting herself primarily to painting in the early 1980s, she has increasingly incorporated media such as film, video and sculptural elements into her practice over the past decade. Norrie deals with the immersive aspects of film, and today investigates interactive forms of cinema. Her works have been shown in Australia and internationally since the mid 1980s, and have been included in numerous museum and gallery collections, among them the Solomon R. Guggenheim Museum, New York; the Museum of Contemporary Art, Sydney; the National Gallery of Victoria, Melbourne; and the Art Gallery of Western Australia, Perth. She lives and works in Sydney.

Pat O'Neill

received an MA in graphic design and photography from UCLA. His first short film was made in 1963 in collaboration with computer-graphics pioneer Robert Abel. In the 1960s and '70s, he taught photography at UCLA, and film and video at the California Institute of the Arts. In 1975 he founded the special-effects company Lookout Mountain Films. He has received grants from the National Endowment for the Arts as well as the Guggenheim and Rockefeller foundations, and was recipient of the prestigious Maya Deren Award

from the American Film Institute. *Water and Power*, his first feature, was a Sundance Grand Jury winner in 1990. Hailed as a touchstone for filmmaking of the future, it was shown at festivals including New York, Berlin, Telluride and London. *Trouble in the Image* followed in 1995, and has likewise been widely screened. Many of the fourteen avant-garde short films he produced between 1963 and 1982 are in the collections of major museums and remain on the international art-film circuit. *The Decay of Fiction*, his most recent film, premiered at the New York Film Festival in 2002.

OnesandZeros
see Philip Pocock

Tony Oursler

born in New York in 1957, studied painting at Rockland Community College and the California Institute for the Arts (BFA, 1979). He teaches at Massachusetts College of Art, Boston. Oursler's works in the mediums of video, sculpture, installation, performance and painting have been shown extensively in the USA, Europe and Japan, among other places at Metro Pictures, New York; MoMA, New York; Portikus, Frankfurt/M, and documenta, Kassel. His work is included in several collections, including MoMA, New York; the Whitney Museum of American Art, New York, and Saatchi Collection, London. Oursler lives and works in New York.

Philip Pocock
Karlsruhe-based artist, born 18.12.1954 in Ottawa, Canada.
Axel Heide
Stuttgart-based datatect, born 21.02.1971 in Schorndorf, Germany.
OnesandZeros
Oliver Kauselmann, Pforzheim-based student, born 26.02.1976 in Pforzheim, Germany; Thorsten Klöpfer, Pforzheim-based student, born 31.08.1974 in Backnang, Germany.
Gregor Stehle
artist based in Weiteswiller, Alsace, born 12.06.1973 in Karlsruhe, Germany.

Alfréd Radok (1914–1976)
worked at the 5th of May Theater in Prague from 1945 to 1948, and later for the Czech state film company. He was stage director of the National Theater in Prague from 1948 to 1968, and participated in Laterna Magika as stage

director and art director (1956–59). From 1968 onward, he was based in Sweden. As a director aiming to synchronize the dynamics of film and theater images, he made a major contribution to twentieth-century Czech theater.

Martin Reinhart

born in Vienna in 1967, studied at the University of Applied Arts, Vienna. While working as a film technician in Munich and Hollywood, he supervised film projects for Martin Arnold, Bady Minck, Günther Selichar and other directors. Reinhart's experimental films were shown at film festivals and exhibitions including Tampere Film Festival (2002); Dutch Electronic Art Festival (DEAF), Rotterdam (2000); Ars Electronica, Linz (1998). He invented the film technique tx-transform used in the eponymous short film (made together with Virgil Widrich). His multimedia projects were showcased at the virtual exhibition "wissen:schaffen," Austrian Academy of Sciences, Vienna, at the Technisches Museum, Vienna and in the scope of the "Skalex" EU projects. Reinhart was a lecturer at the AHS, the Wiener Kunstschule, Vienna, and the University of Linz. He is currently responsible for the Film and Photography department at the Technical Museum, Vienna, and working on two new films (*herzlose filme* and *Urgeräusch*).

Constanze Ruhm

was born in Vienna in 1965. She studied under Peter Weibel at the University of Applied Arts, Vienna, and was a postgraduate student at the Insitute for New Media at the Academy of Fine Arts, Frankfurt/M. In 1996/97, Ruhm was visiting professor for visual media and electronic image design at the Hochschule für Gestaltung in Offenbach/M. Her work has been exhibited internationally since 1986, including one-woman shows at Kerstin Engholm Galerie, Graz and Entwistle Gallery, London (both 2001); Museum moderner Kunst, Stiftung Ludwig, Vienna (1998); Venice Biennial, Austrian Pavilion (1995); Neue Galerie am Landesmuseum Joanneum, Graz, and Grand Palais, Paris (both 1993). Ruhm was the holder of the Wilfried Skreiner Award, Graz (2002), the Media Art Award for Women of the Austrian government (1999), the Schindler Scholarship Los Angeles of the Museum of Applied Arts, Vienna

(1997) and the Austrian State Grant for Visual Arts (1993). She lives and works in Vienna.

Zbigniew Rybczynski

born in Poland in 1949, has been directing films in Europe and the US since the early 1970s. Among the many prestigious industry awards granted to his work were an Academy Award (1983) for *Tango*, a special-effects Emmy (1990) for *The Orchestra*, the Prix Italia, the Golden Gate Award in San Francisco, and awards at the Electronic Cinema Festival Tokyo/Montreaux as well as awards from MTV, American Video Awards, Monitor Awards and the Billboard Music Video Awards. Rybczynski taught at the Lodz Film School, Poland (cinematography), at Columbia University, New York (electronic filmmaking) and was professor of experimental film at the Academy of Media Arts, Cologne. He currently lives in Los Angeles, where he works for the R&D team at Ultimatte Corporation (http://www.ultimatte.com) and runs his own company, Zbig Vision Ltd.

Joachim Sauter

born 1959, lives and works in Berlin. He was a master student at the Berlin Academy of Arts and at the Deutsche Film- und Fernsehakademie, Potsdam. In 1988, he co-founded Art+Com with a group of designers, artists, scientists and technicians. Since 1991, Sauter has been professor for digital media design at the Hochschule der Künste, Berlin and has been an adjunct professor at UCLA since 2001. His work was shown at Ars Electronica, Linz; Centre Georges Pompidou, Paris; NTT Inter-Communication Center (ICC), Tokyo; EXPO 2000, Hanover. His work as an interaction designer and researcher at Art+Com has earned prizes including the Ars Electronica Interactive Award (1992, 1997) and the German Multimedia Award (2001).

Michael Schmid

born in Stuttgart in 1967, graduated in computer science in 1996. He received a PhD for his research in diffractive optics in 2000. He is currently working for Bosch on the fusion of vehicle dynamics and passenger safety.

Jill Scott

was born in Melbourne in 1952. Her video artworks, conceptual performances and interactive environments have been exhibited internationally. After graduating in film, art and design from the Prahran Institute of Technology in Melbourne, she moved to San Francisco and gained an MA in communications from San Francisco State University. In 1982 she returned to Australia to lecture on media at the University of New South Wales, Sydney, where her work with computers led to 3-D animation and interactive art. She was visiting professor of computer animation at the Hochschule für Kunst, Saarbrücken in 1992, and received the Golden Nica for interactive art at the Ars Electronica in 1993. From 1994 to 1997, she was an artist in residence at the ZKM | Karlsruhe, and a research fellow at the Center for Advanced Inquiry into Interactive Art at the University of Wales in the UK, where she earned a PhD in media philosophy. She is currently a professor of installation design at the Media Faculty of the Bauhaus University, Weimar.

Bill Seaman

was born in Kennet, Missouri in 1965. He lives and works in Providence, Rhode Island. He received a PhD from the Centre for Advanced Inquiry into the Interactive Arts, University of Wales, Newport in 1999, and holds a Master of Science in visual studies from MIT. His work explores text, image and sound relationships through technological installation, virtual reality, linear video, computer-controlled laserdisc, and other computer-based media, photography, and studio-based audio compositions. His work has been shown in numerous international festivals, and was awarded prizes at the Ars Electronica in 1992 and 1995, as well as the International Award for Video Art from ZKM in 1995. His exhibitions include "Mediascape," Guggenheim, New York, 1996, "Portable Sacred Grounds," NTT-ICC, Tokyo, 1998, "Body Mécanique," Wexner Center, Columbus, Ohio, 1999. He is professor and head of the Graduate Department of Digital Media at Rhode Island School of Design.

Jeffrey Shaw

born in Melbourne in 1944. He has been a leading figure in new media art since its emergence from the performance, expanded cinema and installation paradigms of the 1960s to its present day technology-informed and virtualized forms. In a prolific oeuvre of widely exhibited works he has pioneered and set benchmarks for the creative use of digital media technologies in the fields of virtual and augmented reality, immersive visualization environments, navigable cinematic systems, algorithmic software techniques, and interactive narrative. He was co-founder of the Eventstructure Research Group in Amsterdam (1969–79), and founding director (1991–2003) of the ZKM | Institute for Visual Media, Karlsruhe, where he initiated, supervised and curated a seminal artistic research program that included the *artintact* series of CD/DVD-ROM publications, the European eSCAPE and eRENA projects, the MultiMediale series of exhibitions, over one hundred artist-in-residence productions, and the invention of new creative technologies such as *EVE* and the Panoramic/Linear Navigators. Shaw is currently the executive director of the iCINEMA Centre for Interactive Cinema Research at UNSW in Sydney (http://www.icinema.unsw.edu.au) and recipient of the prestigious Australian Research Council Federation Fellowship. He is also director of international projects at the ZKM | Institute for Visual Media and visiting professor at the University of Art and Media, Karlsruhe.

Karl Sims

studied computer graphics at the MIT Media Lab, and life sciences as an undergraduate at MIT. He currently leads GenArts, Inc. in Cambridge, MA, where he creates special-effects software for the motion-picture industry. His work and research includes several computer-graphics animations and interactive media installations, as well as technical papers on his work about virtual creatures and interactive evolution. He has exhibited among other places at NTT InterCommunication Center (ICC), Tokyo; Centre Georges Pompidou, Paris; Ars Electronica, Linz. He received a MacArthur Fellowship and numerous other awards for his work. See website for more information (http://web.genarts.com/karl).

Michael Snow

was born in Toronto in 1929. A painter, sculptor, photographer, filmmaker and musician, he studied at the Ontario College of Art. Since his first solo exhibition in 1957, his works of art and films have been shown at retrospectives and film festivals around the world. *Wavelength* (1967) established his reputation as one of the key filmmakers of the American avant-garde. Among the numerous distinctions received by Snow are the title Chevalier de l'ordre des arts et des lettres, the Toronto Arts Award, a Guggenheim Fellowship, a Los Angeles Film Critics' Association Award, and honorary degrees from several Universities. He was visiting professor at Princeton University and at l'Ecole Nationale de la Photographie, Arles. A recent retrospective of Snow's multi-faceted work at the Festival International Nouveau Cinéma Nouveau Médias in Montreal (2002), including the new feature-length film *Corpus Callosum*, a live concert, and the launch of his DVD-ROM *Digital Snow*, testifies to his continued creativity and importance in the field(s) of avant-garde art.

Jan Speckenbach
was born in Münster in 1970. He studied art history, philosophy and film in Munich, Karlsruhe and Paris. His multi-screen installation *Film Essay Black Maria*, created in collaboration with Rebecca Picht, was shown at the Hamburger Bahnhof, Berlin (1999). His *keyframe.org* project, co-founded with Birk Weiberg in 1999, was awarded the Heinrich-Klotz-Stipendium (2000). Since 2001 he has been working on various projects for the Volksbühne theater in Berlin, acting as video director for the video plays *Erniedrigte & Beleidigte* and *Der Meister & Margarita*, as well as for Frank Castorf's production *Der Idiot*. Based in Berlin, Speckenbach is currently working on a documentary about the Volksbühne theater.

Gregor Stehle
see Philip Pocock

Caspar Stracke
was born in Darmstadt in 1967, and has lived and worked in New York as a video artist and filmmaker since 1993. His work has been widely screened and exhibited in the USA, Canada, Europe and Japan. His feature-length experimental cycle *Circle's Short Circuit* featuring Avital Ronell (among other contemporary thinkers) was included in "The American Century," Whitney Museum of American Art, New York (1999) and shown at MoMA's "Cineprobe" (1999). He received a Rockefeller Media Arts Fellowship in

2000. His work (http://www.videokasbah.net) is distributed by Video Data Bank, Chicago and Light Cone, Paris.

Josef Svoboda (1920–2002)
was educated in Prague at the Central School of Housing Industry and the Academy of Applied Arts. After working as stage designer and technical director at various theaters, in 1970 he was appointed director of stage design at the National Theater, Prague, then in 1973 artistic and managing director of Laterna Magika. From 1969 to 1990, Svoboda was professor of architecture at the Academy of Applied Arts, Prague. Among the numerous distinctions awarded to Svoboda were the Légion d'Honneur (1993), the designation Royal Designer of Industry from the Royal Society of Arts, London (1989), the International Theater Award from the American Theater Association (1976), the Chevalier de l'Ordre des Arts et des Lettres, Paris (1976), and the First Prize for Stage Design at the São Paolo Biennial (1961). His work was shown in retrospectives at the Centre Georges Pompidou, Paris (1994) and the Quadriennale, Prague (1995).

Synthetic Characters Group
at the MIT Media Lab was formed in 1997 by Professor Bruce Blumberg. Over the last five years, the group has exhibited installations at SIGGRAPH (98, 99, 2001, 2002), Ars Electronica 2002, E3 2001, the 1999 NY Digital Salon, and a number of other venues. In addition, the group has published widely on topics including real-time learning for virtual characters, interactive cinematography, synthetic perception, and computational modeling of social behavior. The Synthetic Characters Group are: Bill Tomlinson, Marc Downie, Matt Berlin, Jesse Gray, Adolph Wong, Robert Burke, Damian Isla, Yuri Ivanov, Michael P. Johnson, Derek Lyons, Jennie Cochran, Bryan Yong, and Bruce Blumberg.

Tjebbe van Tijen
was born in The Hague in 1944, and studied sculpture in Den Bosch, Milan and London. He was involved in various happenings and expanded cinema projects in London and the Netherlands in the period 1965–68, and from 1973 to 1998 founded and curated the Documentation Center of Social Movements at the University Library of Amsterdam

(now at the IISH). In the 1970s and '80s he designed exhibitions in Vienna, Milan, Copenhagen, Dortmund and Hamburg on the subjects of ecology, urban conflicts and alternative culture. Since 1989, he has been making interactive installations devoted to historical topics, including *Imaginary Museum of Revolution* (with Jeffrey Shaw), *Orbis Pictus Revised* (with Milos Vojtechovsky) and *Neo-Shamanism* (with Fred Gales); these works were shown in Paris, Linz, Karlsruhe, Amsterdam, Prague and Tokyo. Van Tijen is based in Amsterdam, works under the name of Imaginary Museum Projects, and lectures widely on his currently research projects involving "psycho-geography," aerial bombing, visual language, and media history and education.

Time's Up
founded in 1996, undertakes applied research into the behavior of the public individual. From its base in the harbor of Linz, Austria, the group organizes situations that perturb the nature of a given everyday situation, allowing and encouraging altered and enhanced interactions among the public individuals visiting the situations. Major projects include the *Hyperfitness Studio* (Germany, France, Slovenia, Austria, Australia, Netherlands, Vietnam, Belgium) and *BodySPIN* (Austria, Germany, France) as well as smaller projects such as *Sonic Pong* (Australia, France, Germany, Hong Kong) and laboratories such as *Closing the Loop* (Austria, Australia, Portugal).

Thomas Tirel
see BIOS team

Steina and Woody Vasuka
over the past four decades have established both a powerful foundation for a rich and exploratory art practice and a collaborative infrastructure for the sustenance of communities. Founders of The Kitchen, they were at the vanguard of the alternative institutions in the 1970s, working in experimental media, sound, theater, video, computer and performance, and have sustained themselves as the embodiment of integrating technology into artistic work more as necessity than as novelty. Their individual investigations into digital technologies brought, on the one hand, what Woody calls "New Epistemic Space" and, on the other,

what Steina brings to the intersection between technology and both sound, installation, and performance. Their numerous awards and exhibitions demonstrate that their on-going work is both cogent and relevant. As Robert Riley writes: "Engaging the meaning of electronic language, exploring a new definition of space, the Vaslukas' work is fundamental to contemporary expression in video art and instrumental to the emergent fields of electronic media."

Stan VanDerBeek (1927–1984)
a pioneer in the development of experimental film and live-action animation techniques, achieved widespread recognition in American avant-garde cinema. An advocate of an utopian fusion of art and technology, he began making films in 1955. In the 1960s, he produced theatrical multimedia pieces and computer animations. In the 1970s, he constructed the *Movie-Drome* in Stony Point, New York as an audiovisual laboratory for the projection of film, dance, magic theater, sound and other visual effects. His experiments included movie murals, projection systems, planetarium events and the exploration of early computer-graphics and image-processing systems. He was awarded grants by, among others, the Rockefeller Foundation, the Guggenheim Foundation, the Ford Foundation, and the National Endowment for the Arts, and won an American Film Institute Independent Filmmaker Award. Two retrospectives of his work have been mounted in New York, one at the MoMA, the other at the Whitney Museum of American Art.

Peter Weibel
born in Odessa in 1944, was appointed professor of visual media art at the University of Applied Arts, Vienna in 1984. He was head of the digital arts laboratory of the Media Department of New York University from 1984 to 1989. He founded the Institute of New Media at the Academy of Fine Arts, Frankfurt/M. in 1989. From 1986 to 1995 he was artistic consultant and later artistic director of the Ars Electronica in Linz, from 1993 to 1999 curator at the Neue Galerie am Landesmuseum Joanneum, Graz. He commissioned the Austrian pavilions at the Venice Biennial from 1993 to 1999. Since 1999 he has been Chair and CEO of the ZKM | Center for Art and Media Karlsruhe.

Birk Weiberg
was born in Hanover in 1972. After studying art history and media art in Karlsruhe and Berlin, he completed a postgraduate degree in media art. Since 1995 he has been involved in a number of film and multimedia projects and contributed to publications on film and media art. His *keyframe.org* project, co-founded with Jan Speckenbach in 1999, was awarded the Heinrich-Klotz-Stipendium (2000). Together with Margarete Vöhringer he created the video installation *The Homeless Story* (2001) for "Bo01 – City of Tomorrow," Malmö. Weiberg is based in Berlin as a media artist and designer.

Grahame Weinbren
has been working in film and video since the early 1970s and was one of the first artists to apply interactivity to the moving image. His interactive cinema installations have been exhibited widely since 1984 at venues including Centre Georges Pompidou, Paris; Caixa de Pensions, Barcelona; Whitney Museum of American Art, New York; The Kitchen, New York; Museum of Contemporary Art, Los Angeles; Jewish Museum; Hallwalls, Buffalo; Walker Art Center, Minneapolis; Oberhausen Film Festival, Germany. His feature-length documentary *George* (made in collaboration with Henry Corra) was broadcast in 2000 on HBO, the American national cable channel. He has written and lectured internationally on cinema, interactivity and new technology, and his writings have been widely published. Weinbren is also an editor of *The Millenium Film Journal*.

Virgil Widrich
born in Salzburg in 1967, has worked on numerous multimedia and film productions. His first feature film *Heller als der Mond* [Brighter than the Moon] won several awards in 2000. His short film *Copy Shop* won twenty-five awards and was nominated for an Academy Award in 2002.

Maciej Wisniewski
born in Warsaw in 1958, studied in a PhD program at the Institute for General Linguistics and Computational Linguistics at University of Stockholm and holds an MFA from Hunter College in New York. Wisniewski's work focuses on the creative, social and political implications of the Internet, networks, and technology in general. His projects *ne-*

tomat (1999 onward), *metaView, InterSections* (1995), *Fetch-a-Sketch, TeleTouch, Jackpot* (1997), *ScanLink* (1998), and *Turnstile* I and II (1998) were shown at the Whitney Museum of American Art, New York, the San Francisco Art Institute (SFAI) and featured in on- and offline exhibitions at ZKM | Center for Art and Media Karlsruhe; Institute of Contemporary Arts (ICA), London; Walker Art Center, Minneapolis; MASS Moca, Massachussets; Guggenheim Museum, New York; Johannesburg Biennial; "ada" web.

Christian Ziegler
was born in 1963. He joined the ZKM | Center for Art and Media Karlsruhe as an artistic collaborator in 1993, and has produced award-winning CD-ROMs, DVDs and interactive installations such as the CD-ROM *William Forsythe: Improvisation Technologies* for the National Gallery of Canada, Goethe Institute, and Frankfurt Ballet. Ziegler has held a number of teaching posts in Germany, the USA, Singapore, Japan and the Ukraine, and won the "Young Arts and New Media" award, Munich (2001). In the capacity of artist in residence at ZKM since 1999, he has developed several interactive media-art projects, including *scanned I-V*, an interactive media dance environment, and *66movingimages*, an interactive road movie filmed in the USA in May/June 1998.

Notes on the Authors

André Bazin (1918–1959)
was a French film critic who greatly influenced the *nouvelle vague* directors. He wrote for many periodicals and magazines, among them *L'Esprit*, the general periodical founded by the personalist Christian philosopher Emmanuel Mounier, *L'Écran français*, a film journal founded during the Resistance, and *La Revue du Cinéma* (1946–49), the revived version of Jean George Auriol's *Le Parisien libéré*, as well as for *L'Observateur*, *France-Observateur* and *Radio-Cinéma-Télévision*. Bazin was co-founder of the important film journal *Cahiers du Cinéma* and established the movement known as *Objectif 49* and the Festival du Film Maudit, both intended to revitalize and intensify cinema and the related discourse.

Raymond Bellour
is a major contributor to contemporary French thinking and criticism. His writing has been devoted both to literature and film, including his book *The analysis of film* (1979) and several anthologies. In 1963, he founded the film journal *Artsept*, and in 1964 joined the Centre National de la Recherche Scientifique (CNRS). He conducted research into film history and theory as well as nineteenth- and twentieth-century French and English literature at the Institut d'Esthétique et des Sciences de l'Art. Since the early 1980s, Bellour has concentrated on new media and the relation between words and images, a new focus reflected in the exhibition "Passages de l'image" at Centre Georges Pompidou, Paris (1989), the books *L'entre-images* (1990) and *L'entre-images 2* (1999), and the MoMA catalog *Jean-Luc Godard: Son + Image* (1992). He is co-editor of *Trafic: Revue de cinéma*. A professor at the Centre Universitaire Américain du Cinéma in Paris since 1973, he has also acted as visiting professor at New York University and the University of California. He is currently director of research at CNRS.

Michael Bielicky
born in Prague in 1954, emigrated to West Germany in 1969. After studying medicine in Dusseldorf from 1975 to 1978, he traveled and photographed in the USA, and in 1980–81 lived in New York as a photographer and horse-cab driver. From 1981 to 1984 he was a freelance photographer for *mono-chrom* magazine. He acted as assistant to Nam June Paik, under whom he studied at the Dusseldorf Academy from 1984 to 1989. After setting up the new media department at the Academy of Fine Arts, Prague in 1991, he was a professor at that institution until 1997. Over the past twenty years, Bielicky has widely exhibited works based on video-communication military VR technology, leading to a number of scholarships and distinctions.

Jean-Louis Boissier
see Notes on the Artists

Neil Brown
is associate professor of art education and associate dean at the College of Fine Arts, University of New South Wales, Sydney. His research interests focus on the concept of practice and its enactment within design, assessment and artistic authenticity in the arts, and factors relevant to cognitive reasoning in art criticism. He is currently working on an Australian Research Council project investigating the role of critical ascription within interactive narrative.

Philippe Codognet
born in 1963, lives and works in Paris. Since 1998, Codognet has been professor for computer science at the University of Paris 6 and scientific advisor at INRIA (French National Research Institute for Computer Science and Automation). He was a senior researcher at the SONY Computer Science Laboratory, Paris (1997–98) and at INRIA, Rocquencourt Research Center (1990–98). His research concentrates on constraint solvers and constraint programming, concurrent constraint programming, virtual reality, and art and new technologies. He has lectured and published widely on these topics.

Glorianna Davenport
is head of the Interactive Cinema group at the MIT Media Lab. Trained as a documentary filmmaker, Davenport has achieved international recognition for her work in new media forms. Her research explores fundamental issues related to the collaborative co-construction of digital media experiences, where the task of narration is split among authors, consumers, and computer mediators. Davenport's recent work focuses on the creation of customizable, personalizable storyteller systems that dynamically serve and adapt to a widely dispersed society of audiences. Davenport's graduate workshop in multimedia production has been adopted by five international institutions. Her publications on subjects of responsive media, as well as her prototype works, have been included in international symposia, conferences, and film festivals. She serves on the advisory board of IEEE Multimedia, and has served on the boards of several start-up companies launched following initial technological invention at MIT.

Guy Debord (1931–1994)
was a French essayist and filmmaker associated with the Situationiste Internationale, an anti-art movement of café radicals that rose out of the ruins of Surrealism in the 1950s. Debord became one of their leading theorists. The political element of his work followed to some extent from his encounters with a very small but influential group of neo-Trotzkyists founded in 1949 by Castoriadis (Lyotard and Baudrillard were also members). Debord, published relatively little, once remarking that he "drank too much and wrote too little," but his slim critique of the alienation and commodification of consumer capitalism, "Society of the Spectacle" (1967), became the main text of the worldwide student-led cultural revolts in May 1968. His greatest works include the book *The Society of the Spectacle* (1967) and the film *In girum imus nocte et consumimur igni* (1978).

Dennis Del Favero
see Notes on the Artists

Oliver Deussen
graduated from the University of Karlsruhe in 1996, and worked as an assistant at the Institute of Simulation and Graphics at Magdeburg University until 2000, when he was appointed professor of computer graphics and media design at Dresden University of Technology. In April 2003, Deussen transferred to Constance University, where he is in the process of establishing a center for visualization and computer graphics.

Timothy Druckrey
is a curator, writer, and editor living in New York City. He lectures internationally on the social impact of electronic media, the transformation of representation, and communication in interactive and networked environments. He has edited numerous books on media culture, including *Culture on the Brink: Ideologies of Technology* (1994), *Iterations: The New Image, and Electronic Culture: Technology and Visual Representation* (1993), and is series editor for the MIT Press series "Electronic Culture: History, Theory, Practice" including *Ars Electronica: Facing the Future* (1999), *net_condition: art and global media* (2001) and *Dark Fiber* (2002).

Barbara Filser
studied art history, English literature, American cultural history, film and photography in Munich, Atlanta (USA), Aberystwyth (GB), and at the State Academy of Design, Karlsruhe. After receiving her MA in 1998, she worked as assistant at the ZKM | Media Museum and Exhibitions Department. She is currently enrolled in the interdisciplinary postgraduate program at the State Academy of Design, Karlsruhe and working on a doctorate thesis.

Ross Gibson
is recognized by major scholars in the field as Australia's leading digital-media curator and one of the country's foremost digital-media researchers. Gibson's experimental research is backed up by formidable expertise in the field of traditional filmmaking and as a theoretician. His filmmaking includes such works as *Camera Natura* (1985), *Dead To The World* (1990), and *Wild* (1996). His theoretical eminence in the field of cinema and digital theory has been demonstrated over the past twenty years in his regular writing for the publications *Filmnews*, *Art & Text*, *Art-Network*, *Editions*, *Cultural Studies*, *Meanjin* and *Photofile*. A collection of his more recent essays was issued as his second book *South of the West: Postcolonialism and the Narrative Construction of Australia* (1992). From 1997 to 2000 he wrote and directed the interactive installation and CD-ROM story engine *Life After Wartime*, which was funded by the Australian Film Commission and the University of Technology, Sydney.

Richard Hamilton
born in London in 1922, is a pioneer of Pop Art and one of the most influential twentieth-century British artists. After working as an engineering draftsman in the army during WWII, he studied at the Slade School of Art and subsequently taught at the Central School of Arts & Crafts in London and at Durham University. His works comment on contemporary life, politics, literature and popular culture. In 1979, the Tate Gallery in London mounted the first comprehensive Hamilton retrospective, which then traveled to the Kunsthalle, Bern. Since 1974, retrospectives of his work have been shown at the Guggenheim Museum, New York as well as the Städtische Galerie, Munich and the Kunsthalle, Tübingen.

Vít Havránek
born in 1971, is a doctoral candidate at Charles University in Prague, where in 1997 he received an MA in history of art. Since 1998, he has worked as a curator at City Gallery, Prague. In 2000, he co-founded the group pas – produkce aktivit soucasnosti (production of contemporary activities) together with Tomás Vanek and Jirí Skála. In 2002 he became project leader of *tranzit.cz* (an art initiative of the Erste Bank Group), and has since curated and organized numerous exhibitions, among them "action word movement space," City Gallery, Prague (1999); "Glued intimacy," (Prague, 2000), "Otto Piene. The Zero experience," (Prague 2002) and "Lanterna Magika," Espace EDF Electra, Paris (2002). Havránek, who lectures in contemporary art at the Prague Academy of Applied Arts, has published catalog essays on contemporary art and edited several books and magazines, amongst them *Artist*, *Detail*, *Documents sur l'art*, and *art press*.

N. Katherine Hayles
professor of English and design/media arts at the University of California, Los Angeles, teaches and writes on the relations of literature, culture, science, and technology in the twentieth and twenty-first centuries. Her most recent book, *Writing Machines*, appeared in November 2002. Her previous book, *How We Became Posthuman: Virtual Bodies in Cybernetics, Literature and Informatics*, won the Rene Wellek Prize for the Best Book in Literary Theory as

well as the Eaton Award for the Best Book in Science Fiction Criticism and Theory (both for 1998–1999). Her work in progress is entitled *Coding the Signifier: Rethinking Semiosis from the Telegraph to the Computer*.

Edwin Heathcote
is a London-based architect and writer. He writes on architecture for the *Financial Times* as well as specialist architectural and design journals, and is the author of a number of books, including *Monument Builders* (1998), *Bank Builders* (2000), *Cinema Builders* (2001), *Theatre London* (2001) and *Budapest: A guide to twentieth-century architecture* (1998). He spent some years in Budapest and published numerous articles on Hungarian architecture as well as the first English-language monograph on Imre Makovecz. Heathcote is a director of the design company izé, which he co-founded.

Sabine Himmelsbach
born in 1966, studied art history, medieval history and cultural anthropology in Munich. After working for galleries in Munich and Vienna between 1993 and 1996, she was project manager for exhibitions and symposia at the Steirischer Herbst Festival in Graz, Austria. In the capacity of exhibition director at ZKM | Center for Art and Media Karlsruhe since 1999 she has been responsible for shows including "CTRL [SPACE]. Rhetorics of Surveillance from Bentham to Big Brother" (2001) "Iconoclash. Beyond the Image Wars in Science, Religion, and Art" (2002) and "Future Cinema. The Cinematic Imaginary after Film" (2002).

Erkki Huhtamo
born in Helsinki in 1958, works as a researcher, educator and curator in the field of audiovisual media culture. He is associate professor of media history and theory at the University of California, Los Angeles (UCLA), Department of Design / Media Arts. His work as a curator has included the exhibitions "Digital Mediations," Art Center College of Design, Pasadena (1995); "Unexpected Obstacles – The work of Perry Hoberman," ZKM | Center for Art and Media Karlsruhe (1998) and "Alien Intelligence," KIASMA Museum of Contemporary Art, Helsinki (2000). He created the "media archaeological" installation *The Ride of Your Life* (1998), and has

directed and written several TV series, as well as serving on many organizing committees and juries for international media festivals, including Inter-Society for the Electronic Arts, Helsinki (ISEA 1994), the Interactive Media Festival, Los Angeles (1995) and Portraits in Cyberspace, The MIT Media Lab (1995). His writing has been published in twelve languages.

Susanne Jaschko

obtained her PhD in art history, and worked as a gallery assistant in Berlin. She has initiated a number of contemporary art exhibitions, for instance at the Ludwig Forum for International Art, Aachen. She became a curator of the transmediale festival in Berlin in 1997, and is now deputy festival director. She has sat on several juries for international media-art awards, and was in charge of program management for the monomedia conference at the Berlin University of the Arts in 1999/2000. Her work as a curator focuses on interactive media art and the digital image.

Marsha Kinder

chairs the Division of Critical Studies in the School of Cinema-TV at the University of Southern California (USC) where she has been teaching since 1980. She is founding director of The Labyrinth Project, an art collective and research initiative at USC's Annenberg Center for Communication, producing interactive documentaries in collaboration with independent filmmakers (Pat O'Neill, Péter Forgács, Nina Menkes, Carroll Parrott Blue) and writers (John Rechy and Norman Klein). Labyrinth's first CD-ROMs were official selections at the Sundance Film Festival and won design awards from New Media Invision and the British Academy of Film & TV Arts. Also a cultural theorist and film scholar, Kinder has published over one hundred essays and ten books, including *Blood Cinema* (1993), *Playing with power in movies, television, and video games* (1991) and *Kids' Media Culture* (1999). She was co-editor of *Dreamworks* (1980–87), and since 1977 has been serving on the editorial board of *Film Quarterly*.

Norman M. Klein

see Notes on the Artists

Bernd Lintermann

see Notes on the Artists

Scott McQuire

is currently a senior lecturer in the media and communication program at the University of Melbourne, Australia. He is the author of *Visions of Modernity: Representation, Memory, Time and Space in the Age of the Camera* (1998), *Maximum Vision: Large Format and Special Venue Cinema* (1999), and *Crossing the Digital Threshold* (1997). He has collaborated with photo-monteur Peter Lyssiotis on a number of projects published in *Camera Austria*, *Photofile* and *Architectural Design*, as well as the limited edition artists' book *The Look of Love* (1998).

Randall Packer

works as a composer, media artist and producer/curator. He focuses on the integration of live performance, technology and the interdisciplinary arts. As founding artistic director of Zakros InterArts in San Francisco, he has produced, directed, and created many critically acclaimed multimedia theater works. In 1999, on the eve of the new millennium, he moved to the US capital to promote the transformative potential of art and technology. For the ZKM "net_condition" exhibition (1999) he assembled the "Telematic Manifesto," a participatory, collectively-generated Net document that articulates a vision for the future of Telematic Art as a socio-cultural force in the twenty-first century. Formerly director of the San Francisco State University multimedia studies program and director of multimedia at the San Jose Museum of Art, he is currently professor of electronic arts at the Maryland Institute College of Art in Baltimore where he directs the Center for New Media. He is also first secretary of the US Department of Art and Technology.

Michele Pierson

received her PhD in the cultural history of computer-generated special effects in Hollywood science-fiction film. She lectures on film and visual culture at the University of Queensland, and is the author of the book *Special Effects: Still in Search of Wonder* (2002) as well as essays on special effects and science-fiction film in journals such as *Screen* and *Wide Angle*. Her current research project is the relation between

amateur, avant-garde and experimental film (1920 to present), the history of stop-motion animation, and film cultures.

Jeffrey Shaw

see Notes on the Artists

Vivian Sobchack

is associate dean and professor of film, television, and digital media studies at the University of California, Los Angeles (UCLA) School of Theater, Film and Television. She was the first woman president of the Society for Cinema Studies and is on the Board of Directors of the American Film Institute. Her work focuses on film and media theory and its intersections with philosophy, cultural studies and historiography. She has published essays in many anthologies and journals, as well as editing the two anthologies *Meta-Morphing: Visual Transformation and the Culture of Quick Change* (2000) and *The Persistence of History: Cinema, Television and the Modern Event* (1996). Her books include *Screening Space: The American Science Fiction Film* (1997) and *The Address of the Eye: A Phenomenology of Film Experience* (1992), and she is currently completing *Carnal Thoughts: Bodies, Texts, Scenes and Screens*, a volume of her own essays.

Gloria H. Sutton

is in the PhD program in art history at the University of California, Los Angeles, where her research focuses on the correlation between conceptual practices of the 1960 and '70s and contemporary new-media and Net art. Sutton is also a former Helena Rubinstein Fellow in critical studies at the Whitney Museum of American Art's Independent Study Program, and she currently sits on the board of directors of Rhizome.org (http://www.rhizome.org), a non-profit organization that provides an online platform for the creation, presentation, discussion and preservation of new-media art.

Stefan Themerson (1910–1988)

studied physics and architecture in Warsaw. After meeting his wife Francizka (1907–1988) in 1929, the couple jointly made a number of experimental films in the period 1930–37, including *Pharmacy* (1930), *Europe* (1931) and *Adventures of a Good Citizen* (1937). The latter film served as inspiration for

Roman Polanski's *Two Men and a Wardrobe* (1958). Francizka and Stefan Themerson's films played a leading role in avant-garde Polish cinema and in the development of independent experimental film in the pre-WWII era. After serving in the Polish army, the Themersons from 1942 onward made films in London – *Calling Mr. Smith* (1943), *The Eye and the Ear* (1944–45) – and in 1948 founded the Gaberbocchus Press. Stefan Themerson wrote philosophical novellas, children's books, poetry and essays in the 1960s and '70s, while Francizka Themerson worked as an artist and designer.

William C. Wees
is an emeritus professor at McGill University. The author of *Vorticism and the English Avant-garde* (1972), *Light moving in time: studies in the visual aesthetics of avant-garde film* (1992) and *Recycled Images: the art and politics of found footage films* (1993), he has also written numerous articles on experimental and avantgarde film. As curator he compiled programs for the Viper Film and Video Festival in Lucerne, the Impakt festivals in Utrecht, the Cinema de Balie in Amsterdam, the San Francisco Cinematheque, the Anthology Film Archives in New York, and the Maine International Film Festival in Waterville, Maine. He has been editor of the *Canadian Journal Of Film Studies / Revue Canadienne D'études Cinématographiques* since 1997.

Peter Weibel
see Notes on the Artists

Brian Winston
is an active journalist, documentary film-maker and writer. He began his career at Granada Television in 1963 on *World in Action*. He also worked for the BBC's current affairs department (*24 Hours*) and as an independent documentary filmmaker both in the UK and in America. He has produced one feature film in Canada. In 1985, Winston won a US prime-time Emmy for documentary script writing. As an educationalist, he has worked at the National Film and Television School of Great Britain, New York University, Pennsylvania State University, and the universities of Glasgow, Cardiff, and Westminster. He is currently dean of media and communication at the University of Lincoln. His book *Media Technology and Society* was voted the best book of 1998 by the American Association for History and Computing. His recent journalism includes work for *The Independent on Sunday*, *The Scotsman*, *Prospect*, *Sight & Sound*, and regular interviews for BBC Radio 4.

Gene Youngblood
is a theorist of electronic media arts and a respected scholar in the history and theory of experimental film and video art, which he has taught for thirty-two years. He is the author of *Expanded Cinema* (1970), the first book about video as an art medium, which inspired a generation of video artists. Youngblood has lectured widely and published extensively. He has received grants from the Rockefeller Foundation, the Rockefeller Brothers Fund, the National Education Association (NEA), the New Mexico Arts Division, and the New Mexico Endowment for the Humanities. He is also a consultant to the US Library of Congress, the Council of Europe, the J. Paul Getty Trust, the Metropolitan Museum, the Rockefeller Foundation, and the US National Endowment for the Arts. He has taught at The California Institute of Technology, the Columbia University, the School of the Art Institute of Chicago, and at University of California, Los Angeles (UCLA) and the University of Southern California (USC).

Dörte Zbikowski
received her doctorate for a thesis on primitivism. She was curator at the Hamburger Kunsthalle, ZKM | Museum of Contemporary Art, Karlsruhe, and Flick Collection, Zurich, as well as editor-in-chief at ZKM | Center for Art and Media Karlsruhe. She is presently curator and deputy director at the Kunsthalle, Kiel. Her publications concentrate on international contemporary art.

Siegfried Zielinski
was founding rector of the Academy of Media Arts in Cologne (1994–2000), where he holds the chair in media studies/archaeology of the media. He taught media studies at the Berlin University of Technology, and from 1990 to 1993 was professor of audio-visual studies at Salzburg University, where he developed the AUDIOVISIONS teaching, production and research department. He has lectured in more than twenty different countries. The most recent of his numerous books and essays, which focus mainly on the archaeology of the media, are *Audiovisions : Cinema and Television as Entr'actes in History* (1999) and *Archäologie der Medien: zur Tiefenzeit des technischen Hörens und Sehens* (2002).

Works in the Exhibition

Eija-Liisa Ahtila
Consolation Service
1999 / two-channel video projection on DVD-ROM, 35mm film /
23:40 min / collection Chara Schreyer, Tiburon, CA / courtesy Thea
Westreich Art Advisory Services, New York / © & produced by
Crystal Eye Ltd, Helsinki / © VG Bild-Kunst, Bonn 2003

Judith Barry
Imagination, Dead Imagine
1991 / five-channel video projection with mirrored cube / five
video projectors/speakers, five laser-disc players or DVDs, one
controller, mirror, wood / color, sound / 295 x 253.5 x 253.5 cm /
collection of Contemporary Art Fundación "la Caixa," Barcelona /
first exhibited: Fundación "la Caixa," Barcelona in "Savage Garden,"
curated by Dan Cameron / Judith Barry is represented by the
following galleries: Rosamund Felsen Gallery, Los Angeles;
Galerie Xavier Hufkens, Brussels; Galerie Karin Sachs, Munich;
Luis Serpa Galeria, Lisbon; Galerie Hubert Winter, Vienna

Zoe Beloff
The Influencing Machine of Miss Natalija A.
2001 / interactive installation / mixed media, video, computer /
dimensions variable / © Zoe Beloff

Maurice Benayoun
So.So.So. (Somebody, Somewhere, Some Time)
2002 / interactive multimedia installation / internet, VR binocu-
lars, video projection / dimensions variable / © Z–A; Maurice
Benayoun / musical composer: Jean-Baptiste Barrière / photo-
graphy: Laurent Simonini, Pleine Lune / software: VRetina David
Nahon, Z–A.net / web graphic designer: Stéphane Thidet / produc-
tion: Karen Benarouch, Z–A.net / thanks to Florence Benayoun,
Bernard Benhamou, Claudette Bribon, Elisabeth Castro, Eric
Deltour, Herveline Fabre, Qio, Florentine Rey, Franck Antunes, David
Bouhsira, Café le Moderne, … / with the help of the THECIF

Jean-Louis Boissier
La Morale sensitive [The Sensitive Morals]
2001 / interactive installation / table with infrared sensor device,
chair, CD-ROM / 80 x 70 x 60 cm / Centre pour l'image contem-
poraine, Geneva / © Jean-Louis Boissier / director: Jean-Louis
Boissier / literary research: Liliane Terrier / video production:
Maren Köpp / assistant director: Hajime Takeuchi / programming:
Jean-Louis Boissier and Jean-Noël Lafargue / typography:
Jean-François Rey / assistants: Philippe Donadini, Thierry Guibert,
Christine Voto / interface development: Christian Laroche /
furniture design: Alain Cieutat, AHA / production: Centre pour
l'image contemporaine, Saint-Gervais, Geneva (direction: André
Iten / administration: Brigitte Chapuis) / with the participation of
the Studio national des arts contemporains, Le Fresnoy and the
Laboratoire Esthétique de l'interactivité, University of Paris 8 /
special thanks: Éditions Gallimard, Alice Morgaine, Agnès B.,
Comme des Garçons, Dries Van Noten, Vivienne Westwood

Jean Michel Bruyère / LFK-lafabriks
Si Poteris Narrare, Licet
2002 / interactive installation using Jeffrey Shaw's EVE dome /
digital video footage on hard disc, 35mm Vistavision film, EVE
dome, pan-tilt projection system, interface / color, sound / EVE
dome 900 cm ø, 1200 cm high / duration variable, based on a 7-min
film loop / © Jean Michel Bruyère / music: Thierry Arredondo /
with: Fiorenza Menni, Issa Samb, Pape Camara, Mansour Guindo,

Abdoulaye Keïta, Ibé Konaté, Mamadou Lamine Sakho, Assane Sène,
Chérif Soumaré, Babacar Sy, Sada Tangara, Ndatté Ndiaye and his
company / produced by: EPIDEMIC (Richard Castelli); ZKM | Insti-
tute for Visual Media, Karlsruhe; LFK-lafabriks (Jean-Luc d'Aléo,
Nadine Febvre); CICV-Pierre Schaeffer (Patrick Zanoli) / co-pro-
duced by: Théâtre du Merlan; Festival EXIT – Maison des Arts de
Créteil; Festival VIA – Le Manège Scène Nationale de Maubeuge;
Fournos Center For Art and New Technologies, Athens / with the
support of: Ministère de la Culture Français (commision
DICREAM); Fondation BNP-Paribas; Concours du Centre Culturel
Français de Saint Louis du Sénégal // EVE 1993–2002 (Extended
Virtual Environment) / concept: Jeffrey Shaw / production man-
agement: Jan Gerigk, assisted by Andrea Hartinger / application
software: Adolf Mathias / hardware, software integration: Torsten
Ziegler / audio design: Torsten Belschner / projection technology:
hellblau / dome manufacture: Wülfing und Hauck

Jim Campbell
Church on 5th Avenue
2001 / custom electronics, Plexiglas, 768 LEDs / 60 x 80 x 8 cm /
courtesy Hosfelt Gallery, San Francisco / presentation with
support of Goethe Institut, Munich / with financial assistance of
the Daniel Langlois Foundation for Art, Science and Technology

Illuminated Average # 1 Hitchcock's Psycho
2000 / diapositive / 5.7 x 5.7 cm / Jim Campbell /
courtesy Hosfelt Gallery, San Francisco

Janet Cardiff
Playhouse
1997 / video installation / color, sound / 381 x 152 x 244 cm /
courtesy Sammlung Goetz, Munich

YOUNG-HAE CHANG HEAVY INDUSTRIES
seventeen works on the web
2002 / website http://www.yhchang.com /
courtesy YOUNG-HAE CHANG HEAVY INDUSTRIES

Peter Cornwell
MetaPlex
2002 / interactive computer installation / Linux cluster,
projector / dimensions variable / courtesy Street Vision Limited,
London / © Peter Cornwell

Luc Courchesne
The Visitor: Living by Numbers
2001 / interactive video panorama / Panoscope 360, SXGA data
projector, microphone, four amplified speakers / 350 x 150 x 150
cm / collection of the artist / © Luc Courchesne 2001 / cast:
man 1: Yokoyama-sense; man 2: Yamamoto Shiro; man 3: Wayne
Macedo; man 4: Philippe Chatelain; woman 1: Miwa Ikuko; woman 2:
Myokam Hiroko; woman 3: Virginie Lave; woman 4: Miwa Momoco /
screenplay: Luc Courchesne and Blanche Ballairgeon / director,
producer: Luc Courchesne / production designer: Myokam Hiroko /
director of photography: Franco Zoccali / sound engineer: Fuyama
Tsuyoshi / coordination in Japan: Myokam Hiroko / systems for
camera movements: Luc Courchesne, Franco Zoccali, Robert
McNabb and André Jetté / systems architecture and design: Marc
Lavallée, Etienne Desautels / programming of authoring software:
Etienne Desautels / authoring: Luc Courchesne / special thanks to
D'nardo Colucci, Jean Gagnon, Franklyn Joyce, Victoria Lynn, Sakane
Itsuo, Monique Savoie, Takashi Yoko, Heath Watts and Oka-san /

created with support from the Daniel Langlois Foundation for Art, Science and Technology; the International Academy for Media Arts and Sciences; the Canada Council for the Arts; Université de Montréal; Société des arts technologiques (SAT)

Max Dean and Kristan Horton
Be Me
2002 / real-time video animation, interactive video installation / custom software, video cameras, microphone, video projectors, electronic components, table and chair / dimensions variable, approx. screen size 213 x 335 cm / Max Dean, Kristan Horton / courtesy Susan Hobbs Gallery, Toronto / project coordinator: Dean Baldwin

Max Dean
Mist
2002 / three-screen DVD video projection / four DVDs, four DVD players, computer controller, three projectors, audio equipment / approx. 228 x 914 cm / Max Dean / courtesy Susan Hobbs Gallery, Toronto / animation: Kristan Horton / project coordinator: Dean Baldwin

Dennis Del Favero
Pentimento
2002 / five-channel interactive video installation / four projectors, four screens, twenty-two speakers, four surveillance cameras, eight infrared lights, one PC, five amplifiers, one CD player / color, sound / 18 min / 8000 x 8000 x 5000 cm / DVD version published in (dis)LOCATIONS (ZKM digital arts edition, 2001) / producer, director and designer: Dennis Del Favero / application programmer: André Bernhardt / writer: Stephen Sewell / composer: Brett Dean / sound designer: Tony MacGregor / stylist and designer: Karla Urizar / sound engineer: John Jacobs / voiceovers: Lenka Kripac, Matthew Edgerton, James Marshall Napier, Peter Kowitz, Tony MacGregor / actors: sister: Hollie Berrie; brother: Andrew Dalton; father: Thor Thorsen / compositing: Greg Ferris / produced with the assistance of Film Victoria's Digital Media Fund; the Digital Media Fund is funded by Film Victoria as part of the Victorian Government's Connecting Victoria policy, which aims to bring the benefits of technology to all Victorians / commissioned by the Australian Centre for the Moving Image / financially assisted by the Australia Council; the Australian Federal Government's Arts Advisory Body / presented in cooperation with the iCINEMA Centre for Interactive Cinema, University of New South Wales / special thanks to Fiona Bathgate, Jeffrey Shaw, Ian Howard, Ross Gibson for supporting the project

Toni Dove
Sally or the Bubble Burst
2002 / video, audio, and MAX/MSP and JITTER software on DVD-ROM / dimensions variable / Toni Dove / © Toni Dove; Bustlelamp Productions, Inc. / written, designed and directed by Toni Dove / distributed by Cycling '74 / programming: Roger Luke DuBois using MAX/MSP and JITTER software from Cycling '74 / music and sound design: Peter Scherer / actress: Helen Pickett / performers: Shelley Hirsch, Lisa Karrer, Judy Nylon, Eric Mingus, Gregory Whitehead

Daniel Egg
Box 3 "Dialog"
1997 / installation / Novopan, spy mirror, monitor, DVD player, cassette recorder / 180 x 60 x 80 cm / Daniel Egg / © Daniel Egg

Shelley Eshkar and Paul Kaiser
Pedestrian
2002 / 3-D digital animation based on motion-capture data / dimensions variable / 12:50 min, loop / © Eshkar and Kaiser / co-producers: Art Production Fund and Eyebeam / sound design: Terry Pender (Computer Music Center, Columbia University) / installation architect: Marco Steinberg (Graduate School of Design, Harvard University) / motion capture supervisor: Lisa Naugle (Dance Department, University of California: Irvine) / software support: Michael Girard and Susan Amkraut (Unreal Pictures) / Connecting Point Multi Media provided technical support / additional support came from Dancing in the Streets / with public funds from the New York State Council on the Arts, and the University of California: Irvine, School of the Arts, Department of Dance / with funds from the UCI Chancellors Distinguished Fellows Grant

Péter Forgács and The Labyrinth Project
The Danube Exodus: The Rippling Currents of the River
2002 / interactive DVD video installation in three spaces / b/w, color, 5.1 surround sound / dimensions and duration variable / courtesy Péter Forgács; The Labyrinth Project, Annenberg Center for Communication, The University of Southern California / website: http://www.danube-exodus.hu / written, directed and edited by Péter Forgács / the installation was conceptualized by project co-directors Rosemary Comella, Kristy H.A. Kang, and Scott Mahoy, in collaboration with Péter Forgács and Marsha Kinder / executive producer: Marsha Kinder / associate producer: JoAnn Hanley / sound design: Jim McKee / music: Tibor Szemzö / co-author of Forgács's Jewish exodus story on the Danube and original idea for a museum installation: János Varga / interface design: Scott Mahoy / digital compositing: Scott Mahoy, Ariel MacNichol and Adriana Quezada-Beruwen / programming: Rosemary Comella, Laurence Tietz / editing assistants: Jesse Cowell, Broderick Fox, Rebecca Rolnick, Monique Zavistovski / sound editing: Adam King, Robyn Bacon / sound engineer: Christopher Cain / research director: Zaia Alexander / website: Szilvia Seres, C3 – Center for Culture & Communication, Budapest / archival sources and support: Private Photo and Film Foundation, Budapest; Hungarian National Film Archive; Bessarabian Museum of Local History, Stuttgart; Hungarian National Cultural Foundation; Museum of Transportation, Budapest; Lumen Film – Cesar Messemaker / special thanks to the late Mrs. Andrásovits, the Ashkenazi family, Benny Goren-Grünhut, the Fano Family, Helmut Fink, András Forgách, Yehuda Tamir-Gros, Raoul Menzel, Ilse Friedlander-Menzel, Dalia Ofer, Michael Renov and Eliah Turner

Masaki Fujihata
Field-Work@Alsace
2002 / interactive multimedia installation / stereoscopic projection, stereoscopic glasses, interface / dimensions variable, 305 x 228 cm rear projection screen / co-production Masaki Fujihata and ZKM | Institute for Visual Media, Karlsruhe / © Masaki Fujihata / technical collaboration: Masaki Fujihata, Takeshi Kawashima / german-japanese interpretation: Shinobu Nomura

Thomas Fürstner
Waypointing Weibel's Wien
2002 / DVD / courtesy Thomas Fürstner

621

Chris Hales
One-Person Touchscreen Cinema Showing
Fourteen Interactive Movies
1995-2002 / digital video installation /
metal stand, plain-glass touchscreen, various electronics /
200 x 150 x 150 cm / Chris Hales / © Chris Hales

Vít Havránek
Pioneers of Interactive Czech Films (50s–60s)
2002 / DVD of Czech films / compiled by Vít Havránek
on the basis of the following films:

Author/Producer unknown
Laterna Magika
1958 / courtesy CZech Television

Vladimìr Tosek
Laterna Magika
1967 / Expo Montreal / camera: Jan Eisner /
courtesy CZech Television

Vladimìr Tosek
Kinoautomat
1967 / Expo Montreal / camera: Jan Eisner /
courtesy CZech Television

Vladimìr Tosek
Diapolyekrán, Stvoøenì svìta
1967 / Expo Montreal / courtesy CZech Television

These films were originally shown at the "Laterna Magika" ex-
hibition at Espace EDF Electra, Paris, organized by Laterna Magika
Fondation EDF, Paris Musées, AFFA, Bohemia Magica, and through
the research efforts of curator Vít Havránek. Special thanks to
Laterna Magika Foundation EDF, Paris Musées, AFFA, Bohemia
Magica.

Agnes Hegedüs
Their Things Spoken
2001 / interactive DVD / published in (dis)LOCATIONS (ZKM
digital arts edition, 2001) / co-production Agnes Hegedüs; ZKM |
Institute for Visual Media, Karlsruhe; iCINEMA Centre for Interactive Cinema Research, University of New South Wales / concept:
Agnes Hegedüs / phase 1 data acquisition at the "Surrogate"
exhibition, ZKM | Center for Art and Media Karlsruhe, Nov–Dec
1998 / production management: Astrid Sommer / installation
design: Matthias Gommel, Jürgen Galli / object and voice recordings, photography: Nicole Blaffert, Simone van gen Hassend,
Marion Höfel, Claudine Profitlich, Margit Rosen, Sandra Voets //
phase 2 DVD-ROM production / programming, interface design:
Volker Kuchelmeister / voice recordings English and German:
Agnes Hegedüs / voice recordings French: Bernhard Serexhe /
Thanks to those 255 visitors to the ZKM "Surrogate" exhibition
who generously participated in this work.

Agnes Hegedüs, Bernd Lintermann, Jeffrey Shaw
reconFiguring the CAVE
2001 / © Hegedüs, Lintermann, Shaw, Stuck / music: Leslie Stuck /
motion analysis for music: Jonathan Bachrach / produced at the
ZKM | Institute for Visual Media / production in Tokyo: Boctok,
David D'Heilly / production assistants ZKM: Christina Zartmann,
Jan Gerigk, Derek Hauffen / reconFiguring the CAVE is a modified

version of conFiguring the CAVE (1997) which was commissioned for
the collection of the NTT InterCommunication Centre Tokyo

Axel Heide, OnesandZeros, Philip Pocock, Gregor Stehle
Unmovie
2002- / Flash python data weblication at http://www.unmovie.net,
interactive network installation composed of Wall, Stage,
Stream and Bubblecam / wall dimensions 520 x 390 x 190 cm /
© Unmovie / © VG Bild-Kunst, Bonn 2003

Gary Hill
Language Willing
2002 / DVD installation / 20:10 min /
courtesy Donald Young Gallery, Chicago / © Gary Hill

Perry Hobermann
The Sub-Division of the Electric Light
1996 / interactive CD-ROM / published in artintact 3 (ZKM, 1996) /
co-production Perry Hoberman and ZKM | Institute for Visual
Media, Karlsruhe / Perry Hobermann / © Perry Hobermann

Let's Make a Monster
2001–2003 / live-projection performance / Powerbook G3,
custom software (MAX/MSP/JITTER, Macromedia Director), data
projection, CCTV cameras, audio, MIDI, other custom controls /
© Perry Hoberman

Ian Howard
SweetStalking
2001 / interactive DVD / published in (dis)LOCATIONS (ZKM digital
arts edition, 2001) / co-production Ian Howard; ZKM | Institute for
Visual Media, Karlsruhe; iCINEMA Centre for Interactive Cinema
Research, University of New South Wales / © Ian Howard /
concept, developement: Ian Howard, Lucienne Howard / program-
ming: Volker Kuchelmeister / multimedia production: Skye Daley,
Volker Kuchelmeister, Daniel Wright

Paul Johnson
Red v. 2.0, Green v. 2.0, Blue v. 2.0
2002 / networked game consoles / vacuum-formed styrene,
mixed media, hardware and software / each console 71 x 71 cm /
in cooperation with Postmasters Gallery, New York /
Paul Johnson / courtesy Postmasters Gallery, New York

Isaac Julien
The Long Road to Mazatlàn
1999 / triple DVD projection / color, sound / dimensions variable /
18 min / collaboration Isaac Julien and Javier de Frutos / director:
Isaac Julien / choreography, movement material: Javier de Frutos /
courtesy Victoria Miro Gallery, London / performers (in order
of appearance): Javier de Frutos, Phillippe Riera / mariachi violin:
Eric Nunez / violin: Santiago Holguìn / vihuela: Mario Alberto
Murioz / guitarron: Benjamin Santos / chorus girls: Amber
Ortega-Perez, Georgina Morgan, S.T. Shimi / snake: Edgar (Laura
Varela, snake handler) / line producer: Scott Greenberg / produc-
tion management: Rallyard Production and Media / director of
photography: Toshak Ozawa / camera assistants: John Pirozzi,
John Tanzer / location mixer: Laura Varela / boom operator:
James Borrego / makeup: Cynthia Syke / grips: George Gardner,
Robert Diaz / grip equipment: L.D. Systems / craft services:
West Stone Catering / editor: Adam Finch / sound designer:
Ben Young / music composer: Andy Cowton / Mazatlàn music

and lyrics: Eric Nunez / 16mm film processing: Bono Film and Video Service, New Jersey / Super-8 film processing: DuArt Film and Video, New York / post production effects: The Farm, London / off and online editing: The Offline Editing Company, London / shot on location in: San Antonio, Texas / DVD encoding: MITES, Liverpool / installation technician: Tom Cullen / design and construction: Steven Connah / construction assistant: Gary Dyson / special thanks to Nevil Bounds, Dataton (UK Ltd), John Sills, Saville Audio Visual, Mark Nash, John Mason / The artist is represented by Victoria Miro Gallery, London.

William Kentridge
Overvloed
1999 / 35mm animated film transferred to DVD / charcoal-and-pastel drawings, paper cut-out figures / b/w, sound / 6 min / projection dimensions variable / courtesy William Kentridge / © William Kentridge / animation, film, direction: William Kentridge / editing: Catherine Meyburgh / music: Alfred Makgamele

Darij Kreuh and Davide Grassi
Brainscore
2000 / interactive performance in a virtual-reality environment / mixed media / performance duration: c. 45 min / authors, performers: Darij Kreuh, Davide Grassi / computer programming: Tadej Fius / eye tracking system: Iztok Lapanja / sound design: Rainer Linz / production: Forum Ljubljana, Eva Rohrman / co-production: Cankarjev dom, Karmen Klučar / supported by : LRSS – Faculty of computer sciences and informatics of the University of Ljubljana; The Ministry of Culture of the Republic Slovenia; the City Council of Ljubljana – Cultural Department / first shown at Cankarjev dom, Ljubljana

Norman M. Klein, with Rosemary Comella, Andreas Kratky, and The Labyrinth Project
Bleeding Through: Layers of Los Angeles, 1920–1986
2002 / interactive DVD installation / 550 x 550 cm / Co-production Annenberg Center for Communication; ZKM | Institute for Visual Media, Karlsruhe / © Klein, Comella, Kratky / the project was developed under the co-direction of Rosemary Comella (The Labyrinth Project), Andreas Kratky (ZKM), and Norman Klein / executive producers: Marsha Kinder (The Labyrinth Project), Jeffrey Shaw (ZKM) / production managers: Tania Trepanier, Juri Hwang, Liang-Yin Kuo / photography: Rosemary Comella, Andreas Kratky / video production: Norman Anderson, Steven Anderson, Rosemary Comella, Juri Hwang, Andreas Kratky, Liang-Yin Kuo, Scott Mahoy, Jay Majer, Myrton Running Wolf, Tania Trepanier, Matt Witt / interface design: Rosemary Comella, Andreas Kratky / graphic design: Andreas Kratky, Holger Jost / digital compression: Priscilla Pena Ovalle / programming: Andreas Kratky / sound: Juri Hwang, Andreas Kratky, Liang-Yin Kuo / research: Norman Klein, Tania Trepanier, Karen Voss, Liang-Yin Kuo, Andreas Kratky / rights clearances: Myrton Running Wolf

Marc Lafia with Didi Fire
Variable Montage
2002 / digital video / software, QuickTime video, MAX/MSP patch / © Marc Lafia

George Legrady with Rosemary Comella
Slippery Traces
1996 / interactive digital media installation / CD-ROM version published in *artintact 3* (ZKM, 1996) / collection of the artist / courtesy George Legrady / production: ZKM | Institute for Visual Media, Karlsruhe / concept, design, interactive programming: George Legrady / consultant, database, programming: Rosemary Comella / programming support and research: Brent Brooks, Steven Chiem / *artintact 3* CD-ROM programming: Wolfgang Münch / production: Easter Bonnifield, JP Collins, Antje Schlabe / produced with the assistance of a Computer Aided Media Award form The Canada Council, Ottawa, and with the support of a Visual Arts Fellowship, The National Endowment for the Arts, Washington DC

Machinima
program curated by Anke Hoffmann / showing the following films:

Mike Berry
Smart Gun
2002 / USA / Machinima, computer generated 3-D film / produced using Quake II / 1 min / production: Mike Berry

Stomp
2002 / USA / Machinima, computer generated 3-D film / produced using Quake II / 1 min / production: Mike Berry

Thin Ice
2002 / USA / Machinima, computer generated 3-D film / produced using Quake II / 1 min / production: Mike Berry

Dead on Que
Fake Science
2002 / USA/Canada / Machinima, computer generated 3-D film / produced using Half-Life / 5:40 min / production: Dead on Que /
concept, director: Michael Holochwost / producer, editor: Brian Mayberry / music: Daniel O'Neil

ILL Clan, Paul Morino
Hardly Workin'
1998 / USA / Machinima, computer generated 3-D film / produced using Quake II / 11:38 min / production: ILL Clan, Paul Morino

ILL Clinton, Matt Dominianni
Apartment Huntin'
1998 / Machinima, computer generated 3-D film / produced using Quake I / 5:27 min / director, editor: Matt Dominianni (ILL Clinton) / producer, skins artist: Paul Marino (ILL Robinson) / writers, voice talent: Matt Dominanni (ILL Clinton) as Lenny Lumberjack, Harry Hunter / John Olinyk (ILL Rogers) as Larry Lumberjack / Paul Jannicola (ILL Spector) as Reggie Realtor / cameraman, project manager: Frank Dellario (ILL Bixby) / sound designer, editor: Manu Smith (ILL Smith) / music: Alan Schwartz, Jim Sigler, and PXD Musicsoft (http://www.ejay.com)

Jake S. Hughes
Anachronox: The Movie
2001 / USA / Machinima, computer generated 3-D film / produced using Quake II / 137 min / producer, cinematics director, editor: Jake S. Hughes / production: Jake S. Hughes and Anachronox-Team / game designer: Tom Hall / writer: Richard Z. Gaubert / cine tool programmer: Joey Liaw / art director: Lee Perry / programmers: Brian "Squirrel"

Eiserloh, Josh Martel, Henrik Jonsson, Ralph Barbagallo /
lead artist: Lee Perry III / art/level design: Seneca Menard,
Lee Dotson, Jay Hosfelt, Travis Doggett, Don Martinez,
Matt Sophos, Mike Jackson, Josh Jay, John Sheffield,
Brian Patenaude, Luke Whiteside / music & sound:
SoundDeluxe, Will Nevins, Darren Walsh

Peter Rasmussen
Rendezvous
2001 / AUS / Machinima, computer generated 3-D film /
produced using Game 3-DGames Studio A4 / 8 min /
writer, director: Peter Rasmussen /
production: Peter Rasmussen/Nanoflix

Strange Company, Hugh Hancock
Matrix : 4 x 1 : Subway
2000 / Great Britain / Machinima, computer generated
3-D film / produced using Half-Life / 0:52 min /
Hugh Hancock, Gordon Mc Donald, Ben Moss,
Strange Company / production: Strange Company

Julien Maire
Demi-Pas [Half Step]
2002 / live-projection performance / twenty-one mechanical diapositives, Ektachrome, laser-cut / each 12 x 9 cm / color, sound /
22 min / Julien Maire / © Julien Maire

Lev Manovich
Soft Cinema
2002 / computer-generated projection, installation / dimensions
variable / co-production Lev Manovich and ZKM | Institute for
Visual Media, Karlsruhe / Lev Manovich: media database (video-
graphy, 2-D and 3-D animations, narratives), keywords, editing
rules, image-processing software, sound design, screen layout and
installation layout concepts / Andreas Kratky (ZKM): implementation logistics, edit list generation software, display software,
screen layout and installation layout / music database: DJ Spooky /
voice-over: Rachel Stevens / voice-over: Gloria Sutton / voice-
over: Francesca Ferguson / architect: Ruth M. Lorenz. maaskant
Berlin / installation construction, hardware: ZKM | Center for Art
and Media Karlsruhe

Chris Marker
Immemory
1997 / CD-ROM, installation / dimensions variable /
courtesy Centre Georges Pompidou, Musée national d'art
Moderne Centre de création industrielle, Paris

Jennifer and Kevin McCoy
Horror Chase
2002 / multimedia object with projection /
custom hardware and software /
50.8 x 55.8 x 50.8 cm, projection variable /
edition of 3 (1/3) / courtesy Postmasters Gallery,
New York and the artists / © Jennifer and Kevin McCoy and
Postmasters Gallery, New York

Margie Medlin
Miss World
2002 / projected three-screen digital image installation /
three concrete panels, each 240 x 180 cm / installation space
approx. 800 x 800 cm / color, sound / 10:05 min, loop / The work

was realized in the scope of a residency at the ZKM | Institute for
Visual Media, Karlsruhe, funded by the New Media Arts Fund of
the Australia Council for the Arts. It was initiated through the
Victorian Commissions funded by the Victorian Community
Support Fund of the Victorian Government (AUS) / concept, real-
ization: Margie Medlin (AUS) / choreography, dance: Rebecca
Hilton (AUS) / sound design, composition: Stevie Wishart (AUS/B) /
design, realization of the virtual figure: Holger Deuter (DNA-
Digital Nature Arts/D) / camera: Benjamin Speth (USA) / motion-
control camera operator and technician in Germany: Gerald
Thompson (Micronite Film Productions Port Melbourne/AUS) /
motion-control camera operator in Malaysia: Scott Inglis
(Micronite Film Productions APV – Asia-Pacific-Video lab, Kuala
Lumpur, Malaysia; AUS/Malaysia) / motion capture with Polhelmus
StarTrak / soft-image animation: Holger Deuter, Martin Winkler
(DNA-Digital Nature Arts/D) / editor: Martin Fox (AUS)

Michael Naimark
Be Now Here
1995–2002 / laserdisc-based stereoscopic projection /
four-channel audio, rotating floor, input pedestal /dimensions
variable / courtesy Michael Naimark / cooperators: Interval
Research Corporation, Palo Alto, CA, USA; UNESCO World Heritage
Centre, Paris, France

Mark Napier
The Waiting Room
2002 / web project / CD-ROM, interactive software art using
JAVA / dimensions variable / courtesy bitforms Gallery, New York

Werner Nekes
**Was geschah wirklich zwischen den Bildern?
[Film before Film]**
1984 / 35mm film / color, sound / 83 min / © Werner Nekes;
VG Bild-Kunst, Bonn 2003

MEDIA MAGICA I–V
1995 – 1997 / film series in five parts / 35mm film / color, sound /
each film 55 min / © Werner Nekes; VG Bild-Kunst, Bonn 2003
MEDIA MAGICA I
– Durchsehekunst [Beyond the Image]
MEDIA MAGICA II
– Belebte Bilder [Pictures come to Life]
MEDIA MAGICA III
– Vieltausendschau [Multi-Thousand Picture Show]
MEDIA MAGICA IV
– Bild-Raum [The Ambiguous Image and Space]
MEDIA MAGICA V
– Wundertrommel [The Magic Drum]

Susan Norrie
Defile
2001 / interactive DVD / published in (dis)LOCATIONS (ZKM digital
arts edition, 2001) / © Susan Norrie 2001 / co-production Susan
Norrie and ZKM | Institute for Visual Media, Karlsruhe; iCINEMA
Centre for Interactive Cinema Research, University of New South
Wales / concept development, cinematography: Susan Norrie,
Reva Childs / sound design, programmer: Greg White / acknowl-
edgment: Greenpeace Australia / thanks to Jeffrey Shaw,
Ian Howard, Dennis Del Favero, Volker Kuchelmeister

Pat O'Neill, with Rosemary Comella, Kristy H.A. Kang, and The Labyrinth Project

Tracing the Decay of Fiction:
Encounters with a film by Pat O'Neill
2002 / interactive DVD-ROM, three-screen computer installation / color, sound / dimensions and duration variable / courtesy The Labyrinth Project, Annenberg Center for Communication, University of Southern California / © The Annenberg Center, USC / written, directed, filmed and edited by: Pat O'Neill / the interface for the DVD-ROM was designed by project co-directors Rosemary Comella and Kristy H.A. Kang, in collaboration with Pat O'Neill and Marsha Kinder / executive producer: Marsha Kinder / assistant producers: Nsenga Burton, JoAnn Hanley, Alison Trope, Cristina Venegas / production manager: Priscilla Ovalle / sound design: George Lockwood, Adam King / programming: Rosemary Comella / graphic design: Kristy H.A. Kang / digital compositing: Kristy H.A. Kang, Scott Mahoy / digital media compression: Priscilla Ovalle / video editing: Liang-Yin Kuo, Tania Trepanier / additional sound editing: Robyn Bacon, Stefanos Kafatos / sound engineer: Christopher Cain / research and rights clearance: Myrton Running Wolf / commentaries by cultural historians: Michael Dear, David James, Norman Klein, Kevin Starr, Robert Winter and others

Martin Reinhart

tx-dance. motion studies in space and time
2002 / video on DVD / color, sound / 5 min / dance performance by Salvar Sanchis / idea and realization: Golden Girls Film-production, Michael Loebensein, Martin Reinhart, Vienna

Constanze Ruhm

Coming Attraction: X Characters (in search of an author)
2002-2003 / installation / mixed media / © Constanze Ruhm / programming, website: Tom Roscher, Bert-Ulrich Baumann / 3-D visualizing, production: Daniel Classen / research, production assistance: Christine Gloggengiesser / thanks to Fareed Armaly, haus.0 Programm

Joachim Sauter and Dirk Lüsebrink

Invisible Shape of Things Past
1995/2001 / interactive installation / collage, poster, 3-D sculpture, projection mirror, video documentation / dimensions variable / Joachim Sauter, Dirk Lüsebrink / © Sauter, Lüsebrink

Michael Schmid, Jörn Müller-Quade, Thomas Beth

Laserfilm
2000 / interactive sculpture / glass, laser, steel, wood / dimensions variable / © the authors; ZKM | Media Museum, Karlsruhe / The idea for *Laserfilm* was born when Harald Aagedal, Sebastian Egner, Jörn Müller-Quade and Michael Schmid discussed the notion of deploying for film purposes the brightness-pattern translation variance occurring in the Fourier transform of a holographic image. Schmid, who directed and carried out the project, co-developed the methods for computing the *Laserfilm* with Aagedal, and was assisted by Janka Reh in designing the visual content. Markus Graf and Stefan Kölmel devised and implemented the technical set-up on the basis of a concept by Thomas Beth. The project would not have been possible without the support of IAP Jena and the generous R&D advancement and funding afforded by the Institute of Algorithms and Cognitive Systems at Karlsruhe University. Beth, director of the Institute, not only initiated the making of *Laserfilm* but also engineered the productive cooperation with ZKM | Center for Art and Media Karlsruhe.

Bill Seaman

The Exquisite Mechanism of Shivers
1997 / interactive CD-ROM / published in *artintact 1* (ZKM, 1997) / co-production Bill Seaman and ZKM | Institute for Visual Media, Karlsruhe / © Bill Seaman

Jeffrey Shaw

Place-Ruhr
2000 / interactive computer-graphic video installation / circular screen, rotating platform, one projector, custom user interface / 9 m diameter, 3,2 m high / produced at ZKM | Institute for Visual Media, Karlsruhe / collection of the Museen Dortmund / courtesy Museen Dortmund / © Jeffrey Shaw / application software: Adolf Mathias / panoramic video production and post-production: Andreas Kiel / production manager ZKM: Jan Gerigk / platform, screen and user-interface engineering: Huib Nelissen / electronic integration: Torsten Ziegler / production partners Dortmund: hARTware projekte, Hans D. Christ, Iris Dressler, Tabea Sieben / production manager: Astrid Sommer / production assistants: Heike Staff, Franz Wamhof, Derek Hauffen / animation and compositing: Christina Zartmann, Andreas Kiel / camera: Boris Michalski / actors: Ariane Andereggen, Andreas Brüning, Derek Hauffen, Mohsen Hosseini, Matthias Kampmann / props: Frank Prummer

Place-Urbanity
2002 / interactive computer-graphic video installation / circular screen, rotating platform, one projector, custom user interface / 9 m diameter, 3.2 m high / produced at ZKM | Institute for Visual Media, Karlsruhe / produced with financial assistance of Cinemedia's Digital Media Fund; the Digital Media Fund is funded by Multimedia Victoria as part of the Victorian government's Connecting Victoria policy, which aims to bring the benefits of technology to all Victorians / collection The Australian Centre for the Moving Image / courtesy The Australian Centre for the Moving Image / © Jeffrey Shaw / audio design: Torsten Belschner / application software: Adolf Mathias / panoramic video production and post-production: Andreas Kiel / production manager ZKM: Jan Gerigk / platform, screen and user-interface engineering: Huib Nelissen / electronic integration: Torsten Ziegler / production assistants: Christina Zartmann, Derek Hauffen, Franz Wamhof / comedians: Ningali Lawford, Milton White, Lyndia Gibson, Lawrence Leung, Gaurav Gupta, Emad Gurgui, Arthur Sarkatzis, Gabriel Rossi, Tal Brot, Bassem Abousaid, John Naumovski, Greg Ulfan, Dave Ivkovic, Tahir Bilgic, Isabel Nalato, Hung Le, Kathy Lang / Melbourne crew: manager: Liz Baulch / production company: Wild Iris productions / camera: Andreas Kiel / studio camera: Benjamin Doudney / studio sound: Ro Woods / production assistants: Annetta Labb, Danny Decarli / makeup: Tamara Heany, Jane Ormond / rigging: Showtech Australia P/L / studio: Premiere Lighting / DVD-ROM version of Place-Urbanity published in *(dis)LOCATIONS* (ZKM digital arts edition, 2001) / DVD-ROM programming, design, video postproduction: Volker Kuchelmeister

Karl Sims

Evolved Virtual Creatures
1994 / computer animation on video / 4 min, loop / Karl Sims / © 1994, Karl Sims, all rights reserved / Thanks to Gary Oberbrunner and Matt Fitzgibbon for Connection Machine and software help. Thanks to Lew Tucker and Thinking Machines Corporation for supporting this research. Thanks to Bruce Blumberg and Peter Schröder for dynamic simulation help and suggestions. And special thanks to Pattie Maes.

Michael Snow
anarchive 2: Digital Snow
2002 / interactive DVD-ROM / Anarchive, Paris / courtesy
Michael Snow and the Daniel Langlois Foundation for Art, Science
and Technology

Caspar Stracke
z2 [zuse strip]
2002 / unwound 35mm film (approx. 24,000 cm), hole-punch device,
two CPUs, digital converter, 90 interactively controlled animation
sequences, fifteen lines of Lev Manovich text (quote one) and nine
lines of John Chadwick text (quote two), video projector / b/w,
sound / dimensions variable / courtesy hole puncher: Deutsches
Technikmuseum Berlin / Caspar Stracke / © Caspar Stracke /
hardware: The punch hole device is modeled on the existing replica
of the original Z3. Generous help provided by Konrad Zuse's son,
Dr. Horst Zuse and the Konrad-Zuse-Zentrum for Information
Technology (ZIB) in Berlin / software: A modified Vidvox Prophet
2.0 by Johnny DeKam (http://www.node.net) / For their valuable
help and input my thanks go to Horst Zuse, Lev Manovich, and
Simon Singh.

Synthetic Characters Group, MIT Media Lab: Bill Tomlinson,
Marc Downie, Matt Berlin, Jesse Gray, Adolph Wong,
Robert Burke, Damian Isla, Yuri Ivanov, Michael P. Johnson,
Derek Lyons, Jennie Cochran, Bryan Yong, Bruce Blumberg
AlphaWolf
2001 / interactive digital installation / 2 x 5 x 5 m /
courtesy Synthetic Characters Group, MIT Media Lab /
© Massachusetts Institute of Technology

Peter Weibel
The Panoptic Society or Immortally in Love with Death
2001 / interactive DVD / published in (dis)LOCATIONS (ZKM digital
arts edition, 2001) / © Peter Weibel / co-production Peter Weibel
and ZKM | Institute for Visual Media, Karlsruhe; iCINEMA Centre
for Interactive Cinema Research, University of New South Wales /
concept: Peter Weibel / design, programming, image creation:
Daniel Wright, Skye Daley / additional visuals: Franz Wamhof /
cell image: photodisc.com

Maciej Wisniewski
Instant Places
2002 / Net-based installation / custom software / courtesy the
artist and Postmasters Gallery, New York / © Maciej Wisniewski

Christian Ziegler
66movingimages
1998–2002 / interactive road movie / two-channel video /
interactive control with moveable monitor (Linear Navigator
© Jeffrey Shaw) / 1.1 x 1 m / © Christian Ziegler / application
software: Christian Ziegler, Torsten Ziegler / co-production
Christian Ziegler and ZKM | Institute for Visual Media, Karlsruhe

Webcinema
An Historical Anthology of Web Cinema Shorts, 1997–2002
program curated by Nora Barry

1999 and 2000:
Experimentation with Narrative and Visual Formats

Mel Bernstine
Mike
2000 / France / film, Flash / directors: Mel Bernstine and
David Moscovic / written by Jon Perello and Mel Bernstine /
produced by LovestreamS.com / An innovative short film
about a man named Mike, cruising the streets of Manhattan
with a lot on his mind. Originally created as a film, *Mike* was
re-imagined in Flash for the web, and was one of the first
projects of its kind.

Young-hae Chang
**Artist's Statement No. 45,730,944:
"A Perfect Artistic Website"**
2000 / South Korea /
produced by Young-hae Chang Heavy Industries /
A funny, political, tongue-in-cheek artistic statement.
Artist's Statement received an Honorable Mention at the
SFMOMA Webby Awards and has been in the Stuttgart
Filmwinter and the Rotterdam Film Festival, and a finalist
in the trAce/Alt-X New Media Writing Competition.

Joe Chow
Dowager
1998 / USA / video / production and direction: Joe Chow /
director of photography: Mitchell Rosenbaum / makeup:
Donna Fumoso / production assistant: Eva Vives / featuring
Stephanie Jacobs, Gerry Hildebrandt / An Asian woman meta-
morphosizes from gentle lotus blossom to murderous dragon
lady. *Dowager* is the story of how she gets there – and why.

Maya Churi
Letters From Homeroom
1999 / USA / interactive video / written and directed by
Maya Churi / production: Fiona Brandon / web site design:
Ariel Churi / additional web site and film dialogue written by:
Sarah Squire, Julia Frey and Sonja Trauss / This unique web-
based film uses video, audio and text segments to chronicle
the correspondence between two girls in high school. Their
story unfolds in the letters they write to each other during the
school day.

Tom Elsner
Glastonbury 99
1999 / United Kingdom / Flash / A unique Flash-based documentary about Britain's most famous open air music festival.
Created by Artificial Environments of London for Greenpeace.

Xeth Feinberg
Post No Bills
1998 / USA / Shockwave / courtesy Animation Express /
The first of the *Bulbo* series, this episode pays tribute to
the earliest black and white animations. *Bulbo* was one of the
first shorts to debut on Animation Express, which launched
in October 1998.

Andrea Flamini

Waterdream

1999 / USA, Italy / interactive video, Flash / *Waterdream* is an interactive experimental short that lets you choose your own path through the movie … but only one way leads to the end.

Kristoffer Gansing

Wake Interactive

2000 / Sweden / Flash / by David Cuartielles, Elisabet Nilsson and Kristoffer Gansing / produced by Carl-Henrik Svenstedt, The Shift and Imagineering Projects at K3-Malmö University, Art, Culture and Communication / based on the film *The Wake* / (*The Wake* is directed by Michael Kvium and Christian Lemmerz and produced by Dino Raymond Hansen, http://www.wake.dk, Copenhagen, 2000.)

Aleksander Gubas

Belgrade Frozen

2000 / Yugoslavia / video / Filmmaker Gubas employs the stuttering and freezing characteristics of the dial-up web to convey life during the bombings of Belgrade.

Craig Johnson

1000 Moons

1998 / USA / video / *1000 Moons* traces a woman's emotional involvement with her lover, from ecstasy to despair and looks at the tragic conflict that arises when our lovers both adore us and abuse us.

Dave Jones

Teetering

1999 / Australia / Flash / A poignant, black and white Flash animation about finding the right balance in a precarious relationship. *Teetering* brings to mind some of the first silent films in its clean and simple approach to storytelling. It has won awards at the AnimaMundi Web Festival, the FIFI, the Pixies, I Castelli Animati, and has been a finalist in many others.

Richard Lainhart

Haiku

1999 / USA / video, Flash / An elegant realization of a 17th-century Japanese haiku.

Spike Lee

Savion Glover Dances

1997 / USA / video / courtesy Real Networks / Master Savion Glover taps through this mini-documentary about dancing. Created by filmmaker Spike Lee for the debut launch of RealVideo 2.0 in October 1997.

Paul Lincoln

Your Own Personal Audience

2000 / Singapore / video / Created for the world's first Palm Pilot Film Festival in November 2000, this short turns the screen back upon the viewer.

Marco and Antonio Manetti

SCUMS

1998 / Italy / digital video linear / Two suspicious guys, an enigmatic woman and a mysterious bag kick start this action-packed 1960s style series. *SCUMS* is a web episodic, shot in tandem by filmmakers from Italy, Canada and the United States.

Jerome Mouscadet

John Lecrocheur

2000 / France / interactive Flash / created by Mouscadet and I-O Interactif / A stunning noir Flash animation about a fictional photo-journalist in Shanghai in the late 1940s. Each frame is a starting point for multiple panels, allowing the story to expand both visually and narratively.

John O'Brian

Life at Night

2000 / USA / Real / A jazz based composition that merges aural and visual story elements to create a unique web "comic" book, Raymond Chandler style. Created by John O'Brian who recently received a American Composers Forum/McKnight Fellowship supporting the completion of the sequel to *Life at Night*.

Michael O'Reilly

City Halls

1999 / USA / video / *City Halls* is a random configuration film series, that configures a different version of the film each time it is accessed. It is a meditation on loss and redemption.

Christine Panushka

AbsolutPanushka

1998 / USA / animation / A selection of experimental animations that screened on the first Absolut Vodka website, which launched in January 1998.

Picture Projects

360 Degrees

2000 / USA / interactive video / co-producer, creative director and designer: Alison Cornyn / co-producer, creative director and photographer: Sue Johnson / editorial advisor: David Anderson / research and community outreach: Adrienne Fitzgerald / research: Dana Greene / marketing, PR and outreach: Hayley Downs / new technology and programming: Catherine Jhee / photo and art research: Maria Finn / programming and design: Britta Frahm / outreach, social action network coordinator: Kenyatta Belcher / copy editor: Ana Deboo / An innovative, interactive documentary about the American Criminal Justice System, *360 Degrees* goes inside the prisons and emerges with the personal stories about prisoners, and the social workers, judicial representatives and relatives whose lives are intertwined with them. The online doc has won the Batten Award for Innovation from the Pew Center for Civic Journalism and an award for the Most Creative Use of the Medium, from the Online Journalism Award.

Martin Reinhart

Pinocchio

2000 / Austria / video / *Pinocchio* is a short about the Haider campaign in Austria, set to a song about the wooden boy whose nose grow longer every time he lied. Each night people would rip down Haider's posters … but in the morning they had reappeared.

Peter Rose

The Gift

2000 / USA / video / Words become images in this aural story by multimedia artist Peter Rose. Using sound and text, Rose invokes classic oral storytelling techniques to create a digital fairy tale.

Silvia Maria Schopf
mmmloook
1999 / Germany / video / *mmmloook*. loop. *mmmloook* is something between eating and looking. The video moves in your eyes through the sense of taste; it touches your eyes with the tongue. You can see tounge-pictures in your mind. How do pictures taste?

John Serpentelli
Positively Negative
1998 / USA / animation / sound / creation and animation: John Serpentelli / music: Joe Volpe / *Positively Negative* is a black and white, additive and subtractive song and dance which explores the sometimes funny, sometimes fierce interplay between positive and negative. It was the first film that launched on The Bit Screen in June 1998.

Deanne Sokolin
Cooking Chronicles
1999 / USA / interactive Shockwave / Preparing a meal is about more than just eating, and this humorous short chronicles the culture and emotions of food at a holiday repast. It was exhibited in winter 2002 at the International Center for Photography.

Tara Veneruso
Austin
1997 / USA / video / A soap opera about the lives of a group of friends in Austin Texas, *Austin* was the first online streaming video series. It debuted on http://Internetv.com, a streaming site that went online in early 1997 with a mix of music and shorts.

Pierre Wayser
Jolt
2000 / France / video, Flash / A syncopated expressionistic journey through the crowded bustling streets of Paris. The stark black and white compositions create a world that is disorienting yet strangely familiar. Shot in video and output to Flash.

Jason Wishnow
Persona
1997 / USA / Hi-8 / Director Wishnow unveils the person behind the persona in this biting commentary on facades. Created in early 1997 for Wishnow's online venue "Experimental Theater," which became the foundation for The New Venue site, which launched in June of 1998.

2001:
Rise of European Voices

8081
The Island
2001 / Italy / interactive Flash / 8081 is Seba Vitale, Antonio Rollo and Luca Barbeni / 8081, The Valley is a reflective, interactive adventure through several different environments. It is an ideal environment made of different micro-environments such as the beach, the Mediterranean spot, the mountain, valleys and the Palm Grove. *The Island* is a continuous work in progress, an open project that develops following the evolution of the Net and new media, able to change and improve according to the new technologies and exploring the changes through the interaction with the visitor.

Analogiks-Indians
Weird Christmas
2001 / France / Flash / the Analogiks Tribe consists of Erwan Defachelles and Fred Fauquette / Stark images, rendered beautifully in black and white, tell a haunting story about an old woman's confession.

Bechamel
El Fantastico del Paradiso
2001 / France / Flash / created by Sophie Estival and Guillaume Joire for Vector Lounge at the Annency Animation Festival / A spaghetti western that pits a tough cowboy against a deadly … worm.

Bill Cahalan
Golden Boy
2001 / USA / Flash / A beautifully eerie animation about the perceptions of modern deities. A selection of Streaming Cinema 2001, and a finalist in the Sundance 2002 Online Film Festival.

Martin Dalhauser
Badcop
2001 / Germany / Flash / created by Martin Dahlhauser, Mike Tucker, and Tim Freccia / Truth is stranger than fiction. In 1997, the Berlin police department brought in consultants from the New York Police Department to teach German officers how to cope with the new breed of criminals swarming on the city. *Badcop* was developed as a "what if/what would happen" response - that is, what happens when you drop an amoral New York cop into the chaos of the reunified Berlin?

Jeannette Lambert
D'où Viens-Tu? [Where are you from?]
2001 / Canada / video, interactive Flash / A simultaneous window on the past, present and future, this interactive short lays out a family's history and their child's future. A selection of Streaming Cinema 2001, and The Irish Museum of Modern Art's "net.art" exhibition in 2002.

Moccu
The Reef
2001 / Germany / Moccu members are: Jens Schmidt, Christoph Petersen, Heiko Freier, Thomas Walter and Bjoern Zaske / A gorgeously interactive undersea universe of jeweled fish and sunken ships that is filled with treasures such as the "groove-o-meter." Navigate through the reef and make the fish dance; zoom in on the reef and find what's hidden behind it. *The Reef* was the Vivendi Grand Prize at the International Festival of Internet Films (FIFI) in March, 2001. *The Reef* is part of a website, http://moccu.com, that offers multiple environments and multiple experiments, such as allowing viewers to hatch an egg online.

Julie Myers
Julie's Weekend
2001 / United Kingdom / video / commissioned by the Arts Council of England's New Media Project Fund /

edited with Matt White / contributors are: Michaela Freeman for Prague, Kate Gauthier for Sydney, Lahary Pittman for New York, Scott Brightwell for Florence, Nuria W. Soeharto and Enrico Soekarno for Jakarta and Anthony Yau for Hong Kong / Who is Julie and where has she been? Her story is mapped out in episodes shot by seven different directors in seven different cities around the world: Prague, London, Sydney, New York, Florence, Jakarta, Hong Kong.

Submarine
City Tunes
2001 / Netherlands / video, Flash / interviews: Inge Willems / camera and editing: Boris Everts / animation: Zoltan Korai, Yiu-loon Lee / production: Janneke van de Kerhof / produced by Submarine / City Tunes is a series of Flash videos about dating and mating rituals in Amsterdam. This episode, "The Right Place at the Right Time" tells the story of two people who keep missing each other as they travel around the world.

2002 and Beyond:
The Future of Web Cinema

Chris Ferrantello
Twin Towers
2002 / USA / Flash / created and animated by Chris Ferrantello, it was a finalist in the 2002 Sundance Online Festival / A disturbingly beautiful reflection on the World Trade Center attack.

Carlos Gomez de Llarena
Live from Tompkins Square
2002 / Venezuela / video, Flash / A live, interactive webcast documentary about the Lower East Side neighborhood in Manhattan. Shot on April 5, 2002, the live doc intertwined mobile phones, SMS, the Internet and wireless networks, allowing the audience and the broadcaster to be linked in a feedback loop that impacted the content and narrative of the show. This is an edited version of the 40-minute webcast.

Petrie Lounge
Kunst Bar
2002 / Canada / Flash / Petrie Lounge is Steve Whitehouse, Paul Teglas, Chris Labonte, John Halfpenny and Denis Gonzalez / Pollock, Matisse, Van Gogh and Dalí hang out (or get hung out) in this after-hours art bar.

Submarine
Killer
2002 / Netherlands / Flash / © Casterman, Jacamon/Matz / story and illustration: Matz and Jacamon / animation and interactive story design: Fons Schiedon, Dan Lentelink / music and sound: REC Sound Design / producer: Femke Wolting / produced by Submarine Amsterdam / based on the graphic novel Le Tueur - Long Feu / A dark noir story about a professional assassin.

Tara Veneruso
Airports for Beginners
2002 / USA / Super-8 / This Super-8 flick explores the terminals and runways of an airport and draws an analogy between take-offs and landing and scheduled departures and delays, and modern relationships.

Film Program

Martin Arnold
pièce touchée
1989 / Austria / 16mm film / b/w, sound / 16 min / © 1999 Martin Arnold; Amour Fou Filmproduktion

passage à l'acte
1993 / Austria / 16mm film / b/w, sound / 12 min / © 1999 Martin Arnold; Amour Fou Filmproduktion

Alone. Life wastes Andy Hardy
1998 / Austria / 16mm film / b/w, sound / 15 min / © Martin Arnold; Sixpack Film, Vienna

Kathryn Bigelow
Strange Days
1994 / USA / 35mm film on DVD / color, sound / 139 min / director: Kathryn Bigelow / writer: James Cameron, Jay Cocks / original music: Peter Gabriel, Graeme Revell / producer: Lightstorm Entertainment / distributed by: 20th-Century Fox

Noel Burch
Retrospective
curated by Constanze Ruhm / showing the following films:

Le Noviciat
1965 / France / 16mm film / b/w / 17 min

Noel Burch with Christopher Mason
The Impersonator or
A Propos the Disappearance of Reginald Pepper
1983 / Great Britain/Germany / 56 min

Sentimental Journey
1993-1994 / USA / 54 min

Correction, Please or How We Got into Pictures
1979 / Great Britain / 52 min

The Year of the Bodyguard
1981 / Great Britain/Germany / 54 min

What do those Old Films Mean?
1984–1985 / Great Britain/Germany / all 26 min
"Great Britain 1900–1912: Along the Great Divide"
"Germany 1926–1932: Under Two Flags"
"USSR 1925–1928: Born Yesterday"

Gustav Deutsch
Film/Spricht/Viele/Sprachen
1995 / Austria / 35mm film / color, sound / 1 min / concept, realization: Gustav Deutsch / production: Viennel (Vienna International Filmfestival) / © G. Deutsch; Sixpack Film, Vienna

Film ist. (1–6)
1998 / Austria / Tableaufilm. Work in Progress / 16mm film /
b/w, color, sound / 60 min / concept, research, realization:
Gustav Deutsch / sound: Dustav Deutsch, Dietmar Schipek /
trick: Blow Up Filmtechnik, Synchro Trick / production: LOOP TV-
Video-Film / producer: Manfred Neuwirth / supported by:
Bundeskanzleramt, Kunstsektion, Kultur und Wissenschaft des
Landes Niederösterreich / distributed by: Sixpack Film /
© Gustav Deutsch; Sixpack Film, Vienna

Film ist. (7–12)
2002 / Austria / Tableaufilm. Work in Progress / 35mm film /
b/w, color, sound / 93 min / concept, realization: Gustav
Deutsch / research: Gustav Deutsch, Hanna Schimek / music:
Werner Dafeldecker, Christian Fennesz, Martin Siewert,
Burkhard Stangl / production: loop media / producer: Manfred
Neuwirth / supervisory producer: Josef Aichholzer / coopera-
tion partner: Netherlands Filmmuseum / cooperation: Centre
national de la Cinématographie; Cinemateca Portuguesa;
Cineteca di Bologna; Filmarchiv Austria / support: Medien-
werkstatt Wien / financial support by: Wiener Filmfond;
BKA/Kunstsektion; Land Niederösterreich / distributed by:
Sixpack Film / © Gustav Deutsch; Sixpack Film, Vienna

Mike Figgis
TIMECODE
1999 / United Kingdom / 35mm film on DVD / color, sound /
94 min / director, story: Mike Figgis / director of photography:
Mike Figgis, Tony Cucchiari / producer: Mike Figgis, Annie Stewart

Lynn Hershman Leeson
Teknolust
2002 / USA / high definition 24p format, 35mm film /
color, sound dolby sr / 85 min / distributed by Skouras Films,
2002 / producer, writer, director: Lynn Hershman Leeson /
producers: Youssef Vahabzadeh, John Bradford King,
Oscar Gubernati / director of photography: Hiro Narita (A.S.C.) /
editor: Lisa Fruchtman / co-producers: Paul Barnett, Peter
Buchanan, John Nazemian / executive producers: Amy
Sommer / costume designers: Yohji Yamamoto, Marianna
Astrom-DeFina / production designer: Chris Farmer / cast:
Rosetta: Tilda Swinton; Ruby: Tilda Swinton; Marinne: Tilda
Swinton; Olive: Tilda Swinton; Sandy: Jeremy Davies; Agent
Hopper: James Urbaniak; Dirty Dick: Karen Black; Dr. Bea:
Al Nazemian; Tim: Josh Kornbluth; Preacher: Thomas Jay Ryan

Les LeVeque
2 Spellbound
1999 / USA / video / color, sound / 9 min / © Les LeVeque;
Electronic Arts Intermix

4 Vertigo
2000 / USA / video / color, sound / 7 min / © Les LeVeque;
Electronic Arts Intermix

Harmony Korine
Julien Donkey Boy
1999 / USA / 35mm film on DVD / color, sound / 94 min /
director, screenwriter: Harmony Korine / cinematographer:
Anthony Dod Mantle / editor: Valdis Oskardottir / producer:
Cary Woods, Robin O'Hara, Scott Macauley / distributed by:
Independent Pictures

Werner Nekes
Der Tag des Malers [The Day of the Painter]
1997 / Germany / 35mm film / color, sound / 84 min /
© 1997 Werner Nekes; VG Bild-Kunst, Bonn 2003

Michael Snow
*Corpus Callosum
2002 / Canada / video / color, sound / 93 min /
© Michael Snow 2001 /
produced and directed by Michael Snow / script, direction,
design, sound: Michael Snow / special effects supervisor:
Greg Hermanovic / senior animator: Rob del Ciancio /
software: Houdini from Side Effects Software /
on-line editing: Paul Cormack / sound mixing: Ian Haskin /
directors of photography: Robbi Hinds, Harald Bachmann /
casting, line production: Janet Hadjidimitriou /
cast: Kim Plate, Greg Hermanovic, John Massey, Joanne Tod,
John Penner, Tom Sherman, and many others ... /
funding: Telefilm Canada; The Canada Council for the Arts;
The Mississauga Living Arts Centre; and Michael Snow

Aleksander Sokurov
Russian Ark
2002 / Russia / 35mm film / color, sound / 96 min / director:
Aleksander Sokurov / writer: Anatoly Nikiforov, Aleksander
Sokurov / director of photography: Tilman Büttner / produced
by: Hermitage Bridge Studio: Andrey Deryabin; Egoli Tossell Film
AG: Jens Meurer, Karsten Stöter

Virgil Widrich
Copy Shop
2001 / Austria / 35mm film / b/w, sound / 12 min / director,
screenwriter: Virgil Widrich / director of photography: Martin
Putz / music: Alexander Zlamal / cast: Johannes
Silberschneider, Elisabeth Ebner-Haid / production: Virgil
Widrich Film- & Multimediaproduktions G.m.b.H.

RESFEST 2002
Digital Film Festival

By Design

Doug Aitken
Windows
2001 / USA / 2 min

Matt Anderson
Anamorph
2001 / USA / 3:28 min / shot in DV and composited with
After Effects

Eric Augier and Olivier Lipski
Itsu
2002 / France / 3:40 min / director: Eric Augier and Olivier
Lipski / producer: Pleix / editor: Jean-Philippe Deslandes /
composer: Plaid / shot on a Canon miniDV camera and created
using Vegas editing software, After Effects and 3D Studio Max
on a PC

Jorge Cosmen
Spot
2002 / Spain / 4:12 min / director, co-cinematographer, screenwriter, editor: Jorge Cosmen / co-cinematographer: Ivan Luque / sound design, composer: Miguel Angel Paredes / cast: Lucia Draper / shot on miniDV, edited on Premiere, used After Effects and Combustion of effects / animated using 3D Studio Max, Photoshop and Flash / used Reason and Nuendo for sound / computer: PC Dual station and Compaq Edit Plus

Void Cump
Freestile Disco
2001 / United Kingdom / 4 min / director: Void Cump / producer: Richard Bell / sound design/composer: S.I.Futures / used 35mm still photos, composited with After Effects and edited on Media 100 / animation created with Lightwave / using Mac and PC

Richard Fenwick
Untitled
2002 / United Kingdom / 3:15 min / director, screenwriter, editor: Richard Fenwick / producers: Dallas Synnott and Giles Johnson / 3-D artist: Dan Capstick / composer: Chris Clark / used aerial stock footage, composited with After Effects and edited on Media 100 using a Mac G4

Genevieve Gauckler and Jean-Philippe Deslandes
NO
2001 / France / 3 min / directors: Genevieve Gauckler and Jean-Philippe Deslandes / producer: Pleix / editor: Jean-Philippe Deslandes / composer: Bleip / used a Canon miniDV camera, Vegas editing software, Photoshop and Illustrator / audio-sound software: Nuendo / on both Mac and PC

Johnny Hardstaff
Pulk/Pull Revolving Doors And Like Spinning Plates
2001 / United Kingdom / 8 min / director, designer: Johnny Hardstuff / producer: John Payne / cinematographer: Stephan Blackman / editor: J.D. Smith / post production: The Mill / models, animation: Pictures on the Wall / sound design, music: Radiohead / shot on 35mm using an Arri A35, cut on Avid, effects and animation created with Flame, Softimage, Photoshop, After Effects and Illustrator on many Mac G4s

Sei Hishhikawa
Prelude
2002 / Japan / 2:48 min / director: Sei Hishikawa / producer: Drawing and Manual / designer: Nobu Joegano / sound design: Gohji Suzuki / used After Effects, 3D Studio Max, an Apple PowerMac G4 1Ghz Dual, custom-made PC Windows 2000 1Ghz Dual

Ed Holdsworth
King Pylon
2002 / United Kingdom / 3 min / director, animator, designer: Ed Holdsworth / producer: Nicola Black / sound design: Welburn Kisbert / cast: Adam Holsworth, Ed Holsworth / using Final Cut Pro for editing and After Effects for compositing / animation created in Flash and 3D Studio Max, on both Mac and PC

H5
Remind Me
2002 / France / 4:05 min / director: H5 / producer: John Payne / production co.: Black Dog, London

Bill McMullen and Ryan McGinness
North Star
2002 / USA / 3:44 min / directors: Bill McMullen and Ryan McGinness / music: DJ Mehdi / used Final Cut Pro for editing, composited with After Effects and animated in Illustrator on Mac

Brazil Inspired
2002 / USA / 17 min / designers: Pysop, MK12, Freestile Collective, Digital Kitchen, Lobo, Trollbäck & Company, Sticopy, Servicio-Ejecutivo, Jeremy Hollister and more / http://www.brasilinspired.com

Chris Cunningham
Retrospective

Mental Wealth
1999 / director: Chris Cunningham / production: RSA / producer: Cindy Burnay / art director: Bill Bungay / post: Flame: Barnsley and Chris Knight at The Mill / editor: Tony Karns / commissioner: Trevor Beattie at TBWA GGT; Simons Palmer, London

Second Bad Vilbel (Autechre)
1996 (second version 2002) / 4:40 min / director: Chris Cunningham

Come To Daddy (Aphex Twin)
1997 / 5:52 min / director: Chris Cunningham / production: RSA/Black Dog Films, London / producer: Cindy Burnay / director of photography: Simon Chaudoir / post: Glassworks; Marcus Timpson at The Mill / editor: Gary Knight at Itopia / commissioner: Rob Mitchell and Steve Beckett at Warp

Only You (Portishead)
1998 / director: Chris Cunningham / producer: Cindy Burnay / director of photography: Simon Chaudoir / set designer: Chris Oddy / post: The Mill / offline editor: Gary Knight at Final Cut / commissioner: Go! Beat Records

Frozen (Madonna)
1998 / director: Chris Cunningham / production: Black Dog Films, New York / producer: Nick Wrathall / director of photography: Darius Khondji / hair: Peter Savic / makeup: Joanne Gair / post: editor: Gary Knight at Itopia / producer: John Payne at The Mill / personnel: Steve Murgatroyd, Dan Williams, Steve Hiam, Anthony Walsham at The Mill / commissioner: Maverick Records, Warner Bros Records

Africa Shox (Leftfield)
1998 / 4:42 min / director: Chris Cunningham / production: RSA/Black Dog Films / producer: Cindy Burnay / production assistant: Holly Ross / director of photography: Darius Khondji / post: editors: Gary Knight at Final Cut, Chris Cunningham / telecine: Ben Eagleton at Rushes /

Flame: Louise Lattimore / line producer: Frank Linkoff / commissioner: Mark Conway at Sony Music Entertainment

Come On My Selector (Squarepusher)
1998 / 7 min / director: Chris Cunningham / production: RSA/Black Dog Films / producer: Cindy Burnay / director of photography: Alex Barber / set designers: Ivan Unwin, Chris Oddy / post: sound: Adam at Grand Central / telecine: Rushes / editor: Chris Cunningham / assistant editor: J.D. Smith / Flame: Passy at Glassworks / commissioner: Warp Records, Nothing Records

Windowlicker (Aphex Twin)
1998 / 10:33 min / director: Chris Cunningham / production: Black Dog Films / producer: Cindy Burnay / director of photography: James Hawkinson / choreographer: Vincent Patterson / production manager (L.A.): Robyn Lattaker-Johnson / post: sound engineer: Max Butcher at Grand Central / telecine: Ben Eagleton at Rushes / editor: Chris Cunningham / assistant editor: J.D. Smyth / Flame: Pasi Johansson at Glassworks / producer: Sally Mattinson / commissioners: Rob Mitchell and Steve Beckett at Warp

All Is Full Of Love (Björk)
1999 / director: Chris Cunningham / production: Black Dog Films / producer: Cindy Burnay / director of photography: John Lynch / production designers: Chris Cunningham, Julian Caldow / art director: Chris Oddy / robot design: Chris Cunningham / robot builder: Paul Catling / sound: Sam Mendelssohn / post: telecine: Marcus Timpson at The Mill / offline editor: Gary Knight at Final Cut / Flame/online: Pasi Johansson at Glassworks / 3-D: James at Glassworks / commissioner: Paul McKee at One Little Indian

Flex
2000 / director: Chris Cunningham

Monkey Drummer
2001 / installation / director: Chris Cunningham

Drukqs (Aphex Twin)
2001 / director: Chris Cunnigham

Cinema Electronica

Sam Arthur
Poor Leno (Röyksopp)
2001 / United Kingdom / 3:57 min / director: Sam Arthur / producer: Sandra Lawrence / editor: Jones at Swordfish / production co.: RHB / record co.: Wall of Sound

Antoine Bardou-Jacquet
How Does It Make You Feel (Air)
2002 / France / 3:38 min / director: Antoine Bardou-Jacquet / producer: Charlotte Le Pot / first assistant director: Olivier Coulhon / cinematographer: David Ungaro / special effects coordinator: Pierre Le Garrec / production co.: Partizan Midi Minuit / record co.: Source

Geoffroy de Crecy
Tempovision (Etienne de Crecy)
2002 / France / 3:25 min / director: Geoffroy de Crecy / production co.: Partizan Midi Minuit / record co.: Solid/V2

Dom & Nic
The Test (The Chemical Brothers)
2002 / United Kingdom / 6 min / director: Dom & Nic / producer: John Madsen / first assistant director: Marc Wilson / cinematographer: Dan Landin / 3-D/effects: Smoke & Mirrors / production co.: Oil Factory / record co.: Virgin

Michel Gondry
Star Guitar (The Chemical Brothers)
2002 / United Kingdom / 4 min / director: Michel Gondry / producer: Dan Dickenson (UK); Julie Fong (USA) / editor: Twist at Twisted Productions / production co.: Partizan Midi Minuit / record co.: Virgin

Thomas Hilland
Eple (Röyksopp)
2001 / USA/Norway / 3:38 min / director: Thomas Hilland (Mother/London) / editor, effects artist: Knut Helgeland / production co.: Toxic (Oslo) / record co.: Wall of Sound / still images put together in After Effects

Tim Hope
My Culture (1 Giant Leap)
2002 / United Kingdom / 4:11 min / director, cinematographer: Tim Hope / producer: Erika Forzy / live-action producer: Emmy Comley, Marcus Stephenson / animation: John Williams, John Hammer, Ludovik Boden, Katy Hood / compositing: Neil Riley / editor: Kevan O'Brian / record co.: Palm Pictures / shot digital video and digital stills / edited with Speed Razor and Premiere / used Combustion, 3D Studio Max and Pro Tools software on 6x Dual 1Ghz PCs

Rich Kim
Rippin Kittin (Golden Boy with Miss Kittin)
2002 / USA / 4:52 min / director: Rich Kim / co-producers: Alexander Moon, Andrew Kwon / cinematographer: Max Da-Yun Wang / cast: Genie Kim, Andrew Kwon / production co.: The Lab / record co.: Emperor Norton

Nick Knight
Pagan Poetry (Björk)
2001 / United Kingdom / 4:01 min / director: Nick Knight / producer: Sam Gainsbury / production manager: Anna Whiting / first assistant director: Lucas Harding / cinematographer: Simon Chaudoir / sound: Johnny Hose / art director: Andrew Rothschild / record co.: One Little Indian

Logan
Information Contraband (Money Mark)
2001 / USA / 3:58 min / director: Logan / producer: Kevin Shapiro / cinematographer: Eric Foster / editor: Philip Shtoll / animators: Alexei Tylevich, Ben Conrad, Joel Lava, Han Lee / Arya Senboutaraj, Paul Seymour, Craig Tollifson, Brian Won / record co.: Emperor Norton / using After Effects, a 3-D camera and several Mac computers

LynnFox

Hayling (FC Kahuna)

2002 / United Kingdom / 3:53 min / director, producer: LynnFox / record co.: City Rockers / using Premiere, After Effects and Maya, on a "home-made" computer

Monkmus

Extra Track II (Bullfrog)

2002 / Canada / 2:12 min / director, producer, animator: Monkmus / editor: Byron Ropeadope / shot in DigiBeta and edited on Avid / using Flash for animation

Tommy Pallotta

Destiny (Zero 7)

2002 / USA / 3:46 min / director: Tommy Pallotta / producer: Zachary Mortensen / editor: Josh Cramer / animation supervisor: Richard Gordoa / animators: Jason Archer, Randy Cole, Jennifer Drummond, Rahab El Ewely, Holly Fisher, Katy O'Conner, Katie Salen, Divya Srinivasan / record co.: Palm Pictures

Shynola and Ruth Lingford

Eye For An Eye (Unkle)

2002 / United Kingdom / 6:20 min / director: Shynola and Ruth Lingford / producer: Paul Fennelly / production co.: Oil Factory (UK) / co-designer: Robert Del Naja

David Slade

Clubbed to Death (Rob Dougan)

2002 / United Kingdom / 3:21 min / director: David Slade / producer: Barney Jeffrey / production manager: Mathew Alden / cinematographer: Jo Willems / art director: Tracey Collis / production co.: Bullet / co-production: Rolling Picture (Cape Town) / record co.: BMG / shot on 35mm with an Arriflex 434 camera / using Flame v. 7.6. for effects and compositing

Traktor

Where's Your Head At (Basement Jaxx)

2001 / United Kingdom/Czech Republic / 4:11 min / director: Traktor / producer: Philippa Smith (UK), Lida Ordnungova (CZ) / cinematographer: Tim Maurice-Jones / production designer: Chris Oddy / MPC producer: John Murrell / production co.: Partizan Midi Minuit / record co.: XL

Wong Kar-Wai

Six Days (DJ Shadow)

2002 / USA/Hong Kong / 3:41 min / director, editor: Wong Kar-Wai / producer: Alice Chan / cinematographer: Christopher Doyle / art director: William Chang / cast: Chang Chen, Danielle Graham / production co.: Block 2 Productions (Hong Kong); Anonymous Content (USA) / record co.: Universal Island

State of the Art

Geoff Adams

Birdbeat (Fugue)

2002 / USA / 4:08 min / director, cinematographer, animator, editor, composer: Geoff Adams / still shots taken with an Olympus 2100-ZU and digital video shot on a Sony TRV900 / using Photoshop and After Effects / edited with Final Cut Pro

Giada Dobrzenska

Mon Amour Mon Parapluie

2002 / Canada / 2:30 min / director: Giada Dobrzenska / producer: Paul Armstrong / screenwriter: Tara Hungerford / cinematographer: Gregory Middleton / editor: Mark Lemmon / composer: Nick Lloyd Webber / cast: Tara Hungerford, Douglas Coupland, William Gibson, Mark Black, Jeff Seymour / shot on 35mm, b/w

Miki Ii

Birdie

2002 / Japan / 1:40 min / director: Miki Ii / sound design: Hiroshi Ito, Eri Horogami / created with Adobe After Effects and Alias Wavefront Maya on a Windows NT Workstation

Junji Kojima

Japanese Tradition (Sushi)

2002 / Japan / 8:02 min / director: Junji Kojima / screenwriter: Kentaroh Kobayashi / cinematographer: Kazuhisa Sekiya / lighting: Osamu Yamamori / designer: Toru Takahashi / production co.: teevee graphics / using Inferno, After Effects, Combustion, Illustrator, Photoshop and Speed Razor

Stéphane Lavoix and François Vogel

Les Crabes

2002 / France / 5:30 min / directors: Stéphane Lavoix and François Vogel / post production: Alain Cure at Mikros Image / shot on Hi-8 / using Photoshop and After Effects

Stéphane Levallois

Carcan

2002 / France / 2:29 min / director: Stéphane Levallois / producer: Alexandra Arnould / cinematographer: Rémi Chevrin / editor: Frederique Olszak / music: House of Lust, Mathias Potter / production co.: Quad

Todd Lincoln

Leave Luck To Heaven

2002 / USA / 12:46 min / director, screenwriter, co-producer: Todd Lincoln / co-producer: Manabu Nagaoka / cinematographer: Justan Floyd / editor: Chan Hatcher / composer: Toshiyuki Honda / sound design: Jon Huck / visual effects supervisor: Westley Sarokin / titles, animation: Kentaro Fujimoto / shot on Super 16mm, additional footage shot on Super-8, miniDV and generated with 8-Bit Nintendo Entertainment System / compositing and effects created with Flame, After Effects, Photoshop and Illustrator

Mototake Makishima

Soil

2002 / United Kingdom / 1 min / director, editor, composer: Mototake Makishima / shot in digital video on a Sony TRV-9 and took 35mm still photos / used After Effects and Photoshop and edited in Premiere on a Mac G3 / used AKAI MPC 2000 sampler, Roland GP100 preamp and sound edited in Peak TDM 2.53

Alexandre Moors

The Lady Lovelace Deception System

2002 / France / 12:36 min / director, screenwriter: Alexandre Moors / producer: Jonathan Lia /

cinematographer: Aaron Philips / editor: Johnathan Nigro /
sound designer, composer: Murat / shot on 35mm with an
Arriflex BL45 camera and edited on Avid /
used After Effects, Softimage and Pro Tools on a Mac G4

Yard
2002 / USA / 3:36 min / director: Bob Sabiston /
animators: Jason Archer, Randy Cole, Jennifer Drummond,
Holly Fisher, Dan Gillotte, Mike Layne, Travis Lindquist,
Katy O'Conner, Bob Sabiston, Penny Van Horn, Constanze Wood /
used a Sony TRV-900 miniDV camera and edited with iMovie /
produced on Apple Mac G4 computers equipped with Wacom
graphics tablets

Whizeewhig
2002 / USA / 2:15 min / director, editor: Chih-Cheng Peng /
shot on a Canon optura DV camera / used After Effects and
Photoshop / edited in Premiere on a Pentium III 500Mhz computer

Mister Lou in Love
2002 / USA / 2:30 min / director, screenwriter: Blair Thornley /
producer: Wolfgang Astert / cinematographer: Nick Vasu /
editor: Carol Martori / sound design: Jason Lane / composer:
Bebel Gilberto / used an animation stand, Final Cut Pro Tools
and a G4

The Rise And Fall Of The Legendary Anglobilly Feverson
2001 / The Netherlands / 9:45 min / director, screenwriter:
Rosto / producer: Richard Falk, Inc. / cinematographer:
Robbert Jan van der Does / animation: Rosto and Martijn
Paasschens / sound: Kees Kroot / music: Roto

Errata

While writing any book there is no way to avoid mistakes, typographic errors, etc. Therefore we must kindly apologize to the following people and institutions:

p. 116	image bottom left, Edmund Kuppel is represented by VG Bild-Kunst, Bonn 2003.
p. 271	column two, bottom, the author's name should read Grahame Weinbren.
pp. 293–294	a couple of times we misspelled the following institution: Neue Galerie am Landesmuseum Joanneum, Graz.
pp. 356–357	the correct authorship for *Tracing the Decay of Fiction: Encounters with a Film by Pat O'Neill* should mention Pat O'Neill, with Rosemary Comella, Kristy H. A. Kang and The Labyrinth Project.
p. 377	caption on top of the page, should read Sean Wellesley-Miller.

Letter
to Serge Daney
Gilles Deleuze (1986)

[…] It's from cinema that there's come the most radical criticism of information, from Godard for instance, and in a different way from Syberberg (this not just in things they've said but concretely in their work); it's from television that there comes the new threat of a death of cinema. So you've thought it necessary to go and "have a close look" at this essentially uneven or asymmetric confrontation. Cinema met its first death at the hands of an authoritarian power culminating in fascism. Why does its threatened second death involve television, just as the first involved radio? Because television is the form in which the new powers of "control" become immediate and direct. To get to the heart of the confrontation you'd almost have to ask whether this control might be reversed, harnessed by the supplementary function opposed to power: whether one could develop an art of control that would be a kind of new form of resistance. Taking the battle to the heart of cinema, making cinema see it as *its* problem instead of coming upon it from outside: that's what Burroughs did in literature, by substituting the viewpoint of control and controllers for that of authors and authority. But isn't this, as you suggest, what Coppola has in his turn attempted to do in cinema, with all his hesitations and ambiguities, but really fighting for something nonetheless? And you give the apt name of *mannerism* to the tense, convulsive form of cinema that leans, as it tries to turn round, on the very system that seeks to control or replace it. You'd already, in *La Rampe,* characterized the image's third phase as "mannerism": when there's nothing to see behind it, not much to see in it or on the surface, but just an image constantly slipping across preexisting, presupposed images, when "the background in any image is always another image," and so on endlessly, and that's what we have to see.

This is the stage where art no longer beautifies or spiritualizes Nature but competes with it: the world is lost, the world itself "turns to film," any film at all, and this is what television amounts to, the world turning to any film at all, and, as you say here, "nothing happening to human beings any more, but everything happening only to images." One might also say that bodies in Nature or people in a landscape are replaced by brains in a city: the screen's no longer a window or door (behind which …) nor a frame or surface (in which …) but a computer screen on which images as "data" slip around. How, though, can we still talk of art, if the world itself is turning cinematic, becoming "just an act" directly controlled and immediately processed by a television that excludes any supplementary function? Cinema ought to stop "being cinematic," stop playacting, and set up specific relationships with video, with electronic and digital images, in order to develop a new form of resistance and combat the televisual function of surveillance and control. It's not a question of short-circuiting television — how could that be possible? — but of preventing television subverting or short-circuiting the extension of cinema into the new types of image. For, as you show, "since television has scorned, marginalized, repressed the potential of video-its only chance of taking over from postwar modern cinema … taking over its urge to take images apart and put them back together, its break with theater, its new way of seeing the human body, bathed in images and sounds — one has to hope the development of video art will itself threaten TV." Here we see in outline the new art of City and Brain, of competing with Nature. And one can already see in this mannerism many different directions or paths, some blocked, others leading tentatively forward, offering great hopes. A mannerism of video "previsualization" in Coppola, where images are already assembled without a camera. And then a completely different mannerism, with its strict, indeed austere, method in Syberberg, where puppetry and front-projection produce an image unfolding against a background of images. Is this the same world we see in pop videos, special effects, and footage from space? Maybe pop video, up to the point where it lost its dreamlike quality, might have played some part in the pursuit of "new associations" proposed by Syberberg, might have traced out the new cerebral circuits of a cinema of the future, if it hadn't immediately been taken over by marketing jingles, sterile patterns of mental deficiency, intricately controlled epileptic fits (rather as, in the previous period, cinema was taken over by the "then hysterical spectacle" of large-scale propaganda). […]

Excerpt from Gilles Deleuze, "Letter to Serge Daney: Optimism, Pessimism, and Travel," (1986) in *Negotiations*, Columbia University Press, New York, 1995, pp. 75–77.

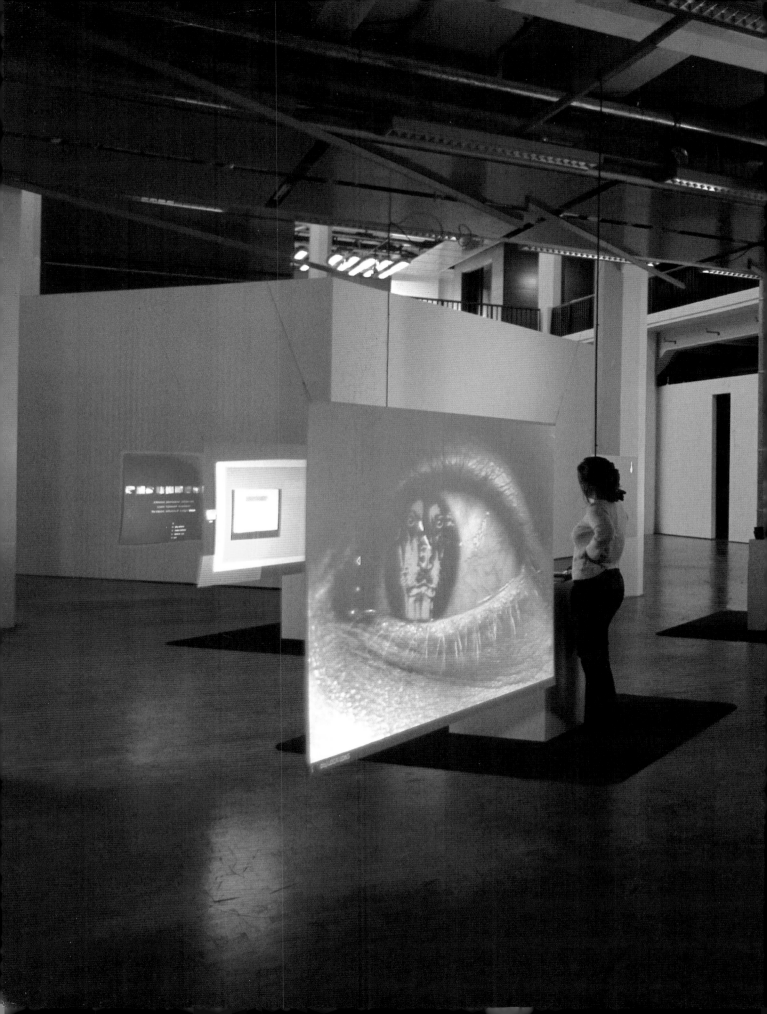